THE IRWIN SERIES IN RISK AND INSURANCE

EDITORS

EDISON L. BOWERS
The Ohio State University

DAVIS W. GREGG
The American College of Life Underwriters

BOOKS IN THE IRWIN SERIES IN RISK AND INSURANCE

ATHEARN *General Insurance Agency Management*
BLACK, KEIR, & SURREY *Cases in Life Insurance*
BRAINARD *Automobile Insurance*
DICKERSON *Health Insurance* Revised Edition
DONALDSON *Casualty Claim Practice*
EILERS & CROWE *Group Insurance Handbook*
FOLLMANN *Medical Care and Health Insurance: A Study in Social Progress*
FRAINE *Valuation of Securities Holdings of Life Insurance Companies*
GOSHAY *Information Technology in the Insurance Industry*
GREGG *Life and Health Insurance Handbook* Second Edition
GREIDER & BEADLES *Law and the Life Insurance Contract*
HABER & COHEN *Social Security: Programs, Problems, and Policies*
HABER & MURRAY *Unemployment Insurance in the American Economy*
LONG & GREGG *Property and Liability Insurance Handbook*
MAGEE *Life Insurance* Third Edition
MAGEE & BICKELHAUPT *General Insurance* Seventh Edition
MAGEE & SERBEIN *Property and Liability Insurance* Fourth Edition
MCGILL *Legal Aspects of Life Insurance*
MCGILL *Life Insurance* Revised Edition
MEHR & CAMMACK *Principles of Insurance* Fourth Edition
MEHR & HEDGES *Risk Management in the Business Enterprise*
MELONE & ALLEN *Pension Planning: Pensions, Profit Sharing, and Other Deferred Compensation Plans*
MYERS *Social Insurance and Allied Government Programs*
REDEKER & REID *Life Insurance Settlement Options* Revised Edition
SNIDER *Readings in Property and Casualty Insurance*
STALNAKER *Life Insurance Agency Financial Management* Revised Edition

PROPERTY AND LIABILITY INSURANCE

Property and Liability INSURANCE

JOHN H. MAGEE
Late Director for Maine of the Federal Housing Administration and Assistant Professor of Economics and Sociology, University of Maine

OSCAR N. SERBEIN
Professor of Insurance
Graduate School of Business
Stanford University

Fourth Edition · 1967
RICHARD D. IRWIN, INC.
Homewood, Illinois

Fourth Edition

First Printing, May, 1967

Library of Congress Catalog Card No. 67-15838

Printed in the United States of America

To

Alice Marie,

Marie,

and

John

Preface

This Book is a revision of *Property Insurance*, first prepared by John H. Magee in 1941 and subsequently revised by him in 1947 and again in 1955, shortly before his death.

Since 1955, the field of property and liability insurance in the United States has undergone fundamental and wide-reaching changes, and now encompasses virtually all forms af insurance except those traditionally associated with life insurers. Perhaps the most significant change that has occurred in the last ten years has been the conversion of more and more specialty insurers to a multiple-line basis, a change greatly enhanced by multiple-line legislation enacted in the various states. A concomitant of this development has been an increased emphasis on multiple-line (or package) contracts in which one insurer has undertaken to provide in one package insurance against a variety of perils that only a few years ago were insured against through separate contracts, often written by more than one insurer. Changes in the direction of multiple-line underwriting are still taking place, and the student of non-life insurance must now be alert to the implications of this development for the product, as well as the internal organization, of the insurer.

The fact of rapid change has necessitated a substantial amount of revision of the older text and the adding of much new material, including new chapters on package contracts for the individual as well as the commercial firm. The aim of the revision has been to view property and liability insurance from a multiple-line standpoint and, at the same time, to take cognizance of the fact that many traditional contracts are still in use and still form a part of many insurance programs. Recognition is also given to the multiple-line character of many older contracts, such as automobile insurance, which have been sold for many years. Thus, multiple-line insurance is in some ways old as well as new.

Every effort has been made to provide a thorough analysis of the principal contract forms now used by insurers in the field of property and liability insurance. The student will find reference to a collection of contracts, such as that provided by the advanced book of property and liabilty contracts issued by the Insurance Information Institute, or the collection from the American Mutual Alliance, helpful in studying this part of the text. The quotations from contracts in the text, unless otherwise indicated, are from the Insurance Information Institute collection. In addition to contracts, the text gives a systematic treatment of the principles of property and liability insurance starting with the meaning and measurement of risk and continuing with legal concepts, types of insurer, marketing, underwriting, adjustment of losses, finance, and other functions of the insurer.

A persistent problem in the study of insurance, and one that often presents difficulty for the student, is the ambiguity that often surrounds insurance terminology. The same word may have different meanings in different branches of the insurance business, and words in common use may have special meanings as they relate to insurance. An effort has been made in this text to follow the recommendations of the Commission on Insurance Terminology of the American Risk and Insurance Association in the use of insurance words, starting with changing the title from "Property Insurance" to "Property and Liability Insurance." Further, certain words have been used in this text in preference to other, perhaps more common, usages. Except for use in quotations "insurer," for example, is preferred to "insurance company" and "contract" to "policy." The word "casualty" has been used sparingly in recognition of the growing tendency to regard contracts in that field as either property or liability coverages.

The text is arranged in such a way that it may be adapted to courses of varying lengths and emphases. For those teachers who want to emphasize multiple-line insurance, Chapters 1–4, all of the chapters in Part IV, plus selected chapters from the other parts of the book should provide ample material for a one-semester or shorter course. In one-semester courses where a more traditional approach is used, Chapters 1–10, 11, 13, and 15, plus selected chapters from the rest of the book, might be used. If the course is a year in length, all of the chapters might well be included.

A number of persons have been helpful during the time this revision has been in preparation in that they have read the text in manuscript form in whole or in part and have given the author the benefit of their suggestions. Although it is not possible to list all of their names here, special mention should be made of Dr. Edison L. Bowers and Dr. John D. Long, both of whom read the manuscript in its entirety and offered valuable comments; of Warren Brockmeier and his associates for many helpful suggestions; and of Dr. Davis W. Gregg for his continuing interest and consideration of various parts of this project. It is a pleasure for the author to extend his thanks to them and to the others who have given generously of their time and experience. The author is also indebted to the American Insurance Association, Central Forms Committee, Courier-Citizens Company, Insurance Information Institute, International Association of Insurance Counsel, and the Western Actuarial Bureau for permission to reprint certain forms and tables.

Stanford, California
March, 1967

OSCAR N. SERBEIN

Table of Contents

PART I. INTRODUCTION TO PROPERTY AND LIABILITY INSURANCE

PART II. MAJOR MONOLINE PROPERTY INSURANCE CONTRACTS

PART III. LIABILITY INSURANCE AND ALLIED CONTRACTS

PART IV. MULTIPLE LINE AND MISCELLANEOUS INSURANCE CONTRACTS

PART V. OPERATIONAL PROBLEMS OF THE PROPERTY AND LIABILITY INSURER

BIBLIOGRAPHY

APPENDIXES

INDEXES

List of Tables and Figures

TABLES

FIGURES

PART I

INTRODUCTION TO PROPERTY AND LIABILITY INSURANCE

CHAPTER • 1

Risk and Insurance

The study of insurance properly begins with a consideration of risk, since it is the presence of risk in business and personal affairs that brings about the need for the institution of insurance.

In every business undertaking, if the management could know exactly and in advance all of the costs it would incur, it could carry on the enterprise without the need of insurance. The fact that a manufacturing plant may burn, a ship may be destroyed, or other unforeseen loss may develop, makes it most desirable in modern business to protect against the financial consequences of unpredictable losses. It is not the fact that a plant burns or that a ship is lost that creates the problem. If the plant were certain to burn or the ship to be lost in a given period, there would be no problem in that loss-cost could be budgeted. The problem is created by the fact that the loss may occur and that no one can know in advance whether it will. The business of insurance undertakes to make costs known in the case of specific perils through a shifting of the burden of the risk from the shoulders of the one to whom it attaches to those of another or a group more willing to bear it.

RISK

Definition. For the purpose of the study of insurance, risk may be defined as uncertainty as to loss or damage and the attendant costs.[1] From the viewpoint of the individual this definition means that with respect to some situation, undertaking, or event there is the possibility of an unfavorable development and that such development will occasion loss. The various factors (or causes of loss) contributing to the

[1] A more general definition of risk is that it is uncertainty. Since uncertainty may attach to gain as well as loss, this definition implies that the general study of risk would embrace all situations where decisions must be made under conditions of uncertainty. In this text only those aspects of risk that relate directly to insurance are considered.

uncertainty are termed "hazards." Ordinarily, there are many separate hazards that contribute to the uncertainty that attaches to any particular object or person. The total of the hazards constitutes the risk.

Risk exists because of unknown or unconsidered forces that may be operative in the happening of a particular event. Strictly speaking, the philosophical concept of an ordered universe finds no place for a theory of risk. It has been pointed out, for example, that lightning strikes where it does as a result of natural laws. Jevons states that ". . . in the greatest storm there is nothing capricious; not a grain of sand lies upon the beach, but infinite knowledge would account for its lying there; and the course of every falling leaf is guided by the same principles of mechanics as rule the motion of the heavenly bodies."[2] Whether, as this statement would indicate, uncertainty does not exist in nature but is merely an expression of ignorance of the causes of an action with the consequent inability to predict results, or whether there is a random and unpredictable element in the world, the fact remains that for individuals there are, from time to time, unpredictable occurrences. Even if the occurrences follow a pattern established by a fixed law, if the law is unknown, any prediction with respect to the operation of the law is impossible. Moreover, it is not always possible to foresee the impact of a known natural law.

Classification of Risk. Risk may be classified in many ways with some of the classifications being more useful to the study of insurance than others. The risks attaching to every sort of human enterprise are multitudinous and range from the unavoidable to those assumed by choice. Disease, accident, the onset of physical incapacity with old age, and death are risks attending human existence. At the other end of the scale are hazardous forms of business enterprise, undertaken through choice for profit, such as investing money in real property that may be destroyed by the forces of nature or through the unsuccessful operation of a business. Between these two categories are many degrees of uncertainty.

Risks of the type considered in the preceding paragraph may be classified as pure or speculative depending on whether financial loss is the only possible outcome of the occurrence of a chance event, or whether gain as well as loss is a possibility. Insurance as a method for providing for the financial consequences of loss is available for certain types of pure risk but is not a method for dealing with speculative risk. Uncertainties surrounding death, illness, loss of property by fire, and similar events are pure risks, whereas risks surrounding the behavior of prices, acceptance of a product, or outcome of an investment are speculative in character.

Another way of classifying risks is to label them dynamic or static

[2] W. Stanley Jevons, *The Principles of Science* (London: Macmillan & Co. Ltd., 1874) Vol I., p. 225.

depending on whether time is or is not a factor in determining the degree of risk. Examples of static risks are uncertainties surrounding loss of buildings by fire, loss of assets through dishonesty of employees, and liability claims. Dynamic risks are illustrated by uncertainties occasioned by population growth changes in the demand for various products, and changes brought about by automation. The two-way classificatory arrangement may be further subdivided according to whether risks are insurable or not insurable, and, if insurable, whether the risks are of the personal or property type.

Burden of Risk. The burden of a loss will rest more heavily upon some than others. A large industrial concern with a utility building valued at $15,000 might well bear its total destruction with virtually no inconvenience. The loss of a $15,000 dwelling to an office worker earning $5,000 a year and without other resources could be virtually catastrophic. The loss of such a building owned by a large municipality would be so light as it touched each citizen that it would not be noticeable. There are some business organizations that could afford to carry a loss of $100,000 or $500,000, or more in a year. The individual in most instances could ill afford to lose a few thousand dollars, or even a few hundred. Thus, the burden of risk is subjective and varies with the individual to whom it attaches. This fact is intrinsic in all insurance planning.

Adjustment to Risk. Once the existence of risk is acknowledged, the next step is to consider methods of dealing with it. With respect to risk in a given situation the person to whom it attaches must determine: (1) to what extent the risk can be eliminated, avoided, or decreased; (2) after all reasonable steps have been taken to eliminate, avoid, or decrease risk, consideration must be given to the financial consequences of bearing the remaining risk; and (3) to the extent that risks cannot be eliminated, avoided, or decreased, and to the extent that it is not financially wise to assume the risk, consideration must be given to shifting the burden.

The attitudes of individuals who are faced with choices among alternatives involving risk are hard to explain. It is sufficient here to point out that attitudes vary with different individuals. There are some who invariably select the choice that involves a minimum of risk. There are others so constituted that they willingly assume large risks particularly when they are associated with the possibility of large gains and the attendant possibility of large losses. Between the two are those willing to assume a moderate degree of risk if extreme losses are not probable, even though there can be no expectation of spectacular profits.[3] It may be pointed out that with respect to choices the safe one with minimum risk and the one offering a few possibly high rewards

[3] Milton Friedman and L. J. Savage, "The Utility Analysis of Choices Involving Risk," *Journal of Political Economy*, Vol. LVI, No. 4 (August, 1948), p. 284.

are both more attractive to larger groups of individuals than the middle course involving a moderate degree of risk and little likelihood of extreme gains.

Of the various ways of meeting risk perhaps the most important are elimination of risk through prevention, and the shifting of the burden of risk by transfer to a professional risk taker such as an insurer or shifting through hedging. The remainder of this book will deal at some length with insurance as a way of providing for the financial consequences of chance losses. In this section prevention and hedging will be discussed.

Prevention. It is only natural that when a pure risk threatens that every reasonable step should be taken to eliminate it or minimize it through the agency of prevention. Thus, fire-resistive structures are built. Protective devices are installed in manufacturing boilers to eliminate accidents. Inspections are made of boilers to detect latent defects. Installations are available to control lightning. Attempts are made to prevent floods through the agency of control projects. Construction is aimed at the elimination of tornado, earthquake, and hurricane losses. Steps to prevent losses extend from efforts of the individual to community undertakings. Some of the larger projects, such as those involving flood control, are carried on by the national government. So far as prevention is effected, it saves the property in question from loss.

In contrast to prevention, insurance as such saves nothing, although it frequently induces prevention efforts; in other situations the mere fact that something is insured may increase the hazard. Insurance indemnifies the owner of the property, and the payment is made out of the fund to which all insured members have contributed. There is a distribution of property following an insurance loss, but the sum total of the property is lessened by the amount of loss. In an effort to reduce the cost of insurance to a minimum, insurance stimulates use of protective measures; and to the extent that it is successful, it is an agency for the preservation of property. On the other hand, insurance contributes to a certain amount of loss through incendiarism, suicide, or other losses instigated in an effort to defraud insurers.

More often prevention and insurance are combined. The owner of capital goods subject to a number of hazards may take every known precaution, install every known safety device, and still there may be hazards that he cannot eliminate. Or it may be that in weighing the costs, insurance up to a certain point is the more attractive. In any instance, insurance begins where prevention ceases. Even though the elimination of hazards in any case materially lessens the cost of insurance, the cost of such prevention cannot be termed a payment for insurance, even though it is a payment for security. The concept of insurance will not extend itself to include prevention but limits itself to the provision of indemnity where the risk to the capital covered remains in existence. The same psychological drive that gives the idea of insurance its momentum has likewise given rise to the development of preventive measures, the two ideas having a common purpose and progressing along parallel lines.

Hedging. The burden of a speculative risk may be shifted by hedging. The risk itself is not transferred to an insurer as in the case of a pure risk, but the burden is canceled out through the creation of another risk of the same magnitude. For example, a manufacturer who buys raw material, to be converted into a finished product to be offered for sale sometime in the future, may suffer a severe loss if the price of the raw materials falls before the finished product is offered on the market. If the price of the raw material rises, he will enjoy a speculative profit. Since a manufacturer is in business to make a profit on his manufactured goods, he is interested in relieving himself of the speculative risk. Here is where the hedge becomes useful. At the time the manufacturer buys the raw material he intends to work into his product, he will sell short an equal amount for delivery at about the time his finished product is offered on the market. "Selling the material short" means selling goods he does not have by obligating himself to make delivery in the future. The transaction is completed by "covering the short sale," that is by a purchase of an amount of goods equal to the amount sold short at or before the time of delivery. If the market goes down after a short sale, the transaction shows a profit, and if the market goes up, there is a loss. Thus, if the manufacturer sells raw material on a current market for delivery in the future and the market advances, he will lose money on his short sale but will make up the difference on the goods in process. If the material sold short declines in price, the manufacturer will make a speculative profit on the short sales but a corresponding loss on the manufactured goods. The net result of the hedge is to eliminate speculative risk and make the cost of the raw material reflect the current market price at the time the goods are offered for sale. The person through whom the short sale is effected may be a speculator whose business is the assumption of speculative risks for a profit.

The term "speculation" is sometimes associated with gambling. The legitimate use of funds in speculative enterprise forms an important part of our economic system; and the speculator who, motivated by the possibility of higher return, is willing to assume a greater risk than the conservative investor contributes to productive enterprise. The gambling or wagering risk, on the contrary, is nonproductive, and in this country is illegal, except in the State of Nevada and in limited instances in some other states, as contrary to public policy. The wagering risk is a risk created by the transaction itself; that is, until a wager is made neither party is subject to the risk in question, but after the wager is made both parties are subject to the risk of loss; also, there is the chance of gain.

A pure risk, because it involves only the possibility of loss, cannot be neutralized by an opposite contract, as in the case of hedging a speculative risk. Take, for example, the case of the manufacturer already cited. His plant may be destroyed by fire, windstorm, or earthquake. He may have taken every means within his power to prevent such losses; but after he has exhausted his resources, destruction still is possible. The temporary shutdown of the property because of the happening of some contingency may interrupt profits. Accidents may involve liability claims. Trusted employees may abscond with company resources. Customers may go into bankruptcy and fail to pay accounts. There are innumerable risks of this nature which cannot be handled by hedging and which cannot be eliminated by prevention. It is the burden of such risks that is shifted by insurance. The insurance business does not minimize or eliminate a pure risk, but it may effect a transfer of the risk from the shoulders of the person to whom it attaches to another willing and able to bear it. The person who transfers the risk is the insured, and the person to whom the risk is transferred is the insurer. A payment is made by the insured to the insurer, and this insurance is said to effect an exchange of a known small loss for a possible large loss. Insurance, then, in relation to pure risk makes certain the cost of loss to the individual.

Risk Measurement. For insurers or other organizations and individuals who wish to plan for the financial consequences of uncertain losses, it is important to measure in mathematical terms the degree of risk that is assumed. The theory of probability provides a way to make mathematical statements about uncertainty or at least a wide range of uncertainties.[4] Any particular event may be certain or it may be impossible. Between these extremes there are varying degrees of probability. The degree of certainty and the degree of probability do not represent the same idea. The measure of probability is expressed algebraically by means of a fraction whose numerator is the number of favorable (or unfavorable) possibilities and whose denominator is the number of all possible outcomes. The equation is $p = a/m$, with p representing the probability of a favorable outcome, with a the number of favorable ways the event can occur, and with m the total number of possible outcomes. If an event is certain to happen, its probability is expressed by 1. If it is impossible for the event to occur, there is no probability; this is represented by 0. Thus, if an event is

[4] In economic theory the word "risk" is usually reserved for describing those situations in which a probability may be attached to the happening of a given event. The word "uncertainty" is used to describe events for which probability statements cannot be made. In this book uncertainty is defined as synonymous with risk, with the understanding that not all risks are measurable in the probability sense.

certain to occur or cannot occur, there is certainty in both cases. As the probability increases from 0, uncertainty likewise increases until the probability reaches a point where it can be measured by ½. Here the chances for and against the occurrence of an event are equal. As the probability continues to increase, the element of uncertainty again begins to decrease. When the probability is expressed by a fraction between 0 and ½, uncertainty increases as probability increases. As probability continues from ½ to 1, uncertainty again begins to decrease, but the probability of the occurrence of the event continues to increase.

Not all probabilities can be computed on an a priori basis. Problems involving tosses of an unbiased coin or an unbiased die or similar situations lend themselves to probability computations that can be carried out by simply determing the outcomes favorable (or unfavorable, as the case may be) and dividing by the total possible outcomes. In the tossing of an unbiased coin, for example, there is only one outcome that is favorable (or unfavorable), since the coin must come up either heads or tails (assuming landing on its edge is ruled out), and there are only two possible ways for the coin to land. Thus, the probability that in a single toss of an unbiased coin heads will appear is ½.

In most practical situations, including insurer operations, probabilities cannot be determined in the manner just described but must be estimated from past experience. The probability that a house of a given type located in a given area will burn within a year can only be estimated through the study of an appropriate statistical record involving a large number of houses having similar characteristics, and a notation as to whether fire did or did not occur. The problem can be further refined by determining whether the losses were total or partial.

Although no effort has been made to discuss probability in all of its aspects, it should be remarked that the interpretation to be placed on probability statements, as far as this discussion is concerned, is frequency in the long run. It is assumed that no probability can be attached to events produced by experiments that cannot be repeated.

The Law of Large Numbers.[5] Probability estimates are often based on a comparatively small amount of experience. Estimates based on less than complete information could lead to serious difficulty, if it should turn out that these estimates were unstable and that future experience might be quite different from the past. The behavior of independent, chance observations, when the number of such observations increases, is described by the law of large numbers. This "law" is

[5] Strictly speaking, this heading should be laws of large numbers, since there is more than one mathematical statement of the idea presented here. The theorem stated in this paragraph is the weak law of large numbers.

a mathematical theorem that states that, as the sample size (of independent, chance observations) increases toward infinity, the probability that the true probability of an event will differ from the estimated probability by a very small amount approaches one. This theorem provides the theoretical basis for the conduct of the insurance business.

Because of the operation of this theorem insurers undertake to include in their portfolios large numbers of similar risks. For this reason, it is the practice of insurers to set a limit on the amount that each will carry on a single risk; likewise risks are distributed geographically in such a manner as to limit large losses occasioned by a single catastrophe. An insurer that would hesitate to write $1,000,000 insurance upon a single building unquestionably worth that sum would without hesitation write $1,000,000 divided into $1,000 lines upon 1,000 buildings where there would be no concentration of the risk. A total loss to the $1,000,000 property would throw the experience of the insurer entirely out of line. A more regular and more accurately predictable loss ratio would unquestionably follow the writing of 1,000 risks for $1,000 each.

Insurer's Advantage. A further illustration of the basic importance of the law of large numbers to the insurance business is provided by the consideration of why an insurer can carry a large risk for a very small premium. In some communities $20,000 of insurance for fire and extended coverage perils may be written on a dwelling house for a period of three years for approximately $75. The risk appears to be entirely out of proportion to the premium. Yet this fact cannot be the case, since protected dwellings are one of the most profitable classes written by fire insurers. The answer to the problem is this: No fire insurer could possible afford to insure one isolated dwelling for a premium of $75 for $20,000 for three years. The property might be destroyed any time during the term, and the amount of the loss would be so far out of proportion to the premium collected that not only would the transaction be unprofitable but the loss would be prohibitive. Because an insurer insures many hundreds of houses and for each collects a premium of $75 and because of the many hundreds of houses insured only a few burn, insurers are able to pay all the losses out of the premiums collected and retain a profit out of which a surplus is built up. It is not, then, the individual risk that is a matter of concern to the insurance underwriter but rather the experience following the accumulation of a great many risks.

Because of the combination of individual risks into groups and because of the ability of insurance underwriters, as a result of experience, to determine with a reasonable degree of certainty the loss experience to be anticipated from a group, the operation of effecting insurance commercially provides for the combination of a large number of uncertainties and reducing them to a reasonable degree of certainty when the entire group is considered. Thus, the insurance underwriter may not know whether any individual risk will be the occasion of a loss, but on the basis of experience he is able to anticipate within workable limits the number of losses from 50,000 to 100,000 like risks. Thus, while the degree of uncertainty for each individual insured remains unchanged, for the insurer the uncertainty is eliminated in a statistical sense and known losses within anticipated limits are provided for by the collection of adequate premiums. It is the responsibility of the insurer to collect premiums adequate to meet anticipated losses. He is not disturbed particularly by the fact that there will be losses, but he is concerned with making a reasonably accurate estimate of their extent as applied to the group.

INSURANCE

In the preceding discussion the word "insurance" has been used and the essential features of insurance as a way of meeting risk have been considered. In spite of the fact that "insurance" is a fairly commonly used word, no definition of it has found universal acceptance. Lack of agreement on a definition often gives rise to legal disputes,[6] and frequently causes misunderstanding in fields where the concept of insurance, as understood by commercial insurers, is modified to meet special conditions. An example of this type of modification is social insurance, a field that has given rise to many important variations of commercial insurance practice. Problems involved not only in defining insurance but in defining many words used in the study of insurance resulted in the establishing of a Commission on Insurance Terminology,[7] which has a number of committees working on basic definitions in the fields of general insurance, health insurance, life insurance, pensions and profit sharing, property and liability insurance, and social insurance. The commission has not completed its work, but preliminary reports from the various committees indicate that progress is being made.

A brief review of some of the definitions of insurance that have been used at various times may be helpful. Insurance has been defined as a contract whereby, for a consideration, the insurer binds himself to compensate the insured if the latter should suffer loss. Legal status has been given the definition: "Insurance is a contract by which the one party, in consideration of a price paid to him adequate to the risk,

[6] For a discussion of the legal problems that result from the lack of an agreed upon definition of insurance see E. W. Patterson, *Cases and Materials on Insurance*, 3d. edition (Brooklyn, New York: The Foundation Press, Inc., 1955), pp. 2–42. See also the discussion in the fourth edition of the Patterson text.

[7] This Commission was established in 1958 by the American Risk and Insurance Association. As of January, 1967, no definition of insurance had been agreed upon. The latest definition to be considered is that insurance is the "protection or promise of service secured by transfer of a risk to an insurer."

becomes security to the other that he shall not suffer loss, damage or prejudice by the happening of the perils specified to certain things which may be exposed to them."[8] As a business institution, insurance has been defined as a plan by which large numbers of persons associate themselves and transfer, to the shoulders of all, risks that attach to individuals. It has as its end the reparation of a serious injury to individuals at a moderate cost by arranging a means whereby, if a certain loss falls upon one, it shall be made good at the expense of many. It should be recalled that the distribution of individual risks over the members of a group is a means for effecting insurance. It is not insurance itself. The shifting of the burden is the insurance function. An adequate definition giving recognition both to the end of insurance and to the means for effecting it has been admirably stated thus: "We should define insurance, then, as that social device for making accumulations to meet uncertain losses of capital which is carried out through the transfer of the risks of many individuals to one person or to a group of persons. Wherever there is accumulation for uncertain losses, or wherever there is a transfer of risk, there is one element of insurance; only where these are joined with the combination of risks in a group is the insurance complete."[9]

In the ordinary course of business the foregoing definition applies; to effect insurance, persons who are exposed to loss from some particular peril agree to contribute to indemnify whichever member of the group shall, because of peril, suffer loss. It is the more usual practice to contribute to a common fund and, out of this fund, to make payments to those who have suffered loss. The payment to the fund represents the individual's share of the losses of the group.

In the strictest interpretation of the term, aside from its customary use in the field of business, contributions to a fund by beneficiaries are not essential. It is conceivable that groups rely entirely upon assessments after losses to indemnify the sufferers and in such instances accumulate no funds in advance. In the case of insurance enterprises in which the government functions as the insurer, a fund may be accumulated, or the beneficiaries may depend for their insurance payments upon the taxing power.[10] As a business, insurance evidences

[8] *Lucena* v. *Crawford,* 2B. and P.N.R. 269 (H.L. 1806).

[9] A. H. Willett, *The Economic Theory of Risk and Insurance* (Columbia University Studies in History, Economics and Public Law, Vol. XIV [New York: Columbia University Press, 1901]), p. 388. See also reprinted edition, published under the auspices of the S. S. Huebner Foundation for Insurance Education (Philadelphia: University of Pennsylvania Press, 1951), p. 72.

[10] For a definition of insurance as it relates to the field of social insurance see Sir William Beveridge, *Insurance for All and Everything, the New Way* (Series VII [London, 1924]), pp. 6–7, and various reports of the Committee on Social Insurance Terminology of the Commission on Insurance Terminology of the American Risk and Insurance Association.

its strength on the basis of a demonstrated ability to pay, and the established practice of accumulating a fund out of which losses are to be paid.

While the applicant for insurance protection may have an academic interest in the means for effecting insurance protection, the purchase of an insurance contract is not itself an agreement to distribute losses over a group. It is a contractual obligation entered into by the insured with an insurer. He makes a payment for the purpose of converting the possibility of an undetermined large loss into a fixed cost. With respect to this transaction he purchases security. The transaction is contractual.[11] As between the parties, the insured and the insurer, the obligations of both are set forth in the contractual document termed the "policy." As an early and distinguished writer in the field has stated: "Policy is the name given to the instrument by which the contract of indemnity is effected between the insurer and the insured; and it is not like most contracts signed by both parties, but only by the insurer, who, on that account, it is supposed, is denominated the Underwriter."[12] He then adds that, notwithstanding this fact, there are certain conditions to be fulfilled by the person not subscribing as the underwriter; otherwise, the contract will be void.

The monetary consideration for the contract is termed the "premium." The limit of liability expressed in the contract, or, in other words, the amount of insurance, is termed the "face of the policy." The company, group, or individual assuming the burden of the risk in the capacity of underwriter is termed the "insurer."

Insurance Distinguished from Gambling. Even assuming the insurer to be faced with the same uncertainties as is the insured in the matter of losses (which is not the case), insurance in its principle is the direct opposite of gambling. It is sometimes said by those who have

[11] Not all insurance codes define the insurance contract accurately. The New York statutory definition is both accurate and comprehensive. This provides: "The term 'insurance contract' shall be deemed to include any agreement or other transaction whereby one party, herein called the insurer, is obligated to confer benefit of pecuniary value upon another party, herein called the insured or the beneficiary, depending upon the happening of a fortuitous event in which the insured or beneficiary has or is expected to have at the time of such happening a material interest which will be adversely affected by the happening of such event. A fortuitous event is any occurrence or failure to occur which is, or is assumed by the parties to be, to a substantial extent beyond the control of either party." Property insurance has been defined as "a contract to indemnify the insured against loss or damage to a certain property named in the policy, by reason of certain perils to which it may be exposed." *State* ex rel. *Sheets, Attorney General* v. *C. C. & St. L. Ry. Company*, 68 Ohio St. 9, 30, 67 N.E. 93: *State* ex rel. *Physicians' Defense Company* v. *Laylin*, Secretary of State, 73 Ohio St. 90, 97, 76 N.E. 567; *State* ex rel. *Duffy* v. *Western Auto Supply Company*, 16 N.E. (2d) 256, 259.

[12] J. A. Park, *A system of the Law of Marine Insurance, with three chapters on bottomry, on insurance on lives, and on insurance against fire* (3d ed.; Dublin: James Moore, 1742), p. 1.

not recognized the operation of risk that the person who owns a house makes a wager with the insurer that the house will burn. Thus, if the house burns, the insured wins the bet, but if the house does not burn, the insurer wins. Such is not the situation. The owner of the house is continually faced with the risk that it may burn. By the payment of a small premium he shifts the burden of the risk to the insurer. The transaction creates no risk but shifts the burden from the person to whom it attaches to a carrier willing to bear it. A wager, on the other hand, of itself creates a risk. If a person bets upon the outcome of a horse race, an athletic contest, or any other like event in which he hitherto had no financial interest in the outcome, the risk is created when the bet is made. There is no shifting of the burden of risk but the actual creation of a risk.

The example of the dwelling serves to illustrate the principle underlying all forms of insurance. To write an insurance contract, if the contract is insurance in a real sense, the element of risk must exist as a condition precedent. This may be the possibility of loss because of liability claims through the operation of an automobile or through ownership of real estate, operation of a factory in which employees or public may be injured, or ownership of wealth in any type or class that is subject to loss or destruction. In the gambling transaction the situation is different. When the agreement is made, a risk is created for both parties where no risk existed before. In certain types of gambling, such as the lottery, the person who buys a ticket assumes a very large chance of losing a small amount (the price of his ticket) plus a very small chance of winning a large amount. There is no certainty in this transaction. The uncertainty lies in whether he will win or lose. If he wins the prize, of which there is a very small chance, there will be no loss. If he does not win the prize, he will lose the price of the ticket.[13] Prior to entering upon the gambling transaction there was no risk.

Reinsurance. The necessity for distributing the risk assumed by an insurer has led to the practice of reinsurance. It is apparent that an insurer will be in a much stronger position with 1,000 individual, widely distributed risks limited to $1,000 than it will be with a single risk of $1,000,000. It often happens that insurers wish to be in a position to afford their customers the maximum in service and protection. It would be awkward if the owner of a valuable property offered a fire insurer a $1,000,000 coverage and that insurer would accept only a small line and suggest to the customer that he shop about until he obtained the coverage he required. Insurers today are in a position to write large lines, and they are able to do this because, through the agency of reinsurance, they can transfer to other insurers as much

[13] Friedman and Savage, *op. cit.*, p. 279.

of the risk as they themselves do not feel that that can safely carry.

Reinsurance is the transferring of insurance business from one insurer to another. The insurer originating the business is termed the "ceding insurer," and the insurer to which the business is transferred by the originating insurer is known in the insurance business as the "reinsurer." The reinsurer assumes all or part of the liability contracted for by the ceding insurer under its contract issued directly to the insured. There is no direct relationship between the insured under the contract written by the ceding insurer and the reinsurers. The reinsurance contract is made by the reinsurer with the ceding insurer. The owner of the property covered by the contract issued to him by the ceding insurer has no interest in the reinsurance. Reinsurance contracts or treaties are typically written on a facultative basis or on an automatic basis. A facultative treaty requires that risks be submitted individually with supporting papers. The ceding insurer is not required to submit any particular proportion of its risks, and the reinsurer is not required to accept. Under an automatic treaty, which may be on an excess or quota-share basis, the primary insurer agrees to cede all or an agreed upon proportion of the excess of each risk beyond the line of retention in the case of an excess treaty and a specified proportion of each risk in the case of a quota-share treaty. The reinsurer agrees to accept the risk thus transferred.

For the purposes of underwriting, an insurer may wish to effect reinsurance for one of the following purposes: (1) the line is undesirable; (2) the line is too large; (3) the insurer wishes to adjust its surplus; (4) the insurer finds that it has a congestion of risks in a conflagration center; and (5) the insurer may wish to limit the effect of many small losses during a given period.

Line Is Undesirable. Under the first heading, the risk may have certain inherent characteristics that make it undesirable from an underwriting standpoint. This may be true because of the nature of the occupancy, the location or structure of the building, or serious neighboring hazards. If the underwriter were free to follow his own best judgment as it affects a particular risk, he would probably reject it, but in the business of insurance there are many collateral reasons why rejection is not always possible. In the first place, this particular risk may belong to a property owner who likewise owns a large number of other valuable properties and his insurance on these properties is actively solicited. Naturally, such a property owner expects the insurer that writes his best properties also to carry the more hazardous lines. The insurer that receives such a line undertakes to reduce its liability to a minimum through the agency of reinsurance. Likewise the insurer that is unwilling occasionally to carry a hazardous line for an agent cannot expect the same agent to give him the high-class, desirable business he obtains. For this reason, insurers are sometimes asked by the agents to carry lines that they would prefer not to have. Such lines, when accepted by insurers at the request of an agent, are known as "accommodation lines," and the liability is reduced by reinsurance.

Line Is Too Large. Excess lines often come to insurers. The insurance agent or broker is not interested primarily in the underwriting details but will make connection with insurers that can offer him adequate facilities for handling his business. Thus, the agent who secures a large line is not interested in the underwriting problems of the insurer but is primarily interested in knowing that the insurer can place the line. In the interests of service, insurers now are prepared to carry amounts far in excess of the amounts that prudent underwriting would permit, if the insurer itself were obliged to carry the entire liability. Contracts are issued and liability is distributed through the agency of reinsurance.

Insurer Wishes to Adjust Its Surplus. State laws set up reserve requirements which an insurer must maintain against all outstanding risks. In the event that this reserve falls below the legal minimum as the outgrowth of excessive losses or as the outgrowth of any other contingency, insurers may resort to the expediency of reinsurance to relieve themselves of a part of the reserve requirements and thereby enable themselves to comply with statutory requirements.

Insurer Has a Congestion of Risks. Insurers, as part of their underwriting procedure, segregate areas in the cities in which they accept business that they believe to be subject to a conflagration. Therefore, if an insurer receives a large number of individual risks located within the limits of this area, it may be, for underwriting purposes, in much the same position as it would be if it accepted a large line for a single insured in a single location. It becomes necessary to scrutinize every risk carefully with a view to determining the limit of liability assumed in any such area. The insurer will, as a result of this examination, determine the amount of liability it is willing to carry in this particular area and reinsure the rest.

Limiting the Effect of Many Small Losses. Although no catastrophe as such may have occurred, many small losses may result in financial problems for the insurer, and it may wish to protect against such an eventuality through reinsurance.

Insurable Risks. As a matter of theory, it might be stated that all risk is insurable. Because of the element of expense in carrying on the business of insurance, premiums are weighted with a charge to provide for this cost. In the case of risks that carry with them a threat of no great consequence, the cost of handling the business would make the rate prohibitive. In order to make a risk insurable, as a matter of business practice, the danger of loss must be sufficiently great to make the cost element a minor factor in the premium charged.

A second, and more important requisite of an insurable risk, is found in the necessity of its being of a nature that permits of statistical commensuration or, failing this, permits of a reasonable estimate based upon conclusions drawn from experience though predicated largely upon judgment. As a corollary to this requirement, the risk must be one of which there are a large number in existence, though insurers occasionally cover isolated risks concerning which there is no previous experience and when the chance of loss is measured by attendant circumstances. But most insurance is written to cover accidental hazards where losses may reasonably be expected and where mathematical treatment or judgment based upon experience permits a sufficiently close estimate of losses to make possible a workable estimate of their probable cost. When experience extends over a number of years and the number of risks is great enough, a premium can be computed that will assure a sum sufficient to pay losses and compensate the insurer; provide stability and permanence in the business; instill confidence in the insured; and, through the promise of stabilized earnings, assure the business of new capital when needed.

While the business of insurance places great emphasis upon statistical data and the use of the mathematical theory of probability, it is not an essential requirement that the probability of the occurrence of the contingency to be covered by insurance be definitely known. In certain of the older forms of insurance, future expectation on the basis of past experience can be computed with a fair degree of accuracy. When new insurance forms are instituted, it becomes necessary to make rates that are dependent upon what is sometimes called "underwriting judgment," and in some instances this is nothing more than an approximation or guess to be adjusted with the accumulation of experience.

In the field of aviation, in many instances, underwriters not only lack a true statistical base but are faced with the necessity of providing insurance that will keep pace with the rapid advances in the field. The advent of jet- and rocket-propelled aircraft, as well as rotary-wing aircraft, created a need for insurance in a field where statistical data were entirely lacking. In a civilian passenger aircraft an amount at risk may be as much as $2 million to $5 million or more. In a field so limited an adequate spread by type of risk is impossible. The insurer assumes the risk on the basis of its best judgment. A severe loss in a classification where the number of risks is limited requires the insurer to draw on the business as a whole to meet its payment. In accepting such risks, the underwriter, to use a Lloyd's phrase, underwrites "against the pot."

Property Insurance. "Property," as synonymous with "ownership," is the right to use and dispose of "an animal or thing" for a legitimate end without the interference of any other person. The "right of use" is the power recognized in law of putting a thing to any use that does not involve its transfer, destruction, or radical transformation. Positive law, as well as economic theory, conceives the right of ownership to carry with it the right of disposal. The modern concept of property does separate the various rights that may attach to a physical object. The owner of real estate in fee simple has the right of use as well as the right of disposal. He may lease the property for a term of years, in which case the lessee has the right of use as set forth in terms of the agreement. A better concept of the property idea is obtained if it is regarded as a "bundle of rights."

In the early agricultural stage of our economic development, property was mainly corporeal; that is, it consisted of physical things. Next, the concept of property was enlarged to include incorporeal property, or the rights involved in negotiable debts. For the purposes of distinguishing property insurance, every form of insurance is included in the category that has for its purpose the protection of persons against loss arising from the ownership or use of property as above defined.

Property insurance includes a great number and variety of coverages. Historically the groupings have included fire and allied lines, marine, aviation, and inland marine insurance. In addition, there are numerous miscellaneous forms including such items as the surety and fidelity coverages provided by bonding companies and the highly specialized forms of insurance, such as the insurance of real estate titles and of credit, that fall into none of the major subdivisions.

Damage to Insured's Property. Marine insurance was devised to furnish protection against the perils of the sea, and it included not only risks growing out of the operation of the forces of nature but those arising out of the acts of man, such as, for example, barratry or piracy. The ship, cargo, freight, profits, and other interests are exposed to a wide variety of hazards during a voyage. It was to protect the owner of the interest against loss that the first marine forms were designed. It soon became apparent that goods in transit were subjected to perils while on land at the beginning and end of a voyage, and the marine contract was extended to include these. It was but a step to extend the insurance idea to land shipments, and today there are two major branches of transportation insurance. The insurance of water-borne risks is known as "ocean marine insurance," and insurance covering risks of land transportation is known as "inland marine insurance."

In the fire group are included not only contracts insuring against loss by fire but fire insurers insure as well against loss from a number of perils closely allied to fire or from which fire may be expected to develop. In this classification are to be found contracts insuring against loss caused by such perils as explosion, earthquake, windstorm, and riot. Damage to property from earthquake, explosion, and similar perils frequently results in serious injury to the property insured, with further damage caused by fire following the disaster. It is not always a simple matter to determine the point where the destruction from one cause ends and that from another begins. To extend the business of fire insurance to cover both classes of risk was a logical step, and the so-called "side lines" form an important part of the business.

There are a number of insurance contracts that protect against loss of or damage to property that are not easily classified and are not properly fire or marine. Included in this group are such direct-loss contracts as burglary and robbery insurance, plate glass insurance, and insurance covering property damage to steam boilers, electrical machinery, steam turbines, and similar items. Comparatively recently many of the traditional coverages have been combined into packages or multiple line insurance contracts, and the insured is able to secure protection from a wide variety of perils in a single document. Because of the rapid growth of this form of insurance, classifications long in use in the insurance business may no longer be fully applicable.[14]

Liability Insurance. The owner of property can readily comprehend the risk of loss occasioned by its possible physical damage or destruction. He is not so readily aware of the fact that he may lose all or part of his property as the outgrowth of its ownership, maintenance, or use. If the property owner infringes upon the civil rights of another, he is liable under the law for damages to the injured party.

There is one serious feature in connection with the liability risk that deserves most careful attention. In connection with the physical destruction of a piece of property, the owner of the property knows the limit of the direct loss. This limit is the value of the property. For example, in the case of an automobile valued at $3,000, if the automobile is destroyed by fire, stolen, or otherwise damaged, the owner's loss is limited to $3,000. If, on the other hand, as a result of operating the car, the owner seriously injures another and the injury is of a permanent nature, the owner of the car may be found liable in damages for a sum many times the value of the automobile. Verdicts running as high as $100,000 or more are to be found in the files of every insurer. Not infrequently they are very much greater.[15] Nor is the liability hazard limited to the ownership and operation of automobiles. In any situation connected with the ownership, maintenance, and operation of property in which the owner or operator may,

---

[14] See Chapter 2 for a discussion of the meaning of multiple line insurance.

[15] Indicative of the nature of disabling injuries from which liability claims arise, see "Verdicts or Awards Exceeding $50,000," published regularly in the *NACCA Law Journal*, compiled by the editors under the supervision of Melvin M. Belli. A verdict of $358,000 awarded to an 18-year old youth injured while diving off a pier into shallow water is indicative of the uncertainty with respect to liability verdicts (9 *NACCA Law Journal* 251; 10 *NACCA Law Journal* 263). In catastrophes involving many injuries the extent of the liability may involve millions.

because of his negligence, cause injury to persons or damage to property, the liability risk is ever present. As a result of an accident in which negligence of the owner of the property is a factor, the entire resources of the property owner may be wiped out in a single verdict. In addition, it is possible in some situations that future earning capacity for many years will be utilized in part in the liquidation of an old damage claim.

Sources of Liability Claims. A liability claim develops as the result of the invasion of the rights of others. A legal right is defined as the power or capacity residing in one person of controlling the action of others, with the assent and assistance of the state. The invasion of such a right is a legal wrong. The wrong may be criminal or civil. A criminal wrong is an injury involving the public at large and is punishable by the state. The action on the part of the state to effect a conviction is termed a "criminal action." Civil wrongs fall into one of two classes: (1) torts, and (2) breaches of contract. Torts are wrongs independent of contract, such, for example, as assault, fraud, libel, slander, and negligence. A breach of contract is the unjustifiable refusal or neglect of a party legally bound to perform the duties imposed by contract. While the state takes action with respect to crimes, civil injuries are remedied by court action instituted by the injured party termed a "civil action." The remedy is, normally, the award of damages. The consequences of a crime are not insurable, but the liability for damages growing out of a civil wrong may be covered.

Breach of Contract. In connection with sales or a contract to sell, the law imposes certain obligations termed "implied warrantees."

It is the law in most jurisdictions that where a buyer, expressly or by implications, makes known to the seller the particular purpose for which goods are required, and it appears that the buyer relies on the skill of the seller or his judgment, there is an implied warranty that the goods are reasonably fit for the purpose for which they were sold. This rule applies whether the seller grew or manufactured the goods or whether they were purchased by him from a supplier. Thus, in any situation where a merchant recommends goods to a customer or selects them for him, there is always a possibility that the seller may be held liable for any injury attributable to the goods so recommended or selected.

Aside from breach of implied warranty a tort liability may develop in connection with sales. A seller may be held liable on the ground of negligence if the thing sold is imminently dangerous to life or health, and, owing to negligent manufacture or construction, injury follows. Again, liability may follow if such products are supplied to a user without giving proper notice of their dangerous qualities. The dividing line between liability growing out of a breach of implied warranty

UNDERWRITING; PRINC + PRAC
ROBERT B HOLTOM
CINCINNATI, NAT UND CO 73
HG8051.H64 4TH FLOOR

MECHANICS of UNDERWR 83
ROB ROSENMAN
KF1440.M4 LAW NY NY

and liability attributable to negligence is not always clear. The point here to be emphasized lies in the fact that the seller of the product may be held liable for injuries that the product may cause after it leaves his hands.

Negligence. Negligence is a tort. Much of the liability imposed by law stems from accidents attributable to negligence. If negligence can be shown to be the proximate cause of an injury to another, the negligent party is liable to the injured party for damages. Negligence is the failure on the part of an individual to exercise the proper degree of care required by circumstances. It may consist in the failure to do what was required under the circumstances, or it may consist in the doing of something that ought not to have been done. Behavior in any circumstances that fails to measure up to that expected of a careful, prudent person in like circumstances constitutes negligence. Faulty judgment may result in liability for negligence, even though the motive behind the act was the best.

If the negligent party acts in the capacity of agent or servant of another, the responsibility may attach to the wrongdoer himself, or the principal or master may be held liable. This point is a matter of tremendous importance because it makes the owner or operator of a property liable personally for the torts of those he employs, if the tort is committed while the agent or servant is acting within the apparent scope of his authority or engaged in the business entrusted to his care. The far-reaching consequences of the rule become at once apparent when it is recognized that the master or principal may be held liable for the acts of his agent or servant if the wrongful act is committed in the course of his employment, even though such act may be a deliberate violation of express instructions. If the owner of a business specifically forbids any of his employees to use their personally owned automobiles in connection with his business, and for their own convenience they disregard the instruction and use their own cars, an accident leading to serious consequences could involve the owner of the business. His liability for damages might be so great as to wipe out all his holdings and bring him face to face with bankruptcy.

SOCIAL SIGNIFICANCE OF INSURANCE

The institution of insurance, as a device for providing certainty in the area to which it is applied, has important social significance. Security is a basic requirement of any economic system that may be expected to endure. The drive for security evidences itself in a desire for personal health and well-being, stability, and the assurance of sufficient resources to enable the individual to maintain his position in the social order not only for the time being but for the future both for himself and for the members of his immediate family. The possession of savings and property is regarded as a means for effecting this security. Insecurity is threatened if the property accumulations, in whatever form they may be, are liable to destruction without any immediate agency for recouping the loss.

Without security there would be a great reluctance on the part of owners of capital to permit that capital to be ventured in hazardous undertakings. If they did permit the capital to find an outlet in such undertakings, the return they would demand for its use would be so great as to increase costs enormously. In almost every form of business enterprise, insurance devices have been effected whereby serious risk is reduced and capital may safely be invested in an enterprise otherwise fraught with danger. Indeed, had the institution of insurance not been devised in a society where free enterprise prevails, some other method of accomplishing the objective would have been necessary.

Insurance provides a basis for credit because owners of capital would be as reluctant to lend it, if it were liable to loss, as they would be to invest it in a hazardous enterprise on their own accounts. Perhaps the most widely known example, because it touches almost everyone at one time or another, is the use of fire, windstorm, and other kindred contracts to cover dwelling houses against loss while they are being paid for. Lending institutions that provide purchase money for homes are universally insistent that the home buyer and borrower protect the property offered with adequate insurance as security for the loan.

Not a direct function of insurance but a matter, nevertheless, of no small significance is the accumulation of insurance resources by means of which large amounts of capital are gathered together. This capital is invested in the basic industries such as public utilities, railroads, and industrials, as well as in real estate.

An indirect consequence of insurance is to be found in the fact that it serves as a stimulus for the installation of protective devices and the elimination of risk. Even though insurance may replace the value of property destroyed to the owner, the property itself can never be restored to society, and such destruction represents a net social loss. Property insurers encourage the installation of protective devices and the use of fire-resistive materials in construction. They have studied the best methods of fire protection, and building codes have been prepared with a view to minimizing fire losses. Liability insurers regularly inspect insured properties, safety devices are tested periodically, and every known device that will have the effect of eliminating a loss is recommended.

All these factors have the effect of increasing business efficiency. With the reduction of risk in business undertakings, there is a vast flow of capital into avenues where it would otherwise be unavailable. With the advent of capital in abundance, a maximum degree of efficiency is essential to survival. Competition tends to reduce prices and eliminate the inefficient producers. The net result is social and economic benefit.

The growth of the business of insurance since the turn of the 20th century has placed it well in the forefront of the important commercial enterprises of the nation. It has successfully survived war, depression, catastrophe, and panic and forms one of the most stable sections of our economic system. The vastness of the institution and its far-reaching importance, a matter of common knowledge to those engaged in the business, is scarcely realized by those who have not troubled themselves to investigate. Entire districts in some of the larger cities are devoted exclusively to insurance, and the ramifications of these financial centers extend to large communities in the country as well as to some of the remotest corners of the globe.

RISK MANAGEMENT[16]

Risk management may be defined as the process for conserving the "earning power and assets" of the firm (or the individual) "by minimizing the financial effect of accidental losses."[17] The risk manager, whose responsibility it is to manage risk for business firms or other organizations, must (1) identify possible types of accidental losses, (2) analyze the possible financial impact on the firm should a fortuitous event occur, (3) recommend the appropriate action to take in order to protect against the possible financial consequences of accidental loss, and (4) relate risk and loss control to cost control. Although these are the major functions of the risk manager, he is also responsible for the maintenance of appropriate records, for coordinating the activities of the risk department with other divisions of the organization, for submitting proper reports, and for the adequate staffing and supervising of the work of his associates.

Organizing for Risk Management. The extensiveness of the risk management function varies considerably among business and non-business organizations. Most large businesses have either risk or insurance managers and the risk (or insurance) department is generally divided into a property and liability insurance section and a loss control (safety and prevention) section. In fairly recent times employee benefits have (in a limited way) become the responsibility

[16] The treatment of risk management here is necessarily brief. For a detailed discussion of this approach see R. S. Mehr and B. A. Hedges, *Risk Management in the Business Enterprise* (Homewood, Illinois: Richard D. Irwin, Inc., 1963) and C. A. Williams, Jr. and R. M. Heins, *Risk Management and Insurance* (New York: McGraw-Hill Book Co., 1964).

[17] James Cristy "Selling Insurance to Risk Managers," *The National Insurance Buyer,* XIII (September 1966), p. 34.

of the risk manager,[18] although historically these benefits were usually managed by the industrial relations division or the personnel department. The risk manager most often reports to the treasurer or the controller of the firm. It is fairly rare for the risk function to be separated from the financial function, even though there is some logic to having a separate department or to associating risk with the management function generally. Most risk departments are centralized, although foreign operations may be handled on a decentralized basis.

Risk Policy. Typically the risk manager is expected to deal with pure or static-type risks and his planning responsibilities are usually limited to risks of these types. Although many pure risks may be transferred to insurers, the risk manager is not limited to insurance as the only tool of risk management. Risks may be assumed or prevented, as well as transferred, and in some situations techniques such as hedging and contracting out may be helpful.

Prevention of loss is an important part of the risk manager's responsibility.[19] Complete elimination of risk through prevention is often unattainable, but protective efforts of various types are usually effective in reducing losses and are a part of all risk control programs. Closely related to prevention and protection, in the sense that they are efforts to eliminate risk, are business forecasting and research. Marketing research is an example of a risk-reduction type of program, although risk managers are not responsible for this activity.

Risk assumption may be on a planned or unplanned basis and, if the former, may be funded or unfunded. Some losses may be paid for out of current funds and little or no planning may take place. Many large firms have adopted a policy of planned no-insurance, wherein they are prepared to withstand losses that do not exceed a pre-determined, substantial figure. Thus, some firms may be willing to pay liability losses, for example, out of current funds if they amount to no more than, say, one million dollars. Risks that might result in losses beyond that figure would be insured. The use of the funding technique for dealing with risk assumption is illustrated by self-insurance. This technique, if it is to be carried out according to basic principles, requires funding as well as a sufficient number and distribution of risks to permit the successful operation of the law of large numbers.

The attitude of the firm toward risk management may be embodied in an official policy statement. This statement ordinarily outlines policy in relation to prevention and safety, risk assumption, and the use of insurance. The policy should be agreed upon by the risk manager, his supervisors, and the board of directors. In those situa-

[18] See David A. Ivry, "The Corporate Insurance Manager and Employee Benefit Plans," *The Journal of Risk and Insurance*, XXXIII (March, 1966), pp. 1–17.

[19] See pages 6 and 7 for a more complete discussion of prevention.

tions where risks are transferred to insurers, the risk manager has the responsibility for knowing types of coverage and for working effectively with agents, brokers, and insurance consultants.

Risk Identification and Analysis. Systematic risk identification and analysis may be carried out in a number of ways. Elaborate schedules have been prepared that enable the risk manager to identify and record sources of accidental loss. Flow charts have been constructed for the production process that help in identifying situations that might cause loss. Accounting statements such as the balance sheet and income statement may be utilized in identifying the source and magnitude of possible loss. Procedures for valuing property are available and are used in conjunction with risk analysis. Careful work in analyzing risks does much toward assuring the effectiveness of the risk management program.

Education for Risk Management. Until quite recently there was no formal educational program available to prospective risk managers. Many of them came from a background of insurance sales or from the home offices of insurers. In 1965 the Insurance Institute of America established a series of six examinations leading to a Diploma in Risk Management. The six examinations cover the following subjects: (1) General Principles of Insurance; (2) Principles of Fire, Marine, and Allied Lines Insurance; (3) Principles of Casualty Insurance and Surety Bonding; (4) Principles of Risk Management; (5) Practices in Risk Management; and (6) Management and Finance. Study programs and outlines are available to assist students in their preparation for the examinations. This program is a substantial part of the professional development of risk managers.

FOR DISCUSSION

1. X, a high school boy, drives a stripped-down automobile for his own personal pleasure. The car has a resale value not in excess of $50. He obtains summer employment in a bank as messenger and is forbidden by his immediate superiors to use his automobile in the course of his work. He disregards these instructions frequently. Today the bank learns that X has been involved in an accident that resulted in the death of three persons. Has the bank any responsibility? If so, under what circumstances?
2. It is stated that the presence of risk is a condition precedent for insurance. Explain the meaning of this statement.
3. Manslaughter is a crime. B, in driving recklessly, kills C, and is held for manslaughter. In the circumstances, is B liable for damages to C's estate? Explain on the basis that manslaughter is a crime.
4. Willett, is his classic study *The Economic Theory of Risk and Insurance*, states: "*Risk,* in the sense in which we are to use the term, is, so to speak, the objectified uncertainty as to the occurrence of an unde-

sired event. It varies with the uncertainty and not with the degree of probability." Explain.

5. Clauses 100 to 103 of the code of Hammurabi (John's translation) read as follows:

   100. . . . The interests of the money as much as he took, he shall write down, and when he has numbered his days he shall answer his merchant.
   101. . . . If where he has gone he has not seen prosperity he shall make up and return the money he took and the agent shall give to the merchant.
   102. . . . If a merchant has given to the agent money as a favour and where he has seen loss the full amount of money he shall return to the trader.
   103. . . . If while he goes on his journey the enemy has made him quit whatever he was carrying, the agent shall swear by the name of God and go free.

   This is used as a basis for the contention that a contract similar to insurance was known to the Babylonians. Explain.
6. The following once appeared in a textbook on economics: "Let us now consider the workings of Insurance. In this case also the contract is a wager. A house-owner pays an insurer fifty dollars in return for which he is to receive five thousand dollars in case his house burns down within a specified time; just as he might pay a book-maker and receive five thousand in case a specified horse wins a race." Explain the fallacy in the statement.
7. There are said to be certain conditions necessary, as far as risk is concerned, in order that a system of insurance function successfully. Discuss.
8. When it is said that insurance is a contract of indemnity what is meant?
9. In *Brownell* v. *Board of Education*, 239 New York 369, it is stated: "In common parlance the buildings are insured; but everyone who stops to consider the nature of the insurance contract understands that they are not." Explain.
10. In placing an insurance contract upon one's life how can one place a money value upon it? If one cannot adequately place a money value, why is not the life insurance contract a gambling contract?
11. A concert artist contends that if for any reason an engagement is broken, there will be a substantial loss of earnings. He wishes insurance against this contingency. Is the risk insurable?
12. There is said to be a relationship between knowledge and risk. Explain.
13. It has been stated that the economic burden of risk may evidence itself in (*a*) the discouragement of enterprise, (*b*) the unproductive use of capital, (*c*) increased costs of economic goods, and (*d*) economic demoralization of individuals with an attendant unfavorable impact on the community. Explain.
14. A group of small boys crowded the sidewalk in front of a grocery store to solicit customers to carry packages. A customer was knocked down by a small wagon owned by one of the boys and seriously injured. The storekeeper disclaims liability. Do you think he has any responsibility?

15. During the publicity given to building up a large army and navy to defend America, it was frequently stated that the vast appropriations amounted to insurance of the security of America. If this is so, in this case, who is the insurer?
16. In effecting reinsurance, the underwriter is concerned not only with the problem of the individual risk but also with the possibilities of conflagration. There are, of course, conflagrations possible that cannot be foreseen. Outstanding in this class is that of the Texas City explosion. However, there are areas throughout the country well known to all insurance underwriters that are believed to be subject to catastrophes. Mention and discuss some of these.
17. The following statement has been made: "Insurance today is an actual guarantee of the perpetuity of existence of industrial and commercial life." Discuss.
18. The disastrous flood in the spring of 1953 in Holland might well have been the cause of great concern to marine underwriters. The possibility of substantial claims in the aggregate from a concentration of cargo shipments, each of a value that called for no reinsurance, is evident. The inundation of a single warehouse would unquestionably involve thousands of marine contracts. How do marine underwriters meet such a situation?
19. All the members of a lodge are insured under an accident contract. Each year a steamboat excursion is held by the organization. From an underwriting standpoint, what is the disadvantage of a large number of insureds together on a boat?
20. Distinguish between the use of reinsurance for agency convenience and as an aid to underwriting.
21. For the purposes of insurance underwriting, indicate the principal reasons for making use of reinsurance.
22. If a risk is undesirable for any reason, what justification is to be found in transferring part of the undesirable line to a reinsurer?

CHAPTER · 2

Development of Property and Liability Insurance

The origin of the idea of insurance is clouded in obscurity, although its development is probably coeval with the earliest development of commerce. Risk bearing, like many of the other ideas that contribute to the safety, comfort, and happiness of the human race, is a development of the process of man's adjustment to his environment. "Man is constrained to adopt the principle of Adjustment, because the Forces of Nature are external to and independent of his will. They may be managed but cannot be disobeyed."[1] The desire for security is recognized by sociologists as one of the basic motives affecting human conduct and has been termed by psychologists "one of the preponderant tendencies in man."[2] It is part of the process of preservation, and it recalls the words of Burke who said that the passions conversant about the preservation of the individual, turning chiefly on pain and danger, are the most powerful of all the passions.[3]

In view of man's need for security, it is not surprising to find the germ of the idea of insurance making its appearance early.[4] The idea was slow to develop, and not until very recent years did it become of great commercial importance. The principle has gradually, steadily, and definitely established itself in the economic structure and has spread its protecting influence to every form of human activity, to all classes and conditions of people, and to the furthermost corners of the globe. It has become a foundation stone of credit and a stabilizer of business, contributing to the wealth, prosperity, high standards of living, and luxuries we now enjoy.

---

[1] Argyll, *The Reign of Law,* chap. ii.

[2] K. Young, *Social Psychology* (New York: A. A. Knopf, Inc., 1930), p. 606.

[3] E. Burke, *On the Sublime and Beautiful,* Part I, sec. 6.

[4] C. F. Trennery, *The Origin and Early History of Insurance* (London: P. S. King & Son, Ltd., 1926), pp. 45 ff. and 107 ff.

When consideration is given to the nicety with which modern business is conducted; the smoothness of operation of the vast, intricate, and delicately balanced system of credits and exchanges; the huge sums of capital invested in every conceivable enterprise, with trade, commerce, and industry bursting through the narrower confines of the past and expanding to ventures whose sizes seem limitless and are world-wide in their extent—in considering these, no undeserved tribute is paid to insurance if attributed to it is a fair share of the credit for the successful operation of this complex, modern business structure.

MARINE AND INLAND MARINE INSURANCE[5]

Transportation risks were the first to receive the attention of the insurers. Aside from the contracts of bottomry and respondentia, which are very ancient indeed, it is not quite clear when the business of transportation insurance became established as a commercial practice. There is reason to believe that it was well established in the 13th century, and numerous ordinances applied specifically to marine insurance have been handed down from the early part of the 14th century. The earliest English contract of marine insurance known today was dated in London, August 5, 1555, and insured the "Santa Cruz." From this early origin, ocean marine insurance has continued its expansion to meet the needs of ocean transportation.

From the original plan of insuring goods against the total loss of the vessel, ocean marine insurance has passed through a gradual period of evolution. First, there was included within the coverage partial losses growing out of sea perils while the goods were aboard ship. It became apparent to shippers that such contracts presented them with a tendon of Achilles. With adequate marine coverage for goods while aboard ship, damage by fire or otherwise on the docks might mean a total loss. To meet this need, marine coverages were extended to include insurance while on docks or quays. It was but a natural step to make the coverage effective at the warehouse of the shipper and terminate at the warehouse at destination. These developments brought into use the "warehouse-to-warehouse clause" and brought ocean marine insurance ashore. Ocean marine contracts are now commonly written to protect merchandise while in transit and include

[5] Inland marine coverages have expanded greatly in recent years and this branch of insurance is now sometimes referred to as the "catch all" of the industry. Marine and inland marine insurance are considered together in this section because they both relate to the risk of transportation. Chronologically inland marine insurance developed fairly late in the history of insurance and was introduced after fire insurance and certain other property contracts had become a major segment of the insurance industry.

the hazards of both land and water conveyances between the warehouse at point of origin and the warehouse at point of destination.

Common Law Liability of a Common Carrier. The liability of common carriers is very ancient, indeed, and comes to us as a part of our inheritance of the common law. Early decisions in the United States were based upon precedent set by the English law.[6] Briefly, it is the duty of a common carrier to transport safely the goods entrusted to it. By virtue of the law he is made an insurer against failure to perform this duty with the exception that he is not liable for losses caused by the public enemy or acts of God.[7]

The doctrine is a harsh one, and its enforcement so stringent that common carriers on land actually regard themselves as insurers of the property entrusted to their custody. This is so because the common law has been modified only in a few respects. A carrier now is still not responsible for a loss occasioned by "an act of God," that is, something which is caused by the exclusive operation of the forces of nature, uninfluenced by the power of man. Nor is he held responsible for a loss caused by an order of the public authority or one occasioned by a public enemy. Acts or defaults of the shipper are exempted, nor is the carrier responsible for losses growing out of the inherent vice or nature of the goods. In no instance may a common carrier be freed from liability because of its own negligence.

Because of this stringent liability, shippers have been accustomed to look to the carrier for reimbursement for loss or damage. While the carrier remains responsible, developments in recent years have tended not to curtail the principle of liability but to limit the amount for which the carrier may be held.

Limitation upon Liability of Carriers by Sea. It has long been recognized that the perils of the sea and the dangers to navigation create risks for which the carrier could not equitably be held responsible if they were the occasion of loss. In this country, the

---

[6] In a widely quoted English case the early doctrine has been thus expressed: "The law charges this person thus entrusted to carry goods, against all events, but Acts of God, and of the enemies of the King. For though the force be never so great, as if an irresistible multitude of people should rob him, nevertheless he is chargeable. And this is a politic establishment, contrived by the policy of the law, for the safety of all persons, the necessity of whose affairs oblige them to trust these sorts of persons, that they may be safe in their ways of dealing; for else these carriers might have an opportunity of undoing all persons that had any dealings with them, by combining with thieves, etc., and yet doing it in such a clandestine manner as would not be possible to be discovered. And this is the reason the law is founded upon in that point." *Coggs* v. *Bernard*, 2 Lord Raymond 909; 1 Smith's Leading Cases 369. Since the early English decisions form part of our inheritance of common law, this citation represents an early formulation of the principle as carried forward in American law.

[7] *Bank of Kentucky* v. *Adams Express Company,* 93 U.S. 174.

Harter Act exempts the owner of any vessel, while transporting property to or from a United States port, from responsibility for loss or damage growing out of faults or errors in navigation, losses arising from the perils of the sea or other navigable waters, and acts of God. The Maritime Law Committee of the International Law Association framed a set of rules now known as "The Hague Rules." It set forth the risks to be assumed by sea carriers under a bill of lading. These rules have been passed into law in their essentials and are widely followed by many countries. Under their terms, the carrier is bound before and at the beginning of a voyage to exercise due diligence to make the ship seaworthy; properly man, equip, and supply the ship; and make the holds, refrigerating and cool chambers, and all other parts of the ship in which goods are carried fit and safe for their reception, carriage, and preservation. The carrier is bound to provide for the proper and careful handling, loading, stowage, carriage, custody, care, and unloading of the goods carried.[8] The rules then provide that the ship shall not be liable for loss or damage arising or resulting from unseaworthiness unless caused by want of due diligence on the part of the carrier to make the ship seaworthy and to see that the ship is properly manned, equipped, and supplied.

It is specifically stipulated that neither the carrier nor the ship shall be responsible for loss or damage arising or resulting from: act, neglect, or default of the master, mariner, pilot, or the servants of the carrier in the navigation or in the management of the ship; fire; perils, dangers, and accidents of the sea or other navigable waters; act of God; act of war; act of public enemies; arrest or restraint of princes, rules, or people, or seizure under legal process quarantine restrictions; act or omission of the shipper or owner of the goods, his agent or representative; strikes, lockouts, stoppage, or restraint of labor from any cause, whether partial or general; riots and civil commotion; saving or attempting to save life or property at sea; inherent defect, quality, or vice of the goods; insufficiency of packing; insufficiency or inadequacy of marks; latent defects not discoverable by due diligence; any other cause arising without the actual fault or privity of the carrier, or without the fault or neglect of the agents, servants, or employees of the carrier. Other immunities of a technical nature include freedom from liability or loss resulting from deviations to save or attempt to save life or property at sea. Provision is made for limiting liability on each package or unit unless a declared value is inserted in the bill of lading. There is also a section providing that the carrier may destroy or render innocuous without liability goods of inflammable or explosive material unless the nature and character have

---

[8] The Hague Rules, 1921, art. III.

been described in writing by the shipper to the carrier before shipment and the carrier has consented to the shipment.[9]

The Hague Rules have no direct bearing upon the contract of marine insurance. Owing to the fact that when the rules are followed the carrier may issue a bill of lading incorporating all or a substantial part of the rights and immunities set forth in the rules, they are of importance to the shipper as indicative of the risks he may be asked to assume, or, if he wishes protection, to cover himself through the purchase of a marine insurance contract.

Released Value Bills of Lading. It was a natural development that carriers would undertake to lessen the severe burden of the common law liability of public carriers. This they undertook from the earliest days of the promulgation of the doctrine. In England, notices were posted limiting the liability of the carrier and indicating that full liability would be assumed only upon the payment of additional charges. In England, the method was held adequate to limit liability, but the situation continued generally unsatisfactory and not until 1854 was the matter definitely settled with the passage by Parliament of the Railway and Canal Traffic Act which provided that the common law liability of carriers could be limited only by a written contract with the shipper. In order to effect this limitation, the carrier was required to accept a lower freight rate than would have been the case had it assumed the full common law liability. Thus, it was early recognized that the carrier acted in a twofold capacity: first, that of providing transportation, and second, that of providing insurance against the hazards of transportation. If the insurance risk was lessened, that part of the rate which represented an insurance premium would naturally be reduced.

In the United States, for a period, developments were the reverse of those in England. The carriers undertook to issue bills of lading limiting their common law liability and limiting their liability for losses that were the outgrowth of negligence, as well. Among other provisions, it was customary to deny liability for loss if it occurred beyond the limits of the line of the carrier issuing the bill of lading. This was the source of great confusion, since it frequently was impossible for the shipper to determine exactly in whose hands the damage occurred. In 1906 the Interstate Commerce Act of 1887 was amended to hold the initial carrier liable for loss or damage caused by it or for loss, damage, or injury to such property caused by "any common carrier, railroad, or transportation company to which such property may be delivered or over whose line or lines such property may pass."[10] This amendment, known as the Carmack Amendment,

[9] *Ibid.*, art. IV.

[10] For a discussion of the effects of the Carmack Amendment see *Adams Express Co.* v. *Croninger*, 226 U.S. 491.

provided that "no contract, receipt, rule or regulation shall exempt such common carrier, railroad, or transportation company, from the liability imposed by the Act."[11]

The Carmack Amendment established the liability of the carrier for any loss, injury, or damage caused by it or a succeeding carrier to whom the property may be delivered. It did not clear up the matter of including provisions limiting liability in the bills of lading. An effort was made to clear this point by the adoption in 1915 of the first Cummins Amendment, which provided that the liability of the common carrier was to be for the loss in full notwithstanding any limitations of liability or limitations of the amount of the recovery set forth in the bill of lading or any other agreement. The effect of this law was to make the initial carrier fully liable for loss or injury caused on its own lines or the lines of succeeding carriers. By making contracts limiting liability for loss unlawful, the initial carrier became an insurer for the full amount of the shipment. Up to and including the enactment of the first Cummins Amendment, the trend in legislation was away from the limitation of liability, with the result that the common carrier became an insurer as well as a carrier. This situation was found to be generally unsatisfactory, and the second Cummins Amendment, which became effective in 1916, completely reversed the position taken by the first Cummins Amendment by permitting limitations of liability or limitations to the amount of recovery, provided rates were predicated upon the values declared by the shipper. An exception was made in the case of livestock. Here it has been definitely established by legislation that the carriers may limit their liability for loss or damage to shipments through the terms of the bill of lading.

With the advent of released liability bills of lading, certain

[11] The Supreme Court of the United States set forth the conditions as they existed at the time of the passage of the Carmack Amendment in the following terms: "Some states allowed carriers to exempt themselves from all or a part of the common law liability by rule, regulation, or contract; others did not. The Federal courts sitting in the various states were following the local rule, a carrier being held liable in one court when, under the same state of facts, he would be exempt from liability in another. Hence, this branch of interstate commerce was being subjected to such a diversity of legislative and judicial holding that it was practically impossible for a shipper engaged in a business that extended beyond the confines of his own state, or a carrier whose lines were extensive, to know, without considerable investigation and trouble, and even then oftentimes with but little certainty, what would be the carrier's actual responsibility as to goods delivered to it for transportation from one state to another. The congressional action has made an end to this diversity, for the national law is paramount and supersedes all state laws as to the rights and liabilities and exemptions created by such transactions. This was doubtless the purpose of the law; and this purpose will be effectuated, and not impaired or destroyed, by the state courts obeying and enforcing the provisions of the Federal Statute where applicable to the Act in such cases as shall come before them." *Southern Power Co.* v. *Crenshaw Bros.*, 5 Ga. App. 675; 63 S.E. 865, cited by the United States Supreme Court in *Adams Express Co.* v. *Croninger*, 226 U.S. 491.

commodities involving high values were frequently shipped with little or no protection. Shipments such as antiques, raw silk, oriental rugs, and other such items run to large sums, and the problem of their protection is a matter of serious concern to the railroad. Under a released liability bill, the insurance risk is reduced to a minimum. Indicative of the problem that carriers face and the necessity for being on guard against new hazards, in the spring of 1940 certain of the railroads engaged in the transportation of airplane engines filed a new freight tariff with the Interstate Commerce Commission which would more than double the then existing rate on engines. It was the contention of the carriers that the proposed increase was necessary because engines, being extremely valuable and subject to sabotage, placed a responsibility upon the railroads greater than was compensated for by the rate. Indicative of the fact that the increase represented an insurance premium, the carriers expressed a willingness to transport the engines without an increased rate under released liability bills of lading. Unquestionably, the released liability bill of lading appealed to the carrier apprehensive of insurance risks; and to the shipper, on the other hand, the lower rate appealed. The shipper, however, did not in all cases recognize the extent to which his shipment was subject to his own risk.

Railroad Shipments Involving Transportation by Water. When a shipment of goods originates with a railroad company and transportation by water is a necessary part of the trip, the question presents itself as to the liability of the initial carrier, if losses occur while the shipment is waterborne. It was natural that carriers should wish to take advantage of the benefits of laws governing movements by water. Early interpretations of the Cummins Amendments made no change in the liability of the carrier, so far as the waterborne portion of the journey was concerned, if damage occurred to shipments moving under through rates and involving sea transportation as part of the journey. While the question was still in doubt, the Transportation Act of 1920 was passed. Its terms provided "that if the loss, damage or injury occurs while the property is in the custody of a carrier by water the liability of such carrier shall be determined by and under the laws and regulations applicable to transportation by water, and the liability of the initial carrier shall be the same as that of such carrier by water."[12] The act does not include lighterage in or across rivers, harbors, or lakes, when performed by or on behalf of rail carriers as "water carriage."

As a result of the situation as it now stands, it is important that the shipper know to what extent there is liability on the part of the carrier, if the shipment moves part way by water, for any loss that

[12] Transportation Act of 1920, Sec. 20.

may occur during the waterborne portion of the trip. It sometimes follows, as a result of competition, that when part of the shipment is carried by water, the carrier provides insurance for the entire trip. Some rates are quoted as insured, and, in such instances, the carrier provides marine insurance for the account of the shipper and the charge therefor is incorporated in the through rate. In other cases, the rates do not provide for marine insurance, although it frequently happens that the shipper may declare a value on all bills of lading and request insurance, in which case the insurance charge is included in the rate cover provided through an open contract carried by the steamship company. It follows that a shipper may not know exactly the extent to which his shipment is protected, unless he carefully studies the tariff to determine whether marine insurance is provided for the waterborne portion of the trip.

Express Shipments. There is a tendency to feel that shipments by express entail a greater liability on the part of the carrier than is the case in freight shipments. Express companies issue a receipt when goods are delivered, and this contains the agreement between the shipper and the carrier in the matter of liability. Express companies have long limited their liability with respect to specific shipments. The shipper has the alternative of paying a higher rate than is required under a limited liability receipt and in return having the express company assume liability for the full value of the shipment. The courts, in passing upon the question, have recognized that the compensation of the carrier is to be commensurate with the risk involved. By limiting the amount recoverable in case of loss or damage to an agreed value and charging a rate proportionate to the value of the property transported, the carrier takes into consideration not only the bulk, weight, and character of the shipment but the value of the property as well.

Liability of Carrier as a Warehouseman. When goods in the hands of a common carrier have reached their destination and have been placed in reasonable safety, the status of the carrier changes to that of a warehouseman. The laws in all jurisdictions are not the same as to precisely when the change becomes effective. Under the Uniform Storage Tariff, the carrier is obligated to send notices of arrival to the consignee and is liable as a carrier or insurer for a period of 48 hours after the first 7:00 A.M. after notice of arrival has been sent to the consignee. In some states no such notice is required. After the expiration of the period set forth limiting responsibility as a carrier, the carrier then becomes a warehouseman and is liable only for losses growing out of negligence. The difference in status is clarified by the knowledge that such losses as are occasioned by fire, burglary, or other hazards that involve no negligence would afford the shipper no protection if his goods were in the hands of a warehouseman, whereas while in the custody of a carrier the common law liability of the carrier would attach. The status of the protection that the shipper may expect from the carrier can automatically change. Failure to provide adequate protection to meet such situations may entail a serious loss to the shipper.

Water Carriers in Competition with Railroads. There has been a tendency for shipping companies engaged in coastwise and intercoastal shipments to provide marine insurance in connection with shipments received so that they would be in a position to compete with the railroads on the basis of security offered the shipper. A confusing situation develops when the same companies provide insurance in connection with shipments to certain designated ports and no insurance in connection with shipments to other ports. It is conceivable that a shipment of 25 automobiles out of New York to be delivered at several different designations could go in some instances under insured rates and in other instances uninsured. In case the ship that carried the automobiles was lost, the carrier would be liable only for those automobiles shipped under insured rates. This situation has tended to create some confusion in the minds of those not thoroughly conversant with shipping practices and tariffs.

The Motor Carrier. The situation with respect to the transportation of shipments by motor carrier is somewhat more complex than is the case of rail transportation. Motor carriers that fall into the category of common carriers have the same liabilities as do other common carriers. Unlike the railroads, however, which are all common carriers, truckmen are not all so classified, and the liability of the truckmen with respect to cargoes differs with their classifications.

With the first appearance of automobiles in the transportation field, there was no regulation of their activities. With the improvement of highways, motor trucks extended their activities to the end that trucking lines were established that became important competitors of the railroads. When it became apparent that a substantial volume of freight had been shifted from the railroads to motor vehicles, in an effort to recover the lost business, the railroads supported legislation requiring of trucks regulation similar to that applicable to railroads. Entirely aside from the contention of the railroads that unregulated competition as it developed was unfair, there was also the question of public interest when the stability of the motor carrier itself became a matter of question. Companies engaged in motor transportation were themselves seriously affected by irresponsible competition from other motor carriers. Before the period of regulation anyone with a down payment on a truck could get into business. Such a trucker could underbid the railroads and established truck lines. Shippers who were cost conscious tended to throw business to the lowest bidder. More often than not the low bidders failed to recognize all the costs of a trucking operation and as their equipment wore out frequently faded from the scene. It was recognized that this type of competition did irreparable damage to the trucking lines having substantial capital investments with a business based on sound practices. Frequently these concerns carried no insurance and, in the event of a serious loss, lacked capacity to meet their legal liability with respect to cargo losses.

Motor Carrier Act of 1935. With the passing of time it became apparent that it would be for the best interests of all parties engaged in the transportation business to bring the trucking industry under some form of regulation. As early as 1934 recommendations to that end were made to the Congress and several bills introduced. The bill that ultimately passed came to be known as the Motor Carrier Act of 1935. The act undertook to bring order out of the nearly chaotic condition that was in the process of development. Its stated objective was the regulation of transportation by motor carriers in such a manner as to recognize and preserve its inherent advantages. It was further stated that the act had for its aim the promotion of adequate and efficient service by motor carriers at reasonable charges without unjust discrimination or undue preferences or advantages. Unfair, destructive, competitive practices were to be eliminated. It was the aim to make the highway transportation system meet the needs of commerce and be available to serve the United States and the national defense.[13]

The act provides for four classes of carriers: (*a*) common carrier by motor vehicle, (*b*) contract carrier by motor vehicle, (*c*) private carrier, and (*d*) brokers. The common-carrier designation applies to those who undertake to transport passengers or property for the general public in interstate or foreign commerce by motor vehicles for compensation. A common carrier may and frequently does operate over a regular route, but a regular route is not a requirement to be included in this category. Also included are the motor-vehicle operations of carriers by rail or water, as well as those of express or forwarding companies. The contract carrier, in contrast, is one who, under special and individual contracts or agreements, transports passengers or property in interstate or foreign commerce by motor vehicles for compensation. The significant difference between a common carrier and a contract carrier is to be found in the fact that the services of the common carrier are available to the general public, whereas the contract carrier serves specific customers on the basis of contract arrangements. A private carrier is one who transports by motor vehicle property of which he is the owner, lessee, or bailee, when such transportation has for its objective the furtherance of some commercial enterprise. A broker is a person who is neither a common

[13] Section 202 (a) of the Motor Carrier Act.

carrier or a contract carrier, not an agent or employee of any such carrier, but is one who negotiates and arranges for transportation for others. For a more concise definition of the types of carriers, reference should be made to the act. It is sufficient here to indicate that the act does distinguish with respect to carriers, and, more than that, the liability that attaches with respect to cargoes transported differs with the different categories.

Liability of Common Carrier by Motor Vehicle. Prior to the enactment of the Motor Carrier Act, there was no uniformity with respect to bills of lading, and numerous forms were adopted. It was virtually impossible to know, without a study of each particular document, the extent of the liability assumed by the carrier. While some assumed common-carrier liability, there were incorporated in others varying degrees of limitation. The Motor Carrier Act incorporates the Cummins Amendment to the Interstate Commerce Act to the end that motor carriers may limit their liability only if expressly authorized by order of the Interstate Commerce Commission. In order to effect this limitation of liability under released-value shipments, application must be made to the commission, and upon authorization tariffs are published based on the commission's approval. Basically, this places the motor carriers in the common-carrier category in the same position as the railroads. Without going into the details of the various classifications, it is sufficient here to point out that motor transportation companies acting as common carriers are now authorized to accept for shipment cargoes that may run to very large amounts with respect to value while limiting liability, with respect to these shipments, to a fraction of their real value.

Liability of Contract and Private Carriers by Motor Vehicles and Brokers. The contract carrier escapes the liability burden of the common carrier to the end that liability imposed by law fixes responsibility only for negligence. This does not prevent the contract carrier from assuming by contract the liability of the common carrier, and this he frequently does. It follows that with respect to contract carriers there is no certainty about liability, which can be determined only by reference to the contract governing shipments. With respect to private carriers and brokers, the situation is the same. Individuals in this latter category are less likely to increase the liability burden by contract, and they will be held liable for loss only when due to negligence.

Exemptions from the Motor Carrier Act. Where the motor vehicle operates in interstate commerce, it is subject to the regulations of the Interstate Commerce Commission. Where it operates within the limits of a single state, unless its operations contribute to interstate commerce, it comes within the purview of the regulations of the Public Utilities Commission of the state in which it operates. There are motor carriers engaged in the transportation of certain commodities that are exempt from the operation of the Motor Carrier Act. Without attempting to give a comprehensive list, it may be pointed out that vehicles used in carrying property consisting of livestock, fish, and certain other agricultural commodities do not come within the operation of the act if they are not used in carrying any other property or passengers for compensation. Exempt from the operation of the act are school buses, taxicabs, or vehicles that transport hotel patrons to and from terminals, with the exception of certain regulations having to do with hours of service and safety. Finally, there are certain zones of operations in which the carrier is exempt. A carrier engaged in the transportation of passengers or property wholly within a municipality or between contiguous municipalities or within a zone adjacent to and commercially a part of any such municipality is exempt. There is an exception to the foregoing if the vehicle is under the control or management of a transportation agency where its operations form a part of a continuous shipment to or from a point outside the exempt zone. The commercial zones exempt from the operation of the act have been established by the commission. Local carriers generally are exempt, as are those engaged in pickup and delivery. With respect to pickup and delivery for railroads, motor vehicles are held not to be operating a common carrier but are merely agents for the railroad furnishing the service. Motor-vehicle transportation forms an extremely complex subject, and with respect to liability for loss, the position of the carrier in every instance must be carefully scrutinized and its cargo liability determined on an individual basis.

Rules for Motor Carriers with Respect to Insurance. The Interstate Commerce Commission has set forth rules with respect to carriers subject to the provision of the Motor Carrier Act with respect to insurance. Unless the carrier can qualify as a self-insurer or otherwise satisfy the commission with respect to securities or agreements in not less than the amounts required for insurance, prescribed amounts of coverage are required. The purpose of the requirement is public protection, since a carrier operating a motor transportation service might well, as the result of a serious loss, be precipitated into bankruptcy and be unable to meet its obligations with respect to the loss or damage.[14] From the point of view of the shipper, it is important to realize that liability protection for the carrier may afford him inadequate cover. A valuable shipment shipped

[14] For bodily injury or death on passenger vehicles the Interstate Commerce Commission requires cover in the amount of $5,000 per person to a maximum of $50,000 with the same limit on each person for vehicles transporting 31 or more passengers. Property damage liability must be in an amount of not less than $1,000 on any one vehicle with an aggregate of $2,000 for any one occurrence. Brokers must file a bond or other security in the amount of $5,000.

under a released-value bill of lading limits the liability of the carrier to a stipulated amount. He is not liable at all for losses attributable to disasters that fall in the category of acts of God. A contract carrier is not liable on the same basis as the common carrier. Where the common carrier would be liable for a fire loss, the contract carrier would be liable only if negligence can be shown. With respect to those carriers exempt from the operation of the Motor Carrier Act, they may, in the absence of state statutes, limit their liability under their bills of lading. Carriers that do not operate in interstate commerce are, in a number of states, required by state law to provide insurance coverage as a condition precedent to a license to operate. Again the question of liability is one for the concern of the shipper.

The implications of the various laws and regulations often prove too complex for the analysis and study of the businessman who has shipments to make as an incident of his business. He prefers to buy transit insurance from an insurer in an amount that will indemnify in the event of loss. He is not then concerned with released values or differences in the liability of the different categories of carriers. If his freight rate is loaded for insurance, this is not a total loss for his own insurer predicates the transit insurance rate on the nature of the shipment and any expected recovery from the carrier with respect thereto.

Need for Transportation Insurance of Land Risks. Because of the exemptions from liability afforded carriers of seagoing transportation, the custom of insuring cargoes aboard vessels and, in fact, the vessels themselves, was established early. With the development of railroads into great systems representing vast investments, shippers tended, for many years, to look to them for reimbursement in the event of loss or damage to the goods shipped. The situation was by no means ideal. Carriers regarded themselves as primarily in the transportation business and not the business of insurance. The adjustment of losses was regarded as a necessary evil. While it may be presumed that it was the intention of the management of railroads to settle equitably all claims for which they were legally liable, questions of fact and law frequently entailed much litigation and delay. The situation as it existed was not entirely satisfactory to shippers, and in some instances it was aggravated by failure on their part to understand thoroughly the effect of limitations of liability incorporated in the bills of lading. Because of these conditions, there developed a growing tendency on the part of shippers to seek transportation insurance from insurers. This demand was crystallized at the time of World War I when the government took over the transportation systems of the country. The delays and disputes that had developed prior to the war were brought into sharp focus when it became apparent that under its operation the government was a factor in any claim for reimbursement. Shippers began to feel that they could expect an increase of any delays that had been experienced heretofore because of the increasingly complex setup of the transportation system. Rather than be faced with the delay and litigation, as well as being disturbed by the element of uncertainty, private insurance was sought as a solution of the problem of transportation risks.

About the same time that the railroad situation was giving stimulus to the insurance of land transportation hazards, the automobile was becoming an increasingly important factor in the transportation system. Large trucking concerns developed. But the trucking business over highways was by no means limited to such companies, and trucking concerns of uncertain financial stability mushroomed almost overnight. While the shipper had a reasonable degree of assurance of the financial responsibility of railroads, in many instances he had little or no assurance of the ability of the trucking concern to meet promptly a heavy claim for loss or damage. With the introduction of trucking, a second feature made its appearance. Many times the shipper himself owned the trucks; therefore, unless the contents were insured by a separate carrier, the goods were in transit with no provision whatever for reimbursement in the event of loss. To a lesser degree, the airplane exerted its influence. Shipments are now made regularly by airplane, but, in the beginning, shippers were apprehensive lest this method of transportation prove particularly hazardous. The sum of all these factors stimulated the demand for transportation insurance written by insurers, and out of this demand inland marine insurance became an established branch of the insurance business.

Insurance of Carrier's Liability. Up to this point, the discussion of the carrier's liability presupposes the ability of the carrier to settle losses for which it is liable. Because of the size and financial strength of railroads, the question of ability has not been an important factor. With the use of motor trucks as carriers, the owners of the trucks have viewed their liability as a very serious risk indeed. It is quite conceivable that the destruction of a shipment might entail a loss far in excess of the value of the truck upon which it was being transported. This led to a demand for insurance covering the legal liability of the carrier for damage to shipments entrusted to his care. The federal government has enacted legislation making adequate automobile insurance coverage a condition precedent for a license to operate in certain fields of business. In addition to federal laws, a number of states require a certificate of insurance on file with the state authority in connection with permits to carry on a motor transportation business.

With the introduction of contracts providing for the legal liability of carriers, it was but a step to provide the same protection for bailees. Not all persons operating transportation facilities come within the legal classification of common carriers. Some truckmen who do not operate regularly established routes, or who work primarily for one or two customers, accept goods as a bailee; in this instance, they are liable for negligence and are not, as in the case of a common carrier, insurers of the goods. The bailee liability has been extended to a wide range of risks.

Development of Inland Marine Insurance. The term "inland marine insurance" does not refer to the insurance of transportation risks on inland waterways. It is, in fact, a comparatively new branch of insurance that developed out of the need for inland transportation insurance involving either land risks or water-borne risks, or both.

When the demand first made its appearance, it is natural that appeal for the coverage should first be made to marine underwriters. These insurers were thoroughly conversant with the problems of transportation risks and under the terms of their charters were authorized to write the business. As the demand for inland marine coverages developed into a veritable boom, fire and casualty insurers were attracted to the business. This, too, was logical. The ocean marine contract required substantial modifications in order to meet the needs of inland hazards. Some of the old marine clauses were retained, but there were also incorporated in the contract features to be found in both fire and some other property insurance contracts. The risks covered involved not only transportation hazards but so many of the fire and other hazards that it was not always easy to determine which were the dominant factors.

Because of the flexibility of the transportation contract, much broader coverages were available under inland marine contracts than could be obtained under fire and related property insurance contracts.[15] A part of the inland marine boom was the outgrowth of the tendency of those attuned to insurance trends to insure their fire, theft, and similar hazards under an inland marine form rather than under the older fire and related contracts. These contracts were particularly desirable when there were concentrated values. In the case of furs, jewelry, art treasures, and similar items, instead of insuring the risks against burglary, fire, accidental damages, malicious mischief, earthquake, and the innumerable list of specific hazards, a single contract covering "all risks" had a tremendous appeal. When, as was usually the case, the all risks contract could be obtained for a premium much less than was required for an accumulation of separate contracts, the appeal of the marine contract to the buyer of insurance was powerfully influenced by the price element.

Because of the transition of inland marine insurance from the competitive and flexible ocean marine field, this new form carried

[15] For a history of fire insurance, see pages 49–53, and for the provisions of the standard fire insurance contract see Chapter 5.

with it an adaptability not to be found in the older established fire field. While the fire insurance business was enlarging the scope of its activities to include perils other than fire, the pattern, as compared to marine business, was comparatively rigid. There was little flexibility with respect to contracts and forms, and business for the most part was written at rates established by inland marine rate-making organizations.

By writing all risk contracts or contracts covering a wide range of named perils, comprehensive forms were early obtainable from marine underwriters. Contracts were written on a valued basis. There was wide-open competition for business both on the basis of form of coverage and premium. More and more the warehouse risk came into prominence, until in some instances the transportation phase of the coverage faded into insignificance. The flexibility of coverage and the competitive spirit with respect to rates attracted business to inland marine underwriters that seemed normally to belong in the casualty and fire fields.

This coverage, as it developed, caused fire insurance underwriters to pause and give serious consideration to the fact that substantial blocks of properties were being written at rates less than the established fire rates. This was accomplished by merging storage risks with transportation risks. A storage risk, before or after shipment, was covered under a transportation contract and frequently at rates less than the fire rate promulgated for the location. Competition flared between fire insurers and the marine underwriters. In some instances, the fire department of an insurer found that it was losing lines written at established rates that were turning up in its own marine department at rates less than the promulgated bureau rates. The opportunity for placing substantial marine lines had its appeal to the larger insurance agencies. The insurer having a marine department with ample facilities was not infrequently able, because of the availability of these facilities, to command the fire lines of an agency that might otherwise be distributed to insurers without these marine facilities. The competition that developed brought about rate decisions and commission allowances to agents that for a time threatened the business.

Nationwide Marine Definition. The first efforts to bring order to the confusion that developed were made by the fire insurers. As a first step, they undertook to provide forms that would parallel the coverage offered by the marine underwriters. They then formed an organization known as the Interstate Underwriters Board which promulgated a definition of marine insurance. This definition became effective July 10, 1929, by virtue of agreements made by insurers which in effect prohibited them from writing as marine or inland marine insurance any risk that did not come within the scope of the definition. These agreements did not have the force of law, and there was a feeling on the part of marine underwriters that they were being forced into a rigid pattern by the fire insurance underwriters and many were out of sympathy with the definition and agreements. There was a tendency on the part of marine underwriters to interpret the decision broadly, and it might even be said in instances that it was ignored. In any case the agreements were held to be ineffective, and an area of conflict between the inland marine business and the older established fire and related lines persisted.

About this time the state supervisory authorities began to view the situation with concern. In the spring of 1931 the Superintendent of Insurance of the State of New York called a general meeting of all interested parties. A committee representing all insurance interests undertook to work out a definition of marine insurance, but it was not until two years later that a definition was presented that seemed acceptable. On June 2, 1933, the definition was published by the Superintendent of Insurance of New York and was approved with slight modification by the National Association of Insurance Commissioners and by resolution was adopted unanimously as the definition of marine underwriting powers. With some modification the definition was adopted became effective in 36 states and was known as the "Nation-Wide Definition and Interpretation of the Insuring Powers of Marine and Transportation Underwriters." In June, 1953, the definition was considerably broadened and modified and in its new draft adopted by the N.A.I.C. In its present form the title has been shortened to "Nation-wide Marine Definition."

This definition is divided into two parts. The first part provides the conditions under which marine and transportation contracts may cover (*a*) imports; (*b*) exports; (*c*) domestic shipments; (*d*) bridges, tunnels, and other instrumentalities of transportation and communication; and (*e*) personal property floater risks. The second part of the definition is known as the "restrictive section." Originally there were eight kinds of risks which were prohibited unless approved under permissive sections. Under the recent revision of the definition the limitations in the restrictive section are reduced to six, and these concern themselves largely with risks where the element of transportation is usually lacking.

When the decision was first formulated, there was a feeling that the older fire insurance interests dominated the negotiations. It was pointed out that no attempt was made to define the underwriting powers of any branch of insurance except marine and inland marine insurance. There were three parties participating: the fire insurance industry, the casualty insurance industry, and representatives of the marine industry. It was felt by some that in the negotiations the marine industry combined to exert pressure in determining how far the inland marine underwriters could go when their interests were in conflict with the marine underwriters. Certain of the lines that the inland marine underwriters were developing were included in the definition as it was formulated, but quite definitely others were not included or were prohibited.[16] Because of the predominating influence of the fire and casualty underwriters, the term "one-way street" has been applied to the definition.[17] In any case, even though the definition is conceded to have limited the area of expansion of the inland marine business, by the same token it prevented unrestricted competition that might have seriously damaged the entire industry.[18]

Inland Marine Insurance Bureau. With the rapid development of transportation insurance and with the extension of the marine contract to the insurance of other hazards not readily insurable by fire and related lines insurers because of the transportation risks, the inland marine business began to develop a sizable volume of premiums. The result was a period of intensive competition. To introduce some stability to this branch and put an end to unregulated competition by adjusting rates and forms to meet needs and experience, a meeting of underwriting executives was called in December, 1929. A committee was appointed to formulate plans for an organization to control the writing of certain specified lines. The outcome of the meeting was the

---

[16] The insurance of consigned goods after arrival was a field in which the inland marine underwriters were developing business. This was prohibited. A second provision was found in the prohibition in the definition of the personal property floater. This contract covered, among other perils, personal property on an all risks basis, including the contents of dwellings. The demand for this protection resulted in exceptions to the definition being allowed in every state to the end that the personal property floater could be written, even though prohibited in the definition. In the revised definition this contract is included as an inland marine cover.

[17] Franklin B. Tuttle, "Inland Marine Insurance," in *Examination of Insurance Carriers* (New York: The New York State Insurance Department, 1953), Vol. 1, p. 294.

[18] Following the release of the original definition, insurers for the most part subscribed to a voluntary agreement which obligated them to apply the principle of the definition in each state in which it was entered for business. In those states where the insurance departments used the definition for the purposes of defining marine and inland marine insurance, the insurers were in a position of being obligated to adjust themselves to the terms of the decision whether or not they were voluntary subscribers to an agreement to do this. This was so since where the insurance department adopted the definition as a basis for defining marine and inland marine insurance, the police power of the state could be brought to bear to effect its enforcement. Hence, insurers that were not signatories to the agreement were, for all practical purposes, in the same position as if they were. The definition in its present form is made effective by state enforcement. If there is doubt with respect to any risk as to whether it falls within the definition, a Committee on Interpretation makes a determination. The committee is appointed by the National Association of Insurance Commissioners "with the advice of the industry" and consists of 15 members of which five are marine and inland marine insurance representatives, five are from the fire insurance business, and five from the casualty and surety insurance field. Members of the committee must be senior executives of insurers or senior officers of insurers' organizations or senior executives of managerial insurance underwriters. In order to be effective in any jurisdiction the definition must be specifically adopted, and this is true, as well, with respect to each interpretation.

formation of an organization known as the "Inland Marine Underwriters Association," and on January 1, 1931, it began functioning. The work of the Inland Marine Underwriters Association was progressing through the development of uniform rates, forms, and commissions throughout the industry when the impact of the Southeastern Underwriters case made itself felt. There probably would have been no serious need for any modification of the work of the association but for the requirement that concerted rate making must now be brought within the purview of state regulation.

The Inland Marine Underwriters Association was within limits reorganized and renamed the Inland Marine Insurance Bureau. It qualified under the new rating laws as a rating body. The I.M.I.B. filed rates and forms, and thus the activities formerly carried on by I.M.I.B. were made subject to the regulations of the various states. Since the time of its organization, I.M.I.B. rates and forms have set the pattern for a substantial area in the field of inland marine insurance. Mutual fire insurers and a few individual insurers make their own filings. The influence of the I.M.I.B., however, has been instrumental in giving uniformity to the contracts and forms of inland marine insurance. Mutual inland marine insurers converted the Mutual Marine Conference into the Transportation Insurance Rating Bureau and this organization also files rates with the insurance supervisory authorities of each state.

In the transportation field many of the contracts are still unregulated. Truckmen's cargo liability, department store floaters, and other inland marine transportation contracts do not lend themselves well to either a rigid form or promulgated rates.[19] There are standardized forms for bridges and tunnels, but no rates have been filed, since the characteristics of each particular risk are determining factors with respect to rates. Pipelines and radio and television towers are all written on tailor-made forms designed to fit the requirements of the particular risk and the needs of the insured, and there are no rate filings. Bailment risks generally are unregulated with the exception of furriers' customers, and garment contractors' contracts. In the floater field salesmen's samples, contractors' equipment floaters, installation risks, and fine-arts and rug dealers' contracts are still in the unregulated area.

As the situation now stands there is one area of the inland marine business where rates and form filings establish for the business much the same rigidity and uniformity found in the field of fire insurance. The transportation area still clings to the original marine pattern. Certain other lines do not lend themselves either to form or rate filings. It has been felt that if in this area forms were to be made

[19] Parcel-post and registered mail contracts are exceptions in the transportation field where form and rate filings have been made.

mandatory and rates promulgated, then in certain situations, if the rate seemed too low to the underwriters, the market for coverage would dry up. If a market for these individualistic risks is to be provided, then the underwriters must have freedom in determining the nature of the cover as well as the premium to be charged. To what extent regulation in the way of form filings and rates will encroach upon the unregulated area cannot be predicted. On the basis of conditions as they exist today, it is generally conceded to be in the public interest that no attempt be made to bring the entire field of inland marine insurance within the regulated area.

Present Status of Transportation Insurance. While the line of demarcation for the purposes of a definition is not a sharp one, for all practical purposes transportation insurance is divided into ocean marine and inland marine coverages, although in view of the rapid development, of multiple line underwriting distinctions of this type are not especially significant. The terms are not strictly descriptive, but, in the industry, inland and ocean marine insurance are sometimes designated, respectively, as "wet" and "dry" marine insurance. The basic ocean marine contract covers sea perils, such as standing, sinking, burning, collision, and damage caused by storms. General average and salvage charges are also included in the coverage. The risks of war, strike, riot and civil commotion, theft, pilferage, nondelivery, breakage, leakage, hook damage, water damage, damage from sweat of vessel's hold, and damage from oil in the cargo may also be included in the contract. Contracts are also written "all risk" when complete protection is essential. The basic contract may be extended to provide land protection by adding the warehouse-to-warehouse clause.

The subject matter of the insurance includes the ship itself, goods in transit, or freight. The terms "ship" and "goods" are self-explanatory. In marine insurance, the term "freight" has a technical significance and represents the compensation of the shipowner for carrying goods to the port of delivery. Freight represents the profits earned by the shipowner. The freight is not considered to be earned until the goods are safely delivered in port. Loss of the ship entails not only the loss of its physical value but the loss of earnings that would have accrued to the owners had the voyage been completed successfully. "Chartered freight" represents the amount paid for the use of a ship either for a voyage or for a period of time. If the ship for any reason is out of condition and there is no provision in the agreement to cover this, the parties to whom the ship is hired will suffer a freight loss. It is true that the owner does not pay himself freight for the transportation of his own goods. On the other hand, the transported goods will have a "place value" in the port of destination greater than in the port of shipment, and this augmented value represents the freight. The cost of the goods at the port of shipment plus a sum equal to the cost of shipment represents an insurable interest.

In the field of ocean marine insurance, entirely aside from ocean-going transportation, there is a substantial volume of hull business, including not only commercial vessels but yachts and motor boats navigating inland waters. Cargo and freight shipments include not only transoceanic travel but coastwise business, intercoastal shipments, and other domestic shipments on rivers and the Great Lakes. In addition to hull and cargo insurance, legal liability for damage done by the owners of hulls is written under a form known as "protection and indemnity insurance." Finally, the workmen's compensation requirements under the Longshoremen's and Harbor Workers' Compensation Act obligate the shipower either to insure his liability for injuries to workmen or to qualify as a self-insurer. Failure to do either subjects the owner of a vessel to fine or imprisonment. Workmen's compensation insurance under the Longshoremen's and Harbor Workers' Compensation Act is ordinarily regarded as a branch of ocean marine insurance.

Inland marine insurance, first of all, covers risks that unquestionably involve an element of transportation. Contracts are issued to cover goods and merchandise while in the hands of carriers such as railroads, express companies, truckmen, and airplane carriers. These contracts insure the goods of the shipper while in the hands of the transportation company. Distinguished from the literal transportation coverage is the "floater." The floater contract is not limited in any sense to coverage for a specific trip but provides insurance upon goods that may fluctuate either as to location or as to amount. For example, radium used by doctors may be transported from place to place for use. The radium floater covers the radium wherever it may be, subject always to any limitations set forth in the contract. A third classification of inland marine coverages is to be found in "bailee and legal liability insurance." Under such a form a laundry may insure its liability for customers' goods. Similar contracts are issued for such organizations as dyers and cleaners, and furriers. Finally, there are contracts that do not themselves involve transportation of the subject matter of the insurance but are regarded rather as instrumentalities of transportation and communication. In this group are to be found contracts insuring bridges and tunnels, as well as other aids to navigation and transportation, including dry docks and marine railways.

Risks that involve a substantial element of storage and only an incidental element of transportation are not to be regarded as marine risks. This is particularly the case when the charge for a marine contract covering transportation hazards, but including the element of storage, is less than the premium for fire would be on the storage portion of the risk, if the standard fire rates were applied.

FIRE INSURANCE

Although the beginnings of marine insurance are not easy to document, it is generally agreed that fire insurance began in 1667 as a result of the Great Fire of London, which had occurred during the previous year.[20] The person responsible for the idea of insuring houses for loss from fire was an English physician by the name of Nicholas Barbon. At first he operated his business as an individual proprietorship, but in 1680, with the help of a few associates, he founded the Fire Office, which was a stock insurer. Barbon's efforts did not prove particularly successful, but the idea of fire insurance was firmly established and other British insurers were formed. Notable among these were the Friendly Society and the Amicable Contributionship, both of which were established before 1700. These organizations were successful and served as a pattern for subsequent insurers of the fire risk. The Amicable Contributionship continued in business on an independent basis until 1905.

Establishment of Fire Insurance in the United States. During the colonial period businessmen and others seeking fire as well as other types of insurance relied heavily on British markets and it was not until 1752 that a fire insurer was founded in the colonies. This company was organized by Benjamin Franklin and his associates and was named The Philadelphia Contributionship for Insurance of Houses from Loss by Fire. This firm is still in existence and has prospered over the years. For approximately thirty years after its founding the Contributionship was the only fire insurer in what was to become the United States. In 1784 a second company was formed and took the name the Mutual Assurance Company for Insuring Houses from Loss by Fire. This organization was better known as the Green Tree because of the circumstances surrounding its formation. The Contributionship had adopted a rule that it viewed trees near a dwelling or any other building as a fire hazard and that it would no longer insure or renew contracts if trees were nearby. There was an objection to this rule by many citizens of Philadelphia and as a result a new insurer that would accept the tree risk was formed. The new firm was successful and insurance in force increased substantially over a fairly short time period.

---

[20] Although 1667 is usually given as the date when fire insurance began, it is known that a fire insurance association was established in Germany in 1591. It was called the Feuer Casse. There is also some evidence that fire associations of a noncommercial type existed in Assyria over 2,500 years ago.

Some 17 years after it began business, the Green Tree began selling perpetual contracts (before that time it had sold seven-year contracts), a practice later adopted by the Contributionship. Perpetual insurance, as the name implies, is not written on a term basis but instead the contracts continue indefinitely or until a total loss occurs. Only one premium or deposit is paid in the amount of 2 or 3 percent of the face amount of the contract. The contract is cancellable and partial losses do not lower the amount of insurance. The insured's deposit may be returned in full if the contract has been in force five years or longer. Insurers operating on a perpetual basis rely heavily on their income from investments in order to meet loss and other costs.

Fire Marks. Municipal fire departments are of fairly recent origin, the first departments having been established in the 1860's. Before this time in the United States reliance was placed on volunteer organizations and some of these organizations were originally responsible for the establishment of the first fire insurers. In order that volunteer firemen would know whether an insurer in which they were interested was on a particular risk, a fire mark was affixed to the insured building. These marks were distinctive and identified the insurer. Many of the earlier fire marks were made of lead or cast iron but later on small metal plates were used. The latter type mark had the name of the insurer on it. The idea of a fire mark originated in Europe. The first American insurer to develop a fire mark was the Philadelphia Contributionship for the Insurance of Houses from Loss by Fire, which adopted a plaque on which was placed four clasped hands. The Mutual Assurance Company for Insuring Houses from Loss by Fire adopted a plaque with a green tree as its fire mark. As new insurers were established they designed distinctive fire marks, which were used until paid fire departments became a reality.[21]

Further Development of Fire Insurance. The development of fire insurance progressed fairly rapidly and by 1800 insurers, mostly mutual, had been started in Maryland, New York, and Virginia. The first stock insurer to be incorporated in the United States was the Insurance Company of North America, which was founded in 1792 as an association and was incorporated in 1794. This firm was and is of particular interest because of the broad underwriting powers that were granted in the original articles of association. The eighth article said that the directors were authorized "To make such Insurances upon Vessels and Merchandize at Sea, or going to Sea, or upon the life or lives of any person or persons, or upon any goods, wares, merchandize, or other property gone or going by land or water; and at such Rates of Insurance or Premium as they shall deem advisable."[22]

[21] See Alwin E. Bulau, *Footprints of Assurance* (New York: Macmillan Co., 1953).

[22] *A History of the Insurance Company of North America* (Philadelphia: Press of Review Publishing and Printing Company, 1885), p. 13.

Although the Insurance Company of North America ceased writing life insurance at an early date, it has continued to the present in the property and casualty field and in the 1950's re-entered the life insurance business through an affiliated life insurer. By its original charter this firm was not only a multiple line insurer but also an all risk insurer.

Very early in the history of fire insurance concern was expressed over the high cost of contracts and efforts to lower costs through underwriting and prevention were made. Notable among these attempts were the development of class mutuals. These insurers were organized to insure primarily certain kinds of businesses such as factories and milling and grain operations, although firms were established to insure lumber and allied lines, hardware and similar risks, drugs, and other types of operation. While many of these insurers have expanded their operations to the end that they may be regarded as general-writing insurers, since they still give emphasis to the special line contemplated when they were organized, the term "class mutual" is still used in referring to them. Factory mutuals and mill mutuals will be considered as examples of the class mutual type of insurer.

The insurance of factories is one of the important fields covered by class mutuals. Loss prevention as a means to low-cost insurance was the motivating idea of the organizers. The first insurer in the group, later to develop into the important Factory Mutual System, was organized in 1835 to insure manufacturing properties, and from the beginning it gave practical application to the idea of prevention.[23] There are, as of 1967, seven factory mutuals in operation and two wholly owned stock subsidiaries. The seven are, with their dates of incorporation, as follows: Manufacturers Mutual Fire Insurance Company of Providence, Rhode Island (1835), Boston Manufacturers Mutual Insurance Company, Waltham, Massachusetts (1850), Fireman's Mutual Insurance Company, Providence, Rhode Island (1854), Arkwright Mutual Insurance Company, Boston, Massachusetts (1860), Blackstone Mutual Insurance Company, Providence,

---

[23] The Factory Mutual Fire Insurance System is the outgrowth of the idea of a New England manufacturer who interested other manufacturers in a plan to share losses on their factories on a mutual basis. The originators of the plan undertook a careful study of the causes of fire, and through the inauguration of a program of prevention, members of the group were able materially to reduce the cost of their insurance protection. A mutual insurer was formed, and later other similar insurers were organized. As the size of lines increased, insurance was distributed among the different insurers of the group. Insurers cooperate in engineering and inspection work, adjustment of losses, or other phases of the business with resultant efficiency and economy. There are monthly meetings of insurer officers at which matters of common interest are considered. The group is known as the "Conference," and its functions are concerned primarily with inspections, though it reviews other matters of interest. The findings of the conference are mainly advisory, each insurer being free in the conduct of its own affairs.

Rhode Island (1868), Philadelphia Manufacturers Mutual Insurance Company, Philadelphia, Pennsylvania (1880), and Protective Mutual Insurance Company, Park Ridge, Illinois (1887).

As the idea grew, a technical staff of trained engineers studied the problem of prevention, and a laboratory for research and testing was maintained. Slow-burning construction was advocated; special hazards were studied with a view to providing safeguards; and when new fire prevention developments appeared, their adoption was encouraged. It was this group that was largely responsible for the adoption of the automatic sprinkler.

The Factory Mutuals limit their commitments to the highest grade of protected properties and insist that their insureds meet their standards before acceptance. More recently these insurers have shown a tendency to enlarge the scope of their operations and, instead of limiting them strictly to factories, have written other classes of risk, including hospitals, churches, and schools.[24]

The cost of administration in the Factory Mutual System includes the cost of inspection and engineering services. Because of the cost of inspections, surveys, consultations, and conferences pending improvement of the risk, the insurance plan, and other services rendered, companies in the group do not solicit small risks.

Contracts of the Factory Mutual System are broad in their scope and especially adapted to the needs of their insureds. Full insurance coverage, amounting ordinarily to 90 percent of the value of the property above the foundation, is usually required, though it is not the practice to make this requirement a part of the contract. Thus, while it is desired that full insurance be carried, a failure to keep insurance up to changing values, when an increase in costs goes unnoticed, does not penalize the insured.

Insurers in the Factory Mutual System make their contracts in their home offices. Manufacturers in states other than the home state of the insurer concerned are considered as having come to that state for insurance. On this basis it has been held that the insurer does business

---

[24] The procedure for placing insurance with the Factory Mutuals requires the filing of an application with one of the insurers of the group by the prospective insured. The insurer then undertakes an examination of the property, and if it is found to conform to requirements, a detailed survey is undertaken. Frequently the services of trained experts are necessary to complete a survey and if necessary make recommendations for required improvements to bring the property up to standard. This work is done at no cost to the applicant. When the findings of the inspection department are sent to the owner of the property, he may then proceed, if he wishes, to effect the recommended changes. If the owner elects to comply with the recommendations, insurance may be written when the improvements have reached a stage approved by the insurer. When the risk is ready for insurance, the insurer that has been supervising the preliminary survey distributes the insurance among the insurers of the group. The insurer placing the insurance checks all contracts of associated insurers, and when all are found ready and in order they are sent by this insurer to the insured.

in its own state, and accordingly there exists no need for formally entering other states. It is the policy of the Factory Mutuals to become licensed in all states where a sufficient volume of business is developed.

The Association of Mill and Elevator Insurance Companies is the outgrowth through association of member insurers originally formed to write insurance on mills or grain elevators. Because of this they are generally known as the "mill mutuals." The first insurers in the group were organized to write flour mill risks. To secure insurance in the mill mutuals, the insured was required to maintain his flour mill up to high standards. For a considerable period of time owners of grain elevators were unable to secure adequate insurance, and because of the unsatisfactory standards maintained, the mill mutuals were generally uninterested in carrying the risk. As a consequence, grain dealers organized their own mutual insurers. These were designed to specialize in elevator risks and were, at the outset, organized to insure risks within a fairly circumscribed area. Over the years they tended to extend their activities to include increasingly greater territories. In time they abandoned the idea of limiting their activities to mill and elevator risks and included within the scope of their operations insurance on various kinds of property. They now insure dwellings as well as manufacturing and mercantile risks. The insurers comprising the group have organized the Mill Mutual Fire Prevention Bureau which has for its purpose the development of standards and specifications that will contribute to loss prevention in the industry. The organization has made outstanding contributions to loss prevention, particularly in the fields of dust control and in the safeguarding of mechanical hazards. It carries on its activities by means of an extensive program of inspection and education.

CASUALTY INSURANCE

Until late in the 19th century the principal types of insurance sold in the United States were fire, life, and marine. In spite of the broad underwriting powers given to early insurers, insurance in the United States developed along specialty lines. This type of development was encouraged by state legislation which, after the formation of the New York Insurance department, increasingly limited the types of insurance that could be written by any one insurer and by the inclination of many persons in the insurance business who were of the opinion that specialization was desirable in order to provide responsible and informed underwriting. Prior to the opening of the 20th century virtually all property insurance in the United States could be categorized as either fire or marine.

With the introduction of workmen's compensation insurance into the United States in the early 20th century and with the advent of the automobile, impetus was given to the development of types of insurance dealing primarily with indirect losses or those situations where loss fell on a party other than the insured but where the insured was legally responsible. Additionally types of direct loss such as damage from explosion and the breakage of plate glass were being considered as appropriate for insurance coverage. The various types of property insurance other than fire or marine were labeled casualty. The first casualty insurer was formed in 1864 to write travel accident contracts. Many casualty insurers were formed after this date and many of them still limit the type of risks that they will take. Increasingly the current trend (as of 1965) is away from specialization and toward multiple and all lines insurance. Many of the modern, large casualty insurers write all types of insurance except life, and some of these handle the life risk through wholly owned subsidiaries.[25] The word "casualty" is gradually becoming obsolete and is no longer particularly descriptive of current practice.

LIABILITY INSURANCE

The recent trend toward the combining of lines of insurance has resulted in the use of the expression "property insurance" as being descriptive of fire, marine, inland marine, and those casualty lines dealing directly with losses to real and personal property. "Liability insurance" includes those coverages dealing with third party losses where the insured has some legal responsibility. Historically, liability insurance has been a part of casualty insurance and its development closely parallels that field.

Liability insurance was first sold in the United States in the latter part of the 19th century. One of the first insurers to sell this type of insurance was the Mutual Boiler and Machinery Insurance Company. The main impetus for liability insurance came from the passing of employer liability statutes in the various states, and the first liability insurance contracts sold in the United States in 1886 were limited to the employer's liability risk. Early in the 20th century in the United States workmen's compensation laws were introduced, and, as these laws became common, the workmen's compensation risk was assumed by insurers, and contracts combining employer's liability and workmen's compensation were widely sold. The Employers Mutual Liability Insurance Company of Wausau, Wisconsin, wrote one of the first workmen's compensation insurance contracts in the United States.

Once employer's liability insurance became well established, other types of liability insurance contracts followed in fairly rapid succes-

[25] For further details on the development of casualty insurance see John Bainbridge, *Biography of an Idea* (Garden City, N.Y.: Doubleday & Co., Inc., 1952), pp. 257–335. Many of the facts on fire insurance were also based on this source.

sion. By 1889, insurers began to write business, elevator, and public liability insurance, and by 1896, a general liability contract was available which could be used to cover owners of dwellings and apartments. About 1912, automobile liability insurance contracts were introduced. Approximately ten years later, a residence liability insurance contract was developed, and this contract was followed in 1932 by a personal liability contract. A major development in residence contracts occurred in 1943, with the introduction of a comprehensive personal liability contract which was revised substantially in 1944, 1946, and 1950. The main provisions of this contract are now a part of the various homeowner's contracts.[26]

MULTIPLE LINE INSURANCE

By "multiple line insurance" we mean the system under which a single corporate entity may write all types of insurance except life and health. Multiple line insurers may write multiple line insurance contracts such as the homeowners, a contract that contains liability, fire, and other property coverages. All states now permit the incorporation of multiple line insurers and multiple line contracts are becoming more and more common. Multiple line insurance should be distinguished from all lines insurance, which is a system whereby one insurer writes property and liability and life and health insurance. With the possible exception of one state, all lines insurance is not authorized, although the result may be essentially achieved through the formation of groups of insurers. The operation of more than one type of insurer through common ownership is not unusual. Where life insurance is not involved, the insurers may be called a multiple line insurer group. If a life insurer is a part of the group, then the arrangement is an all lines group.

The idea of multiple line insurance is not new. Great Britain has long permitted multiple line as well as all lines insurance, and, as noted above, the charters of many of the early insurers in the United States granted underwriting powers without restriction. From 1799 to 1859, a period before extensive state regulation, insurers in the United States operated without legal restriction on the types of insurance that they might write. In spite of this freedom early insurers showed a reluctance to write all lines and specialization was common. With the advent of state insurance departments during the middle of the 19th century the limitation of underwriting powers by statute became common with New York State taking the lead. The New York attitude was further strengthened by the Appleton Rule, which was promulgated around 1900 by Appleton, who was then Deputy Superintendent of the New York Insurance Department. This rule estab-

[26] See John Eugene Pierce, *Development of Comprehensive Insurance for the Household* (Homewood, Ill.: Richard D. Irwin, Inc., 1958).

lished the principle that to be licensed to do business in New York a foreign or alien insurer had to agree that it would not sell in New York any insurance that could not be sold by insurers domiciled in New York and that it would not sell such insurance outside New York. Likewise domestic insurers could not sell outside of New York any type of insurance prohibited to them within the state. Because of the influence of the New York Insurance Department the monoline insurance principle became firmly established in the United States.

Although specialization on the part of insurers seemed to be generally accepted, almost from the first there were those who questioned the wisdom of limiting insuring powers so severely. In 1860 Superintendent Barnes of the New York Insurance Department recommended multiple line legislation, and this recommendation was followed some 30 years later by discussion of multiple line powers by a committee of insurance commissioners. Discussion of the desirability of multiple line insurance continued over the years and in the 1920's interest centered around marine and inland marine insurance. A step toward multiple line insurance was taken about this time when multiple line groups or fleets were authorized by the states. The acquisition of subsidiaries by an insurer became a way to increase the lines of business written. Perhaps the greatest impetus to multiple line insurance came about as a result of the formation of the Diemand Committee. This committee headed by John A. Diemand was a committee of the National Association of Insurance Commissioners. After thorough study the Diemand Committee in 1944 recommended multiple line insurance, and after accepting the report, the National Association recommended that each state legislature pass multiple line laws. The Committee recommended a gradual change from monoline to multiple line laws and the first laws conferred partial multiple line authority. Gradually the states conferred full multiple line powers on insurers and by 1955 all of the states had full multiple line insurance laws. In view of the importance of this legislation and its subsequent influence on the insurance industry, the remainder of this book will emphasize the developments in insurance, particularly multiple line contracts, that have resulted from multiple line operation. Particular attention will be given to homeowners' and commercial multiple line contracts.[27]

A BASIC INDUSTRY

Ranking in importance with agriculture, commerce, banking, manufacturing, transportation, and communication, insurance is

[27] For further discussion of the development of multiple line insurance see D. L. Bickelhaupt, *Transition to Multiple Line Insurance Companies* (Homewood, Ill.: Richard D. Irwin, Inc., 1961).

classed today in the United States as one of the basic industries. Insurance is the principal occupation for 1,200,000 persons and insurers have invested over $188 billion of assets. Property and liability insurers employ on a part or full-time basis approximately 600,000 persons and they have over $39 billion of invested assets. There are over 4,800 insurers domiciled in the United States of which in the neighborhood of 3,200 sell property and liability insurance.[28] In 1964, the largest insurers in the property-liability field in the United States, from the viewpoint of net premiums written, were State Farm Insurance Company, Travelers Insurance Company, All State Insurance Company, Hartford Fire Insurance Company, Continental National American Insurance Companies, The Fireman's Fund-American Insurance Company, The Aetna Insurance Company, Continental Insurance Company, Insurance Company of North America, and Liberty Mutual Insurance Company.

In the field, aside from agents and brokers and their employees who make direct contact with insureds in producing business, there are insurer field representatives, general and special agents, and adjusters. Specialized groups include chemists, electricians, and engineers who test material and devices used in the construction and protection of buildings. Aside from the number gainfully employed at full-time occupations, thousands are employed part time. In this category are to be found local physicians who make examinations for life insurers, attorneys who assist in difficult or litigated adjustments, independent adjusters, and credit investigators. To such a point has insurance developed as an economic institution that in 1944 the Supreme Court said of it: "Insurance touches the home, the family, and the occupation or the business of almost every person in the United States."[29]

FOR DISCUSSION

1. Explain the term "transportation insurance" as used by inland marine insurers.
2. If the transportation company as a common carrier is liable as an insurer for goods entrusted to it for transportation, explain the need for transportation insurance.
3. The following clause, or one similar, usually appears in railroad sidetrack agreements: "And the Railroad Company agrees to switch to and from said sidetrack carload freight consigned to and from the Contractor over the railroad of the Railroad Company, at such times as shall be convenient to the Railroad Company, the placing upon said sidetrack of any car containing freight consigned to the Contractor to

---

[28] *Insurance Facts* (New York: Insurance Information Institute, 1965), p. 2.

[29] *United States* v. *South-Eastern Underwriters Association* et al., 64 Sup. Ct. 1162 (1944).

be deemed a full delivery of such freight to the Contractor." What danger is to be found in this clause in connection with inland marine insurance of shipments via the railroad?

4. B is the owner of a plant whose principal business is packing sardines and clams. He sells in carload lots upon orders placed by brokers. He does not insure his shipments, relying upon the liability of the carrier to reimburse him in event of loss. On a given day he is notified that a carload of sardines consigned to a dealer in the Middle West was destroyed by a fire in the freight sheds of the railroad. Why is the time of arrival of the shipment of vital importance to the shipper?
5. In *Stevenson* v. *Hartman* (231 N.Y. 378) the court stated: "As we have indicated it seems to us perfectly clear that the business thus described was that of a common carrier of goods. Defendant was either a private carrier carrying occasionally for some particular person under some particular agreement or he was a common carrier engaged in the general business of carrying goods generally for those who desired his services. It seems plain that his case is not fitted by the former description but that he comes within the latter definition." What is the significance of this decision?
6. It was early contended that the limitation of liability of a carrier based upon an agreed value for the purpose of adjusting rates was in conflict with sound public policy in that the limitation as to value had the tendency to exempt the carrier from liability for negligence. The courts have decided that this is not the case. In your opinion, is the decision logical? Explain.
7. Many transportation contracts contain the following clause or one similar in effect: "This insurance covers from the time the property insured passes into the custody of any railroad, express company or public truckman, transfer and/or transportation companies for transportation only by land and/or while on ferries and/or cars on transfers, in connection therewith, until delivered by railroad, express company or public truckman, transfer and/or transportation companies at destination but only while in due course of transit." What is the significance of the phrases "the custody of" and "in due course of transit"?
8. X consigned a shipment of goods to an express company with instructions that they be held at the place of destination until called for by the shipper or his agent. The express company held the goods in its warehouse for four months. While the goods were in the warehouse an unusually heavy rainstorm occurred. Part of the shipment was on the floor of the warehouse. Because of the seepage of water into the building, the goods on the floor were damaged. The express company made every effort to minimize the damage. The damaged goods were removed to another room, dried, and repacked. Advise the express company of its liability.
9. X ships a package weighing 15 pounds valued at $200, receiving a receipt limiting the liability of the express company to $50. Upon receipt of the package, the consignee notices it to be damaged. May

he refuse to accept it on the grounds that it is insured and make a claim against his insurance company for the full value of the package? In the above case, what is the liability of the express company?

10. Define "bailee," and distinguish between the responsibility of a gratuitous bailee and that of a paid bailee.
11. A common carrier by water is defined as a shipowner who holds himself out to the public generally as offering his service of carrying goods for hire. Except as modified by statute the common carrier is almost in the position of an insurer. What is the significance of the phrase "modified by statute" and the word "almost" as used above?
12. In July, 1951, thousands of shippers located in all parts of the country were affected by the devastating flood that occurred in Kansas. Losses to goods in transit running to many millions of dollars were irrecoverable from the carriers. Shippers would not anticipate flood losses in the Middle West in July. Why are the carriers not liable?
13. Discuss the development of multiple line insurance and distinguish this type of insurance from all lines insurance.
14. What is the origin of the word "casualty" as it is used in the insurance business? Is the word now as descriptive of insurance practice as it may once have been? What trends seem to be developing in this area?
15. The insurance business has grown substantially over the years. Look up figures on premium volume for property and liability insurers in the United States and discuss the nature of the trends that you observe.
16. In your opinion, is the rolling stock of a railroad properly the subject matter of an inland marine insurance contract?
17. Select one multiple line insurer and undertake a detailed study of its historical development, current status, and financial strength.
18. Discuss the history of fire marks. What purpose did they serve?
19. B contends that most of his shipments are made by railroad and that he is quite satisfied with the responsibility of the railroad in the event of loss or damage. X asks if he has ever given thought to the difference in the responsibility of the railroad as a common carrier and as a warehouseman. Indicate the difference in the liability of the railroad in the two situations.

CHAPTER • 3

Basic Concepts and Practices of Property and Liability Insurers

In succeeding chapters considerable attention will be given to a variety of insurance contracts in terms of their provisions and legal nature. Before entering on that discussion it is useful to review certain insurance practices that are related to the contract and that have some bearing on its nature, the way it is administered, and the extent of settlement in the event of loss.

TREND TOWARD UNIFORMITY

In the process of the evolution of insurance, several important factors have established a trend toward uniformity. These are competition, cooperation, and regulation.

In the early days of insurance there were a wide variety of contracts. In the field of marine insurance, Lloyd's of London was a dominant factor, and the Lloyd's contract early became a model for the ocean marine contract. While the contract today contains many clauses and phrases that seem hardly to apply to the present-day needs of marine insurance, the rich background of legal interpretation operates in favor of the retention of much of the ancient phraseology. State legislatures do not require a standard marine contract or uniform provisions. Competition in the field is international in its scope, and the requirements of shippers and competition among insurers have tended to establish in the generally offered contracts certain basic principles, with extensions that the exigencies of modern business require. While, then, no standard marine contract and no standard provisions are required by our state legislatures, there is a degree of uniformity in marine insurance practices that is the outgrowth of tradition and custom.

There was for may years a confusion in the field of fire insurance, created by the wide differences in the phrasing of the contracts issued. The insurance business itself recognized the need for standardization, and the first step was undertaken by the New York Board of Fire Underwriters prior to the enactment of any legislation. In all jurisdictions in this country standard fire contracts are required today, either the outgrowth of specific legislation or as a result of the ruling of the insurance department.

The idea of standardization has not resulted in legislation in all fields of insurance, although most insurance departments require that contract forms be submitted to them before a contract may be issued. Because many insurers operate on a nationwide basis, this requirement has given rise to a necessity for uniformity. Competition between insurers has resulted in the issuing of contracts that are alike in their essentials, as far as liberalization of the coverage forms a feature of the contract.

SPECIFIED PERILS AND ALL RISKS CONTRACTS

Insurance contracts are, for the most part, issued to indemnify the insured against loss occasioned by some specified peril or group of perils. For example, the standard fire insurance contracts undertake to indemnify the insured "against all direct loss and damage by fire, lightning, and by removal from premises endangered by the perils insured against. . . ." A building insured against loss by fire might be destroyed by earthquake, windstorm, or one of many other causes and the loss be outside the coverage of the fire contract.

In the field of marine insurance, the early contracts were written to "cover all risks and perils of transportation." Such a contract included within the scope of its coverage all losses occasioned by perils *of* the sea. It was early determined that even as comprehensive a coverage as this did not extend to all perils, and fire was early determined to be not a peril *of* the sea but a peril *on* the sea. From marine insurance there has risen the tendency to incorporate a large number of perils within the scope of a given contract, and when this is done the contract is known as an "all risks" contract. The practice has been widely accepted in the field of inland marine insurance, and the tendency to extend into other fields has already manifested itself.

There are those who have suggested that the term "all risks" is comprehensive enough to cover all loss of any nature whatever to the property insured. This is not the case. The principle has been generally accepted in the field of insurance, and consequently, even though the contract is written for all risks, there must be "some casualty, something which could not be foreseen as one of the necessary incidents of the adventure" in order that there be a loss. Our courts have quite definitely established the rule.[1] Risks are distinguished from inherent vice, and an all risks contract covers exactly as it states and the loss to be included within the scope of the coverage must be attributable to a risk. To meet this requirement all risk contracts are limited to fortuitous physical loss from external causes. Under an all risks contract the insurer is not liable for loss or damage to the insured property attributable to decay. In the case of an opal, for example, which has an inherent tendency to crack, a loss attributable to such a crack would not be covered under an all risks jewelry contract. In discussing a loss of this character, the courts state: "Because the contract must be considered as one against damage from fortuitous and extraneous damage, it is not permissible to resort to an ultra-literal interpretation which will convert it into a contract of warranty against loss resulting wholly from inherent susceptibility to dissolution."[2] Even in those contracts where the term "all risks" is followed by such comprehensive phraseology as "other causes of whatsoever nature of and/or damage to the above described property or part thereof from any cause whatsoever," it has been held that the term "any cause whatsoever" in an insurance contract refers to risks and does not apply to losses attributable to wear and tear, inherent vice, or losses to be expected in the normal course of use. The rule has been succinctly summarized in the following: "I have followed the English authorities because I think them right in holding that even under an 'all-risks policy,' there must be a fortuitous event—casualty—to give rise to liability."[3] The loss to be covered by an all risks insurance contract must be attributable to an accident or fortuitous event and not something that is an outgrowth of the nature of the subject of the insurance.

All risks contracts usually contain a number of qualifying clauses excluding perils which the insurer does not wish to cover. In the fine-arts contract, it is customary to exclude losses due to war risks, strikes, and riots. These exclusions are usual to most property contracts. In addition, in this particular coverage, there are exclusions for losses due to wear and tear and damage due to restoration or retouching.

---

[1] *Mellon* v. *Federal Insurance Company*, 14 F (2d) 997.

[2] *Chute* v. *North River Insurance Company*, 172 Minn. 13, 214 N.W. 473.

[3] *Mellon* v. *Federal Insurance Company*, 14 F (2d) 997. The principle was laid down in an old English case, *Wilson* v. *Owners of Cargo per "Xantho,"* 12 L.R. App. Cas. 509, when the court stated that insurance against perils of the sea does not provide protection "against that natural and inevitable action of the winds and waves which results in what may be described as wear and tear. There must be some casualty, something which could not be foreseen as one of the necessary incidents of the adventure. The purpose of the policy is to secure an indemnity against accidents which may happen, not against events which must happen."

AMOUNT OF THE CONTRACT

One of the most important functions of insurance underwriting is to limit the face of the insurance contract to an amount that will reasonably indemnify the insured. In a great majority of cases this presents little or no difficulty. The value of the property, the subject of the insurance, can be determined within reasonably narrow limits, and the amount of the insurance is limited to the amount of the loss that the insured may suffer. There are cases, however, in which values as represented by replacement costs and the probable loss represent widely divergent figures. To cite a specific example: In some sections of the country there are in existence elaborate stables built years ago at great cost when horses were maintained in connection with the dwelling. These stables have been converted into garages and in the event of their total destruction would probably never be replaced. Stables that might cost $15,000 or more to replace if destroyed by fire would probably be replaced by a small two- or three-car garage. Insurance underwriters, in placing insurance on a building of this sort, disregard entirely the replacement cost of the property and give consideration rather to its functional value. If a building with a replacement cost of $15,000 is rendering no more service to the insured than would a new building valued at $5,000, the careful underwriter will be unwilling to insure the building for an amount in excess of $5,000.

There are properties that, because of their nature, are extremely difficult to appraise accurately. In this category fall works of art, curios, rare and unusual collections, family portraits, and heirlooms. Because of the difficulty of arriving at any satisfactory agreement as to value following a loss, it is deemed advisable in underwriting this class of business that the insurance underwriter and the insured agree upon a value at the time the contract is issued. From an underwriting standpoint, this value must be one that unquestionably will make the preservation of the property more attractive to the insured than would be its loss accompanied by the payment of the insurance.

In the field of liability insurance, the face of the contract is ordinarily an amount which the insured feels will adequately provide protection. It is quite possible that a judgment will be rendered against a policyholder in excess of the face of his contract. This is true because the value of the property covered by the contract and the loss or damage for which the owner may be held liable bear no relationship, one to the other, and hence the face of the contract cannot be written with any advance knowledge as to a definite liability limit. The amounts written take into consideration judgments awarded by the courts and the laws governing recovery. Insurers issue contracts based upon this experience, with limits known as standard. It is quite customary for insureds to buy contracts with limits considerably above the standard limits, and insurance underwriters emphasize the importance of higher limits if, because of the financial standing of the insured or the nature of the risk, large judgments are probable.

CONTRACTS OF INDEMNITY VERSUS VALUED CONTRACTS

Property insurance contracts are generally regarded as contracts of indemnity, inasmuch as the insurer typically agrees to pay only the cash value of the loss at the time of loss subject to the face amount of the contract. Contracts are written in some cases that provide that the amount of insurance shall be regarded as the true value of the property, and as the amount of loss and damage in the event the property, the subject of the insurance, is destroyed. Such contracts are said to be valued. The practice at first thought might seem to be a direct contradiction to the indemnity rule and valued contracts may, in fact, be written so that they do create an element of speculation. It is not the intention of insurers that this be the case. When valued contracts are written, careful underwriting tends to limit the amount of the face of the contract to a sum that, in the minds of all the parties interested, fairly represents the value of the property insured. Certain types of property, such as works of art, curios, and other objects possessing a unique value, may be the subject of an honest difference of opinion at any particular time. To forestall the possibility of such a difficulty, it is not unusual for the insured and insurer to agree in advance on the value of the property with the understanding that this value shall be accepted as the basis of settlement in the event of loss or damage. The valued contract is widely used in the insurance of works of art, as well as collections of coins and stamps, rare books and manuscripts, dies, patterns, and, in fact, any items whose value at the time of loss is difficult to determine or subject to a possible difference of opinion. In writing a contract of this type there is no violation of the indemnity idea. Rather, an agreement is made in advance as to the amount necessary to indemnify the insured in the event of loss or damage to his property. The use of the valued contract in such situations is regarded as sound underwriting.

From time to time there develops a demand by the public for valued contracts in connection with the insurance of other types of property. The necessity for careful and painstaking underwriting and the opportunity to use such contracts to overinsure have caused insurance authorities to frown upon the general use of this contract. Nevertheless, statutes have been enacted that make valued contracts mandatory. When such laws have been enacted, the statutes provide that, whenever an insured property shall be totally destroyed, the amount of insurance in force shall be taken as conclusive evidence of the true value of the property and the true amount of the loss or damage, regardless of the actual value of the property. Such laws are based upon the reasoning presented by the property owner that it is unjust for him to pay for insurance over a number of years and then, if his property is destroyed, to get less than the face of the contract. The reasoning has its appeal. The fact remains, however, that experience in the insurance business has shown that there is less injustice if the responsibility for fixing a reasonable amount of insurance is placed upon the insured than is the case if the insured is permitted to make a profit through the destruction of his property if he is successful in effecting its overinsurance. This being the case, the valued contract laws, as they apply to property in general, are believed to invite carelessness and fraud and in many instances to stimulate overinsurance. In a specific case in which the property insured is carefully appraised by both the parties at interest prior to the issuance of the contract and an agreement is reached, the valued contract will not violate the indemnity rule.

Liability contracts, as they were formerly written, were contracts of indemnity. If the insured were held to be legally liable in any given case, the contract undertook to indemnify him for his loss. In the case of bankruptcy, if the insured could not settle the claim, the insurer was not obligated to do so because in such a situation the insured suffered no loss. Insurers later offered contracts containing the so-called "bankruptcy clause." This provided that, regardless of whether judgment was enforceable against the insured, the insurer assumed the obligation to pay a claimant, if the insured was legally liable for damages that came within the scope of a contract. The liability contracts as now issued are regarded not as contracts of indemnity against loss but as contracts of indemnity against liability.[4]

ANNUAL AND TERM CONTRACTS

The time specified in the contract during which the coverage is effective is its *term.* A contract written for one year is called an *annual* contract, while a contract written for a longer period is called

[4] The difference between a liability contract and an indemnity contract has been clearly set forth in the language of the courts in the following terms: "There is a well-recognized difference between contracts of indemnity against loss and contracts of indemnity against liability. In the former the insurer does not become liable until loss has actually been suffered and the amount of the insurance does not become available until the insured has paid the loss, whereas in the latter case the obligation of the insurer becomes fixed when the liability attaches to the insured." (*Klotzbach* v. *Bull Dog Auto Fire Association,* Mo. App. 267 S.W. 39.)

a *term* contract. Certain types of risks are accepted on an annual basis only; others are written for a term with a concession in the rate.

When contracts are written on a term basis, with a three-year term being the maximum in virtually all states, a discount is allowed if the entire three-year premium is paid in advance. The discount is generally 10 percent, and the amount of premium paid for a three-year contract would be 2.7 times the annual premium. For some contracts, term rates are allowed permitting installment payments.

Contracts may also be written for a period less than a year. Short-

TABLE 3–1

SHORT-RATE TABLE

Days Policy in Force	*Percentages to Be Charged or Retained*	*Days Policy in Force*	*Percentages to Be Charged or Retained*	*Days Policy in Force*	*Percentages to Be Charged or Retained*
1	2	18	16	105	45
2	4	19	16	120 (4 mo.)	50
3	5	20	17	135	55
4	6	25	19	150 (5 mo.)	60
5	7	30 (1 mo.)	20	165	65
6	8	35	23	180 (6 mo.)	70
7	9	40	26	195	73
8	9	45	27	210 (7 mo.)	75
9	10	50	28	225	78
10	10	55	29	240 (8 mo.)	80
11	11	60 (2 mo.)	30	255	83
12	12	65	33	270 (9 mo.)	85
13	13	70	36	285	88
14	13	75	37	300 (10 mo.)	90
15	14	80	38	315	93
16	14	85	39	330 (11 mo.)	95
17	15	90 (3 mo.)	40	360 (12 mo.)	100

term contracts are ordinarily written for a special purpose, such as to bring about an expiration date at a particular time or to add to insurance during the period of a temporary inventory increase. Contracts written for less than a year are often charged for on what is termed the *short-rate* basis. Table 3–1 is a short-rate table used for computing short-term fire premiums.

Some fire insurers write business on a weekly collection or "industrial system."[5] A continuous-form contract is issued, and this, in turn, is extended from week to week as payments are made. The form of insurance is available only for limited classes of business, and the maximum risk assumed on any one policy is low. There are only eleven states in which this type of insurance is written.

[5] The term "industrial" is derived from weekly payment life insurance that was originated during the 19th century and designed for the needs of industrial workers. Because of the weekly payment feature the term "industrial" has been applied to this form of insurance.

DEDUCTIBLE CLAUSES AND EXCESS INSURANCE

Insurance contracts are written to pay a sum less than the full amount of the loss. These are termed "deductible" contracts and "catastrophe" or "excess-of-loss" contracts. At first thought both forms of insurance might appear to differ only in degree. There is, however, a fundamental difference in the two forms.

Deductibles. Marine underwriters early recognized that certain types of goods were particularly susceptible to small losses. The losses themselves could easily be carried by the owners of the goods. If the insurer were to be responsible, the necessity was created of adding to the insurance rate a definite sum to cover the damage that was almost sure to happen. There seemed to be little point in adding to a rate the amount of a loss that could reasonably be anticipated. This being the case, the marine underwriters provided in their contracts that they were to be relieved of all partial losses on certain types of goods, and in other classifications the loss to be collectible must exceed a designated percentage of value. The provision was first attached to the policy in the form of a memorandum, and for that reason such clauses to this day are referred to as "memorandum clauses."

The principle has found its way into other branches of insurance. In the field of automobile insurance, the owner of an automobile might be perfectly satisfied to have small damages repaired himself. If the insurer is liable for the repair of minor losses, not only is the cost of handling the claims entirely out of proportion to the damage sustained, but there is a tendency on the part of the insured to ask for more extensive repairs if insurance is involved than would be required if he were making the damage good. For this reason, automobile insurance involving loss or damage to the car of the insured is frequently written with a deductible clause providing that the insurer is not liable unless the loss exceeds an amount named in the clause, and then the liability is only for such amount as the loss exceeds the specified deduction.

Deductible insurance as offered by insurers is based upon sound theory. It is predicated upon the assumption that minor losses do not lend themselves logically to insurance because of the increased cost that must inevitably attach because of the cost of handling the business. If the property which is the subject of the insurance is exposed to heavy losses, the heavy losses may well be insured. Insuring the risk of large losses and at the same time eliminating the insurance of small losses is effected through the use of deductible clauses, although different names may be applied to them in actual practice in the various branches of insurance.

Recently sizable deductibles have been introduced in the field of fire insurance. Some insurers offer forms allowing deductibles at the insured's option ranging from $5,000 up to $250,000. These contracts are written without any relation whatever to the probable loss expectancy. A schedule of rate credits is applicable according to the percentage of value represented by the deductible amount which the insured selects. Some insurers are averse to writing this kind of deductible insurance because of a conviction that it would encourage self-insurance, reduce insurer income generally, and endanger the rate structure by injecting an element of uncertainty and inaccuracy into premium and loss data. These insurers distinguish sizable fire deductibles from the $40- and $100-deductible coverages designed to eliminate nuisance claims.

Excess Insurance. Under excess-of-loss insurance, the insured stands each loss up to the maximum damage reasonably to be expected on any item embraced by the contract. This type of insurance may at first sight appear to differ from deductible insurance only in degree. Such is not the case. Deductible insurance permits the insured to select the amount of loss or damage that develops because of the peril covered by the contract. In the case of excess-of-loss insurance, determination of the probable maximum loss is not left to chance or the insured's preference, but must be made by the insurer after careful consideration of the construction, occupancy, protection, value distribution, and the loss history of the properties themselves. The normal loss expectancy of a frame, unprotected building is 100 percent; upon a large industrial plant, scattered over a considerable area, the probable maximum loss is determined through the application of ordinary underwriting principles. Whatever this figure may be, it follows that any loss in excess of the one reasonably foreseeable represents the unexpected or unusual and takes on the character of a catastrophe.

The basis of excess-of-loss insurance is the assumption by the insured of each and every loss up to the amount of the probable loss upon his properties; the contract then affords indemnity only for the loss in excess of that normally expected. This type of coverage is especially important in liability insurance and in reinsurance, and is discussed further in connection with each of these topics.

AVERAGE AND COINSURANCE

In the development of marine insurance, contracts were issued for a premium, and the coverage was expected to equal the full value of the subject of the insurance. When rates were promulgated, it was understood that the amount designated in the contract represented the full value of the risk. Failure to designate full value had an effect upon the insurance in the case of total loss, and the full amount of the insurance was paid. In the event of partial loss, however, the insurer was obligated to pay only that portion of the partial loss that the amount of insurance bore to the value of the risk. To illustrate: If a cargo valued at $50,000 is insured for $25,000 and there is a loss of $10,000, even with $25,000 insurance the full amount of the loss cannot be collected. Since the amount of insurance to value is one half, the amount for which the insurance carrier is liable is likewise one half. It follows that in the case of any partial loss, unless full insurance to value is carried, the insured must contribute to any loss an amount proportionate to the deficiency. This principle is thoroughly established in marine insurance and is so universally followed that mention of it in the contract is regarded as unnecessary.

In other fields the situation is not the same. Insurance may be written for a specific amount regardless of the value of the property. A building valued at $100,000 may be insured for 5 percent of the value, 50 percent of the value, or any other percentage that may be agreed upon between the owner and the underwriters. Experience has shown that in many types of risk a large proportion of payments are for partial losses and not total losses. It follows that if a group of property owners carry but a small proportion of insurance to value and another group is insured for full value, in the long run, because of the prevalence of partial losses, those insured for small amounts collect more from the insurers than those who are insured for full value in relation to the premium paid. From the viewpoint of insurance theory, this creates an inequitable situation. As a remedy, insurers have introduced the idea of a lower rate in return for an agreement on the part of the property owner to carry an agreed amount of insurance.

In the earlier attempts to incorporate a condition in the contract providing for higher limits of insurance, the contract was so worded as to make it appear that the insured had no alternative except to carry the amount of insurance indicated, if he was to comply with the condition of the contract. The clause stated in effect that the insured must carry insurance in a stipulated percentage of the value insured. To overcome an opposition to what appeared to many to be an effort on the part of the insurers to increase their business rather than to establish an equitable rate structure, a new clause known for some time as an "average clause" and later as a "coinsurance clause" was worked out.[6]

Contracts are now written in such a way that the insured will bear as much of the loss as is represented by the insurance deficiency. For this reason, the clauses in contracts covering the agreement are refer-

[6] Although the expressions "average clause" and "coinsurance clause" are often used interchangeably, a distinction is sometimes made. See A. H. Mowbray and R. H. Blanchard, *Insurance* (5th ed.; New York: McGraw-Hill Book Company, Inc., 1961), pp. 113–14.

red to as "coinsurance clauses." A coinsurance clause—sometimes known as the "contribution clause," the "reduced-rate average clause," the "reduced-rate contribution clause," and in some states the "standard average clause"—states that, in consideration of the reduced rate or form under which the policy is written, it is stipulated and made a condition of the contract that, in the event of loss, the company shall be liable for no greater proportion thereof than the amount insured under its contract bears to a designated percentage of the actual cash value of the property described at the time when such loss shall happen. Thus, in the case of a building valued at $100,000, an insured with an 80 percent coinsurance clause obligates himself to provide $80,000 in insurance in order to collect the full amount of a partial loss. In the event that he fails to do this, he is presumed to be an insurer himself to the extent of the deficiency. If the insured in the foregoing example carries $40,000 insurance instead of $80,000, he carries one half as much insurance as is required for full protection. He is presumed to be carrying the other half himself. In the event of a $10,000 loss with $40,000 in insurance, the insurers would pay one-half the loss and the owner would be a coinsurer for the balance.

In the fire insurance field covering direct loss, a reduced rate is allowed on specified classes of property if the owner carries insurance equal to 80 percent of the value. If he carries a higher percentage, additional reductions are allowed. In other types of contract, reduced rates are allowed if the insured agrees to carry 10, 25, or other percentages ranging upward. In the case of a blanket contract covering the mortgage interest of a mortgagee, the exposure on a single loss might be $5,000 but the total risk $5,000,000. In order to derive sufficient premium to create an equitable contract, the insurer might provide a rate based upon the insured carrying 10 percent of the total risk, or $500,000.

MINIMUM PREMIUMS

If a contract is written and then canceled, it is usual to provide for a minimum earned premium. There are certain fixed costs that attach to the issuing of an insurance contract. A fire insurance rate may call for $0.27 for each $1.00 of insurance written for a period of one year. If one asked for $100 of insurance, the insurer could not profitably issue a contract for $0.27. A certain amount of expense is involved in the preparation of the rates and in the purchase of supplies. Likewise, there is the expense of office labor required in preparing the contract. For this reason it is customary to require a minimum premium. In such instances the minimum premium is designed to cover minimum expenses in connection with the issuance and processing of the contract, including expenses such as are entailed in making audits and handling reporting forms, where the usual provision in the rate for a percentage of premium would be insufficient to cover such expenses.

In some fields of insurance a large part of the expense in connection with the carrying of the risk involves inspections or other such services. This is always true in connection with the acceptance and processing of casualty risks. In some instances an inspection must be made and a credit report obtained. Files are established for each risk, and provision must be made for accounting and statistical records. With respect to these risks certain of the expenses have little or no relationship to the size of the account or the premium resulting from it. In connection with losses some of the claim expenses such as the adjusters' time and traveling expenses do not vary with the size of the risk. In the field of workmen's compensation insurance, certain administration and audit expenses are basic with every contract. Unless the payroll produces a premium of a given amount, the insurer will lose if the contract is canceled before such a premium is earned. The minimum premium aims to get the minimum dollars needed, based on an assumed minimum payroll, plus a flat charge representing a minimum cost for issuing and servicing the contract.

Minimum premiums are used to indicate whether a risk is eligible for a certain type of rating plan. High minimums are required in connection with reporting forms and premium adjustment plans. These plans cannot economically be adapted to small risks. In certain of these plans high processing costs and the nature of the coverage granted require that the line develop a sizable premium to cover these costs. By requiring a sizable minimum premium the companies automatically eliminate the small risks for which the plans are not adaptable.

Again minimum premiums are provided to catch what is termed the "high flash point of exposure" in connection with certain types of insurance. Particularly in the case of riot and civil commotion it is the practice of insureds to take out insurance when an emergency appears imminent. When the emergency is past, the insurance is canceled. In order to cover the flash point of exposure, it is the practice to require substantial minimums in order to protect the insurers and to prevent selection against the insurer when the risk is particularly high. If such insurance were written at the manual rate in smaller amounts, there would be a tendency to create a situation of adverse selection against the insurer. Hence, the minimum premium in such instances is ordinarily in an amount sufficiently large to reimburse the insurer for the risk.

CANCELLATION

If an insurance contract is terminated before its expiration by either the insured or the insurer, the contact is said to be canceled. The basis of cancellation is usually made a part of the contract. The insured may cancel without notice. The contract ordinarily stipulates the length of notice that the insurer must give before cancellation becomes effective.

When cancellation is initiated by the insurer a pro rata return premium is the usual rule. If the insured cancels the contract, the short-rate table (Table 3–1) is made the basis for computing the premium earned for the period the contract is in force. This difference in return premium is based on the reasoning that the insured should not be penalized when a contract is canceled for the convenience of the insurer. On the other hand, it is held to be equitable to charge the insured the same premium he would be required to pay had he bought insurance for less than a year at the outset.

In the case of insurance written for a term longer than a year, the same rule holds for a pro rata return of premium if the contract is canceled by the insured. A short-rate table that penalizes the insured has been computed for term insurance, and return premiums are computed on the basis of this table if the insured initiates the cancellation.

Various attempts have been made to justify the use of a short-rate table. It has been stated that the various factors considered in allowing term discounts, particularly expense and interest elements, should operate to make short-term contracts somewhat more expensive than term contracts. It is doubtful whether these factors have been carried out with any degree of scientific accuracy for the purposes of computing the short-rate table. The fact remains that it is now accepted in the business that some expense and inconvenience accrue to the insurer when an insured cancels a contract and the short-rate table compensates for this.[7]

RENEWAL OF INSURANCE

It is the practice in the insurance business for the agent or broker with whom the line of insurance has been placed to solicit renewal some time before the expiration date. Many agencies have a form termed an "expiration notice" which is mailed to the insured usually about 30 days prior to the expiration of the contract in question. Notices are usually worded to read that in the absence of contrary instructions a new contract will be issued and delivered before expiration of the present coverage. Some agencies have dispensed entirely with the notice and forward a contract to their insureds renewing the old contract as of its expiration date. This gives the insured the

---

[7] The short-rate formula now in general use dates from 1947 and was developed to correct inequities and inconsistencies in the short-rate practices in effect in different branches of the business. Stock and mutual property and liability insurers generally follow the same formula for short-rate cancellation.

opportunity to retain the contract if he elects to do so, or otherwise to return it for cancellation or modification.

This practice of automatically renewing contracts has led many insureds to rely upon their agents for notice with respect to expirations or for the automatic renewal of outstanding contracts. In the absence of express agreement, there appears to be no obligation on the part of the agent to notify an insured with respect to expirations. The notice or renewal is primarily for the purpose of carrying on the business of the agent. The insured should keep a careful record of his own expirations, and if the contract is not renewed prior to expiration, he should take active steps himself to see that the continuous coverage is maintained. There are records of situations where agencies have changed hands and the transfer of records has been inadequate or incomplete and expiring contracts have not been renewed. Actually, the responsibility of placing the business is that of the property owner buying the insurance. Fortunately, the pressure for business on the part of the insurance agent tends to jog his memory. This reminder is purely a gratuitous service. A simple expiration record in the hands of the insured, upon which he will rely, is always indicated.

RECORDS

Contracts covering property insurance do not have a cash or surrender value as do life insurance contracts. While it is important for an insured to retain his contracts and have them available in the event of loss, it is not a serious problem if a contract is, in fact, lost or destroyed.

When contracts are issued, it is the custom to make at least three copies. The copies are not complete duplicates of the original contract, but a form is inserted when the contract is typed and spaces appear on this form where all pertinent data particular to the risk are copied by means of a carbon. The form is known as a "daily report," deriving its name from the fact that one copy is sent at the end of each business day to the home office of the insurer as a record of the risks assumed and the business transacted. A second copy of the daily report, sometimes referred to as the "agent's record," is maintained by the agent in his files. Where brokers or other intermediaries are involved or interested, additional copies of the daily report or agent's record are made for their accommodation.

In the event that a contract is lost or destroyed, as might be the case with the destruction of a fire insurance contract in a fire, all the pertinent data with respect to the contract are immediately available both at the office of the agent and the home office of the insurer. Upon notice of loss, the insured is asked to sign a "lost contract receipt," and a new contract replacing the original is issued. Since, as stated, the contract has no cash value, no bond or other indemnity agreement other than the lost contract receipt is required. It follows that if a conflagration should wipe out a community and an insured lose his contracts, even if the records of the agencies are destroyed, copies of the contracts may always be obtained from the home office of the insurer. It is a remote contingency that both the home office and the agency would be destroyed simultaneously with the loss of an insured's contracts.[8]

GUIDING PRINCIPLES

The insurance industry has established a procedure for the prompt adjustment of losses when the insured finds himself with two or more applicable insurance contracts affording similar coverages but so written as to create grave uncertainty as to which of the contracts was liable in the loss. Another situation develops when the contract of the insured covers a loss on property in the hands of a bailee and where again he would have been covered in the absence of his own insurance by the contract of the bailee.

In the early history of insurance, when an insured covered property at a given location, he expected his loss to be covered at that location. Today, there are numerous extensions under certain contracts, and other contracts are written as floaters to cover anywhere in a designated territory. An example of the contract written with an extension is to be found in the dwelling contents contract that extends 10 percent of the face of the contract to cover personal property temporarily away from the permanent dwelling. This would mean that a suit at a tailor's shop for alteration or at a cleaning and dyeing establishment for pressing and cleaning would be covered under the owner's dwelling contents contract. It would also mean a bailee's inland marine contract written for the tailor or cleaning establishment, covering the goods of customers in his hands, would also provide coverage. Some contracts have divested themselves of liability where there is other insurance. When this situation developed with respect to two contracts, each covering identical lost or damaged property, the insured found himself in an extremely difficult position and, from a public relation standpoint, the position of the insurers each denying liability was intolerable.

To correct such a situation the fire insurers that ordinarily wrote the dwelling contents contract and the inland marine insurers that wrote the bailee's contract entered into an agreement that became

[8] Some insurers have prepared for the remote contingency that a catastrophe, such, for example, as an atomic attack, might destroy the entire home office plant. With this thought in view, they have made microfilm copies of all important records and have sent them to a remote depository in an area far distant from the home office.

known to the industry as "Agreement of Guiding Principles, Fire-Inland Marine."[9] There are many other situations where a literal interpretation of the insurance contracts leaves the liability of the insurers in doubt. A great many casualty contracts contain clauses intended to make the contract in which they appear excess insurance with respect to other insurance covering the same perils. Such "other insurance" provisions may have the apparent effect of negating all of the contracts. For instance, a contract may be written with a clause that provides, in effect, that the insurance will not cover if the insured has "other valid and collectible insurance" covering the same loss. Two contracts covering the same loss with the same identical clause will prove at least confusing to the layman. The situation is, likewise, confusing if there is a clause in all of the contracts covering a given loss providing that each contract shall cover only "excess" if there is other insurance. It might appear that each contract will pick up the loss when the other insurance is exhausted but none, under the literal terms of its contract, constitutes primary insurance. Fortunately, the courts, in situations such as this have held that where there are two contracts covering the same loss, each providing that "the insurance does not apply if the insured has other insurance covering the loss," the clauses cancel each other out. The contracts are interpreted as if the clause appeared in neither. Each insurer is liable to contribute to the loss up to the limit of its liability. Each contract covers in proportion to the amount at risk. There are a great many similar situations where the courts have not always been called upon to establish a principle. Here is where the agreements of guiding principles have filled a need. These agreements, in substance, provide in cases of duplicate coverage, regardless of whatever technical situations the contract provisions may create, that the insured shall receive first consideration. All insurers on the risk settle the loss in accordance with the formula provided in the agreement. It is to be pointed out that these agreements are not a part of the contract nor is the insured by law entitled to their benefits. They represent formulae resolving overlapping coverages, and agreements have been made between insurers with respect to their use. Signatory

---

[9] The first agreement of guiding principles was an agreement made January 1, 1936, between signatory members of the Inland Marine Underwriters Association. This agreement was designed to resolve conflict betweeen Inland Marine Underwriters where one insurer covered a property under a personal floater and the same property was insured under a bailee's contract. The most recent statement of guiding principles entitled, *Guiding Principles: Casualty-Fidelity-Fire-Inland Marine: First-Party Property Losses and Claims*, was published November 1, 1963. The statement was prepared under the auspices of The Association of Casualty and Surety Companies, Inland Marine Underwriters Association, National Automobile Underwriters Association, National Board of Fire Underwriters, National Bureau of Casualty Underwriters, and the Surety Association of America. The Association of Casualty and Surety Companies and the National Board of Fire Underwriters are now part of the American Insurance Association.

insurers are bound to follow the pattern established in the agreements. Other insurers may and frequently do elect to do so.

FOR DISCUSSION

1. The residence of B is covered for $10,000 under a valued contract. A fire in the roof causes $1,000 damage, and in the process of adjustment it is brought out that the value of the building is not over $5,000. What is the measure of the insurer's liability, if it is determined that the building is 20 percent destroyed?
2. As a condition precedent to a contract of indemnity, the insured must have an insurable interest in the subject of the insurance. Define "insurable interest."
3. It is sometimes stated in insurance literature that when the loss is total, the coinsurance clause is inoperative. This is the outgrowth of the fact that in a total loss the insured collects the full amount of insurance as represented by the face of his contracts regardless of percentage of insurance to value carried. The statement that the clause is inoperative is not correct. The clause is operative in every loss. Reconcile this with the fact that in a total loss the insured collects the face of his contracts.
4. Economic changes in communities result in properties being offered for sale at a fraction of their replacement cost. When the contract value is very much below the replacement value, the question of coinsurance becomes confusing. Assume a building costs $40,000 to rebuild and yet is offered for sale for $10,000. Explain the position of the purchaser as coinsurance applies to his insurance needs.
5. What is meant by the statement that liability insurance is not accident insurance? Is it not true that payments made under a liability contract are paid for accidental injuries?
6. B purchases a dwelling house for $40,000 and insures it in X insurer for $38,000. He pays the premium for a term of three years. At the end of six months, he sells the house to C and, as part of the transaction, gives him the three-year fire insurance contract. C files the contract with his deed. At the end of a year the property is totally destroyed by fire, and X insurer refuses to make any payment whatsoever. Upon what grounds may it do this?
7. B, while traveling abroad, purchases an oil painting which he believes to be an authentic old master. The purchase price is $100,000 and, in good faith, B insures the work for that amount. The premiums are paid over a period of ten years, and then in a destructive fire the painting is completely destroyed. B makes claim under his insurance for $100,000; but, following an investigation, it develops that the painting which he purchased was a fine copy valued at probably $500, and it is proved beyond any doubt that the original, which B supposed he had, is still in existence in Europe. B feels that his loss is still $100,000 and that he has paid insurance premiums for ten years to

cover the risk. The contract may be written one of two ways; in one situation he will collect $100,000 and in another, $500. Explain.

8. X carries a valued contract on a picture in the amount of $10,000. The picture was destroyed by fire, and upon investigation it is found to be worth but $1,000. The insurer denies liability on the ground that the owner of the picture knew that it was overvalued and contends that the contract was fraudulently obtained. Discuss from the point of view of the valued contract laws.
9. M is the sole heir of his father's estate. The father owns considerable real property. M believes it to be inadequately insured but cannot convince his father. May M insure the property to protect his interest?
10. Distinguish between the theory of the small deductible, such as the $50 deductible in windstorm insurance, and the theory of deductibles in sizable amounts found in contracts written for large business organizations.
11. Some insurers like to maintain a personal contact with insureds in the event of loss. Why is this not feasible in the event of a catastrophe?
12. Suggest some of the principal advantages to be found in the all risk approach to insurance coverage as compared with the named peril contract.
13. To fall within the scope of an all risk cover, the loss or damage must be accidental or fortuitous. Not only must the loss be attributable to an accident but the cause of the loss must be extraneous to the subject matter. This being so, there are property losses that an all risk contract does not cover. Give examples of such losses and explain the logic of the underlying principle.
14. Under an all risk contract it is stated that loss or damage contributed to by the insured's wilful or fraudulent act is under no circumstances insurable and, moreover, the loss or damage must be due to a lawful risk. Justify the statement.
15. Is there any possibility of an applicant for insurance receiving a counterfeit insurance contract?

CHAPTER · 4

Legal Basis of Property and Liability Insurance Contracts

The rights and obligations of the parties to an insurance agreement are determined largely by the law that governs contracts. There are certain essential elements that must form a part of every contract in order that it be held binding by law. These essential elements are an offer and an acceptance, marks required by law for legality, a capacity of the parties to contract, and the legality of the object of the contract. A lack of any of the essential elements is fatal to the enforcement of the agreement.

The contract will show: (*a*) the name of the insurer, (*b*) the name of the party that is insured, (*c*) the risk to be covered, (*d*) the premium, (*e*) the term of the insurance, and (*f*) the amount of insurance. The contract is executed and delivered in accordance with the application. While the insurance, by agreement, may become effective prior to the delivery of the contract, the contract evidences the terms of the agreement.

Insurance developed as a custom among merchants long before it became a subject of positive law; and accordingly, there are certain principles that apply to the interpretation of an insurance contract that do not apply to other contracts generally. Because of this, the insurance contract has been referred to by the courts as an "exotic in the common law." It is essential to consider the application of the usual rules of law that apply to contracts in general and also the rules that apply to the insurance contract in particular.

GENERAL CONSIDERATIONS

An insurance contract may be described in general terms as a contract that requires an insurable interest, utmost good faith, and is conditional in nature. In addition it is a contract of adhesion. The significance of these characteristics will now be considered.

Insurable Interest Essential. In order to take the property insurance contract out of the category of a wager or gamble, it is essential that the person who purchases the insurance have a sufficient interest in the property to cause him a loss if it is destroyed. In insurance terminology the term "insurable interest" is applied to that interest.

The Supreme Court of the United States has stated that insurable interest is not easy to define "with precision."[1] In the broadest possible terms, an insurable interest exists when the insured will suffer a disadvantage if the contingency insured against happens and will enjoy a benefit if the contingency fails to happen. A contract of insurance is "unequivocally unenforceable" without the prerequisite of an insurable interest.[2] The requirement is not one that the insurer may waive but is essential to every contract of insurance if the contract is to be enforceable. Without insurable interest any insurance contract, like a wager, is contrary to public policy and, therefore, void.[3]

Any definition of insurable interest to include within its scope all specific instances must of necessity be broad. Every interest in property, or liability concerning it, when the nature of the interest or liability is such that the insured may suffer loss from the destruction of the property, constitutes an insurable interest, sufficient to warrant valid insurance thereof.

Good Faith Required. The insurance contract is known as an "aleatory agreement" in contrast to the more usual type of contract termed a "commutative agreement." The commutative agreement provides an exchange of benefits that are reasonably equivalent. An aleatory contract incorporates in its terms an uncertain event or contingency. The happening of the contingency is a matter of chance, and the payment to one party may be entirely out of proportion to the payment to the other. Aleatory contracts include lottery agreements, wagering, and insurance. Insurance involves chance. Where there is an insurable interest, the contract is socially constructive, even though it embraces a contingency, and the benefits and premium constitute not even a semblance of equality. Because the

---

[1] *Warnock* v. *Davis,* 104 U.S. 775.

[2] B. Harnett and J. V. Thornton, "Insurable Interest in Property," *Columbia Law Review,* December, 1948; reprinted in *Insurance Law Journal,* June, 1949, p. 420.

[3] When the idea of insurance in England first began to take on commercial importance as a socially constructive enterprise, it was fast being converted into a means to satisfy a mania for gambling. Wagering contracts, at common law, were valid; and insurance contracts, even though the insured had no interest in property or life of the subject of the contract, were enforceable. When the gambling mania reached a point to create public revulsion, it drew the attention of the legislators. The earlier statutes dealt with wagering contracts in general. A series of statutes had the effect of making wagers unenforceable. Ultimately the statutes dealt specifically with insurance. But, again, the intent was to take insurance out of the category of a gambling contract.

insurance contract is an aleatory contract, it involves a possible payment of benefits entirely out of line with premium payments.

The insurer enters into the agreement having made certain assumptions. If the insured has any knowledge that might preclude the issuance of the contract, he is required to exercise good faith with the insurer throughout the entire transaction. This brings the insurance contract into a category sometimes said to be *uberrimae fidei.* Contracts of this class require for their validity the most perfect good faith of the contracting parties, because each party to the agreement must depend upon the other for his information or knowledge. Basically, an insurance contract as a contract is governed by the same principles that govern other contracts. When it is said to be a contract *uberrimae fidei,* it means that the good faith which is the basis for all contracts is more especially required in that species of contract in which one of the parties is supposed to be necessarily less acquainted with the details of the subject of the contract than the other.[4] Contracts *uberrimae fidei* are exceptions to the rule governing ordinary contracts not coupled with expressed guarantees to which the maxim *caveat emptor* applies. In the case of insurance, it is the general rule that "whether a policy be effected on a life, or a ship, or against fire, the underwriter has a right to expect that everything material should be communicated to him."[5]

Conditional Nature of the Contract. The insurance contract is conditional in that it obligates one party of the contract to fulfill certain conditions before the other party incurs an obligation. In the case of property and liability insurance, even though the contract

---

[4] *Gates* v. *Madison County Mutual Insurance Company,* 5 N.Y. 469. Grotius covers this point in referring to insurance contracts thus: "Contracts for guarding against danger, which are called insurances, will be deemed fraudulent and void, if the insurer knows beforehand that the thing insured is already safe, or has reached its place of destination, and the other party that it is already destroyed or lost. And that not so much on account of the equality naturally requisite in all contracts of exchange, as because the danger and uncertainty is the very essence of such contract. Now the premium upon all insurances must be regulated by common estimation." (*De Jure Belli,* Book II, chap. xii, Campbell translation.) Campbell cites Blackstone in a footnote: "Insurances being contracts, the very essence of which consists in observing the purest good faith and integrity, they are vacated by any the least shadow of fraud or undue concealment; and, on the other hand, being much for the benefit and extension of trade, by distributing the loss or gain among a number of adventurers, they are greatly encouraged and protected both by common law and acts of parliament." (Blakst. Com. b. ii, chap. xxx.) Christian's note on the same passage is added, as follows: "The contract of insurance is founded upon the purest principles of morality and abstract justice. Hence it is necessary that the contracting parties should have perfectly equal knowledge or ignorance of every material circumstance respecting the thing insured. If on either side there is any misrepresentation or *allegatio falsi,* or concealment, or *suppresio veri,* which would in any degree affect the premiums, or the terms of the engagement, the contract is fraudulent and absolutely void."

[5] *Lindman* v. *Desborough,* 3 Car. & P. 353.

undertakes to indemnify the insured for loss growing out of certain risks, invariably the contract places an obligation to perform on the part of the insured, and this obligation requires full compliance before the insurer is called upon to act. In the standard fire insurance contract, for example, the insured must file a proof of loss as a requirement that must be satisfied before the insurer is obligated to pay the loss. A clause in an insurance contract requiring such a performance is usually referred to as a "condition." In contract law a condition is distinguished from a promise in that a promise creates a duty in the promisor, while a condition qualifies a promise but creates no duty of performance. In the field of insurance this means simply that where there is a condition in a contract requiring some action on the part of the insured, the insured is under no legal obligation to perform that action but he must perform it in order to obligate the insurer to fulfill its part of the agreement, that is, the adjustment and payment of a loss.

Strict Compliance Rule. The insurance contract is said to be a contract of adhesion. This is so because in the case of insurance the insured has no part in drawing up its clauses or determining its wording. It is not a contract drawn after a period of negotiation in which both parties to the agreement insist upon or require certain features to appear. Rather the insured accepts the standard form of contract or, in any case, accepts a contract prepared by the insurer. It is true, property and liability insurance contracts are modified in particular cases to meet the requirements of individual applicants, but even when so modified the contract is prepared by the insurer and written on standardized forms.

Since the insurer has the advantage in drawing up the agreement and is expected to be able to represent clearly the intent of all parties, it is now a rule, generally enforced, that where the terms of the contract are ambiguous, obscure, or susceptible of more than one construction that one most favorable to the insured must prevail.[6] The rule is predicated on the assumption that the insurer, in drawing up its contract, is under a duty to make its meaning clear. When the insurer has failed to be clear, the insurer, and not the insured, must suffer. In cases of ambiguity or doubt it is not presumed that the terms of the contract are changed. The parties may have resort to the courts, and the courts in turn attempt a fair and reasonable interpretation.[7]

Where there is no ambiguity, the contract is to be enforced in

[6] *Knouse* v. *Equitable Life Insurance Company of Ohio*, 181 Pac. (2d) 310.

[7] The rule has thus been expressed: "No rule of interpretation of an insurance contract is more firmly imbedded than that which declares that where the language of the policy is without violence susceptible of two interpretations, one of which being that contended for by the insured, it should be most strongly construed against the insurer for the language is that of the insurer." G. Richards, *Laws of Insurance* (4th ed.; New York: Baker, Voorhis & Co., 1932), p. 115.

accordance with its terms. Nothing may be added to the contract, nor may its meaning be distorted by interpretations. Consideration must be given to the entire context to determine the nature and extent of coverage. If the contract is clear and understandable, it is to be enforced in accordance with the generally understood meaning of the terms used. Again, some courts have held that the rule that the terms and provisions of an insurance contract are to be construed more strictly against the insurer and more favorably to the insured does not apply when the wording is not that of the insurer but is taken from the statutes.[8] This appears to be sound reasoning, since the strict compliance rule is predicated on the assumption that the insurer that draws the contract is in a better position to know its meaning than the insured and, hence, interpretation should be in favor of the insured. Again, if the ambiguity can be resolved where the intent can be gathered from the entire contract, then the courts have interpreted the agreement on the basis of intent as so determined. Where intent is not clear and an ambiguity exists with respect to an insurance contract prepared by an insurer, the rule here definitely applies, and the terms and conditions of the contract are construed against the insurer in favor of the insured.

DOCTRINES PECULIAR TO THE INSURANCE CONTRACT

There are certain rules of law that apply specifically to the insurance contract. Certain customs that have grown up and been associated over a long period of time with the business of insurance are presumed to form part of the contract whether written specifically into the agreement or not. Among the fundamental doctrines that must be recognized are: (1) indemnity, (2) concealment, (3) representation and warranty, (4) substantial performance, (5) implied warranties, (6) fraud, (7) subrogation, and (8) waiver and estoppel.

Indemnity. Insurance undertakes to provide compensation for loss or damage sustained. It looks toward the future, with a view to reimbursing the insured in the event that loss shall occur. Thus, obligation to make payment rests upon the insurer only in the event that loss or damage has been incurred as a result of the happening of the unfavorable contingency covered in the contract. This last point is to be emphasized. When it is stated that the fire insurance contract is a contract of indemnity, it does not mean that every fire loss up to

---

[8] *Funk* v. *Aetna Life Insurance Company*, 96 F. (2d) 38; *Coyne* v. *American Policyholders Insurance Company*, 120 Conn. 645; *Haitner* v. *Aetna Casualty & Surety Company*, 189 So. 365; *Brown* v. *Great American Indemnity Company*, 298 Mass. 101.

the contract limits is covered. The contract covers direct loss. Thus a consequential loss, such as loss due to interruption of business, would not be covered unless the peril is specifically insured. The rule of indemnity, then, allows only within the limits of the coverage of the contract that the insured be fully reimbursed for any loss sustained. Any reimbursement in excess of actual loss or damage is a contradiction of the principle. The general rule is set forth in an old English case in the following terms: "The very foundation, in my opinion, of every rule which has been applied to insurance law is this, namely, that the contract of insurance contained in a marine or fire policy is a contract of indemnity, and of indemnity only, and that this contract means that the assured, in case of a loss against which the policy has been made, shall be fully indemnified, but shall never be more than fully indemnified."[9]

As a contract of indemnity, the face of the property insurance contract has no immediate bearing upon the amount payable in the event of a loss but rather represents a limit to the liability of the insurer. Under the indemnity rule, in the case of a property valued at $5,000 and insured for $10,000, the insurer would be liable only to pay the insured who suffered a total loss the amount of the value of his loss, or $5,000. If, for any reason, the insured receives reimbursement for the loss from any other source, or reimbursement in part, the liability of the insurer is reduced in the same amount.[10] The destruction or damage of the property described in the contract of insurance is not the contingency upon which the insurer promises to indemnify the insured; it is only when the insured has suffered a loss that the insurer may be called upon to make a payment under the contract.[11]

Doctrine of Concealment. Since the insurance contract is a contract *uberrimae fidei*, that is, a contract calling for the utmost good faith, it has become a fundamental doctrine of insurance law that both parties to the agreement must stand upon equal footing so far as the knowledge of either with relation to the risk is concerned. The contract is one involving the uncertainty with reference to an unfavorable contingency. It is essential that both parties to the contract enter on equal terms. Information unknown to both parties involves no obligation, since lack of information enters into the risk. On the

[9] *Castellain* v. *Preston,* L.R. 11 Q.B.D. 380.

[10] This rule was set forth in a decision of the United States Supreme Court as follows: "The general rule of law (and it is obvious justice) is, that where there is a contract of indemnity (it matters not whether it is a marine policy or a policy against fire on land or any other contract of indemnity), and a loss happens anything which reduces or diminishes that loss reduces or diminishes the amount which the indemnifier is bound to pay," *Chicago, St. Louis & New Orleans R. R. Co.* v. *Pullman Southern Car Co.*, 139 U.S. 79.

[11] *Draper* v. *Delaware State Grange Mutual Fire Insurance Co.*, 91 Atl. 206.

other hand, secret information in the part of either party that would, if known to the other party, deter him from entering into the agreement would, unless revealed, constitute a concealment.

The doctrine of concealment imposes a general duty of disclosure upon the applicant for insurance. This is an exception to the usual requirement with respect to contracts. The doctrine takes its point of departure from the English common law of marine insurance as it was developed in the latter part of the 18th century. It held that in insurance, being a contract upon speculation, it was mandatory upon the part of the insured to disclose to the insurer all material facts which are the exclusive knowledge of the applicant for insurance.[12] It was the outgrowth of an effort on the part of the courts to encourage the insurance industry. The promulgation of the doctrine tended to throw a mantle of protection around the insurers. The marine insurance business of the day involved many hazards, and it was the applicant for insurance who was possessed of a superior knowledge with respect to any particular risk. In order to foster the insurance business it became a legal requirement that a ship owner, applying for insurance, who knew of any fact that was material to the risk should disclose that fact in connection with his application for insurance.

The law as it developed provided that there was concealment, and the insurance contract could be voided, if (1) the fact in question was known to the insured, (2) the insured did not disclose the fact to the insurer and the insurer was not chargeable with its knowledge, and (3) the fact was material. There is no requirement that the insured know the fact to be material. If there is a fact known to the insured but not disclosed because it does not appear material, the failure to make disclosure amounts to an innocent concealment. Since the rule thus established in England makes no requirement for fraud or bad faith, an innocent concealment is grounds for denying liability. In marine insurance the rule still holds. There is a concealment if the insured fails to disclose a fact within his knowledge (of which the insured is not chargeable), if the fact is material. The United States Supreme Court in 1882 upheld this rule when it stated: "The duty of communication, indeed, is independent of the intention, and is

[12] In commenting upon insurance as a contract upon speculation, the reasoning behind the concealment doctrine was admirably set forth in the following terms: "The special facts, upon which the contingent chance is to be computed, lie most commonly in the knowledge of the insured only: the underwriter trusts to his representation, and proceeds upon confidence that he does not keep back any circumstances in his knowledge, to mislead the underwriter into a belief that the circumstance does not exist, and to induce him to estimate the risque, as if it did not exist. The keeping back (of) such circumstances is a fraud, and therefore the policy is void. Although the suppression should happen through mistake, without any fraudulent intention; yet still the underwriter is deceived, and the policy is void; because the risque run is really different from the risque understood and intended to be run, at the time of the agreement." *Carter* v. *Boehm*, 3 Burr 1905; 97 Eng. Rep. 1162 (1776).

violated by the fact of concealment even where there is no design to deceive."[13] Thus in the application of this rule, sometimes known as the "marine rule," in order to serve as grounds for voiding a contract, it was not necessary to show the concealment to have been intentional or tainted with fraud. If one party to the contract suppressed any facts or circumstances, whether by design, mistake, or ignorance, and if these were facts that, in justice, ought to be known to the other party, the effect in every instance allowed for the voiding of the contract. The strict interpretation of the doctrine continues to hold in marine insurance presumably because the original grounds for the doctrine to a large degree continue to prevail.

In the case of fire insurance, the situation is not always the same. Since the property subject to the insurance is ordinarily available for inspection, and, as a result, the material facts essential for the appraisal of the risk are within the range of the insurer's observation, the doctrine as it applies to marine insurance has been modified to the extent that matters not made the subject of express inquiry must be intentionally concealed in order to avoid the risk. In the case of fire insurance, it has been held that if the insured answers fully and in good faith all inquiries made by the insurer, there is no concealment. This is sometimes known as the "nonmarine rule" and sometimes as the "ordinary rule."

The change with respect to fire insurance grew out of the fact that conditions in this field were to a large degree reversed from those that applied with respect to marine insurance when the concealment doctrine was first promulgated. In the field of fire insurance the applicant for insurance was not possessed of the expert knowledge of fire insurance underwriter. At the same time, because of the fixed location of the subject of the insurance, the insurer was able at any time to make inspections and appraise the risk. Thus, the "nonmarine rule" introduced a fourth factor that placed upon the insurer the responsibility of showing that the insured knew the fact concealed to be material if the insurer is to deny liability on the ground of concealment.[14] Such facts or circumstances, to constitute grounds for voiding the contract, must be of such a nature "as could not, with reasonable diligence, be discovered by the insurer, or reasonably anticipated by him, as a foundation for specific inquiries."[15] In the case of a dwelling house in an area exposed by a forest fire, there would be a concealment if the owner of the property attempted to buy new insurance or

[13] *Sun Mutual Insurance Company* v. *Ocean Insurance Company*, 107 U.S. 485.

[14] The four factors are summarized as follows: (1) the insured must have known the fact; (2) the insured did not disclose this fact to the insurer, and the insurer was not chargeable with its knowledge; (3) the fact was material; and (4) the insured had knowledge of the material nature of the fact.

[15] *Protection Insurance Co.* v. *Harmer*, 2 Ohio St. 473.

increase his present insurance without explaining to the insurer or agent the unusual and extraordinary threat of a conflagration growing out of the forest fire.

Representation and Warranty. A representation is a statement as to past or present fact made by the insured to the insurer at the time of, or previous to, the formation of the contract. A misrepresentation is an incorrect, unfair, or false statement. Misrepresentation is closely akin to concealment. In the case of concealment there is a silence when there is an obligation to speak. In the case of misrepresentation, whether occurring through negligence, mistake, oversight, or otherwise, there is an untrue or improper representation. It is a positive statement that is untrue. A representation does not become a substantive part of the contract. It affects the contract only if material. A matter is material if it would serve as a basis for declining a risk or if it would modify the basis for its acceptance.

A warranty, in contrast to a representation, is a statement by the insured which is inserted in the contract and becomes part of it; or, it may be a condition inserted by the insurer. The significant feature of a warranty is to be found in the fact that it is a term of the insurance contract itself. As a part of the contract it requires strict compliance. It is a term of the contract "which has the effect of requiring, as a condition precedent of the taking effect of such contract or as a condition precedent of the insurer's liability thereunder, the existence of a fact which tends to diminish, or the nonexistence of a fact which tends to increase, the risk of the occurrence of any loss, damage, or injury within the coverage of the contract."[16]

A statement made in connection with the issuance of a contract, in order to constitute a warranty, not only must be intended as such but also must be definitely indicated as a warranty, either through its incorporation into the contract or by specifically being referred to as such. In cases of doubt, statements are regarded as representations and must be shown as material in order to defeat the contract. If any subject matter is of sufficient importance to the insurer to avoid the necessity of showing whether the fact is material, he may make it a provision of the contract that statements concerning the matter so made shall be deemed warranties. Provision may also be made that statements made in an application shall be deemed warranties; and when such a provision is incorporated in the contract, the application for insurance is held to be a part of the contract. The answers to specific questions on the application, unless the harsh rule is modified by legislative action, are deemed warranties which, if false, void the contract.

The strict rule that a warranty must be literally fulfilled in order

---

[16] New York Insurance Law §150.

not to defeat the contract has been modified in several states by acts of the legislatures. The tendency in such acts is to provide that the insurance will be voided if a loss occurs during a breach or is caused thereby, or if the breach materially increases the risk. Such legislative enactments tend to operate in the interests of the insured in cases in which a warranty has been breached and a loss occurs which can in no way be traced to the breach.

Doctrine of Substantial Performance. Not to encourage the tampering with warranties but to point out a possible defense in a situation where it may appear that a contract has been voided because of breach of warranty, it is well to be familiar with the equitable doctrine of substantial performance. By virtue of this doctrine the courts have undertaken to provide protection and relief for those who have faithfully and honestly endeavored to perform their contracts in all material and substantial particulars.

A situation can be envisaged where an insured warrants to keep a protective device in good condition and operation, and for some reason beyond his control an accident to the device makes it inoperative. It would be a severe hardship if, while the device is inoperative, a loss occurred, yet the insurer be permitted to deny liability. Assume the insured had agreed to maintain an alarm system for his business premises and was unable to do so because of total power failure in the area. Certainly this inability to maintain an alarm system would be an intolerable burden on the insured if it had the effect of voiding the contract for a breach of warranty. The courts have held that the insurance protection may not be forfeited by reason of mere technical, inadvertent, or unimportant omissions or defects. In this respect it has been pointed out: "It is incumbent on him who invokes its protection—the equitable doctrine of substantial performance—to present a case in which there has been no willful omission or departure from the terms of his contract. If he fails to do so, the question of substantial performance should not be submitted to the jury."[17]

Doctrine of Implied Warranties. The effect of custom on the development of maritime law and marine insurance has resulted in the introduction of certain legal principles that apply particularly to marine insurance. Because of the nature of the risk, there are conditions with respect to marine insurance that apply between the insured and the underwriters which are not mentioned in the contract but which, nevertheless, are as binding as if they were definitely written into every agreement. These are the "implied warranties," of which there are three.[18] There is an implied warranty that at the commence-

---

[17] *Gillespie Tool Company* v. *Wilson,* 123 Pa. 19, 16 A 36.

[18] The Marine Insurance Act of 1906 recognizes two implied warranties only, namely, seaworthiness and legality.

ment of the voyage the ship shall be seaworthy for the purpose of the particular adventure insured. The second implied warranty provides that the vessel insured must not deviate from the proper course of the voyage. Finally, there is an implied warranty that the adventure insured is a legal one and, so far as it is within the control of the insured, carried out in a lawful manner.

Seaworthiness. The implied warranty of seaworthiness attaches to all voyage contracts. It can readily be seen that the application of the principle to time contracts would result in an unworkable situation, since time contracts frequently attach when a ship is at sea or otherwise not in a position where it would be possible to refit her at the time the insurance becomes effective. Whereas there is no implied warranty in a time contract that a ship shall be seaworthy at any stage of the adventure, it is nevertheless true that if a ship were sent to sea in an unseaworthy state with the knowledge of the insured and without his making the facts known to the insurer and obtaining his consent, the insurer would have grounds for denying liability, since the law will not permit an insured to take advantage of his own wrong when that wrong has resulted in a loss.

There is no specified set of conditions that may be set forth as complying with the warranty of seaworthiness. The standard is not the same for every port, and, as a rule, the acceptable standard is that of the port where the vessel belongs. Nor is the standard the same for all types of vessels and for all voyages. A vessel is considered to be seaworthy when it is able to encounter whatever perils of the sea a ship of her kind, laden as she is, may be expected to encounter on the contemplated voyage. This assumes that the vessel must be tight, properly equipped to withstand common dangers to be anticipated, with the cargo properly stowed and not in excess of safe carrying capacity. There must be necessary food, fuel, water, and other stores as well as a competent master, officers, and crew, and a pilot, when one is required by law or usage. If the voyage is divisible into stages and a different class of equipment is required for each stage, the implied warranty of seaworthiness requires that at the commencement of each stage the ship be adequately equipped.

The implied warranty of seaworthiness operates regardless of the knowledge of the insured. If a vessel leaves port in an unseaworthy condition and the insured has every reason to believe that she is seaworthy, there is, nevertheless, a breach of warranty. The rule applies with the same force when a cargo is shipped in a vessel. Since many cargo shipments are made in vessels over which the shipper has no control, a clause is frequently attached to the contract eliminating the warranty in the following terms: "Seaworthiness of the vessel as between the assured and the underwriter is hereby admitted." This clause serves to protect the insured from having his contract voided by a condition over which he has no control and of which he has no knowledge. Without such a clause, there would be many instances in which the insured would be uncertain as to the effectiveness of his coverage.

Deviation. The implied warranty that a ship insured for a voyage shall not deviate from the proper course is based upon the reasoning that the insurer is entitled to have sufficient knowledge of the voyage contemplated to judge the perils involved. To vary the voyage amounts to a variation of the risk.

It is not necessary that there be an actual change in the course of the voyage to effect deviation. It is held that there is a deviation if the risk insured against be materially changed without just cause. Likewise, if there is unnecessary delay in the commencement of the voyage after the insurance has been effected, the delay may be held to be a deviation. This is notably true when insurance is effected during a season of favorable weather and the delay brings all or part of the voyage into the winter season or a season when cyclonic storms are prevalent. The vessel is expected to follow the recognized route and the one that custom justifies the insurer in assuming that the insured would follow. If there is no usual course, the insurer has a right to assume that the vessel will follow the safest and most advantageous course. The vessel is expected to proceed directly to her destination and may not touch a port not in the voyage unless justified by usage.

A deviation is a voluntary act. It follows that if a vessel is driven off the course there is no deviation. Likewise, any act that has the effect of changing the risk is not technically a deviation if it is the result of compulsion. When necessity is the compelling motive, the change in risk is not regarded as voluntary. Therefore, when by necessity the voyage is changed for repairs, water, or provisions, the change in course is not held to be a deviation. Nor are delays occasioned by efforts to save life or give aid in cases of distress regarded as deviations, although changes made solely in the interests of saving property do not come under this rule.

As in the case of the implied warranty of seaworthiness, the warranty concerning deviation may be waived by agreement. This procedure is ordinarily followed in the case of merchandise shipments when the insured does not wish to be in a position of having his insurance terminated by some act over which he has no control. The warranty may be eliminated from any contract by agreement with the insurer, and in such instances the following or a similar clause is used: "It is hereby agreed to hold the insured covered should the vessel deviate from the terms and conditions of this policy, at a premium to be arranged as soon as the deviation is known." It is apparent from the foregoing clause that the insurance remains effective in the event of a deviation, but the increase in risk is to be appraised immediately and the insurer compensated accordingly.

Legality. This is the only one of the implied warranties that may not be waived by agreement. In the case of every marine contract issued, there is annexed by law to the contract the warranty that the adventure insured is a lawful one and that, so far as the insured can control the matter, the adventure shall be carried out in a lawful manner.

A contract issued on a ship engaged in smuggling would be void because of the operation of the warranty of legality. Likewise, in time of war, to violate any law prohibiting trading with the enemy or governing the neutral position of a nation would bring a voyage within the illegal category. As to what constitutes illegality in the case of an American ship and American insurance is determined by American law. Insurance effected to cover any illegal undertaking is void and without effect.

Fraud. A false representation of a material fact, or the disclosure of a material fact under circumstances that make it tantamount to a misrepresentation, with the intent that it be acted upon by another party and is acted upon to his injury, may constitute fraud. A misrepresentation, to constitute fraud, must be false in fact and the party making the representation must know or believe it to be false. While usually a false representation is required, it is true that a nondisclosure or concealment amounts to a false representation if active steps are taken to prevent discovery of the truth. The same is true if a representation is made that is in part truth but certain facts are suppressed. The same is true if there is a duty to disclose facts and failure to disclose them implies that they do not exist.

To constitute fraud the representation must be of past or existing fact. Expressions of opinion, belief, expectation, or expressions of intention, if not false at the time they are made, do not constitute fraudulent statements. The representation must be of material fact and of a character that would lead to reliance upon it by the party to whom it is made. Commendatory expressions of value or false representations made where the parties deal on equal footing and have equal means of knowledge are not held to be fraudulent. The person to be held for fraud must know that he is not telling the truth, that he is definitely telling an untruth, or that he is practicing concealment. This knowledge is what is termed in the law *scienter*. Knowledge is imputed if the person making the statement does so in reckless disregard as to whether it is true or false.[19] Finally in order to constitute

[19] If a statement is recklessly made by a person who has no knowledge as to whether it is true or false, in order to induce a person to act in making a contract the party acting upon such a statement has grounds for rescission. ". . . If a party to a bargain avers the existence of a material fact recklessly, or affirms its existence positively, when he is consciously ignorant whether it be true or false, he may be held responsible for a falsehood; and this doctrine is especially applicable when the parties to a bargain are not upon equal terms with reference to the representation. . . ." *Whitehurst* v. *Life Insurance Company of Virginia*, 149 N.C. 273, 62 S.E. 1067.

fraud the misrepresentation must be relied upon by the party intended to be injured and action by him must result in his injury.

To constitute fraud, then, there must be an active attempt to deceive and the attempt must be successful to the extent that prejudice or injury results to the party relying on the misrepresentation. There are five essential elements to fraud: (1) a representation, (2) a fact that is not true, (3) the person making the statement must know it to be untrue, (4) the statement must be made with the intent to be acted upon or in a manner designed to induce action, and, finally, (5) the person defrauded must have acted in reliance on the statement to his damage.[20]

Subrogation. Subrogation has been defined as the "mode which equity adopts to compel the ultimate payment of a debt by one who in justice, equity and good conscience ought to pay it."[21] Subrogation, as it applies in the field of insurance, is the substituting of the insurer who paid the loss for the claimant so that, if there is any responsibility on the party primarily liable for the loss, the insurer may reimburse itself. If the insured could collect his loss from the insurer and then collect again from the parties responsible for the loss, this would amount to double payment and would be contrary to the principle of indemnity.

The subrogation rule has been expressed by the United States Supreme Court in the following terms:

> In fire insurance, as in marine insurance, the insurer, upon paying to the assured the amount of a loss of the property insured, is doubtless subrogated in a corresponding amount to the assured's right of action against any other person responsible for the loss. But the right of the insurer against such other person does not rest upon any relation of contract or of privity between them. It arises out of the nature of the contract of insurance as a contract of indemnity, and is derived from the assured alone, and can be enforced in his right only. By the strict rules of the common law, it must be asserted in the name of the assured. In a court of equity or of admiralty, or under some state codes, it may be asserted by the insurer in his own name; but in any form of remedy the insurer can take nothing by subrogation, but the rights of the assured, and if the assured has no right of action none passes to the insurer.[22]

Subrogation is a right of the insurer. It follows that if a property owner has in any way waived his rights to a claim for damages, in the event of a loss growing out of the peril covered in the contract, he may jeopardize the effectiveness of his insurance. The insurer has a right to anticipate that, after paying the loss, it will succeed to any

---

[20] *Small* v. *Dorsett*, 223 N.C. 754, 28 S.E. (2d) 514.

[21] *Arnold* v. *Green*, 161 N.Y. 566.

[22] *St. Louis, I. M. & S. Ry. Co.* v. *Commercial Union Ins. Co.*, 139 U.S. 223, 235.

claims for damages that would normally accrue to the insured. If the insured has no rights of action, because he has waived them, the insurer cannot succeed to them. In order that the matter be entirely outside the realm of doubt, subrogation is now ordinarily made the subject of a clause in the contract. Such clauses obligate the insured to protect the right of subrogation to the insurer and have the effect of serving notice that any act or agreement tending to defeat subrogation has the effect of voiding the insurance.

There is a second type of subrogation clause that sometimes appears in insurance contracts. This type of clause *permits* the insured to enter into a written agreement waiving his rights against a third party prior to a loss, without impairing the insurance contract. This release prior to the existence of a cause of action in effect destroys subrogation but may be willingly agreed to by the insurer.

Waiver and Estoppel. Estoppel prevents one from alleging or denying a fact the contrary of which, by one's own previous action, one has admitted. A waiver is the voluntary relinquishment of a known right. An insurer may by some act before a loss "induce the insured to do or not to do some act, contrary to the stipulations of the policy, and thereby be estopped from setting up such violation as a forfeiture."[23] In cases in which insurers have led an insured, to his prejudice or to his expense, to understand that forfeitures, breaches of warranties, or conditions would not be insisted upon, the insurers are estopped from asserting these particular breaches as defenses to defeat recovery under the contracts.

The difference between waiver and estoppel may be illustrated by the following example: If an insurer that has a rule against writing insurance on a building situated on land not owned by the insured accepts an applicant and issues a contract with full knowledge that the applicant owns a building but does not own the land upon which it is situated, it would be manifestly unfair for the insurer at the time of the loss to deny liability on the ground that the owner of the building did not own the land. This would be true even though the contract stated that the insurance would not cover if the insured was other than sole and unconditional owner of the property. In such a situation the law holds that the insurer by accepting the premium, with full knowledge of the nature of the ownership, waived the contract requirement with respect to ownership. Waiver is sometimes the express "abandonment of a right."[24] More often, waiver is implied from acts that are inconsistent with the continued assertion of a right. As has been said: ". . . if the words and acts of the insurer reasonably justified a conclusion that with full knowledge of all the facts it intended to abandon or not to insist upon the particular defense

---

[23] *Ruddock* v. *Detroit Life Ins. Co.*, 209 Mich. 638, 177 N.W. 242.

[24] *Johnson* v. *Aetna Insurance Company*, 123 Ga. 404, 51 S.E. 339.

afterwards relied upon, a verdict or finding to that effect establishes waiver, which, if it once exists can never be evoked."[25] The purpose of a waiver, then, is to relieve against forfeiture. "Where, after knowledge of the forfeiture of a policy the insurer recognizes its continued validity, does acts based thereon, and requires the insured by virtue thereof to do some act or incur some trouble or expense, the forfeiture is as a matter of law waived, and such a waiver need not be based upon any new agreement or upon estoppel. It exists when there is an intention to waive unexpressed, but clearly to be inferred from the circumstances, or when there is no such intention in fact, but the conduct of the insurer has misled the insured into acting upon a reasonable belief that the company has waived some provision of the policy."[26] If, in the circumstances just indicated, an insurer should undertake to deny liability, the courts would afford the insured protection. An insurer is estopped from setting up a defense of no liability where, after knowledge of a forfeiture of a contract, the insurer, by some act, recognized its continuance. "Estoppel is the shield of justice interposed for the protection of those who have not been wise or strong enough to protect themselves. It is the special grace of the court, authorized and permitted to preserve equities that would otherwise be sacrificed to cunning and fraud."[27]

There are three periods generally recognized in the consideration of waiver and estoppel in which there are some differences in the operation of the doctrines. These are: (1) period of negotiation, and up to and including the time of the delivery of the contract; (2) period from the delivery of the contract until the time of the loss; and (3) period from the occurrence of the loss through the time covering all subsequent negotiations.

The first period is concerned with information in the hands of the insurer that would serve as a ground for denying liability. The discussions of the courts are based upon the contention that it would be unjust to issue a contract and take the insured's money, knowing that the insured could not realize upon his contract. It is held that if the insurer has any knowledge of a fact that would void the contract and, in the face of this information, issues the contract, it waives the defense and is estopped from denying liability.[28]

---

[25] *Kiernan* v. *Dutchess County Mutual Insurance Company*, 150 N.Y. 190, 44 N.E. 698.

[26] *Draper et al.* v. *Oswego County Fire Relief Association*, 190 N.Y. 12, 82 N.E. 755.

[27] *Johnson* v. *Aetna Insurance Company*, 123 Ga. 404, 51 S.E. 339.

[28] "To permit this defense now would be in effect to hold that this insurance company purposely perpetrated a fraud upon these plaintiffs, accepted their money for the premium, and issued to them a policy that it had no intention whatever of paying in case of loss. That, of course, was not the purpose and intent of this insurance company. It was not organized, and its business is not conducted, for the purpose of defrauding widows and orphans, or for that matter any one else, by accepting money for the premium and issuing a policy that it has no intention

In the second period, that is, the period from the delivery of contract until the time of the loss, there are several situations in which the doctrine of estoppel may be evoked. It has been held that if an agent has full knowledge of a situation that would void the contract but takes no steps to cancel it, the insurer is estopped from denying liability because of the violation. Emphasis is given to a situation in which knowledge of the violation comes to the agent after the delivery of the contract but prior to the collection of the premium. The collection of the premium with a knowledge of a violation of the terms of the contract is held to waive the violation. This is on the ground that an insurer could not accept a premium on a voided contract, and, by so accepting the premium, indicates the contract to be valid. To serve a cancellation notice indicating that the contract is to be canceled at the end of a designated period of time has the effect of validating the contract during the period indicated. Finally, if an agent endorses a contract with knowledge of a violation, it is held that the violation is waived.

The third period, commencing with the loss and carrying through the period of adjustment, is regarded by insurer representatives as the most difficult to handle. A move on the part of an insurer representative that appears most innocent may have far-reaching and costly effects. A denial of liability under a contract waives the conditions of the contract requiring the filing of proofs and gives the insured an immediate right of action. Grounds for a waiver of a defense are established if an insurer, with knowledge of a defense, asks an insured to pay a premium or file proofs. In fact, almost any act taken by the insurer's representative toward the ascertaining of the amount of the loss and its adjustment may be construed as a waiver of a violation of a contract condition. If the insurer wishes to stand on its rights, it may refuse to cooperate in any way in the adjustment until the insured has complied with all contract requirements. Since this procedure is not always feasible, a nonwaiver agreement is frequently taken. This agreement provides that the rights of both parties are not waived by any action taken in arriving at an agreement as to the amount of the loss or damage.

ADDITIONAL CONTRACT PRINCIPLES

Void and Voidable Contracts. The terms "void" and "voidable" come into frequent use in connection with the insurance

---

whatever of paying in case of loss; yet there is absolutely no theory upon which the conduct of the insurance company can be reconciled with honesty and fair dealing, except upon the theory that it intended to insure this property, regardless of the defect in the title of which it then had full knowledge." *Hartford Fire Ins. Co.* v. *Nance,* 12 F. (2d) 575.

contract. They are sometimes used interchangeably, but such use is not correct. A void agreement is one that is entirely without legal effect. The law makes certain requirements essential for the validity of a contract, and in the absence of these essentials the contract is void. In the case of insurance a contract issued without insurable interest is void, as would be a contract having an illegal object.

A voidable contract is one that may be affirmed or rejected at the option of one of the parties but is binding on the other. In the case of insurance a situation may develop in which the insured has failed to comply with a condition of the contract. The insurer may elect, nevertheless, to fulfill its part of the agreement or, on the other hand, may elect to avoid the contract and revoke the insurance coverage. There are frequent instances where the insurer has a technical right to claim a forfeiture but in the interests of equity and good public relations will recognize a claim.

Presumption of Intent. The law holds a person to be bound by the terms of a written contract which he signs or accepts, regardless of whether he has taken the trouble and pains to acquaint himself with all of its terms and conditions.

Too many insurance contracts are complicated and difficult to understand. It is probably safe to state that, regardless of the clarity or obscurity of the terminology, more people do not, than do, read their contracts. The insured assumes that the contract meets his needs and lets it go at that. It is no defense when the loss occurs to claim ignorance of the terms of the contract because of failure to read the agreement. Summarizing a line of decisions, the court said in the case of *Grace* v. *Adams* (100 Mass. 505): "It has often been decided that one who accepts a contract and proceeds to avail himself of its provisions is bound by the stipulations and conditions expressed in it whether he reads them or not."

In connection with the insurance contract, the question of admissibility of parole evidence frequently presents itself. The rule of law applying to parole evidence has thus been expressed in a leading case: "It is a fundamental rule, in courts both of law and equity, that parole contemporaneous evidence is inadmissible to contradict or vary the terms of a valid written instrument."[29] To the same end, the distinguished insurance authority Richards, referring to the contract of insurance as best evidence, states: "In the absence of fraud or mutual mistake the written contract, if there be one, is the best and only admissible evidence of what the contract is as to all matters which it purports to cover."[30] While the contract usually is not subject to modification by parole evidence, the language of the contract is

---

[29] *Northern Assurance Co.* v. *Grand View Building Assn.*, 183 U.S. 308 (1902).

[30] Richards, *op. cit.*, p. 105.

nevertheless not binding in clear cases of mutual mistake of fact or where there is a mistake on one side and fraud inducing it on the other. In instances in which fraud or mutual mistake enters into the transaction, the injured party has relief in equity and may ask that the written contract be reformed to correspond to the real agreement.[31] The effect of waiver and estoppel upon the operation of the insurance contract has already been discussed; and this in so many instances has the effect of varying the terms of the written instrument that a literal interpretation of the instrument, it is sometimes said, is the exception rather than the rule. This seems an overstrong statement. In securing a contract the insured should satisfy himself that its literal terms provide the coverage he requires. On the other hand, it is well to know under what circumstances relief is available when the written contract is not in fact a statement of the actual agreement.

FOR DISCUSSION

1. A great deal of the reinsurance in this country has, from time to time, been placed abroad in alien insurers. It was felt that in the event of a great disaster calling for liquidation of securities, the resources of foreign insurers would be of benefit. What would be the effect of a declaration of war with the country in which the reinsuring company was located?
2. Is there any difference, so far as insurance is concerned, between a civil war and a war with a foreign state?
3. It has been stated that every interest in property or liability concerning it, when the nature of the interest or liability is such that the insured may suffer loss from the destruction of the property, constitutes an insurable interest sufficient to warrant valid insurance thereof. On the basis of this definition, make as complete a list as possible of situations in which an insurable interest exists.
4. Distinguish between a "warranty" and a "representation"; between a "misrepresentation" and a "concealment"; and between an "affirmative" and a "promissory" warranty.
5. It has been stated that the face value of an insurance contract covering against property loss "is not the measure but the extreme limit of recovery." Explain.
6. X operated a toll road. The income from the road depended upon the existence of a bridge. X insured the bridge under a valued contract, and after its destruction the insurer denied liability on the ground that X could demonstrate no ownership in the bridge. Did X have an insurable interest, and is the insurer's contention correct?
7. X goes to the office of his agent and orders $50,000 coverage on his mill. The agent is pleased with the new line, and after some friendly conversation the owner of the mill leaves. When he reaches the street

[31] *Ibid.*, p. 107.

he hears a fire alarm and upon inquiry learns that his mill is burning. He rushes back to the office of the agent to advise him of the circumstance and to learn with what insurers the new insurance was placed. The agent is just about to enter the coverage on his binder. What is the status of all the parties?

8. It has been stated that the right of subrogation is a corollary incident to the doctrine of indemnity. What does this statement mean?
9. Is an oral contract of insurance enforceable?
10. There is a case on record of an agent of an insured at Smyrna who learned that a vessel containing goods belonging to his principal had stranded. Instead of wiring him he sent notice of the loss by mail with the thought that the owner might possibly place insurance in the meantime. Before receipt of the letter the owner as a matter of fact did take out insurance on the goods. He had no knowledge of the loss, and the contract was purchased in good faith. He was, nevertheless, unable to collect. Upon what sound legal basis does this decision rest?
11. B carries a fire insurance contract in which certain warranties are written to provide protective features for dangerous materials used on the property. He becomes ill, and during the period of his illness the warranty is broken. He dies, and shortly after a fire occurs destroying the entire property. The estate in attempting to effect a settlement claims that, because of the illness and subsequent death of the insured, he cannot be held responsible for compliance with the requirements of the warranty. Have the insurers a case?
12. It has been argued that a valued contract statute legalizes a contract that otherwise would be a wagering contract. What is your opinion?
13. B owns a pearl necklace consisting of three strings with a total of approximately 300 pearls. As a result of an accident, 250 pearls were destroyed. The value of the necklace new was $5,000. What is the amount of the loss?
14. In a case involving an inland marine risk where the decision hinged on whether the marine or nonmarine rule with respect to concealment should be applied, what rule, in your opinion, will the courts follow? Justify your conclusion.
15. Where a contractual obligation is subject to a condition, the condition may be either (*a*) precedent, (*b*) concurrent, or (*c*) subsequent. Give examples from an insurance contract.
16. Edward and Annie, husband and wife, own a building as community property. They insure it against fire. Before the expiration of the policy, they are divorced. No disposition of the property is made as a result of divorce proceedings. Shortly after the divorce proceedings, the husband, as a matter of revenge, sets fire to the property. It is completely destroyed. The wife has no connection with the burning of the property or no knowledge of the felonious intent of her former husband. The wife files claim for half of the value of the insurance covering the property, and the insurer denies liability. Do you think the insurer is on firm ground?

17. X, an agent, issues a contract which he knows on its face to be unenforceable because he knows the owner of the property is breaching a warranty and will continue to do so. A fire occurs, and an independent adjuster who is sent to settle the loss denies liability. What are the rights of the parties?
18. M purchased a piece of property for $5,000 and shortly thereafter insured it for $15,000. He told a credit agency that he had paid $15,000 for the property and listed it for that amount on a financial statement made to a lending institution for the purpose of obtaining financing for his business. Within a few months, the property burned, and M, in order to protect his reputation with the credit company and the lending institution, made an identical statement known to be false to the insurers. M contended that the statements were not material to the insurers and were made only to protect his name and reputation with the credit agency and lending institution. Does such a statement constitute fraud and will it operate to bar recovery of the insurance?

PART II

MAJOR MONOLINE PROPERTY INSURANCE CONTRACTS

CHAPTER · 5

Standard Fire Insurance Contract[1]

The earliest fire insurance contracts written in this country or abroad represented agreements, ordinarily drawn up by the insurer, to provide indemnity to the insured in accordance with the terms of the contract. In the very earliest days, such agreements were probably satisfactory. As the business developed, the practice of buying insurance from several insurers led to a necessity for some degree of uniformity in the contracts as they were issued. If this were not so, contradictory clauses would tend to nullify all or part of the insurance which the insured believed himself to be carrying.

Apart from the need for uniformity, there also developed a necessity of drawing up a contract that treated both the insurer and the insured fairly. The possibility was always present that in a long and complicated contract there might be hidden features that adversely affected the interests of the insured. So complex were some of the documents that few but insurance experts knew exactly the extent of the coverage. Because of this, after fires, there were many disputes giving rise to intense dissatisfaction and much litigation.

Those associated with the business of insurance as well as the insuring public gradually came to realize that the situation was intolerable and that steps had to be taken for its correction. The matter was brought to the attention of the New York legislature. While the legislature was giving consideration to it, the New York Board of Underwriters took action. A committee was appointed, and

[1] Although this chapter and the next five chapters deal with the contractual aspects of fire insurance on a monoline basis, the student should be aware that the vast majority of fire insurance on residential and on many commercial properties is sold on a multiple line basis via the homeowner's contract or some type of commercial package (see Part IV). Since the standard fire contract and many parts of the forms usually attached to it are reproduced in the homeowner's and other package contracts, the material in these chapters should serve as background information for the more comprehensive contracts. The student should also be aware that the standard fire contract (plus its many endorsements) is still in use in many situations where multiple line contracts are not needed or are inapplicable or, perhaps for underwriting reasons, are not available.

a contract form was drawn up and adopted by many of the insurers represented on the board. Its use was by no means universal, and to correct the situation it was felt that legislation was necessary. A bill to require a uniform contract was introduced into the New York legislature and passed in 1886.

The New York contract did not represent the first step in this direction. The Massachusetts legislature had adopted a contract as early as 1873. This contract did not meet with general approval, and, accordingly, its form has not been generally accepted outside of New England. The Massachusetts contract was shorter and more liberal than that subsequently adopted by New York. The first New York form, known as the "old" New York standard to distinguish it from a later standard contract known as the "new" New York standard, was widely accepted and ultimately adopted by 27 states.

As time went on, there were certain features of the old New York contract that were held to be unduly severe. Some of the features were held by the courts to be unfair to the insureds; and, as the result of the decisions of the courts, it was not possible to interpret the contract in an identical manner in different jurisdictions. Confusion again presented itself, and the need for further legislation was recognized. In 1916 the National Association of Insurance Commissioners recommended the revision of the 1886 policy. Fourteen of the conditions that would void the coverage found in the old contract were reduced to five, and the remainder had the effect of suspending the coverage rather than terminating it. A change in the arrangement of the contract was recommended, and its length was reduced from 112 lines to 100 lines. The new contract was drafted in two columns instead of having the lines run the length of the page. The new contract is sometimes referred to as the "200-line" contract to distinguish it from the old contract, which is referred to as the "112-line." The new contract was adopted by the New York legislature in 1918, and until the adoption of the 1943 contract of 165 lines was widely used as the standard contract in approximately 15 states.[2]

The net result of the adoption of the new (1918) New York form was less rather than more uniformity. There were then three basic standard forms: the old New York standard, the new New York standard, and the Massachusetts or New England standard. In an effort to find a means for correcting this situation, at the meeting of the National Association of Insurance Commissioners held in 1936, it

---

[2] The contracts used for many years in Maine, New Hampshire, and Minnesota followed the original Massachusetts form, and these contracts as a group were sometimes referred to as the "New England standard." The terms "forms," clauses," "and endorsements" are sometimes used loosely in insurance literature. Committees on terminology of the American Risk and Insurance Association are attempting to clarify this situation.

was recommended that a special committee be appointed to study the problem and to make a recommendation as to the advisability of preparing a new and simplified contract to be recommended in all jurisdictions.

The outgrowth of this study was the adoption by act of the New York legislature of the new standard contract now known as the "1943 New York form." The form, also sometimes known as the "Revised Standard," became mandatory in New York, July 1, 1943, and was soon adopted by a wide majority of the states. Figure 5–1 shows the insuring clause from the first page of this contract; Figure 5–2 shows the stipulations and conditions. The new form is much simpler and considerably shorter than any of the other forms, and the contract covers lightning damage in the insuring clause as well as fire. The language of the older forms is generally retained, though a number of conditions and prohibitions that have become obsolete have been eliminated entirely from the contract.

When reference is made to the "standard fire contract" in this text, the "1943 New York form" is meant. This contract has been adopted in its entirety or subject to certain minor statutory differences in 47 jurisdictions. Included among these are the District of Columbia and Puerto Rico. There are variations in the insuring clause in the states of Michigan, Georgia, Kansas, Vermont, California, and Indiana. Other significant departures are few. Texas and Maine have statutory forms based on the 1943 New York form. In 1951 Massachusetts adopted a new form mandatory after 1952 that includes features of both the old form and the 1943 New York form. In 1955 Minnesota adopted a new form retaining some provisions of the old form, but incorporating much of the 1943 New York form. New Hampshire, with a valued policy form, alone of all the states continues to follow the old New England pattern.

Before the adoption by the states of a standard contract form, an insured might carefully study the conditions of one or all of his contracts and be satisfied that his needs for insurance coverage were satisfactorily met. But before renewal, some happening in the insurance business might have given rise to a change in contract forms, and when the new contracts were delivered some obscure change in wording might have materially altered the coverage. Eternal vigilance was necessary in order to be sure that the coverage remained as desired. The standard contract eliminates this danger and provides a uniform continuity of coverage from contract to contract.

Discrepancies in the wording of contracts, often considered of trifling importance by the insured, frequently gave rise to questions of coverage and to difficulties in adjustment. With a standardized form such discrepancies are reduced to a minimum, with a consequent simplification of adjustment problems.

In Consideration of the Provisions and Stipulations herein or added hereto and of

.... **Dollars Premium**

this Company, for the term from the .... day of ...., 19.... at noon, Standard Time, at
of .... to the .... day of ...., 19.... location of property involved,

to an amount not exceeding .... Dollars

does insure ....
and legal representatives, to the extent of the actual cash value of the property at the time of loss, but not exceeding the amount which it would cost to repair or replace the property with material of like kind and quality within a reasonable time after such loss, without allowance for any increased cost of repair or reconstruction by reason of any ordinance or law regulating construction or repair, and without compensation for loss resulting from interruption of business or manufacture, nor in any event for more than the interest of the insured, against all DIRECT LOSS BY FIRE, LIGHTNING AND BY REMOVAL FROM PREMISES ENDANGERED BY THE PERILS INSURED AGAINST IN THIS POLICY, EXCEPT AS HEREINAFTER PROVIDED, to the property described hereinafter while located or contained as described in this policy, or pro rata for five days at each proper place to which any of the property shall necessarily be removed for preservation from the perils insured against in this policy, but not elsewhere.

Assignment of this policy shall not be valid except with the written consent of this Company.

This policy is made and accepted subject to the foregoing provisions and stipulations and those hereinafter stated, which are hereby made a part of this policy, together with such other provisions, stipulations and agreements as may be added hereto, as provided in this policy.

Fig. 5–1. Insuring clause from first page of 1943 New York Standard Fire Policy.

A body of insurance law, as reflected in court decisions, tends to develop under a uniform contract. The meanings of the terms used are clarified and fixed; the conditions of the contract and the meaning of terms tend to become well understood by businessmen. The misunderstandings thus eliminated tend to reduce litigation to a minimum.

Concealment, fraud. This entire policy shall be void if, whether before or after a loss, the insured has wilfully concealed or misrepresented any material fact or circumstance concerning this insurance or the subject thereof, or the interest of the insured therein, or in case of any fraud or false swearing by the insured relating thereto.

Uninsurable and excepted property. This policy shall not cover accounts, bills, currency, deeds, evidences of debt, money or securities; nor, unless specifically named hereon in writing, bullion or manuscripts.

Perils not included. This Company shall not be liable for loss by fire or other perils insured against in this policy caused, directly or indirectly, by: (a) enemy attack by armed forces, including action taken by military, naval or air forces in resisting an actual or an immediately impending enemy attack; (b) invasion; (c) insurrection; (d) rebellion; (e) revolution; (f) civil war; (g) usurped power; (h) order of any civil authority except acts of destruction at the time of and for the purpose of preventing the spread of fire, provided that such fire did not originate from any of the perils excluded by this policy; (i) neglect of the insured to use all reasonable means to save and preserve the property at and after a loss, or when the property is endangered by fire in neighboring premises; (j) nor shall this Company be liable for loss by theft.

Other Insurance. Other insurance may be prohibited or the amount of insurance may be limited by endorsement attached hereto.

Conditions suspending or restricting insurance. Unless otherwise provided in writing added hereto this Company shall not be liable for loss occurring
(a) while the hazard is increased by any means within the control or knowledge of the insured; or
(b) while a described building, whether intended for occupancy by owner or tenant, is vacant or unoccupied beyond a period of sixty consecutive days; or
(c) as a result of explosion or riot, unless fire ensue, and in that event for loss by fire only.

Other perils or subjects. Any other peril to be insured against or subject of insurance to be covered in this policy shall be by endorsement in writing hereon or added hereto.

Added provisions. The extent of the application of insurance under this policy and of the contribution to be made by this Company in case of loss, and any other provision or agreement not inconsistent with the provisions of this policy, may be provided for in writing added hereto, but no provision may be waived except such as by the terms of this policy is subject to change.

Waiver provisions. No permission affecting this insurance shall exist, or waiver of any provision be valid, unless granted herein or expressed in writing added hereto. No provision, stipulation or forfeiture shall be held to be waived by any requirement or proceeding on the part of this Company relating to appraisal or to any examination provided for herein.

Cancellation of policy. This policy shall be cancelled at any time at the request of the insured, in which case this Company shall, upon demand and surrender of this policy, refund the excess of paid premium above the customary short rates for the expired time. This policy may be cancelled at any time by this Company by giving to the insured a five days' written notice of cancellation with or without tender of the excess of paid premium above the pro rata premium for the expired time, which excess, if not tendered, shall be refunded on demand. Notice of cancellation shall state that said excess premium (if not tendered) will be refunded on demand.

Mortgagee interests and obligations. If loss hereunder is made payable, in whole or in part, to a designated mortgagee not named herein as the insured, such interest in this policy may be cancelled by giving to such mortgagee a ten days' written notice of cancellation.
If the insured fails to render proof of loss such mortgagee, upon notice, shall render proof of loss in the form herein specified within sixty (60) days thereafter and shall be subject to the provisions hereof relating to appraisal and time of payment and of bringing suit. If this Company shall claim that no liability existed as to the mortgagor or owner, it shall, to the extent of payment of loss to the mortgagee, be subrogated to all the mortgagee's rights of recovery, but without impairing mortgagee's right to sue; or it may pay off the mortgage debt and require an assignment thereof and of the mortgage. Other provisions relating to the interests and obligations of such mortgagee may be added hereto by agreement in writing.

Pro rata liability. This Company shall not be liable for a greater proportion of any loss than the amount hereby insured shall bear to the whole insurance covering the property against the peril involved, whether collectible or not.

Requirements in case loss occurs. The insured shall give immediate written notice to this Company of any loss, protect the property from further damage, forthwith separate the damaged and undamaged personal property, put it in the best possible order, furnish a complete inventory of the destroyed, damaged and undamaged property, showing in detail quantities, costs, actual cash value and amount of loss claimed; **and within sixty days after the loss, unless such time is extended in writing by this Company, the insured shall render to this Company a proof of loss,** signed and sworn to by the insured, stating the knowledge and belief of the insured as to the following: the time and origin of the loss, the interest of the insured and of all others in the property, the actual cash value of each item thereof and the amount of loss thereto, all encumbrances thereon, all other contracts of insurance, whether valid or not, covering any of said property, any changes in the title, use, occupation, location, possession or exposures of said property since the issuing of this policy, by whom and for what purpose any building herein described and the several parts thereof were occupied at the time of loss and whether or not it then stood on leased ground, and shall furnish a copy of all the descriptions and schedules in all policies and, if required, verified plans and specifications of any building, fixtures or machinery destroyed or damaged. The insured, as often as may be reasonably required, shall exhibit to any person designated by this Company all that remains of any property herein described, and submit to examinations under oath by any person named by this Company, and subscribe the same; and, as often as may be reasonably required, shall produce for examination all books of account, bills, invoices and other vouchers, or certified copies thereof if originals be lost, at such reasonable time and place as may be designated by this Company or its representative, and shall permit extracts and copies thereof to be made.

Appraisal. In case the insured and this Company shall fail to agree as to the actual cash value or the amount of loss, then, on the written demand of either, each shall select a competent and disinterested appraiser and notify the other of the appraiser selected within twenty days of such demand. The appraisers shall first select a competent and disinterested umpire; and failing for fifteen days to agree upon such umpire, then, on request of the insured or this Company, such umpire shall be selected by a judge of a court of record in the state in which the property covered is located. The appraisers shall then appraise the loss, stating separately actual cash value and loss to each item, and, failing to agree, shall submit their differences, only, to the umpire. An award in writing, so itemized, of any two when filed with this Company shall determine the amount of actual cash value and loss. Each appraiser shall be paid by the party selecting him and the expenses of appraisal and umpire shall be paid by the parties equally.

Company's options. It shall be optional with this Company to take all, or any part, of the property at the agreed or appraised value, and also to repair, rebuild or replace the property destroyed or damaged with other of like kind and quality within a reasonable time, on giving notice of its intention so to do within thirty days after the receipt of the proof of loss herein required.

Abandonment. There can be no abandonment to this Company of any property.

When loss payable. The amount of loss for which this Company may be liable shall be payable sixty days after proof of loss, as herein provided, is received by this Company and ascertainment of the loss is made either by agreement between the insured and this Company expressed in writing or by the filing with this Company of an award as herein provided.

Suit. No suit or action on this policy for the recovery of any claim shall be sustainable in any court of law or equity unless all the requirements of this policy shall have been complied with, and unless commenced within twelve months next after inception of the loss.

Subrogation. This Company may require from the insured an assignment of all right of recovery against any party for loss to the extent that payment therefor is made by this Company.

FIG. 5–2.

Standardization unquestionably reflects both to the benefit of insurer and insured.

PARTS OF THE STATUTORY CONTRACT

The 165-line New York standard contract is divided into two parts: (1) the agreement, and (2) the provisions and stipulations. The "agreement," or "contract proper," as it is sometimes called, contains the insuring agreement and could of itself serve as a complete fire insurance contract. In the interest of clarification the "provisions and stipulations" are added. These are found on the second page of the contract and constitute the "165 lines." Not only do they serve to clarify where areas of doubt might occur but, as well, place certain obligations on both the insurer and the insured.

The Insuring Agreement. The insuring agreement establishes two basic principles of fire insurance: (1) the contract is personal; and (2) it is a contract of indemnity. Since the agreement is a contract it must have the attributes of a contract and it becomes necessary to establish offer, acceptance, competency of parties, and legal purpose.

With respect to the terms of coverage, insurance is provided against direct loss by (*a*) fire, (*b*) lightning, and (*c*) removal.

The contract (*a*) limits the right of assignment, (*b*) excludes consequential loss, (*c*) excludes allowance for increased costs attributable to an ordinance or law, and (*d*) establishes the contract as an "interest" contract.

Stipulations and Conditions. The second part of the contract, the stipulations and conditions, covers (*a*) fraud, (*b*) uninsurable property, (*c*) property now covered unless specifically mentioned, and (*d*) perils not covered.

Provision is made for (*a*) limiting or prohibiting other insurance; (*b*) conditions suspending or restricting insurance; (*c*) including perils other than loss by fire, lightning, or removal; (*d*) the waiver of contract provisions; and (*e*) cancellation of the contract.

Special provisions cover the interest and obligations of the mortgagee. The contract contains instructions to be followed in the event of loss, including reference to the right of the insurer to subrogation.

GENERAL ASPECTS OF THE INSURING AGREEMENT

Inasmuch as the insuring agreement establishes a contract between the insurer and the insured, it is useful to consider in some detail the meaning and implications of the agreement. This section will deal with certain general aspects of the agreement while later sections in this chapter will deal with the perils covered and with limitations on recovery in the event of loss.

Personal Contract. The fire insurance contract follows the person rather than the property covered. Because a named insured is the party to be indemnified and because the insurance does not automatically follow the property that is the subject of insurance, the contract is said to be a personal one. The contract agrees to indemnify the insured against loss in accordance with its terms. It makes no agreement to make any payment whatever for loss or damage to the property, the subject of the insurance, unless the named insured has an interest that results in his suffering a loss. Although it is common to refer to the insuring of a house, an automobile, or other property, it is apparent that the insurance contract in no way minimizes losses that may arise. Nor can the insurance contract guarantee to replace the property destroyed with material of like kind or quality. This becomes apparent if a rare picture or object of art is insured. Properties of this kind are frequently impossible to replace. The insurer does not undertake to replace the property, nor does it undertake to make a payment if the property is injured or destroyed. Payment may be made only if the person carrying the insurance suffers a loss as a result of the loss or damage to the property. If the owner of a dwelling house, or similar property, carries insurance upon it and transfers title to a second party, the insurance does not automatically follow the property. If the property is destroyed without having the insurance properly transferred to the new owner, the person in whose name the contract is written has no claim whatever for loss or damage under the contract since, not owning the property, he suffered no loss. The person who purchased the property has no claim under the contract, since he is not the person insured. While the contract is referred to as personal, the insured may be an individual, partnership, or corporation. Guardians, executors, administrators, trustees, or receivers holding property in their various capacities may be insureds.

There is one instance where insurance is provided automatically at the termination of protection for the named insured. Under the terms of the contract, in the event of the death of the insured, protection is continued for his legal representatives.

Assignment. Ordinarily, one party to a contract may not assign his interest to another without the consent of the other contracting party. This is the case with respect to the fire insurance contract, since the contract itself provides "assignment of this policy shall not be valid except with the written consent of the company." Because of this provision an assignment of a fire insurance contract without the consent of the insurer is ineffective.

The usual assignment of a contract carries with it only such rights as are possessed by the assignor. In the case of a fire insurance contract the transfer is not, in the strict sense of the word, an assignment but rather a novation. A novation is a new contract, in this case between the insurer and the assignee. The relationship between the two original parties is terminated, and a new contractual relationship is established.

The purpose of limiting the right of assignment centers around the problem of moral hazard. Insurers very carefully scrutinize the reputation of the owners of property offered for insurance. They reserve the right to select the persons whom they will insure, and for this reason there is no provision, typically, for fire insurance to follow the property, without the consent of the insurer, when a transfer of ownership has been effected.

A Contract of Indemnity. The fire insurance contract undertakes to indemnify the insured "to the extent of the actual cash value of the property at the time of loss. . . ." It was the intent of the framers of the standard contract to incorporate into the contract by means of this clause the idea of indemnity. The amount collectible is limited to the actual cash value of the damaged property, but in no event for more than the face of the contract. Actual cash value at the time of loss is also subject to the following five limitations: (1) The loss cannot exceed the amount which it would cost to repair or replace the property with material of like kind and quality within a reasonable time after the loss. (2) There is no allowance for any increased cost of repair or reconstruction by reason of any ordinance or law regulating construction and repair. (3) There can be no compensation for loss resulting from interruption of business or manufacture. (4) The loss cannot exceed the interest of the insured. (5) The amount of loss paid by any one insurer is also subject to the pro rata clause, which is a part of the stipulations and conditions, and is not mentioned in the insuring agreement.

The older standard fire contracts, in referring to the actual cash value of the property, provided that it should be ascertained or estimated "with proper deduction for depreciation however caused." Reference to depreciation is omitted in the 1943 standard contract, since it is believed to be superfluous. It is now held that actual cash value cannot be determined without giving full consideration to depreciation. The inference that the omission of reference to depreciation presumed that depreciation was not to be taken is an error. Depreciation which includes not only physical depreciation but the loss in value due to obsolescence must logically be taken into consideration before any figure representing actual cash value can be reached. This is so since depreciation means by derivation and common usage "a fall in value; reduction of worth."[3] It is this depreciated value that the standard fire insurance contract contemplates.

---

[3] *McAnarney* v. *Newark Fire Insurance Company* et al., 159 N.E. 902. The word "depreciation" as used here is used in a nonaccounting sense. It does not refer to the systematic write-off of historical cost over the object's estimated useful life.

Consideration. A consideration is defined in law as something of a detriment to the promisee or of benefit to the promisor. It is the price which the offeror, in this case the insurer, demands for his promise, that is, the promise to insure. Consideration does not necessarily mean a payment of money. It may be a payment of money, or it may be that and something more, or it may be simply the waiving of, or the promise to waive, a legal right. This distinction is important, because there is a tendency to regard the payment of the premium as the sole consideration for the insurance. The contract provides "in consideration of the provisions and stipulations herein or added hereto and of ...... dollars premium." This is important because it places directly upon the insured the necessity of observing the obligations he assumes under the stipulations. It is essential to understand that both the payment of the premium and the fulfilling of any obligations under the stipulations, taken together, constitute the consideration under the contract.

The prior payment of the premium is not essential to the validity of the agreement. The delivery of the contract to the insured and his acceptance of it implies his obligation to pay. The insurance agent may, and frequently does extend credit. A contract delivered to an insured, and credit extended for the payment of premium, may not be canceled except by following the procedure for cancellation outlined in the contract itself. The fact that the premium has not been paid does not in any way change the situation nor operate to work a forfeiture of the contract. If the agent, or insurer, elects to cancel a contract for nonpayment of premium, it may be done by giving the required notice. The insured then is liable to the insurer for premium earned from the inception of the contract to the date of cancellation.

Inception and Termination of Coverage. Under the standard fire insurance contract, the insurance becomes effective at a given day at noon, and it is written for a term to expire likewise at noon on a specified day. Contracts ordinarily are written for periods of one or three years. Where the convenience of the insured requires it, contracts may be written for less than one year or for terms of two or four years. There is nothing to prevent the insurance becoming effective at a time other than noon, and where this is required, it is usually effected through a binder.

No particular time was designated in the older contracts, and there was considerable uncertainty as to whether standard time or local sun time was meant. Courts were inclined to an interpretation favorable to the insured, as when a fire broke out at 12:02 P.M. standard time, which was 11:45 A.M. sun time; and, it not being shown that the parties had intended standard time, it was held that the insurance had not expired at the time of the fire and that the insurer was liable. In the New York standard form, this uncertainty has been eliminated by providing in the agreement that the insurance becomes effective "at noon, Standard Time, at location of property involved." This phrasing applies as well to the termination of the coverage.

There has been, in years past, some doubt as to whether a contract covered for loss after the time of the expiration of the contract if the cause originated before that time. It is now held that if a fire causing damage breaks out before the contract expires, the insurer is liable for all the damage that comes within the limits of the coverage, even though most of the damage was occasioned by continuance of the fire after the time for the contract to expire.

When the day and time indicated in the contract arrive, if there is no happening of the contingency insured against, the coverage automatically terminates. Under a fire contract, a loss does not cancel the contract and any loss paid will not reduce the amount of the contract. Since the amount of the contract is not reduced by the payment of a loss, the cancellation of a contract is handled as though no loss had occurred, and the return premium is based on the amount of insurance before the loss.

The fact that the amount of insurance is not reduced in the event of loss enables the insured to keep his contract record and expiration dated unchanged. He may, if he wishes, cancel the unexpired portion of his contracts and have a new set written dating from the loss.

The Binder. A contract of insurance need not be in writing. Every day in the fire insurance business there are literally thousands of fire insurance contracts entered into between insured and insurer without as much as a scrap of paper being given to the insured to evidence the agreement. This is not the safest practice to follow. It is far better for the insured to have in his possession some memorandum of the agreement, but this is not necessary. When insurance coverage is effected prior to the delivery of a standard contract, it is ordinarily for a short period, pending the drawing up and delivery of the formal contract. Insurance in such an instance is said to be "bound."

In every insurance agency, a record is provided of bound risks. No particular form is required, and ordinarily a blank record book suffices. Upon receiving an order for insurance, the agent will enter in his book, known as a "binder," the date and hour. He will then enter the name of the insured, the date and hour the insurance is to become effective, the property to be covered, all pertinent information and conditions to be incorporated in the policy, and the amount of insurance. He will then apportion the insurance among the insurers he intends to commit to the risk, with the amount at risk for each insurer indicated. From the moment the insurers are committed, their liability begins, unless a future time is indicated.

The custom of binding insurance is a great convenience to the business. A telephone call is sufficient to increase a line or change a coverage. It is quite in accordance with custom to bind insurance in this manner and let it run without any written evidence of the contract until the policy is delivered days later. Insurance exchanges, however, have provided a printed form that an agent may fill out with a few strokes of the pen or pencil, sign, and forward to the insured. Or, instead, a letter stating that the insurance is bound and naming the insurers committed and the amounts would be sufficient evidence to show the existence of the binder in case of dispute. Ordinarily, insurers take great pride in honoring binders, whether in writing or not, and no difficulty whatever is to be anticipated. However, recognizing that human weakness gives rise to errors and misunderstandings, and even though misunderstandings are extremely infrequent, it represents the part of prudence and safety on the part of the insured to ask the agent binding the risk to send him at once a copy of the binder. This the agent will gladly do.

While many individuals, in the conduct of their own affairs, have been willing to dispense with the formality of a written binder, trustees, administrators, agents, and others, acting in representative capacity that makes them conscious of their responsibilities, ordinarily dispense with no formality and require a written binder. There are agencies who, anxious that there be no misunderstanding and unwilling to entrust important insurance coverages to memory and the spoken word pending entry in the office binder, immediately upon entry have copies sent to the insured for verification, even though not requested to do so.

Binders are ordinarily issued for a definite period of time, and the coverage automatically expires at the termination of that period. Insurers usually incorporate the right to cancel on shorter notice than provided in the standard contract, one or two days being the customary period allowed. It is believed that in the absence of a clause definitely bearing on this point, the contract conditions would govern. Finally, if the insurer deals with a broker instead of directly with the insured, it may incorporate in the binder a privilege of canceling upon notice to the broker. When a binder is issued pending the drawing up of a contract, the binder is canceled upon delivery of the contract.

A satisfactory binder form, used as standard in New England, follows:

.... 19..

Each of the undersigned Companies, for itself only, in consideration of a premium at the rate of ...... percent for ...... year promised to be paid by the insured hereinafter named does hereby insure .... against loss or damage by fire or lightning to the amount set opposite its signature on .... at .... from noon of date below named either until the expiration of thirty days thereafter, or until the issue by such Company of a Standard Policy covering said property, or until twelve o'clock noon of the second business day after written notice of cancellation to the insured or to . . . . . ., the Broker placing this insurance, whichever of said three events shall first occur.

This contract is made upon the terms of the Standard Policy and of an application filed with each undersigned Company which are incorporated herein by reference, except the provisions for cancellation, the right to cancel the contract as above being expressly reserved by each Company. Other insurance permitted.

Subject to condition of the {80 / 90% / 100} Reduced Rate Contribution Clause.

When a contract is issued following a binder, it is customary to date the contract back to the date of the original binder. Hence, the term begins in such a case with the date of the binder. This procedure is by no means necessary, and a binder may be carried for a certain time and paid for separately, to be followed by the issuance of the contract at a new and later date.

The Lost Contract. The loss of a fire insurance contract has no effect upon the liability of the insurer. Copies of all contracts are retained in the office of the issuing agent, and duplicates are forwarded to the home office of the insurers concerned. It is a simple matter to issue a duplicate of a lost fire contract, and, even if the contracts of an insured are destroyed in a fire, the loss may cause some little delay; yet it is not of major importance.

When a contract is lost and a new one is to be issued in its place, steps must be taken to render the lost contract void and ineffective. The same procedure is necessary when an insured wishes to cancel a contract but finds he has lost or mislaid it. To take care of this situation, insurers have prepared a printed form known as a lost contract receipt which, when executed by the interested parties, is filed; then a new contract is issued to replace the one lost or mislaid.

PERILS COVERED

The standard fire insurance contract is a named peril contract, and the perils insured against are listed in the insuring agreement. These perils are fire, lightning, and loss by removal.

Fire. Since the contract provides insurance "against all direct loss and damage by fire," it is essential to know what constitutes fire within the intent of the contract. First, it must be understood that the purpose of insurance would be defeated if the contract covered loss or damage caused by fires intentionally started by the insured or his agents. Hence, to bring the fire within the coverage of the contract, the fire must be, as far as the insured is concerned, accidental in its origin. Thus we have the terms "friendly" and "unfriendly" fires. A friendly fire is a fire deliberately kindled and remaining within the limits intended for it and within control. Any damage such a fire may do is not covered by the fire contract. An unfriendly fire is one accidental in its origin, or a friendly fire that spreads beyond the control of its custodian.

The flame of a lighted lamp, a gas jet, a fire in a stove, a fireplace, an oil burner, or a furnace is regarded as a friendly fire. Damage from such fires in the form of smoke, heat, or similar items does not come within the coverage of the fire contract. If the fire escapes from the confines in which it is intended that it remain and accidentally ignites other property, the fire becomes unfriendly, and the damage thus done is covered.

Exactly what constitutes fire within the intent of the contract is not always easy to establish. If there is a flame and an actual burning, there can be little doubt. On the other hand, it is not the intent of the fire contract to cover such items as the scorching of property by cigarettes, heat from stoves, or electric irons. Again, when food placed on the stove for cooking becomes overheated and becomes charred, this is not held to be a fire as defined in the contract, and consequently smoke damage arising therefrom does not constitute a loss. The mere presence of heat is not evidence of fire. Combustion may develop heat, but, unless it is sufficiently rapid to produce ignition, there is no fire as contemplated by the fire insurance contract. One of the more frequently quoted cases affording an authoritative delineation of the dividing line between combustion and fire is that of *Western Woolen Mills Co.* v. *Northern Assurance Co.* The contract in question covered wool. As result of a fire, the wool was submerged for eight days in a flood. Spontaneous combustion followed, with smoke, steam, and heat, and the fiber of the wool was destroyed. Claim was made for a loss under the fire contract. The court held that spontaneous combustion in the wool was not a fire within the intent of the fire insurance contract. It is now generally held, on the basis of this and similar decisions, that heat, itself, cannot create a loss under a fire contract. There must be some evidence, in addition, that there was a "flame or glow."[4]

---

[4] On this point the court stated in part: "Spontaneous combustion is usually a rapid oxidation. Fire is oxidation which is so rapid as to either produce flame or a glow. Fire is always caused by combustion, but combustion does not always cause fire. The word "spontaneous" refers to the origin of the combustion. It means the internal development of heat without the action of an external agent. Combustion or spontaneous combustion may be so rapid as to produce fire, but until it does so, combuston cannot be said to be fire.

"No definition of fire can be found that does not include the idea of visible heat or light, and this is also the popular meaning of the word. The slow decomposition of

Lightning. Under the provisions of the older standard contracts, damage from lightning is not covered unless fire ensues, and in that case the coverage extends only to the damage caused by the fire. In other words, if lightning succeeded in wrecking a building, and the wreckage were then to catch fire, the fire insurance contract would cover the loss of the wreckage but not the lightning damage.

Lightning is frequently the cause of serious loss, though there is neither indication of fire or, for that matter, evidence of the presence of heat. When the contract was endorsed to include damage for lightning, "whether fire ensues or not," such losses fell within the limits of the coverage afforded by the contract. The 1943 New York standard contract obviates the necessity for such endorsement by specifically including loss by lightning as well as by fire in the insuring clause of the contract.

Loss by Removal. The loss incurred by removing property endangered by fire has been definitely assumed under the terms of the New York standard contract. While the insured is obligated to do everything reasonable to save threatened property, and costs thus incurred are not insurance losses, it is now specifically provided in the contract, that, if damage is sustained in the operation of removal, fire is the direct and proximate cause, and the insurer therefore is liable.

In order to charge the insurer, the removal must be deemed reasonably necessary, and the threatened danger must be of a nature that would prompt a careful and prudent uninsured person to take a like action in his own interest. Losses caused by breakage and exposure, when there is no element of gross negligence, as well as cost of removal, are cause for proper claims. Losses by theft are specifically excluded from the coverage.

The insurance follows the property to whatever point it is removed and continues in effect in the new location, covering pro rata on the old location and on each location to which the goods may be removed, for a period of five days after the fire. After the five-day period has elapsed, the insured must make provision for new or continued coverage in the new locations, or he will be without insurance. If a contract expires shortly after the inception of a fire, all the damage caused by that fire is chargeable to the insurance in effect when the fire started. Carrying the reasoning to removal, exposure losses that are not preventable by the insured may be charged to the

---

animal and vegetable matter in the air is caused by combustion. Combustion keeps up the animal heat in the body. It causes the wheat to heat in the bin and in the stock. It causes hay in the stack and in the mow of the barn to heat and decompose. It causes the sound tree of the forest, when thrown to the ground, in the course of years to decay and molder away until it becomes again a part of Mother Earth. Still we never speak of these processes as fire. And why? Because the process of oxidation is so slow that it does not produce a flame or glow." *Western Woolen Mills Co.* v. *Northern Assurance Co.,* 139 Fed. Rep. 637, 92 U.S.C.A. 1.

insurer, if caused by a fire for which the insurer is liable, even though the exposure loss occurs after the expiration of the contract.

Direct Loss. To be covered by the standard contract the loss must be directly caused by one of the perils covered by the contract. Some interesting efforts have been made to establish the causal relationship between a peril covered by the contract and the resulting damages. In the case of fire, the loss must be caused by an unfriendly fire and there must be actual damage as a result to the property that is the subject of the insurance. The fire must be the immediate or proximate cause of the loss, as distinguished from the remote cause.[5] In a train of circumstances, culminating in a loss, the proximate cause is held to be the efficient cause; that is, the one that sets intervening agencies in motion. The courts have held that causes that are merely incidental to a superior or controlling agency are not proximate causes, even though they be nearer in time to the result. Hence, a fire may be the direct cause of a loss or damage, even though some intervening agency may form part of the chain of circumstances set in motion by the fire. For example, it was held that a fire in a tower of a building, where it was confined with but slight damage, was the proximate cause of a large machinery loss in a part of the building remote from the fire. The fire in the tower damaged the building's electric wires and caused a short circuit. This act in turn set in motion a train of circumstances causing a general breakdown of the machinery. The entire loss was held to be by fire. The fire causing the loss, therefore, need not of necessity, originate on the premises of the insured. It is sufficient if an unfriendly fire is the proximate cause of the loss within the contemplation of the parties to the contract at the time the contract is drawn.

A leading case, and one most often quoted, in reference to the question of the friendly and unfriendly fire is the English case of *Austin* v. *Drewe* (4 Campbell 360, 6 Taunt. 436) decided in 1816. A building containing sugar in the process of being refined, was heated by a huge chimney. A register at the top was closed each night and, through neglect, was not opened on a particular morning. As a result, sparks and smoke made their way into one of the rooms, some of the walls were slightly blistered from the heat, and the sugars were accidentally damaged and discolored. There was no fire in the building

[5] The following definition of proximate cause is frequently quoted in insurance cases: "The question is not what cause was nearest in time or place to the catastrophe. That is not the meaning of the maxim, *causa proxima non remota spectatur*. The proximate cause is the efficient cause, the one that necessarily sets the other cause in operation. The causes that are merely incidental or instruments of a superior or controlling agency are not the proximate causes, and the responsible ones, though they may be nearer in time to the result. It is only when the causes are independent of each other than the nearest is, of course, to be charged with the disaster." *The G. R. Booth*, 171 U.S. 450.

other than that intentionally started, and it had not spread from the confines intended for it. The damage was caused by sparks, heat, and smoke. There was no hostile fire and no claim for a loss under the fire insurance contract.

LIMITATIONS ON AMOUNT OF RECOVERY

The insuring agreement of the standard fire insurance contract places specific limits on the amount to be recovered in the event of loss from one of the named perils. Since the contract is one of indemnity, an effort is made to prevent more than the recovery of the monetary value of the loss. The insurer agrees to insure "to an amount not exceeding the amount(s) above specified . . . to the extent of the actual cash value of the property at the time of loss, but not exceeding the amount which it would cost to repair or replace the property with material of like kind and quality within a reasonable time after such loss, without allowance for any increased cost of repair or reconstruction by reason of any ordinance or law regulating construction or repair, and without compensation for loss resulting from interruption of business or manufacture, nor in any event for more than the interest of the insured. . . ." The interpretation of these limits is discussed in the following paragraphs.

Face Amount. The face amount of the contract serves as an upper limit to recovery and the insured will in no event receive more than this amount.[6] There is no assurance that the face amount will be paid, since the other limitations on recovery may be the determining factors in deciding upon the amount to be paid.

Actual Cash Value. Value, as used in insurance terminology, undertakes to establish a measure of the injury to the owner of insured property as the result of its destruction or damage. To determine the actual cash value of destroyed property at the time of loss or damage might, at first sight, seem a simple and easy task. The problem, however, is a difficult one. The term "value" is one of the most elusive with which economists have to deal, and its different uses tend to confusion. There are, for example, valuations made for tax purposes, for appraisals of estates, for rate making in public utilities, as a basis for issuing bonds, for condemnation purposes, or for sale.

A number of courts have held "actual cash value" to be the cost of replacing the property at the time of loss less depreciation.[7] There are situations where this rule will apply, and the courts have been quite

---

[6] These amounts are placed on the face of the contract immediately below the space for the insured's name and mailing address and above the insuring agreement. The items insured would normally be (1) the dwelling and (2) contents. An amount of insurance would be noted for each item.

[7] *Svea Fire and Life Insurance Company* v. *State Savings & Loan Assn.*, 19 (F2d).

correct in using it. In the case of a dwelling recently built, replacement cost less physical depreciation usually serves as a basis for determining value. The rule cannot be given universal application, for there are many situations where it is inapplicable. This is particularly the case where there is a wide difference between a fair market value of the property and the cost of replacement new less physical depreciation. Where market value is substantially less than replacement value less depreciation, the market price may determine value. There are many properties that have a limited market value but a high value to the owner. This is true with respect to many properties that have been built for a special purpose. Market value may be a determining factor in reaching actual value, but it is not necessarily so. If the objective of the insurance is the placing of the insured in as good a financial position following the loss as he would have been had no loss occurred, a rule that fails to accomplish this must be disregarded. Actual value now is generally held to depend upon all the conditions and circumstances surrounding a property and need not necessarily be either market value or replacement cost.[8] As defined by the New York Court of Appeals, actual cash value becomes the economic value as distinguished from its replacement value. Through the operation of what has now come to be known as the *McAnarney rule*, the measure of loss is to be determined from all available evidence.[9] All of the available factors which may have any relationship to value may be brought into the picture as evidence tending to demonstrate the actual value of the property destroyed, but no one factor of itself may determine it.

An extreme case may serve to illustrate the point. An art collector purchases what he supposes to be an old master. He pays $100,000 for the picture and hangs it in his home. Assessments in his community run about 50 percent of value, so the assessor, in computing personal property values, includes the picture at a figure of $50,000. As the years go by, the owner, watching sales, believes that his picture has increased in value, and for the purpose of adjusting his insurance coverage writes the dealer from whom the purchase was made for his opinion. He receives a reply that the picture would bring $200,000

---

[8] *Canal National Fire Insurance Co.* v. *Colonsay Hotel* 3 D.L.R. 1001.

[9] The New York Court of Appeals in *McAnarney* v. *Newark Insurance Company*, 247 N.Y. 176, 159 N.E. 902, in rejecting both market value and replacement cost less depreciation as the basis for determining the measure of damages, covered the situation in the following terms: "Where insured buildings have been destroyed, the trier of fact may, and should, call to its aid, in order to affectuate complete indemnity, every fact and circumstance which would logically tend to the formation of a correct estimate of the loss. It may consider original cost and cost of reproduction; the opinions upon value given by qualified witnesses; the declarations against interest which may have been made by the assured; the gainful uses to which the buildings might have been put; as well as any other fact tending to throw light upon the subject."

easily at a sale, and as a result of this letter he increases his insurance coverage accordingly. Shortly afterward his home burns, and the picture is totally destroyed. His claim for $200,000 is received by the insurers, who find upon investigation that the picture supposedly lost in the fire is still in existence and that the picture, which was purchased for $100,000 and upon which insurance in that amount or greater had been paid for many years, was nothing more than a cleverly executed copy worth perhaps $500.

Now, what is the liability of the insurer carrying a policy of $200,000 on the picture? The price paid is evidence of value. The assessor's valuation may be presented, with the statement that it was customary to underestimate and that the assessment remained unchanged for many years. The opinion of the expert is evidence. But none of these determines value. If they are all wrong, and the picture is a copy worth $500, then that is the limit collectible under the contract.

On the other hand, a shrewd buyer may recognize a value that the vendor does not see, and the price paid for an article may be considerably less than would have been the case between two equally well-informed parties. In such an instance the buyer is entitled to the benefit of his bargain, and the value of purchase may be in a sum in excess of the purchase price.

In the case of household furniture, it has been held that what a junk shop or secondhand dealer would have given for the property is no measure of its value. Nor is the price it would have brought at a forced sale. The owner who needs it and is using it would not part with it at such a price, and, therefore, since no such sales would have been made, what it might have brought does not govern the value. If the owner had offered it for sale at a given price, this would be evidence to set an upper limit to his claim, but nothing more.

Cost to Repair or Replace. The second limitation on the amount collectible under a fire insurance contract has to do with the cost to repair or replace the damaged property. There are two factors that have a bearing: (*a*) the kind and quality of the material and (*b*) cost attributable to an ordinance or law.

Kind and Quality of Material. It is not expected that the insured will profit as a result of his loss by charging to the insurer the cost of repairs if better or more expensive material is used. If a wooden roof burns from a building and the insured elects to replace it with tile, the limit of his loss is still the cost of the wooden roof. If the insured elects to rebuild out of entirely different materials, the extra cost of building cannot be charged in any way to the loss.

Cost Attributable to Law. It sometimes happens that insured property, within areas in a municipality restricted to specific requirements as to construction, fails to meet the requirements of the local building ordinance because of adoption of the ordinance after the building in question was constructed. Fire contracts as now written do not cover the increased cost of repairs when the increase is made necessary as the outgrowth of a building code. Frequently, the ordinance makes mandatory the demolition of a building when a substantial part of it is destroyed by fire. Before the incorporation into the contract of the clause "without allowance for any increased cost of repair or reconstruction by reason of any ordinance or law regulating construction or repair," it was a matter of doubt whether a property was a total loss under the fire contract if demolition was necessary as an outcome of the fire. The New York form definitely settles this question.[10]

Business Interruption. The standard fire contract undertakes to indemnify the insured for loss or damage to the physical property that is the subject of the insurance. By limiting the loss to the cost of repairing or replacing damaged property with materials of like kind and quality, the element of profit is eliminated. The contract goes one step further and specifically eliminates from the scope of the coverage consequential loss attributable to the interruption of business.

When a fire loss occurs that makes necessary the partial or total suspension of business operations at a location, a loss to the owner of the business materializes. It might well be argued that such a loss is directly attributable to the fire and consequentially within the scope of the fire insurance contract. To clearly delineate the intent of the coverage, loss resulting from the interruption of business or manufacture is excluded and a clause to this effect is incorporated in the contract. Business interruption losses are insurable but only under a contract specifically drawn to insure this risk.

Interest of the Insured. There is no warranty as to ownership in the New York standard contract of 1943. The insuring clause limits the amount that may be recovered to the "interest of the insured." If the insured is something less than sole and unconditional owner, he may not collect in the case of loss to the property for the full amount of the damage unless his interest in the property is such that the amount of the damage will represent loss to him. It is the intent of the contract to provide indemnity for loss sustained. It is no longer essential that the insured be the sole and unconditional owner of the property, nor need the building stand on ground owned in fee simple as was heretofore the case. (See, for example, the New York standard fire contract of 1918.) Foreclose proceedings will not adversely affect the insurance, nor does the existence of a chattel mortgage. Any

---

[10] That the situation involves a real risk that is insurable can readily be recognized. To provide for the consequent loss when demolition is required by the ordinance, a clause (to be discussed in more detail later) may be added to the contract providing for the payment of a total loss. For this coverage an additional premium is charged.

change of interest during the term of the contract will make no difference in the effectiveness of the insurance, other than the amount collectible will, in every instance, be limited to the value of the interest. Should any change take place which leaves the insured without an interest, he would have no claim under the contract in the event of loss or damage to the property covered.

REPLACEMENT COST CONTRACTS

Although the fire insurance contract provides for payment of the "actual cash value of the property at the time of loss," it is possible for the insured to obtain replacement cost insurance where this type of insurance would be appropriate.

FOR DISCUSSION

1. There are two main divisions to the statutory standard fire contract. Name them.
2. There are two elements essential to cause a direct loss as covered by the standard fire insurance contract. Name them.
3. B is pressing a garment and scorches it. Claim is made for a loss under the fire insurance contract on the ground that the scorching is accidental. Is this a direct loss under the fire contract?
4. What is the meaning of the term "indemnity" as it is used in the standard fire contract?
5. It is stated that the fire insurance contract may be liable for several different amounts if the same type of goods is damaged; that is, it may be obligated to pay A one sum, but if B owned the same goods, it might be obligated to pay him another. Explain.
6. Reference is frequently made to "actual cash" value and to "sound" value. Is there any difference between the two?
7. It has long been contended by fire insurance underwriters that it was the intent of the framers of fire insurance contracts to reimburse insureds only to the extent that the property insured was actually destroyed. With the advent of building laws requiring demolition if certain types of property were destroyed to the extent indicated in the law, the problem presented itself as to the liability of insurance carriers for the value of the property to be demolished as well as the cost of demolition. Some courts have held the insurance companies to be liable. Explain.
8. The contract of fire insurance is said to be a personal contract. In one particular instance there is an exception. Explain.
9. Fire insurance contracts provide that they are not valid until countersigned. Is this provision binding?
10. Railroad companies permit a reduction in rate on raw materials when, as part of the agreement, a manufacturer obligates himself to ship the

finished product by the same railroad. Such rates are known as "transit rates." B is a manufacturer of pulp. Large quantities of pulpwood have been shipped under transit rates, but before the finished product can be shipped, B's plant burns and the railroad claims an increase in freight on the incoming raw material. Is this increase covered by the standard fire policy?

11. X spills acid on a valuable oriental rug, and a hole is burned through the rug. Is this covered under a fire insurance contract?
12. A steampipe bursts in the storehouse of X causing considerable damage to packaged breakfast food. X claims that a fire is the proximate cause of the loss since steam is generated by a fire. May he collect under his fire insurance contract?
13. Firemen in an effort to extinguish a fire on the premises of A direct a line of hose in such a way that the windows of B's house are broken and serious water damage results. There is no fire in B's property. May he collect for the water damage under his fire insurance contract?
14. A fire engine responding to a call to a fire collides with the automobile of B. Is this a fire loss that will permit B to collect damages under his fire insurance contract?
15. B in using a blowtorch to thaw a frozen water pipe sets fire to the floor timbers in his cellar. The fire spreads upward through a partition and before it is extinguished by the fire department causes substantial damage. Since the blowtorch was deliberately used by the owner of the property, has he a claim against his fire insurer? May he call the fire an unfriendly fire?
16. A housewife places a roast in an oven and sets an electric clock to time the shutoff at an hour when the roast is expected to be properly cooked. Through some error in judgment the oven is set so that it overheats and the roast is badly burned, and not only the kitchen but the entire house is saturated with a greasy smoke. The roast is exactly where it was intended to be, though the smoke is the result of too much heat. Does the fire insurance contract cover?
17. In working around the sprinkler system in B's department store, a workman using a blowtorch accidentally sets off a sprinkler head. Before the system can be turned off the water pours down from the building causing damage in the amount of hundreds of dollars. A claim is made under the fire insurance contract, and liability is denied. Is the denial justifiable, and on what grounds? Do you think there is a case for a claim? This is in fact regarded as a borderline situation. Give arguments pro and con.
18. X deliberately sets fire to the property of a member of the family to seek revenge. Is this a fire loss for which the insurers are liable?
19. An insane person sets fire to his own home. Here the act was unquestionably deliberate. Must the insurers bear the loss?
20. B orders a fire insurance contract from Agent X, and before the contract is delivered a loss occurs. B contends that because the

contract has not actually been issued he is not bound by the provisions of the standard contract requiring the filing of a proof of loss. There is no such requirement in the binder form. If you were called upon to advise the insured, what advice would you give?

21. There is a legal maxim which states: "The words of the instrument are construed strongly against the one who drafts them." What is the significance of this maxim with reference to the standard fire insurance contract?
22. X has a contract expiring with the Blank Agency on June 15. He decides to transfer it to another agency and orders a contract effective June 16 discontinuing the contract to expire on the 15th. He feels in the circumstances that there is no lack in the continuity of coverage. At 3:00 P.M. on June 15, the property is destroyed by fire. Discuss.
23. B, the owner of a restaurant, secured fire insurance in the amount of $25,000 on his furniture and fixtures. They were totally destroyed by fire. The insured was not satisfied with the adjustment and brought action. The Court found the loss to be $21,361.60. The insurers appealed. They contended that there was actually no market for used equipment of the nature insured. Admitting this to be the case, what coverage does the standard fire insurance contract provide? Do you feel the companies are on strong ground in appealing? Explain.
24. On July 30, 1916, fire broke out beneath some freight cars in the Lehigh Valley company freight yards at Black Tom in New York harbor. The cars were loaded with explosives, and after the fire had burned approximately one-half hour the contents of the cars exploded. The explosion caused another fire, which in turn caused another and much greater explosion of a large quantity of dynamite. The last explosion caused a concussion of the air which damaged a vessel situated about 100 feet distant. Claim was made for damage to the vessel under a fire policy on the ground that fire was the proximate cause of the loss. Do you think the owner of the vessel has a claim?
25. The building of X is insured for $10,000. The policy contains an 80 percent coinsurance clause. In the process of adjustment, it is found that it would cost $39,453.83 to reproduce the building exactly as it was just before the fire. However, because of the aging condition of the building, a deduction of 60 percent was taken for depreciation in order to arrive at an actual cash value of $15,774.34. Assuming the actual cash value so determined to be correct, the insured was obligated under the terms of his insurance contract to carry $12,619.46, or 80 percent of $15,774.34, in order to be fully covered up to the face amount of the contract. It was further found, in the course of adjustment, that the cost of labor and materials to repair the damage to restore the building to its prior use was $17,225.44. Must the 60 percent depreciation figure used in obtaining sound value be applied to the cost of restoring the building to obtain the amount of the loss?

CHAPTER · 6

Standard Fire Insurance Contract (Continued)

In addition to the insuring agreement the standard fire insurance contract contains 165 lines of stipulations and conditions (see Figure 5–2). This part of the contract provides the insured with a detailed statement of the limitations placed on the contract, as well as information on such items as cancellation, procedure to be followed in the event of loss, and conditions surrounding the interests of the mortgagee.

CONCEALMENT AND MISREPRESENTATION

The first of the stipulations in the 1943 New York Standard fire insurance contract deals with concealment, misrepresentation, and fraud in the following terms:

1 **Concealment,** This entire policy shall be void if, whether
2 **fraud.** before or after a loss, the insured has wil-
3 fully concealed or misrepresented any ma-
4 terial fact or circumstance concerning this insurance or the
5 subject thereof, or the interest of the insured therein, or in case
6 of any fraud or false swearing by the insured relating thereto.

Fraud is ordinarily defined as an intentional misrepresentation of material existing facts which induces another to act in reliance thereon to his damage. To constitute fraud, therefore, there must be the intention to mislead, and the injured person must have relied upon the misleading statements and have been injured thereby. The misrepresentation in such an instance must have been material.

A material fact is held to be any fact which, if known to the insurer, would influence it either to reject the risk or to accept it on different terms than those contemplated in the contract under consideration. In the light of this definition, a misrepresentation without intent to mislead would typically not be sufficient ground to void a contract for fraud. To cover this contingency, it is stipulated that the contract shall be void for wilful concealment or misrepresentation if the subject matter is material to the risk. Even though the concealment may be prompted by some other motive than fraud upon the insurer, it will not operate to prevent voiding the contract.

As far as fire insurance is concerned, there is no concealment in the event of failure to disclose facts material to the risk that typically are readily available to the insurer. The applicant for insurance is expected to answer truthfully any inquiries that may be made by the insurer or its representative. If he answers fully and in good faith such inquiries as are directed to him, he is not expected to go beyond this unless there is some information of an extraordinary nature which the insurer ought to know and "could not, with reasonable diligence, be discovered by the insurer, or reasonably anticipated by him, as a foundation for specific inquiries."[1]

Fraud and false swearing are coupled in the stipulation in such a manner as to permit the conclusion that their effects are the same. In a Maine case the court held that if an insured knowingly and purposely makes a false statement on oath concerning the subject matter of the insurance and the contract contains a clause similar to the one now under discussion, the false statement has the effect of voiding the contract and bars the insured's right of recovery.[2] This is true whether or not it was the purpose of the insured to deceive the insurer.

Concealment or false swearing has the same effect whether made before or after a loss. It may happen that an insured who knowingly and wilfully makes a false answer relating to any matter material to a loss, or makes a false oath, may void the contract. Attempts have been made in cases of false swearing to show that there was no attempt made to deceive the insurer and that the false statements were made to cover like statements made for other purposes. Because of this, it has been contended that lack of intention to deceive the insurer takes the false swearing out of the category of fraud. The courts, on the other hand, have held that false swearing knowingly and intentionally done is evidence of fraud and shows an intention to injure.[3]

Swearing to an instrument that contains an honest mistake does not come within the category of false swearing. In the case of a column of figures added incorrectly by mistake, if it can be shown that the mistake was in every sense honest, the error will not have the effect of

---

[1] *Protection Ins. Co.* v. *Harmer*, 2 Ohio St. 473.

[2] In this case the court stated: "False swearing is fraud. False swearing consists in knowingly and intentionally stating upon oath what is not true. A false statement intentionally and knowingly, or fraudulently made, certainly constitutes fraud, and the statement of a fact as true which a party does not know to be true, and which he has no reasonable ground for believing to be true, is fraudulent." *Tinscott* v. *Orient Ins. Co.*, 88 Maine 497.

[3] *Claflin* v. *Commonwealth Ins. Co.*, 110 U.S. 81.

voiding the insurance on the grounds of false swearing. An insured is not responsible for the acts of an agent that might void an insurance contract under the aforementioned stipulation unless the acts of the agent were carried out at the instigation of the insured or unless he knew of their import and acquiesced in the agent's act.

EXCEPTIONS AND LIMITATIONS

The standard fire insurance contract contains a number of exceptions and limitations. These provisions range from a statement about property and perils excluded to a statement about conditions under which the basic agreement may be changed through endorsements or waiver. Statements of the type here considered serve to limit the liability of the insurer and a thorough understanding of them is essential to an evaluation of the contract.

Uninsurable and Excepted Property. Uninsurable and excepted property consist of (1) property that cannot be insured, and (2) property that is not covered by the contract unless there is a specific statement that provides coverage. The distinction between these classes of property is made in the following terms:

> **Uninsurable and excepted property.** This policy shall not cover accounts, bills, currency, deeds, evidences of debt, money or securities; nor, unless specifically named hereon in writing, bullion or manuscripts.

The items listed as uninsurable are not usually regarded as property but rather as evidences of ownership or media of exchange.[4] The two items that may be covered only if specifically mentioned are properties that may have almost any degree of value, ranging from the very rare to the virtually valueless. Because of this, and because of the grave possibility that misunderstanding might arise in the event of a claim, it has been felt that, before accepting liability on such properties, insurers should have a right to determine whether they wish to cover on the risk.[5]

---

[4] Accounts receivable insurance may be written to cover loss growing out of inability to collect because of destruction of records.

[5] The list of uninsurable and excepted properties has been greatly reduced in the 1943 contract as compared with the older contracts. In the old New York contract and the 1918 contract, properties that are not insurable include accounts, bills, currency, deeds, evidences of debt, money, notes, or securities. In the old New York contract the list of properties exempt from coverage, unless liability is specifically assumed, was somewhat longer than the list in the 1918 contract and included: awnings, bullion, casts, curiosities, drawings, dies, implements, jewels, manuscripts, medals, models, patterns, pictures, scientific apparatus, signs, store or office furniture or fixtures, sculpture, tools, or property held in storage or for repairs. The 1918 contract shortened this latter list to include only bullion, manuscripts, mechanical drawings, dies, or patterns. The 1943 contract drops the item "notes" from the list of uninsurable items and reduces to two the items not covered unless specifically named in the contract.

Hazards Not Covered. Although the 1943 New York standard fire insurance contract generally covers losses by fire from any cause, there are a few causes that are excluded. The contract provides:

> **Perils not included.** This Company shall not be liable for loss by fire or other perils insured against in this policy caused, directly or indirectly, by: (a) enemy attack by armed forces, including action taken by military, naval or air forces in resisting an actual or an immediately impending enemy attack; (b) invasion; (c) insurrection; (d) rebellion; (e) revolution; (f) civil war; (g) usurped power; (h) order of any civil authority except acts of destruction at the time of and for the purpose of preventing the spread of fire, provided that such fire did not originate from any of the perils excluded by this policy; (i) neglect of the insured to use all reasonable means to save and preserve the property at and after a loss, or when the property is endangered by fire in neighboring premises; (j) nor shall this Company be liable for loss by theft.

The possibility of loss from certain of these causes has been considered so remote as to warrant little or no consideration from many insurers. It is important to recognize the limitations placed upon the coverage by this clause and to know to what extent these limitations may be eliminated from the contract by endorsements or special contracts.

Invasion has been defined as "the entrance of an armed force from abroad with hostile intent."[6] Fires caused by military occupation come within the exclusion of the contract, and it has been held that military or usurped power was the proximate cause of a loss when the fire spread to the insured property through several buildings.[7] Insurrection, on the other hand, carries with it no implication of invasion from the outside but is defined as an armed and organized resistance to established authority.

The exemption "by order of any civil authority" has the effect of excluding from the coverage of the fire contract property destroyed by public officers, with the exception that destruction to prevent the spread of a fire is covered if the fire did not originate from perils excluded in the contract. When the exemption did not appear in the contract, such losses were covered: "Whether it be the result of accident or design—whether the torch be applied by the honest magistrate, or the wicked incendiary—whether the purpose be to save a city, as at New York, or a country, as at Moscow—the loss is equally within the terms of the contract."[8]

---

[6] G. Richards, *The Law of Insurance* (4th ed.; New York: Baker, Voorhis & Co. 1932), p. 369.

[7] *Royal Ins. Co.* v. *Martin*, 192 U.S. 149.

[8] *City Fire Ins. Co.* v. *Corlies*, 21 Wend. (N.Y.) 347, 34 Am. Dec. 258.

If the police, properly authorized, were to set fire to a building to dislodge a fugitive, the fire contract would not cover; but the authority of the police in such situations has been questioned many times. There have been cases in which property was burned to check bubonic plague; and such a loss is eliminated by the civil authorities exception. In the past it has been held that, if a fire is in progress and it is definitely apparent that the insured property is already doomed, fire is the proximate cause of the loss even though the authorities blow up the building to check the spread of a conflagration.[9] This is the doctrine that has now been incorporated in the contract.

The reference to neglect of an insured to use reasonable means to save and preserve the property at and after a fire, or when property is endangered by fire in the neighboring premises, brings in, for the first time, the element of neglect as a factor in determining liability. The obligation of determining whether there has been neglect rests with the insurer if it wishes to deny liability upon these grounds.

While the contract definitely places the obligation upon the insured to use all reasonable means to save property threatened by fire, insurance authorities hold that the clause places no additional liability upon the insured that he would not have had in any case, since the duties it imposes are said to arise from the nature of the insurance contract. As a matter of practical information, the insured is interested in learning to what extent he is obligated to go to comply with the requirements of his contract. The insured must follow a line of conduct reasonable in the circumstances. Indicative of one extreme, it has been held that the duty of caring for family or saving life takes precedence over the obligation to care for threatened property. If a policyholder gives his entire attention to the care of his family or to the saving of life, at the expense of the property insured, he is not to be charged with negligence. On the other hand, the insured may not sit complacently by and, in the knowledge that his property is insured, allow it to burn without making such efforts to save it as in the circumstances seem reasonable.

Theft during the time the premises are ablaze is excluded. A loss by theft as a result of a fire would, in the absence of a specific exclusion, come within the protection of the contract, since fire would be held to be the proximate cause of the loss. The expressed exception sets forth theft as one of the perils not covered, although theft as a result of removal of the property from the endangered premises is not excluded.

Other Insurance. The stipulation with reference to other insurance is based on the assumption that excess insurance tends to enhance moral hazard. Formerly, other insurance was prohibited unless

[9] *Foster* v. *Fidelity F. Ins. Co.*, 24 Pa. Sup. Ct. 585.

consent was endorsed on the contract. It had become customary automatically to endorse such consent by including it in the form. The new contract covers the matter thus:

> **Other insurance.** Other insurance may be prohibited or the amount of insurance may be limited by endorsement attached hereto.

If insurance is prohibited, it has been held by the courts that this condition becomes effective as soon as new insurance is issued protecting the same interests. "When temptation is invited, the penalty is earned."[10] When there is grave danger from the point of view of negligence, if the property is overinsured, the insurers may wish to make use of the stipulation as to other insurance by placing a definite limitation upon the amount that may be carried instead of giving carte blanche. The clause is designed to protect the insurer from overinsurance in the event that it has no knowledge of such overinsurance. If the fact of overinsurance is known, the insurer would probably reduce its line.

When the element of other insurance is important, it is essential to know precisely what is meant by the term. There can be other insurance only when there is a duplication of insurance on the same interests. There is no other insurance within the scope of the condition if the coverage of one contract is on an interest entirely separate from a second interest. If the owner of a property carries insurance on his interest and the mortgagee likewise insures his own interest, there is no violation of the stipulation. "Neither the policy of the law nor the contracts of insurance forbid, but on the contrary permit as many several insurances upon the same property as there are separate interests."[11] It has been equally settled that other insurance may not be taken by using a "dummy" to effect a subterfuge. A frequently quoted rule is set forth by Lord Mansfield in the following terms: "If the same man really and for his own proper account insures the same good doubly, though both insurances be not made in his own name, but one or both of them in the name of another person, yet that is just the same thing; for the same person is to have the benefit of both policies."[12] The courts have held that since the additional insurance is prohibited because of the moral hazard, the temptation and hazard are increased whether the contract be taken in the name of the real owner or of another acting in his stead. If only one person is, in the end, to profit by the two contracts in the event of a loss by fire, there is held to be other insurance.

---

[10] *Sutterlein* v. *Northern Ins. Co. of New York*, 251 N.Y. 72, 167 N.E. 176.

[11] *DeWitt* v. *Agricultural Ins. Co.*, 157 N.Y. 353, 51 N.E. 977.

[12] *Godin* v. *Landon Assur. Co.*, 1 Burr. 489, quoted in *Sutterlein* v. *Northern Ins. Co. of New York*, 251 N.Y. 72, 167 N.E. 176.

Excepted Conditions. There are certain situations which have been written into the contract and have the effect of suspending the coverage unless the insurer authorizes the insurance by agreeing in writing thereto on the contract. These are covered in the following manner:

> **Conditions suspending or restricting insurance. Unless otherwise provided in writing added hereto this Company shall not be liable for loss occurring**
>
> (a) while the hazard is increased by any means within the control or knowledge of the insured; or
>
> (b) while a described building, whether intended for occupancy by owner or tenant, is vacant or unoccupied beyond a period of sixty consecutive days; or
>
> (c) as a result of explosion or riot, unless fire ensue, and in that event for loss by fire only.

The important point in connection with the foregoing clauses is that the coverage is voided during the period in which the prohibited conditions exist. Similar conditions appear in the old New York form, but under the terms of the contract, violation of any one of the conditions voided the contract and there was no automatic reinstatement. Since the courts did not always follow the stipulations of the contract, it is important to recognize the difference between the 1943 form, which follows the 1918 form, and the old form. A violation of any one of the conditions quoted above suspends the coverage during violation but does not have the effect of terminating the insurance.

Increase in Hazard. The intent of this clause is evident, and it has long been recognized that a literal interpretation is virtually impossible. If it were true that the insurer were not liable for loss or damage occurring while the hazard is increased by any means within the control or knowledge of the insured, it would follow that any slight or temporary condition that tended in any way to increase the hazard would have the effect of suspending the insurance. This situation was not the intent of the framers of the contract, nor have the courts followed such an interpretation in their decisions. They have recognized that any hazard whatever varies within certain limits. The use of fires, the presence of workmen, and many other daily incidents may have the effect of increasing the hazard for a short period. The intent of the clause is not to suspend the coverage for changes that would ordinarily be anticipated in connection with the use of the property. It does undertake to obligate the insured to maintain the risk in essentially the same condition as to structure and use as it was when the insurance was placed. If the hazard becomes greater and is immediately different and is not simply a temporary variation, then the insurance coverage is suspended. This point has been well set forth in the following terms: "The general rule seems to be that there must be something in the nature of a permanent change either in the premises themselves or in the manner of their use, to justify a court in declaring the policy void for increase of physical hazard."[13]

The clause provides that the insurer shall not be liable for loss or damage while the hazard is increased. This fact has been held to mean that the insurer is not liable for a loss that originates during the period that the hazard has increased, even though the hazard in no way contributed to the loss. What constitutes an increase in hazard is regarded as a question of fact. Changes may sometimes take place that do, in fact, increase a hazard but were within the contemplation of the parties when the contract was placed. The increase in hazard contemplated by the clause must be actual and substantial. In the matter of dispute, the question is determined by the jury, giving due consideration to customary use.

Vacancy and Unoccupancy. Reference to the terms "vacancy" and "unoccupancy" in the contract indicates a difference in meaning between the two terms. A building is said to be vacant when it is empty, that is, when furnishings are entirely lacking and nothing, unless waste or rubbish, is contained therein. A building completely furnished is unoccupied if not tenanted in the customary way by human beings. A dwelling house entirely furnished, but closed, is unoccupied. It is vacant when the furniture has been removed. Under the terms of the standard contract, a property vacant or unoccupied beyond a 60-day period suspends the coverage during the continuance of this situation. Insurance on certain types of property would be of little use if this condition of the contract remained unmodified. In the forms used on the contracts insuring summer or seasonal dwellings, it is necessary that a clause be inserted granting permission for the property to remain vacant or unoccupied for a portion of each year. While no limit is ordinarily set on a period of unoccupancy, vacancy is usually limited to a definite period, depending upon the nature and character of the property insured. Vacancy and unoccupancy are without effect upon the coverage when so stated in the form. The vacancy clause in the form may be thus expressed: "Vacancy for not exceeding thirty (30) consecutive days, in addition to the period permitted by the policy conditions in any one policy year shall not vitiate this policy." Other variations of the clause fit particular needs and in some instances call for the payment of an additional premium. Clauses to cover for a considerable period and for which a premium is charged read as follows:

In consideration of $...... additional premium, permission is hereby given for the building described in the ...... items of this policy to

[13] H. Cabell, "Increase in Hazard" in *The Fire Insurance Contract* (Indianapolis: The Rough Notes Co., 1922), p. 126.

be unoccupied and/or vacant for a period of .... from the .... day of .... 19.. to the............. day of .... 19.., at 12 o'clock noon.

A building is not considered vacant if, for a temporary period, there are no humans present. If the entire family leave a building for the day, it is not unoccupied. If it is being used as a dwelling and at a customary time the members of the household habitually return, the dwelling is occupied. Likewise, a church may be without the presence of humans for a considerable period of time, such as, for example, during the week, yet if used regularly for service it is considered occupied. A school closed for vacation is not unoccupied if it is used in the school term. Caretakers are not ordinarily considered occupants, although a house kept open and in running order by a servant, even though the owners have been for a considerable period elsewhere, is occupied.

Explosion and Riot. For the purpose of determining coverage under a fire insurance contract, explosion falls into one of two categories. If, as a result of an unfriendly fire, an explosion causes damages, the explosion is construed to be a part of the fire. The damage which it causes, whether concussion damage or the result of burning, is now held by most authorities to be a fire loss. On the other hand, if an explosion is the cause of the fire, the concussion damage is not covered; but the contract does cover for whatever loss the ensuing fire causes.[14] In this case it is important to recognize that if a building is seriously damaged by explosion and fire ensues, the amount for which the fire contract is liable is only that which the fire itself caused to property already damaged. In other words, if the property should be already worthless as a result of an explosion and the wreckage should catch fire, there would be no fire loss. If the wreckage had some value, the extent of the loss would be the value of the wreckage as such, not its value before the fire.

In order to establish a fire loss for concussion damage following an explosion, the explosion must have occurred as a result of an unfriendly fire. The fact that the explosion is accidental will not bring fire damage which it may cause within the coverage of the contract if, as a result of a friendly fire, an explosion is precipitated. It has been frequently held that the lighting of a match which results in an explosion is not an unfriendly fire, and, therefore, the explosion damage, even though caused by a fire, does not come within the protection of the contract. Fire damage, caused by an unfriendly fire following the explosion, would be covered.

Losses caused by the explosion of water-heating coils in ranges and boilers, by the explosion of heating boilers, hot water tanks, or other

[14] The explosion risk may be covered by a specific contract.

like installations are not property losses assumed by the standard fire contract unless the risk is endorsed on the contract.

In connection with exposure losses there is a point to be considered. If an unfriendly fire in progress is the cause of an explosion, fire is considered the proximate cause of the loss caused by both the explosion and the fire on the premises where the explosion occurs. But if the concussion from this same explosion is severe enough to break neighboring windows, or causes an adjoining building to collapse, then the loss to the adjoining property is deemed to be a concussion loss caused by an independent explosion, and not a fire loss. Hence, the same explosion may do damage covered by one set of fire contracts and not by another.

The rule as to riot is the same as that for explosion. A "riot" is defined as a violent disturbance of the peace by three or more persons. In some states the definition finds a place in the statutes; in others it is the outgrowth of decisions. There is a general agreement that the following three factors are essential for a riot: (1) disturbance of the peace; (2) three or more persons; and (3) violence, turbulence, or disorder. To constitute a riot then, the act, in which three or more persons are engaged, may be either a lawless act or a lawful act carried out in an unlawful manner. In either case, violence or a breach of public peace is a requisite in some states, though in others a breach of public peace is a requisite only in the case of a lawful act. In the case of a riot, therefore, unlawfulness of purpose is not a factor.[15] One of the most frequent sources of loss growing out of riots is to be found in fires caused by rioting incident to strikes. Such losses are covered, but only to the extent of the fire loss. Damage caused by riot, if fire is not a factor, is not covered by the standard contract.[16]

As a result of riot and explosion, the contract is not suspended, but loss is restricted to damage by fire only. This has been the general rule in the case of explosion, but until the 1943 New York contract, loss caused directly or indirectly by riot was not covered. This created a serious gap in the fire coverage and left an important source of doubt in instances where it was not altogether clearly established whether the fire could be attributed to a riot. The contract does not cover sabotage, vandalism, and other like damage that might originate from a riot, but it does include within its scope losses caused by fire.

---

15 A frequently cited definition from Kentucky provides: "A riot is a tumultuous disturbance of the peace by three persons or more assembling together, of their own authority, with an intent actually to assist each other against any who shall oppose them in the execution of some enterprise of a private nature, and afterwards actually executing same in a violent and turbulent manner, to the terror of the people. *Spring Garden Insurance Co.* v. *Imperial Tobacco Co.*, 132 Ky. 7, 116 S.W. 234. Also quoted in *American Central Ins. Co.* v. *Stearns Lumber Co.*, 145 Ky. 255, 140 S. W. 148.

16 Riot and civil commotion insurance is widely written to cover the risk of riot damage.

In the case of both riot and explosion, if there is loss prior to the inception of the fire, the liability of the fire insurer extends only to the value of the property at the time the fire started. In other words, if the property is partly demolished by explosion and a fire follows, the fire contract is not responsible for the wreckage caused by the explosion but only for the loss caused by the fire to the property in its wrecked condition. The rule is similar in the case of riot. If the property is sabotaged, and the fire follows, the fire contract picks up on the property in its condition at the inception of the fire.

Optional Coverages. The insuring clause of the contract provides insurance against loss by fire, lightning, and by removal. The contract provides for the inclusion of other perils in the following terms:

38 **Other perils** Any other peril to be insured against or sub-
39 **or subjects.** ject of insurance to be covered in this policy
40 shall be by endorsement in writing hereon or
41 added hereto.

The effect of these lines is to broaden enormously the usefulness of the contract. It may now be used to write any of the allied fire lines. In some states the contract is prepared with windstorm conditions included to the end that both fire and windstorm may be included in a single contract. The insured elects whether he will purchase the additional coverage. Perils other than windstorm may be included by means of an endorsement attached to the contract. Taken in connection with the provision for added clauses, the contract as now drawn has great flexibility.

Added Provisions. To draw up an insurance agreement that would fairly treat both the insured and the insurer and be comprehensive enough in its scope to satisfy every situation was a task that the framers of the standard contract recognized to be virtually unattainable. Knowing that the standard contract must be used in insuring all classes of property and extending coverage to a multiplicity of insurable interests, it was anticipated that many of the clauses in the contract would be found either burdensome or entirely inapplicable.[17] The framers of the contract incorporated permission for added provisions in the following manner:

42 **Added provisions.** The extent of the application of insurance
43 under this policy and of the contribution to
44 be made by this Company in case of loss, and any other pro-
45 vision or agreement not inconsistent with the provisions of this
46 policy, may be provided for in writing added hereto, but no pro-

[17] Standard forms, used with the fire insurance contract (see Chapter 7) may and frequently do alter conditions in the basic contract. Such changes are authorized in this section dealing with added provisions.

47 vision may be waived except such as by the terms of this policy
48 is subject to change.

This section permits additions so long as the final agreement is "not inconsistent with the provisions of this policy." Thus, it would not be permissible by the use of a rider to nullify any of the mandatory features of the contract. It does permit, however, endorsement of the contract to extend the coverage to those situations in which the contract provides that the insurer shall not be liable for loss or damage "unless otherwise provided by agreement in writing added hereto."

Waiver. One of the most confusing of all the clauses of the standard contract is the following:

49 **Waiver** No permission affecting this insurance shall
50 **provisions.** exist, or waiver of any provision be valid,
51 unless granted herein or expressed in writing
52 added hereto. No provision, stipulation or forfeiture shall be
53 held to be waived by any requirement or proceeding on the part
54 of this Company relating to appraisal or to any examination
55 provided for herein.

The intent of the clause is perfectly apparent. The doctrine of waiver, as it applies to insurance, and the accompanying doctrine of estoppel were deemed to be fraught with so much danger that the framers of the New York standard contract undertook to nullify their effects through the insertion of two clauses touching upon the matter.[18] In the new form, the matter is covered in a single paragraph just cited. Regardless of this attempt to exclude by a clause of the contract the element of parole waivers, and hence estoppel, the framers of the contract have met with, at best, but partial success. The principle is based upon the theory that whoever has the authority to conduct oral negotiations for the insurer may waive the waiver clause quite as freely as he may waive any other clause. To curtail in any way the power of an authorized agent to waive a condition of the contract, unless such waiver shall be in writing, is held by many courts to be

[18] The clause in the old standard contract reads as follows:

". . . And no officer, agent or other representative of this Company shall have power to waive any provision or condition of this Policy except such as by the terms of this Policy may be the subject of agreement endorsed hereon or added hereto; and as to such provisions and conditions no officer, agent or representative shall have such power or be deemed or held to have waived such provisions or conditions unless such waiver, if any, shall be written upon or attached hereto, nor shall any privilege or permission affecting the insurance under this Policy exist or be claimed by the insured unless so written or attached."

In another part of the old contract, the following clause appears:

"This Company shall not be held to have waived any provision or condition of this contract or any forfeiture thereof by any requirement, act, or proceeding on its part relating to the appraisal of to any examination herein provided for."

The clause in the 1918 contract covers virtually the same ground as these two clauses but brings the material together in a single section of the contract.

impossible. Insurers may not rely upon the clause to protect them against waiver; however, the insured will do well, so far as possible, to comply with the written terms of the agreement. On the other hand, the insured should not lose sight of the fact that, when he is justified in presenting a claim under waiver, the wording of this clause will not of necessity prevent recovery.

CANCELLATION

Under the terms of the contract, cancellation may be effected by either the insured or the insurer. Contractual provisions relating to cancellation are stated in the following terms:

56 **Cancellation** This policy shall be cancelled at any time
57 **of policy.** at the request of the insured, in which case
58 this Company shall, upon demand and sur-
59 render of this policy, refund the excess of paid premium above
60 the customary short rates for the expired time. This pol-
61 icy may be cancelled at any time by this Company by giving
62 to the insured a five days' written notice of cancellation with
63 or without tender of the excess of paid premium above the pro
64 rata premium for the expired time, which excess, if not ten-
65 dered, shall be refunded on demand. Notice of cancellation shall
66 state that said excess premium (if not tendered) will be re-
67 funded on demand.

The clause as it applies to the insured is simple. It states that the contract may be canceled at any time at his request, and the insurer is obligated *upon demand and surrender of the contract* to refund any premium in its hands in excess of the amount due at short rates for the term that the contract has run. In the case of cancellation by the insurer, five days' written notice is required. The form does not require a return of the unearned premium as a condition precedent to cancellation, but the notice of cancellation must state that the excess of premium, computed for the term the contract has to run, on a pro rata basis, will be refunded on demand. The excess of premium may be tendered when notice is given but if not so tendered must be refunded on demand.

Depending upon who initiates the cancellation, there is a difference in the amount of premium return to the policyholder. If the contract is canceled by the insured, he pays for the term he has been covered on a short-rate basis. If cancellation is initiated by the insurer, the insurer is entitled to retain only a pro rata share of the premium for the term the insurance remained in effect.

Cancellation and Substitution. In dealing with a local agent who represents a number of insurers, the insured rarely specifies the particular insurer or insurers that are to carry his line. He leaves that to the discretion of the agent.

It may happen that an insurer is given a particular line in a building or congested locality where it is already carrying its maximum liability. For this or some other reason, it may desire to be relieved of the line and may write or wire its agent instructions accordingly. The agent is bound to act with reasonable dispatch in such an instance and take steps to see that the insurer is relieved of liability. If the risk is a desirable one, he will wish to retain it on his books and will prepare a substitute contract for the one ordered canceled by the insurer.

In the usual course of business, the transaction presents no difficulty. It is in the rare case, when a fire intervenes between the binding of the risk with a second insurer and notification of the insured, that anything of a problem is presented. It is held that the entry of a binder of the risk by an agent, with the intent to relieve the first insurer and commit the second, does not accomplish this purpose unless the insured has been notified of the change and has given his consent thereto.

Should an insured find himself in possession of a contract which had been, according to the agent's records, canceled, with another substituted but not delivered before the loss, the insured will be following the path of wisdom if he does not permit any change or substitution thereafter until the entire question of liability has been settled at the time of the adjustment. He cannot benefit by both contracts, and the contract he holds is effective if he had no notice to the contrary.

There is one other combination of circumstances. If an insured has been given five days' notice of cancellation and has as yet not acceded to the substitution through some act that might be interpreted as acceptance and if in this period a fire occurs, it is held that the insured may elect which of the insurers he will hold; but, as indicated previously, he may not hold both.

Intervening Liability. The question is sometimes raised as to the rights and obligations of an insurer that wishes to cancel after a loss has occurred but before it has been paid. The question is presented as to whether in tendering the return premium the insurer is likewise obligated to tender the intervening liability. There is nothing in the standard contract that makes such a tender a condition precedent to cancellation, and it is held that, while a tender of the unearned premium is mandatory, a tender of intervening liability is not. It follows that an insurer may, after a fire and before payment of the loss, cancel a contract in the usual manner; the settlement of the claim and the payment of the loss are, of course, to follow the terms and conditions of the contract as it was in effect at the time of the fire.

What Constitutes Notice. To cancel a contract effectively the insurer must notify the premium payer, all parties named as insureds, and all parties named as mortgagees. The notice must state unconditionally the insurer's determination to cancel at a specific time. Notice of cancellation does not become effective until received. The time will not run on the notice until it is in the insured's hands. Nor is the time computed from the instant of receipt. The first day, that is, the day the notice is received, is excluded in the computation of the time, and, beginning with the next midnight, the days are then counted running from midnight to midnight.

When it is not convenient to reach the insured and make a personal service of the notice, it is the custom of insurers to send a notice by registered mail. Elaborate forms have been prepared for the purpose. Some are printed on a form that itself folds into an envelope, thereby avoiding the possibility of the insured's claiming to have received an empty envelope. Sometimes these notices are made in duplicate, and the postmaster is asked to witness the inclusion of the notice in the envelope. Finally, a demand is made for a "personal return receipt." The letter containing the notice should bear, plainly marked or printed, the name of the agent or insurer sending the notice, because failure to do so was deemed grounds for claiming no notice when an insured received the envelope containing it but carelessly laid it aside unopened. It was held that, had he seen the agent's or insurer's name, he might have been warned that the communication pertained to insurance and given it attention. An insured may waive the requirements as to notice and surrender his contract for immediate cancellation.

MORTGAGEE INTERESTS

In the event the insured property is subject to a mortgage, the rights and obligations of the mortgagee must be considered. The standard fire insurance contract deals with these interests in the following manner:

Mortgagee interests and obligations. If loss hereunder is made payable, in whole or in part, to a designated mortgagee not named herein as the insured, such interest in this policy may be canceled by giving to such mortgagee a ten days' written notice of cancellation.

If the insured fails to render proof of loss such mortgagee, upon notice, shall render proof of loss in the form herein specified within sixty (60) days thereafter and shall be subject to the provisions hereof relating to appraisal and time of payment and of bringing suit. If this Company shall claim that no liability existed as to the mortgagor or owner, it shall, to the extent of payment of loss to the mortgagee, be subrogated to all the mortgagee's rights of recovery, but without impairing mortgagee's right to sue; or it may pay off the mortgage debt and require an assignment thereof and of the mortgage. Other provisions **relating to the interests and obligations of such mortgagee may be added hereto by agreement in writing.**

This section of the contract deals with a set of conditions in which the named insured has only a secondary interest. The mortgagee is made a party to a contract with three conditions that affect him directly. They are: (1) provision for cancellation of the mortgage interest, (2) provision for filing of proofs of loss by the mortgagee, and (3) provision that mortgagee be subject to contract conditions governing appraisal, time of payment, and time of bringing suit. The section further provides for adding other conditions by agreement. This clause permits the endorsement of the contract to cover the interest of the mortgagee. While the interest of the mortgagee may be covered by a separate contract of insurance or by naming the mortgagee as an insured, the more usual practice is to effect this protection by the attachment of the standard mortgagee clause. This clause will be considered in detail in the next chapter.

LOSS

Lines 86 through 165 of the second page of the standard fire contract contain a number of provisions that relate to the rights and responsibilities of the insured and the insurer in the event that loss occurs. These provisions cover contribution, requirements in case of loss, appraisal, insurer's options, abandonment, payment of loss, suit, and subrogation.

Contribution Clause. The contribution, or pro rata, clause applies when two or more insurers are on a risk and the amount of the loss is less than the sum total of the insurance. The clause has the effect of limiting the liability of the insurer in any particular loss to a proportionate part rather than, as would be the case without the clause, permitting the insured to proceed against any particular insurer for the full amount and leaving that insurer with the necessity of attempting to effect an equitable adjustment as between the insurers.[19] The clause is designed to eliminate what has been termed

[19] In the earlier days, it was the practice in marine insurance to exhaust the first contract written and then collect from each successive contract written until the loss was paid in full. Walford cites a number of old ordinances bearing upon the subject. One of the briefest of these is an Amsterdam Ordinance of 1744, which admirably illustrates the point. The ordinance provides: "But if more than one policy is used and underwrote upon for one and the same parcel of goods and interest, then the first policy, in date, without regarding the following policy shall take place for the amount of the sum insured, for the value of the goods and effects; and the reduction shall fall on the policy of later date: as well in case of returns as of average losses." The fire

"circuity of action."[20] The new New York contract reads:

> **Pro rata liability.** This Company shall not be liable for a greater proportion of any loss than the amount hereby insured shall bear to the whole insurance covering the property against the peril involved, whether collectible or not.

Under the terms of the clause, in addition to providing that each contract shall be liable only for its proportionate part of the loss, it is provided that, for the sake of the adjustment, insurance shall be considered contributing insurance even though it is not collectible. This feature of the clause is based upon the contention that one insurer does not wish to be responsible for the solvency of the others. If the strong insurers were obliged to make good that part of a loss apportionable to insolvent insurers, they would, to a degree, be guaranteeing the solvency of the weak insurers that an insured might place on the risk.

It is likewise true that if one or more of the contracts are uncollectible because of some act of the insured that constitutes a breach of warranty, the other insurers are not obligated to make up the difference in the loss. It follows that a contract subject to forfeiture for breach of warranty is included in the total amount of insurance in determining the coverage before the proportion to be paid is determined for each of the insurers. The insurers covering on the risk are not obligated to determine the validity or invalidity of other existing contracts but are obligated only to pay their pro rata proportion of the loss as set forth in the clause. It is quite possible, that a contract might be voided because of breach of warranty and the remaining collectible insurance exceed the amount of the loss, but because of the operation of the pro rata clause, the insured would be obligated to bear that proportion of the loss that would have been assigned to the insurer whose contract is voided.

In the event, for example, that a property valued at $125,000 carries fire insurance in the amount of $100,000 with four insurers as follows: Insurer A, $40,000; Insurer B, $30,000; Insurer C, $20,000; and Insurer D, $10,000. And in the event there is a loss of $5,000, each

---

insurance business early recognized the necessity of pro rata contribution and long before the inauguration of our standard contracts incorporated a clause covering the point. Indicative of this practice is one of the earliest clauses of which we have a record, which appeared in a Sun contract of 1798 and was phrased as follows: "To prevent fraud, persons insured by this office, shall receive no benefit from their policy if the same houses or goods, etc., are insured in any other office, unless such insurance be first specified and allowed by an indorsement on the back of the policy; in which case this office will pay their (its) rateable proportion on any loss or damage." C. Walford, *Insurance Cyclopaedia* (London: Charles & Edwin Layton, 1871), Vol. II, pp. 394–97.

[20] Richards, *op. cit.*, p. 456.

insurer pays a pro rata part of the loss. This loss would be apportioned as follows:

Company	*Insurance*	*Pays*
A.	$40,000	$2,000
B.	30,000	1,500
C.	20,000	1,000
D.	10,000	500
Insured collects		$5,000

Now let us assume the same amount of insurance but that for some reason Insurer A refuses to pay. Assume the insurer is in financial difficulties and the loss is uncollectible. There is a loss now of $5,000 as before. There is, however, $60,000 of valid insurance. With $60,000 contributing insurance, a $5,000 loss, and with $40,000 uncollectible insurance, the apportionment is as follows:

Company	*Insurance*	*Pays*
A.	$40,000	0
B.	30,000	$1,500
C.	20,000	1,000
D.	10,000	500
Insured collects		$3,000

The insurers that contribute pay exactly the same amount in both of the foregoing instances. Even though the insured has insurance far in excess of the amount of his loss, the fact that part of the insurance is uncollectible operates to penalize the insured rather than the contributing insurers.

To constitute contributing insurance and thus participate in any apportionment, contracts must cover not only on the same property but on the same interest in the particular property. The insurance must be in force at the time of the loss. While the insurance must cover on the same property and the same interest, it is not necessary that the persons whose interests are covered be named specifically in the contract.

As to what constitutes the same property, the courts have not insisted that the descriptions be identical. Even though one contract covers less or more than the other, there is, nevertheless, contributing insurance. Thus, it is quite possible for a party to be insured under a contract held by another if the contract in question is written with one of the "in trust" or "commission" clauses. For example, it would be possible for the owner of grain in a warehouse to insure it and find that he also had an interest in a blanket contract taken out by the warehouseman in his own name but containing a clause "his own or held in trust." The process is also reversed, and sometimes to the discomfort of the policyholder. He may write his insurance with a commission or in trust clause, thinking that this gives him simply a broader coverage, in case he might happen to be liable for some particular loss; but what he finds is that there are many claimants under his contract with the result that sometimes he may not have insurance enough to meet his own requirements.

Requirements in Case of Loss. The fire insurance contract undertakes to provide for the named insured indemnity for loss sustained in accordance with the terms of the contract. The contract, however, requires that initial action be taken by the insured to set the process of adjustment in motion. Generally, the insured is required to give prompt written notice of loss, take all necessary steps to minimize loss or damage, and then within a period of 60 days file a claim with the insurer. This claim must be supported by evidence that will establish a loss, indicate its amount, and establish the right of the have been set forth in the contract in the following terms:
insured to collect it from the insurer. The obligations of the insured

Requirments in case loss occurs The insured shall give immediate written notice of this Company of any loss, protect the property from further damage, forthwith separate the damaged and undamaged personal property, put it in the best possible order, furnish a complete inventory of the destroyed, damaged and undamaged property, showing in detail quantities, costs, actual cash value and amount of loss claimed; **and within sixty days after the loss, unless such time is extended in writing by this Company, the insured shall render to this Company a proof of loss,** signed and sworn to by the insured, stating the knowledge and belief of the insured as to the following: the time and origin of the loss, the interest of the insured and of all others in the property, the actual cash value of each item thereof and the amount of loss thereto, all encumbrances thereon, all other contracts of insurance, whether valid or not, covering any of said property, any changes in the title, use, occupation, location, possession or exposures of said property since the issuing of this policy, by whom and for what purpose any building herein described and the several parts thereof were occupied at the time of loss and whether or not it then stood on leased ground, and shall furnish a copy of all the descriptions and schedules in all policies and, if required, verified plans and specifications of any building, fixtures or machinery destroyed or damaged. The insured, as often as may be reasonably required, shall exhibit to any person designated by this Company all that remains of any property herein described, and submit to examinations under oath by any person named by this Company, and subscribe the same; and, as often as may be reasonably required, shall produce for examination all books of account, bills, invoices and other vouchers, or certified copies thereof if originals be lost, at such reasonable time and place as may be designated by this

Company or its representative, and shall permit extracts and copies thereof to be made.

The foregoing stipulations obligate the insured to (1) immediately notify the insurer if a loss occurs; (2) file a proof of loss with the insurer within 60 days after a loss, setting forth the information outlined in the foregoing stipulations; (3) be prepared to supply plans and specifications of buildings, fixtures, or machinery destroyed or damaged; (4) exhibit the remains of property damaged; (5) submit to examination under oath; and (6) produce for examination books of account and other supporting documents.

Even though the contract undertakes to indemnify the insured for losses from specified perils, until the insured takes the first step, the insurer is under no obligation to make any move to effect an adjustment. In addition to giving notice and filing proof of loss, the insured is further obligated to take all necessary steps to protect the property from further damage, as well as to separate the damaged and undamaged goods, place them in the best possible order, and make an inventory showing the cost and claim as it applies to each item. Other than this, the insured is under no obligation unless a request originates with the insurer to furnish plans, specifications, and other data set forth in the stipulations. Upon request from the insurer, the insured must submit to examination under oath and produce books and records at a reasonable time and place.

Notice of Loss. The requirement as set forth in the stipulations that notice of loss be "immediate" has been the occasion of some concern. The purpose of notice is to convey to the insurer information that a loss in which it has an interest has occurred, thus enabling it to take whatever steps seem necessary in the circumstances. Any unreasonable or undue delay might have the effect of seriously jeopardizing the position of the insurer. If circumstances beyond the control of the insured prevent notice within a period which would, in ordinary circumstances, be termed "immediate," the courts have tended to interpret the exercise of due diligence as meeting the contract requirements.

Thus, if the situation of the insured is such that in the light of the circumstances he could not have given notice immediately after the fire, and notice was given as soon as he was able to do so, this has been held to be sufficient compliance. In a case in which a contract was in a safe in a building that was destroyed by fire and could not be obtained until 53 days after the fire, notice when the contract was obtained was held sufficient. What constitutes reasonable diligence must in every instance be determined in the light of the circumstances surrounding the fire. If there is nothing to prevent it, notice should ordinarily be given the day the fire occurs or at the least the day following.

The contract requires that the notice be given in writing. It is the usual custom in the business for the insured to notify his agent using whatever means of communication proves to be most convenient. If the insured does not give a written notice to the insurer, the agent or broker immediately forwards such a notice when he becomes cognizant of the loss. It is generally held that, as far as the insured is concerned, the requirement of a written notice is waived if knowledge of the loss comes to the insurer or its agent and steps have been taken to effect an investigation. As a matter of general practice, if notice is given to the insurer or its agent within a reasonable time, whether in writing or not, this is all that is required of the insured if steps are taken to effect an adjustment. In the absence of such steps the insured should adhere meticulously to the literal requirement of the contract.

Nature of Proof. The proof of loss has for its purpose the supplying of information to be used as the basis of the settlement of a loss. It is a statement of fact concerning the property, the nature and extent of the loss, and the nature and extent of the insurance coverage. It furnishes, in addition, sufficient information to indicate whether the insured has complied with the contract terms and conditions. Specifically the proof accomplishes two things: (1) it furnishes evidence that the insured is entitled to collect a certain amount from the insurer, and (2) it supplies the sworn statement setting forth the detailed information required by the contract. In this respect as part of the proof the insured states his knowledge and belief as to the following:

1. The time and origin of the loss.
2. The interest of the insured and of all others in the property.
3. The actual cash value of each item thereof and the amount of loss thereto.
4. All encumbrances thereon.
5. All other contracts of insurance, whether valid or not, covering any of said property.
6. Any changes in the title, use, location, possession, or exposures of said property since the issuing of this contract.
7. By whom and for what purpose any building herein described and the several parts thereof were occupied at the time of loss.
8. Whether it then stood on leased ground.

The document thus required must be signed and sworn to by the insured. Blank forms designed to meet the requirements of the insurer in the matter of proof of loss are obtainable, and their use to a considerable degree lessens the possibility of technical error or deficiency. The agent through whom the insured purchased the contract, as well as adjusters assigned to settle the loss, are often helpful to the insured in the matter of filling out blank forms and preparing other documents.

The Appraisal. The framers of the standard contract, knowing the extent to which judgment plays a part in the settlement of losses, realized the frequency with which disagreement originating in errors of judgment might be expected. To relieve the courts of the burden of a large number of disputes that might readily be settled by arbitration, the contract provides that before court action may be taken in a disputed claim the parties must resort to arbitration.

> **Appraisal.** In case the insured and this Company shall fail to agree as to the actual cash value or the amount of loss, then, on the written demand of either, each shall select a competent and disinterested appraiser and notify the other of the appraiser selected within twenty days of such demand. The appraisers shall first select a competent and disinterested umpire; and failing for fifteen days to agree upon such umpire, then, on request of the insured or this Company, such umpire shall be selected by a judge of a court of record in the state in which the property covered is located. The appraisers shall then appraise the loss, stating separately actual cash value and loss to each item; and failing to agree, shall submit their differences, only, to the umpire. An award in writing, so itemized, of any two when filed with this Company shall determine the amount of actual cash value and loss. Each appraiser shall be paid by the party selecting him and the expenses of appraisal and umpire shall be paid by the parties equally.

The option to require appraisal or arbitration to determine the amount of a loss is the right equally of both parties to the contract. To make the clause operative, the party who requests the appraisal must make his demand within a reasonable time. An appraisal may not be demanded until an attempt has been made to settle the loss and a disagreement develops as to its amount.

The clause requires that the appraisers be "competent and disinterested." This requires that the appraisers have neither a financial interest in the loss settlement nor a prejudice for, or against, either of the parties.

In making an appraisal, the appraisers must be given the right to examine the damaged property, and if the insured sells or otherwise disposes of it he does so at his peril. It has been held that if an insured after a disagreement filed proofs and, before their receipt by the insurer, advertised and sold the property in spite of the insurer's protest, the insurer, being deprived of its right of appraisal, was released from liability under the contract. Again, when an insured revoked an appraisal agreement and himself had the properties appraised and sold, the contracts were held forfeited. An insured whose patience is short may sometimes feel that, in the case of delay or disagreement, he is badly treated. He may labor under the misconception that an inventory and appraisal made by disinterested parties at his request are sufficient evidence to substantiate a claim to be made later in court. With this in mind, he proceeds to salvage the damaged goods to the best advantage possible and is sincere in his belief that circumstances justify the procedure. If such action is based upon nothing more than a disagreement, the insured places himself in a position that may result in forfeiture.

If the insurer refuses to appraise, it has been held that the insurer cannot afterward compel an appraisal. On the other hand, the insurer, after demanding an appraisal at given time and place and then failing to appear, has been held to have waived its right to an appraisal. The contract requires that appraisers be chosen but once, and if the appraisal fail through no fault of the insured, he may bring suit. If the failure is due to no fault of the insurer, the insured cannot proceed with suit until after another appraisal.

Awards made by the appraisers determine the amount of the loss, and from their findings there can be no appeal except for fraud or corrupt practices involving one or more of the appraisers, or for mistake, or for wilful misconduct. If one of the parties attempts to set aside the findings of the appraisers, the burden of proof rests upon him to show cause; and until the evidence is very clear that there has been some form of partiality, conspiracy, fraud, or palpable error, the presumption is in favor of fairness, and the findings stand. It has been held that when the award is an amount so far out of line with the facts as to shock the moral sense, this fact may be presented as evidence of fraud, corruption, partiality, or bias. It may be stated that of the vast number of cases in which insurance adjustments go to appraisals, the appeal from the findings of the appraisers is comparatively rare.

Insurer's Options. In order to simplify the adjustment of loss, the contract provides alternate modes of settlement. The insured may make a payment for the amount of the loss, or it may, if it elects to do so, take all or any part of the damaged articles at the agreed or appraised value, or it may elect to restore the subject matter of the insurance to its former condition. The contract provides:

141 **Company's options.** It shall be optional with this Company to
142 take all, or any part, of the property at the
143 agreed or appraised value, and also to re-
144 pair, rebuild or replace the property destroyed or damaged with
145 other of like kind and quality within a reasonable time, on giv-
146 ing notice of its intention so to do within thirty days after the
147 receipt of the proof of loss herein required.

In the interests of effecting a prompt and equitable settlement and maintaining the good will of all parties at interest, the insurer may, in the face of an extravagant claim made in good faith, elect to pay a total loss on damaged merchandise and undertake to work out the salvage itself.

It is very rare that an insurer elects to rebuild the damaged property. This is so because, among other reasons, once the insurer indicates his intention, he his held to have abandoned the alternative mode of settlement and the insurance contract is converted into a building contract. The amount of the insurance liability thereafter is not limited to the amount of insurance since the insurer, once having elected to rebuild, must complete the operation and is liable for damages, including rent, resulting from delay. Because of these disadvantages, companies prefer to settle all losses by cash payment, and this is, indeed, the common practice. In connection with the time limitation set forth in the clause, the right of the insurer to exercise its option to repair and rebuild expires in 30 days after filing of the proofs. In the case of damaged merchandise, the courts have generally held that the time limitation will extend until after the award has been made, if there is resort to an appraisal.

It has been held that, if an insured sells goods without giving the insurer the right to exercise the option to take the goods, he renders the contract void. Even though the option to take the damaged goods may extend beyond 30 days from the filing of the proofs, it has been held unreasonable to expect the insured to wait for 30 days after an appraisal if the insurer takes no steps to indicate its intention to exercise the option. The option contained in the policy extends rights to the insurer. The insured cannot insist upon the insurer exercising any of these rights.

Abandonment Prohibited. The contract provides that there can be no abandonment to the company of any property.

148 **Abandonment.** There can be no abandonment to this Com-
149 pany of any property.

This fact is important since in the field of marine insurance there is a precedent for abandonment. Marine insurance antedates fire insurance; and, because of the nature of the business and the difficulty in effecting adjustments under certain circumstances, the insured was allowed to abandon his entire interests in the property and make a claim for a total loss.[21]

[21] For example, if a ship were captured the property itself was not destroyed; under early maritime codes the insured was permitted to abandon the insured ship to the underwriters and claim a total loss. The principle was carried further, and in England the courts held that: "If a prudent man not insured would decline any further expense in prosecuting an adventure, the termination of which will probably never be successfully accomplished, a party insured may, for his own benefit, as well as that of the underwriter, treat the case as one of a total loss and demand the full sum insured." *Roux* v. *Salvador*, 3 Bing. N.C. 266.

From the earliest days, abandonment was never made a part of the law of fire insurance. The nature of the property insured permits its owner to salvage it quite as well as the insurer; but, although the insurer may exercise its option with regard to taking the property, the insured cannot compel it to do so. This early principle has been incorporated definitely into the standard policy in lines 148 and 149. Thus, there are no circumstances, however unattractive to the insured, which will permit him to claim a total loss under his contracts and leave the work of salvaging to the insurer.

When Loss Is Payable. After the insured has complied with the requirements of the contract as to the filing of proof of loss, the contract provides that he may expect payment of his loss as follows:

150 **When loss** The amount of loss for which this Company
151 **payable.** may be liable shall be payable sixty days
152 after proof of loss, as herein provided, is
153 received by this Company and ascertainment of the loss is made
154 either by agreement between the insured and this Company ex-
155 pressed in writing or by the filing with this Company of an
156 award as herein provided.

Under the terms of this clause, the loss becomes payable within 60 days after notice and the filing of formal proofs which meet the requirements of the contract. There is an exception in the instance of an appraisal, in which case the loss is payable 60 days from the making of the award, or 60 days from the filing of the proofs, if proofs were filed after the making of the award. It is a custom of the business not to take advantage of the full 60 days allowed the insurer under the terms of the contract, although an insurer is perfectly within its rights to do so. In some states the statutes have set up a requirement for a waiting period before losses may be paid. Insurers are obligated to comply with the statutory requirement even though, in the interests of a prompt adjustment and settlement, they may wish to make an immediate cash payment.

Limitation of Time to Sue. The standard contract makes compliance with all the provisions of the contract a condition precedent to initiating a suit under the contract. In addition to this, there is a restrictive limit of 12 months within which litigation may be started. The contract provides:

157 **Suit.** No suit or action on this policy for the recov-
158 ery of any claim shall be sustainable in any
159 court of law or equity unless all the requirements of this policy
160 shall have been complied with, and unless commenced within
161 twelve months next after inception of the loss.

It has been held that without this clause an insured might proceed with the suit without complying with the requirements having to do with the ascertainment of loss, appraisal, and the like. As the clause operates, the insured must give notice of loss, file proofs of loss, and comply with the conditions as to appraisal and examination under oath before he may bring his case to court.

There is one important point in the foregoing clause that has been subject to some question. Some authorities hold that the period of limitation begins to run from the date of the fire, as stated in the contract. In some of the older contracts, the question "after the loss occurs" appeared instead of the phrase as now used. There are numerous decisions that favor the doctrine that the "loss occurs" not as of the date of the fire but when loss is ascertained and established.[22] The substitution of the word "fire" for the expression "after the loss occurs" was made in the 1918 contract with the intention of fixing the beginning of the period of limitation at the time of the fire. There was still a tendency on the part of some to contend that "twelve months next after the fire" meant 12 months after the liability is fixed. It was argued that since the insured was obligated to comply with all the conditions of the contract before legal action could be taken, it must have been the intent of the contract to give the insured 12 full months after his right of action matures. The court said no. The wording, it was held, was plain and unambiguous. " 'Twelve months next after the fire' has one certain meaning and but one."[23] Thus, it was held that the period of limitation runs from the time of the fire and not the date when the loss is ascertained. Whatever doubt may have existed in the past, the wording of the 1943 contract "after inception of loss" seems to clarify the situation. The inception of the loss can be no other time than the time of the fire or happening of other peril insured against. Certainly it cannot be construed to mean the date that the loss is established.

Subrogation. The clause governing subrogation to be found in the last four lines of the stipulations does not, as a matter of law, increase the rights of the insurer. The insertion of the following clause in the contract does have the effect of obligating the insured to assign his rights to the insurer so that the insurer may institute action in its own name:

162 **Subrogation.** This Company may require from the insured
163 an assignment of all right of recovery against
164 any party for loss to the extent that payment therefor is made
165 by this Company.

If this right of assignment were not incorporated in the contract and the insurer were compelled to rely upon the strict rules of common

---

[22] Cases cited in *Hart* v. *Citizens' Insurance Company*, 56 N.W. 332. Contrary decisions are also cited.

[23] *Hamilton* v. *Royal Ins. Co.*, 156 N.Y. 327, 50 N.E. 863.

law, any action to be brought would have to be instituted in the name of the insured.

While the common law rule has been modified in the equity courts and under some of the state codes to the end that the insurer may bring action in its own name, it is felt that the situation is simplified if the insured assigns his rights. The clause, at the same time, has the effect of putting the insured on notice not to take any steps that would affect the insurer's right of subrogation.

FOR DISCUSSION

1. The insured, under a contract in X Insurer, habitually used kerosene to kindle the fire in his kitchen range. The kerosene container was accidentally dropped on one occasion, and a fire started that soon enveloped the premises in flames. Investigation brought out that the insured was negligent in the handling of the kerosene, and because of this the insurer denied liability on the ground that the action of the insured constituted an increase of risk not contemplated when the risk was assumed by the insurer. In your opinion, has the insurer a case?
2. B owns an undivided interest in a stock of merchandise and procures insurance to the extent of his interest. C, the owner of the remaining interest, procures separate insurance. The *forms* provided "no other insurance without consent of the company." Neither contract was endorsed to permit "other insurance." In the event of loss, what is the status of the policyholders?
3. The standard fire contract provides that under no circumstances shall certain items be covered and, again, that other items shall be covered only if they are specifically named and liability is assumed in writing. Indicate examples of each type of property.
4. B purchases a rain insurance contract providing an indemnity of $5,000 if a certain event has to be abandoned. It later develops that B had no insurable interest whatever in the event. Rain falls during the period covered by the insurance, and B makes claim for $5,000. The insurer denies liability on the ground of no insurable interest, and B contends that the matter has been waived because the agent did, in fact, know that B had no insurable interest in the event and was taking the contract as a speculation. It is contended that knowledge of the agent is knowledge of the insurer and that the insurer is estopped from denying liability. Discuss.
5. If added clauses may modify or change the standard contract, may not the whole effect of the standard contract be nullified by the addition of such clauses?
6. B carries five contracts on his property in an amount of $2,000 each. On a certain day he mailed two of the contracts to the insurer for cancellation. After the contracts had left his hands, but before they arrived at their destination, the insured property was totally destroyed by fire. The question arises as to whether the contracts now in the

hands of the insurer are canceled or they should be required to contribute to the loss.

7. B carries insurance in the X insurer for $5,000. At the time the contract is written B is carrying $15,000 with three other insurers. This insurance he later cancels. The X insurer contends that it relied upon B carrying the other insurance and, in the case of a $4,000 loss, claims that its pro rata contribution is $1,000. The insurer contends that it should have been advised of the cancellation of the other insurance. What is your opinion?
8. Following a loss on B's property there are found in his strong box ten insurance contracts for $5,000 each. Investigation brings to light the fact that two of these contracts had been canceled by the insurer through the agency of registered mail. X claims that the words "whether collectible or not" make these contracts contributing insurance, and, therefore, the remaining contracts must pay one tenth of the loss each, instead of one eighth. What is your opinion?
9. B, acting as a broker for A, secures five insurance contracts for $5,000 each in as many different insurers. Before the contracts are delivered to A, he is notified by one of the insurers that it does not wish to retain the line and orders the contract canceled. The broker surrenders the contract, and before he can place new insurance there is a loss. Is the cancellation effective?
10. X, the insured, holds fire insurance contracts on a property covered under five different items. One item covers a certain type of merchandise in storage; and, at the time of the fire, most of this merchandise has been sold and not replaced. X makes a willful misstatement of the amount of merchandise under this item with the intent to defraud the insurer. The insurer claims the contract to be void because of fraud. The attorneys for X deny the fraud and claim an innocent mistake, but they contend, even if there were a fraud, that the contract would be voided only as to the merchandise item. Is this correct?
11. If the United States were to be invaded and an officer in charge of our defenses were to destroy the property of B by fire to prevent it falling into the hands of the enemy, would B have any recourse for indemnity under his standard fire contract?
12. An armed mob pursued by a United States marshal took refuge in the property of X. The marshal, to dislodge them and effect their capture, set fire to the property. Liability is denied on the insurance on the ground that the fire was "by order of a civil authority." Has X any recourse under his contract?
13. Does B violate the contract condition (lines 31–32) touching upon *increase in hazards* if he allows a tent to be set up temporarily in his yard for the sale of fireworks during the week preceding the Fourth of July?
14. B files a proof of loss, stating therein that the value of the destroyed house is $54,000. Evidence is produced to show its value to be $50,000.

The insurer undertakes to deny liability on the grounds of fraud and false swearing. What is the position of the claimant?

15. The X insurer had a policy issued to B on a stock of merchandise. B takes a partner who acquires one-fourth interest in the business. The stock is damaged by fire, and the insurer contends that the insurance does not cover. In your opinion, does it cover three fourths for B and one fourth suspended, or is the entire coverage suspended?
16. There is a line of decisions holding an explosion of gunpowder to be, in its nature, fire, even though such explosion is occasioned without hostile fire or antecedent conflagration. Can this line of decisions be reconciled with the provision in the standard contract that exempts from coverage loss by explosion unless fire ensues, and, in that event, for loss or damage by fire only?
17. A schedule covering institutional property is written for $13,219,000. There are 200 items on the schedule. Under Item 84F there is a small loss to a dwelling caused by the faulty operation of an oil burner. This loss occurred on December 16. It is agreed between the adjusters that the amount of the loss is $15. On January 15 a dwelling having a replacement cost of $17,580 with a depreciation of $5,860 and insured under Item 121C on the schedule for $7,000 is totally destroyed. Contents having a depreciated value of $2,234 and covered under the schedule under Item 121D for $1,000 is a total loss. There is an exposure loss to a brick school building. The school building has a sound value of $25,000 and is covered for this amount under the schedule with 80 percent coinsurance applying. The exposure loss to the school includes $150 for painting exterior trim, $100 for interior trim and painting, $200 for lath and plaster work, and $125 for plumbing and heating. Covering on the loss the A Company has three contracts: one for $1,906,000, a second for $1,000,000, and a third for $2,653,000. The B Company covers with three contracts in the amounts of $1,936,000, $2,138,000, and $1,000,000. The C Company covers for $93,000, $110,000, and $70,000. The D Company has contracts for $313,000 and two separate contracts each for $1,000,000. Make up a statement of the loss and show the amount for which each insurer is liable and the amount of the liability attached to each insurer. Combine both losses.
18. The X manufacturing plant carries blanket insurance covering stock and machinery for $2,000 with specific insurance coverage on stock for $1,000. How would you apportion the loss on stock only in the amount of $750?
19. The Y manufacturing plant carries blanket insurance covering stock and machinery for $2,000 and specific insurance on machinery in the amount of $1,000. Following a fire there is a loss on stock amounting to $1,000 and loss on machinery amounting to $1,000. Work out an adjustment.
20. Sometimes properties are sold with the vendor handing the vendee a fire insurance contract indicating to him that the property is covered

and intending thereby to give the new owner the benefit of the insurance. What are the dangers in this transaction?

21. Following a fire loss the insurer and the insured failed to reach an agreement, and the case was submitted to appraisers in accordance with the contract provision. The appraisers could not agree, and an award was made by the insured's nominee and the umpire. The award was based solely upon the replacement cost of the property less physical depreciation. The insurer contended that there were other pertinent factors bearing upon the matter, but these the insured's representative refused to consider. The insurer contended that this deliberate refusal constituted misconduct. Do you feel that the findings could be set aside on the basis of misconduct?

22. X owned a property upon which there was a mortgage. The property was insured for $3,000 with insurer A. Later the amount of the mortgage was increased, and two new insurance contracts were purchased in insurer B and C for the amount of $2,500 each. When the new insurance for $5,000 was written with the consent of the insured, the agent requested the mortgagee to return contract A for cancellation. X agreed and the mortgagee sent the contract to the agent who, in turn, mailed it to insurer A. Apparently, the letter and the contract never reached insurer A. A fire occurred resulting in a loss in excess of the $5,000 insurance written by insurer B and insurer C. Since the contract mailed for cancellation did not reach insurer A, do you believe that this insurer should contribute to the loss?

23. X rented a building that has formerly been used as a motion-picture theater and turned it into a warehouse. He used it to store merchandise and placed $60,000 insurance on the contents, which were said to have a value of $75,000. As a result of heavy snowstorms during the following winter, part of the roof collapsed. The side walls bulged and left openings at the corners. The following spring the building was destroyed by fire. The insured made claim under the contract and the insurer denied liability on the ground that the insurance had been suspended because the hazard had been increased. Do you believe the insurers have a case or do you believe the insured, who was a tenant of the building, can collect his insurance?

24. The standard fire contract requires the insured to perform certain acts whether or not the insurer asks him to do so. There are other acts which he must perform only upon specific request or notice made by the insurer. Name the acts to be found in each of the classifications.

CHAPTER · 7

Dwelling Property and Related Forms

The statutory fire insurance contract consists of two parts: (*a*) the insuring agreement, and (*b*) the stipulations and conditions. Not all of the information essential to the completion of the agreement between the insured and the insurer is contained in the statutory contract. The contract is completed through the addition of a form or rider. The form contains a description of the property to be insured, as well as a number of clauses pertinent to the particular contract. The insuring clause and stipulations and conditions are general in their application. By means of the form the contract is tailored to the specific needs of the insured.

The statutory contract specifically makes provision for such a form. The insuring agreement does not describe specifically the property to be covered by the insurance. Rather, it makes provision for this description by attachment in the following terms: ". . . to the property described hereinafter while located or contained as described in this contract. . . ." This clause, taken together with the stipulations touching upon other perils or subjects (lines 38–41) and added provisions (lines 42–48), definitely contemplates the addition of a property description and location and permits the modification of the statutory contract by means of added provisions. Forms may provide also for the inclusion of perils other than those specifically mentioned in the insuring clause.

After the description of the property to be insured, the typical form contains a number of provisions called "clauses." These have the effect (*a*) of extending or limiting the coverage provided by the statutory wording of the standard contract, and (*b*) modifying the statutory provisions to meet the insured's requirements with respect to the perils covered. The first few words of each clause are printed in bold face, and this bold face printing is usually the name by which the clause is known. There are, for example, the electrical apparatus clause, the loss clause, the removal of debris clause, and mortgage clause. These clauses find their way into the forms where they are required. There are numerous other clauses, and these are added depending upon the type of coverage and the particular needs of the insured.

The wording of the form is not prescribed by statute. If the form is specially prepared for an individual insured, it may be, and usually is, printed in its entirety. Standard forms are prepared by the various rating organizations and are printed and distributed to agents. There is no requirement that the form be printed, and where it satisfies the needs of the insured it may be mimeographed, typed, or even handwritten. Since standard forms are available for the more usual type of risk, it is the general practice to use them. If there is no standard form available to meet the needs of a special situation, the insured may have his own form prepared.

It is quite customary in the case of sizable risks to prepare and print a special form. Where this is done, the approval of the rating authority must be obtained before the form can be used. This approval serves two purposes. The form must afford the insured the protection he contemplates and give him the benefits of the various liberalizing clauses to which his premium entitles him. On the other hand, the form must also be checked to prevent discrimination against other insureds through an extension of cover not provided for in the rating structure. While forms specially printed are not at all unusual, by far the greater number of contracts are written making use of the standard forms provided by the rating organizations.

Insureds who have familiarized themselves with the conditions of standard forms and contracts are sometimes inclined to confuse the modifications permitted in the form with the terms and conditions of the contract. This gives rise to the opinion that the standard contract affords coverages that, as a matter of fact, it does not afford. It is of the utmost importance to recognize that certain coverages and privileges, as well as certain restrictions and conditions, originate in the form attached to the contract as a rider, and not in the contract itself. It is highly essential for an insured, whose plan of insurance requires a number of contracts on the same property, to have his contracts carefully checked and to see that the forms are identical. The insured should also realize that the provisions in the form when at variance with those in the basic contract take precedence over the contract provisions.

DESCRIPTION AND LOCATION OF THE PROPERTY

The first page or face of the standard fire insurance contract provides a space for a recording of the description and location of the property covered. The instructions on the contract require that the person filling out the contract should indicate type of construction, type of roof, and occupancy of the building or buildings covered. If the building covered is a dwelling, the number of families must also be stated. The address where the property is situated is also given. Although the description of the property on the first page of the contract describes and locates the property in a general way, it is not a complete description, and in order to clarify the nature of the property covered, additional description is given on the form. Space is provided on the face of the contract for recording the numbers of the forms to which the standard contract is subject.

The first essential in the preparation of the form is an adequate description of the subject matter of the insurance. Length and excessive verbiage are not indicative of the most desirable form of description; nor are vague and general terms. The description should be short and concise, clear-cut, accurate, and inclusive enough to describe adequately the property intended to be covered. Obviously, the task is not a simple one, and much care and thought have been exercised in the preparation of the forms in general use.

A specific amount of insurance is usually written on a building and a specific amount on contents. The exception is the blanket contract, which must be written subject to rules promulgated by the rating authority and these rules vary from one rating jurisdiction to another. In the case of mercantile property, permanent fixtures are included with the building.[1] Store fixtures are written separately, and separate coverage is required for stock. In the case of dwellings, a specific amount is written on the building; and the contents, that is, the furniture, is written as a separate item. If there is other personal property than that which comes under the category of household and personal property, such as farm machinery, these are written with a specific amount assigned to each category or in separate contracts. In the case of manufacturing risks, the rule closely parallels that of merchantile property. The building is written as one item, which includes fixtures that form a permanent part of the building and are necessary for its operation. The machinery is written separately; this item includes tools used in connection with its operation. Finally, stock and materials are written as a separate item. In all cases, the rules promulgated by the rating agency are followed. They are not uniform in every jurisdiction but, in general, are based upon the same underwriting principles.

The description of the building, so far as the needs of the insured

---

[1] The statements in this paragraph are illustrative and do not apply in every rating jurisdiction. In general, fixtures used for the service of the building are building items and insured under the building rate. All other fixtures are insured under the contents rate.

are concerned, should be sufficiently accurate to indicate exactly the property the insured wishes to cover. Building descriptions will generally follow the fire divisions established by the rating bureau. Extensions to existing buildings are automatically covered during the construction period under the existing building form. If such additions constitute a separate fire division after completion, they will be separately rated and should be separately described on the face of the contract.

The method of describing buildings is to a considerable degree standardized by rating classifications. Reference is usually made to height, roof, construction, and occupancy. Contents are described in as comprehensive a manner as possible, and the description is followed by the statement "while contained in." The construction type and location of the building are indicated. Illustrative examples of descriptions are given in the typical forms in the following sections.

The location of the property is a matter of little difficulty in the built-up sections of the city. Usually the street address, with an indication of the side of the street, is sufficient. Thus: "Located at No. 130 on the Westerly side of Cedar Street, in Bangor, Maine." When buildings are not numbered, any indication that is clear and will serve to indicate location is sufficient, thus: "Located on the Northerly side of the River Road, about three hundred yards in an Easterly direction from Grange Hall, in the Town of, etc." Indicating a side of a given road, particularly if a long one, without tying in with some permanent landmark is considered undesirable. A railroad crossing, standpipe, crossroads, local store, or public building such as a hall or church, anything that is distinctive, will indicate within sufficiently narrow limits the location of the property insured.

DWELLING PROPERTY FORM

The Dwelling Property Form[2] serves as an illustration of the method used to provide a statement of covered property and extension or limitations of the standard contract. Forms of a similar type that are frequently used and which will be described in the next chapter, are the Dwelling Buildings and Contents Broad Form, and Dwelling Buildings Special Form. The Dwelling Property Form is divided into eleven sections. The first sections deal with various matters concerning the type of property covered. Specific reference is made to dwelling coverage; contents coverage; outbuilding coverage; trees, shrubs, or plants coverage; and rental value coverage. The remaining sections of the form contain for the most part various clauses such as the

[2] The form described in this section is the one provided in *Sample Insurance Policies for Property and Liability Coverages* (New York: Insurance Information Institute, 1965). Quotations in this section are from this form.

mortgage clause and electrical apparatus clause, as well as a detailed statement about insurance against a number of perils not included in the standard contract.

Dwelling Defined. In Section I of the Dwelling Property Form the term "dwelling" is defined as "a building occupied exclusively for dwelling purposes by the number of families stated in this policy, but in no event by more than four families." This definition may be modified by endorsement, or occupancy may be otherwise described on the first page of the contract.

Dwelling Coverage. In the absence of a specific statement about what constitutes a building intended for a dwelling, some question might arise as to whether buildings attached to the principal residence or buildings not attached but located on the same premises were insured. Section II of the form clarifies this matter through a statement on dwelling coverage and an extension to the statement. In part A of Section II of the form the insurer agrees that "When the insurance under this policy covers a dwelling, such insurance shall include additions in contact therewith." Also included in this agreement, if the property of the owner of the dwelling and if not otherwise covered, are building equipment, fixtures, and outdoor equipment used in the service of the described premises "and while located thereon but not lawns, trees, shrubs or plants." Coverage is further extended to include "materials and supplies located on the described premises or adjacent thereto, intended for use in construction, alteration or repair of structures covered hereunder."

In paragraph two of Section II dwelling coverage is extended to "private structures other than the described dwelling and additions in contact there with appertaining to the described premises and located thereon." The amount of the extension is limited to 10 percent of "the amount of insurance applicable to the principal dwelling item." This amount is regarded as additional insurance to cover private structures. Structures used for commercial, manufacturing, or farming purposes are excluded from coverage. Structures, except those used primarily as private garages, that are wholly "rented or leased to other than a tenant of the principal dwelling" are not covered under this extension.

In paragraph three of Section II dwelling coverage is further extended to cover rental value. The amount of additional insurance allowed for this purpose is limited to 10 percent of the amount "specified for the principal dwelling item," but no more than one twelfth of the 10 percent is allowed for "each month the principal dwelling or appurtenant private structures or parts thereof are untenantable as a result of physical damage to the described building(s) or the equipment therein, or the equipment on the described premises, caused by a peril insured against." Structures used for commercial, manufacturing, or farming purposes are excluded from this coverage.

Contents Coverage. Section III of this form provides a definition of dwelling contents, which is useful in those instances where the contents of the dwelling are insured as well as the dwelling itself. Contents are defined as "all household and personal property usual or incidental to the occupancy of the premises as a dwelling . . . belonging to the Insured or for which the Insured may be liable . . . while contained in the described dwelling or appurtenant private structures . . . or while in the open on the described premises." Also included as contents, if the insured chooses, and subject to the foregoing definition, is the household and personal property of members of the insured's family and of servants of the insured. Certain types of personal property are excluded from coverage. The exclusions are: animals, birds, aircraft, motor vehicles (unless they can be classified as motorized equipment used on the premises for maintenance), and boats and their equipment except rowboats, canoes, and their equipment. Household and personal property located in appurtenant private structures would not be covered if these structures were used for commercial, manufacturing, or farming purposes.

When the contents insured under the contract, and during the term of the contract, are moved from one location to another within the state in which the insured lives, and if the new location is used in whole or in part as the insured's residence, the contract "shall cover such property while at such new location up to the amount applicable to contents and shall cease to cover at the former location." During the time the property is being moved, it is covered at each location on a pro rata basis. It should be emphasized that the permit does not cover perils of transportation, and if protection on the way is desired, a transportation coverage becomes necessary.

Coverage is provided in Section III for household and personal property, as defined in the contract, of the insured or members of his family of the same household while in locations other than the described premises. This coverage is not regarded as an additional amount of insurance and is limited to 10 percent of the amount of insurance applicable to contents under the contract. Rowboats and canoes are not covered under this extension. Geographical limits are placed on this extension. They are: "that part of Continental North America included within the United States of America and Canada and in the State of Hawaii." Further, this extension of coverage is not intended to benefit directly or indirectly any carrier or other bailee.

Another extension under contents coverage, which is also limited to 10 percent of the amount of insurance carried on contents, is the provision that covers "improvements, alterations or additions to the described dwelling and private structures appertaining thereto." The 10 percent is not regarded as an additional amount of insurance, and the coverage does not apply to commercial, manufacturing, or farming purposes.

Other Coverages. Through use of a dwelling and contents form specific coverage may be provided for outbuildings; trees, shrubs, or plants; and rentai value.

Outbuilding Coverage. When specifically described appurtenant private structures are covered, insurance is provided not only for the structure but also for "building equipment, fixtures, and outdoor equipment all pertaining to the service of the described premises and located thereon." These items must be the property of the owner of the structures. Lawns, trees, shrubs, and plants are excluded from this coverage.

Trees, Shrubs, and Plants. Trees, shrubs, and plants may be specifically covered if located on the described premises and if they are not grown for commercial purposes. The insurer limits its liability for any one tree, shrub, or plant to the limit stated on the first page of the contract.

Rental Value Coverage. When specific rental value coverage is provided, the insurance covers not only the dwelling but appurtenant private structures as well. There is the usual exclusion of buildings used for commercial, manufacturing, or farming purposes. Rental value is defined as "the fair rental value of the building(s) or parts thereof, as furnished and equipped by the owner whether rented or not." Loss of rental value is limited to the loss that results from physical damage to the structures and equipment that is caused by an insured peril. It is computed for "the period of time, following loss, which would be required with the exercise of due diligence and dispatch, and not limited by the expiration date of this policy, to restore the property to a tenantable condition, less such charges and expenses as do not continue." Rental value is provided whether the building is owner occupied or tenant occupied.

Miscellaneous Provisions. The Dwelling Property Form contains a number of miscellaneous provisions some of which are in the nature of permits, some place limitations on the liability on the insurer, and some serve further to clarify other parts of the contract.

Permits. Permission is granted (*a*) "to make alterations, additions, and repairs, and to complete structures in course of construction"; and (*b*) for vacancy "or unoccupancy without limit of time, except as provided in any endorsement attached to this policy." A building under construction is not regarded as vacant. A provision that is somewhat in the nature of a permit is the section of the form (Section IX) that provides for deferred premium payment. The insured may elect "to pay the premium in equal annual payments . . . provided that no payment shall be less than the Minimum Premium applicable."

Limitations on Liability. In Section IV of the form the insurer limits its liability under the 10 percent optional provisions in the situation where there is more than one contract covering the described property and where not all of the contracts contain identical optional provisions. This section of the contract reads as follows: "This Company shall not be liable for a greater proportion of any loss than would have been the case if all policies covering the described property had contained identical optional provisions and the same election were made under all policies." In the event the extended coverage endorsement applies to the contract the insurer is not liable under Section VIII "for loss caused by wind or hail to metal smokestacks, or, when outside of buildings, cloth awnings, signs, radio or television antennas including their lead-in wiring, masts or towers, unless liability is assumed as a separate item(s) by endorsement to such Extended Coverage Endorsement and additional premium(s) paid therefore."

Clarification of Contract. Certain items in the form provide additional information to the insured about matters that should be of interest to him. These items are: (*a*) loss under the contract does not reduce the face amount of the contract; (*b*) if the insured requests cancellation of the contract, the total premium retained by the insurer must not be less than the minimum provided by the short-rate table; and (*c*) the insurance provided under the contract is not prejudiced "by any act or neglect of any person, other than the named insured, when such act or neglect is not within the control of the named insured."

Clauses. There are a number of clauses included in the form covering matters felt to be pertinent to the insurance of a dwelling. Among these are: mortgage clause, debris removal clause, electrical apparatus clause, inherent explosion clause, liberalization clause, nuclear clause, pro rata clause, and subrogation clause. A number of these clauses such as the mortgage clause, pro rata clause, and liberalization clause are not peculiar to the dwelling and contents form and may appear in other types of form. For purposes of continuity they will be discussed at this point, although the pro rata clause will receive additional attention later in the chapter.

Debris Removal Clause. This clause is in a strict sense an extension of the insurance coverage. It obligates the insurer to pay expenses incurred in the removal of debris of the property insured occasioned by a loss caused by any of the perils covered in the contract. The clause does not add to the amount of the insurance. If the face amount of the contract is exhausted in the payment for loss or damage to the building insured, there is nothing left to pay for removal of debris. If other insurance contracts apply to the property, the insurer is responsible for no more than the "proportion of such debris removal expense as the amount of insurance under this policy bears to the total amount of insurance on the property covered hereunder, whether or not all such insurance includes this clause." If a coinsurance clause applies to the contract, the amount of debris removal expense is not included in the determination of actual cash value. Unless there is a specific endorsement to the contrary the insurer is not responsible for debris removal expense "occasioned by the enforcement of any state or municipal law or ordinance which necessitates the demolition of any portion of a building covered hereunder which has or has not suffered damage by any of the perils insured against."

Electrical Apparatus Clause. It is not the intention of the insurer to cover defective electrical equipment in the fire contract. The electrical apparatus clause excludes from coverage any loss resulting from any electrical injury or disturbance to electrical appliances unless fire ensues. If fire ensues the insurer is liable only for loss caused by the ensuring fire. Thus, if a motor should burn out and from the sparks fire spread with resulting minor damage to nearby furniture, the fire contract covering dwelling and furniture would pay for the furniture damage but not for rewinding the motor. If loss to electrical appliances, devices, fixtures, and wiring is covered under the contract and is caused by lightning, the insurer is liable only "when such loss exceeds $50.00 in any one occurrence and then only for its proportion of such excess."

Inherent Explosion Clause. The Standard Fire Insurance Contract in lines 36 and 37 of the stipulations excludes explosion damage unless fire ensues and then only fire damage is covered. The inherent explosion clause extends the contract to cover direct explosion loss to property caused by hazards inherent in the dwelling risk. This fact means, for example, that if gas should leak from a stove or fixture and accumulate to the point where an explosion followed, the damage would be covered. The clause excludes explosions originating within steam boilers and similar items and provides that electrical arcing, a water hammer, or bursting of water pipes are not to be regarded as explosions. Further, "nuclear reaction or nuclear radiation or radioactive contamination, all whether controlled or uncontrolled, is not 'inherent explosion.' "

Liberalization Clause. This clause gives the insured the benefit of any changes that may be made in form that serve to extend or broaden the insurance without increase in premium. These changes must have been filed with and approved by the insurance commissioner either during the time the insurance is in force under the contract or within 45 days prior to the inception of the contract.

Nuclear Clause. The nuclear clause contains a specific limitation on the meaning of the word "fire" as it relates to nuclear reaction. Fire as contemplated by this contract does not include "nuclear reaction or nuclear radiation or radioactive contamination, all whether controlled or uncontrolled, and loss by nuclear reaction or nuclear radiation or radioactive contamination is not intended to be and is not insured against by this policy or said endorsements, whether such loss be direct or indirect, proximate or remote, or be in whole or in part caused by, contributed to, or aggravated by 'fire' or any other perils insured against by this policy or said endorsements." Direct loss by fire that results from nuclear reaction or radioactive contamination is covered and is subject to all of the provisions of the contract.

Pro Rata Clause. The pro rata clause reads as follows: "If this policy covers on two or more items for which specific amounts are shown, the amount of this policy applies to each item in the proportion that the specific amount shown for each item bears to the sum of all items." This clause follows the general pro rata procedures found in fire insurance and is consistent with the basic principles of indemnity.

Subrogation Clause. This clause, sometimes known as the "subrogation waiver clause," provides that any written agreement of relief from liability entered into by the insured prior to loss shall not affect the contract or the right of the insured to recover. In the case of leased property the insured may in his lease agree to some condition with respect to the property that would act as a limitation on the subrogation rights of the insurer. At one time it was the custom to cover each situation by a specific endorsement to a contract. The brief subrogation clause, when made a part of the form, automatically takes care of any agreement made by the property owner that might otherwise void the contract through a waiver of subrogation rights.

The Dwelling Property Form described in the preceding paragraphs also contains an extended coverage endorsement (Section XI). This endorsement will be discussed in the next chapter. It should be emphasized that the purpose of this discussion is to indicate the pattern of a typical form and the extent to which the form may be used to modify the statutory contract rather than to give a complete analysis of all possible types of form. The specific provisions vary to some extent from one jurisdiction to another and the printed form used in any particular situation should be checked carefully.

INDICATING THE INSURED[3]

When the insured is an individual, his name in full, or as he is ordinarily known, should appear in the contract. If he carries the

---

[3] In this section the standard fire insurance contract is treated as a "form" and should not be confused with such forms as the Dwelling Property Form, which is used to complete, modify, or extend the standard contract. The name of the insured usually does not appear on these forms except for purposes of identification.

insurance in some capacity other than as sole owner, such as administrator, executor, or trustee, this relationship should be indicated. It sometimes happens that more than one interest is to be covered, such as owner and contractor, owner and lienor, or when there is an undivided ownership. The names of the interested parties may in this instance be inserted in the contract, to be followed by the phrase "as interest may appear." When the interest is a changing one, as in the case of a contractor constructing a building and from time to time receiving payments, the contract covers the interests as they are shown at the time of the fire.

Uncertain or vague descriptions are frowned upon and may be a source of considerable confusion and annoyance. A contract written for the heirs, or the estate, of a deceased individual, without specifically naming them, may cause difficulty in effecting an adjustment. From the standpoint of adjustment, the procedure is simpler if the contract names definite persons as insureds rather than a group whose membership must be determined in order to learn with whom to negotiate in order to effect a settlement. The possibility of omitting an interested party is always a matter of grave concern. The proper procedure in the case of an estate is to name the heirs as insureds, and if there are minors, to name their legal representative and the minors as well, for example, "John Doe, Guardian of Richard Doe, infant." If it is impracticable to insert the names of all the insureds or when all the names are inserted, if there are a number of heirs, it is the better part of wisdom to indicate a representative with whom adjustments are to be made. The following form has been suggested: "Loss, if any, to be adjusted with, payable to and recoverable by John Doe, and by him only."

Partnerships present a minor problem in that any additions to the firm are held to amount to a change of interest under the contract and, therefore, terminate the coverage. Retirement of a partner does not have the same serious consequence. In order to have the insurance remain effective in spite of a change in personnel and to secure the coverage to the firm as constituted at the time of the loss, the phrase "as now or may be hereafter constituted" is frequently inserted in the contract after the firm name. In the case of corporations, the exact corporate name is to be used. It is the custom here, likewise, to designate a representative with whom the loss is to be adjusted and paid. The officer ordinarily designated is the treasurer of the company.

Vague and uncertain expressions as "for whom it may concern" are considered to be undesirable, and the end sought by the insurer can usually be effected in some other and more satisfactory manner. The aforementioned clause is sometimes used by the owner of a warehouse or storage plant to cover the contents stored there, regardless of who the owner may be. When this form is used, owners of goods for whom the coverage was contemplated may ratify the insurance after a loss and proceed to collect under the contract as if they were specifically indicated as insureds. If contracts are so written, confusion and uncertainty will be eliminated if the purchaser of the insurance has himself named as the one with whom adjustments are to be made and to whom losses are to be paid, using the form indicated for estates.

Commission Clause. Another clause that has been the source of considerable difficulty and annoyance is the "commission clause." Inserted in the form, the clause reads in the following or similar terms: "His own or held by him in trust, or on commission or consignment, or on storage or for repairs, or sold but not removed, or for which he may be liable."

This clause was intended when first used to cover the named insured and to bring within the scope of the coverage goods not actually owned by him but for which he was legally liable, and for which he would have to pay in the event of its destruction. It sometimes happens that this form best serves the purpose of the insured, as, for example, the owner of a warehouse who is also a dealer in the commodities handled, and when title frequently changes by bookkeeping entries.

When the commission clause is used, the purchaser of the insurance should be certain that the amount of insurance is sufficient to provide adequate coverage not only for his own property but also any property on the premises that might be brought under his contract by means of the clause. He should also incorporate a clause excluding property upon which there is specific insurance. This can be done by inserting the phrase: "This policy does not cover property specifically insured." Finally, the purchaser of the insurance should name himself as the one with whom the adjustment of losses is to be made and to whom they are to be paid.

The danger of the commission clause is to be found in its inclusion in contracts when not necessary, with a view to providing for coverage on goods for which the insured is legally liable. Court decisions have established that the clause does much more than this. As a matter of fact, it is now held that, regardless of whether a bailee has assumed liability for property on his premises and whether he is legally liable, if the commission clause is found in his contracts, the owners of such property may, upon learning of the fire and the form of contract, at once ratify the insurance and proceed to collect under it as if they were named insureds. An insured who contemplated covering, in addition to his own property, only that for which he has assumed liability or for which he is legally liable may find himself forced to share his insurance with others. This may exhaust so much of the insurance as to leave himself sadly underinsured.

Instead of using the commission clause, it is considered the better practice to divide the insurance when it is possible to do so. The property of the policyholder should be covered under a single form restricted to his property only. Another contract could then be written covering the legal liability and the assumed liability of the insured for the property of others. In this way, as far as his own coverage is concerned, there should be no encroachment upon it by unforeseen and unexpected claimants.

PERMANENT FIXTURES

In connection with the description of the property to be insured, it should be emphasized that permanent fixtures may be insured with the building. The significance of this information to the insured lies in the fact that the building rate is ordinarily less than the contents rate. A saving in premium is effected when the building form is extended to cover permanent fixtures. Machinery having to do with the service of the building, such as fans and ventilator systems, as well as the heating plant, may be thus included, as may be refrigerating apparatus and equipment in cold storage plants. In school buildings, seats may be included in the coverage as part of the building, as may pews, altars, confessionals, shrines, and pulpits in church buildings. In apartment buildings, stoves, refrigerators, floor coverings, cleaning apparatus, and other equipment used by the janitor, as well as fuel, heating plant, and other property of the owner designed for permanent use in the building may likewise be included in the building form.

METHODS OF PROVIDING INSURANCE ON PROPERTY

There are three basic methods of insuring property: (1) specific, (2) blanket, and (3) reporting. Combinations of these methods are customary. Although the three methods just listed are the ones usually cited, in practice five methods are employed: (1) specific, (2) blanket, (3) floater, (4) automatic, or (5) schedule. These last five categories are an extension of the three, since they are methods in constant use. Although a "form" will be used with each of these methods, it should be distinguished from such forms as the Dwelling Property Form.

Each type has its particular use, and a more extensive description of their operation will be given with the description of certain coverages to which the forms are adapted. A brief description of each will indicate their particular characteristics.

Specific Coverage. This form covers one kind of property in one definite location. When the building and contents are insured under a single policy, with definite amounts covered on each, the contract continues to be specific. The following is an example of a specific form:

Item 1. $......On the building and additions structurally attached and communicating, occupied as and for purposes incident thereto, including foundations (except as hereinafter specifically excluded), vaults, stacks, elevators, hoists, chutes and their appurtenances; engines, boilers, pumps, their settings and appurtenances; electrical, heating, lighting and ventilating equipment pertaining to the building service; piping and plumbing of every description; landlord's storm and screen doors, storm windows, screens and awnings, whether in place or stored in said building; and on all property fastened to and made a part of the building , situated

Item 2. $......On stock consisting principally of and on stock materials, and stock supplies, including packages, labels, packing materials and supplies for same, the property of the Insured; all while contained in the above described building and additions structurally attached and communicating.

Item 3. $......On furniture and fixtures of every description, useful and ornamental incident to the business of including manuscripts; and when the property of the building occupant and not the property of the building owner, on storm and screen doors, storm windows, screens and awnings, whether in place or stored in said building; and on supplies, signs, tools and implements, machines and their parts, which do not pertain to the building service; all while contained in or attached to the above described building and additions structurally attached and communicating.

In many states the style of the contract has been arranged so that the description of the hazard and the location of the property may be typed on its face. There is also space for the number of standard printed forms. The use of this type of contract cuts down filing space, since it makes it unnecessary to attach copies of the form to the agent's or insurer's record. Where this type of contract is used, the form defines the exact nature of the coverage and contains the applicable clauses and permits. The specific amounts of coverage appear on the face of the contract instead of on the form.

Blanket Coverage. A blanket contract covers the same kind of property at different locations, or different kinds of property at a single location. Several buildings in different locations may be insured under a blanket contract, as may stocks of goods or merchandise located in different warehouses or stores, or building and contents at a single location. The following form is designed to cover building and contents:

$...... On the .... building and additions there adjoining and communicating, occupied as ....

....

and for purposes incident thereto, including foundations, exterior attachments, vaults, stacks, elevators, hoists, chutes and their appurtenances; engines, boilers, pumps, their settings and appurtenances; heating, lighting and ventilating equipment; automatic sprinkler and other piping and plumbing of every description; electrical wiring for lighting and power service; landlord's storm and screen doors, storm windows, screens and awnings, whether in place or stored in said building(s); and on all permanent fixtures therein or thereon; also on all fixed and movable machines and machinery of every description incident to the business, including dynamos, motors, electrical machinery, apparatus, appliances and devices; machinery parts and supplies, implements and tools; patterns, models, dies and drawings in use; shop, factory and office furniture and fixtures, advertising matter, books of account (not exceeding their value blank), printed books, pictures, signs, wearing apparel (the property of the insured), equipment and supplies usual to the business of the insured; stock, merchandise and material wrought, raw or in process, including packages, labels, packing materials and supplies for same, the property of the insured; and on the interest of the insured in and/or legal liability for similar property belonging in whole or in part to others, and held by the insured either sold but not removed, on storage or for repairs, or otherwise held; all while contained in the above described building(s) and additions thereto adjoining and communicating, situated

Floating Coverage. A floating contract, termed in the insurance business a "floater," is used to cover goods in different locations when it is difficult or impossible to furnish an accurate description of location. One form of floater covers certain specific goods wherever they may be, usually within certain prescribed limits as to territory. For example, the personal effects, theatrical costumes, and equipment of a traveling stock company are located week after week and night after night in different hotels, theaters, and trains, boats, automobiles, and terminals. A floater would cover this equipment wherever it might be so long as it remained within limits prescribed. Such limits might be a single state, they might be within the continental limits of the United States, or worldwide coverage could be secured.

Another form of floater sometimes used, although not so frequently with the advent of automatic coverages, has to do with excess coverages. A floater covering in excess of specific insurance may be secured, or a similar contract covering only when the loss exceeds a specified amount. The floater form is used if the insured wishes to protect a number of locations and desires the excess contract to extend its coverage to all of them. The following form illustrates a coverage by means of a floater:

CONTENTS POTATO WAREHOUSES

Floater for Maine

On Potatoes in Maine for himself alone or as Agent for whom it may concern, as interest may appear, as now or hereafter be constituted: Loss, if any, to be adjusted with and payable to .... $........ On Merchandise consisting principally of Potatoes, Fertilizer, Sacks and Barrels containing same or empty, or other merchandise not more hazardous; storehouse supplies and fixtures of every description, including lumber for car linings, the property of the insured; and on the interest of the insured in the legal liability for similar property belonging in whole or in part to others, and held by the insured either sold but not removed, on storage or for repairs, or otherwise held.

All while contained in farm storehouses and/or warehouses or shipping stations along the line of any railroad in Maine.......................... .... more particularly defined by maps on file with the insuring company and as per list filed with the company by the assured as hereinafter provided.

This policy is also extended to cover in cars on tracks and not accepted by the railroad company, and also including legal liability of the assured for railroad cars on sidings under their control.

This Company shall not be liable for loss in any one potato house for any greater sum than its proportion of 30% of the total amount of value last reported, as provided below, except that such limit shall not be effective where it amounts to less than $15,000.

It is understood and agreed that by the term potato house is meant a distinct building not communicating with any adjoining building.

Automatic Coverage. Automatic coverages are written with the "reporting forms." They are used when it is difficult, if not impossible, to provide the insurer with an accurate statement of values because of changes or fluctuations, yet a full insurance coverage is desired. The contract limit remains the same and the insured is freed from the burden of determining his values before a loss in order to avoid coinsurance penalties. Losses will be paid up to the limit of the contract provided there is no under-reporting of values or delay in reporting of values.

The multiple location contracts, utilized by chain stores and others having varying values in different locations, fall within this category. As long as the required reports are accurately made, within the limits of the contract, the insurance automatically adjusts itself to intervening inventory changes. The automatic builder's risk has the same effect. A building in the process of construction accrues value day by day. Monthly reports are required, but a loss at a point between two reports will be protected by full insurance.

Another type of automatic coverage is frequently incorporated in the contracts of institutions holding property in widely scattered areas. To obviate the danger of the institution having acquired a property and suffering a loss because of failure to provide insurance coverage, the following clause is inserted:

On property (as described by specific forms and certificates hereinafter referred to) to the extent of the insured's insurable interest as OWNER, TRUSTEE, MORTGAGEE, or other interest, while located anywhere in the State of Maine.

AUTOMATIC PICK-UP CLAUSE. If, during the term of this contract, the insured shall acquire any property as described herein not already included in the list of locations, or shall increase the value by additions to construction or equipment, located on the premises described as covered by this policy, this insurance shall be increased automatically subject to the terms and conditions of this policy, to apply and cover at such point, or points, to an amount not exceeding $25,000 at any one location, and the insured hereby agrees to notify the insurance company within sixty days of such new location, or increase of value at locations already specified in this form, and the company shall issue an endorsement to care for its proportionate part thereof. This additional insurance shall not extend to cover any value covered by endorsement or any value added to any location involved prior to the effective date of any endorsement covering such item nor shall it, in any event, extend to cover any value added prior to sixty days before the date of any fire that may occur.

Schedule Coverage. Schedule contracts are indicated for certain large organizations. All the buildings and their contents belonging to an insured may be grouped on a single form instead of written as specific insurance on separate forms. While specific amounts of insurance are indicated for each unit of the property, the contracts as written cover blanket on every unit. An organization, such as a state, a municipality, a church with widely scattered properties, or a public utility company, frequently finds this form to be desirable as a means for simplifying the clerical supervision of insurance detail. The following schedule illustrates a form suitable for a municipality:

PORTLAND WATER DISTRICT

$...... On buildings, additions and connections (structurally attached), including all permanent fixtures, and on personal property, including books, wearing apparel, plate, jewels, medals, patterns, models, scientific cabinets and collections, paintings, sculpture and curiosities, tools, appliances, machines, belting, meters, motors, plans, blueprint records, water meters in process of repair or in storage, including parts for the same and all other personal property, tools, machines or materials used or useful in the conduct of a water works business and contained in said buildings (excluding automobiles, bills of exchange, notes, accounts, evidences and securities of property of every kind and money);

To apply to and cover at locations described in the following Schedule; this policy covering pro rata on each

Item No.		Item:
1.	$ 99,000	Office and Laboratory, 16–18 Casco Street, Portland, Maine.
2.	127,600	Shop and Garage, 199–221 Douglass Street, Portland, Maine.
3.	4,700	Dwelling and Office, Brackett Avenue, Peaks Island, Portland, Maine.
4.	29,500	Pumping Station, Sheridan Street, Portland, Maine.
5.	500	Pumping Station, Elizabeth Street, Peaks Island, Portland, Maine.
6.	500	Pumping Station, Church Avenue, Peaks Island, Portland, Maine.
7.	500	Pumping Station, off Pleasant Street, Peaks Island, Portland, Maine.
8.	3,700	Pumping Station, Main Street, Gorham, Maine.
9.	2,500	Pumping Station, North Windham, Maine.
10.	11,000	Office, 630–634 Main Street, Westbrook, Maine.
	$279,500	

An enormous amount of detail work, checking a great many different forms, as well as keeping track of many expirations, is eliminated through the use of a schedule form.

SCHEDULE REINSURANCE

Where the desire for simplicity in paper work in the office of the insured calls for an irreducible minimum in contract checking, it is possible for an agent to write the entire line on a single contract and deliver it to the insured. Or, when the business is to be given to several agents, a single contract may be requested from each agent. The agent, in turn, issues contracts in such amounts as he sees fit, reinsuring with other insurers he wishes to commit. Thus, if an agent gets a line of $100,000 with the request for a single contract, he may write it in one insurer and deliver it. Then he may, if he chooses, issue, say, nine contracts for $10,000 each with nine other insurers. The net result will be a liability of $10,000 in each of ten insurers, yet the insured has but one contract and one insurer with which to deal. This type of reinsurance is effected by means of the following form:

Reinsurance of .... Insurance Company of .... $...... On its liability as Insurers under its Policy No..... of ...., Agency issued to and covering the property of .... as per schedule on file.

This policy of reinsurance is subject to the same risks, privileges, conditions and endorsements (except changes of location), assignments, changes of interest or of rate, valuations and modes of settlement, as are or may be assumed or adopted by the .... Insurance Company of ....

The amount payable under this policy shall bear the same ratio to the amount payable by the reinsured Company under any and all policies upon the property specified and contained within the limits described herein, that the amount of this reinsurance in force at the time of loss shall bear to the total amount insured by the reinsured Company upon such property in force at the time of such loss, and shall be paid at the same time and in the same manner as payment shall be made by said reinsured Company.

Other reinsurance is permitted without notice until required.

Attached to and forming part of Policy No. .... of the .... Insurance Company of ....

While it is not to be denied that this procedure simplifies matters for the insured, the plan is not wholly without its shortcomings. The insured's loss of contact with the carrying insurer is a matter for regret, and, when it serves the purpose as well, the practice of accepting directly the contracts covering on the risk seems most desirable from the standpoint of both insurer and insured.

THE VALUED CONTRACT

In the case of personal property, there frequently develop situations that call for a valued contract. When a contract is so written, it is customary to make a schedule of the items to be covered and then to add the following clause: "It is understood and agreed that the amount stated opposite each item in the foregoing schedule, shall for the purpose of this insurance, be considered the value thereof." When personal property is insured under such a form, the necessity of arriving at a value of the property destroyed by fire is eliminated. The insured is obligated to demonstrate that the property is the identical property insured under the contract.

EXTENSIONS AND LIMITATIONS OF COVERAGE

It frequently happens that merchandise or raw material is located on or near the property of the insured but not actually within the premises. Sometimes it is located on cars, switches, and sidetracks on or within a specified area near the premises. Likewise, it may be on loading platforms or neighboring streets. To bring such property within the scope of the contract, the following, or similar, clause is used. "This contract covers also personal property similar to that hereby insured while (*a*) in cars on switches or sidetracks when such cars are on premises described or within 100 feet of buildings described in policy; (*b*) on platforms in contact with buildings described in policy; (*c*) on sidewalks, streets, alleys or detached platforms, when within 50 feet of buildings described in policy; (*d*) while temporarily in the open on premises."

It sometimes happens that there is personal property in which parties other than the insured have an insurable interest and the insured's interest in the property is covered by other insurances. In such an instance, if the property of others is excluded from the coverage, there is no double insurance. Again, automobiles are usually the subject of separate insurance, and for this reason it is customary to exclude them from coverage under the ordinary fire contract covering personal property of the insured. The following form is typical: "This policy does not cover the insured's interest in personal property in which parties other than the insured also have an insurable interest when the insured's interest in said property is otherwise covered. This policy does not cover automobiles, including all self-propelled vehicles and machines using gasoline."

The insured frequently agrees in his contract to carry insurance to comply with the requirements of a coinsurance clause. It is, therefore, to the advantage of the insured to eliminate from coverage those parts of the building not exposed to loss or of which the loss, if any at all, will be negligible. If such exclusions are deemed desirable, it is customary to eliminate, by means of a clause in the form, the cost of excavations, brick, stone, or concrete foundations, piers, or other supports, below the undersurface of the lowest floor or basement or, when there is no basement, piers that are underground, as well as buried flues, pipes, or drains. Other exclusions may be added when they particularly apply.

If the insured obligates himself to adjust on the basis of a designated percentage of insurance to value, and cost of excavations, buried foundations, and other costs that enter into the construction of the building not subject to a fire loss are included in estimating the value, the insured may find himself forced to carry insurance upon a part of his property on which little or no loss is possible.

CLAUSES THAT LIMIT PAYMENT

There are a number of clauses not previously discussed that may appear on fire insurance forms and that may serve to limit the amount to be recovered from the insurer. Chief among these clauses are the coinsurance clause, the waiver clause, the pro rata distribution clauses, the three-fourths value clause, the three-fourths loss clause, and the two-thirds vacancy clause. The last three of these clauses are somewhat rare in present-day practice.

The Coinsurance Clause. When coinsurance is a factor in the fire insurance contract, the clause appears in the form. Because of the usual requirement of insurance equal to 80 percent of the value, the clause is frequently referred to as the "80 percent clause," or sometimes as the "80 percent coinsurance clause." The clause in use at the present time is the reduced rate contribution clause; and percentages other than 80 are frequently used. The form makes no requirement concerning the amount of insurance the insured must carry, but instead, in consideration of a reduced premium, sets forth the proportion of the loss the insurer is obligated to pay. The following clause is an example of the one now in use:

> In consideration of the reduced rate and (or) form under which this policy is written, it is expressly stipulated and made a condition of this contract that in the event of loss this Company shall be liable for no greater proportion thereof than the amount hereby insured bears to ...... percent of the actual cash value of the property described herein at the time when such loss shall happen, nor for more than the proportion which this policy bears to the total insurance thereon.
>
> In the event that the aggregate claim for any loss is *Both Less than Ten Thousand Dollars ($10,000)* and less than five percent (5%) of the total amount of insurance upon the property described herein at the time such loss occurs, no special inventory or appraisement of the undamaged property shall be required.
>
> If this policy be divided into two or more items, the foregoing shall apply to each item separately.

The operation of the clause may be expressed by means of the following formula:

Let L = loss,
I = insurance,
P = percentage indicated in clause,
V = sound value,
X = amount the insurer pays.
Then $X = LI/PV$.

It is sometimes stated that when the loss under any contract is total, the coinsurance clause is inoperative. This is not the case. The clause operates in the event of every loss, but whenever the loss is total the percentage of loss that limits the amount the insurer is required to pay will exceed the face of the contracts. This being the case, the full face of the contract is payable whenever the loss is total. For example, a $100,000 value insured with an 80 percent clause calls for $80,000 insurance. If the insured carries $40,000, he becomes a coinsurer for every loss to the extent of 50 percent. In the event of a total loss, 50 percent of $100,000 exceeds the insurance. Therefore, the full amount of insurance is payable.

However, in the case indicated above, if the loss were $10,000 the formula would operate as follows:

$$L = \$10{,}000,$$
$$I = \$40{,}000,$$
$$P = \$80\%, \text{ and}$$
$$V = \$100{,}000,$$
$$\text{Then } X = \frac{\$10{,}000 \times \$40{,}000}{80\% \times 100{,}000} = \frac{\$400{,}000{,}000}{80{,}000} = \$5{,}000.$$
$$X = \$5{,}000, \text{ the amount the insurance pays.}$$

The Waiver Clause. In the field of fire insurance, it is customary to incorporate in the reduced-rate contribution clause a second clause which has the effect of relieving the insured of the necessity of taking a physical inventory of the undamaged property in the event of small losses. This clause is, in fact, not a part of the reduced-rate contribution clause; but, since it has been so universally associated with it, the two clauses are generally regarded as one.

The waiver clause does not have the effect of suspending the operation of the coinsurance feature of the contract in small losses. Instead, it relieves the insured of the necessity of verifying the figures shown in his books by an actual inventory at the time of the loss. The statement frequently heard that small losses are outside the operation of the coinsurance clause is not correct. Even if an inventory is not taken, if the figures as submitted show insufficient insurance as to value, the insured becomes a coinsurer.

Pro Rata Distribution Clause. The pro rata distribution clause has the effect of dividing the total coverage under a blanket contract to apply specifically upon each separate location in proportion that the value at each location bears to the sum of the values at all locations. Sometimes referred to as the "average clause," the following example is typical: "It is a condition of this contract that the amount insured hereunder shall attach in or on each building, shed and other structure and (or) place in that proportion to the amount hereby insured that the value of the property covered by this policy in or on each said building, shed and other structure and (or) place shall bear to the value of all the property described herein."

If no coinsurance clause is used under a blanket form, a pro rata distribution clause is usually mandatory. The reason for this is at once apparent. If an insured owned a number of properties in widely different locations, he could insure them under a blanket form for an amount that would be full insurance in any one location. Without the pro rata distribution clause, in the event of any loss the full amount would be paid until the insurance becomes exhausted. In other words, barring the catastrophe hazard, if an insured carried insurance in an amount equal to his most valuable property under a blanket form, all his properties would be covered in full. This situation would be manifestly unfair. To preclude the possibility of writing such contracts, the insurance exchanges usually offer the alternative of using the 90 percent reduced-rate contribution clause on blanket contracts or, instead, the pro rata distribution clause. This is not always the case, however, and sometimes both a coinsurance clause and the pro rata distribution clause are required. It is to the advantage of the insured to carry insurance to value with a 90 percent coinsurance clause and without the pro rata distribution clause. This is so for in any loss the insurance will apply until exhausted if the coinsurance requirement has been met. With the use of the pro rata distribution clause, recovery in full is possible only with 100 percent insurance. This fact is illustrated by the following example. Assume stock in three locations as follows: $100,000 at X, $60,000 at Y, and $40,000 at Z, with a total loss at X and a 90 percent coinsurance clause with $180,000 insurance. The insured would collect $100,000. In other words, the full amount of the insurance would apply to the loss until the insurance was exhausted. In the case of the same loss with a pro rata distribution clause we have:

Values at X	$100,000
Values at Y	60,000
Values at Z	40,000
	$200,000

With the pro rata distribution clause the insured is entitled to recover:

$$\frac{\$100,000}{\$200,000} \times \$180,000 = \$90,000.$$

If both the 90 percent coinsurance clause and the pro rata distribution clause are used with $180,000 insurance the limit of liability at location X would still be $90,000. In other words, with both clauses the insured may recover the lower limit of liability of both clauses. In case of partial losses the rule is the same, though where both the 90 percent coinsurance clause and the pro rata distribution clause are both used the coinsurance clause would in all probability control the amount of liability of the insurers. This is not necessarily so, though it is to be expected that the pro rata distribution clause would allocate adequate insurance for partial losses *provided always* that adequate insurance to meet the coinsurance requirement is carried.

The clause is used principally in connection with the blanket contract in which stocks are carried in a number of locations with values constantly shifting from one location to the other. The insured may have a comprehensive idea of his total values but may be uncertain from time to time as to the inventory in each specific location. If the subject of insurance is being shipped constantly or in the process of manufacture is shifted from building to building, a blanket contract with a pro rata distribution clause automatically shifts the coverage as the relative values shift. There is little point in using the clause in insuring buildings, because the value of the buildings may be easily be determined and is not subject to sharp fluctuations.

Three-Fourths Value Clause. This clause limits the amount of the insurer's liability on a given property to three fourths of the cash value of the property at the time of the loss or damage. Premium concessions are sometimes made when the clause is used. It has for its purpose counteracting the element of moral hazard in the form of carelessness by requiring the insured to assume a substantial share of the risk. The clause is used primarily in communities where the facilities for fire protection are few and where, if a fire once starts, the loss may reasonably be expected to be total. The clause does not have the effect of limiting the amount to be paid in the event of partial losses, unless the partial loss exceeds three fourths of the value of the property. In other words, in the case of a property valued at $60,000, a $10,000 loss would be paid in full. On the other hand, a $50,000 loss with full insurance would obligate the insurers to pay but $45,000.

Three-Fourths Loss Clause. This clause limits the insurer's liability to three fourths of any loss. A loss of $12,000 with full insurance would obligate the insurer to pay $9,000. The purposes of the clause are much the same as those of the three-fourths value clause, but from the point of view of the insured, they are much more stringent.

Two-Thirds Vacancy Clause. This clause has been used to some extent in insuring unprotected property when there is a hazard from tramps and marauders. The clause has the effect of suspending one third of the insurance during the period of vacancy or unoccupancy. Two forms of the clause have been used. On suspends one third of the insurance during vacancy or unoccupancy; the second clause is far more stringent for, in addition, it limits the amount payable under the insurance to two thirds of the amount of any loss or damage. In connection with the writing of the two-thirds vacancy clause, it is not unusual to incorporate other requirements in the contract. For example, the agreement may require that doors and windows be adequately secured during the period of vacancy, and in some instances it may be required that the property be regularly visited by some person entrusted with its supervision.

SPECIALIZED FORMS

There are a number of specialized forms used with the standard fire insurance contract. Forms are available for churches, schools, colleges, public buildings, art dealers, telephone exchanges, lodges, elevators, warehouses, clubs, and there are many other types. Probably the most widely used form is that covering dwellings and their contents. This form was described earlier in this chapter. Next in importance, and the form that produces the greatest volume of premiums for the insurers, is that covering buildings, stock, and fixtures for mercantile risks. These forms contain many of the clauses previously discussed. In addition there will be provisions that apply to the particular type of property being insured. As an illustration of a special form, the main features of the mercantile building, fixtures, and stock form will be summarized. The clauses described are those pertinent to the mercantile risk. The list is not intended to be exhaustive.

Mercantile Building, Fixtures, and Stock Form. This form provides a specific amount of insurance on the three named items: (*a*) building, (*b*) stock, and (*c*) furniture and fixtures.

The building item covers the basic structure and all additions attached and communicating. It also covers building service equipment, such as screen doors, storm windows, screens, and awnings. These last items, at first thought, might appear to be regarded as contents rather than a part of the building. This is particularly the case if they are in storage and not attached to the building. These items are treated in a fashion similar to machinery having to do with the service of the building which may be covered as part of the building and the description is written so to provide.

The furniture and fixtures description is written to cover everything that possibly could be included in this category. It will be recalled that lines 9 and 10 of the stipulations exclude manuscripts and bullion unless mentioned in writing in the contract. Manuscripts are mentioned to include them within the coverage. Bullion ordinarily would not be owned by a mercantile firm, and if it were, specific insurance would be provided for it.

The item of stock is all-inclusive. The form provides a space to indicate its general character. For example, it could be the stock of a wholesale grocery store, a hardware store, a drugstore, or other known class of business. Stock of every character pertaining to the particular business mentioned in the form would be covered.

Coinsurance Clause. A coinsurance clause is usually printed in the form. A space is left to indicate the coinsurance percentage to be used. If the clause does not apply, it is stamped void at the time the policy is written.

Property Not Covered Clause. This clause provides that the contract will not cover cost of excavations; brick, stone, or concrete foundations; piers; or other supports below the lowest basement floor. Other items such as the cost of underground flues, pipes, or drains are excluded. The purpose of excluding these items is to reduce the total insurable value of the building by the cost of items that probably would not be destroyed as a result of a fire. This reduces the amount of insurance necessary to meet the coinsurance requirement. The clause also excludes from cover any interest the insured may have in personal property in which others have an interest when the interest of the insured is otherwise covered. This precludes double insurance and also reflects to the advantage of the insured with respect to the coinsurance requirement. Automobiles, including all self-propelled vehicles and machines, are excluded, since it is the custom that these be specifically insured.

Automatic Sprinkler Clause. This clause makes it a condition of the contract that so far as the sprinkler system and its water supply are under the control of the insured due diligence shall be used to maintain both in working order. The insured is obligated to get consent in writing of the insurer, or the rating association, before a change is made either in the system or the water supply. If the system is connected with an approved central station sprinkler advisory service, the same rules apply with respect to the service.

Bituminous Coal Clause. Where this clause applies, it is made a condition of the contract that no claim will be made for loss or damage to bituminous coal, or for salvaging such coal on the insured's premises, because of fire or heat caused by fire originating in the coal. Bituminous coal frequently heats with resulting spontaneous combustion. It is loss originating from this source that the clause excludes. This clause is used primarily with coal yard and other situations where there is a large supply of coal exposed to possible loss. It does not apply to situations with a normal coal exposure.

Alterations and Repairs Permit. This permit allows the employment of mechanics to make alterations, additions, and repairs to the building without adversely affecting the insurance. It also extends the insurance to cover alterations and additions, as well as all materials and supplies used in connection therewith. If the building is equipped with automatic sprinklers, the same rule holds except that it does not permit the enlargement or reconstruction of any building. If the building having the sprinkler system is to be reconstructed or enlarged, the nature of the change should be reported to the insurance company and permission therefor endorsed on the contract.

Work and Materials Clause. This clause permits the use of such appliances, devices, or materials as are usual and incidental to the type of business. It will be recalled that the standard contract provides that the insurance shall not apply while the hazard is increased by any means within the control or knowledge of the insured. It is entirely conceivable that some material used, or piece of equipment installed, might be regarded by some as increasing the hazard. To preclude any possibility of such an interpretation, this clause is inserted in the form.

In addition to these clauses, which are the more usual in the mercantile form, there may be found as well as the divisible contract clause, the electrical apparatus clause, the inherent explosion clause, the loss clause, the removal of debris clause, and the warrantly endorsement already noted in connection with the dwelling form. The wording of the clauses in both forms is not always identical, but the objective is the same. Other clauses may be included where required by the nature of the risk.

ENDORSEMENTS

A form is to be distinguished from an endorsement, though the line of demarcation is sometimes a nebulous one. The form is essential to the completion of the contract and is attached when the contract is prepared. The term "endorsement" developed from the practice of adding clauses to a contract after it had been issued for the purpose of modifying it in some way. And endorsement is, in a strict sense, a provision added to the insurance contract whereby the scope of its coverage is restricted or enlarged. It presumes a change in the conditions of the policy after its preparation. Certain endorsements, such as those that extend the perils covered, may be as long as the form and may be attached when the contract is issued. Even here, the endorsement may be presumed to be an extension of the scope of the original contract, although prepared at the inception of the agreement and attached to the contract before delivery.

An endorsement may be added to the contract changing its amount or term. Errors may be corrected in the same manner. If a property is sold, the insurance may be continued for the benefit of the new owner by means of an endorsement. Clauses may be added to the contract in the form of an endorsement when the form does not of itself meet the needs of the insured. Such endorsements are frequently in the nature of permits. For example, a permit may be added to the contract authorizing removal of the insured property and providing for coverage in another location. Endorsements may be used to effect changes in the contract, such as amount, rate, location, and interest insured. The only limitation bearing upon added clauses is to be found in the requirement that they may not be inconsistent with, or a waiver of, any of the conditions or provisions of the contract.

CONCURRENCY

In the preparation of the forms, a serious defect may develop that will, to a greater or less degree, defeat the purposes of the insurance.

Contracts designed to cover identical properties should be exactly alike as to form. When there are discrepancies, the insurance is said to be "nonconcurrent," and this may have the effect of complicating the problem of adjustment, or providing inadequate coverage under permits and clauses even though the face of the insurance may be sufficient.

Nonconcurrency most frequently manifests itself in the form of a combination of specific and blanket contracts. The owner of several buildings forming part of one establishment may take out specific insurance on certain of the buildings and blanket insurance covering several or all of the buildings. Another form of nonconcurrency is to be found when there are several contracts covering on a given property, but some written with coinsurance and others without the clause. Contracts sometimes cover the contents of a building and extend to cover in adjacent yards, while other policies covering on the same property do not provide the protection in the yards.

For all practical purposes, it is not essential that forms be absolutely identical. Contracts are regarded as concurrent if the coverage is identical so far as terms and conditions affecting the liability are concerned. When contracts are identical line for line and word for word, the ideal situation is attained. In the instance of many large and important risks, to arrive at this ideal, special forms are printed, and the use of these forms only is permitted in writing contracts of the insured.

FOR DISCUSSION

1. X wishes to do some work on his property which will involve extensive alterations and repairs. His contract is endorsed accordingly, but now the question presents itself as to whether, because of the nature of the work contemplated, there will be an increase in hazard which will suspend the contract for this cause. Should he also have the contract endorsed with a clause authorizing the specific operations which he believes will tend to increase the hazard?
2. At one time the property of one of our political subdivisions was covered by approximately 1,800 separate insurance contracts expiring at all times during the year. It was the wish of those in authority that all agents writing the business retain their lines but that some method of simplifying the handling of expirations and the accounting of premiums be worked out. Suggest a plan.
3. B wishes to insure, in connection with his furniture contract, the face value of certain notes that he keeps in a strong box in his desk. He contends that if the notes are destroyed, the account is not collectible. He wishes the contract endorsed to include the notes. If the insurer is willing to do this, may the contract be so endorsed?
4. It does not always suit the needs of the insured to eliminate bullion or

manuscripts from the coverage of the fire contract. A clause somewhat along the lines of the following has been suggested: "The term 'contents' as used herein shall be construed to mean contents of every nature and description except property specifically excluded, but including all articles upon which liability must be specifically assumed as mentioned in the contract." This form was satisfactory for use with the old New York standard contract. Why is it defective in connection with the new contract?

5. Contracts are sometimes written to read: "John Doe, on his interest in, etc." Is the insurance valid in such an instance if John Doe is not the sole and unconditional owner, or must John Doe's interest be specifically described? Give reasons for your answer.
6. X, a trustee of his church, wishes to include in the form covering on a church building, the following clause: "This item covers all pews, pulpits, altars, lecterns, choir stalls and confessionals attached to the building, window, plate and ornamental glass, frescoing, gilding, painting, gas, water and heating apparatus, connections and appurtenances, signs, awnings, gas and electrical fixtures and all appliances appertaining thereto, bells and tower clocks, doors and window screens and storm doors and windows, belonging to the above described building, while attached thereto or stored therein." B, another trustee, contends that the above items represent furniture and should be written on a contents form instead of a building form. What is your opinion?
7. X claims that A owes him $5,000. He goes to his insurance agent and orders a contract in this amount to protect himself in the event that A's property should be destroyed by fire. The property as a matter of actual fact burns and is fully insured by the owner. May the debtor also collect under his contract?
8. X owns a dwelling house valued at $40,000 with a mortgage in the amount of $30,000 payable to the Ninth National Bank. He insures his house for $32,000. In the course of time while the contract is still in effect, he sells the property to C subject to the mortgage. Before C actually places insurance, the property burns. The insurer denies liability on the ground that, since the contract is a personal one and C no longer owns the property, there can be no liability on the part of the insurer. What is your opinion?
9. X carries a line of merchandise consisting principally of boots and shoes. He adds a line of stockings. Will the stockings be covered without having them specifically mentioned in the contract covering boots and shoes? What steps, if any, should he take to be fully protected?
10. In insuring personal property indicate the information that should appear in the form with relation to the nature of the property.
11. B owns a summer hotel. For the last two seasons he has been unable to obtain a tenant for it and because of ill health did not operate it himself. His insurance contract reads "occupied as a summer hotel." In the circumstances is this a correct description?

12. B owns a tenement house providing separate dwelling units for 14 families. In insuring the property the description in the form indicates the coverage to apply to a property "occupied as a 14 family brick structure." If several of the apartments are vacant when a fire occurs, would the description in the contract be regarded as inaccurate?
13. X has a building located on the bank of the Penobscot River. In the winter months ice is harvested and stored in the building packed in sawdust. The insurance contract covering the building states that it is used for the storage of ice. By early fall the entire supply of ice has been sold and the building is empty. A fire occurs, and the property is totally destroyed. Under the terms of the form can the owner collect if at the time of the fire the building is not actually used for the storage of ice?
14. Distinguish between a form and an endorsement.
15. What are the functions of the form, and what does it include in supplementing the standard contract? Discuss.
16. The term "inherent explosion," as used in fire insurance, is that explosion occurring within a structure caused by a hazard inherent in its occupancy. Is the peril covered by the fire insurance contract?
17. It has been stated that the form may extend considerably the coverage provided by the insurance agreement by adapting the coverage to the particular risk. How can the form modify the coverage provided by a standard contract, every line of which is prescribed by statute?
18. B issues a contract for the account of C. X is named in the policy as mortgagee. The premium is $1,000, and at the end of 60 days B attempts to collect the premium but is unable to do so. He, therefore, takes a note from C for $1,000 payable in 30 days and discounts the note in the bank. At the end of 30 days the note is unpaid, and B is obliged to take it up. He attempts to effect cancellation of the insurance and serves notice on the mortgagee of his intention. The mortgagee holds the contracts and refuses to deliver them on the ground that, when B accepted the note, the contracts were fully paid for and the fact that B has been unable to collect on the note is not material so far as he is concerned. What is your opinion?
19. A owns a property with a mortgage payable to the Blank National Bank in the amount of $3,000. Insurance in the usual course is deposited with the bank with the mortgage clause. The mortgage is in default, and A has apparently lost all interest in it. Following a fire, A ignores the bank and refuses to take any action whatever. After some weeks of attempted negotiation in which the bank undertakes to get A to take action with a view to effecting an adjustment, a representative of the bank comes to you and asks your advice. What will you tell him?
20. Read the mortgage clause carefully, and see whether, in your opinion, the mortgagee is obliged to pay the premium if the mortgagor refuses or fails to do so.

CHAPTER 8

Dwelling Property and Related Forms (Continued)

In a strict sense any endorsement to the fire insurance standard contract that provides insurance of perils specifically excluded by the terms of the standard contract[1] or extends the insurance to include perils that, because of their nature, do not fall within the scope of the protection provided by the statutory phraseology, is an extended coverage endorsement. Not all exclusions are insurable.[2] However, the contract does provide for including perils other than the perils of "fire, lightning, and by removal." This is accomplished in the stipulations by providing: "Any other peril to be insured against or subject of insurance to be covered in this policy shall be by endorsement in writing hereon or added hereto."[3] This is the statutory authority for extending the coverage under the fire contract. The more usual extended coverage contracts are written to cover the hazards of windstorm, hail, explosion, riot, not attending a strike, civil commotion, aircraft, smoke, and vehicle damage. Contracts are also written to include the earthquake hazard, vandalism, and malicious mischief. Certain of these perils may be written as separate contracts. The practice of extending the fire insurance contract by endorsement, however, has become well established in the insurance business and is a generally accepted method of providing coverage for additional perils.[4]

---

[1] Standard contract, lines 7–10, 10–25.

[2] *Ibid.*, lines 7–10.

[3] *Ibid.*, lines 38–40.

[4] Extended coverage contracts are distinguished from consequential loss contracts in that the damage under an extended coverage contract represents a direct loss, but from a hazard other than the hazard covered by the fire insurance contract. Consequential loss contracts cover indirect losses. Consequential losses due to fires are insurable, and extended cover contracts may likewise be endorsed to include consequential losses occasioned by the hazard covered in the contract.

THE SEPARATE CONTRACT

Before considering at length the various extension endorsements, a discussion of the methods of writing perils in addition to fire as separate contracts is in order. This can be accomplished in two ways: (*a*) by use of the standard fire contract with a conversion endorsement, and (*b*) by a special contract form designed for the peril or the use of the optional perils contract, although this contract now has very limited use.

When the standard fire contract is used as a separate contract for a particular peril without fire coverage, this is accomplished by attaching a form describing the perils to be covered to a standard fire insurance contract. This is known as a conversion form. Windstorm and hail insurance may be written on the standard fire contract, and where only windstorm and hail perils are to be covered, the conversion form is attached. In some instances, as in the case of earthquake and volcanic eruption, a contract designed to insure the perils is available. In a few instances, a contract form designed to cover one of several perils, known as the "optional perils policy," is used.

Windstorm and Hail Insurance. This coverage has for its purpose the indemnification of the insured for loss or damage directly caused by windstorm of any nature. Windstorm insurance is written (*a*) by an extension of the fire contract, (*b*) by a separate windstorm contract, and (*c*) by a conversion of the fire contract to cover the weather risks without covering fire. If a separate contract is required, this last method is preferable to (*b*).

Earthquake Insurance. There are three methods of writing earthquake insurance: (*a*) by endorsing the fire contract, (*b*) by using the fire contract as a separate contract with a conversion endorsement, and (*c*) by using a contract designed for the purpose known as the "earthquake and volcanic eruption contract."[5]

---

[5] In the Pacific territory, earthquake insurance is written either by endorsing the coverage to the fire insurance contract, or by means of the earthquake assumption endorsement. This latter method extends the fire insurance contract to cover earthquake damage in the same amount as does the fire contract and is, therefore, in the true sense an extended coverage endorsement. It adds nothing to the total amount of insurance but simply spreads the insurance to include earthquake losses as well as fire losses. While the assumption endorsement is the more usual method in the Pacific territory of providing earthquake insurance, as noted, earthquake insurance is sometimes provided by attaching a conversion endorsement to the fire insurance contract. This endorsement, known as the "earthquake policy form," converts a fire insurance contract into an earthquake insurance contract. The provisions of the conversion endorsement are similar to that of the assumption endorsement. The difference lies in the fact that the assumption endorsement attaches to a fire contract providing fire insurance for the property in question, whereas the conversion endorsement simply takes a fire contract form and adapts it for use as a separate earthquake contract. See discussion of earthquake insurance at the end of this chapter.

Explosion Insurance. Explosion insurance may be provided (*a*) as a separate contract, and (*b*) as part of the extended coverage endorsement to the fire insurance contract. By far the greater part of explosion insurance is written as extended coverage. When written as a separate contract, until recently, explosion insurance was made available on a standard form designed for these purposes. This standard explosion form is now held to be obsolete.

Riot and Civil Commotion Insurance. Riot and civil commotion insurance is, in fact, an extension of explosion insurance to cover losses when there is no explosion but the damage originates as the outgrowth of a riot. The coverage is provided: (*a*) by the extended coverage endorsement, and (*b*) possibly through the use of the optional perils contract.

Vandalism and Malicious Mischief. This coverage is always written in connection with riot and civil commotion insurance. It is never written as separate insurance. It is usually written by an endorsement to the fire insurance contract with extended coverage, although it is possible to use an optional perils contract for this purpose.

A specific type of separate contract, such as the optional perils contract, will not be considered in detail here because of its limited use and because discussion of its contents would duplicate to a large extent the provisions of the various extended coverage endorsements which will be discussed at some length in this chapter.

DWELLING PROPERTY FORM (NOT FARM)—SECTION XI

An example of the usual type of extended coverage endorsement is Section XI of the Dwelling Property Form (not Farm) (see pages 186 and 187). The various sections of this form, except for Section XI were discussed in Chapter 7. Section XI will now be considered in some detail. Although the extended coverage endorsement is presented here as a part of the Dwelling Property Form, its use is not limited to dwellings and it may be added to a variety of specialized forms.

The first uniform extended coverage endorsements appeared in 1937. Through a process of evolution the endorsement has been generally broadened and extended. The endorsement, in its present form, when attached to the fire insurance contract, extends the contract to include the following perils: (*a*) windstorm; (*b*) hail; (*c*) explosion; (*d*) riot, riot attending a strike, and civil commotion; (*e*) aircraft damage; (*f*) vehicle damage; and (*g*) smoke damage.

The extended coverage endorsement does not increase the amount of insurance provided in the contract to which it is attached. The coverage is effected by a clause that substitutes the new perils to be covered

SECTION XI — EXTENDED COVERAGE ENDORSEMENT

(Perils of Windstorm and Hail [$50 Deductible Applicable], Explosion, Riot, Riot Attending a Strike, Civil Commotion, Aircraft, Vehicles and Smoke)

Effective only when rate and premium for Extended Coverage is inserted in the space provided on the first page of this policy, or endorsed hereon after the effective date of this policy.

THIS POLICY IS EXTENDED TO INSURE AGAINST DIRECT LOSS BY WINDSTORM, HAIL, EXPLOSION, RIOT, RIOT ATTENDING A STRIKE, CIVIL COMMOTION, AIRCRAFT, VEHICLES, AND SMOKE, EXCEPT AS HEREINAFTER PROVIDED.

Deductible: The sum of $50 shall be deducted from the amount of loss resulting from each windstorm or hailstorm. This deductible shall apply separately to each building or structure and separately to all personal property in the open. This deductible does not apply to contents in any building.

This Deductible Clause shall not apply to insurance covering Business Interruption, Tuition Fees, Extra Expense, Additional Living Expense, Rent or Rental Value or Leasehold Interest.

Provisions Applicable only to Windstorm and Hail: This Company shall not be liable for loss caused directly or indirectly by frost or cold weather, or ice (other than hail), snow or sleet, whether driven by wind or not.

This Company shall not be liable for loss to the interior of the building(s) or the property covered therein caused: (a) by rain, snow, sand or dust, whether driven by wind or not, unless the building(s) covered or containing the property covered shall first sustain an actual damage to roof or walls by the direct action of wind or hail and then shall be liable for loss to the interior of the building(s) or the property covered therein as may be caused by rain, snow, sand or dust entering the building(s) through openings in the roof or walls made by direct action of wind or hail; or (b) by water from sprinkler equipment or from other piping, unless such equipment or piping be damaged as a direct result of wind or hail.

Unless liability therefor is assumed in the form attached to this policy, or by endorsement hereon, this Company shall not be liable for damage to the following property: (a) grain, hay, straw or other crops outside of buildings; or (b) windmills, windpumps or their towers; or (c) crop silos (or their contents); or (d) metal smokestacks or, when outside of buildings, cloth awnings, signs, radio or television antennas including their lead-in wiring, masts or towers; or (e) lawns, trees, shrubs or plants.

Provisions Applicable Only to Explosion: Loss by explosion shall include direct loss resulting from the explosion of accumulated gases or unconsumed fuel within the firebox (or combustion chamber) of any fired vessel or within the flues or passages which conduct the gases of combustion therefrom.

This Company shall not be liable for loss by explosion of steam boilers, steam pipes, steam turbines or steam engines, if owned by, leased by or operated under the control of the Insured.

The following are not explosions within the intent or meaning of these provisions:

(a) Shock waves caused by aircraft, generally known as "sonic boom,"

(b) Electric arcing,

(c) Rupture or bursting of rotating or moving parts of machinery caused by centrifugal force or mechanical breakdown,

Nuclear Exclusion: Loss by nuclear reaction or nuclear radiation or radioactive contamination, all whether controlled or uncontrolled, or due to any act or condition incident to any of the foregoing, is not insured against by this Extended Coverage Endorsement, whether such loss be direct or indirect, proximate or remote, or be in whole or in part caused by, contributed to, or aggravated by windstorm, hail, explosion, riot, riot attending a strike, civil commotion, aircraft, vehicles or smoke; and nuclear reaction or nuclear radiation or radioactive contamination, all whether controlled or uncontrolled, is not "explosion" or "smoke."

War Risk Exclusion: This Company shall not be liable for loss caused directly or indirectly by (a) hostile or warlike action in time of peace or war, including action in hindering, combating or defending against an actual, impending or expected attack, (1) by any government or sovereign power (de jure or de facto), or by any authority maintaining or using military, naval or air forces; or (2) by military, naval or air forces; or (3) by an agent of any such government, power, authority or forces, it being understood that any discharge, explosion or use of any weapon of war employing nuclear fission or fusion shall be conclusively presumed to be such a hostile or warlike action by such government, power, authority or forces; (b) insurrection, rebellion, revolution, civil war, usurped power, or action taken by governmental authority in hindering, combating or defending against such an occurrence.

Water Exclusion: This Company shall not be liable for loss caused by, resulting from, contributed to or aggravated by any of the following—

(a) flood, surface water, waves, tidal water or tidal wave, overflow of streams or other bodies of water, or spray from any of the foregoing, all whether driven by wind or not;

(b) water which backs up through sewers or drains;

(c) water below the surface of the ground including that which exerts pressure on or flows, seeps or leaks through sidewalks, driveways, foundations, walls, basement or other floors, or through doors, windows or any other openings in such sidewalks, driveways, foundations, walls or floors;

unless loss by explosion as insured against hereunder ensues, and then this Company shall be liable for only such ensuing loss.

Other Provisions:

A claim for loss by any peril insured against by this endorsement shall not be barred because of change of occupancy, nor because of vacancy or unoccupancy.

This endorsement does not increase the amount(s) of insurance provided in this policy.

If this policy covers on two or more items, the provisions of this endorsement shall apply to each item separately.

Apportionment: This Company shall not be liable for a greater proportion of any loss less the amount of deductible, if any, from any peril or perils included in this endorsement than (1) the amount of insurance under this policy bears to the whole amount of fire insurance covering the property, or which would have covered the property except for the existence of this insurance, whether collectible or not, and whether or not such other fire insurance covers against

(d) Water hammer,
(e) Rupture or bursting of water pipes,
(f) Rupture or bursting due to expansion or swelling of the contents of any building or structure, caused by or resulting from water,
(g) Rupture, bursting or operation of pressure relief devices.

Any other explosion clause made a part of this policy is superseded by this endorsement.

Provisions Applicable Only to Riot, Riot Attending a Strike and Civil Commotion: Loss by riot, riot attending a strike or civil commotion shall include direct loss by acts of striking employees of the owner or tenant(s) of the described building(s) while occupied by said striking employees and shall also include direct loss from pillage and looting occurring during and at the immediate place of a riot, riot attending a strike or civil commotion. Unless specifically endorsed hereon, this Company shall not be liable for loss resulting from damage to or destruction of the described property due to change in temperature or humidity or interruption of operations whether or not such loss is covered by this policy as to other perils.

Provisions Applicable Only to Loss by Aircraft and Vehicles: The term "vehicles," as used in this endorsement, means vehicles running on land or tracks but not aircraft. Loss by aircraft or by vehicles shall include only direct loss resulting from actual physical contact of an aircraft or a vehicle with the property covered hereunder or with the building(s) containing the property covered hereunder, except that loss by aircraft includes direct loss by objects falling therefrom. This Company shall not be liable for loss: (a) by any vehicle owned or operated by an Insured or by any tenant of the described premises; (b) by any vehicle to fences, driveways, walks or lawns, trees, shrubs or plants; (c) to any aircraft or vehicle including contents thereof other than stocks of aircraft or vehicles in process of manufacture or for sale.

Provisions Applicable Only to Smoke: The term "smoke" as used in this endorsement means only smoke due to a sudden, unusual and faulty operation of any heating or cooking unit, only when such unit is connected to a chimney by a smoke pipe or vent pipe, and while in or on the described premises but not smoke from fireplaces or industrial apparatus.

the additional peril or perils insured hereunder, nor (2) for a greater proportion of any loss less the amount of deductible, if any, than the amount hereby insured bears to all insurance whether collectible or not, covering in any manner such loss, or which would have covered such loss except for the existence of this insurance; except if any type of insurance other than fire extended to cover additional perils or windstorm insurance applies to any loss to which this insurance also applies, or would have applied to any such loss except for the existence of this insurance, the limit of liability of each type of insurance for such loss, hereby designated as "joint loss," shall first be determined as if it were the only insurance, and this type of insurance shall be liable for no greater proportion of joint loss than the limit of its liability for such loss bears to the sum of all such limits. The liability of this Company (under this endorsement) for such joint loss shall be limited to its proportionate part of the aggregate limit of this and all other insurance of the same type. The words "joint loss," as used in the foregoing, mean that portion of the loss in excess of the highest deductible, if any, to which this endorsement and other types of insurance above referred to both apply.

Provisions Applicable Only When This Endorsement is Attached to a Policy Covering Business Interruption, Tuition Fees, Extra Expense, Additional Living Expense, Rent or Rental Value, Leasehold Interest or Other Consequential Loss: The term "direct," as applied to loss, means loss, as limited and conditioned in such policy, resulting from direct loss to described property from the peril(s) insured against; and while the business of the owner or tenant(s) of the described building(s) is interrupted by a strike at the described location, this Company shall not be liable for any loss due to interference by any person(s) with rebuilding, repairing or replacing the property damaged or destroyed or with the resumption or continuation of business.

CAUTION

WHEN THIS ENDORSEMENT IS ATTACHED TO ONE FIRE POLICY, THE INSURED SHOULD SECURE LIKE COVERAGE ON ALL FIRE POLICIES COVERING THE SAME PROPERTY.

for the word "fire" as it appears in the insuring clause of the statutory contract. The clause provides that, in the application of the provisions of the contract to the perils covered by the extended coverage contract, wherever the word "fire" appears there shall be substituted therefor the peril involved. If a loss is caused by one of the perils named in the extended cover contract, the same substitution is made for the purposes of applying the contract coverage. All of the contract provisions are applied with respect to a loss attributable to a peril covered by the extended coverage endorsement exactly as they would be applied to a fire loss.

While the extension of coverage provided by the endorsement is very broad, it contains certain limitations to the coverage. These limitations are designed primarily to exclude from cover risks with features that are unusually hazardous that should be insured only for the payment of an additional premium. In other instances, the endorsement excludes losses that are not attributable to the perils covered by the contract. It is not the intent of insurance, for example, to pay for repairs in the nature of maintenance.

Windstorm and Hail. With respect to windstorm or hailstorm losses, there is a $50 deductible required in approximately one half of the states. In most of the other states the deductible is available for optional use, although there are several areas where deductible coverage is not available as yet. The application of the deductible to other than dwelling properties is much more limited. The intent of the deductibles is to eliminate maintenance claims. In the case of a dwelling, for example, where the roof is not properly maintained, a few shingles might blow off in a storm. If the insurance covered, and the insured in every instance made claim for windstorm damage where such repairs are required, there would be an excessive cost attributable to adjustment and settlement. Moreover, the sum total of claims, each insignificant in nature, would tend to build up the cost of the insurance to everyone. In some jurisdictions full coverage is available for additional premium, but the $50 deductible is the more usual. The deductible applies to each structure separately and to personal property in the open. In some jurisdictions the deductible applies to both a building and its contents. Other provisions applicable to windstorm and hail appear in the contract in the endorsement in the following terms:

> This Company shall not be liable for loss caused directly or indirectly by frost or cold weather, or ice (other than hail), snow or sleet, whether driven by wind or not.
>
> This Company shall not be liable for loss to the interior of the building(s) or the property covered therein caused: (a) by rain, snow, sand or dust, whether driven by wind or not, unless the building(s) covered or containing the property covered shall first sustain an actual damage to

roof or walls by the direct action of wind or hail and then shall be liable for loss to the interior of the building(s) or property covered therein as may be caused by rain, snow, sand or dust entering the building(s) through openings in the roof or walls made by direct action of wind or hail; or (b) by water from sprinkler equipment or other piping, unless such equipment or piping be damaged as a direct result of wind or hail.

Unless liability therefor is assumed in the form attached to this policy or by endorsement hereon, this Company shall not be liable for damage to the following property: (a) grain, hay, straw or other crops outside of buildings; or (b) windmills, windpumps or their towers, or (c) crop silos (or their contents); or (d) metal smokestacks or, when outside of buildings, cloth awnings, signs, radio or television antennas including their lead-in wiring, masts or towers; or (e) lawns, trees, shrubs or plants.

The exclusions with reference to cold are self-explanatory. Ice and snow claims are sometimes made where weight causes the damage and not windstorm. These claims are not covered, but a loss caused by hail is covered in every instance whether there is a storm that could be characterized as a windstorm. Damage to the interior of a building or its contents is covered by loss attributable to rain, snow, sand, or dust whether driven by wind, but only if wind or hail causes actual damage to the roof or walls by direct force. In other words, wind or hail must have made an opening through which the other elements have entered to cause damage. If rain, snow, or dust should enter a building through an open window, there would be no coverage. Damage to a sprinkler system or piping caused by windstorm or hail is covered. Loss attributable to leaking water, where the damage could not be traced to wind or hail, would not be covered. Crops outside of buildings, windmills, silos, and property under construction are excluded as being particularly hazardous. The insurer reserves the right to elect whether it will insure these items and whether a premium will be charged therefor. When the extended cover endorsement is attached to a builder's risk contract, it is customary to endorse the contract waiving the requirement that the building be entirely closed and the windows and doors in place.

Explosion. Unlike the fire insurance contract that covers fire damage only in the case of an unfriendly fire, explosion damage is covered even though it may not be accidental. Many explosions are attributable to carelessness and negligence or even design. Such explosion losses are covered, but the contract extends to protect only the property described in the contract and at the location covered. Thus, an extended coverage endorsement on the dwelling of an insured would not cover explosion damage to contents. The endorsement conditions with respect to explosion follow:

Loss by explosion shall include direct loss resulting from the explosion of accumulated gases or unconsumed fuel within the firebox (or combustion chamber) of any fired vessel or within the flues or passages which conduct the gases of combustion therefrom.

This Company shall not be liable for loss by explosion of steam boilers, steam pipes, steam turbines or steam engines, if owned by, leased by or operated under the control of the insured.

The following are not explosions within the intent or meaning of these provisions:

a) Shock waves caused by aircraft, generally known as "sonic boom,"
b) Electric arcing,
c) Rupture or bursting of rotating or moving parts of machinery caused by centrifugal force or mechanical breakdown,
d) Water hammer,
e) Rupture or bursting of water pipes.

Any other explosion clause made a part of this policy is superseded by this endorsement

Explosions within the contemplation of this endorsement include those caused by dust risks in woodworking plants and flour mills, escaping gas, the explosion of pressure cookers, the explosion of inflammable liquids such as gasoline or benzine sometimes used for cleaning, and explosions attributable to the defective operation of air compressors or refrigerating units, to mention a few.

Riot and Civil Commotion. This section provides insurance coverage for riot, riot attending a strike, and civil commotion. The statutory fire contract excludes loss caused by riot but as in the case of explosion provides coverage for fire loss if fire ensues. All physical damage attributable to riot is covered by the endorsement. Fire losses attributable to civil commotion are covered by the statutory contract without the benefit of the extended coverage endorsement. The endorsement broadens the coverage to the end that it provides protection for any physical damage caused by a civil commotion. The endorsement provides this coverage in the following terms:

Loss by riot, riot attending a strike or civil commotion shall include direct loss by acts of striking employees of the owner or tenant(s) of the described building(s) while occupied by said striking employees and shall also include direct loss from pillage and looting occurring during and at the immediate place of a riot, riot attending a strike or civil commotion. Unless specifically endorsed hereon in writing this Company shall not be liable for loss resulting from damage to or destruction of the described property due to change in temperature or humidity or interruption of operations, whether or not such loss is covered by this policy as to other perils.

In order to constitute a loss attributable to riot or civil commotion, there must be (*a*) violence, (*b*) open defiance, and (*c*) the ability to make a threat. This means that an act of sabotage made in the darkness or by stealth without creating a disturbance is neither a riot nor a civil commotion. Losses due to business interruption or temperature change are excluded. Theft losses are covered if they occur at the time of the disturbance.

Aircraft and Vehicles. The provisions of the endorsement applicable to loss by aircraft and vehicles follow:

> The term "vehicles," as used in this endorsement means vehicles running on land or tracks but not aircraft. Loss by aircraft or by vehicles shall include only direct loss resulting from actual physical contact of an aircraft or a vehicle with property covered hereunder, or with the building(s) containing the property covered hereunder, except that loss by aircraft includes direct loss by objects falling therefrom. This Company shall not be liable for loss: (*a*) by any vehicle owned or operated by the Insured or by any tenant of the described premises; (*b*) by any vehicle to fences, driveways, walks or lawns, trees, shrubs, or plants; (*c*) to any aircraft or vehicle including contents thereof other than stocks of aircraft or vehicles in process of manufacture or for sale.

The insurer is not liable for losses by any vehicle owned or operated by the insured or by any tenant occupying the insured premises. This exclusion with respect to ownership does not apply to aircraft. If an automobile owned by the insured seriously damages his property, there is no loss, but if his airplane crashes and does an equal amount of damage, the loss is covered. The exclusion with respect to walks and lawns includes trees, shrubs, or plants.

Smoke. The clause reads: "The term 'smoke' as used in this endorsement means only smoke due to a sudden, unusual and faulty operation of any heating or cooking unit, only when such unit is connected to a chimney by a smoke pipe or vent pipe, and while in or on the described premises, but not smoke from fireplaces or industrial apparatus." This clause is largely self-explanatory. It provides for certain types of smoke damage but does not contemplate complete protection regardless of cause.

The standard fire contract covers smoke damage if the damage is the consequence of an unfriendly fire. With the advent of oil as a fuel, properties have been seriously damaged by smoke or smudge owing to the improper operation of a burner. If the fire does not escape beyond its original confines and the smoke or smudge is due to the faulty operation of the burner or explosion, the standard fire contract does not cover. This endorsement provides protection if the smoke damage is due to a "sudden, unusual and faulty operation of any heating or cooking unit . . . but not smoke from fireplaces or industrial apparatus."

The interpretation of the words "sudden, unusual, and faulty" is not always easy. In the clear-cut cases where the loss or damage comes unexpectedly, is without previous notice and not prepared for, and is rapid and unforeseen, there is little room for doubt. To be unusual means uncommon or rare. This means that the loss should be attributable to some occurrence not to be expected in the ordinary course of the operation of the unit. A happening attributable to a fault implies a failure. A fault is a defect or weakness, and the faulty operation of a unit would mean that the unit failed in its operation or its operations were imperfect. Smoke losses attributable to furnace explosions or the breakdown of oil burners offer no problem, and it is against losses of this type that the insurance is written.

In addition to direct loss and damage from the perils included in the endorsement, this endorsement may also be attached to contracts covering consequential loss. It is regularly used in connection with business interruption, extra expense, additional living expense, rents, leasehold interests, tuition fees, profits and commissions, or other consequential loss forms. There is a special clause in the extended coverage endorsement to adapt it for use with consequential loss covers.

The extended coverage contract is a package deal. The insured is not permitted to select coverage for certain perils and omit others. If insurance is required for one or more of the perils, this is obtainable only by a separate endorsement or by a separate contract. A separate contract is indicated where the insured desires insurance for the extended cover peril in an amount less than the face of his fire insurance. If the insured carries his building and contents insurance together with the same insurers and wishes extended coverage only, for example, on the building, it is necessary to write separate contracts with one group of contracts covering the building and another group covering contents. All of the building contracts are then endorsed with the extended coverage endorsement.

Exclusions. The extended coverage endorsement contains three specific exclusions: (1) nuclear exclusion, (2) war risk exclusion, and (3) water exclusion.

Nuclear Exclusion. This exclusion specifically states that loss by "nuclear reaction or nuclear radiation or radioactive contamination, all whether controlled or uncontrolled . . . is not insured against by this Extended Coverage Endorsement." It doesn't matter whether the loss is direct or indirect or caused by or contributed to by any of the perils included in the endorsement. It is also emphasized that "nuclear reaction or nuclear radiation or radioactive contamination, all whether controlled or uncontrolled, is not 'explosion' or 'smoke.' "

War Risk Exclusion. This exclusion relieves the insurer from liability for loss caused directly or indirectly by "hostile or warlike action" or by "insurrection, rebellion, revolution, civil war, usurped power, or action taken by governmental authority in hindering, combating or defending against such an occurrence." The clause contains a fairly lengthy description of "war perils." Notable is the reference to weapons of war, employing atomic fission or radioactive force. By agreement in the stipulations, a loss attributable to such a weapon is to be conclusively presumed as a hostile or warlike action and hence not covered by the contract.

Water Exclusion. The water exclusion states that the insurer

> shall not be liable for loss caused by, resulting from, contributed to or aggravated by any of the following: (*a*) flood, surface water, waves, tidal water or tidal wave, overflow of streams or other bodies of water, or spray from any of the foregoing, all whether driven by wind or not; (*b*) water which backs up through sewers or drains; (*c*) water below the surface of the ground including that which exerts pressure on or flows, seeps or leaks through sidewalks, driveways, foundations, walls, basement or other floors, or through doors, windows or any other openings in such sidewalks, driveways, foundations, walls or floors; unless loss by explosion as insured against hereunder ensues, and then this Company shall be liable for only such ensuing loss.

Although this exclusion is fairly common in windstorm insurance, it is often misunderstood, and the insured frequently assumes that the damage from water driven by wind is covered. To meet the needs of insureds subject to the perils of tidal wave or other water damage, an endorsement is available that includes, in addition to the extended coverage endorsement providing windstorm protection, coverage for loss or damage caused by waves or overflow of tidal waters. With the use of this endorsement, it is usual to provide $100 deductible with respect to both wind and high-water losses.

Other Provisions. This section of the extended coverage endorsement serves to clarify certain matters that relate to occupancy, amount of insurance, and items covered. Change of occupancy, vacancy, or unoccupancy do not prevent recovery under the endorsement. The amount of insurance provided is not increased by the endorsement, and if two or more items are covered, the provisions of the endorsement shall apply to each item separately.

Apportionment. The apportionment clause sets forth the rules to be followed in determining the liability of the insurer in the event there is other fire insurance covering the property or in the event there is more than one type of insurance covering the loss. Loss from any peril covered by the extended coverage endorsement must be prorated with all fire insurance covering the same property. This means, for example, that if there were two contracts, each for $20,000 covering on a building and only one endorsed for extended coverage, the insured could collect only one half of any loss attributable to an extended coverage peril. Thus, the insurer is not liable "for a greater proportion of any loss less the amount of deductible, if any, from any peril or perils included in this endorsement than the amount of insurance under this policy bears to the whole amount of fire insurance covering the property, or which would have covered the property except for the existence of this insurance, whether collectible or not, and whether or not such other fire insurance covers against the additional peril or perils insured hereunder."

The second part of the apportionment clause applies to the situation where there is more than one type of insurance covering a loss. In this situation the "limit of liability of each type of insurance for such loss, hereby designated as 'joint loss,' shall first be determined as if it were the only insurance. . . ." Each type of insurance, though, is liable for no greater proportion of the joint loss than the limit of its liability for such loss bears to the sum of all such limits. To illustrate the workings of this clause, assume a building valued at $100,000 with $40,000 insurance written with an 80 percent coinsurance clause. Assume that the contract is endorsed to cover explosion, riot, and civil commotion. Assume an optional perils contract with the same coverage in the amount of $20,000.

In the event of a $20,000 explosion loss, since the insured under the fire contract would be a 50 percent coinsurer, the total liability of the fire insurance on this loss would be $10,000. The optional perils contract, in the absence of other insurance, would be $20,000. The loss would be apportioned as follows:

Joint loss	$20,000.00
Limit of liability fire insurance	10,000.00
Limit of liability explosion insurance	20,000.00
Explosion insurance pays ⅔, or	$13,333.33
Fire insurance pays ⅓, or	6,666.67
	$20,000.00

The liability of each insurer is limited to its proportionate part of the aggregate limit of the same type of insurance. In the case just cited if there were two explosion policies for $20,000, the aggregate limit for the explosion coverage would still be $20,000, but each company would pay half of the explosion insurance liability. In this instance the apportionment would work out as follows:

Explosion Company A	$ 6,666.67
Explosion Company B	6,666.67
Fire	6,666.67
	$20,000.01

The last two lines of the clause have to do with deductibles. In the foregoing case, assuming the limit of liability of the fire insurers to be the full $20,000 but the limit of liability on the part of the explosion insurer to be $19,000 by virtue of a $1,000 deductible, the joint loss would be $19,000 instead of $20,000. The explosion insurance pays half or $9,500. The $1,000 deductible is added to the half to be paid by the fire insurance, making the liability of this insurer $10,500. In the event that two or more fire insurers cover the line, the $10,500 would be apportioned between or among them.

In brief, when the joint loss clause becomes operative in the settlement of a loss, it becomes necessary to consider each type of contract as a group. The amount of loss for which each group would be liable, had there been no other insurance, is determined. The loss is then apportioned to each group in proportion to the established limits of liability. If there is more than one insurer in a group, the total liability allocated to that group is distributed among the insurers in proportion to the amount of insurance written by each insurer. This is, of course, the usual pro rata distribution of liability.

MODIFICATIONS OF THE DWELLING PROPERTY FORM

The appeal of the extended coverage endorsement has prompted the development of special forms for dwellings that insure these and additional perils. There are a number of these forms. Two of them, the Dwelling Building(s) and Contents Broad Form and the Dwelling Building(s) Special Form are widely used and will be considered here.

Dwelling Building(s) and Contents Broad Form. This form provides insurance coverage for 19 separate perils.[6] In addition to a specific listing of perils, there are sections dealing with exclusions, deductibles, definitions, extensions of coverage, and other provisions.

The perils insured against are fire and lightning; windstorm; hail; explosion; sudden and accidental tearing asunder, cracking, burning or bulging (not by wear and tear, deterioration, or rust) of a steam or hot water heating system; vandalism and malicious mischief; burglars; riot, riot attending a strike, and civil commotion; aircraft; vehicles; sudden and accidental damage from smoke; falling objects; weight of ice, snow, or sleet; collapse (not settling, cracking, shrinkage, bulging, or expansion) of building(s) or any part thereof; accidental discharge, leakage or overflow of water or steam; sudden and accidental tearing asunder, cracking, burning, or bulging (not by wear and tear, deterioration, or rust) of appliances for heating water for domestic consumption; breakage of glass; freezing of plumbing, heating, and air conditioning systems and domestic appliances; sudden and accidental injury from artificially generated electrical currents to electrical appliances, devices, fixtures, and wiring. Thirteen of these perils are subject to deductibles and all of them are subject to one or more specific exclusions including the war risk exclusion clause, the nuclear clause, and nuclear exclusion.

The extent to which the deductibles apply varies. In the case of windstorm or hailstorm the $50 deductible applies to each windstorm or hailstorm and separately to "each building or structure and

---

[6] This is the coverage provided by Form No. 49D (January, 1964).

separately to all personal property in the open." The deductible that applies to vandalism and malicious mischief and buraglars is effective only for seasonal dwelling property. Additional details in regard to deductibles associated with other perils may be obtained by a careful reading of the form. Rental value and additional living expense are not subject to deductibles. It is fairly common to eliminate deductibles from these forms by the use of an appropriate rider (or riders). One such rider reads as follows: "In consideration of the rate and premium for which this policy is written, the $50.00 deductible Provision forming a part of Form No. 490 attached to this policy and applicable to Perils 12 to 19 inclusive is hereby voided and of no effect as to Perils 12 to 18 inclusive, but remains in effect as to Peril 19."

The list of exclusions contains some items that are applicable to all of the perils and some that pertain to particular situations. In general the contract does not insure against loss caused by war; nuclear reaction; local or state ordinances regarding construction, repair, or demolition; earthquake and other earth movements; flood, tidal waves, water backing up through sewers or drains, or underground water that may seep through foundations, walls, or similar structures. In the event of earthquake or water damage, if fire or explosion ensues, the insurer is liable for the damage caused by fire or explosion but not for the earthquake or water damage. An example of an exclusion to a specific peril is provided by the provision in regard to vehicles. Damage to "driveways, walks, lawns, trees, shrubs or plants caused by any vehicle owned or operated by an insured or any tenant of the described premises" is not covered. There are other exclusions depending on the nature of the peril, but they do not serve to limit severely the protection provided by the contract.

After listing perils and exclusions the form contains a section which provides definitions of dwelling; private structures; contents; rental value; additional living expense; and trees, shrubs, or plants. These definitions are similar to those found in the Dwelling Property Form that was discussed in the last chapter. Following the definitions is a section providing for extension of coverage to trees, shrubs, plants, lawns, debris removal, off premises contents, and similar items. These extensions are similar to those found in the basic dwelling form except for replacement cost coverage. This coverage provides the following benefits:

This extension of coverage shall be applicable only to a building structure covered hereunder, but excluding carpeting, cloth awnings, domestic appliances and outdoor equipment, all whether permanently attached to the building or not:[7]

---

[7] In most middlewestern states roof surfacing is now excluded from replacement cost coverage.

1. If at the time of loss the whole amount of insurance applicable to said building structure for the peril causing the loss is 80% or more of the full replacement cost of such building structure, the coverage of this policy applicable to such building structure is extended to include the full cost of repair or replacement (without deduction for depreciation).
2. If at the time of loss the whole amount of insurance applicable to said building structure for the peril causing the loss is less than 80 per cent of the full replacement cost of such building structure, this Company's liability for loss under this policy shall not exceed the larger of the following amounts (*a*) or (*b*).
   a) The actual cash value of that part of the building structure damaged or destroyed.
   b) That proportion of the full cost of repair or replacement (without) deduction for depreciation of that part of the building structure damaged or destroyed, which the whole amount of insurance applicable to said building structure for the peril causing the loss bears to 80% of the full replacement cost of such building structure.
3. This Company's liability for loss under this policy including this extension of coverage shall not exceed the smallest of the following amounts (*a*), (*b*), or (*c*).
   a) The amount of this policy applicable to the damaged or destroyed building structure.
   b) The replacement cost of the building structure or any part thereof identical with such building structure on the same premises and intended for the same occupancy and use.
   c) The amount actually and necessarily expended in repairing or replacing said building structure or any part thereof intended for the same occupancy and use.

   When the full cost of repair or replacement is more than $1,000 or more than 5% of the whole amount of insurance applicable to said building structure for the peril causing the loss, this Company shall not be liable for any loss under paragraph (1) or subparagraph (*b*) of paragraph (2) of this extension of coverage unless and until actual repair or replacement is completed.
4. In determining if the whole amount of insurance applicable to said building structure is 80 percent or more of the full replacement cost of such building structure, the cost of excavations, underground flues and pipes, underground wiring and drains, and brick, stone and concrete foundations, piers and other supports which are below the under surface of the lowest basement floor, or where there is no basement, which are below the surface of the ground inside the foundation walls, shall be disregarded.
5. The Insured may elect to disregard this extension of coverage in making claim hereunder, but such election shall not prejudice the Insured's right to make further claim within 180 days after loss for any additional liability brought about by this extension of coverage.

The extensions of coverage listed on page 197 that are provided in this form are optional and if elected, the insurer is not liable for more than it would have been liable for if all insurance contracts covering the property had provided the same optional provisions and if the insured had made the same election under each.

The final section of this form contains a number of miscellaneous provisions such as the subrogation clause, liberalization clause, pro rata clause, apportionment clause, and similar items. Space is left for appending the standard mortgage clause. These clauses have been described elsewhere in this text.[8]

Dwelling Building(s) Special Form. This form provides all risk protection for items specifically described in the contract for which a definite amount is listed. The provisions of the contract apply to each separately listed item and do not apply to seasonal dwellings unless the dwelling is so described. The amount of the contract is not reduced by loss.

The "special form" follows much the same pattern as the "broad form" and many of the provisions in the two forms are identical. The principal difference is that the special form extends coverage "to insure against all risks of direct physical loss, except as hereinafter provided, subject to the provisions and stipulations in this form and subject to the provisions in the policy to which this form is attached including endorsements thereon" while the broad form extends coverage on a named peril basis.

The insuring clause in the special form is subject to a fairly long list of exclusions. In addition to the war risk exclusion clause, the nuclear clause, and the nuclear exclusion, there are nine specific exclusions. These exclusions are similar to those found in the Broad Form and provide that the contract does not insure against loss caused by wear and tear; earthquake (unless loss by fire or explosion ensues and then liability is only for the ensuing loss); flood (and several other types of loss from water); enforcement of local or state ordinances regarding construction; theft (if property lost is not an integral part of dwelling or if loss is from a building in process of construction); vandalism and malicious mischief, if the dwelling has been vacant for more than 30 days; and loss to certain types of property by freezing and thawing and by hail, ice, and snow. Some of the exclusions are modified by the expression "unless loss from a peril not excluded in this policy ensues." In such event the insurer is liable for the ensuing loss.

Provision is made for a deductible although loss from certain perils is not subject to the deductible clause and in particular rental value and additional living expense are not subject to deductibles.

The sections of the special form that provide for definitions, extensions of coverage, and other provisions are virtually identical with the

[8] See, for example, pages 193–94.

broad form. The major difference is that the special form does not provide a definition for contents and extensions of coverage relating to contents are not provided.

Other "All Risk" Forms. Other "all risk" coverages are now available in addition to the Dwelling Building(s) Special Form, including the Special Extended Coverage Endorsement, Office Contents Special Form, and Commercial Property Coverage Form. These forms are written on a nonnamed peril basis and provide insurance against all risks of direct physical loss subject to various limitations and exclusions (see Appendixes B to E).

Special Extended Coverage Endorsement. The Special Extended Coverage Endorsement when added to the standard fire insurance contract extends the contract to "insure against all other risks of direct physical loss . . . ." In a typical form a deductible of $100 applies to any peril except windstorm, hailstorm, fire, lightning, aircraft, vehicles, smoke, explosion, riot, or civil commotion. There are 20 exclusions, some of which exclude particular perils such as flood, and others which exclude loss to certain types of property. Examples are electrical appliances, lawns, trees, and shrubs. An apportionment clause is included on the form.

Office Contents Special Form. The Office Contents Special Form provides "all risk" coverage for "business personal property of the insured usual to the office occupancy of the insured. . . ." There are a number of limitations and exclusions as well as extensions of coverage. The form is divided into nine parts including the insuring agreement, property covered, limitations, extensions, exclusions, coinsurance, deductible, valuation, and special agreements. No effort will be made to describe the provisions of each contract. These provisions are stated in Appendix C.

Commercial Property Coverage Forms. The Commercial Property Coverage Forms are issued on a reporting and nonreporting basis. The property covered includes "the personal property usual to the conduct of the Insured's business, consisting principally of . . . the property of the insured, or similar property of others held by the Insured for which the Insured is liable except as provided elsewhere in this policy" and tenants improvements and betterments not legally subject to removal by the insured. As with the other forms there are numerous limitations, exclusions, and conditions.

OTHER ENDORSEMENTS TO THE FIRE INSURANCE CONTRACT

Other perils not previously considered, or considered only briefly, may be provided for by appropriate endorsement (or in some cases separate contracts) of the fire insurance contract. Chief among these perils are earthquake, tidal wave and high water, sonic boom, and radioactive contamination.

Earthquake Insurance. Earthquake insurance on the Pacific Coast[9] provides for a deduction of 5 percent of the value of the property, and in some cases minimum deductibles as high as 15 percent are prescribed. The insured may elect to have his contract written with deductibles higher than the prescribed minimum in which case a reduction in rate is provided. The earthquake endorsement provides for the same coinsurance or average requirements as are set forth in the fire contract; in any case, with the exception of dwellings, the coverage must be equal to 70 percent of the value of the property. No average clause is mandatory in the case of dwellings, but if a clause is used requiring insurance to value of 33 1/3 percent or more, a reduction in rate is provided. In many fire contracts particularly if written with a coinsurance clause, foundations, excavations, and other parts of the building presumably not subject to serious fire damage are excluded from the coverage. Since foundations and other parts in or under the ground may be damaged by earthquake, earthquake insurance includes these items within the coverage. With respect to the deductible, it is important to recognize this fact. The deductible is computed upon a cash value of the property, including foundations and other items that may be excluded from the fire coverage.

If earthquake insurance is provided by endorsement, the clauses are so written that all contracts contribute on the basis of the total amount of the fire insurance. Thus, if there is $100,000 insurance on a given property and only $50,000 is endorsed with earthquake coverage, the $50,000 insurance so endorsed would contribute to one half of any loss. In the case of a $10,000 loss, even with $50,000 insurance endorsed with earthquake coverage, the collectible loss would be only $5,000. Therefore, to obtain full contribution, it is essential that every fire contract covering the risk be concurrently endorsed with earthquake coverage.

Earthquake coverage for dwelling properties is available in many states by use of an endorsement to the fire insurance contract. The content of the endorsements varies somewhat in different parts of the United States. The endorsement used in the Middle West is shown in Appendix A.

Coastal Extended Coverage Endorsement. Windstorm insurance invariably excludes damage caused by tidal wave, high water, or overflow. This exclusion is to be found in the extended coverage endorsement as well as in the separate contracts. Shoreline properties have suffered heavy losses when, during a windstorm, the surf and heavy waves wash inland leaving a train of destruction in their wake.

---

[9] The Pacific territory embraces the states of Arizona, California, Idaho, Montana, Nevada, Oregon, Utah, and Washington.

With respect to the windstorm coverage, there was considerable misunderstanding. Even in the face of the aforementioned exclusion, it was felt that if the water was driven by a windstorm, the loss was properly covered either by the windstorm insurance or the extended cover endorsement.

To meet the needs of insureds subject to the perils of tidal wave or other water damage, an endorsement is available which includes, in addition to the extended cover endorsement providing windstorm protection, coverage for loss or damage caused by waves or overflow of tidal waters. The endorsement is identical with Extended Coverage Endorsement No. 4, except that in addition to the perils covered by that endorsement there is provided also protection against loss by waves or overflow. This endorsement, sometimes termed "wave-wash insurance," definitely brings wave damage within the scope of the fire insurance contract endorsed to cover extended coverage perils. With the contract so endorsed, both windstorm and wave damage are covered in the same contract, and there is no necessity for establishing a line of demarcation between the damage caused by wind and the damage caused by water. With the use of the wave-wash endorsement, it is usual to provide a $100 deductible with respect to both wind and high water losses.

Sonic Boom. An endorsement is available to provide insurance against "direct loss caused by sonic shock waves generated by aircraft. The endorsement carries a $500 deductible, which applied "separately to each building or structure and separately to personal property."

Radioactive Contamination. Contamination assumption endorsements may be written on a limited coverage basis or broad basis. They are intended to provide coverage against direct loss by sudden and accidental radioactive contamination. These are given in Appendix F.

FOR DISCUSSION

1. Indicate as many methods as you know to cover the explosion hazard.
2. B installs an oil burner in the heating boiler of his residence. He is told that sometimes a slight explosion in the firebox will blow the door of the heater open, and if smoke thereafter escapes and damages the property, the fire insurance contract does not cover. B is advised to provide an inherent explosion endorsement to obtain this protection. Is this good advice?
3. X, who is later determined to be insane, feels that he has a divine mission to wreck a manufacturing plant by throwing foreign substances into delicate machinery. He causes a breakdown in the plant, with heavy resulting damage. Does the extended coverage endorsement cover, and if not, is the risk insurable?
4. Early in December, 1908, there was a strike at the Stearns Coal Company. Warrants were issued for the arrest of certain employees,

and on December 24 a deputy marshal, accompanied by a number of persons to assist him, undertook to make the arrest. On the morning of December 25, three of the men for whom they were searching were reported to be in a hotel building. One of the deputy marshals was shot and killed by one of the three men inside the building. Shooting continued, and the deputy marshal announced that unless the men surrendered he would burn the building. He finally made a fagot, soaked it in oil, and turned it over to a member of his posse who, in turn, under his command set fire to the building and burned it down. The insurance company claimed it was not liable for the loss. What is your opinion?

5. The riot and civil commotion contract covers fires caused by a riot, but the vandalism and malicious mischief endorsement excludes liability for such fires. Explain the logic of the exclusion.
6. If a bomb is dropped accidentally by an army airplane during peacetime maneuvers and explodes, causing damage to property, what type of insurance should the owner have to secure adequate protection?
7. In the event of an accidental crash of an army airplane during peacetime maneuvers, what contract will reimburse the owner of the damaged property?
8. The secret agent of a foreign government with which this government is not at war places a bomb in a munitions factory. The bomb explodes, causing a huge fire which spreads to a neighboring property. B owns a neighboring factory which is completely destroyed. He carries neither riot and civil commotion, explosion, extended cover, nor vandalism insurance. Has he any recourse under his standard fire contract?
9. B does not wish to carry the full extended cover endorsement but, because he has an oil burner, feels that he should have a smoke damage endorsement. Just exactly what extension of the coverage does a smoke damage endorsement provide?
10. Is vandalism and malicious mischief coverage provided under the extended coverage endorsement?
11. Certain types of business, such as newspapers, milk distributors, and laundries often continue to carry on business as nearly normal as possible in order to retain their customers even in the face of a fire or other loss. To carry on business under the adverse circumstances that follow a fire may mean a considerable loss to the owner of the business or, at least, a substantial reduction in his profits. What form of insurance does he need to protect him against this type of loss? Discuss.
12. B has ten contracts covering on his dwelling—each for $1,000. He feels that any damage that may develop under the items covered in the extended cover contract will not exceed $1,000, so he decides that it would be unsound to pay the premium for endorsing all of his contracts. He develops a windstorm loss that figures exactly $1,000 and determines himself fortunate that the contract is equal to the loss.

You are called upon to advise him in the circumstances. Explain the bad news, and tell him why his coverage is inadequate.

13. Mr. and Mrs. X had a special savings account for a long-planned vacation. On the given day they were standing near the main line in the railroad station of the small community in which they lived. Their baggage had been packed, with the exception of two suitcases which they planned to carry with them. While they were waiting a through-express train roared by. The vacuum created by the passing cars sucked one of the suitcases under the train, and the suitcase and its contents were ground to shreds about the size of confetti. The unfortunate couple had neglected to purchase any form of insurance covering their trip, and they did not have any of the marine floaters, such as personal property, personal effects, or tourist baggage. What inquiry would you make with respect to their other insurance with a view to helping them?
14. In your opinion would the acts of sit-down strikers fit the legal definition of a riot?
15. In certain parts of Florida, the extended cover contracts contain a clause excluding windstorm and hail damage to exterior paint and water proofing. There is also a 2 percent hail deductible clause. Assume the wall of a building is blown down. It is expected that the insurer will pay the cost of replacement. What is the insurer's position with respect to paint in a loss such as this?
16. During the "big wind" of 1950 in settling windstorm losses, the following line of reasoning was frequently presented to the insurance companies: (*a*) a radio or television set is part of the contents of the building, and (*b*) it follows, therefore, that the television antenna which is a part of the television set is, in fact, a part of the contents of the building. Following this line of reasoning, full coverage was afforded on the television antenna damaged by the windstorm. This was so because the deductible in the extended coverage endorsement applied to buildings and personal property in the open and not to contents in any building. Do you believe the reasoning in this instance to be sound and do you believe a television antenna should not be subject to the $50 deductible because it is to be construed as contents of the building?
17. One of the early all risk dwelling forms contained this exclusion: "The insurance herein provided does not cover loss caused by mechanical breakdown." This clause, of course, was designed to eliminate maintenance claims such as those necessary to repair a refrigerator, electric stove, or other mechanical equipment in a dwelling house. The clause was considered defective, however, and extremely dangerous. Explain why.
18. What reason can you advance for increasing the deductible for a windstorm policy?
19. Under the extended coverage endorsement, protection is provided for smoke damage caused by a friendly fire but only under certain circumstances. What type of smoke damage is not covered?

CHAPTER · 9

Allied Fire Lines

There are a number of risks insured by property and liability insurers that pay indemnity without regard to direct loss or damage to physical property. These contracts are known as consequential loss coverages, and they indemnify the insured for such losses as grow out of the interruption of business and the failure of a service such as heat or refrigeration. There are, as well, a number of risks that involve neither extensions of the standard fire contract nor the insurance of consequential hazards. They are so closely associated with the fire business that inclusion of the lines in the general field of fire insurance was probably inevitable. For example, the writing of sprinkler leakage insurance is a natural accompaniment of fire insurance. Water damage insurance has no immediate relationship with fire coverage but, having included the water damage from sprinkler leakage within the scope of the fire business, it was a logical step to the writing of a straight water damage contract. The sprinkler leakage contract, rain insurance contracts, and similar contracts fall within the category of allied lines.

Two types of consequential loss coverage are written: (*a*) time element contracts, and (*b*) contracts covering losses where time is not a factor. Time element contracts protect the insured for loss growing out of the loss of use of property. In contrast there are certain types of losses where the measurement of loss does not involve a time element. Collateral fire lines and consequential loss coverages that do not involve a time element will be considered in this chapter. Time element coverages associated with the interruption of business will be considered in Chapter 10.

COLLATERAL FIRE LINES

The collateral fire lines here considered are: sprinkler leakage, water damage, tenant's improvements and betterments, deferred payment, yard improvements, coinsurance deficiency, builder's automatic and open binder, contract of supply, fire apparatus, and standing timber.

Sprinkler Leakage Insurance. The installation of automatic sprinkler systems as a protective device serves to reduce the fire hazard but, at the same time, introduces a new hazard growing out of the precipitation of water from the system itself. The sprinkler system is designed as an automatic watchman, and the fire hazard against which it is placed on guard sets the system in operation. A sprinkler system provides for the piping of water throughout the building it is designed to protect, and at given intervals "heads" are provided which open if the temperature rises to a predetermined point. If a fire occurs in the vicinity of a sprinkler head, the head is opened and water is released on the fire. Water damage caused by the opening of a sprinkler head to extinguish an accidental and unfriendly fire is covered under the direct-loss fire contract. Water damage caused by leakage of the sprinkler system or by collapse of a tank used in connection therewith is not covered under the fire contract.

Sprinkler leakage insurance covers the hazard thus created. It provides indemnity for all direct loss or damage to property caused by accidental discharge or by leakage of any part of the system or by the collapse or precipitation of a sprinkler tank or any part thereof. The coverage is provided, in most areas, by a special form to be attached to a fire contract with or without fire insurance.

Sprinkler Leakage Coverage. The sprinkler coverage may be written to cover buildings, their contents, stock only, furniture and fixtures, machinery, property and employees, and improvements and betterments. Manufacturing, mercantile, residential, or other occupancies are insurable. The contract insures against "all direct loss by Sprinkler Leakage subject to the provisions and stipulations in the policy, except as otherwise provided in this endorsement." By "sprinkler leakage" is meant "leakage or discharge of water or other substances from within any 'Automatic Sprinkler System' or direct loss caused by collapse or fall of tank(s) forming a part of such system." Nonautomatic sprinklers, hydrants, standpipes, and base outlets, if supplied from an automatic sprinkler system, are included in the definition of automatic sprinkler system. Since the contract does not cover leakage from nonautomatic systems independent of a sprinkler system, insurance of loss from this source is covered by a water damage contract. Damage caused by the collapse or fall of tanks, or the component parts or supports thereof is a very important coverage, since water tanks located on the roof of manufacturing plants have been known to cause substantial loss when the supports collapsed.

The sprinkler leakage contract does not cover damage caused directly or indirectly by seepage or leakage of water through building walls, foundations, sidewalks, or sidewalk lights unless the loss is caused specifically by sprinkler leakage. Nor does the contract cover for loss caused by condensation of deposits on the sprinkler leakage system itself. Loss by flows, inundation, or backing up of sewers or drains, or by the influx of tide water or water from any source other than from the sprinkler system is excluded, as well as loss caused by hazards for which special insurance forms are provided and specifically mentioned in the form, including hazards of fire, lightning, cyclone, windstorm, earthquake, explosion, including explosion or rupture of steam boilers and flywheels, blasting, invasion, insurrection, riot, civil war, and commotion. Likewise excluded are losses occasioned by usurped power or by order of any civil authority. Coverage is limited on "books of account, drawings, card index systems, and other records (except film, recording tape or wire), for not exceeding cost of blank books, blank cards and other materials plus cost of labor for actually transcribing or copying such records" and "on film, recording tape or wire (except stock) for not exceeding the cost of unexposed film or blank tape or wire." Loss by sprinkler leakage or by collapse or the fall of a tank caused directly or indirectly by fire, lightning, windstorm, earthquake, blasting, explosion, rupture of a steam boiler, flywheel explosion, riot, civil commotion, or any water damage except from within the automatic sprinkler system are all excluded. These last mentioned exclusions are all insurable under other forms and to include them in the sprinkler leakage contract would constitute duplication.

Not only may sprinkler leakage insurance be written to cover direct damage but it may also cover all of the consequential losses for which fire insurance is written.

Sprinkler Leakage Liability. The installation of a sprinkler system in a building may, because of an accident to the system, result in serious loss or damage to the property of others, and if any element of negligence can be shown on the part of the owner of the system, he may be held legally liable for the damage. One of the most frequent causes of sprinkler leakage loss is freezing. This may be the result of failure of the heating system, or it may be the outgrowth of negligence on the part of the person entrusted with the operation of the plant. A window may be carelessly left open or accidentally broken. An unexpected change in temperature may find the building inadequately heated. There are numerous other causes of accident which may introduce the element of liability. It may be contended that the system has not been properly maintained, that parts are faulty, or that the construction, particularly of parts bearing great weights, such as the support of tanks, was unsafe. If the element of negligence can be shown by a third party having suffered a loss because of sprinkler leakage, the property owner having the sprinkler system is faced with a liability claim.

Protection against sprinkler leakage liability imposed by law may be obtained by adding an appropriate endorsement to a fire insurance contract (with or without fire insurance). The insurer agrees "to pay on behalf of the Insured all sums which the Insured shall become legally obligated to pay as damages because of injury to or destruction of property owned by others, including the loss of use thereof (except property in the portion of a building occupied by the Insured) caused by "Sprinkler Leakage," and arising out of the ownership, maintenance or use of the described premises, subject to the provisions herein." Defense, settlement, and supplementary payments are provided and various conditions are placed in the endorsement. Liability assumed by the insured is not covered, and unless there is some agreement to the contrary, the insurer is not liable while the insured building is vacant or unoccupied.

Water Damage Insurance. The sprinkler leakage contract excludes liability for water damage losses except for water leaking from inside the sprinkler system. To provide complete water damage insurance, the water damage contract is essential. The contract covers direct loss or damage caused by the accidental discharge, leakage, or overflow of water or steam from plumbing systems, tanks, heating systems, elevator tanks and cylinders, standpipes for fire hose, industrial and domestic appliances, and refrigerating systems and air-conditioning systems. The contract also covers loss or damage caused by rain or snow admitted directly to the interior of the building through defective roofs, leaders, or downspouts, or by open or defective windows, show windows, transoms, ventilators, or skylights.

The coverage is fairly comprehensive. Except in special situations, the contract does not cover seepage, leakage, or influx of water through building walls, foundations, lowest basement floors, and sidewalks, nor does it cover flood, surface water, and similar types of damage. Gases, fumes, or vapors other than steam are not covered; nor are losses attributable to fire, lightning, windstorm, earthquake, and explosion. Such losses as fire and related perils are expected to be covered by the contracts written for that purpose. Theft losses are not covered, and losses due to failure of the insured to use all reasonable means to protect property after damage are excluded. Unless specifically covered, leakage from underground mains or leakage of refrigerants is not insured. There is no coverage to any part of a sprinkler system, since this is covered by the sprinkler leakage contract. Direct damage caused by the water leakage is covered, but there is no coverage for damage to the system, tank, or other source of the water damage loss.

There are three additional coverages available for the payment of an additional premium. These are coverage for (*a*) leakage from street water supply mains or hydrants, (*b*) leakage of refrigerants, and (*c*) liability imposed by law. The contract contains clauses providing coverage for the first of these two items on an optional basis. Protection is provided if a premium is inserted in the blank clause. Liability imposed by law may be covered by adding a "water damage liability imposed by law form" to the water damage contract. (In the Middle West this is form W.D. 602, Edition 1963. See Appendix I.)

The underground water supply mains and fire hydrants clause extends the insurance afforded by the contracts to include the hazard of accidental discharge or leakage of water from underground water supply mains and fire hydrants. The protection of the clause does not extend, however, to branch piping installed to supply a sprinkler system. Such a branch would be part of the sprinkler system and covered by that contract. With respect to supply mains and fire hydrants, the contract exclusion of loss or damage by seepage or leakage through building walls and the like does not apply.

The refrigerant leakage clause extends the insurance to include the hazard of accidental discharge or leakage of a chemical refrigerant from any refrigerating or air-conditioning system. Leakage or discharge of water from such systems is covered in any case. With respect to refrigerant leakage, the exclusion of loss or damage by gases, fumes, or vapors does not apply.

Descriptions of coverage for nonliability water damage situations are given in a form to be attached to the water damage contract. This form provides definitions, as well as a statement on limitations on coverage and other provisions.

Water Damage Liability Forms. The extent of the protection of the property of others afforded under the standard fire property damage form is identical to that provided by the sprinkler leakage property damage contract. Legal liability of the insured for property similar to his own held in trust or on commission in storage is covered with a contents item.

The form providing for liability imposed by law protects the insured for liability obligations imposed by law for loss of or damage to property of others caused by water damage. As in the case of the sprinkler leakage, contract liability for loss or damage to property in the portion of the building occupied by the insured is excluded. While the loss must originate as the result of ownership or occupancy of premises described in the contract, liability is not limited to property damaged on these premises. For example, if a supply tank on the roof of the insured collapses through negligence in maintaining supports and a neighboring building is damaged, the contract covers the liability.

Liability assumed by contract must be insured as a coverage in addition to the contract providing protection for liability imposed by law. Again, this coverage follows the pattern of the sprinkler leakage form. It must be recalled that in a situation where a lessee assumes responsibility under a lease for damage to the premises in which he is a tenant, only a contract covering assumed liability will afford him protection for a water damage loss.

Tenant's Improvements and Betterments. It is quite customary for a tenant planning a business establishment to lease real estate in a condition quite unsuitable to his needs. After the lease has been obtained upon suitable terms, the property may be partly or entirely renovated and reconstructed, involving substantial expenditure of money. To have an insurable interest in improvements or betterments, it is not necessary that the tenant have a written lease nor is it necessary that the improvements be installed during the term of the lease in force at the time of the loss. To constitute tenant's improvements or betterments, it is required that they be installed at the expense of the tenant who is the insured and that after installation the tenant has no legal right to remove them.

Insurable tenant's improvements are of a nature that make them a part of the building and, hence, are absorbed into the realty. In such an instance, they cease to be the property of the lessee and instead are the property of the owner of the building. Nevertheless, they represent a substantial outlay on the part of the tenant, and the outlay is made in contemplation of their use over the period of his tenancy. They are within his control and available for his use as long as the rental agreement remains effective, and the loss of their use would represent a substantial loss indeed. It is this use interest in the improvements that the tenant's improvements and betterments contract covers.

Nature of Improvements and Betterments Coverage. It is not always possible to work out an equitable or satisfactory agreement with the owner of the real estate in which a business is located with respect to loss of or damage to improvements and betterments. Insurance is now written frequently as an endorsement to the fire insurance contract to include improvements and betterments in the contents item of the fire insurance coverage. This permits recovery by the tenant entirely independent and apart from recovery by the owner of the real estate. Improvements and betterments provide that in the event improvements and betterments are damaged or destroyed during the contract term by the perils insured against, liability of the insurer shall be determined as follows:

a) If repaired or replaced at the expense of the Insured within a reasonable time after such loss, the actual cash value of the damaged or destroyed Improvements and Betterments.

b) If not repaired or replaced within a reasonable time after such loss, that proportion of the original cost of the damaged or destroyed

Improvements and Betterments which the unexpired term of the lease at the time of loss bears to the period(s) from the date(s) such Improvements and Betterments were made to the expiration date of the lease.

c) If repaired or replaced at the expense of others for the use of the Insured, there shall be no liability hereunder.

d) If cloth awnings, signs and metal smokestacks, which qualify as Improvements and Betterments, are damaged or destroyed by windstorm or hail, there shall be no liability therefor unless the 80% or higher Coinsurance Clause applies.

e) If radio and television equipment on the outside of the building is damaged or destroyed by windstorm or hail, there shall be no liability therefor.

There is coverage under this form for two situations: (*a*) where the landlord refuses to restore but the lease is not canceled, and (*b*) where the lease is canceled. Awnings, signs, and metal smokestacks are not covered unless there is 80 percent coinsurance, if there is damage by windstorm or hail. These items are particularly susceptible to damage, and a small contract written flat on betterments could easily absorb several times the premium with a small loss affecting them. With respect to radio and television equipment, because of their nature, it is expected that where coverage is desired they will be separately insured. Inland marine contracts are available for the coverage.

Landlord Refuses to Restore. If the landlord in rebuilding the damaged premises restores the improvements at his own expense, the tenant has suffered no loss. The landlord secures title to the improvements once they become part of the real estate, and it is entirely in order for him to insure them. He is required to give consideration to their value if his insurance is written with a coinsurance clause. If the landlord restores the improvements without cost to the tenant, then there is no liability on the part of the tenant's improvements and betterments contract. If the landlord refuses to replace the betterments, whether he collects insurance for them, and the tenant replaces them at his expense, then his contract covers. Settlement is made on an actual cash value basis of the damaged improvements or betterments.

Where the Lease is Canceled. There are two situations with respect to improvements and betterments where the lease is canceled under a fire clause. The improvements and betterments may be damaged or destroyed, or they may be uninjured or only partly injured. If the premises are sufficiently damaged to warrant cancellation of the lease, then from the standpoint of the insured the betterments are a total loss. If the lease is canceled, it follows that the betterments can not be repaired or replaced within a reasonable time after the loss. In these circumstances, settlement is made by determining how much longer the lease has to run from the time of the loss. The loss is settled then by paying the insured pro rata for the unexpired term of the lease based on the original cost of the improvements. In contrast to the situation where the improvements and betterments are replaced at the expense of the tenant and adjustment made on an actual cash value basis, when the lease is canceled, original cost is the basis of adjustment. No consideration is given to either depreciation or increased costs. The pro rata cost of the improvements determined by the unexpired term of the lease is the sole criterion.

Deferred Payment Insurance. Many types of business have large amounts of merchandise in which they have an interest located in widely different sections of a territory. These are items that have been sold on a partial payment basis. In this category are washing machines, radios, vacuum cleaners, refrigerators, pianos, fur coats, and many other different types of merchandise. Since regular payments are a part of the sales agreement, the interest of the seller in each item of merchandise differs from month to month. The problem of specifically insuring the interest at the various locations is complicated and cumbersome. To provide adequate coverage, a form has been devised that insures merchants who sell goods on a partial payment plan against loss of their interest in the goods while in the hands of customers. In addition to fire, the usual allied fire coverages, such as windstorm, earthquake, and explosion, are written.

The contract is written under three forms: (*a*) dual- or multiple-interest form, (*b*) the unpaid-balance form, and (*c*) the single-interest form. The first two forms cover the interest of the seller and the purchaser. The third form covers only the interest of the seller.

Dual- or Multiple-Interest Form. This form covers the interest of the seller and the purchaser for the actual value of the merchandise until it is paid for. If the transaction is financial, the interest of the finance company is covered. Certificates of insurance are available and may be supplied by the insured to the purchaser in connection with the installment sales transaction.

Unpaid-Balance Form. This form, like the foregoing form, covers both the interest of the seller, or, as the case may be, the finance company, and the purchaser. It covers only for the unpaid balance due the merchant or the finance company at the time of the loss. It may be written to exclude unpaid balances that are past due. When so written it is usual to provide that the portion of unpaid balances 120 days past due are not covered.

Single-Interest Form. The form is written to cover only the interest of the seller or the finance company. As in the case of the unpaid-balance form, the insurer is liable only for the amount of the balance due at the time of the loss. It is usually written to exclude liability for unpaid balances more than 120 days past due. The form provides no protection for the purchaser. It is intended to reimburse the insured only in the event he is unable to collect a balance due him because of the loss of the item sold. The insured is required to make every reasonable effort to collect the account or repossess the damaged merchandise before the insurer is liable. The insured is not required to bring suit.

Deferred payment insurance is what is known as "excess" coverage. Thus, if a purchaser of the article has, himself, placed specific insurance, the deferred payment contract will not cover until the amount of the specific insurance has been exhausted. Deferred payment contracts do not cover failure of the merchant to secure payments as set forth in the contract. Nor do they cover against any losses other than those growing out of the perils specifically set forth in the agreement.[1]

Yard Improvements Insurance. Unless specifically insured or included by endorsement in the fire, windstorm, or other hazard contract, contracts on buildings do not include damage to trees, hedges, shrubs, plants, fences, pergolas, arbors, ornamental steps, bridges, bird baths, seats, benches, or permanent yard betterments of any sort. Special coverage is available to indemnify the insured in the event of loss or damage to yard improvements.

The contract is ordinarily written by attaching a form to the fire contract. The scope of the coverage may be extended to include certain of the hazards covered by the extended coverage endorsement. Notable in this category are the hazards of loss to property from falling aircraft, as well as explosion, riot, and windstorm. A usual exclusion is loss or damage caused by sleet or freezing, as well as loss or damage to any tree unless the trunk or main branch is destroyed, and a limit of $100 is placed for each tree. In some jurisdictions, a pro rata distribution clause or a coinsurance clause is mandatory. In other jurisdictions, such a clause is optional.

Some forms limit the coverage to an area within a designated number of feet, usually 250, of the main building insured by the contract. Forms also frequently provide a clause limiting the loss or damage under the contract in question to such proportion of the loss or damage as the amount of insurance to which the form is attached bears to the total insurance of the same kind and nature. This is the

---

[1] The contract described here provides insurance against loss or damage caused by fire and may be written to provide protection against extended cover perils. The contract never covers the perils of transportation. An inland marine form may be written on a named perils basis and include transportation coverage, which provides insurance while the goods are in transit from the store or warehouse of the seller to the location on the premises of the buyer. Such forms ordinarily cover interests of both the vendor and the vendee, though the single-interest coverage may be written on an inland marine form if required.

usual contribution clause and it is essential, when the coverage is endorsed on a fire or similar contract, that all other identical contracts be likewise endorsed. Not to do so will result in incomplete coverage.

The property description in the dwelling form is usually written to include coverage, not only for the buildings but, as well, for outdoor equipment pertaining to the services of the premises but excluding "trees, shrubs and plants." Trees, shrubs, and plants may be specifically covered under a separate clause. Some forms limit the liability of the insurer to $300 on any one tree, $25 on any one shrub, and $5 on any one plant. Other forms do not print a limitation in the form but provide a blank so that limitations may be inserted consistent with the circumstances.

Coinsurance Deficiency Insurance. In some jurisdictions insurance is obtainable which is devised to protect the insured against becoming a coinsurer because of fluctuating values covered under specific or blanket insurance. The contract protects the insured against loss if his values increase to a degree that makes him a coinsurer. The coinsurance deficiency contract does not contribute to the loss, but if the insured is a coinsurer under his specific insurance, the deficiency coverage makes up what would otherwise be the insured's contribution. The deficiency coverage is limited to not more than 10 percent of the total value of the merchandise insured and is issued typically only with insurance having a 90 percent reduced-rate contribution clause.

Builder's Risk. A building in the process of construction presents a situation in which values are constantly changing. Several forms are available for covering these risks. The four considered here are automatic builders' risk, builders' risk form, builders' risk reporting form, and builders' risk completed value form. The automatic builders' risk form now has fairly limited use.

Automatic Builders' Risk. If insurance is placed at infrequent intervals, it follows that there will be periods of overinsurance and others in which the insurance is inadequate. To eliminate such a situation and at the same time provide an equitable insurance plan, the automatic builder's risk form has been devised.

When the contractor is prepared to commence construction, a binder is issued, and as soon as there is any insurable property on the location a contract is issued for a period of a year covering this value. The form covers not only the building under construction but also temporary or permanent buildings, sheds, fences, tool houses, builder's machinery, tools, implements, apparatus, supplies, and materials of every description used in connection with the construction of the insured building, if located on the premises or adjacent thereto.

The insured is required on the first day of each month to furnish the insurer with a statement setting forth the insurable value of the property as of the last day of the previous month. Upon receipt of the statement, an endorsement is attached to the contract showing the increase in the insurable value of the property and charging an additional premium therefor. Upon receipt of subsequent reports, the insurance is increased to meet the new values reported. The contract undertakes to protect the insured automatically against loss or damage by fire as the value at risk increases, pending the attachment of the monthly endorsements. This form provides the insured with full protection during the process of construction of a building up to the limit stated in the contract. To illustrate its operation: If at the time of the last report values were $50,000 and just before time for the next report they have increased to $55,000 and a fire occurs, the contract covers for the full value of $55,000, even though this amount is not endorsed on the contract. The 100 percent coinsurance clause is mandatory. The interest of the contractor or owner, or both, may be covered under the contract, and the usual extended cover hazards may be included in addition to the regular fire coverage.

Builders' Risk Form. A builders' risk form is available for attachment to a fire insurance contract and covers on the building or structure "while in course of construction, including foundations, additions, attachments, and all permanent fixtures . . . belonging to and constituting a part of said building or structure. . . ." When the contract to which the form is attached covers the perils of windstorm and hail, cloth awnings and metal smokestacks are not protected from these perils unless an 80 percent or higher coinsurance clause applies. The consent of the insurer must be obtained before the premises are occupied.

Materials and supplies needed in the construction of the building are also covered by the form, and if the 80 percent coinsurance clause applies, temporary structures are covered. Unless there is other insurance covering them, "builders' machinery, tools and equipment owned by the Insured or similar property of others for which the Insured is legally liable" are protected by the contract, although these items must be on the premises or in the buildings thereon or within 100 feet. A coinsurance clause appears on the form and is applicable if a percentage is placed in the blank provided. Among the other clauses contained on the form are the liberalization clause, nuclear clause, debris removal endorsement, subrogation clause, loss clause, and electrical apparatus clause.

Builders' Risk Reporting Form. This form is similar to the one just considered and is designed to provide similar coverage. The differences relate mainly to the reporting requirement. The amount of insurance listed on the form is provisional, as is the premium. The amount of insurance clause reads as follows: "The provisional amount of insurance is for the purpose of determining the premium. The actual amount of insurance hereunder shall equal this Company's percentage of the total value of the property described herein, but this Company shall not be liable for any loss in excess of this Company's percentage of the stated limit of liability notwithstanding the requirement that the premium shall be adjusted on the basis of full values reported."

The insured is required to report monthly to the insurer and to state the total value of the property covered. The day of the month on which reports are to be made is selected by the insured. The contractural requirement is: "Within thirty days after inception of this policy the Insured shall select a day of the month as of which the first and all succeeding monthly reports shall be made; each of such reports to this Company shall be due within thirty days after the day of the month selected." Full reporting is required and the insurer's liability does not exceed "that proportion of any loss hereunder which the last reported value filed prior to the date of loss bears to the actual value on the date for which the report was made." The reporting form also contains such clauses as occupancy, electrical apparatus, liberalization, subrogation, debris removal, and nuclear.

Completed Value Builder's Risk. The builders' risk completed value form, like the reporting form, calls for a provisional amount of insurance, but monthly reporting is not required. Since the rate and premium are based on an average amount of liability during the period of construction, at any date while the contract is in force, "the actual amount of insurance hereunder is that proportion of the provisional amount that the actual value of the described property on that date bears to the value at the date of completion, but shall not in any case exceed the provisional amount." Partial losses are paid in full only if the provisional amount of insurance stated in the contract is equal to the value of the described property at the date of completion. For further details see Appendix J.

Automatic and Open Binders. Under an automatic binder, the insured is automatically covered for an amount up to a stipulated limit against loss or damage by fire to any property passing into his control in the capacity of an executor, administrator, trustee, guardian, or conservator. The purpose of the binder is to cover the interim period between actual transfer of title and the time that knowledge of the transfer comes to the insured and he has an opportunity to place specific insurance.

The insured is obligated within 60 days to take steps to ascertain the insurance in effect on the property and to have any deficiency written with the insurer writing the automatic binder. The contract is particularly attractive to financial institutions serving in fiduciary capacities. The contract protects the institution from the time the property passes into its control and makes good any deficiency in insurance pending a period within which it has an opportunity to check existing coverages.

Open binders are issued to financial institutions and are designed to indemnify them against loss sustained through impairment of their mortgage interests because of fire when the loss is covered by specific insurance in an insolvent insurer. The open binder provides insurance automatically for a period of 30 days. If an insurer placing specific insurance on the mortgage interest of an insured becomes insolvent, the insured has a period of 30 days within which to discover this fact and to replace the insurance in the insolvent insurer with a like amount of insurance with the insurer issuing the binder.

These binders are issued by insurers for a nominal premium, usually a dollar.

Contract of Supply Insurance. This contract, written very often under contingent business interruption forms, is designed to provide protection for a favorable contract for material or goods. If, for example, a manufacturing plant is receiving raw material at a favorable price that cannot be duplicated either because of an advance in market prices or because, if bought elsewhere, freight or other charges would advance the price, the loss that would accrue because of the interruption or delay, if the interruption is caused by an insurable hazard, may be made the subject of an insurance contract. The usual hazards covered by contracts as issued include fire, windstorm, explosion, and riot. The risk of riot is covered if it is felt that the strike hazard is a serious one.

The contract of supply contract takes for granted that the raw material or goods will be readily obtainable in the open market but obtainable only at a higher price than that being paid under the present contract. The contract is a direct-loss cover and is to be distinguished from the consequential loss contract that pays for the interruption of business due to inability to get the raw material or goods.

Fire Apparatus Charges. Under the New York standard contracts, the insurer is not liable for expenses incurred by the insured either in protecting property from threatening fire or even in putting fire out when discovered. There are a number of situations in which property is located far from built-up communities and, therefore, without the protection of established fire departments. Since fire departments in neighboring communities are supported by taxpayers, when called upon to assist property owners elsewhere than in the community that supports them, these departments expect and demand remuneration.

Rarely will an insured stand idly by and see his property burn if the services of a fire department are available. Insureds not infrequently are bitterly disappointed when, at the expenditure of a few hundred dollars for the services of a neighboring fire department, they have saved a possible loss to the insurers of several thousand dollars and find the insurers unwilling to reimburse them for their outlay. The loss simply is not covered by the contract unless the contract is specifically endorsed to include the risk.

Fire apparatus charges are included by endorsing one or more of the fire contracts covering the property in question. Unlike the extended cover endorsements, there is not a contribution or pro rata clause in the endorsement, and, accordingly, not all the contracts need be made concurrent. It is necessary to indicate a specific amount that will represent the limit for which the insured is to be liable, and it is sufficient if one contract only is endorsed, although more than one may be endorsed if the insured prefers it this way.

Standing Timber Insurance. Insurance against loss or damage caused by fire to standing timber has been written by a number of property and liability insurers. The demand made its appearance in connection with the requirements of financial institutions that tracts of standing timber be insured when these tracts were included as an important part of the assets of a borrower.

The line has not been regarded by fire insurers as a particularly attractive one due to the fact that a forest fire ordinarily amounts to a catastrophe and any loss stands a very substantial chance of being total.

Standing timber insurance contemplates two types of risk: (1) merchantable lumber, and (2) reforestation plantation. Whereas the contract is written on an annual basis, the major fire hazard is during the summer months. For this reason, the insurers regard the months from April to November as the dry season and make for that period what is known as a "dry season charge." If the contract is in force during any part of the dry season, the dry season charge is regarded as fully earned, and no return premium for any part of it is allowed. This charge represents 80 percent of the annual premium.

NO TIME ELEMENT CONSEQUENTIAL LOSS

There are five forms in general use covering consequential loss where the time element is not a factor in determining the amount of the loss. These are: (1) profits, (2) change of temperature, (3) matched sets or parts, (4) errors and omissions, (5) replacement cost (depreciation), and (6) rain. In this category there are certain types of losses that have come to be regarded as consequential losses primarily because they are so defined. Included are losses attributable to temperature change or loss to the remaining part of a matched set because of the destruction to the other part. It may be argued that such losses are direct losses, but the business of insurance covers the situation by either definitely assuming such losses under the terms of the contract or excluding them by means of an endorsement known as the "consequential loss and damage exemption clause."

Profits Insurance.[2] Profits insurance indemnifies the insured for loss of profits on finished goods. It is written by attaching a special form to the fire, windstorm, explosion, earthquake, or other peril insurance contract. Under the fire or other direct loss contract, the measure of the damage to the insured is the cost to repair or replace. In the case of manufactured goods, this is limited to the manufacturing costs. It may happen, therefore, that if a warehouse is filled with completed goods not yet delivered, their destruction will result in a substantial loss to the insured because his direct damage loss will be settled on the basis of cost to him rather than on the basis of the price for which the goods may be sold. In the case of seasonable goods, the profits of an entire year may be lost if fire occurs just before it is time to deliver the finished product. Calendars are ordinarily delivered during the month of December, but the manufacturing process takes place during the entire year. If the year's stock of calendars of a manufacturing establishment is destroyed late in November, the loss of profits will be serious. Nor is the loss of profits serious only to business establishments that make seasonable deliveries. Any business that has substantial amounts of finished stocks in storage is faced with a possible loss of profits.

Two forms of profits insurance are written. One limits the liability of the insurer for loss of profits to the percentage of loss ascertained and adjusted under the property loss or damage contracts. This form provides that if the direct loss on stock is determined to be 50 percent, the loss of profits is limited by the same percentage.

A second form, known as the "unlimited form," adjusts the profits item without regard to the percentage of loss on stock. It is quite possible that a partial loss on stock might so damage the merchandise as to eliminate the profit item entirely. Under the unlimited form, there could be a percentage loss under the direct damage contracts with a total loss of profits. The unlimited form is regarded as the most satisfactory protection. From an underwriting point of view, the risk is greater and the premium charge correspondingly higher.

Profits insurance is usually written only for a manufacturer and not for merchandise held for sale by a retail merchant. Loss of profits for a retailer is covered in business interruption indemnity. It is expected that the retail merchant can replace damaged stock and resume business in the period during which the building, where his business is located, is being restored. If profits to his entire stock on

[2] Profits insurance is discussed here for completeness, although it is rapidly becoming obsolete and may in the future be replaced entirely by market value clauses.

hand were to be paid for a short business interruption and the stock could be replaced, the merchant would collect in a lump sum from his insurance profits that would require an extended period to earn. On the other hand, the manufacturer is in quite a different position. He has on hand merchandise completed and ready for delivery. The finished goods cannot be replaced by the manufacturer at the cost to him. The manufacturer would have realized his profit on this merchandise had there been no loss and time is not a factor. Profits insurance covers the loss of this profit.

Delayed Profits Insurance. Contracts have been issued covering the loss of profits due to unusual delay in the completion of a contract. Ordinarily, this risk would be written only in the face of the most unusual circumstances. In wartime, for example, the construction of ships is feverishly carried on, and a completed ship is often worth substantially more than its replacement cost. Here the time element is of great importance. It follows, in such instances, that if a ship near completion were totally destroyed, its value would be considerably in excess of the cost of building a new ship.

It is conceivable that destruction of a ship built for a specific purpose might result in a substantial loss to its owners if they were unable to fulfill an agreed contract because of its destruction. The hazard is insurable under the delayed profits form.

Contingent Profits Insurance. This form is used by insurance agencies whose commissions are contingent upon the loss experience of the agency. It sometimes happens that the agreement between the agent and the insurer provides for an agreed commission and a contingent commission if the loss experience does not exceed an agreed percentage of premiums. As the year's end approaches and the contingent commission is earned, there is ever present the possibility of a serious loss or even a conflagration that might have the effect of wiping out the contingent earnings of the agency. It is quite the usual procedure for an insurance agency to provide insurance against the loss of anticipated contingent earnings.

The purpose of a contingent commissions agreement is to encourage the agent to select a high class of business. If the agent rejects questionable or doubtful business during the year and thereby reduces his commissions, he does not wish to be in a position of losing his contingent commission at the end of the year through the happening of some last minute serious loss.

Temperature Damage. If a temperature change follows a fire loss and the fire originated in the insured premises, any loss to stock caused by the change is generally held to be covered by the fire insurance contract. The situation is not so clear if the stock is located in a building that secures its heat or refrigeration from a plant located some distance away. Because of the uncertainty that exists, insurers usually attach to the contract issued on cold storage warehouses, breweries, packing plants, greenhouses, creameries, and other such risks where there is a liability for loss or damage by interruption of power or change of temperature, a clause exempting the insurer from liability for loss due to temperature change.

Because of the nature of stocks of merchandise or material in process located in buildings where temperature change may be one of the most serious hazards, contracts may be endorsed to cover consequential damage caused by failure of heat or refrigeration. The rules covering the attachment of the endorsement are not the same in all jurisdictions. In some instances no premium is charged if the source of heat or refrigeration is located within the insured premises. An additional premium may be charged if the source is located outside the premises.

Matched Set or Parts. Another source of consequential loss is found where one part of a matched set is damaged or destroyed. The risk is one that is peculiar to the garment trade. Here it is customary to send different parts of a garment to several locations for a part of the processing. It becomes apparent that if a manufacturer of suits should lose all the vests of a large lot of goods in process, the value of the coats and trousers would be materially lessened, entirely aside from the amount of loss or damage that would apply directly to the vests. Insurers writing contracts on garment manufacturers' stock eliminate the possibility of consequential loss claims by endorsing the contract to provide that the insurance will not cover any loss or damage due to the reduction in value of remaining parts of clothing or parts of suits resulting from the destruction of, or damage by fire or by lightning to, any other part or parts of such clothing or parts of suits unless such other part or parts are in the same fire section. If it is desired that the consequential damage risk be assumed by the insurer, an endorsement is provided which includes consequential damage to clothing whether caused by fire at the insured's location or elsewhere.

Errors and Omissions. Financial institutions that make a practice of lending money with real estate as security are always faced with the possibility that, through some neglect on the part of the owner of the property, insurance in force when the loan was made will not be renewed. Painstaking care in checking expirations still leaves a loophole—the outgrowth of an error on the part of the employees to whom this responsibility has been assigned.

The errors and omissions contract protects the insured against losses arising out of failure to have in force proper insurance to protect the mortgaged property as a result of error or omissions. The contract protects the insured's mortgagee interest including his mortgagee interest in any legal fiduciary capacity in "real property arising by reason of error or accidental omission in the operation of the

Insured's customary procedure in requiring, procuring and maintaining valid insurance against . . . all risks and perils against which the Insured customarily requires its mortgagor's to provide policy (ies) in insurance covering real property." This agreement is subject to exclusions and limitations and conditions involving requirements in case loss occurs, appraisal, suit, subrogation, and abandonment.

Additionally in Section II of the errors and omissions form (see Appendix K) the insurer agrees, subject to certain exclusions and conditions, "to pay on behalf of the Insured all sums which the Insured shall become legally obligated to pay as damages in any mortgagee, mortgage fiduciary or mortgage servicing agency capacity arising by reason of error or accidental omission in the operation of the Insured's customary procedures in procuring and maintaining valid insurance against . . . all risks and perils against which the mortgagor customarily obtains policies of insurance except policies of title, life, sickness or accident insurance."

It is to be emphasized that errors and omissions insurance is designed to protect the insured from loss due to the destruction of its security if insurance through error has not been placed or renewed. The insurer after paying a loss is subrogated to the rights of the insured. The debt of the mortgagor remains unchanged; and, if it is collectible, the insurer must be reimbursed. This has a bearing upon the nature of the forms available.

It is not the purpose of the errors and omissions contract to relieve the insured of his obligations regarding the careful supervision of the contracts held. As a matter of fact, it would be difficult, if not impossible, to secure the coverage if the institution could not demonstrate a carefully worked out plan of follow-up for insurance contracts and their renewals. The number of technical problems involved, however, indicate the danger of error and the loss that might arise therefrom.

The most prevalent errors from which losses arise involve the elements of carelessness, delay, or oversight. It may happen that the mortgagor has agreed to deliver his insurance contracts to the bank. Before he can do so, a loss occurs. After the loss, it develops that his insurance is insuffiicent to cover the mortgage debt. The errors and omissions contract indemnifies the mortgagee to the extent of his loss. When property is sold and the deeds are passed but the insurance, through oversight or inadvertence, is not transferred, the errors and omissions coverage would step into the breach to protect the mortgagee. Changes in ownership, incorrect description, errors in entering expirations at the bank, failure to report change of occupancy or increase of hazard when known, errors in ordering or binding coverage, incorrect statement of ownership, oversight in ordering renewal—these and scores of other errors that might invalidate the coverage or jeopardize the protection are covered by the contract.

Replacement Cost Insurance. The fire insurance contract covers the insured for loss or damage to the extent of the actual cash value of the insured property at the time of the loss. Cash value is determined by giving consideration to depreciation. An insured property whose value is lessened by age and use, changing business conditions, neighborhood, and other changes may be covered for full value under a fire insurance contract and yet the insurance be less than the amount necessary to replace the loss or damaged property.

Availability of replacement cost coverage is now nationwide. Until fairly recently many insurers felt that there was an element of moral hazard in providing insurance that would replace in its entirety an old and partly obsolete building in a new condition. Now there seems to be considerable agreement that in most instances the element of moral hazard is negligible and that an insured has every right to buy insurance that will place him back in business after a fire without contributing to the replacement cost of his building an amount measured by depreciation.

Replacement cost insurance undertakes to replace loss or damage to the insured property without deduction for depreciation. It provides indemnity for the expenditures the insured is obliged to make over and above the amount of the loss covered by full insurance under the standard fire contract in order to restore the property to its full usefulness as before the loss or damage. Replacement cost insurance substitutes the term "actual cash value" at the time of the loss, which means the cost to replace less depreciation, for a figure representing the cost of replacement new.

Coinsurance is invariably required in replacement cost insurance. Some underwriters insist upon 100 percent of value, though in some instances contracts are written on an 80 percent basis. The coinsurance percentage applies to the full replacement cost and not to the actual cash value, as would be the case with ordinary fire insurance. Typically, liability under the contract accrues on an actual cash value basis until repair or replacement has actually been effected. This means that if the property is not repaired or replaced, the only liability of the insurer will be on an actual cash value basis. Some insurers specify a time limit within which repair or replacement must be completed. It is usual to provide that repairs or replacements shall be undertaken with due diligence and dispatch. The period within which completion must be effected is ordinarily 12 months. In some jurisdictions 24 months may be allowed, and, depending upon the circumstances, this time may be extended by the insurer. It is usual to require that replacement be made on the same site as that occupied by the insured property. Exceptions to this requirement are made, but it is not the general practice. The coverage specifically excludes losses which are the outgrowth of zoning ordinances or municipal building regulations. Losses in this latter category are covered by demolition insurance. (See Appendix L.)

Rain Insurance. It would seem to be a far cry from covering direct loss or damage to property by fire to include within the scope of fire insurance loss of profits due to rainfall. The extension of the fire insurance contract to include within its scope loss or damage growing out of unfavorable weather conditions followed a logical sequence. The first step included fire damage in the windstorm and earthquake contracts when the damage caused by those hazards was sufficient to collapse the building and under the older contracts terminate the direct-loss fire coverage. To this end, the earthquake and windstorm contracts are logical extensions of fire insurance. With the development of windstorm and earthquake business interruption coverages, indemnity was provided for loss growing out of the interruption of the business rather than for property damage. It was but a logical step to provide indemnity for losses due to the interruption of a business activity or the lessening of the profits of that activity when only a single day or single event is concerned and unfavorable weather is the cause of the loss. The result has been to extend the coverage provided by fire insurers to rain insurance which indemnifies for loss incurred as result of rain, hail, snow, or sleet. It indemnifies for loss of funds advanced for expenses and for loss of income on events when unfavorable weather such as rain, hail, snow, or sleet is the cause of the loss.

Unlike other forms of insurance, rain insurance attaches for a very brief period, usually for only a few hours in a single day. The contract provides that, if rainfall occurs within certain specified hours, the indemnity is payable. There are two types of coverage available. One provides for the measurement of the amount of precipitation, and the findings of an established weather station are usually relied upon for these readings. If there is no such station within a reasonable distance of the event for which coverage is provided, a rain gauge is set up at some convenient location, and the reading is under the supervision of some responsible person agreed upon by the parties. The nonmeasurement contract provides that payment shall be made under the policy if rain in any amount shall fall during the specified hours.

There are six different forms of rain insurance coverage all of which are strict contracts of indemnity. Each undertakes to pay only for loss sustained. If a certain event is insured against loss due to the fall of rain but there is a full attendance and no loss can be demonstrated, the insurer is under no liability to make payment. This is an extreme situation, for ordinarily any event insured against loss due to rain would suffer some lessening of income because of rain. The measure of damages is the amount of loss that the rain actually caused. This is determined in different ways for different types of events.

Form A—Income Expectancy. This form, known as the "income expectancy form," covers indoor or outdoor events for which there are certain fixed expenses and the income expectancy may be determined on the basis of the experience of a previous year. The amount of indemnity that may be collected is limited by the falling off in receipts from those of the previous year. If there is no previous experience, the limit of indemnity is the amount of money disbursed for expenses.

Form B—Abandonment. Form B is written for events that will have to be abandoned or postponed in case of rain. Under this form the amount of insurance may not exceed the fixed charges or expenses. The contract is ordinarily issued without specification of the amount of rainfall on the theory that if the day is rainy at all the project will have to be abandoned. Where the insured elects, the insurance may be written with a minimum rainfall requirement instead of "the no specific measurement" basis. If the insured is able to effect any salvage from fixed charges and expenses, these are applied to reduce the liability of the insurer.

Form C—Experience. This form is used largely to cover annual events, such as fairs, races, meets, and similar events. The contract covers the difference between the gross income received and the anticipated income set forth under the terms of the contract. It is ordinarily not written to cover an event unless the event has been held at least three consecutive years.

Form D—Valued. This form, unlike the other rain insurance forms, pays the face amount of the contract in the event of the prescribed amount of rainfall designated in the contract. When the contract is written, the amount of insurance provided is based upon expenses or the gross income for a similar day not affected by rainfall, or gross profits for a similar day not affected by rainfall. The form provides that a specific amount of rain shall fall during the hours specified in order to establish a loss, and it is used only if readings may be obtained from a self-recording United States government rain guage or a government cooperative observer equipped with a standard rain gauge. This form is termed "nondeductible" because in making the adjustment, no deductions are made for possible income. A specific amount of insurance is set forth and payable, but the amount is limited as already indicated. Coverage may not exceed one of the three following limits: (*a*) the full amount of expenses incurred, (*b*) 60 percent of gross income received on the last similar day not affected by rainfall, or (*c*) 60 percent of the gross income of the last similar day not affected by rainfall if the insured is a mercantile establishment or other class of business where profit will serve as the criterion for loss based on previous experience.

Form E—Advance Ticket Sales. There are certain types of events that rely for patronage on an advance sale of tickets. Where the tickets are subject to refund in the event of rain, form E protects the insured against loss from refunds. The form may be written on an individual ticket basis, or it may cover on all redeemable tickets. There is no liability on the part of the insurer unless the performers or other participants in the event are available and prepared to appear as scheduled.

Form F—Advertising Sales. This form is sold only to publishers and provides a specialized type of coverage. It undertakes to reimburse the publisher for refunds for any advertising space sold for a special event under an agreement to make a refund in the event of rain. It has an appeal to publishers, since it can be used as a sales argument for space. Sometimes the publisher agrees to a refund and sometimes, in other instances, to reprint the advertisement at a reduced cost or without any additional charge. The coverage may be written in an amount equal to the full value of the insured advertising accounts, or the insurance may be limited to the amount of the refund or the cost or rerunning the advertisement. As in the case of form D, this contract is written only where rainfall readings are available from a United States Weather Station or a government observer.

To place rainfall insurance, an application for the contract must be made at least seven days before the contract attaches. Local agents are not authorized to bind rainfall insurance without authorization from the home office of the insurer, and the business is not accepted until the premium has been paid in advance. Contracts may be written to provide indemnity for rain during the period covered for (*a*) 1/20-inch rainfall, (*b*) 1/10-inch rainfall, (*c*) 2/10-inch rainfall, and (*d*) rainfall, no amount specified. Because, within limits, weather conditions may be forecast, the seven-day limit has been set for filing applications. For the same reason, rain insurance contracts may not be canceled. Thus, once a seven-day period has commenced to run, the insurer may not relieve itself of liability if rain seems to threaten, nor may the insured call up at the last minute and cancel his insurance if the indications are that the weather is fair.

FOR DISCUSSION

1. Under a contract covering on a tenant's improvements, does it matter whether the lease contains a cancellation clause? Assume improvements and betterments costing $100,000 that have been in place for 15 years. Their present value after depreciation is $40,000. Assume the

lease to have been written for 20 years when the betterments were installed. In the case of a $20,000 loss, how much ought the insurers pay to the tenant in the event (*a*) that the lease is canceled because of a fire clause, and (*b*) in the event that the lease is not canceled?

2. Can you contemplate a situation where tenant's improvements are not damaged at all and yet the insured can collect total loss under his contract?
3. B has a tenant's improvement contract that has been running concurrently with a 20-year lease. The lease expires, and he has arranged for renewal for an additional 10 years at the same monthly rental. He wishes, therefore, to continue his tenant's improvement contract until the present lease expires. Is the risk insurable?
4. The X university holds a football game each year for which thousands of tickets are sold weeks and months in advance. One of the members of the athletic association is of the opinion that it would be a good gamble to insure the receipts against rain. Since few reservations are ever canceled because of poor weather, in the event of rain, taking into consideration the expected payment from insurance, he contends the receipts might be doubled. Is this reasoning correct?
5. The water damage contract covers direct loss or damage caused by accidental discharge, leakage, or overflow of the water system from which of the following: (*a*) water or plumbing system; (*b*) steam from heating system; (*c*) water from elevator tanks; (*d*) standpipes for fire house; (*e*) refrigerating systems; (*f*) air-conditioning systems; (*g*) rain or snow admitted through defective roofs; (*h*) rain or snow admitted through windows, doors, transoms, or skylights; and (*i*) overflow of tanks of standpipes connected with the sprinkler system?
6. Are losses caused by the freezing of water in the sprinkler system, with resulting bursting of the pipes, covered under the sprinkler leakage policy form?
7. B is the owner of a large building located in the retail district of the city and carries sprinkler leakage insurance. After a loss, he is faced with a suit by one of the occupants of the building who claims that the janitor of the building negligently left a window open, causing the sprinkler system to freeze with a resulting break. Does B's sprinkler leakage contract afford him any protection in this instance if it is proved that he is legally liable for the loss?
8. In the case of standing timber insurance, explain the logic of the "dry season charge."
9. The owner of X department store carries a water damage contract. On an unusually cold night the heat from the boiler is low with the result that a water pipe freezes. The pipe bursts and water discharged therefrom seriously damages both the building and the merchandise. Is this loss recoverable under a water damage contract?
10. In the case of a water damage contract, do you think that the contract would cover loss to merchandise damaged by the penetration of snow and water around the edges of a show window?

11. X purchased a water damage contract which insured against all direct loss and damage "solely by the accidental discharge, leakage or overflow of water from within the following source or sources: [Plumbing, heating, air-conditioning systems and similar systems were listed.]. . . and rain or snow admitted directly to the interior of the building through defective roof leaders or spouting." The roof of the insured building sloped toward a drain or rainspout which carried off rain water from the roof. The drain became clogged, causing a pool of water to form on the roof 12 or 13 inches in depth. The water overflowed the flashings of an elevator well flowing down the shaft and flooding all the floors in the building. The insurer claimed that the contract did not cover the loss since the water was not admitted *through* a defective spout. What do you think? Give reasons for your answer.
12. What effect may a local ordinance have upon the right of a property owner to rebuild a partially destroyed property? Discuss the application of fire insurance to losses where the cost to rebuild is increased because of such an ordinance.
13. In some parts of the country, it is customary to build buildings on leased land. Leases are commonly written for a period of 99 years. Does the owner of a 99-year lease have an insurable interest in the lease? Describe the interest and how it should be covered.
14. Has a local agent authority to issue a binder for rain insurance?
15. A sudden change in the temperature of a building causes heavy condensation on the pipes of the sprinkler system. Water dripping on a stock of silks and laces causes severe damage. Is this loss covered under a sprinkler leakage contract?
16. A tornado severely damages a building and, among other effects, causes a sprinkler system to open. Is the water damage so caused covered by the sprinkler leakage contract?
17. Water damage contracts are never issued until a careful inspection has been made by the insurance writers of the property to be covered. Has this inspection any value to the insured?
18. The supports of a water storage tank give way, with the result that the collapsing tank itself causes terrific damage in addition to the damage caused by the released water. Is the loss covered by the sprinkler leakage contract?
19. Through negligence of the janitor, the fires of a building are allowed to go out. Owing to freezing, parts of the sprinkler leakage system burst, with resulting damage to the building of the insured and the stocks of merchandise belonging to the tenants. Are the losses covered under the sprinkler leakage contract?

CHAPTER · 10

Business Interruption and Related Agreements

In the insuring agreement of the standard fire insurance contract it is provided that loss shall be determined "without compensation for loss resulting from the interruption of business or manufacture. . . ." It is also provided that the liability of the insurer shall not exceed "the amount that it would cost to repair or replace the property with material of like kind and quality. . . ." The first of these quotations excludes business interruption losses from the standard fire insurance contract protection. The second excludes profits on finished goods from the protection of the contract by limiting loss to replacement cost and not selling price.

A method of insuring profits, widely used before market value clauses became common, was discussed in the preceding chapter. The insurance of profits is a consequential loss coverage where the time element is not a factor. Losses attributable to the interruption of business, on the contrary, depend for their extent upon the period of interruption. There are eight forms involving time element as the factor vital in measuring the loss. These are: (1) business interruption (use and occupancy), (2) contingent business interruption, (3) rent and rental values, (4) selling agents' commissions, (5) tuition fees, (6) extra expense, (7) additional living expense, and (8) leasehold interest.

BUSINESS INTERRUPTION

Business Interruption Insurance. Business interruption indemnity protects against the loss of prospective earnings because of the interruption of business by fire or other hazards insured against, to the extent of the net profits prevented, plus such fixed charges and expenses as necessarily continue during the interruption, but only to the extent that such fixed charges and expenses would have been earned had no interruption due to an insured peril occurred. The contract is one of indemnity and undertakes to keep the business in the position that the business could have maintained for itself had there been no interruption.

The form is said to have originated in England where it was known as "consequential insurance." First written in this country in 1880, it was called at the time "use and occupancy insurance." While the term "use and occupancy" continued in use for many years and is still used by many, particularly in the abbreviated form, referring to the coverage as "U and O insurance," more recently the coverage has come to be known as "business interruption insurance."

The terms "use and occupancy" and "business interruption insurance" are, to a large degree, used interchangeably, and the appeal of abbreviations has given some preference to the U and O designation. There is some logic in the earlier terminology in that the insurance was written to protect the insured from loss growing out of the destruction of his premises or the inability to occupy them due to damage. It has been contended, however, that the actual purpose of protecting the insured against loss of profits due to business interruption is only implied in the name. "Prospective earnings insurance" has been suggested as a logical term and is, in fact, sometimes used. The more direct designation, "business interruption insurance," is generally accepted today, though the traditional "use and occupancy" term is still widely used.

No Relationship between Property Damage and Business Interruption Losses. During the period of business suspension attributable to an insured peril, the business interruption contract undertakes to do for the business what the business would have done for itself had there been no loss. In doing this the contract provides indemnity for net profits prevented and for fixed charges and expenses that of necessity must go on during the suspension, to the extent that such profits would have been earned but for the loss. Losses occasioned by interruption to business during the rebuilding period after a property loss are often heavy and not infrequently of greater consequence than the loss occasioned by the destruction of the physical plant or material. When a fire makes it necessary for a business to discontinue operations, or to continue at less than the normal rate, business interruption insurance fills the breach and provides the business with uninterrupted income until the damage has been repaired and normal operations have been resumed.

There is no fixed relationship between property damage loss or value and business interruption loss or value. The importance of business interruption insurance is appreciated when it is recognized that a small property loss in a vital section of a plant may result in total suspension of operations, with the resulting consequential loss far in excess of the property damage loss. There is an example in a paper mill that was forced to suspend business because of damage to a boiler. When the replacement was ordered, it was found that a bridge would have to be strengthened before delivery could be made. As a result, the plant was closed for an abnormally long period. Fixed charges, such as interest on bonded indebtedness and taxes, continued to mount and essential personnel were continued on the payroll, with the result that by the time the plant was finally opened the loss of profits for the period of shutdown plus the drain for fixed charges found the business, upon reopening, with its quick assets seriously depleted and much of its business irreparably lost to competitors. Business interruption insurance would have reimbursed the business for lost profits and continuing expenses and would have sustained its financial credit. It could not have prevented loss of accounts to competitors, but it would have enabled the business to reopen strong financially and in a position to enter the field aggressively and bid for a recovery of the lost business. A weakened financial structure following an uninsured business interruption is not unusual.

Earliest Forms Written on a Per Diem or Weekly Indemnity Basis. Business interruption insurance when it first made its appearance provided indemnity on a per diem basis. The per diem basis was held to be too rigid, and with a view to introducing some degree of flexibility because earnings varied on different days, the weekly form was introduced. The forms are still authorized in a few states and could be written in any state if the insurer wished to take the necessary steps to make a special filing, but they are, for the most part, obsolete.

Coinsurance Forms. Coinsurance forms make no daily or weekly limitation of payment but require coinsurance based upon the annual business interruption value of the business. These forms have an advantage over the older and now obsolete per diem and weekly forms in that they automatically adjust to fluctuating earnings. The insurer is liable for any loss during the period of coverage, whatever the amount, provided the face of the contract is equal to the coinsurance percentage of the business interruption value.

There are two primary coinsurance forms that are known as (1) the two-item contribution form (now virtually obsolete in most parts of the United States), and (2) the single-item gross earnings contribution form. Since it is necessary, because of the nature of the two classes of business, to use different terminology for mercantile or nonmanufacturing plants in one instance and manufacturing establishments in another, there are two forms available for each of the primary classifications. This being the case, it is sometimes stated that there are four coinsurance forms, and these are designated as follows: (1) the two-item form for mercantile or nonmanufacturing plants,

(2) the two-item form for manufacturing plants, (3) the gross earnings form for mercantile or nonmanufacturing plants, and (4) the gross earnings form for manufacturing plants. Hence, from the two basic coinsurance forms, there are two single-item gross earnings forms, one for manufacturers and the other for mercantile risks. Likewise, there is a two-item contribution form for manufacturers and another for mercantile establishments.

Under the coinsurance forms, loss is paid without any per diem or weekly limitation, thereby taking care automatically of seasonal or daily fluctuations in earnings. The forms take into consideration the prospective insurable interest as one lump sum and pay the actual loss sustained as it appears at the time of the business interruption. In the case of a department store, this would mean a high amount of indemnity for Saturdays, with lower amounts for the less active days, as well as higher sums for the periods of greatest activity, such as during the Christmas shopping season, and lesser sums for the dull periods between seasons. Likewise, department store operators contend that in order to keep their organizations intact during short periods of suspension, they must continue all or part of their force of employees and, for this reason, may wish to include in the coverage the item of ordinary payroll. This increases the insurable value and with the operation of the coinsurance clause requires additional insurance. On the other hand, a business establishment, such as a manufacturing plant, that hires a large number of that class of employees known as ordinary labor may exclude such payroll from its insurable value or it may insure it for a limited period or for the entire contract period, whichever coverage best meets its needs.

It is necessary to have separate forms for mercantile and for manufacturing risks because of the different nature of their operations. A manufacturer sells merchandise but before he can sell it he must produce it. The shutdown of a manufacturing plant interrupts production. The manufacturer's loss, therefore, stems from inability to produce. Coverage for the manufacturer is for the total net sales value of production less the direct cost of raw stock from which production is derived in contrast to the mercantile coverage which insures annual gross earnings less discontinuing expenses.

The Two-Item Contribution Form. This form was originally designed to meet the needs of department store and mercantile risks. Its adoption followed the requests of mercantile interest for a form that would eliminate all fixed limits except that of the year's earnings. The aim was to provide a form of insurance that would cover the requirements of the insured at the time of the loss, whether the loss occurred at a period of maximum business activity or during a period of lull.

With respect to mercantile risks, particularly where the interruption was for a short period, not only were they obliged to continue all fixed expenses but, as well, to maintain on the payroll not only key employees but the salaries of the entire sales force if they expected to reopen in normal order. Therefore, these establishments required a form that would cover profits and all fixed charges and, as well, salaries of all employees for a limited period at least. In the case of an indefinite shutdown, part of the payroll might be discontinued, but this was certainly not the case for periods of brief interruption. This led to the development of the two-item coinsurance form.

This form proved useful, but has now largely been eliminated. Coverage comparable to that formerly provided by the two-item forms is now provided by using the gross earnings form and a payroll limitations or exclusion endorsement.

Gross Earnings Forms. Two gross earnings forms are now widely used. One of these forms is for manufacturing and mining risks and the other for mercantile or nonmanufacturing risks. There are two endorsements that may be attached to these forms, one of which is the "ordinary payroll exclusion endorsement" and the other the "ordinary payroll—limited coverage endorsement." (See Appendix G.)

Mercantile or Nonmanufacturing Risks. The form for mercantile or nonmanufacturing risks is written for one specified amount and provides:

1. Subject to all its provisions and stipulations, this policy covers only against loss resulting directly from necessary interruption of business caused by damage to or destruction of real or personal property by the peril(s) insured against, during the term of this policy, on premises occupied by the Insured as. . . .
2. In the event of such damage or destruction this Company shall be liable for the *actual loss sustained* by the insured resulting directly from such interruption of business, but not exceeding the reduction in Gross Earnings less charges and expenses which do not necessarily continue during the interruption of business, for only such length of time as would be required with the exercise of due diligence and dispatch to rebuild, repair or replace such part of the property herein described as has been damaged or destroyed, commencing with the date of such damage or destruction and not limited by the date of expiration of this policy. Due consideration shall be given to the continuation of normal charges and expenses, including payroll expense, to the extent necessary to resume operations of the Insured with the same quality of service which existed immediately preceding the loss.

Insurable value is based on gross earnings, determined as follows:

3. For the purposes of this insurance "Gross Earnings" are defined as the sum of:

a) Total net sales, and
b) Other earnings derived from operations of the business, less the cost of:
c) Merchandise sold, including packaging materials therefor,
d) Materials and supplies consumed directly in supplying the service(s) sold by the Insured, and
e) Service(s) purchased from outsiders (not employees of the Insured) for resale which do not continue under contract.

No other costs shall be deducted in determining Gross Earnings. In determining Gross Earnings due consideration shall be given to the experience of the business before the date of damage or destruction and the probable experience thereafter had no loss occurred.

The entire payroll is covered as are other continuing expenses. The loss adjustment is simple in that the contract covers any reduction in gross earnings, due to the interruption of business through a peril covered in the contract, less discontinuable expenses. This form requires that insurance shall equal either 50, 60, 70, or 80 percent of the gross earnings determined as the insurable value. These coinsurance requirements give the insured a wide latitude in the event of fluctuating earnings.

Manufacturing and Mining Risks. The manufacturing and mining risks form is similar to the mercantile form with necessary changes being made for the differing characteristics of the risks. For example, gross earnings are defined as:

a) Total net sales value of production,
b) Total net sales of merchandise, and
c) Other earnings derived from operation of the business, less the cost of:
d) Raw Stock from which such production is derived,
e) Supplies consisting of materials consumed directly in the conversion of such raw stock into finished stock or in supplying the service(s) sold by the Insured.
f) Merchandise sold, including packaging materials therefor, and
g) Service(s) purchased from outsiders (not employees of the Insured) for resale which do not continue under contract.

No other costs shall be deducted in determining Gross Earnings. In determining Gross Earnings due consideration shall be given to the experience of the business before the date of damage or destruction and the probable experience thereafter had no loss occurred.

Certain clauses have been added to the form that deal specifically with manufacturing and mining risks. The insurer is not liable for any loss resulting from damage to or destruction of finished stock nor for the time required to reproduce said finished stock." There are definitions of "raw stock," "stock in process," "finished stock," "merchandise," and "normal." Two special conditions apply to mining risks only: (*a*) Losses occurring in mines by the perils insured against are not covered unless superstructures above ground are damaged; and (*b*) the contract applies "only to buildings and machinery that contribute to the production of the mining plant."

Ordinary Payroll Exclusion Endorsement. Ordinary payroll expense is defined in this endorsement as "the entire payroll expense for all employees of the Insured, except officers, executives, department managers, employees under contract, and other important employees." This endorsement serves to exclude payroll expense from the business interruption coverage and affords a way (along with other limiting endorsements) of providing coverage comparable to that provided formerly by the two-item form.

Ordinary Payroll—Limited Coverage Endorsement. The limited coverage endorsement is similar to the ordinary payroll exclusion endorsement except that coverage for ordinary payroll is limited "to such expense which must necessarily continue during the interruption of business for not exceeding 90 consecutive calendar days immediately following the date of damage to or destruction of the described property." The ninety-day limit is subject to increase.

Earnings Insurance. This is a form of gross earnings business interruption insurance. In some areas it is known as the "gross earnings short form." It is, in fact, shorter than the standard forms of business interruption insurance in general use. It is drawn in simple understandable language and designed to meet the needs of smaller business establishments.

The contract is written without a coinsurance clause, and unlike the business interruption form described above, it may be written as an item of a multiple peril physical damage contract or it may be endorsed to an outstanding fire insurance contract covering building and contents. In lieu of a coinsurance clause, the contract limits recovery of loss of gross earnings to a maximum of 25 percent of the face amount of the contract in any one month. Thus, if an insured wishes to be covered for at least $500 a month, he must carry a minimum of $2,000 insurance. If there is a possibility of an interruption of business for a period longer than four months, the face amount of the contract must be increased accordingly.

The contract covers against loss of earnings caused directly by one of the perils insured against. Earnings are defined as net profit plus payroll expense, taxes, interest, rents, and all other operating expenses earned by the business. The insurance may be written to cover the perils of fire and lightning or, at the option of the insured, may be extended to include the perils covered by extended coverage No. 4 or, as well, vandalism and malicious mischief. The contract provides the usual business interruption coverages and limitations.

This contract appeals particularly to small shopkeepers or

merchants. It is not available to manufacturers but may be written for the service risks, such as garages, restaurants, banks, and theaters.

Agreed-Amount Endorsement. The operation of a coinsurance clause in a business interruption contract takes into consideration the period immediately following a loss and not a period of past experience. It follows, particularly in the case of a concern with an expanding business, that the insured, in spite of carefully estimating his insurable value, may become a heavy coinsurer. To avoid becoming a coinsurer, there are two alternatives. The first requires a careful and continued checking of the operations of the business with adjustments of insurance amounts giving full consideration to trends. Even here, because of the tendency to conserve premium outlay by avoiding overinsurance, there is still danger. The other alternative method, where permissible, is the use of the agreed-amount endorsement.

Both coinsurance forms may be written with a stipulated agreed amount instead of a percentage of coinsurance if the insured files annually a statement of income and expenses with the rating bureau. Not all risks are eligible for this endorsement. In some territories all mercantile risks are acceptable, but in others only risks rated as fire resistive or equipped with automatic sprinklers may be so covered. In the case of manufacturers, the endorsement may not be used except with specific permission, and the form is usually restricted to superior risks in the sprinklered fire resistive category.

The agreed-amount endorsement has the effect of nullifying the application of the coinsurance by establishing a value based upon a profit and loss statement as a basis for determining the amount of insurance required under the coinsurance clause. The clause effects this by providing that in the application of the coinsurance clause attached to the contract, the percentage of gross earnings referred to in the coinsurance clause is agreed to be a flat sum. This means that instead of requiring 50, 60, 70, or 80 percent of gross earnings in a given case, a flat sum such, for example, as $100,000 could be agreed upon.

Premium Adjustment Endorsement. This form represents another attempt to avoid coinsurance penalties and, at the same time, provides adequate coverage for the insured and premium income commensurate to the risk for the insurer.

The form allows the insured to place coverage that he feels will, in all respects, be adequate. The coverage is effected by an endorsement added to the gross earnings form. The coinsurance requirements remain the same, and the insured may elect 50, 60, 70, or 80 percent coverage based on an estimate of the earnings of the insured immediately following a loss. The insurer's liability is limited to the same percentage of gross earnings for one year as the percentage appearing in the coinsurance clause.

The contract when written provides for a provisional premium based upon the amount of insurance determined upon. At the expiration of the contract term a report of gross earnings for the year is submitted to the insurer. This report is made on a form supplied for the purpose. The actual earned premium for the period is computed on the basis of this report. If the provisional premium exceeds the earned premium, the insurer will refund the excess paid but the total retained premium must not be less than fifty dollars. This means that so much of the provisional insurance that was originally written as is needed will apply in the case of a loss, and upon the basis of report of gross earnings at the end of the contract term, the insurer determines the amount of the provisional premium to be retained. No additional premium is assessed in the event the additional premium turns out to be too low.

Business Interruption Value. In business interruption insurance the principle of indemnity operates as in other insurance coverages. A business establishment is operated for its earnings. The amount of insurance collectible under a business interruption contract is limited to the loss sustained through the interruption of the business because of fire or other hazard insured against.

Every going business at any given time finds itself in one of three situations: it is being operated at a profit, at cost, or at a loss. While business interruption indemnity aims primarily to indemnify the insured for loss of profits because of an enforced cessation or limitation of operations, it does not follow that an insured has no loss if the business is not making a profit. When a plant is shut down, certain fixed charges must go on if the business is to continue to function. The contract, therefore, not only covers loss of net profits on business prevented from being carried on but also includes the payment of such fixed charges and expenses as must continue during the business interruption, to the extent that they would have been earned had there been no fire. Finally, the coverage makes allowance for expenses necessarily incurred for the purpose of reducing the loss.

It follows from the foregoing, then, that if a business is operating at a profit, and a fire causes suspension, the loss includes both the profit item and the fixed charge item, plus any costs incurred for minimizing the loss. If the business is operating at cost, and a fire occurs, the loss is the same, less the profit item. If the business is operating at a loss, it may still be earning part of its fixed charges, and to the extent that these are earned they represent a loss if business is suspended. The insurable value under a business interruption coverage, then, represents the profits for a year that would have been earned had there been no suspension or cessation of operations plus a year's fixed charges and expenses.

Work sheets have been devised to simplify the determination of the

BUSINESS INTERRUPTION WORK SHEET

For Use with Gross Earnings Contribution on Mercantile Risks

ALL ITEMS TO BE ON AN ANNUAL BASIS		Column 1 Actual Values for Year Ended................	Column 2 Estimated Values for Year Ending.........
A. Total Annual Net Sales (Gross sales less returns and allowances)		$.....................	$.....................
B. Add Other Earnings Derived from Operations of Business (other than Sales):			
1. Cash Discounts received	$....................		
2. Commissions and Rents from Leased Depts.	....		
3.	....		
4. Total Other Earnings		....	....
		....	....
C. Deduct Only:			
1. *Cost of Merchandise Sold, including packaging materials	$....................		
2. *Cost of materials and supplies consumed in services sold	....		
3. Cost of services purchased for resale (not employees)	....		
4. Total Deductions		....	....
D. Gross Earnings		....	....
E. Take 50%, 60%, 70% or 80% of Item D, Column 2, as amount of insurance required, depending upon percentage Contribution Clause to be used in policy	(.................%)		$.....................
*Explanatory Note:			
To obtain invoice cost of merchandise sold (or of materials and supplies consumed), the following procedure is recommended:			
1. Inventory at beginning of fiscal year	$....................		
2. Add invoice cost of merchandise purchased (or of materials and supplies purchased) during fiscal year (including cartage and transportation charges on incoming merchandise or on materials and supplies)	....		
	....		
3. Deduct inventory at end of fiscal year	....		
4. Amount for Item C.1 (or C.2)	$....................		

Fig. 10–1.

insurable value for a going concern. In the case of the gross earning form, it is necessary to reach a figure that will represent the gross earnings, and the amount of insurance to be carried should equal the percentage of value required in the coinsurance clause adopted. To indicate the nature of a work sheet, an example is given in Figure 10–1 of the form for use in computing gross earnings for a mercantile establishment.

In the case of the two-item 80 percent coinsurance form, the amount of insurance should equal 80 percent of the annual value of the insured's output less the annual sales cost and the cost of such items as raw materials, labor, light, heat, power, freight, and supplies. This is broken down to show (*a*) the sum of the annual net profits plus the annual amount of all charges and other expenses that would have been earned had no loss occurred for a period of 12 months, and (*b*) the insured's entire payroll expense. The amount of insurance to be carried is 80 percent of the sum of (*a*) and (*b*).

Since the insurer assumes liability for fixed charges and expenses, the insured is faced with the necessity of segregating those charges that are continuing. A study of the usual business establishment will reveal two types of continuing expenses: (1) full continuing, and (2) variable continuing. Thus, such items as salaries of officers and superintendents must be paid during a shutdown. Rent of undestroyed property, branch offices, distributing points, ground rents, and similar items must be paid in full. Bond interest, interest on notes and other obligations, taxes, insurance premiums that must be continued, such as liability coverage, business life insurance contracts, and insurance upon other property—all are fully continuing expenses.

In the category of variable-continuing expenses, the range is wider. Salaries of key employees, such as foremen and others necessary to keep the organization intact and ready to resume operations, must continue. The remainder of the payroll may be discontinued. Part of the annual depreciation and maintenance charges should be classified as continuing, though the amount that could be figured in a loss would depend upon the property damage loss. Charges such as electricity and telephone are variable, the minimum service of meter charges continuing. Noncancellable contracts, such as those for advertising, membership in trade associations, professional retainer fees, and similar items are to be included as continuing to the extent that they must be paid because of legal liability to do so or because they are necessary to maintain the business organization as a going concern. Fully continuing expenses offer but little difficulty in estimating use and occupancy values. To appraise the second group properly requires a careful analysis of the entire overhead expense of the business.

In addition to the items provided in the work sheet, operating income from any unusual source should appear. Bad debts, commissions paid, and sales discounts should be added. It should be recognized that the work sheet merely establishes a pattern as an aid. The objective should be maintained clearly in mind, and any contributing factors that will affect the end result should receive consideration. The rigid adherence to a work sheet can easily result in overinsurance with the unnecessary expenditure of premium or underinsurance with a resultant coinsurance penalty in the event of a loss.

Manufacturing and Mercantile Forms Distinguished. The once widely used two-item business interruption form was first devised for mercantile risks and later was adopted for manufacturing risks. The same process of development followed in the case of the gross earning form. This form was planned originally for mercantile business establishments, though, like the two-item form, through a process of revision it now is used for manufacturing as well as mercantile risks.

The principal requirement for changes in terminology originates from the differences in the nature of the stocks of the two classes of risks. A manufacturing risk may suffer a loss to either raw stock or stock in process. For a mercantile institution there is no reference to raw stock or stock in process in the form, since the stock of such an institution would be limited to merchandise held for sale. With this difference in the treatment of the stock items, there is some difference in the terminology of the forms. In the case of the manufacturing risk the value of the completed goods as a basis for determining profits is the "total sales value of production," and the cost is based upon the "cost of raw stock." In the mercantile form the corresponding terms are "total sales" and "cost of merchandise sold."

Blanket Business Interruption. Where a business is conducted at a number of locations and because of the nature of the business one plant is dependent upon another for the smooth and continued operation of the business, blanket business interruption insurance may properly be written covering at all the premises contributing to the operation of the business. It is logical to provide blanket insurance in such a situation, since damage or destruction at one plant may make itself felt in the final experience of the business. It is not a requirement that there be an interdependence with respect to locations to write blanket insurance. If there are several locations all under common ownership or operation, they may be covered by blanket insurance, even though some or all of them operate independently.

Blanket insurance appeals in that with one contract covering all locations the contract limit will apply to any location. This is in contrast to several separate contracts on independently operated locations each with a lower limit of insurance. A disadvantage to be found is the requirement that the operations of all plants must be studied and the books examined in case of a loss to determine whether coinsurance requirements are satisfied. This, of course, is not the case where specific insurance is carried at each location. Whatever the advantages and disadvantages, blanket insurance is indicated where there is an interdependency with respect to locations. Where there is no interdependency, the accounting involved in settling a loss at a single location may be the determining factor in making a choice.

Length of Coverage. Standard forms at one time limited liability to a period of 12 months from the date of the loss. This was so even in partial losses where the face amount of the insurance was not exhausted. The use of this form necessitated a longer contract period than a year if the business was of such a nature that the property might not be restored in a period of 12 months. With the exception of certain contracts written with the premium adjustment endorsement the 12 months' limitation does not appear in the contract or if it is in, the form used may be deleted without charge.

Under present-day contracts the insured may collect "actual loss sustained" until the insurance is exhausted regardless of the length of shutdown. The coverage now extends over the actual time required to build "with due diligence and dispatch." There is actually no requirement that the damaged building be rebuilt but if it is not rebuilt the measure of liability is still the amount of income lost during the time it would have taken to rebuild or to find new permanent quarters whichever is the less.

Expenses Incurred in Reducing Loss. In addition to providing indemnity to the insured for loss sustained because of the interruption of his business as a result of fire or other hazard insured against, the contract agrees to pay, in addition, such expenses as are necessarily incurred for the purpose of reducing the loss under the contract. This element is not computed in arriving at the business interruption insurable value for, as a matter of fact, it adds nothing to the insurer's risk. The operation of this clause is illustrated by the following example. Assume that a seasonal business suffers a fire just as it is about to fill a number of large orders. The loss is estimated to be $80,000, and work will probably be totally suspended for 90 days. As the insured does not wish his customers to go to another concern, he rents a neighboring property, sets up machinery, and is operating at full capacity in 30 days. Although the accomplishment of this feat involves working night and day shifts at increased labor costs, as well as other extraordinary expenses, and the total cost amounts to $20,000, the insured considers it worth while since it is thereby able to keep its contact with valuable customers.

If by the expenditure of $20,000 the insured is able to reduce the business interruption loss to $40,000, for example, the insurer is obligated to pay the $40,000 business interruption loss plus the expediting expense item of $20,000. This makes the total outlay of the insurer $60,000 instead of $80,000 had the expediting expense not been incurred. If the expediting expense of $20,000 had reduced the business interruption loss by only $15,000, the liability of the insurer would not exceed the $80,000 for which it would have been liable had no expediting expense been insured.

Expediting expenses covered by the business interruption contract are not to be confused with the benefits payable under an extra-expense contract. Extra-expense insurance pays the extra expense required to prevent business interruption, in excess of the expense that would normally be incurred had there been no loss or damage. Extra-expense insurance may be written as an alternative to business interruption insurance, or in other instances it is written as a supplementary cover.

This clause is not affected by a coinsurance clause in the contract. As the clause originally appeared in the older contracts, there was doubt in the minds of adjusters as to the application of coinsurance to expediting charges, and there was no agreement among underwriters. It was argued by some that the insured benefited equally with the insurer by incurring expenses to reduce loss, and on this basis extraordinary expense incurred was added to the business loss and the coinsurance clause was applied to the total figure. Thus, if the loss was reduced by the application of the coinsurance clause, the item of extraordinary expense was reduced accordingly.

Contracts as now written definitely provide that expense incurred in reducing loss shall not be subject to the operation of the coinsurance clause. The expense incurred cannot bring the loss to an amount greater than the anticipated loss would have been computed by the application of the coinsurance clause. In other words, in the case just cited the expenditure of $20,000 was able to reduce the business interruption loss to $40,000. If the insured were a 25 percent coinsurer, the business interruption loss would have been reduced to $30,000. The settlement then would have been $50,000 instead of $60,000, since to the interruption loss there is added the extraordinary expense item without reduction by the application of coinsurance. Without extraordinary expense to reduce loss, the $80,000 anticipated loss with the application of the coinsurance clause, with the insured a 25 percent coinsurer would reduce the liability of the insurer to $60,000. If the expenditure of $20,000 reduced the loss to $60,000 before the application of coinsurance, the liability of the insurer would not be $60,000 reduced to $45,000 by the application of coinsurance plus $20,000 for extraordinary expense, or a total of $65,000. The liability of the insurer would be limited to $60,000, the outside amount for which the insurer would have been liable without the extraordinary expense item but with the application of the coinsurance clause.

Civil Authority Clause. This clause affords a valuable additional coverage to the business interruption contract in that it provides for indemnity in situations where there may be no actual damage to the premises or equipment of the insured business. It is entirely possible that damage in the vicinity of the insured business may result in areas being closed to traffic as a safety measure. Sometimes a block or more may be destroyed in a conflagration, and, while walls and chimneys are standing, areas closed to the public may interfere with businesses that have suffered no actual damage. Hurricane areas are partially susceptible to such losses.

The civil authority clause provides that the insurer shall be liable for loss for a period not exceeding two weeks if access to the premises described in the contract is prohibited by order of civil authority as a result of fire or lightning or other covered peril in the vicinity of the insured premises. In order that the insurer be liable for such an interruption, the order preventing access to the premises must originate from the police or other comparable governmental authority.

Special Exclusions. The business interruption forms contain a number of special exclusions, and the nature of these depends upon whether the contract is designed for a mercantile or manufacturing risk. Certain of these exclusions that are applicable to both classes of risk appear in all forms. In the category of special exclusions the contract provides that there shall be no liability for (*a*) the destruction of any finished stock, (*b*) any increase of loss which may be occasioned by any ordinance or law regulating construction or repair of buildings, (*c*) suspension, lapse, or cancellation of any lease or license, contract, or order, (*d*) increase of loss due to interference with rebuilding by strikers, and (*e*) consequential or remote loss.

Destruction of Finished Stock. It is the intent of this exclusion not only to remove all doubt with respect to the liability of the insurer for direct damage to finished merchandise but to eliminate as well any claims for loss of profits on finished stock. Damage or destruction to finished stock is a loss under the property damage contract. The property damage contract will not, however, cover profits, and the insured under a business interruption contract might reach the conclusion that fixed charges and profits with respect to this stock amounted to a business interruption loss. The fixed charges and net profits with respect to finished goods are a matter of past history as soon as the manufacturing process is completed. The interruption of business did not interfere with the manufacturing process for finished stock; hence, the business interruption contract does not cover and the exclusion appears to obviate any uncertainty. Profits can be covered only by profits insurance.

Impact of Ordinance or Law. The exclusion of liability for increase of loss occasioned by ordinance or law regulating construction or repair of buildings has the effect of limiting the period of interruption to such a time as buildings destroyed or damaged could reasonably be replaced. Thus, if a frame building in an area now restricted to fire-resistive construction should be destroyed, the insurer would be liable for loss for a period necessary to replace the frame building. Any extra time that would be needed to replace the type of building required by the law or ordinance is not a business interruption loss. If the insured himself elects to build a structure larger or more substantial than the damaged structure, any increase in the time required for replacement is not covered. The limit of liability is the time required to replace the original buildings or equipment insured under the contract. On the other hand, if some alternative type of construction is selected that permits building in a shorter period than it would take to replace the type of structure destroyed, then only the actual time that elapses during the reconstruction period may be considered for the purpose of measuring the business interruption loss.

Impact of Cancellation. By providing that the insurer shall not be liable for loss which is the direct result of the suspension, lapse, or cancellation of any lease or license, contract, or order, there is no liability for payment for interruption beyond the normal period of time it would take to replace or repair buildings and equipment if for any reason the insured is unable to effect such replacement. If by virtue of the terms of a lease or governmental license the insured is unable to reoccupy the damaged property, this fact of itself will not increase the loss. If the insured is obliged to rent in another location or purchase another building, the time element will not contribute to increase his loss. As before, the limit of liability is the time required to repair or replace the original buildings.

If as a result of business interruption, contracts are canceled that could easily have been filled on time, this is still not a direct loss, and only the losses due to the interruption of business while the premises and equipment are being replaced and restored are covered. It is conceivable that word might get abroad that the X Manufacturing Company has suffered a severe fire loss. Not knowing when it would be back in production, customers might send in a wholesale cancellation of orders. The fact that these orders might, for the most part, be filled upon reopening will not increase the loss if they cannot be retained.

Impact of Strikers. If building or replacement is delayed due to a strike on the part of workmen, the delay in the restoration of the property will not increase the loss. Reference to interference by "other persons" excludes as a loss factor delay caused by an unauthorized strike or by any interference that would prolong business interruption. A delay caused by a strike on premises other than those of the insured will increase the loss. If the builder cannot get material because his source of supply is cut off by a strike, then the delay will increase the business interruption loss. Liability for delays caused by strikes is excluded only where the interference occurs at the premises of the insured.

Consequential or Remote Loss. If the insured is back in business, having his building and equipment fully restored, but for some reason attributable to the loss his business does not fully recover, this is not a direct but a remote loss and excluded from the coverage. Assume, for example, a druggist whose prescription records are destroyed by fire. Duplications are obtained and filed with a competitor. If, after three months' business interruption the druggist is open for business and many of the former customers continue their prescription business with the competitor, this is a consequential loss. It is possible to extend coverage by endorsement (within limits) to the time required to "restore the business."

Contingent Business Interruption Insurance. This form is available to indemnify the insured in the event of loss due to damage or to the destruction of property not owned or operated by the insured but upon which the insured is dependent in whole or in part for the continued operation of his business. There are two forms of contingent business interruption included in the business interruption category. These are: (*a*) contributing properties coverage, and (*b*) recipient properties coverage. The first form provides indemnity in the event that the insured suffers a business interruption loss due to the destruction of or damage to other plants furnishing materials, parts, or services to the plant of the insured. The second form insures against loss caused by damage to or destruction of other plants to which the product of the insured plant is sold. Recipient properties coverage is a required form for the manufacturer who as a subcontractor supplies materials or parts to a prime contractor. In the event that the plant of the prime contractor, termed in the contract the "recipient property," is damaged or destroyed so that the prime contractor is no longer able to take the product of the insured, his (the insured's) business interruption losses are covered under his recipient properties coverage.

Off-Premises Power Plant Insurance. Closely related to the contingent business interruption coverage is a specialized contingent form covering the continued flow of utilities. Insurance may be written to cover loss attributable to the interruption of the supply of electricity, heat, gas, or water. The source may be either a public utility or a privately operated source. Since the coverage applies with respect to utilities received from plants outside the premises of the insured, the coverage is, in fact, a form of contributing properties business interruption indemnity. Coverage may be provided for the interruption of the supply of any one or of several named utilities. Coverage may be written to protect the insured against interruption of power, light, or other utility due to fire damage at the source of supply. It may also be written to cover against tornado, explosion, vehicle damage, and all the other hazards insurable under the fire and extended coverage endorsement. Interruption due to damage to transmission lines may be covered, as well as property damage at the generating plant.

RENTS AND RENTAL VALUE INSURANCE

If a property is rendered untenantable by fire, in addition to the direct loss or damage there is a loss of use if occupied by the owner, or a loss of rental income if occupied by a tenant. Losses from this source are insurable under a rents or rental value form.

Rents insurance indemnifies the owner of a property in the event that his rental income is cut off or interrupted by fire or other hazard included in the coverage. Rental value insurance covers the occupant and indemnifies him for the loss of use of the premises. The occupant may be the owner, in which case his indemnity represents the rental he must pay to secure premises similar to those destroyed or damaged. On the other hand, if the occupant is a tenant under a lease so drawn that his payments must continue during the untenantable period, he too is indemnified on the same basis as if he were the owner.

Rents insurance is a particularly important coverage for estates whose holdings are largely real estate, the beneficiaries of which would be seriously inconvenienced if their income should be interrupted for any lengthy period. Trustees might personally be willing to assume the risk on their own property but are frequently unwilling to take the risk as trustees if the beneficiaries of the trust depend largely upon the income from the real estate in question.

Rental forms in common use are written with coinsurance. The requirements vary from 60 percent to 100 percent. The rate is less as the ratio of insurance to value required by the coinsurance clause increases.

If the form is based upon the rental value for the length of time required to rebuild the property if totally destroyed, the amount of insurance necessary for full coverage is the amount of income received during the estimated period. If the form contains the 100 percent coinsurance clause, the period estimated as the time required to rebuild should be generous; otherwise, when a loss occurs, the insurance may be found to be inadequate.

In seasonal risks, the months of customary occupancy are incorporated into the form, and the contract is written to limit its liability for loss of rental value only during this period. A summer home, with a rental value of $1,500 for the months of June, July, and August, would be insured for $1,500 for one year under a seasonal form. If damaged in September and repairs could reasonably be completed before the following June, there would be no liability under the contract. Damage in May that could not be repaired until September would require the payment of the face of the contract. When a property is untenable for a month or fraction thereof during the indicated usual period of occupancy, indemnity is paid on a pro rata basis—that is, at the rate of $500 for each month so vacant.

The period for which a loss may be collected begins with the happening of the fire, or other contingency insured against, and runs for the period required with the exercise of reasonable diligence to restore the property. The loss must originate during the term of the contract, though the liability may continue beyond its termination.

Wherever rent is a continuing expense and must be paid by the insured, this loss is covered under the business interruption contract. It will be recalled that rental value insurance indemnifies a tenant for rent payments he is obligated to make under a lease during the period the property he occupies is untenantable. The question presents itself as to whether there is not duplication in the two coverages. To an extent there is, and sometimes the business interruption contract is endorsed to provide that if the insured's interest is otherwise insured under a rent or rental value contract, then rental value is to be eliminated from all consideration under the business interruption contract. The purpose of eliminating the rental coverage from the business interruption contract is a premium savings. The need for rental coverage in addition to business interruption is only in that situation where the insured knows or fears his business is not earning fixed charges. Under the business interruption contract the insured recovers rent only to the extent that he would have earned fixed charges during the period operations are suspended. Rental value insurance is not dependent upon whether the rent is earned but makes payment to the insured during the period he is obligated to pay.

LEASEHOLD INTEREST

This form is closely allied to rent and rental value insurance. Leases as they are ordinarily written contain a "cancellation clause" which provides that either party to the lease may terminate it at option if a designated percentage of the property is destroyed. It follows that if a tenant possesses a long-term lease particularly advantageous to him, the lease will in all probability not be continued if the owner has the option of terminating it under his cancellation clause.

Leasehold value represents the increased rental value of premises to a lessee in excess of the actual rental paid by him under the terms of his lease. Thus, if 10 years ago a lease was executed on a property calling for $1,000 monthly rental to run for a period of 20 years, it might be quite possible that, owing to a change in business conditions, the same property would today bring $2,000 a month. If this is so, the holder of the lease has a leasehold interest in the property valued at $1,000 a month for 10 years. Assuming the property to be destroyed to an extent that permits the owner of the property to cancel the lease, the holder of the lease has lost the equivalent of $1,000 a month for 120 months. This, it will readily be recognized, is not $120,000 but rather the present value of $1,000 a month for 120 months. The amount of the loss is determined by the use of a compound interest table computed at varying percentages that will give the present value of $1.00 a month for a period of years. By entering the table and determining the proper factor to be applied, an amount can be determined which, if invested at the agreed upon percentage, would yield an income equivalent to $1,000 per month for the period in question. The leasehold interest contract does not cover losses growing out of the loss of the use of a building, potential profits, good will, or other types of consequential loss. Its coverage is limited strictly to the leasehold value. If the owner of the property has the right to cancel the lease but does not elect to do so, the insured may not collect under his leasehold interest contract. If the insured has the right to cancel the contract and elects to do so, there is likewise no loss. The contract does not cover in the event of cancellation of the lease for any reason other than the happening of a loss, the outgrowth of one of the perils insured against. If the loss is occasioned by any act of the insured, there is no coverage under the contract.

In addition to the situation where a tenant is paying a rental less than the actual rental value measured by the current market for the property, there are other situations that create an insurable interest in a lease. These are: (*a*) the payment of a bonus to secure a location, (*b*) advance rent payments, and (*c*) expenditures for betterments and improvements. It often happens where good locations are scarce and held under long-term leases that a concern may find it profitable to pay a substantial lump sum to a present tenant to secure his location. This sum would be lost entirely if the premises were destroyed and his lease canceled. The bonus is amortized over the period of the lease and may be insured under a special form designed for the purpose. The contract is written for a face amount equal to the bonus with the amount of insurance decreasing monthly to reflect the amortization of the bonus.

Tenants' improvements are insured for physical loss or damage under a tenants' improvements form. There is no conflict between this form and the leasehold interest form covering an amount invested in betterments. The leasehold interest form covering benefits follows the pattern of the bonus form. It defines leasehold interest as the insured's interest in improvements and betterments to a particular building during the unexpired term of his lease. If the building is destroyed or damaged to the extent that the lease is canceled, then the leasehold improvements and betterments coverage indemnifies the insured. In the case of partial destruction of the premises, with no lease cancellation, the leasehold improvements and betterments coverage pays nothing. Here the insured requires tenants' improvements insurance to pay the cost of repairing physical damage to the property. To obviate double insurance the improvements and betterments leasehold form provides that in the event of the cancellation of the insured's lease by fire, any amount payable to the insured under property damage contracts for the direct loss or damage to improvements and betterments is to be deducted from the amount recoverable under the leasehold contract.

In some situations substantial amounts of rent are payable in advance. Without any interest in the betterments, a property owner may agree to make certain renovations for a prospective tenant and, as an aid to financing them, require the advance payment of rent for a year or more. In other instances the owner, as a convenience to himself, may require rent paid annually in advance with no provisions for refund under any circumstances. The cancellation of such a lease would leave the tenant without the use of the property for the unexpired term of the lease and accordingly he would lose a pro rata share of the advance rent. This form of advance rent may be covered, as in the case of the bonus and improvements, with the amount of insurance decreasing over the term of the lease.

In writing a leasehold-interest contract, the fire clause in the lease furnishes the key to the entire underwriting problem. When the clause is vaguely stated and gives one or both parties the right to terminate the lease in the event of a fire, a leasehold interest under such an agreement is uninsurable. A satisfactory form of fire clause will require that the property be over 50 percent destroyed by fire before the lease may be canceled. Discounts from the rate are sometimes allowed if the fire clause requires a 75 percent or more destruction before the right of cancellation arises. From the point of view of the underwriter, the higher the percentage indicated, the more favorable the risk. If no fire clause appears in the lease, statutes in the state where the property is located govern in case of fire. When the statute is considered adequate from the insurer's viewpoint, a leasehold-interest policy may be written, incorporating into the form the stipulation that the statute of the state is to be followed in the matter of right to cancel.

Rates for leasehold interest are governed by the building rate. Since a leasehold interest reduces in value from month to month as the term of the lease runs toward expiration, with no value left at expiration, it will be seen if one follows the idea of indemnity that regardless of the amount written in the face of the contract, the amount collectible is less each month. For this reason the form itself provides for this continued reduction in the amount payable, decreasing the amount as the contract approaches expiration. The premium, so that it may be equitable, is based upon an average of the amount of the insurer has at risk during the contract term. The average is found by adding the insurable value at the beginning of the contract term to the insurable value at its termination and dividing by two the sum so found. The average thus obtained is multiplied by the rate, and the resulting amount is the premium for the contract term. The face amount of the contract is the value of the lease the day the contract is written.

Loss under the contract is payable only if the lease is terminated. As in the case of other fire insurance contracts, the contract is one of indemnity. There are a number of forms covering leasehold interest, but they all follow much the same pattern. A widely used form provides, in the case of cancellation of the lease, for the payment of the gross leasehold value for a period of three months. The leasehold value for the balance of the term is discounted on the basis of a discount rate established in the contract. In other words, the benefits to be derived in the future over the term of the lease are reduced to their present value and paid in a lump sum. It is usual to provide that if the premises become uninhabitable but the lease is not canceled, the contract will indemnify the insured for such excess rental as he is obliged to pay for the time required to restore the premises.

Leasehold-interest contracts may be written on an annual basis or for a term, as may the fire contract covering the direct loss. Upon renewal, or at any time during the contract term, if a change in the leasehold value takes place, the insurance may be adjusted to cover accordingly. A leasehold interest may run to great value, and executors or trustees particularly should recognize their obligation to protect and preserve this value as an asset, just as they would protect an asset represented by ownership of physical property. This value, however, is frequently overlooked.

EXCESS RENTAL VALUE

A converse of the leasehold-interest contract is found in the excess rental value contract which undertakes to protect the owner of buildings who has an advantageous lease which, if canceled, could not be renewed on equally favorable terms. This is in contrast to the leasehold-interest contract, which provides indemnity if the lessee is obliged to cancel a lease that is worth more than the price he is paying.

The excess rental value contract operates in the following manner. Assume a lease written 10 years ago for a period of 20 years and calling for a monthly payment of $2,500. Assume further that on the present market the most the property would bring is $1,500. Under these circumstances, the property owner has an insurable excess rental value in the lease of $1,000 a month for 10 years. If the property should be so destroyed by fire that the lessee could elect to cancel, it is apparent that this would be the logical procedure for him to follow. In these circumstances, if the owner of the property restored it and offered it for rent, his income would be reduced by $1,000 a month.

As in the case of leasehold interest, the insurable value is determined by discounting the monthly payments and finding their present lump-sum value.

SELLING AGENTS' COMMISSIONS INSURANCE

The commission lost where goods already manufactured and sold but not delivered are damaged or destroyed may be insured under the profits form. The loss is identical to the loss of profits to the owner of the goods but is measured by the commission earned through the sale but lost through inability to secure delivery of the goods sold. In contrast to this type of commission is the selling agent who handles large quantities of the output of one or more manufacturing establishments. He does not purchase for his own account but secures his income from placing orders. He may be a commission agent, broker, or factor. A person or concern operating in one of these capacities is not concerned solely with goods manufactured but not delivered. He is concerned with the interruption of a continuous flow of the goods he undertakes to sell and may suffer a severe loss if this flow of goods is interrupted. The loss may be covered under a selling agents' commission form.

The selling agents' commission form is actually a type of contingent business interruption insurance. It has a particular appeal when a substantial volume or all of the business of the selling agent is derived from the output of a single plant. It also appeals to the agent or salesman who spends the entire year on the road taking orders for a future seasonable delivery. Orders for calendars and advertising novelties are taken the year around, but deliveries are made about December 1. If a representative working on a commission basis were to have orders in for a year and the plant were destroyed before delivery of the goods, he might, depending upon his contract, suffer a substantial loss. Under a commissions coverage, the goods need not have been completed, since it is sufficient to support a claim if the concern for which the goods were sold is unable to make deliveries because of a hazard covered by the contract.

Commissions insurance is written with a coinsurance clause with the usual requirement at least 80 percent of insurance to value. The rate charged is the rate for business interruption insurance at the location where the goods sold by the agent are manufactured.

TUITION FEES INSURANCE

Private schools, run for profit, are dependent upon the income derived from tuition fees for their maintenance. A fire that destroys any substantial part of the property of the school might necessitate a temporary suspension of operations, with a consequent obligation to refund tuition collected or to cancel charges already made. Nor is there any assurance, with the work of reconstruction and repair completed, that all the students formerly enrolled will return. Thus, the consequences of the fire from this angle alone may be far-reaching enough to disorganize the entire program of the school.

The insurance, as written, indemnifies the insured for loss occasioned by the necessity to return, or the failure to receive, tuition fees as the outgrowth of a fire. If a fire occurs during the summer vacation, the loss is computed on the basis of the attendance for the previous year. The contract pays for the loss of tuition fees sustained after the expiration of the contract if the fire occasioning the loss occurred during the contract term. Recovery is not limited to the time required to restore the damaged property. Protection extends to the day preceding the beginning of the first school year following the date that restoration and repairs have been completed. If a school building is destroyed or damaged during a school term, resulting transfers may not be determined until the opening of the next school year. The contract further provides that if the reconstruction period runs to a date within 30 days of the opening of the next school year, loss of tuition due to uncertainty of the plans for reopening are covered. This provision covers a loss where rebuilding is possible during the vacation period but transfers result because of the students' uncertainty regarding the completion date.

It follows that even though the building or buildings destroyed may have been completed in their entirety and ready for occupancy on the day the school was scheduled to open, unless ready at least 30 days prior to the opening date, any loss of tuitions sustained by the school is covered by the contract. If a part of the damaged property is completed, any loss attributable to incomplete facilities with a resulting curtailment in enrollment under the normal roster is covered.

Under the tuition fees coverage the insured is required to carry insurance in an amount equal to the normal tuition fees for the fiscal year covered by the contract. If a loss occurs and the insured fails to carry the required amount of insurance, the insurer is liable only for that proportion of the loss which the insurance bears to the normal tuition fees for the fiscal year in which the loss occurs. This is in effect a 100 percent coinsurance requirement.

The insured is obligated immediately following the loss to take all reasonable steps to eliminate any expense which does not necessarily continue. He is expected to make use of other available property or take advantage of any other reasonable steps that will reduce the amount of the loss. The cost of this procedure as well as the savings effected are taken into consideration in arriving at the amount of the loss for which the company is liable. The insurer is not liable for any increase in loss sustained occasioned by an ordinance or law regulating or prohibiting construction or repair of buildings. Neither is it liable for any increase in loss attributable to the cancellation of any license or lease or for any other consequential or remote loss. These limitations are identical to those of business interruption contracts.

Tuition fees insurance does not lend itself for the insurance of schools that operate continuously throughout the year. For such institutions, one of the standard business interruption contracts is better adapted to provide protection. On the other hand, for a school operated on a seasonal basis the tuition fees form appeals since, unlike business interruption insurance, it makes the recovery in no way contingent upon the time required to replace or restore the damaged property. If school buildings are destroyed to such an extent that it will take three months to replace them, the measure of the loss is not one fourth of the year's income, but, it will be such income as was lost due to the necessity of suspending school operations.

EXTRA-EXPENSE INSURANCE

Extra-expense insurance covers, subject to the contract limits, all extra-expense or additional charges incurred by the insured in order to continue as nearly as practicable the normal conduct of his business following damage or destruction of buildings or contents by an insured peril. This may cover the cost of doing business at a location other than the usual premises of the insured, if the move is necessitated by a hazard covered by the insurance contract. It is sometimes confused with business interruption insurance, but when it is recalled that business interruption insurance covers loss against interruption of the business and extra-expense insurance covers the additional cost of carrying on a business following a loss, the difference in the two forms of insurance is quite apparent.

The business interruption contract does contain an extraordinary expense item, and for many classes of risk the business interruption contract satisfies the needs of the insured. It should be recalled that extraordinary expenses under the business interruption contract are covered to the extent that loss under the contract is reduced. Extra-expense insurance provides for the extraordinary outlay to get a business in operation immediately without regard to any reduction in the business interruption loss. The insurance is sometimes referred to as "additional charges and expense insurance" or "surplus charges and expense insurance." The tendency is developing to use the shorter form, "extra-expense insurance."

The extra-expense form provides insurance for necessary extra expense over and above normal operating costs to provide the means to permit the insured to continue as nearly as practicable normal business operations immediately following damage or destructions to buildings or contents by the perils insured against. The contract does not cover loss of income in any respect.

Additional Living-Expense Insurance. There is a form of extra-expense coverage, known as the "additional living-expense form," available for residents of dwellings and written in connection with rental value insurance.[1] This form bears the same relationship to rental value insurance that extra-expense insurance bears to business interruption. As before, one supplements the other. Rental value coverage indemnifies the insured for the rental value of the home during the period it is unfit for occupancy because of a loss caused by a peril covered by the insurance. The additional living-expense form reimburses the insured for excess expenses necessitated by securing temporary living quarters during the period the property is not habitable.

The additional living-expense contract covers *necessary* living expenses. To establish a claim the expenses must be *incurred*. An insured may not create excessive charges to provide quarters more luxurious than those which he occupied. There must be a reasonable relationship between the two. Conversely, he may not move in with relatives or occupy less desirable quarters on a temporary basis and collect on the ground that he *could have* obligated the insurer for the better quarters under the terms of his contract. The insurer undertakes to indemnify the insured for excess payments which the insured himself has made to house his family adequately.

The contract provides payment for such a period as is required to restore and make habitable the damaged property, subject always to the contract limits. If the family establishes itself in permanent quarters other than those vacated because of the loss, the insurance payments terminate.

This insurance is not written with a coinsurance requirement, but the payment in any one month under the contract is limited to 25 percent of the face of the contract. This means that with excess costs of $100 monthly and an interruption of use of the premises of one month, $400 insurance would be required. This same insurance would pay $100 monthly for four months, but not $400 for one month even if a necessary incurred expenditure could be shown. It follows that insurance should be at least four times the first monthly anticipated claim and should be in an amount sufficient to last for such a time as the family may at the outside be expected to occupy substitute quarters. It is to be remembered that the insurance does not pay the full cost of substitute quarters but only the excess cost of the new quarters

[1] Additional living expense coverage is no longer available in some areas, except in connection with the dwelling broad and special forms and in the homeowner's program.

per month above the usual costs of living in the uninhabitable damaged property.

FOR DISCUSSION

1. B has a contract with C to supply certain parts for a machine that he manufactures. The contract has been running for a long time and is most favorable to B. Should C's plant burn or otherwise be put out of operation, B would suffer a very substantial loss. Could this loss be covered under a business interruption contract?
2. It is a part of the business of the operators of grain elevators to purchase grain as well as to handle, store, and clean it, after which it is delivered for the account of the owner. If the warehouse burns, the owner, in addition to losing his grain, would also lose charges for storage and other services. May the charges that have accrued on the grain belonging to others be insured under a business interruption contract?
3. Business interruption forms now provide that for the purposes of ascertaining the amount of loss sustained, or for the purpose of the application of the coinsurance clause, due consideration shall be given to the insured's business before the loss and the probable experience thereafter. Explain.
4. D operates a newspaper in the city of X. In the event of a fire, the newspaper would not suspend publication but would hire outside facilities to continue operations. This in almost every conceivable instance would involve a heavy extra expense to D. Is this extra expense insurable under a business interruption contract?
5. B carries riot and civil commotion insurance and in connection therewith provides business interruption coverage. He is particularly interested in this coverage because he is fearful of the interruption of his business as a result of a strike. To what extent does the contract provide him coverage, if any, against strike losses?
6. X carries a broad vandalism endorsement on his business interruption contract. In a strike some years ago, he suffered great production losses caused by inefficient strike breakers, as well as the deliberate wasting of materials, mislaying of tools, and deliberate inefficiency. He wishes to know to what extent his contract covers losses of this nature.
7. X owns a large apartment building upon which he carries both business interruption indemnity and rent insurance. He is advised that his cover is duplicated, because, in the case in question, both furnish essentially the same cover. Is this so? Explain your answer.
8. The city of X inquires of you whether it may put business interruption indemnity and rental value insurance on its school buildings. It may put one but not the other. Explain which may be carried and the logic of your answer.

9. The Livonia fire of August 12, 1953, resulted in a physical damage loss to the General Motors Corporation in excess of $50 million. There has been said to have been no business interruption coverage. It has been suggested that the production of some 300,000 automotive units was stopped as a result of the fire. Discuss the business interruption implications, both direct and contingent.
10. The Port of New York Authority carries blanket business interruption insurance on its three Hudson River crossings. Why do the insurers require blanket insurance rather than insuring each facility separately?
11. It is sometimes stated that contingent business interruption insurance provides protection against the interruption of the business of another. This is not correct. Why?
12. May business interruption insurance be written to cover an individual who is not a proprietor of a business enterprise?
13. Tuition fees insurance differs from the usual business interruption forms in one very important respect. Loss payable under business interruption insurance ends when the property covered by the insurance is restored to operating condition. How does the tuition fees coverage differ?
14. A simplified gross earnings business interruption form designed for small business enterprises is sometimes known as the "no-coinsurance" form. What are the important characteristics of this form?
15. The B manufacturing company has automatically renewed its business interruption indemnity contract without change for several years. For the last three years the concern has been losing money. What is your recommendation to the insured?
16. What are the particular features that make the coinsurance business interruption form attractive to certain types of business organizations?
17. A manufacturing plant is made up of five separate units, each in charge of a vice-president. You are asked to review the coverage and, upon examination of the contracts, discover that each unit carries an adequate business interruption coverage. What recommendation would you make and why?
18. Is business interruption indemnity coverage limited to the fire risk, or may it be extended to include other hazards?
19. It is obvious that consequential losses can be serious. It is a natural tendency for owners of property to insure the physical property and neglect intangibles. Discuss impact of failure to insure consequential risks.
20. The problem of determining a business interruption value for a new business enterprise is at once apparent. The establishment of a new business carries with it immediately all the fixed charges and continuing obligations that attach to a long-established enterprise. The item of prospective net profits is the enigma. Because of the difficulty of arriving at this figure, it is not always easy to underwrite a contract

for a new business. What factors would you consider in determining the insurable value for such a risk?

21. A building in the process of construction to be occupied by a business establishment can be covered by the prospective occupant under a business interruption form to compensate him for loss attributable to an insurable peril. How would you determine the insurable value?

CHAPTER · 11

Ocean Marine Contracts

The ocean marine business is highly specialized and is carried on in the United States primarily by large multiple line insurers who participate in underwriting syndicates. The principal non-American insurer is Lloyd's of London. Ocean marine insurance is concerned primarily with insuring against loss caused by maritime perils. Every lawful maritime adventure may be the subject of an ocean marine insurance contract; there is said to be a maritime adventure when:

a) Any ship, goods, or other movables are exposed to maritime perils. Such property is in this Act referred to as "insurable property";
b) The earning or acquisition of any freight, passage money, commission, profit, or other pecuniary benefit, or the security for any advances, loan or disbursements, is endangered by the exposure of insurable property to maritime perils;
c) Any liability to a third party may be incurred by the owner of, or other person interested in or responsible for, insurable property, by reason of maritime perils.[1]

Stated somewhat differently, it may be said that the principal interests in a maritime venture are hull, cargo, freight, and third party liability, and that these interests form the subject matter of various marine insurance contracts.

TERMINOLOGY AND RELATED MATTERS

The practices in marine insurance differ in many ways from other forms of property insurance. The protection against various perils is typically "all risk," and the contracts are relatively free of exclusions and limiting clauses. Further, marine insurance tends not to be regulated by governmental authority, relies more heavily on tradition, informal methods of rate making, and the utmost good faith of the parties to the venture. Many words and phrases are different in marine

[1] Marine Insurance Act, 1906 (6 Edw. 7, c. 41), sec. 3.

than in other forms of insurance, and before considering typical contracts, a consideration of specific terms is essential.

"Ocean marine insurance," as the term is now used, is understood to mean "sea insurance." The term applies to insurance made upon ships or vessels, or upon machinery, tackle, merchandise, or other property on board a ship or vessel, or upon the freight of, or any other interest relating to, a ship or vessel. Ocean marine insurance may include, in addition to the sea risk, other incidental risks which attach from the commencement of the transit to the ultimate destination covered by the insurance.[2] It has been more simply defined as "a contract whereby the insurer undertakes to indemnify the insured in a manner and to the extent thereby agreed, against marine losses; that is to say, the losses incident to marine adventure."[3] It may, by its express terms or by usage of trade, be extended to protect the insured against losses "on inland waters or on any land risk which may be incidental to any sea voyage."[4] "Marine perils" are defined as "the perils of the sea, fire, war perils, pirates, rovers, thieves, captures, seizures, restraints, and detainments of princes and people, jettisons, barratry, and any other perils, either of the like kind or which may be designated by the policy."[5]

The term "average" has become by general acceptance in marine insurance to mean loss or damage. The etymology of the word is not altogether clear, but the most logical theory, and one widely advanced, is that the word is a derivation of the French word *avarie*, meaning loss or damage.

"Particular average" refers to loss upon any one interest that is not a total loss. Particular average is distinguished from general average in that particular average remains where it falls, whereas in the case of a general average loss, all interests at risk in a given voyage must bear it proportionately. Damage to a ship by fire or storm must be borne entirely by the shipowner, and the loss is a particular average loss. If a proportion of the cargo is jettisoned in the face of danger to save the ship and the balance of the cargo, the owners of the ship and the cargo so saved must contribute to make good to its owner the loss of the property jettisoned. The contributions thus made are general average contributions.

If the subject of the insurance is covered in such a way that there is no liability on the part of the insurer until the loss reaches a designated percentage of value, the percentage limitation is termed "average limitation." In the case of average limitation, if the loss equals the

---

[2] The Stamp Act, 1891 (54 and 55 Victoria, c. 39), sec. 92.

[3] Marine Insurance Act, 1906 (6 Edw. VII, c. 41), sec. 1.

[4] *Ibid.*, sec. 2.

[5] *Ibid.*, sec. 3.

designated percentage, the insurer is liable for the loss in full. Another situation is to be found when the insured bears a given percentage of every loss. The amount he assumes is termed "deductible average."

TYPES OF CONTRACT

Marine insurance contracts are largely constructed to protect against the financial consequences of the perils that may affect the marine interests of hull, cargo, liability, and freight. Contracts covering these interests may be written on a time or voyage basis and they may be valued or unvalued.

A voyage contract covers the subject matter for the voyage named in the contract, while a time contract provides coverage for a fixed period of time. Most marine insurance contracts are valued; that is, the parties agree at the time the insurance is placed upon the value of the thing insured, and this value is set forth in the contract. Unvalued contracts, rarely used in marine insurance, provide that the value of the thing insured be ascertained following a loss.

Hull Contracts. Hull contracts cover on the various types of ship for which marine insurance is written. There are a number of subdivisions in the hull classification in which the contract is adapted to a particular type of risk, such as ocean steamers, sailing vessels, builders' risks, port risk contracts, and fleet contracts. Contracts covering the liability risk may be one of the foregoing with the liability hazard incorporated in the form of a collision or running-down clause.

Cargo Contracts. Cargo contracts may be written under a single risk form providing insurance for a particular shipment, or they may be written under floating or open forms, providing coverage for goods of a certain class up to a certain limit, with provision for the specific thing insured and its value to be declared subsequently. Contracts covering on freight protect the insured for loss of money due him if, as result of the perils covered in his contract, he is unable to complete the delivery of merchandise and secure the amounts due therefor. Freight coverage may be included in contracts covering other interests.

Single Risk Forms. This form is now rarely used, and virtually all of the cargo insurance written in this country is insured by an open contract. Since the form is available and does have an occasional use, it will be considered briefly. When such protection is required the owner of the interest to be insured must submit to the insurer a statement of the kind of merchandise to be insured, how it is packed, the places of shipment and destination, the name of the steamer, and the nature of connecting conveyances. Finally, the owner must indicate the perils against which he wishes coverage. With this information the insurer submits a rate, and not until it is indicated as acceptable is the risk bound. In due course, a single risk certificate is issued and delivered to the insured.

Open Cargo Forms. Open cargo forms, which will be discussed in greater detail in Chapter 12, are designed to accommodate exporters or importers who are constantly shipping goods throughout the entire period of the year. It often happens in the case of such businesses that goods consigned to them have been shipped prior to their actual receipt of notice, and goods on the dock ready for shipment may be placed aboard ship and underway before notice is in the hands of the owner. To provide the automatic attachment of insurance, open cargo forms are written. These contracts may cover on either imports or exports, and the insurance is effected by attaching a special "import" or "export" form to the cargo contract. Both forms are very much alike and are modified only to the extent necessary to distinguish between the needs of the importer and those of the exporter. To illustrate, under the export form, provision is made for the insured to issue certificates of insurance so that he may be able to furnish without delay evidence of the fact that insurance has been effected upon shipments covered by the open contract. On the other hand, the import contract is sufficiently broad to attach coverage even before the insured knows that the cargo is shipped. From the time it becomes effective the contract attaches on all shipments consigned to the insured, or other parties, if an insurable interest exists in the insured. Shipments insured under open contracts covering imports are reported to the insurer as required in the contract. With respect to this insurance, individual certificates of insurance are not required, since it is the interest of the insured in shipments consigned to him that is covered.

Cargo contracts are sometimes written before the insurable interest of the insured attaches. It is essential that the insured be interested in the subject matter insured at the time of the loss. In the absence of an insurable interest on the part of the insured, a contract may be written to cover shipments which the insured is under instructions to insure for the account of others. The requirement of insurable interest is the same for both open and single risk contracts.

Protection and Indemnity Insurance. The exclusions that found their way into the collision clause (see page 268) were designed to set limitations upon the extent of the collision liability that insurance underwriters were willing to assume. The demand, however, presented itself for a more comprehensive coverage, and, as a result, the collision liability provided in the running down clause may be augmented by the protection and indemnity contract known as protection and indemnity (P. & I.) insurance. The coverage is usually provided in a separate contract, though in some instances it is attached to the hull contract by means of an endorsement. It provides a comprehensive liability protection against losses excluded under the hull collision liability.

The collision clause, as originally written, obligated the underwriters to assume only three fourths of the collision liability. Other exclusions, such as liability for loss of life or personal injury and damage to docks and piers were excluded and continued to be excluded under the collision clause in the contract. When the running down clause was written only to cover three fourths of the liability of the vessel owner, efforts were made on the part of owners to share this one-fourth portion of collision liability on a mutual basis. To do this they grouped together in clubs. Vessel owners contributed to the expense of the club and to losses incurred on the basis of tonnage to be protected by the club. While this type of arrangement is no longer necessary, the exclusions still in the clause with respect to liability for persons and property leaves the vessel owner with a wide area of liability unprotected. With the development of legislation in the nature of employers' liability, owners became increasingly conscious of the need for insurance protection other than that provided by the running down clause. This additional insurance was first provided by the groups organized to carry the one-fourth liability uninsured under the earlier running down clause. When the clubs began to assume liability for personal injury, the basis for P. & I. insurance was laid.

The coverage is a highly specialized form of protection. It concerns itself with marine legal liability insurance with respect to vessel operations. The contract "protects" and "indemnifies" the vessel owner with respect to his legal liability as the owner and operator of the insured vessel. The contract covers liability with respect to (*a*) crew members, (*b*) persons other than employees, (*c*) cargo, (*d*) other vessels and fixed objects, and (*e*) miscellaneous claims including liability for customs or other fines or penalties.

Liability to Crew Members. Coverage is provided for liability of the insured for personal injury to and death of crew members. This is a source of a large number of claims. This phase of the coverage differs considerably from other liability contracts, since negligence is not necessarily a condition precedent for liability. A seaman who is injured or becomes ill while in the service of a vessel is entitled to wages to the end of the voyage, maintenance, and medical care plus transportation. While, as stated, negligence is not a factor, the vessel is not liable if injury or illness is the result of wilful misconduct. If the injury or illness is so severe that the injured seaman must be left in a foreign port, the shipowner is obligated to pay cost of transportation to the port where the seaman joined the voyage. If negligence of the vessel is a factor, the seaman may bring suit against his employer.

Persons Other than Employees. Liability of the vessel to persons other than employees for bodily injury and death is covered. This protection extends to include claims of passengers, stevedores, and any other persons who may be working on the vessel or who may be on board. Claims of persons injured in a collision are covered. Briefly, under this heading any claim for personal injury to persons other than employees that establishes liability on the vessel owner arising out of its ownership, operation, or maintenance is covered.

Cargo. Any responsibility on the part of the vessel owner for damage to cargo carried by it is covered. Cargo damage frequently arises when a ship is not in proper condition to accept it or if it is improperly stowed. There are laws that provide certain immunities with respect to claims for cargo damage, but if damage is attributable to negligence then the cargo owner may proceed against the ship and recover his loss. Claims resulting from improper stowage, contamination, unseaworthiness of the vessel, and shortages are all covered.

Other Vessels and Fixed Objects. There are certain exemptions with respect to docks, piers, breakwaters, and similar items, which limit the protection of the collision clause. Damage to other vessels for which the insured vessel is liable where actual collision is not a factor is covered. Damage to fixed objects as piers, docks, bridges, and aids to navigation is covered. Damage resulting from collision with a bridge or marine cable may run to very sizable sums. If a negligently operated vessel causes another vessel to run aground or collide with a third vessel, protection and indemnity on the negligent vessel responds for damages.

Miscellaneous Claims. Liability for customs, immigration or other fines, or penalties for the violation of the law, for which the owner, master, or agents of the vessel are liable are covered. If the owner of the vessel suffers a loss due to a deviation for the purpose of landing an injured or sick seaman, the contract covers port charges, insurance, fuel, stores, and provisions consumed as a result of the deviation. Extraordinary expenses incurred as a result of quarantine are covered, as are reasonable expenses in defending claims under the contract.

The P. & I. contract contains the same "sister ship clause" found in the collision clause. Moreover, unlike the usual liability contract, the coverage will pay damages if property belonging to the insured, such as docks and wharves, is damaged. The P. & I. contract is written on a deductible basis with deductibles ranging from $250 to as high as $15,000 or more a claim.

Freight Contracts. Contracts issued to cover freight are usually designed to cover some special interest as well. In the case of hull contracts the freight interest is usually included, and in the case of cargo contracts the freight is included in the valuation. If a ship undertakes a voyage, since the freight to be earned is not payable until the cargo is delivered, the total loss of the ship will involve as well the loss of the freight to be earned on the cargo. In insuring the hull for a voyage, it is a normal procedure to include the income expected from freight for the voyage. In the case of a cargo shipment, the shipping charges will represent part of the value at the port of destination. In cargo shipments it is customary to add shipping costs, that is, freight, to the value at the port of embarkation.

Builders' Risk Coverage. The builders' risk form covers the hazards peculiar to ship construction. The contract attaches from the laying of the keel and, while usually written for a period of a year, may be written for the estimated period of construction. The coverage terminates upon the expiration date of the contract or, if the vessel is finished earlier, upon the delivery of the completed vessel to the owner. The builders' risk contract covers against the perils found in the usual hull contract and covers not only the hull itself but tackle, apparel, ordinance, munitions, artillery, engines, boilers, machinery, boats, and all furniture and fixtures as well as all material in the yard, buildings, workshops, on docks, quays, and pontoons, and similar items to be used in the work of construction. The contract covers against fire, and risks of launching may be included if required. General average and salvage charges are covered, together with liability risks assumed under the collision and P. & I. clauses. Excluded are claims originating from loss of life and personal injury, whatever the cause, including claims under workmen's compensation and employers' liability acts. The contract does not cover losses originating in strikes, riot, civil commotion, earthquake, or war risks. Consequential damage through delay is not covered, nor is damage to boilers, engines, and material while in transport, except in the port where the construction is taking place.

Officers' Protective Contract. This contract is available to officers of the merchant marine service and covers the insured against loss or damage to personal effects, instruments, and equipment resulting from stranding, sinking, burning, or collision of a vessel. The contract may also be written to provide protection to the insured officer against loss which he incurs if his license should be suspended or revoked as a result of a marine casualty.

Longshoremen's and Harbor Workers' Compensation. Under the terms of the Longshoremen's and Harbor Workers' Compensation Act, every employer is obliged to secure the payment of compensation either by insurance or by qualifying as a self-insurer for the "disability or death of an employee resulting from an injury occurring upon the navigable waters of the United States (including any dry dock), if recovery for the disability or death through Workmen's Compensation proceedings may not be validly provided for by state law." This requirement does not extend to include the master or crew of any vessel. Failure to secure payment of compensation carries with it a penalty of fine not more than $1,000 or by imprisonment for not more than a year, or both. The insured's liability for compensation may be endorsed upon the fire and marine contract that has been extended to cover P. & I. risks.

War Risks. The practice now in vogue in this country is to insure marine perils and war risks under separate contract. The war perils have been dropped from the perils clause of cargo contracts, but in connection with hull risks the clause continues to include the war perils. There is a free of capture and seizure (F.C.&C.) clause printed on the form. This clause states that unless the clause is physically deleted by the underwriters, it shall be paramount and supersede and nullify any contrary provision of the contract.

The ocean marine contract covering perils of the sea includes such perils as sinking, collision damage, stranding, damage from storms, and as well includes fire damage. These particular hazards are increased during wartime because of the necessity to run without lights, removal of guides to navigation, and danger of collision in convoys. Even though the increase in hazard was due to war, for many years it was held that such increase was not to be regarded as war risk within the meaning of ocean marine war risk insurance. War risks included only cover against losses caused by acts of an enemy such as torpedoing, bombing, and damage from shell fire. More recently, the war perils clause has been enlarged to include certain losses resulting from wartime conditions, such as collision in convoy, collision resulting from vessels running without lights, stranding occasioned by removal of lights, buoys or other aids to navigation, or by navigating without a pilot. Simultaneously, these perils were excluded from the marine contract by the revised F.C.&C. clause.

On the basis of a leading English case growing out of a seizure during World War I, it was held that underwriters covering under the usual war risk clause which included "restraint of princes" as a peril were liable in case of loss of voyage or frustration of voyage if it could not be completed because of the orders of governmental authority.[6] It was held that not only the thing insured but the voyage for which it is insured together formed the subject matter of the insurance and, therefore, the insurance covered against loss by frustration of the voyage. Because of this, when insurers are prepared to cover war perils but do not wish to cover losses which amount to loss of market owing to inability to complete the voyage, the policy is endorsed with the so-called "frustration clause." This clause has the effect of eliminating losses based upon failure to complete the voyage due to the orders of governmental authority.

---

[6] *British and Foreign Marine Insurance Company* v. *Sanday* (1916), 1 App. Cas. 650; 85 L.J.K.B. 550; 114 L.T. 521; 32 T.I.R. 266; 60 Sol. Jo. 253; 21 Com. Cas. 154; 29 Digest 276, 2236.

CLAUSES OF THE MARINE CONTRACT WITH SPECIAL REFERENCE TO HULL AND CARGO

It is not practical to review the details of all of the clauses of all possible marine insurance contracts and their endorsements. In this section some of the more important clauses of the hull and/or cargo contracts will be reviewed, since they serve to illustrate a number of principles of marine insurance.

Perils Clause. Marine insurance contracts, as issued today, are based upon the Lloyd's contract of 1779. The perils clause in Lloyd's marine contract form as it is used today follows the original pattern and reads as follows:

> Touching the Adventures and Perils which we the Assurers are contented to bear and do take upon us in this Voyage, they are, of the Seas, Men-of-War, Fire, Enemies, Pirates, Rovers, Thieves, Jettisons, Letters of Mart and Countermart, Surprisals, Takings at Sea, Arrests, Restraints and Detainments of all Kings, Princes and People, of what Nation, Condition, or Quality soever, Barratry of the Master and Mariners, and of all other Perils, Losses and Misfortunes that have or shall come to the Hurt, Detriment or Damage of the said Goods and Merchandises and Ship, &c., or any Part thereof.

The foregoing perils clause covers three classes of risk: (*a*) fire, (*b*) perils of the sea, and (*c*) war.

Fire is not regarded as a peril of the sea but rather a peril *on* the sea. Therefore, fire requires specific mention in the contract in order to be covered.

Perils of the sea include sinking, capsizing, stranding, collision of the vessel, and unusually heavy weather. Contact of insured goods with sea water due to any of the foregoing causes, resulting in damage, is a loss under the contract. The contract is not liable for damage that is the outgrowth of ordinary wear and tear. In order to establish a loss, it must be shown that the damage was the outgrowth of some accidental and unexpected cause. Pirates and rovers, while formerly important hazards, are of little or no importance today as perils. Thieves when stated as perils against which the insurance is written are interpreted in the United States to mean those who bring about losses where there is no element of violence, and may apply not only to strangers but also to the passengers and the crew. When the term "assailing thieves" is used, clandestine theft and pilferage are not covered, nor is theft which has been committed by the ship's company, whether passengers or crew. Under this term the peril covered is theft by force originating from the outside. Barratry includes within its scope any wilful misconduct or wrong done by the master or the crew against the interests of the owner. To constitute barratry, the wrongful act must be committed without the knowledge of the owners, and any complicity on the part of the owners with the perpetrators of the act removes it from the category. Jettison is the deliberate sacrifice of property. It includes throwing overboard part of the cargo, or any other property aboard ship, as well as cutting away the masts or rigging to relieve the ship in an emergency.

"Letters of Mart and Countermart, Surprisals, Takings at Sea, Arrests, Restraints and Detainments of all Kings, Princes and People" are perils of little concern today and are frequently not found in the contract. These perils together with "Men-of-War" constituted the war perils when the Lloyd's contract was drawn. Letters of Mart were commissions granted by a sovereign power to persons whose property had been seized by subjects of other states. They authorized their holders to make reprisals in order to indemnify themselves for their loss. Letters of Countermart authorized the holder to resist threatened reprisals. Capture and restraint when insured against are covered whether the act is a public enemy, a belligerent, or the assured's own government. The word "people" has been defined to mean "the power of the country," and hence would not include an armed mob. Capture or seizure means the taking with intent to keep. Arrest or detention is the taking with the intent to return. Takings at sea is a broad term and includes the loss of control or possession of property by force, regardless of whether the act be legal or illegal, such as by mutiny, pirates, or by mistaken seizure. Reference to men-of-war and enemies refers to those authorized by governmental authority to make war. The war perils, which included the lawless acts of individuals such as pirates, rovers, and thieves, were invariably covered in the older contracts. This was so because risk of loss from these sources was always imminent. News travels slowly, and a state of war could exist for considerable periods of time without becoming known to the owner of a ship or cargo at sea. It is customary today in this country to insure war risks under a contract entirely separate and apart from the contract that covers fire and sea perils.

The Lloyd's form appears in the first schedule of the Marine Insurance Act of 1906, in which Great Britain codified its marine insurance law.[7] It is notable that even there the Lloyd's form is not mandatory. In the United States, the Lloyd's contract serves as the general frame around which the various contracts offered by insurers have been built. The contracts have been enlarged and extended, and many of the clauses that first found their way into the Lloyd's contract as endorsements are now included in the printed forms as permanent parts of the contract. Because of the international nature

[7] Marine Insurance Act, 1906 (6 Edw. VII, c. 41), sec. 3.

Touching the Adventures and Perils which we, the said Underwriters, are contented to bear and take upon us, they are of the Seas, Men-of-War, Fire, Lightning, Earthquake, Enemies, Pirates, Rovers, Assailing Thieves, Jettisons, Letters of Mart and Counter-Mart, Surprisals, Takings at Sea, Arrests, Restraints and Detainments of all Kings, Princes and Peoples, of what nation, condition or quality soever, Barratry of the Master and Mariners and of all other like Perils, Losses and Misfortunes that have or shall come to the Hurt, Detriment or Damage of the said Vessel, &c., or any part thereof; excepting, however, such of the foregoing Perils as may be excluded by provisions elsewhere in the Policy or by endorsement. And in case of any Loss or Misfortune, it shall be lawful and necessary for the Assured, their Factors, Servants and Assigns, to sue, labor and travel for, in, and about the Defense, Safeguard and Recovery of the said Vessel, &c., or any part thereof, without prejudice to this Insurance, to the Charges whereof the Underwriters will contribute their proportion as provided below. And it is expressly declared and agreed that no acts of the Underwriters or Assured in recovering, saving or preserving the property insured shall be considered as a waiver or acceptance of abandonment.

This insurance also specially to cover (subject to the Average Warranty) loss of or damage to the subject matter insured directly caused by the following:

Accidents in loading, discharging or handling cargo, or in bunkering;

Accidents in going on or off, or while on drydocks, graving docks, ways, gridirons or pontoons;

Explosions on shipboard or elsewhere;

Breakdown of motor generators or other electrical machinery and electrical connections thereto, bursting of boilers, breakage of shafts, or any latent defect in the machinery or hull, (excluding the cost and expense of replacing or repairing the defective part);

Breakdown of or accidents to nuclear installations or reactors not on board the insured vessel:

Contact with Aircraft, rockets or similar missiles, or with any land conveyance;

Negligence of Charterers and/or Repairers, provided such Charterers and Repairers are not Assured(s) hereunder;

Negligence of Master, Charterers other than an Assured, Mariners, Engineers or Pilots:

Provided such loss or damage has not resulted from want of due diligence by the Assured, the Owners or Managers of the Vessel, or any of them. Masters, Mates, Engineers, Pilots or Crew not to be considered as part owners within the meaning of this clause should they hold shares in the Vessel.

FIG. 11–1. Hull Contract Perils Clause.

of marine insurance and because of the exigencies of competition, coverages have assumed a considerable degree of uniformity. In the United States the American Institute of Marine Underwriters has developed a number of standard cargo clauses reflecting the generally accepted practice in the American marine market. These clauses have met with considerable approval on the part of underwriters, brokers, and insureds. The hope has been expressed that this development may lead to the adoption of a uniform ocean marine contract. The fact remains, however, that in the field of marine insurance there are no standard forms made mandatory by law.

The modern American ocean marine contract covers (*a*) fire, (*b*) perils of the sea, and (*c*) such additional perils as meet the requirements of the insured. Such a clause from an American Institute hulls contract is shown on page 267.

War risks still appear in print in the perils clause of the hull contract, but, notwithstanding this, war perils are usually not covered in the contract issued to cover fire and perils of the sea. The war perils are excluded by virtue of a clause known as the "free-of-capture and seizure" clause printed into the form. Thus, there is the example of war perils appearing in one part of the document and nullified by a clause further on in the contract. The F.C.&S. clause may be canceled out, and, when this is done, the perils clause is restored to its complete form and covers war perils. In the United States when it is the intent to cover war perils, it is not the usual practice to delete the free-of-capture and seizure clause but rather to write a separate war risks contract with a perils clause indicating in detail the war perils to be covered and the conditions applicable to this particular contract.

That part of the clause which follows the recitation of fire, war risks, and sea perils which reads "and of all other like perils, etc.," might seem to carry with it the implication that the ocean marine contract is an all risks agreement. This is not the case. Even before the word "like" found its way into the clause and the list of perils concluded with the phrase "and of all other perils," it was held that the clause applied only to perils of the same nature as those previously enumerated. All losses which are the outgrowth of perils *ejusdem generis* with those described in the contract are covered, but here the extent of the "other perils" clause ends.

Collision Liability. Damage to an insured ship as a result of collision constitutes one of the perils covered under the marine contract. The contract without special provision does not cover the liability of the shipowner for damage he may do to the craft with which his ship collided. To cover this liability, the "collision," or "running down" clause is made a part of the hull contract. One such clause reads partially as follows:

And it is further agreed that if the vessel hereby insured shall come into collision with any other ship or vessel and the Assured or the Charterers or the Surety in consequence of the insured Vessel being at fault shall become liable to pay and shall pay by way of damages to any other person or persons any sum or sums in respect of such collision, we, the Underwriters will pay the Assured, or the Charterers, or the Surety, which ever shall have paid, such proportion of such sum or sums so paid as our respective subscriptions hereto bear to the value of the Vessel hereby insured, provided always that our liability in respect to any one such collision shall not exceed our proportionate part of the value of the Vessel hereby insured. . . .

In case both vessels in a collision are found to be responsible, liability of each vessel is fixed in proportion to the degree in which each vessel is determined to be at fault. The collision clause is limited to provide indemnity only in the case of liability for physical damage to another vessel and its freight and cargo, including loss of use of the damaged vessel. The clause does not assume liability for damage to cargo in the custody of the insured vessel, or damage to persons, or damage to such items as docks, piers, and breakwaters.

A problem early presented itself in providing collision insurance for fleets under a common ownership. It is a basic principle of liability law that an owner cannot recover damages in the case of a collision of two ships owned by himself, since he cannot sue himself as a wrongdoer. This being the case, there is no right of action known to the law and, therefore, under the ordinary collision clause the underwriter would not be obligated to make any adjustment. The situation is covered by the "sister ship clause." This provides that in case of collision between two ships the property of a single shipowner, or two ships under the same management, the insured shall have the same rights under the contract as he would were the other vessel the property of owners having no interest in the vessel insured.

The Sue and Labor Clause. In case of loss or misfortune the insured or his representives are both permitted and obligated to take certain designated steps to prevent, limit, or reduce loss. This clause, known as the "sue and labor clause," not only affords the insured the privilege, without prejudice to his rights, to take such steps as are reasonable to minimize or avert loss but likewise places upon him a definite obligation to do this. The clause is, in fact, an independent contract and operates as a collateral agreement separate and apart from the provision to indemnify for loss or damage from the named perils. Payment made to an insured for expenses incurred under the sue and labor clause are not regarded as a partial loss and therefore, are not subject to percentage restrictions that may apply to particular average claims. Likewise, it is quite conceivable in the case of a total loss that compensation under the sue and labor clause might sometimes be payable over and above the face of the contract.

To establish a claim under the sue and labor clause, the expenditure must have been made for the benefit of the particular property covered by the contract. The expenditure must have been made to avert a loss for which the underwriters would be liable, and, finally, the steps taken in the interests of the property for which compensation is claimed must be the act of the insured or his agents.

Money expended and recoverable under the sue and labor clause must definitely be spent to save the ship or goods insured from damage by the perils insured against in the contract. It has been held, for instance, that money expended to defend a collision suit when collision was covered by the contract does not come within the scope of the clause. Money expended to save the property from a peril not covered in the contract would, of course, not be included as a sue and labor charge. Salvage charges may not be paid by the clause when voluntary salvors act to save the insured property. If the salvors act under contract with the insured, the situation is different, and the charge is a proper one.

The Inchmaree Clause. A decision having a lasting influence upon the contract of marine insurance was rendered in the case of the steamer "Inchmaree." A check valve had become closed with salt, with the result that a donkey pump was damaged. Claim was made to the underwriters on the ground that the loss was covered under the "and all other perils, losses, and misfortunes" clause. This was held not to be the case. In appeal to the House of Lords it was held that whether due to negligence or accident the loss had not been caused by any of the perils set out in the contract, or perils *ejusdem generis*, and, therefore, the loss was not covered. To counteract the effect of this decision and to provide indemnity for the insured for damage to the hull or machinery resulting from the negligence of the master or crew, as well as from explosion or latent defects, a machinery clause, more commonly known to insurance underwriters as the "Inchmaree clause," was introduced into hull contracts. It is used in hull contracts insuring steam vessels or others using machinery and adds new perils to those incorporated in the perils clause.

The reference in the clause to latent defects has been the source of some confusion. Claims have been made for losses due to latent defects when such defects have been discovered. The courts have held that it is not the intention of the underwriters to assume liability for making good a latent defect if the defect makes its appearance without its being the cause of loss or damage. Thus, a preexisting latent defect, if it becomes apparent as result of wear and tear, will not support a claim against the underwriters. It has been held that a crack discovered in the tail shaft of a vessel created no liability for the insurers because the crack had been developed from a latent flaw over a period of years and there was no damage other than the latent defect itself. On the other hand, if damage is caused by a defect, even though the defect existed before the inception of the coverage, such damage is covered.

Negligence Clause. The final section of the recitation of perils to be covered deals with the question of negligence and errors of navigation. At first reading, the purpose of the clause is not altogether clear, since ordinarily negligence is no defense to relieve underwriters. The purpose of the clause is to place negligence in the list of perils insured against; in other words, to make the underwriters liable when negligence is the proximate cause of the loss. To make the situation clear: if, as a result of negligence, a member of the crew sets fire to the ship, the contract covers if it insures against the peril of fire. If, however, insufficient fuel is placed aboard a ship and the master is obliged to burn spars and furniture to bring her into port, this is not a fire loss within the terms of the marine contract. Negligence in providing the proper fuel is the proximate cause of the loss, and negligence of this nature is covered under the clause. Neglect properly to batten down hatches might result in a serious loss, and yet there would be no accident that would bring the damage within the scope of the contracts covering perils of the sea. Negligence of this nature is brought within the scope of the insurance through the use of the clause here described.

Limitations to Perils Clause. The marine insurance contract undertakes to cover only losses that are accidental in their nature and beyond the control of the insured. This fact being the case, the underwriters are not liable for loss to the subject of insurance growing out of inherent vice or improper methods of shipment. Losses the outgrowth of decay, leakage, or evaporation do not come within the scope of the perils clause. More particularly, and this is a point frequently brought up in connection with transportation insurance, the contract does not cover wear and tear due to packing and unpacking or due to the vibration of the vessel. The test as to whether there is liability under the contract is to be found in determining whether the cause of the loss is a fortuitous happening of an extraordinary and abnormal nature. If the cause of the loss is a normal and customary incident of the voyage that might reasonably have been foreseen, the underwriters are not liable. The dividing line between the accidental, fortuitous, and unexpected must of necessity be established. Borderline cases may, and frequently do, give rise to some doubt. It is true, however, that the contract does not cover ordinary wear and tear, ordinary leakage, and breakage or the ordinary action of the winds and waves.

"Lost or Not Lost." The phrase "To be insured lost or not lost" appeared in the early marine contracts when, among other reasons, because of limited communication facilities, it was impossible to know the exact status of the subject of the insurance when the contract was written. Under the terms of the clause, the insured is protected if the thing insured is lost before the insurance become effective. The phrase continues in modern contracts of marine insurance and is particularly useful to the merchant importing stocks of merchandise. Upon receipt of notice that a consignment has been made to him, he can provide insurance immediately, and if by chance the merchandise is damaged prior to the time the contract attaches, the underwriters are liable for the damage. An important condition in connection with the operation of this clause is to be found in the requirement that the underwriter be acquainted with all information available. If the owner of merchandise offered for insurance "lost or not lost" heard even a rumor indicating possible loss or damage and did not make this information fully available to the underwriters, the concealment not only would have the effect of rendering the contract void but would also effect a forefeit of the premium to the underwriters.

"At and From." Contracts usually provide that the insurance shall cover "at and from." A contract may read: "At and from London to New York" or "At and from Liverpool to New York and Baltimore, via New York." The word "at" in the contract provides protection for the risk *in* the port of departure, whereas "from" covers the risk only after sailing. The combination of both terms has the effect of covering the risk not only in the port of departure but on the voyage as well. The omission of the word "at" requires that the ship must have sailed upon the voyage before the insurance attaches. The contract, if written for a single voyage, usually provides that the insurance "shall continue and endure until the said merchandise shall be safely landed." In the case of an "at and from" contract or a contract written "from" covering on a hull, the insurance terminates 24 hours after the arrival and safe mooring of the vessel at her destination. The period of 24 hours, then, will not commence to run until the ship has been moored, and she must then have been moored in good safety. The safety clause may be varied, and frequently is, in hull contracts to the end that the insurance coverage extends considerably beyond the 24-hour limit.

Contracts written on goods frequently become effective "from the loading thereof." This clause is likewise subject to wide variations. The warehouse-to-warehouse clause may be attached (see page 289), and when coverage as extensive as this is not desirable, the coverage may become effective from the time the goods are placed upon the dock for shipment and may continue while on the dock at the port of destination. Shipments of goods are covered until "safely landed." Goods so insured are protected while they are being discharged and landed in a manner customary in the particular port. Thus, where it is customary to use lighters, the insurance extends to the goods while being so handled.

Strikes, Riots, and Civil Commotions. The marine contract as ordinarily written does not include strikes, riots, or civil commotion in the scope of the contract. To avoid any possible confusion of including losses from this source within the war risks covers, it is usual to incorporate a clause, known as the "S.R.&C.C. clause," which provides as follows: "Warranted free of loss or damage caused by strikers, locked out workmen, or persons taking part in labor disturbances, or riots, or civil commotions."

As in the case of goods in storage on land, the riot and civil commotion hazard is a very real one. This hazard, of course, exists entirely apart from the war risks hazard. In time of peace, when goods may be shipped insured under contracts which contain the warehouse-to-warehouse clause, it is quite possible that losses might develop resulting from the action of strikers, locked-out workmen, or other persons involved in riots or civil conflicts. The marine contract does not cover this hazard, but the risk may be written when specifically accepted by the underwriter and made part of a special agreement incorporated in the contract.

The Memorandum Clause. It was early recognized that, under the broad coverage of the marine contract, insurers would be continually harassed by claims for trifling losses whenever shipments of certain susceptible types of merchandise were covered. In 1749, in an effort to solve the problem, a clause was added to the contract in the form of a note or memorandum designating certain goods upon which the underwriter was relieved of all partial loss and other goods less susceptible to damage on which no loss was to be paid unless the damage amounted to a certain percentage of the value. In the early Lloyd's contracts the memorandum, now known as the "memorandum clause," was attached following the signatures. The clause is now no longer attached in the form of an additional note but is inserted in the body of the contract itself. The list that appears in modern cargo contracts has been considerably enlarged since the days of the early Lloyd's contract. The old terminology continues generally in use, although clauses as used today are by no means uniform. Risks mentioned in the clause are referred to as "memorandum risks," and we refer to "memorandum articles" and "memorandum rates."

Under the memorandum clause, that a loss must equal a certain percentage of the value before liability exists, the claim is paid in full without deduction once liability is established. The percentage mentioned in the memorandum clause is known as the "average limitation." There is no provision for an average limitation in the event of general average claims.

Under the terms of the Lloyd's contract, the memorandum clause does not operate if the ship be stranded. The memorandum clause does not generally appear in modern cargo contracts. The objective is attained by the use of free of particular average clauses. These are closely related to the memorandum clause but differ in that items pertinent to the particular shipment or risk are mentioned rather than a long list designed to foresee every eventuality.

Free of Particular Average (F.P.A.). Rather than extend or modify the memorandum clause as it appears in the different forms of contract, and particularly because the memorandum clause is not sufficiently specific to meet all situations, a clause may be attached to the contract definitely effecting the more specific limitation. Some insurances are issued with the intention that a loss shall be paid only if total. In such an instance, an F.P.A. clause is attached, providing that no partial losses shall be paid. The following is an example of the clause known as the "free of particular average American conditions" clause (F.P.A.A.C.); it includes a jettison and washing overboard clause and provides: "Free of particular average unless caused by the vessel being stranded, sunk, burned, or in collision but including Jettison and/or washing overboard irrespective of percentage." The foregoing clause is used particularly when the insurer is willing to issue a contract on a cargo shipped on deck. In the case of underdeck shipments, approved merchandise is ordinarily covered under the following clause: "Free of particular average under 3 percent unless the vessel be stranded, sunk, burned or in collision, each package separately insured." This clause has the effect of relieving the insurer of the burden of paying petty claims, but if the loss to any package equals 3 percent it is paid in full. This second clause follows the "free of particular average English conditions" form (F.P.A.E.C.) and is the one most frequently used. By the terms of the American conditions clause, there is no liability on the part of the insurer for a partial loss unless caused by one of the enumerated accidents. Under the English conditions clause, the underwriters are liable if one of the casualties enumerated happens during the voyage, whether it is or is not the cause of the loss. It has been contended that it was the intent of the English clause to cover as the American clause in fact does cover; that is, particular average claims were to be paid only if caused by the enumerated accidents. Court decisions have nullified this interpretation by ruling that the happening of one of the accidents has the effect of nullifying the average clause but restoring the original contract conditions. Under the English clause, if a vessel is stranded early in a voyage and the cargo insured under the F.P.A. clause is in no way injured but is later injured from some cause in no way related to the stranding, the insurer is liable for a particular average loss. Under the American conditions clause, this would not be the case, since the stranding would have to be the cause of the loss. Notwithstanding the fact that the American conditions clause seems to accomplish what was originally attempted when the clause was worded, shippers prefer the English form, and this is the one that finds general acceptance.

Janson Clause. Under the terms of the various F.P.A. clauses, the damage is paid without deduction in case of loss provided the loss equals the percentage stipulated in the clause. Under the terms of the Janson clause, a proportion of the loss falls upon the insured in any case. The clause is so written that only the excess of loss upon the stipulated percentage shall be paid by the underwriters. In the case of a valuation of $5,000, with the use of the 5 percent Janson clause, a loss of $300 would obligate the underwriters to a payment of but $50. This is true because, under the terms of the clause, 5 percent of the value is deductible from any loss.

Hull Average Clauses. With a view of reaching an end the same as that accomplished by the F.P.A. clause in the case of merchandise, hull average clauses are written providing that no liability shall rest upon the underwriters unless the damage to a ship caused by the peril insured against shall reach a designated percentage. No reference is made to stranding, sinking, or collision. The average form most frequently to be found limits the liability of the insurer under a minimum franchise form, and the percentage used is ordinarily 3 percent, though it may sometimes be as high as 5 percent. This type of clause is not always entirely satisfactory in the case of large steamships. In the case of a steamer valued at $500,000 insured under a minimum 3 percent franchise form, in order that the underwriters may be liable a loss must equal $15,000. To provide for the elimination of minor claims and at the same time provide adequate coverage, a specific amount may be inserted in the clause instead of a designated percentage.

Another practice frequently followed is to divide the value of the vessel into subdivisions. For example, valuations may be assigned to (*a*) hull and materials, (*b*) machinery and boilers, (*c*) electric lighting apparatus, and (*d*) cabin fittings and furniture. In such instances, the average clause is applied to each separate valuation. Under a 3 percent clause, damage equal to 3 percent or more to any one of the subdivisions has the effect of making the underwriters liable for the loss.

A second form of clause, known as the "deductible average coverage," provides that a designated deduction shall be made from any loss. This is in contrast to the minimum franchise form which provides that no claim shall be made unless the loss reaches a certain limit, but if it reaches or exceeds the designated limit the loss is paid in full. Under the deductible average form, any sum agreeable to the parties may be written into the contract. Contracts may be written providing for deductions from every claim of a few hundred dollars, or the sum may run into many thousands, all depending upon the amount of the risk the insured is willing to carry.

Cancellation and Premium Credits. Because of the nature of marine insurance, it is held that, in the usual situation to provide for cancellation of a contract and the return of a part of the premium might frequently develop inequitable situations. If the underwriter for a given premium assumes the risk of a voyage and the ship sets forth and the contract attaches, the full premium is held to be earned. If the ship shortly after departure is lost and the cause of the loss is not one of the perils insured against, the underwriters are obligated neither to make a payment under the contract nor to return any part of the premium. In the case of transfer of ownership, the same general rule applies and underwriters are not obligated to make a return of premium. On the other hand, the insurer may not cancel once the insurance attaches. It can readily be seen that if the underwriters learned of the development of hazardous conditions and could cancel the insurance on notice, the owner of the ship or goods insured might be left in a position in which new insurance would not be obtainable or, if obtainable at all, at a prohibitive cost. Indicative of the extent to which the rule is carried, if a contract is issued and, unknown to the parties at the time, the voyage had successfully terminated, no return premium is due the policyholder. It is true that if the insurer should accept a premium knowing the voyage had successfully terminated, he would be perpetrating a fraud and in such circumstances could not retain the premium.

While the foregoing is the basic rule, as a matter of practice, clauses have been incorporated into contracts providing for its modification. It is sometimes provided that, in case of the sale of a ship, a return premium will be allowed at an established rate per month. It is also frequently provided that in case of a lay-up for repairs, or, if for any reason the vessel is out of service, there shall be a return premium for each 15 or 30 consecutive days in port. A delay in port while the ship is in commission is not a lay-up warranting a return premium. To come within the meaning of the clause, the ship must be deliberately taken out of commission for a definite reason, as for overhauling or lack of business. The underwriters may also cancel the contract on five days written notice in the event the premium has not been paid within 30 days after the inception of the contract, but the premium earned to the date of cancellation is due and payable.

Assignment. Marine contracts are assignable unless under the terms of the contract assignment is specifically prohibited. The protection under a marine contract extends in the first instance only to those for whose account the contract was issued. In the case of an assignment, the assignment is without effect because of lack of insurable interest unless the subject matter of the insurance is likewise transferred. The assignment may be clouded with doubt when the interests of the assignee are such as to change materially the character of the risk. This is not the case if the subject matter of the insurance has been destroyed. If, after a loss covered by the contract the policyholder wishes to assign his right of action to another, he may do so.

Marine cargo insurance contracts are drawn in such a manner as to permit assignment before a loss and without the consent of the insurer. The matter is covered in the contract so that assignment may be made without question by writing the insurance "on account of whom it may concern." The frequent assignment of such cargo contracts with a change of ownership of merchandise is the outgrowth of commercial development. In the case of hull contracts, the situation is not the same, because underwriters, foreseeing the importance of underwriting moral hazard, have definitely settled the question of assignment by incorporating in the contract a clause making the contract void if assigned without the consent of the underwriter.

Warranties. The more important implied warranties have to do with (*a*) seaworthiness, (*b*) deviation, and (*c*) legality. Warranties of this class need not be, and seldom are, incorporated into the contract for, by law, without any expression on the part of the parties, they are made a part of the agreement.

Express warranties are written into contracts to cover particular situations and operate in the case of marine insuancer as in other forms of coverage. Express warranties are rarely found in marine contracts covering on goods. Occasionally an underwriter, in order to limit his liability under an open contract, may provide for a limitation in the following terms: "Warranted not more than $10,000 by any one steamer." In the case of hull contracts, the use of express warranties is common. A warranty must be literally complied with, and in the event of a breach of warranty, the insurer is discharged of all liability from the date of the breach but not from liability incurred before that date. Warranties frequently found in contracts have to do with the date of sailing, the position of the ship, and the number of the crew, and in time of war it is usual to warrant that vessels shall sail under the protection of an armed convoy. Likewise, warranties of nationality and neutrality are frequently met with in wartime.

A warranty sometimes used when the insurer wishes the insured to bear a part of the loss provides: "Warranted $ . . . uninsured." In the case of a cargo valued at $10,000 insured under a cargo contract with the clause attached providing "Warranted $2,500 uninsured," the insurer knows that the insured will bear 25 percent of any loss. If the insured were to purchase a contract covering the full value of the cargo, this would be a breach of the warranty and the entire insurance would cease to cover.

To constitute an expressed warranty it is not necessary in every instance that the word "warranty" be used. As a matter of fact, frequently the word "warranty" appears in a clause where it is not a warranty at all. A simple statement in the contract with respect to the nationality or construction of the ship constitutes a warranty. On the other hand, the clause in the contract which reads "warranted free of particular average unless 3 percent" is not in the true sense a warranty but rather a stipulation indicating a limitation of the liability of the underwriter. There is no limitation with respect to subject matter covered by a warranty. It is only required that it be a matter concerning which the underwriters demand a warranty and concerning which the assured is willing to warrant. There are certain areas in which it is customary to provide limitations by means of expressed warranties. Few assureds would be willing to accept a contract containing warranties over which they had no control. This being the case underwriters ordinarily limit warranties to matters within the control of the insured.

Certain warranties are known as "trading warranties." Certain vessels that are built to operate in a particular area are not always safe for worldwide operations. A case in point is to be found in vessels constructed for operation on the Great Lakes. When contracts are issued on such vessels, it is usual to designate definitely the geographic areas in which they will operate. Because of weather conditions, as in the case of the Great Lakes operations, contracts may contain a warranty that the vessels will operate only in the open season of navigation. Another group of warranties are known as "loading warranties." These concern themselves with the nature of the cargo to be handled. In the case of extra heavy cargo, such as lead, coal, iron, or the like, the contract will contain a warranty that the vessel will not load in excess of registered under-deck capacity. Other loading warranties concern themselves with cargoes that are inherently dangerous.

THE MARINE MARKET

The principal markets for marine insurance are the London market (mainly Lloyd's) and the American Hull Insurance Syndicate. These two markets have the capacity to insure ships whose value are great and in general have served shipping interests well. Since the American Hull Insurance Syndicate is dominant in the American market, its history and present status will be briefly reviewed.

American Hull Insurance Syndicate. The American Hull Insurance Syndicate was formed December 1, 1943, and has its headquarters in New York City. It is the successor to the American Marine Insurance Syndicates A, B, and C. The original organizations and their successor were developed for the purpose of encouraging the American Merchant Marine through an organization that was American in origin and was designed to give inspection and survey services for American-owned ships, as well as to provide an adequate insurance market in the United States for ships of American register. For the American Hull Insurance Syndicate to be effective, it was necessary for it to have the capacity to insure ships whose value might be very high without reinsuring abroad, and it must be sufficiently strong to compete vigorously with foreign insurance markets.

Currently the American Hull Insurance Syndicate consists of 78 insurers whose combined assets are approximately $6.5 billion. The organization has the capacity to insure each ship for as much as $10 million, and now insures some 3,000 ships of both American and foreign register. Domestic insurers provide about two thirds of the total capacity. The rest is provided by insurers admitted to do business in the United States.[8]

FOR DISCUSSION

1. It is stated in a contract of marine insurance that the ship insured is to sail on August 1. The ship actually sailed on August 5. The insured claims that since it was not stated in the contract "warranted to sail on or before August 1" and since the risk was not materially increased, the contract covers. What is your opinion?
2. A ship was insured "warranted neutral ship and property" and was lost from the perils of the sea. There was no question of there being a warranty loss. Investigation proved that the ship was not neutral property. Since a warranty risk did not contribute to the loss, is the contract binding?
3. The ship X sailed from Baltimore in a seaworthy condition but encountered a storm off Cape Hatteras and, as a result, became unseaworthy. What effect does this have upon the insurance with relation to the implied warranty of seaworthiness?
4. A contract was issued covering a ship, and in the printed terms of the contract it was provided that coverage should continue 24 hours after the ship was safely in port. However, there was attached to the contract a written clause providing protection for 30 days in port. State a rule to apply in this and other situations in which terms have

[8] See *The Insurance Almanac* (New York: Underwriter Printing and Publishing Co., 1965), and *Cyclopedia of Insurance in the United States* (Paterson, N.J.: Index Publishing Co., 1965).

been added to a printed contract that can conflict with the printed conditions.

5. The ship A is at sea and in difficulty. It is decided to jettison part of the cargo. The jettison meets with all the requirements for a general average claim. Later the ship is lost as a result of a collision, and the loss has no relationship to the peril which prompted the jettison. Is the owner of the jettisoned goods entitled to a general average contribution? Explain.
6. In the case of combined values on a voyage of $100,000, values to the extent of $10,000 are jettisoned. Assume there are at the beginning of the voyage ten owners with a value at risk of $10,000 each. B claims that if all of A's goods are jettisoned, he will be better off than those whose goods have been saved because the contribution will put him in the position he was before the loss, whereas the contribution of the others will result in a loss to them. Explain the error in this reasoning.
7. Marine insurance is classified (*a*) as to subject matter of the interest, and (*b*) as to the form of the interest. Distinguish by example the difference between the two forms of classification, and point out which determines the contract form to be used.
8. Explain what is meant in marine insurance by the insurance of freight.
9. A steamer is insured for $500,000 at the beginning of a contract term. Just before the contract expires, the ship is caught in a gale, with the result that it is a total loss. Investigation brings to light that the ship at the time of the loss was probably worth $450,000. What is the liability of the underwriters?
10. B insured a steamship for $500,000. As a result of a gale, damage in the amount of $50,000 forced the ship to put into port for repairs. The repairs were made and paid for, and the ship proceeded on the voyage. Before completion of the voyage, the ship was lost. The owner of the ship claims the insurance company to be liable for a partial loss of $50,000 and a total loss of $500,000, or a total liability of $550,000. What is, in fact, the liability of the insurer?
11. It has been stated (*Brough* v. *Whitmore* [1791], 4 Term Rep. 206): "Without commenting on the words of the contract, it is sufficient to say that a contract of assurance has at all times been considered in courts of law as an absurd and incoherent instrument." Over and over the courts have held the marine contract to be founded on usage and it must be governed and construed by usage. Explain.
12. The Green Arrow Line owns a fleet of steamships. One of them, the "Star of the Sea," collides with another, the "Excalibar." Both ships are seriously damaged, although, from the investigation, the "Excalibar" is at fault. The owners are told that, since they cannot sue themselves, they cannot collect under their contract covering collision liability. What will you look for in the contract to determine whether or not there is any liability on the part of the insurers?
13. Which of the following losses are recoverable under the Inchmaree clause:

a) Actual total loss of a part of the hull or machinery, through a latent defect coming into existence and causing the loss during the period of the contract.

b) Constructive total loss under the same circumstances, as where, though the part of the hull survives, it is by reason of the latent defect of no value and cannot be profitably repaired.

c) Damage to other parts of the hull happening during the currency of the contract through a latent defect, even if the latter came into existence before the period of the contract.

14. It has sometimes been considered strange that the ancient Lloyd's marine contract form should remain the basic contract of marine insurance. The contract in its insuring clause provides many coverages that are eliminated before issue by endorsement. Clauses are written, stamped, or attached to the contract which extend or limit the coverage and, not infrequently, definitely contradict the terms of the contract itself. In fact, so varied and confusing are the clauses that appear in the marine contract that Sir Douglas Owen in his work, Ocean Trade and Shipping, has stated: "If such a contract were to be drawn up for the first time today it would be put down as the work of a lunatic endowed with a private sense of humor." The question at once presents itself as to why the old form persists. Can you give the answer?

15. The liner "United States" was said to have a total value of over $273 million. It was insured by the owners for $31 million. In the light of the requirement that insurance to value is required under the marine contract, explain the difference.

16. Indicate an underlying philosophy that characterizes marine insurance and on the basis of this philosophy indicate some features of the ocean marine contract that distinguish it from the standard fire insurance contract.

CHAPTER · 12

Marine Open Cargo Contract

Marine open cargo insurance contracts are not standard contracts in the sense that all of them follow an identical pattern in printing or have exactly the same clauses. A number of the clauses, however, are so universally used that they are in a sense standard for this type of contract.[1]

PRELIMINARY CLAUSES

The upper half of the first page of the contract gives the contract number, the name of the insurer, and the insured. The parties to whom loss is to be payable are indicated, and the nature of the goods to be covered is described briefly. Contract limits are set in the valuation clause, and the conveyance clause indicates the extent of the coverage with respect to types of ship. The geographical limits are also specified.

Parties to the Agreement. The name of the insurer is printed in the contract. It is provided in "consideration of the premium as agreed, payable monthly in cash" that the insurer will insure the party or parties designated. There is a blank space in the contract in which the name of the insured is inserted. Next is the "for account of" clause. Here the name of all parties interested in the insurance may be inserted. When, as in the case of the usual open contract, it is the intent to make the insurance assignable, and, because of this, it is not possible at the time the contract is written to insert the name of all parties who may be interested in the insurance, the contract may provide: "For the account of whom it may concern."

Loss Payable Clause. The contract may provide for payment of loss to the named insured. In the case where goods covered by insurance may pass from one owner to another with the certificate of

[1] The contract discussed in this chapter is the one contained in the kit of advanced contracts published by the Insurance Information Institute.

insurance assigned, it is customary to provide: "Loss, if any, payable to the assured or order."

Goods Insured. A blank space left in the contract provides for a description of the goods to be shipped. It may, for example, describe the merchandise as "incidental to the business of the assured." To provide for incoming shipments, and to exclude shipments which the assured is under no obligation to cover, the clause may provide:

> Under and/or on deck, consigned to, or shipped by the Assured, or consigned to or shipped by others for their account or control and in which they may have an insurable interest but excluding shipments sold by the Assured on F.O.B. [free on board], F.A.S. [free along side], Cost and Freight or similar terms whereby the Assured is not obliged to furnish ocean marine insurance and excluding shipments purchased by the Assured on terms which include insurance to final destination; also to cover all shipments which the Assured may be instructed to insure, provided such instructions are given in writing prior to sailing of vessel and before any known or reported loss or accident.

The reference to "lawful goods and merchandise" has the effect of excluding from coverage shipments that for any reason are prohibited by law.

Conveyances. Here, it is the intent to permit the insurer to exercise a reasonable degree of control over the conveyances in which it elects to insure cargos. Specifically, it is the intent to exclude, as conveyances, wooden vessels, sailing vessels, or similar ships that are deemed unusually hazardous. Following is a wording by which the conveyance clause may be completed: "Per iron or steel steamer or steamers, iron or steel motor vessels (but excluding all auxiliary engined vessels) and connnecting conveyances, including shipments by air freight and/or air express and/or air mail and/or parcel post." Reference to air freight, air express, air mail, or parcel post brings these methods of conveyance within the scope of the contract protection without the necessity of separate endorsements. If the insured has no need for protection for air shipments, the reference to these conveyances may be dropped from the clause. The insurer may establish, in the clause limiting insurance, separate limits for the various types of conveyance. Separate limitations may also be established with respect to on-deck shipments. The conveyance clause is normally limited to certain Lloyd's classes of ship.

Geographical Limits. This section of the contract affords the insurer an opportunity to limit the coverage to certain geographical areas. If coverage is to be worldwide, the clause may be completed "at and from ports and/or places in the world to ports and/or places in the world." The clause may cover shipments "lost or not lost." In the open cargo form, the words "at" and "from" lose considerable of their significance when read in connection with the warehouse-to-warehouse clause. With both clauses the insurance covers the shipment while in transit and is not limited to ocean-going conveyances. The phrase "lost or not lost" protects the insured in the event that an incoming shipment has already been lost by the time he becomes aware that the shipment has been made and is in a position to report it to the insurer.

INSURING AGREEMENTS, TERMS, AND CONDITIONS

The clauses discussed above, when completed, tailor the contract to the particular needs of the insured. On the second half of the first page and on the following page are the insuring agreements and certain terms and conditions.

Perils. The perils clause in the open-cargo contract provides coverage under five divisions: (*a*) of the seas, (*b*) fire, (*c*) assailing thieves, (*d*) jettisons, and (*e*) barratry. These perils are set forth in a short simple clause of which the following is an example:

> Touching the adventures and perils which said Assurers are contented to bear, and take upon themselves, in this voyage, they are of the seas, fires, jettisons, assailing thieves, barratry of the Master and Mariners and all other like perils, losses and misfortunes that have or shall come to the hurt, detriment or damage of the said goods and merchandise, or any part thereof except as may be otherwise provided for herein or endorsed hereon.

Damage due to unusual weather, strandings, and collisions are all covered as "perils of the seas." Most marine losses fall in this category. Fire damage to cargo, including consequential damage caused by smoke or steam, as well as loss from efforts to extinguish a fire, are covered. Assailing thieves provides protection where force is used in effecting the theft and is to be distinguished from pilferage or sneak thievery. The voluntary throwing overboard of cargo to protect other property from a common danger would constitute a jettison loss. Loss attributable to any illegal act or breach of duty by the ship's captain or crew would be a barratry loss. In order not to create the impression that the perils clause indicates the extent of coverage under the open-cargo contract, at the risk of repetition it may be pointed out here that additional coverages to those noted in the perils clause are provided under other sections of the contract. These include: (*a*) explosion losses, (*b*) losses covered by the Inchmaree clause, (*c*) fumigation losses, (*d*) warehousing and forwarding charges incurred as a result of perils insured against, (*e*) total loss of a package in loading or unloading, (*f*) general average and salvage charges, and (*g*) shore perils providing protection while on inland transit and elsewhere ashore. The contract also covers the collision liability which the cargo owner is legally liable to pay the shipowner as the result of a collision.

The perils clause would not extend to cover illegal ventures of any sort. Such coverage would be contrary to public policy. The open-cargo contract does not cover loss of market or damage or deterioration arising from delay. Neither are losses arising from inherent vice of the goods themselves covered. Losses attributable to acts of war, strikes, riots, and civil commotion are not covered, but coverage for these last named risks may be provided by endorsement, though in the case of war perils, a separate contract is now the practice.

Some insureds have felt the need for a more comprehensive coverage than afforded by the clause described here. For an additional premium a contract may be endorsed to cover, in addition to the usual fire and sea perils, such perils as fresh water damage, breakage, leakage, theft and pilferage, contact with fuel oil or other cargo, and sweat damage, to mention a few. Where coverage on a named peril basis is not comprehensive enough, an all risks coverage is available. Such a form, known as the "external cause clause" reads as follows:

> To cover against all risks of physical loss or damage from any external cause irrespective of percentage, but excluding, nevertheless the risks of war, strikes, riots, seizure, detention and other risks, excluded by the F.C.&S. (Free of Capture and Seizure) Warranty and the S.R.&C.C. (strikes, Riots and Civil Commotions) Warranty in this policy excepting to the extent that such risks are specifically covered by endorsement.

Another form widely used provides virtually an all risks protection on both land and sea. The external cause clause reads as follows:

> To pay for physical loss or damage from an external cause (but excluding those risks excepted by the Free of Capture and Seizure and Strikes, Riots and Civil Commotions clauses, unless otherwise provided herein) arising during transportation between the points of shipment and of destination named in the policy irrespective of percentage.

It is to be noted that war risks and strikes and riots are not covered unless specifically included by endorsement.

Sue and Labor Clause. This clause was discussed in the preceding chapter. It appears in the open cargo contract in the following form:

> In case of any loss or misfortune, it shall be lawful and necessary to and for the Assured, his or their factors, servants and assigns, to sue, labor and travel for, in and about the defense, safeguard and recovery of the said goods and merchandise, or any part thereof, without prejudice to this insurance; nor shall the acts of the Assured or Assurers, in recovering, saving and preserving the property insured, in case of disaster, be considered a waiver or an acceptance of an abandonment; to the charges where-

of, the said Assurers will contribute according to the rate and quantity of the sum hereby insured.

Payments made under this clause are not regarded as partial losses and are not subject to percentage restrictions applicable to particular average claims. With respect to a cargo contract, the insured may take action under the terms of the clause to enforce rights against a carrier, bailee, or other third party who may be liable for damage to the shipment. Expenses so incurred would properly constitute a claim under the sue and labor clause.

Average Terms and Conditions. These clauses in a cargo contract determine the amount of particular average loss recovery. For the purposes of underwriting cargo shipments, a different consideration is given to on-deck shipments and shipments excepting while on deck. Underdeck cargo refers to cargo stowed below the weather deck of a vessel. On-deck shipments usually constitute certain kinds of goods that, because of their dangerous nature, are not safe to carry stowed in the hold.

The average clauses as they appear in the contract are:

A. Except while on deck of ocean vessel:
B. On Deck: Merchandise and/or goods shipped on deck are insured: Free of particular average unless caused by the vessel being stranded, sunk, burnt, on fire, or in collision, but including jettison and/or washing overboard irrespective of percentage.
C. On Deck: Notwithstanding the above, merchandise and/or goods shipped on deck under an Under Deck Bill of Lading without the knowledge and consent of the shipper shall be treated as Under Deck cargo and insured as in A above.

On-deck shipments are written free of particular average American conditions (F.P.A.A.C.). It will be recalled that this is the most limited of the average clauses in general use, but it is used, since it is the intent not to cover partial losses of *on-deck* cargo, although jettison and washing overboard losses are fully covered. With respect to underdeck shipments, the average terms or conditions vary with each risk and are written into the blank space in the contract provided for the purpose.

For merchandise particularly susceptible to partial loss, the F.P.A.A.C. clause may be used. Losses attributable to stranding, sinking, fire, or collision are paid in full, and this is logical since such losses are in no way associated with the nature of the shipment. If the F.P.A.E.C. clause is used, the coverage is broadened to the extent that loss resulting from any peril of the sea is recoverable provided the vessel has suffered any of the disasters mentioned without requiring that the damage be caused by one of the perils mentioned. A usual clause for approved merchandise stipulates: Free of average under three percent (3%) unless general, or the vessel be *stranded*, *sunk*, *burnt*, *on fire* or *in collision*, each case or shipping package separately insured." This clause provides protection from partial loss by sea perils if the partial damage amounts to 3 percent. The percentage indicated is not a deductible but represents a minimum allowable claim. If the vessel is involved in a fire, stranding, sinking, or collision, the percentage is waived. General average claims are paid in full. The foregoing clause is usually known as the "3 percent W.A. clause." This means that the coverage is written "with average" terms of 3 percent. The average terms refer to the insurance coverage provided in the perils clause. This clause may add to the perils covered in the perils clause. This is accomplished by adding such words as "including the risks of theft and pilferage." Other perils may be included, such as leakage and breakage, fresh water damage, contact with fuel oil, ship's sweat, and the like.

Valuation. The space left on the front page of the contract for indicating the basis of value for the purpose of adjusting losses allows for considerable flexibility. In the case of a single shipment the contract might read "valued at sum insured," or a definite sum might be inserted. In the case of the open cargo contract, it is not possible to insert a specific amount. A clause similar to the following is customary:

> The Value of shipments insured under this policy shall be the amount of invoice, including all charges therein plus any prepaid and/or advanced and/or guaranteed freight not included in the invoice, plus Ten (10)%.

It is the intent of the cargo contract to reimburse the insured for his loss. In the case of marine shipments, when the cargo is placed in transit, it is beyond the control of the insured and for all purposes has a value equal to the amount due the shipper. In addition to the cost of the goods, the shipper will have invested in the shipment insurance premiums, all costs such as inland freight, packing for export, and like charges as well as ocean freight which may either be prepaid or guaranteed. To all the charges which are added to the invoice, to obtain a value of the shipment at the time of shipment, a flat percentage is added to represent the increased value of the shipment at the point of destination. In open cargo contracts 10 percent is quite customary, though, in some instances, there is no added percentage, and in others the percentage may be as high as 100 or 150 percent. In some contracts different percentages may be indicated for different ports of destination. In case of loss the insured is not obligated to prove the amount of loss with respect to the particular shipment. The valuation established in this clause represents the amount to be paid in the event of a total loss. Partial losses are settled as a percentage of the amount so established, depending, of course, on the extent of damage.

Sometimes a clause reading: "Foreign currency to be converted into dollars at banker's sight rate of exchange applicable to each invoice and/or credit and/or draft" may be inserted in the valuation clause. This provides for the immediate conversion of losses payable abroad into United States dollars.

Limit of Liability. This clause establishes the limits of liability that the underwriters will accept with respect to shipments on any one vessel. Such a clause reads:

> To cover 100% interest not exceeding $100,000.00 by any one vessel or in any one place at any one time or in any one distaster or accident unless otherwise agreed upon in writing; it being further understood and agreed that in respect of shipments on deck, this insurance shall not be liable for more than $10,000.00 while on board the vessel.
>
> Notwithstanding the foregoing, this insurance shall not be liable for more than $10,000.00 by any one aircraft, nor for more than $500.00 per package by parcel post.

It is customary to establish a generous limit of liability, so that it will always exceed the aggregate value of any number of separate shipments that may be expected on a single vessel. It is customary to make the "on-deck limit 10 percent of the total limit of liability, though this is not a hard and fast rule and the on-deck limit may be increased by agreement.

Accumulation. A typical accumulation clause reads as follows:

> Should there be an accumulation of interests beyond the limits expressed in this contract by reason of any interruption of transit beyond the control of the Assured, or by reason of any casualty or at a transshipping point or on a connecting steamer or conveyance, this contract shall attach for the full amount at risk (but in no event for more than twice the policy limit) provided written notice be given to this Company as soon as known to the Assured.

This provision has the effect of protecting the assured against developments beyond his control, such as the interruption of a shipment with its transfer to another vessel with the result that the total cargo at risk exceeds the limit of liability named in the contract. In such situations the contract covers accumulations up to an agreed amount. In the case of the clause here cited, there is coverage up to twice the limit of liability.

Attachment and Termination. This clause indicates the date that the insurance becomes effective and the conditions under which the contract may be canceled. The following example will serve to indicate the provisions of such a clause.

> Covering all shipments described herein made on and after ______________ but this contract may be canceled by either

party giving thirty days written notice to the other, but such cancellation shall not affect any risk on which this insurance has attached prior to the effective date of such notice.

The word "all" is significant in that it indicates that all shipments made on and after the designated date are covered. Not only are they covered for insurance but the insured is likewise obligated to pay the agreed premium for each shipment. In other words, in the case of an incoming shipment, the fact that it arrived safely before the assured knew of it does not relieve him of the obligation to report it and pay a premium. The shipment is automatically covered, and had it been lost the insurer would have been obliged to settle.

Ocean marine contracts covering cargo are deemed continuous and remain in force until positive steps are taken by one part or the other to effect cancellation. While any number of days' notice may be required in the contract, a cancellation notice of 30 days is usual.

The phrase "shall not affect any risk on which this insurance has attached prior to the effective date of such notice" is significant. If a 30-day notice of cancellation is given, the contract nevertheless covers all shipments that have been made prior to the cancellation date. The insurance covers even though shipments have not arrived at destination when the contract terminates and continues with respect to such shipments until they arrive. Thus, a shipper is not in jeopardy of having a shipment uninsured while in transit if the contract was in force when the shipment started. This is no hardship on the insurer since each shipment is, in effect, a separate coverage for which a premium is charged. The insurer considers the premium earned for insurance protection to destination once the insurance attaches, and it is this protection that is provided by covering all insured shipments that remain undelivered at the cancellation date.

AMERICAN INSTITUTE CARGO CLAUSES

The American Institute cargo clauses include the warehouse-to-warehouse clause, the deviation clause, the craft clause, and similar clauses. Because of their importance a number of these clauses will be briefly described.

Warehouse-to-Warehouse Clause. In the case of voyage cargo contracts, the insurance attaches "immediately following the loading on board," unless another point of attachment is designated, and coverage terminates when the goods are safely landed. Numerous modifications of this provision are common, such as insuring from warehouse to warehouse, in which case not only sea perils but also truck, railroad, dock handling, and perils of like nature are covered during transportation to and from the warehouses. In the interest of uniformity the American Institute of Marine Underwriters has developed a warehouse-to-warehouse clause for use in cargo contracts. By virtue of this clause the insurance attaches from the time the goods leaves the hands of the shipper until delivered to the warehouse of the consignee. The American Institute clause reads as follows:

This insurance attaches from the time the goods leave the Warehouse and/or Store at the place named in the policy for the commencement of the transit and continues during the ordinary course of transit, including customary transshipment if any, until the goods are discharged overside from the overseas vessel at the final port. Thereafter the insurance continues whilst the goods are in transit and/or awaiting transit until delivered to final warehouse at the destination named in the policy or until the expiry of 15 days (or 30 days if the destination to which the goods are insured is outside the limits of the port) whichever shall first occur. The time limits referred to above to be reckoned from midnight of the day on which the discharge overside of the goods hereby insured from the overseas vessel is completed. Held covered at a premium to be arranged in the event of transshipment, if any, other than as above and/or in the event of delay in excess of the above time limits arising from circumstances beyond the control of the Assured.

The phrase "during the ordinary course of transit" is significant. It is not the intent to cover delays not caused by insured perils. The 15-day and 30-day limitations in the clause have the effect of preventing shippers from leaving cargoes in storage on piers or in custom sheds indefinitely and claiming coverage on the ground that the shipment is still in transit. The "held covered" provision in the concluding sentence of the clause enables an insured to secure an extension of coverage in the event the goods are awaiting transit longer than the limitations established in the clause. If the transshipment is necessary, the insurance may likewise be extended to cover. To effect this extension the insurer must be notified. The insured is billed for such additional premium as the extension of the risk requires. It is not always possible for the shipper of merchandise to know of delays and transshipments in advance. Notice, therefore, need not be given in advance, but such notice is expected and the premium paid when the information becomes available to the insured.

Craft Clause. In some ports it is necessary that goods be transported by lighter from the shore to the vessel upon which they are shipped. At one time there was some doubt as to whether cargo contracts attached while the goods were being transported in a lighter from the shore to the vessel. To remove all doubt the following clause now appears in the policy:

Including transit by craft and/or lighter to and from the vessel. Each craft and/or lighter to be deemed a separate insurance. The Assured are not to be prejudiced by any agreement exempting lightermen from liability.

The reference to each craft as separate insurance has the effect of applying any franchise in the contract to the value on the lighter. A 5 percent franchise would mean a loss equal to 5 percent of the value of the cargo before the insurers are liable for loss. The sinking of an entire lighter might not bring the claim to 5 percent of the shipment. But if the lighter is regarded as a separate insurance, a loss of 5 percent to the lighter cargo creates liability. Under the terms of the contract as usually written, the insurer agrees to pay for total loss of any package or packages while loading, transshipping, or discharging.

The insured is not to be prejudiced by any agreement exempting lightermen from liability. Where such agreements are necessary or customary, the insured in entering into them might be held to waive subrogation rights of the insurer and, hence, void his coverage. The clause as written precludes such a development.

Deviation. In ocean marine contracts there is an implied warranty that there shall be no deviation from the specified voyage for which the contract was written. Since under export and import cargo forms, the shipper can exercise virtually no control over the voyage, it is provided that in case of change of voyage, or deviation, or unintentional omission in the description of the interest, vessel, or voyage, the insurance will continue to cover at a premium to be arranged, provided notice of the deviation, change, or error is communicated to the insurer as soon as known to the insured. The contract provides:

> This insurance shall not be vitiated by any unintentional error in description of vessel, voyage or interest, or by deviation, overcarriage, change of voyage, transshipment or any other interruption of the ordinary course of transit, from causes beyond the control of the Assured. It is agreed, however, that any such error, deviation or other occurrence mentioned above shall be reported to this Company as soon as known to the Assured, and additional premium paid if required.

The clause has the effect of providing protection with respect to situations that develop in the ordinary course of the marine transportation business that technically would terminate the insurance. By virtue of the clause the insured is "held covered." At the same time a direct obligation is placed upon the insured to report the changed conditions to the insurer as soon as they become known. He is likewise obligated to pay such additional premium, if any, as the insurer may elect to charge.

Labels Clause. In case of damage from perils insured against affecting labels only, loss is limited to an amount sufficient to pay the cost of new labels and relabeling the goods. The clause provides:

> In case of damage affecting labels, capsules or wrappers, these assurers, if liable therefor under the terms of this policy, shall not be liable for more than an amount sufficient to pay the cost of new labels, capsules or

wrappers, and the cost of reconditioning the goods, but in no event shall this Company be liable for more than the insured value of the damaged merchandise.

The intent of this clause is to prohibit the insured from making a claim for a total loss when the only loss to the merchandise is damage to labels or packaging. The insurance assumes liability for the cost of reconditioning the damaged merchandise. This, it is felt, saves the insured from loss without obligating the insurer to salvage the damaged shipment.

Machinery Clause. The purpose of this clause is to prevent a claim for a whole machine when only a part is damaged. Payment is limited to the value of the part and thus prevents abandonment of the machine to the insurer. The clause reads:

When the property insured under this policy includes a machine consisting when complete for sale or use of several parts, then in case of loss or damage covered by this insurance to any part of such machine, these Assurers shall be liable only for the proportion of the insured value of the part lost or damaged, or at the Assured's option, for the cost and expense, including labor and forwarding charges, of replacing or repairing the lost or damaged part; but in no event shall these Assurers be liable for more than the insured value of the complete machine.

At first thought it might seem unreasonable to make a claim for a part in excess of the value of the whole. It will be recalled, however, that this might well happen in the case of secondhand machinery. Regardless of what a part may cost, the liability of the insurer is limited to the insured value of the complete machine.

General Average and Salvage. For the purposes of a general average contribution, cargo is valued at its gross wholesale value at destination. Salvage is the compensation due to those who voluntarily assist in saving a ship or cargo in peril. Whether there is insurance, the owner of a cargo is liable for general average and salvage charges. The open cargo policy assumes this liability in the following terms:

General Average and Salvage Charges payable according to United States laws and usage and/or as per Foreign Statement and/or per York-Antwerp Rules (as prescribed in whole or in part) if in accordance with the Contract of Affreightment.

Adjusters place a value on every interest concerned in a venture involving general average or salvage. Since the laws in the various countries with respect to general average differ and since, in the absence of other agreement, general average adjustments are made according to the law and usages of the port of destination, it is customary to insert in the bills of lading the basis for such adjustment. It is frequently provided that general average claims shall be adjusted in accordance with the York-Antwerp Rules, and by virtue of the above or a similar clause, the policy covers where the bill of lading so provides. There are some occasions where the calculation of general average, in accordance with a law of a foreign country, provides a heavier assessment upon a cargo owner than the calculation in accordance with the York-Antwerp Rules would provide. In order to protect the cargo owner with full reimbursement for general average charges which are reasonably calculated in accordance with the law of any country, the words "as per Foreign Statement" are inserted in the contract.

Explosion Clause. Explosion is not covered in the ordinary perils clause. The peril is assumed by the following:

> Including the risk of explosion, howsoever or wheresoever occurring during the currency of this insurance unless excluded by the F.C.&S. Warranty or S.R.&C. Warranty set forth herein.

By virtue of this clause, losses from all types of explosions are covered, with the exception of those attributable to war or strikes, riots, and civil commotion. Explosions arising from war risks are covered under the war risks contract, and those arising from strikes, riots, or civil commotion may be covered by an endorsement to the contract.

Shore Clause. By virtue of the warehouse-to-warehouse clause, as well as the deviation clause, goods are insured from the time they leave the warehouse at point of shipment, during the ordinary course of transit, until they reach the final warehouse at destination. There is coverage for reshipment, transshipment, or any variation of a shipment beyond the control of the assured. Coverage is provided while the insured cargo is on inland transit or elsewhere on shore if lost or damaged because of any of the perils listed. Since land perils differ considerably from fire and sea perils, it becomes necessary to indicate perils covered while the cargo is being transported on shore. Following is a typical clause:

> Where this insurance by its terms covers while on docks, wharves or elsewhere on shore, and/or during land transportation, it shall include the risks of collision, derailment, overturning or other accident to the conveyance, fire, lightning, sprinkler leakage, cyclones, hurricanes, earthquakes, floods (meaning the rising of navigable waters), and/or collapse or subsidence of docks or wharves, even though the insurance be otherwise F.P.A. [free of particular average].

If the contract provides broader coverage than the terms of this clause, as, for instance, where the perils clause is all risks, the broad coverage applies equally on shore. Warehousing and forwarding charges are paid if incurred as a result of a peril covered by the contract.

Bill of Lading, Etc., Clause. The contract covers the implied warranty of seaworthiness. If a cargo is shipped in a vessel that proves for some reason beyond the control of the shipper to be unseaworthy, this fact will not have an adverse effect on his insurance. The "seaworthiness admitted" provision in the bill of lading clause covers the situation. This clause reads as follows:

The Assured are not to be prejudiced by the presence of the negligence clause and/or latent defect clause in the Bills of Lading and/or Charter Party. The seaworthiness of the vessel as between the Assured and the Company is hereby admitted and the wrongful act or misconduct of the shipowner or his servants causing a loss is not to defeat the recovery by an innocent Assured if the loss in the absence of such wrongful act or misconduct would have been a loss recoverable on the policy. With leave to sail with or without pilots, and to gow and assist vessels or craft in all situations, and to be towed.

Sometimes the clause is more limited and provides that seaworthiness of the vessel is admitted as between insured and insurer *unless* the insured is a charterer or owner or is chargeable with some fault or negligence contributing to the unseaworthiness of the vessel. This form does not ordinarily appear in contracts issued to shippers who are not owners or who do not charter vessels in the ordinary course of business. Clauses in the bill of lading or charter party relieving the carrier from liability because of negligence or latent defects will not adversely affect the insured's protection. To sail without a pilot where it is customary to carry one breaches the warranty of seaworthiness. Even though seaworthiness is admitted, the clause provides permission to sail without pilots, as well as permits towing and being towed, and otherwise rendering assistance that might possibly be construed a deviation.

Actually the implied warranty with respect to seaworthiness does not apply to cargo. A cargo improperly packed or otherwise in bad condition that might imperil the ship will not void the insurance covering either the hull or cargo. While the condition of the cargo will not void the contract, if the owner of the cargo was aware at the time that the insurance was placed that the cargo was in a precarious condition, and knew that if this information were brought to the attention of the underwriters they would not accept the contract, then the underwriters may deny liability. Likewise, the underwriters are not liable for losses due to deterioration or other injuries attributable to inherent qualities of the goods shipped.

Inchmaree Clause. It has only been comparatively recently that the Inchmaree clause has been placed in cargo contracts. Because of the possibility of machinery damage to cargoes, shippers have asked for the inclusion of the clause. The Inchmaree clause in the cargo contract reads as follows:

This insurance is also specially to cover any loss of or damage to the interest insured hereunder, through the bursting of boilers, breakage of shafts or through any latent defect in the machinery, hull or appurtenances, or from faults or errors in the navigation and/or management of the vessel by the master, mariners, mates, engineers or pilots.

The clause has the effect of providing coverage where there is loss or damage to cargo attributable to negligence of the crew or latent defect of machinery. The contract covers, as specified, even though there are statutes relieving the carrier of responsibility. The clause reserves for the underwriters, as subrogation, any rights of the shipper against the carrier. The perils excluded elsewhere in the contract with respect to delay, deterioration, or loss of market are not covered under the Inchmaree clause.

Delay Clause. Losses attributable to delay may be covered in the open cargo contract. Unless the contract is so endorsed, such losses are not covered. In this respect the contract provides:

Warranted free of claim for loss of market or for loss, damage or deterioration arising from delay, whether caused by a peril insured against or otherwise, unless the risk of delay is expressly assumed in writing hereon.

There are a number of cargos, fresh fruit to mention one, that are susceptible to deterioration if a voyage is unduly prolonged. Where protection against such losses is required, the contract may be endorsed to cover deterioration losses resulting from delay, not only caused by the perils insured against but, as well, if caused by the breakdown of machinery, the failure of the rudder, and similar causes.

Both-to-Blame Clause. The "both-to-blame clause" in ocean carriers' bills of lading, permits the carrying vessel to recover from the owner of cargo in both-to-blame collisions the amount which the carrier pays the noncarrying vessel for damages to cargo under the rules of divided damages. The following clause protects the shipper of cargo with respect to such claims:

Where goods are shipped under a Bill of Lading containing the so-called "Both to Blame Collision" Clause, these Assurers agree as to all losses covered by this insurance, to indemnify the Assured for this policy's proportion of any amount (not exceeding the amount insured) which the Assured may be legally bound to pay to the shipowners under such clause. In the event that such liability is asserted, the Assured agree to notify these Assurers who shall have the right at their own cost and expense to defend the Assured against such claim.

The Supreme Court has declared both-to-blame clauses in the ocean carriers' bills of lading to be invalid. The clause still appears in the contract, and in the event the insured is called upon to make a defense against asserted liability, the insurance is available for his protection.

Constructive Total Loss. In marine insurance there are two kinds of total loss. When the insured property has been destroyed, there is an actual loss. When the property cannot be preserved from actual loss without an expenditure that would exceed its value when the expenditure has been incurred, there is a constructive total loss. The constructive total loss clause reads into the contract a long-established practice and one that has been enacted into law in the English Insurance Act of 1906. The clause reads:

> No recovery for a constructive total loss shall be made hereunder unless the property insured is reasonably abandoned on account of its actual loss appearing to be unavoidable, or because it cannot be preserved from actual total loss without an expenditure which would exceed its value when the expense had been incurred.

If it appears that the insurer is liable for a constructive total loss, in order to make a claim the insured makes a statement of the existing condition and abandons the cargo to the insurer. The insured must tender the abandonment to the underwriter promptly, and thereafter the underwriter, upon acceptance, has the right to take possession and institute such steps as he deems feasible to minimize the loss. The insured receives payment in full for the insured cargo. Salvage, if any, belongs to the underwriters.

Carrier Clause. This is a very important clause and is typically found in ocean marine and inland marine contracts. It provides that cargo insurance shall be null and void as concerns loss or damage while on docks, wharves, or elsewhere on shore to the extent that responsibility for loss rests with a carrier or bailee or with insurance carried by them. A typical carrier clause reads as follows: "Warranted that this insurance shall not inure, directly or indirectly, to the benefit of any carrier or bailee."

It is the intent of the insurer to cover risks for the insured but to retain for itself subrogation against the carrier. Insurers recover substantial sums under subrogation from carriers, and if this recovery were closed to them marine rates would be higher.

Paramount Warranties. It was the intention, in preparing the perils clause of the cargo contract, to omit war risks. Because of the broad nature of the coverage provided by the contract, there was apprehension on the part of the underwriters that certain features of the protection designed to extend only to marine perils might be held to cover, in certain instances, war damage that the underwriters did not intend to cover. Likewise, to establish clearly the limits of protection with respect to strikes, riots, and civil commotion, loss or damage attributable to these perils is excluded. The paramount warranties as they appear follow:

> The following warranties shall be paramount and shall not be modified or superseded by any other provision included in this Policy or stamped or endorsed hereon unless such other provision refers specifically to the risks excluded by these warranties and expressly assumes the said risks:

(A) F.C.&S. Warranty Notwithstanding anything herein contained to the contrary, this insurance is warranted free from capture, seizure, arrest, restraint, detainment, confiscation, preemption, requisition or nationalization, and the consequences thereof or any attempt thereat, whether in time of peace or war and whether lawful or otherwise; also warranted free, whether in time of peace or war, from all loss or damage caused by any weapon of war employing atomic fission or radioactive force; also warranted free from all consequences of hostilities or warlike operations (whether there be a declaration of war or not) but this warranty shall not exclude collision, explosion or contact with any fixed or floating object (other than a mine or torpedo), stranding, heavy weather or fire unless caused directly (and independently of the nature of the voyage or service which the vessel concerned or, in the case of a collision, any other vessel involved therein, is performing) by a hostile act by or against a belligerent power; and for the purpose of this warranty "power" includes any authority maintaining naval, military or air forces in association with a power.

Further warranted free from the consequences of civil war, revolution, rebellion, insurrection, or civil strife arising therefrom, or piracy.

(B) S.R.&C.C. Warranty Warranted free of loss or damage caused by or resulting from strikes, lockouts, labor disturbances, riots, civil commotions or the acts of any person or persons taking part in any such occurrence or disorder.

The use of the F.C.&S. clause definitely eliminates the question of liability of underwriters for loss or damage growing out of war or a state of war. It follows, therefore, that with the use of the F.C.&S. clause an insured who wishes his ship or goods to be protected against the perils of war must provide specific insurance covering these hazards, and this is the custom today. Likewise, coverage for loss or damage arising from strikes, riots, and civil commotion is excluded by virtue of the S.R.&C.C. clause. In contrast to war perils, the perils excluded by the S.R.&C.C. clause may be added to the marine perils policy by endorsement.

INSURER'S CLAUSES

The insurer's clauses (company's clauses) cover such matters as payment of loss, other insurance, partial loss, breakage and leakage, decay, reporting, and inspection of records. The contract provides that losses will be paid "not later than thirty days after proof of loss and proof of interest in the property insured" has been demonstrated. In the case of partial losses the insurer declares that "the loss shall as far as practicable, be ascertained by a separation and a sale or appraisement of the damaged portion only of the contents of the packages so damaged and not otherwise." Breakage, leakage, loss of weight, and loss of contents are not covered unless caused by stranding or collision or unless the "insurance has been expressly extended to include such losses." The clauses relating to decay, reporting, and other insurance require more extended comment and will now be considered.

Decay Clause. There are certain types of shipment that, because of their nature, are particularly susceptible to damage caused by moisture. Sweat damage follows condensation of moisture in the hold which in turn may drip from the vessel structure to the cargo. Sometimes there is damage caused by contact with fuel oil or oil carried as a cargo. It is the intent of the decay clause to exclude losses due to wet or dampness or other causes that may affect the flavor or otherwise adversely affect the marketability of perishable goods. This clause reads as follows:

> Warranted by the Assured free from damage or injury from dampness, change of flavor or being spotted, discolored, musty or mouldy, except caused by actual content of sea water with the articles damaged, occasioned by sea perils unless . . . this insurance has been expressly extended to include such losses.

It is the intent of the clause to eliminate small claims with respect to merchandise that is almost certain to suffer some change due to moisture, but losses directly attributable to sea perils are covered. Where the risk of loss attributable to dampness may involve substantial amounts, the contract may be endorsed to provide coverage. Commodities such as coffee or cocoa, which move from a warm to a cool climate, may suffer considerable sweat damage. Modern cargo vessels are equipped with air-conditioning systems designed to reduce the probability of such losses. Shippers may require insurance against the peril, and the coverage may be provided with particular average terms.

The contract is written "with average" since, due to the nature of the cargo, some loss is almost certain. Protection is provided under the "skimmings clause." Damaged coffee or cocoa is separated from the undamaged in the bags that are wet or stained by water. Loss is paid on that part of the cargo that is segregated as damaged. Where, however, the loss is not expected to be great, the decay clause is the occasion of no hardship. It is the intent definitely to eliminate from coverage minor damage that is more or less inevitable.

Declarations. Since the open cargo contract is an agreement whereby the insurer agrees to insure all shipments of the insured of the nature described in the contract and within the territorial limits set forth, the contract requires the insured to declare all covered shipments whenever notice is received or as soon thereafter as practicable. This agreement obligates the insured to act promptly and with due diligence. Failure to act promptly without some reasonable excuse may prejudice the position of the insured to such a degree that he will not be allowed to recover. The matter is covered in the following terms:

> It is a condition of this insurance that all shipments coming within the terms hereof shall be reported to this Company as soon as known to the Assured and amounts declared as soon as ascertained, and failure to make such reports shall render this policy null and void if this Company shall so elect; provided, however, that unintentional error or omission in making such report shall not avoid this insurance provided the same be reported to this Company as soon as known to the Assured.

The premium for a shipment is earned whenever the shipment becomes at risk. The obligation placed on the assured to notify the insurer and pay premiums is a heavy one. The right given in the clause to permit the insurer to render the contract void for failure simply puts in words the right that the insurer would have in any case by virtue of placing the obligation to report and pay on the level of a warranty. The consequences might be serious if a contract were declared null and void as of a given date and subsequent shipments were at risk without insurance. If the contract covers imports, it is entirely possible that shipments might be made without the knowledge of the insured and these could be without insurance.

Other Insurance. In the event there are other insurance contracts covering the same interest the loss is collected under the various contracts "in the order of the date of their attachment." The complete statement about other insurance follows:

> In case the interest hereby insured is covered by other insurance (except as hereinafter provided) the loss shall be collected from the several policies in the order of the date of their attachment, insurance attaching on the same date to be deemed simultaneous and to contribute pro rata: Provided, however, that where any fire insurance, or any insurance (including fire) taken out by any carrier or bailee is available to the beneficiary of this policy, or would be so available if this insurance did not exist, then this insurance shall be void to the extent that such other insurance is or would have been available. It is agreed, nevertheless, that where these Assurers are thus relieved of liability because of the existence of other insurance, these Assurers shall receive and retain the premium payable under this policy and, in consideration thereof, shall guarantee the solvency of the companies and/or underwriters who issued such other insurance and the prompt collection of the loss thereunder to the same extent (only) as these Assurers shall have been relieved of liability under the terms of this clause, but not exceeding, in any case, the amount which would have been collectible under this policy if such other insurance did not exist.

The specific reference to the carrier or bailee is important and should be read in connection with the Carrier Clause.

MARINE EXTENSION CLAUSES

Under the open cargo contract the insurance becomes effective at the time the material to be shipped leaves the warehouse until it is delivered to the warehouse at the final destination. Although no delay, deviation, reshipment, or similar contingency is contemplated, it is possible that such events will occur and will be beyond the control of the insured. It is also possible that the shipowner carrying the insured cargo will take advantage of some authorization in the shipping agreement and might, for example, terminate the voyage at a place other than the destination of the insured shipment. The open cargo contract continues to cover in these circumstances. The following excerpts from the marine extension clauses are especially pertinent:

> In the event of the exercise of any liberty granted to the shipowner or charterer under the contract of affreightment whereby such contract is terminated at a port or place other than the original insured destination, the insurance continues until the goods are sold and delivered at such port or place; or, if the goods be not sold but are forwarded to the original insured destination or to any other destination this insurance continues until the goods have arrived at final warehouse.
>
> If while this insurance is still in force and before the expiry of 15 days from midnight of the day on which the discharge overside of the goods hereby insured from the overseas vessel at the final port of discharge is completed, the goods are resold . . . and are to be forwarded to a destination other than that covered by this insurance, the goods are covered hereunder while deposited at such port of discharge until again in transit or until the expiry of the aforementioned 15 days whichever shall first occur. If a sale is effected after the expiry of the aforementioned 15 days while this insurance is still in force the protection afforded hereunder shall cease as from the time of the sale.
>
> Held covered at a premium to be arranged in case of change of voyage or of any omission or error in the description of the interest vessel or voyage.
>
> This insurance shall in no case be deemed to extend to cover loss damage or expense proximately caused by delay or inherent vice or nature of the subject-matter insured.

In case of short shipment of merchandise in whole or in part by the vessel reported for insurance, or if the goods are transshipped by another vessel or vessels or are carried beyond or discharged short of destination, or in the event of deviation or change of voyage, or in the event of any interruption or variation beyond the control of the insured, it is provided that the insurance shall cover until the goods arrive at final destination or until the subject matter insured is no longer at the risk of the insurer, whichever first may occur. To effect this continuity of coverage, notice must be given to the insurer immediately by the insured when such facts are known to him and an additional premium must be paid if required.

STRIKES, RIOTS, AND CIVIL COMMOTION

Losses attributable to strikes, riots, sabotage, vandalism, and similar actions are eliminated from the contract covering marine perils in the S.R.&C.C. warranty. As in the case of hull contracts the coverage may be provided for cargo risks and the open cargo contract may be endorsed to provide the additional coverage.

An additional premium is required, and the same cancellation provisions prevail as in the war perils clause. War risk rates may and frequently do provide for the strike, riot, and civil commotion perils.

CERTIFICATES

The insured under the open cargo form may issue certificates that indicate that a shipment identified on the certificate has been insured with the insurer named for a specified sum. The conveyances by which the shipment is to be transferred are indicated, as well as the point of shipment and the point of destination. There is a blank space in the certificate for inserting marks and numbers identifying the shipment. Another space is provided to indicate the perils covered and applicable clauses. The certificate refers by number to the open contract under which it is issued and states "this Certificate is subject to all the terms of the Open Policy, provided, however, that the rights of a bona fide holder of this certificate for value shall not be prejudiced by any terms of the Open Policy which are in conflict with the terms of this certificate." Virtually, all of the important contract conditions are printed in the certificate. The provision relieves the holder of a certificate of any apprehension with respect to terms concerning which he may have no information. The certificate conveys the right of collecting any loss as fully as if the property were covered by a special contract direct to the holder. Like the bill of lading the certificate is a quasi-negotiable instrument and transfers the insurance to the holder to whom it has in good faith been endorsed. Certificates of insurance provide for the adjustment of losses in all parts of the commercial world and usually indicate the cities in which settling agents and claim agents are permanently located.

FOR DISCUSSION

1. Assume a cargo shipped by X is insured for $5,000 under the usual valued marine cargo form. As a result of an accident during transit, the

cargo is damaged to the extent of 50 percent. Suppose during the course of transit, the market for the products fell so that when the ship arrived it had a sound value of $3,500. What would the insurer be liable to pay? In the foregoing situation, assume a rising market so that the sound value amounted to $8,500. What, then, would be the liability of the insurer?

2. X shipped a cargo of cotton from San Francisco to the Orient. The contract covered the ordinary marine perils, but war risks were excluded under the F.C.&S. clause. The ship was damaged in a gale, and the hold was flooded with sea water. While the ship was in distress and unable to maneuver, it was sunk by the raider of a belligerent nation. Has the insured a claim for a total loss or a partial loss, or has he any claim at all? How would you arrive at the liability of the insurer?
3. X in 1939 had a shipment of goods bound for a China seaport. As a result of the hostilities between Japan and China, the goods were destroyed. In the ordinary course, the loss would have been attributed to a war risk, but X claims that since Japan never formally declared war against China, a state of war does not exist. In your opinion would an insurance contract excluding war risks be liable for the loss?
4. There is a shipment of European steel products shipped from Liverpool through the St. Lawrence River and Great Lakes. It is consigned to a concern in Chicago. Before the shipment reaches its destination, part of the water route is closed by ice. The vessel is obliged to tie up at St. John, Newfoundland, or Halifax, Nova Scotia. In such an occurrence, where does the consignee in Chicago stand, with respect to the cargo insurance covering the shipment?
5. A ship loaded principally with timber, as a result of a collision, becomes partially filled with water. Because of the nature of the cargo, it is impossible for the ship to sink to bottom. To bring memorandum items aboard within the operation of the memorandum clause, could this be termed a sinking?
6. The vessel X, proceeding up the Cork River, took ground on three occasions. Her voyage was suspended for three full days, yet the courts held that this grounding did not constitute a stranding. Can you give a logical reason for the decision?
7. The "Petersham" was sailing during World War I in convoy at night without lights. The loss was the outgrowth of a collision, and it was contended that the collision would not have happened but for the conditions made necessary by the warlike operations of the belligerent nations. In your opinion, would a marine insurance contract without war risk cover be liable for this loss?
8. The usual terms of average under which approved merchandise is shipped are as follows: "free of particular average under 3 percent unless the vessel be stranded, sunk, burnt, or in collision, each shipping package separately insured." What is the significance of the term "each package separately insured?"
9. B shipped a cargo from San Francisco to China insured against sea

perils but with war risks excluded by the F.C.&S. clause. The ship was long overdue, and the owners, apprehensive of the war risk exclusions in the policy, sought war risk insurance "lost or not lost." The premium charged by the underwriter in the circumstances was 50 percent of the value. Five days after insurance was effected, the owner learned that the ship had been driven from its course by a storm and damaged to some extent by sea perils, but was otherwise safe and ready, following minor repairs, to proceed on the journey. The owner attempted to cancel the policy covering war risks, since the premium involved approximately $25,000. What is his position?

10. With respect to the purchase and financing of shipments from overseas, whether or not an importer should insure his interest in a particular cargo depends upon the terms of the sale. The bill of sale has been consummated, and such contracts fall into one of three categories: (a) cost contracts; (b) cost and freight contracts; and (c) cost, insurance and freight contracts. In which of the foregoing instances does the importer have an insurable interest?
11. By means of the open cargo contract and the certificate issued with it, it is possible to secure credit for the financing of international trade transactions that otherwise might present considerably more complex problems. Explain the use of the open cargo contract certificate in such a transaction.
12. X sells an American car to a customer in France. Upon delivery, it is found that one of the fenders is seriously damaged. Explain the application of the machinery clause with respect to the repair of this automobile.
13. A shipment of champagne from France comes in contact with sea water with the result that all the labels are damaged. The consignee claims the goods to be unsalable and will not permit relabeling. What is his position?
14. A shipment of a number of valuable machines was made from this country to France. In the course of shipment many of the machines were seriously damaged, and the cost of repairs ran into a very substantial sum. There was considerable delay in working out the claim. The policy was insured in United States dollars. When all the documents relating to the claim were presented to the company, the currency had been considerably devalued. The claimants argued that they should receive United States dollars in an amount that would be the equivalent of the amount of the claim at the time of the loss. The underwriters, on the other hand, argued that they are entitled to convert the foreign currency into dollars at the rate in effect at the time the claim is paid. Is this contention correct?
15. B is expecting a large consignment of chestnuts and proposes to sell them for the Thanksgiving market. If the consignment arrives too late for this market, the consignee will suffer a large loss. If there is a delay on the part of the cargo carrier, may the consignee make a claim against his insurance carrier for the loss attributable to the delay in shipment?
16. X makes a shipment under an opencargo form and realizes that under

the terms of warehouse-to-warehouse clause coverage is provided from the port of transportation to the final warehouse for 15 days, unless the warehouse is outside the limits of the port and then coverage is provided for 30 days. Because of a strike on the dock at the port of destination, goods do not reach the warehouse and are destroyed by fire 45 days after the arrival of the ship. What is the position of the consignee?

CHAPTER · 13

Inland Marine Transportation Contracts

The need for protection from inland transportation risks resulted from the development of cargo shipments within the continental United States and Canada, some of which were by land while others were waterborne. Insurance contracts were developed to provide the required financial protection and a number of these contracts will be considered in this chapter. An inland marine transit contract will be analyzed in some detail as an example of typical contractual provisions.

INLAND TRANSIT CONTRACT

An inland transit contract, which is nonstandard, typically lists neither perils nor exclusions. These appear in the form or endorsement attached. The contract is designed so that it may be modified to fit the particular needs of the insured. There are standardized forms to cover goods, wares, and merchandise shipped by common carrier. Contracts may be issued to cover a single shipment or, as in the case of the open cargo form, merchants, manufacturers, or others who ship and receive goods continuously may cover all shipments under an open form. In certain instances, contracts are prepared for specialized risks. Even where these contracts are printed in their entirety, they are based on the inland transit floater contract.

The form attached to the contract lists the perils covered, as well as the exclusions; and if there are any features peculiar to the type of risk that make additional conditions necessary, these are made part of the form and referred to as "special conditions." If, on the other hand, a special contract is prepared, as is the case for many classes of risk, the basic clauses, as well as the special clauses, are printed as a part of the contract, and the perils covered and exclusions are all incorporated in the one document. Within the limits available, consideration cannot be given to the details of all the different forms. Significant features of some of the more important of these will be pointed out. First, certain of the clauses in a sample contract will be described.

Misrepresentation and Fraud. This clause in the contract states the principle with respect to misrepresentation and fraud that applies to every insurance contract. The clause reads as follows:

> This policy shall be void if the assured has concealed or misrepresented any material fact or circumstance concerning this insurance or the subject thereof or in case of any fraud, attempted fraud or false swearing by the assured touching any matter relating to this insurance or the subject thereof, whether before or after a loss.

It will be recalled that in the matter of misrepresentation there is an *ordinary* rule and a *marine* rule. In marine insurance the insured is required, although no inquiry is made, to disclose every fact material to the risk, within his knowledge. The applicant for marine insurance must state all material facts which are known to him and are unknown to the insurer. The ordinary rule allows the insured to remain silent, in the absence of fraud, with respect to matters that the marine rule would obligate him to divulge. The question presents itself with respect to inland marine insurance as to whether the ordinary rule or the marine rule applies.

The question was resolved in 1949 by the New York Court of Appeals in a lengthy decision which set forth the distinguishing features of the two rules. It pointed out that the reasons that brought into being the strict marine insurance doctrine did not apply with respect to inland marine risks. Historically, as well as logically, marine insurance always involved some sort of a vessel, and a marine insurance contract always involved a maritime risk. The court held that notwithstanding the use of the term "marine," the ordinary rule with respect to misrepresentation applied to inland marine insurance and not the marine rule.

Machinery Clause. This clause is similar to the machinery clause in the open cargo form but has been modified and shortened so that it is applicable to merchandise insured under an inland marine contract. The clause provides that if one part of a machine made up of several parts is lost or damaged, the insurer will not be liable for the value of the entire machine but only for the insured value of the part lost or destroyed. The purpose of this clause is at once evident. Insurers do not wish to be in a position of having to pay a total loss on a large and expensive machine simply because some small part has been damaged and the machine abandoned to the insurer as result thereof. The clause as written in the inland marine contract has been held to limit the liability of the insurer to the value of the lost or damaged part, even though that part cannot be replaced. The operation of this clause, while intended originally only for machinery, has been found so satisfactory that the clause is now inserted in contracts covering shipments other than of machinery when there is a possibility that a part only may be injured and a claim made for the whole.

Label Clause. The clause provides that in case of loss or damage to labels only, the loss shall be adjusted on the basis of an amount sufficient to pay the cost of new labels and relabeling the goods. This clause is likely to be the occasion of serious misunderstanding in connection with certain shipments. It is the intent of the clause to limit the liability of the insurer to the relabeling cost if the labels are damaged or destroyed and this is the extent of the damage. An insured frequently is not satisfied with relabeling. Sometimes there is no immediate apparent damage to the merchandise but the insured as a matter of policy will not take the risk of letting goods with only labels damaged to go on the market as new goods; nor is he willing to take a total loss and allow the insurer to salvage the goods. If the goods go on the market and because of the damage create dissatisfaction, the reputation of the insured will suffer. It is to be pointed out that under the terms of the contract containing a label clause, the insured has no alternative with respect to the determination of his loss or damage. If his shipments are of a nature that will not permit relabeling, an agreement should be made and endorsed on the contract nullifying the label clause and providing a method for the disposition of damaged property.

Bailee Clause. The bailee clause in the inland marine transit contract, as in the open cargo form, provides that "this insurance shall in no wise inure directly or indirectly to the benefit of any carrier or other bailee." There is no agreement in the clause indicating that the insurer will advance funds in the form of a loan in the event of a loss. This, nevertheless, is the practice. If an insured suffers a loss, he makes a claim against the insurer, and after the loss has been investigated, the insurer advances to the insured funds equivalent to the amount determined upon as the loss. In return the insured is obligated to reimburse the insurer for any funds recovered from the carrier. The loan procedure has been considerably formalized.

Notice of Loss Clause. The notice of loss clause obligates the insured to notify the insurer or its agent with respect to any loss "as soon as practicable." The insured is obligated to use every care in bringing prompt notice to the insurer so that the insurer in turn may take whatever steps are necessary in the circumstances to protect its interest. If in the case of a burglary loss the contract requires evidence of force and violence to sustain a claim, the insured may not satisfy the insurer by contending that such evidence was there and has disappeared, if he could well have given notice before the evidence disappeared. There are situations where prompt notice may be of assistance in tracking down thieves and others where delay may contribute to the further damage of the insured merchandise. If the insured acts expeditiously and stands prepared to cooperate fully with the insurer, he cannot be criticized. If there is a loss and the insured, even without any intent to defraud but purely through negligence and inertia, fails to get around to notifying the insurer promptly, he may well jeopardize his coverage.

The notice of loss clause requires the filing of a proof of loss within a period of 90 days. Failure to file the proof has the effect of invalidating a claim. In some states the statutes modify the contract requirement by providing that the insurer must first make a formal demand for a proof, and the time within which the proof must be filed commences to run with the demand. It is well to remember, however, that notice should be given as promptly as possible and proof of loss, in the ordinary course, filed within the time limit specified in the contract.

Sue and Labor Clause. Inland marine transit contracts all contain a sue and labor clause patterned after that found in the contract of ocean marine insurance. The purpose of the clause in both contracts is the same. It will be recalled that by virtue of the clause in the ocean marine contract, the insured is both permitted and obligated to take necessary steps to protect the insured property against further loss; the same is true in the inland marine form. The obligation is particularly important and is sometimes not recognized by inland marine insureds. For example, in the case of a damaged truck cargo shipment the insured may not carelessly leave the shipment with the thought that he has no further responsibility since it is fully insured. He must take every possible step to protect and salvage the wreckage.

As in the case of the ocean marine contract, the sue and labor clause is a contract separate and apart from the contract of indemnity. There may be, and frequently are, legitimate claims under the sue and labor clause that must be paid by the insurer, even if there is no actual loss caused by a peril insured against. This situation follows when the insured, through his efforts, has succeeded in averting a loss threatened by one of the perils covered in the contract. In the case of a total loss, it may likewise follow that the insurer will be obligated for an additional liability for expenses incurred under the sue and labor clause.

Reinstatement Clause. The reinstatement clause restates the accepted practice in marine insurance of reducing the amount of insurance by the amount of every claim paid. The significance of the clause is to be found in that the contract is automatically reinstated to its full face amount without the requirement of any action on the part of the insured. Reinstatement takes effect immediately upon the occurrence which occasioned the loss, though reinstatement is typically not made without charge as is now the case with fire insurance contracts. The insured is obligated, in most instances, to pay an additional premium at pro rata rates on the amount of reinstated losses.

Not all reinstatement clauses have the effect of automatically reinstating insurance. Clauses have been written providing that each claim reduces the amount of the insurance by the sum paid unless the same be reinstated by the payment of an additional premium at pro rata rates. The automatic reinstatement clause is the broader coverage, and unless the property is destroyed with no further need of insurance, it is necessary to provide continuous and complete coverage.

Since most of the transportation contracts provide for the payment of a premium on the basis of reported values, and it is customary when this practice is followed to waive the reinstatement clause, the clause now only finds occasional use in connection with the writing of transportation insurance. It is of interest to the insured, if the clause does form a part of his contract, to know whether reinstatement is effected automatically or whether under its terms he is obliged to take the initiative to effect a full restoration of his insurance.

Coinsurance. Inland marine contracts, following the custom of ocean marine, are usually written contemplating full insurance to value. When the subject of the insurance is of such a nature that the value can easily be determined, the matter of coinsurance does not always find a place in the contract. When the goods are of such a nature that the value cannot readily be ascertained by the underwriters, a clause is frequently inserted in the contract covering the matter of coinsurance. When such a clause is inserted, it is usual to require full insurance to value; therefore, the 100 percent coinsurance clause is made a part of the contract. This rule, while general, is not without exception, and in particular cases a clause for less than 100 percent is sometimes used.

Other Contract Conditions. The inland marine transit contract contains certain other clauses that parallel to a considerable degree clauses discussed in connection with other contracts. It is provided that adjusted claims shall be paid within 60 days, but no loss shall be paid if the insured has collected for the loss from others. No suit or action may be sustained in any court unless commenced by the insured within 12 months after discovery of the occurrence which gives rise to the claim. If the laws of a state allow a longer time for bringing suit, the state law prevails. Provision is made for appraisal if the insured and insurer fail to agree on the amount of loss. Provision is made for cancellation by either the insured or the insurer. Cancellation may be effected by means of a written notice. If the insurer cancels, notice may be mailed to the last known address of the insured and at least five days' notice must be given. The usual short-rate premium is charged if the insured cancels, otherwise the return premium is computed on a pro rate basis.

War Risk. As was the case with ocean marine insurance, the advent of World War II focused the attention of inland marine underwriters upon war risk hazards. Some inland marine contracts already contained exclusions to war risk, but in others, no such exclusion appeared in the contract. Effective March 1, 1940, the Inland Marine Underwriters Association adopted the following clause as the approved association war exclusion clause: "This contract does not insure against loss or damage arising from War, Invasion, Hostilities, Rebellion, Insurrection, Seizure or Destruction under quarantine or Customs regulations, Confiscation by order of any Government or Public Authority, or risks of Contraband or Illegal Transportation and/or Trade." The clause follows to some extent the pattern of the F.C.&S. clause in use at the time by ocean marine underwriters. With the passing of time the clause has been broadened. The present Inland Marine Insurance Bureau form reads as follows:

> **War Risks Exclusion.** This policy does not insure against loss or damage caused by or resulting from:
> (1) hostile or warlike action in time of peace or war, including action in hindering, combating or defending against an actual, impending or expected attack, (a) by any government or sovereign power (de jure or de facto), or by any authority maintaining or using military, naval or air forces; or (b) by military, naval or air forces; or (c) by an agent of any such government, power, authority or forces; (2) any weapon of war employing atomic fission or radio-active force whether in time of peace or war; (3) insurrection, rebellion, revolution, civil war, usurped power, or action taken by governmental authority in hindering, combating or defending against such an occurrence, seizure or destruction under quarantine or Customs regulations, confiscation by order of any government or public authority, or risks of contraband or illegal transportation or trade.

This form follows the pattern in the fire insurance extended coverage endorsement. It differs from the older form and from the war perils exclusion of the standard fire contract in two respects. Specifically excluded are all losses attributable to weapons of war employing atomic fission or radioactive force. Secondly, a formal declaration of war by a recognized government is not essential to bring a loss within the exclusion. Losses attributable to undeclared wars, police actions, or, in fact, any hostile action by an authority maintaining or using armed forces are excluded. All of the exclusions of the older clause are incorporated in the newer form, and in addition atomic fission and radioactive force losses are excluded in both peace and war. Any uncertainty that may heretofore have been felt with respect to the meaning of hostile or warlike actions has been clarified.

Inception and Termination of Cover. Contracts as usually written provide insurance upon the goods shipped "while in due course of transit." They cover from the time the shipment passes into the custody of the carrier, and the insurance continues while the goods remain in the hands of the carrier as such. An agency of transportation may hold goods either as a common carrier or as a bailee. When goods are shipped and the insurance covers only while in the hands of the transportation company in the capacity of a carrier, a loss of the goods in storage after the carrier status of the transportation agency has changed to that of bailee would find the insured without protection. If, in connection with shipments, there is a possibility that the goods will remain in storage, the insurance should be endorsed to cover not only while in transit but for such period at destination as in the circumstances seems necessary.

Territorial Limits. All transportation contracts provide territorial limits within which the coverage is effective. As usually written, they cover "within the limits of the United States and Canada." These limitations, of course, can be extended as the needs of the insured require. In the event that goods are to be shipped beyond the limits set forth, it is important that the insured secure immediate authority from the insurer so that the territorial limits may be extended. To fail to do this may have the effect of developing a loss without insurance, since once the goods pass beyond the limits set forth in the contract the insurance ceases to cover.

TRIP TRANSIT INSURANCE

Single shipments between specified points are covered by the trip transit contract. The usual form covers, in the United States and Canada, shipment of approved goods made by freight, express, motor truck, and inland or coastwise steamers. The trip covered need not be confined to any one of these carriers, but it may involve a combination of one or more of them. Household furniture and personal effects are frequently insured under this contract, as are shipments of machinery, merchandise, and livestock.

The perils insured against include, while on land, loss or damage caused by fire, lightning, cyclone, tornado, flood, earthquake, landslide, collision of the conveyance on which the goods are carried, derailment, overturning of trucks, collapse of bridges, and collapse or subsidence of docks or platforms. While waterborne, the contract covers loss or damage caused by stranding, sinking, burning, or collision of the vessel, including general average and salvage charges for which the insured is liable. It is provided that coupling of cars shall not be considered a collision and that the company shall not be liable for loss caused by theft, robbery, civil commotion, strikes, lockouts, riots, or war. There is, moreover, no liability for loss or damage to goods occasioned by delay, wet, or dampness, or being spotted, discolored, rotted, or changed in flavor. Leakage, breakage, marring, and scratching are not losses under the contract unless caused by a peril insured against.

Theft may be included within the scope of the protection on approved property when shipped by railroad, express, steamer, truck, or any responsible public carrier. When so written, the contract covers only theft of an entire shipping package and does not include pilferage losses. Items such as silks, tobacco, and jewelry are rarely insured against theft unless shipped by express. Shipments by express may be covered against all risks of transportation and navigation, including fire, lightning, cyclone, tornado, flood, earthquake, landslide, theft, pilferage, short delivery, and nondelivery. Here is a very broad protection, and the coverage as to theft and pilferage is particularly liberal. In the case of express shipments made by airplane, a special endorsement excludes losses caused by the breakage of fragile goods unless such loss is the direct result of a fire or accidental or forced landing.

The exclusions as to strikes and lockouts may be modified by endorsement to the extent that destruction of the property or damage done to it by strikers, locked-out workmen, or others taking part in riots or civil commotion may be covered. Loss or damage caused by deterioration, loss of market, or delay as a consequence of a strike or lockout is not covered. Goods held for packing may be insured against fire while held temporarily in a warehouse by the payment of an additional premium. Works of art or other objects in which there are large concentrations of value usually require an endorsement on the contract "warranted packed by expert packers." In the case of livestock insured while in transit by rail or motor truck, it is usual to provide that the contract cover only against accident causing death or rendering death necessary in consequence of an insured peril.

ANNUAL AND OPEN TRANSPORTATION FORMS

For shippers who have a continuous need for transportation insurance, the insuring of each shipment under a trip transit contract would involve enormous detail, and, in addition, it would not always be possible to provide an individual contract before the shipment was actually subject to a transportation hazard. Transportation contracts are as varied as the needs of individual shippers. They are written to cover either incoming or outgoing shipments, or both, while in the custody of one or a combination of carriers.

A broad form covering the hazards of rail and water provides insurance on the property of the insured at and in transit between specified points. Transportation may be by railroad or express, licensed public trucks, ferries or inland steamers, and coastwise steamers. Insurance is provided:

> Against all risks of fire, lightning, cyclone, tornado, flood (meaning rising waters) and navigation and transportation, including risks in and/or on docks, wharves, piers, and/or bulkheads, landing sheds, depots, stations and/or platform awaiting shipment and/or after arrival, from the time of leaving the warehouse, store or factory of shipper until safely delivered to warehouse, store or factory of consignee, or arrival at seaboard for export, whichever may first occur, covering only while goods are actually in transit and at the risk of the assured.

When there is no waterborne risk, the form may be written to provide land cover only. There are both a rail and a water form and also a form limited to land cover written to exclude theft protection. There is a limited form rail and water cover that insures only against the risks of fire, collision, or derailment while on land and the perils of the seas, lakes, rivers, or inland waters while waterborne. This form includes the same cover for dock risks as is found in the broad form. As in the case of the broad form, this limited cover is available covering land hazards only. Exclusion of the waterborne risk does not exclude cover for shipments on ferries or transfers in connection with railroad shipments. When shipments are handled solely by licensed trucks, there is a form which provides insurance against the risks of fire, lightning, cyclone, tornado, flood, collapse of bridges, collision, and perils of seas, lakes, and inland waters while on ferries.

The principal difference between the annual and the open form is to be found in the method of collecting the premium. Under the annual form, the contract is written for a period of one year and at the time the contract is issued a deposit premium is paid, based upon an estimate of the value of the shipments to be covered during the contract term. At the end of the contract term an audit is made, and if, on the basis of the audit, the actual shipments exceed the estimate, the insured pays the insurer an additional premium. If, on the other hand, the estimate proves to be in excess of actual shipments, a return premium is paid. In the case of the open form, the contract is issued without a deposit premium, but monthly reports are required, and the premium is paid monthly on the basis of the reports as submitted.

POSTAL INSURANCE

Parcel-Post Insurance. The insurance of packages shipped by parcel post, whether registered or unregistered, is covered by either of two forms that provide insurance upon merchandise from the time it is delivered into the custody of the postal authorities for shipment until it reaches the address of the consignee.

For the convenience of shippers handling a small volume of shipments, the coupon form has been prepared. In connection with the contract, books containing 100, 200, 500, or 1,000 coupons are provided. Insurance on a package is effected by enclosing either in the package or with the invoice the number of coupons required and entering upon the stub provided for the purpose in the book: (*a*) the name and address of the consignee as it appears on the package, (*b*) a description of the contents of the package, and (*c*) the class of mail by which the merchandise was sent. In addition to this, the date of mailing and valuation of the property are entered. There is no necessity to report to postal authorities or to anyone outside the insured's place of business.

The premium on this type of contract varies, but the rate of five cents per coupon is generally required. The number of coupons to be used on each package depends upon the value and the class of mail used.

The open form is designed for shippers handling parcel-post shipments in large volume. The insured keeps a record of all shipments in a special book provided for this purpose and makes monthly reports of shipments to the insurer. Premiums are based upon rates promulgated for the particular risk, and the rate is applied to the total monthly premiums. A deposit premium of $50 is required when the contract is issued. In some cases the deposit premium may be waived by an endorsement on the contract, but in such a case the endorsement states that the contract shall be subject to an annual minimum premium of $50. When such an endorsement is provided, monthly premiums are paid to the insurer as earned, but if during 12 continuous months the earned premium is less than $50, the difference between the earned premium and the minimum premium becomes due and payable to the insurer. If the insurance is for any reason discontinued before the expiration of a 12-month period, the minimum premium on a monthly basis is charged.

Since the rate is applied to the total monthly business, there is an economy in this form for the insured. Under the coupon form, one coupon is required to send a package valued at $25; but to send five packages each valued at $5.00, five coupons must be used. The same value is at risk in both cases. Under the open form, all values are added together and a rate applied to the aggregate.

Rates for the open form are based upon experience if this is available. In any case, the type of goods to be insured, the volume of business, and the limits for each package are taken into consideration. If no experience is available when the contract is first written, an arbitrary rate is used, and as time goes on the rate is then modified by an upward or downward adjustment as the experience on the risk warrants.

Under both forms, an all risk cover is provided. The exclusions are few and include the following:

Accounts, bills, currency, deeds, evidence of debt, money, notes or securities;

Merchandise shipped on consignment, memorandum or approval unless shipped in fulfillment of an order or request, or consigned to parties to whom the Assured has previously sold merchandise;

Merchandise such as green fruit, butter, eggs, lard or such other articles as are perishable in their own nature, except against the risks of fire, theft, pilferage and non-arrival only;

Loss or damage or the non-arrival of any package or any part of the contents thereof, which is incorrectly or insufficiently addressed; improperly or insecurely wrapped, packed or fastened; or on which the postage is not fully prepaid;

Shipments destined to transients at hotels unless sent by registered mail or government insured parcel post;

Packages bearing descriptive labels or the outside of which tends to describe the nature of the contents;

Packages that do not bear a stipulation, "Return requested";

War, invasion, hostilities, rebellion, insurrection, confiscation by order of any Government, Public Authority, or risks of Contraband or Illegal Transportation and/or Trade.

With reference to the foregoing exclusion bearing upon descriptive labels, it is now provided in the contract that descriptive labels may be permitted on merchandise which by reason of the United States postal laws must be described on the outside of the parcel. Labels also may be used in shipping merchandise which, under the postal laws, may be sent at a reduced rate when the contents are indicated. This reduced-rate regulation applies particularly to parcels marked "book" or "books."

A modification of the open form regulations provides that the contract may be amended by attaching an endorsement covering return shipment of property originally shipped by the insured and incoming shipments of property owned or purchased by the insured or in which the insured has an insurable interest. There is a small additional premium for this extension of coverage. As in the case of outgoing shipments, the insured is required to make an entry of incoming shipments to be covered and the value of such shipments, the name and address of the shipper or consignee, and the class of mail by which shipped. The entry is to be made as soon as practicable after the insured has knowledge thereof, and a statement of such shipments must be made to the insurance company monthly.

Registered Mail Insurance. This contract covers shipment by registered mail and by express. The contract may be written to cover incoming and outgoing shipments, and air shipments are covered if so declared. The contract is designed for business institutions having large values at risk in the process of transportation. Such values are usually concentrated in shipments of securities or currency. The contracts are used primarily by banking institutions, brokers, dealers in investments, and others handling securities in large amounts. Since the maximum protection obtainable under post-office regulations is $10,000, the need for insuring registered mail is a very real one.

The contract covers registered mail or express shipments of bonds, coupons, stock certificates, and securities of all kinds. In addition, postage and revenue stamps, postal express and money orders, certificates of deposit, checks, drafts, notes, bills of lading, warehouse receipts, and all other types of commercial papers are covered. Shipments of gold, silver, platinum, coin and paper money, jewelry, and precious stones likewise may be insured under this form. There are three methods of providing the cover: (1) daily reporting, (2) monthly reporting, and (3) annual premium adjustment. The form to apply in a particular case depends upon the nature of the business and the volume involved.

The contract provides an all risks coverage subject only to the exclusion of war risks. A package may be packed and sealed in any manner satisfactory to the post office. The contract also requires that the insured shall endeavor to have contents verified by two persons, but verification by only one person will not prejudice the insurance.

As to territory, coverage is worldwide and becomes effective from the premises of the senders to the premises of the addressees or until returned to the senders in the event of nondelivery. Risks of messengers or any conveyance used to and from the post office or express office at places of sending or delivery are covered. In other words, coverage attaches from the time the property is accepted by a messenger or carrier. It continues while the shipment is in transit and while in the custody of the post office. Coverage continues while the shipment is in transit from the post office or express office until delivered to the addressee.

Theft losses attributable to employees of either the sender or the addressee while in transit to and from the post office or express office are covered. Under the monthly and daily reporting forms, incoming shipments may be covered if entry is made prior to loss as required by the terms of the contract. Incoming shipments may be covered under the annual premium adjustment form, but in this case, only if the contract is so endorsed and an additional premium paid. The contract places the limit of $250,000 on each individual shipment of currency, jewelry, and precious stones. There is no limit placed upon shipments of securities, although in the event that shipments are made to one addressee during one day in excess of $2.5 million in the case of the annual adjustment form and of $5 million in the case of the reporting forms, notice to the insurer by telephone, telegram, or messenger is required. The excess is covered only after the insured receives confirmation of acceptance by the insurer. The requirement of notice is not for the purpose of permitting any additional check by the insurer, but it enables the insurer, if it wishes to do so, to relieve itself of part of the liability by effecting reinsurance.

A feature of this contract is to be found in the fact that it insures not only shipments belonging to the insured but shipments of others, either outgoing or incoming, if the insured elects to bring such shipments within the protection of the contract. Insurance is effected in all cases by making a record of the shipment in accordance with the conditions of the contract prior to the loss. It sometimes happens that a shipper has only an occasional need for insurance of this type. In the event that he has no need for an open contract, shipments may be insured on a single-trip basis.

With respect to express shipments, this contract has an appeal in that it allows the shipper to take advantage of the expeditious service of the express agency and at the same time avail himself of minimum express rates. Under the terms of the express company's tariff, an excess value charge is made on each $100 or any fraction thereof of value declared. Unless this excess charge is paid upon a value declared by the shipper, the express company limits its liability to $0.50 for each pound of actual weight for any shipment over 100 pounds and $50 in case of the loss of any one shipment. The rates charged for the express transit contract vary with the percentage of value declared, as well as with the type of merchandise to be covered in the shipment. Business institutions carrying this type of contract make it a practice when incoming shipments are covered to notify those with whom they do business to declare no value on express shipments made to them.

First-Class Mail Insurance. Banks, insurers, investment firms, security brokers, and other business institutions handling securities in volume pointed out the relative safety of first-class mail and the convenience entailed in mailing shipments without the necessity of the registration process at the post office. Moreover, certain shipments involving modest values make the cost of shipment proportionately high when fees for registered mail are considered. These considerations have prompted the demand for insurance covering shipments sent unregistered by first-class mail. There are three different types of first-class mail contracts in general use at the present time in addition to certified mail coverage. The three types are: Form A, Form B, and the Transfer Agents' Mail contract. Form B differs from Form A mainly in that only shipments made by the insured are covered under

Form B. The transfer agents' contract is useful for persons or organizations serving as trustees. Form A will be described in a little more detail by way of illustration.

The first-class mail contract (Form A) covers only securities and detached coupons with the exception of United States government securities or coupons which are not covered. The contract is written on a monthly reporting basis and covers all risks on the shipments listed for insurance by the insured. As in the case of registered mail insurance, war, along with such perils as insurrection and nuclear energy, is the only peril excluded. Form A protects interoffice shipments of both negotiable and nonnegotiable securities and other types of shipment of nonnegotiable securities.

Since the risk is greater with respect to first-class mail than is the case with registered mail, the premium is higher, the limit for a single package is $110,000, and the maximum limit, without prior confirmed acceptance by the insurer, is $1,110,000 from any one shipper to the same addressee in a given business day. Rates differ for negotiable and nonnegotiable securities and coupons.

Since the government limits its liability for registered mail shipments of negotiable instruments to $1,000 per package when commercial insurance exists and to $10,000 when there is no commercial insurance, but imposes a mailing surcharge for values in excess of that amount, the first-class mail contract offers shipping cost advantages for securities eligible for coverage within certain areas of value. Fiduciaries handling substantial security shipments will usually carry both the registered mail and the first-class mail forms. It will be a matter of determination in each instance, giving consideration to the nature of the shipment, its value, postage rates, and insurance premium, which contract is to be used in any particular instance.

ARMORED-CAR AND MESSENGER INSURANCE

This contract is issued to financial institutions such as banks and investment houses and provides much the same protection as that found in the registered mail contract, except that it provides insurance for shipments of money, securities, and other valuables made by armored motorcars and messengers. There are contract limits for different classes of shipments, varying according to the safeguards to be provided.

The insurance is effected as a separate contract, or, if the insured already carries a registered mail contract, the additional cover may be provided by an endorsement attached to that contract. The contract as usually written covers the continental limits of the United States and Canada but excludes Alaska. Contracts are written on a daily reporting or monthly reporting basis. A third form available is known as the "annual excess form." This is used when the insured has other insurance covering on such shipments. It is written for a flat premium and covers shipments of the insured subject to a specified deductible. The usual rule is to write the contract with $100,000 deductible, thereby providing protection for shipments in the event that losses run in excess of the amount deductible. The contract provides the same broad protection afforded under the registered mail contract.

It contemplates the insured as the owner of the property or as representing the owner in placing the insurance. Contracts may also be written to cover the liability of the operators of armored cars for property of others placed in their custody for transportation.

PROCESSORS' FLOATER

A processors' floater covers the goods of the insured while in the custody of bailees for the purpose of performing work thereon including the treatment of, or assemblage of, property. Forms used for this type of insurance vary among insurers and for the processing being covered. The coverage granted is determined by the inland marine definition.

There has developed in many lines of business the custom of sending goods and merchandise from the premises of the owner to various locations for processing. A part of the work may be completed at one location and the goods then moved along to another for further work. In the process of manufacturing the finished product, the goods may be in transit several times and temporarily located from time to time in one of several locations. The problem of keeping an accurate account of values in each location, as well as determining values in transit from time to time between the different locations, has given rise to the need for a contract that will provide protection of the goods in process from the time it leaves the premises of the owner until it is returned. Protection is required not only while in transit but while temporarily located in the hands of processors.

A contract, to meet this need, may cover property such as yarns, cloth, metals, plastics, leather, rubber, paper, glass, foods, and other similar properties when (*a*) the property is owned by the insured and is being processed by others, and (*b*) while such property is in transit. Property owned by the insured on the insured's own premises is not covered, or are stocks of merchandise not undergoing processing operations wherever located.

GARMENT CONTRACTORS' INSURANCE

The garment contractors' floater is closely related to the type of coverage provided under the processing floater. The form is adapted to the particular needs of the garment maker, jobber, or dealer who ships materials or unfinished clothing for processing by contractors or subcontractors. The contract covers garment materials and partly finished garments, such as suits, coats, dresses, jackets, and other wearing apparel or materials. The property is covered while temporarily detained on the premises of contractors or subcontractors during cutting, sewing, embroidering, or other similar work performed by the insured. Transit coverage is provided between the premises of the insured and contractors or subcontractors, or while in transit from mills or other suppliers to contractors or subcontractors doing work for the insured.

The contract covers (*a*) while in transit against all risks of direct physical loss or damage from external causes, and (*b*) while on the premises of contractors or subcontractors against named perils which include loss or damage by fire, the perils included in the extended cover contract, water damage, burglary, holdup, and in some instances boiler explosion. Consequential loss damage may be covered by endorsement. Under this endorsement the insured receives the difference between the amount for which the insurer is liable for direct loss and the amount he is able to realize through sale of the undamaged garments. There is an optional consequential damage coverage broader than the foregoing which provides coverage for loss attributable to broken lots, sizes, or color ranges. This coverage is purchased by manufacturers who sell in lots or ranges of sizes or colors. Damage to garments or parts that constitute a lot would result in a loss to the undamaged items if a complete lot following damage could not be reassembled. In the case of consequential damage, there is no liability on the part of the company for 21 days after the loss. During this period the insured is obligated to make every effort to replace the lost or damaged goods. The contract may be also extended to cover explosion, riot, and malicious damage. Burglary and holdup are included in the regular form, but the contract may be extended to cover theft while on the premises of contractors or subcontractors.

The usual marine exclusions such as war risk, neglect of the insured, and delay or loss of market are included. Mysterious disappearance or inventory shortages are not covered, nor is infidelity or dishonest acts on the part of the insured or his employees or the contractor or subcontractor or his employees.

The contract insures against named perils including loss or damage caused by fire or lightning and may include the perils ordinarily included in the extended coverage endorsement provided by property and liability insurers. Sprinkler leakage is covered as well as burglary from the premises. While in transit, the theft of an entire shipping package is covered, as well as losses occasioned by collision, overturn, or derailment of the carrying conveyance.

The exclusions are those found in the usual marine transit contract, including war risks and loss or damage growing out of delay, deterioration, temperature change, or similar items. Because of the wide range of risks that may be covered under this contract, special forms are frequently prepared to meet the needs of an individual insured. Where necessary the exclusions may be adjusted to meet the requirements of the particular risk.

The contract covers all shipments described at the risk of the insured from the time the property leaves the premises of the shipper, while in transit, while in the custody of the processor or processors, and until arrival at the warehouse, store, or factory of the consignee.

BAILEES' INSURANCE

Insurance to meet the needs of persons who have temporary custody of the goods or property of others has resulted in the inland marine field in the development of several forms known as "bailee coverages." Originally the insurance was written on a liability basis, and the insurance today is sometimes known as "bailee liability." Many bailees, however, do not wish, in the event that property entrusted to them has been lost or damaged, to make adjustments based strictly upon the elements of legal liability. To do so many have the effect of involving them in legal disputes, and, in any case, failure to reimburse a customer for property left in charge of the bailee, even in the absence of legal liability, might tend to create bad will. For this reason, bailees frequently secure an inland marine contract covering goods entrusted to their care if damaged by perils designated, whether or not the element of legal liability is present. Bailee insurance may be written not only on a liability basis but to cover direct damage to the insured property regardless of liability.

The term "bailment" pertains solely to personal property. For a bailment to arise, it is necessary that personal property pass temporarily into the possession of a person or persons other than the owner. A bailee may be a carrier, a laundryman, cleaner, dyer, garagekeeper, or other person having possession of goods whose title is in another.

Bailments have been classed as exceptional and ordinary. In the first category are public carriers and innkeepers, who are subject to exceptional duties and liabilities.

Ordinary bailments include business transactions with the element of hiring, such as hire of services, hire of custody, and hire of carriage. Services are hired where goods are entrusted to another who is to use labor and skill upon them, as in the case of a dyer or cleaner. Custody can be illustrated by the business of a warehouseman. Hire of carriage is effected when goods are entrusted to a carrier to be transported from one place to another for a compensation.

In dealing with bailments the degree of care required of the bailee differs. An innkeeper would be expected to handle money in quite a different manner than a truckman would be expected to handle a bag of coal. What constitutes ordinary diligence in one set of circumstances would be construed as gross negligence in another. In ordinary business contracts, in the absence of special agreement, a bailee is obligated to take reasonable or ordinary care of the property bailed to him. This is held to be such care as a reasonably careful owner of similar goods would exercise with respect to them.[1]

With respect to bailees there are various statutory liabilities that apply in specific cases. Included in the category are carriers, warehousemen, and public garagekeepers, among others. Bailees are invariably liable for negligence. Negligence is defined as "failure to exercise the care that the circumstances justly demand." The negligent performance of a required duty, or failure to perform the duty, will create a legal liability for damages on the part of the bailee. Any element of negligence in the care of the property entrusted to the bailee makes him responsible for the loss to the bailor.

The first step in providing insurance to protect the bailee is to cover his legal liability for loss. Under such a contract in order to establish a loss, there must be (1) legal liability on the part of the bailee, and (2) loss or damage due to a peril covered by the contract. It is obvious that many losses would involve no legal liability, yet the bailee, because of his relationship with his customers, would wish to make good for loss of property while in his custody. There are now three forms of bailee contracts written: (*a*) for the sole benefit of the bailor, (*b*) for the sole benefit of the bailee, and (*c*) for the benefit of both. The legal liability type of coverage affords limited protection. It is more usual today and more satisfactory to provide direct damage insurance which pays for damage to the property in the hands of the bailee even though there is no element of legal liability.

Many forms of insurance are written that have a bailee interest. There are three such major inland marine forms: (1) motor-truck carriers, (2) bailee's customers, and (3) furrier's customers.

Truckmen's Legal Liability Interest. With the recent increases in volume of shipping by truck, legislatures have given consideration to the question of the ability of trucking concerns to settle claims for loss or damage for which they may become liable. The owners of the trucking business may not wish to insure against losses from this source, but as time goes on, statutory enactments are compelling public truckmen to provide themselves with a prescribed minimum coverage before a license is granted.

The legal liability of a truckman may be written under a blanket

[1] *Levine* v. *Wolff*, 78 N.J.L. 306; 73 Atl., 73; *Mortimer* v. *Otto*, 206 N.Y. 89; 99 N.E. 189.

form or under a gross receipts form. Under the blanket form a list is made of the trucks operated by the insured and a limit of liability set for each truck. The premium is computed by applying the rate to the aggregate liability. Under the gross receipts form the rate is applied to the total receipts of the business. This form is considered to have an advantage in that a percentage of every charge goes for insurance, and when the trucks are idle or empty, no insurance costs accrue. Under the blanket form an estimated annual premium is paid, with the usual adjustment at the end of the contract term. Under the gross receipts form an advance premium is paid, and earned premiums are payable thereafter monthly on the basis of the monthly report. Both forms are subject to 100 percent coinsurance.

Perils insured against are fire; perils of seas, lakes, and rivers while on ferries; collision and overturning of truck; and collapse of bridges. The contract assumes no liability for loss or damage caused by neglect to use reasonable means to save insured property at or after an accident, loss due to rough handling, damage to goods carried gratuitously or as an accommodation. The usual exclusions of losses due to riot, strikes, and the like are a part of the contract, as are the usual stipulations relating to wet, dampness, or spotting. Damage to the truck itself is not covered. In the case of breakage of eggs, damage must equal 50 percent of the value of the package and be caused by the perils insured against before liability attaches to the insurer.

The risk of theft of an entire load may be covered, but insurers are reluctant to accept the risk of theft of packages from a truck unless conditions are such as to afford a reasonable degree of protection. Theft of packages from open, unprotected trucks is ordinarily not written, and in any case pilferage is not covered. When especially valuable shipments are forwarded in locked and guarded cars, the theft risk may be covered.

Bailees' Customers Contracts. This insurance, sometimes called "customers' goods insurance," is written on a named perils basis and covers direct damage, without regard to legal liability, to goods in the custody or control of the insured for services such as cleaning, repairing, or laundering. While the contract may be adapted to the needs of any business institution accepting goods of its customers where the bailor is to render services to the bailed property involving labor and skills, there are three forms that have attained wide acceptance: the first for laundries, the second for dyers and cleaners, and the third for rug and carpet cleaners.

The three forms are alike in their essentials, varying in details to fit the needs of the particular business. The usual perils insured against are fire, explosion, collision, theft, burglary, holdup, tornado, cyclone, windstorm, flood, sprinkler leakage, transportation risks by public carriers or mail service, earthquake, strikes, riots, civil commotion, and, in the case of laundries and carpet cleaners, the confusion of goods resulting from any of the foregoing perils.[2] The usual exclusions are theft or shortage of individual pieces or articles unless by burglary or holdup; loss or damage to goods in the custody of other laundries; loss or damage to goods held in storage; or loss if other insurance covers.

Protection is provided on all kinds of lawful goods or articles that are the property of customers and accepted by the insured for cleaning, pressing, laundering, or other like service while contained in the premises occupied by the insured or used by its agents, and while being transferred to and from its customers or between its own branches or agencies. The liability of the insurer is limited to the actual cash value of the property destroyed, with no limit set for any one disaster. Provision is made in the contract to cover the insured's charges for services rendered on the lost or damaged items.

The premium is based upon the gross income of the business insured, and monthly reports are required indicating the gross earnings for the previous month, whether collected or not. The contents fire rate is used as a basis for establishing a rate.

Furriers' Customers Insurance. Furriers and department stores accepting furs for storage offer as part of their service insurance protection on the stored items. The contract is written on a special inland marine form, and insurance certificates are furnished the dealer to issue to customers. The dealer is named in the contract as the insured, and all furs or garments for which certificates have been issued are covered. The coverage is for all risks and provides not only legal liability coverage up to the valuation on the receipt issued to the owners of the furs but as well direct loss or damage without regard to legal liability. If the insured elects to purchase the coverage, the contract may be endorsed with the excess legal liability endorsement which covers the insured for any legal liability for which he may be held in excess of the receipt valuations.

The contract does not cover stocks belonging to the insured or to any subsidiaries or affiliates of the insured. The exclusions are few. In addition to the exclusion of war risk and seizure or confiscation by any government or public authority, the contract does not cover loss or damage occasioned by gradual deterioration, moth, vermin, inherent vice, or damage sustained due to any process or to being worked upon unless caused by fire or explosion. It will not cover liability assumed by the insured under any agreement to guarantee the results of processing or any work to be performed. The contract will cover no liability incurred by the insured to provide other insurance. The insured may have the contract endorsed to cover accrued storage charges and service charges, such as those made for alterations,

[2] All risk contracts are also available and the present trend is toward the all risk type of coverage.

repairs, or remodeling, either paid or unpaid, which may become uncollectible or which may have to be refunded by reason of loss or damage to property in the custody of the insured.

Rates for this class of business depend upon the construction of the vault used by the insured for storing the furs, its location, burglary protection, valuation of the items, and amount of risk. The premium is paid by the dealer, and no premium charge is made directly to the owner of the garment insured, this being included in the general charge for service. The policyholder is required to keep a record of all receipts issued and to make a report each month to the company showing the total amount at risk as of the last day of the preceding month. The values so reported form the basis for computing the premium.

The furriers' customers contract may be written to cover specifically the legal liability of the furrier without regard to the insurance that may be carried by the customer. It is of the utmost importance that a furrier place no reliance upon the insurance of customers unless the contract is written to include the furrier as well as the customer. It is quite possible that an insurer would pay the insured owner for furs lost while in the custody of a furrier, and then under its right of subrogation hold the furrier responsible to the extent that liability could be established. It is to cover this hazard that legal liability is available.

BLANKET MOTOR CARGO INSURANCE

This contract is issued in the name of the shipper and covers the owner of the goods against loss or damage growing out of the perils against which the insurance is written. It is to be distinguished from the contract insuring truckmen for loss or damage growing out of their legal liability. In the case of goods shipped by owners of their own trucks, the contract provides insurance upon the property of the insured or goods sold by them and in course of delivery within the continental limits of the United States and Canada while the insured property is on trucks owned by the insured. The usual perils covered by the contract include fire; flood; cyclone and tornado; perils of the seas, lakes, rivers, inland waters; collision or overturn of the truck; and collapse of bridges. This contract specifically excludes from coverage goods hauled under a contract or agreement of hauling as bailee for hire and, therefore, would not be issued to licensed public truckmen. The contract contains the usual exclusions of war, strike, civil commotion, and the other exclusions found in transportation contracts bearing upon delay, breakage, or leakage. All risk contracts are also available and named peril contracts are gradually being superseded.

A blanket contract is available to cover the owner of goods for shipments made on public automobile trucks. The same perils as indicated above are covered, and the exclusions are essentially the same as those in other transportation contracts. This contract is frequently found to be desirable, even though the trucking concern by which the goods are shipped is known to carry protection for its legal liability as carrier or bailee. The truckman's contract insures against specific perils, and it is not always possible in the case of accident to establish liability or to show that his contract covered against the exact peril that caused the loss. There is always the possibility that the truckman's insurance may have lapsed or have been canceled, that his insurance may be uncollectible because of a breach of warranty, or that the insurance may be insufficient to provide complete protection. Since the shipper has no control of the insurance of the truckman and relies entirely upon the statement that insurance is carried, many shippers find it in their interests to carry a contract in their own name.

BRIDGES, TUNNELS, AND INSTRUMENTALITIES OF TRANSPORTATION AND COMMUNICATION

Insurance of bridges, tunnels, and instrumentalities of transportation and communication excludes buildings, their furniture and furnishings, as well as fixed contents and supplies held in storage. The contract is written "all risks," and provides comprehensive coverage from the standpoint of causes of loss.

Instrumentalities of transportation are insured under three forms: (*a*) property damage, (*b*) builders risk, and (*c*) business interruption. The following risks are listed in the Nationwide Definition as insurable:

1. Bridges, tunnels, other similar instrumentalities, unless fire, lightning, windstorm, sprinkler leakage, hail, explosion, earthquake, riot or civil commotion are the only perils to be covered.
2. Piers, wharves, docks and slips, but excluding the risks of fire, lightning, windstorm, sprinkler leakage, hail, explosion, earthquake, riot or civil commotion.
3. *a*) Pipelines, including on-line propulsion, regulating and other equipment appurtenant to such pipelines, but excluding all property at manufacturing, producing, refining, converting, treating, or conditioning plants.
   b) Power transmission and Telephone and Telegraph lines, excluding all property at generating, converting or transforming stations, substations, and exchanges.
4. Radio and Television Communication Equipment in commercial use as such, including towers and antennae with auxiliary equipment, and appurtenant electrical operating and control apparatus but

excluding buildings, their improvements and betterments, furniture and furnishings, and supplies held in storage therein.

5. Outdoor cranes, loading bridges, and similar equipment used to load, unload, and transport.

Bridges are owned not only by the various governmental units, such as states and their political subdivisions, but also by carriers, such as railroads, and not infrequently by companies which have built the bridges and operate them for profit from the tolls. Enormous sums are invested in a single structure, and sometimes the financing of the enterprise involves the floating of bonds and stocks. If the bridge represents the major asset of the company, the purchasers of securities are interested in the steps taken by the authorities to preserve the value of the assets. Likewise, state, county, and municipal authorities, as well as corporation directors, are impressed with the concentration of value in a single risk.

Insurance on tunnels and other instrumentalities of transportation and communication is written to cover essentially the same risks as those provided for bridges, and the policy forms are similar.

Bridge insurance covers direct loss or damage to the bridge and its approaches "however caused" with a limited number of exceptions. The contract does not cover, typically, losses caused by, or resulting from, strikes, lockouts, labor disturbances, riots, civil commotions, sabotage, vandalism, malicious mischief, or the acts of any person or persons taking part in any such occurrence or disorder. The contract may be extended at an additional premium to include these perils.

The usual contract does not cover loss arising from any act of government, from the violation of law, or from war risks. The coverage is terminated in the event of a suspension of use of the insured bridge through the operation of any ordinance or law, through injunction or court procedure, cancellation of license, or like cause. Losses occasioned by failure of the insured to maintain the structure properly are excluded, as are losses caused by neglect of the insured to use reasonable means to save and protect the property at or after any disaster covered by the contract. The insurance is written subject to an agreed deduction in the case of all losses, which in the usual course is not less than $1,000, and an 80 percent coinsurance clause is required. Use and occupancy losses are not covered under the contract, but the coverage may be written covering against loss due to the total or partial suspension of use of the bridge necessitated because of a property loss or damage caused by perils insured against. In the use and occupancy cover, contracts are written with a deductible clause, and no liability for loss arises unless the period under suspension exceeds the period indicated, and then only for the period in excess. The deductible is, usually, at least seven days; each accident is considered a special claim, and the seven-day waiting period runs in each case. The perils named are ordinarily the same as those recited in the property damage contract. The form in general use excludes from cover loss or damage arising from capture, seizure or detention, or any attempt thereto, or from any consequence of hostility.

A builder's risk form is available to cover structures under construction. The cover includes, in addition to the structure, materials at the site to be used in construction work during the period of actual construction and until the work is completed, accepted by the owners, or until the contract expires. Ordinarily, the contract is written calling for a monthly report showing total values at risk at the end of each monthly period. However, completed value forms, without the need for monthly reports, may be written for small projects. The contract is written to cover against specifically named perils, and these usually include: fire, lightning, flood, rising waters, ice, explosion, tornado, windstorm, earthquake, and collision. The collision coverage excludes loss or damage caused by collision with construction material or construction equipment. The same rules with reference to strikes, lockouts, vandalism, and the like apply in the case of builder's risks as apply in the direct damage contract; that is, these risks may be endorsed on the contract for the payment of an additional premium, but they are not otherwise included.

FOR DISCUSSION

1. A contract issued to the X theatrical company contained the clause which provides that the insured shall not enter into any special agreements whereby the carrier's common law or statutory liability is waived. A fire broke out in the baggage car in which the goods were being shipped, resulting in a damage of approximately $90,000. Upon investigation, it was found that the insured did, in fact, violate the contract condition by entering into a special agreement. The underwriters contended that this agreement violated an important contract warranty, and, therefore, there was no liability. The court held for the insured. Can you explain why?
2. In his manual on marine insurance, one of the important inland marine underwriters states the underlying principle of transportation insurance to be "insurance, service, and guarantee of solvency." Explain this in the light of your knowledge of the carrier's own liability for loss or damage.
3. In your opinion, is a boardwalk erected at a seashore contiguous to the ocean insurable as an inland marine risk?
4. X operates a plant that sells oxygen and acetylene gas in cylinders. The cylinders are transported from place to place and remain for a considerable period in the hands of customers. In your opinion, are the cylinders an inland marine transportation risk?

5. Floodlights and code beacons, used as aids to aerial navigation and transportation, are without question permanently fixed in a given location. Are they insurable under an inland marine form?
6. B operates a bookbinding plant and from time to time receives books from colleges and schools for rebinding. B asks if he may insure his liability, assumed under receipts issued to owners of the books, from the time the books leave the hands of the owners until they are returned, under an inland marine form. In your opinion, is this a transportation risk, or should the books be insured at the location of the binder and again separately to and from the bindery?
7. X claims that he may avoid high insurance premiums in a given location by insuring the goods, when ordered, under an inland marine contract to cover in transit and at the location indicated. It is his claim that the marine rate is less than the fire rate at the given location. Is this possible?
8. May water pipelines and transmission pipelines be insured as marine risks?
9. In your opinion, would dams to check or control the flow of water fall in the same category as water pipelines; that is, are they insurable under an inland marine form?
10. The second bridge over San Francisco Bay was built parallel with the first bridge to Oakland. A recent commentator made the remark that the idea was one which makes underwriters shudder. Can you tell why?
11. The New Jersey Turnpike Authority's bond resolution contains a stipulation that three turnpike bridges which span the Hackensack, Passaic, and Raritan Rivers must be adequately covered by insurance from risks of direct loss or damage by: fire, lightning, flood, rising waters, ice, explosion, strikes, walkouts, locked-out workmen or persons taking part in labor disturbances, riots and civil commotions, vandalism, malicious mischief, tornado, cyclone, windstorm, earthquake, collision from or by water, and airplane or automotive traffic and collapse. Also required under the bond resolution is use and occupancy insurance covering loss of toll revenue and income from concessions affected by the reason of necessary interruption, total or partial, resulting from a direct physical loss or damage to any of the three bridges from any of the causes just listed. The requirements of the turnpike authority were unique, and there was no standard form available to exactly meet the requirements. What recommendations would you make in order to effect a solution and provide a form?
12. A carload of flour shipped from Minnesota to Frankfort, Kentucky, was destroyed in the 1937 flood. Is this covered under a marine contract?
13. X, a truckman, carries the truckmen's legal liability coverage in the amount of $5,000. While carrying a shipment of oriental rugs valued at $15,000, his truck overturns and catches fire. He is able to save

part of the shipment, and the actual loss is $4,000. What is the collectible amount of insurance?

14. B, a truckman, agrees to move a piano for a friend without charge. Owing to the collapse of a bridge, the piano is destroyed. Is the risk covered by the truckmen's legal liability contract?
15. You have been asked to examine the insurance contracts of a shoe manufacturer. You find that from time to time he has large values in leather in the hands of tanners. He carries fire insurance on this material up to 100 percent value with a 90 percent coinsurance clause. What marine coverage furnishes adequate protection, and to what extent is the coverage broader than the fire contract?
16. X, an employee of B's hotel, allowed a truck being transported from the railroad terminal to become wet, destroying $300 worth of clothing. B denies liability on the ground that the truckman was negligent. Is B liable, and, if so, is the risk insurable?
17. B is a branch manager of a large brokerage house. Late in the afternoon he receives a shipment of $50,000 in negotiable securities. It is too late to place these securities in the vault of the bank, and the safe in the local office is not designed to protect such values. Advise the manager of the branch how, through the agency of insurance, he may adequately protect these securities until morning at comparatively small expense.
18. Recent floods in this country have brought forcibly before property owners the danger of damage to property by flood and rising waters. What form of flood insurance may be obtained?
19. The famous captured German submarine, the U–505, was insured while in transit from Portsmouth to its final berth outside the Museum of Science and Industry in Chicago. Replacement value was approximately $15 million, but the submarine was insured on an hour-to-hour basis until it reached its final destination. At Buffalo, insurance was $45,000. At Evanston, $85,000, and the aggregate amount of insurance continued to increase. Explain the logic of this type of valuation.

CHAPTER · 14

Inland Marine Floaters

As used in inland marine insurance, the term "floater" does not lend itself to strict definition. The term "floater" is used in the sense that it provides insurance to follow the insured property wherever it may be located, subject always to the territorial limits of the contract. Inland marine floaters may be used to provide insurance upon property so located that specific insurance is either inconvenient or impossible, and the term is sometimes used to apply to the transportation contracts discussed in the previous chapter.

The term "personal property floater" as used in inland marine insurance generally refers to contracts to insure property that, because of the transportation element inherent in its use, it is difficult, if not impossible, to insure in a given location.

The Nationwide Definition separates personal property floaters into two main divisions: (1) contracts covering individuals, and (2) contracts covering individuals or generally. In the first category are to be found the contracts that insure the personal effects of individuals such as furs, jewelry, or other personal property. In the second classification are included contracts covering risks on movable property that may belong to an individual but frequently belongs to, or is used by, a business enterprise. In this category are to be found contracts covering theatrical property, radium, salesmen's samples, contractors' movable equipment, and similar types of property. Personal property floaters are written to cover not only the interest of the owner but also the interest of a bailee.

Floater contracts may also be classified as (*a*) personal, and (*b*) commercial. In the personal category are to be found the contracts covering personal effects of every nature, including specifically such items as jewelry, furs, silverware, and works of art, to mention but a few. In the commercial floater category are to be found contracts covering property such as contractor's equipment, farm equipment, theatrical property, and salesmen's samples. Also included in the commercial category are the stock floaters which include processing risks, stocks of fine-art dealers, and motion-picture firms, among others. Finally, there are the consignment and sales floaters which cover such risks as property on consignment, installment sales, and installation risks.

The scheduled property floater contract is the basic contract for all floaters. It is a very simple contract that states on its face the usual insuring clause indicating that the contract covers "on property described below or in schedule attached." It is then stated that the contract is made and accepted subject to the foregoing provisions and stipulations and those hereinafter stated, which are hereby made a part of this contract, together with such other provisions, stipulations and agreements as may be added hereto. . . ." With this basic contract the property to be covered may be listed and forms with additional clauses and stipulations attached, depending upon the extent and nature of the cover.

The standard clauses that appear in the basic property floater are in many cases repetitions of clauses that have appeared in contracts that have been discussed previously.

TYPES OF PERSONAL PROPERTY FLOATER CONTRACTS

There are a number of important floater contracts covering personal effects that are prefixed by the term "personal." The contracts are so different and their names are so similar that it is important at the outset to distinguish the different forms. Those most likely to be confused are: (*a*) the personal property floater, (*b*) the personal effects floater, and (*c*) the personal articles floater. Closely akin to the foregoing are the tourists baggage form and similar contracts.

The personal property floater is perhaps the most important contract in this group and provides an all risks coverage for the personal property of the insured, not only while away from his residence but in the residence as well. The personal effects floater provides protection for the insured on personal property away from his residence. It is broader than the tourists baggage contract in that it does not specifically list the personal effects to be covered. The coverage is all risks. The personal articles floater provides coverage in a single contract for furs, jewelry, cameras, silverware, and other classes of property formerly insured under separate contract. The coverage is all risks. The tourists baggage floater is a restricted form of personal effects floater and covers specifically certain named articles such as are usually carried by travelers while the property is outside and away from the permanent residence of the insured.

It is the intent at this point to distinguish between forms that either because of the nature of the coverage or the name of the form might easily lead to confusion. In order to avoid repetition in treatment, detailed consideration will be given to the more comprehensive personal property floater.

PERSONAL PROPERTY FLOATER

The personal property floater is the broadest and most comprehensive contract available for the insurance protection of personal effects. Sometimes termed the "householder's comprehensive," the contract covers the personal property of the insured and members of his family of the same household on an all risks basis. The several forms of personal property floater all follow the basic pattern of the inland marine schedule property floater. There are some differences in the coverages of the various contracts offered, but the general pattern of providing all risks, subject to specific exclusions, and worldwide protection is common to all of them.

Because of the broad coverage afforded, the contract occupies an important position in the property insurance field with major emphasis upon coverage in fixed locations. From the standpoint of comprehensive coverage for the household, the practice is now that of including the essential features of the personal property floater into the most comprehensive of the homeowner's contracts (Homeowners Number 5), and the contract analysis here given should be considered in its relation to package contracts for the household. The importance of this coverage is mainly in its relationship to package programs. Though still listed as an inland marine coverage, the marine aspects of the contract are tending to become more and more incidental. For the homeowner with valuable furnishings and personal effects, the contract offers an extraordinary all risk coverage.

Insuring Clause and Coverage. The personal property floater is written in three sections: (*a*) a blanket section covering unscheduled personal property, (*b*) schedule section covering specific items of personal jewelry, watches, furs, fine arts, and other similar properties, and (*c*) blanket coverage on jewelry, watches, furs, and similar items. There is no coinsurance clause in the contract, but scheduled articles must be covered for 100 percent of value. An approximate value of unscheduled articles appears on the face of the contract, and on these insurance equal to 80 percent of this valuation is normally required.

With respect to property covered, the contract provides protection for "personal property owned, used or worn by the person in whose name this policy is issued and members of assured's family of the same household, while in all situations, except as hereinafter provided." The contract thus covers virtually every piece of personal property owned by the insured. The exceptions are animals, motor vehicles, boats, aircraft, or other conveyances or property used in the conduct of a business. The equipment or furnishings of a conveyance are covered if removed from the conveyance and located on any residence premises belonging to the insured. Bicycles, tricycles, baby carriages, invalid chairs, and similar conveyances are covered. Professional books, instruments, and other professional equipment belonging to the insured are covered while within a residence. Otherwise property pertaining to a business or occupation must be specifically scheduled in order to be covered.

The all risks protection afforded is subject to but very few limitations. For example, fragile articles, such as glassware, statuary, bric-a-brac, porcelains, or articles such as eye glasses, are not covered against breakage unless caused by a peril named in the exclusions. Wear and tear losses are excluded, as well as losses to property on exhibition and losses due to war. The exclusions appear in the contract in the following terms:

a) Animals; automobiles, motocycles, aircraft, boats or other conveyances (except bicycles, tricycles, baby carriages, invalid chairs and similar conveniences), or their equipment or furnishings except when removed therefrom and actually on the premises of residences of the Assured; property of any government or subdivision thereof;

b) unscheduled property pertaining to a business, profession or occupation of the persons whose property is insured hereunder, excepting professional books, instruments and other professional equipment owned by the Assured while actually within the residences of the Assured;

c) against breakage of eye glasses, glassware, statuary, marbles, bric-a-brac, porcelains and similar fragile articles (jewelry, watches, bronzes, cameras and photographic lenses excepted), unless occasioned by theft or attempt thereat, vandalism or malicious mischief, or by fire, lightning, windstorm, earthquake, explosion, falling aircraft, rioters, strikers, collapse of building, accident to conveyance or other similar casualty, nor unless likewise occasioned, against marring or scratching of any property not specifically scheduled herein;

d) against mechanical breakdown; against loss or damage to electrical apparatus caused by electricity other than lightning unless fire ensues and then only for loss or damage by such ensuing fire;

e) against wear and tear; against loss or damage caused by dampness of atmosphere or extremes of temperature unless directly caused by rain, snow, sleet, hail, bursting of pipes or apparatus and provided further that such loss or damage is not specifically excluded under subsection (h) hereof; against deterioration, moth, vermin and inherent vice; against damage to property (watches, jewelry and furs excepted) occasioned by or actually resulting from any work thereon in the course of any refinishing, renovating or repairing process;

f) property on exhibition at Fairgrounds or on the premises of any National or International Exhibition unless such premises are specifically herein described;

g) against loss or damage caused by or resulting from: (1) hostile or warlike action in time of peace or war, including action in hindering, combating or defending against an actual, impending or expected attack (a) by any government or sovereign power (de jure or de facto), or by any authority maintaining or using military, naval or air forces; or (b) by military, naval or air forces; or (c) by an agent of any such government, power, authority or forces; (2) any weapon of war employing atomic fission or radioactive force whether in time of peace or war; (3) insurrection, rebellion, revolution, civil war, usurped power, or action taken by governmental authority in hindering, combating or defending against such an occurrence, seizure or destruction under quarantine or Customs regulations, confiscation by order of any government or public authority, or risks of contraband or illegal transportation or trade:

h) unscheduled property at premises owned, rented, occupied or controlled by the Assured or any other party whose property is insured hereunder, against loss caused by, resulting from, contributed to or aggravated by any of the following:

(1) flood, surface water, waves, tidal water or tidal wave, overflow of streams or other bodies of water, or spray from any of the foregoing, all whether driven by wind or not;

(2) water which backs up through sewers or drains;

(3) water below the surface of the ground including that which exerts pressure on or flows, seeps or leaks through sidewalks, driveways, foundations, walls, basement or other floors, or through doors, windows or other openings in such sidewalks, driveways, foundations, walls or floors;

unless loss by fire or explosion ensues and this Company shall then be liable only for such ensuing loss;

i) against loss or damage caused by animals or birds owned or kept by an insured or by a residence employee of an insured unless loss by fire, explosion or smoke ensues and this company shall then be liable only for such ensuing loss;

j) against loss by nuclear radiation or radioactive contamination, all whether controlled or uncontrolled, and whether such loss be direct or indirect, proximate or remote, or be in whole or in part caused by, contributed to, or aggravated by the peril(s) insured against in this policy; however, subject to the foregoing and all provisions of this policy, direct loss by fire resulting from nuclear reaction or nuclear radiation or radioactive contamination is insured against by this policy.

The contract may be issued with a deductible at a substantial savings in cost. The usual deductible is $50. Contracts are also written with a partial limitation clause instead of a deductible. Like the franchise in ocean marine insurance, there is no liability on the part of the insurer unless the loss exceeds the limitation, and then, if it does, the loss is paid in full. Neither deductible nor partial limitation clauses apply to losses caused by fire, lightning, perils covered under the extended coverage endorsement, and burglary and holdup. Deductibles apply only to unscheduled articles. Scheduled items such as jewelry, furs, or works of art are covered in full regardless of the deductible.

Limitations. There are three limitations in the contract, and they concern themselves with (*a*) unscheduled personal property at other than the principal residence; (*b*) unscheduled jewelry, watches, and furs; and (*c*) money and numismatic property.

Unscheduled personal property ordinarily situated throughout the year at residences other than the principal residence of the insured is covered for an amount not in excess of 10 percent of the total amount of insurance listed in the contract under item 3a as covering on unscheduled personal property. For the payment of an additional premium the Secondary Location Additional Amount Endorsement may be attached. This endorsement increases the 10 percent limitation to an agreed amount at named locations; it does not increase the amount of insurance applying on unscheduled property but only provides that the 10 percent limitation with respect to dwellings other than the principal residence shall be increased by the amount designated.

With respect to unscheduled jewelry, watches, and furs, the liability of the insurer is limited to $250 in any one loss whether one or more of these classes of property is involved. This limitation may be extended by inserting an amount in item 3c of the contract. By extending this limitation in this manner the additional insurance does not cover all risks but only against the perils of fire and lightning. The extension does cover, however, wherever the property is located, and the protection may be further extended to cover loss by the extended coverage perils. If all risks coverage is desired, the procedure is to schedule the items separately. It is also possible through an endorsement to increase the $250 limit by $750.

As respects money and numismatic property the contract limits the liability of the insurer to $100 in any one loss. As respects any one loss of notes, securities, stamps including philatelic property, accounts, bills, deeds, evidences of debt, letters of credit, passports, documents, and railroad or other tickets, the liability of the insurer for any one loss is limited to $500 whether one or more of these classes of property is involved. There is a separate endorsement for money and numismatic property and another for securities and philatelic property. For an additional premium for each, the limit indicated in the contract applicable to the type of property is increased to an agreed amount. As before, however, the total amount of insurance applying to unscheduled property is not increased.

Scheduled Property. Jewelry, furs, fine arts, cameras, musical instruments, stamp collections, and, in fact, any article of personal property which may be insured separately under an inland marine contract may be covered as scheduled property under the personal property floater. Articles of jewelry or of fur are covered as unscheduled property up to $250. Even then the $250 limitation applies to one loss and not to one item. Where items run to considerable value, they should be scheduled, since the loss of several might run the aggregate value to an amount considerably in excess of the contract limitation.

If professional books, instruments, and equipment are scheduled, they will receive the same broad protection as other scheduled items. Otherwise protection for property in the professional classification applies only while in the residence of the insured. Property pertaining to the business of the insured is not covered unless scheduled.

Scheduled property is covered for 100 percent of its value. While the contract does not so specifically provide, the scheduled value is usually accepted as the basis for an adjustment. Some insurers, with respect to scheduled items, treat the contract as a valued contract.

There is an advantage in including as many items as possible in the scheduled category. By so doing they receive broader protection, and at the same time their value may be removed from the total of unscheduled property. Much of the scheduled property is covered at the same rate that applies to a separate floater. This is usually lower than the rates used for unscheduled property; hence, with respect to scheduled items there is a broader coverage at a lower rate.

Extensions of Coverage. The personal property floater protects primarily the insured and his family against loss or destruction of personal property. The contract will also cover the personal property of guests while on the premises of the insured, and it covers as well the personal property of servants while they are actually engaged in the service of the insured. It is to be pointed out that guests and servants have no rights under the contract. Whether the coverage is effective or not is solely at the option of the insured. That guests and servants should be protected is highly desirable, and it is a source of considerable satisfaction to an insured to know that such protection is available. The coverage is provided in the following terms:

a) Subject otherwise to all of the conditions of this policy, Item (a) Paragraph 3, includes, at the sole option of the Assured, personal property of others while on the premises of the residences of the Assured, and personal property of servants while they are actually engaged in the service of the Assured and while in the physical custody of such servants outside such residences;

The contract also provides protection for damage to the interior of the residence of the insured. Fire damage is excluded because it is expected that this damage will be picked up by the fire insurance contracts. However, damage caused by theft or attempted theft, or by vandalism or malicious mischief, is covered, even though it is real and not personal property that is damaged. The contract provides:

> *b*) The Company will also pay:
>
> (1) The actual loss of or damage (except by fire) to the property of the Assured not specifically excluded by this contract caused by theft or attempt thereat; or by vandalism or malicious mischief to the interior of the residences of the Assured.
>
> (2) Actual loss of or damage to improvements, alterations or additions made by the Assured to buildings occupied as residences by but not owned by the Assured caused by fire, lightning, windstorm, cyclone, tornado, hail, explosion, riot, riot attending a strike, smoke, damage by vehicles or aircraft, but as respects such loss or damage the liability of the Company is limited to 10% of the amount of insurance under item (a) paragraph 3.
>
> These extensions do not increase the amount of the insurance but simply extend the coverage conditionally in one instance to include owners of personal property other than the insured and in another instance to include loss or damage to property other than personal property.

Also included under extensions is a clause providing for the automatic reinstatement of unscheduled property losses. The clause provides that "Any loss payment hereunder shall not reduce the amount of insurance on" unscheduled personal property or on unscheduled personal jewelry, watches, or furs in excess of the $250 limitation. It is further provided that the insurer's combined liability for loss or damage will not exceed the amount listed for unscheduled personal property not including any additional coverage for unscheduled jewelry, watches, and furs.

Boats, Equipment, and Outboard Motors. Boats, equipment, and outboard motors are excluded from coverage under the personal property floater contract. They may be included under the optional coverage stipulations of the contract by the payment of an additional premium. The perils included are: "direct loss by fire, lightning, explosion, smoke, riot, riot attending a strike, civil commotion, falling aircraft and other falling objects, vandalism and malicious mischief, collapse of a building, theft, and collision, upset or overturning of land vehicles." Direct losses by windstorm or hail are covered in respect to row boats and canoes "while on the premise(s) of residence(s) of the Assured" and to boats, equipment, and outboard motors while inside a fully enclosed building.

Residence, Burglary, and Holdup Coverage. There is an endorsement, known as the "burglary and holdup coverage at residence endorsement," that for an additional premium extends the coverage on unscheduled personal jewelry, watches, and furs against direct loss occasioned by holdup or burglary at the residence or residences of the insured. This contract increases the limitation of $250 placed on these items in the contract, with respect to burglary and holdup perils, to an agreed amount in excess of that sum.

The contract defines burglary as "the felonious abstraction of the insured property from within the residence(s) referred to herein by any person or persons making felonious entry therein by actual force and violence of which there shall be visible marks made upon the exterior of the premises at the place of such entry by tools, explosives, electricity or chemicals." This is the usual type of burglary definition and requires some evidence of forcible entry.

Credit for Existing Specific Insurance. The transition from specific coverages to the personal property floater might involve considerable expense to the insured if it were necessary to cancel existing insurance on a short-rate basis. Existing insurance need not be canceled at all. The personal property floater contract may be endorsed at its inception to allow credit for specific insurance, provided the insurance has been in effect 60 days or more prior to the effective date of the personal property floater contract.

The endorsement is an agreement between the insurer and the insured that certain specified contracts will be carried in force until expiration. The insurer writing the personal property floater, as respects loss or damage caused by perils covered by the specific insurance, is liable only for the amounts of loss or damage in excess of the specific insurance. The personal property floater liability is limited by the endorsement to an amount measured by the difference between the face of the specific contracts covering a peril and the amount for which the personal property floater would have covered had there been no specific insurance. If any of the unexpired specific contracts carry a coinsurance clause and the total amount of the insurance under the personal property floater is sufficient to meet that coinsurance requirement, the personal property floater assumes the insured's proportion of the loss, if any, under the provisions of such coinsurance.

The credit for existing specific insurance is equal to the unearned premium calculated on a pro rata basis from the inception date of the personal property floater to the expiration date of the specific insurance or of the personal property floater, whichever comes first. Since the personal property floater allows full premium credit for specific insurance, it is, in fact, carrying this insurance at full rates. It is for this reason that the personal property floater covers as excess over specific insurance for which it allows a credit and not as contributing insurance.

Other Insurance. It is expected that no other insurance on personal property will be written in connection with the personal property floater with the exception of outstanding insurance at the time of the inception of the contract. This is permitted and a premium credit allowed by attaching a credit for existing insurance endorsement to the contract. It is possible to write more than one personal property floater covering on the same risk, and when this is done, it is stipulated in each contract the interest which each assumes.

Certain property, however, may be specifically insured without going into a personal property floater contract. Included in this category are the following: (*a*) personal property belonging to other than the insured; (*b*) real property; (*c*) jewelry, watches, and furs; (*d*) money, notes, or securities; (*e*) equipment or furnishings of conveyances; and (*f*) professional books, instruments, and other professional equipment owned by the insured. If the specific insurance written on any of the above categories provides for indemnification that is at the same time provided by the personal property floater, the two insurances do not contribute. The personal property floater applies only as excess insurance. This is true even though the specific insurance may not be valid. Expressed differently, if the insured carries $5,000 specific insurance on his professional library and has a loss of $10,000, if the specific insurance proved to be uncollectible the personal property floater would, notwithstanding this, be liable only to the extent that the loss exceeded $5,000.

BLANKET PERSONAL PROPERTY FORMS

There are many classes of personal property that involve in the aggregate substantial values but include no single item or items sufficiently valuable or distinctive to require scheduling. Such properties are insured under the blanket form. While a number of inland marine contracts cover blanket on unscheduled items and leave it to the option of the insured whether the more valuable items of the category covered will be scheduled and insured for a specific amount, there are some contracts that cover blanket without any scheduling. Examples of contracts covering blanket include the military and naval effects floater and the golfer's equipment contract.

Military and Naval Effects Floater. Under this form the personnel of the army, navy, marine corps, air corps, and diplomatic corps may secure broad protection for their personal property. Personal effects of all kinds are covered, including household furniture and military equipment of every description, belonging to the insured and dependent members of his family. The contract covers all risks of fire, lightning, navigation, transportation, theft, pilferage, and larceny in the continental United States and its insular possessions, the Panama Canal Zone, the Dominion of Canada, British North America possessions, and Haiti. When required, the coverage can be extended. The theft, pilferage, and larceny coverage in the case of furs, jewelry, watches, and other like items is limited to 40 percent of the contract amount. Theft of coats, hats, caps, and similar items from an automobile is excluded.

Golfer's Equipment. This is a blanket contract covering all risks to the property of the named insured used in connection with the game of golf. The contract may be extended to cover the effects of the spouse and children of the named insured for an additional premium if this coverage is desired. The contract may not be issued to a group such as the members of a country club providing blanket coverage for the equipment of all its members. Open contracts are not issued to dealers, clubs, golf professionals, or others who would in turn undertake to provide insurance for customers or club members through the issuance of certificates. No schedule is required with respect to any of the equipment, and the protection extends to include as well as golf clubs, balls, bags, clothing, and other equipment owned by the insured wherever situated. The contract also covers street clothing of the insured while located in the club house. The usual exceptions of war and wear and tear are found in the contract. Loss to golf balls is covered only if the loss can be traced to burglary or is caused by fire. Watches, jewelry, and property held for sale are not covered.

SCHEDULED PERSONAL PROPERTY FORMS

Scheduled property floaters are used to cover properties involving a number of items each of substantial value. To effect insurance on property when blanket contracts have not been sufficiently comprehensive to provide adequate coverage, the scheduled property floater provides broad and adequate protection. Assuming correct valuation of the scheduled items, the contract provides full insurance to value for each separate item included in the schedule. Such contracts may be written on an all risks basis with the few exclusions that are typical of all inland marine contracts. These, as has previously been noted, include war, wear and tear, gradual deterioration, moth, vermin, and inherent vice. With respect to certain items, the exclusions may vary. They are reduced to a minimum to the end that the contracts provide a very broad coverage. Almost any type of floating property may be covered under the form, although for certain classes, such as musical instruments and objects of art, a special contract is used.

To be covered under this contract, the property must be carefully scheduled. It must be described in sufficient detail as to indicate clearly the item to be covered, and, when more than one item is covered, each must be separately valued. Some of the more usual classes of property for which special riders are available and for which the coverage is more or less standardized will be discussed.

Musical Instruments Floater. This contract is designed to provide a comprehensive coverage for musical instruments. The coverage is written on a broad form providing an all risks protection, and on a limited form insuring against loss or damage caused by fire, lightning, cyclone, tornado, flood, theft, and transportation hazards.

The coverage was originally designed to cover rare and costly instruments owned either by professional concert artists or by private individuals. The business has now extended to cover all types of instruments, whether owned by amateurs or professionals. Miscellaneous equipment used in connection with the instruments, such as music, cases, and racks may be insured with the instruments blanketed, with the 100 percent coinsurance clause and limited to 10 percent of the face of the contract. Otherwise, each item must be scheduled and valued.

The all risks contract excludes loss or damage caused by any process of refinishing, renovating, or repairing; by dampness or atmosphere or extremes of temperature; by wear and tear or gradual depreciation; by infidelity of the insured's employees or persons to whom the property is entrusted; and by civil commotion, riots, and war. In addition to the foregoing, the limited form excludes loss or damage to the property insured while in an automobile unless in the custody of a common carrier.

A 100 percent coinsurance clause may be used in blanket forms covering such institutions as schools and colleges. When no coinsurance requirement is written into the contract, insurers require insurance in an amount approximately equal to the values insured. In preparing the schedule, some substantiation of values, such as a bill of sale or appraisal, is necessary. Depreciation is deducted when instruments are not new, with the exception of violins and cellos, which may be covered up to the cost price to the insured. If the instrument is old and rare, an appraisal is the satisfactory way to establish values.

For professional musicians the professional clause is deleted and a professional rate is charged. The contract issued to nonprofessionals becomes void if during its term the insured plays any instrument covered by the contract for remuneration. This clause is deleted on contracts issued to bands, orchestras, and similar groups, as well as to professional musicians.

Cameras, Projection Machines, and Equipment Floater. This form provides an all risks coverage on cameras, projection machines, and equipment for both professionals and amateurs. The usual exclusions apply.

Furs and Jewelry. Individual fur pieces or fur coats which belong to the insured, or to members of his family residing permanently with him, are insured under a worldwide fur floater contract covering the property wherever it may be, in the home or elsewhere. The contract covers against all risks. The only exclusions are gradual wear and tear, moth, vermin, inherent vice, or damage due to any process, war risks, and loss due to government order.

Each piece of fur insured must be specifically scheduled in the contract and carefully valued. When new, the cost price is acceptable as a valuation; otherwise, an appraisal by a reliable furrier is preferable, unless the insured is willing that a valuation be fixed as between himself and the insurer, taking into consideration age and depreciation. It is an underwriting practice not to insure furs for an amount greater than their cost, regardless of what an appraisal will show or through what agency the insured was able to secure a price less than the current market value.

When both furs and jewelry are insured, they may be covered under a single contract. The rate will depend to a large extent on territory with higher rates applying to urban areas. A reduction in the premium may be obtained if a $50 deductible clause is made a part of the contract.

Because of the element of moral hazard, the insurance of furs and jewels is most carefully underwritten. Persons known to be careless are never acceptable as insureds, or are those living in sections where there have been frequent burglaries. The integrity of the insured must be unquestioned. In every case involving the insurance of jewelry or expensive furs, a confidential report is made on the insured by sources entirely independent of the agent placing the business.

Outboard Motors and Motorboats Floater. This contract covers both the boat and the motor. The boat is covered on an all risk basis as is the motor. Forms and rates vary among the insurers. In addition to the usual exclusions, the contract is void if the boat is rented, used to carry passengers for hire, and used in illicit trade or in any official race or speed test.

Sportsmen's Floater. This is an all risks form covering against *direct physical* loss or damage to the property insured. The usual wear and tear and war risks exclusions are in the contract. Losses attributable to dishonesty of persons to whom the insured property may be loaned or rented are not covered. Loss or damage attributable to derangement or breakdown, rust, fouling, marring, or scratching are not covered, nor is loss due to breakage while the insured article is being used in the sport for which it is designed. Territorial limits include continental United States and Canada, but the limits may be extended on request.

Equipment and paraphernalia that may be insured include that used in hunting, fishing, hiking, camping, bowling, tennis, archery, badminton, swimming, shuffleboard, volleyball, baseball, football, basketball, boxing, fencing, skiing, skating or hockey, and tobogganing. Beach paraphernalia may be insured in connection with swimming equipment. The same is true of articles of clothing and personal effects worn in connection with sports. All insured equipment must be scheduled.

This contract does not cover golfer's equipment. A special form is provided for the purpose. The same is true of harness, saddlery, and blankets covered under the horse and wagon floater. Special contracts are also provided for canoes, kayaks, and outboard motorboats, as well as outboard motors. These are not covered under the sportsmen's floater.

The foregoing coverages for which special forms have been devised by no means limit the scope of usefulness of the scheduled property floater. Other property insured under this form includes guns, trophies, false teeth, and artificial limbs. Unless for some reason the property is deemed to be uninsurable or unless a special form has been designed to meet the need, the scheduled property floater may be utilized to provide whatever coverage is needed. The coverage may be for all risks. It may, however, be limited to designated perils, depending upon the nature of the property and the needs of the insured.

SCHEDULED AND BLANKET PERSONAL PROPERTY FORMS

There are certain types of personal property that lend themselves, for the most part, to blanket coverage. If there are included in the properties to be covered certain items that have an unusual value, these may be scheduled. Some of the more usual contracts that may be written on a scheduled and blanket form will be discussed. The personal property floater, considered earlier in this chapter, is an example of scheduled and blanket personal property forms. Following are a few other examples:

Fine-Arts Contract. Under this form, the owner of paintings, tapestries, sculpture, and other articles of rarity, historical value, or artistic merit may secure an all risks coverage. In addition to the usual exclusion of war risks, strikes, and riots, other exceptions are limited to wear and tear and damage due to restoration or retouching.

The contract is used in insuring private or public collections of paintings, etchings, pictures, tapestries, valuable rugs, statuary, marbles, bronzes, antique furniture, rare books, antique silver, manuscripts, rare procelains, rare glass, and other rare and valuable items. Special forms adapted to particular needs are available for museums, art galleries, dealers, or other commercial enterprises.

In the case of works of art, so much value is concentrated into comparatively small and easily damaged items that fire and burglary coverages are entirely inadequate. Friendly fires have caused losses not covered under the fire contract. Malicious mischief, prompted by revenge or other reason, is a frequent source of loss. Water and steam damage, explosion, windstorm, carelessness, damage caused by pets, defective building construction, accidents of various types, and hundreds of other unavoidable happenings may result in severe loss. Protection not otherwise obtainable is afforded by the fine-arts contract.

There is no coinsurance requirement in the contract; but the form is valued, and each article to be insured must be described and scheduled with a separate valuation. Valuations are based upon an appraisal made by competent parties, by the original bill of sale, or by the catalogue price of the article. Blanket coverage is written in special situations.

Silverware Floater. Silverware, silverplate, and pewter ware can be insured against all risks under this contract. In addition to the usual exclusions, the contract does not cover claims arising from denting unless caused by fire, tornado, burglary, or theft, or loss occasioned by breakage of glass or brittle parts. Flasks, smoking implements, pens, and pencils are ordinarily not covered. When loss or damage occurs to any item that forms one of a pair or set, the company assumes liability only for the parts actually lost or damaged and not for the value of the pair or set. Historical or antique value is not covered. This form is designed to insure private property, and while no coinsurance requirement is written into the contract, insurers require the insurance carried to represent approximately the actual values. Contracts are written on either a scheduled or a blanket basis or a combination of both. Scheduled items are listed with a specified amount of insurance applying to each item. Property covered blanket must show the amount of insurance applying to (*a*) silverware and silverplated ware, (*b*) gold ware and gold-plated ware, and (*c*) pewter ware.

Wedding Presents Floater. In order to protect wedding presents, wherever they may be and until permanently located, the wedding presents floater provides a worldwide coverage against all risks. The contract is written in two forms. The first of these is written with the 80 percent coinsurance clause; the second, at an advanced rate, reduces the coinsurance requirement to 50 percent. In addition to the usual exceptions, loss or damage by moths or vermin is excluded, as is loss or damage occasioned by breakage, unless such breakage is caused by fire, burglars, thieves, or a transportation peril.

The breakage exclusion may be deleted by endorsement, but loss by marring or scratching of fragile articles, unless caused by named perils, is not insurable. Losses due to processing or repairing items or caused by mechanical breakdown or electrical disturbance of electrical apparatus is not insurable. The contract excludes loss or damage to accounts, bills, deeds, currency, money, notes, securities, livestock, automobiles, bicycles, aircraft, motorcycle, boats, motors, and other conveyances or their appurtenances. To comply with the Nationwide Marine Definition, the contract must be written to expire not over 90 days after the wedding. As in the case of the silverware floater, the contract may be written on a scheduled, blanket, or combination basis. It is usual to cover wedding gifts blanket with unusual and highly valued items scheduled.

COMMERCIAL FLOATERS

Property used in connection with a business or profession that is moved about may be insured under a commercial floater. Some commercial floaters are prepared as modifications of the transportation contract. Others, because of the nature of the property covered, are written on a form prepared for the particular form of risk. Some of the more widely used commercial forms will be described.

Physicians' and Surgeons' Equipment Floater. This form is designed to cover professional instruments and equipment used by the insured in the practice of medicine or dentistry. It is an all risks contract covering in the territorial United States and Canada. It is the intent to cover instruments and equipment carried by the insured from place to place, and such instruments not customarily carried are excluded from the protection. Office equipment including furniture and fixtures but excluding radium is covered. If radium is to be insured, it is covered under a floater designed for the purpose. There are the usual exclusions of wear and tear, gradual deterioration, inherent vice, mechanical breakdown, or derangement. Losses caused by breakage of glass and articles of brittle nature are not covered unless caused by theft or attempt thereat, vandalism or malicious mischief, fire, lightning, windstorm, earthquake, flood, explosion, falling aircraft, rioters, strikers, collapse of building or other structure, or by accident to a transporting conveyance. The exclusion as to breakage does not apply to lenses of scientific instruments. War risks are excluded as usual. Losses to electrical apparatus caused by electricity, other than lightning, are excluded, unless fire ensues and then the fire damage is covered. If there is a loss or damage to insured property due to any process or work being done upon it, there is no coverage unless the loss is caused by fire or explosion. These limitations leave a broad and comprehensive protection. If there are any unusually valuable instruments, they may be scheduled, though for most physicians or surgeons blanket insurance is adequate.

Contractors' Equipment Floater. This contract covers the floating property of a contractor, such as steam shovels, cranes, derricks, hoisting machines, compressors, power drills, stone crushers, concrete mixers, engines, boilers, pile drivers, tractors, wagons, chains, ladders, scaffolding, hand tools, and similar equipment. A complete schedule of each item is required, except that hand tools and small items may be grouped. The perils insured against vary but may include fire, explosion, flood, cyclone, earthquake, collapse of bridges, theft, collision, including upset or overturning of steam shovels and similar equipment. In addition to the usual exclusions, the contract does not cover loss from excessive loading, loss to automobiles or underground property, or electrical damage to dynamos and the like.

Salesmen's Floater Contracts. Substantial sums of money are invested in samples to be transported from place to place for display to prospective customers. There are as many classes of samples as there are types of business. Obviously, a case of shoe samples, with only one shoe of a kind, is less of an attraction to thieves than is a case of jewelry. Some samples are shipped by railroad or other transportation company, while others are transported in the automobile of the salesman. Again, extremely valuable items are carried in cases constantly in the care of the salesman or in charge of another responsible custodian. Salesmen's floater contracts are written under one of three general forms, though any form may be modified within limits to meet a particular need. The forms are referred to as "limited," "broad," and "all risks."

The limited form covers the samples, and the trunks and containers in which they are transported, against the perils of fire, lightning, explosion, cyclone, tornado, flood and the perils of navigation and transportation, as well as theft of an entire trunk or shipping package in the custody of any common carrier, on while checked against receipt with any hotel or public checking room. Losses caused by riot, civil commotion, and strike are excluded. Neither are losses by pilferage covered, nor theft losses of jewelry or like valuables, nor losses by theft while the property is in the custody of the insured or his salesman. Losses by leakage, breakage, and scratching are covered only when caused by a peril insured against; and there is no liability if damage is caused by delay, improper packing, or inherent defect in the property.

The broad form covers all risks, subject to limitations to be noted. Unrestricted theft coverage is provided, except in the case of theft from automobiles left unattended. In the case of approved commodities, the contract may be extended to cover pilferage from locked, closed cars.

The all risks form includes theft from unattended automobiles subject to the locked-car and forcible entry warranty. Under this coverage the insured warrants that all the automobiles in which the insured property is carried are equipped with closed bodies and suitable locks. The insurer usually approves the type of lock before it will issue the contract. Loss from such cars is covered only if there is visible evidence of a forcible break, or if the entire automobile is stolen or driven away.

The exclusions under the broad and all risks forms are substantially the same as for the limited form, except that there is no theft exclusion. It is provided that the contract does not cover the infidelity of the employees of the insured or persons to whom the insured property is entrusted. When the locked-car and forcible entry warranty is used, it does not cover theft of property from cars in garages overnight. All contracts exclude coverage on the premises of the insured.

Radium Floater Contract. Radium is one of the most peculiar types of property ever made the subject of insurance. It is a rare substance, now widely used by the medical profession, particularly in the treatment of cancer. Because the substance is extremely rare and the world's known supply widely distributed, infinitesimal amounts have a high value.

In spite of the great care exercised in handling so valuable a substance, losses frequently occur. It is to idemnify the owner of radium in the event of its loss from any cause, war risks and gradual deterioration excepted, that the all risks radium floater is written.

Because of the nature of the substance and the use to which it is put, it is important to review certain clauses and conditions that are peculiar to this particular contract. The first of these is the requirement as to notice in case of loss. Although in most cases, the interpretation of the word "immediate" in connection with the requirement as to notice in case of loss allows for some leeway, if radium is involved, the contract requires strict compliance with the requirement of immediate notice by telephone or telegraph, usually to the home office of the insurer. The reason for this requirement becomes apparent when it is realized that a trained radium expert with proper instruments may locate the lost radium. In some cases immediate action may make recovery possible, where delay would have put the lost radium beyond possible reach. Among instances of losses in which the radium was subsequently located by an expert with an electroscope are those resulting from accidents, such as throwing out the container with bandages or allowing it to be washed down a drain. The frequency with which lost radium is recovered in wastepipes, when a brief delay would have meant total loss, indicates the necessity for quick action.

The contract is usually written with the patient-supervision clause. This clause requires uninterrupted care and supervision of each patient under radium treatment by a doctor, nurse, or other person specially designated for the purpose. Insurers are reluctant to insure radium without this clause, and they issue such a contract, with an increase in the premium charge, only after satisfying themselves as to the care exercised in using the radium and the precautions taken to prevent loss. Radium covered by the contract must be individually itemized and so described that the insured item can be identified. Blanket insurance covering miscellaneous items is not written. Full coverage insurance equal to 100 percent of the value must be carried; otherwise, the insured becomes a coinsurer for the deficiency.

Stamp Collection Floater. Privately owned stamp collections are covered under this contract against all risks, subject to exclusions. In the form as usually written the contract covers postage stamps, including due, envelope, official, revenue including match and medicine stamps, covers, locals, reprints, proofs, and other philatelic property of the insured, including books and mountings.

Individual stamps may be scheduled, and when so covered, as to them the contract is valued. When the contract covers the collection under a blanket form, there is a limit of liability on any one item fixed at $250. If the collection is ordinarily kept in a fireproof safe equipped with combination lock, a credit of 10 percent off the total premium is allowed provided the following warranty is attached to the contract: "In consideration of the reduced rate at which this policy is issued the insured agrees to keep the property insured in a fireproof safe with combination lock when not in use or on exhibition."

In addition to exclusions relating to such matters as war and insurrection, the contract does not insure against infidelity of persons to whom the property is entrusted; loss or damage while on an aircraft during flight; or while in the hands of transportation companies unless sent by express, insured parcel post, or registered mail. "Mysterious disappearance" of individual stamps is not covered unless the stamps are specifically scheduled or unless mounted in a volume and the page to which they are attached is lost. With reference to injury to the stamps, the form specifically states that damage that is the result of fading, creasing, tearing, thinning, transfer of colors, wear, tear, dampness, extremes of temperature, moths, vermin, gradual depreciation and deterioration, or damage done during handling or while being worked upon and resulting therefrom is not covered. Contracts are usually written for a year, but when insurance is desired for a shorter period, it may be written at the usual short rates. When insurance is desired to cover special exhibitions of stamps held by clubs or like organizations, it is necessary to submit in detail all the attending circumstances, and a special rate applying to the particular risk is promulgated.

Theatrical Floater Contract. The producing of plays is a type of business involving substantial sums of money invested in scenery, costumes, and other theatrical properties that are continually transferred from place to place while the production is on the road. The theatrical floater contract covers goods of this description while in theaters and other business buildings, except the customary business premises of the insured, against loss or damage by fire and lightning and against the risks of fire, lightning, collision, overturn, or derailment while in transit.

The contract exempts from coverage loss from riots, strikes, and the like; a falling building; explosion; or neglect of the insured to use reasonable means to save the property at or after an accident. Theft is not covered, nor is loss of money, notes, securities, and the like. Livestock is insured against loss by fire only.

Installation Risks. There are a number of concerns whose business is of a nature that requires the complete installation of their product in working, or serviceable, order in the premises of the customer before delivery is completed. Houses specializing in store fixtures contract to remodel a given location, which may require anything from a new front to interior decoration. Again, pipe organs sold to churches, public buildings, and residences are delivered installed, as are heavy machines, carillons, and similar items. A given business at any time will have goods in numerous locations and in transit, and installation in all degrees of completion.

Such risks may be insured covering the goods against fire and transportation perils and perils on the premises to which they have been consigned until installation is complete. A deposit premium is paid and monthly reports are required indicating the average daily values upon which the insurance has covered.

Conditional Sales and Merchandise on Approval. Floater contracts may be written covering department stores and other business houses against loss of goods sold on the installment plan, loaned, leased, or sent on approval. The development of merchandising during the past decade has made it a usual practice to send out to prospective customers on approval or for trial such commodities as rugs, radios, refrigerators, furniture, and washing machines. Sales frequently involve installment payments. The contract covers the goods while in transit against the perils of fire, collision, cyclone, flood, theft, sprinkler leakage, and breakage when the damage exceeds a specified minimum. It covers in buildings, excluding premises owned, rented, leased, or used for storage or exhibition purposes by the insured, against fire, lightning, and any of the aforementioned perils required by the insured. Exclusions are wear and tear, wrongful conversion by persons to whom the insured property has been entrusted, and war risks. When there is other insurance, the floater does not contribute but applies as excess coverage after the specific insurance has been exhausted.

The contract is written on an open form and may cover the interest of the dealer only or cover the interests of both dealer and purchaser. In the case of loss under the first plan, the liability of the insurer is limited to the unpaid balance at the time of the loss. In cases in which both interests are covered, however, the dealer receives the amount of the unpaid balance, and the purchaser the amount paid by him as installments up to the time of the loss.

When both interests are covered under the contract, a certificate form is available under which the dealer may issue a certificate to the purchaser to hold as evidence of the insurance. This form is particularly desirable when the purchaser pays for the insurance in the sales agreement. Copies of the certificates as issued are mailed to the company, and the premium is payable at the end of each month for the business reported during the preceding month.

When certificates are not required under either plan, a monthly reporting form is used. At the end of each month a report is made of the total values at risk under partial payment sales, plus full value of all merchandise loaned, leased, or sent out on approval.

It sometimes happens that under the terms of the sales agreement the purchaser is obligated to keep the goods insured, covering the interest of the seller as well as his own. The purchaser may inadvertently allow the contract to lapse, or for some other reason the protection may be inadequate. In case the property in question is destroyed and no insurance is forthcoming, the purchaser is obligated to continue the payments, which he is frequently unable to do. For such situations the dealer may purchase a contingent form at greatly reduced rates. Under this form the insurer is obligated to pay only so much of the amount due the dealer as proves, after reasonable effort, to be uncollectible. In no case is the purchaser freed from his obligation. The insurer takes the rights of the seller by subrogation to the extent of its payment.

THE BLOCK CONTRACT

Originally written for jewelers, and said to have originated with the underwriters at Lloyd's of London, the block contract provides in a single instrument a number of insurance coverages that but for this type of contract would cover as separate contracts. The contract is now available under five forms: (1) jewelers' block contract, (2) fur dealers' contract, (3) camera dealers' contract, (4) musical instrument dealers' contract, and (5) equipment dealers' contract. Contracts are usually written on an all risks basis with the list of exclusions tailored to meet the particular class of business to be covered.

The exact meaning of the term "block" is not always clear. As an English word it has no logical meaning as an insurance term. It is generally conceded to be an Anglicization of the French "en bloc" meaning altogether.[1] Whatever the meaning of the term the coverage provided under a block contract is very broad. Particularly important is the fact that the insured's goods are covered without limitation as to time on his own premises. This is in contrast to the usual marine contract. In addition, the block contract provides in a single package coverage for: (*a*) goods on premises of others; (*b*) goods in transit, including salesmen's samples; and (*c*) goods of others in the custody of the insured. With the exception of the jewelers' block contract where forms have been standarized, there are variations in the terms of other inland marine forms. Because the jewelers' form is the oldest and has become standardized, this will be considered as an example of a block contract.

Jewelers' Block Contract. This form is written to provide comprehensive coverage for retail and wholesale jewelers, manufacturing jewelers, watch dealers, pawnbrokers, silverware dealers, and diamond wholesalers. The contract provides an all risk cover, but in this, as in other block contracts, there are a number of exclusions. These exclusions are not, in fact, serious curtailments of the cover but, rather, list perils that are to be specifically insured or perils not ordinarily insurable in any case, such as inherent vice or insufficient or defective packing. A complete list of the exclusions is not given here, but in addition to the usual inland marine exclusions the examples here cited indicate their nature.

There are five specific limitations in the contract with respect to coverage. The limitations apply as follows: (1) to property at the premises named in the contract; (2) to property shipped by first-class registered mail, railway express, or armored-car service "deposited in the safe or vault of a bank or safe deposit company; in the custody of a dealer in property of the kind insured hereunder not employed by or associated with the Assured, but property deposited for safe keeping with such a dealer by the Assured or its authorized representatives while traveling is subject to the limit expressed for property included in (5) below"; (3) to registered air mail or express shipments in a given day to one recipient at the same address; (4) to

---

[1] In an editorial comment the *National Underwriter* points out that in spite of the fact that the word "block" is neither a definitive or suggestive one it has nevertheless found its way into the lexicon of the insurance business to be used uncritically by generation after generation. The comment quotes Federal Judge D. J. Byers as commenting on the term: "This is an action upon a so-called jewelers block policy, but what the adjective means has not been explained. Its office may be merely to preserve the cryptic traditions of the calling pursued by underwriters." The editorial writer then referring to the theory of the derivation of the term from the French adds: "Be that as it may, the term 'block' is about as far removed from 'en bloc' as 'Bob Blow' is from 'Dois Blanc' or 'Skilligalee' is from 'Isle au Galets' which are Anglicizations that are in common use in northern Michigan." *National Underwriter*, July 23, 1953, p. 24.

property handled by customer parcel delivery service and parcel transportation services; and (5) to property away from the premises and not included in the above categories.

The contract covers pearls, precious and semiprecious stones, jewels, watches and watch movements, gold, silver, platinum, precious metals, alloys, and other stock usual to the business of a jeweler against loss or damage "arising from any cause whatsoever" but subject to the exclusions indicated in the contract. Specifically, the contract provides insurance as follows:

a) Pearls, precious and semiprecious stones, jewels, jewelry, watches and watch movements, gold, silver, platinum, other precious metals, and alloys and other stock usual to the conduct of the assured's business, owned by the assured;

b) Property as above described, delivered or entrusted to the assured, belonging to others who are not dealers in such property or not otherwise engaged in the jewelry trade;

c) Property as above described, delivered or entrusted to the assured by others who are dealers in such property or otherwise engaged in the jewelry trade, but only to the extent of the assured's own actual interest therein, because of money actually advanced thereon, or legal liability for loss of or damage thereto.

From the foregoing, it can readily be seen that in addition to property as described belonging to the insured himself, the policy provides protection against loss of property such as is covered by the contract if owned by customers of the jeweler but entrusted to him for some purpose such as for repair. To this extent the contract provides a bailee's customers' protection. The third paragraph covers the insured's liability, whether legal or contractual, for property entrusted to him by dealers who are in the jewelry trade. Thus, if the insured during the holiday season has a consignment of diamonds sent him for a period of 10 days and, as a result of a fire, they are lost or destroyed, the insured's liability to the lender is covered. If the insured has no interest or liability in connection with such consignments, the block contract does not cover, and the consignor must look to his own insurance for reimbursement.

Contracts as written generally cover "in or upon any place or premises whatsoever" in the United States and Canada and while being carried or in transit by land or sea between any ports or any places within these limits. The in-transit cover may extended or limited, depending upon circumstances and the requirements of the insured. In spite of the fact that in-transit coverage is provided, the contract is essentially a location cover, and because of the inherent hazard of burglary and theft and the high values involved, underwriting is very carefully done.

Conditions and stipulations found in the contract are lengthy and comprehensive. Particular emphasis is given to a number of warranties that appear. The insured is required to keep an accurate inventory of his property, including traveling salesmen's stocks, in such a manner that the exact amount of loss can be determined therefrom. Again, the insured warrants that he will maintain during the life of the contract protective devices and watchmen's service described in the proposal. The contract also provides that the insured will submit to examinations under oath relative to any matters in connection with a claim and, so far as he is able to do so, will cause all other persons interested in the property and members of their households and employees to submit to such examination. This clause is not unique to the jeweler's block contract and appears in other inland marine contracts as well as in other types of insurance contracts. Because of the nature of the coverage afforded by the jeweler's block contract, the right to examine the insured and other persons interested in the property under oath is regarded as essential. The usual clauses relative to misrepresentation and concealment appear, and because of the emphasis given in the contract to reliance upon the proposal and declarations of the insured, it is of utmost importance that the proposal and declarations be carefully prepared and that all warranties meet with strict compliance.

FARM EQUIPMENT AND ANIMAL FLOATERS

There are six forms in general use for the insuring of agricultural machinery and farm animals. These forms all contain the basic conditions of the schedule property floater. Each is designed for a particular class of risk. The contracts for which standard forms are available are: (*a*) the mobile agricultural equipment floater, (*b*) the equipment dealers' floater, (*c*) the livestock floaters, (*d*) the mobile agricultural equipment and farm livestock floater, (*e*) the monthly reporting livestock floater, and (*f*) the horse and wagon floater.

In addition to the foregoing, where the conditions of the schedule property floater have been modified, is the winter range livestock floater. Some insurers also write livestock mortality insurance on valuable animals and cover chickens, turkeys, and other poultry, and, in some instances, dogs or other animals on a named perils basis.

Mobile Agricultural Equipment Floater. This contract provides all risks coverage on farm machinery and equipment in use or intended for use on a farm. Dealers' stocks accordingly may not be covered under this contract.

Equipment Dealers' Floater. This contract is designed to insure dealers in mobile agricultural construction equipment. It fits the definition of a block, in that it is an all risks contract and covers property of the insured or goods of others in his custody both on the premises of the insured without limitation as to time and goods in transit. The contract is designed to cover property held for sale, display, or demonstration.

The Livestock Floater. This is a named perils contract and covers cattle kept for feeding, dairy, breeding, or show purposes. Other animals may be covered, including hogs, horses, or mules.

The Mobile Agricultural Equipment and Farm Livestock Floater. This contract, as its name would indicate, is a combination of the livestock floater with the mobile agricultural equipment floater. It is listed as a separate contract only because the combination has become standard and the contracts in their combined form find wide acceptance as a single contract document.

The Monthly Reporting Livestock Floater. This contract is identical to the livestock floater with respect to coverages. There is no coinsurance clause, but the insured is required before the 15th of each month to report values as of the last day of the previous month. Where there is a wide range in values, reports more frequently than once a month may be required.

Horse and Wagon Floater. This contract insures horses, mules, vehicles, harness, blankets, and similar equipment used exclusively for delivery purposes on a named perils basis.

Winter Range Livestock Floater. This contract covers death of cattle or sheep while being fed at range locations. The contract covers also while the insured animals are in transit to and from ranges to any place in the United States. The contract is written on a named perils basis and provides generally the same protection with respect to perils as is afforded by the livestock floater. This is a specialized form and is written only in the areas where livestock are fed on winter crops at range locations. The livestock floater is the more generally accepted form for insuring livestock.

Livestock Mortality Insurance. Some insurers will write a contract covering on livestock that is, in fact, a form of life insurance protection. The contract covers only the peril of death. Valuable animals, such as race horses, saddle horses, hunters, polo ponies, and the like, are all insurable. Coverage is not limited to such animals, however, and farm and work horses, commercial draft horses, dairy cattle, and family milk cows to mention a few other classifications may all be covered.

FOR DISCUSSION

1. B purchases a piano on a monthly payment basis and, under the terms of the agreement, is obligated to carry full insurance on the instrument. He takes the matter up with his insurance agent, who advises him that his household furniture contract affords full protection on the piano. Is this correct?

2. Under what inland marine forms would you insure the following property: (*a*) paintings, works of art; (*b*) musical instruments; (*c*) religious articles; (*d*) paintings, statutary; (*e*) transits; (*f*) radium; (*g*) scientific instruments; (*h*) paraphernalia, instruments, trophies; (*i*) customers' goods; (*j*) cameras, projecting machines; (*k*) guns, trophies, collections; (*l*) jewelry; (*m*) outboard motors; (*n*) wedding presents; and (*o*) stock of jewelry?
3. Indicate the property which the following insureds logically would cover under inland marine contracts, and indicate the form of contract to be used: (*a*) art galleries, museums; (*b*) bands and orchestras; (*c*) banks; (d) churches; (*e*) civil engineers; (*f*) contractors; (*g*) doctors; (*h*) furriers; (*i*) hospitals; (*j*) investment houses; (*k*) lodges; (*l*) milk companies; (*m*) motion picture producers; (*n*) theatrical producers; (*o*) undertakers; and (*p*) warehousemen.
4. In your opinion, may stained glass windows installed and used as such be insured under an inland marine form?
5. X operates a commercial circulating library. The total value of the books amounts to several thousand dollars. Because of the wide circulation, the owner asks that all the books be covered under an inland marine form. In your opinion, is such a risk logically an inland marine risk?
6. Abstracts, tract index sets, abstract books, plat books, maps, and similar books and notes, used in connection with abstract and title insurance, represent a substantial investment in money. They are moved about from time to time, and the question arises whether the proper coverage for insurance would not be an inland marine contract. What is your opinion?
7. There is a building in New York located at Canal, Varick, and Vestry Streets known as the Tunnel Field Office Building. This building is used in connection with the operation of the Holland Tunnel. In your opinion, may it be covered by a tunnel contract as an instrumentality of transportation?
8. The question has been raised whether ancient and historic residences such as Mount Vernon, Monticello, and the like may be insured against all risks under a fine-arts contract. What is your opinion?
9. It would certainly seem that rolling stock of railroad and traction companies would logically fall into the category of risks covered by inland marine contracts. In your opinion, should they be insured as instrumentalities of transportation as described in Section D of the Nationwide Marine Definition? If not, upon what basis should they be covered by a marine contract, if at all?
10. M lends four dozen sterling silver knives and forks to a friend for use at a party. They are destroyed by fire, and she is advised that under a tourists baggage contract, since the damage occurred outside of her domicile, the loss is covered. What is your opinion?
11. B claims that because he does no traveling, he has no need for a personal effects contract. How can the personal effects contract serve the interests of the stay-at-home?

12. Indicate the principal differences in the coverage afforded by the three following contracts: (*a*) tourist baggage, (*b*) personal effects, and (*c*) personal property.
13. When the statement is made that flood insurance is not practicable, it is sometimes pointed out that inland marine floaters provide coverage. Is this an important feature of the coverage?
14. A young girl, the daughter of X who carries a personal property floater contract, laid down a fur coat near a ticket window while opening her purse in the process of purchasing a ticket. During the brief interval, the coat was stolen. Is the loss covered?
15. A homeowner is in the habit of having hot waffles for breakfast. The waffle iron, on one occasion, blistered the dining room table. The damage was such that the entire table had to be refinished. Is this a fire loss? Does the personal property floater cover?
16. X, a contractor, in the process of installing a transformer, meets with an accident. Just as the transformer is being lowered into position, one of the jacks kicked out and the transformer toppled, damaging the building, destroying a 16-inch gate valve. At the same time, the transformer itself was wrecked. Damage to the transformer amounted to $22,000. X files a claim with his liability insurer. He is advised that the liability contract covers damage to the building and to the gate valve but the $22,000 damage to the transformer is not covered. Why? If this were a new building in which the transformer were being installed, would the builder's risk contract cover?

CHAPTER · 15

Theft Insurance Contracts

The amount of money and the value of the various classes of property lost each year because of criminal activities involving robbery, burglary, or larceny run to many millions of dollars. Millions more are lost through the dishonest acts of employees. Making the fullest use of modern inventions and keeping pace with scientific development, criminals are constantly plotting to possess themselves by illegal means of the money, securities, silverware, jewels, merchandise, or valuables of every sort belonging to others.

Notwithstanding the expensive devices designed for the protection of property and the enormous expenditures for judicial and protective officials, audits, and checks, losses continue. The activities of the criminals are as varied as the types of property that attract them. There are housebreakers, holdup men, sneak thieves, warehouse robbers, and other criminal groups confining their operation to specialized activities. As in other instances in which the security of property is threatened, resort is made to insurance for protection. The present status of theft insurance may be gauged by reference to premiums written. In 1950 premiums written amounted to \$82,890,000. By 1964 this figure stood at \$120,000,000 (estimated the largest amount in the history of this type of insurance).[1]

There are two divisions of the insurance business that are concerned with insurance protection against theft losses. These are: nonemployee or burglary-theft dishonesty insurance, and employee or fidelity dishonesty insurance. The first of these categories may be further subdivided into residence, commercial, financial, and miscellaneous. The burglary-theft dishonesty coverages, usually known in the business as "burglary insurance," provide insurance against pecuniary losses resulting from the dishonesty of persons who are not employed by the insureds. Dishonesty coverage for employees is known as the "fidelity bond business" and provides protection for the insured

[1] *Insurance Facts* (New York: Insurance Information Institute, 1965), p. 23.

resulting from the dishonesty of persons employed by him. The two branches are quite commonly known in insurance terminology as "burglary insurance" and "fidelity bonds." Only burglary and related insurance will be considered in this chapter. Fidelity bonds will be discussed in Chapter 16.

Crimes involving offenses against property, such as robbery, burglary, and larceny, are not always defined identically in the statutes of different jurisdictions. To eliminate any element of uncertainty, the insurance contract covering burglary, robbery, and larceny losses incorporates in the contract definitions of the crimes to be followed when the question of loss arises. When the statutory definition or a decision of a court in a particular jurisdiction differs from the definition of the crime as given in the contract, courts have upheld the right of the insurer to follow the contract definition.

Robbery is a common law felony and is defined as "the carrying away of the personal property of another, from his person or in his presence, by violence or by putting him in fear." In the messenger or paymaster robbery contract, the definition reads:

> Robbery, within the meaning of this policy, is limited to a felonious and forcible taking of property—(*a*) By violence inflicted upon the person or persons in the actual care and custody of the property at the time; or (*b*) by an overt felonious act committeed in the presence of such person or persons and of which they were actually cognizant at the time; or (*c*) from the person or direct care or custody of a custodian, who, while conveying property insured under this policy, has been killed or rendered unconscious by injuries inflicted maliciously or sustained accidentally.

The different definitions have points in common. When it is understood, however, that the contract definition varies in some detail with different types of coverage, the danger of confusion without a careful reading of the contract becomes apparent.

At common law, burglary was the breaking and entering of the dwelling of another at night with the intent to commit a felony. A contract definition limits burglary losses to those "occasioned by any person or persons (except a person whose property is covered hereby) making felonious entry into the premises by actual force and violence, of which force and violence there shall be visible marks made by tools or explosives at the place of such entry." As in the case of robbery, burglary definitions differ with the type of risk. In contracts covering vaults and safes, an attempt to open the safe by means of gas, electricity, or chemicals constitutes burglary.

Theft is any act of stealing or taking of another's goods and includes robbery, burglary, and larceny. Larceny at common law is the taking and carrying away of the personal goods of another with felonious intent to steal. Larcenies are divided in some jurisdictions, according to the value of the property stolen, into *grand* and *petit*, or "petty" larceny. Contracts covering larceny losses protect the insured for loss when the property is taken by sneak thieves, servants, tradesmen, mechanics, or others having access to the premises of the insured. Such losses are not covered under a burglary contract. Inasmuch as "theft" is an inclusive word, it might seem unnecessary to have insurance contracts involving less complete coverage. Many insureds are unwilling to carry full theft coverage because they feel that the probability of certain types of theft is low and they do not want to pay the premium for a comprehensive type contract. Thus they insure only certain types of theft.

ANALYSIS OF BURGLARY CONTRACTS

Contracts in the burglary-theft category follow the pattern of liability contracts. There are four sections: (1) declarations, (2) insuring agreements, (3) exclusions, and (4) conditions. Every contract has four pages. The printed contract is included in the first three pages, and the fourth which is virtually blank is reserved for endorsements.

Declarations. The first page of the contract contains the declarations. At the top of the page, following the name of the insurer is a reference to "the assured named in the declarations forming a part hereof" instead of the actual name of the insured. The declarations then follow and consist of all the essential statements and specifications required for the particular risk. They contain the name and address of the insured and, where pertinent, his business. The contract period is given and a statement of the coverage together with limits of insurance. The premium to be charged will appear, and the premises to which the contract applies will be indicated. The declarations may call for the total amount of insurance to be carried. The declarations will state whether a burglar alarm system is maintained, pertinent information with respect to the premises, whether or not a private watchman will be on duty, or any other feature in the nature of a warranty or with respect to special protective features that reflect in a reduction in premium. Finally, there is a statement with respect to a history of previous losses. A statement is also required with respect to any cancellation of theft insurance issued to the insured or whether any such insurance has been declined by any insurer. The period with respect to losses for which the insured has received indemnity is five years, and the statement with respect to cancellations or declinations of insurance covers a similar period.

Insuring Agreements. The insuring agreements are preceded by a short paragraph in which the insurer agrees with the insured named in the declarations, in consideration of the payment of the premium and in reliance upon the statements in the declarations and subject to the limits of liability, exclusions, conditions, and other terms of the contract, to indemnify the insured for certain losses. The insuring agreements then describe the perils against which the insurance is written and the property covered.

The insuring agreement may consist of one or more parts, and insurance may be granted under one or more or all of them. While the insuring agreement establishes in a broad way the nature of the perils to be covered, the extent of the protection can be determined only in connection with the exclusions, definitions, and conditions contained in the contract.

Exclusions. The exclusions in theft coverages are designed primarily to establish limits to the coverage. By so doing the insured is saved from paying twice for the same coverage. Damage to premises caused by burglary is ordinarily covered with fire damage excluded. This exclusion appears because fire losses are in any event covered by the fire insurance contract. Losses caused by theft of an aircraft or automobile are excluded, since such vehicles are ordinarily specifically insured. Other exclusions deal with features that apply to the particular type of coverage. Most contracts, but not all, exclude losses attributable to war, insurrection, and similar perils.

Conditions. The conditions for the most part follow the pattern of other property insurance contracts. They provide for notice and proof of loss, subrogation, assignment, cancellations, other insurance, action against the insurer, changes, special statutes, declarations and a clause covering payment, replacement, and recovery. These clauses are to be found in one form or another in all theft contracts. The notice of cancellation when the insurer elects to cancel, while in most instances is five days, is longer in some forms. The conditions peculiar to an individual contract are concerned primarily with definitions and ownership of the property covered. There is a difference is statutory definitions of various forms of theft. To avoid confusion and misunderstanding, the extent of the coverage for a given form of theft is clarified by definition in the conditions. Other terms such as custodian, guard, messenger, and premises are carefully defined. Loss is defined to include damage, and business to include trade, profession, or occupation. Other specific definitions appear where the coverage requires it. Following the definitions is a condition with respect to the ownership of the property insured. Some contracts provide that the insured property may be owned by the insured or held by him in any capacity even though he may not be liable for the loss. Burglary contracts undertake to provide coverage for both the property of the insured and property for which he may be held liable. A broader contract affords coverage for all property held by the insured regardless of liability.

RESIDENCE THEFT CONTRACTS[2]

The earliest attempts to insure householders against theft losses provided insurance only against loss by burglary. Contracts are now written furnishing a broad coverage and covering in addition to burglary the hazards of robbery, theft, and larceny. Since so many residence losses are due to sneak thieves and others who enter the premises without the use of force, the broad coverage is desirable because there is less likelihood of misunderstanding.

The two most widely used theft forms for residences are the broad form personal theft insurance and personal theft insurance. The first of these furnishes a very broad coverage. There is no restriction as to the nature of the theft. It may be attributable to burglars, servants, occasional employees, or for that matter, anyone except a relative permanently residing with the insured. In contrast, the personal theft contract is designed to provide theft protection to homeowners who either do not require the broad protection afforded under the broad form personal theft contract or are not in a position to afford it. The broad form (but only the premises part of the coverage) may be written to cover burglary only at a discount of 20 percent.

Broad Form Personal Theft Insurance. This contract provides two major types of coverage: (1) theft from premises or a depository, and (2) theft away from premises anywhere in the world. The second type of coverage is optional, and the insured must carry at least $1,000 of insurance of the first type before being permitted to carry the second type. An extra premium is required, and an additional amount of insurance is provided. The coverage is very broad in that the word "theft" is defined to include larceny, burglary and robbery, and the mysterious disappearance of any insured property except a precious or semiprecious stone from its setting. This means that theft of every character is covered, and it also means that if any piece of insured property is missing, with the exception referred to above, and there is no explanation for its disappearance, then the loss is presumed to be due to theft and covered by the contract. The reason for the exception with respect to the disappearance of a stone from its setting is obvious. It is more reasonable to presume that such a stone is lost due to a defective setting rather than to theft. There has been some criticism of the mysterious disappearance coverage. It is contended that the coverage is broader than necessary to be useful, and the claims that are presented are costly. There is a feeling that a theft loss should be substantiated by some evidence of theft and that it is not the purpose of the insurance to cover losses caused by careless-

[2] Theft insurance is provided by the various homeowners' contracts, the most comprehensive coverage being found in Homeowners' 5 (see Chapter 22).

ness. A contrary argument holds that sneak thieves may well steal valuable items leaving no evidence to substantiate an actual theft. The definition of theft, then, that provides that mysterious disappearance shall be presumed to be due to theft furnishes the broadest conceivable theft protection.

Coverage includes the property of the insured, members of his family, relatives, guests, residence employees, and other permanent members of the household. The property is covered not only in the residence or apartment of the insured, and on the porches, grounds, in the garage or other outbuildings but also while in any bank, trust or safe deposit company, public warehouse, or occupied dwelling not owned, occupied, or rented by the insured where the property is placed for safekeeping. The premises part of the contract also covers damage caused by burglars, robbers, and thieves to the insured property or to the premises occupied by the insured, or loss or damage within the residence caused by vandalism or malicious mischief.

Property for the purposes of insurance is divided into the following three classes: (*a*) jewelry and furs; (*b*) other property including silverware not specifically insured; and (*c*) specified articles described and insured for specific amounts. Specified limits of insurance are applied to the first two categories; and, as indicated, specified amounts are applied to each article in the third category. If certain particularly valuable items of jewelry or furs are specifically insured, a specific amount may still be applied under the first group to unscheduled items in the category. Property not specifically insured in the second category includes such personal property as household furniture, clothing, rugs, plated ware, musical instruments, cameras, money, and securities. It is the practice to place separate amounts of insurance upon jewelry, watches, gems, and similar items, and another amount upon household goods and personal property generally. Any particularly valuable items are specifically insured.

It is not necessary to separate jewelry and furs. When this is done the coverage is said to be divided. An alternative to divided coverage is one of two forms of combined coverage referred to usually as "blanket coverages." The insured may elect to have covered theft losses of personal property from a private automobile.

Personal Theft Insurance. Personal theft insurance may be written as a separate contract or it may be added by endorsement to another contract. This type of theft insurance now forms a part of Homeowners' 1, 2, and 4, and theft coverage is fairly widely provided by these package contracts.

The contract is a limited version of the broad form personal theft contract and provides both on-premises and away from premises coverage with one insuring clause. Money is covered up to $100, and securities up to $500. These limits may be increased.

Where increased coverage applicable to money and securities is required or where additional outside protection seems desirable, the broad form may be preferable. In contrast to the broad form personal theft contract, the personal theft form does not cover: (*a*) property in dormitories or fraternity or sorority houses; (*b*) mysterious disappearance; (*c*) property in automobiles unless there is forcible entry into locked cars; (*d*) servant's property except on premises occupied exclusively by the insured.

COMMERCIAL THEFT CONTRACTS

A variety of insurance contracts have been designed to protect the business firm from losses caused by burglary and robbery. Chief among these contracts are the mercantile open stock contract; mercantile safe-burglary contract; mercantile robbery; paymaster robbery insurance; broad form money and securities; comprehensive crime insurance; comprehensive dishonesty, disappearances, and destruction contract; and storekeepers burglary and robbery.[3]

Mercantile Open Stock Policy (M.O.S. Contract). In its more usual form this contract provides burglary insurance and property damage insurance attributable to burglary. The burglary risk is defined in the contract, and by means of an endorsement in connection with certain carefully underwritten risks, the contract may be extended to cover the undefined risks of larceny and robbery.

Unlike insurance coverages for money and securities that are written on all risks or broad forms, all risks contracts are never written to cover mercantile open stock, and the contract does not apply to money and securities. The contract then is a specified risks contract covering burglary, attempted burglary, robbery of a watchman, property damage, and in some instances, theft.

Burglary. The contract undertakes to indemnify the insured for loss of the insured property caused by burglary while the premises are not open for business. The contract covers all merchandise in the insured premises as well as furniture, fixtures, and equipment, but not money and securities. To be within the protection afforded by the contract, the property must be on the premises of the insured as defined in the contract. Show windows inside the premises are covered, and other show windows are covered if "located outside the premises but inside the building line of the building containing the premises or attached to said building." There is a $100 coverage limit per case or window for outside windows as defined above, although the limit may be increased through an additional premium. The term

[3] The comprehensive dishonesty, disappearance, and destruction contract is discussed at length in the next chapter (Chapter 16). Also theft coverage is provided in many commercial package contracts. These will be discussed in Part IV.

"premises" is defined to mean only the interior of that part of the building described in the application as occupied solely by the insured in conducting his business.

Under the terms of the contract there is no coverage for loss or damage to furs or articles made entirely or principally of fur caused by burglary of such merchandise from within any show window in the premises after glass has been broken from the outside. The risk is insurable; but if this class of merchandise is to be covered in show windows, the coverage must be supplied by means of a separate endorsement attached to the contract, for which an additional premium is charged. The contract further provides a limit of $50 for loss or damage to any one article of jewelry. This limit may be increased upon the payment of an additional premium. Property held as a pledge or as collateral for a loan is insured to the extent of "the value shown by the insured's records when he arranged the transaction." If this information is not available, the insurer's liability is the "unpaid portion of the advance or loan" plus accrued interest at the legal rate. Under its terms the contract excludes liability if the insured, a partner, an associate, a director, a trustee, or an employee is connected with the burglary either as a principal or as an accessory.

If the merchandise covered is stored in a public storage warehouse, the contract may be extended to cover, in addition to burglary, loss by theft and larceny. Pilferage from packages may be covered; but if this risk is excluded, there is a very substantial reduction in the rate. This type of cover is most carefully underwritten, and many insurers require home office authorization prior to the binding of a risk.

Robbery of a Watchman. Robbery of a watchman is included as one of the perils against which coverage is provided. The watchman must be a private employee and must work only for the insured. The watchman is covered only while on duty within the premises.

Property Damage. As is usually the case in burglary insurance, property covered by the insurance and damaged by a burglary or an attempted burglary is covered. Under this contract this includes not only merchandise but furniture, fixtures, and equipment in the premises. Damage to the premises is covered if the insured is the owner or is liable for the damage. Losses caused or contributed to by fire, or occurring during a fire in the building in which the premises are located, are excluded. The fire exclusion is usually well understood, since the losses are covered by the fire contract.

Theft Coverage. Theft coverage is provided by an endorsement to the mercantile open stock burglary contract. There is a $50 mandatory deductible applying only to this endorsement. Also, the amount of insurance applying to theft must not be greater than the amount of burglary insurance and must equal at least the coinsurance limit. Insurers are unwilling to insure merchandise against the shoplifter type of loss unless "the insured can produce some evidence of theft and then only in excess of the normal shortage." Theft risks are underwritten as a rule only for those types of manufacturing and wholesale establishments that handle bulk merchandise, such as textiles and fabrics in bales or bolts. The endorsement would be carefully underwritten for any establishment where there are inevitable stock shortages due to breakage, shrinkage, and spoilage. Mysterious disappearance losses are never covered, and wherever a theft is suspected as a result of any shortage of insured merchandise brought to light by an inventory, there is no coverage unless it can reasonably be shown that the shortage was occasioned by theft. The theft coverage provided by the endorsement excludes, as does the burglary coverage, liability of a loss by theft committed by an employee or servant of the insured. Because of the restrictions and imitations which surround the theft endorsement, it provides only a limited extension to the basic M.O.S. burglary contract.

The coverages apply only while the premises of the insured are closed to business. This being the case, the contract is sometimes said to be a "nighttime, Saturdays, Sundays" contract. Moreover, because of the restriction that limits liability to losses committed by nonemployees, it can be seen that the scope of the coverage is fairly limited. The M.O.S. contract provides important insurance protection to nonfinancial business institutions, but to avoid misunderstanding and disappointment it is important to have a clear understanding of the limitations of the coverage.

The exclusions are few. They provide that there is no coverage (*a*) for loss in excess of actual cash value or cost to repair or replace, (*b*) for loss of manuscripts, records, or accounts. (*c*) for losses contributed to by a change in the condition of the risk (*d*) for loss of furs in a show window from the outside, (*e*) for loss attributable to dishonesty of employees, (*f*) for loss or damage that cannot be ascertained from the records of the insured and (*g*) vandalism or malicious mischief. The exclusion relating to change of conditions, as well as the ones relating to furs in a show window and vandalism and malicious mischief may be either deleted or modified by endorsement where conditions warrant. The exclusion with respect to dishonesty eliminates duplication with fidelity coverages. Glass losses are covered by a specific glass contract, and again the exclusion eliminates duplication.

Coinsurance Clause. The mercantile open stock burglary form introduces a feature peculiar to this type of contract. The contract contains an average clause sometimes known as the "coinsurance clause." The rating manual provides for a classification of risks according to the type of business carried on and establishes a limit known as the "coinsurance limit" for each classification. In addition to the coinsurance limit for the classification there is established a coinsurance percentage based upon location. For the purpose of determining the coinsurance percentage with respect to location the country is divided into four territories. Territorial requirements vary from 80 percent to 40 percent. New York City and Los Angeles are included in the highest percentage group. The states of North Carolina and Vermont are in the lowest. By territories, the coinsurance requirement for territory I is 80 percent; territory II, 60 percent; territory III, 50 percent; and in territory IV, 40 percent. The method of rating for all the territories is the same. The rate for different groups varies in the same territory, and the amount of insurance mandatory under a contract varies. The coinsurance requirement for each territory is uniform within the territory.

The coinsurance limit expressed for a class of business is in a dollar amount. The coinsurance requirement for a territory is expressed as a percentage of the value of the stock insured. To determine the amount of insurance to be carried for a given risk and therefore to avoid a coinsurance penalty, it is necessary to know the value of the stock, the coinsurance limit, and the coinsurance percentage determined by rating territory. Take, for example, a stock of musical instruments valued at $20,000 located in New York City. New York is located in territory I and requires insurance to 80 percent of value, subject to the requirement that the amount of insurance need not exceed the coinsurance limit. The coinsurance limit for musical instruments is $10,000. The contract must be written for at least $10,000 to avoid a coinsurance penalty but need not be written for more. Expressed differently, to avoid penalty through the operation of the average clause, the insured must carry an amount of insurance which equals or exceeds the coinsurance limit or equals or exceeds the amount determined by applying the coinsurance percentage to the value of merchandise at the time of loss. The operation of the coinsurance clause under the foregoing condition may be illustrated by the following example:

Value of inventory	$60,000
Coinsurance percentage for territory II, 60 percent	36,000
Coinsurance limit for territory II	30,000

To comply with the coinsurance clause, the insured must carry 60 percent of the value of the inventory; but since the coinsurance limit is less than 60 percent of the value of the inventory, the coinsurance requirement is fully satisfied if $30,000 of insurance is carried. The average clause adversely affects the position of the insured in a loss settlement only when the amount of insurance covering the merchandise is less than both the coinsurance limit and the amount determined by the application of the coinsurance percentage. The amount of insurance carried may be less than one of these figures, but it may not be less than both if the insured is not to be penalized.

Specific insurance not subject to a coinsurance clause may be written with no specific limit on single articles.

Mercantile Safe-Burglary Contract. The insuring agreement of this contract provides indemnity to the insured for all loss to the insured property caused by burglary. The term "burglary" is defined to mean the felonious abstraction of insured property from the covered safe when all doors of the safe are duly closed and locked by all combination locks and time locks that are a part of the safe. In addition to the insuring agreement there is a supplemental agreement that obligates the insurer to pay for damage to the safe or chest covered by the contract or to any property contained therein caused by the commission or attempted commission of burglary as defined in the contract. The property damage coverage also extends to include furniture, furnishings, fixtures, equipment, or other property of the insured. Property insured includes money, securities, and other property. The coverage is not limited to strictly mercantile risks but may be issued to any person or organization owning a safe or vault.

Under this form, money is defined as "currency, coins, bank notes, and bullion." Securities, as defined in the contract, include all negotiable or nonnegotiable instruments, such as checks, drafts, bonds, and stock certificates or contracts representing either money or other property. Included in the category are revenue and other stamps in current use. In addition to covering money and securities in the safe, the contract covers "other property." Other property of any kind kept by the insured in the safe is covered; and personal property, such as jewelry owned by the insured or employees, is covered provided always that there is a sufficiently adequate record to permit a determination of the amount of the loss or damage in the event of a burglary.

Burglary. In order to establish a loss under a mercantile safe contract, it must be shown that a burglary was actually effected or attempted. Entry to the safe or vault must have been effected by the use of tools, explosives, electricity, gas, or other chemicals upon the exterior of the safe, at a time when it was properly closed and locked by at least one combination or time lock. Evidence of the force used must appear on the exterior of the safe. An adequate set of books must be maintained from which the value of the lost or damaged items can be determined.

Under the safe-burglary contract, the insurer is not liable for loss or damage to manuscripts, records, or accounts; or is it liable for losses brought about by fraudulent, dishonest, or criminal acts of insureds or partners. This exclusion is not applicable to employees of the insured. Losses caused by nuclear reaction, nuclear radiation, radioactive contamination, war, insurrection, rebellion, and revolution are not covered. Losses effected by opening the door of the safe, vault, or chest by manipulation of the lock are also excluded.

Losses attributed to manipulation of locks are regarded as theft losses but not in the burglary category. If the manipulation is performed by an employee of the insured, the protection is available through a fidelity bond coverage. Kidnapping coverage is not available in connection with safe-burglary insurance. If an employee of the insured is forced to return to the premises under threat of violence and opens a safe or vault, the loss is not regarded as a burglary loss. If the insured feels that this hazard should be covered, he may obtain protection through providing inside robbery insurance with the kidnapping coverage included.

Property Damage. As in other burglary contracts, the contract extends to cover damage to property, with the exception of fire, caused by burglary of the insured's safe or any attempt at a burglary. Property damage coverage extends to the insured's safe or vault together with the insured's property within. It also covers property damage to furniture, equipment, and merchandise in the premises, but not in the safe or vault if the loss is attributable to a burglary. If the insured is liable for damages to the premises, this coverage also comes within the scope of the contract.

Rates for safe insurance are quoted per thousands of insurance carried and depend upon the following features: type of safe, territory, class of business, and property covered. Safes are classified as fire resistive, semiburglarproof, burglarproof, and double burglarproof. Discounts are allowed for features that tend to minimize the risk, such as a private watchman, safes equipped with an approved relocking system, premises protected with an approved burglar alarm system, and safes or vaults equipped with certified tear-gas systems. Discounts are allowed when there is more than one safe in a single location. If the insurance covers "merchandise only," or "securities and merchandise only," a discount of 25 percent is allowed. If the insurance covers loss to securities only, a 50 percent discount from the manual rate is allowed.

Mercantile Robbery Insurance. Stores, offices, and other places of business are not immune from robbery during business hours, and messengers carrying money and valuables are held up and robbed on the city streets. Mercantile robbery insurance (formerly messenger and interior robbery insurance) has two optional insuring clauses. The two clauses are: (*a*) robbery inside the premises, and (*b*) robbery outside the premises which covers the risk of messenger robbery. Either coverage is available separately. A mercantile robbery coverage form is also available, but is generally used with other form of protection.

The interior holdup contract covers loss or damage to the insured property through robbery or attempted robbery and loss or damage to furniture, fixtures, and other property. The coverage is effective on a 24-hour basis and furnishes protection only within the insured's premises. Loss or damage to merchandise stolen from a show window by a person who has broken the glass from the outside, or by his accomplice, is covered while the premises are regularly open for business.

Kidnapping is sometimes resorted to by robbers to hold the owner of the property or his employee, later forcing the person detained to open the premises or supply information, keys, or other means of admission. Kidnapping usually occurs off the premises. The contract provides protection to the insured if a loss is attributed to the kidnapping of a custodian, defined as "the insured, a partner therein or an officer thereof, or any employee thereof who is in the regular service of and duly authorized by the insured to have the care and custody of the insured property within the premises, excluding any person while acting as watchman, porter, or janitor."[4]

The outside holdup feature of the contract covers the insured for robbery losses if the robbery or attempted robbery takes place outside the premises of the insured. This feature of the contract covers not only messenger robbery but, as well, damage to money, securities, or merchandise in the possession of the messenger resulting from robbery or attempted robbery. Protection is afforded also for damage to the wallet, bag, satchel, or other container in which the money or other property is being carried by the messenger. The protection applies outside the insured's premises anywhere within the United States or Canada and provides a 24-hour protection. A messenger is defined as "the insured, a partner therein or an officer thereof who is in the regular service of and duly authorized by the insured to have the care and custody of the insured property outside the premises."

When both robbery inside the premises and outside the premises are carried, losses are covered whether they occur inside the building or outside of it. Robbery inside the premises, if written without messenger coverage, does not cover outside the building. In certain types of risk this coverage is desirable when the messenger contract is unnecessary. In cases in which custodians meet customers outside the building, as at filling stations and other roadside places of business, upon the payment of an additional premium equal to 50 percent of the charge for inside robbery, the coverage may be extended to include the ground immediately surrounding the store, office, or structure used by the insured in serving his customers.

Again, there is a type of risk in which it is the usual practice for the manager or owner to take the cash home that accumulates after

---

[4] *The Fire, Casualty, and Surety Bulletins* (Cincinnati, Ohio: National Underwriter Co., 1965). This quotation and subsequent ones in this chapter are from this source.

banking hours and up to closing time. This is usually the custom if there is lacking safe means for leaving the cash on the premises of the business. Where this is the custom, burglary, robbery, theft, and larceny coverage in the home of the custodian may be endorsed to the messenger or interior robbery contract. This extended coverage may be limited to burglary only, if this more limited protection is desirable.

Robbery outside the premises insurance covers the insured for robbery losses if the robbery or attempted robbery takes place outside the premises of the insured. Factors affecting the premium on robbery outside the premises are the territory, the number of guards accompanying the custodian, the nature of the property covered, and any other protective measures approved as tending to reduce the hazard.

There are not many exclusions in the mercantile robbery contract. Losses due to nuclear reaction and radiation are excluded as are war and allied risks. Manuscripts, books of account, and records are not covered, and the contract does not cover "any fraudulent, dishonest, or criminal acts by any insured or by a partner."

Paymaster Robbery Insurance. Many concerns pay their employees in cash and, in the course of effecting the transaction, transfer large sums of money from point to point. The contract to cover this is similar to the robbery outside the premises section of the mercantile robbery contract, but contains features to fit the particular needs of payroll risks. Paymaster robbery insurance is now written as an endorsement rather than as a separate contract. It applies mainly to payroll funds.

The contract provides day and night protection for the insured from loss by robbery from a custodian outside the insured's premises of money or checks held solely for payroll purposes. It covers as well, outside the premises, for an amount not exceeding 10 percent of the amount of the insurance, for loss of, or damage to, money and securities not intended solely for payroll purposes if the loss is the consequence of a robbery or attempted robbery from a custodian. As in the case of messenger robbery, the bag, satchel, safe, chest, or other container in which money is being transported is covered against loss or damage attributable to robbery or attempted robbery.

Differing from the robbery outside the premises section of the mercantile, robbery contract, the paymaster robbery form covers inside the insured's premises for loss of, or damage to, money or checks intended for payroll purposes and extends also to cover damage to the premises, furniture, fixtures, or other property within the control of a custodian provided the custodian at the time is engaged in his regular duties in handling payroll funds. Employees of the insured are protected, while on the premises of the employer, against loss of money or checks in their possession if such loss is the outgrowth of a robbery on the day or night on which they were paid. Payroll funds taken by robbery from a safe do not come within the protection of the contract. Losses to payroll funds after the premises are closed for business are covered if attributable to the kidnapping of a custodian.

If the paymaster takes funds to his home during the night, the same type of extended coverage for such funds may be provided as is provided under the mercantile robbery contract in like situations.

A paymaster broad form endorsement is available to provide an all risks coverage. When so endorsed the contract covers, in addition to robbery, the destruction, disappearance, and wrongful abstraction of payroll funds. The endorsement may be written to cover inside the residence of the insured to provide both inside and outside coverage. War risks and forgery are excluded from the protection. The surrendering of the money or securities in any exchange or purchase is not covered under the broad form, or are fraudulent or dishonest acts of the insured or officers or employees of the insured.

Money and Securities Contract—Broad Form. The broad form money and securities contract is designed to provide all risks coverage on money and securities. Money includes currency, coins, bank notes, bullion, travelers checks, registered checks, and money orders; and securities includes "negotiable or nonnegotiable instruments or contracts representing either money or other property, including revenue and other stamps in 'current use.'" The money and securities coverage is also available in the 3–D (comprehensive dishonesty, disappearance, and destruction) contract and in the blanket crime contract.

The coverage applies to loss of money and securities while on the premises and in certain situations outside the premises. Premises include the described premises, banking premises, or "similar recognized places of safe deposit." The losses contemplated are those caused by "actual destruction, disappearance, or wrongful abstraction." Within premises coverage is extended to include other property when lost by safe burglary or robbery or attempts thereat. Damage to the premises, if they are owned by the insured or if he is liable for the damage, is also included, if such damages are caused by safe burglary or robbery or "by burglarious entry or attempt." The outside section of the contract covers money and securities against "actual destruction, disappearance, or wrongful abstraction" in three situations: "(1) While the property is being conveyed by a messenger; (2) While it is being conveyed by an armored car; (3) While it is within the living quarters in the home of any messenger." The contract has certain territorial limits which are: the United States, the District of Columbia Virgin Island, Puerto Rico, Canal Zone, and Canada.

The money and securities contract contains a number of exclusions, most of which are not particularly restrictive. Coverage ordinarily provided by a fidelity bond is excluded with the exception of safe burglary or robbery by an "officer, employee, director, trustee, or representative," which is covered under the contract. Accounting and arithmetical errors or omissions are excluded, as is the surrendering of money and securities for the purposes of exchange or purchase. This latter exclusion is intended to cover situations in which a customer has been given too much change or where swindling losses have occurred. Manuscripts, books of account, or records are not covered, nor is the loss of money in a "coin operated amusement device or vending machines," unless the amount of money deposited is recorded on a continuous recording instrument." There is the usual war and related perils exclusion and the exclusion of nuclear reaction, nuclear radiation, and radioactive contamination. Losses by fire are excluded with the exception of fire losses to money, securities, and a safe or vault. In general, the exclusions serve to eliminate situations where losses are normally covered under other contracts, or where a peril, such as war, is not usually assumed by insurers.

The contract may be written with a deductible that varies from $50 to $1,000. The resulting discounts vary from 5 percent to 10 percent. Since the money and securities contract provides very limited protection to other types of property, an insured may need to carry a mercantile open stock burglary contract as well as open stock theft. This may be done by endorsement to the money and securities broad form.

Storekeepers Burglary and Robbery Contract. The storekeepers burglary and robbery contract is a combination form that is widely sold. It contains seven coverages and meets the needs of small, retail establishments. The seven coverages are: (1) premises robbery (inside holdup); (2) messenger robbery (outside holdup); (3) kidnapping; (4) safe burglary and limited burglary; (5) theft—night depository or residence; (6) mercantile open stock burglary; and (7) all damage (property damage is excluded from the other six items). The meaning of these terms has been discussed in connection with other contracts. The exclusions are similar to those found in other burglary and robbery contracts and include employees' dishonesty; manuscripts, records, and accounts; war risks; nuclear risks; and fire.

The limit of recovery on jewelry is $50 per piece with a like limit applying to "burglary of money and securities from outside a locked safe or vault." Money and securities coverage of a more comprehensive sort may be endorsed on the contract.

Storekeeper's Contract—Broad Form. A broad form storekeepers contract is available and was first introduced to the public in 1956. It is similar to the storekeepers burglary and robbery contract but is more comprehensive and is, in fact, a "package crime contract for small and medium-sized retail and service businesses." Small amounts of coverage (a maximum of $1,000 per insuring agreement) are available for nine coverages: (1) employee dishonesty; (2) loss inside the premises; (3) loss outside the premises; (4) merchandise and counterfeit paper currency; (6) residence theft (applies only to money and securities); (7) depositors forgery; (8) damage by vandalism or malicious mischief; (9) other damage.

Blanket Crime Contract. The blanket crime contract is designed to provide protection against financial loss caused by various acts of dishonesty. It provides five dishonesty coverages in one "package" under a single limit. These coverages are: (1) fidelity insurance (on the same basis as the commercial blanket bond); (2) premises coverage; (3) outside coverage; (4) money orders and counterfeit paper currency coverages; and (5) depositors forgery insurance. The premises coverage gives the same protection for loss of money and securities as that found in the broad form of the money and securities contract. Other types of property "within the insured's premises (not including banking premises) is insured against loss or damage by safe burglary and inside holdup." Damage to the premises from specified types of dishonesty is also covered. The outside coverage is the same as that provided by the outside section of the broad form of the money and securities contract. Other property is protected "against loss by robbery if the property is being conveyed by a messenger or an armored car company and against theft from the home of a messenger." In order for the fourth type of coverage to be effective, the acceptance of counterfeit instruments must be during the regular course of business. The forgery coverage is the same as that provided by the depositors forgery bond and applies to outgoing instruments.

The comprehensive dishonesty, disappearance, and destruction contract and the blanket crime contract are much alike. There are some differences in the language of the contracts, and the 3–D contract is not written with a single limit. Separate limits apply to each insuring agreement. Also, the blanket crime contract may be issued for small amounts (but not below $1,000), whereas the 3–D contract has a minimum limit for fidelity coverage of $10,000.

FINANCIAL THEFT CONTRACTS

Financial institutions, particularly banks, are vulnerable to losses from robbery, burglary, and theft. A number of contracts have been devised to protect these institutions against the effects of losses from these perils.

Bank Burglary and Robbery Insurance. Since the greatest concentration of money and securities is in banks and other financial institutions, it is natural that these institutions should early have been a target for burglary and holdup. Bank burglary and robbery insurance was one of the first forms of this type of coverage to be written. Institutions carrying blanket bond coverage are protected for burglary and robbery losses. The individual burglary and robbery contract is still used for institutions that do not require the broad protection furnished by a blanket bond or do not elect to pay the premium for such a bond, and as excess cover for large institutions that require more burglary and robbery insurance than the blanket bond provides.

The bank burglary and robbery contract provides four distinct coverages: (1) burglary, (2) robbery, (3) property damage caused by either burglary or robbery, and (4) property damage caused by vandalism or malicious mischief. The last two coverages are not provided in distinct sections of the contract but rather are a part of the burglary and robbery insuring clauses.

Burglary and robbery, together with the attendant property damage, may be covered under a single contract. It is possible to cover losses from either burglary or robbery with attendant property damage. When burglary and robbery are carried together, a separate limit of liability is designated in the contract for each hazard, and property damage losses from either hazard are subject to the contract limit designated for that particular hazard.

Burglary. The burglary protection furnishes indemnity for loss of money or securities by burglary of safes or vaults. As in other burglary coverages, in order to establish the liability of the insurer one must prove that entry was made by force. This is to be demonstrated by the presence of marks caused by the use of tools, explosives, electricity, gas, or other chemicals. It follows that money, securities, and other property taken from safes while open are not covered. If the vault is forced open and a money box or safe carried away and opened off the premises, the burglary coverage is effective.

Robbery. The robbery coverage provides indemnity for loss of money or securities by robbery from within any part of the premises occupied exclusively by the insured or his officers or employees.

Property Damage. The property damage feature provides indemnity for loss sustained as the result of damage to money and securities or to the premises, furniture, fixtures, vaults, safes, and money boxes when caused by burglary or robbery or any attempt thereat. Vandalism and malicious mischief coverage takes within its scope any intentional wrongful injury to money or securities or the fixtures of the insured. Providing protection for vandalism losses eliminates the possibility of a dispute as to whether the damage in a particular case is actually an attempted burglary. In the property damage coverages, loss caused either by burglary, robbery, vandalism, or malicious mischief, or by fire damage to money and securities is not excluded.

There is no fire damage exclusion here because damage to money and securities is not covered under the fire contract. Fire losses to premises, and such items as furniture and fixtures are never covered under the bank burglary and robbery insurance contract regardless of how the fire loss is caused.

The contract provides that there is no liability on the part of the insurer for loss or damage to securities unless the insured takes active steps and exercises due diligence in preventing negotiation, sale, or retirement. It is also mandatory upon an insured to keep adequate records to the end that the amount of any loss can be accurately determined. There is no loss under a burglary contract, if the vault is left unlocked or if it is opened through a manipulation of the combination. The contract does not cover transit risks or property stolen away from the premises of the bank. Neither are the contents of safe-deposit boxes covered unless the loss involves the contents of a specified vault for which a record is maintained. Unobserved sneak-thief losses are not covered, or are losses due to mysterious disappearance. Losses that are the outgrowth of dishonest, fraudulent, or criminal act of employees of the bank are excluded, except in the instances when an employee is an active participant in a burglary or robbery.

Bank burglary and robbery rates are computed separately. Burglary coverage is based upon a classification of safes and vaults. A rate is quoted, and the premium is determined by multiplying the rate by the thousands of dollars of insurance to be carried. From this sum certain deductions are allowable. Discounts are based upon: the territory, the population of the town or city, the use of an approved alarm system, watchman service, the division of insurance so that not more than 50 or 75 percent applies to any one safe or vault at any one place, and the limitation of contract to cover securities only or securities and subsidiary coin only. A discount is allowed for the use of certain designated locks and for insurance if written for a term.

Bank robbery rates are based upon a territorial classification. Discounts are allowed for daytime guard or watchman, daytime burglar alarm, and limitation of insurance to securities, silver, and subsidiary coin. Banks in cities where the population is 1,000,000 or more and where 25 or more persons are employed are allowed a special discount on the rate.

Safe-Deposit Boxes Insurance. In the absence of negligence it has been generally held that there is no liability on the part of a bank for loss to the contents of rented safe-deposit boxes. In those cases in which the decisions of the courts have held the banks liable, the question has been presented as to whether the bank had furnished the holders of safe-deposit boxes the same protection as the bank gave its own property. With the question of liability to this extent uncertain, the owners of securities or other valuables in rented boxes are interested in providing insurance against loss of the contents. Banks are likewise interested in providing the same insurance protection for property in boxes as they provide for their own property. Two forms of burglary and robbery contracts are offered: to the bank that wishes to insure all the boxes, and to the individual who wishes to insure his own box only.

Bank Forms. Insurance written for the bank is available in two forms: a blanket safe-deposit box burglary and robbery form, and a safe-depository liability form or the two types of coverage may be purchased through a combination safe-depository contract. The blanket burglary and robbery contract covers against the risks of loss of property in customers' safe-deposit boxes through burglary or robbery. The contract also covers damage or destruction caused by these hazards or attempts thereat, as well as that caused by vandalism or malicious mischief. All property is covered, including money in the customers' safe-deposit boxes. Damage to the premises, safes, vaults, and other furnishings of the insured institution are covered under this form as under other burglary and robbery forms. The measure of loss is the pecuniary loss. This precludes making a claim based upon a sentimental value.

Damage to the premises, equipment, or furnishings of the lending institution is paid for first, and the balance of the insurance is prorated among the boxes. While this contract is not a legal liability form and the interest of the box renters is covered regardless of the liability of the bank, the protection afforded may be limited to legal liability by endorsement. The contract then covers, for a reduced rate, legal liability for burglary and robbery losses only.

The second safe-depository form issued to banks, the safe-depository liability contract, covers only the legal liability of the insured for loss to the property of a lessee. Under this contract there are no restrictions as to how the loss or damage must occur, or is there any limitation as to the amount applicable to each box. The contract is in the nature of a defense contract, and the insurer is liable to pay only in the event that it can be established that the insured is obligated to pay the amount of the claim because of liability imposed by law. This is in contrast to the burglary and robbery form, which does not require that the bank be legally liable in order that the insurer be liable under the contract. The weakness in the liability contract is found in the fact that it does not protect the lessee. Unless liability can be established, the bank may suffer loss of good will through its failure to provide insurance protection for the boxes.

Lessee Form. This form issued to individual lessees undertakes to indemnify the insured for loss or damage to his own property or to property for which he is liable. The burglary coverage is effective while such property is contained in leased or rented boxes in a designated vault. The robbery feature provides coverage inside the premises of the bank while at least one officer or employee of the bank is on the premises.

The most recent development in this classification is an all risk securities safe-deposit form. This form is issued to lessees and provides protection against all risk of loss, damage, or destruction caused by burglary and robbery only, and only securities are covered. In addition, the contract provides insurance against any form of theft or larceny and includes within its protection the unexplainable disappearance or misplacement of securities. Losses originating through dishonesty or the criminal act of an agent of the insured would fall in the fidelity category and are not covered, although the contract does extend to cover losses occasioned by carelessness or negligence. This form is particularly desirable for the use of institutions that have large security holdings.

Depositor's Forgery Contract. This contract, sometimes referred to as a "forgery bond," is issued to individuals, firms, or corporations. It is not issued to banks and building and loan associations.

The contract is divided into two sections: covering outgoing items, and covering incoming items. It is the intent of the contract to protect the insured against forgery losses on commercial paper issued or presumed to have been issued by the insured or an authorized agent and to provide forgery protection on incoming paper received by the insured. The insured may elect to cover his own paper only; but if he wishes to insure incoming items, he must provide a combined coverage insuring both outgoing and incoming items. Incoming items are not insured separately.

Coverage of Insured's Paper Only. This is the form most commonly used and serves the requirements of the insured when the hazard from incoming items is not regarded as great. Therefore, checks, drafts, or other instruments accepted by the insured that may be the occasion of loss because of alteration or forgery are not insured under this form. On the other hand, the banks in which the insured maintains his accounts enjoy the same protection as the insured with respect to forged instruments of the insured. This protection to the bank has the effect of eliminating the question of liability between the bank and the insured.

The insurance covers whether the forged signature purports to be that of the insured in the capacity of the drawer of a draft, check, or bill of exchange; the maker of a note; or the acceptor of a draft, bill of exchange, or trade acceptance. The coverage affords protection against forgery of the endorsement of any payee or other person upon a check or draft drawn by the insured upon his bank.

Combined Coverage. Retail establishments that in the ordinary course of business take large numbers of checks find the danger of losses from forgery a very real one. Business establishments where the incoming hazard is regarded as important find adequate insurance protection through coverage for both incoming and outgoing items.

The insurance provided for incoming items covers losses caused by the taking by the insured of forged or altered instruments in the course of business operations in exchange for merchandise or services. It follows, therefore, that checks cashed by the insured as an accommodation are not within the scope of the coverage. Cash may be given as change when a check is paid whose face value is in excess of the price charged for the article or service without affecting the coverage. The coverage does not extend to indemnify the insured for losses when the check is drawn on an account with insufficient funds, or when the check is returned marked "no account." Such losses are not regarded as due to forgery or alteration and are to be guarded against by the ordinary precautions of those in charge of credits.

With respect to incoming items the insured is required to carry 25 percent of every loss. This is due to a provision in the contract limiting the amount of the insurer's liability for any one instrument to 75 percent of the insured's pecuniary interest in the instrument. This is to be determined by the amount paid for property sold and delivered, or for services rendered, fixed at the time of the transaction, to which may be added any sums delivered against the instrument in question in excess of the amount paid for goods or services. The contract does not cover losses which are the outgrowth of receiving that class of instrument known as a "traveler's check."

Family Forgery Contract. This contract is designed to cover the named insured, his spouse, and children residing permanently in his household against forgery losses. Contrary to the depositor's form, it applies only to personal financial transactions. Business and professional activities are not covered.

There are three forms of protection: outgoing items, incoming items, and counterfeit money. The protection afforded under outgoing items is similar to that provided in the depositor's forgery contract. Incoming items receive considerably broader coverage than that provided by the depositor's contract in that protection is afforded not only for loss attributable to the acceptance of forged or altered checks but for loss resulting from forged or altered incoming coupons, drafts, money orders, real estate mortgages, stock certificates, or other negotiable instrument ordinarily traded in the securities market. If the insured gives value or extends credit on the strength of a forged or counterfeit instrument, or one that has been altered or stolen, or one that has been acquired under a lost or stolen transfer, assignment, guarantee, or endorsement, the contract covers the loss. Under the section covering counterfeit money, the insured is protected up to $100 aggregate if he accepts counterfeit United States paper currency in good faith. Liability is limited to $50 for counterfeit currency accepted in any one transaction.

Bankers' Limited Forgery Contract. Lending institutions, as a rule, cover the forgery hazard under a blanket bond. For those institutions that do not elect to carry forgery protection under a blanket bond, the bankers' limited forgery contract may be written. It is particularly attractive to those who deem the coverage satisfactory because its cost is moderate.

The form provides for the banking institution essentially the same protection upon its own paper, such as checks and drafts, savings account withdrawal orders, and certificates of deposit as is afforded individuals and firms under the section insuring outgoing items of the depositors' forgery form. The contract protects the insured banks and the interests of other banks (but not individual depositors) from forgery or alteration losses.

Under the terms of the insuring clause, the insurer agrees to indemnify the insured against direct loss, not exceeding the limits set in the face of the contract, which may be sustained through the payment during the contract term of any instrument or instruments as defined in the contract which shall have been raised or altered in any other respect or upon which the name of the drawer, maker, acceptor, or endorser thereof shall have been forged.

Important contracts affording a forgery and alteration protection to bankers are known as "bankers' blanket bonds." These bonds offer, in addition to forgery, a wide range of coverage, including the various classes of theft losses. Since an important part of the cover has to do with dishonest acts of employees, the bankers' blanket bond is, in large part, a fidelity coverage. This bond is merely mentioned here because many large banking institutions obtain their forgery coverage under it.

Forged-Securities Contract. This coverage is provided for banks, brokerage houses, corporations, or other business organizations whose business is concerned largely with issuing securities or with investing or dealing in them.

The coverage offered under the forged-securities contract is very broad. Two forms are in general use. The coverage afforded under both forms is broken down into a number of insuring clauses. These are optional, and the protection the contract affords may be adjusted to meet the particular needs of the individual insured.

MISCELLANEOUS THEFT CONTRACTS

There are a number of contracts in the miscellaneous category, such as the money and securities destruction contract and certain liability contracts written for insureds such as innkeepers and warehousemen providing third-party liability protection in the event of the theft of property left in their custody. By way of illustration the liability forms will be reviewed here.

Liability Forms. Contracts covering the liability of the insured imposed by law upon custodians, similar in many respects to that made available to lending institutions with respect to safety-deposit box lessees, are written as burglary forms, although the protection is considerably broader. They are included in the burglary category presumably because burglary and robbery are among the principal sources of loss. Two widely used forms are: innkeepers' liability, and warehousemen's liability.

Innkeepers' Liability. This form protects the innkeeper in the event he is held liable for the loss of property of guests. The contract provides no protection directly for the guests. The liability of an innkeeper is considerably greater than that of a bailee. At common law, an innkeeper was at one time absolutely liable as an insurer of the property of his guests if brought *infra hospitum.* Property is said to be *infra hospitum* when it is the property of a guest and comes within the care and charge of the innkeeper. Originally, innkeepers were held liable for all losses whether by reason of burglary, theft, fire, or negligence, unless the loss was occasioned by negligence or misconduct of the guest or by an act of God or the public enemy. The common law liability has been modified by statute in all jurisdictions in the United States, but the liability resting upon the innkeeper is still severe. The status of the hotel man may in one instance be that of an innkeeper, in another that of a landlord, and in a third that of a bailee or warehouseman. To provide protection against the various liabilities that may arise, the hotel and innkeepers' contract provides insurance against loss from the liability imposed by law upon the insured for damages on account of loss of, or injury to, property of guests of the insured's hostelry.

Contractual liability is excluded with the exception that written agreements made with a guest before a loss do not fall within this exclusion. Coverage does not apply if the insured has released any third party from its legal liability. Losses caused by spilling or upsetting food or loss of or damage to automobiles or property in automobiles, as well as property in the insured's custody for laundering or cleaning, or merchandise for exhibition, sale, or delivery by guests, are not covered. These liability losses with respect to food, automobiles, and other property in the custody of the insured may be covered by endorsement upon payment of an additional premium.

Warehousemen's Liability. This form covers warehousemen, packers, and other similar bailees for their liability for loss of property in their custody. Coverage is against liability regardless of cause, unless restricted by state laws. The contract is written with a required deductible which may be as little as $50 or as much as $10,000 or more. The deductible applies to each occurrence giving rise to one or more claims and not to each claim. Thus, in the case of robbery with loss to several owners of merchandise, the deductible would apply once to the aggregate of all claims. The exclusions include war risks, money, securities, and perishable goods. In some states, because of legal requirements, fire and sprinkler leakage losses are not covered, and these risks are in such circumstances insured separately. There are also the usual liability exclusions with respect to contractual liability.

FOR DISCUSSION

1. B has a stock of merchandise valued at $20,000 located in a territory where the coinsurance requirement is 80 percent and the coinsurance limit on the particular class is $40,000. With $10,000 insurance, how much are the insurers obligated to pay if the loss is $8,000?
2. In the foregoing situation, suppose the value of the merchandise had been $100,000 with $50,000 insurance. How much would the insurer pay in the case of an $8,000 loss?
3. A loss occurred in a Western city, and investigation brought to light that the burglars were assisted by someone inside the property who was familiar with the layout of the vault and in a position to make ineffective the burglary alarm system. In the circumstances, the insurer writing the burglary insurance denied liability. In your opinion, is such a denial justified in view of the fact that the safe was forcibly opened and jewels valued in a large amount stolen?
4. There is a case on record in which the lessee of a safe-deposit box made a claim against the bank for loss of $5,000 worth of United States Savings Bonds which the renter claimed disappeared from his box. An investigation brought to light the fact that the claimant never owned $5,000 worth of United States Savings Bonds and, therefore, could not have lost them out of his box. How does safe-deposit burglary and robbery insurance assist a bank in a case like this?
5. In the case of safe-deposit claims against lending institutions, it has been stated that, in order to sustain a claim for loss or damage, the claimant must prove negligence on the part of the depository. Obviously, if a customer is able to prove negligence, he can recover. In the circumstances, how is it possible for fraudulent claimants to involve banks in expensive defense actions?
6. Is the lessee security safe-deposit box contract a burglary contract, a robbery contract, or both?
7. Why should a bank give consideration to safe-deposit burglary and robbery insurance to apply to the contents of safe-deposit boxes if it carries adequate bank burglary and robbery insurance?
8. X bank carries a blanket safe-deposit box contract and a robbery contract for its own protection and for the protection of the contents of customers' boxes. From the standpoint of the bank, there are

certain limitations which only the legal liability contract can meet. What are these?

9. Which of the following types of losses would you expect to be excluded under a mercantile open stock burglary contract: (*a*) losses caused by an officer or employee of the insured, (*b*) loss of records and accounts, (*c*) loss occurring during a fire in the premises, (*d*) loss or damage due to vandalism or malicious mischief, and (*e*) losses due to war risks?
10. How is the amount of the insurer's liability determined under an M.O.S. contract?
11. Insurance underwriters advise an insured to take every precaution to have his premises equipped with adequate bars and locking devices. What advantage does the insured derive if he carries full insurance?
12. In what circumstances is a loss by theft not covered by the broad form personal theft contract?
13. If an insured moves from one residence to another, how does his broad form personal theft contract cover?
14. X possesses a ring set with a large diamond. He called at the office of a doctor for a physical examination. Believing that doctors charge on the basis of the financial ability of the patient, and assuming the diamond ring to be evidence of affluence, X removed the ring from his finger and placed it in his pocket. After leaving the doctor's office, X purchased a newspaper and in reaching in his pocket for change he found the ring to be missing. He returned to the doctor's office, but the ring could not be found. X carried a broad form personal theft contract. X brought an action on the contract, claiming the loss of the ring was a "mysterious disappearance." Do you think the insurer should be held liable? Why?
15. Many people would like to buy burglary insurance. They have not done so because they did not feel that their need for the broad theft protection provided by the broad form personal theft contract warranted the premium required for this coverage. The personal theft contract, has been developed to meet this market. What is included and what is excluded from this coverage? Discuss. To what extent have the various homeowners' contracts obviated the need for separate theft insurance contracts?

CHAPTER · 16

Bonds

Perhaps the earliest form of the transfer of risk is that of suretyship, and the earliest records of society contain references to going bond for another. A surety is a person or corporation who agrees to accept responsibility in the event of the failure of another. The agreement (or contract) embodying the conditions surrounding the acceptance of responsibility is known as a "bond."

Historically, the earliest sureties were persons, and personal suretyship was commonplace for many centuries. The Bible contains a number of references to suretyship and provides warnings against the practice of assuming financial responsibility for the performance of another. It is also known that surety contracts were in the library of Sargon I as early as 2750 B.C. These instances, as well as other references to suretyship throughout recorded history, serve to establish that the practice of personal suretyship has been known to civilization for a long time.

There are several problems associated with personal suretyship. The principal, whose performance is being guaranteed, might have problems finding a surety and might be reluctant to impose on family and friends. Likewise, the situation for the surety under personal suretyship has some disadvantageous aspects. For one thing, the surety is vulnerable to financial disaster, which might well lead to bankruptcy, unless his personal financial resources are particularly strong. Similarly, the beneficiary under the bond (the obligee) could easily lose under personal suretyship—particularly if the surety was unable to respond because of difficult financial circumstances. Although the beneficiary might try legally to enforce his rights, recovery is made difficult by the favored treatment given personal sureties in the courts.

The difficulties associated with personal suretyship resulted in the idea of having corporations serve as sureties, and this form of suretyship was first tried in England in the 18th century. The first corporate surety to do business in the United States was the Fidelity Insurance Company, which was founded in 1865. The first surety to write contract bonds was the American Surety Company (1884). Corporate suretyship has flourished over the years and as of 1964, surety bond premiums written amounted to approximately $265 million, and fidelity bonds premiums written were approximately $130 million. Comparable figures for 1940 for both classes of business were about $50 million and $41 million respectively. Although these figures are large, they represent a small proportion of the potential for these coverages. In the case of fidelity bonds, it has been estimated that "only about 15 to 20 percent of business firms bond their employees against fraud and embezzlement."[1]

INSURANCE AND SURETYSHIP CONTRASTED

In its pure form suretyship is not insurance, although many bonds currently in use are essentially insurance contracts. The principal difference between insurance and suretyship is that in the former the insurer assumes the entire risk and losses are paid out of the premiums that are collected. In the latter, in theory, the surety does not expect loss, and if it occurs, recovery is made from the party who defaults, and it is only after failure to collect that premiums are used for the payment of losses. In this sense bond underwriters do not contemplate taking the entire risk and the premiums collected are fees for service.

There are three parties to a bond in contrast to the insurance contract where there are only two. These parties are the principal, the obligee, and the surety. The principal is the party whose performance is being guaranteed such as a builder, a public official, or an employee. The obligee is the beneficiary of the bond and might be a firm for whom a building is being constructed. The surety is the organization issuing the bond and it agrees to pay the obligee in accordance with the terms of the bond in the event that the principal fails to perform.

Other differences cited by Denenberg between insurance and suretyship center around such matters as salvage, rating, type of contract, and problems in underwriting.[2] Salvage probably plays a more important role in suretyship than in insurance, although it has considerable importance in marine insurance too. The use of past experience in predicting future losses may not be as reliable in suretyship because the various rating classifications may not have sufficient numbers to bring about stability in loss ratios and cyclical swings may have a greater effect on surety experience than is the case with most lines of

---

[1] *Insurance Facts* (New York: Insurance Information Institute, 1965), pp. 21–22. For additional facts on the history of suretyship, see John D. Long and Davis W. Gregg (eds.), *Property and Liability Insurance Handbook* (Homewood, Ill.: Richard D. Irwin, Inc., 1965), pp. 803–6.

[2] Herbert S. Denenberg, "History, Nature, and Uses of Suretyship" in *ibid.,* pp. 810–11.

insurance. Contracts in suretyship differ in many ways from typical insurance agreements and are more often prepared than in the case of insurance by persons or agencies not acting as the surety. The fact of a three-party contract complicates underwriting in the sense that both the principal and the obligee may need to be reviewed from the standpoint of their conformity to selection criteria. It is easy to overemphasize the differences between suretyship and insurance. In practice it is frequently difficult to make a real distinction between the two.

CLASSIFICATION OF BONDS

There are many types of bond sold by corporate sureties. Although there is no official classification of bonds, the publishers of the *Fire, Casualty, and Surety Bulletins* suggest that bonds can be divided into four groups: (1) financial guarantee, (2) fidelity, (3) blanket, and (4) forgery and miscellaneous. Financial guarantee bonds, which in some classifications are called "surety bonds," in spite of the fact that the word "surety" properly refers to the entire field, include contract, completion, bid, court, license and permit, and last instrument bonds. Fidelity bonds include such items as individual, name schedule, position schedule, blanket, statutory, and public official bonds. Blanket bonds, as a separate classification, refer to contracts such as the banker's blanket bond and the broker's blanket bond where the agreement goes beyond the usual type of fidelity coverage to include losses often insured under a theft contract. Illustrations of forgery and miscellaneous bonds are the bankers forgery bond, depositors forgery bond, and various protective contracts that are probably more insurance than suretyship. There are some contracts that combine surety concepts with traditional insurance coverages. Two of these, the blanket crime contract and the comprehensive dishonesty, disappearance, and destruction contract (3–D) are of major importance. The blanket crime contract was discussed on page 274. The 3–D contract will be analyzed at the end of this chapter.

No attempt will be made in this chapter to analyze all of the different bond forms that are sold by corporate sureties nor to cover all of the bonds mentioned in the above classification. The contracts selected for discussion are those that are fairly commonly used by business and industry.

FINANCIAL GUARANTEE BONDS (SURETY BONDS)

A financial guarantee bond is an agreement that secures an expressed obligation. This obligation is ordinarily in writing, and a typical example would be a building contract.[3] The nature of the guarantee provided by surety bonds is best illustrated by a consideration of the content of typical bond forms. These forms are not standard, and a great variety of forms are in existence. A bid bond, a performance bond, a labor and materials bond, and a court bond will be analyzed in this section and other financial guarantee bonds will be briefly described. The forms on which the analyses are based are those published by the Insurance Information Institute.

Bid Bond. Bid bonds are often required of building contractors when they bid (usually competitively) for construction contracts. The bond begins with the salutation "Know All Men By These Presents" and this greeting is followed by spaces for the recording of the names of the principal, the surety, and the obligee. The face amount of the bond is then stated followed by the words "for the payment of which sum well and truly to be made, the said Principal and the said Surety, bind ourselves, our heirs, executors, administrators, successors and assigns, jointly and severally, firmly by these presents." After this statement space is provided for a brief description of the type of construction for which a bid has been submitted.

Following these preliminaries is a paragraph in which the essential nature of the agreement is recorded. The principal agrees, that if his bid is accepted by the obligee, that he will "enter into a contract with the Obligee in accordance with the terms of such bid, and give such bond or bonds as may be specified in the bidding or contract documents with good and sufficient surety for the faithful performance of such contract and for the prompt payment of labor and material furnished in prosecution thereof. . . ." If the principal fails to enter into a contract with the obligee and fails to provide the required bond or bonds, he is required to pay the obligee the difference "between the amount specified in said bid and such larger amount for which the Obligee may in good faith contract with another party to perform the work covered by said bid. . . ." The amount paid is not to exceed the face amount of the bond. If the principal carries out this part of the agreement or pays in accordance with the terms of the bond, the bond becomes null and void. If he does not, the bid bond remains in full effect, and the obligee may look to the surety for a proper settlement under the agreement.

Space is provided on the bond form for the signatures of the principal and surety and witnesses for the date of the agreement, and for a seal, if this is required by state law. To be binding the agreement should be signed by both the principal and the surety.

---

[3] G. W. Crist, Jr., *Corporate Suretyship* (2nd ed.; New York: McGraw-Hill Book Co., Inc., 1950), p. 22.

Performance Bond. A performance bond undertakes to guarantee that a contractor (or principal) will "promptly and faithfully" perform the duties specified in a contract entered into by him and the owner (or obligee). A bond of this type often enables a contractor to qualify for a construction project out of which he may make a profit. The owner or obligee in turn is assured that the contractor will perform in accordance with the plans and specifications and will in general complete the work according to the terms and obligations of the construction contract.

The bond form is similar to that of the bid bond. There is the usual salutation and place for the naming of the principal, the surety, and the obligee, as well as space for a recording of the face amount of the bond. There is space at the bottom of the form for signatures. After the usual and important statement that the contractor and surety firmly bind themselves, their heirs, executors, administrators, successors, and assigns, there is reference to the written agreement between the contractor and owner and the statement that this contract is made a part of the bond. There is space for a brief description of the type of construction and the address of the proposed building, as well as a record of the name or names of the architect.

The conditions surrounding the issuance of the bond are carefully set forth as follows:[4]

> Now, therefore, the condition of this obligation is such that, if the Contractor shall promptly and faithfully perform said contract, then this obligation shall be null and void; otherwise it shall remain in full force and effect.
>
> The Surety hereby waives notice of any alteration or extension of time made by the Owner.
>
> Whenever Contractor shall be, and declared by Owner to be in default under the Contract, the Owner having performed Owner's obligations thereunder, the Surety may promptly remedy the default, or shall promptly
>
> 1. Complete the Contract in accordance with its terms and conditions, or
> 2. Obtain a bid or bids for submission to Owner for completing the Contract in accordance with its terms and conditions, and upon determination by Owner and Surety of the lowest responsible bidder, arrange for a contract between such bidder and Owner, and make available as work progresses (even though there should be a default or a succession of defaults under the contract or contracts of completion arranged under this paragraph) sufficient funds to pay the cost of completion less the balance of the contract price; but not exceeding, including other costs and damages for which the Surety may be liable hereunder, the amount set forth in the first paragraph

[4] This wording is not standard and variations are to be expected.

hereof. The term "balance of the contract price," as used in this paragraph, shall mean the total amount payable by Owner to Contractor under the Contract and any amendments thereto, less the amount properly paid by Owner to Contractor.

Any suit under this bond must be instituted before the expiration of two (2) years from the date on which final payment under the contract falls due.

No right of action shall accrue on this bond to or for the use of any person or corporation other than the Owner named herein or the heirs, executors, administrators or successors of Owner.

The conditions as set forth fully protect the Obligee in the event of the default of the principal. Essentially the agreement is that if the principal carries out his obligation the bond becomes null and void; if not, then the Surety may take the specific types of action recorded in the above quotation, or other types of action depending on the form used.

Labor and Material Payment Bond. The labor and material payment bond is issued simultaneously with a performance bond and is designed to guarantee that the "Principal shall promptly make payment to all claimants . . . for all labor and material used or reasonably required for use in the performance of the Contract. . . ." In basic form this bond is similar to the bid and performance bonds and is sometimes included as a part of the performance bond. Except for the amount of the bond, which is often the same as for the Performance bond, and the condition of the obligation, the wording is identical to that used in the performance bond. Further, the labor and material payment bond is furnished free when a performance bond is bought.

If the principal makes the payments for labor and material as required under the construction contract, the bond becomes null and void. Otherwise the bond is operative and is subject to four conditions. The first condition[5] defines a claimant "as one having a direct contract with the Principal or with a subcontractor of the Principal for labor, material, or both, used or reasonably required for use in the performance of the contract. . . ." Labor and material include water, gas, power, light, and similar items to the extent that they apply directly to the contract. The second condition provides that any claimant who has not received payment within 90 days for work performed or materials furnished may sue for the amounts that are properly due. The owner or obligee does not have to pay the costs of the suit. The third condition sets forth the requirements that have to be met before a claimant may enter suit. No action may be commenced under the bond unless the claimant has given written notice to any two of the principal, owner, or surety "within ninety

[5] The wording quoted here is not standard and is often determined by statute. In Illinois, for example, on federal works projects the Miller Act rules.

(90) days after such claimant did or performed the last of the work or labor, or furnished the last materials for which said claim is made. . . ." A claimant having a direct contract with the principal need not follow this procedure. The written statement must state the amount claimed as well as name the person for whom the materials were furnished. The bond also prescribes the manner in which the written notice is served. A suit or action may not be brought after one year has expired from the date the principal ceased work on the contract unless there is a law governing the minimum period in which case the bond is brought into conformity with the law. Any suit or action must be brought in a "state court of competent jurisdiction in and for the county or other political subdivision of the state in which the project, or any part thereof, is situated, or in the United States District Court for the district in which the project, or any part thereof, is situated and not elsewhere." The fourth condition provides for the reduction in the amount of the bond in the event payments have been made to persons supplying labor and materials.

Court Bonds. Court proceedings very often require the placing of bonds. Court bonds are of two general types: (1) fiduciary, and (2) litigation. Fiduciary bonds are designed to guarantee the performance of those persons who care for the property of others such as executors and administrators; and litigation bonds are designed for various legal actions where a guarantee of the payment of court costs and damages is desired in the event a suit is unsuccessful. Court bonds remain in effect until the case is closed.

Fiduciary Bonds. Fiduciary bonds may be used in a variety of situations where persons acting in a fiduciary capacity are required to be bonded. Although sureties have their own bond forms, they are not often used because the form of the bond is usually determined by the court or by statute. The administrator's bond is an example of a fiduciary bond and seeks to guarantee that the person appointed to such a post will faithfully discharge his duties. The administrator is an appointee of the court and has the duty to conserve and to account for the assets of the deceased and to accomplish a proper settlement of the deceased's estate.

One form of the bond is not especially complex. After the usual greeting the names of the parties to the bond and the amount of the bond are stated with the proviso that "we bind ourselves, our and each of our heirs, executors and administrators, and the said Company binds itself, its successors and assigns, jointly and severally, firmly by these presents." The condition of the bond is that it will be null and void if the administrator performs his duties faithfully and obeys "all lawful decrees and orders" of the court of jurisdiction that apply to the settling of the estate of the deceased. If there is a breach of trust, then the surety will be called upon to respond.

There are spaces for the usual signatures and seal and in addition a place for the signature and seal of a notary public. A notary signs in two places. First, the administrator must appear before the notary, and second, the person who signs for the corporate surety must swear that he is authorized to do so and that the seal affixed is that of the corporation. He must also affirm that the liabilities of the surety do not exceed its assets, that it has obtained a certificate of solvency from the insurance commissioner which has not been revoked, and that he knows the assistant secretary of the surety who has also signed the bond and that this person is authorized to affix his signature. Also contained in the bond is a transcript of the resolution contained in the minutes of the board of trustees of the corporate surety that authorizes certain officers to act for the corporation.

Litigation Bonds. Litigation bonds are of various types, and the form of the bond varies throughout the United States and is usually prescribed by a court or other jurisdiction. Bonds may be required of plaintiffs or defendants. In the case of plaintiffs, the bonds may be, for example, cost bonds, attachment bonds, replevin bonds, sheriff or marshal bonds, or garnishment bonds. All states require a nonresident plaintiff to post a bond guaranteeing the payment of court costs, if assessed against the principal. Cost bonds are sometimes required of resident plaintiffs, although this depends on the state and the type of legal action. Attachment bonds are appropriate when the plaintiff wants to be certain that the defendant will not remove property, and wants to tie up the defendant's property at the beginning of a legal action. Replevin bonds are used when specific property is the subject of legal action or suit, and the plaintiff is given immediate possession. The replevin bond guarantees that the property will be returned to the defendant if the plaintiff loses the case. Sheriff or marshal bonds are appropriate in situations where a court officer may be held liable in the event he seizes the wrong property. In this case the plaintiff would have to pay the damages levied against the officer. Garnishment bonds are used when the property of a defendant is put in the hands of a third party.

The bonds that are required of defendants are such instruments as: release attachment bonds, counter replevin bonds, appeal bonds, and bail bonds. Release attachment bonds are appropriate when the defendant's property has been released from attachment by the court and he is required to post a bond guaranteeing the entire judgment and court costs in the event the plaintiff wins. Counter replevin bonds guarantee return by the defendant of specific property to the plaintiff in the event the plaintiff is successful in his suit. There is also a guarantee that court costs and other damages will be paid and that the property will be returned in the same condition. Appeal bonds are needed when the defendant appeals a decision to a higher court and is required to guarantee that he will pay the entire judgment plus interest and court costs. Bail bonds guarantee that the person posting a bond will appear in court at the time and place required.

License and Permit Bonds. Various governmental jurisdictions may require the posting of a bond before issuing a license or permit to engage in a particular type of business. Real estate brokers, plumbers, insurance agents, and security dealers are examples of persons who are required to obtain bonds. The nature of the guarantee provided by the bond varies from assuring that the business will be conducted according to governing laws, to protecting against physical damage and fraud.

FIDELITY BONDS

Fidelity bonds are "usually given in security of an implied obligation,"[6] such as the obligation of an employee to perform his work honestly. In recent years, embezzlement loss payments have been at an all-time high. Each year approximately $1 billion is lost by employers through the dishonesty of employees who take cash and merchandise that do not belong to them.

Fidelity coverages are a part of the corporate surety business. Fidelity bonds may be written to indemnify an employer who is either an individual, a firm, a corporation, or the public. Fidelity coverage may extend to include any loss attributable to a dishonest act of an employee, though there is a difference in the scope of the coverages as written. Fidelity bonds are classified as to extent of protection offered into those affording protection against (1) larceny and embezzlement, and (2) dishonesty. For the purposes of underwriting, bonds are classified as: (1) bonds required by private employers to cover loss through dishonesty of employees, and (2) bonds required of public officers for the faithful performance of their duties. As to form, bonds are written as follows: (1) individual bonds, (2) schedule bonds, and (3) blanket bonds. Schedule bonds are written as (*a*) name schedule or (*b*) position schedule. Blanket bonds are subdivided into (*a*) commercial blanket, primary or excess; and (*b*) blanket position. In addition, a large number of blanket bonds are written for financial institutions in which the fidelity coverage forms only a portion of the protection afforded.

Analysis of Fidelity Bond Form. In contrast to the direct obligation of the insurer under an insurance contract, in the surety contract the undertaking of the surety is secondary. The agreement is drawn in such a form that the surety is not liable until after the failure of the principal to perform a specified obligation. Failure may be

---

[6] Crist, *op. cit.*, p. 22.

occasioned by dishonesty, incompetence, or lack of resources. In the case of a fidelity bond, the bond undertakes to reimburse the obligee for loss of the money or property growing out of the dishonest acts of the principal. To prove a claim under a fidelity bond, it follows, therefore, that the principal must have been guilty of a dishonest act which is the cause of a loss to the obligee.

The two principal features of the fidelity bond are: the insuring clause, and the conditions and limitations. There is ordinarily no place for declarations. The statements upon which the corporate surety relies to issue the bond are included in an application and are not made a part of the bond.[7]

Insuring Clause. This clause defines the scope of the coverage. It names the party or parties bonded, the type of property insured, and the kind of losses covered. If the bond contains a restoration clause, it may but usually does not follow the insuring clause and appear just before the section devoted to conditions and limitations.

Conditions and Limitations. Here is to be found a statement concerning continuation of the bond. A definition of "employee" follows and any other definitions essential to the coverage. There are clauses dealing with limits of liability, other insurance, cancellation, loss, notice, proof, legal proceedings, and similar items. Certain of these clauses are common to all fidelity bonds, and there are clauses that are added to certain of these bonds where, because of the nature of the insuring clause, they are required to delineate the coverage completely.

Types of Fidelity Bond. The scope of the coverage provided by fidelity bonds is best delineated by considering the content of some of the contracts. Individual, schedule, and blanket bonds will be briefly discussed.

Larceny and Embezzlement, and Dishonesty Fidelity Forms. The larceny and embezzlement form is a restricted cover and limits indemnity of the surety to an amount indicated in the bond for losses growing out of larceny and embezzlement committed by the employee named in connection with his duties in a specified position.

In contrast to the more limited form, the dishonesty bond binds the surety to pay the employer for pecuniary loss sustained either of money or of property, including property for which the employer is responsible, growing out of fraud, dishonesty, foregery, theft, embezzlement, wrongful abstraction, misappropriation, or any form of dishonesty committed by the bonded employee while the employee holds any position at any location.

Individual Fidelity Bonds. Individual bonds, as the name implies,

---

[7] See discussion of commercial blanket bond and blanket position bond on pages 396–97 as an illustration of a situation in which the declarations are a part of the bond.

are written to guarantee the employer against loss growing out of dishonest acts of a named individual. An application is required of the principal, and on the basis of this application an investigation is made by the surety. If the risk is acceptable, the surety signs the bonds, and this in turn is delivered to the employer. In the beginning, fidelity bonds were all individual; and if there were a number of persons to be bonded in the employ of a given concern, a separate bond was written for each. The bonds ran for a period of one year, with the result that considerable confusion was experienced in keeping all employees covered and bonds renewed as they expired. To overcome this difficulty, the schedule bond was devised.

Name Schedule Bonds. The name schedule bond was the first of the schedule forms to be developed. It was a simple step to list the names of all the employees to be covered and provide surety protection in a single document. The name schedule bond, as in the case of the individual bond, guarantees the employer against dishonesty losses and extends the protection to all the employees listed in the schedule attached. The insuring clause indicates the acts of dishonesty to be covered and limits the coverage to the amount indicated in the schedule as applying to the particular employee concerned. The name of each bonded employee is listed in the schedule, and the limit for which he is bonded is set after his name. This permits compactness in the contract itself and, at the same time, flexibility in the amount of coverage. For example, the treasurer of a concern may be bonded on a name schedule bond for $25,000, while outside salesmen may be provided with satisfactory coverage in the amount of $1,000. As new employees are added to the staff, their names may be included in the coverage by endorsement; and if an employee severs his connection with the organization, coverage for him may be removed from the schedule upon notice to the surety. It follows that at any time the original bond taken in connection with endorsements showing additions and decreases will at all times indicate the names of the employees bonded and the amount for which each is covered.

As is the custom in writing schedule bonds, the persons named in the schedule are not required to sign the bond. Each employee is required to sign an application in which he agrees to indemnify the surety against any loss caused by him once his name is included in the schedule.

Position Schedule Bonds. The principal difference between the name schedule bond and the position schedule bond is to be found in the method of preparing the schedule. In the name schedule bond, defaults of persons designated by name are covered. Under the position form, instead of designating the persons to be covered by name, the list of positions appears in the schedule, and persons holding those positions are covered by the bond. This bond appeals particularly to business concerns having a considerable turnover in personnel. In the schedule, every position to be covered is listed; and if there are more than one occupying the same position, the number in that position must be listed. It would be logical that a schedule show the position of treasurer, but it might show 20 positions of outside salesmen. If there is more than one person concurrently occupying the same position, each must be bonded for the same amount. If the number of employees concurrently occupying a position is not correctly stated in the schedule, the employer is obliged to contribute to the loss to the extent that the bond does not cover every employee. If there are 20 outside salesmen and only 15 positions are listed on a schedule under this heading, in the case of a loss of $2,000 the bonding company will be liable for only three fourths of the loss since only three fourths of the positions are covered.

Under the position schedule bond, an automatic coverage is provided which protects the employer in the event that additional positions are added to the same designation as positions already included in the schedule. The automatic coverage continues for a period of 90 days. Within that time the employer is expected to file a written request that the new position be included in the schedule, and failure to do so will result in termination of the automatic coverage. New positions of a class not already designated in the schedule may also be automatically added, but in this case it is usual to set a limit for the liability of the surety. As before, the automatic coverage continues for a period of 90 days and is terminated at the end of that period unless written request for continuation is filed by the employer and the coverage accepted by the surety.

Blanket Fidelity Bonds. There are three classes of blanket bonds: blanket commercial bonds, blanket bonds for financial institutions, and public official blanket bonds. There are a number of different forms under the blanket commercial classification. These include: commercial blanket bond, and blanket position bond, both of which are designed for a wide number of commercial or industrial enterprises. There are, as well, limited forms designed for special types of business enterprises. In this category are to be found the insurance companies' blanket bond and the railroad blanket bond. Public official blanket bonds are written patterned after the commercial blanket bond and the blanket position bond.

Several of the bonds have features in addition to the fidelity protection. The fidelity feature of the comprehensive dishonesty, disappearance, and destruction contract (the 3–D policy) is a blanket commercial fidelity cover; but the contract is, in fact, a combination of coverages that may be purchased as separate contracts. Only the first insuring clause provides fidelity cover. The blanket commercial forms are fidelity coverages; but the blanket bonds for financial institutions contain, in addition to the fidelity feature, a number of other forms of protection written originally as separate insurance contracts. Additional coverages are afforded, as well, with the insurance companies' blanket bond.

Commercial Blanket Bond. The Commercial Blanket Bond is a commonly used type of bond and the form of the agreement is standard for insurers who are members of the Surety Association of America. A bond of this type is not issued to financial institutions or to public officials. The agreement is in four parts and consists of declaration, insuring agreement, general agreements, and conditions and limitations.

Declarations. The declarations consist of five items: (1) the name and address of the insured; (2) the bond period, which is continuous until canceled by the surety or obligee; (3) limit of liability; (4) riders to which the liability of the underwriter is subject; and (5) notice to the underwriter terminating prior bonds or contracts.

Insuring Agreement. The insuring agreement reads as follows:

> The Underwriter, in consideration of the payment of the premium, and subject to the Declarations made a part hereof, the General Agreements, Conditions and Limitations, and other terms of this Bond, agrees to indemnify the Insured against any loss of money or other property which the insured shall sustain through any fraudulent or dishonest act or acts committed by any of the Employees acting alone or in collusion with others, to an amount not exceeding in the aggregate the amount stated in Item 3 of the Declaration.

According to this agreement, the surety will respond even though the employees involved in the loss cannot be individually identified. Thus, the coverage is quite general and applies to all employees.

General Agreements. There are three general agreements applying to consolidation-merger, joint insureds, and loss under prior bond or contract. If additional persons become employees as a result of consolidation or merger, the insured (obligee) is required to give the insurer (surety) written notice and pay an additional premium computed on a pro rata basis. New employees not acquired by merger are automatically covered without additional premiums. More than one insured may be covered under the bond, and when this is the case, the first named "shall act for itself and for every other Insured for all purposes of this Bond." Likewise, knowledge possessed by any insured constitutes knowledge possessed by all insureds. The third general agreement sets forth the conditions under which this bond will cover loss sustained under a prior bond that was canceled at the time the present bond was substituted.

Conditions and Limitations. The conditions and limitations section of the bond contains 13 sections dealing with territorial limitations, exclusions, definitions, cancellation, limits of liability, other insurance, and similar items. Under "exclusion" it is stated: "This Bond does not apply to loss, or to that part of any loss. . . . the proof of which, either as to its factual existence or as to its amount, is dependent upon an inventory computation or a profit and loss computation. . . ." However, if the insured can prove apart from such computations, that money or property was lost from dishonest acts of employees, the bond will apply. Another limitation relates to employees and states: "The coverage of this Bond shall not apply to any employee from and after the time that the Insured or any partner or officer thereof not in collusion with such Employee shall have knowledge or information that such Employee has committed any fraudulent or dishonest act in the service of the Insured or otherwise, whether such act be committed before or after the date of employment by the Insured."

Blanket Position Bond. The blanket position bond is virtually identical to the commercial blanket bond. The contract form contains the same divisions and the declarations, insuring agreement, general agreements, and the conditions and limitations are, with a few exceptions, the same. The principal differences relate to the bond period and to the limits of liability. In the case of the commercial blanket bond, loss is covered under the bond "if discovered not later than one year from the end of the Bond period." Under the blanket position bond, the time period is two years. The bond penalty under a commercial blanket bond is aggregative with regard to any one loss, even though more than one employee is involved. The blanket position bond is a multiple penalty bond, and the amount named in the bond applies to each employee. The commercial blanket bond may be issued for a minimum of $10,000. Higher amounts are permitted, and no maximum is specified. The blanket position bond may be issued for amounts as low as $2,500 and will not be issued in amounts greater than $100,000.[8]

OTHER BLANKET BONDS

There are a number of bond forms that go considerably beyond the usual type of fidelity bond and provide insurance coverage for dishonest acts not only of employees but of other persons as well. These bonds are typically sold to financial institutions and undertake to provide broad coverage in the area of dishonesty risks.[9] Perhaps the best known of these coverages is the bankers blanket bond.

[8] See Long and Gregg, *op. cit.*, p. 818.

[9] See *Fire, Casualty, and Surety Bulletins* (Cincinnati, Ohio: National Underwriter Co., 1965). There are 12 different forms regularly used for insuring financial institutions of various kinds.

Bankers Blanket Bond. There are six forms of blanket bond that may be issued to banks. One form is written for savings banks only; another for Federal Reserve banks only; another for Federal Land banks; and still another for Federal Home Loan banks only. Two forms (Number 2 and Number 24) are available for commercial banks. The first of these forms (Number 2) gives limited protection against "dishonesty, holdup, theft, robbery, larceny and misplacement on the insured's premises and in transit, and burglary, damage and destruction on the premises." Form Number 24 provides the broadest protection.

The usual bankers blanket bond is divided into five sections (A through E). Section A is the fidelity cover; section B covers premises, "including premises of correspondent banks"; section C covers "in-transit" items; section D provides optional coverage "against forgery and alteration of checks, drafts and other instruments—not securities"; and section E is an optional coverage providing protection against forgery and alteration of securities. It is possible to provide coverage in some bonds for counterfeit money, redemption of United States savings bonds, and court costs and attorneys' fees by adding additional clauses.

The most comprehensive of the bankers blanket bonds cover under fidelity any dishonest, fraudulent, or criminal act of employees including directors "while performing the usual duties of employees or acts specified by the board of directors." Premises coverage is quite comprehensive under all forms and includes "burglary, robbery, holdup, theft, larceny, misplacement, mysterious unexplainable disappearance, and damage or destruction of property covered by the bond." Form Number 24 covers "property in transit anywhere in the world except while in the mail or a carrier for hire." Other forms (except Number 5) provide somewhat less complete transit coverage. Other details of coverage may be obtained through a careful reading of the various blanket bond forms.

The exclusions to be found in bankers blanket bonds are ones that are fairly common in insurance contracts. Losses from war and related perils are excluded with some exceptions, and both forms Number 2 and Number 24 exclude loss due to "windstorm, earthquake, volcanic eruption, and similar disturbances of nature."

COMPREHENSIVE DISHONESTY, DISAPPEARANCE, AND DESTRUCTION CONTRACT

The comprehensive dishonesty, disappearance, and destruction contract, familiarly known as "the 3–D policy," is designed to provide the broadest possible coverage for business firms. Since it combines in a single document coverages that may be purchased separately and at one time were available only as separate contracts, this form serves as an admirable vehicle for a more detailed consideration of certain of the dishonesty forms heretofore analyzed.

Dishonesty coverages may be broken down into four categories: (1) dishonest acts committed by employees (*a*) at insured's premises, or (*b*) elsewhere; (2) dishonest acts by nonemployees committed at premises of the insured; (3) dishonest acts other than forgeries committed away from the premises of the insured; and (4) forgeries wherever committed by either employees or nonemployees. The various exposures of an insured may be covered by individual contracts. By means of the basic 3–D contract and available endorsements, any or all of these exposures may be incorporated into a single document. Full fidelity coverage, as well as completed burglary-theft insurance, written in the 3–D contract makes available complete dishonesty coverage for the insured.

The basic form contains five separate insuring clauses. These are: (a) employee dishonesty, (*b*) loss inside the premises coverage, (*c*) loss outside the premises coverage, (*d*) money orders and counterfeit paper currency coverage, and (*e*) depositors forgery coverage.

In addition to the foregoing five basic insuring clauses, the following 12 coverages may be added to the contract by endorsement: (1) forgery insurance on incoming instruments; (2) burglary coverage on merchandise; (3) paymaster robbery coverage; (4) paymaster broad form coverage—inside and outside premises; (5) paymaster broad form coverage—inside premises only; (6) burglary and theft coverage on merchandise; (7) warehouse receipts forgery coverage; (8) securities of lessees of safe-deposit boxes coverage; (9) burglary coverage on office equipment; (10) theft coverages of office equipment; (11) paymaster robbery coverage; (12) credit card forgery coverage.

Any of the 17 coverages may be written alone. It is not required that the coverages be written for a uniform amount. The contract is flexible and may be adapted to the needs of the insured with each insuring clause written to provide a separate amount of protection with the premium adjusted accordingly.

Because of the breadth of this coverage, protection is extended to every conceivable type of dishonesty loss.

Form of 3–D Contract. The 3–D contract, since it incorporates both fidelity and forgery bond coverage and burglary-theft coverage, merges the salient features of both the fidelity bond and the burglary contract. The face of the contract contains the name and address of the insured and a space for inserting the limits of liability for the five coverages included on the basic form.

The contract does not have a uniform penalty applying to each of the insuring clauses; an optional amount may be elected to apply to each of the various clauses, subject always to the underwriting rules of the insurer. Moreover, the insured is not required to carry protection under all of the insuring clauses but may elect to adjust the protection under the contract to his own immediate requirements.

Insuring Agreements. Immediately following the declarations on the first page of the contract, there is a section devoted to the five basic insuring agreements. The coverage provided under these agreements is carefully described. Losses sustained through robbery of messengers including armored cars, as well as losses of money and securities and other property by safe burglary and robbery within the premises as well as damage to premises through burglary are covered. Additionally employee dishonesty, losses from counterfeit money, and fraudulently drawn checks are included as risks accepted by the insurer.

General Agreements. This section of the contract follows the insuring agreements and contains sections dealing with consolidation-merger, joint insureds, and a clause in which the bond assumes certain liabilities with respect to prior coverage.

Conditions and Limitations. The third part of the contract provides that the insuring agreements and general agreements shall be subject to certain conditions and limitations. There are 19 sections in this part of the contract. The first of these deals with policy period, territory, and discovery. Other sections have to do with such subjects as exclusions, ownership of insured property, definitions, requirement with respect to records, other insurance, and cancellation.

Insuring Agreements. The five insuring agreements available under the 3–D form and printed in the basic contract require careful study.

Fidelity Coverage. Fidelity coverage is available under one of two forms. The first of these forms, known as Form A, provides protection identical with that afforded in the primary commercial blanket bond. The alternative, Form B, provides fidelity protection identical with that in the blanket position bond. The clause here reproduced is from Form A:

I. EMPLOYEE DISHONESTY COVERAGE—FORM A

Loss of Money, Securities and other property which the Insured shall sustain, to an amount not exceeding in the aggregate the amount stated in the Table of Limits of Liability applicable to Insuring Agreement I, through any fraudulent or dishonest act or acts committed by any of the Employees, acting alone or in collusion with others.

The coverage under either form is complete and extends to cover any fraudulent or dishonest act of any employee. Inventory shortages are covered if the insured can conclusively establish a dishonesty loss. This means that not every shortage of inventory will constitute a loss under the form, but every inventory shortage that can be shown apart from an inventory computation or profit and loss computation to be attributable to the dishonest act of any of the employees is covered. All salaried or commissioned employees are covered. Reference to the definition of employee will indicate that brokers, factors, commission merchants, and certain others are not regarded as employees. Territorial limitations are given in Section One of conditions and limitations. It may be noted in passing that this insuring agreement is the only one that differs in the two contract forms. With respect to all other insuring clauses, there is no difference whatsoever.

Premises Coverage. This clause provides protection against destruction, disappearance, or wrongful abstraction of money or securities from within the premises. It includes, as well, loss or damage to other property by actual or attempted robbery or safe-burglary within the premises. The protection is identical with that supplied by the premises section of the money and securities broad form contract. The agreement, as it appears in the contract, follows:

II. Loss Inside the Premises Coverage

Loss of Money and Securities by the actual destruction, disappearance or wrongful abstraction thereof within the Premises or within any Banking Premises or similar recognized places of safe deposit.

Loss of (*a*) other property by Safe Burglary or Robbery within the Premises or attempt thereat, and (*b*) a locked cash drawer, cash box or cash register by felonious entry into such container within the premises or attempt thereat or by felonious abstraction of such container from within the premises or attempt thereat.

Damage to the Premises by such Safe Burglary, Robbery or felonious abstraction, or by or following burglarious entry into the premises or attempt thereat, provided with respect to damage of the Premises the insured is the owner thereof or is liable for such damage.

Losses due to any fraudulent, dishonest, or criminal act of an insured or an officer or other member of the organization are excluded under Insuring Agreement II. Notwithstanding this, the exclusion of "insider" or employee dishonesty losses does not extend to robbery losses or safe burglary losses, even though an employee or officer of the insured is involved. Another limitation contained in the exclusions section of the contract touches upon "the giving or surrendering of money or securities in any exchange or purchase" and excludes any claim based upon a loss attributable to the exercise of poor business judgment in making an exchange transaction or to accounting or arithmetical errors or omissions. This risk is held by underwriters to be uninsurable. Money is not excluded from coverage, but money in coin-operated vending machines and amusement devices is excluded unless the machine provides a method for recording the money deposited. The reason for this is obvious. It is the intent to cover money, but it would be impossible to pay a money loss attributable to theft from a coin-operated machine with no record or way of determining the amount stolen. Losses due to war and related perils are excluded, as is loss due to nuclear reaction, nuclear radiation, and related conditions.

Messenger Coverage. This clause provides protection for money and securities while being conveyed by a custodian outside the premises, as well as loss or damage to the wallet, bag, safe, or chest in which the money is being conveyed. The protection here is the same as that afforded by the outside section of the broad form and money and securities contract. The agreement reads:

III. Loss Outside the Premises Coverage

Loss of Money and Securities by the actual destruction, disappearance or wrongful abstraction thereof outside the Premises while being conveyed by a Messenger or any armored motor vehicle company or while within the living quarters in the home of any messenger.

Loss of other property by Robbery or attempt thereat outside the Premises while being conveyed by a Messenger or any armored motor vehicle company, or by theft while within the living quarters in the home of any messenger.

The exclusions are identical with those that apply to Insuring Agreement II. Reference to the definition of "messenger" will indicate the coverage is very broad, since "messenger" is defined to mean not only the insured or his partner but any employee of the insured authorized to have custody of the property outside the premises. The term "securities" includes negotiable and nonnegotiable instruments or contracts and includes revenue or other stamps but does not include money.

Money Orders and Counterfeit Paper Currency Coverage. This clause provides protection against losses that occur because of the acceptance of money orders not subsequently paid and because of the acceptance of counterfeit paper money. The agreement reads:

IV. Money Orders and Counterfeit
Paper Currency Coverage

Loss due to the acceptance in good faith, in exchange for merchandise, Money or services, of any post office or express money order, issued or purporting to have been issued by a post office or express company, if such money order is not paid upon prsentation, or due to acceptance in good faith in the regular course of business of counterfeit United States or Canadian paper currency.

Except for the general limitations in the contract, there are no specific exclusions that apply to this insuring agreement.

Except for the general limitations in the contract, there are no specific exclusions that apply to this insuring agreement.

Forgery Coverage. This clause provides forgery insurance on outgoing instruments. It includes the forgery of an endorsement and is identical to the depositors' forgery bond. The clause is a long one and only the first paragraph outlining the coverage is quoted here:

V. Depositors Forgery Coverage

Loss which the insured or any bank which is included in the insured's proof of loss and in which the insured carries a checking or savings account, as their respective interests may appear, shall sustain through forgery or alteration of, on or in any check, draft, promissory note, bill of exchange, or similar written promise, order or direction to pay a sum certain in money, made or drawn by or drawn upon the insured, or made or drawn by one acting as agent of the Insured, or purporting to have been made or drawn as hereinbefore set forth, including

a) any check or draft made or drawn in the name of the insured, payable to a fictitious payee and endorsed in the name of such fictitious payee;
b) any check or draft procured in a face to face transaction with the insured, or with one acting as agent of the Insured, by anyone impersonating another and made or drawn payable to the one so impersonated and endorsed by anyone other than the one so impersonated; and
c) any payroll check, payroll draft or payroll order made or drawn by the Insured, payable to bearer as well as to a named payee and endorsed by anyone other than the named payee without authority from such payee;

whether or not any endorsement mentioned in (*a*), (*b*), or (*c*) be a forgery within the law of the place controlling the construction thereof.

The agreement then goes on to state that mechanically reproduced facsimile signatures are treated the same as handwritten signatures. The forgery or alteration of checks, drafts, promissory notes, bills of exchange, or other negotiable instruments is covered. The forgery or alteration of registered or coupon bonds or the coupons of these obligations is not included within the scope of this coverage. As is customary with forgery contracts, the interest of a bank in which the insured has an account is covered. The insured has priority of payment over the loss of any bank. Losses whether sustained by the insured or by the bank are paid directly to the insured in its own name, except in cases where the bank shall have already fully reimbursed the insured for a loss covered by the contract. The liability of the insurer to the bank for forgery losses is part of and not in addition to the amount of insurance to which such loss would have been allocated had it been sustained by the insured without the involvement of a bank. In the event of a forgery involving an employee of the insured, the forgery section carries the loss unless it is in excess of the amount of forgery insurance. In this instance the forgery section pays until exhausted, and the loss in excess of the amount of the forgery insurance is carried by the fidelity coverage. Insuring Agreement V may be endorsed to exclude forgery by employees. When this is done, there is a 50 percent reduction in premium for the forgery protection.

FOR DISCUSSION

1. Banks ordinarily carry primary burglary and robbery coverage under the form known as a "banker's blanket bond." Banks that need more coverage than is provided under the blanket bond ordinarily carry a bank burglary and robbery contract as an excess form. The blanket bond covers against damage caused by actual or attempted burglary or robbery but does not cover vandalism or malicious mischief. How does this operate when the bank burglary and robbery is written as an excess cover?
2. There are a number of surety bonds in addition to the ones considered in this chapter. By consulting reference sources prepare a classification of the various types of surety bond and write a description of the main provisions of each bond that you include in your list.
3. Write a brief history of suretyship. Include in your discussion an account of the development of corporate sureties and analyze the operations of at least one of these organizations.
4. James Doe is a salesman for the Blank Manufacturing Company and has as his territory the state of Maine, with headquarters at Bangor. He is covered under a position schedule bond that covers 30 salesmen. A new branch is opened in the Middle West, and Doe is appointed sales manager, with headquarters at Chicago. Is the employer protected in the event that Doe is responsible for a dishonesty loss? Explain.
5. By means of a diagram, show how the following coverages operate: \$100,000 bankers' blanket bond as primary coverage; \$200,000 burglary and robbery insurance on money and securities at main office—excess over blanket bond; \$1 million robbery insurance on securities only at main office—excess over blanket bonds; and \$50,000 burglary and robbery on securities only at D Branch—excess over blanket bonds.
6. B has purchased a small brokerage business and has 15 employees. The employees have never been bonded before, and he decides to purchase a position schedule bond. Could he purchase such a bond on a discovery basis?
7. B is seeking employment with X, and X has learned that B has been involved in some irregularities with his former employer. He, therefore, decides to have B bonded but says nothing to the bonding company about his suspicions. Discuss.
8. X is an employee of the B bank. He is also a relative of one of the directors and a leading stockholder. A shortage is discovered for which X is responsible. The amount is comparatively small and is

immediately replaced. It is believed that X has learned his lesson and will continue to be honest in the future. Does this situation have any bearing upon the bond written for the bank?

9. Under the "General Agreements" in the 3–D contract are three sections dealing with consolidation-merger, joint insured, and loss under prior bond or policy. What are the essential contractual provisions contained in these three sections?
10. What are the meanings of the following terms as used in the 3–D contract: money, securities, employee, premises, banking premises, messenger, custodian, robbery, safe burglary, loss?
11. What are the duties and responsibilities of the insured under the 3–D contract after loss has been incurred?
12. State the provisions of the 3–D contract in respect to the following items: limits of liability, other insurance, subrogation, cancellation, assignment, and changes.
13. The following is one of the exclusions in the 3–D contract:

    "Under insuring agreement I, to loss, or to that part of any loss, as the case may be, the proof of which, either as to its factual existence or as to its amount, is dependent upon an inventory computation or a profit and loss computation; provided, however, that this paragraph shall not apply to loss of Money, Securities, or other property which the insured can prove, through evidence wholly apart from such computations, is sustained by the insured through any fraudulent or dishonest act or acts committed by any one or more of the Employees."

    What is the rationale of this exclusion?
14. Write a brief summary of the insuring agreements of the 3–D contract.
15. Distinguish between the commercial blanket bond and the blanket position bond. Under what circumstances is one to be preferred over the other?

PART III

LIABILITY INSURANCE AND ALLIED CONTRACTS

CHAPTER · 17

Liability Insurance Contracts

Every person is to some degree in danger of suffering loss because he may be held legally liable to pay damages because of bodily injury or property damage caused by his negligence. Liability for loss and damage may arise in manufacturing and construction operations, in the maintenance of property, in the operation or use of property—including one's home, in the course of rendering professional services, and while engaging in recreational activities, selling or serving goods, and entertaining guests. In fact, in business, recreation, or entertainment, casualties may and do occur giving rise to huge liability claims. If a negligent act or omission interferes with the rights of any individual, the party responsible for the negligence is liable for damages to the injured party. Liability claims (and consequently liability insurance) have become increasingly significant over the years both in terms of number of claims and in the amounts of the settlements. Liability insurance premiums written (other than automobile liability) were somewhat over $100 million in 1940, and by 1964 had reached approximately $1.10 billion. If automobile liability insurance premiums written were included, the total liability insurance premiums written for 1964 would be over four times as large.[1]

THE BASIS FOR LIABILITY CLAIMS

Liability claims arise basically because a person or other legal entity has acted negligently or has failed "to do what a reasonably prudent individual would ordinarily do under the circumstances of a particular case, or doing what a prudent person would not have done."[2] Determination of negligent behavior is basically a question to

[1] *Insurance Facts* (New York: Insurance Information Institute, 1965), pp. 13–15.

[2] L. E. Davids, *Dictionary of Insurance* (Patterson, N.J.: Littlefield, Adams, & Co., 1959), p. 146.

be settled through a legal process, such as a trial before a jury. The field of law involved is the law of torts (a tort is, according to Webster, a wrong act not involving a breach of contract) the precise nature of which varies among the fifty states. Kimball[3] suggests that torts may be classified as intentional torts, torts arising from negligence, and strict liability. Intentional torts are such items as assault or libel (which may be damaging to reputation); negligence actions arise from the failure to maintain appropriate standards of care; strict liability is illustrated by workmen's compensation laws, which place liability on the employer for employee injuries regardless of who is at fault.

Typically, insurance contracts are not available to protect against the financial consequences of deliberate torts. Since events to be insurable should be fortuitous, deliberate injuries fall outside the range of insurable risks. Negligent acts are generally insurable, and a wide variety of insurance contracts are available for risks of this type. Insurance contracts are available in situations involving strict liability, although the concept of imposing liability without regard to fault departs from the usual concepts of negligence and from the common-law notion that financial responsibility should fall on the person who caused the injury. The basic social reasons for departing from the common-law theory will be discussed in the next chapter.

In order for liability insurance to have maximum usefulness, it has become necessary to broaden the coverage to include many types of business and professional situations even though in some instances direct liability may not be involved. Liability assumed by contract is insurable, as is product liability and liability arising from the alleged errors and omissions of professional persons. Contracts are written on "contingent liability" which covers the insured in cases in which the liability might reasonably be expected to attach to another directly liable for the accident but when, because of the nature of the situation, the insured might still be held liable indirectly. Such a situation might arise in the relationship of contractor and subcontractor. A subcontractor might be liable for an accident, but the injured party, having no knowledge of the relationship, would in such case proceed against the general contractor.

In this chapter a number of liability insurance contracts will be analyzed by way of illustrating the basic principles of liability insurance.[4] But before undertaking this discussion, it is necessary further to explore the nature of liability claims.

---

[3] See J. F. Long and D. W. Gregg (eds.), *Property and Liability Insurance Handbook* (Homewood, Ill.: Richard D. Irwin, Inc., 1965), p. 449.

[4] Employer liability and liability arising out of the use of automobiles, aircraft, and other special situations are treated in separate chapters. See, e.g., Chapters 18, 19, 20, and 21.

NATURE OF LIABILITY CLAIMS

In the adjustment of both bodily injury and property damage liability claims, the claimant is not the insured. The adjuster, in representing the insurer, is not dealing with a customer of the insurer, as is the case in settling the usual direct damage property loss.

From the outset the fact that a liability claim exists carries with it a element of conflict with respect to the measure of damages. Mental attitudes frequently intensify the degree of conflict. Different individuals have a different approach and attitude to a given situation. The owner of a new Cadillac car may take great pride in its appearance. He might require a scratch on a fender to be removed at considerable expense even though the damage may not fall within the protection of insurance.[5] Such a man is a perfectionist. To another individual a scratch on the fender is but an incidental injury to be expected as part of the wear and tear attendant upon the use of the car. This second individual would neither spend a substantial sum to repair the scratch nor expect an insurer to do so. There are those who are unreasonable in their demands where insurance is involved. Frequently, for example, where a damaged fender could be repaired the insured will insist upon a new one. Again, the nature of the repairs required may depend upon the coverage. A scratch caused by a collision with a $50 deductible may concern an insured much less than would be the case if the loss may be brought within the full coverage of the comprehensive form. Finally, a difference in the attitude of a claimant from that of a defendant may be expected as a natural course with respect to the extent of the injury. This is particularly the case if bodily injury is involved. Persons involved in accidents tend to exaggerate the nature and extent of the injury, while it is natural for the person alleged to be at fault to discount or minimize its importance. In adjusting a claim or in a court action, such divergent opinions are not held to be motivated by dishonesty. They rather represent different approaches to a matter that does not lend itself readily to any accurate measurement. In settling such claims the insurance adjuster undertakes to make the best possible settlement on behalf of his insurer and his insured.

Measure of Personal Injury Liability. The determination of an adequate amount to compensate for a personal injury is not always a simple process. This statement is supported by the number of verdicts in widely different amounts for seemingly identical injuries. In no other area of loss adjustment are there so many imponderables and uncertainties. Even where all the factors are known and some of them are readily reducible to a monetary amount, there will be others

[5] For a discussion of automobile insurance see Chapter 19.

where the measure of damages will to a large degree be influenced by the fallibilities and prejudices that are characteristic of human nature.

While it is to be expected that a defendant in a liability suit will tend to minimize the amount of the value of a claim, and this is true of the insurance adjuster attempting to settle such a claim, the difficulties involved become apparent when disinterested witnesses, jurymen, and judges attempt to assign a monetary value to a severe personal injury. It can be argued that a disabling injury is the occasion of a more severe financial loss to a wage earner than to a housewife. Who can measure the loss of the housewife's care of small children? Who will differentiate with respect to the nature or amount of pain suffered? What impact will social position, financial circumstances, and reputation of the claimant have upon the amount of the settlement? Finally, what will be the contribution of the ability, resourcefulness, forensic talents, and persuasiveness of the claimant's attorney if the case goes to trial? All of these factors, particularly those that represent uncertainties, must be weighed by the adjuster in an attempt to reach a settlement that he feels he can conscientiously recommend to his insurer.

Injuries that involve primarily a loss of time are not too difficult to handle. The value of the time is easily ascertainable. The same is true with respect to medical bills and hospital expenses, if any. The area of uncertainty in such cases involves suffering and inconvenience. Since the claimant tends to be conscious of loss of time and out-of-pocket expenditures, when these are taken care of, particularly if the injury is not severe, no great difficulty may be anticipated in closing the claims. These cases are usually settled on the basis of a generally accepted formula. This gives consideration to wages lost because of the injury, wages that may be expected to be lost, age of the injured person at time of accident, number of dependents, amount of doctor and medical expenses, nature of the injury, extent of pain suffered (pain, suffering, and mental anguish), and social status of the injured person. For a person suffering from a broken leg where recovery may be expected, time lost, as represented by income lost together with expenses plus a settlement for suffering, is the usual measure of damages.

The situation is quite different with more serious injuries. In the case of death some states limit recovery by statute. In other states there is no limitation. Where there is a statutory limitation for death, the law may specify "instantaneous death." In such an instance claim may be made for the statutory limit for death with an additional amount, if the injured party is not killed instantaneously, for "conscious suffering." The amount to be claimed for conscious suffering will, of course, depend upon the magnitude of the injury and the length of time covered by the conscious suffering. Where death is not instantaneous, in addition to the statutory limitations and the award for conscious suffering, damages will include a sum for loss of wages, medical expenses, and the loss to dependents of the support of the deceased. Where the injured party lives and suffers permanent injury, the problem of damages becomes increasingly complex. A comparison of verdicts where cases have gone to trial affords only a partial solution. Some states are known as "low-verdict states," and the findings in these states vary substantially from those where the verdicts appear to be based upon a more realistic approach to the conditions surrounding the injured person.

What, for example, is the amount to be awarded in the case of a person who, as the result of his injuries, loses his mind and must be confined for the remainder of his life to an asylum? What is the measure of damages in the case of an injury where the mind is uninjured but the injured person will never work again? Take the case of a young man, 27 years of age, who lost two arms and one leg. In this case the court stated that if the courtroom were filled with gold as an award, no rational human being would change places with the injured. The court goes on to state that no one "would contend that such is the legal measure of damages."[6] These is no way exactly to fix an amount in such cases. The principal elements for consideration are: physical and mental suffering caused, and to be caused, by the injury; and partial or total impairment of earning capacity caused by the injury. With respect to the impairment of earning capacity, the law attempts to apply a measure of damages. This is predicated on the extent of the partial loss of earning capacity, the total loss of earning capacity, and the earning capacity of the injured person. These, it is pointed out, can be approximated with reasonable exactness. With respect to physical and mental suffering, the situation is not the same. It is difficult to put a monetary value on pain and suffering.

Measure of Property Damage Liability. The extent of a claim for damages for injury to property is measured by the amount of the loss occasioned the property owner. As a point of departure the same procedure is followed in measuring damages in third-party liability losses as is used in claims where the insured has suffered the damage. The measure of loss to any property is the difference in value between the property undamaged and the property in its damaged condition. While the cost of repair may serve as a measure of damage, there is no obligation to restore a property to its original condition if the cost of repair exceeds the value of the property before the accident giving rise to the claim. An old automobile virtually demolished is worth as a claim the value of the car before the accident less its salvage value. It

---

[6] *Heddles* v. *Chicago and Northwestern Railway*, 74 Wis. 239, 42 N.W. 237.

may cost considerably more than this figure to restore the car, but such a cost is not a proper claim for damages.

There is one point in respect to property damage liability claims that must be differentiated from direct-loss insurance claims. There is no limitation with respect to consequential loss sometimes found in direct damage contracts. It follows that in any liability damage claim loss of use may be a factor in determining the amount of the claim where this would not enter in the case of a claim made by an insured under a physical damage contract. In this last instance the liability of the insurer is limited by the contract coverage. In the case of a third-party liability claim, there are no limitations with respect to the makeup of a claim if the factors entering into it are attributable to a covered accident.

Review of Verdict. If a claim for damages, based upon negligence, goes to trial, the authority to fix the amount of damages rests almost entirely with the jury. The law establishes a safeguard against the dangers of excessive verdicts in that the judge of the trial court may set aside a verdict if he feels it to have been awarded under the influence of passion or prejudice. In the event of a motion for a new trial, the position of the trial judge has been likened to that of a 13th juror. He weighs the evidence, gives consideration to the credibility of witnesses, and attempts to resolve conflicts. If the verdict appears to be against the weight of evidence, the trial judge not only has the discretion but the duty to set aside the verdict on motion for a new trial. If the judge believes the damages awarded by the jury to be excessive, and the amount is questioned, it is his duty to reduce them. If the question of the amount of the verdict is raised, and the judge denies a motion for a new trial, this is held to indicate approval of the amount of the award.

In the case of an appeal from the findings of the trial court, there is a mistaken conviction that the appellate court may review the verdict and reduce it if it appears excessive. This is not the case. The denial of a motion for a new trial by the court is held to constitute judicial review and is frequently final. An excessive verdict cannot be corrected on appeal, except when the facts are such that the excess appears to involve a matter of law or suggests prejudice or corruption on the part of the jury. This is true even though the amount of the verdict is higher than an appellate court would have itself awarded. Unless intemperance, passion, partiality, or corruption on the part of the jury can be shown or the verdict is beyond all measure unreasonable, there is no hope of a reduced verdict on appeal.

GENERAL CONSIDERATIONS IN LIABILITY COVERAGES

A wide variety of liability insurance coverages is available to the prospective insured, and these coverages undertake to protect against the financial consequences of liability obligations of many types. Examples of types of coverage are: (1) contractual liability, (2) elevator liability, (3) manufacturers' and contractors' liability, (4) owners' landlords' and tenanants' liability, (5) owners' or contractors' protective liability, (6) product liability, (7) druggists' liability, (8) hospital professional liability, (9) miscellaneous medical professional liability, (10) physicians', surgeons', and dentists' professional liability, (11) lawyers professional liability, (12) errors and omissions liability for real estate and insurance agents, (13) comprehensive personal liability, (14) farmers' comprehensive liability, and (15) comprehensive general liability.

Before considering specific types of coverages, it is useful to review some contractual provisions that tend to be common to all liability insurance coverages regardless of the particular liability risk that may be under consideration.

Contract Form. As of February 1, 1966, a new format for liability insurance contracts was adopted which obviated the need for a series of separate liability insurance contracts. As in the case of homeowners and similar contracts, a contract jacket is provided "which contains the common provisions, definitions, and conditions."[7] The contract is completed by adding forms of standard provisions for such coverages as owners, landlords and tenants; manufacturers and contractors, and comprehensive general.

Liability insurance is generally written on a schedule basis or a comprehensive basis. In the case of the former, the coverages such as bodily injury, property damage, medical payments, and specified types of contractual liability, divided as to premises-operations, elevators, or other appropriate divisions, are listed and space is provided for stating limits of liability (each person, each accident, or a single limit) and for stating premiums. Thus the insured may select the operation for which he wants specified types of coverage. The comprehensive form provides protection against virtually all types of situations out of which liability claims may arise subject to certain exclusions. The new contract format enables the insured to combine schedule insurance with comprehensive insurance. Thus, schedule general liability insurance could be combined with comprehensive automobile liability coverage.[8]

Features Common to All Liability Contracts. The following common features may be noted:

Insuring Agreement. The insurer agrees to pay on behalf of the insured all sums which the insured shall become legally obligated to pay as damages because of the hazards insured against. In the case of

---

[7] See *Fire Casualty and Surety Bulletins* (Cincinnati, Ohio: National Underwriter Co., 1966). The new provisions became effective in most states on October 1, 1966.

[8] *Ibid.*

bodily injury liability, the coverage extends to include liability for care of losses of services for which the insured may be legally liable. Property damage liability, "which is defined as injury to or destruction of tangible property," specifically covers liability for loss of use of the damaged property.

Definition of Insured. Wherever the word "insured" is used in the contract without qualification, it includes any director, executive officer, stockholder, or partner of the insured, if the named insured is a corporation or partnership. It also includes "any organization or proprietor with respect to real estate management for the named insured." The coverage to directors, executive officers, stockholders, or partners applies only while they are acting within the scope of their duties as such. By virtue of this limitation a director, executive officer, stockholder, or partner of a business enterprise is not covered by the contract in connection with his general affairs. Coverage is specifically limited to acts performed in connection with the furthering of the interests of the business of the insured in his particular capacity. If the insured is a person, the contract covers the named insured, persons residing with him such as his spouse, and relatives of either, as well as anyone under 21 who is cared for by the insured.

Investigation, Settlement, Defense, and Payment of Cost. All general liability contracts provide that in addition to the payment of damages up to the contract limits, the insurer will also obligate itself with respect to the investigation and settlement of the claim, including defense of "any suit against the insured alleging such injury, sickness, disease or destruction and seeking damages on account thereof, even if such suit is groundless, false, or fraudulent." Additionally, the insurer agrees to pay premiums on certain court bonds, pay all expenses incurred by the insurer, as well as costs taxed against the insured, pay for first aid that may be essential at the time of the accident, and pay for expenses incurred by the insured at the request of the insurer.

Notice of Accidents. As in the case of other liability contracts, the contract provides that upon the occurrence of an accident, written notice shall be given by or on behalf of the insured to the insurer or any of its authorized representatives "as soon as practicable." The notice is required to contain particulars sufficient to identify the insured and also reasonably obtain information respecting the time, place, and circumstances of the accident and the names and addresses of the injured and of available witnesses.

Notice of Claim or Suit. If a claim is made or a suit is brought against the insured, the insured is required immediately to forward to the insurer every demand, notice, summons and complaint, or other process received by him or by his representatives. The word "immediately" takes on considerable significance. Any undue delay in notifying the insurer with respect to any legal action brought against the insured may seriously jeopardize his position with respect to the insurance.

Assistance and Cooperation of the Insured. The assistance and cooperation of the insured are required. The insured may not wash his hands of the claim once he has turned it over to the insurer. This clause imposes very definite obligations upon him to render every reasonable cooperation in connection with the settlement of a claim and to attend hearings and trials if required to do so. As before, the insured may not, except at his own cost, make voluntary settlements or payments nor assume any obligations or incur any expense other than for first aid that appears imperative at the time of the accident.

Action against the Insurer. "No action shall lie against the insurer unless, as a conditon precedent thereto, the insured shall have fully complied with all of the terms of the contract, nor until the amount of the insured's obligation to pay shall have been finally determined either by judgment against the insured after actual trial or by written agreement of the insured, the claimant, and the insurer." This precludes an injured party suing the insurer directly prior to an adjustment, and it precludes any legal action by an insured against the insurer until he has complied with all the contract conditions. After a settlement is made, any person or organization or legal representative thereof who has secured such judgment or written agreement may, thereafter, take action to recover under the contract to the extent of the insurance supported by the contract. If an action is brought against the insured and another person or organization, the contract specifically precludes any right of such person or organization to join the insurer as a codefendant in any action against the insured to determine the insured's liability.

The final section of this condition provides that bankruptcy or insolvency of the insured or of the insured's estate shall not relieve the insurer of any of its obligations thereunder. This clause now appears in all liability contracts. A strict contract of indemnity would relieve the liability insurer of any payment if the insured were bankrupt and unable to pay. As a matter of public policy the laws now require liability insurers to pay where liability is determined, even if the insured would not have been able to pay in the absence of insurance.

Other Insurance. The contract covers as contributing insurance if there is other insurance covering the loss. The contract contributes on an equal shares basis if the contracts are written on this basis in regard to other insurance. Assume, for example, the contract has an applicable limit of liability of $10,000. Assume two other contracts have like limits. That means that there are three contracts with an applicable limit of $10,000 covering on the loss. Assume the loss is finally adjusted for $6,000. Each insurer then would contribute $2,000 to the payment of the loss. When the insurance is primary, the insurer must pay according to the limits of the contract. There is no proration with excess insurance.

Subrogation. This condition protects the rights of subrogation of the insurer and places certain obligations on the insured to render cooperation with respect thereto. Subrogation gives the insurer whatever rights the insured possesses against responsible third parties. With respect to any payment under the contract, the insurer is subrogated to all the insured's rights of recovery. The insured is required to execute all papers required and to do everything that may be necessary to secure to the insurer such rights. It is important here to mention that any action that the insured might take in the way of executing releases that might defeat the right of subrogation of the insurer with respect to such claims would also jeopardize the insurance protection of the named insured and might provide a basis for voiding the coverage.

Contract Changes. It is provided that changes in the contract may be effected only by endorsement.

Cancellation. The usual cancellation clause provides that the insured may cancel the contract at any time on a short-rate basis. If the insurer elects to cancel, it must pay a return premium on a pro rata basis and give ten days' notice of cancellation.

Terms (Statutory Conflict). It is usual to provide that if any of the terms of the contract are in conflict with statutes of the state in which the contract is issued, it is automatically amended to conform to such statutes.

Declarations. The declarations are made a part of the contract either by means of the insuring agreement or as one of the conditions of the contract. When named in the insuring agreement, the insurer agrees, in consideration of the payment of the premium and of the statements contained in the declaration, to pay, on behalf of the insured, all sums which the insured shall become obligated to pay by reason of the liability imposed upon him by law for damages arising out of the hazards covered by the contract. A condition covering declarations provides that the named insured, by accepting the contract, agrees that the statements in the declaration are his agreements and representations; that the contract is issued in reliance upon the truth of such representations; and that the contract embodies all agreements entered between the named insured and the insurer or any of its agents relating to the insurance.

"Occurrence" versus "Accident." Formerly most liability contracts were written on an "accident" basis. As of 1966, these contracts are issued on an "occurrence" basis. An "occurrence" is defined as "an accident, including injurious exposure to conditions, which results, during the policy period, in bodily injury or property damage neither expected nor intended from the standpoint of the insured." By way of distinguishing between the two insuring clauses, an accident is defined as "a sudden and unforeseeable event." An occurrence may be any event. Thus, anything that happens is an occurrence. An accident must happen at a definite time. Thus, gradual damage cannot be construed as an accident. A contract written on an occurrence basis is broader than the contract covering damage caused by accident in that it provides for gradual damage.

A contract written on an occurrence basis covers injury caused by a lotion sold as a cosmetic. Damage from the use of a lotion is rarely instantaneous, though its use over a continued period might cause damage. Fumes escaping from a manufacturing plant might kill crops. Airplanes flying over a fur farm have frightened the animals and prevented breeding. There have been claims because of the lessening in value of property caused by a manufacturing process. There have been sickness and disease claims, the outgrowth of unsanitary conditions where no accident has been involved. Another example is to be found in claims growing out of the gradual pollution of a stream. Unquestionably, a contract written on an "occurrence" basis is broader than a contract written on a "caused by accident" basis, even with the limiting language that appears in the definition.

Exclusions. Liability contracts invariably exclude liability for injury imposed by workmen's compensation laws. This peril is covered by workmen's compensation insurance. There is also an exclusion extending to bodily injury, sickness, disease, or death of any employee while engaged in the employment of the insured. Such claims as do not fall within the purview of workmen's compensation are covered by employer's liability insurance. Liability assumed by the insured under any contract or agreement is excluded, except that some contracts provide a limited contractual liability coverage. Contractual liability may be covered by endorsement with respect to any liability contract. Elevator liability is excluded unless coverage is specifically provided in the declarations.

There is no liability with respect to the ownership, maintenance, or use, including loading or unloading of power-driven vehicles, draft or saddle animals, watercraft, or aircraft, though nearly all forms cover the premises hazard for automobiles and watercraft. Nor is there any liability for injury to or destruction of property owned, occupied, or used by, rented to, or in the care, custody, or control of the insured. Damage to buildings or their contents from causes originating within the premises, such as water damage that may be covered by water damage or sprinkler leakage insurance, is excluded. Injury to or destruction or premises alienated by the insured out of which the accident arises is excluded. The exclusions vary with the coverage, but the foregoing appear in one form or another in all general liability contracts.

Medical Payments. Medical payments coverage may be written with most forms of bodily injury liability insurance. The medical payments coverage in a general liability contract provides necessary medical, surgical, ambulance, hospital, professional nursing, and funeral expenses for a person injured or killed in an accident covered by the liability contract. The coverage provides a per-person limit, payable for injuries caused by an accident regardless of negligence on the part of the insured or on the part of his employees.

The payment is made regardless of liability, and no release is required of the injured party. The medical payments coverage, in addition to having a per-person limit, has a limit per accident. The limit thus established is independent of bodily injury liability limits.

Under the medical payments contract for general liability coverages, there is no coverage for injury to the named insured, any partner of the insured, or any employee while engaged in his employment. With respect to tenants there is no coverage for injury to a tenant or other person residing regularly on the premises covered by the liability contract; and there is no coverage for an employee of a tenant or resident while engaged in his employment.

TYPES OF LIABILITY INSURANCE

The broad scope of liability insurance is best illustrated by a consideration of some of the provisions of specific types of coverage. These provisions will be reviewed in the sections that follow:

Owners', Landlords', and Tenants' Public Liability Insurance. This contract assumes the risk for loss or expense, or both, resulting from claims upon the insured for damages on account of bodily injuries or death alleged to have been suffered by any person or persons not employed by the insured, if the occurrence is alleged to have been caused by reason of the ownership, maintenance, ordinary alterations and repair, or use of the premises occupied by the insured and described in the contract. Stated differently, the contract covers the insured's legal liability for loss or damage to persons or property arising through ownership or control of real property and arising out of the hazards listed in the contract.

The hazards mentioned and defined in the contract are premises, operations in progress, and elevators. The schedule type contract, formerly used has been abandoned. The premises-operation hazard includes "the ownership, maintenance or use of the premises, and all operations necessary or incidental thereto." Similarly the elevator hazard involves the ownership, maintenance or use of any elevator designated in the declarations.

There are four coverages in the typical owners', landlords', and tenants liability contract. These coverages are: (1) bodily injury liability, (2) property damage liability, (3) medical payments, and (4) contractual liability of a specified type.

Bodily Injury Liability. Under this protection the insurer agrees to pay on behalf of the insured "all sums which he becomes legally obligated to pay because of bodily injury, sickness, or disease including death" suffered by members of the public arising out of the hazards defined in the contract. To be covered, the injury must be the outgrowth of an occurrence while the contract is in force arising out of ownership, maintenance, ordinary alterations and repairs, or use of the premises described in the declarations. Protection is provided for operations carried on at and from the premises of the insured. Coverage, therefore, extends to accidents off the premises if caused by employees of the insured engaged in the same type of operation as conducted at the premises. Automatic coverage on newly acquired locations or undertakings is provided if the insurer is notified within 30 days after acquisition of the new risk. This feature does not apply if the insured is covered by other valid and collectible insurance.

Premises Property Damage Liability. Protection is afforded under this cover for legal liability for injury to or destruction of property, including loss of use. It provides property damage protection under the same conditions that bodily injury protection is afforded. Excluded are losses to buildings or contents caused by discharge, leakage, or overflow from plumbing, heating, refrigerating or air-conditioning systems, or from automatic sprinkler systems. Rain or snow losses caused by defective roofs, open window skylights, or the like on premises of the insured are excluded.

The contract is not limited to the use of business establishments but may be used in connection with the operation or ownership of any type of real estate. Apartment houses, for example, are a source of claim from falling plaster and similar accidents. Signs, pipes, dark stairways or stairways with insufficient guards, torn carpets or coverings, defective railings, and similar items are sources of other accidents from which claims may develop. All classes of property, not even excepting churches, have been the sources of very substantial claims.

Medical Payments. In addition to bodily injury and property damage liability, the contract agrees "to pay all reasonable expenses incurred within one year from the date of accident for necessary medical, surgical, and dental services, including prosthetic devices, and necessary ambulance, hospital, professional nursing and funeral services, to and for each person who sustains bodily injury, sickness or disease . . . arising out of the ownership, maintenance or use of the premises, or operations necessary or incidental thereto." Legal liability is not involved in this coverage.

Contractual Liability of a Specified Type. Certain types of contractual liability are covered as follows: (1) a sidetrack agreement; (2) an easement agreement in connection with a railroad grade crossing; and (3) an agreement required by municipal ordinance in connection with work for the municipality. The insurer agrees "to pay on behalf of the insured all sums which the insured, by reason of the liability assumed by him" under these agreements shall become legally obligated to pay as damages because of bodily injury or property damage liability.

Trustee's Blanket Liability Coverage. The protection afforded by this contract is the same as that coverage provided by the standard owners', landlords', and tenants' contract, with the addition of coverage for an insured who is interested as neither a beneficial owner or tenant. The trustee's blanket contract is useful not only to individuals acting in the capacity of trustees but particularly so to banks and trust companies. The contract is written to cover all properties held in trust at the time the contract is effected, and a special endorsement provides the same coverage on newly acquired properties and automatically excludes properties no longer held by the trust.[9]

Rates are based upon the manual rates for each property covered. There is no charge for including the trustee as an additional interest, and the charge for each beneficial ownership is indicated so that each estate may be charged with its proper portion of the cost.

Manufacturers' and Contractors' Liability Insurance. This contract is issued to provide protection for the manufacturer similar in nature to that afforded under the owners', landlords', and tenants' coverage but adapted to meet the needs of the manufacturer.

The manufacturers' and contractors' liability contract covers all premises and operations of the insured in situations where the insured may be held legally liable to pay damages because of bodily injury or property damage. Separate limits are written for each hazard, and it is optional whether the insured carries property damage coverage. The contract establishes a limit for each occurrence and an aggregate limit establishing the total liability of the insurer during the contract period. In the case of contracting operations the aggregate limit applies to a project.

Bodily injury liability covers the legal liability of the insured on account of bodily injury, sickness, disease, or death sustained, or alleged to have been sustained, by members of the public caused by an occurrence arising out of operation of the insured's business. The clause is extended to cover the legal liability for such accidents occurring in

---

[9] Because trustees have been held responsible for damages growing out of injuries caused by accidents involving property in their charge, the need for an insurance contract covering blanket the liability of trustees for all property under their control and management brought about the development of the trustees' blanket contract. The contract covers the liability of owners or beneficiaries or trusts and covers the trustees as an additional interest.

or about the premises described in the contract and includes accidents caused by the insured's employees in his business. It also covers losses (except automobile) caused by such employees while engaged in the insured's business away from the premises. Property damage coverage, when carried, provides protection of the same nature with respect to injury to or destruction of property, including loss of use of such property, for which the insured is held legally liable.

Employees are not regarded as members of the public while engaged in the performance of their duties, but it is possible for an employee to be injured on the premises in such circumstances as to be classed as a member of the public. Applicants for employment, visitors to the plant, salesmen, collectors, deliverymen, employees of contractors, children, and trespassers—all form a part of the public.

The insured is protected under this form against accidents that occur in the factories or other buildings, yards, and adjacent walks, whether caused by an act of an employee or otherwise in the course of the insured's business operations. Accidents away from the premises connected with necessary or incidental operations are covered.

Liability for accidents for which another form of insurance is designed is excluded. Such accidents are those caused by automobiles, or elevators. Accidents caused by the employee of a contractor or subcontractor are not covered.

Liability for accidents for which another form of insurance is designed is excluded. Such accidents are those caused by automobiles, or elevators. Accidents caused by the employee of a contractor or subcontractor are not covered.

When written to cover the liability of a contractor, the protection applies at specified locations, or a blanket contract may be written to cover all locations. Included in the contract is liability for loss when the accident is caused by the use of hoists, elevators (subject to exclusions), teams, or automobiles on the premises. Contractors engaged in road paving and street construction are protected in the setting up, taking down, and operation of the machinery and equipment used in their work while they are at the place and while they are being taken to and from the place of work. This includes such equipment as power shovels, concrete mixers, road rollers and graders, tractors, and other similar equipment.

Elevator Liability. The elevator liability contract undertakes to provide protection to the insured for his legal liability to the public growing out of accidents contributed to by the ownership, care, maintenance, or operation of the insured elevator. The coverage extends to claims originating in accidents to persons while entering or leaving the elevator or caused by elevator wells or equipment.

The elevator liability contract may be written to cover bodily injury liability, property damage liability, and collision. The first two of these coverages are liability forms. The third is a form of physical damage coverage and provides insurance against loss through accidental damage to the insured elevator.

The greatest source of elevator claims is found in elevators of the passenger-carrying type, such as those used by hotels, apartment buildings, office buildings, stores, and other properties where elevators are installed to carry members of the public. It is also true that in factories, warehouses, garages, and other properties where elevators are installed only for freight, accidents often occur which involve members of the public. In this respect is may be noted that bodily injury to any employee of the insured engaged in the course of his employment is not covered, and the insurance does not apply to structural alterations or new construction or demolition operations.

Elevator liability protection may be made a part of the owners', landlords', and tenants' form. The elevator liability is not so covered unless the elevators are described in the application for the contract and specifically written into the contract. If no owners', landlords', and tenants' contract is carried, the elevators may be separately insured under an elevator liability contract.

Accidental damage to the insured elevator itself is provided by an endorsement. This is known as the "elevator collision endorsement" and is made part of the liability contract. This is not itself a liability coverage, although it is written only in connection with property damage insurance and covers loss or damage to the insured elevator resulting from collision of the elevator or objects carried in the elevator with other objects. The coverage extends to indemnify the insured for loss or damage to other property owned, leased, occupied, or used by the insured if the loss is occasioned as the result of a collision of the insured elevator.

Collision coverage is not typically written as a part of the elevator liability contract. Some insureds are concerned only with bodily injury liability. If the insured carries property damage liability, he may have the coverage extended to cover damage to property of the insured including the elevator itself under the collision form.

Owners' or Contractors' Protective Liability Contract. This contract covers the insured for his liability claims growing out of work performed for him by an independent contractor. This contract is designed to provide owners of property a protection for the contingent liability that may develop as the result of an accident caused by the negligence of a contractor. Contractors purchase the coverage to provide themselves the same protection for claims that develop as the result of alleged negligence of subcontractors.

The owners' or contractors' protective liability contract is primarily a "defense" contract. There are numerous recorded cases in which judgments have been awarded against an owner or against a contractor when it would appear that the primary liability should attach elsewhere. Hence, the contract is used by contractors carrying on a big project in which substantial parts of the operation are sublet to other contractors. Members of the public frequently recognize only the general contractor and file their suit for damages against him; or, if they do recognize the subcontractor, they file a joint suit. The purpose of the protective liability contract is to provide defense for the general contractor in the event that he is drawn into litigation of this character. When, because of the surrounding circumstances, the line of demarcation of liability is not clear and judgment is rendered against the insured, the contract indemnifies him, subject to the contract limits, to the extent of the judgment plus expenses incurred in investigation and defense.

The protective contract, while primarily purchased for its investigation and defense provisions, provides direct liability protection in those situations where the law holds the owner or principal contractor liable in spite of the negligence of an independent contractor. These situations develop in connection with unlawful work, responsibility that cannot be delegated, and inherently dangerous work. The violation of a municipal ordinance bringing about an accident would fall in the first category. The principal contractor cannot delegate to others duty to the public, such as maintenance of a sidewalk in safe condition. Where an extremely hazardous operation, such as for example, blasting, is a part of an operation, the principal contractor may not escape responsibility for injury to the public on the ground that the dangerous work was let to a subcontractor.

As in the case of other liability contracts, the contract may be written to cover bodily injury liability with property damage coverage optional.

Principal's Protective Contract. This form provides insurance protection in an area where the liability is uncertain. There are business establishments that carry on their operations in such a manner as to leave the status of their operators in question. While from the point of view of the business they may be regarded as independent contractors, in some instances it is quite possible for determining liability that their status be construed as that of an employee. Whatever determination is made will require liability protection for the owner of the business establishment. If the status of the worker is that of independent contractor, the business, nevertheless, may be responsible to the public for his negligent acts performed in the course of his operations in behalf of the business.

For business establishments that employ canvassers and distribute their products under arrangements whereby the products are purchased by an individual and resold to the public, the principal's protective contract covers the insured whether the canvassers are determined to be employees or independent contractors. It accomplishes this by stating in the contract that the persons concerned are to be regarded as independent contractors or employees of independent contractors. The contract provides protection under two insuring clauses: liability to independent contractors, and liability for independent contractors. Thus, if the insured is held liable for injury or damages to a person described in the contract as an independent contractor, the insurance covers. If the insured is held liable for injuries to members of the public because of an accident arising out of the activities of his business operations carried on by a described independent contractor or his employee, protection is afforded.

The contract is tailored to meet borderline situations such as confront newspaper publishers in their distribution arrangements, as well as bakeries, ice cream manufacturers, milk distributors, and others who operate on a basis that is ostensibly that of an independent contractor.

Products Liability Insurance. Claims for damages caused by or alleged to be caused by the consumption, use, or handling of goods away from the premises of the insured are often excluded from the coverage of the public liability contract issued to merchants and manufacturers or is included in a limited way for an additional premium. To meet the needs of insureds in various lines of business, products liability coverage has been developed. Liability protection is provided under this form against loss caused by sickness or disability due to the consumption, handling, or use away from the insured's premises of any article manufactured, handled, or distributed by the insured. While bodily injury liability is the more usual form of protection carried, property damage liability is written if the insured requires this coverage. The protection is available as a separate contract or may be a part of another contract, such as the general liability contract, the garage liability, or the farmer's comprehensive personal liability contract.

The products liability contract covers claims for damage caused by mistakes, imperfect ingredients, or foreign substances, as well as improper handling, labeling, packing, or delivering. The contract does not cover products consumed on the premises of the insured, except in the case of restaurants and similar establishments, or any liability for injury to employees. Goods manufactured, sold, or distributed in violation of law are never covered. It is the intent to provide liability protection for defects, errors, or mistakes made in connection with the manufacture or preparation of products offered for sale. The protection extends to include losses attributable to defective materials. It is not necessary that the product actually be sold since injury attributable to samples or souvenirs is covered.

The contract covers only for amounts for which the insured shall become legally obligated to pay as damages if the occurrence causing the loss occurs: (*a*) away from the insured's premises, and (*b*) after the insured has relinquished possession of the product to others. The contract is written with three limits: (1) a limit per person, (2) a limit per accident, and (3) an aggregate limit. The limit per person injured in a given accident applies to each person. The per-accident limit fixes a total liability for claims from one common cause, such as from one prepared or acquired lot of goods. The aggregate limit is the total liability for all damages under the contract. Basic limits are $5,000 for each person, $10,000 for each accident, with an aggregate limit of $25,000.

Retailer Protection by Manufacturer. The manufacturer's contract may be endorsed to protect the retailer against claims resulting from the manufacturer's negligence. Retailers sometimes require this protection in connection with a sales agreement. Protection limited to the manufacturer's negligence is limited in its nature. Full liability for vendors of a manufacturer or distributor may also be written.

Purchase-order agreements are sometimes written with a "hold harmless" clause under the terms of which the manufacturer agrees to hold the retailer harmless for liability claims attributable to the handling of his product. The hold-harmless agreement is an assumed liability and excluded under the products liability contract. The contract may be extended by agreement to cover this form of assumed liability.

Completed Operations. The manufacturers' and contractors' liability contract excludes coverage on accidents that occur after an operation has been completed. Contractors have been held liable on the grounds of defective work after a job has been completed and turned over to the owner. Formerly products liability and completed operations were written together, but adverse court decisions brought about a separation of the coverages. Completed operations may now be obtained as a separate cover or as a part of the comprehensive general liability contract.

Contractual Liability. Since liability insurance contracts cover in general only against loss occasioned by legally imposed damages and typically excludes coverage when the liability is specifically assumed by the insured, it follows that in cases of assumed liability specific insurance is necessary if adequate protection is to be provided. The comprehensive liability contract automatically covers certain assumed liability, such as "switch-track" agreements, and other assumed liability agreements may be included by endorsement. Separate contractual liability contracts may be issued, but it is considered preferable to write contractual liability in connection with the liability coverage carried. When a contractual liability endorsement is attached to another liability contract, no additional insurance limits are provided, but the insurance protection afforded by the contract is extended over a broader area of risk. With a separate contract additional insurance for the contractual risk is provided.

Under the terms of the contract, the insurer agrees with the insured to provide liability insurance for personal injuries or property damage that may grow out of claims that the insured has agreed to assume. The contract covers only liability assumed by the insured under a written contract, and the agreement under which liability is assumed is identified in the contract usually by reference but in some instances a copy of the idemnity provisions of the contract is attached to the insurance contract. The party with whom the idemnity agreement is made is referred to in the contract as the "indemnitee." Any liability that the indemnitee may incur as a result of the operations of the insured and which is covered in the agreement between the indemnitee and the insured is included within the scope of the contract protection. The contract does not cover any liability assumed by the insured other than to the indemnitee indicated in the agreement. Further, professional liability insurance is not included under contractual liability.

This contract finds frequent use in providing protection for contractors who are required to assume the responsibility for all liability of a municipality growing out of his operations before a permit is issued to use city streets to store material, to bridge sidewalks, or otherwise to use the streets in connection with his operations. Again, it is the custom of railroads to insert a clause in agreements with property owners, when a siding or spur track is built for their convenience and use, requiring that the parties for whose convenience the siding is built shall assume all responsibility for injuries to persons or loss to property arising out of the use, existence, or maintenance of the siding. If the policyholder insuring his liability under an owners', landlords', and tenants' contract is not aware of the limitations placed on contractual liability and does not take steps to provide the needed coverage, he may find his insurance cover sadly inadequate.

The Comprehensive General Liability Contract. As one of the more recent developments in the liability field, property and liability insurers are now writing a comprehensive contract designed to include in a single contract insurance protection against all the noncontractual liability perils to which an insured may be subject. Contractual liability may be included through the use of a separate coverage part. Prior to the introduction of this contract, it was necessary for the insured, in building up his liability protection, to select such of the single peril contracts as he felt met his needs. The danger of this procedure is to be found in the possibility of gaps in the coverage of the contracts or of an unforeseen exposure for which no coverage has been provided. Finally, claims sometimes develop as the result of exposures that do not come within the scope of any of the named perils contracts. With a comprehensive contract, covering all public liability, the insured has the most complete liability protection that can be purchased.

The comprehensive contract is so broad that it covers virtually all third-party liability because of bodily injury, sickness or disease, and injury to or destruction of property. The contract provides full automatic coverage for all included exposures: that is, if a claim arises because of the acquisition of some property creating a liability peril subsequent to the writing of the contract, the coverage automatically attaches.

The contract is written to include the hazards ordinarily insured by the following separate contracts or endorsements: (*a*) owners', landlords', and tenants'; (*b*) manufacturers' and contractors'; (*c*) elevator; (*d*) contractual (subject to conditions noted above); (*e*) products and completed operations; and (*f*) protective. Provisions are also made for the "unknown hazard" when the insured may be subject to some peril about which he knows nothing or a peril which usually would not be covered by any named perils contract.

With respect to contractual liability (when included), the contract covers: warranty of goods or products; liability assumed under written lease, easement, or sidetrack agreements; written agreements required by municipal ordinances; and written escalator or elevator maintenance contracts. Other types of assumed liability are excluded. Forms not automatically covered may be included by endorsement.[10]

Exclusions under the contract have been reduced to a minimum. While all contracts are not identical, the following exclusions are found in one form or another: assumed liability as discussed above; employees of the named insured; automobiles away from premises; watercraft away from premises; aircraft on or away from premises; property in the care, custody, and control of the insured; and water damage liability including sprinkler leakage. Not all contracts include the water damage exclusion; but when water damage liability is not to be covered, the contract is endorsed accordingly. On the other hand, if the exclusion is found in the contract, water damage protection may be included by endorsement.

Automobiles away from the premises are excluded. It is expected

[10] In spite of the term "comprehensive" that applies to the general liability contract, there are limitations to the contractual liability coverage provided. The general liability contract may be indorsed, for an additional premium, to provide complete automatic contractual liability coverage. This point is important since the insured ordinarily assumes that the comprehensive liability contract covers all liability known and unknown. This is true regarding legally imposed liability, but true only with respect to liability assumed under a contract if complete automatic contractual liability is endorsed on the policy.

that the automobile hazard will be covered by an automobile liability contract. A comprehensive automobile cover may be included in the same contract that provides the comprehensive general liability, and where necessary other liability exclusions may be covered by endorsement. It is the intent to make the contract available as a combination of all the known liability contract forms that would apply to the risk plus an overall coverage designed to make the protection complete. An exception to this statement is that workmen's compensation and employers' liability protection are not included in the basic contract or by endorsement. The hazard regarding employees is covered under the workmen's compensation contract.

The relationship between comprehensive contracts and the more limited forms of liability insurance often causes a certain amount of confusion. In most forms of business operations the comprehensive general liability contract provides the broadest coverage. In order to save premiums or because of the nature of special needs, the less comprehensive forms may be selected.

Personal Comprehensive Forms. There are two forms designed to provide comprehensive liability protection for individuals. These are: the comprehensive personal liability contract, and the farmers' personal comprehensive liability contract. Both contracts are designed to provide comprehensive liability protection for a named insured and members of his household. There are certain hazards in the farm risk not found in the usual household, and the farmers' comprehensive form is adapted to them. The comprehensive personal liability contract is not written for farm risks. If the insured engages in farming and requires personal comprehensive liability protection, the farmers' comprehensive liability form is mandatory.

Both of these forms incorporated in a single document the risks that were at one time separately insured under such forms as the sports liability contract, residential liability, and a number of others.

In the liability insuring clause, the comprehensive personal liability contracts, unlike most liability contracts, cover under a single limit the liability of the insured for damage on account of bodily injury to members of the public and to employees and for damage to the property of others caused by an occurrence. The minimum single limit is $10,000, but, as in the case of other liability coverages, contracts for larger limits are written. The single limit represents the maximum liability of the insurer regardless of the number of persons injured or the extent of the property damage attributable to a single occurrence. The contract excludes assumed liability, but the exclusion states that the contract does not apply to liability assumed by the insured under any contract or agreement except liability assumed under a written contract relating to the premises. The intent of this wording of the insuring clause taken together with the exclusion is to provide protection to an insured who has assumed certain liabilities in a "hold harmless" clause under a lease.

The comprehensive contract provides protection for many types of losses that happen rarely but, when they do happen, may involve the parties in serious litigation and frequently heavy damages. For example, children playing with firearms sometimes shoot and kill one of their group. Injuries attributable to mechanical devices, such as lawnmowers, sewing machines, and power tools result in serious injuries to children. In the type of claim based upon the injury of children, there is the ever-present danger, in the absence of negligence, of liability under the "attractive nuisance" doctrine. The liability of a child for torts is not clearly established, but in most states responsibility attaches to the child sometime between the ages of five and seven. Injuries caused by children riding bicycles; throwing rocks; engaging in sports, coasting, Halloween pranks; and damage to parked cars—all may originate a claim. Whether the child is liable or whether the parent is liable, the ability to meet medical payments with insurance—with additional insurance to satisfy judgments if liability is established—is a source of satisfaction.

Comprehensive Personal Liability Contract. Under this form there are three basic coverages: (1) liability including bodily injury and property damage, (2) medical payments, and (3) physical damage to property.

The liability protection afforded by the contract covers an insured against claims from bodily injury to members of the public or to employees and from damage to the property of others. The liability is, therefore, a combination of public liability and employers' liability insurance within the limits of a single insuring clause. The employers' liability coverage provides protection for the insured but not benefit to the injured employee unless the insured is legally liable for the injury under the common law. Liability under workmen's compensation law is excluded; and, where such law applies, the risk should be covered by workmen's compensation insurance. The medical payments protection provides reasonable medical expense in connection with injuries to employees and to members of the public injured on the premises of the insured and elsewhere if attributable to the activities of the insured, to an employee while engaged in the employment of the insured, or to an animal owned by or in the care of the insured. The physical damage to property protection provides payment for loss to the property of others caused by an insured under circumstances wherein the insured is not legally liable. "Loss" means damage or destruction but does not include disappearance, abstraction, or loss of use.

Premises protection applies to accidents that happen on the premises of the insured, such as his permanent residence, whether a dwelling owned by him or an apartment that is rented; a summer cottage, whether owned or rented; and even a cemetery lot. The contract extends to provide protection for injuries attributable: to pets or the use of saddle horses, bicycles, and small boats; to sports, such as golfing, hunting, or fishing; and to any type of accident away from home for which the insured or any member of his household is held responsible. The contract covers liability of the insured and the members of his family and household for loss or damage the outgrowth of personal activities but not including losses attributable to an automobile accident off premises or to business or professional acts.

Business pursuits of the insured are not covered in the contract, but the contract may be extended to include them if the insured is employed on a salary, or operates a business in his residence. Medical payments coverage in connection with the business pursuits endorsement is optional.[11]

Farmer's Personal Comprehensive Liability Contract. This form is written with three insuring clauses: liability, medical payments, and animal collision.

The liability coverage affords not only bodily injury and property damage liability insurance protection similar to that afforded under the comprehensive personal liability form but as well provides product liability. The medical payments coverage follows the same pattern as that provided in the comprehensive personal liability form.

A new departure is found in the animal-collision cover. This feature is an optional cover. It is not, in fact, liability insurance but provides a limited form of livestock mortality insurance for the insured. The contract undertakes to pay the insured for loss by death of cattle, horses, sheep, hogs, and the like if death is caused by collision between the animal and a motor vehicle not owned or operated by the insured or by any of his employees. The animal collision applies only to animals killed in a public highway while not being transported. The protection does not extend to dogs. Animal-collision coverage is, in many respects, similar to automobile collision insurance in that it protects the property of the insured. Unlike automobile

[11] Comprehensive personal liability coverage may be endorsed on marine contracts. The combination of marine and liability coverage is based on the theory that the personal liability of an individual tends to follow his possessions. It is because of the existence of such possessions that the causes of accidents develop. It is logical, therefore, that the contract that covers the insured's personal possessions on an all risks basis might well be extended to provide personal liability on the same basis. The endorsement is available, of course, only from insurers that operate on a multiple line basis. Also, the provisions of the comprehensive personal liability contract are now a mandatory part of the various homeowners' contracts. The student should consider the contents of this section in their relationship to these contracts. The great majority of comprehensive personal liability provisions are also available for farmers and professional persons.

collision insurance, there is no liability for injury comparable to a partial automobile loss—loss by death only is covered.

Contractual liability with respect to liability assumed under written contracts with relation to the premises or with respect to warranties of goods and products is covered. Otherwise, as in the case of the comprehensive personal contract, assumed liability is excluded.

Employees on the farm are not covered. If coverage is desired, it is required that the employees covered be declared and employers' liability insurance protection be included in the contract. There is no liability or medical payments coverage applying to any employee who, because of his employment, is entitled to benefits under a workmen's compensation law.

Legal liability cover for damage to nonowned premises and furnishings caused by fire, explosion, or smoke loss caused by the faulty operation of a heating or cooking unit may be provided by endorsement. This protection appeals to tenants, particularly those who rent valuable seasonable properties. It protects them from damage suits growing out of injury to or destruction of home or home furnishings which have been rented to them if the loss is caused by one of the hazards noted.

Watercraft, with more than 24 horsepower or exceeding 25 feet in overall length, owned or rented to an insured away from the premises are excluded. As in the case of automobiles, larger craft are expected to be specifically insured.

The automobile exclusion states that the contract does not apply to automobiles while away from the premises or the ways immediately adjoining, except that liability and property damage protection covers with respect to operations by independent contractors for nonbusiness or nonfarming purposes. The wording of this exclusion makes the contract provide legal liability coverage for an insured if he is sued because of an accident involving an independent contractor, such as, for instance, a furniture mover using an automobile on behalf of the insured.

The fact that personal liability claims are infrequent tends to make the rate for the comprehensive personal liability forms moderate. The protection is a valuable one when a claim does, in fact, materialize. The modest premium prompts the purchase of this insurance, which provides protection against a very real possibility of heavy damages.

Comprehensive Catastrophe Liability Insurance. There is often need for liability insurance that will serve as excess over basic coverage or that will cover situations not usually insured under basic programs. Catastrophe liability insurance of this type is sometimes called "umbrella" coverage and serves to offer rather complete protection on a single limit basis in amounts that vary depending on the needs of the insured. A limit of $500,000 or $5 million or more is not uncommon. A typical, although not necessarily standard, insuring agreement provides that the insurer "agrees to indemnify the insured for ultimate net loss in excess of the retained limit hereinafter stated, which the insured may sustain by reason of the liability imposed upon the insured by law or assumed by the insured under contract. . . ." The situations for which coverage is provided under the insuring agreement are: (1) personal injury liability, which includes such things as bodily injury, sickness, disease, shock, mental anguish, false arrest, wrongful eviction, malicious prosecution or humiliation, libel, slander, and assault and battery not committed by or at the direction of the insured; (2) property damage liability, which includes "property of others in the care, custody, or control of the insured;" and (3) advertising liability "for damages because of libel, slander, defamation, infringement of copyright, title or slogan, piracy, unfair competition, idea misappropriation or invasion of rights of privacy arising out of the named insured's advertising activities."

As excess insurance the comprehensive catastrophe contract applies over, for example, automobile liability, products and completed operations liability, contingent liability, aircraft liability, watercraft liability, and premises-operations. In the case of liabilites that are often not included in basic programs, the catastrophe contract covers such items as personal injury, property rented or occupied, blanket contractual, water damage legal liability, and fire legal liability. Coverage is worldwide and applies "to occurrences happening anywhere during the policy period." Lack of territorial limitations tends now, as a result of recent changes, to be true of virtually all liability insurance contracts. Also, as is typical, the comprehensive catastrophe contract provides for legal defense including payment of premiums on bonds and other expenses.

There are not many exclusions. Obligations that the insured may have under workmen's compensation and similar laws are not covered, nor is damage to property owned by the insured. Also excluded is "property rented to, occupied or used by or in the care, custody or control of the insured, to the extent the insured is under contract to provide insurance therefore." There is a broad form nuclear energy liability exclusion and a war exclusion applying to occurrences outside the United States, its territories, possessions, or Canada.

Professional Liability Insurance. This type of coverage was first written to indemnify professional practitioners for loss or expense arising or resulting from claims on account of bodily injuries or death resulting from malpractice, error, or mistake committed, or alleged to have been committed, by the insured in the practice of his profession. Professional practitioners in every field find themselves defendants in heavy damage suits, and frequently the claims are made with a justifiable cause. More recently, professional liability insurance has been extended into fields to cover losses where monetary damages are a consequence of the professional services of the insured attributable to negligence and involving no bodily injury. The original malpractice contracts were written to cover physicians, surgeons, hospitals, and other medical practitioners. Contracts are now written to cover accountants, attorneys, real estate and insurance agents, surveyors, and morticians.

Malpractice liability—that is, the coverage written for doctors, hospitals, and other practitioners—indemnifies the insured, subject to the contract limits, for loss because of any legal liability for bodily injury or death and in addition provides for the payment of all costs of defense, investigation, and other expenses of settlement. Property damage insurance is not written under a malpractice coverage.

Limits of liability under the malpractice contract differ from the usual liability coverage. Standard limits are $5,000 and $15,000. In the case of the professional contract, the lower limit of $5,000 is the maximum liability under a single claim, and the upper limit of $15,000 represents, subject to the same limits, the maximum liability during the contract term. Many liability contracts set no limit for the contract term, but the upper limit applies to any single accident.

Insurers write malpractice liability under several different forms designed to meet the particular needs of a particular group. All insurers writing professional liability insurance do not issue contracts for all the covers. There are four professional liability programs for which the National Bureau of Casualty Underwriters exercises jurisdiction and for which standard provisions for professional liability contracts have been developed. These are : (*a*) physicians, surgeons, and dentists; (*b*) hospital; (*c*) druggists; and (*d*) miscellaneous medical. The professional liability contracts that provide insurance to indemnify the insured for monetary damages attributable to his negligence, in contrast to malpractice liability, are more in the nature of errors and omissions coverages. These contracts are not standardized, and in some instances they are available only from insurers that specialize in the coverage. There are contracts in this category offered to accountants, architects, adjusters, advertisers and advertising agencies, attorneys, collection agencies, directors of corporations, insurance brokers, agents and general agents, public notaries, real estate agents, stock brokers, surveyors, civil engineers, and title abstractors. Contracts are also written for the operators of beauty parlors and for morticians.

Druggists' Malpractice Form. This, as the name indicates, is a malpractice coverage but extends to provide, as well, a product liability coverage. It is, therefore, a combination of malpractice insurance and product liability.

The contract provides insurance against loss and expense arising or resulting directly from claims upon the insured for damages on account of bodily injury or death as the result of actual or alleged error on the part of the insured or his employees in preparing, compounding, dispensing, selling, or delivering any of the drugs, medicines, or merchandise customarily kept for sale in drugstores. Coverage is also provided for claims arising out of the consumption or use of beverages, food, or other products, including merchandise of every character. This extends to losses caused by errors in labeling or delivering. A claim originating because two correctly compounded prescriptions were accidentally exchanged in delivery is covered. Likewise, errors in reading or interpreting the physician's prescriptions and carelessness on the part of a clerk referring to a wrong number on a refill are covered.

The contract does not cover (*a*) bodily injury or death suffered by an employee of the insured in the course of his employment, (*b*) claims arising directly or indirectly from the wilful violation of a penal statute, ordinance, or regulation committed by or with the knowledge or consent of an insured or of a store manager employed by the named insured, (*c*) liability assumed by contract, and (*d*) damage to insured's own property or that in his care, custody, or control.

The exclusions for the most part are those to be found in all liability contracts and have to do with claims that are ordinarily covered by workmen's compensation insurance together with the usual exclusions covering assumed liability and property of the insured or that in his care, custody, or control. The exclusion in respect to claims attributable to illegality assumes some significance in connection with this coverage. For example, the illegal employment of clerks, sales of prohibited drugs, or sale of drugs contrary to statutory regulation, or the compounding of a prescription by a person other than one legally qualified, unless by an assistant in his presence and under his direction, will in each instance void the coverage so far as these acts give rise to claims. Violation of the Medical Practice Act by prescribing treatment or violation of the Harrison Narcotic Act or of statutes or ordinances governing the sale of alcoholic liquors has the same effect. If the insured or his manager does not intentionally violate the law, the contract protects him from the illegal actions of his employees who may knowingly commit an illegal act.

Coverage is on an occurrence basis. The injury to be covered must happen during the contract period, though claims attributable to the use of goods or products sold prior to the inception date of the contract, at the premises covered by the contract, are covered.

Hospital Liability. As in the case of the druggists' contract, this form is a combination of malpractice and product liability. It is designed for use by hospitals, clinics, dispensaries or infirmaries, convalescent or nursing homes, homes for the aged, mental-psychopathic institutions, sanitariums, and health institutions other than osteopathic hospitals, institutions, or clinics.

Coverage is provided for liability arising out of malpractice, error, or mistake made in rendering or failing to render medical, surgical, dental, or nursing treatment, including the furnishing of food or beverages in connection therewith. Product liability insurance is included, both on and off the premises, for drugs or medical, dental, or surgical supplies or appliances furnished or dispensed by the insured. Insurance is afforded for liability arising out of the performance of autopsies or other handling of deceased human bodies. Coverage includes bodily injury and property damage liability, but it is not limited to these. For example, a claim based on mental anguish would be covered. As in the case of the physicians' and surgeons' form, coverage is on an occurrence basis. The source of the claim must have occurred during the contract period, but there is no time limit on the appearance or discovery of the injury.

The exclusions are concerned with the following: (*a*) liability arising out of the performance of a criminal act; (*b*) liability on account of injuries to employees; (*c*) liability of an insured, if an individual, for his personal acts or omissions of a professional nature; (*d*) liability assumed under any contract or agreement; and (*e*) liability arising out of motor vehicles, watercraft, or aircraft.

Miscellaneous Medical Form. This coverage is provided by endorsing one of the other professional liability contracts. The contract to be used depends upon the professional classification of the applicant for insurance. The physicians', surgeons', and dentists' form is used to cover chiropodists, chiropractors, nurses, optometrists, physiotherapists, and veterinarians, whether self-employed or employed by others, and, when employed by others, pharmacists, opticians, dental hygienists, and laboratory, X-ray, or physiotherapy technicians.

The hospital form is used for blood banks and medical or X-ray laboratories. Proprietor opticians are covered by endorsement of the druggists' form.

The basic limits of liability for each of the four forms are $5,000 for each claim with an aggregate of $15,000 for a contract year. As in the case of other liability policies, increased limits are available.

Physicians', Surgeons', and Dentists' Malpractice Liability. This form provides coverage for liability arising out of malpractice, error, or mistake made in rendering or failing to render professional services in the practice of the insured's profession that are committed by the insured or by any person for whose acts or omissions the insured is legally responsible.

The insuring clause providing payment on behalf of the insured of all sums which the insured becomes legally liable to pay as damages because of malpractice or mistake is very broad. Any claim whatever arising from injuries either real or alleged comes within the scope of the contract. The insured is covered whether the act occasioning the claim is his own or the act of any assistant acting under the insured's instructions. An assistant need not necessarily be in the insured's presence to be deemed to be acting under the instructions of the insured. A specialist called in to cooperate in the care of a patient or to perform an operation is not an assistant. The contract covers such claims as loss of services of husband, wife, or other member of the family; errors in prescribing or dispensing drugs or medicines; and claims arising through the performance of autopsies. It also defends counterclaims in suits brought for the collection of fees.

Physicians and other professional practitioners have not infrequently been victimized by claims based upon alleged moral turpitude while engaged in professional practice. Such claims are covered by this contract, as are claims based upon undue familiarity, anesthesia, hallucination, assault, slander, libel, and malicious persecution. The contract also covers counterclaims in suits for collection of fees. In short, the contract covers claims for personal injury, for property damage, for care and loss of services, and losses of an intangible nature such as those just listed. The contract is a very broad professional coverage, but the contract is not broad enough to cover the personal liability of the insured for claims that cannot be traced to the professional practice of the insured.

The physicians', surgeons', and dentists' liability contracts, as usually written exclude liability for any partner of the insured unless the liability is specifically assumed. X-ray therapeutic work is specifically excluded under all contracts, although protection is obtainable through endorsement of the coverage on the contract with the payment of an additional premium. X-ray used for diagnosis and the taking of pictures does not fall in the therapeutic exclusion. The contract excludes claims in cases in which it shall have been legally established that the damage was caused by the insured, or any assistant of the insured, while under the influence of intoxicants or narcotics or while engaged in or in consequence of the performance of a criminal act. Finally, the contract excludes claims arising by reason of the liability of the insured as proprietor in whole or in part of any hospital, sanatorium, dispensary, clinic, or other business enterprise.

A feature peculiar to this contract is the requirement that the insurer secure the consent of the insured before compromising any claim. When the insured feels his professional reputation is at stake, he may require the insurer to resist the case to the court of last resort, even though the claimant offers to compromise on a basis satisfactory to the insurer. The insurer obligates itself to defend the insured's reputation at the risk of huge verdicts and to pay, subject to the contract limits, such award as may be made against the claimant plus the full costs of the defense.

Contracts are written on an occurrence basis with a limit per claim and an aggregate limit of liability for the contract period. The per-claim limit is in contrast to the per-person limit to be found in certain of the other liability contracts, and the aggregate limit has no reference to a single accident. Basic limits for which manual premiums are quoted are $5,000 per claim with a $15,000 aggregate. The premium is based on a flat charge for the insured plus other additional flat charges to cover professional assistance, if any.

In addition to the contract written for an individual, contracts are written to cover groups and partnerships.

Sports Liability Insurance. With the advent of comprehensive personal liability contracts, individual sports liability forms for nonprofessional individuals are seldom written. The comprehensive form provides sports protection. An insured conscious of the sports liability hazard is likewise interested in the broader protection furnished by the comprehensive contract. Sports liability contracts are still issued to professionals, since the comprehensive personal liability excludes business or occupational pursuits.

Employee Benefit Programs Liability Insurance. Employee benefit programs liability insurance is a fairly recent development in the liability insurance field and seeks to protect the employer against claims that may arise from the administration of employee benefit programs. Although contracts are not standard, a typical insuring agreement reads: (1) "To pay on behalf of the Insured, all sums which the Insured shall become legally obligated to pay on account of any claim made against the Insured by an employee, former employee or the beneficiaries or legal representatives thereof and caused by any negligent act, error or omission of the Insured, or any other person for whose acts the Insured is legally liable in the administration of the Insured's Employee Benefit Programs as defined herein. (2) It is agreed that in the event of a claim, $1,000 shall be deducted from the amount of each claim when determined, and the Company shall be liable for loss only in excess of the amount. . . ." The deductible feature contained in the insuring agreement is a fairly new concept for liability insurance, although it has been employed in various types of property insurance for many years.

Other features of the contract are similar to other liability agreements analyzed in this chapter. There is provision for defense, settlement, and supplementary payments; definitions; and conditions. Under the exclusions section it is stated that this contract does not apply "(1) To any dishonest, fraudulent, criminal or malicious act, libel, slander, discrimination, or humiliation; (2) to bodily injury to, or sickness, disease, or death of any person, or to injury to or destruction of any tangible property, including the loss of use thereof; (3) to any claim for failure of performance of contract by any Insurer; (4) to any claim based upon the Insured's failure to comply with any law concerning Workmen's Compensation, Unemployment Insurance, Social Security, or Disability Benefits; (5) to any claim based upon: (*a*) failure of stock to perform as represented by an Insured; (*b*) advice given by an Insured to an employee to participate or not to participate in stock subscription plans."

FOR DISCUSSION

1. X owns an apartment house, and he is advised that the law places an obligation upon him to keep his premises in a safe and suitable condition for those who come upon them or over them. B, a trespasser, is injured, and X claims that as to a trespasser he has no liability. Is that correct?
2. A fireman, while fighting a fire in an apartment building, fell off a defective stairway and was seriously injured. He sued the owner of the building for damages, but it was claimed that the fireman was injured primarily because of the fire. Would the liability of the owner of the property extend to the injuries of the fireman?
3. Frequently, in connection with the issuance of a license or permit, the municipal authority requires a bond which is designed to provide protection to the public in the case of injury. X claims that, in the circumstances, a liability contract is unnecessary. Explain the error of his reasoning.
4. B, in connection with a lease, assumes the liability of the owner of the property for any accidents that may happen during his occupancy. He purchases an O.L.&T. (owners', landlords' and tenants') contract but is told that he should also purchase a contractual liability contract. A friend, in an effort to save him money, advises that his present contract may be endorsed to make the owner of the building a named insured. What defect does this plan have?
5. Why is malpractice liability insurance as written for doctors sometimes referred to as "physician's defense" insurance?
6. What are the hazards confronting the operator of a drugstore, and what insurance is available to provide protection?
7. X operates a freight elevator in his premises, and its use is forbidden to all but employees. He states that his workmen's compensation contract covers employees and he, therefore, has no need for public liability protection. Is this correct?
8. B, a trustee for a large estate, claims that the estate has adequate funds to meet any claims for negligence and, accord-

ingly, a public liability policy is unnecessary. The reasoning is fallacious and may vitally affect B. How?

9. B goes to the store to purchase a loaf of bread. A loaf made by a large baking concern is delivered to him by the grocer in the original wrapping. A member of B's family is later injured by a pin found in the loaf of bread. B brings suit against the grocer, but the grocer contends that he gave B exactly what he asked for and that if anyone is liable it is the baking concern. Has B a case against the grocer?
10. X, a bottler of soft beverages, is sued because it was contended that B found a mouse in a pop bottle. It is pointed out that the efficiency of the manufacturer's machinery made it impossible for the mouse to get into the bottle in its plant. It is also pointed out that the cap could easily be moved after the bottle was outside the hands of the bottler. In your opinion, has the claimant a case against the bottler?
11. There is a case on record where a fisherman, when casting, caught his hook in the face of another fisherman, with the result that he was faced with a judgment in the amount of $12,500 for damages. Is this risk insurable?
12. Y, rushing from the building in which he was employed to catch a bus, collided with a woman walking on the sidewalk. She was knocked down and injured. Suit was brought for $15,000. Has she a claim and is the risk insurable?
13. C, a young woman, was paddling a canoe in a lake. As a result of a collision when the canoe was struck by an outboard motorboat she was thrown into the lake and seriously injured. Under what contract could the risk to the owner of the motorboat be insured?
14. A servant employed by B is knocked down by B's dog and injured. Is B responsible for the damage caused by the dog and, if so, can the risk be insured?
15. In a malpractice action brought by Mrs. X and her husband who claimed that Mrs. X was negligently treated at a clinic, three insurance contracts were involved. Each contract had a $50,000 limit of liability, one protecting the clinic and its partners individually and two (group form) separate certificates covering doctors. The clinic contract contained an "other insurance" provision; the group contracts had a similar "concurrent insurance" provision. All the contracts were in one insurer. The insurer contends its limit of liability to be $50,000, since one occurrence is involved. Is this correct? Explain.
16. How do you as an insured determine the upper limits of liability to be carried in connection with the liability risk of a specific business or profession?
17. X owns a department store and makes deliveries by truck. He carries an O.L.&T. contract with a $20,000 limit, and the truck is

covered with liability limits of $50/100,000. In delivering a roll of linoleum, the roll slid from the truck onto the ground. The driver was unable to move the roll and was assisted by a neighbor in standing it upright on the porch. Sometime after, the roll fell and injured a little girl. Claim was made for $200,000 and was settled before suit for $25,000. The insurer is willing to pay under the O.L.&T. contract up to the contract limit. What would you advise the insured?

18. The H Company operated a retail furniture business. It made a contract with the M Company to do repair work on its roof. The repairs involved opening the roof, and the repair company secured the services of a second company to close and seal the roof. The company that was to close the roof was slow in reporting, after notice, to the end that rain damaged the merchandise of H. Action was brought against M as the contractor responsible. M's liability insurer denied liability and was upheld by the courts. Why?
19. A boat owned jointly by X, Y, and Z foundered with a loss of 16 lives. The owners carried a general liability contract with limits of $100,000 for each person and $300,000 for each accident. As a result of the loss of the boat, suits amounting to several millions of dollars were filed. The insurer argues that after claims amounting to $300,000 have been settled, it owes no further obligation to the insureds. What is your opinion?
20. In the foregoing question, there are three insureds. They contend that each of them is entitled to the contract limit, and the aggregate coverage for all three, therefore, is $900,000. Is this contention sound?
21. With the same facts set forth in the foregoing questions, when it is apparent that the insurance has been exhausted, may the attorneys representing the insurer, in order to save defense expenses, undertake to negotiate settlements?
22. Indicate the type of business where the catastrophe owners', landlords', and tenants' hazard is great.
23. X is a contractor, and he carries a liability contract covering him and his business against liability imposed upon it by law for damages because of injury to property "caused by accident." The usual exclusion is found in the contract which provides no coverage with respect to property in the "care, custody, or control" of the insured. The insured while in the process of resurfacing the roof of an apartment building was unable to complete work on a partially finished job because of a snowstorm. After the work was interrupted the snow turned to rain. Water collected on the partially finished roof, leaked under the felts, and entered the interior of the building. There was serious damage to the interior of the building itself, as well as to personal property of tenants. Action was brought by the owner of the building and tenants against the contractor for damages. The insurer denied liability on the ground that the damage was not caused by an accident but was caused by improper workmanship of the contractor. It was also contended that the damaged property was in the care,

custody, and control of the insured. Do you think the insurer has a case? What is the position of the insured?

24. There is a record of two men moving furniture and fixtures into a store. While carrying a heavy piece of furniture up a flight of stairs, one of the men slipped and fell two stories. He was severely injured and brought suit for $35,000. Damages were allowed in the amount of $7,800. Insurance covered the loss. What contract is involved?
25. A young girl, passing a building in the business section of her community, was struck by a piece of masonry. She brought suit for $25,000, and the claim was defended and settled for $3,000. What kind of a contract did the owner of the building carry to secure this protection?

CHAPTER · 18

Employers' Liability and Workmen's Compensation Insurance Contracts

At common law an employer is liable to employees for damage due to injury when the negligence of the employer is the cause of the injury. The burden of proof in the case of accidental injuries rests upon the employee to show that there was negligence on the part of his employer, that this negligence was the cause of the accident, and that the employee was not guilty of contributory negligence.

Although the common law theoretically provided a satisfactory remedy for work injuries, in practice difficulties arose. Beginning with the decision of *Priestley* v. *Fowler* in 1837 and a number of subsequent judicial decisions that supported the decision in that case, it became more rather than less difficult for an employee to win damages in a negligence suit. As a result of judicial opinion employers acquired, in addition to the defense of contributory negligence, two additional defenses. It was held that when a servant has knowledge of the ordinary risks involved in his work, he is paid for assuming those risks and cannot recover for injuries caused thereby. The doctrine has been extended to apply in cases in which the employee continues to work without complaint after the discovery of failure on the part of his employer to afford proper protection. The defense against claims thus afforded is referred to as the "assumption of risk rule." The second acquired defense relieved the employer of responsibility when the cause of the injury was the wilful wrongdoing or negligence of a fellow servant. This defense is known as the "fellow-servant rule."

The difficulty of an injured employee's establishing a case of liability can readily be understood. Through statutory enactment and a tendency on the part of the courts to interpret the rules favorably to employees, the position of the worker has been considerably bettered. The class of fellow servants has been narrowed to include only those who work with the injured person, not the foreman or manager. A statute in 1856 abolished this defense in the case of employees of railroads. Other laws followed but were to a degree nullified by employers who required workmen to sign contracts releasing them from liability.

With the changes brought about by industrial development and the widespread substitution of machinery for hand labor, it became increasingly apparent that the problem of loss due to industrial accidents was still far from a satisfactory solution. In an effort to correct the situation, there were adopted by a number of states, employers' liability acts by which the position of the employee was immeasurably improved. These laws were followed by workmen's compensation legislation which completely revolutionized the law of liability as between employer and employee.

EMPLOYERS' LIABILITY LEGISLATION

Employers' liability legislation was the outgrowth of a recognition of the need of liberalizing existing law in favor of the employee. The English laws of 1875 and 1880 mark a turning point in liability legislation. Under the law of 1880 the employer was held responsible for defective machinery when it was the cause of an accident, as well as for the negligence of foremen and others in authority. The old rules of liability were otherwise broadened. This law is important as serving as a model for the laws subsequently adopted in the United States.

Employers' liability acts were fought every inch of the way in the courts, and certain of the earlier acts were declared unconstitutional on one ground or another. Defects in the earlier laws were corrected. The Federal Employers' Liability Act of 1906 was held unconstitutional, but upon its reenactment in a new form it was upheld by the United States Supreme Court. This law abrogated the fellow-servant rule and modified the operation of the rules of contributory negligence and assumption of risk. Finally, the law provided that contracts or other devices intended to exempt the employer from liability created by the act were void.

Employers' liability acts in all jurisdictions in the United States have now been superseded by workmen's compensation laws. Even though the liability acts were designed to improve the position of the employee, and in fact did accomplish this, they were, nevertheless, far from satisfactory. Negligence on the part of the employee was still a factor, and many accidents occurred where the employer's negligence could not be shown. Great expense was occasioned by both employer and employee in litigation, and the award of a jury in any case was beyond anticipation. Even when the legal liability of the employer was covered by insurance, the injured person enjoyed no benefit under the policy, and the insurer assumed the obligation of defending suits as a basis for determining the insured's liability, if any, to the claimant.

WORKMEN'S COMPENSATION LAWS

The theory behind workmen's compensation legislation completely disregards the old idea of liability based upon negligence. Rather, the theory is based upon the idea that neither the employer nor the employee is to be burdened with the cost of accidents, but that this cost is to be charged as a part of the cost of production to be borne by the consumer.

As a first step to the accomplishment of this end, compensation laws make the employer responsible for indemnity to the injured employee without regard to the matter of fault or negligence. The amount of indemnity to apply in particular cases is predetermined by the law and is sufficient to provide relief for the injured workman, although it does not equal the compensation received while employed. The laws undertake to make indemnities correspond to injuries; and if the injuries are fatal, benefits are provided for the employee's dependents.

Development of Compensation Legislation. Compensation laws are either compulsory or elective. A compulsory statute makes it mandatory that every employer within the scope of the compensation law accept the act and pay the compensation specified. On the other hand, an elective act gives the employer the option of either accepting or rejecting it, but with the additional proviso that he loses the common-law defenses of (1) assumed risk of employment, (2) negligence of fellow servants, and (3) contributory negligence. The differences in the laws are attributable to constitutional difficulties encountered in early legislation.[1]

Where compensation acts are compulsory, they do not ordinarily

[1] As of January 1, 1964, 30 workmen's compensation acts were compulsory. These are: Alaska, Arkansas, California, Connecticut, Delaware, District of Columbia, Hawaii, Idaho, Illinois, Maryland, Massachusetts, Michigan, Minnesota, Mississippi, Nevada, New Hampshire, New York, North Dakota, Ohio, Oklahoma, Puerto Rico, Rhode Island, Utah, Virginia, Washington, Wisconsin, Wyoming, Longshoremen's and Harbor Workers' Act, and United States Civil Employees Act. There are 26 acts that are elective. These are: Alabama, Colorado, Connecticut, Florida, Georgia, Indiana, Iowa, Kansas, Kentucky, Louisiana, Maine, Missouri, Montana, Nebraska, New Jersey, New Mexico, North Carolina, Oregon, Pennsylvania, Rhode Island, South Carolina, South Dakota, Tennessee, Texas, Vermont, and West Virginia. Some types of elective laws presume acceptance by employers or employees unless specific notice of rejection is filed. In the absence of this presumption, if the law is elective, the employer must accept the law in writing. Two of the compulsory laws, Arizona and New Hampshire, permit the employee to reject the coverage. In some states the laws are part elective and part compulsory. This is the case where laws are elective as to private employment and compulsory as to public employment. See *State Workmen's Compensation Laws* (Washington, D.C.; U.S. Department of Labor, Bureau of Labor Standards, Rev., 1964), Bulletin No. 212.

extend to include all employees or every class of injury. Domestic servants are almost universally an excluded classification and the employees of farmers engaged in farm labor generally fall into the same category. Some statutes provide that small establishments shall not come within the operation of the act. It may be provided that unless an employer has five or more employees he may elect to come within the operation of the act but is in no way penalized for failure to do so. The minimums vary with the different states. In 24 of the laws there are no numerical exemptions. In the remaining 28 jurisdictions the range is from two employees to 15. In states where voluntary acts are in force, the same exclusions generally apply.

Terms of the Laws. The earliest compensation laws were enacted to protect employees engaged in particularly hazardous industries. The trend of legislation has been such that the scope of benefits has been enlarged.

Compensation is provided for all accidental injuries and many occupational diseases arising out of and occurring in the course of employment. No benefits under compensation acts are allowed for the injury or death of an employee when it is proved that such was occasioned by the wilful intention of the employee to bring about the injury or death, or that the injury or death resulted from the intoxication of the employee while on duty. An exception to the regulation covering intoxication is sometimes made if the employer knew that the employee was intoxicated, or that he was in the habit of being intoxicated while on duty.

While the benefits differ in different states, there are points of similarity in all the acts. Definite schedules of benefits are provided for different types of injury. While in certain cases lump-sum settlements may be made, it is usual to provide for the payment of benefits on a weekly basis. To discourage malingering, the weekly benefit is set at a percentage of the injured employee's weekly wage. This ranges from approximately 50 to 90 percent of the average weekly wage, subject to a sum set as a maximum and another set as a minimum. Thus, a state might allow 66⅔ percent of the injured employee's average weekly wage, but would in no case allow a benefit in excess of $70 or below $30 per week. In most states the maximum benefit is below $50 per week for temporary total disability. Although 66⅔ percent is the typical percentage of the average weekly wage that is allowed, the operation of the maximum is such that many workers do not receive the statutory percentage. In only six jurisdictions are "maximum weekly benefits equal to two thirds of the state's average weekly wage." In 1963, "twenty-five states had weekly benefit levels less than 50 percent of the average weekly wage."[2]

---

[2] *Ibid.*, p. 34.

In order to eliminate the excessive expense of handling small losses and to prevent malingering when the injury is of no serious consequence, most laws provide a period of from a few days to two weeks during which no compensation is paid. This interval is called a "waiting period." Some laws provide that in cases of serious injury involving a protracted period of payments, indemnity shall be payable from the date of the injury, regardless of the waiting period.

An important feature of compensation legislation is the fixing with as much detail as possible the exact benefit due in each specific type of injury. Substantial variations appear in the provisions of the acts of the various states, but the following injuries or disabilities are usually specifically provided for: (*a*) fatal, (*b*) temporary total disability, (*c*) permanent total disability, (*d*) temporary partial disability, and (*e*) permanent partial disability. Some laws provide benefits in the case of such disfigurements as might be a handicap in securing employment, while others make provision for disability due to an occupational disease.

Medical benefits are provided in all jurisdictions for injuries covered by the workmen's compensation laws. For accidental injuries these benefits are unlimited as to time and amount in approximately three fourths of the states. The remaining states place limits on either time or monetary amount or both. In the case of occupational diseases about one half of the states place limits on the benefits. Wyoming is the only state that has no specific occupational disease coverage. Eighteen jurisdictions have a rehabilitation agency that is a part of the workmen's compensation agency.

The schedule of benefits does not appear in the compensation contract; but since the compensation contract incorporates by its terms the state act, the insurer is liable for whatever benefits are provided by the act in the jurisdiction in which the contract covers.

Covered Injuries. As compensation laws are generally worded, to bring an injury within the scope of the compensation insurance protection, it is necessary not only to show injury in connection with an accident but it is necessary also to show that the injury was "in the course of" and "arising out of" employment. There has been little difficulty in determining what constitutes a personal injury or what constitutes an accident. It has not always been easy to determine that the accident or injury was one "arising out of and in the course of employment."[3] The interpretation of the phrase has resulted in a mass

[3] "The statutory phrase 'arising out of and in the course of the employment' which appears in most workmen's compensation acts is deceptively simple and litigiously prolific." Mr. Justice Murphy in *Cardillo* v. *Liberty Mutual Insurance Company*, 330 U.S. 469, 67 Sup. Ct. 801. Again the point has been succinctly covered thus: "A few and seemingly simple words, 'arising out of and in the course of the employment' have been the fruitful (or fruitless) source of a mass of decisions turning upon nice distinctions and supported by refinements so subtle as to leave the

of legal decisions. It is the now generally accepted rule that if the employee's position or situation is such that it is a contributory or cooperative cause of the injury, then the injury is compensable.

Occupational Diseases. Occupational diseases are defined as "diseases peculiar to the occupation in which the employee is engaged and due to causes in excess of the ordinary hazards of employment." Within recent years, suits claiming compensation for diseases developing from exposure to chemical fumes, dust, skin abrasions, frostbite, to name a few, have come increasingly to the attention of employers.

Workmen's compensation acts treat occupational diseases differently. In some states, disease that arises out of, and in the course of, employment is covered by the act. In other states, the act so defines the term "accident or injury" that disease, unless resulting from accident or injury, is excluded. There are other acts which cover all, or some, occupational diseases by specific provision. In some states, only those diseases that are mentioned specifically by name or description or by designating the process from which they are contracted are covered. Thus, we have a situation in which all diseases are covered in some states. In other states, diseases are covered only if they follow an injury and in other states only specifically listed diseases are covered.

WORKMEN'S COMPENSATION INSURANCE

There is no standard workmen's compensation contract in the sense that a standard form is required by statutory enactment. Because of the diversity of the compensation laws as enacted in the various states, it was at first feared that a large number of different forms would be necessary to meet all requirements. This, the insurers feared, would create confusion, and in an effort to solve the difficulty the insurer executives undertook to develop a standard form sufficiently broad to meet the requirements of insureds and at the same time meet the legal demands in each jurisdiction. Insurance executives, after many conferences with representatives of the various industrial accident commissions, developed the form that came to be known as the "standard workmen's compensation and employers' liability policy." That the contract served well is evidenced by the fact that since its introduction it has been revised infrequently. A substantial revision occurred in 1954, which was designed to simplify and clarify the older form. The revision undertook to reduce to a minimum the

---

mind of the reader in a maze of confusion." *Herbert* v. *Fox,* A.C. 405, 419, 9 B.W.C.C. 164. A number of recent court decisions have awarded compensation under circumstances in which it would formerly have been denied; the definition of employment has been expanded to include leisure periods not directly connected with the job. For example, an award recently went to the widow of an auto salesman who died of a heart attack after dancing the twist at a company party.

number of endorsements that developments in the field made necessary with respect to the original contract. With the revision the majority of contracts may be issued to the average risk without endorsements. There are a few situations, due to statutory requirements, manual rules, or underwriting practices where endorsements are still required.

The Form of the Workmen's Compensation Contract. The standard provisions for workmen's compensation and employers' liability contracts follow the pattern of liability contracts with four main divisions: (1) declarations, (2) insuring agreements, (3) exclusions, and (4) conditions. Efforts have been made to follow the language of comparable provisions in liability contracts. This makes for consistency and contributes to the understanding of both forms of insurance.

Declarations. The declarations cover such pertinent information as the name of the insured, contract period, states where operations are carried on, and liability limits for employers' liability. Premium information and certain other data that may be required by the insurer appear here. Basically the declarations provide the underwriting data relied upon by the insurer for the issuance of the contract.

Insuring Agreements. There are four sections to the insuring agreements. They are designated by roman numerals and are known as Agreement I, II, III, and IV. Insuring Agreement I concerns itself with coverages known as coverage A and coverage B. Coverage A provides coverage for the insured's liability under the workmen's compensation law of the state or states indicated in the declarations, and coverage B provides an employers' liability coverage with respect to injuries arising out of and in the course of employment. Insuring Agreement II covers the matter of defense, settlement, and supplementary payments. Insuring Agreement III provides for definitions. Insuring Agreement IV is concerned with the application of the contract by limiting liability to disease or injury that originates within the contract term.

Exclusions. The exclusions, in the light of the importance of the coverage, are few. There are six in number. They are designed primarily to clarify coverage and to prevent overlapping.

Conditions. The conditions follow closely corresponding conditions to be found in contracts making use of the national standard provisions program for liability contracts. In some instances minor changes have been made in the interest of editorial consistency. Certain of these conditions have been discussed in substance in connection with the discussion of automobile liability insurance. Those that have particular application to workmen's compensation and public liability insurance will be considered in detail.

The Declarations. The page of the contract devoted to the declarations is divided into six items, number 1 to 6. Certain of the information common to all insurance coverages is to be found here. Other declarations are those peculiar to this contract.

Item 1. The first declarations call for the name of the insured, the address, and the form of business organization; whether the business is carried on as an individual proprietorship, partnership, corporation, or other form. Then are to be listed all usual work places of the insured at or from which operations covered by the contract are located. The requirement of listing "usual work places" calls for the listing only of permanent locations and does not require that every place where work may be carried on appear in the declarations.

Item 2. Here the contract period is given. The contract runs from 12:01 A.M. standard time at the address of the insured. This reference to the address of the insured as stated in Item 1 of the declarations is very important. In the case of a risk that extends to a number of states and includes more than one time zone, the time of an accident at the place of occurrence would not coincide with the time used to determine the inception and termination of the contract period.

Item 3. This is perhaps one of the most important of all declarations. It states that coverage A of the contract applies to the workmen's compensation law and any occupational disease law of the state or states listed. The entries on this item indicate the extent of coverage. By listing a state in Item 3 the contract extends to provide insurance for the entire liability of the insured under compensation and occupational disease laws of that state. The contract covers all operations of the insured in the state or states listed that are not specifically excluded or otherwise insured. In the case of a concern operating on a nationwide basis, Item 3 may list the states to be covered by inserting: "All states except. . . ." The excepted states are then listed. When this practice is followed, states with monopolistic state funds, states in which the insurer is not qualified to write compensation insurance, and states where the insured has not complied with the formal requirements necessary to bring himself and his employees within the provisions of the workmen's compensation law must be listed as exceptions.

Item 4. Here the operations of the insured are classified. The estimated total annual remuneration of all employees is given as a premium basis. The rates per $100 of remuneration are listed together with the minimum premium for the contract and the total estimated annual premium. The deposit premium is given. If premium adjustments are to be made on a semiannual, quarterly, or monthly basis, this is indicated. Contracts may be written without reference to an interim premium adjustment in the declarations by an endorsement known as the "periodical audit endorsements."

Item 5. A single limit is entered under this item to apply to the employers' liability feature of the coverage. Sometimes provision is made for a different limit of liability for certain operations, and in some states there are special requirements touching upon this matter. In such instances the limit of liability is clarified by endorsement. This limit applies only to employer's liability coverage and not to workmen's compensation. Compensation benefits are all fixed by the law, and the contract provides full coverage.

Item 6. This declaration may not appear in all contracts, since it is optional with the insurer. It is designed to provide notice to the insurer of locations not intended to be covered by the contract. It is to be noted that the listing of these excluded locations in this item provides underwriting information only. Actually to exclude a location not intended to be covered and not otherwise insured would require a contract endorsement. Some states require that the entire compensation obligation of an employer be insured in a single contract. Except where such a requirement exists, locations not intended to be covered, whether they are otherwise insured or not, may be excluded by endorsement. It is important to emphasize here that listing excepted locations in Item 6 is for the information of the insurer only and whether or not Item 6 appears in the contract locations otherwise covered by the contract may only be excluded by specific endorsement.

The Risk Covered. The standard workmen's compensation and employers' liability contract affords the insured a twofold coverage. It undertakes, first of all, to assume the insured's liability under the workmen's compensation law of the state or states in which the coverage is effective by reading the law into the contract. The contract in addition provides employers' liability coverage with respect to injuries arising out of the course of employment. The coverages are provided by insuring Agreement I and appear in two parts as follows:

I. Coverage A—Workmen's Compensation

To pay promptly when due all compensation and other benefits required of the insured by the workmen's compensation law.

Coverage A refers to the benefits of the "workmen's compensation law." This is defined in insuring Agreement III and applies with respect to the state or states indicated in the declarations. By inserting the name of a state in the declaration, the contract extends to cover the liability of the insured under the workmen's compensation law of that state. If a state has a separate occupational disease law, coverage A of the contract covers the liability of the insured under that law. In a state where there are separate laws for occupational disease and workmen's compensation, it is possible to use the contract to provide coverage only under the compensation law. When this is the intent, coverage under the occupational disease law is specifically excluded from the contract by endorsement.

Coverage B, which provides the employers' liability protection, appears in the contract as follows:

Coverage B—Employers' Liability

To pay on behalf of the insured all sums which the insured shall become legally obligated to pay as damages because of bodily injury by accident or disease, including death at any time resulting therefrom, sustained in the United States of America, its territories or possessions, or Canada by any employee of the insured arising out of and in the course of his employment by the insured either in operations in a state designated in Item 3 of the declarations or in operations necessary or incidental thereto.

Coverage B has the effect of providing protection for the employer, even though he may be operating under the compensation law, who may find himself faced with a common-law or employers' liability claim. It is quite possible that such a claim might be filed, particularly in those states providing employees with the option of coming within the operation of the compensation act. It is not altogether clear in some states whether the workmen's compensation acts have the effect of repealing employers' liability laws and terminating common-law liability, though this is generally regarded to be the case in most jurisdictions. In addition to liability coverage for injury, a broad common-law disease coverage is afforded. The word "disease" appears in coverage B and not "occupational disease." Thus coverages are afforded with respect to a liability claim attributable to any disease to which the employment may be alleged as a contributing cause. Coverage B has the effect of complementing the compensation protection and affords the insured the satisfaction of knowing that liability claims for injuries not covered by the compensation laws, even though groundless, will be defended by his insurer. Coverage B affords protection only with respect to injuries "arising out of and in the course of employment." This means that a claim for coverage must be traceable to the operations of the insured in a state specified in the declarations. Other claims would be covered by one of the standard liability contracts. To avoid duplication in coverage, there is usually an exclusion in liability contracts with respect to employers' liability. The exclusion in the liability contract specifically refers to injuries "arising out of and in the course of employment."

Since compensation benefits are fixed by law, there is no limitation with respect to them in the contract. A contract limit for coverage B is established in the declarations. A widely used limitation is $25,000, though for many business institutions this limit is not considered adequate. The insured may elect higher limits, but coverage B is always written with a definite limitation established in the declarations.

Defense, Settlement, and Supplementary Payments. This clause as it appears in the workmen's compensation and employers' liability contract is similar in effect to similar clauses in the liability insurance coverages. It appears in the contract as follows:

II. Defense, Settlement, Supplementary Payments

As respects the insurance afforded by the other terms of this policy the company shall:

a) defend any proceeding against the insured seeking such benefits and any suit against the insured alleging such injury and seeking damages on account thereof, even if such proceeding or suit is groundless, false or fraudulent; but the company may make such investigation, negotiation and settlement of any claim or suit as it deems expedient;

b) pay all premiums on bonds to release attachments for an amount not in excess of the applicable limit of liability of this policy, all premiums on appeal bonds required in any such defended proceeding or suit, but without any obligation to apply for or furnish any such bonds;

c) pay all expenses incurred by the company, all costs taxed against the insured in any such proceeding or suit and all interest accruing after entry of judgment until the company has paid or tendered or deposited in court such part of such judgment as does not exceed the limit of the company's liability thereon;

d) reimburse the insured for all reasonable expenses, other than loss of earnings, incurred at the company's request.

The amounts incurred under this insuring agreement, except settlements of claims and suits, are payable by the company in addition to the amounts payable under coverage A or the applicable limit of liability under coverage B.

As in the case of liability contracts, the clause obligates the insurer to undertake the defense of the insured and places the matter of negotiation and settlement with the insurer alone. There is the usual requirement to pay bond premiums and expenses incurred by the insurer in effecting a settlement. Likewise, the insurer is obligated to reimburse the insured for reasonable expenses incurred at the insurer's request. Amounts paid for bonds, investigations, and other expenses incurred in connection with a claim are all in excess of the limit of liability with respect to liability coverages and in addition to the amounts required to be paid under a compensation law. The insurer always pays the full amount of the benefits provided by the compensation law, regardless of the amount of expense incurred in effecting a claim settlement. If the action is brought under coverage B, the insured has the benefit of the full amount of the limit of liability for the adjustment of claims. Expenses incurred in effecting the adjustment are in excess of that limit of liability.

Definitions. The third of the insuring agreements is concerned with definitions. These definitions are closely coordinated with the coverages provided under insuring Agreement I. This agreement uses such broad terms as "the workmen's compensation law," "states," and "bodily injury by accident or disease." Insuring Agreement III clarifies the meaning of these terms with respect to coverage. It appears in the contract as follows:

III. Definitions

a) **Workmen's Compensation Law.** The unqualified term "workmen's compensation law" means the workmen's compensation law and any occupational disease law of a state designated in Item 3 of the declarations, but does not include those provisions of any such law which provide non-occupational disability benefits.

b) **State.** The word "state" means any State or Territory of the United States of America and the District of Columbia.

c) **Bodily Injury by Accident; Bodily Injury by Disease.** The contraction of disease is not an accident within the meaning of the word "accident" in the term "bodily injury by accident" and only such disease as results directly from a bodily injury by accident is included within the term "bodily injury by accident." The term "bodily injury by disease" includes only such disease as is not included within the term "bodily injury by accident."

d) **Assault and Battery.** Under coverage B, assault and battery shall be deemed an accident unless committed by or at the direction of the insured.

Definition (*a*) ties the term "workmen's compensation laws" as found in coverage A with the state or states indicated in Item 3 of the declaration. In other words, by the designation of a state in Item 3 of the declarations, the contract provides coverage for liability of the insured under the workmen's compensation law of that state. Moreover, if the state has a separate occupational disease law, by virtue of insuring Agreement III, coverage A provides occupational disease coverage. In the circumstances, in a state having separate laws for compensation and occupational disease, if it is the intent of the insured to provide coverage for accidental injuries only and not for occupational disease, the coverage not to be provided must be specifically excluded from the contract by endorsement. The definition of "workmen's compensation law" does not include the United States Longshoremen's and Harbor Workers' Compensation Act. It follows that no insurance is automatically afforded for the insured's obligation to employees subject to this act, even if the operations are carried on in the state designated in Item 3 of the declaration.[4] Finally, the

[4] Because of the wide difference in longshoremen's risks, they are not automatically included in the definition. The insurer is thus afforded an opportunity to underwrite maritime risks apart from other lines. If they are to be insured, such risks are included in the contract by endorsement.

definition states that it "does not include those provisions of any such law which provide nonoccupational disability benefits.[5]

Definition (*b*) makes the word "state" mean any state or territory in the United States and the District of Columbia. This precludes limiting the term to its more restricted use. Risks in a territory or the District of Columbia may be covered on the same basis as a state if listed in the declarations.

Definition (*c*) clarifies the meaning of "bodily injury by accident" and "bodily injury by disease" in such a way that there cannot possibly be any overlapping. This prevents accumulation of limits. Hence, it would be impossible under the definition for an injured employee to claim an accidental injury and then if a disease followed as a result of the injury to hold the insurer liable for an occupational disease. Under the terms of the definition any given injury must be one or the other but it cannot be both.

Definition (*d*) is usual to liability policies and provides that with respect to coverage B, assault and battery shall be deemed an accident unless committed by or at the direction of the insured.[6]

Application of the Policy. Insuring Agreement IV limits coverage by the contract to injury by accident or disease that occurs during the contract period and clarifies liability with respect to an occupational disease that has been developing over a considerable period of time. This agreement provides:

IV. Application of Policy

This policy applies only to injury (1) by accident occurring during the policy period, or (2) by disease caused or aggravated by exposure of which the last day of the last exposure, in the employment of the insured, to conditions causing the disease occurs during the policy period.

The first part of the agreement is simple and easily understood. It states that the contract applies only to an injury occurring during the

---

[5] By virtue of an extension of the New York Compensation Law, nonoccupational disability benefits are brought within the purview of that law. Whether other states follow or not, the clause is incorporated in the contract to exclude coverage for nonoccupational disabilities.

[6] An assault to be compensable, as in the case of all other accidents, must be one "arising out of and in the course of employment." The Court of Appeals in affirming an award to the claimant in *Heiz* v. *Ruppert*, 218 N.Y. 148, touched upon the necessity that the assault arises out of the claimant's employment in the following terms: "Altercations and blows may, however, arise from the act of a fellow-servant while both are engaged in the employer's work and in relation to the employment. The employer may be badly or carelessly served by two men engaged in his work, and yet it may be inferred, when one injured the other in a quarrel over the manner of working together in a common employment, that the accident arose out of the employment and was not entirely outside of its scope, if it was connected with the employer's work and in a sense in his interest." If the assault is not compensable and suit is brought against the insured for the purpose of coverage B, the assault is held to be an accident and the insurer will provide defense.

contract period. The second part requires a brief word of explanation. An occupational disease may develop over a long period of time. In the case of silicosis, for example, an employee may be exposed over a period of years. During this period of time the workman's lungs are gradually becoming affected. Finally, he becomes disabled. Insuring Agreement IV incorporates into the contract the obligation of the insurer to provide benefits. In a disease case, the insurer that is covering at the time of the last injurious exposure of the employee is liable for the benefits provided in the law. If A has been working in a granite quarry all his life and is now found to be disabled, even though several insurers provided coverage over the years, the insurer covering when the last injurious exposure developed assumes the liability.[7]

Exclusions. Exclusions in a workmen's compensation law cannot establish limitations with respect to the extent of coverage. They do have the effect of delineating the area of the coverage. There are six exclusions, and they appear in the contract as follows:

This policy does not apply:

a) to operations conducted at or from any workplace not described in Item 1 or 4 of the declarations if the insured has, under the workmen's compensation law, other insurance for such operations or is a qualified self-insurer therefor;

b) unless required by law or described in the declarations, to domestic employment or to farm or agricultural employment;

c) under coverage B, to liability assumed by the insured under any contract or agreement;

d) under coverage B, (1) to punitive or exemplary damages on account of bodily injury to or death of any employee employed in violation of law, or (2) with respect to any employee employed in violation of law with the knowledge or acquiescence of the insured or any executive officer thereof;

e) under coverage B, to bodily injury by disease unless prior to thirty-six months after the end of the policy period written claim is made or suit is brought against the insured for damages because of such injury or death resulting therefrom;

f) under coverage B, to any obligation for which the insured or any carrier as his insurer may be held liable under the workmen's compensation or occupational disease law of a state designated in Item 3 of the declarations, any other workmen's compensation or occupational disease law, any unemployment compensation or disability benefits law, or under any similar law.

---

[7] This is not the case in all states. For example, California and Connecticut, in occupational disease cases, require contributions from successive insurers of the same employee. In these states the contract is endorsed amending insuring Agreement IV, so that this contract condition complies with the state law.

The first of these is designed to prevent double coverage. Since, under the terms of the insuring agreement, the contract provides coverage for all operations within a state designated in the declarations, if an insured had more than one operation in a state each covered by different contracts, every contract, by virtue of its terms, would extend to each operation. Exclusion (*a*) has the effect of excluding coverage for operations in any state named in the declarations which are otherwise insured or self-insured. In other words, a contract taken out by an insured to cover a particular operation excludes any other operation in the state where other insurance is written or where the insured has qualified as a self-insured. If this exclusion did not appear, each contract would cover all the operations of the insured in every state named in the declarations.

Exclusion (*b*) has the effect of preventing coverage of farm laborers and domestic servants when coverage is not required under existing law. Secondly, it prevents the purchase of a compensation contract from becoming an automatic election by the insured to bring himself within the workmen's compensation law with respect to the types of employees mentioned. There are situations where an insured engages in a commercial undertaking and covers the operations of that business with a compensation contract. He may also have in his employ domestic or farm labor, but it is not his intention to cover such employees with compensation insurance. By virtue of Exclusion (*b*), the contract does not apply to any domestic, farm, or agricultural employment not described in the declaration unless by law the contract is required to apply to such employment. If the insured wishes employees in these categories to be covered, this is accomplished by including them in the declarations.

Exclusion (*c*) applies only with respect to coverage B. It is the usual exclusion found in all contracts covering liability imposed by law and excludes liability assumed by the insured under any contract or agreement.

The contract is designed to provide insurance protection for the insured for his liability growing out of industrial accident or disease. An illegal act of the insured is not within the purview of such coverage. Under exclusion (*d*) there is no liability under coverage B if the claim is attributable to a violation of the law.[8]

Exclusion (*e*) sets up a time limit for bringing occupational disease claims under coverage B.[9] This is, in fact, a liberalization of the older

[8] For the application of the contract with respect to illegal acts as they apply to coverage A, see discussion of statutory provisions on page 465.

[9] Prior to the adoption of the standard provisions for workmen's compensation and employers' liability contracts that are now in use, occupational disease coverage was provided by means of an endorsement attached to the standard contract. This endorsement provided that no employers' liability for disease was afforded unless incapacity from such disease developed within 12 months after the end of the

contract form. Protection is provided for a full three-year period after the end of the contract term.

Exclusion (*f*) accomplishes two purposes. Coverage A undertakes to pay promptly, when due, benefits required of the insured under the workmen's compensation law and coverage B undertakes to pay on behalf of the insured "all sums which the insured shall become legally obligated to pay as damages because of bodily injury by accident or disease." Exclusion (*f*) prevents the assumption under coverage B of liability that is properly the subject of coverage A. If one of the states named in the declaration has an unemployment compensation or a disability law not attributable to employment, such benefits are not within the purview of the coverage.[10]

Premium. Compensation premiums are computed as a percentage of the payroll of the insured. The premium that an employer must pay for his workmen's compensation coverage depends on (1) the classification of business operations, and (2) the total amount of remuneration paid. This information is found in the declarations. Condition 1 of the contract deals with the manner of premium computation. It is a rather long condition of five paragraphs. The first of these incorporates by reference "the manuals in use by the company" as follows:

> The premium bases and rates for the classifications of operations described in the declarations are as stated therein and for classifications not so described are those applicable in accordance with the manuals in use by the company. This policy is issued by the company and accepted by the insured with the agreement that if any change in classifications, rates or rating plans is or becomes applicable to this policy under any law regulating this insurance or because of any amendments affecting the benefits provided by the workmen's compensation law, such change with the effective date thereof shall be stated in an endorsement issued to form a part of this policy.

By virtue of this clause the preparation of the contract is enormously simplified. If an employer should carry on operations not mentioned in the declarations, it is clear that the premium will be computed for those operations by the use of manual rates. The insured, moreover, agrees that any change in classifications, rates, or rating plans or any changes in benefits provided by the workmen's compensation law all become a part of the contract and effective by the issuance of an endorsement by the insurer.

---

contract period. Instead there is now no requirement that incapacity be shown after 12 months, but exclusion (*e*) does rule out coverage for disease claims under coverage B unless brought within 36 months after the contract period.

[10] The definition of the term "workmen's compensation law" excludes nonoccupational disability benefits. Exclusion (*f*) in the contract has the same effect with respect to coverage B.

The second paragraph of Condition 1 then goes on to describe what is meant by "remuneration." This appears in the contract as follows:

> When used as a premium basis, "remuneration" means the entire remuneration, computed in accordance with the manuals in use by the company, earned during the policy period by (a) all executive officers and other employees of the insured engaged in operations covered by this policy, and (b) any other person performing work which may render the company liable under this policy for injury to or death of such person in accordance with the workmen's compensation law. "Remuneration" shall not include the remuneration of any person within division (b) foregoing if the insured maintains evidence satisfactory to the company that the payment of compensation and other benefits under such law to such person is secured by other valid and collectible insurance or by any other undertaking approved by the governmental agency having jurisdiction thereof.

This part of the condition is easy to understand. Sometimes there are those who feel that the payroll of officers of a corporation should not be included in determining the compensation premium. Unless otherwise provided by endorsement, the contract provides specifically that the renumeration of all employees *engaged in operations covered by the contract*, whether executive officers or not, shall be included in the payroll submitted for determining the compensation premium. A maximum of $300 per week is considered as remuneration of corporate officers and other employees.

The second section of the paragraph includes all other persons "which may render the company liable under this policy for injury to or death of such person." This would mean, for example, that if an employer sublet work to a subcontractor he must include the payroll of that subcontractor in his compensation premium unless that subcontractor already carries compensation insurance. This exception is set forth in the latter part of the paragraph. The paragraph provides that the insurer shall be entitled to a premium based on every dollar of remuneration paid to employees who will have a right to benefit under the compensation law of the state in which the operations are carried on.

Workmen's compensation premiums, since they are based on the payroll, cannot be computed until the end of the contract term. The contract is written with an estimated payroll. At the end of the contract term an audit is made, and if the estimated premium is in excess of the actual premium developed by the audit, the difference is returned to the insured. If the estimated premium is less than the premium developed by the audit, the insured is billed for the difference. If the risk is a particularly large one, arrangements may be made to determine the premium due on a periodic basis shorter than a year.

The third paragraph of the condition deals with premiums and covers this situation as follows:

> If the declarations provide for adjustment of premium on other than an annual basis, the insured shall pay the deposit premium to the company upon the inception of this policy and thereafter interim premiums shall be computed in accordance with the manuals in use by the company and paid by the insured promptly after the end of each interval specified in the declarations. The deposit premium shall be retained by the company until termination of this policy and credited to the final premium adjustment.

This means, briefly, that if a deposit premium is paid at the beginning of the contract term, the deposit is retained in its entirety until the end of the contract term and an adjustment is made at that time. If an estimated premium of $2,000 is paid at the beginning of a contract term and an audit at the end of six months indicates a premium of $1,500 for that period, the insured is billed for the full amount of the $1,500. No credit is allowed for the $2,000 deposit premium. If a $1,500 premium is developed for the second six months, then the $2,000 deposit is credited to that premium and a balance of $500 returned to the insured. On the other hand, if during the second six months period the audit develops a premium of $2,500, then the $2,000 would be credited to that premium and the insured billed for the additional $500.

The next paragraph of Condition 1 places an obligation on the insured to maintain all the necessary records for the purpose of computing the premium. The contract sets forth the requirement as follows:

> The insured shall maintain records of the information necessary for premium computation on the bases stated in the declarations, and shall send copies of such records to the company at the end of the policy period and at such times during the policy period as the company may direct. If the insured does not furnish records of the remuneration of persons within division (b) of the definition of remuneration foregoing, the remuneration of such persons shall be computed in accordance with the manuals in use by the company.

The insurer may elect to ask the insured to forward those records at such times as the insurer may direct for the purposes of computation of premium. As a matter of actual practice in risks, other than the smaller ones, it is the practice of the insurer to send an auditor to the office of the insured and there check payrolls and records. It is to be noted, in this respect, that the right of the insurer to records of the insured is limited to "the information necessary for premium computation." The insurer has no right of access to any other records or files.

The final clause of Condition 1 deals with the method of premium computation. In this respect the contract provides:

The premium stated in the declarations is an estimated premium only. Upon termination of this policy, the earned premium shall be computed in accordance with the rules, rates, rating plans, premiums and minimum premiums applicable to this insurance in accordance with the manuals in use by the company. If the earned premium thus computed exceeds the premium previously paid, the insured shall pay the excess to the company; if less, the company shall return to the insured the unearned portion paid by the insured. All premiums shall be fully earned whether any workmen's compensation law, or any part thereof, is or shall be declared invalid or unconstitutional.

The clause precludes any misunderstanding with respect to the premium indicated in the declaration. It clearly states that the premium is an estimated one. It again incorporates the rules, rates, and rating plan to be found in the manuals of the insurer as part of the contract. There is a saving clause at the end of the paragraph that provides that the premium due the insurer shall be dependent neither on the validity of the compensation law nor its constitutionality. In other words, if the insurer assumes the risk, even though all or part of the law may be declared invalid, the right of the insurer to retain the premium is not thereby jeopardized.[11]

Partnership or Joint Venture as Insured. There is a condition designed to clarify a situation where individuals operate in the capacity of both members of a partnership and also as individual proprietors. It reads as follows:

Partnership or Joint Venture as Insured If the insured is a partnership or joint venture, such insurance as is afforded by this policy applies to each partner or member thereof as an insured only while he is acting within the scope of his duties as such partner or member.

If A and B are engaged in the operations of the Blank Company, a partnership, it is logical that their remuneration from the partnership appear in the company payroll for the purpose of computing the partnership compensation premium. However, if both A and B carry on businesses at other locations entirely apart from the operation of the partnership, it is not expected that the insurance of the partnership will cover accidents other than those originating in the insured activ-

[11] There is an optional condition that may be inserted in the contract following Condition 1 covering the matter of contracts written for a period longer than one year. It makes all the provisions of the contract apply separately to each consecutive 12-month period. If the first or past period is less than 12 months, the shorter period is treated on the same basis that a short-term contract would be treated had it been written separately. Premiums for each 12-month period are computed as provided in Condition 1.

ity. This clause clarifies this intent by providing that the contract will apply to a partner or member of a joint venture only while acting within the scope of his duties as such partner or member.

Inspection and Audit. The insurer undertakes to inspect the workplaces covered. The purpose of the inspection is twofold: (*a*) to check the classifications and see to it that the insurer is getting proper premium for the risk, and (*b*) to suggest to the insured such changes and improvements that may operate to reduce the number and severity of accidents. The right to make these inspections and to check the insurer's books is incorporated in the contract. It is provided that such examinations may be made at any time during the contract term or extension thereof and for three years after the termination of the coverage. The contract provides:

Inspection and Audit The company and any rating authority having jurisdiction by law shall each be permitted to inspect the workplaces, machinery and equipment covered by this policy and to examine and audit the insured's books, vouchers, contracts, documents and records of any and every kind at any reasonable time during the policy period and any extension thereof and within three years after termination of this policy, as far as they relate to the premium bases or the subject matter of this insurance.

When the audit has been completed, if the auditor finds that the risk has not been properly classified, he picks up the changes in classification. After the audit has been made, the insured is charged with any excess over the estimated premium that has developed or is credited with a refund if the earned premium for the contract period proves to be less than the estimated premium.

Requirement as to Notice. Compensation laws require that injured employees give notice of an injury within a specified period, usually 30 days. The notice is required to include the time, place, and cause of the accident, and the nature of the injury, together with the name and address of the person injured. The notice is to be given by the injured employee or by a person in his behalf; or in the event of his death, by his legal representative, or by a dependent, or by a person in behalf of either.

The laws require that notice be given to the employer. If the employer is a corporation, the requirement as to notice is satisfied if notice is given to any official of the corporation or to any employee designated by the employer as one to whom reports of injuries to employees should be made. In this category are included general superintendents or foremen in charge of the particular work being done by the employee at the time of the accident. In giving notice, inaccuracy or unintentional misstatements do not reflect to the disadvantage of the injured employee. Neither is such a notice held to be invalid unless it can be shown that it was the intention to mislead and the employer was, in fact, actually misled by such a notice. The acts provide extensions where the employee is unable by reason of physical or mental incapacity to give the notice within the specified time in the act. Extensions are also allowed where there has been a delay on account of mistake of fact. In the case of a death of an employee within the period required for giving notice, the time for giving notice of death extends beyond the limitations of the requirements for notice of the injury. Formal notice of injury is not ordinarily required where it can be shown that the employer or his agent had knowledge of the accident.

Upon receiving notice of the injury of an employee, the employer proceeds immediately to notify the insurer and the industrial accident commission. The contract requirement with respect to notice reads:

Notice of Injury When an injury occurs written notice shall be given by or on behalf of the insured to the company or any of its authorized agents as soon as practicable. Such notice shall contain particulars sufficient to identify the insured and also reasonably obtainable information respecting the time, place and circumstances of the injury, the names and addresses of the injured and of available witnesses.

In the event of claim or suit, the requirements follow the pattern usually to be found in liability contracts. In this respect the contract provides:

Notice of Claim or Suit If claim is made or suit or other proceeding is brought against the insured, the insured shall immediately forward to the company every demand, notice, summons or other process received by him or his representative.

Notice to the industrial accident commission of an injury is not of itself to be regarded as an admission of compensable injury. The notices given to the commission and to the insurer contain the same information. In addition to the employer's name, address, nature of business, and location of plant or place where accident occurred, the report is confined to data with respect to the injury and the injured employee. The name, address, age, sex, and marital status of the person injured, as well as the occupation in which he was engaged at the time of the injury, is reported. The date of the accident and all pertinent data, as well as the nature of the injury, form part of the first report. Wage data upon which compensation is to be based are included, as well as a report of all medical attention provided by the employer. The employer indicates the time he was notified of the accident or the time he or one of his supervisors first had actual knowledge of the injury. He is finally required to indicate whether there are any questionable features with respect to the accident or the injury.

Statutory Provisions. This is a rather long condition divided into five paragraphs and is designed primarily to incorporate into the insurance contract certain provisions of the law applicable to compensation cases. The first paragraph has to do with the right of action of an injured employee against the insurer and reads as follows:

Statutory Provisions Coverage A — The company shall be directly and primarily liable to any person entitled to the benefits of the workmen's compensation law under this policy. The obligations of the company may be enforced by such person, or for his benefit by any agency authorized by law, whether against the company alone or jointly with the insured. Bankruptcy or insolvency of the insured or of the insured's estate, or any default of the insured, shall not relieve the company of any of its obligations under Coverage A.

The insured in a compensation contract and the insurer are the immediate parties to the agreement. The employee is a third-party beneficiary. Unlike the liability contract this paragraph in the compensation contract introduces a condition that permits direct action against the insurer by a person not actually a contracting party. The usual liability contract requires an injured party to seek redress against the insured. The insurer undertakes the defense and settlement. The injured party has no right of action against the insurer. On the contrary, in the compensation contract, the injured employee may proceed immediately for redress against the compensation insurer of his employer. This clause reflects the usual compensation statute and in effect makes the injured employee a party to the contract by making the insurer directly and primarily liable to any person entitled to compensation benefits. This feature applies to coverage A only. There is no direct right of action with respect to liability claims insured under coverage B. This paragraph contains also the usual bankruptcy paragraph now found in liability contracts. In case of a judgment, it provides that in the event of bankruptcy or insolvency of the insured, or the insured's estate, the insurer will not be relieved from the payment of any compensation claims.

The second paragraph of the condition sets forth the statutory obligations of the insurer with respect to notice. Ordinarily insurers incorporate requirements with respect to notice in their contracts. Where bodily injury is involved, great emphasis is placed upon promptness. If an injured employee should have his right jeopardized by failure of the insured to notify the insurer promptly, injustice might follow. Therefore, it is provided that notice or knowledge of injury on the part of the insured shall constitute notice or knowledge on the part of the insurer. This appears in the contract as follows:

As between the employee and the company, notice or knowledge of the injury on the part of the insured shall be notice or knowledge, as the case may be, on the part of the company; the jurisdiction of the insured, for the purposes of the workmen's compensation law, shall be jurisdiction of the company and the company shall in all things be bound by and subject to the findings, judgments, awards, decrees, orders or decisions rendered against the insured in the form and manner provided by such law and within the terms, limitations and provisions of this policy not inconsistent with such law.

It is important to point out the difference between notice and knowledge. If an employee is injured and fails to make formal notice of the injury to the employer, knowledge of the injury, however obtained, on the part of the employer is sufficient to make the insurer liable under the compensation law. The jurisdiction of the insured with respect to compensation is accepted by the insurer and the insurer binds itself to abide in all respects with the terms and conditions of the law.

The next paragraph writes into the contract, in effect, all of the terms and conditions of the applicable compensation law. In this respect the contract provides:

> All of the provisions of the workmen's compensation law shall be and remain a part of this policy and fully and completely as if written herein, so far as they apply to compensation and other benefits provided by this policy and to special taxes, payments into security or other special funds, and assessments required of or levied against compensation insurance carriers under such law.

The following paragraph has to do with wilful misconduct on the part of the insured or obligations which the insurer is obliged to meet attributable to illegal acts. The paragraph reads:

> The insured shall reimburse the company for any payments required of the company under the workmen's compensation law, in excess of the benefits regularly provided by such law, solely because of injury to (*a*) any employee by reason of the serious and wilful misconduct of the insured, or (*b*) any employee employed by the insured in violation of law with the knowledge or acquiescence of the insured or any executive officer thereof.

The insured is obligated by virtue of this paragraph to reimburse the insurer if it is required to make payment to an injured employee that may be traced to wilful misconduct on the part of the insured or to an employee of the insured in violation of the law with his knowledge and acquiescence. If the statutes require that payments in such instance be made, the insurer will make them but it will then charge the payments back to the insured. An assault by an employer upon an employee constitutes wilful misconduct of the insured. The question of legality makes its appearance in the case of employees who are under the legal age limit provided by the statutes. The responsibility of determining that employees are of proper age as provided by law rests squarely upon the employer. The employer cannot rely for defense upon the statement of the youth that he is of the proper age. If a person employed is of illegal age and is seriously injured or killed and the insurer is obligated to pay compensation, the insured in turn may be encumbered with a heavy obligation to the insurer.

Finally there is a short paragraph that has the effect of stating that statutory provisions do not narrow the scope of the coverage provided in the contract. This clause states:

> Nothing herein shall relieve the insured of the obligations imposed upon the insured by the other terms of this policy.

This means that there are obligations that the insurer undertakes in the contract that are not specifically required by the compensation act. The compensation act requires that certain benefits be paid. It makes no provision for the cost of investigation. The insurance contract, under insuring Agreement II, assumes liability for these investigation costs. It is the intent here to show that by complying strictly with the statutory provisions of the various compensation acts the insurer may not relieve itself of any obligations, over and above the requirements, that are elsewhere included in the contract.

Limits of Liability. There is no limit of liability with respect to workmen's compensation coverage. The applicable compensation act determines the nature and extent of payments to be made. With respect to common-law liability, the situation is different. A claimant for bodily injury damages at common law may collect to the extent of the damage he is able to establish. Verdicts for serious bodily injuries run to very substantial amounts. No limit is required with respect to coverage A. The insurer's liability with respect to liability protection afforded under coverage B is set forth in the declarations. A limitation frequently used is $25,000 and this limitation has been felt by many to be inadequate. The limit may be increased by the payment of an additional premium equal to a small percentage of the coverage A premium. The limit of liability under coverage B is the total amount available for the payment of liability claims from all sources originating from one accident. With respect to bodily injury by disease, the situation is slightly different. The limit in this instance is expressed as a contract year limit by state. The application of the limitation is set forth in the contract in the following terms:

Limits of Liability Coverage B — The words "damages because of bodily injury by accident or disease, including death at any time resulting therefrom," in coverage B include damages for care and loss of services and damages for which the insured is liable by reason of suits or claims brought against the insured by others to recover the damages obtained from such others because of such bodily injury sustained by employees of the insured arising out of and in the course of their employment. The limit of liability stated in the declarations for coverage B is the total limit of the company's lability for all damages because of bodily injury by accident, including death at any time resulting therefrom, sustained by one or more employees in any one accident. The limit of liability stated in the declarations for coverage B is the total limit of the company's liability for all damages because of bodily injury by disease, including death at any time resulting therefrom, sustained by one or more employees of the insured in operations in any one state designated in Item 3 of the declarations or in operations necessary or incidental thereto.

The inclusion herein of more than one insured shall not operate to increase the limits of the company's liability.

The condition clarifies two other important features of protection. The measure of "damages because of bodily injury" includes "damages for care and loss of services." It is important to clarify this point because these two items are important contributing factors in determining extent of damage. The condition also clarifies the matter of liability for the "liability over" type of claim. The condition definitely makes the insurer liable with respect to suits for damages brought by third parties who have paid the claims of the insured's employees injured in the course of employment.

There is no duplication with respect to limits. If there is more than one insured, the limit does not apply to each insured but to both collectively. In other words, if a contract is issued to cover the Doe Construction Company, a corporation, and John Doe, as an individual, and a common-law action is brought against both the corporation and John Doe, the liability section of the contract would cover up to the limits named in the declarations and no more. This would be true regardless of the amount of damages assessed against either the corporation or John Doe as an individual, or both.

Other Insurance. A condition of the contract provides that the insurance afforded is contributing insurance with other valid and collectible insurance. The clause reads:

Other Insurance If the insured has other insurance against a loss covered by this policy, the company shall not be liable to the insured hereunder for a greater proportion of such loss than the amount which would have been payable under this policy, had no such other insurance existed, bears to the sum of said amount and the amounts which would have been payable under each other policy applicable to such loss, had each such policy been the only policy so applicable.

Since compensation insurance covering a given risk is ordinarily written in a single insurer, the question of other insurance is more likely to appear with respect to coverage B. This clause takes into consideration the possibility of contributing insurance written without any specific limit of liability. Where one or more contracts are concerned, the liability is determined with respect to each contract as if there had been no other insurance. The contract is apportioned then on the basis of the liability so determined rather than on the basis of the limits of liability. In the case of one contract with the limit of liability of $50,000 and another contract with a limit of liability of $100,000, in the event of an award of $200,000 each insurer would be liable for its limits. If the award had been $100,000, one insurer would be liable for the full amount and the other would be liable for half the amount, or its limits of liability. In this instance there is $150,000 of liability to pay $100,000. The contract with the $50,000 limit would pay one-third the loss and the insurer with the $150,000 limit would pay the balance.

Assignments. In the matter of assignments, the workmen's compensation policy follows the situation generally to be found in insurance contracts and provides:

Assignment Assignment of interest under this policy shall not bind the company until its consent is endorsed hereon. If, however, during the policy period the insured shall die, and written notice is given to the company within thirty days after the date of such death, this policy shall cover the insured's legal representative as insured; provided that notice of cancellation addressed to the insured named in the declarations and mailed or delivered, after such death, to the address shown in this policy shall be sufficient notice to effect cancellation of this policy.

No assignment of interest under the contract can bind the insurer unless the consent of the insurer shall be endorsed thereon. It has been felt by some that because of the social implications of the compensation act, protection to the employee was the primary function of the insurance. Without underestimating in any way the importance of the insurance in protecting the employee, it is nevertheless true that the insurer, in writing the risk, weighs the reputation of the insured and wishes to protect itself against the change of an insured without its knowledge.[12]

Employees' Benefits Protected by Laws. The rights of the employee himself to his compensation benefits are protected by the law.

---

[12] The reasoning has thus been lucidly set forth: "A compensation policy, such as is involved here, is peculiarly personal. In the issuing of such a policy much depends upon the character of the insured employer relative to his integrity, prudence, caution, and ability, in the management and operation of his business, and in the selection and supervision of his employees. It would seem, therefore, that such a policy, on principle, is not assignable without the assent of the insurer. Aside from this, the assignment of such a policy, giving it the effect insisted upon by the appellants, creates an entirely new contract. It changes both the insured and the subject of the insurance. The policy as originally written insures the employer named in the policy against his liability to his employees. The assignment substitutes the assignee as the insured employer, so as to insure him against his liability to his employees, thus wholly changing the coverage of the policy. It takes the policy from the original risk insured, and makes it cover upon an entirely different risk. We are unwilling to rule that this may be done without the assent or knowledge of the insurer." *Rendelmann* v. *Levitt* (1930), Mo. App., 24 S.W. (2d) 211.

They are held to be personal and beyond the reach of creditors through attachment or other legal proceedings. Nor may the employee voluntarily assign or transfer his rights to compensation to a third party. Furthermore, the laws customarily provide that any agreement made by an employee, unless approved by the commission or commissioner, to waive any rights to compensation under the provisions of the act is invalid.

Cancellation. Condition 15 makes provision for the cancellation of the contract in its entirety. The condition is divided into three paragraphs. The first of these deals with the requirement as to notice. This paragraph, with certain permitted alternative phrasing included in brackets, reads as follows:

> **Cancellation** This policy may be cancelled by the insured [by surrender thereof to the company or any of its authorized agents or] by mailing to the company written notice stating when thereafter the cancellation shall be effective. This policy may be canceled by the company by mailing to the insured at the address shown in this policy written notice stating when not less than ten days thereafter such cancellation shall be effective. The mailing of notice as aforesaid shall be sufficient proof of notice. The [time of the surrender or the] effective date [and hour] of cancellation stated in the notice shall become the end of the policy period. Delivery of such written notice either by the insured or by the company shall be equivalent to mailing.

The insured may elect to cancel the contract at any time, and the insurer may cancel the contract by giving ten days' notice. The provision with respect to what constitutes notice is important. In the absence of such a clear definition of notice, it has sometimes been difficult, if not impossible, for the insurer to serve adequate notice on an insured.

The second paragraph of the condition is concerned with the premium adjustment in the event of cancellation. As is the practice in the business of insurance, if the contract is canceled by the insured, the insurer pays a return premium on a short-rate basis. If the contract is canceled by the insurer, the return premium is computed on a pro rata basis. This paragraph of the condition dealing with cancellation reads:

> If the insured cancels, unless the manuals in use by the company otherwise provide, earned premium shall be (1) computed in accordance with the customary short rate table and procedure and (2) not less than the minimum premium stated in the declarations. If the company cancels, earned premium shall be computed pro rata. Premium adjustment may be made at the time cancellation is effected and, if not then made, shall be made as soon as practicable after cancellation becomes effective. The company's check or the check of its representative mailed or delivered as

aforesaid shall be a sufficient tender of any refund of premium due to the insured.

The insurer's check delivered or mailed constitutes a tender of a refund of the premium. This forestalls the possibility of interposing legal technicalities by demanding that the premium be paid in legal tender or otherwise claiming that the cancellation is ineffective because of the nature of the refund offered.

The concluding paragraph of the condition is the shortest but in effect one of great importance. It requires full compliance, before cancellation can be effected, with any provisions with respect to cancellation incorporated in the workmen's compensation law. This paragraph provides:

> When the insurance under the workmen's compensation law may not be canceled except in accordance with such law, this condition so far as it applies to the insurance under this policy with respect to such law, is amended to conform to such law.

Where a copy of the contract is on file with the state and the state requires notice before cancellation, even if the steps just indicated are taken, there can be no cancellation until the insurer meets all the formalities required in the statute.

Contract Conforms to Statute. A short but important condition of the contract guarantees conformity of the contract with the workmen's compensation law in the applicable state. Since the laws of the various jurisdictions vary, and since they may be changed at any session of a legislature, it is conceivable that a standard contract could be written containing some feature that, with changing laws, might be in conflict with a particular statute. This eliminates the need for endorsement to make the standard form comply with the workmen's compensation law of the particular state in virtually all jurisdictions. The condition reads as follows:

Terms of Policy Conformed to Statute Coverage A	Terms of this policy which are in conflict with the provisions of the workmen's compensation law are hereby amended to conform to such law.

By virtue of the condition the contract is brought in harmony with the provisions of any workmen's compensation law in any jurisdiction where insurance is to be provided.[13]

---

[13] This condition in the contract eliminates the necessity for endorsement to adjust the contract to conflicts that arise due to lack of uniformity of workmen's compensation laws. There still are a few states where the statutes require a verbatim recital of certain prescribed provisions in the contract. To meet these situations, there are special state endorsements still in use. These state endorsements have been developed by the Policy Forms Committee of the National Council on Compensation Insurance.

Other Standard Conditions. There are other conditions to be found in the workmen's compensation and employers' liability contract that are not discussed here in detail that are in substance similar to clauses already considered. These have to do with the requirement for assistance and cooperation of the insured, right of action against the company, subrogation, requirements with respect to policy changes, and, finally, a condition dealing with declarations in which the insured agrees that statements in the declarations are his agreements and representations and that the contract is issued in reliance upon their truth. It is further provided that the contract embodies the entire agreement. Further treatment of these conditions is omitted here in the interest of avoiding repetition.

Extra-Legal Medical Coverage. The compensation laws in the various states differ with respect to the amount of medical benefits provided. The compensation insurer is obligated to pay no more than the benefits provided in the law. In those jurisdictions where the act provides only for limited medical payments, it frequently happens that an injured employee is obliged to go without certain expensive treatments and in some instances may become a dependent or public charge without further recourse to insurance benefits. Where employers feel that the law should be more generous, particularly in recognition of the increasing cost of medical and hospital care, the employer may elect to provide benefits more liberal than the act provides.

The insurers writing workmen's compensation coverages make provisions for these extra benefits by allowing the insured to provide additional protection by what is known as "extra-legal medical coverage." This form has a wide appeal, particularly among large employers. They feel it to be good public relations to see that all injured employees are provided with adequate medical and hospital care even though the requirements in a particular situation extend beyond any legal obligation.

All-States Coverage. The workmen's compensation contract covers in only those states indicated in the declarations. Insureds operating in more than one state would ordinarily list the states in which operations were to be carried on, or in which there was a reasonable probability that operations would be carried on during the contract term. It sometimes happens that an employer carries on business in one or more states and, in an effort to make his coverage comprehensive, lists all the probable states, even though there may be some doubt with respect to some of them. In some instances even this procedure is not adequate. Where there is some uncertainty with respect to the compensation exposure, insurers have provided an endorsement known as the "all-states" endorsement. This endorsement has certain advantages but also some limitations. An insured with a contract endorsed with an all-states endorsement has an agreement with the insurer that it will provide legal compensation as soon as an exposure develops and the insurer has knowledge of the exposure.

By means of this endorsement legal compensation cannot be effected in those states where certain formalities such as filings and acceptance of the act are required under the law. These formalities are a condition precedent to actually bringing the employer within the compensation act of the particular state. By virtue of the endorsement, an injured employee in a state not named in the declarations will be offered protection under the compensation feature of the contract to the extent that he would have been protected had the insured actually complied with all of the requirements of the law. It is always possible that an employee may refuse compensation in such circumstances and bring suit for damages without regard to compensation. In this event the liability section of the contract would cover the insured.[14]

EMPLOYERS' LIABILITY INSURANCE

Workmen's compensation insurance is now by far the most important of the coverages written to insure industrial accidents. Employers' liability coverage is provided in the standard compensation contract. A separate employers' liability contract is still used occasionally by an employer to protect himself when his employees do not come within the scope of the compensation law.

The insuring clause covers the insured's legal liability for personal injuries sustained by employees. The contract undertakes to indemnify the policyholder against loss or expense arising, or resulting, from claims upon him for damages on account of death or of bodily injuries accidentally suffered, or alleged to have been suffered, by his employees. Under this form the employee has no rights against the insurer but makes his case directly against the employer, as if insurance were not a factor. The insurer defends the case in the name of the insured and effects a settlement or pays judgment and costs, subject to the contract limits.

FOR DISCUSSION

1. The compensation contract obligates the insured to maintain records of the information necessary for premium computation and make

[14] Even though the endorsement is known as an all-states endorsement, no protection can be provided in states where compensation is provided by monopolistic state funds. Further, the endorsement does not cover penalties for not having workmen's compensation insurance or penalties for violations, such as when minor children hired in violation of child labor laws are injured.

them available to the insurer. Usually the check is made on the premises of the insured by an insurer auditor. B contends that he is willing to supply the total payroll as a lump sum but objects to a detailed payroll breakdown. What advantages may accrue to the insured from a careful audit of his payroll by an experienced representative of the insurer?

2. Compensation insurance is said to have social implications and is essentially personal insurance. Justify, if you can, its consideration in connection with property insurance coverages.
3. Sometimes the statute providing compensation for occupational disease is so worded that to be covered the disease must be "peculiar" to, or "inherent" in, the employment. X is making a claim for compensation for a disease which he claims to be inherent in the employment. His claim is being contested on the ground that many others were employed without contracting the disease. Do you think this precludes X from getting compensation? Discuss.
4. B is employed in a factory. He contracts tuberculosis but does not become totally incapacitated until two years after leaving the plant in which the disease was contracted. There is no coverage under the occupational disease law. If claim is filed two years after the termination of employment, will the liability and compensation contract provide any protection?
5. The compensation laws of a number of states provide for only a limited amount of medical payments. From a legal standpoint the insured has no obligation to pay more. If he wishes to assist the employees to meet increased costs of hospitalization and medical treatment, should he buy a separate disability contract or may he provide the coverage under his compensation contract?
6. The use of atomic energy as a source of power for peacetime activities has created a situation in the field of workmen's compensation and liability where insurance requirements are taxing the market to the limit. In this early stage of peacetime development of atomic energy why is this so?
7. X, an employer, is told that the workmen's compensation contract affords a coverage as broad as the act. He conducts a business at B Street. A new location is shortly opened in another part of the city, and the employer expects to report the payroll at this location at the time it is audited. Is he protected at the new location?
8. Are occupational diseases covered by the standard compensation contract under Coverage A without special endorsement?
9. In some states all occupational diseases are under the compensation act. In others the act includes certain specified diseases. In a third group there are no occupational diseases under the act. In the last two instances, should the insured have his contract endorsed to provide full occupational disease coverage? May he secure as full protection as the contract provides when the occupational hazard is included in the compensation act?

10. A. B. filed suit against his employer for $60,000. He claimed that he had contracted silicosis because the plant in which he worked was not properly equipped with health-protecting devices. The compensation law provided no occupational disease coverage. He was awarded $10,000. The award was followed by a flood of suits from other employees. How would the position of the employer be bettered if the disease were covered by the compensation act?
11. In a state in which occupational disease is not within the workmen's compensation law, may an employer, entirely aside from any humanitarian element that may enter the situation, disregard the question of occupational disease liability, if he elects to accept the compensation act?
12. Give an example of the following types of disability: (*a*) temporary total, (*b*) permanent total, and (*d*) occupational disease.
13. J, a mechanic employed in the X Manufacturing Company, completes his day's work at 4:00 in the afternoon. At 4:15 he is washed up and ready to leave the plant. On the way through the yard he is injured by a truck driving to the plant. In your opinion, did this accident happen in the course of employment, and is the injured employee entitled to workmen's compensation benefits?
14. B arranges for compensation insurance with the X company and indicates that he employs a crew of men to do landscape gardening. The payroll is estimated at $15,000 annually. When the audit is made, it is found that the payroll works out almost exactly as it was estimated, but the auditor finds that many of the members of the crew are engaged in much more hazardous work than grading and landscape work. Among other things, they are engaged in tree surgery which involves hazardous climbing. Although the payroll is no greater because of a change in classification, the premium is much greater as result of the audit. Has the insurer a right to change classifications at the end of the contract period?
15. One of the problems that confronts the carriers of workmen's compensation insurance is malingering. It frequently happens that employees attempt to continue disability payments long after actual disability is past. Sometimes there is no injury, but an employee contends he has suffered an accident. In other instances, the injured employee may aggravate a legitimate injury to postpone recovery. To what extent is the problem of malingering a problem for the insured as well as the insurer?
16. An employee who contracts a disease not specifically covered under the compensation law may, if he can show the disease was aggravated by the employer's neglect, file suit at common law against the employer. Does Coverage B of the compensation contract afford any protection if the disease is of a nature that precludes definition as "occupational"?
17. B, while in the course of his employment for A, is injured by an automobile driven by X. He feels that if he were to bring suit against

X he could collect more than is provided for him under the terms of the compensation act. May he bring a suit, and what is his legal position?

18. What is the status of an injured employee who refuses to undergo an operation that medical advice indicates will cure his disability?
19. An employee of the E Corporation broke through a gas main maintained by the W Utility Company in a public street and enclosed the break in a drain laid to a house on an abutting lot. Another employee of the E Corporation, working in the house, was asphyxiated. The administratrix of his estate secured judgment against the utility company. The utility company, maintaining that it was in no way negligent, brought action against the E Corporation as employer of the deceased. Does the compensation contract help the insured in an instance such as this or is it a public liability claim?

PART IV

MULTIPLE LINE AND MISCELLANEOUS INSURANCE CONTRACTS

CHAPTER · 19

Automobile Insurance Contracts

In view of the nature of inland marine insurance, it might be assumed that the insurance of automobiles would fall logically into the inland marine category. Strictly speaking, automobile insurance is a marine coverage, but as the business has developed, automobile insurance has come to be regarded as a branch entirely apart from inland marine insurance and is treated by insurers as a separate department. Since modern automobile insurance is essentially multiple line in nature, the automobile contract is classified here as a multiple line contract.

Automobile insurance falls into four major classifications: (1) liability, (2) physical damage, (3) medical payments, and (4) uninsured motorist protection. The liability coverages include bodily injury liability and property damage liability. Physical damage insurance protects the insured from loss or damage to the car itself. The physical damage coverages are fire and related perils, theft, and collision. In addition, a number of miscellaneous coverages may be included, such as windstorm, hail, earthquake, explosion, water damage, flood, riot and civil commotion insurance, and insurance against loss by aircraft damage. Insurance against damage caused by vandalism and malicious mischief may be written as well as coverage protecting the insured against loss growing out of dishonesty not covered by the theft contract, such as wrongful conversion or embezzlement. Many of these perils may be provided for under the comprehensive coverage found in the typical automobile contract. Ordinarily this coverage is used by the insured instead of named perils.

For the purposes of insurance, automobiles are classed as (1) private passenger, (2) commercial, (3) public, (4) garage, and (5) miscellaneous.

Private passenger automobiles include motor vehicles of the private passenger type, unaltered, and station wagons and jeeps used for pleasure or business purposes. In this category are included motor vehicles of the private passenger type even though altered by the attachment of a small box and used to transport tools or materials or to carry samples but not used for wholesale or retail delivery. Regardless of the type of the car, motor vehicles used for renting, livery work, or carrying passengers for compensation do not fall in the private passenger category, nor do motor vehicles owned and held for sale or used for demonstrating purposes by a dealer or manufacturer.

Commercial automobiles are motor vehicles of the truck type, including truck-type tractors, trailers, and semitrailers, used for the transportation or delivery of goods or merchandise or for other business purposes. Private passenger cars that have been altered and motor vehicles of the pickup body or delivery type used for wholesale or retail delivery are classified as commercial automobiles.

Public automobiles include automobiles, regardless of type, used to carry passengers for a consideration. Private passenger cars rented to individuals who drive them themselves are classified as public automobiles. In this group are to be found taxicabs, jitneys, livery automobiles, driverless-for-rent cars, rented auto homes, buses, and cars of employers used to transport employees.

Garage automobiles are all automobiles owned by dealers and held for sale or used for demonstrating purposes or in repair service or automobiles owned by persons who are a part of the firm. The dealer's equity in new automobiles consigned to him, even though title is held by another, is insurable under the dealer's form. Service and towing automobiles are also included in this category.

There are a number of a automobiles designed for special purposes that are included in the miscellaneous category. Examples are fire department automobiles; fire department apparatus; salvage corps automobiles; ambulances; hearses; invalid cars; police department automobiles; police patrol wagons; armored cars; auto homes; motorcycles; industrial, railway station, and dock trucks; snow plows; street flushers; street sweepers; tar spreaders; tractors (not of truck type); station cars; trailers; semitrailers; and dollies. Automotive equipment not insurable under the automobile contract includes lawn mowers, power shovels, and trench diggers. Risks of this type are normally insured under general liability and inland marine contracts.

The economic consequences of automobile accidents and the resulting need for automobile insurance may be estimated from a consideration of some of the facts about motor vehicle deaths and injuries, and facts about economic losses from traffic accidents and claim costs. In 1940, deaths in the United States caused by motor vehicle accidents totaled 34,501; and in 1964, the comparable figure was 47,700. Although these figures show an increase in absolute amounts, as a percentage of the population resident in the United States during those years, deaths have remained fairly stable with .026 percent of the population dying as a result of an automobile accident in 1940, and

.025 percent in 1964. The number of automobile injuries in 1940 totaled 1,320,000, and 3,840,000 in 1964, or 1 percent of the population in 1940, and 2 percent in 1964. Economic losses from traffic accidents, which include property damage even though not insured, legal, medical, surgical, and hospital costs, some of which may be insured, loss of income from work, and administrative costs of insurance, increased from approximately $2 billion in 1940, to almost $10 billion in 1964. In population terms, this represents an increase from about $15 for each person resident in the United States in 1940, to slightly over $51 for 1964.[1]

THE FAMILY AUTOMOBILE CONTRACT

The automobile insurance contract may take a variety of forms depending on the needs of the insured. Brainard has identified the following major contract forms: "(*a*) the Family policy, (*b*) the Special policy, (*c*) the Massachusetts statutory policy, (*d*) the Basic policy, (*e*) the Garage Liability policy, and (*f*) the Comprehensive Automobile Liability Policy."[2] The physical damage coverages are provided under the family, basic, and special contracts. No effort will be made to discuss all of these forms, although later in this chapter some consideration will be given briefly to the provisions of contracts for special purposes. The family automobile contract will be used as an illustration of the coverages normally provided for private passenger cars. This contract is divided into the following parts: (1) declarations, (2) liability, (3) expenses for medical services, (4) physical damage, (5) protection against uninsured motorists, and (6) conditions. It should be kept in mind that the liability coverages may be written separately and insured by a liability insurer and the physical damage coverages may be covered by a fire and marine insurer. It is the practice today, in view of multiple line underwriting, for the insurance of private passenger automobiles to be written on a combined form with one insurer undertaking the entire risk.

The Declarations. The first page of the automobile contract contains the "declarations." The declarations contain the basic information required by the insurance underwriter to effect the coverage. There is the name of the insured, his address, and occupation. The contract period and coverages are listed and a description of the automobile to be insured. The purposes for which the automobile is to be used are given. The insured declares himself to be sole owner of the

---

[1] *Insurance Facts* (New York: Insurance Information Institute, 1965) pp. 48–49.

[2] C. H. Brainard, *Automobile Insurance* (Homewood, Ill.: Richard D. Irwin, Inc., 1961), p. 65.

automobile and that, unless stated, no insurer during the past three years has canceled any automobile insurance.

The insured elects the coverages he wishes to carry. Provision for this is made in the declarations. Protection is provided where a premium charge appears on the declaration page of the contract for the coverage. The declarations contain a description of the automobile and factual data respecting its purchase.

Liability. Liability insurance contracts undertake basically to pay, on behalf of the insured, all sums that the insured shall become legally obligated to pay as damages as a result of bodily injury, property damage, or some related cause. Liability imposed by law stems from some negligent action attributable to the insured or for which the insured is responsible. The liability section of the family automobile contract provides for bodily injury liability, property damage liability, and supplementary payments. In addition this part of the contract contains a list of definitions, a list of exclusions, and statements about financial responsibility laws, limits of liability, and other insurance.[3]

Bodily Injury and Property Damage Liability. Bodily injury and property damage liability protection is provided in the liability section of the family automobile contract under coverages designated as A and B. Under A the insurer agrees "to pay on behalf of the insured all sums which the insured shall become legally obligated to pay as damages because of bodily injury, sickness or disease, including death resulting therefrom . . . sustained by any person" and under B, "injury to or destruction of property, including loss of use thereof . . . arising out of the ownership, maintenance or use of the owned automobile or any nonowned automobile. . . ." The insuring clause also contains a provision that the insurer will "defend any suit alleging such bodily injury or property damage and seeking damages which are payable under the terms of the policy, even if any of the allegations of the suit are groundless, false or fraudulent." It is further provided that the insurer may investigate and settle any claim as it deems expedient. This affords the insurer an important right but carries with it a corresponding obligation. It places the control of the settlement in the hands of the insurer and takes it entirely out of the hands of the insured. The insurer is thereby obligated to use every reasonable means to effect a settlement within contract limits.

Supplementary Payments. In addition to paying damages imposed by law the insurer agrees to assume responsibility for certain supplementary payments. These obligations are set forth in the contract as follows:

[3] The form of contract followed here is the one given in the kit of contracts prepared by Insurance Information Institute. Other automobile contracts may follow a somewhat different pattern but the same basic information is included.

To pay, in addition to the applicable limits of liability:

a) all expenses incurred by the company, all costs taxed against the insured in any such suit and all interest on the entire amount of any judgment therein which accrues after entry of the judgment and before the company has paid or tendered or deposited in court that part of the judgment which does not exceed the limit of the company's liability thereon;

b) premiums on appeal bonds required in any such suit, premiums on bonds to release attachments for an amount not in excess of the applicable limit of liability of this policy, and the cost of bail bonds required of the insured because of accident or traffic law violation arising out of the use of an automobile insured hereunder, not to exceed $100 per bail bond, but without any obligation to apply for or furnish any such bonds;

c) expenses incurred by the insured for such immediate medical and surgical relief to others as shall be imperative at the time of an accident involving an automobile insured hereunder and not due to war;

d) all reasonable expenses, other than loss of earnings, incurred by the insured at the company's request.

If the insured is arrested for an alleged violation of a traffic law, resulting in an automobile accident, and bail is required for his release, or if as a result of an automobile accident a claimant secures a writ of attachment on any property of the insured including the automobile, the cost of the bail bond or the release of attachment bond not to exceed $100 is paid by the insurer. In the case of an appeal from a judgment to a higher court, a bond is required, and the premium for the bond is paid. This feature is more important than the actual cost of the bond. While the insurer is not obligated to apply for or furnish bonds, it usually does this, relieving the applicant of any obligation to deposit cash or bonds as collateral to the surety.

The cost of investigating a claim, the negotiations for settlement, and the cost of defense are all paid by the insurer. This is true, even in case of a false or fraudulent claim or in the case of a claim excessive in amount. Defense costs frequently run to sizable amounts. In the case of an appeal, interest on the amount of the judgment not in excess of contract limits is covered.

In the case of an automobile accident involving personal injury, an insured may feel obligated to secure first-aid medical or surgical treatment without exploring the matter of liability, or even regardless of liability. Where treatment of injured is imperative, the cost is covered.

If it becomes necessary as part of the adjusting procedure to ask the insured to incur some expense, the contract provides for reimbursement. This clause clarifies any doubt where it might be construed under the cooperation clause that the insured should bear certain or all such expenses. Loss of earnings on the part of the insured due to the interruption of his personal affairs is not covered. Actually, it is the intent of this clause to reimburse the insured for actual cash outlay made at the request of the insurer presumably to further its interest. Loss of earnings might not be easy in some instances to determine, and in many instances there would be no such loss.

The coverages provided under this insuring agreement, if the claim is one the insurer is liable to defend or settle, is in addition to applicable contract limits. Assume, for example, a claim of an individual amounts to $10,000 with a contract limit of $5,000. If the insurer spends time and money in investigation, provides appeal bonds, and otherwise runs up expenses to $2,000 for the purposes of effecting a $5,000 settlement out of court, the insured is fully protected. The $5,000 claim is paid, and the insurer bears all settlement costs in addition. Moreover, if at the time of the accident the insured provided first aid, this is not used to reduce the insurer liability but is assumed by the insurer in excess of the liability limit of the contract. A variation of the foregoing situation is to be found, with a contract limit of $5,000 as before. In the case of injury to any one person, if, as a result of defending a suit, expenses were $1,000 and a verdict is rendered for $7,000, the insurer will pay its limit of $5,000 under the bodily injury liability coverage of the contract and will pay, in addition, the $1,000 defense costs.

Persons Insured. The insured named in the declarations and the insurer are the contracting parties under the automobile contract. Over a number of years the contract has been broadened to include within the scope of its protection the family of the insured and others driving with the permission of the insured. The clause that defines the word "insured" is often called the "omnibus clause." In the case of owned automobiles the persons insured include the "named insured and any resident of the same household and any other person using such automobile, provided the actual use thereof is with the permission of the named insured." For nonowned automobiles the persons insured include the "named insured and any relative, but only with respect to a private passenger automobile or trailer, provided the actual use thereof is with permission of the owner." The persons insured also include any person or organization legally responsible for the use of an owned or nonowned automobile, "if such automobile is not owned or hired by such person or organization provided the actual use thereof is by a person who is an insured as described above with respect to such owned or non-owned automobile." Where the insurance is extended to cover others than the named insured the insurance coverage is not enlarged but insures more persons for the same contract limits. The extension to persons or organizations legally responsible for the use of an owned or nonowned automobile covers such situations as sending a volunteer worker on an errand in a borrowed car, and should he meet with an accident, his own insurance would cover not only himself but any liability that might attach to the organization or person in whose interests the errand was performed.

Definitions. Under definitions the meanings of such expressions as named insured, insured, relative, owned automobile, temporary substitute automobile, nonowned automobile, private passenger automobile, farm automobile, utility automobile, trailer, automobile business, use, and war are given. Of particular interest here is that an owned automobile includes a temporary substitute automobile and that a nonowned automobile "means an automobile or trailer not owned or furnished for the regular use of either the named insured or any relative, other than a temporary substitute automobile."

Exclusions. There are nine exclusions that apply to the liability section of the contract. These exclusions are not particularly restrictive and cover items that are often excluded in liability contracts. The exclusions are:

This policy does not apply under the liability section:

a) to any automobile while used as a public or livery conveyance, but this exclusion does not apply to the named insured with respect to bodily injury or property damage which results from the named insured's occupancy of a non-owned automobile other than as the operator thereof;

b) to bodily injury or property damage caused intentionally by or at the direction of the insured;

c) to bodily injury or property damage with respect to which an insured under this policy is also an insured under a contract of nuclear energy liability insurance issued by the Nuclear Energy Liability Insurance Association or the Mutual Atomic Energy Liability Underwriters and in effect at the time of the occurrence resulting in such bodily injury or property damage; provided, such contract of nuclear energy liability insurance shall be deemed to be in effect at the time of such occurrence notwithstanding such contract has terminated upon exhaustion of its limit of liability;

d) to bodily injury or property damage arising out of the operation of farm machinery;

e) to bodily injury to any employee of the insured arising out of and in the course of (1) domestic employment by the insured, if benefits therefor are in whole or in part either payable or required to be provided under any workmen's compensation law, or (2) other employment by the insured;

f) to bodily injury to any fellow employee of the insured injured in the course of his employment if such injury arises out of the use of an automobile in the business of his employer, but this exclusion does not apply to the named insured with respect to injury sustained by any such fellow employee;

g) to an owned automobile while used in the automobile business but this exclusion does not apply to the named insured, a resident of the same household as the named insured, a partnership in which the named insured or such resident is a partner, or any partner, agent or employee of the named insured, such resident or partnership;

h) to a non-owned automobile while used (1) in the automobile business by the insured or (2) in any other business or occupation of the insured except a private passenger automobile operated or occupied by the named insured or by his private chauffeur or domestic servant, or a trailer used therewith or with an owned automobile;

i) to injury to or destruction of (1) property owned or transported by the insured or (2) property rented to or in charge of the insured other than a residence or private garage.

Most of these exclusions are self-explanatory, although the limitations surrounding accidents involving employees and property owned or in charge of the insured may need further clarification. The purpose of the clause relating to accidents involving employees is to exclude risks that are ordinarily covered under workmen's compensation insurance. The exemption applies to employees only while engaged in the business of the insured. If, for example, a car owned by the insured were to strike an employee and injure him while he was away from the premises of the insured and not engaged in the business of the insured, the claim of the employee would not fall within the scope of workmen's compensation and the insured would be protected in the case of such a claim by the automobile contract.

There are situations in which an insured may not carry workmen's compensation insurance and he feels that this exclusion creates a loophole in his insurance protection. For such situations, the insured's liability may be written under a separate contract covering either the workmen's compensation risk or the employer's liability if the Workmen's Compensation Act does not apply.

The exclusion relating to property owned or in charge of the insured is intended to clarify any doubt as to whether the property damage coverage operates if the insured injures his own property or property in his custody. In the first place, it is the intent of the contract to pay for losses for which the insured is legally liable. If the insured damages his own property, quite obviously he is not subject to suit for damages, for he cannot sue himself. If the insured leases property, he is responsible for its return to its owner at the termination of the lease; but during the period in which it is in his custody, if he injures the property he occupies the same position as one injuring his own property. To clarify any doubts that might possibly exist, this exclusion makes perfectly clear that the contract is not responsible for property damage losses to property owned by, rented to, leased to, in charge of, or transported by the insured. It is to be pointed out that the term "insured" means any insured within the meaning of persons insured although legal interpretations have varied on this point. Thus, if A damages an automobile belonging to B and B sues A, A is protected by B's policy and B may get paid by his own insurer.

There is one exception to this exclusion. If there is injury to or destruction of a residence or private garage, if such injury or destruction is by a private passenger automobile covered by the contract, then the liability coverage applies. This exception covers situations where a tenant might be liable for injury to the property of a landlord. Other than this one exception, the contract is not liable for damage to property owned, rented to, in charge of or transported by the insured.

Financial Responsibility Laws. Under the financial responsibility laws of the various states an automobile driver may be required to demonstrate financial responsibility in order to continue driving, if he is involved in an automobile accident and someone is injured or there is property damage of a certain amount. The family automobile contract provides that when the contract "is certified as proof of financial responsibility for the future under the provisions of any motor vehicle financial responsibility law" the insurance provided for bodily injury or property damage liability "shall comply with the provisions of such law to the extent of the coverage and limits of liability required by such law, but in no event in excess of the limits of liability stated in the contract." Once certification has occurred the insurer is obligated to pay the injured party under the terms of the contract even though the insured has in some manner not complied with the contract. In the case of contract violation the insurer may proceed against the insured for reimbursement of "any payment made by the insurer which it would not have been obligated to make under the terms of the policy" in the absence of the financial responsibility section of the contract.

Limits of Liability. This section of the contract sets forth that the limit of bodily injury liability expressed in the declarations as applicable to "each person" is the limit of the insurer's liability for all damages, including damages for care and loss of services arising out of bodily injury to, or death of, one person in any one accident. The limit applicable to "each accident" is subject to the same limit applying to each person. Automobile contracts may be written with standard limits of $5,000 for each person and $10,000 for each accident, although almost all policies now have limits of liability of at least $10,000 for each person and $20,000 for each accident.

In the case of property damage, the standard limit is ordinarily set at $5,000. It is also provided that if more than one named insured appears in the contract, this fact does not operate to increase the limits of the insurer's liability. Excess bodily injury liability limits are now usual because $5,000 as a limit on each person often proves to be inadequate. Since the majority of claims may be settled within the standard limits, insurers write excess limits for an additional premium proportionately much less than that charged for the standard limits. The cost of excess limits varies with the nature of the risk.

Other Insurance. Although it is not usual for an insured to carry automobile insurance with more than one insurer, situations do arise where there is duplication of coverage. For example, the comprehensive personal liability contract provides coverage for automobile accidents occurring on the premises of the insured, as does the family automobile contract. Newly acquired automobiles are automatically covered under the family automobile contract but the insured might not be aware of this and take insurance with a different insurer. If there is other insurance applicable to the loss, each insurer contributes a proportionate share. The proportion is determined by dividing the applicable limit of liability for a particular contract by the total "applicable limit of liability of all valid and collectible insurance against such loss." In the case of a temporary substitute automobile or a nonowned automobile the insurance "shall be excess insurance over any other valid and collectible insurance."

Expenses for Medical Services. The part of the family automobile contract providing expenses for medical services was designed historically to enable the insured to reimburse persons injured while occupying his car (or struck by him) as a result of his driving his car in those situations where no liability appeared or where liability was doubtful. Now the medical services clause has been extended to include the driver even if he is the named insured. The insurer agrees:

> To pay all reasonable expenses incurred within one year from the date of accident for necessary medical, surgical, X-ray and dental services, including prosthetic devices, and necessary ambulance, hospital, professional nursing and funeral services:
>
> Division 1. To or for the named insured and each relative who sustains bodily injury, sickness or disease, including death resulting therefrom, hereinafter called "bodily injury," caused by accident, while occupying or through being struck by an automobile;
>
> Division 2. To or for any other person who sustains bodily injury, caused by accident, while occupying
>
> *a*) the owned automobile, while being used by the named insured, by any resident of the same household or by any other person with permission of the named insured; or
>
> *b*) a non-owned automobile, if the bodily injury results from (1) its operation or occupancy by the named insured or its operation on his behalf by his private chauffeur or domestic servant or (2) its operation or occupancy by a relative, provided it is a private passenger automobile or trailer.

The definitions given in the contract under the heading "liability" apply to medical payments. Additionally by occupying is meant "in or upon or entering into or alighting from" and an automobile includes "a trailer of any type."

Payment is made under the contract up to the designated contract limit regardless of who is at fault. If the insured is struck by another car, he is under no obligation to sue the owner or driver of the car to collect under his medical payments protection. Injuries caused by all land motor vehicles designed to be used principally on public roads are covered. This provision includes trucks, trailers, and semitrailers but does not include farm-type tractors or vehicles or equipment designed for nonpublic road use. The contract limit applies to each injured person covered. If an insured is driving his car and his wife, two children, and another person who qualifies as a member of his household are all injured with a contract with $5,000 limits, the insurer has a liability limit for that accident of $25,000, or $5,000 for each person.

There are five exclusions that limit recovery under the medical payments section of the contract. These exclusions are designed to deny coverage for various uses of the automobile including situations where workmen's compensation applies. The war risk is excluded. Another exclusion relates to situations where an owned automobile may not be covered under the contract. In this situation there is no coverage for medical payments when the owned automobile, which may be an additional car, is not listed in the contract and a suitable premium has not been paid.

Physical Damage. The physical damage part of the contract provides six coverages. These coverages are: comprehensive and personal effects; collision; fire, lightning, and transportation; theft; combined additional coverage; and towing and labor costs.

Comprehensive and Personal Effects. The comprehensive automobile coverage is, with the exception of collision losses, virtually an all risks coverage. It is now widely substituted for the named perils forms that were the first to be offered. Protection is afforded for any direct and accidental loss of, or damage to, the automobile covered and equipment usually attached thereto. It is difficult to list all the hazards that the comprehensive part of the contract covers, but among them are the following: fire, theft, windstorm, pilferage, earthquake, strike, flood, spray from trees, attempted theft, malicious mischief, submersion in water, acid from battery, riot, falling aircraft, civil commotion, rising water, breakage of glass, leakage of water pipes, explosion, hail, robbery, and lightning. There have been many strange cases involving the comprehensive coverage. There was a case involving damage to a fender kicked by a horse, damage to the finish of an automobile caused by arsenic tree spray, damage by Fourth of July firecrackers, and Halloween vandals. The damage to be covered must be accidental. To break a window to get into a car with the keys locked inside is not an accidental damage. Vandalism losses are specifically covered. Breakage of glass and losses caused by missiles, falling objects, fire, theft, explosion, malicious mischief, and other named perils are not deemed collision losses. This means that the collision exclusion of the comprehensive cover does not extend to exclude damage caused by missiles, falling objects, or losses attributable to malicious mischief, windstorm, or other such perils. The personal effects coverage pays "for loss caused by fire or lightning to robes, wearing apparel and other personal effects which are the property of the named insured or a relative, while such effects are in or upon the owned automobile." The limit of the coverage on personal effects is $100.

Collision. Collision insurance reimburses the insured for damage to "an owned automobile or to a non-owned automobile but only for the amount of each such loss in excess of the deductible amount. . . ." The collision may be with another car or with any other object, movable or fixed. Collision insurance written in connection with the comprehensive coverage provides the broadest available physical damage protection. Comprehensive insurance may also be sold with a deductible.

Fire, Lightning, and Transportation. Physical damage by fire, lightning, and transportation covers loss by fire, whatever the cause, as well as losses caused by lightning. Included in the coverage are losses growing out of the stranding, sinking, burning, collision, or derailment of any conveyance in or upon which the automobile is being transported on land or water. This coverage affords a smudge damage protecton similar to that added to the standard fire contract by endorsement. Accidental direct loss caused by smoke or smudge due to a sudden, unusual, and faulty operation of any fixed heating equipment serving the premises in which the automobile is located is covered.

Theft. Theft insurance is written only in connection with the fire insurance coverage and protects against loss of the insured car or damage thereto caused by theft, larceny, robbery, or pilferage.

Combined Additional Coverage. This is an extension of the fire coverage. Insurance is provided not only against loss caused by windstorm, hail, earthquake, or explosion but includes as well riot and civil commotion losses, losses attributable to forced landing or the falling of any aircraft or their parts or equipment. Flood or rising waters, malicious mischief or vandalism, the external discharge or leakage of water are covered, but, as before, losses resulting from rain, snow, or sleet are not covered. There is a $25 deductible that applies to loss caused by malicious mischief or vandalism.

Towing and Labor Costs. At the election of the insured this coverage may be included in any contract. When the coverage is provided the insurer obligates itself to pay for towing and labor costs necessitated by the disablement of the insured automobile provided the labor is performed at the place of disablement. A claim must be supported by receipted bills or other acceptable evidence of loss. There is no coverage for costs of parts or replacements, gasoline, oil, batteries, or tires.

Supplementary Payments. The insurer agrees to pay, in addition to any payments under the physical damage coverages, for loss of use by theft and for general average and salvage charges.

In the section of the contract providing for reimbursement for transportation expenses in the event of theft, it is provided that the insurer is liable for amounts that the insured has disbursed for rental or hire during the period that he has been deprived of his automobile. There is a limit of $10 per day and an aggregate limit of $300. Liability for payment terminates when the stolen car has been "returned to use or the insurer pays for the loss." There is no coverage if the automobile is used as a public or livery conveyance or is held for sale by an automobile dealer. There is no liability on the part of the insurer until 48 hours after the theft has been reported to the insurer and the police.

The fire, lightning, and transportation coverage includes loss caused by the stranding, sinking, or burning of a conveyance upon which the automobile is being transported. As in the case of other marine cargoes, an automobile without damage to itself might become liable for either general average or salvage charges or both. Under supplementary payments the insurer agrees to pay "general average and salvage charges for which the insured becomes legally liable."

Definitions. The definitions in the physical damage section of the contract are similar to those listed under liability. The words "insured," "nonowned automobile," "loss," "collision," and "trailer" are defined somewhat differently as follows:

"Insured" means (*a*) with respect to the owned automobile (1) the named insured and (2) any person or organization, other than a person or organization engaged in the automobile business or as a carrier or other bailee for hire, maintaining, using or having custody of said automobile with the permission of the named insured; (*b*) with respect to a nonowned automobile, the named insured and any relative provided the actual use thereof is with the permission of the owner;

"Nonowned automobile" means a private passenger automobile or trailer not owned by or furnished for the regular use of either the named insured or any relative, other than a temporary substitute automobile, while said automobile or trailer is in the possession or custody of the insured or is being operated by him.

"Loss" means direct and accidental loss of or damage to (*a*) the automobile, including its equipment, or (*b*) other insured property.

"Collision" means collision of an automobile covered by this policy with another object or with a vehicle to which it is attached or by upset of such automobile.

"Trailer" means a trailer designed for use with a private passenger automobile, if not being used for business or commercial purposes with other than a private passenger, farm or utility automobile, and if not a home, office, store, display or passenger trailer.

Exclusions. The automobile physical damage coverage contains a number of exclusions. There is no protection for

(*a*) any automobile while used as a public or livery conveyance; (*b*) loss due to war; (*c*) loss to a nonowned automobile arising out of its use by the insured in the automobile business; (*d*) loss to a private passenger, farm or utility automobile or trailer owned by the named insured and not described in this policy or to any substitute automobile therefor, if the insured has other valid and collectible insurance against such loss; (*e*) damage which is due and confined to wear and tear, freezing, mechanical or electrical breakdown or failure, unless such damage results from theft covered by this policy; (*f*) tires, unless damaged by fire, malicious mischief or vandalism, or stolen or unless the loss be coincident with and from the same cause as other loss covered by this policy; (*g*) loss due to radioactive contamination; (*h*) under collision, to breakage of glass if insurance with respect to such breakage is otherwise afforded.

The livery exclusions afford the insurer an opportunity not only to select or reject this class of risk on the basis of the application but, as well, to secure an adequate premium if a livery risk is assumed. The war risk exclusion, while brief, follows the general pattern of physical damage coverages and undertakes to exclude all losses due to warlike activities. The exclusion is made particularly to apply to those actions where military operations are carried on without an actual declaration of war. Wear and tear losses and losses attributable to mechanical defects follow the usual pattern to be found in marine contracts. A flat tire or other tire damage is not within the contemplation of the coverage. The exclusion makes this clear. But for the exclusion an insured might well call a flat tire a comprehensive or collision loss. If a tire is damaged by fire, is stolen, or is otherwise lost or damaged coincident with another loss covered by the contract, there would be coverage. For example, if tires were slashed by vandals or damaged by a flying missile, the damage would be part of a loss covered under the comprehensive contract and, hence, the insurer would be liable.

Theft losses whether under the comprehensive coverage or under the coverages specifying theft, larceny, robbery, or pilferage definitely do not cover the unlawful disposal of the insured car by a person who is in lawful possession of it. The exclusion with respect to glass breakage clarifies a situation where there might otherwise be doubt as to coverage. If collision insurance were written with one insurer and comprehensive physical damage with another insurer, the comprehensive contract would cover glass losses. The exclusion with respect to illicit trade is clear. An automobile used for smuggling or the illicit sale of narcotics or liquor would, by virtue of its illegal use, terminate the insurance while so used. The confiscation exclusion is optional. To become operative, the confiscation must be by "duly constituted" governmental or civil authority. If a public official, without legal right to do so, should confiscate a car for public use, the insurance would still be effective.

Limit of Liability. In the event of loss the insurer's liability does not exceed the cash value of the property or part thereof at time of loss or what "it would then cost to repair or replace the property or such part thereof with other of like kind and quality, nor, with respect to an owned automobile described in this policy, the applicable limit of liability stated in the declarations." The insurer's liability for loss to personal effects is $100 for any one occurrence, and its liability for loss to a nonowned trailer is $500.

Other Insurance. The contribution rule applies in the event of other insurance except with respect to a temporary substitute automobile or a nonowned automobile, in which case the insurance is excess over any other valid and collectible insurance.

Protection against Uninsured Motorists. A serious problem that arises in the field of automobile accidents is that of the failure of some drivers to carry insurance or otherwise to make provision for the financial consequences of accidents. Thus an insured driver may be legally entitled to damages because of the negligence of another driver but unable to collect because of the financial inability of the driver of the second car to respond. Part IV of the family automobile contract provides protection against uninsured motorists and is frequently referred to as "Family Protection." The insuring clause states that the insurer will "pay all sums which the insured or his legal representative shall be legally entitled to recover as damages from the owner or operator of an uninsured automobile because of bodily injury, sickness or disease, including death therefrom . . . caused by accident and arising out of the ownership, maintenance or use of such uninsured automobile. . . ." Thus an insured may recover under his own contract in the event that he has been injured in an automobile accident through the negligence of an uninsured driver. The insurance granted by this clause is subject to exclusions, definitions, and other provisions specified in Part IV of the contract.

Definitions. The definition of the word "insured," as it applies to the uninsured motorists section of the contract differs from that given in the liability part of the contract. Insured means "(*a*) the named insured and any relative; (*b*) any other person while occupying an insured automobile; and (*c*) any person, with respect to damages he is entitled to recover because of bodily injury to which this Part applies sustained by an insured under (*a*) or (*b*) above. By an "uninsured automobile" is meant a hit-and-run automobile and "an automobile or trailer with respect to the ownership, maintenance or use of which there is, in at least the amounts specified by the financial responsibility law of the state in which the insured automobile is principally garaged, no bodily injury liability bond or insurance policy applicable at the time of the accident with respect to any person or organization legally responsible for the use of such automobile, or with respect to which there is a bodily injury liability bond or insurance policy applicable at the time of the accident but the company writing the same denies coverage thereunder. . . ." Although this definition makes an insured with insufficient limits an uninsured motorist, it is generally held that this is so only to the extent of the insufficiency.

Exclusions. There are not many exclusions applying directly to the uninsured motorist coverage. If an automobile owned by the named insured or by a person residing in his household is at fault, coverage is denied, since not to exclude this situation would be simply providing coverage without a premium for an automobile that the insured owns but for some reason didn't insure. The contract also excludes situations wherein a settlement may have been reached with the person at fault without the written consent of the insurer. Another exclusion provides that the contract must now "insure directly or to the benefit of any workmen's compensation or disability benefits carrier or any person or organization qualifying as a self-insurer under any workmen's compensation or disability benefits law or similar law."

Limits of Liability. The contract states that the limits of liability for uninsured motorists given in the declarations for each person and for each accident constitute the insurers total limit of liability for all damages as the result of any one accident. The amount paid to the insured because of bodily injury may be reduced by any payments made on "account of such bodily injury by or on behalf of the owner or operator of the uninsured automobile and any other person or organization jointly or severally liable together with such owner or operator for such bodily injury including sums paid under Coverage A" and "the amount paid and the present value of all amounts payable on account of such bodily injury under any workmen's compensation law, disability benefits law or any similar law." Further, if the insured receives payment under the uninsured motorists coverage, this payment "shall be applied in reduction of the amount of damages which he may be entitled to recover from any person insured under the Coverage A (Bodily Injury Liability)." Finally, "The Company shall not be obligated to pay under this Coverage that part of the damages which the insured may be entitled to recover from the owner or operator of an uninsured automobile which represents expenses for medical services paid or payable" under the part of the family automobile contract dealing with expenses for medical services.

Other Insurance. If an insured receives bodily injury as a result of occupying an automobile not owned by the named insured, the insurance under this part of the contract "shall apply only as excess insurance over any other similar insurance available to such insured and applicable to such automobile as primary insurance, and this insurance shall then apply only in the amount by which the limit of liability for this coverage exceeds the applicable limit of liability of such other insurance." In other circumstances, other similar insurance is treated as contributing insurance on a proportional basis.

Arbitration. In the event of disagreement between the insured and the insurer as to whether the claimant is legally entitled to recover damages or if there is disagreement on the amount, the contract provides that the matter may be settled by arbitration "in accordance with the rules of the American Arbitration Association. . . ." and the claimant and the insurer "each agree to consider itself bound and to be bound by any award made by the arbitrators pursuant to this part."

Trust Agreement. If the uninsured motorists insurer makes payment to any person under the provisions of Part IV, the person, under the requirements of the trust agreement, agrees to the following: (*a*) that the insurer "shall be entitled to the extent of such payment to the proceeds of any settlement or judgment that may result from the exercise of any rights of recovery of such person against any person or organization legally responsible for the bodily injury because of which such payment is made"; (*b*) to "hold in trust for the benefit of the company all rights of recovery which he shall have against such other person or organization because of the damages which are the subject of claim made under this part"; (*c*) to "do whatever is proper to secure and shall do nothing after loss to prejudice such rights"; (*d*) if the insurer makes written request, "such person shall take, through any representative designated by the company, such action as may be necessary or appropriate to recover such payment as damages from such other person or organization . . . the company shall be reimbursed out of such recovery for expenses, costs and attorneys' fees incurred by it in connection therewith"; and (*e*) "execute and delivery to the company such instruments and papers as may be appropriate to secure the rights and obligations of such person and the company established by this provision."

Compulsory Aspects of the Uninsured Motorist Provision. In two states that have compulsory automobile insurance (New York and North Carolina) the law requires that the uninsured motorist provision be included in automobile liability insurance contracts. In Massachusetts the insurance commissioner has proposed a law to include it in every automobile liability insurance contract, although 85 percent of the drivers in his state already have such protection. The following fourteen states (although only two of the fourteen have compulsory automobile insurance) require by law that the uninsured motorist protection be offered in all automobile liability insurance contracts: California, Florida, Georgia, Illinois, Louisiana, Nebraska, New Hampshire, New York, North Carolina, Oregon, Pennsylvania, Rhode Island, South Carolina, and Virginia.

Conditions. In addition to the fundamental doctrines of insurance practice centering around the principles of indemnity, insurable interest, subrogation, fraud, inception, and termination of the coverage, which remain the same in the automobile contract as in other contracts insuring property, features of the contract present new questions because of the nature of the property insured. Certain salient features of the conditions will now be reviewed, but no effort will be made to discuss each condition in detail, since many of them follow a pattern that has already been described in respect to other physical damage coverages.

Notice. When an accident occurs the contract requires written notice. This is given by or on behalf of the insured to the insurer or any of its authorized agents as soon as practicable. The contract provides that the notice shall contain particulars sufficient to identify the insured, as well as reasonably obtainable information respecting the time, place, and circumstances of an accident, together with the name and addresses of the owner or driver of the car involved in the collision and all available witnesses. If a claim is made or a suit is brought against the insured, he is obligated immediately to forward to the insurer every demand, notice, summons, or other process received by him or his representative.

It follows that in the event of an accident that may involve a claim for damages, even though the insured feels himself not to be liable, notice should be given the insurer as promptly as possible. Insurers, as a rule, have printed forms indicating the nature of the data they require. This varies to some degree with the nature of the coverage. It may be stated that the insurer will require all pertinent information bearing upon the accident. The insured will be expected to use reasonable discretion and initiative in acquiring and recording this information.

In every instance where there is personal injury, an estimate of the extent of the injury is required. Whether the injured persons received first aid or medical attention is significant information. If injured parties receive medical attention, the name of the attending physician should be ascertained. If they are hospitalized, the name and location of the hospital should appear in the report. The names and addresses of all witnesses are required, and if an automobile is involved, the name and address of the owner, as well as the car license number, should be taken. If the driver is someone other than the owner, his name, address, and driver's license forms an essential part of the report. It is important to note the exact location of the accident, together with weather conditions. Again, if a car is involved, the condition of the highway should be noted and a detailed sketch made showing the relative positions of the cars just before and after the collision. In complying with the state requirements for reporting accidents, insureds will at the same time make a duplicate copy of any written forms or reports and a copy will be held for the insurance adjuster. If one or more members of the police force are present, a notation should be made of their names or badge numbers. It is important that the insured make no admission as to liability and make no effort at the scene of the accident to negotiate a settlement of the claim. The insurer by virtue of the contract has exclusive control over the adjustment of the claim, and the insured may make no attempt to effect a settlement without the consent of the insurer. By doing so he runs the risk of placing himself outside of the protection of the contract.

Duties When Loss Occurs. The condition governing duties when loss occurs requires protection of the insured automobile from further loss, notice as soon as practicable, and a proof of loss within 91 days. Due to the nature of an automobile that may be damaged at some remote place, the obligation to protect the damaged property is significant. An insured is expected to use all reasonable care and treat the property as he would had there been no insurance. Negligence on the part of the insured to exercise reasonable care in preserving the damaged property and protecting it from further loss may result in loss or damage not collectible under his contract. The contract undertakes to reimburse the insured for all reasonable expense incurred in protecting and preserving any salvage, and the insured is obligated to take all reasonable steps to this end. In the case of theft losses, immediate notice should be communicated to the public authorities. The insured is not obligated to offer any reward for the return of his property, and if he does so without the specific authorization or direction of the insurer, such a disbursement is not collectible under the contract. The contract covers reasonable expense incurred to provide such protection. The insured is also obligated to make the damaged property available for inspection by insurer representatives. The insured may also be required to submit to examination under oath and make available to insurer representatives records and invoices that may have a bearing on the loss.

Appraisal. This condition is patterned after a similar one contained in the fire insurance contract. A request for an appraisal is to be made within 60 days after receipt of proof of loss by the insurer. It is also a part of the condition that participation in an appraisal by the insurer in no way is a waiver of any rights. Thus, an insurer having a defense under the contract may participate in an appraisal without waiving that defense. This makes it unnecessary to take an agreement that no defense is waived as is sometimes the practice where such a clause does not appear in the contract.

Payment of Loss. The insurer is never liable beyond the actual value of the insured automobile, but in the case of a car written for a stated amount, this amount represents a limit of liability. If the actual value is less than the stated amount, actual value prevails as the limit. When an automobile has become damaged, an insured frequently feels that it cannot be replaced in a manner to satisfy him or restored to a condition reasonably approximating that before the loss. In such a case, he feels it not at all unreasonable to ask from the insurer the full value of the car, leaving the salvage to the insurer. Under the contract, the insured has no right of abandonment, nor has the insurer any obligation to settle on such a basis. Regardless of the lack of any right on the part of the insured to abandon, the insurer has the right to take any part or all of the salvage at the appraised value. The measure of the insured's loss represents the difference between the value before the loss and the value of the salvage. It does not matter that salvage is beyond repair, nor is it necessary that the amount of loss be sufficient to repair the damage.

Action against Insurer. Liability contracts when first offered were indemnity agreements between the insurer and the insured. Under the terms of the contract, the insurer agreed to indemnify the insured for any expenditures he was obligated to make because of his legal liability arising out of an accident covered by the contract. Injured parties under such contracts had no remedy so far as the insurance was concerned, if a judgment obtained against the insured was uncollectible. Thus, in a situation where an insured became insolvent, or was declared bankrupt following an accident, his insurance made no contribution to the injured party. There was no obligation to satisfy the damages.

As time went on, the situation was held to be intolerable and legislatures took steps to effect a correction. By virtue of statutory enactment, injured parties may now bring direct action against the liability insurer of a negligent insured. Most states have adopted remedial statutes which require in substance that liability contracts shall contain a provision that the bankruptcy or insolvency of the person insured shall not release the insurer from the payment of damages for injuries sustained or loss that developed during the effective period of the insurance. Such statutes require a contract provision to the effect that an injured party may maintain an action directly against the insurer if, after judgment the execution against the insured is returned unsatisfied. Some statutes provide the right of action for the injured party in case the judgment remains unsatisfied for the specified period. In some instances the right to sue the insurer is conditioned both upon his bankruptcy or insolvency and upon the existence of a final judgment which establishes his liability. The family automobile contract provides as follows:

Action against Company—Liability: No action shall lie against the company unless, as a condition precedent thereto, the insured shall have fully complied with all the terms of this policy, nor until the amount of the insured's obligation to pay shall have been finally determined either by judgment against the insured after actual trial or by written agreement of the insured, the claimant and the company.

Any person or organization or the legal representative thereof who has secured such judgment or written agreement shall thereafter be entitled to recover under this policy to the extent of the insurance afforded by this policy. Nothing contained in this policy shall give any person or organization any right to join the company as a co-defendant in any action against the insured to determine the insured's liability.

Bankruptcy or insolvency of the insured or of the insured's estate shall not relieve the company of any of its obligations hereunder.

Action against Company—Medical Payments, Property Damage, and Uninsured Motorists: No action shall lie against the company unless, as a condition precedent thereto, there shall have been full compliance with all the terms of this policy, nor until thirty days after the required proofs of claim have been filed with the company.

By virtue of the foregoing condition it is provided that any person who has secured either judgment or written agreement of the insured's liability may recover under the contract to the extent of the insurance afforded. This provision allows the injured judgment creditor to sue the insurer without the necessity of demonstrating the insured's insolvency through an unsatisfied execution.

Not only is it the general rule that the claimant has no right of action against the insurer until he has secured a written agreement of the insured's liability or until judgment has been allowed but, more than this, to indicate in a legal action against the insured that he is covered by insurance may result in a mistrial or the judgment for the plaintiff be reversed. The rule is based upon the assumption that if the jury knows that an insurer is to pay the damages and not the individual defendant, there will be a temptation to be generous with the insurer's money and in borderline cases sympathy rather than the facts at issue may be the determining factor. It follows, therefore, that reference to "insurance" or "insurance protection" directly or by inference may jeopardize the case of the plaintiff. The rule is not viewed as an entirely logical one in the light of the wide distribution of insurance and the practice of the use of defense counsel that came to be known as "insurance company attorneys." Where, however, the rule is in full force and effect, insurer attorneys conducting a defense will be on the alert to turn it to their advantage wherever the opportunity presents itself. This is entirely proper in a legal action, and it is, therefore, the responsibility of the plaintiff so to conduct himself with respect to the rule that he will not be responsible for a mistrial or a reversal on appeal of any judgment in his favor.

No Benefit to Bailee. This clause is found in one form or another in all marine contracts. The contract expressly excludes liability for loss or damage to the insured automobile when in the possession of a carrier or bailee if the proceeds of the insurance is to inure directly or indirectly to the benefit of such carrier or bailee. The insured is expected, as in the case of all marine contracts, to proceed against the carrier or bailee. In the process of adjustment the insurer may advance to the insured, by way of a loan, money equivalent to his loss or damage. The money is to be repaid to the insurer to the extent of the net amount collected by, or for, the account of the insured for the carrier or bailee after deducting the cost and expense of collection. This condition prevents railroads or steamship lines, otherwise liable, from taking advantage of a shipper's insurance.

Assistance and Cooperation of the Insured. The insured is required to give all reasonable assistance to the insurer to the end that a satisfactory settlement may be effected. The insured may not stand by and rely upon his insurance for reimbursement and refuse to testify at a hearing or otherwise give reasonable help to insurer representatives. This clause assumes great importance in connection with liability claims.

Assignment. An assignment of the contract will not bind the insurer until the insurer consents. Because of the nature of automobile coverages, the insurer wishes to underwrite its insureds carefully. The clause contains provisions as to the application of insurance in the event of the named insured's death. It is provided that the contract shall cover, in such a case, the named insured's spouse, if a resident of the same household at the time of death. Legal representatives of the named insured are covered following his death. Bodily injury liability and property liability extend to persons in temporary custody of the automobile. Medical payments coverage applies to such a person while the automobile is used by him up to the time of the appointment and qualification of the insured's legal representative. Notice of cancellation addressed to the named insured that appears in the declaration and mailed to his address as shown in the contract will serve to cancel the coverage.

Declarations. This part of the contract incorporates the declarations into the agreement. It is stated that the contract embraces all agreements existing between the insured and the insurer or any of its agents relating to the insurance. Thus it is important that all material information called for appear in the declarations. Particularly if the insured is other than sole owner of the car covered, this interest should be indicated. Any encumbrances, lien, or mortgage should be indicated, as should any change of interest of the insured through sale or otherwise.

Subrogation. As in the case of other insurance contracts with respect to liability claims but not with respect to medical payments, the insurer is subrogated to all rights of recovery which the insured may have. The insured is obligated to execute and deliver instruments and papers and do whatever else is necessary to secure the subrogation rights of the insurer. In this respect the contract provides:

Subrogation—Liability and Physical Damage: In the event of any payment under this policy, the company shall be subrogated to all the insured's rights of recovery therefor against any person or organization and the insured shall execute and deliver instruments and papers and do whatever else is necessary to secure such rights. The insured shall do nothing after loss to prejudice such rights.

It is important that the insured do nothing whatever after a loss to prejudice the subrogation rights of the insurer. It is particularly important in gathering information required for the loss notice that the insured make no statement that would in any way prejudice the position of the insurer either by relieving another of liability or assuming responsibility himself. The insured may feel himself to be to blame for an accident but he quite well may be mistaken. He will gather his facts and such admissions, if any are to be made, will be made after due deliberation and after consultation with his insurer. No insured is required to testify to an untruth or contend that which is false. He may, unless careful, unwittingly prejudice the position of the insurer and, hence, violate a contract condition.

OTHER TYPES OF CONTRACTS

The family automobile contract is not suitable for all of the situations where automobile insurance may be desirable. A brief outline of some of these situations and the available coverages will give an indication of the possibilities.

Forms of Collision Coverage. Collision insurance is written to provide full cover or may be written on a deductible basis or on one of several special forms devised in the interest of reducing the cost of the coverage. Some of these forms now have limited use but for reasons of completeness are defined below. It is fairly rare for complete coverage collision to be written. The most common deductible is now $100 and there is a possible trend toward higher amounts.

Full-Cover Collision. Under the full-cover form, the insurer pays the full amount of any collision loss or damage.

Deductible Collision. The deductible collision form provides that there shall be no liability on the part of the insurer unless the loss exceeds a named amount, and then the amount of the liability is only so much of the loss as exceeds the deductible amount. Thus, if a contract is written under a $50 deductible form, there would be no liability on the insurer until the loss exceeds $50. In the case of a $200 loss, the insurer's liability would be $150.

Deductible collision coverage is usually written under one of three forms: $25 deductible, $50 deductible, or $100 deductible. In some instances, contracts are written for $150 deductible, and even for $250. In special cases when values run to large amounts as, for example, in the insurance of buses, $500 and $1,000 deductible contracts may be written.

Convertible Collision. Convertible collision, sometimes known as "retention collision," is written providing for an initial payment to be made when the contract is written and the balance to be paid in the form of an additional premium if a claim is made. In some jurisdictions the initial premium represents 50 percent of the full coverage premium, while in other jurisdictions an initial premium is quoted in the manual; but even here the premium is approximately 50 percent of the full coverage premium. Under this form, the insured is protected for full coverage at all times, but in the event that he has no claim, his insurance will cost him for the year only the amount of the initial premium. In the event a collision claim is made to the insurer, regardless of the size of the claim, the additional premium becomes due. If the insured has a small collision loss and elects to pay it himself rather than incur the liability to pay the additional premium and later has a sizable collision loss which he reports to the insurer, it is not possible to back-date the coverage and include payment for the earlier loss. The contract provides that loss or damage occurring previous to the first reported accident shall not be covered.

80 Percent Collision. This form sometimes known as the "80–20" form provides collision coverage for all losses but pays only 80 percent of a loss of $250 or less. Losses in excess of $250 are paid in full. In the case of a $10 loss the insurer is liable for $8. In the case of a $200 loss the insurer is liable for $160. In the case of a $300 loss the insurer is liable for the full amount.

Cumulative and Participation Collision. This form is used in some jurisdictions where convertible collision is not permitted. The insured pays 50 percent of the full coverage premium and assumes all losses up to this sum. After losses have reached or exceeded the amount of the premium paid, the insurer is liable for all collision losses in full.

Progressively Diminishing Collision. This form provides that losses less than a stipulated amount will impose no liability on the insurer. If a loss is twice the stipulated amount or more, it is paid in full. Losses between these two figures pay twice the amount that the loss exceeds the stipulated sum. With a stipulated sum of $100 there is no liability for losses under that amount. A loss must be $200 or more to paid in full. A loss of $150 represents $50 more than the stipulated amount and, hence, the $50 is doubled. For $150 loss the insurer is liable for $100.

Reducing Deductible Collision. This is a deductible form that reduces during the contract term if the collision experience is favorable. A deductible is selected by the insured, usually $50 or $100, and this applies in full at the inception date of the contract and for six months thereafter. If after six months there are no collision claims, the deductible is reduced by $5. Like deductibles are made for each six-month period free from collision claims. After 60 months no further reductions are allowed. This means that an insured may reduce a $50 deductible collision to full coverage or $100 deductible collision to $50 deductible if no claim is reported for 60 months. Since it requires more than one contract term to earn the maximum reduction on a deductible, deductions earned in one contract term are carried over to succeeding terms. If a claim is made, the deduction developed applies, but the contract then reverts to the full amount of the original deductible and the insured must then earn again reductions on the basis of subsequent experience. This form is sometimes known as "safe driver reward" collision insurance.

Single Interest Collision and Conversion Insurance. This is a form of insurance made available to dealers and finance companies to protect them against loss occasioned by the hazards incident to financed automobiles. Not all cars carry comprehensive or collision insurance, and a financed car seriously damaged by collision might deplete the security of the finance company and might possibly result in a situation in which collection of the amount due is impossible.

Single interest collision insurance protects the interest of the insured finance company or automobile dealer only. In the event of an accident, the owner of the automobile is expected to make necessary repairs, and if he does this, there is no liability on the part of the insurer writing the single interest collision insurance. If, following a collision damage to a financed car, the purchaser of the car fails to make necessary repairs and discontinues making his payments under the terms of the sales contract, the insurer is obligated to repair the collision damage or make good to the insured the loss occasioned by the collision.

When conversion coverage is attached to the contract, it has the effect of protecting the insured against the illegal disposal, embezzlement, or concealment of the automobile by a purchaser in lawful possession under a conditional sales contract or lease. The standard theft contract provides no protection for conversion losses of this type. Consequently, even though the owner of the car protects the interest of the finance company under a fire and theft contract, the theft coverage affords the finance company no protection against conversion losses. To establish conversion loss, it must be shown that the act upon which the claim is predicated is illegal and committed with intent to defraud the insured finance company or dealer. Conversion insurance is a form of theft cover protecting the creditor against the wrongful acts of the debtor.

Single Interest Fire and Theft. While it is usual in connection with the financing of the purchase of automobiles for the party providing the funds to require the purchaser of the car to insure it for fire and theft and have the contract endorsed to cover the interest of the mortgagee, there are, nevertheless, situations in which a single interest fire and theft contract meets a need. Automobile dealers and finance companies in the chattel loan business that advance money with automobiles as security frequently find the single interest fire and theft contract advantageous. The contract provides a cover similar to that afforded by the single interest collision contract but limited to the risks of fire and theft. Thus, the party advancing funds in connection with the purchase of an automobile or a loan secured by an automobile is the named insured. This party alone benefits from the insurance; under no circumstance is the purchaser or owner of the car a participant in its benefits. In the event of a loss by fire or theft, the insured is obligated to make every effort to collect from the borrower the amount due, but if this is impossible and the automobile which represents the security is so damaged that the security is destroyed or impaired, the insurer is liable to the mortgagee for any difference that may exist between the salvage value of the damaged car and the amount due on the funds advanced.

Dealers' Direct Damage Insurance. Direct damage insurance for automobile dealers is written under several forms, each adapted to meet a particular need. The contracts are usually written to cover fire and theft, although collision is frequently included. The comprehensive contract is not available for dealers, but riot and civil commotion, hail, earthquake, explosion, vandalism, windstorm, water damage, and flood insurance each may be written. If insurance against all these risks is desired, the special combined additional coverage endorsement may be used.

The various contracts cover automobiles owned by the dealer and held for sale or used in repair service. The insurance does not extend to automobiles sold under a conditional sale, mortgage, or other similar agreement. The contract covers the equity of the insured in new automobiles consigned to him for sale, even though actual title may remain in the name of another. Automobiles in service stations, salesrooms, or garages are covered, although it is usual to exclude automobiles while in any building or on premises occupied by the insured as a factory or assembly plant. If automobiles are in transit, coverage is limited to four on any single lake or river boat, harbor barge, or lighter. This limitation does not apply to automobiles in transit by railroad if the cars are being transported on a ferry. The contract excludes transportation losses while the automobile is being conveyed in or on a motor vehicle or trailer. The contract covers for 48 hours at unnamed locations if such locations are owned, rented, or controlled wholly or in part by the insured. A limit of liability applies with respect to any loss at an unnamed location; if unnamed locations are not reported within the 48 hours of coverage, the coverage terminates. There is coverage for seven days from the date liability could first attach for locations not owned, rented, or controlled by the insured. Open-lot storage is covered under one of two bases: standard lots, and nonstandard lots. If the lot is enclosed on all sides by metal cyclone fencing, or the equivalent, not less than six feet high with all openings securely locked when unattended, the lot is regarded as standard. All other open storage spaces fall in the nonstandard category. The coverage extends without deduction to standard lots, but for nonstandard lots a $25 deductible applies to theft losses not occasioned by theft of an entire automobile.

The theft coverage under dealers' forms is limited in that the term "theft" as defined in the contract is not as broad as the generally accepted legal definition of the term. This is so because under the so-called "trick and device clause" the insurer excludes liability growing out of loss occasioned by the voluntary parting of possession of the insured car by the insured "whether or not induced so to do by any fraudulent scheme, trick, device, or false pretence." Thus, under the terms of the contract, if the owner of the car delivers it to a third party for sale or for any other purpose and the automobile is not returned or the proceeds of sale accounted for, there is no loss under the contract. Again, if the owner of a car delivers it to a person as a result of a sale and receives in payment therefor a forged check, there is no loss under the theft contract. Finally, there is no loss if the theft is made by persons in the insured's household, service, or employment. It is not the intention of the contract to provide fidelity coverage upon employees or to provide protection against fraudulent schemes or tricks. Rather, it is the intent to cover the taking of the car itself by a thief without the knowledge of the owner. The contract does not cover the theft, robbery, or pilferage of tools or repair equipment unless the entire automobile is stolen.

Nonownership Liability. It has become well settled in law that liability for damages resulting from negligence on the part of employees or agents in the use of their automobiles in furthering the interests of their employer's or principal's business may attach to the employer or principal. The principle not only applies to chauffeurs and other employees driving cars in connection with the employer's business with their knowledge and consent but also applies when any employee uses his car with or without the consent or knowledge of the employer in carrying on the work for which he is engaged.

The nonownership contract is undertaken to protect the named insured against all legal liability for bodily injuries or property damage arising out of the use or operation of automobiles not owned by him. Under the nonownership form the person, copartnership, or corporation named in the contract is the insured, and there is no extension to others, as is found in the omnibus clause of the private passenger coverage issued to individuals. The nonownership coverage applies to the use of passenger cars and the occasional use of commercial cars.

In writing this coverage, employees are divided into two classes. Employees who are known to use individually owned cars when on the business of the employer are class 1 employees. All other employees are class 2 employees; their status is not known, and they may or may not use their cars in their employer's business. Contracts may be issued providing a blanket coverage for class 1 and class 2 employees, or they may be written covering specific class 1 employees or specific class 2 employees. Under the blanket form, there is complete coverage on all classes of employees.

Fleet Liability Plan. For the purposes of liability rate making, five or more automobiles owned by one insured under one direct operating management constitute a fleet. Discounts from the manual rate are based upon the size of the fleet, the discount increasing with the number of car increases. The discount is based on the theory that when a single concern operates a large number of cars, a percentage of them will be out of operation part of the time for repairs or other reasons.

If there is any possibility that hired cars will be used during the contract term, the hired-car liability hazard can be covered by extending the fleet plan contract on owned cars by endorsement to cover all cars and trailers hired by the insured. Careful insureds frequently incorporate the hired-car endorsement into the coverage, even though they do not customarily hire cars. By paying the minimum premium charge they are protected if, in the event of an emergency, a car is hired and the matter of insurance overlooked.

Deductible Liability and Property Damage. Fleets of five or more are eligible for bodily injury liability and property damage insurance on a deductible basis. The plan is usually more attractive to owners of large fleets willing to assume small claims themselves. Bodily injury deductible insurance is written with a deductible figure ranging from $250 upward, depending upon the requirements of the insured, and in some cases the amount is several thousand dollars. The deductible feature is written in two ways. It may be made to apply to each individual claim or to all claims arising out of any one accident. On property damage coverage the deductible amounts are usually lower; standard coverages being offered with a deduction of $25, $50, and $100 per accident.

The deductible feature applies only to the loss portion of the claim and not to the expenses of investigation and settlement. The insurer, through its adjusters, handles all claims and settles them in full, charging the deductible amount against a deposit made for that purpose by the insured.

Garage Liability and Property Damage. To meet the needs of automobile dealers, garages, repair shops, and service stations, a garage liability contract is available which is, in fact, a combination of the automobile liability and property damage contract covering the operation of automobiles and a general liability contract covering the hazards due to maintenance of the premises and the operation of the business. Under the automobile section of the contract, the automobile bodily injury and property damage liability coverage is provided. In addition, nonownership bodily injury and property damage liability is covered. The contract covers a manufacturer's liability on the premises and business operations on or away from the premises. Liability for defective workmanship or repairs is covered as well as liability growing out of the use or existence of hoists for greasing or otherwise servicing cars.

The liability for damage to property of others in the custody of the insured is excluded in the basic contract. Since accidents sometimes happen to automobiles while in the custody of the insured, the property damage coverage under such circumstances is required. The contract may be endorsed to provide insurance in the case of accidental collision. Such contracts invariably are written on the $100 deductible basis. They exclude fire and theft losses, elevator losses, and collision losses on drive-away or haul-away cars from a factory or distribution point.

Garage liability contracts are written to provide a premium computed on a payroll basis, on a named driver basis, or on a specified car basis. The first of these forms is the broadest and the one most generally used. The other forms are used only in the case of small risks when the names of the drivers or the designation of the cars is sufficient to cover the automobile liability exposure. In the case of the named driver and the specific car bases, the premises hazard is not covered in the contract but is covered by a separate contract specifically assuming this part of the risk.

The garage liability contract does not cover the liability hazards of cars rented without drivers, taxicabs, omnibuses, sight-seeing automobiles, school buses, and cars used in transporting property for others. Coverage on this type of risk is secured by specific insurance.

Livery operations are likewise excluded, although in the case of a garage where livery operations form a minor part of the business, livery coverage may be endorsed on the contract and the premium based upon gross livery receipts.

Garage Keepers' Legal Liability. The contract provides protection against the perils of fire, explosion, theft, collision, and riot or civil commotion, as well as malicious mischief or vandalism. It undertakes to cover the legal liability of garage keepers and applies to cars which they have in their custody for safekeeping. It is not necessary that the car for which the insured is responsible be located in his garage at the time the loss occurs. The contract covers the insured's liability for loss or damage to cars temporarily removed from his premises. The coverage is on a named perils basis and not all risk. In addition to fire and explosion the insured may elect at his option theft, collision, and riot or civil commotion, including malicious mischief or vandalism. The last named coverage is written with a $25 deductible. The contract may be written not only for garages but also to cover the legal liability of operators of parking lots.

The coverage is not to be confused with the garage public liability policy which provides bodily injury and property damage liability on a premises basis. The garage keepers' legal liability covers only the legal liability of the insured for loss or damage to automobiles of others in his custody.

Suspension Endorsement. In areas where, because of inclement weather, owners consider it to be not feasible to drive their automobiles for part of the year, a plan was worked out for providing a return credit if the automobile was placed out of use during the winter months. The rule now no longer applies to winter months; and in any case in which an insured has occasion to lay up his automobile for 30 days or more a premium credit is allowed. Under the plan, when the insurer is notified, coverage is terminated under the suspension endorsement and does not again become effective until notice to reinstate is received from the insured by the insurer or its agent. When the contract is reinstated, a pro rata credit is allowed the insured, provided always that the coverage has been suspended for 30 days or more. If the insurance is not reinstated, insurance is regarded as having been canceled as of the date of the suspending endorsement and a short-rate return premium is allowed. Liability, property damage, and collision coverages are eligible for suspension.

Comprehensive Automobile Liability Contract. In line with the development of comprehensive insurance covers, the National Bureau of Casualty and Surety Underwriters and the American Mutual Alliance have drawn up a contract form known as the "comprehensive automobile liability policy." This contract differs from those covering specific exposures in that it covers all the liability of the insured from the maintenance or use of any automobile irrespective of the kind of car or by whom it is owned. The insuring clause providing bodily injury liability and property damage liability undertakes "to pay on behalf of the insured all sums which the insured shall become legally obligated to pay as damages because of . . . accident and arising out of the ownership, maintenance or the use of any automobile."

The comprehensive liability contract makes a particular appeal to the individual or concern which has a number of automobile exposures. To insure separately the drive-other-car hazard, the garage risk, the nonownership risk, hired car risk, and other like exposures with the attendant possibility of overlapping coverages in some instances and failure to complete coverage in others has given rise to a serious problem that the comprehensive contract admirably solves. In addition to covering all known automobile exposures, it covers as well any loss that may develop from an unknown and unforeseen exposure.

CHANGING NATURE OF AUTOMOBILE LIABILITY INSURANCE

Events of recent years have changed to some extent the nature and functions of automobile liability insurance. When automobiles were few in number and personal injuries and property damages resulting from their operation were far less significant than they are today, an automobile liability insurance contract served principally to protect its purchaser against liability imposed by laws arising out of the operation of his automobile. Automobile liability insurance was an institution for the protection of the motorist.

Today, the motorist's need for automobile liability insurance is much greater than ever before, but this coverage is being looked upon more and more as an institution for the protection of the public. This change is being reflected in several ways, particularly in court decisions involving automobile accident cases. If the insured defendant is in any degree responsible for an automobile accident, his insurance company probably will make a settlement, the amount varying with the degree of negligence of the insured.

Although settlements are now being made in approximately 70 percent of the accident cases where the defendant carries automobile liability insurance, the public seeks still more protection. Through financial (or safety) responsibility laws, states seek to secure the solvency of motorists. Such legislation has had the effect of increasing automobile liability coverage very appreciably. Several Canadian provinces have attempted to apply still more pressure to motorists to purchase liability insurance by incorporating in their safety responsibility laws an "impounding" provision which may result in an uninsured motorist losing his car in addition to license suspension.

Massachusetts, New York, and North Carolina require, under compulsory laws, automobile liability insurance for all motorists licensed in the state. In addition, several states have set up such a requirement for young drivers.

A few states and Canadian provinces have attempted to reinforce the voluntary automobile liability insurance system by providing unsatisfied judgment funds through which successful plaintiffs in automobile accident cases may, under certain conditions and within certain limits, collect the judgment account which the defendant cannot meet.

It has been suggested that the workmen's compensation principle of payment regardless of fault should be adapted to automobile accidents. Such a plan is in operation in the Canadian province of Saskatchewan. The medical payments benefit referred to earlier are based upon the compensation principle. The substitution of the compensation for the negligence principle creates many problems.

While opinion is divided in respect to the merits of the various measures just discussed, there appears to be a very large majority which holds that no motorist should venture forth in today's traffic without the protection afforded by an automobile liability insurance contract with adequate limits.

FOR DISCUSSION

1. How would you interpret the meaning of the words "each person" in the limit of liability clause of a liability contract? Explain the relationship with the total liability of an insurer in any one accident.
2. A and B are riding together in an automobile. A owns and is driving the car, and B is a passenger. The car collides with another at a street intersection, and while the passengers appear slightly shaken up, there are no apparent injuries. Shortly afterwards, B makes a claim against A stating that he has a strained back and other injuries as a result of the accident. B quite frankly tells a friend that he was not injured in the accident but sees no reason why he cannot get a little easy money from the insurer. The insurance adjusters, in their investigation, bring this information to light. Therefore, the insurer denies liability and refuses to give any consideration to B's claim. B files suit, but the insurer contends that it is not liable and will not defend A. What is the position of the insured, and also what is the position of the insurer?
3. D, the owner of a car insured under a family automobile policy, had frequently loaned it to CS. It had always been returned promptly. At six o'clock one evening CS asked for the use of the car to collect

money owed him. D agreed on the understanding that CS would use it only to go on the errand and would be back in less than an hour. CS failed to find his debtor. In the meantime he met a friend and they drove out of town together to a bar. On the way home, the car struck and injured PC. This was more than five hours after CS had borrowed the car. The injured party won a judgment against CS. The insurer refused to pay. The car was not stolen, and the claimant argued that the insurer was liable under the omnibus clause. The court held differently. Can you tell why?

4. Following a collision X, the insured, got out of his car to make himself known to the other party. While returning to his own car, the car was struck by a third car. The car of X was set in motion, striking X and injuring him. X made a claim to recover under the medical payment provision of his liability contract. Liability depended upon whether the injury was caused by an accident which occurred "while in or upon or while entering into or alighting from the automobile." Do you think the insurer is liable?

5. X, the owner of an automobile, allows his son to use the car from time to time. The son, while out with friends, has been in the habit of lending the car to a girl friend without the special permission of his father. An accident occurs while the friend is driving the car with the express permission and consent of the son. The injured party brings suit. The father's insurer denies liability. Is the insurer on firm ground? Explain.

6. X, a banking institution, carries a nonownership liability contract. B, an employee of the bank, states that in the circumstances an individual liability contract is unnecessary. Is this correct?

7. The legal doctrine "respondeat superior" provides that "a master is responsible for acts committed by his servants in pursuit of his business." What is the significance of this doctrine in the field of automobile liability?

8. B is a sales agent compensated on a commission basis. Following an automobile accident, his employer contended that B was an independent contractor and not, in fact, an employee. Do you think this would change the situation so far as the application of the doctrine "respondeat superior" is concerned?

9. The automobile liability policy does not cover when the insured car is used as a public or livery conveyance unless such use is specifically declared and described in the policy and a premium charged therefor. X, who permitted some friends to share expenses on a trip is told that he received a "consideration" and therefore jeopardized his liability coverage. Clarify the matter for us.

10. X had a policy with $100,000/300,000 bodily injury liability limits and $5,000 for property damage liability for each accident. His truck was negligently driven into a train, damaging 16 railway cars belonging to 14 owners in amounts ranging from $349 to $4,015, the total damage to the 16 cars being $41,371. Contents belonging to various shippers were damaged in an aggregate of $7,638. The roadbed of the

railroad suffered $9,000 damage. The insurer contends its limit of liability to be $5,000, since this was the limit for each accident. Suit was instituted against the insured for damages totaling $75,000. Is this one or several accidents?

11. B purchased an automobile on June 15 and some months later had an expensive radio installed in his automobile. To what extent will this radio be covered, if at all, by the insurance covering the automobile?
12. In the following list, indicate the losses that would come within the scope of the comprehensive automobile cover: (a) horse kicks in fender of new car; (b) dead skunk lodges in springs, rendering car uninhabitable until fumigated; (c) acid in tree spray ruins paint job; (d) foul ball breaks windshield; (e) cloudburst inundates car; (f) thieves break window and damage car interior; (g) Halloween vandals slash car tires and deface top and sides with chalk; (h) sand in dustbowl storm ruins the finish; (i) firecracker under hood damages ignition; (j) dog left in car chews up upholstery; (k) lighted cigarette discarded by driver lodges in rear seat and garaged car ultimately burns up.
13. An automobile, owned by B, was hit from the rear and was damaged to the extent of $250. The owner of the other car was quite apparently at fault. B's insurer paid him, under the $50 deductible collision contract, $200. He then took subrogation rights and proceeded against the person responsible for the accident. The insurer collected the $250. The cost of collecting the $250 from the party responsible for the accident was $50. The insured has already been paid $200. Is he entitled to all or any part of the $50 in excess of that collected by the insurers where the cost of collection is $50?
14. B parks his car on a public highway. When he returns, he finds the lock badly damaged and the wiring tampered with. As a result, he is unable to start his car. The damage appears unquestionably to be the outgrowth of an attempted theft. To what extent may he appeal to his insurance for reimbursement for his loss?
15. B maintains a garage in which he rents space for the storage of privately owned automobiles. Because of the nature of his business, he feels confident that all his customers carry fire and theft insurance, and he is of the opinion, therefore, that it is unnecessary for him to carry garage keeper's legal liability, insuring his liability for losses originating from these risks. Indicate the fallacy in this line of reasoning.
16. B carries a comprehensive contract on his automobile with a $100 deductible applying to collision. He has a collision loss amounting to $500. In computing the loss, it is found that $15 of the damage is attributable to glass breakage. For how much is the insurer liable?
17. How would the settlement in the foregoing problem differ if the collision coverage were the same but, instead of comprehensive insurance, a fire and theft contract were written?
18. X on the way home from a shopping trip stops to make a call on a friend. She leaves a valuable package in the automobile and the auto-

mobile is attended by a chauffeur. While the owner of the car is making the visit, the chauffeur leaves temporarily to purchase a package of cigarettes. In the interval the package containing the purchase at the store is stolen as well as a valuable robe. Are these items covered by the family automobile contract?

19. The owner of an automobile left his car parked near a hotel. The ignition was locked and the owner of the car retained the key. At some time later the 20-year-old son of the owner secured possession of the key or in some other means was able to get the car under way and, while driving at 100 miles per hour, overturned the car and demolished it. The boy had previously been confined to a state hospital, and there was evidence that he had been drunk. The father had no collision coverage and filed a claim for damage on the grounds that it was vandalism. Has he a claim?
20. The special automobile contract is frequently sold. In what way does it differ from the family automobile policy? In what circumstances is its use appropriate?

CHAPTER · 20

Aviation Insurance Contracts

Aviation insurance is that branch of the insurance industry which provides coverage for loss growing out of the hazards involved in the ownership, operation, care, repair, maintenance, or sale of aircraft. Aviation insurance, from a small beginning has developed into an important branch of the industry. Insurance protection is afforded not only to the plane owner, the pilot, and the passenger, but to students, instructors, base operators, airport owners, and airlines and aircraft manufacturers, to mention but a few beneficiaries. Strictly speaking, aviation insurance is not multiple line insurance. The intent here is to classify it under the miscellaneous part of the general heading "multiple line and miscellaneous insurance contracts."

In many ways, aviation insurance and automobile insurance are similar. Both are concerned with physical damage to the vehicle itself, as well as with the problem of third-party liability arising out of ownership, operation, and use. In some respects both are marine-type coverages. But there are a number of differences, and these differences account for many of the problems surrounding the aviation risk. As compared with automobile insurance, for example, aviation direct-loss insurance involves much larger sums. Planes valued at $9 or $10 million are not at all unusual, and in some instances, the value is far in excess of this sum. Three or four or five jets may be in one hangar at one time with numerous other expensive hulls on the same airfield. This concentration, with the concomitant exposure to catastrophic loss, is one of aviation insurance's largest problems. Because of the amounts involved, the peculiar nature of the risk, and the fact that the number of risks covered is comparatively small,[1] interested insurers have tended to form into groups or pools to write aviation risks, and the underwriting problems are handled by agents or managers who are

[1] It has been estimated that as of 1964, all of the airlines in the world account for no more than 3,700 aircraft and that there are fewer than 150,000 nonmilitary aircraft of all types. See Davis W. Gregg and John D. Long (eds.), *Property and Liability Insurance Handbook* (Homewood, Ill.: Richard D. Irwin, Inc., 1965), p. 317.

specialists in aviation coverages. Within recent years insurers are insuring, on an individual basis, planes that are privately owned or are owned by aircraft dealers or industrial concerns using aircraft in connection with their operations. In those fields where there is a heavy concentration of risk, such as the insurance of airlines or aircraft manufacturers, the business is still largely handled by pools or syndicates.

With the continued use of aircraft in industry and the establishment of regular transportation lines, together with the passage of federal regulatory legislation, the business of aviation attained stability. Notwithstanding the strides that have already been made by the industry, aviation insurance is still comparatively new. The control of aviation activities exercised by the federal government through the Civil Aeronautics Authority and the Civil Air Board has tended to give stability to the industry and to make mandatory safety measures that might otherwise be disregarded. Control is exercised with respect to the certification of pilots, and regulations are promulgated covering aircraft flights in the United States. Adequate insurance facilities now exist for handling aviation risks of every description. Contracts have been carefully constructed and competition is a factor with respect to rates and liberality of coverage.

The problems associated with aviation insurance vary to some extent with the use that is to be made of the aircraft. Some airplanes are designed to be used in the regularly scheduled passenger service of large airlines; others, and usually smaller craft, in private business and pleasure; and still others in large commercial and industrial enterprises. Although aviation insurance contracts have not been standardized, it is possible to identify contract forms of wide applicability to various uses. These forms will be analyzed in this chapter in sufficient detail to bring out some of the basic principles of this type of insurance.

CONTRACT FORMS

The contract forms in aviation insurance include: (*a*) the hull contract, which covers the risks of loss or damage to the insured aircraft itself, (*b*) aircraft liability written to cover public and passenger liability and property damage liability; (*c*) hangar keeper's liability that covers the bailee's liability with respect to aircraft stored for safekeeping or repair; (*d*) admitted aircraft liability that provides for voluntary settlements to injured passengers; (*e*) medical payments that provide medical expenses regardless of liability; (*f*) airport and airmeet liability contracts that provide protection similar to the owners', landlords', and tenants' forms generally written for property owners; (*g*) products liability covering manufactures, sales, or repair organizations against liability claims attributable to defective products or work; (*h*) aircraft workmen's compensation and employers' liability; (*i*) aviation personal accident insurance; and (*j*) cargo liability covering legal liability for loss or damage to cargo or baggage.

Cargo liability is to be distinguished from cargo insurance. Cargo insurance is not classed as an aviation line but is written by property and liability insurers in their inland marine departments. The hangar fire risk, windstorm hazard, and theft losses come within the scope of ground coverages. Accidental damage or "crash insurance," public liability, passenger liability, and property damage form the important coverages of the flying classification.

THE AIRCRAFT HULL CONTRACT

Physical damage to aircraft may be written to include one or more of the hazards listed above or it may be written to cover on an all risk basis with exclusions. Hull coverages, therefore, are said to be on a named perils basis, or an all risks basis. Largely due to competition, hull coverages for risks other than airlines and factories are fairly similar as far as contract working is concerned. Contracts may be written on a specified perils basis to pay for any loss or damage caused by such perils as fire, explosion, lightning, theft, and windstorm. When fire insurance is written, coverage is provided for loss or damage to the insured plane attributable to an accident to the conveyance in or upon which the aircraft when dismantled is being transported by land or by water.

There are three optional insuring agreements that are often used in aircraft hull contracts, although these contracts are not standard. The three coverages are: (1) all risks ground—limited in flight; (2) all risks ground and flight; and (3) fire, explosion and lightning, and transportation. Some insurers also offer a coverage that is all risks except while in flight and another that is all risks except while in flight or taxiing. Flight is defined as the period from the time the aircraft moves forward in taking off or attempting to take off for air transit, while in the air and until the aircraft completes its landing run, or has attained normal taxiing speed, after contact with land or water. The aircraft is said to be taxiing when it is moving under its own power, or momentum generated thereby, on land or water while in motion other than for the purpose of taking off or landing.

Some of the more usual established patterns of protection may be described as follows:

Coverage A: All risks—Limited In Flight. This coverage provides all risk protection while the aircraft is on the ground and named perils coverage while in flight. The flight perils are fire, explosion, lightning, theft, robbery, or vandalism. Losses by fire or explosion caused by crash or collision are not included.

Coverage B: "All risks" Ground and Flight, to pay for any loss of or damage to the aircraft, including disappearance, provided the aircraft is unreported for sixty (60) days after take-off.

Coverage C: Fire, Explosion, Lightning, and Transportation, to pay for any loss of or damage to the aircraft, except while In Flight or while Taxiing caused by (*a*) Fire, lightning, or explosion; (*b*) An accident to the conveyance in or upon which the aircraft when dismantled is being transported by land or water.

Coverage may apply in one of three circumstances: (1) while the aircraft is not in motion, (2) while the aircraft is not in flight, and (3) whether the aircraft is on the ground or in flight.

When insurers first undertook to write hull aviation risks, they imposed heavy deductibles upon the insured. These deductibles were designed to eliminate small losses and to place part of the burden of loss on the insured. With a heavy deductible there never could be an actual total loss. Whatever merit the deductibles may have possessed, they were placing serious limitations upon the adequacy of the insurance protection. Whatever deterrent they may have exerted toward the elimination of moral hazard losses or whatever effect they may have exerted with respect to loss ratios, there were many who felt that in the hazardous field of aviation the deductibles were too great to provide the protection required. A small plane valued at $5,000 and insured with a 10 percent deductible would involve the insurer in no liability until a loss exceeded the amount of the deductible. In other words, in the case of a $600 loss, the insurer would be liable for only $100. There were many who felt that they could not assume such losses. This was particularly the case with new and growing business establishments. A few losses that could be entirely justified as free of any moral-hazard taint could, nevertheless, result in seriously crippling the business undertaking.

Today policy with regard to deductibles varies among insureds. On business of high desirability, there are often no deductibles, while with respect to less desirable hulls, deductible may be required as a consideration in underwriting. If a deductible is included as part of the contract, it is normally (especially for in-motion losses) based on a percentage of the amount of insured value. The percentages used for this purpose are 2½ percent, 5 percent, or 10 percent. The minimum deductible amount of 2½ percent is $50; at 5 percent, $75; and at 10 percent, $100. Two sets of deductibles may apply; one set for in-motion losses, and the other set for not-in-motion losses. Flat deductibles are often used in the latter case.

Hull risks use the same contract form regardless of the perils covered. The insuring clause indicates that, in consideration of the premium stated, and subject to the stipulations and general conditions included in the contract, insurance is granted, in respect to the aircraft listed in the schedule of particulars, against direct loss or damage from the perils defined in the schedule of coverage. This is usually attached to the contract in the form of an endorsement.[2] The insuring clause further states that the contract itself embodies all agreements between the insurer and the insured. This is in contrast to the contract that previously prevailed by which the application was made a part of the contract. The schedule is attached in the form of a rider and indicates the perils against which the insurance is written. There are variations in detail in both the hull and liability contracts offered by the different aviation markets. Much of the business is handled by groups. Some of these groups are composed of 50 or more insurers. Others are smaller and include as few as three insurers. In addition, the foreign market is important. The underwriters at Lloyd's represent a most significant hull capacity. The coverages offered by the various markets are basically the same, though the contracts do contain differences and it is important to recognize that two contracts, each obtained from a different insurer, may not be identical.

Responsibility of Insurer under Hull Contract. The first of the conditions in the hull contract sets forth the liability of the insurer. The insuring clause of the contract indicates that, in consideration of the premium stated and subject to the stipulations and general conditions included in the contract, insurance is granted, in respect to the aircraft listed in the schedule of particulars, against direct loss or damage from the perils defined in the schedule of coverages. The first of the general conditions in the contract defines the liability of the insurer. This appears in the contract as follows:

> **Liability of Insurer.** The Insurer will pay, subject to the terms and conditions of this policy: In respect to TOTAL LOSS, the Insured Value less the deductions stated in the Schedule of Coverage;
>
> In respect to PARTIAL LOSS,
>
> *a*) If repairs are made by other than the Insured, the cost to repair the damaged property with material of like kind and quality, plus reasonable transportation charges, as herein defined, less deductions, if any.

---

[2] Some insurers provide contracts that follow the pattern of the automobile contract. The coverages appear on the face of the contract and are defined therein. As in the case of the automobile contract, the insurance is in effect with respect to only such coverages are are indicated by a specific premium charge. The limit of the insurer's liability is indicated against each coverage. There are also contracts available similar in effect to the combination automobile contract that provides both physical damage and liability coverages. The contract that provides for the definition of the extent and nature of the coverage by the attachment of an endorsement allows for greater flexibility, even though the endorsements are to a degree standardized.

b) If repairs are made by the Insured, the total of the following items, less deductions, if any:
   I. Actual cost of material or parts of like kind and quality.
   II. Actual wages paid for labor at current rates with no additional for overtime.
   III. 50% of Item II in lieu of all overhead including supervisory services.
   IV. Reasonable transportation charges as herein defined.

Notwithstanding the above, the amount due under this policy in respect to a partial loss shall not exceed the amount due were the loss payable as a total loss. In any event where the amount paid hereunder is equal to the amount payable as a total loss, any salvage value remaining shall inure to the benefit of the Insurer. There shall, however, be no abandonment without the consent of the Insurer.

Where theft, robbery or pilferage is insured against hereunder, the Insurer shall have the right to return the stolen property, at any time before actual payment of the claim hereunder, with payment for physical damage thereto sustained.

First of all the contract provides that the insurer will pay the insured value of the plane in the event of total loss subject to whatever deductions are provided in the schedule of coverages. In the case of partial loss the liability of the insurer is limited to the cost of repairing the damaged property plus transportation charges and less any applicable deductions. If the insured makes the repairs, a provision is made so that the insured will realize overhead costs. Thus, he is reimbursed for the cost of the material or parts and actual wages paid. To the sum of these items he may add 50 percent of the wage item. In addition, if there are transportation charges, these are covered as before. From the sum of these four items is deducted the amount of any deductions provided in the contract.

The condition provides that the liability of the insurer in the event of a partial loss shall never exceed the amount due if the loss payable were a total loss. Moreover, if the insurer is called upon to pay a total loss and the aircraft is, in fact, not totally destroyed, the insurer is entitled to whatever salvage remains. As in the case of other similar contracts, the contract provides that there shall be no abandonment to the insurer without his consent. If insured property is stolen the insured may not claim replacement with new. The insured must pay for any physical damage attributable to the theft and return the stolen property if it is recovered. If the property appears irrevocably lost and payment is made for it, the insured is not obligated to accept it if it is subsequently found and return the sum received in settlement.

Exclusions in Hull Contract. There are few exclusions in the contract and they vary greatly among insurers. Only two apply with particular reference to aircraft coverages. An example of a possible set of exclusions follows:

Exclusions. This policy does not cover Loss or Damage:

a) Occurring while the aircraft: (1) is being used for any unlawful purpose with the consent of the Insured, or of an executive officer if the Insured be a corporation; (2) is outside the Standard Geographical Limits, as herein defined; (3) is being operated for or in connection with any purposes other than specified in this policy; or (4) is being operated by any person other than the pilot or pilots specified in Item 5 of the declarations of this policy, excluding the starting and running of engine(s) and taxiing by mechanics and pilots certificated by the Civil Aeronautics Administration when so authorized by the Insured.

b) Occurring in flight while: (1) the terms of the Civil Aeronautics Administration Airworthiness Certificate, or Operational Record, of the insured aircraft or terms of the Pilot Certificate are violated; (2) the insured aircraft is being used for closed course racing, crop dusting or any form of hunting; or (3) the insured aircraft is being operated with the consent of the Insured in violation of the Civil Air Regulations applying to acrobatic flying, instrument flying, repairs, alterations and inspections, night flying, minimum safe altitudes and student instruction.

c) Due to and confined to wear and tear, deterioration, freezing or mechanical, structural, or electrical breakdown or failure, unless such damage is the result of other loss covered by this policy.

d) To tires, except where such damage results directly from other loss covered by this policy.

e) Due to conversion by any person in lawful possession of the Aircraft, or otherwise.

f) Resulting from: (1) captures, seizure, arrest, restraint or detention or the consequence thereof or of any attempt thereat, or any taking of the property insured or damage to or destruction thereof by any Government or governmental authority or agent (whether secret or otherwise) or by any military, naval or usurped power, whether any of the foregoing be done by way of requisition or otherwise and whether in time of peace or war and whether lawful or unlawful; (2) war, invasion, civil war, revolution, rebellion, insurrection or warlike operations, whether there be a declaration of war or not; or (3) strikes, riots or civil commotion.

The first of these dealing with the use of the aircraft may be summarized as providing no coverage in the following circumstances: unlawful use, operations outside standard geographical limits provided in contract, used for purposes other than for which insurance was provided, and operated by pilots other than specified in declarations. The second exclusion deals with occurrences while in flight. These include violation of the terms of certain documents essential to legal flight, particularly hazardous uses of aircraft, and violation of certain civil air regulations.

The remainder of the exclusions have been discussed in one form or another in the automobile contracts and in marine coverages. Loss due to wear and tear, tire damage, conversion, and war risk are all excluded.

Conditions Rendering Contract Void. This condition provides that the contract shall be void: in case of misrepresentation or fraud, and if the ownership is other than indicated in the declarations. This condition reads:

Conditions Rendering This Entire Policy Void. This entire policy shall be void:

a) If the Insured has concealed or misrepresented, in writing or otherwise, any material fact or circumstance concerning this insurance or the subject thereof; or in the case of any fraud, attempted fraud or false swearing by the Insured touching any matter relating to this insurance or the subject thereof, whether before or after a loss.

b) If the interest of the Insured in this insurance or the subject thereof be or become other than unconditional or sole ownership thereof unless specifically endorsed herein.

Particular emphasis is given to misrepresentation and fraud because of the nature of the risk. The statement with respect to misrepresentation and fraud that appears in the contract appears in more or less the same form in other contracts. It takes on particular significance since unlike the fire or automobile insurance contracts that are issued without a written application, a signed application is required for aviation coverages and considerable detailed information is called for. It is important to emphasize that painstaking care should be exercised in the completion of the application. It is certainly not a routine matter, and a question whose answer might appear immaterial to the applicant could have an entirely different import to the underwriter. Aside from a complete description of the aircraft and its uses, the name, age, licensing information, and hours of flight for each pilot named in the contract are required. If any pilot has any physical disability, this must be described fully. The following general questions then must be answered:

The interest of the Insured in the Aircraft is sole-unconditional ownership except .... If aircraft is mortgaged, name and address of mortgagee .... Amount of mortgage $........ Number of installment payments .... Amount of each $........ Date of final installment .... Name of last Aviation Insurance carrier (if none so state) .... To the Insured's knowledge no damage has been sustained during the past five years by aircraft owned by or in the custody of the Insured except .... No claims have ever been made by or against the Insured or by others in connection with an aircraft owned or operated by the Insured or otherwise except .... No insurance company or underwriter has at any time:

a) Canceled or declined to issue or renew insurance; or
b) Declined an application for insurance of, because of, or for any of the pilots listed herein, to the Insured's knowledge except ....

All particulars herein are warranted true and complete to the best of my/our knowledge and no information has been withheld or suppressed and I/we agree that this Application and the terms and conditions of the policy in use by the Insurer shall be the basis of any contract between me/us and the Insurer.
Date .... Applicant's Signature ....

The requirement that the contract will be void if the insured is other than unconditional or sole owner unless specifically endorsed prevents a change of ownership during the contract term without the consent of the insurer. If an aircraft is encumbered when the contract is written and it is so stated in the application, this will appear in the contract. To encumber a contract or sell an interest after the contract is written and without securing approval of the insurer by endorsement on the contract would have the effect of voiding it. The condition is drastic, but it is deemed to be necessary for the protection of the insurer.

Insured's Responsibility at Time of Loss. In the event of loss or damage giving rise to a claim against the insurer, the contract places a duty upon the insured to give notice and file proof, protect salvage, and make available insured property and records.

With respect to notice some insurers require written notice be given by or on behalf of the insured to the insurer "as soon as practicable." Other insurers require telegraphic notice. Following is an example of this latter form.

Insured's Duties When Loss Occurs. In the event of loss or damage the Insured shall as soon as possible telegraph the company giving the estimated extent of loss or damage and identifying by license number or otherwise the aircraft involved, and, in the event of theft, robbery or pilferage, the Insured shall also give immediate notice to the police. Within 60 days, unless such time be extended in writing by the Insurer, the insured shall execute and render to the Insurer a Proof of Loss stating the place, time and cause of the loss or damage, the interest of the Insured and all others in the property and the amount of loss or damage thereto, all encumbrances thereon and all insurance, whether collectible or not, covering said property.

The requirement of telegraphic notice gives emphasis to the requirement of promptness. Certainly a delay of days followed by a telegram without some sound reason for the delay would not satisfy the requirement as to notice. The notice should supply location or scene of accident, an estimate of damage or extent of injuries, address where insured may be reached by the adjuster, and location where damaged aircraft may be inspected. In case of theft losses the contract requires as well that "immediate" notice be given to the police. The usual proof of loss is required within 60 days, though this time may, of course, be extended and provision for the extension is mentioned in the contract.

This section of the contract then treats of the matter of salvage. It provides that in the event of loss or damage to the insured plane, whether the particular loss is covered by the contract, the insured shall protect the property from other or future loss so far as he is able to do this. Salvage is covered as follows:

> In the event of any loss or damage whether or not insured against hereunder the Insured shall protect the property from further loss or damage and in his failure to do so any such further loss or damage shall not be recoverable under this policy and, whenever requested by the Insurer, the Insured shall assist in the recovery of property insured hereunder either by means of replevin proceedings or otherwise, in effecting settlement, securing evidence, obtaining the attendance of witnesses and prosecuting suits to such an extent and in such a manner as is deemed desirable by the Insurer. Any such act or acts of the Insured, the Insurer or its Agents, including recovering, saving or preserving the property described herein shall be considered as done for the benefit of all concerned and without prejudice to the rights of either party and where loss or damage suffered constitutes a claim under this policy then all reasonable expenses thus incurred shall also constitute a claim under this policy, provided that the Insurer shall not be responsible for the payment of a reward offered for the recovery of the insured property unless authorized by the Insurer.

If the insured fails to take steps to provide adequate protection for the salvage, any further loss or damage that may be attributed directly or indirectly to the insured's failure is not recoverable under the contract. Thus, if an airplane should become disabled, it is the duty of the insured to use every means in his power to guard against theft losses. To abandon the plane, unless absolutely necessary, would prevent recovery for the theft of instruments or parts because of the insured's failure to protect the property.

It is provided that whatever efforts the insured or the insurer makes in recovering, saving, or preserving the insured property shall be considered as made for the benefit of all concerned. If the loss or damage suffered constitutes a claim under the contract, all reasonable expenses incurred in preserving or saving the property constitute a claim. The insurer assumes no responsibility for the offer of a reward unless such a reward is previously authorized by the insurer. Aviation insurance underwriters urge upon insureds the importance of not committing the insurer to any liability without definite authorization in advance.

Finally this section of the contract provides that all claims must be supported by logbooks, one each for the pilot, airplane, and engine, kept in order as required by the Civil Aeronautics Authority. Such a section reads as follows:

Claims must be made separately for each section, each accident and each aircraft and must be supported by the exhibit as often as required, and at any reasonable time during the currency of this policy or thereafter, of aircraft or insured property or remains thereof and of logbooks, one each for pilot, airplane and engine, kept in order as required by Federal Regulations; and by the exhibit at such reasonable place as may be designated by the Insurer for the purpose of making extracts or copies or otherwise of all books of accounts, bills, invoices or other vouchers, or certified copies thereof if originals be lost. The Insured shall further submit to examination under oath by any person or persons named by the Insurer and subscribe the same.

The logs must be made available to the insurer, and it must be allowed to make extracts or copies if it elects to do so. The insured property must be available for examination, and the insurer has the right to examine the insured under oath.

Reinstatement. Airplane contracts do not follow the fire and automobile pattern for reinstatement following a loss. One form of reinstatement clause is given herewith:

Reinstatement. In the event of loss or damage, whether or not covered by this policy, the amount hereby insured shall be reduced by the amount of such loss or damage until repairs have been completed, but shall then attach as originally written unless the Insured make written request to the contrary to the Insurer, provided, however, that if such damage is covered by this policy and is reinstated, the proper pro rata additional premium shall then be payable.

This clause provides for the automatic reinstatement of insurance following a partial loss unless the insurer shall make a contrary request. Up to this point the contract follows the pattern of automobile insurance. If the contract is reinstated, however, a pro rata additional premium is required. Some contracts are written with a loading in the premium to provide for the automatic reinstatement following a partial loss but with no provision for a return premium in the event of a total loss.

Requirement for Insurance to Value. There is no requirement in the hull form for insurance to value, nor does the contract contain a coinsurance clause. It is true that as an underwriting practice, aviation insurance underwriters attempt to obtain full coverage to value. A basic amount of premium is required for certain coverages, and if the insured wants to take a reduced amount of coverage, this will prove to be to his disadvantage and the actual cash value provisions of the contract will always benefit the insurer.

Component Parts Endorsement. A problem arises with respect to aircraft risks that are either very old or have a market value substantially less than replacement cost. Converted military surplus planes have been found to be in this category. Where this situation is found, partial losses may well result in claim payments that constitute an unreasonably large percentage of the total amount insured.

Insurance underwriters have met the problem by means of an endorsement known as a "component parts endorsement." This is attached to the basic contract stating that the component parts of the aircraft will not exceed such proportion of the insured values represented by indicated percentages. The percentages used are based upon underwriting judgment. The following is an example:

Fuselage	16%
Engine	17
Propeller	4
Wings	28
Ailerons	6
Landing gear	8
Fin	2
Rudder	2
Stabilizers	4
Elevators	4
Instruments (including radio equipment)	5
Tail wheel assembly	2
Miscellaneous	2
	100%

When this endorsement is used there is no loading in the basic rate for underinsurance.

Endorsements Establishing Conditions for Insurability. There are two endorsements that are attached to the basic hull contract that establish conditions for insurability. These are: the hangaring endorsement, and the tie-down endorsement.

The first of these endorsements deletes coverage for windstorm, hail, sleet, or snow while the aircraft is unhangared, except for reasonable parking between flights or away from the home airport.

The tie-down endorsement does not require the aircraft to be hangared but instead requires that the plane be tied down as an insuring requirement. In both of these endorsements if the condition set forth is not met, damage from tornado, cyclone, or the other named weather perils is not covered. The purpose of these endorsements is to minimize the weather perils. Consequently, when they are used, the premium is less than would otherwise be the case.

Fleet Plan Endorsement. An insured who is a fixed-base operator may have his hull contract endorsed to extend its coverage to additional aircraft purchased. The endorsement provides for a pro rata premium on the newly acquired aircraft from the date of acquisition.

The endorsement requires that the insured notify the insurer of the acquisition of the additional aircraft within a specified time. If a loss occurs prior to the time the additional aircraft is rated, the liability of the insurer is limited to the contract purchase price to the insured or, if a trade-in, the actual amount allowed by the insured; or a limit of liability can be stated in the endorsement. This endorsement provides for a deductible. Two aircraft must be continuously insured under the contract in order for the premium eliminated or added to the contract to be computed on a pro rata basis.

Reporting Forms of Coverage. Contracts written for fixed-base operators may be covered on a reporting form. The hull contract is endorsed and provides for a monthly report of values. The contract when so written covers airplanes acquired during the contract term, and premium credits are automatically reflected for contracts disposed of during the contract term by means of the monthly report of values.

The contract is written with an initial deposit premium. This may not be less than 25 percent of the flat annual premium nor less than the total annual premium on the three aircraft carrying the highest premium, whichever is greater. This rule may be modified in instances where because of the operations of the insured it would involve hardships. If the fleet is one where the change of aircraft is so frequent that a monthly report will not reflect an equitable premium, the contract may be written on a reporting form at per diem rates. The per diem rate is 1/365 of the annual premium. The premium on reporting forms is adjusted annually.

Excess Insurance. Values in hull contracts are so great that premiums represent very substantial sums. Airlines are sometimes in a position to assume substantial losses and in the interest of premium reduction frequently buy hull insurance on an excess basis. When this is done, the insured assumes a net retention and provides insurance for the excess.

Where insurance is written on a net retention basis, the plan works as follows. Assume, for example, an airline provides hull coverage with a net retention of $1 million. Assume coverage is written with a 5 percent deductible. In the event of $100,000 loss, the full amount of the loss is borne by the insured. Since the insurance is written with a 5 percent deductible, the insurance loss is considered to be $95,000. The amount of the net retention from this point on is $905,000. Thus, the insurer writing the contract will not be liable for a claim until the first $1 million in losses, computed on the basis here rated, have been borne by the insurer.

A second method of providing excess insurance utilizes an escrow fund. The airline contract is endorsed accordingly. The fund is set up in escrow, and all losses are settled by the insurer. If and when the escrow fund becomes exhausted, then the insurer becomes liable for losses over and above that amount.

AIRCRAFT LIABILITY COVERAGES

There are six optional coverages in the aircraft liability contract. These are: (1) bodily injury liability excluding passengers, (2) passenger bodily injury liability, (3) property damage liability, (4) medical payments, (5) bodily injury and property damage liability on a single limit basis excluding passenger liability, and (6) bodily injury and property damage liability on a single limit basis including passenger liability. The coverages are much the same as the liability coverages of automobile insurance. A principal difference is to be found in a separate insuring clause for passengers. As in the case of automobile insurance, the insured selects the coverage he elects to carry and the contract limits. It should be kept in mind that aircraft contracts are not standard and variations in coverage are to be expected.

The contract provides for the first four coverages listed above in the following terms:

> **Coverage A—Bodily Injury Liability, Excluding Passengers.** To pay on behalf of the Insured all sums which the Insured shall become legally obligated to pay as damages, including damages for care and loss of services, because of bodily injury, sickness, disease or mental anguish, including death at any time resulting therefrom, sustained by any person, excluding any passenger, caused by an occurrence and arising out of the ownership, maintenance or use of the aircraft.

The contract assumes liability imposed by law *caused by an occurrence* arising out of the ownership, maintenance, or use of the insured aircraft. There is some question as to the distinction between an "accident" and an "occurrence." The substitution of the term "occurrence" for "accident" is intended as a broadening of the coverage. The term "occurrence" which literally means an event is limited by definition in the contract. By definition the word "occurrence" whenever used in the contract means either an accident or a "continuous or repeated exposure to conditions, which results in injury during the contract period, provided the injury is accidentally caused." The definition then goes on to state that all damages arising out of exposure to substantially the same general conditions shall be deemed to arise out of one occurrence. The requirement that the injury be accidentally caused is designed to exclude claims resulting from the wilful intent of the insured. The use of the term "occurrence" provides coverage for gradual damage. If, for example, an insured knew that some action of his would result in bodily injury and he committed the act in any case, the contract would not cover since the injury would not be accidentally caused. On the other hand, if an occupant of a plane was forced to bail out and landed without injury but contracted pneumonia due to exposure, such a sickness or disease claim would be attributable to the occurrence.

Coverage with respect to passengers is provided as follows:

> **Coverage B—Passenger Bodily Injury Liability.** To pay on behalf of the Insured all sums which the Insured shall become legally obligated to pay as damages, including damages for care and loss of services, because of bodily injury, sickness, disease or mental anguish, including death at any time resulting therefrom, sustained by any passenger, caused by an occurrence and arising out of the ownership, maintenance or use of the aircraft.

This clause is identical in wording with coverage A, except that the word "passenger" is substituted for the phrase "person, excluding any passenger." The two clauses together provide the same protection as the liability insurance on an automobile. A principal reason for separating the coverages is to be found in the fact that seating capacity in a plane varies more than with an automobile. For the purposes of determining a premium based on seating capacity, passengers are covered separately. A second reason that separate bodily injury liability insurance on passengers is written is found in the fact that this practice permits a different limit for each of the coverages.

Property damage liability is covered as follows:

> **Coverage C—Property Damage Liability.** To pay on behalf of the Insured all sums which the Insured shall become legally obligated to pay as damages because of injury to or destruction of property, including loss of use thereof, caused by an occurrence and arising out of the ownership, maintenance or use of the aircraft.

Medical payments coverage is available in the following terms:

> **Coverage D—Medical Payments.** To pay the reasonable expense of necessary medical, surgical, ambulance, hospital and professional nursing services and, in the event of death resulting from such injury, the reasonable funeral expense, all incurred within one year from the date of occurrence, to or for each person, except the pilot unless specifically stated as "Included" in the Declarations, who sustains Bodily Injury caused by an occurrence while in or upon, entering or alighting from:
>
> 1. The aircraft described in the Declarations provided injury arises out of the use thereof by or with the permission of the named Insured and the purposes of use described in the Declarations are not other than "Industrial Aid" or "Private Business and Pleasure."
> 2. Any other aircraft with respect to which insurance is afforded under Agreement V of the policy provided such other aircraft is operated by the named Insured or spouse, or, if not so operated, such

medical payments coverage shall not apply in respect to injuries to or death of any person other than the named Insured or spouse.

The insurance afforded with respect to such other aircraft shall be excess insurance over any other valid and collectible medical payments insurance applicable thereto.

One point of significance needs to be emphasized. The medical payments coverage does not apply to the pilot unless specific insurance for him is provided. There is a space in the declarations in the medical payments coverage where the word "included" or "excluded" is to be inserted, depending upon whether or not medical payments coverage for the pilot is to be written.

Omnibus Clause. When aviation liability contracts were first offered, they contained no omnibus clause. The insurance extended to cover only the person specifically named in the contract. There is now a clause similar to that to be found in the automobile liability contract. The following is an example:

Definition of "Insured." The unqualified word "Insured" wherever used in this policy, except in respect to Coverage D, includes not only the named Insured, but also any person while using or riding in the aircraft and any person or organization legally responsible for its use provided the actual use is with the permission of the named Insured. This Insuring Agreement does not apply:

a) to any person or organization with respect to bodily injury, sickness, disease, mental anguish or death of any person who is a named Insured;

b) to any employee of an Insured with respect to any action brought against said employee because of bodily injury, sickness, disease, mental anguish, or death of another employee of the same Insured, injured in the course of his employment, caused by an occurrence arising out of the maintenance or use of the aircraft in the business of such Insured;

c) to any person or organization or to any agent or employee thereof (other than agents or employees of the named Insured) engaged in the manufacture of aircraft, aircraft engines or aircraft accessories, or operating an aircraft repair shop, airport, hangar, aircraft sales agency or flying school with respect to any occurrence arising out of the manufacture or the operation thereof.

The pattern of this clause follows that of the automobile contract in that it provides protection for other than the named insured if the person or organization operating the plane does so with permission of the named insured. The limitations in the clause are brief. The named insured may not make a claim for himself against another insured who becomes so by virtue of the omnibus clause. If one employee of an insured is injured by another, there is no coverage. Such injuries are expected to be covered by compensation insurance. Finally, organizations or their agents or employees engaged in manufacturing aircraft or otherwise in a business associated with the aviation industry are not covered. Persons or organizations in the business category are expected to be covered by their own insurance.

Liability Exclusions. Through a process of evolution the aviation liability contract that once contained a long list of exclusions now provides a coverage that is very broad, as indicated by the small number of exclusions. These appear in the contract as follows:

a) to liability assumed by the Insured under any contract or agreement;

b) to bodily injury, sickness, disease, mental anguish or death of any employee of the Insured while engaged in the duties of his employment or to any obligation for which the Insured or any Company as his Insurer may be held liable under any Workmen's Compensation or occupational disease law;

c) to injury to or destruction of property owned, rented, occupied or used by, or in the care, custody or control of the Insured or carried in or on any aircraft with respect to which insurance is afforded by this policy;

d) in respect to any aircraft while being operated, except while not in flight, by other than the person(s) approved in Item 5 of the Declarations;

e) to any Insured who operates or who permits the operation of the aircraft: (1) in violation of its Civil Aeronautics Administration Airworthiness Certificate or operational record or in violation of the terms of any Civil Aeronautics Administration Pilots Certificate; (2) in violation of any regulations of the Civil Aeronautics Administration applicable to acrobatic flying, instrument flying, repairs, alterations and inspections, night flying, minimum safe altitudes and student instruction: (3) for any unlawful purpose or for the purpose of closed course racing, crop dusting, spraying, seeding or any form of hunting.

Certain of these exclusions follow the pattern established in the automobile coverages. This is true with respect to liability assumed under contract and with respect to injuries to employees of the insured. If assumed liability is to be covered, the contract must be so endorsed and injuries to employees are expected to be covered by compensation insurance. The exclusion with respect to the destruction of property of the insured or in his care, custody, or control is typical of liability insurance. The exclusion with respect to property carried on an insured aircraft should be noted. By virtue of this exclusion there is no liability for a loss of the baggage of passengers. An extension of coverage to include baggage is available. The other exclusions have to do with the operation of the aircraft. There is no coverage unless the aircraft is operated by an approved pilot. Nor is there coverage if the plane is operated in violation of Civil Aeronautics Administration regulations. Coverage does not apply if the plane is operated for an unlawful purpose and certain dangerous uses such as racing, crop dusting, or hunting.

Limits of Liability. Rates for standard limits are quoted. For bodily injury liability, standard limits are $5/10,000. For passenger liability, the standard limit is $5,000 per seat, and $5,000 is the standard limit for property damage. Medical payments coverage is written only in connection with passenger liability with a standard limit of $500. With respect to liability limits the contract provides:

> **Limits of Liability.** (*a*) The limit of liability stated in the Declarations for Coverages A and B as applicable to "each person" is the limit of the Insurer's liability for all damages arising out of bodily injury, sickness, or mental anguish, including death at any time resulting therefrom, sustained by one person in any one occurrence; the limit of such liability stated in the Declarations as applicable to "each occurrence" is, subject to the above provision respecting each person, the total limit of Insurer's liability for all damages arising out of bodily injury, sickness, disease or mental anguish, including death at any time resulting therefrom sustained by two or more persons in any one occurrence.
>
> (*b*) The limit of liability stated in the Declarations for Coverage D as applicable to "each person" is the limit of the Insurer's liability for all expenses incurred by or on behalf of each person who sustains bodily injury, including death resulting therefrom, in any one occurrence; the limit of such liability stated in the Declarations as applicable to "each occurrence" is, subject to the above provision respecting each person, the total limit of the Insurer's liability for all expenses incurred by or on behalf of two or more persons who sustain bodily injury, including death resulting therefrom, in any one occurrence.
>
> The inclusion herein of more than one Insured shall not operate to increase the limits of the Insurer's liability.

Because of the values involved and the possibility of catastrophic accidents, limits higher than standard are the rule. Rate manuals quote liability limits for bodily injury, other than passenger liability, as high as $100/300,000 and passenger liability to $100,000 per seat. Property damage rates are quoted with $100,000 limit. Needs of an insured are often such that requests are made for limits beyond those provided for in an insurer's rating schedule. Insurers are willing to consider such higher limits and have developed a formula for computing the premium charge.

Passenger liability coverage is written with a standard limit of $5,000 per passenger seat. The lower standard limit of passenger liability coverage is $5,000, and the upper limit is the lower limit multiplied by the number of passenger seats. In determining the limits of insurance the pilot seat is not counted. In a four-passenger plane, one seat would be allocated to the pilot and the limit per passenger would be multiplied by three. Higher limits, as in other liability coverages, are available. In the case of transport lines in particular, the higher limits are invariably recommended. It has become increasingly the practice to carry high limits in connection with privately owned planes as well. Unlike the automobile contract that pays for far more injuries for temporary disability than for death, injuries to airplane passengers are very likely to be fatal. Passenger injuries are usually the outgrowth of a collision or crash, and few such accidents occur without one or more deaths. While injury claims do develop, it is the mortality hazard that could develop claims to catastrophic proportions.

Cancellation. Avaiation contracts provide for cancellation on the usual basis. The insured may cancel on notice, and the insurer may cancel by giving five days' notice. If notice is mailed to the insured at the address shown in the contract, this meets the contract requirements.

One significant point with respect to cancellation should be mentioned here. It is customary in some branches of the business of insurance to permit the flat cancellation of a contract. This means that when a contract is written and has run for a short period of time, it may be canceled "at date" with no premium charge. In the course of business, contracts are frequently written and for some reason canceled flat. Such contracts are usually reported as "not taken." In the field of aviation insurance, because of the huge amounts at risk and even where smaller contract limits are involved because of the hazardous nature of the business, flat cancellations are not permitted. It is possible to make a transoceanic flight in the matter of hours. A contract in force for only a few hours or a few days could quite possibly be liable for large amounts. It is also true that during a short period some extra hazardous operation might be performed. It is not felt to be equitable to have a contract or binder outstanding covering the exposure to be followed by cancellation at its successful termination. It is a practice in the aviation business to charge an earned premium on every contract once it is in force, regardless of how short a time may have elapsed before it is offered for cancellation. The same rule holds with respect to binders. Once a binder is issued and the insurance attaches, a premium becomes due. Aviation insurance agents are instructed not to issue binders without a firm order for insurance, and if a binder is canceled, the same rule applies with respect to earned premiums as would apply had the contract been issued.

Single Limit Liability Contracts. While most aircraft liability contracts are written showing separate limits for each coverage, a contract is available providing protection for the three liability coverages on a single limit basis.

The single limit liability contract protects the insured with respect to liability imposed by law for bodily injury, sickness, disease, or death suffered by any person or persons and for damages because of injury to or destruction of property due to an occurrence arising out of the ownership maintenance or use of the insured aircraft.

The contract is written with only one limit. This represents the maximum liability of the insurer for one coverage or any combination of coverages which may be involved in a claim attributable to one occurrence. Underwriting requirements make mandatory both bodily injury and property damage liability. Passenger liability is optional. When passenger liability is written, the premium is based on the number of seats, but there is no corresponding increase in the liability limit of the contract because of the number of seats.

This form appeals to corporations having an aviation exposure and fearful of a catastrophe loss. It may be written with high limits such, for example, as a half million dollars to cover planes used by salesmen. It is also a form frequently used to cover nonownership aviation liability.

Admitted Liability. This form, sometimes known as "guest voluntary settlement coverage," provides that the insurer will pay voluntarily the amount of admitted liability insurance to passengers suffering dismemberment or to dependents of passengers sustaining fatal injuries in an insured aircraft. The coverage is provided only in connection with the usual legal liability insurance. Underwriting requirements call for legal liability coverage in an amount at least equal to the amount of admitted liability insurance.

The form has a wide appeal as an extension of the aircraft liability coverage for the industrial aid classification. Corporate owners of aircraft who carry customers or employees of customers provide this form of protection as a means for retaining good will in the event of an accident involving injury to, or death of, a passenger where for business reasons a voluntary settlement seems desirable without investigating the question of legal liability.

When the coverage was first made available to insureds, an upper limit of $10,000 was usual. With the emphasis given to large liability claims, the demand for larger limits evidenced itself. Contracts with a limit of $25,000 per passenger are quite customary, and many contracts are written with limits as high as $50,000 per passenger.

The admitted liability endorsement requires a full release of all liability under the contract from the claimant when a payment is made. If the claimant fails to sign such a release, no payment is made under the endorsement. Instead the insurer undertakes a settlement under the legal liability coverage, and protection is afforded up to the legal liability limits of the contract. Usually a claimant would accept an adjustment based upon a voluntary payment. The exception would be, of course, where the voluntary payment limits are less than the claimant feels he is in a position to collect. In such an instance the insured is faced with a claim in excess of contract limits, since legal liability and guest voluntary settlement coverages must be equal. Here the defense, settlement, and supplementary payments feature of the contract may keep the amount of the claim within contract limits. Admitted liability coverage is akin to medical payments protection. The similarity is found in the fact that payment is offered the injured passenger without the necessity of establishing liability. In contrast to medical payments coverage where the limits are low, under the admitted liability coverage, limits are high enough to satisfy a liability claim in the ordinary course.

Nonownership Liability. While nonownership automobile liability coverage is regarded as essential for an employer where there is a possibility that an employee may use his car in the furtherance of the business of his employer, the need in the aircraft field has not been so readily recognized. The contract is written to provide protection for insureds in connection with aircraft used in their interest but which they do not own.

It is pointed out particularly that crews employed by corporations to operate aircraft may move the plane of another owner under circumstances that will precipitate a claim against the employer. Whether there is actual liability, the cost of defense may be substantial. The defense feature of the contract is a prime motivating reason for the purchase of this coverage.

In the case of corporations with a large number of employees, some of whom may own their own airplanes, there is always the possibility of a situation where actual liability may develop and where the insurance will be required for the payment of claims. Nonownership liability insurance is obtainable at a comparatively low cost. This is so because the chance of claim is remote. Without this protection a serious exposure to loss may remain uninsured.

Cargo Liability. Contracts are written covering the legal liability of the carrying plane for loss or damage to cargo or baggage. Cargo liability is written as a separate form and covers the liability of the aircraft owner to shippers for loss or damage to merchandise for which the airline may be legally liable. Passenger baggage liability covers aircraft owner's liability for loss or damage to passengers' baggage.

Both of these forms are third-party, or liability, coverages and are to be distinguished from the inland marine cargo cover written for the account of merchandise owners against loss or damage caused by agreed perils of air transportation.

AIRPORT LIABILITY

Airport liability coverage has many of the characteristics of the owners', landlords', and tenants' liability contract; but because the risk is peculiar to the business of aviation, it is usually written by insurers specializing in aviation risks.

Airports, whether individually owned, the property of private corporations, or under municipal management or ownership, may be insured under this form. The contract covers the insured's liability for bodily injury and may likewise be written to include property damage. The coverage protects the insured, not only for his liability for loss to persons or property of visitors to the airport and patrons but also for claims if planes using the airport meet with accident that may be attributed to his negligence or that of his employees.

In the case of airport liability insurance, an application is required in the case of each risk, and the insurer willing to assume the risk bases his premium charge upon the data supplied in each individual case. The following data are required before fixing a rate: (1) area of the airport in acres; (2) number of lineal feet on highway; (3) how fenced; (4) average number of aircraft located at airport; (5) automobile parking space and whether or not charge is made for parking; (6) list and description of all buildings on the airport; (7) whether there is student instruction; (8) approximate population within ten-mile radius of airport; (9) effective landing length in four directions; (10) description of bleachers or group-seating structures on the airport; (11) system of air traffic control; (12) number of daily stops made by scheduled airlines; (13) whether repair work is done by insured; and (14) estimated total dollar-amount of sales, and description of all products sold. A plan or sketch may be required showing all pertinent features of the airport.

The airport liability contract is designed to meet primarily the aviation hazards incidental to the operation of an airport. Coverage for air meets for which an admission charge is made is excluded in the contract, but there is a special form of contract to cover this risk issued by the aviation companies after making appraisal of the hazard involved.

The airport liability contract may be written to cover both bodily injury and property damage liability claims. This follows the pattern of the usual owners', landlords', and tenants' liability form. The basic limits in both contracts are the same. The bodily injury limits are $5,000 for each person and, subject to the same limit, $10,000 for each accident. The standard limit for property damage is $1,000. These limits are likely to be misleading since the liability for loss in connection with the operation of an airport may run to several times the standard limits. An accident that results in the complete demolition of a sizable airplane with death or injury to a number of passengers could develop claims that would aggregate many thousands of dollars. Insurance advisers suggest the estimated total of claims that a single accident could produce as the minimum limits for this type of insurance.

The airport liability contract may be written to include incidental liability hazards other than those strictly associated with aviation. These include, in addition to the premises coverage which provides liability protection for claims growing out of the maintenance, ownership, or use of the premises, the following: (*a*) elevators, (*b*) alterations, (*c*) products, and (*d*) contractual liability. Any or all of these coverages may be written in a single contract. Hangar keeper's legal liability may be written as an endorsement to the airport liability contract.

Hangar Keepers' Liability. Hangars are frequently owned or leased by airlines, flying services, aviation schools, and aircraft and engine manufacturers. In the course of business operations, aircraft, the property of others, is taken in for storage or repair. The hangar keepers' liability contract covers the legal liability of the hangar owner or lessee for loss or damage to aircraft in his custody and not owned by him. The perils insured against are fire and such other perils as may be agreed upon. It is strictly a legal liability form and affords essentially the same protection as the garage keepers' legal liability form. The contract covers the liability imposed by law upon the insured for damage or destruction of any aircraft, including resultant loss of use, which is the property of others and which at the time of the loss is in the custody of the insured for storage, repair, or safe-keeping in the premises set forth in the declarations. The following exclusions are substituted for those contained in the basic liability contract and provide that the contract will not cover:

a) Loss of or damage to robes, wearing apparel, personal effects or merchandise of any description, whether the aircraft in which they are contained is stolen or damaged or not;

b) Loss of or damage to any aircraft owned by, hired by or loaned to the Insured or his family or employees or if the Insured be a co-partnership, by any member thereof or his family or if the Insured be a corporation, by any officer or his family.

c) Loss of or damage to any aircraft while in flight (the term "In Flight" shall mean that period of time commencing with the actual take-off run of the aircraft and continuing thereafter until it has safely completed its landing run, or has attained normal taxiing speed, after contact with the land or water).

d) Loss of or damage to any material furnished by the Insured or any work done by the Insured, out of which the accident arises.

e) Liability assumed by the Insured under any contract or agreement not identified specifically or by definition under this policy.

The contract is written with two limits. It is provided that at each of the listed premises the liability of the insured shall not exceed the limit established (*a*) in respect to any one aircraft, and (*b*) in respect to a casualty or disaster or loss or series of losses arising out of one event involving a number of aircraft. The lower of the two limits, therefore, establishes the maximum liability of the insured for any one aircraft. The second, and higher limit, establishes the maximum liability for any one loss. Hence, in writing a contract the insurer must be supplied with information giving the highest valued aircraft for which the insured may be held responsible during the contract year. Then the insurer must have a figure that represents the total value of all aircraft that may at any one time be placed in the care and custody of the insured.

Air Meet Liability. The airport liability contract does not extend to cover the premises during the conduct of an air meet or air show for which admission is charged. The coverage is obtainable by endorsing the airport liability contract to provide for the risk created by holding the air meet or air show. As in the case of airport liability, the underwriters quote special rates for each risk, depending upon the size of the air meet, the nature of the exhibit, and other pertinent data.

Products Liability. This form is similar to the products liability forms offered for other classes of business. It provides protection for the insured growing out of the handling, use, or existence of goods or products in any condition that are manufactured, sold, handled, or distributed at the premises by the named insured if the accident occurs after the insured has relinquished possession thereof to others and away from premises owned, rented, or controlled by the insured. This protection picks up where the premises liability coverage terminates and provides protection growing out of the use of goods or products when the accident occurs away from the premises of the insured and after the insued has relinquished possession.

Products liability is ordinarily written to cover personal injury. With respect to aviation insurance both personal injury and property damage liability are important hazards. Defective repair work or misdelivery of gasoline might cause a serious accident to a plane with resulting personal injuries and heavy property damage.

Fixed-Base Liability Contract. This form covers risks that are usually classified as commercial and operate out of one airport. It is purchased by insureds that charter, rent, and instruct in aircraft that operate from a fixed base. The contract provides the same liability coverages that are found in the usual aircraft liability contracts. The contract is unique in that it is a package contract and provides in a single contract the following coverages:

Aircraft Third-Party Liability. The coverage is to insure against losses for liability imposed by law (other than passenger) due to ownership, maintenance, or use of any insured aircraft.

Property Damage Liability. This coverage is to insure against losses for liability imposed by law for damages and loss of use to property caused by the maintenance, use, and ownership of any insured aircraft.

Passenger Liability. This coverage is to insure against losses for liability imposed by law due to the use and operation of an insured aircraft.

Premises Operations. This coverage is to insure against losses due to ownership maintenance and use of the premises. This is the coverage generally referred to as "airport liability."

Alterations and Repairs. This coverage is to provide insurance against loss caused by the airport operator's employees and independent contractors for extraordinary alterations, such as repairing or extending runways.

Contractual. This would insure against losses due to liability assumed by the insured.

Products. This would insure against losses due to the handling, use, or the existence of any condition in goods manufactured or handled or distributed by the insured in connection with operations.

Hangar Keepers' Liability. This coverage is to insure against loss caused by liability imposed by law or for loss or damage to aircraft which are the property of others and in the custody of the insured for storage and repairs.

In addition to the foregoing coverages included in the contract, baggage liability may be included by endorsement.

AVIATION ACCIDENT INSURANCE

Aviation accident insurance is insurance purchased by individuals who wish to protect themselves or their beneficiaries against financial loss caused by aviation accidents. Ordinarily these individuals are persons who fly as passengers or they may be students or pilots. A brief reference to workmen's compensation insurance is included in this section, although it is insurance purchased by employers for the benefit of employees.

Workmen's Compensation and Personal Accident. Because of the nature of the employment of those connected with the aviation industry, personal accident and workmen's compensation coverages for members of this group are sometimes classed as aviation coverages.

In addition to those actually engaged in flying, the aviation industry employs large numbers of workers engaged in many forms of ground work. Compensation insurance is written in accordance with the requirements of each particular state.

Personal accident contracts are available, but they are issued only after careful underwriting. Contracts issued to cover pilots are more acceptable to insurers than are those required by passengers who do not wish to be subject to any restrictions as to the type of flying to be covered. Many personal accident contracts today cover the risk of travel on domestic scheduled airlines. Pilots, students, and passengers, in aircraft as well as those flying on established lines secure accident insurance coverage in the aviation insurance market, and the coverages are regarded as aviation lines.

Trip-Ticket Personal Accident Contract. Insurance covering personal injury due to accidents is offered to passengers in licensed planes piloted by duly licensed pilots. The coverage is issued in two forms and covers the flying, day by day. The first form covers the perils of death and dismemberment only, while the second form provides the same coverage as the first, plus a weekly indemnity feature for accidental injuries. Rates for this insurance vary with the coverage, and the charge is made for each day of flying.

MANUFACTURER'S RISKS

Aircraft in production are insured under a blanket contract, and the coverage attaches automatically to each plane as it comes at risk. The contract is written on a reporting form. Premiums are collected on a flying-hour basis for the flight risks and on a per diem basis for the ground risks.

In the case of a new model, before it has completed its test and received its approval certificate from the Inspection Department of the Civil Aeronautics Administration, special premiums are fixed governing the trial period. A manufacturer may have an enormous investment in a model plane that will not reflect in subsequent like models once the plane is in production. The perils during the test period involve great uncertainty, and insurance covering the replacement cost of the model is of paramount importance to the manufacturer. Crash risks and liability coverages on such planes are usually written to cover for a specific number of flying hours with provision for an additional charge at a predetermined rate for additional hours. The ground coverages are written on a per diem basis. Before a contract is written covering a test risk, a complete survey is made of all the factors that may bear upon the situation and the rate determined on the basis of this survey.

FOR DISCUSSION

1. X, a barnstorner, goes from place to place with his airplane and takes up passengers for short flights for a fee. In the course of one flight, A is injured. X's lawyer contends that the passenger assumed the risks of the flight and has no claim. A's attorney contends that X is a public carrier and is accordingly liable for the injury. What is the importance of the contention that X is a public carrier and, in your opinion, is the contention correct?

2. Explain the doctrine of *res ipsa loquitur* as it applies to aviation liability.
3. To what sources would you go to secure evidence of legal standards of aviation? Would you expect to find a carefully detailed list of specifications for air safety?
4. Aircraft tort liability is, for the purpose of classification, frequently divided into four divisions. Can you name them?
5. As a rule, do aviation underwriters inspect the aircraft they insure?
6. Distinguish between employers' indemnity insurance and workmen's compensation insurance.
7. What forms of aviation insurance are written to protect the owner against damage to his own aircraft?
8. What are the coverages provided in the aircraft liability insurance contract?
9. What is the liability of an insurer writing an aircraft bodily injury liability contract for injury to passengers being carried in the insured plane?
10. Aviation insurers contend that they should have a wide flexibility in quoting rates and that their rates should be exempt from departmental rate approval required of most other forms of insurance under state regulatory procedure. In your opinion, have aviation underwriters a case?
11. B, when attempting to land in a municipal airport, damaged his plane through collision with a road roller on a runway under construction. Action was brought against the city on the ground that it was negligent. The roller was a piece of equipment used in maintaining the field. Do you believe the owner of the damaged plane has a claim against the city?
12. The employees of an airport removed B's plane from a hangar and failed to stake it properly. Shortly thereafter, as a result of a windstorm the plane was destroyed. Does the owner of the plane have cause for action against the owner of the airport?
13. A carries full crash insurance, and as a result of an obstruction on a runway his plane is badly damaged. He collects in full from his insurer. What is the position of the owner of an airport with respect to liability?
14. An accident occurs on an airport owned by a municipality. There is little question regarding negligence, and if the airport had been privately owned, the injured party could unquestionably collect. It is a general rule of law that municipalities are immune from suit for damage committed in the exercise of a governmental function. Do you think this rule will operate to relieve a municipal airport from liability? Explain.
15. Aviation insurance furnishes another example where it is virtually impossible to compute a premium upon loss experience alone. What is your explanation of this?

16. Distinguish between the coverage afforded by an airplane liability contract written on a "caused by accident" basis and that of a contract written on an "occurrence" basis.
17. Is there a standard airplane contract?
18. Are all classes and types of airplanes insurable?
19. X purchases an airplane for $8,000. The list price of this plane is $12,000. In the event of a partial loss requiring the expenditure of $3,000 or parts and labor, what is X's position?
20. B owns an airplane which, when not in use, is kept in a hangar at a public airport. A windstorm blows open the doors and damages the plane. Is this a windstorm loss contemplated in the windstorm contract?

CHAPTER · 21

Boiler and Machinery Insurance Contracts

With the introduction of use of steam as an agency for developing power, destructive explosions caused enormous damage. Not only were power plants demolished but other property losses were involved, as well as injuries to persons and loss of life. Safety devices designed to make disasters impossible failed to detect latent or hidden defects, and the devices themselves frequently became defective and inoperative.

Operators of power boilers early recognized the destructive force of an exploding boiler. In an effort to minimize the risk, they provided for regular and systematic inspections to bring to light any signs of weakness. In the early days of industrial development in England, the boiler inspections were regularly carried out before the idea of providing indemnity by means of boiler insurance had made its appearance. It is not surprising that the idea of inspections for the purpose of loss prevention should be carried over and become an important feature of boiler insurance. While other types of insurance coverages have made use of the inspection idea to prevent losses, in no other form has it been carried to a higher degree of specialization or efficiency.

With the advances made by invention in the fields of power, the steam boiler has increased in size and in some cases has been entirely supplanted. Machinery of a size and power undreamed of a century ago is the commonplace of today. With the increase in power and new forms of machinery came new risks followed by new forms of insurance. Power plant insurance not only includes within its scope the insurance of steam boilers and pressure vessels of other types but also there are contracts covering engines, flywheels, electrical machinery, and turbines. Contracts are also written on boilers used for heating purposes, and indemnity is obtainable under a contract covering loss occasioned by the interruption of electric current or other power supplied by a public utility.

Contracts issued upon boilers, turbines, flywheels, electrical machinery, and other objects covered by power plant insurance provide two classes of insurance: direct loss, and indirect loss. A single contract may cover boilers, machinery, or both.

Direct loss provides indemnity in the following cases: damage to the insured's property, whether to the insured object or other property; damage to the property of others for which the insured may be liable; liability for loss of life and injury to employees when coverage is not provided by the compensation laws of the jurisdiction; and liability for loss of life and injury to members of the public, that is, not employees.

Indirect loss is covered as follows: business interruption; indemnity for indirect losses caused by an accident when there is no business interruption, under the outage form; and consequential loss to perishable materials when caused by accident to the boiler or other object insured.

The explosion contract written by fire insurers excludes all losses due to "explosion of steam boilers, steam pipes, steam turbines, or steam engines." The insured who carries a straight explosion contract must guard against the misapprehension that power plant losses are covered. There is one exception to the statement that steam explosion damage is covered only under a boiler contract. A marine insurer may issue an all risks contract which will cover steam pressure explosion unless excluded. A bailee's customers contract such as is purchased by dyers and cleaners contains such an all risks explosion coverage. A marine all risks contract may not be written on all forms of property, and never on permanently located buildings.

THE BOILER AND MACHINERY CONTRACT

In the course of the development of power plant insurance there was at the outset one contract form used for all available coverages. With the advent of boiler business interruption insurance a new contract was developed by some insurers for use in connection with this coverage. Other insurers provided identical coverage by an endorsement attached to the direct damage contract. In the course of time with the development of new lines there were special contract forms prepared to cover flywheel insurance, engine coverages, and later an electrical machinery contract. For each of these lines there was a corresponding business interruption contract. The multiplicity of contracts tended to create some confusion, since all contracts issued by the different insurers were not identical. As a result, a standard form was developed. For a number of years, the standard form that found wide acceptance was a copyrighted form.

More recently, instead of a standard form, standard provisions have been adopted. The arrangement of the contract has been altered to the end that the contract now in use follows the pattern of other contracts providing liability coverage. This basic contract, now known as the "general boiler and machinery contract," or more simply "the general contract," is used for all but a few boiler and machinery contracts. It is also used by all but a very small percentage of the insurers writing this class of business. Since standard provisions replace a standard contract, it follows that the contract issued by the different insurers writing boiler and machinery business need not be identical, even though the contracts make use of the standard provisions. The variations are for the most part matters of form rather than matters of coverage. The general boiler and machinery contract is available for use in connection with any kind of direct damage, boiler, and machinery insurance coverage.[1] It is also used for indirect loss.

All contracts that make use of the standard provisions are made up of four parts: declarations, insuring agreements, exclusions, and conditions. Not printed as part of the standard form but constituting an important part of every contract is one or more schedules. Every boiler insurance contract consists of the basic contract and one or more schedules to it.

Declarations. Frequently the declarations are combined with schedule page A and are attached to the contract. Unlike other liability contracts or physical damage contracts, the declarations do not set forth in detail the property to be insured. Rather, reference is made to schedules, endorsements, or pages which are attached to the basic contract and which determine the nature and extent of the coverage. There are seven sections to the declarations. The information contained in the declarations is as follows:

DECLARATIONS

Item 1. Name of Insured ....
....

Item 2. Address of Insured ....
....

Item 3. The word "loss" in the first paragraph of the Insuring Agreement means loss under Coverages A, B, C, D, E, and F of the Insuring Agreement except as otherwise stated herein: ....

Item 4. Policy period is from noon of .... to noon of .... standard time as to each of said dates, at the place where the accident occurs.

Item 5. Premium is $...............

[1] There are two lines of coverage where the general form is not used. These are: power interruption insurance, and nonownership insurance. While these lines are part of the boiler and machinery business, the form of contract is entirely different from that used for direct damage and liability coverages.

Item 6. The following are made a part of this Policy at inception date.
Schedules: ....
Riders: ....
Endorsements: ....

Item 1 calls for the name of the insured. Here are stated all of the interests to be protected by the contract. Item 2 gives the address of the insured. This address is not necessarily the location of the insured property but is the address to which all notices may properly be mailed. This includes reports of inspections, cancellation notices, notices of suspension of coverage when dangerous conditions materialize, and similar matters. Item 3 provides space for stating any exclusions to the basic coverages. Item 4 indicates the contract period which runs from noon of the inception date to noon of the termination date. Standard time at the place where the accident occurs governs. Item 5 of the declarations indicates the premium to be charged for the insurance under the contract. A contract is not complete without one or more schedules. A contract must have one schedule, but it may possibly have a hundred or more. There may also be endorsements or additional pages attached to the general form modifying or clarifying the coverage. Item 7 of the declarations lists the serial numbers of schedules, riders, and endorsements, and pages that form a part of the contract at its inception date. Immediately following the "items" and under the heading, "Schedule No. 1," is space for stating the location of objects described in the schedule and also space for stating the limit per accident. This limit is set forth in dollar amount. This sum represents the insurer's total liability under the contract for all loss or damage resulting from one accident. This single limit applies to the sum total of both physical damage to property and bodily injury liability. The insured takes all six of the coverages provided and the limit is used in turn for the various coverages.

The Insuring Agreement. Following the declarations on the front page of the contract appears the insuring agreement. This agreement consists of an introductory clause and six sections labeled A, B, C, D, E, and F.

The introductory clause reads as follows:

In consideration of the Premium, the Company named on declarations and schedule page A agrees with the Issured named on declarations and schedule page A respecting loss from an Accident, as defined herein, occurring during the Policy Period, to an Object, as defined herein, while the Object is in use or connected ready for use at the Location specified for it in the Schedule, subject to the Declarations, to the Limit per Accident specified for it in the schedules to the Exclusions and the Conditions, to other terms of this policy and to the Schedules, Riders and Endorsements issued to form a part thereof, as follows:

The words "object" and "accident" appear for the first time in the contract. Reference is made only to insurance against an accident to an object. What constitutes an accident and what constitutes an object is not defined. These definitions are set forth in detail in the schedule. Since this clause applies to all forms of insurance provided under the general contract, an accident, in order to create a liability on the part of the insurer, must happen while the object is in use or connected ready for use at the location specified for it in the schedule. This means that an accident to an object in the process of being installed, or disconnected while in the process of repair, is not covered. It also means that an object installed in one part of a plant and later removed to another location would not be covered. It is necessary with respect to location to have the contract properly endorsed if an insured object is moved from one location to another.

Following the introductory clause are the six sections of the insuring agreement which specifically define the extent and nature of the coverage provided.

Loss on Property of Insured (*Coverage A*). This section of the insuring agreement is an undertaking on the part of the insurer to pay the insured for loss or damage to his own property directly traceable to a covered accident. Coverage A of the contract reads as follows:

COVERAGE A **Loss on Property of Assured** To PAY for loss on the property of the Insured directly damaged by such Accident (or, if the Company so elects, to repair or replace such damaged property), excluding (*a*) loss from fire concomitant with or following an Accident or from the use of water or other means to extinguish fire, (*b*) loss from an Accident caused directly or indirectly by fire or from the use of water or other means to extinguish fire, (*c*) loss from a combustion explosion outside the Object concomitant with or following an accident, (*d*) loss from flood unless an accident ensues and the Company shall then be liable only for loss from such ensuing accident, (*e*) loss from delay or interruption of business or manufacturing or process, (*f*) loss from lack of power, light, heat, steam or refrigeration and (*g*) loss from any other indirect result of an Accident.

This section delineates the extent of the property damage coverage provided. It accomplishes this by means of six exclusions. There is no coverage for losses that a fire insurance contract will cover or for indirect damage.

The first exclusion refers directly to losses from fire. If a fire loss occurs at the time of an accident covered by the contract, or following it, there is no contribution on the part of the boiler and machinery contract. Such losses are covered under all fire insurance contracts. (The schedule modifies this exclusion in connection with certain electrical machinery losses where the fire insurance contract would not cover.) Exclusion (*b*) applies to a type of accident directly attributable to fire. If a fire cause an explosion, the insurer is not liable for any property damage loss attributable to the explosion. Again, all such losses are covered by the fire contract. Exclusion (*c*) is important and is sometimes the occasion for misunderstanding. If there is a combustion explosion outside the insured object at the time of the accident, or following it, there is no coverage for property damage caused by this explosion. If an insured object contains inflammable gas and ruptures causing property damage, the damage caused by the explosion is covered. If the gas that escapes following the rupture mixes with the air and there is a subsequent explosion, the property damage caused by this subsequent explosion is not covered. This is not considered to be an explosion of the insured object. By virtue of this exclusion, even though the rupture of the insured object is construed to be the direct cause of the subsequent explosion, the contract will not cover. Combustion explosions of this sort are expected to be covered by an extension of the fire insurance contract. Finally, since this section of the insuring agreement is designed to cover direct damage, the three final exclusions (*e*), (*f*) and (*g*) make it perfectly clear that all forms of indirect loss are excluded from coverage under this section. The contract may be amended by endorsement to provide for indirct damage coverages. The insurer reserves the right to repair or replace the damaged property. Under this right certain advantages may, in some circumstances, accrue to the insurer. Ordinarily, the insurer does not take advantage of the right but allows the insured to proceed with repairs or replacements as soon as possible. If the circumstances are such that the insurer can place the insured back in the position that he found himself before the loss at a cost less than the insured estimates the cost of replacing the damaged property, the contract specifically gives the company the right to do so.

Expediting Expenses (*Coverage B*). The provision for expediting expenses was, at one time, optional in the boiler and machinery contract. It is now a part of the general contract. The section as it appears in the contract reads as follows:

COVERAGE B **Expediting Expenses** To PAY, to the extent of any indemnity remaining after payment of all loss as may be required under Coverage A, for the reasonable extra cost of temporary repair and of expediting the repair of such damaged property of the Insured, including overtime and the extra cost of express or other rapid means of transportation, but the Company's liability under Coverage B shall not exceed $1,000.

The coverage provided under this section includes reimbursement for expediting the repair of damaged property by the use of overtime labor, express, or airplane shipment of parts and other steps taken to effect the speediest possible replacement of the damaged property.

Payments for expediting charges constitute a part of the limit per accident and are not regarded as additional insurance.

Expediting expense coverage does not provide for the substitution of one object for the damaged object for the sole purpose of preventing the interruption of business. Such a substitution is not an expense incurred in the repair of the damaged property and accordingly is not regarded as an expediting expense. Losses attributable to the interruption of the business of the insured is an indirect loss and is covered only under some form of indirect damage insurance.

Property Damage Liability (Coverage C). If an object owned by the insured explodes and damages the property of others, his liability for such loss is covered under this section of the boiler and machinery contract. This is distinctly a liability coverage. The section extends only to property now owned, operated, or controlled by the insured and for which there may be liability imposed by law, if the damage caused by the accident is covered by the contract.

COVERAGE C **Property Damage Liability** To PAY, on behalf of the insured to the extent of any indemnity remaining after payment of all loss as may be required under Coverages A and B, such amounts as the Insured shall become obligated to pay by reason of the liability of the Insured for loss on property of others directly damaged by such Accident, including liability for loss of use of such damaged property of others;

To establish liability on the part of the insurer, it must be shown that the property was directly damaged by the accident. The section also undertakes to pay for loss of use of the damaged property.

In Coverage C there is no exclusion with respect to loss resulting from an accident caused by fire. If there is an accident caused by fire covered under the contract and the accident causes damage to the property of others, the liability claim is provided for under Coverage C.

Bodily Injury Liability (Coverage D). Very broad bodily injury liability coverage is provided in this part of the insuring agreement. It undertakes to give liability protection for bodily injury or death sustained by any person with the exception of that liability imposed under any workmen's compensation law. The section reads as follows:

COVERAGE D **Bodily Injury Liability** To PAY, on behalf of the insured, to the extent of any indemnity remaining after payment of all loss as may be required under Coverages A, B, and C, such amounts as the Insured shall become obligated to pay by reason of the liability of the Insured, including liability for care and loss of services, because of bodily injury, sickness or disease, including death at any time resulting therefrom, sustained by any person and caused by such Accident, except that the indemnity hereunder shall not apply to any obligation for which the Insured or any company as insurer of the Insured may be liable under any workmen's compensation, unemployment compensation or disability benefits law, or under any similar law; to pay, irrespective of the Limit per Accident, for such immediate medical and surgical relief to others as shall be rendered at the time of the Accident;

Under this section, all common-law liability of the insured is covered, whether the injured person is an employee or member of the public. This means that if an employee can trace an injury to a covered accident and the injury is not covered by workmen's compensation, the section gives the insured the same protection with respect to the employee that is afforded with respect to members of the public. The usual provision for first-aid relief appears. Such first-aid does not have the effect of reducing the coverage available for settling a claim.

Defense, Settlement and Supplementary Payments (*Coverage E*). This section of the contract provides coverage similar to that provided in general liability coverages. In the boiler and machinery contract the coverage is provided in the following terms:

COVERAGE E **Defense Settlement Supplementary Payments** To DEFEND the Insured against claim or suit alleging liability under Coverage C, and under Coverage D if insurance under Coverage D is included, unless or until the Company shall elect to effect settlement thereof; and to pay, on behalf of the insured, all costs taxed against the Insured in any legal proceeding defended by the Company in accordance with such Coverages, all interest accruing after entry of judgment rendered in connection therewith up to the date of payment by the Company of its share of such judgment, all premiums on appeal bonds required in such legal proceedings, all premiums on bonds to release attachments for an amount not in excess of the applicable limits of liability for Coverages C and D, and all expenses incurred by the Company for such defense; the amounts incurred under Coverage E are payable by the Company irrespective of the Limit per Accident, except settlements of claims and suits.

As is usual in liability contracts, the insurer agrees to defend the insured against claims or suits alleging liability. The protection is provided with respect to coverage C in any case, and with respect to coverage D only if included in the declarations. Expenses incurred in connection with investigation and legal proceedings are paid irrespective of the limit of liability expressed in the contract. This means, in the case of a contract written with a limit per accident of $25,000 and a claim of $30,000 is settled, the insurer would be liable for $25,000 for the settlement of the claim. If the insurer incurred $2,000 expense in the investigation and defense proceedings, this amount would be payable as provided in the section over and above the limit per accident expressed in the contract.

The phrase "to the extent of any indemnity remaining" that appears in coverages B, C, and D means that if the limit of liability after adjusting claims under coverage A has not been exhausted, then the amount left will be applied to reimbursing the insured for expediting expenses. When these two items have been settled, any remaining liability on the part of the insurer will be directed to the settlement of property damage liability. If the contract covers bodily injury liability, there will be no coverage available to pay such claims until after the liability under coverages A, B, and C have been adjusted.

Coverage E covering defense, settlement, and supplementary payments is not concerned with this phraseology. Any liability incurred under coverage E, over and above the cost of settlement of claims and suit, is payable irrespective of the limit per accident. This phrasing makes it perfectly clear that the limit per accident does not apply separately to each insuring agreement. In a contract written with a limit per accident of $25,000, with a loss on property of the insured in the amount of $25,000 and a similar loss under coverage D covering bodily injury liability, the insurer would be obligated to pay only $25,000, the loss to property of the insured. In an accident with a contract having the same limits, involving a loss under coverage A of $10,000, and a loss under coverage D of $25,000, the insurer would be liable for the $10,000 under coverage A and for only $15,000 under coverage D. In other words, coverages B, C, and D of the contract are so worded that, even though all the coverages are effective, there is no protection under any one of the coverages until all claims under preceding coverages have been settled. An insured is not covered under any section, except coverage E, if the total amount of insurance, as evidenced by the limit per accident, is exhausted by any previous coverage.

Automatic Coverage (Coverage F). Automatic protection for newly acquired objects is covered under this section. The clause requires written notice to the insurer within 90 days after the newly acquired object is put in operation. The coverage for the new object dates from the time of its operation, and the premium is computed accordingly. Coverage already in effect for similar objects applies with respect to the newly acquired object. The clause reads as follows:

COVERAGE F **Automatic Coverage**	That any Object within the continental United States (except Alaska), similar to any Object designated and described in any Schedule forming a part of this policy

a) hereafter installed by the Insured at any location specified in any of the Schedules of this policy shall be considered as added to this policy as of the time said Object is first placed in operation by the Insured, subject to

(1) the Limit per Accident specified for the location where the Object is installed, and

(2) the insurance (excluding Outage Insurance) applicable to another similar Object at the location where the Object is installed, except that if there are no other similar Objects at said location, such Object hereafter installed shall be subject to the insurance (excluding Use and Occupancy, Outage, Consequential Damage, and any other indirect insurance) applicable to another similar Object at any location, or

b) hereafter installed by the Insured at any location owned or leased by the Insured and not specified in any Schedule or Endorsement of this policy or existing in any property hereafter acquired by the Insured shall be considered as added to this policy as of the time said Object is first placed in operation by the Insured, subject to the insurance (excluding Use and Occupancy, Outage, Consequential damage and other indirect insurance applicable to any similar object insured under this policy) and all subject to the highest limit per Accident applicable to any similar Object at any specified location,

provided that the Insured notifies the Company in writing within ninety days after said date of first operation, but not otherwise, and agrees to pay the required additional premium for insurance on said Object in accordance with the Company's Manual of Rules and Rates in force on the date said Object is first placed in operation by the Insured.

Insuring Clause Variations. Virtually all insurers writing boiler and machinery insurance include all of the six coverages of the insuring agreement in their printed general contract forms. Some of the insurers, and this includes insurers that are identified with writing a major portion of the boiler insurance business, use a contract containing only the six sections here described.

Contract Schedules. A boiler and machinery insurance contract is not complete without one or more schedules. Each schedule contains a definition of object, and a definition of accident. It may contain special provisions or other clauses pertinent to the coverage.

All definitions of accident to be found in schedules have certain characteristics. This is true whether they apply to boilers, pressure vessels, or machinery. To be covered, the damage must be caused by an occurrence that is "sudden and accidental." The use of this phraseology eliminates the possibility of claims for damage, which are the outgrowth of slowly developing occurrences that are maintenance items. The definitions of accident make a positive statement with respect to coverage and follow this with a limited number of exclusions to eliminate routine operating occurrences. Boiler and pressure vessels schedules so define the term "accident" that for coverage the accident must be caused by pressure of contents. With respect to machinery objects, the definition invariably measures accidents by effects rather than causes. To this end, they follow a pattern that is the reverse of definitions for boiler and pressure vessels.

By way of illustration a copy of the face of a boiler insurance schedule is reproduced in Figure 21–1. Reference is made to the

SCHEDULE

BOILERS

This Schedule forms a part of Policy No.......... and is effective from noon of.....................

Assured...

A. The Objects covered under this Schedule are designated and described as follows:

Location...
(Street and Number) (City) (County) (State)

Designating Number of each Object	Description of Object	Class	Size	Coverage	Furnace Explosion / Fuel

Paragraphs B, C, D and E printed on the back of this sheet are hereby made a part of this schedule.

FIG. 21–1.

contract to which the schedule is attached and its effective date, the name of the insured, and the location of the insured objects. Each object is described. In the column headed "coverage" it will be indicated whether broad or limited coverage is provided. Reference is made to paragraphs B, C, D, and E printed on the back of the schedule. Paragraph B gives a definition of the object, paragraph C gives a definition of accident, paragraph D defines furnace explosion, and paragraph E is concerned with special provisions applicable to the schedule. There are many schedules. Each is designed for a particular class of object to be insured. The boiler schedule, since it is perhaps the most widely used, is cited here as an example.

The Boiler Insurance Schedule. The boiler schedule defines an accident to provide two forms of cover—the first known as "limited" and the second known as "broad." The limited cover provides explosion cover only while the broad cover includes losses that do not involve the violence of an explosion as described by the terms "accidental tearing asunder." Following is the definition of object as it appears in the boiler schedule:[2]

Object shall mean any complete vessel designated and described in this Schedule, and shall also include

1. Any steel economizer used solely with such vessel,
2. Any indirect water heater used for hot water supply service which is directly in the water circulating system of such vessel and which does not form a part of a water storage tank, and
3. Any piping on the premises of the Insured, or between parts of said premises, with valves, fittings, traps and separators thereon, which contains steam or condensate thereof, generated in whole or in part in such vessel, and any feed water pipping between such vessel and its feed pump or injector;

but Object shall not include

a) any part of such vessel or piping which does not contain water or steam;
b) any reciprocating or rotating machine;
c) any electrical apparatus;
d) any piping not on the premises of the Insured, used to supply any premises not owned by, leased by or operated under the control of the of the Insured; nor
e) any other piping, any radiator, convector, coil, vessel or apparatus except as included in Sections 1, 2, and 3 above.

"Premises" shall mean the premises of the Insured where the Object is located and the premises of the Insured which would be continuous with said premises except for the presence of one or more roadways, streams or rights of way between said premises, except that if the Object is a track locomotive boiler the Premises of the Insured, for the purpose of this definition, shall mean only the track locomotive.

The schedule then defines an accident as follows:

As respects any Object designated and described in this Schedule, "Accident" shall mean a sudden and accidental breakdown of the object, or part thereof, which manifests itself at the time of its occurrence by physical damage to the Object that necessitates repair or replacement of the Object of part thereof; but Accident shall not mean

a) depletion, deterioration, corrosion, or erosion of material;
b) wear and tear;
c) leakage at any valve, fitting, shaft seal, gland packing, joint or connection;
d) the breakdown of any vacuum tube, gas tube or brush;
e) the breakdown of any structure or foundation supporting the Object or any part thereof; not
f) the functioning of any safety device or protective device.

---

[2] The definition of "object" may vary somewhat among schedules. The definition of "accident" given of page 546 is used in virtually all schedules.

Under the broad form one of the most important coverages is known as "cracking of sections." In the case of a cast-iron boiler, sections are frequently found to be cracked, and it is not always clear what is the occasion of the difficulty. When it becomes necessary to take the entire boiler down to replace a section, the cost of repairs frequently runs to substantial sums of money. While the damage ordinarily is limited to the cost of replacement of the section and there is not the danger that is inherent in the explosion risk, nevertheless the frequency of cracked sections has made the coverage an attractive one for boiler owners. Insurance against cracking of sections is obtainable only in connection with the broad form explosion cover. It may not be written separately and apart from explosion insurance.

Furnace explosion is covered only if specifically included. With respect to furnace explosion the Schedule provides:

> As respects any Object which is designated and described in this Schedule and for which the word "Included" is inserted in the column headed "Furnace Explosion—Fuel," but not otherwise, "Accident" shall also mean a sudden and accidental explosion of gas within the furnace of the Object or within the gas passages therefrom to the atmosphere, provided said explosion occurs while the Object is being operated with the kind of fuel specified for it in the column headed "Furnace Explosion—Fuel."

Special provisions that follow declare that there shall be no liability while an object is undergoing a hydrostatic pressure test, provide for certain minimum premiums, and declare the furnace and gas passages to be "outside the object" unless the word "included" is inserted in the proper column on the face of the schedule.

Exclusions. There are four exclusions listed in the contract. The first of these exclusions deals with the war risk. The insurer does not agree to pay for losses caused "directly or indirectly by hostile or warlike action . . . insurrection, rebellion, revolution, civil war or usurped power. . . ." In the second exclusion the insurer will not pay for loss whether "direct or indirect, proximate or remote, from an Accident caused directly or indirectly by nuclear reaction, nuclear radiation or radioactive contamination, all whether controlled or uncontrolled; or from nuclear reaction, nuclear radiation or radioactive contamination all whether controlled or uncontrolled, caused directly or indirectly by, contributed to or aggravated by an Accident." The insurer also denies liability for any loss "covered in whole or in part by any contract of insurance, carried by the Assured, which also covers any hazard or peril of nuclear reaction or nuclear radiation." The third exclusion repeats the exclusions listed in Coverage A dealing with the loss of property of the insured. Exclusion four relates to bodily injury (Coverage D) and provides that the contract does not apply "to any obligation for which the Assured or any company as insurer of the Assured may be liable under any workmen's compensation, unemployment compensation or disability benefits law, or under any similar law."

Conditions. A number of conditions appear on the second and third pages of the general contract form. A number of them are usual to all contracts covering physical damage and liability lines. Particularly there are the provisions relating to cancellation, handling claims, action against the insurer, changes, assignments, and subrogation. The other conditions are particularly concerned with boiler and machinery coverages and will now be considered.

Limit per Accident. This condition defines term "one accident." By virtue of this condition it is established that the term shall be understood to include all resultant or concomitant accidents, regardless of the number of insured objects involved. This condition reads as follows:

The Company's total liability for loss from any One Accident shall not exceed the amount specified as Limit per Accident. . . . The term "One Accident" shall be taken as including all resultant or concomitant Accidents whether to one Object or to more than one Object or to part of an Object. The inclusion herein of more than one Assured shall not operate to increase the limits of the Company's liability.

The limit per accident applies to every general occurrence during the contract term and applies even though more than one insured object is involved. If two or more objects are involved, the highest limit applying to any one of the objects governs. If one accident involves both engine breakdown and boiler explosion, and the limit per accident for each object is $50,000, the insured would not have $100,000 protection but $50,000. Any general occurrence which involves one or several insured objects is considered one accident. The maximum limit per accident applying to any of the insured objects is the maximum amount of insurance available for the accident.

Other Insurance—Bodily Injury. The following condition applies to bodily injury:

In the event there is in effect any insurance or any agreement to pay the Insured, or on his behalf, for loss of the kind described in Coverage D, the insurance afforded under Coverage D, if any, shall not be considered as contributing insurance and shall become effective and applicable only with respect to any part of the loss of the Insured for bodily injuries for which there is not in effect such other insurance or agreement. If there is not in effect any insurance or agreement with respect to such loss, the insurance, if any, under Coverage D may be applied to any part of said loss.

By virtue of this condition, bodily injury liability provided by the boiler and machinery contract is considered excess and not contributing insurance where there is other bodily injury liability coverage. It is applicable only to that portion of the insured's loss that is in excess of other valid and collectible indemnity required to be paid under a contract of other similar insurance. If an insured carries liability insurance on an excess basis, that is, if he assumes liability claims up to a given amount, and then has insurance to cover catastrophe losses in excess of that amount, the bodily injury liability of the boiler machinery contract will pay the loss up to the amount where the excess liability insurance becomes effective. If the liability insurance is then exhausted and there is still a remaining unpaid balance on a claim, the boiler and machinery insurance would then apply. If an insured were carrying liability insurance with a $10,000 deductible, the liability contract would pay claims only in excess of $10,000. If the limit of liability on the general liability contract was $100,000 and there were $125,000 in claims attributable to the one accident, the boiler and machinery insurance would pay the first $10,000 in claims. The general liability contract would then cover up to the contract limit. The boiler insurance then would pick up and pay the remaining unpaid claims until the limit of liability under the contract has been exhausted. Bodily injury liability insurance then is not contributing but is excess insurance.

Other Insurance—Property. Unlike the protection afforded under bodily injury liability which is excess over other liability insurance protection available to the insured, property damage liability is contributing insurance. There are two methods for determining the amount of contributions: (1) if the other insurance provides for settlement on a joint loss basis, and (2) if there is no such provision in the other insurance. The clause reads as follows:

> The words "joint loss," as used herein, mean loss to which both this insurance and other insurance carried by the Insured apply. In the event of such "joint loss,"
>
> *a*) The Company shall be liable under this policy only for the proportion of the said joint loss that the amount which would have been payable under this policy on account of said joint loss, had no other insurance existed, bears to the combined total of the said amount and the amount which would have been payable under all other insurance on account of said joint loss, had there been no insurance under this policy, but
>
> *b*) In case the policy or policies affording such other insurance do not contain a clause similar to Clause (*a*), the Company shall be liable under this policy only for the proportion of said joint loss that the amount insured under this policy, applicable to said joint loss, bears to the whole amount of insurance, applicable to said joint loss.

Assume a furnace explosion loss covered under a boiler and machinery insurance contract with a limit per accident of $10,000 and a fire insurance contract with extended coverage in the amount of $25,000. Assume a loss of $2,000. Without other insurance each insurer would be liable for the full amount of the loss. The extended coverage contract provides for settlement on a joint loss basis. Since each insurer is liable for the full amount of the loss, each would pay half of the loss. On the other hand, with $25,000 insurance without a joint loss clause, each contract would cover the loss in full in the absence of other insurance. There would be $10,000 under the boiler policy and $25,000 other insurance. The total insurance covering would be $35,000, and the boiler insurance policy would be liable for $^{10}/_{35}$ of the loss.

Property Valuation (Coverage A). This condition is similar to that found in the insuring clause of the fire insurance contract and in inland marine contracts. It provides:

The limit of the Company's liability for loss on the property of the Insured shall not exceed the actual cash value thereof at the time of the Accident. If, as respects the damaged property of the Insured, the repair or replacement of any part or parts of an Object is involved, the Company shall not be liable for the cost of such repair or replacement in excess of the actual cash value of said part or parts or in excess of the actual cash value of the Object, whichever value is less. Actual cash value in all cases shall be ascertained with property deductions for depreciation, however caused.

By virtue of this condition the liability of the insurer with respect to property of the insured that is destroyed is limited to its actual cash value at the time of the accident. Actual cash value is determined by taking proper deductions for depreciation. In the event of a partial loss the insurer is not liable for the cost of repairs if this cost is in excess of the value of the object as a whole. Where repair costs exceed the value of the damaged object, the lower figure is the limit of liability. For example, an older boiler that has all but served its useful life may be damaged by a cracked section. The boiler has some value. The insurer will pay this value but is not obligated either to replace the damaged boiler new or to pay more than its value before the accident to repair it.

Inspection and Suspension. The insurer has the right of access to the property at reasonable times to make inspections. This right is set forth as follows:

The Company shall be permitted at all reasonable times during the Policy Period to inspect any Object and the premises where said Object is located. Upon the discovery of a dangerous condition with respect to any Object, any representative of the Company may immediately suspend the insurance with respect to an Accident to said Object by written notice mailed or delivered to the Assured at the Address of the Assured, as specified in the Declarations, or at the Location of the Object, as specified for it in the Schedule. Insurance so suspended may be reinstated by the Company, but only by an Endorsement issued to form a part of this policy and signed by an officer of the Company. The Insured shall be allowed the unearned portion of the premium paid for such suspended insurance, pro rata, for the period of suspension.

No right is given the insured to demand inspections, though the inspection reports are regarded as one of the most valuable features of the insurance. If an inspector finds a dangerous situation he may give written notice to the insured and immediately suspend coverage. This is not the hardship it seems. Where dangerous conditions are shown to exist, insureds are usually willing to shut down the object. Only where insureds fail to cooperate will the insurer resort to suspension. The insurer has no right to suspend an object in this manner unless it finds a dangerous condition to exist. To cancel coverage otherwise it must comply with conditions with respect to notice found in the cancellation clause.

Schedules and Endorsements. The definitions of "accident" and "object" do not appear in the contract itself but are rather to be found in the schedules. The schedule contains the location and description of the objects covered, as well as the applicable coverages. This condition makes the insurance under the contract apply with respect to accidents and objects described in the schedule. The condition reads:

> The insurance afforded hereunder shall apply only to loss from an Accident to an Object designated and described in a Schedule forming a part hereof, countersigned by a duly authorized agent of the Company, and containing the description of such Object, the definition thereof, the definition of Accident and other provisions as applicable to the said Object, in accordance with provisions of the specified Rider.

The clause designates the schedules as a part of the contract.

OTHER CONTRACTS AND ENDORSEMENTS

A number of contracts and endorsements other than the basic boiler and machinery contract are available to the prospective insured. These instruments provide for indirect losses arising out of boiler and machinery accidents as well as direct and indirect losses to engines, turbines, and similar items.

Business Interruption Insurance. Business interruption coverage is written as a separate contract covering any of the objects insured under power plant forms or may be added to the direct damage contracts by endorsement. In principle, the coverage is the same as the other business interruption forms previously considered, having as its purpose the payment of continuing fixed charges and indemnification for loss of profits due to shutdown as a result of accident.

Power plant contracts provide a daily indemnity, which is the amount payable for each day business on the premises is entirely suspended. A valued form is often used for small risks and occasionally for medium and large risks, thus eliminating the necessity upon the part of the insured to prove his loss. Upon the happening of an accident to the insured object covered by the contract, the full daily indemnity is payable in accordance with the contract provisions. Contracts are in some instances written on an "actual loss sustained" basis. This form is more in line with the established practices in other fields.

Indemnity may be provided from the time of the accident, or a contract may be written at a reduced premium, if losses are excluded for a designated number of days following the accident. With the increased use of the actual loss sustained form, a stated amount of deductible is very often used. When indemnity begins with the accident, the matter of notice is of great importance, since the contract provides that under this form indemnity shall not commence earlier than 24 hours prior to the arrival of the notice of loss to the insurer.

The coverage excludes liability for any day that the plant would not have been in operation had the accident not occurred. The insured is required to use all reasonable means to avert or minimize loss. Surplus machinery, duplicate parts, or other equipment or supplies owned or controlled by the insured must be used in placing the property in condition for operation. There is no liability for a daily indemnity if the plant could have been restored with reasonable diligence or the functions of the insured object could otherwise have been performed.

Part-Time Operation. When a contract is written covering objects that are in operation only a part of the year, a saving in premium is effected by endorsing the contract to suspend coverage during the period of shutdown. The endorsement is not used for objects in reserve or for objects indefinitely out of service but is designed to allow a credit for an object seasonally operated when the period of suspension can be designated in advance. The endorsement may be issued at any time during the contract term, in which case a return premium is payable to the insured.

Indefinite Suspension. On some occasions, boilers or other objects are shut down for periods of considerable length that cannot be predetermined. For such situations, an endorsement is issued indefinitely suspending the insurance, and when operations are resumed another endorsement reinstating the coverage is issued. In some plants it is necessary that objects be operated occasionally for short periods in order to care for and maintain the plant properly. Operation for maintenance during suspension is sometimes on a weekly and sometimes on a monthly basis. This matter may be handled by an appropriate endorsement.

Consequential Loss. Power plant contracts may be written to cover consequential losses as well as direct damage. Consequential damage insurance provides payment for actual loss on specified property of the insured and also for such amounts as the insured is obligated to pay by reason of his liability for loss on specified property of others, when any such loss is due to spoilage from lack of power, light, heat, steam, or refrigeration, at a specifically described plant, caused solely by an accident to an object, which is described in the schedule for direct damage. The coverage may be provided by endorsement of the direct damage contract.

Under the rules governing this insurance, the term "plant" is construed to mean the complete business or enterprise at one location. If there are several units or departments, each manufacturing or storing a marketable product, each such unit or department may be considered a separate plant. This insurance applies particularly to losses from spoilage. The breakdown of a small motor operating a pasteurizer in a dairy might result in a very small loss to the motor itself but a large consequential loss from spoilage of the cream or milk. It is also provided that admission fees, tuition fees, or similar fees which do not vary with the period of suspension may be brought within the coverage of the consequential damage endorsement.

In writing this type of coverage, it is necessary to state in the endorsement the nature of the risk. The endorsement must contain a description of the stock, materials, or other property to be insured, and it must provide a limit of liability for any one accident. This type of coverage may be written to provide protection from accidents to objects located outside the insured's premises. Objects supplying power, light, heat, steam, or refrigeration may be brought within the scope of the coverage. Spoilage resulting from an accident to outside objects forming a part of a public utility system may not be included within the scope of a consequential loss endorsement, but the risk may be insured under the form known as "power interruption insurance."

Power Interruption Insurance. An accident to a power plant causing loss to a user of power through interruption of service is not covered by the electrical machinery contract. Indemnity for this type of loss is available under the power interruption contract, which provides insurance on an hourly indemnity basis for loss of use of the plant caused by the deprivtion of power and also provides a coverage for property loss due to spoilage. Power interruption insurance provides indemnity against loss arising from the total or partial deprivation of usable service (electric current, steam, water, gas, or refrigeration) furnished by a public utility. In order to constitute a loss under the contract, such deprivation must be caused by an accidental occurrence to the physical equipment of a public service system which immediately prevents, in whole or in part, the delivery of usable service to the premises. The general contract form is not used for this coverage. A separate contract form has been prepared for the purpose.

Under the hourly indemnity form, the contract provides for the payment of a specified sum termed the "limit per hour" for each hour of that part of a period of deprivation which is in excess of five minutes. There is also a provision for "limit per day," which is the maximum amount payable in any one day, a day representing a period of 24 consecutive hours and beginning at midnight. There is also a "limit per accident," which is the amount of insurance available for each accident during the contract period. Under the form of coverage for property loss due to spoilage, the contract provides payment for actual loss on specified property of the insured and also for amounts for which the insured is liable as the result of loss to the property of others when such loss is occasioned by the deprivation of such service as electric current, steam, water, gas, or refrigeration. The contract provides for a limit per accident and may be written to provide indemnity for deprivation of power from the time of accident or for deprivation of power after a period has elapsed known as a "waiting period." Thus, in some types of operations a short interruption of power would be the occasion of little or no loss, but after the interruption extends a certain period of time, losses will begin to develop. In such risks, a contract providing for a waiting period would be ample.

Power interruption contracts may be written for varying limits for different periods of the contract term. Thus, a contract may be written with $100 hourly indemnity during certain months of the year and a $200 hourly indemnity during the balance of the year. The same rule holds true in the case of a contract covering against loss due to spoilage. If the business is of a nature that calls for big inventories during certain periods of the year, the contract may provide for a high limit per accident during such periods and a lower limit during the remainder of the year.

The insurance may apply to losses from "time of accident" or may be written at a lesser rate providing a "waiting period." Under the second form, there is no loss unless the deprivation exceeds the waiting period specified in the contract. Under power interruption forms, the insured is obligated immediately to notify the public utility company upon any interruption of service, and the insurer assumes no liability for any part of a period of deprivation preceding the giving of notice to the utility. Notice must be given the insurer "as soon as practicable." Liability is excluded for loss or damage caused by the interruption of service if the interruption is directly or indirectly occasioned by strike, riot, or civil commotion.

Engine Risk. The principal hazard in connection with the operation of a steam engine is the flywheel. A heavy flywheel rotating at a high speed creates a centrifugal force with a heavy outward strain on the metal of the wheel. If the wheel revolves at the speed for which it is designed and there is no defect in its construction, there need be no occasion for alarm. The speed of a flywheel is regulated by a governor. But the governor is a mechanical device and sometimes fails to operate. Again, there may be a hidden defect in the wheel causing a rupture at a speed calculated to be safe. Wheels improperly put together often become unsafe after being operated for a time. Whatever the cause, it frequently happens that a wheel breaks while in operation with disastrous results. Sometimes a rapidly moving wheel disintegrates with such force that the break is referred to as a "flywheel explosion."

The damage caused by such a break is often terrific. The force generated by a wheel racing at a runaway speed is tremendous. The momentum of a mass of metal weighing 16 to 30 tons and rotating about a mile a minute over a path 20 to 30 feet in length can be imagined. Upon a break, such a wheel can entirely wreck plant, machinery, and neighboring property and cause injury and loss of life.

Engine losses are not limited to those caused by flywheels. Cylinders explode, hurling fragments with terrific force. Moving parts become crystalized from "fatigue" and give way. Improper lubrication, loosened parts not promptly discovered, or other cause may result in some part of the engine giving way. Because of the great force involved, a comparatively slight break of a part may start a chain of events that will end in complete destruction of the plant.

Engine Insurance. This coverage may be written to insure engines that derive their power from steam, oil, or gas. Pumps, compressors, and refrigerating machines are objects insurable under the form. The definition of "accident" is drawn broad enough to include every form of breakdown. When the engine is insured, all wheels mounted on it are covered. The engine contract is the same contract as that used for the insurance of boilers, with the difference that the schedule attached to the contract is designed to meet the requirements of engines. On the reverse of the schedule designed for reciprocating engines, pumps, and compressors, the object to be insured is defined. Thus, the same types of protection are afforded under the engine contract as are afforded under the boiler contract.

Flywheel Insurance. Flywheels mounted on an engine and forming a part of the complete unit are covered under the engine contract. Flywheels may also be separately insured. Flywheel insurance may be written on many types of revolving machinery, such as pulleys, shaft wheels, gear wheels, fans, blowers, centrifugal dryers, separators, and other rotating objects. In connection with wheel insurance, an object is defined to include the rotating part, or parts, of the apparatus described but not to include the shaft upon which the wheel is mounted.

Electrical Machinery Insurance. The investment in electrical machinery is very large. Insurance, following the coverage afforded by the engine breakdown contract, is provided under the electrical machinery form to provide protection against losses from breakdown. Motors, generators, and exciters are insurable, as are power and distribution transformers. Miscellaneous electrical apparatus that may be covered includes such objects as switchboards, oil switches or circuit breakers, and units of electrical control and starting for motors.

Turbine Insurance. The protection afforded under the turbine contract is essentially the same as that provided in the other power plant contracts. Direct and consequential loss to property may be covered, as well as liability for personal injury. Four kinds of coverage are written, each furnishing a different degree of protection. These are (1) breakdown insurance, (2) explosion insurance, (3) limited breakdown, and (4) combined coverage.

Breakdown Insurance. This is the most complete form of insurance obtainable on a turbine, since it covers all the major hazards, including all types of explosions, the burning out, short-circuiting, or breakdown of electrical equipment, as well as accidents to the rotor, such as the stripping of the blades or other breakdown.

Explosion Insurance. This form is designed to protect the insured from catastrophe losses. Accidents involving the breaking or rupturing of the shaft or rotor and explosions due to steam pressure are covered. Losses caused by breaking, cracking, stripping, or loosening of gears or couplings or of movable or stationary blades are not covered. Likewise, the contract does not cover losses caused by short-circuiting, burning, breaking, or loosening of electrical conductors.

Limited Breakdown. Under this form the broad breakdown coverage is provided, with the exception that electrical burnouts on the generator rotor are excluded from coverage.

Combined Coverage. This form provides a combination of turbine explosion and generator breakdown. The steam end of the equipment is provided with explosion coverage only, while full breakdown insurance is provided for the generator and exciter.

Nonownership Explosion Insurance. This form provides coverage for direct loss of the property of the insured resulting from an explosion of objects not owned by the insured.

This contract is not written on the general form. An insured with property located near high-pressure boilers over which he has no control, either as owner or as lessor or operator in any other capacity, uses this form to cover the explosion hazard from the boilers. Since the insured neither owns nor operates the boilers, no provision can be made for inspection, and the contract makes no requirement with respect thereto.

Residence Coverage. A special rate is promulgated for objects ordinarily used in connection with the heating and plumbing systems in dwellings. The contract covers all of the broad form losses and is written for a term; and, while it may be canceled at any time under the usual conditions, there is no provision for part-time suspension of operations.

In order to be covered at the residence rate, the object must be located in a building designed for residential purposes occupied as the living quarters of one or more families, provided the number of heated rooms, excluding bathrooms, pantries, and halls, is not in excess of thirty. Objects located in apartment buildings and buildings of the two-family house or the three-family house type are not classed for the purposes of this coverage as residences. Houses of the duplex, semidetached, or row type, when the living quarters of each family group are side by side and not one above the other, are classed each as individual residences. Residential coverage of the type here described is now widely provided for through homeowners' contracts. The provisions of these contracts will be considered in the next chapter.

FOR DISCUSSION

1. What is the necessity of having a limit per hour, a limit per day, and a limit per accident under the power interruption form? Are they not all, in fact, the same thing expressed differently?
2. Apply the rule for the settlement of a loss under an endorsement covering expediting charges when the direct damage loss is $500 and the expenses for overtime and extra costs amount to $1,000. What will the difference be in the expediting charges settlement if the direct damage loss is $5,000?
3. As a result of an explosion, the insurer expends $500 defending a suit. A verdict is brought in, in excess of the limit for the accident. Does the $500 expended for the defense come out of the limit for the accident, or is this paid in addition to the limit?
4. X, a manufacturer, carries a liability contract with a provision that he shall bear all losses up to $500 and after that his liability contract will assume the excess. He is faced with a claim of $5,000. His liability insurer agrees to pay $4,500 but points out to him that since the accident originated as a result of a boiler explosion, his boiler contract ought to pay the other $500. What is your opinion?

5. Business interruption, outage, consequential damage, and power interruption forms all provide insurance for protection from indirect loss. How do the coverages differ?
6. When it is stated that the power plant business interruption contract is valued, what does this mean? Are all power plant business interruption forms valued?
7. B carries consequential damage insurance in connection with his fire and windstorm coverage. He operates a cold-storage plant and is fearful lest he suffer a loss due to failure of his refrigeration plant. Because of his consequential loss coverage, he feels that he is adequately protected and does not expect to repeat the protection in connection with his power plant insurance. Is the reasoning correct?
8. X carries a steam boiler contract written with a limit per accident of $10,000. Following a serious explosion there is a property damage loss of $9,000 and liability claims, by a coincidence, amount to $9,000. Who gets paid by the insurer?
9. B carries a general liability contract on his plant with $10,000 limits. Assume all the conditions in the foregoing question. How would the loss be settled?
10. Boiler insurers claim that they do not sell an inspection service. Nevertheless, the inspection service which they render is highly valued by the purchasers of insurance, and in many instances it is primarily for the inspection that the insurance is purchased. What is the significance of the statement that boiler insurers do not sell inspection service?
11. Boiler and machinery contracts provide for insurance against an "accident to any kind of object" listed in the schedule. What is the significance of the terms "accident" and "object"?
12. In what circumstances where outage insurance is required will not a use and occupancy contract fill the need as well?
13. Power interruption insurance provides indemnity against loss arising from the total or partial deprivation of usable service, such as electric current, steam, water, gas, or refrigeration furnished by a public utility. Coverage may be written for hourly indemnity for loss of use, but there is a situation in which such a contract might be entirely inadequate. Indicate the type of contract that would fit better.
14. B is convinced of the necessity for insurance on his boilers, and he orders a contract. Because he is concerned about the fact that several large steam lines carry steam under heavy pressure, he makes inquiry as to the situation if a steam line bursts and causes damage. Will the boiler contract cover?
15. The boiler insurer has the right to make inspections but is not obligated to do so. Some feel, in spite of this, that the inspection service is of equal value, if not more valuable, than the indemnity provided by the contract. Explain.

16. State briefly the type of machinery that may be covered by a company writing power plant insurance and indicate briefly the hazards covered.
17. A steam or hot-water heating boiler in a residence, or any hot-water tank or heater, may, as a result of accidental overpressure, cause a violent explosion with serious loss. How should this risk be insured?
18. Distinguish between "furnace explosion" and "boiler explosion" as the terms are used in the field of power plant insurance. Are both covered under the boiler explosion contract?
19. Compare the protection afforded by furnace explosion and that afforded by the extended cover endorsement of the fire insurance contract.
20. Are smudge losses, caused by soot or smoke, the result of imperfect combustion covered by the power plant insurance contract?

CHAPTER · 22

Personal and Residential Insurance Contracts

A number of multiple line insurance contracts have been analyzed in preceding chapters. Among these contracts are the family automobile, the boiler and machinery, the jeweler's block, and marine contracts of various types, although these latter contracts were not specifically classified as multiple line. In this chapter areas in which multiple line contracts are especially important will be considered. Major emphasis will be given to the residential coverages represented by the homeowner's contract, but variations on these contracts will also be discussed. In addition, certain miscellaneous coverages that relate to the personal and residental category but are not multiple line contracts and are not included in residential packages will be briefly considered.

HISTORICAL BACKGROUND

Most multiple line insurance contracts covering real and personal property, as well as liability, in a single package have been developed since 1950, although prior to this date a number of multiple peril contracts had been issued. In 1913, a combination residence contract was written by a casualty insurer which provided certain types of physical damages protection along with liability insurance. Before this time, the fire contract with the extended coverage endorsement was perhaps the best example of a multiple peril contract. Although multiple line contracts, in contrast to multiple peril contracts, were not generally written in the United States, they were fairly common in Great Britain, and as early as 1915 British insurers had issued an "all-in" or comprehensive household contract.[1] Although develop-

[1] For further details see John E. Pierce, *Development of Comprehensive Insurance for the Household* (Homewood, Ill.: Richard D. Irwin, Inc., 1958).

ments in the United States in the direction of comprehensive contracts have been recent, the growth of this type of insurance in this country has been substantial. In 1955, approximately $68 million in premiums were written by insurers in the United States for multiple line contracts including homeowner's and commercial package contracts. In 1964, the comparable figure was $1,657 million.[2] It is likely that this growth will continue, since many insurers are now extending their interest in package contracts to the commercial field and many more homes now qualify for this type of insurance.

GENERAL CONSIDERATIONS IN HOMEOWNER'S CONTRACTS

Homeowner's contracts are now sold in every state except Mississippi and Oregon, and the overwhelming majority of individual homes are insured under these contracts. There are five types of homeowner's contracts available. These contracts are numbered one through five, and each is distinguished from the other mainly in terms of the extensiveness of coverage. When they were first developed, homeowner's contracts were labeled A, B, and C.[3] Under the new system adopted in 1958, homeowner's 1 and homeowner's A are alike. Homeowner's 2 and homeowner's B are the same, and homeowner's 5 corresponds to homeowner's C. Homeowner's 1 provides minimal coverage and is essentially a combination of fire and extended coverage plus personal liability and theft. Personal property as well as real property is insured. Plants, trees, and shrubs are covered within limits. The coverage is on a named peril basis and the insured should note carefully the limitations of the list of perils. Homeowner's 2 is similar to homeowner's 1, except that it adds eight perils against which insurance is provided. These perils include such items as damage from frozen pipes, falling objects, weight of ice or snow, explosion of a water heater, structural collapse (except if damage is from landslide, flood, tidal wave, termites, or earthquake). Homeowner's 3, which is never written by itself but always in connection with homeowner's 4, is an all risk form on the building with exclusions for such perils as flood, back-up of sewer, war and nuclear radiation, mechanical breakdowns, landslide, earthquake (although this peril may be added by endorsement). It is a named perils contract as far as contents are concerned. Homeowner's 4 is designed for renters. It provides the same coverage as homeowner's 2, except that the structure itself is not insured. Homeowner's 5 is the most comprehensive of the various

---

[2] *Insurance Facts* (New York: Insurance Information Institute, 1965), p. 17.

[3] Homeowner's A, B, and C and comprehensive dwelling contracts are still written in some of the states.

forms. It provides all risk coverage, subject to comparatively few exclusions, and covers personal property in much the same manner as the personal property floater.

Principles Underlying Homeowner's Contracts. For a number of years prior to the development of homeowner's contracts, there was a feeling among those persons interested in insurance that the principle of separate lines of insurance and separate contracts written by specialty insurers was not conducive in many situations to the best development of insurance theory and practice and was not the most efficient way to provide effectively for the insurance needs of the public. The necessity for securing a number of contracts often led to uncoordinated insurance programs, inadequate coverage, and a piecemeal approach to buying insurance. Nowhere were these difficulties more apparent than in the realm of personal and residential coverages.

After much discussion and thought insurers developed the homeowner's package contract as an answer to the need for an integrated and effective property and liability insurance contract for the household. From the beginning the fundamental principle was "a combination of coverages in a single policy, the coverages being mandatory and the amounts of each rigidly controlled by the amount of insurance on the dwelling building."[4] Although there has been some liberalization over the years, the principle of adequate protection still exists. The contracts were designed to be appealing to the mass market, and from the outset, the premium was an indivisible one.

Not all residences are eligible for "complete package policy protection," although eligibility rules very somewhat among the states. Typically, only owner-occupied or one- or two-family houses may be covered. This fact "puts the owner-occupant of a three or four family dwelling or larger apartment building in the same position as a tenant." Farm property is generally not eligible for homeowner's protection, since a separate package contract is available for that purpose.

Structure of Homeowner's Contracts. There is a standard framework that forms the basis for all homeowner's contracts. This basic contract consists ordinarily of four pages, but the exact arrangement of the pages may vary among insurers. The declarations are found on page one. Space is provided for recording the name of the insured, location of property, term of the contract, facts about the premium, types of coverages, and similar kinds of information. There are seven possible coverages labeled A through G and are as follows: A, dwelling building; B, private structures; C, personal property; D,

---

[4] See *Fire, Casualty, and Surety Bulletins* (Cincinnati, Ohio: The National Underwriter Company, 1966). The quotation in the following paragraph is also from this source.

additional living expense; E, comprehensive personal liability; F, medical payments; and G, physical damage to property. Toward the lower part of the first page is the insuring agreement of the standard fire insurance contract and the second page contains the 165 lines. Pages three and four are reserved for provisions and conditions that may be found in all homeowner's contracts.

There are five standard forms that may be attached to the basic contract.[5] The first is the standard form; the second, the broad form; the third, the special form; the fourth, the residence contents broad form; and the fifth, the comprehensive form. Various endorsements may also be added. The distinguishing characteristics of the five forms were briefly described earlier in this chapter. Form 2 (the broad form), which is probably the most popular of the five forms, will be discussed in some detail later in this chapter, and this discussion will be followed by an analysis of form 5 (the comprehensive form).

Amounts of Insurance. Minimum amounts of coverage are specified for the various contractual forms. For the property coverages these minima are related to the amount listed for the dwelling building. The following limits are generally applicable:[6] "Homeowners Form 1, Coverage A, Dwelling Building, $8,000 minimum; Coverage B, Private Structure, 10 percent of Coverage A; Coverage C, Personal Property, 40 percent of Coverage A (10 percent of this amount, with a minimum of $1,000 applies away from premises); Coverage D, Additional Living Expense, 10 percent of coverage A; Coverage E, Comprehensive Personal Liability, $25,000 per occurrence; Coverage F, Medical Payments, $500 per person, $25,000 per accident; Coverage G, Physical Damage to Property, $250 per occurrence." Form 2 has the same limits as form 1, except that additional living expense must be 20 percent of coverage A. Form 4 has a minimum coverage of $4,000 based on the "personal property on the premises"; Coverage D in this form is 20 percent of the personal property limit. The combination of form 3 and form 4 must have a limit for coverage C that is at least 40 percent of coverage A. Under form 5, the minimum amount for coverage A is $15,000, for coverage C, 50 percent of coverage A, and coverage D must be at least 20 percent of coverage A. The amount of insurance carried for unscheduled personal property may be increased, and in certain instances the rules allow for decreases in the amount of this coverage in forms 1 through 4. If there is incidental office, professional, or similar occupancy, the personal property limit is subject to a mandatory increase.

Endorsements. Homeowner's contracts may be modified by endorsement. There are various underwriting rules relating to these

---

[5] The reader will recall that form 3 is not issued separately.

[6] These limits are from the *Fire, Casualty and Surety Bulletins, op. cit.*

modifications and additional premiums are often charged.[7] There are over 20 standard endorsements. Examples are: changes in limits, location, and similar items; extended theft (forms 2 and 4 only); office, professional, private school, and studio occupancy; earthquake damage; credit card and depositors forgery coverage; additional limits on money and securities; watercraft; business pursuits; and secondary location. Credit card and depositors' forgery insurance is of increasing importance in view of the widespread use of credit cards, and many of the other endorsements are often essential, depending on the needs of the insureds.

THE BROAD FORM (FORM 2)

Homeowner's form 2 insures the dwelling, appurtenant private structures, and unscheduled personal property against a variety of named perils. There is also coverage for additional living expense. As a second part of the contract, comprehensive personal liability insurance is provided to cover situations in which the insured may become legally obligated to pay damages because of bodily injury or property damage. There is also coverage not involving legal liability for personal medical payments and physical damage to the property of others. The entire package is intended to provide adequate insurance against the risks normally arising out of the ownership of a home.

Property Section of the Contract. The property section of the contract describes the insurance protection afforded the homeowner relative to the dwelling and its contents. The coverage descriptions are virtually the same as those found in the forms attached to the standard fire insurance contract.

Property Insured. Coverage A of form 2 "insures the dwelling described in the declarations. . . ." The precise content of the paragraph setting forth this coverage has been analyzed previously and will be considered again later in this chapter. Coverage B is closely related to coverage A and insures "private structures" appertaining to the described premises and located thereon. . . ." Business, professional, and farming structures are excluded. Trees, shrubs, and plants are not included in the coverage, although "the insured may apply up to 5 percent of the amount of insurance applying to Coverage A to cover trees, shrubs and plants not grown for commercial purposes. . . ." against certain perils listed under extensions of coverage. No more than $250 is payable for any one tree, plant or shrub.[8]

Unscheduled personal property is insured under coverage C. All personal property is covered "except property which is separately

[7] *Ibid.*

[8] *Ibid.*

described and enumerated and specifically insured in whole or in part by other insurance." The homeowners' contract may not be used as excess insurance for personal property nor does it contribute to a loss insured under another personal property contract. Specifically excluded are "live animals and birds; vehicles required by law to be licensed for road or air use; and articles carried or held as samples, or for sale, or for delivery after sale or for rental to others." Not only is personal property owned, worn, or used by the insured covered, but also personal property of "members of the name Insured's family of the same household and at the option of the named Insured, personal property of others, while situated on the described premises." Personal property belonging to a tenant is not covered, nor is personal property "rented to others except while on the described premises or in that portion of a dwelling customarily occupied exclusively by the insured."

Much of the detail surrounding personal property covered including extensions and limitations, such as dollar limitations on such items as bullion, accounts, and manuscripts, is the same for both forms 2 and 5. Additional discussion of these matters is included in the discussion of the latter form (see pages 574–82). An important difference between the two forms is that protection for personal property is on a named peril, somewhat limited basis in form 2 and on an all risk worldwide basis in form 5. An important extension of coverage in form 2 permits the insured to apply 10 percent of the amount specified for coverage C (but not less than $1,000), "on personal property as described and limited while elsewhere than on the described premises, anywhere in the world. . . ." Insureds other than the named insured, such as a member of the insured's family living with him, are also included in this extension.

Additional living expense (coverage D), which includes rental value coverage, relates to coverages A, B, and C. If loss occurs under any of these coverages that makes the dwelling or appurtenant structures untenantable, the insured needs protection against the additional expenses incurred in finding temporary quarters.

Perils Insured Against. The perils insured against in form 2 are similar (but not exactly the same) as those found in the dwelling building and contents broad form. The perils apply to coverages A, B, and C, although in some variations of form 2, coverages A and B may be provided on an all risks of physical loss basis with the named perils applying to coverage C. The perils typically listed are: fire and lightning; windstorm and hail; explosion; sudden and accidental tearing asunder, cracking, burning, or bulging of a steam or hot water heating system; vandalism and malicious mischief; riot and civil commotion; aircraft and vehicles; sudden and accidental damage from smoke; falling objects; weight of ice, snow, or sleet; collapse of buildings or any part thereof; glass breakage; theft; removal; water escape; sudden and accidental tearing asunder, cracking, burning, or bulging of appliances for heating water for domestic consumption; freezing of plumbing, heating, and air-conditioning systems and domestic appliances; and sudden and accidental injury to electrical applicances, devices, fixtures, and wiring resulting from electrical currents artificially generated.

Many of these perils are subject to limitations that are specifically mentioned in their contractural description. Deductibles may be applicable to some or, depending on the wording of the deductible clause, almost all of them, and such perils as vandalism and malicious mischief, glass breakage, freezing of systems and appliances are subject to restrictions on vacancy. Mysterious disappearance is neither excluded nor insured in forms 1, 2, and 4.

Exclusions. The contract makes reference to certain specific exclusions. There are the typical exclusions of losses caused by war or war-like action, nuclear reaction, radiation, or radioactive contamination, and losses caused by deterioration and related action, which are not fortuitous and might be alleviated through proper maintenance. Two exclusions, in addition to those already considered should be mentioned.[9] First, loss caused by earthquake, volcanic eruption, landslide, mudflow, earth sinking, shifting, or other earth movement is excluded. This exclusion is specifically related to such perils as sudden or accidental tearing asunder, falling objects, and collapse of building or parts. Second, losses caused by flood, surface water, and related activity are not insured. The exclusion reads as follows: "This policy does not insure against loss caused by, resulting from, contributed to or aggravated by any of the following: (*a*) flood, surface water, waves or tidal wave, overflow of streams or other bodies of water, or spray from any of the foregoing, all whether driven by wind or not; (*b*) water which backs up through sewers or drains; (*c*) water below the surface of the ground including that which exerts pressure on or flows, seeps or leaks through sidewalks, driveways, foundations, walls, basement or other floors, or through doors, windows or any other openings in such sidewalks, driveways, foundations, walls or floors; this exclusion, however, shall not apply to loss by fire or explosion caused by perils excluded in this paragraph nor to loss by theft." This exclusion, like the earthquake exclusion, is particularly applicable to certain perils. These perils are the same as for earthquake with the addition of windstorm and hail, weight of ice, and snow or sleet and glass breakage.

Conditions. There are a number of conditions, listed in form 2,

---

[9] This listing of exclusions is not complete. The reader should consult a contract for a detailed statement.

that relate specifically to the property coverages. One of these conditions that is of particular importance is the one relating to replacement cost. The discussion of this condition, as well as the other conditions will be deferred and considered in the analysis of form 5.

Comprehensive Personal Liability. The comprehensive personal liability section of the contract follows the pattern of the comprehensive personal liability contract that was discussed in Chapter 17. The insuring agreement defines three coverages: coverage E, personal liability; coverage F, personal medical payments; and coverage G, physical damage to property. In addition, there is a statement about supplementary payments and definitions of automobile, midget automobile, undeclared outboard motor, residence employee, insured, bodily injury, property damage, insured premises, business property, and business. There are a number of exclusions and the usual conditions.[10]

THE COMPREHENSIVE FORM (FORM 5)[11]

The comprehensive form of the homeowner's contract, like the broad form is divided into two sections. Section I contains the provisions applicable to the dwelling, appurtenant private structures, unscheduled personal property, and additional living expense. Section II contains the agreement relating to comprehensive personal liability, medical payments, and physical damage to the property of others. Space is provided for a deferred premium payment endorsement, and spaces for increasing the limits on money and securities and personal property in a secondary residence.

Section I. Since Section I covers real and personal property, considerable space in the contract is given to a description of the property covered, the perils insured against, extensions of coverage, special limits of liability, special exclusions, and special conditions.

The property and interests covered include the dwelling (coverage A), appurtenant private structures (coverage B), unscheduled personal property (coverage C), and additional living expense (coverage D). The insurance provided is similar to that found in the special dwelling and all physical loss form.

Dwelling. A dwelling is defined as the building described in the declarations, "including additions in contact therewith occupied principally for dwelling purposes." Building equipment, fixtures, and outdoor equipment are included as a part of dwelling coverage as are

---

[10] For additional discussion, see pages 430–31 and pages 580–82.

[11] Since form 5 and form 2 are similar in much of their contractual detail, some duplication in the discussion of the two forms is unavoidable. An effort has been made to keep repetition to a minimum. Where provisions are the same, or virtually so, the detailed discussion will be found in this section.

materials and supplies intended for construction or repair. Equipment, fixtures, and similar items must be owned by the insured and not covered by other insurance contracts and must be located on the premises, although temporary locations elsewhere are permitted. Likewise materials and supplies must be on the premises or close by. Appurtenant private structures located on the premises and related to the use of the premises as a dwelling along with materials intended for construction are covered under the contract. Any structures used for manufacturing or other commercial purposes or for farming are excluded as are structures "wholly rented or leased to other than a tenant of the described dwelling." Buildings used primarily as private garages are not included as a part of this latter provision.

Unscheduled Personal Property. Unscheduled personal property is insured "while in all situations anywhere in the world." The personal property must be of the type that is related to the use of the building as a dwelling and be "owned, worn, or used by an insured." The coverage is similar to that of the personal property floater that was discussed in Chapter 14. If the named insured so elects, personal property owned by other persons may be covered, if such persons are on the premises where the insured is living. Likewise personal property owned by residence employees comes within the purview of the contract while the employee is not on the premises but nevertheless in the course of his employment. Certain types of property are excluded from Coverage C. Not included are "animals, birds, automobiles, vehicles licensed for road use and aircraft, property of roomers or boarders not related to the insured, articles carried or held as samples or for sale or for delivery after sale or for rental to others, or any business property away from the premises, and property which is separately described and specifically insured in whole or in part by this or any other insurance."

Additional Living Expense. Additional living expenses often arise as the result of loss to property from one of the perils insured under the contract. In providing for additional living expenses the insurer undertakes to provide funds to enable the named insured to maintain his usual standard of living. The amount of coverage is limited by the figure named in the declarations, and the period during which these additional expenses will be paid is restricted to "the time required with the exercise of due diligence and dispatch to repair or replace such damaged or destroyed property; or the time required for the named insured's household to become settled in permanent quarters." This coverage extends also to the fair rental value of the structure or any part which is "rented or held for rental" for the "period of time required with the exercise of due diligence or dispatch to restore the same to tenantable condition less such charges and expenses as do not continue." This period is not limited to the expiration of the contract.

There are situations where an insured is denied access to his home because a neighbor's house has been damaged by a peril insured under this contract. The insurer in this circumstance accepts liability under coverage D for a period not to exceed two weeks.

All Risk Contract. The comprehensive form of the homeowner's contract is an all risk contract and "insures under Section One against all risks of physical loss to the property covered (and additional living expense resulting from such loss)" subject to certain exclusions. These exclusions are the ones that tend to be typical in property insurance contracts and have been discussed in earlier chapters. Losses from depreciation, insects, and mechanical breakdown are excluded, as are flood, backing up of water from sewers and drains, seepage of water, theft of supplies or materials from a building under construction, and loss by nuclear reaction, nuclear radiation, or radioactive contamination. Special exclusions applying to personal property are losses caused by breakage of eyeglasses, glassware, statuary, and similar fragile articles; losses by vermin, dampness of atmosphere, and related cause of loss. These exclusions do not apply to "direct loss caused by fire, lightning, windstorm, hail, smoke (other than smoke from agricultural smudging or industrial operations), explosion, riot attending a strike, civil commotion, falling aircraft, vehicle collision, vandalism and malicious mischief, collapse of a building or any part thereof, earthquake, water not otherwise excluded, theft or attempted theft, or sudden and accidental tearing asunder, crackling, burning or bulging of a steam or hot water heating system." Losses caused by the insured's animals or birds are excluded unless fire, explosion, or smoke results from the damage. In such cases only the loss from fire, explosion, or smoke is covered. The exclusions relating to real property and additional living expense are such items as loss by smog, earthquake, landslide, freezing of plumbing and heating systems, loss by vandalism and malicious mischief, if building has been vacant beyond 30 days.[12]

Extensions of Coverage. An important feature of Section I is the provision relating to extensions of coverage. These extensions apply to trees, shrubs, plants, and lawns; debris removal, consequential loss, and replacement cost of real property. They do not serve to increase the limits of liability applying to the items insured.

Limited coverage for trees, shrubs, plants, and lawns is provided for direct loss from certain named perils. These perils are fire, lightning, smoke (with a few restrictions), explosion, riot, riot attending a strike, civil commotion, aircraft, vehicles (except vehicles operated by an occupant of the premises), vandalism and malicious mischief, and theft. Windstorm and hail are specifically excluded. The amount of liability that the insurer will assume is limited to 5 percent of the

[12] See homeowner's contract for complete listing of exclusions.

amount of coverage provided for the dwelling and is further limited to the insurer's "proportion of $250 on any one tree, shrub or plant." Plants grown for commercial purposes are excluded.

Debris removal is provided for under extensions of coverage for any loss to property occasioned by a peril insured against under the contract. Also, consequential loss to unscheduled personal property is covered while the property is "contained in a building at the described location" and if the loss is "due to a change of temperature as a result of physical damage to such building or equipment therein, caused by a peril insured against."

Coverage C (unscheduled personal property) is extended to residences of the insured other than the dwelling described in the declarations for direct loss except by fire caused by "theft or attempt thereat or vandalism and malicious mischief to the interior of such residences, or loss to improvements, alterations, or additions made by an insured to residences occupied but not owned by the insured." The amount of coverage may not exceed 10 percent of the amount of coverage for unscheduled personal property as recorded in the declarations.

Replacement Cost. A feature of the homeowner's contract that is somewhat unique is that replacement cost is provided for dwellings and appurtenant private structures under the extensions of coverage. The specific provision is:

As respects building structures (meaning thereby only property which at the time of loss is an essential part of any building structure):

a) In the event of loss to such a building structure covered under this policy, when the full cost of repair or replacement is both (1) less than $1,000 and (2) less than 5 percent of the whole amount of insurance applicable to such building structure for the peril causing the loss, the coverage of this policy is extended to include the full cost of repair or replacement (without deduction for depreciation).[13]

b) If at the time of loss the whole amount of insurance applicable to said building structure for the peril causing the loss is 80 percent or more of the full replacement cost of such building structure, the coverage of this policy applicable to such building structures is extended to include the full cost of repair or replacement (without deduction for depreciation).

c) If at the time of loss the whole amount of insurance applicable to said building structure for the peril causing the loss is less than 80 percent of the full replacement cost of such building structure, this Company's liability for loss under this policy shall not exceed the larger of the following amounts (1) or (2):

---

[13] In approximately 20 states this part of the replacement cost provision has been changed. There is now reference to the 80 percent requirement. A claim may be paid under this section even if repairs or replacement has not been made.

(1) The actual cash value of that part of the building structure damaged or destroyed;

(2) That proportion of the full cost of repair or replacement (without deduction for depreciation) of that part of the building structure damaged or destroyed, which the whole amount of insurance applicable to said building structure for the peril causing the loss bears to 80 percent of the full replacement cost of such building structure.

d) This Company's liability for loss under this policy including this Extension of Coverage shall not exceed the smallest of the following amounts (1), (2), or (3):

(1) The limit of liability of this policy applicable to the damaged or destroyed building structure;

(2) The replacement cost of the building structure or any part thereof identical with such building structure on the same premises and intended for the same occupancy and use;

(3) The amount actually and necessarily expended in repairing or replacing said building structure or any part thereof intended for the same occupancy and use.

This Company shall not be liable under paragraph (*b*) or subparagraph (2) of paragraph (*c*) of this Extension of Coverage for any loss unless and until actual repair or replacement is completed.

e) In determining if the amount of insurance on the building structure insured equals or exceeds 80 percent of its replacement cost the value of excavations, underground flues and pipes, underground wiring and drains, and brick, stone and concrete foundations, piers and other supports which are below the surface of the ground shall be disregarded.

f) The named insured may elect to disregard this Extension of Coverage in making claim hereunder, but such election shall not prejudice the Named Insured's right to make further claim within 180 days after loss for any additional liability brought about by this Extension of Coverage.

This extension provides replacement value of the structure as the basis for settlement under two conditions: (1) if the full cost of repair or replacement is less than $1,000 and less than 5 percent of the whole amount of insurance "applicable to the structure and (2) if at the time of loss the face amount of the insurance applicable to the structure is 80 percent or more of full replacement cost of the structure." If the insured does not have insurance on the building equal to 80 percent of replacement value at the time of loss, the insurer's liability is determined by taking the larger of either the "actual cash value of that part of the building structure damaged or destroyed" or that proportion of the "full cost of repair or replacement" determined by dividing the amount of insurance applicable to the structure by 80 percent of the replacement cost of the structure. The amount of settlement is subject, in addition to the limits already specified, to the three limits listed in part (*d*) of the preceding quotation. These are the types of restrictions that are to be expected, since the insurer in no event would pay more than the face of the contract, nor would it be expected to pay more than was expended in repairing or replacing a structure. In determining 80 percent of replacement cost "the value of excavations, underground flues and pipes, underground wiring and drains, and brick, stone and concrete foundations, piers and other supports which are below the surface of the ground" are disregarded.

Deductibles. In addition to the limits placed on insurer liability that have already been considered, there are special limits that apply to certain of the coverages. There are two loss deductible clauses that are applicable if provision has been made in the declarations for them. They do not apply to the coverage that provides additional living expense. These clauses are in effect a combination of a deductible clause, a franchise clause and a disappearing deductible. The first loss deductible clause states that in the event of "loss by windstorm or hail to buildings, structures, or personal property in the open, this Company shall be liable only when such loss in each occurrence exceeds $100." If the loss is between $100 and $500, the insurer will pay 125 percent of the loss that exceeds $100. If the loss is $500 or greater, the deductible does not apply. The second deductible clause applies to perils other than fire, lightning, windstorm, or hail. The financial arrangements are the same as for the first deductible clause.[14]

Limitations on Personal Property. There are three special limits that apply to personal property. The first of these limits the insurer's liability on such items as money, bullion, numismatic property, accounts, bills, deeds, passports, manuscripts, articles of jewelry, and similar items. These limits vary from $100 on money and bullion to $1,000 on manuscripts. Jewelry has a $250 limit unless the loss is occasioned by fire, lightning, windstorm, hail, smoke, explosion, riot, and perils of a similar type. The second limit relates to personal property in residences that are not the dwelling described in the declarations. The insurer is not liable for more than 10 percent of the value of unscheduled personal property normally located in these other residences. The third restriction places a limit of $500 on the amount of any one loss that the insurer will bear on "watercraft, including their trailers whether licensed or not, furnishing, equipment and outboard motors." Property of this type is covered only for such named perils as fire, lightning, explosion, smoke, falling aircraft, theft, collision, and upset or overturning of land vehicles.

Special Conditions. There are five clauses listed under the general heading "Special Conditions." The first of these conditions provides

[14] A $50 deductible with a 111 percent adjustment factor is available as an option on the homeowner's 5. This option is regarded as the standard type deductible in other homeowner's forms in most states.

that losses under the contract shall not reduce the limits stated in the declarations. The second condition places the responsibility on the insured to notify the insurer and the police in the event of loss by theft or mysterious disappearance. The third condition declares that the insurer is not willing to assume the nuclear risk. The fourth condition is a nonfarming clause that is applicable only in New Jersey and the fifth condition is the mortgage clause. This clause is void if the mortgagee's name is not placed in the declarations. Since this clause has been discussed at length in Chapter 7, it will not be considered here.

Section II. Section II contains the insuring and other agreements relating to coverages E, F, and G. Coverage E provides comprehensive personal liability insurance, coverage F, medical payments, and coverage G, physical damage to property.

Two aspects of comprehensive personal liability are provided for—bodily injury and property damage, and fire legal liability. Under bodily injury and property damage the insurer agrees "to pay on behalf of the insured all sums which the insured shall become legally obligated to pay as damages." As in the comprehensive personal liability contract, the insurer agrees to defend suits even if groundless, false, or fraudulent. An additional charge is made for any swimming pool covered under personal liability, if the pool can be "filled to a depth of more than 30 inches at any point." The fire legal liability provision states that the comprehensive personal liability coverage "applies with respect to injury to or destruction of, including loss of use of, the premises or house furnishings used by, rented to or in the care, custody or control of the insured, if such injury or destruction arises out of (1) fire, (2) explosion, or (3) smoke or smudge caused by sudden, unusual and faulty operation of any heating or cooking unit."

The medical payments coverage is independent of legal obligation and is similar to that provided in other liability contracts. The bodily injury requiring medical care must be accidental and sustained on the premises of the insured with care for off-premises injuries being provided if the bodily injury "(1) arises out of the premises or a condition in the ways immediately adjoining, (2) is caused by the activities of an insured, (3) is caused by the activities of or is sustained by a residence employee and arises out of and in the course of his employment by an insured, or (4) is caused by an animal owned by or in the care of an insured."

The physical damage to property coverage is designed to pay for losses of property belonging to others that have been caused by the insured. Again, legal liability is not involved. Loss does not include "disappearance, abstraction or loss of use." Losses covered under Section I are excluded from this part of the contract.

The insuring agreement in Section II includes, in addition to a statement of the coverages, several paragraphs that serve to enlarge the coverage (supplementary payments), to define such words or expressions as "premises," "automobile," and "bodily injury," and to state the conditions under which newly acquired outboard motors will be insured. The supplementary payments provision is the same as that previously discussed in relation to the comprehensive personal liability contract. Newly acquired outboard motors are included if the insured "notifies the insurer within thirty days after acquiring ownership of such motor, did not own an undeclared outboard motor at the inception of the contract period, and has no other valid and collectible insurance applicable thereto."

There are ten exclusions that are applicable to Section II. Four of these exclusions relate to both comprehensive personal liability and medical payments, four to comprehensive personal liability, one to medical payments, and one to physical damage to property. The four exclusions applicable to both comprehensive personal liability and medical payments are:

a) to any business pursuits of an Insured other than under Coverages E and F, (comprehensive personal liability and medical payments), activities therein which are ordinarily incident to non-business pursuits, (2) to the rendering of any professional service or the omission thereof, or (3) to any act or omission in connection with premises, other than as defined, which are owned, rented or controlled by an Insured, but this subdivision (3) does not apply with respect to bodily injury to a residence employee arising out of and in the course of his employment by the Insured;

b) under Coverages E and F, to the ownership, maintenance, operation, use, loading or unloading of (1) automobiles or midget automobiles while away from the premises or the ways immediately adjoining, except under Coverage E with respect to operations by independent contractors for non-business purposes of an Insured not involving automobiles owned or hired by the Insured, (2) watercraft owned by or rented to an Insured, while away from the premises, if with inboard motor power exceeding fifty horsepower or if twenty-six feet or more in over-all length and a sailing vessel, with or without auxiliary power, (3) watercraft while away from the premises and powered in whole or in part by an Insured, or (4) aircraft; but, with respect to bodily injury to a residence employee, arising out of and in the course of his employment by the insured, parts (1), (2), and (3) of this exclusion do not apply, and part (4) applies only while such employee is engaged in the operation or maintenance of aircraft.

c) under Coverages E and F, to bodily injury or property damage caused intentionally by or at the direction of the insured.

d) under Coverages E and F, to bodily to any person (1) if the insured has in effect on the date of the occurrence a policy providing workmen's compensation or occupational disease benefits therefor, or (2) if benefits therefor are in whole or in part either payable or required to be provided under any workmen's compensation or occupational disease law, but this subdivision (2) does not apply with respect to Coverage E unless such benefits are payable or required to be provided by the Insured.

The four exceptions applicable to comprehensive personal liability are:

e) under Coverage E, to liability assumed by the Insured under any contract or agreement except under Insuring Agreement 1 (*a*) (liability) liability of others assumed under a written contract relating to the premises;

f) under Insuring Agreement 1 (*a*) of Coverage E to property damage to property used by, rented to or in the care, custody, or control of the Insured, or property as to which the Insured for any purpose is exercising physical control;

g) under Coverage E, to sickness or disease of any residence employee unless prior to 36 months after the end of the policy period written claim is made or suit is brought against the Insured for damages because of such sickness or disease or death resulting therefrom;

h) under Coverage E, to bodily injury or property damage with respect to which an Insured under this policy is also an Insured under a nuclear energy liability policy issued by Nuclear Energy Liability Association, Mutual Atomic Energy Liability Underwriters or Nuclear Insurance Association of Canada, or would be an Insured under any such policy but for its termination upon exhaustion of its limit of liability.

An exclusion relating solely to medical payments is:

i) under Coverage F (Medical Payments), to bodily injury to (1) any Insured within the meaning of parts (1) and (2) of Definition of Insured in the Basic Policy or (2) any person, other than a residence employee, if such person is regularly residing on the premises, or is on the premises because of a business conducted thereon, or is injured by an accident arising out of such business.

The single exclusion that applies to physical damage to property is:

j) under Coverage G (Physical Damage to Property), to loss (1) arising out of the ownership, maintenance, operation, use, loading or unloading of any land motor vehicle, trailer or semitrailer, farm machinery or equipment, aircraft or watercraft; or (2) of property owned by or rented to any Insured, any resident of the Named Insured's household or any tenant of the insured; or (3) caused intentionally by an Insured over the age of 12 years."

Although the exclusions seem fairly extensive and detailed, they are not seriously limiting, and for the most part, simply serve to exclude situations normally covered under separate contracts such as the family automobile and various contracts applicable to business situations.

Other Conditions Applicable to the Homeowner's Contract. There are 24 conditions that appear on the last pages of the homeowner's contract. Eight of these conditions apply to the contract as a whole, six to Section I, and ten to Section II. Additionally, there is the war risk exclusion, which states that the contract does not cover "hostile or warlike action in time of peace or war. . . ." nor does it apply to "insurrection, rebellion, revolution, civil war, unsurped power, or action taken by governmental authority in hindering, combating or defending against such an occurrence; seizure or destruction under quarantine or Custom's regulations, confiscation by order of any government or public authority, or risks of contraband or illegal transportation or trade."

Under "General Conditions" are contained such items as definitions (insured, premises, residence employee, and business), other insurance apportionment, liberalization, and cancellation. Many of these provisions are similar to those considered in other contracts and have been discussed in previous chapters. A condition somewhat unique in this particular contract is one which provides that on the death of the named insured the contract "shall cover the Named Insured's spouse, if a resident of the same household at the time of such death, and legal representative as Named Insured's from the date of such death." In general, the legal representative is regarded, in the event of the death of the named insured, as an insured in respect only to the premises of the named insured.

The conditions that apply to Section I are brief. The insured is allowed to leave his home vacant or unoccupied without any restriction as to time, although any provision in the contract to the contrary supersedes this permission. The named insured is also permitted to "make alterations, additions and repairs, and to complete structures in the course of construction." There is a subrogation clause, a bailee clause, and a pair and set clause. Under the latter clause the insurer establishes that the loss of one item from a pair or set does not mean the total loss of the pair or set.

The ten conditions applicable to Section II relate mainly to requirements in the event of losses under coverages E and F. The following items are included: limits of liability, settlement options, coverage G; severability of interests, coverages E and F; notice of occurrence, notice of claim or suit, coverage E; assistance and cooperation of the insured; coverage E; medical reports—proof and payment of claim, coverage F; notice—proof and payment of loss, coverage G; action against company, coverage E; and action against company, coverages F and G. These conditions are the ones that ordinarily apply to liability and medical payments coverages and they present no new considerations.

PERSONAL PACKAGES VARIATIONS

Homeowners contracts and forms are fairly uniform, regardless of whether the insurer uses bureau forms and rates or files independently, and major differences in contractual provisions are not common. Competition is mainly in the area of rates. Some insurers write three types of homeowner's contracts corresponding roughly to the homeowner's 1, 3 plus 4, and 5. Form 2 is not written. Other insurers offer slightly different benefits such as all risk insurance on the dwelling and appurtenant private structures, although the form itself may be essentially named peril. The Texas homeowners program is illustrative of these and other variations.[15] Another variation offered by one large insurer is term life insurance in combination with a homeowners contract.

Homeowner's Life Insurance Contract. The homeowner's life insurance contract is issued in conjunction with a regular homeowner's form without medical examination, although the insured is required to answer three questions that relate to his present state of health and to his medical history. The agent cannot bind the coverage if any of these questions is answered negatively. The contract is of the decreasing term type and is available to persons between ages 20 and 54. A level annual premium is charged, even though the amount of insurance based on the premium for a unit of coverage decreases from $13,500 at age 20 to $2,000 at age 54. People of certain occupations, such as boxers, jockeys, rodeo riders, and test pilots, are not acceptable. Double indemnity is available and proceeds are normally paid as a monthly benefit, although a lump-sum settlement option is available.

CAREER COVERAGE

Numerous special contracts are available which provide an indemnity in the event of the happening of an accident that would terminate the career of the insured. The contracts partake to a large degree of the nature of a personal accident contract but differ from the contract ordinarily written in that they are designed to protect one particular feature or physical characteristic that is an important factor in the career of the insured.

It is reported that a well-known novelist insured her hand. It was her contention that she was unable to produce fiction on a typewriter and was unable successfully to dictate. She, therefore, obtained a contract covering her right hand, contending that her occupation would be terminated if she were unable to write in longhand. A dancer insured her feet for $100,000. There is recorded the case of a

[15] See *Fire, Casualty and Surety Bulletins, op. cit.,* for a discussion of the Texas program.

band leader who insured his Russian accent for $100,000, and it is reported that clauses in the contract forbade his taking diction lessons in any form, attempting to present or introduce any dialect other than Russian in his performances, or living with anyone who would have a negative effect upon his accent. It was also provided that, in the event of his marriage, the coverage terminated. Applications for this type of coverage are common. A few years ago, a radio actor sought a $100,000 contract against loss of his British accent, including the loss of his voice or change in its tone. An actress insured her film career through a clause attached to a life and accident contract which guaranteed her earnings to be $125,000 for a period of three years. Another film actress carried a contract insuring her back in the amount of $50,000, providing payment for disfigurement "by reason of marring, mauling by crowds, or affectionate friends, sunburn, scratches or burns." A well-known skater obtained a contract providing that any accident or injury to her legs which would prevent her from skating made the insurer liable for $5,000 weekly for a maximum period of 52 weeks. Perhaps one of the most unusual contracts ever written was that obtained by Prince Sukhadava. When he was King Prajadhipok of Siam, he is said to have taken out insurance against the risk of loss of his throne. In 1935 the first payments were made by French and British firms. Under the terms of the contract, he was to receive about $40,000 a year for the rest of his life.

For underwriting purposes, contracts of this class fall in the same category as that of insurance written against isolated contingencies. The amounts of insurance are ordinarily high and involve a risk usually peculiar to itself. There is no group experience available as a basis for determining rates, and the underwriter is forced to rely upon his best judgment. A severe loss in a classification where the number of risks is limited requires the insurer to draw on the business as a whole to meet its payment. In accepting such risks the underwriter, to use a Lloyd's phrase, underwrites "against the pot."

TITLE INSURANCE[16]

Title insurance is a type of property insurance designed to protect the insured from losses that may arise through a defective title to land and improvements. This insurance was first written in the United States in Philadelphia in 1876. Although a system for the transfer of title to real property has been carefully worked out through the use of deeds and abstracts, it is still possible for a defective title to be transferred to the purchaser of real estate. Abstracts cannot be fully relied

[16] Title insurance is here classified as a personal and residential coverage, since most persons first encounter it when purchasing a home. It is applicable, of course, to property purchased for business use.

upon, since they depend on the public record, and there is no guarantee that every transaction affecting the title to a parcel of land has been fully and accurately recorded. Invalid wills, dower claims, defective foreclosures, undiscovered heirs, and similar items may give rise to defects in title. Even though an attorney is retained to prepare an abstract, he simply gives an opinion as to whether the title is clear and in no way guarantees that it is free of defects. The difficulties encountered in a title search should not be underestimated. Records involving the transfer of real property extend over many years and omissions and inaccurate entries are always possible.

Title insurance contracts differ in certain ways from the typical property insurance contract. The term of the contract is indefinite and runs into the future without a specific termination date. The premium is payable only once and, unless a change in the title occurs, no new premium becomes due. Insurance is provided against defects in the title that existed prior to the time the contract is entered into and there is no protection against defects that may originate in the future. Defects that are known at the time the contract is purchased are not assumed. One of the services rendered by the insurer is a careful title search, and firms that sell this type of insurance maintain extensive records.

The typical title insurance contract contains declarations, insuring clause, exclusions, and conditions as do other property insurance contracts. The insuring clause agrees to protect the owner of the property or others for an amount not to exceed the face of the contract because of a defective title. The insuring clause refers to Schedule A and Schedule B. The first of these schedules contains such items as the date, amount, and number of the contract as well as information on the interest of the insured, the deed, and the description of the property. The second provides a list of defects, liens, and other items that the insurer does not agree to assume. Transfer of the contract is permitted but usually only if the insurer approves and so endorses the contract. In addition to indemnifying against losses the insurer agrees to defend the insured in the suits that may be brought for the purpose of ejecting the insured (or other proceedings) which arise out of difficulties encountered because of defects in the title that are covered by the contract. Other parts of the contract deal with such matters as transfer, settlement of claims, duties of the insured, and subrogation. These items follow the general pattern found in other contracts with such changes as are appropriate to title insurance.

FOR DISCUSSION

1. List the contracts in preceding chapters that may be classified as multiple line. In what way, if any, do they differ from the contracts considered in this chapter?

2. Discuss the growth of homeowner's contracts over the last ten years.
3. Mr. X, while eating in a cafeteria, took off his wrist watch and placed it on the table. After leaving the cafeteria he realized that he had forgotten his watch and went back to get it. The watch could not be found and the cafeteria owners said no one had reported finding it. Would a homeowner's 5 contract cover this loss? Why or why not?
4. List the property and property interests covered by the homeowner's 5 contract. To what extent do these differ from the property interests insured under a fire insurance contract with extended coverage?
5. Under what conditions would an insured receive replacement cost for a home destroyed by fire if the building were insured under a homeowner's 2 contract?
6. While cleaning her employer's home a maid accidentally broke several china vases that had considerable value as antiques. Would the loss be covered under a homeowner's 5 contract? Why or why not?
7. To what extent is it possible to increase the liability and medical payment limits in homeowner's contracts?
8. Some insurers believe that a collection of "standard" contracts is to be preferred as a package to a single integrated-type contract. What reasons could you give in justification of this point of view?
9. A enjoys a moderate income but employs no servants. He lives with his wife in a dwelling valued at $15,000. B is a professional man who lives with his wife and two children in a residence valued at $30,000 and contents valued at $10,000. They have a part-time servant and occasionally hire a man for outside work. They have a dog. The wife plays golf and the husband does not participate in sports. Outline insurance coverages for each.
10. What are some of the advantages of title insurance?
11. The following article appeared in the *Boston Sunday Herald*, December 29, 1946: ". . . was well known in his lower East Side neighborhood for his distinguished Van Dyke beard and mustaches, but no more. He dozed over an early morning cigar, police reported today, and awakened to find the beard was burning briskly and had ignited the bedclothes and mattress. Five fire engines and 20 firemen answered the alarm neighbors sent in. The beard was a total loss." Is this an insurable risk?

CHAPTER • 23

Farm Insurance Contracts

Premiums on insurance contracts protecting farm property are substantial and amount to well over $100 million annually. Approximately 60 percent of these premiums apply to fire insurance, 25 percent to extended coverage, and approximately 15 percent to farmowner's contracts.[1] The need for farm insurance continues to be substantial in spite of the fact that the farm population is declining.

Many of the contracts that were considered in earlier chapters may be adapted to farm needs, and historically monoline contracts have been typical in farm insurance. More diversity has existed in this field than in many of the other areas of insurance, at least partly because of the popularity of county mutuals and other specialized insurers that were formed for the purpose of providing insurance for farm property over a relatively small geographical area. The contracts issued by these organizations tend to be nonstandard and somewhat more restrictive than the more common types of property and liability insurance contracts.

Since a detailed analysis of monoline contracts issued to farmers would involve a considerable amount of repetition, the only monoline contracts that will be analyzed in this chapter are those relating to crops, greenhouses, and livestock. Major emphasis will be given to the farmowner's program, which is the farm counterpart of the homeowner's program.

FARMOWNER'S CONTRACTS[2]

Farmowner's contracts first became available in 1961, when they were introduced by the Inter-Regional Insurance Conference. These

[1] Dean E. Matthews, "Is Farm Market Untapped?" *American Agency Bulletin*, Vol. 63, No. 8 (April, 1966), p. 28.

[2] See *Fire, Casualty, and Surety Bulletins* (Cincinnati, Ohio: National Underwriter Company, 1966), Miscellaneous Fire Section. The facts on farmowner's contracts are based on this source.

contracts were designed to provide comprehensive insurance for the farm through a package covering the farm residence, farm buildings, and farm personal property. The farm need not be owner occupied in order for a farmowner's contract to be written, but must not be vacant. The farm dwelling must be of a one- or two-family type used solely for residential purposes, although a limited number (2) of roomers or boarders per family may also reside in the farm home.

Structure of the Farmowner's Contract. The farmowner's contract is similar structurally to the homeowner's contracts. The basic contract has four pages that contain the declarations, the standard fire insurance contract, and the conditions that are applicable to the contract in general. The declarations cover such items as the description of the farm premises, limits of liability, premium information, type of construction, statement that dwelling is not seasonal, coinsurance, deductibles, and information pertaining to the liability section of the contract. The contract is completed by the adding of forms and endorsements.

The basic farmowner's contract is divided into two sections; the first section provides physical damage coverage along with time element and theft coverage, while Section II covers farmers comprehensive personal liability insurance. Physical damage protection may be afforded in varying degrees of comprehensiveness. One type of form that may be added as Section I provides fire and extended coverage plus vandalism, malicious mischief, and theft, and is regarded as the standard form. There is also a broad form and a tenant's form. Property covered includes, in addition to the dwelling and farm buildings, appurtenant private garages, unscheduled personal property, additional living expense, and, optionally, farm personal property (equipment, feed, livestock, and similar items).

Depending on the type of physical damage form that is used, farmowner's contracts may be identified as farmowner's 1, 2, or 4. Farmowner's 1 is the most limited and provides fire insurance, extended coverage, vandalism and malicious mischief, and theft insurance for the farm dwelling. Farmowner's 2 corresponds to homeowner's 2 and includes the optional coverage of farm personal property. It is written on a named peril basis with the broad form perils applying to the dwelling and to additional living expense. Farm personal property and farm buildings are insured against fire, lightning, extended coverage perils, vandalism and malicious mischief, overturn, and theft. Farmowner's 4 is the tenant's form and is similar to homeowner's 4. Farm personal property may be included on an optional basis, as well as the tenant's interest in improvement and betterments in farm buildings and structures. As in farmowner's 2, the broad form perils apply to the dwelling and additional living expense. The form is intended for the tenant who is farming on a full-time basis. Unscheduled personal property, additional living expense, and farm personal property are mandatory coverages under the tenant's forms. Coverage on farm buildings is optional, and if elected, applies only to improvements and betterments. The minimum amount of insurance that may be carried for unscheduled personal property is $3,000. There is also a farm-owner's 3 that is the same as the farmer's comprehensive personal liability contract.

Property Covered. There are nine coverages detailed in the contract. They are: (A) farm dwelling; (B) appurtenant private structures; (C) unscheduled personal property; (D) additional living expense; (E) farm personal property; (F) farm barns, buildings, and structures; (G) farmer's comprehensive personal liability; (H) personal medical payments; (I) physical damage to property of others.

The minimum amount of insurance for coverage A is $8,000. Included as a part of the dwelling are such items as materials and supplies that are intended for construction or repair and are located on the premises or adjacent thereto; additions in contact with the dwelling; building equipment, fixtures, and outdoor equipment, if they are used in the maintenance of the building and if they are the property of the insured. Appurtenant private structures are insured under coverage B, although the only structures covered are private garages that are not used for commercial purposes and are not rented to others. The minimum amount of insurance that may be carried under this coverage is 10 percent of the amount of insurance on the dwelling.

Unscheduled personal property and additional living expense are insured under coverage C and D, respectively. Unscheduled personal property refers to family personal property or that property usually associated with the ownership and operation of a dwelling. Farm personal property is specifically excluded, as is business personal property, and property separately and specifically insured in whole or in part by other insurance contracts. Both on premises and off premises coverage is provided with the latter being worldwide. The minimum amount of insurance permitted for unscheduled personal property is 40 percent of the dwelling amount with 10 percent subject to minimum limit of $1,000 of coverage C amount applying to personal property while away from the premises. There are special limits of liability that apply to money, securities, philatelic property, and similar items. These limits are similar to those found in the homeowner's forms. The limits for money and securities may be increased to a maximum of $500 for money and a $1,000 for securities. Ten percent of the amount of insurance covering the dwelling is applicable to additional living expense insurance coverage D, which also includes rental value coverage. Coverage D does not apply to farm buildings or to farm personal property. The principal reason for this restriction is that the insurer does not want to provide business interruption insurance or extra expense insurance.

Coverage E provides on premises and off premises insurance for farm personal property. If the insured meets the requirements for discounted rates,[3] the minimum amount of coverage is $10,000. The "on premises" part of the coverage excludes tobacco, cotton, and similar items as well as property separately described and covered by other insurance. There are also a number of other exclusions. Off premises coverage applies to certain types of farm personal property such as livestock; farm implements, machinery, and vehicles; and grain, threshed seeds, and other property of this type. These items are subject to exclusions. There are three extensions under coverage E: (1) Ten percent of the amount of insurance applicable to this coverage may be used for the loss of certain standing crops. The only peril insured against under this extension is fire. (2) Grain in stocks and shocks is insured against fire only. No percentage of the amount of insurance applicable to farm personal property is stated. (3) Livestock coverage is extended to include loss by electrocution.

Farm buildings used in farming operations are insured under coverage F. This coverage is optional, and a schedule is required. If discounted rates are to apply, the total of the schedule must be at least $10,000, and any single building or structure must be insured for at least $500. Further, any additional farm dwelling must be covered for a minimum of $2,500. As is the case generally for buildings insured under property and liability insurance, the coverage includes materials and supplies intended to be used for construction and certain types of building equipment.

Perils Insured Against. Farmowner's contracts are named peril contracts, and the perils vary somewhat, depending on the form. The perils insured against under farmowner's 1 are fire and lightning; windstorm and hail; explosion; riot, riot attending a strike, and civil commotion; aircraft; vehicles; smoke; vandalism and malicious mischief; theft and overturn. Under farmowner's 2 there are two sets of insured perils. The broad form perils found in homeowner's 2 apply to coverages A, B, C, and D and the homeowner's 1 perils apply to coverages E and F. There are various exclusions and limitations that relate to the perils and to the property covered, and they may be ascertained by referring to the contract.

Extension of Coverage. Certain extensions of coverage have already been considered, particularly those extensions relating to farm personal property. Two additional extensions are of considerable

[3] If the insured does not meet these requirements, the insurance may still be issued, but the full rates of the fire rating bureau are the only rates used.

importance. First, there is a replacement cost extension that is limited to the main farm dwelling building (coverage A). There is no replacement cost provision for private garages or other farm buildings. Second, coverage is extended to include up to $100 for fire department service charges in those situations where such a charge is applicable. Unlike the homeowner's forms there is no extension covering trees, shrubs, plants, and lawns.

Deductibles. Deductible clauses that are included in farmowner's forms are very similar to those found in other multiple line contracts such as the homeowners. The clauses are a combination of a deductible clause, a franchise clause, and a disappearing deductible clause. A typical clause reads as follows: "The deductible amount is $50, with no deduction being made on losses of $500 or more and 111 percent of the excess of $50 being paid on losses between $50 and $500." Some variations on this clause exist in some of the independent versions of the farmowner's contracts.

VARIATIONS ON THE FARMOWNER'S CONTRACT

Although package insurance contracts covering farm property are not highly variable in terms of content and follow the farmowner's contract for the most part, there are some variations in contractual provisions among insurers. The farm contract of a large insurer, which will be analyzed below, is an example of an independent-type contract. It will also serve as an elaboration of some of the points made in the discussion of the farmowner's contract in the preceding section.

Independent Farmowner's Contract. The independent farm contract under consideration here has three sections and 20 coverages in addition to the declarations. Section I provides for farm property interests, Section II is a farm comprehensive liability coverage, and Section III covers the automobile hazard. The 20 coverages are: (A) farm dwelling; (B) appurtenant private garages; (C) unscheduled personal property; (D) additional living expense; (E) farm personal property (may be insured on a blanket or scheduled basis); (F) barns, buildings, and structures; (G) farmers comprehensive liability; (H) medical payments; (I) physical damage to property of others; (J) bodily injury liability (automobile); (K) property damage liability (automobile); (L) medical expense; (M) accidental death benefit; (N) protection against uninsured motorists; (O) comprehensive (automobile physical damage); (P) collision; (Q) fire, lightning, and transportation; (R) theft; (S) windstorm, hail, earthquake, or explosion; (T) combined additional coverage.

Declarations. The declarations part of the contract is fairly lengthy because of the large number of coverages and the necessity for obtaining information on many property items. Page one of the declarations contains space for listing the named insured and his address, the term of the contract, and a description and location of the farm and/or ranch premises. Also, on page one is a listing of the coverages with spaces for limits, premiums, coinsurance percentages, deductibles, endorsement numbers, and the name of the first mortgagee (if any) and his address. At the bottom of the page is the insuring agreement of the standard fire insurance contract. Page two contains the 165 lines.

Page three of the declaration provides space for scheduling farm personal property; farm barns, buildings, and structures; and specifically insured livestock. Under personal property are such items as grain; hay-in-barns, sheds, and silos; tractor; crop drier; corn picker; hay baler; poultry; dairy cattle; feeder cattle; swine; sheep; and horses. Examples of property other than personal property that may be scheduled are: additional farm dwellings, garage, barns, granary, crib, silo, hoghouse, implement shed, and henhouse. The specifically insured livestock schedule contains spaces for the descriptions of the animals to be covered.

Section III declarations are on page 4. Space is provided for the name of the insured, a description of the vehicles covered (model year, trade name, body type, identification numbers, and similar information), and purchase information. On the last one third of the page is a listing of the automobile coverages, and space is provided for stating limits of liability, premiums, and deductibles.

Section I: Description of Property and Interests Covered. The property and interests covered by this contract include the farm dwelling, appurtenant private garages, farm barns, and other buildings common to farms and ranches, personal property (including farm personal property), and additional living expense. Each of these coverages is described in the contract and the extensions, limitations, exclusions, and conditions are carefully outlined.

Buildings. Buildings normally found on farms or ranches may be classified as dwellings, garages, barns, and other buildings such as hog houses that are a part of the farming operation.

A farm dwelling is defined in the following way:

> This policy covers: (*a*) the building described, including additions in contact therewith, occupied principally for dwelling purposes; (*b*) if the property of an insured and when not otherwise covered, building equipment, fixtures, and outdoor equipment, all pertaining to the service of the dwelling premises and while located thereon or temporarily elsewhere; and (*c*) materials and supplies located on the dwelling premises or adjacent thereto, intended for use in construction, alteration or repair of such dwelling. Trees, shrubs, plants, or lawns are not covered.

Appurtenant private garages are provided for in a separate coverage (coverage B), although garages used "in whole or in part for commercial, manufacturing or farming purposes" are excluded, as are garages "rented or leased to other than the occupant of the farm dwelling." The wording of this coverage makes an attached garage a part of the farm dwelling, and thus it is not treated as a separate structure.

Farm barns, buildings, and structures are included in coverage F and are insured only if a limit of liability for such buildings is stated in the declarations. Building equipment is included as a part of the structure, and outdoor equipment "pertaining to the service of the building while located on the premises described" is also covered. Sheds attached to farm buildings are included, although silos, whether attached or not, are excluded unless specifically declared. There is a limited provision for new construction and also for rental value. Improvements and betterments are insured in the situation where the named insured is not the owner of the buildings.

Personal Property. Two types of personal property are distinguished in the contract. Farm personal property includes such items as grain, livestock, and tractors. The second type of personal property is that property "usual or incidental to the occupancy of the premises as a dwelling, owned, worn or used by an Insured. . . ." This type of personal property is treated in the contract in much the same manner as it is in the homeowner's contracts, and is typically unscheduled. Farm personal property may be scheduled or provided on a blanket basis. Regardless of the method selected, there is coverage on premises, away from premises (for some types of property), and there are a number of extensions of coverage.

When farm personal property is insured on a blanket basis and is on the premises, it does not include:

(*a*) personal property covered under Coverage C; (*b*) property that is separately described and specifically insured in whole or in part by this or any other insurance; (*c*) tobacco, cotton, vegetables, root crops, bulbs, and fruit; (*d*) contents of potato, onion, bulb or fruit cleaning, grading, sorting, packing or storage buildings; (*e*) race horses, show horses, and show ponies; (*f*) contents of chicken fryer or broiler houses, laying houses, poultry brooder houses, duck or turkey houses including fowl therein, except the contents of small unheated hen houses and poultry brooder houses incidental to ordinary farm operations; (*g*) fences, windmills, wind chargers and their towers; (*h*) automobiles, vehicles licensed for road use, house trailers, watercraft, aircraft and sawmill equipment; (*i*) animals other than livestock; (*j*) bulk milk tanks, bulk feed tanks, barn cleaners, pasteurizers, boilers, and any permanent fixtures attached to or within a building; (*k*) private power and light poles and outdoor wiring; (*l*) crops in the open (standing or otherwise) except as specifically provided for in the Extension of Blanket Coverage.

Certain types of farm personal property that is insured on premises may be protected by the contract while away from the premises. Among such property are "farm implements, machinery, and vehicles, not otherwise excluded, while within 100 miles of the described premises." Livestock and grain may also be insured off premises under certain conditions.

Blanket coverage may be extended to include standing grain; grain, hay, straw, and fodder; and farm machinery, vehicles, and equipment of others. Standing grain is insured against loss by fire only, and 10 percent of the limit of liability for farm personal property may be used for this purpose. Grain in stacks, baled hay, straw in stacks, and similar items are insured against loss by fire only. If the named insured wishes, coverage may be extended to include, "for not exceeding in the aggregate $1,000 as an additional amount of insurance, farm machinery, vehicles not licensed for road use, and equipment in which the insured has no interest, while in the care, custody, or control of the insured."

Scheduled coverage of farm personal property may be effected by stating (in the declarations) a specific limit of liability for the following types of property: grain and silage; hay, straw, and fodder in stacks and bales; machinery, vehicles, tools, supplies, and equipment; poultry, and livestock. There are various limitations that apply to each of these categories, and they are specifically stated in the contract. There is coverage away from premises for certain types of property and there are extensions (with limitations) of scheduled coverage to standing grain, with the same restrictions as for blanket coverage); specifically insured machinery, vehicles, and equipment; newly acquired farm equipment, machinery, and vehicles; and farm machinery, vehicles, and equipment of others.

Perils Insured Against. Property and property interests are insured against named perils, which are: fire and lightning, removal, windstorm or hail, explosion, riot and civil commotion, aircraft, vehicles, sudden and accidental damage from smoke, vandalism and malicious mischief, theft, overturn, collision, electrocution of livestock, attack on livestock, and accidental shooting of livestock. There are numerous limitations that are specified in the description of the perils. If stated in the declarations, the dwelling broad form perils are applicable and the list of perils is extended to include: sudden and accidental tearing asunder, cracking, burning, or bulging of a steam or hot water heating system; falling objects; weight of ice, snow, or sleet; collapse (not settling, cracking, shrinkage, bulging, or expansion) of building(s) or any part thereof; accidental discharge, leakage or overflow of water or steam from within a plumbing, heating, or air-conditioning system or domestic appliance; sudden and accidental tearing asunder, cracking, burning, or bulging (not by wear or tear, deterioration, or rust) of appliances for heating water for domestic consumption; breakage of glass; freezing of plumbing, heating, and air-conditioning systems and domestic appliances; and sudden and accidental injury from artifically generated electrical currents. These additional perils are also subject to various restrictive clauses.

Exclusions, Limitations, and Conditions. The contract contains some special exclusions in addition to the ones mentioned in the definitions of each of the perils. Among these exclusions are nuclear reaction, earthquake, landslide, flood, and war. There are two loss deductible clauses which do not apply if the loss per occurrence is $200 or more, nor do they apply to additional living expense. The first clause provides for a deductible of $50, which is applicable to losses from windstorm or hail. The second clause also has a $50 deductible, which applies to all of the perils except fire or lightning, windstorm, or hail to buildings or structures, and collision. The insurer is not liable for more than $100 on bullion, money, and numismatic property; $500 on accounts, bills, deeds, and similar property; $1,000 on manuscripts; by theft for "more than $1,000 on any single article or jewelry, including watches, necklaces, bracelets, gems, precious and semiprecious stones and any article of gold or platinum or any article of fur or any article containing fur which represents its principal value;" $500 on watercraft.

There are 28 additional extensions of coverage and special conditions. These include such items as debris removal, replacement cost, coinsurance clause, cancellation, other insurance, definitions, nuclear clause, pair and set clause, and subrogation. This list is only a partial enumeration of conditions and extensions. A detailed discussion of them will not be undertaken here, since most of these items have been discussed in connection with other contracts.

Section II: Liability. There are three coverages listed in Section II: farmers comprehensive liability, medical payments, and physical damage to the property of others. The insuring agreements, in addition to defining these coverages, provide for supplementary payments, and also define the insured and such words or expressions as automobile, bodily injury, business, business property, farm, farm employee, insured farm employee, medical services, midget automobile, premises, property damage, and residence employee. Farmers comprehensive liability covers the usual type liability plus fire legal liability. The medical payments coverage reads as follows:

> This Company will pay all reasonable expenses for medical services performed within one year from the date of accident to or for each person who sustains bodily injury caused by accident
>
> *a*) while on the premises with the permission of an insured, or

b) while elsewhere if such bodily injury, (1) arises out of the premises or a condition in the ways immediately adjoining, (2) is caused by the activities of an Insured or of any farm or residence employee in the course of his employment by or in the care of an insured.

The exclusions and conditions will not be listed here. They are similar to those found in most liability contracts.

Section III: Automobile Coverage. Section III is in two parts. Part 1 provides bodily injury liability and property damage liability "arising out of the ownership, maintenance or use of an owned automobile or non-owned automobile . . ." medical expense, accidental death benefit, and protection against uninsured motorists. Supplementary payments are also included. There are the usual definitions and exclusions. The accidental death benefit is payable if death is caused by accident "(*a*) while occupying an automobile, or through being struck by an automobile, if death occurs within 90 days of the accident."

Part 2 is the automobile physical damage coverage and includes comprehensive; collision; fire, lightning, and transportation; theft; windstorm, hail, earthquake or explosion; and combined additional coverage. Supplementary benefits such as general average and salvage charges, towing and labor costs, loss of robes and wearing apparel, and transportation charges are included.

There are 17 special conditions that are applicable to Section III. They are: policy period and territory, modification of terms, other automobile insurance in this company, notice, assistance and cooperation of the insured, action against company, medical reports and proof and payment of claim, insured's duties in the event of loss, appraisal, payment of loss, loss payee, no benefit to bailee, subrogation, assignment, cancellation, liberalization, and premium. Each of these items is carefully defined in the contract and the duties of the insured are fully explained.

Endorsements. A variety of endorsements may be added to the contract. One, in particular, should be mentioned. This endorsement is the special building endorsement, and insures the property outlined in Section I "against all risks of physical loss or damage. . . ." Following the insuring agreement there are a number of exclusions that make the coverage something less than all risk, but considerably broader than named peril.

CROP INSURANCE

It was a natural progression from one weather coverage to another to recognize the damage to growing crops attributable to unfavorable weather conditions. The distress resulting from widespread crop failure and the urgent necessity for relief have focused the attention of agricultural interests upon the necessity for crop insurance as a social measure. In providing insurance, it was recognized that hazards other than weather constituted a serious threat. These include, among others, floods, insects, and disease.

All risk crop insurance is not generally available from insurers, although all risk insurance is written on a limited basis by the Federal Crop Insurance Corporation, a division of the United States Department of Agriculture. Insurance is written covering losses which are the outgrowth of specified hazards. In this category are to be found hail insurance and insurance written on fruit and vegetable crops against frost loss and freeze hazards. Not all insurers eligible to do so write even these lines, and some insurers that have written crop coverages in one classification or another have, because of unsuccessful experience, withdrawn from this class of business. A number of nongovernmental insurers are currently experimenting with a "weather perils" coverage. This insurance covers a number of specified perils including drought, frost, excessive heat, excessive moisture, and others.

Hail insurance protects against direct loss to growing crops from hail. Considerable demand for the coverage manifested itself in connection with the tobacco crops in the Connecticut River valley, but more recently it has been expanded to include more than 80 different types of crop. Substantial lines have been written on wheat, corn, cotton, and soybeans. Other crops covered are fruits, grapes, strawberries, peas, and sugar beets.

A contract is entered into by means of a binder that becomes effective 24 hours after the application for insurance has been signed by the applicant and the agent, or when the crop comes to a stand, whichever is later. The 24-hour period is a waiting period before the binder takes effect and is designed to prevent someone from binding insurance because he has heard a weather forecast. The binder is in effect for ten days and during this period the insurer may decline the business if it wishes. After ten days have elapsed the contract is in full effect. When the crop is harvested, the insurance terminates and is reduced pro rata as harvesting progresses. In any case, the insurance terminates with the expiration of the time limit set forth in the contract.

If the contract covers tree fruits, bush fruits, beans, grapes, or strawberries, no liability is assumed for loss or damage resulting in injury to trees, vines, leaves, bushes, plants, blooms, or blossoms. In the case of beans, vine vegetable crops, and similar crops, there is no liability for damage to blooms or blossoms or for damage to vines, plants, bushes, or leaves unless it can definitely be shown that such damage was caused by hail causing a loss to the product itself. There is liability in this case only to the extent that the product itself has been affected. Limitations are set for other crops with a view to limiting the liability of the insurer to situations in which a real risk has developed. A limit of liability per acre is set for certain crops, and contracts may provide a clause similar to the memorandum clause found in marine contracts setting forth that there shall be no liability on the part of the insurer unless the crop is damaged more than a certain designated percentage—5 percent is a figure frequently used. If the crop can be reset or reseeded, the liability of the insurer is limited to actual cost of these operations. The contract specifically provides that there shall be no abandonment to the insurer of any insured crop.

Underwriting insurance on growing crops presents numerous difficulties. At the planting season it is impossible to know what the market will be at the time of harvest. A solution that has seemed to be equitable provides that if there is a loss covered by the contract, the insurer will pay the farmer on the basis of the percentage of crop destroyed. This plan provides indemnity to the insured for a partial loss, even though he is able to sell as much of the crop as may be salvaged and show a profit for the year's operation.

Frost and freeze coverages are written for owners of orchards or growing citrus fruits or those engaged in marketing crops that are particularly susceptible to frost damage. One of the major difficulties that has presented itself in connection with writing this form of insurance is to be found in the effects that serious frost losses have upon the market price of the balance of the crop. If the frost losses throughout a wide territory are severe enough to reduce the entire crop seriously, then part of the loss is regained by the increased value in the part of the crop that is marketable. This increased value is of no assistance to the orchard owner whose entire crop is destroyed. If, however, he is able to salvage part of his crop, the scarcity reflects to his benefit. Attempts have been made to take this factor into consideration by providing for only a partial settlement at the time the damage occurs and a final settlement based upon the income received when the salable crop has been marketed.

Crop insurance written on an all risks basis and designed to cover such hazards as blight, insect pests, and drought has been attempted from time to time but has met with only mediocre success. The insurance is not generally available, and the reluctance of insurers to continue the line is based, among other reasons, upon the element of moral hazard. It has been found that the contract holder, knowing that his insurance will idemnify him fully if his crop fails, will tend to neglect the crop by failing to take the necessary precautions to minimize the loss. Efforts have been made to eliminate the element of moral hazard by reducing the amount of insurance to a percentage of the average yield. Three fourths of the yield has been a widely accepted maximum in the past, and such a contract leaves the farmer a coinsurer for one fourth of any loss.

Crop Hail and Fire Combination Contract. This contract was originally introduced as a broad coverage tobacco contract. The contract covers tobacco from the field until arrival on the warehouse floor. While the crop is in the field, it insures against the peril of hail, wind when accompanied by hail, fire, lightning, livestock, and aircraft. In the curing and packing barn, there is protection under the standard fire and extended cover contracts.

Weather Perils Crop Insurance. A weather perils crop insurance contract was introduced in 1964 by capital stock insurers and it has been approved in a number of states. This contract insures corn and soybean growers against the perils of hail, fire, drought, excessive heat, excessive moisture, wind, frost, freeze, hurricane, tornado, snow, and sleet. The contract may be written as an endorsement to the hail insurance contract, in which case it does not change the conditions of that contract, or it may be written as a separate contract. One of the basic requirements of the contract is that all of the acreage of corn and/or soybeans grown on the farm unit must be included.

GREENHOUSE INSURANCE

A special form is available to cover greenhouse structures against the perils of windstorm and hail. The contract does not cover hot bed sash but does include glass in the greenhouse structures and covers office buildings, potting houses, boiler rooms, and attached masonry stack and auxiliary buildings. Metal stacks are not covered under the basic contract, but they may be specifically insured.

The contract excludes coverage for brick, stone, or concrete foundations and other supports below the basement floor. These and other items not susceptible to windstorm or hail damage are excluded, thereby lessening the amount of insurance required with a coinsurance clause. The contract is ordinarily written with an 80 percent coinsurance clause. When so written with adequate insurance, the cost of broken glass and all damage caused by wind or hail is covered up to the face amount of the contract. Within the scope of the protection, losses attributable to tree branches or other articles blown against the property by the force of the wind are covered.

LIVESTOCK INSURANCE

The need for livestock insurance has been recognized from the earliest times. Coverages of one type or another were provided by the early guilds and more recently by mutual associations. The need for livestock insurance is emphasized from time to time by banking institutions who hesitate to make loans on livestock because of the various hazards involved in the maintenance of the animals. The epidemic some years ago of foot and mouth disease worked havoc in a number of herds and focused attention of financial institutions upon the need for this type of insurance as a basis for farm credit.

In spite of the need for the cover, livestock insurance is written only by a limited number of commercial insurers. The problem of moral hazard has created the major difficulty to underwriting this class of risk. Adequate coverage is, however, obtainable from insurers that have given the problem specialized study and have developed contract forms to meet all ordinary needs. Insurance is obtainable to protect against loss by death resulting from fire, lightning, windstorm, disease, and accidental death. This type of insurance is, in fact, a form of term life insurance and does not indemnify for depreciation in value, loss of services, theft, or disappearance. Since the contract covers death resulting from disease or accident, coverage extends to death from any causes except intentional slaughter without the consent of the insurer. These contracts are to be distinguished from the animal floaters in inland marine forms. The animal floaters provide blanket coverage on a named perils basis for flocks and herds belonging to livestock producers. The livestock contracts described here in many respects provide coverage parallel to that afforded by the animal floaters. Generally, the coverage of the livestock contract is broader than that afforded by the animal floaters and are adopted to cover either on an individual or group basis particularly valuable animals such as race horses or polo ponies.

The following contracts are issued: (1) general livestock contract, (2) mortality floater contract, (3) floater coverage, (4) limited coverage, and (5) trip-transit contracts. The general livestock contract provides protection against loss by death resulting from disease, accidental injury, fire, lightning, and windstorm covering on the premises of the insured or while temporarily in the vicinity thereof. The following is a typical clause describing the extent of the coverage:

Against loss resulting only from death, occurring within the term of this policy, of any or all of the animals insured hereunder, but only when such death is caused directly by disease, accidental injury, fire or lightning, while on the premises described in the above mentioned application or applications or while temporarily elsewhere in the immediate vicinity thereof, and also when liability therefor is specifically assumed by endorsement written hereon or added hereto, but not otherwise, wherever they may be within the limits of the United States or Canada, also to include liability in the event it shall become necessary, for humane consideration, to destroy any animal insured hereunder, because of its having been accidentally crippled or maimed, and a certificate from a licensed veterinarian, certifying that the destruction of such animal was immediately necessary because of its having been accidentally crippled or maimed, shall have been obtained prior to the destruction of such animal or animals, or where this company shall consent to such destruction in writing signed by its general agent.

The mortality floater contract provides protection against loss by death resulting directly from disease, accidental injury, fire, and lightning, including while in transit by rail, ferry transportation, or properly equipped motor vehicle in the United States and Canada. No mention is made in the contract of windstorm as a hazard, but since death caused by windstorm is construed as a loss by accident, such a loss comes within the protection of the contract. The floater coverage is provided by extending the general livestock contract by endorsement to include the hazards of transportation anywhere within the limits of the United States or Canada. The coverage is broad, and the contract has a wide appeal.

Limited coverage provides insurance against death caused by specifically named hazards. The contract is issued primarily to exhibitors and breeders. There are two principal forms, known as "proposition No. 1," and "proposition No. 2." Proposition No. 1 provides insurance against the hazards of fire, lightning, and tornado, while proposition No. 2 is broadened to include accidental death, "meaning death resulting from external, accidental and violent means only."

A herd contract is available covering all the insurable animals of a given kind when there are ten or more animals in a herd. This contract is written to cover commercial dairy herds and breeding herds of either pure breed or grade cattle. Horses also may be covered under the form. Cattle being fed for market and slaughter are not insurable. A deductible herd contract may be written requiring the insured to pay half the premium required for full coverage. Under the terms of the contract, the insured must then stand the full loss or losses as they occur until the losses equal the amount of cash premium paid to the insurer. Under this form, the insured gets protection at a low premium if there are no losses, and if there are losses, his contribution represents only the amount that he would have paid in any case for full cover. Under the terms of the contract, the insured's loss can never exceed the deductible sum stated in the contract, and this is so irrespective of the number of losses that occur.

The trip-transit contract is a special form designed to cover valuable stock while in transport only. The coverage becomes effective when the animals are loaded on the cars for shipment in good condition and expires when the cars are unloaded. This contract is a form of inland marine insurance, although the coverage is largely written by specialists covering livestock risks. There are two forms—one covering fire, derailment, and collision only, and the other providing full coverage. The contract is issued only to cover valuable or registered livestock and is not available to cover cattle going to market for slaughter. Where the perils of transportation are the only concern this contract is adequate.

FOR DISCUSSION

1. To what extent are minor injuries, depreciation in value, and injuries incapacitating an animal to perform the requirements for which he is kept covered by a livestock contract?
2. Broken legs, colic, indigestion, heart failure, pneumonia, shipping fever, fire and lightning are some of the causes of death to a horse. A race horse valued at $10,000 is insured under the general livestock cover. Which of these hazards is covered?
3. How may the life of an animal be insured?
4. Contrast the liability coverage found in the homeowner's 2 contract with that found in the farmowner's broad form contract.
5. In which states is crop hail insurance of special importance? To what extent does hail damage vary with topography.
6. What are the essential features of the Federal Crop Insurance Program? When was this program put into effect? To what extent is it competitive with private programs?
7. List the basic differences between the contracts offered under the homeowner's program and those issued as part of the farm owner's program. Which of the contracts are the most complex?
8. Jewelry, watches, necklaces and similar property are often insured under separate contracts. If these items are separately insured, what type of protection is offered by the farmowner's forms? Why?
9. The *National Underwriter* for February 4, 1966, reported that "Automobile insurers, which are examining all phases of their underwriting to plug loopholes previously missed, are taking a new look at the farm discount. The long-held precept that farmers are better risks than city drivers is undergoing examination on several fronts." The article went on to say that the "Southern Farm Bureau Casualty of Jackson, Mississippi, a large big farm writer, has cut its farm discount in Mississippi from 30 to 20 percent. One other major insurer has taken similar action, and others have indicated that they plan to do so in the near future." What are the factors that have led to a worsening of farm automobile insurance experience?
10. Coverage B of the farm owner's contracts is labeled appurtenant private structures, but it is clear from the wording of the contract that coverage is limited to private garages only. There is no statement to the effect that the garage must be detached from the house. What problems, if any, might arise from this seeming lack of clarity?
11. On what basis may a package weather perils contract be written? What are the perils covered? Why was this contract developed?

12. What proportion of property and liability insurance written on farms and ranches is represented by farm owner's and related contracts? Are any trends discernible in this area? What would you expect the situation to be in 1970?

CHAPTER · 24

Insurance Contracts for Commercial Enterprises

The need that commercial enterprises have for property and liability insurance has been met over the years by a variety of contracts designed to protect against the financial consequences of fire, theft, legal action, and other perils. Currently there is a trend toward protecting the business firm through multiple line contracts, although certain monoline contracts are still used. In this chapter types of package contracts that are important to commercial enterprises will be discussed. Several miscellaneous monoline contracts not previously considered will also be analyzed.

COMMERCIAL PACKAGE CONTRACTS

By 1959 homeowner's contracts were well established and received and in that year the Insurance Company of North America extended the package concept to contracts involving commercial property, and liability coverages were written on motels, apartment houses, and similar properties. Subsequently contracts were developed for retailers, manufacturers, and wholesalers. Originally package contracts were established by those insurers who filed independently and were not available from insurers that relied on rates supplied by rating bureaus. It was not long, however, before the bureau insurers developed the special multiple peril contract, which sought to accomplish the same purposes as the earlier packages. Following the introduction of this contract a number of variations were developed by property insurers. The packages carry a variety of names such as professional package, merchant's policy, all-in-one plan, business insurance comprehensive policy, business owner's policy, commercial package policy, comprehensive business policy, comprehensive insurance policy, credit bureau package policy, portfolio policy, funeral director's policy, business insurance comprehensive policy, multicover plan policy (Mark III) semi-policy, service station policy, and store owner's policy.[1]

Commercial packages for business risks take various forms but basically are designed to cover almost any type of business. One form currently used may be adapted to the needs of apartment owners, dry cleaners, funeral directors, motels, office buildings, and wholesalers and retailers. In most of these forms certain coverages are mandatory while others are optional. Property insurance covering buildings and contents is typically required, although within this general category there may be options such as boiler and machinery, elevator collision, and sprinkler leakage. It is not unusual to find seven or eight parts to a package contract, each part providing a different type of coverage such as basic property insurance, business interruption, inland marine insurance, automobile liability insurance, automobile physical damage insurance, comprehensive liability, and crime. Some of the typical provisions of a contract of this type will serve to illustrate some of these points.

Since fire is one of the perils covered under the part insuring property, the standard fire insurance contract is contained in the package and is printed in its entirety. A schedule is provided for listing and describing the property to be insured. Following the fire contract there is a form that serves to define the meaning of building and contents and other terms and extends the coverage to perils other than fire. Of some importance in this form, as provided by most insurers, are the paragraphs that provide automatic coverage for newly acquired buildings, contents at newly acquired locations, and property temporarily at other locations. One such clause reads that for newly acquired buildings the contract "covers, subject to all terms and provisions, for not more than $100,000 on any building within any State of the United States except Alaska and Hawaii, or within the District of Columbia, owned by the insured and acquired by him after the inception date of the policy." The insurance on the new building expires after 60 days, unless specific insurance for the building is taken. Coinsurance does not apply to the newly acquired building during the time of automatic coverage. Similarly contents are automatically covered for a period not to exceed 60 days to an amount of not more than $25,000. Automatic coverage for property temporarily located elsewhere may be provided by a clause that reads as follows:

This policy covers, subject to all its terms and provisions, for not more than $10,000 on personal property used by the insured in the conduct of

[1] See *Fire, Casualty and Surety Bulletins, Companies Coverages* (Cincinnati, Ohio: National Underwriter Company, 1966). The contracts discussed are those contained in this publication. Although these contracts are not standard, they are assumed to be fairly typical. The special multiple peril plan was revised considerably in October, 1966.

the insured's business, including the Insured's interest in and legal liability for property of others, held by the Insured in the course of such business, while such property is temporarily in a building not owned by, rented to or regularly used by the Insured within a State of the United States excluding Alaska or Hawaii, or within the District of Columbia.

This statement is subject to a few minor restrictions.

Following the part of the contract that provides property coverage for buildings and contents is a general statement of the conditions and exclusions that pertain to the various parts of the agreement. If desired, business interruption insurance, automobile liability, and other coverages may be added to the contract by a series of schedules that require appropriate descriptions of property or interests to be covered. The automobile schedule provides a listing of coverages such as comprehensive, collision, fire, windstorm and towing, and space is provided for stating limits of liability. Also the automobile or truck must be described in terms of year, model, trade name, and other identifying features. Under comprehensive general liability, limits of liability must be stated depending on the coverages selected under bodily injury, for each person, each accident, and aggregate products. Similarly for property damage, liability limits may be stated for each accident, aggregate operations, aggregate protective, aggregate products, and aggregate contractual liability.

Some insurers have approached the comprehensive business contract in a somewhat different manner. They have elected to provide the various coverages through the use of "standard" or, if not standard, at least commonly used contracts, and to bind these contracts together into a single package. One insurer that uses this approach makes the property and liability coverages mandatory and makes provision for a variety of optional coverages. The package can be tailored to the needs of different types of business. Under liability forms, such contracts as owner's, landlord's, and tenant's, comprehensive general, and store keepers's liability may be used. Likewise, crime coverages, including a number of different bonds, may be included. Since many different contracts may appear in one group, considerable flexibility in coverage is provided with the added advantage that producers and insureds are familiar with contracts that have been used for many years apart from the package concept.

SPECIAL MULTIPERIL CONTRACT

The structure of the special multiperil contract is similar to that of the homeowners. The first page consists mainly of declarations, although the insuring agreement of the standard fire insurance contract appears near the bottom of the page. The second page contains the 165 lines of the fire insurance contract and the third and fourth pages list the conditions applicable to both Section I (property coverage) and Section II (liability coverage), to Section I only, and to Section II only. The conditions applying to both sections are: war risk exclusion, liberalization clause, inspection and audit, cancellation, deferred premium payment plan, subrogation, impariment of recovery, conformity with statute, other insurance, policy period, and territory. The conditions that apply only to Section I are: nuclear clause, nuclear exclusion, no control, protective safeguards, no benefit to bailee, loss payable clause and report to police. Those conditions applying to Section II only are: modification of terms; premium; limits of liability coverage C; limits of liability, coverage D; notice of occurrence; notice of claim or suit, coverage C; assistance and cooperation of the insured, coverage C; medical reports, coverage D; proof and payment of claim, coverage D; action against insurer, coverage C; action against insurer, coverage D; and nuclear exclusion. These conditions are not unlike those found in other contracts and have been discussed in connection with other contracts.

The special multi-peril program is a combination of six multiple line contracts covering such organizations as apartment houses, offices, mercantile establishments, institutions such as schools and hospitals, processing or service groups, and the motel-hotel combination. When the program was first developed, there was a separate form for each type of organization. Recent revisions eliminated this set of forms, and now there is one basic general property and liability form that is used for all the organizations making up the program. The new program is effective in over 50 percent of the states. Endorsements of various types may be added to the contract for purposes of extending coverage or in other ways modifying the contract and special forms may be added. In this discussion the basic contract plus the special building form have been selected for analysis.

Special Multiple Peril General Property Form. The general property form is the basic form and is Section I of the special multiperil contract. This form contains nine subdivisions dealing with such subjects as property covered, property not covered, perils insured against, extensions of coverage, exclusions, coinsurance clause, deductible clauses, valuation, and conditions.

Property Covered and Limitations. Property covered includes buildings, personal property, and debris removal in connection with buildings and personal property. The coverage for buildings includes additions and extensions as well as fixtures, machinery, and like items that are a permanent part of the building. Personal property includes business personal property, as well as "bullion, manuscripts, furniture, fixtures, equipment, and supplies." Property of others may be covered with some limitations. Tenants' improvements and betterments are also included as a part of the personal property coverage. Some types of property are specifically excluded. Examples of such exclusions are animals and pets; aircraft; watercraft; outdoor swimming pools; cost of excavations; outdoor signs; household and personal effects; growing crops and lawns; trees, shrubs, and plants with certain exceptions; and property of tenants or guests subject to certain extensions of coverage.

Perils. The basic form is a named perils type of contract and insurance is provided for direct loss to the property insured, if that loss is caused by fire; lightning; windstorm and hail; explosion; sudden and accidental damage from smoke; vehicles or aircraft; and riot, riot attending a strike, and civil commotion. A number of these perils such as windstorm and hail and explosion are qualified in various ways and damage to some types of property is excluded as is damage to the interior of buildings caused by rain, snow, and similar elements. A detailed reading of the contract is necessary to obtain complete knowledge of the precise nature of the restrictions.

Extensions of Coverage. There are seven extensions of coverage and these include newly acquired property; off-premises coverage; personal effects; valuable papers and records; trees, shrubs, and plants; extra expense; and replacement cost. These extensions are similar to ones discussed in connection with other contracts; however, a few special features should be noted. Replacement cost coverage is limited and is provided only if the replacement cost is less than $1,000 and the insured has met the coinsurance provisions of the contract. If more complete replacement cost coverage is desired, a special endorsement is necessary. Personal effects of others may be covered up to $500 of the limit of liability specified for personal property. There is a limit of $100 for any one person and the extension is inapplicable if there is other insurance covering such property. A limit of $500 is placed on the extension to valuable papers and records, and there is a $1,000 limit for trees, shrubs, and plants (but only $250 for any one tree, shrub, or plant). Although coverage is extended to a number of areas, a review of the limits indicates that the dollar amount of coverage is not large.

Exclusions and Other Provisions. The exclusions in the form are fairly typical and relate to such items as earthquake, landslide, flood, water seepage, loss caused by power failure, and similar problems. The coinsurance clause and the deductible clauses serve to place limits on the amount of recovery unless certain conditions are met. The valuation section makes clear the basis for the valuation of loss and includes a specific statement about tenant's improvements and betterments, books of account and related items, and such property as film and tape. The last page of the form lists the conditions, which are relatively few. The mortgage clause appears in this part of the form.

Special Building Form. The special building form provides insurance "against all risks of direct physical loss to Coverage A—Building(s), subject to the provisions herein and in the policy to which this form is attached." There are nine parts to the form which are: insuring agreement, property covered, property not covered, extensions of coverage, exclusions, coinsurance clause, deductible clauses, and conditions. Most of these clauses are similar to those found in typical property insurance contracts. Some of the more salient features will be reviewed.

Property Covered and Limitations. The property covered, as indicated in the insuring agreement, is either a building or buildings, "including additions and extensions thereto, fixtures and detachable parts thereof, materials and supplies intended for use in construction, and alteration or repair of the building(s)." These items are covered while situated at the locations described in the declarations. Included in coverage, while in the described location, are such items as "floor coverings, refrigerating, ventilating, cooking, dishwashing, laundering equipment, shades, and outdoor furniture." Other types of furnishings are excluded.

The special building form places limitations on property that may pose special problems in regard to loss. For example, "plumbing, heating, air conditioning or other equipment or appliances (except fire protective systems) are not covered against loss caused by or resulting from freezing while the described building(s) is vacant or unoccupied, unless the Insured shall have exercised due diligence with respect to maintaining heat in the building(s) or unless such equipment and appliances had been drained and the water supply shut off during such vacancy or unoccupancy." Similarly, steam boilers, steam pipes, steam turbines, hot water boilers, glass, fences, swimming pools, buildings in the process of construction, and like items are all subject to certain restrictions.

Certain property is not covered. Lawns, trees, shrubs, and plants are not insured, although the section of the contract called "extensions of coverage" provides in a limited way for these items. "The cost of excavations; foundations of buildings which are below the under surface of the lowest basement floor; or where there is no basement, which are below the surface of the ground; foundations of machinery or boilers and engines which are below the surface of the ground; underground flues, pipes, wiring, and drains; sidewalks or driveways; and piling for buildings, or wharf property below the low water mark" are excluded. Another exclusion deals with property "more specifically insured" in whole or in part under this or any other contract of insurance. Such property is not covered by the special form.

Extensions of Coverage. There are five extensions of coverage: off-premises; extra expense; trees, plants, and shrubs; newly acquired property; and replacement cost. Ten percent of the amount for coverage A, but not to exceed $10,000 in any one occurrence, may be applied toward loss to property "covered under this form while temporarily away from the premises (not exceeding 30 consecutive days)." If extra expense is incurred by the insured in order to keep the building in normal operation after loss by an insured peril, the contract provides for reimbursement "for an amount not exceeding $1,000." It is assumed that every effort will be made as rapidly as possible to restore the building in order that services and operations may be carried on.

Trees, plants, and shrubs not grown for commercial purposes may be covered "for an amount not exceeding $1,000 in any one occurrence." Liability is limited to $250 for any one tree plant or shrub. This extension applies only if loss is caused by the perils of fire, lightning, explosion, riot, civil commotion, or aircraft. Newly acquired property may be covered subject to a limit of 10 percent of the building coverage with a maximum of $25,000. The new property may be of two types: (1) New additions, new buildings, and structures built on the premises described in the declarations; and (2) "buildings acquired by the insured at any other location and used by him in connection with his principal business operations within the territorial" limits of this contract. If the insured wishes continuing coverage, he must report the newly acquired property within 30 days. Additional premiums are charged for the new coverage. The replacement cost extension is similar to that contained in the homeowner's forms and has been discussed in Chapter 22. These extensions are not additional amounts of insurance and do not increase the amounts of insurance listed on the declarations.

Exclusions. The exclusions contained in the special building form are the ones that are fairly typical in contracts of this type. Wear and tear, deterioration, mechanical breakdown, and similar losses are not covered nor is theft of property that is not an integral part of the building. "Unexplained or mysterious disappearance of any property, or shortage disclosed on taking inventory; or caused by any wilful or dishonest act or omission of the Insured or any associate, employee or agent of any insured" is excluded. Vandalism, malicious mischief, theft or attempted theft are excluded if the building or buildings described in the declarations have been vacant for 30 consecutive days or more immediately preceding the loss. Leakage or overflow from plumbing, explosion of steam boilers, flood, water that backs up through sewers or drains, and similar causes of loss are also excluded. Losses caused by the "enforcement of any local or state ordinance or law regulating the construction, repair or demolition of buildings or structures" are excluded unless "specifically assumed by endorsement." Losses resulting from artificially generated electrical currents are also excluded "unless loss by fire ensues, and then only for such ensuing loss."

Other Clauses and Conditions. The last three sections of the special building form are made up of the coinsurance clause, deductible clauses, and conditions in addition to the ones in the basic contract. The mortgage clause is reproduced as a part of the conditions. There are two deductible clauses; one called "loss deductible clause No. 1," and the other "special loss deductible clause." These deductible clauses are similar to those found in homeowner's contracts.

Liability Coverage (Section II). Section II of the special mercantile form contains coverages C and D. The former is a liability coverage and the latter medical payments. There are three parts to Section II: (1) insuring agreements, (2) definitions, and (3) exclusions. In the part of the insuring agreement dealing with liability the insurer agrees to "pay on the behalf of the Insured all sums which the Insured shall become legally obligated to pay as damages because of bodily injury or property damage to which this Section applies arising out of the ownership, maintenance or use of the premises, and all operations necessary or incidental thereto. . . ." The insurer agrees further, as in all liability contracts, to defend the suit even if it is groundless, false, or fraudulent and to pay the various expenses associated with a lawsuit. The medical payments coverage is like that found in most liability contracts.

The definitions section has ten parts and words such as automobile, bodily injury, premises, named insured, occurrence, and products are defined. An insured includes the named insured, any partner, executive officer, director, or stockholder, and "any organization or proprietor with respect to real estate management for the named insured."

The exclusions are divided into three parts with some of them applying to Section II in its entirety and others applying to either coverage C or coverage D. Section II does not apply, in general, to automobiles away from the premises or to "bodily injury or property damage for which coverage is provided under a comprehensive personal liability endorsement." Contractual liability is generally not covered, except for sidetrack agreements, warranties about goods or products, and related agreements. Injuries compensable under workmen's compensation are not covered, nor does the contract apply to bodily injury to the "named insured, any partner therein, any tenant or other person regularly residing on the premises. . . ." These exclusions, as well as others not discussed here, are similar to those found in other liability contracts.

ADDITIONAL EXAMPLES OF COMMERCIAL PACKAGES

Consideration of packages that have been developed for particular types of businesses will serve to illustrate some of the variety that exists in the commercial package field.

Store Owner's Contract. The store owner's contract is divided into several parts including declarations, general conditions, provisions applicable to property and liability interests, broad perils endorsement, and a boiler and machinery supplement. Contracts of this type are not standard, and there are variations among contracts, depending on the insurer.

Under property and related interests three general coverages are provided—building (coverage A), contents (coverage B), and business interruption and rental value (coverage C). By a "building" is meant "the building described in the declarations and building service equipment or machinery, owned by the insured and used for maintenance or service of the building (including fire extinguishing apparatus, floor coverings, refrigerating or air conditioning equipment, signs and awnings), while on the premises or temporarily elsewhere." Excluded from the term "building" are cost of excavations, foundations, and other supports below the ground, "underground flues, pipes, or drains, and driveways, curbing, walks, fences, retaining walls and lawns, trees, plants, and shrubs" unless provided elsewhere.

Coverage D provides insurance on contents, which is fairly comprehensive but subject to minor restrictions. The provision reads as follows:

Personal property of the Insured usual or incidental to the Insured's business while on the premises or within 100 feet of the premises, including:

1. stock of merchandise, supplies and materials;
2. furniture and fixtures, machinery and equipment;
3. at the option of the Insured, personal property of others usual or incidental to the Insured's business while in the care, custody or control of the Insured and for which the Insured is liable, including (unless the policy is otherwise endorsed) personal property of the Insured's customers; and
4. improvements and betterments to buildings, not owned by the Insured at the premises, but only to the extent of the Insured's interest therein."

Property not covered under B includes:

1. automobiles, motor trucks, trailers (except trailers held for sale and designed for use with private passenger vehicles for general utility purposes or carrying boats) and similar vehicles; motorcycles,

motor scooters and similar vehicles all while licensed for highway use; aircraft, watercraft (including motors, equipment and accessories thereof) while afloat;

2. money and securities;
3. outdoor television equipment, owned by others; and
4. any property insured in whole or in part under Coverage A or more specifically under any other contract of insurance.

The third coverage includes the business interruption and rental value risks. Under the former the reduction in gross earnings occasioned by the interruption of business caused by a loss to real or personal property from one of the perils insured against is covered as are expenses incurred in reducing such loss. These expenses must not exceed the amount by which the loss is reduced, if they are to be reimbursable by the insurer. Coinsurance does not apply to expenses. Not covered are increases in loss brought about by such matters as lease cancellation or interference of strikers or persons engaged in repairing or replacing property.

The particular type of contract under discussion here is a named peril contract and insures against the following items: fire and lightning, removal, windstorm or hail, explosion, riot and civil commotion, aircraft, vehicles, sudden and accidental discharge of smoke, and vandalism and malicious mischief. The fire and lightning coverage excludes damage of an electrical sort such as damage to electrical appliances but this coverage does apply if fire ensues but only to the fire damage. The windstorm and hail coverage does not include damage to the interior of a building from rain, snow, sand, dust, or water from sprinkler systems unless wind or hail is a proximate cause in the sense of first causing damage to the roof or the walls of a building. Explosion does not include bursting of steam boilers and related types of machinery, although losses of this type may be provided for by special endorsement. Vehicle coverage does not include "vehicles which are owned or operated by the Insured or any occupant of the premises." Vandalism and malicious mischief excludes loss "to glass (other than glass building blocks) constituting a part of the building; to outdoor signs; by pilferage, theft, burglary or larceny; or while the building is vacant beyond a period of 30 consecutive days, but a building under construction shall not be deemed vacant."

There are a number of extensions of coverage applicable to property interests. One form provides eight of these extensions and includes such items as personal belongings not incidental to the business, debris removal expenses, costs involved in reproduction of valuable papers, trees and shrubs, consequential loss caused by changes in temperature and humidity (for certain perils), and additional amounts of insurance for new buildings. Except for the last item these extensions do not raise the limits of liability for the various coverages.

The exclusions listed in the store owner's contract are the usual ones and do not serve to limit the usefulness of the contract. Damage from flood, surface water, and similar items is excluded as is damage caused by war, insurrection, and nuclear reaction or radiation.

A considerable amount of space is given in the contract to a discussion of the basis for loss payment. This discussion includes a detailed statement of the determination of liability in the event of losses to building and contents including the basis for determining the value of stock sold but not delivered, property of others, and valuable papers and records. Replacement cost is available if certain conditions are met, and a coinsurance clause is included. Fairly lengthy statements concerning the limit of liability for business interruption are included, a coinsurance clause for this coverage is added, and a set of definitions are provided, including explanations for such terms as "gross earnings" and "ordinary payroll expenses." In the event of disagreement between the insured and the insurer, the usual procedures for arranging for an appraisal are included as a part of the contract. The content of this clause is the same as the appraisal section of the standard fire contract.

Included among special conditions are such items as the mortgage clause, nuclear clause, increase of hazard clause, definitions, benefit to bailee clause, permission granted clauses, and divisible contract clause. These provisions have been explained elsewhere in the text and do not require exposition here. They appear in the "conditions" section of the usual type of property insurance contract.

An essential feature of the store owner's contract is the section that outlines the liability coverages. There are two such coverages; one is called "store owners liability" and the other "store owners medical payments." Included also in the insuring agreement is the usual statement about supplementary payments and a definition of the insured. These statements provide no new situations, since the agreement is of the type that is typical of all liability contracts.

There are 18 exclusions in the contract that cover the situations that might arise under liability and medical payments for which the insurer does not want to accept responsibility. These exclusions appear in liability contracts generally and do not raise any new problems. The contractual conditions include definitions of designated premises, incidental premises, newly acquired premises, and alienated premises. Also defined are words and expressions such as bodily injury; property damage; occurrence; contract; elevator; products-completed operations hazard; war; hazardous properties; nuclear material; source, special, special nuclear, and byproduct materials; spent fuel, waste, nuclear facility, and nuclear reactor. There is a statement about limits of liability and medical reports. An injured person must give the insurer authorization to obtain medical reports and copies of records and submit to examination by physicians selected by the insurer.

The store owner's contract like other insurance contracts may be modified by endorsement. A broad perils endorsement extends coverage to falling objects; weight of ice, snow, or sleet; collapse of building; water damage or sprinkler leakage; burglary or robbery; and extended explosion. A significant extension of coverage applies to contents and insures, subject to a maximum amount, property that is away from the premises and in the "care, custody, or control of any salesman of the insured." Another endorsement, which is essentially a supplement to the contract, provides boiler and machinery insurance. The insuring agreement covers direct damage as well as prevention of occupancy. There are the usual exclusion conditions, definitions, and special provisions.

Service Station Contract. Another example of a package contract for a particular type of business is the service station contract. This contract follows the form of the store owner's contract and includes many similar provisions. The differences center around the specific nature of the service station. In the discussion of this contract emphasis will be placed on the provisions that represent departures from the store owner's form.

Property and Property Interests. Two coverages are offered under the heading of property and property interests; one covers the building and the other personal property. The building coverage is similar to that provided by the store owner's contract. The personal property provision reads as follows:

> Personal property, owned by the Insured, usual or incidental to the use of the premises as a gasoline service station while on or within 100 feet of the premises, including:
>
> *a*) at the option of the Insured, personal property of others while in the care, custody or control of the Insured and for which the Insured is liable; and
>
> *b*) improvements and betterments to buildings not owned by the Insured at the premises, but only to the extent of the Insured's interest therein.

Excluded property follows a pattern similar to the store owners but excludes additionally gasoline pumps, household furnishings and personal effects, property sold under installment and similar arrangements, and animals and birds.

Contractual provisions under the property coverage in regard to the perils insured against, extensions of coverage, loss deductible clause, losses excluded, basis of loss payment, and special conditions are similar to the store owners and in most instances are identical. They do not require extensive comment.

Liability. The liability section of the service station contract is in three parts—liability, expenses for medical services, garage keepers' legal liability, and fire legal liability. These parts are labeled coverages C, D, E, and F.

The liability section of the contract that deals with bodily injury or property damage "arising out of the service station operation hazard" is quite lengthy and includes statements about supplementary payments, persons insured, definitions, exclusions, and limits of liability. The service station operation hazard is defined as:

The ownership, maintenance or use of the premises for the purposes of a gasoline service station, and all operations necessary or incidental thereto, herein called "service station operations," including with respect to automobiles, only the use in connection with service station operations of any automobile which is neither owned nor hired by the Named Insured, a partner therein or a member of the same household as any such person, herein called the "non-owned automobiles hazard."

The supplementary payments provision is similar to that of other liability contracts. The persons insured include, in addition to the named insured,

With respect to service station operations other than the non-owned automobiles hazard;

a) any employee, director or stockholder of the Named Insured while acting within the scope of his duties as such,

b) if the Named Insured is a partnership, any partner therein but only with respect to his liability as such,

c) any person or organization having a financial interest in the service station operations of the Named Insured;

With respect to the non-owned automobile hazard:

a) any person while using, with the permission of the Named Insured, an automobile to which the insurance applies provided such person's actual operation or (if he is not operating) his other actual use thereof is within the scope of such permission,

b) any other person or organization but only with respect to his or its liability because of acts or omissions of the Named Insured or of an insured under paragraph (*a*) above."

Certain persons are specifically excluded from the insured category. These include employees with respect to bodily injury of other employees; persons or organizations acting as independent contractors (except for the named insured; directors, and similar persons while within the scope of their duties); persons or organizations in respect to owned automobiles; and "any partner, employee or spouse thereof with respect to property damage to property owned by, rented to or held for sale by the Named Insured, or property in the care, custody or control of or transported by the Named Insured." There are a number of specific exclusions to coverage. Some of them are: contractual liability; liability arising out of ownership, maintenance, or use of elevators; intentional bodily injury and property damage; and obligations arising out of workman's compensation, unemployment compensation, or disability benefits law.

The medical payments coverage is available on the usual basis to persons who are injured because they are in automobiles covered under the liability section of this contract or because they are injured accidentally as a result of the ownership, maintenance, or use of the gasoline service station. The war, nuclear, and workman's compensation risks are excluded.

Garage keeper's legal liability is designed to cover losses that may occur as the result of the custody of automobiles by the insured while they are left for repair, service, storage, or safekeeping. Loss may be at a specific location named in the contract or at a temporary location elsewhere or while "away from the premises if the insured is attending the automobile." Loss is payable under the contract only if the insured is legally obligated to pay damages. The situations giving rise to loss that are covered by the contract are: fire or explosion; theft; riot, civil commotion, malicious mischief or vandalism; and collision or upset. Exclusions are as follows:

1. Liability of the Insured under any agreement to be responsible for loss;
2. Loss to an automobile
   a) owned by or rented to
      (1) the Named Insured or a partner therein, or a spouse of either if a resident of the same household,
      (2) an employee of the Named Insured or his spouse if a resident of the same household, unless the automobile is in the custody of the Named Insured under an agreement for which a specific pecuniary charge has been made, or
   b) in the custody of the Named Insured for demonstration or sale;
3. Loss by theft due to any fraudulent, dishonest or criminal act by the Named Insured, a partner therein or employee, trustee or authorized representative thereof, whether working or otherwise and whether acting alone or in collusion with others;
4. Loss arising out of the use of any elevator, or any automobile servicing hoist designed to raise an entire automobile.
5. Loss from defective parts, accessories or materials furnished or to faulty work performed on an automobile, out of which loss arises;
6. Loss to an automobile while operated in any prearranged or organized racing or speed contest;
7. Loss due to war.
8. Loss due to radioactive contamination;
9. Under fire, explosion, riot, civil commotion, malicious mischief or vandalism, to damages for loss of use of the automobile.

Coverage of more than one person or more than one location does not increase the limits of liability stated in the contract.

Miscellaneous Coverages. A third section of the contract extends the insurance to such perils as employee dishonesty and burglary and robbery. Employee dishonesty is subject to a deductible and covers "loss of money, securities and other property by any fraudulent or dishonest act committed by any of the employees. . . ." Burglary and robbery coverage includes robbery inside the premises, robbery outside the premises, kidnapping, safe burglary, theft from night depository or residence, and burglary including robbery of watchman. Fraudulent and dishonest acts by the insured or his partners are excluded as well as losses of manuscripts, records, or accounts. Under burglary and robbery losses due to war and related perils as well as nuclear losses are not covered. Other exclusions may be obtained by reference to the contract. There are a number of special conditions including definitions and provisions relating to property interests, books and records, limits of liability, cancellation, and the rules relating to bailees.

GENERAL CONSIDERATIONS

The trend toward multiple line contracts is now firmly established and the combination of coverages is in accord with the basic principle of the insurance of all types of peril in a single contract. Package contracts have proved less expensive than the same type of coverage in a variety of separate contracts. Since the package concept represents a considerable departure from the older methods of speciality underwriting, numerous problems have arisen, some of which are still in the process of being solved. Package contracts require more home office or at least branch office underwriting and problems of rating are more difficult. Organizational and training problems arise within the home office, since conversion to combination contracts tends to blur the concept of organization according to lines of insurance. The competitive situation is different, too, since sales representatives tend to do more shopping for their clients when package contracts are involved. Although these problems exist, they do not seem insuperable and much progress has already been made.

PLATE GLASS INSURANCE

The widespread use of glass, particularly expensive plates in large commercial structures, for light, display, or ornamentation has tended to concentrate large values that are, because of the peculiar nature of glass, subject to substantial losses caused by accidental breakage.

Other forms of hazard insurance protect glass only if injured by the particular peril covered under the specific contract, and even in such cases the protection afforded to glass is often limited. If glass is to be adequately protected against the many hazards to which it is subject, this protection must be effected through the use of a specific contract providing a broad coverage. To provide this coverage, the insurance business has developed the plate glass contract.

Glass set in show windows is particularly susceptible to breakage. Crowds, riots, strikes, runaway automobiles, rocks hurled by passing cars, window dressing, or falling awnings are some of the factors that contribute to the risk. Other hazards to which this and other glass is subject include breakage caused by burglars, defective settings, explosions, sudden temperature changes, hail, snow, ice, windstorms, sudden jar of building, settling of building, and falling articles.

That the owner of valuable glass is subjected to a very real risk of loss is readily apparent. Based upon the loss experience of insurers of plate glass, it has been estimated that somewhere in the United States a valuable plate glass is broken every five minutes. When it is realized that the value of a single large plate is measured in hundreds of dollars, the reason for the development of this form of insurance becomes clear.

Comprehensive Glass Contract. Although the comprehensive glass contract provides broad coverage, it is not an all risks contract but rather covers the perils of breakage and chemical damage subject to a limited number of exclusions. The contract is succinctly written and is one of the least complicated of property insurance agreements.

Declarations. The declarations are contained on the first page of the contract and provide for the name and address of the insured, the contract period, and for the description of the glass including lettering and ornamentation. Unless exceptions are stated it is assumed that the "glass is plain flat glass with all edges set in frames."

Insuring Agreement. The insuring agreement provides protection against broken glass, damage by acids or chemicals, damage to frames and bars, installation of temporary plates, and removal of obstructions. As an alternative to replacing the glass the insurer may pay for the replacement in cash. When a replacement of a broken plate is made, the contract automatically covers the new plate and no additional premium is required. Damage caused by acids or chemicals to the insured glass and lettering or ornamentation insured under the contract is covered whether the damage is caused accidentally or maliciously.

The cost, not to exceed $75, of repairing or replacing window sashes immediately in casings and contiguous to the insured glass is covered if the repairing or replacing is made necessary by damage to or breakage of the insured glass. In addition to the $75 limitation, cost is also limited to replacement with sashes of like material. Coverage is provided for the cost of boarding up or installing temporary plates in openings in which any broken insured glass or glass damage by chemicals is located. The limitation is $75, and it is the requirement of the contract that the boarding up or the temporary installation is made necessary by unavoidable delay in replacing any broken glass insured under the contract. If it becomes necessary to remove or replace fixtures or any other obstruction, in order to replace the broken or damaged glass, the cost of such removal is covered by the contract. The limitation is $75. The contract does not cover the cost of the removal of show window displays.

Exclusions. There are two exclusions listed in the contract. There is no coverage from loss by fire or from loss due to war, invasion, insurrection, rebellion, or revolution.

Conditions. There are nine conditions in the comprehensive glass contract as follows: limits of liability and settlement options, insured's duties when loss occurs, other insurance, action against company, subrogation, cancellation, assignment, changes, and declarations. These conditions are similar to those found in other property insurance contracts. The contract does not make the filing of a formal proof of loss within a stipulated period a condition precedent to recovery, but the insurer may require the insured to file such a proof under oath on forms provided for the purpose. Immediate written notice to the insurer in the event of loss is not required. Rather the contract states that the insured "shall give notice thereof as soon as practicable to the company or any of its authorized agents."

Unless otherwise described in the schedule, each plate insured is covered as plain plate, flat glass set in frames, and adjustment is made accordingly. Liability of the insurer is limited to the actual cost of the glass, including its replacement, at the time of the breakage. If lettering or ornamentation is insured, the insurer is liable for the cost of replacement at the time of the breakage. In no case does the liability of the insurer exceed the amount of insurance stated in the schedule.

Miscellaneous Considerations in Glass Insurance. Glass is not limited to the protection of plate glass. The comprehensive glass contract may cover ordinary window glass or many special types of glass. Contracts may be written to cover structural glass, such as glass bricks and blocks, flexiglass, carrara, opalite, vitrolite, and other building glass. Since the comprehensive glass contract covers only breakage and chemical damage, a broader form is sometimes preferred. Stained glass set in leaded sections, such as the glass used in church and memorial windows, may be covered under an all risks contract. This form excludes only wear and tear, deterioration, and war risks. Marring, scarring, scratches, theft, breakage, or injury caused by fire would be covered under the all risks contract; whereas scratching, defacement, and disfigurement are not covered under the glass comprehensive contract unless caused by breakage or chemical damage.

Halftone screens and lenses, as well as rotogravure screens, may be insured against all risks. Neon signs are insurable under a comprehensive glass contract, and the coverage may be extended to all risks by endorsement. Neon signs are written on either a deductible or full-cover basis. The deductible varies from $10 to $100 for each insured object with a corresponding reduction in premium as the deductible increases.

The replacement of the glass, the lettering or ornamentation covered by the insurance, or the payment in money for any loss, does not have the effect of reducing the coverage. Upon replacement, the glass is covered automatically to the end of the contract period without the payment of any additional premium.

FLOOD INSURANCE[2]

The term "flood insurance" is applied to forms covering against direct loss by flood, such as the overflowing of a river or a tidal wave. The coverage is to be distinguished from insurance against leakage or rain. Flood insurance applying to real property is not easily obtainable, and the statement is frequently heard that the coverage is unobtainable. The reason flood insurance is difficult to obtain is to be found in the fact that there are certain areas in the country where floods may be expected and other areas where they never occur. For this reason, it is impossible to get a wide spread of risks, such as is possible in the case of fire insurance. If only those located in an area susceptible to floods were to buy flood insurance, the premiums would be inordinately high. In addition to this, and particularly as an outgrowth of the necessity for high premiums, when the immediate danger of floods disappears, the flood insurance is generally canceled. With threatened high water, the demand again appears. Obviously, flood insurance can be written on such property, if at all, only at premium rates that would make it seem prohibitive. For this reason, little flood insurance is written. Such flood risks as insurers are willing to accept are carefully underwritten with respect to the nature of the contents of buildings insured, as well as the structure of the buildings. They usually require warranties covering storage and make the insured a participant in every loss through the use of high deductibles. On the other hand, flood insurance has been sucessfully written in the case of

---

[2] Flood insurance does not apply solely to commercial enterprise. Its inclusion in this chapter is somewhat arbitrary although dollar-wise, losses from flood are more important to commerical concerns than to individuals.

all risks contracts covering the perils of transportation.[3] Such contracts ordinarily provide coverage for loss or damage from the rising of navigable waters. Baled cotton in the Mississippi flood area has been successfully insured against flood loss, and insurers sometimes form pools to carry the risk. Bridges and their approaches are insured against the hazards of flood. Growing crops, land, and buildings are not ordinarily acceptable risks.

ACCOUNTS-RECEIVABLE AND VALUABLE PAPERS INSURANCE

These are two separate forms. When written as an inland marine contract, a form is attached to the basic schedule property floater. Separate forms are available for each coverage: (*a*) the valuable papers and records form, and (*b*) the accounts-receivable form. The forms are very much alike but are modified to meet the requirements of the property insured. Both provide all risks coverage.

The valuable papers and records form provides insurance under two headings: specified articles, and all others. Specified articles are listed and valued, and the amount per article is the agreed value for the purposes of loss adjustment. All other papers and records are covered blanket, and a limit of liability is established. The insurance covers only while the papers and records are contained in the premises named in the contract. It is required that the insured papers and records be maintained in a fireproof safe or receptacle named and described in the contract at all times except when they are in actual use. There is an extension of the coverage not exceeding 10 percent of the combined limits of insurance but in no case in excess of $5,000 while the papers and records insured are being conveyed outside the premises or temporarily within other premises for any purpose other than storage.

The accounts-receivable form contains the same provisions noted above, except that insurance is written for a lump sum covering as follows: all sums due the insured from customers, provided the insured is unable to effect collection thereof as the direct result of loss of or damage to records or accounts receivable; interest charges on

[3] The usual marine contracts covering the perils of transportation include loss or damage from the rising of navigable waters, and flood losses are covered under the all risks transportation floaters. Indicative of the flood problem, the 1951 Kansas and Missouri flood is reported to have resulted in the largest single marine loss in history. Yet, out of a total property damage of nearly $750 million, only 2 percent or $15 million was covered by insurance. There were cargo losses of all kinds, including 2,500 carloads of grain. There were losses under other types of inland marine insurance, such as installation floaters, contractor's equipment, locker plants, storage warehouses, furrier's customers forms, and personal property forms. It is probably true that many insureds under a marine form did not anticipate loss from flood at the time the insurance was placed.

any loan to offset impaired collections pending repayment of such sums made uncollectible by such loss or damage; collection expense in excess of normal collection cost and made necessary because of such loss or damage; and other expenses, when reasonably incurred by the insured in reestablishing records of accounts receivable following such loss or damage.

Both contracts exclude loss attributable to fraudulent or criminal acts of any insured or any such act committed in collusion with an insured or a partner or officer of the named insured if a corporation or copartnership. The usual war damage exclusion appears, as well as the exclusion applying to wear, tear, vermin, or inherent vice.

CONTINGENCY COVERAGES

The practice of issuing contracts providing for the payment of loss in the event of the happening of some isolated contingency has proved fascinating to the layman, and the coverages have frequently been the source of misunderstanding. Numerous examples are to be found and, because many of the contracts have been issued by Lloyd's of London, the popular notion has developed that Lloyd's are writing insurance contracts covering any conceivable risk. This is not the case. Insurance contracts issued by Lloyd's or any other reputable insurer involving the payment of loss in the event of the happening of some particular contingency require a condition precedent that the insured shall be placed in such a position by the happening of the contingency that financial loss will follow.

Several examples may be appropriate. When war threatens, contracts are issued covering the hazard and paying an indemnity if war does, in fact, break out within the term and between the countries specified in the contract. Prior to the advent of World War II, contracts were issued by Lloyd's insuring the income of businessmen who were reservists against the possibility of being called to the colors. The premiums on such contracts ranged from 5 to 10 percent of their face value. The premium depended upon the age and nationality of the applicant for the insurance. In 1935, an American insurer is reported to have paid an indemnity of approximately $300,000 to the national organization of the Boy Scouts of America which had taken out a contract of $400,000 against the cancellation of the Jamboree scheduled that year in Washington. The Jamboree was, in fact, canceled because of the prevalence of infantile paralysis. According to the report, the Scouts had been able to cancel $100,000 of contracts for foodstuff and equipment, and the loss represented primarily expenses incurred in preparing the camp site on a 400-acre tract in the city of Washington. Contracts have been issued on an athletic event covering training expenses to pay an indemnity if the insured loses the event. A manufacturer, paying a royalty to the Canadian government for the privilege of manufacturing dolls resembling the Dionne quintuplets, secured a contract from Lloyd's which undertook to pay him the face amount of the contract in the event that any one of the quintuplets should die during the period of 12 months covered by the contract. Immediately preceding the death of King George V, contracts were issued covering against his death. As his condition became more critical, rates increased from 25 percent to 60 percent, and contracts were issued to trades which would suffer from a long period of official mourning. A period of court mourning in England affects unfavorably the business of hotels, theaters, caterers, dress shops, and similar businesses. Some of these institutions regularly purchase annual contracts protecting against the death of any member of the royal family which would have the effect of interrupting social activities. When no serious illness threatens, rates for this type of coverage vary from 10 to 12 percent.

When King Edward VIII selected May 12, 1937, as the date of his coronation, there developed three possible contingencies: marriage, postponement, and abandonment due to death or other causes. Developments indicated that placing insurance covering these hazards was not without reason, for losses were paid when the abdication of Edward VIII became effective. Other contracts were taken out covering simply the postponement of the coronation. Such contracts insured the owners of grandstands put up along the line of march of the procession and other similar concessions. George VI was crowned on the day scheduled for Edward VIII, and there was no postponement of the coronation and no losses were paid. The question of marriage or possible abdication did not present itself in connection with the coronation of Queen Elizabeth II set for June 2, 1953. Contracts were issued on her life. There were hundreds of such contracts. As it developed, no losses were paid.

In this country, insurance is frequently effected when there are heavy advanced reservations for the appearance of a particular star performer. Should anything happen that would require a cancellation of the performance, the promotors would be heavy losers because of expenses incurred. In 1933, contracts were issued on the theory that President Roosvelt's death would have an adverse effect on the stock market. In 1937, a musical comedy entitled, "I'd Rather Be Right," mimicked important public personages, and among those burlesqued were President Roosevelt, his family, his cabinet, and the Supreme Court. The burlesque had a tremendous appeal, and the play drew capacity audiences. It was recognized that the death of the President or any serious misfortune to any member of his family would have been disastrous and terminated the play's run. The producers were said to have insured against this contingency. In England, contracts have been issued paying an indemnity if taxes are increased.

CREDIT INSURANCE

Credit insurance was developed for the purpose of protecting creditors from financial losses occasioned by the failure of debtors to pay for merchandise or service that they purchased and received on credit. The need for insurance of this type stems from the nature of commercial transactions in an economy accustomed to the extension of credit. Credit insurance is sold to advertising agencies, manufacturing concerns, wholesalers, and some service organizations but not to retailers. It was first developed in Great Britain with the founding in 1869 of the London Guarantee and Accident Company, Limited, of London, England. Starting in 1887, various efforts to establish firms in America authorized to write credit insurance were attempted, many of which were later abandoned, but it was not until 1893 with the founding of the American Credit Indemnity Company of New York that credit insurance was firmly established in the United States. This company, which is still in operation, has written a substantial part of all of the credit insurance contracts issued in this country.[4]

Credit insurance contracts may be divided into two classes: (1) contracts of indemnity (back coverage) and (2) forward coverage contracts.[5] Contracts written on an indemnity basis provide that the insurer will pay the insured for losses that occur during the term of the contract. A rider is attached wherein the insurer agrees to cover unpaid, current invoices that appear on the insured's books on the effective date of the contract. A similar rider is attached on renewal and covers the term of the previous contract. These riders are automatically attached and are without additional cost to the insured. The forward coverage contract provides protection during the term of the contract (12 months) and does not cover back sales, although there is a provision that provides coverage for a limited period after the contract has expired. Credit insurance contracts may be further classified as regular and combination contracts; collection and noncollection contracts; and general and specific contracts. Regular contracts are those covering accounts that have preferred credit ratings according to the standards of a mercantile agency such as Dun & Bradstreet. Combination contracts include both preferred and inferior accounts. Under a collection contract past due accounts may be filed with the

---

[4] See Joseph T. Trapp, *Credit Insurance a Factor in Bank Lending* (Baltimore, Md.: American Credit Indemnity Co. of New York, 1953), pp. 5–13.

[5] *Ibid.*, pp. 14–15.

insurer, whereas noncollection contracts do not so permit. The latter type contract only covers legal insolvency or its equivalent. General credit insurance contracts provide coverage for all or a large percentage of the insured's accounts in contrast to specific contracts, which are designed to cover individual debtors who are listed in the contract or subsequently approved by the insurer. Specific contracts may be helpful in cases where the insured has a few large or unusual accounts for which specific coverage is desired.

Because of the inherent difficulties in the underwriting of credit insurance, insurers place certain limits on the extent of their liability. If the insurer agreed to give unlimited protection, loss experience might deteriorate in that the insured would have a tendency to grant credit without careful investigation and would not administer the affairs of the credit department in an efficient manner. The principal limitations on insurer liability are known as coverage, the primary loss, and coinsurance. Typically the credit insurer will limit the amount it is willing to pay for losses on any one account. The amount of coverage is related to the debtor's mercantile agency rating. The maximum limits for various ratings are set forth in a schedule in the contract. Credit insurers are essentially excess insurers and they do not agree to bear the primary or "normal" annual credit losses of business firms. By imposing this limitation credit insurers are able to charge lower premiums and the insurance protection is efficiently used. Coinsurance in credit insurance is not used in the fire insurance sense. The requirement is that each insured must bear 10 or in some cases 20 percent of the net loss. This feature of the contract tends to limit overinsurance and the moral hazard may be reduced.

FOR DISCUSSION

1. Select a commercial package, other than one considered in this chapter, and analyze its provisions.
2. Contrast the service station contract and the store keeper's contract.
3. B owns a plant valued at $100,000. The value of the glass in the plant is $5,000. He carries a windstorm contract for $5,000 and a plate glass contract insuring specifically ground-floor glass particularly liable to damage. It is his contention that the only hazard threatening remaining glass is windstorm. Criticize this.
4. Can you indicate a reason for preferring to insure a neon sign under a plate glass contract rather than under an inland marine contract?
5. Which of the following losses are covered by the plate glass contract: (*a*) damage to frames; (*b*) installation of temporary plates; and (*c*) removal of obstructions made necessary by replacing broken or damaged glass?

6. It has been the experience that in severe fires the contents of fireproof safes may sometimes become so charred that securities contained therein fall to pieces and disintegrate when exposed to the air. B is advised that a money and securities destruction contract should be purchased to care for securities contained in his safe. He argues that destroyed securities may be replaced by duplicates and that such a contract is unnecessary. Discuss.
7. May a glass plate which has already been cracked be covered by plate glass insurance?
8. The owner of a drugstore has been in business for a great many years, and he places a high value upon his record of prescriptions. In the event that he should sell out his business, because of the repeat orders from his prescription file that would go to whoever has possession of the file, he feels that he could sell the records for $15,000. Could he collect $15,000 under his fire insurance contract if the records were destroyed by fire?
9. Life insurance contracts usually exclude death by suicide during the first two years that the insurance is in force. Corporations, banks, and trust companies that arrange life insurance as collateral for loans, or for reimbursement for loss of service, are without protection under ordinary life contracts for the period of limitation. Do you think the risk of suicide to be insurable?
10. Loch Ness in Scotland is said to be inhabited by a dreadful monster. Reports of its appearance circulate from time to time. In 1936 the Loch Ness monster found its way into the newspapers of Britain and the United States, and the owner of a London circus advertised a £20,000 reward to any one who could produce the monster before a definite date. Indicate an insurable risk created by the advertisement.
11. List and discuss the benefits that credit insurance offers to the insured.
12. Discuss the problems encountered by insurers in marketing commercial package contracts. To what extent do you expect the package concept to replace the older monoline contracts?

CHAPTER · 25

Insurance Contracts for Industrial Property[1]

The trend in modern business has been in the direction of larger and larger organizations, each controlling subsidiaries or branches, frequently with property values distributed among many locations and substantial values more or less constantly in transit. Insurance has had to adapt to this trend by developing special coverages. Two forms of particular importance are: (*a*) the manufacturer's output, one of the earliest package contracts to be developed, and (*b*) multiple location and reporting forms.

Manufacturing establishments usually have property in all stages of progress located not only in the plants but elsewhere. This may include raw materials in storage or in transit and manufactured products after they have left the premises of the insured. Products are sent to others for processing or installation. There are tools, patterns, automobiles, rolling stock, samples, carriers, in fact an almost unlimited number of items and classes of property owned by a manufacturing establishment, at risk at all times in a number of locations or in transit. The manufacturer's output contract is a comprehensive coverage written to cover personal property of manufacturing risks off the plant property. It is a broad, comprehensive multiperil contract, designed to cover physical damage but not the third-party liability of the named insured.

Then there are those business establishments other than manufacturing concerns that have a wide number of locations with constantly changing inventories. In this category are to be found notably chain stores, though other establishments with warehouses and distribution points that do not operate on the chain basis have fluctuating inventories at numerous locations.

---

[1] In the preceding chapter the main emphasis was on nonmanufacturing, commercial enterprises. In this chapter major consideration will be given to contracts of particular importance to manufacturers that have not been discussed previously.

There is the situation where values fluctuate sharply at a single location. The amounts are sizable enough to make overinsurance for safety unduly expensive, and a conservative insurance practice based on averages might result in a disastrous uninsured loss if it occurs when values at risk are higher than the average. The multiple location contracts satisfy the requirements of insureds having contents at a number of locations with fluctuating values throughout the year. Finally, there is a multiple location form that adapts itself to fluctuations but does not necessarily require that the risk extend to more than one location.

The forms to be discussed below are designed to adjust insurance to fluctuating values and to follow the values with respect to different locations. In some instances, other insurance is written applying to one or more specific locations covered by the contracts. Such insurance is termed "specific insurance." Specific insurance may be either permitted or required. Both the manufacturer's output contract and the multiple location contracts are always excess over specific insurance.

Contributing insurance is insurance written upon the same plan, terms, conditions, and provisions as are to be found in the reporting form. Where such insurance is written, it contributes with other similar contracts for losses after all specific insurance, if any, has been exhausted. This means that if a reporting form covers at ten locations and there is specific insurance at each location for $100,000, the reporting form is not liable for loss until a loss at a given location exceeds $100,000, the amount of the specific insurance.

MANUFACTURER'S OUTPUT CONTRACT

The manufacturer's output contract originated with the automobile industry and was first called the "automobile output contract." The original contract has been expanded to include other industries and in its present form is known as the "manufacturer's output contract." It is written for, among others, automobile manufacturers and manufacturers of automobile tires, business machines, corn products, electronics, and heating appliances. The contract is a comparatively new departure in both coverage and rating methods. In adjusting the contract to the needs of manufacturers, it was not the intent to overlook wholesalers and retailers, since their needs are well served by the multiple location contracts. An effort was made to adjust the multiperils contract to the needs of one particular group. It is the expectation that with continued success and acceptance of the contract for insuring businesses engaged in manufacturing that the idea will spread and find use with groups in other categories.

The coverage afforded is all risks in the sense that the term is known to the insurance industry. It covers against all direct physical loss to the insured property, subject to a limited number of exclusions. Unlike the multiple location forms, this coverage is provided by means of a special contract designed for the purpose and is not written by the attachment of a form to the standard fire insurance contract. The form is a reporting form and is continuous. In other words, it is not term but covers from its inception indicated by an hour and date inserted in the contract and remains in effect until canceled. Subject to the limited exclusions that the contract contains, the coverage is very broad in that it provides protection for property damage loss caused by unpredictable occurrences or those that may be foreseen but with a probability so remote that the peril remains uninsured.[2]

Entirely aside from the burden of setting up a comprehensive insurance program through the purchase of a variety of types of coverage, the department or person responsible for the placing of the coverage is relieved through the use of this contract of detail and paper work, since it is no longer necessary to keep records of a number of expirations and to approve and clear premium payments for renewals.

Interests and Property Insured. Property covered by the manufacturer's output contract consists of personal property of the insured while away from his manufacturing premises. This contract does not cover real property, except that the interest of the insured in improvements and betterments is covered. There is provision for bringing within the scope of the insurance property of others. With respect to interest and property insured the contract provides:

Interest and Property Insured: Except as hereinafter excluded, this policy insures:

a) The interest of the Assured in all personal property owned by the Assured;

b) The interest of the Assured in improvements and betterments to buildings not owned by the Assured;

c) The interest of the Assured in, and legal liability for personal property of others in the actual or constructive custody of the Assured;

d) Personal property of others

1. Sold by the Assured which the Assured has agreed prior to loss to insure for the account of the purchaser during course of delivery;

[2] Prior to the use of the present multirisk bridge and tunnel property damage form, in an effort to provide complete coverage on a named perils basis for the George Washington Memorial Bridge, falling meteors were named as a peril. The happening of a remote contingency may be as disastrous as a more probable one, though insuring against every conceivable contingency on a named perils basis is cumbersome, expensive, and sometimes impossible. The output contract affords peace of mind in that it covers remote contingencies without unduly burdening the premium.

2. In the custody of the Assured which the Assured has agreed prior to loss to insure;
3. Sold by the Assured under an installation agreement whereby the Assured's responsibility continues until the installation is accepted by the purchaser.

If the manufacturer sells property but agrees to keep it insured during course of delivery, the coverage applies. The same is true with respect to property of others in the custody of the insured. Again property sold under an installation agreement covers the insured's responsibility until the installation is accepted by the purchaser. There is no exclusion with respect to automobiles. Automotive equipment is covered against physical damage loss.[3] With respect to licensed automobiles, coverage applies at any location within the territorial limits set forth in the contract.

Interests and Property Excluded. The contract does not cover certain types of risk for which clearly defined insurance coverages are available. One or more of the interests or properties excluded might be found as a part of any risk. There would be no uniformity in this respect. These exclusions do not in any way impair the coverage, since they are clearly delineated and insurance where desired is obtainable. The contract provides:

Interest and Property Excluded: This policy does not insure:

a) Currency, money, notes, securities, growing crops or standing timber;
b) Property while covered under import or export ocean marine policies;
c) Animals, aircraft or watercraft;
d) Property sold by the Assured under conditional sale, trust agreement, installment payment, or other deferred payment plan;
e) Loss resulting from interruption of business or other consequential loss extending beyond the direct physical loss of or damage to the insured property.

Currency, money, notes, and securities are insurable under the money and securities destruction forms. Growing crops are insured under a specialized form, as is standing timber. The exclusion with respect to property covered under import or export ocean marine contracts avoids duplication. To the extent that animals are insurable, a special form is required. Aircraft are covered by the various aircraft insurance forms, and watercraft requires a marine form. Conditional sales and installment plans vary so with different business establishments that property so sold is excluded on the assumption that the insured will handle his risk under one of the various conditional sales

[3] There is an exclusion applicable to automotive equipment that applies to collision losses.

contracts available. Business interruption and other consequential losses must form the subject of separate insurance.

These various interests and properties will differ so much with each class of risk that any effort to merge them in a single premium that already covers physical damage would result in a loading that would in many instances be inequitable. The indivisible premium for physical damage with properties and interests excluded that admirably adapt themselves to insurance under readily available forms produces the most equitable result.[4]

Insured and Excluded Perils. Since the contract is an all risks form, it insures against all perils except those expressly excluded. This coverage is expressed as follows:

Perils Insured: This policy insures against all risks of direct physical loss of or damage to the insured property from any external cause (including general average and salvage charges on shipments covered while waterborne) except as hereinafter excluded.

The more important exclusions are infidelity, flood and earthquake at location, war, and mysterious disappearance. The flood and earthquake exclusions do not apply to property on which flood and earthquake coverage is usually granted in the marine and automobile physical damage markets. Since many of the perils excluded are identical with the wording of the same perils excluded in other property insurance contracts, they will not here be repeated in the language of the contract but noted briefly. The contract does not insure against:

War Perils or Public Authority. War perils are excluded, as are losses attributable to confiscation or destruction by public authority, except destruction to prevent spread of fire or explosion. Risks of contraband or illegal trade are not covered.

Infidelity Losses. There is no coverage for loss or damage caused by or resulting from any dishonest act or acts committed alone or in collusion with others by any of the partners, officers, or employee of the insured. The same is true with respect to any proprietor, partner, director, trustee, or any elected officer of any of these organizations engaged by the insured to render services in connection with insured property. Losses attributable to infidelity of officials or other employees of a common carrier are covered.

Earthquake or Flood. Loss or damage caused by or resulting from

[4] Consequential loss coverages are available with respect to loss caused by the destruction or damage of parts of a set or other marketing combination. This is provided by endorsement for the payment of an additional premium. The exclusion with respect to animals, aircraft, and watercraft may likewise be removed by endorsement for an additional premium. The coverage when required as part of the output contract is available, but the perils are separately insured. The experience with respect thereto is not absorbed in the statistics used as a basis for computing the indivisible all risks basic premium.

earthquake or flood is not covered. This exclusion is modified to provide the same flood and earthquake coverages that could have been obtained for part of the risk by using inland marine or standard automobile forms. In this respect the contract provides that the exclusion with respect to loss or damage resulting from earthquake or flood shall not apply:

1. To licensed automotive vehicles, rolling stock, salesmen's samples, patterns and dies, cameras and camera equipment, scientific instruments, and other similar property of a mobile nature not intended for sale; or
2. To property which is in due course of transit; or
3. Imports and exports; or
4. Property in the custody of processors; or
5. To damage caused by ensuing fire, theft or explosion not otherwise excluded by this policy.

The term "flood" shall mean waves, tide or tidal water, and the rising (including the overflowing or breaking of boundaries) of lakes, ponds, reservoirs, rivers, harbors, streams and similar bodies of water, whether driven by wind or not.

Explosion. Explosions attributable to the rupture or bursting of steam boilers or machinery are not covered. This peril would normally be covered under a power plant contract. The explosion exclusion does not apply to locomotives, rolling stock, conveyances, or other property insured under the contract. This exclusion with respect to explosions applies only to boilers and machinery owned by the insured away from his own premises. In any case, boilers and machinery located on the premises of the insured would require specific insurance, and it is likely that boilers and machinery located elsewhere would be covered in this contract.

Electrical Equipment. Electrical injury or disturbance due to electrical appliances or devices, including wiring, caused by electrical currents artificially generated are not covered. The exclusion includes mechanical breakdown, structural failure, latent defects, or faulty workmanship. If fire or other accident covered by the contract ensues, then the loss or damage covered by the fire or ensuing accident is covered. This exclusion is the same as that found in virtually all property damage contracts.

Collision or Overturning. Loss or damage caused by collision or overturning of automobiles, trucks, and trailers operated under their own power or towed is not covered with the one exception that damage from ensuing fire is covered. The exclusion applies to the vehicles only and not to property carried on a vehicle. If the contract is written with a deductible of $500 or more applicable to all items, the collision exclusion may be removed by endorsement.

Inherent Vice. This exclusion is the same as found in all inland marine contracts and provides that there shall be no liability for loss or damage caused by or resulting from delay, loss of use, loss of market, inherent vice, gradual deterioration, wear and tear, moth, or vermin.

Losses Attributable to Dampness or Temperature Change. Here again is an exclusion similar to that found in inland marine contracts. The contract provides there shall be no loss attributable to dampness or dryness of atmosphere or extremes or changes of temperature, shrinkage, evaporation, loss of weight, rust, contamination, change in flavor, color, texture, or finish unless caused directly by fire or other named perils.

Work Damage. There is no coverage while the property is actually being worked upon and directly resulting therefrom other than damage from ensuing fire or explosion. This again is a typical exclusion in inland marine contracts. It is the intent to take out of the realm of protection defective workmanship or accidental injury for which the party doing the work may be liable.

Mysterious Disappearances. There is no coverage for unexplained loss, mysterious disappearance, or loss or shortage disclosed on taking inventory.

While the list of exclusions appears long, they are for the most part similar to those found in the fire and inland marine contracts. The exclusion of flood coverage at permanent locations is perhaps one of the most significant features, since the contract does, in fact, afford considerable flood damage protection. It is important to understand where the coverage ends.

Territorial Extent of Cover. The contract covers property of the insured anywhere within the continental United States or Alaska, except on the premises of the insured, and this exception is subject to some modification. Property airborne or waterborne between points and places in either the United States or Alaska is covered, but such shipments to or from Alaska are not covered. Property in Canada in due course of transit originating or terminating in the United States or Alaska is covered. With respect to territorial exclusions the contract provides:

Territory: Except as hereinafter provided, this policy covers while the property is (1) within the Continental United States or Alaska, (2) airborne or waterborne between points and places therein, or (3) in Canada in due course of transit originating or terminating in the United States or Alaska:

a) Coverage is excluded on all property, other than licensed automotive vehicles owned by the Assured, while on any premises used by the Assured for manufacturing purposes except such premises and such kinds of property as are specifically included by endorsement hereon;

b) Coverage is excluded on waterborne shipments via Panama Canal;
c) Coverage is excluded on waterborne or airborne shipments to and from Alaska;
d) Coverage on export shipments not insured under ocean marine policies does not extend beyond the time when the property is loaded on board overseas vessel or aircraft; coverage on import shipments not insured under ocean marine policies does not attach until after discharge from overseas vessel or aircraft.

By virtue of exempting licensed automobiles from the exclusion of property while on the premises of the insured, it follows that licensed automobiles are actually covered both on and off the premises of the insured. Airborne or waterborne shipments between points in the United States or Alaska are covered but not such shipments to and from Alaska. Coverage is also excluded on shipments via the Panama Canal. There is no coverage on transoceanic shipments whether waterborne or airborne. The contract does cover up to the time the shipment is loaded on an overseas vessel or aircraft and attaches with respect to imports when the goods is discharged from the vessel or aircraft. The exclusion with respect to property on the premises of the insured for manufacturing purposes may be modified by endorsement to include such property as cameras, tools, patterns, dies, scientific instruments, or other similar equipment of movable nature not intended for sale.

Limits of Liability. The contract establishes limits of liability for loss or damage arising from any one loss or disaster. These limits have to do with property at any one location, on conveyances, and property at a convention or fair. There is also a limitation with respect to property insured against loss or damage by flood. The contract provides limits as follows:

Limits of Liability: The Company shall not be liable under this policy for more than the following limits for loss or damage arising from any one loss or disaster:

a) $ on property at any one location, loaded on coveyances or otherwise. Location is defined as any building, dock, wharf, pier, bulkhead (or groups thereof) bounded on all sides by public streets or open waterways or open land space, each of which shall be not less than fifty feet wide (any bridge or tunnel crossing such street or waterway or open space shall render such separation inoperative for the purpose of this definition).
b) $ on property in or on any one conveyance or individual unit thereof outside the confines of any location covered hereby, not exceeding however $ for any one disaster
c) $ on property (refer to Section 4c) insured against loss or damage by flood at any one location (as defined above) from loss due to flood.
d) $ on property at any convention or fair.

There is a limitation applying to each conveyance and a second limitation with respect to any one disaster. An insured might be within the contract limits as far as values to carload lots are concerned, but at the same time he might exceed the limit for one disaster if a number of conveyances were destroyed in a catastrophe such as a windstorm or flood.

Valuation. There are so many different kinds of property covered under the output contract that to preclude misunderstanding a basis of valuation for loss adjustments is incorporated in the contract. Following is a copy of the valuation clause:

Valuation: In case of loss, the adjustment, unless otherwise endorsed hereon, shall be as follows:

a) Stocks of merchandise, at actual cash value;

b) Improvements and betterments at replacement cost less physical depreciation at time and place of loss if actually replaced at Assured's expense within two years from date of loss; if not so replaced, at the unamortized value;

c) Accounts, manuscripts, mechanical drawings and other records and documents at value blank, plus cost of transcribing;

d) Exhibitions and displays, at cost to Assured;

e) Patterns and dies, at replacement cost if actually replaced; otherwise, at actual cash value;

f) Automobiles, trucks, machinery, equipment and any other property not otherwise provided for, at actual cash value at time and place of loss.

When rendering reports as provided in Section 11, values are to be reported on an equivalent basis.

When rendering reports of values for the purposes of premium computation, values are always reported on a basis equivalent to the values here set forth. Betterments and improvements are valued at replacement cost less depreciation if replaced. Otherwise the insurer is liable only for the unamortized value. Manuscripts, drawings, and records are covered only for their value blank plus the cost of transcribing. Patterns and dies are included at replacement cost only if actually replaced. With respect to all of these items it is possible to amend the valuation clause to provide for any other basis of valuation agreed upon between insured and insurer. When such a change is made, the contract is endorsed to require the reporting of insured values and payment of premiums upon an equivalent basis of valuation.

Replacement and Repairs—Insurer Options. In the event of loss or damage the insured is obligated, where feasible and if requested by the insurer, to make the necessary repairs and furnish the necessary parts of their own manufacture. When parts are so furnished, the insured may make the same charge as it would charge any purchaser plus transportation charges and taxes. In the event of damage to or loss of any part of a machine or article consisting when complete for sale or use of several parts, the insurer is liable only for the cash value of the part lost or damaged. If the damaged part is available in normal channels of commerce, the insured may require the insurer to pay the cost and expense of repair. This cost may never exceed the cost new of the damaged machine or article or the cost of its replacement, whichever is less.

The insurer has the right to take all or any part of damaged property at the agreed or appraised value. It may also elect to rebuild or replace the damaged property within a reasonable time. If the insurer elects to exercise its option to repair or replace, it must give notice to the insured of its intention to do so within 30 days after receipt of proof of the loss. While the insurer may elect to exercise one of these options, as in the case of fire insurance, the insured has no right to abandon damaged property to the insurer.

Insureds sometimes object to the placing of damaged merchandise bearing their names or labels on the market. The output contract approaches this problem by providing that if branded or labeled merchandise covered by the contract is damaged and the insurer elects to take all or any part of it at the agreed or appraised value, the insured may, at his own expense, stamp "salvage" on the merchandise or its containers, or he may remove the brands or labels, if such stamp or removal will not physically damage the merchandise.

Specific and Other Insurance. Insurance in the name of and for the benefit of the insured applying to any location covered by the output contract is termed "specific insurance." Other identical insurance may be written, but it is regarded as "other insurance" and treated differently in the case of adjustment.

The output contract is excess to specific insurance, and the same is true with respect to other insurance. If specific insurance is required, the insured agrees to effect and keep in force the required amount until otherwise agreed to in writing by the insurer. Failure to keep such insurance in force relieves the insurer of liability for any loss which would have been recoverable under such specific insurance. The insured under the output contract is reimbursed to the extent of the difference between the amount recoverable or due from specific insurance and the amount of the loss subject always to the limit of liability for the location.

In respect to other insurance, the output contract is excess insurance. There is no obligation on the part of the insured to keep such other insurance in force. Moreover, in case of loss, the insurer agrees to advance the insured as a loan the amount payable under the output contract were the other insurance not a consideration. The insured is obligated to repay the loan at the time of recovery under the contracts providing other insurance. This feature is particularly advantageous where there is duplication of insurance and uncertainty with respect to coverage. If the output contract would have paid had there been no other insurance in force, then it pays anyway. If the insured collects the other insurance, then the insurer writing the output contract is reimbursed. It is important to emphasize that this provision does not apply with respect to insurance in the specific category, and whether valid or not the output contract is liable only for an amount in excess of the specific insurance.

Cancellation. Since the contract is written without an expiration date, it follows that coverage can be terminated only by cancellation. Under its terms the contract may be canceled either by the insured or by the insurer by mailing to the other at an address included in the contract written notice stating, not less than 90 days after notice, when cancellation is to be effective.

The mailing of the notice is all that is required, and the effective date and hour of cancellation stated in the notice becomes the end of the contract period. Delivery of the written notice by either the insured or the insurer is permitted in lieu of mailing. The insured, in the event of cancellation, is required to report the values at risk and pay a premium on these valuations up to the date of cancellation.

Reports and Premiums. The contract requires that within 60 days after the end of each month a report shall be made to the insurer showing the total values of all properties at risk under the contract on the last business day of the month. Once a year a report is required showing the values of property at risk by locations. This report must show separately the values in transit unless they are incorporated otherwise in the report.

In reporting values the same basis is used as for loss adjustments. Premiums are paid on full values adjusted for permitted specific insurance. When specific insurance is against more limited perils than covered by the output contract, provision is made for a corresponding premium adjustment. If specific insurance is against the perils of fire and lightning, only 50 percent of the final rate is applied to the amount so covered. If the specific insurance is against the perils of fire and perils covered by the extended coverage endorsement, only 33⅓ percent of the final rate is applied to these values. A minimum annual premium of $5,000 for all contributing insurance is required. In the event of cancellation, the minimum premium for that portion of the year during which the contract is in force is computed on the basis of $417 for each month or part thereof. If the earned premium based on the application of rates to values reported for a period of less than a year is less than the minimum premium, the insured is required to pay the difference the date the contract is terminated.

MULTIPLE LOCATION CONTRACTS

The multiple location contracts cover property at one or more of the locations of the insured. They are designed to provide insurance that follows values where the values at the different locations fluctuate. This is in contrast to the output contract that covers property of the insured, with some exceptions, only when located elsewhere than on the premises of the insured.

Unlike the output contract, which is a special form, the multiple location contracts are not special contracts, but the contracts are written by attaching forms, setting forth the terms of the contract, to the standard fire insurance contract. The usual perils provided by the fire insurance contract may be written. The extended coverage endorsement may be used with or without vandalism or malicious mischief coverage. Where required, sprinkler leakage protection may also be endorsed on the contract providing fire coverage. The contracts, as in the case of the output contract, are not all risks, although on a named perils basis a fairly comprehensive contract may be written. Again in contrast to the output contract written on an indefinite term basis, multiple location contracts are written for a definite term, as provided for in the standard fire insurance contract.

Property Eligible for Coverage. Since the multiple location forms are designed to provide protection for fluctuating values, they do not lend themselves to the insurance of buildings. Coverage is provided for merchandise and materials, though betterments and improvements to buildings may be covered in the same contract. This is an important feature, since chain stores frequently make long-term leases followed by extensive improvements. The improvements are regarded not in the category of real estate owned but rather as an investment to be amortized over the term of the lease. It simplifies the entire insurance problem to allow betterments values to be covered under the same contract that covers other values of the business.

Generally speaking, stocks, materials, and supplies including packages, as well as patterns and dies, may be covered. Consigned stocks, wherever located, are insurable. The same is true with respect to furniture and fixtures when covered in the same policy with the stock. Leased machinery or other machinery incidental to a business operation may be covered in the same contract with the stock. This does not apply to machinery located on the premises of a manufacturing plant owned or controlled by the insured. Machinery in this last named category is expected to be insured specifically like the real estate. There are certain classes of risk that might appear to be eligible for coverage by a multiple location contract that may not be so covered because of existing rules. Certain of these either have values sufficiently stabilized or other forms have been provided for their needs. The rule provides that banks, barber shops, beauty shops and beauty parlors, cotton risks, grain risks, hotels, laundries, shoe repairing shops, and theater furniture, fixtures, and betterments may not be covered under a multiple location form.

Multiple Location Forms. Insurance is written under two general types of coverage: (1) reporting, and (2) coinsurance. There are five available forms. Some of the forms are reporting, and some are not. One form may cover as a multiple location form, but it may also cover fluctuating values in a single location. The forms are known as: form No. 1, form A, form No. 2, form No. 4, and form No. 5. The forms differ with respect to the number of locations required and whether they are reporting forms. There are also differences with respect to rating plans and requirements for minimum premiums.

Form No. 1. This form, designed for sizable risks, requires at least two locations. Values away from the principal location must equal at least 10 percent of the total values, or values at any location other than the principal location shall amount to at least $50,000. Form No. 1 is a reporting form and is to be distinguished from a contract providing for a specific amount of insurance. If form No. 1 is used, the original application for insurance specifies the locations to be covered and states a value for each location. This stated value represents the average value of the contents which the insured expects will be located there during the contract year. An average rate is computed based upon these stated values. The insured is then required once each month to report separately the value of the contents for each location. At the end of the year the monthly reports are averaged for the purpose of determining the total average value at risk at all locations. A provisional premium is charged at the inception of the contract based on the total of estimated values. Upon the expiration of the contract, the final premium is computed on the basis of the average of the reported monthly values, and an adjustment is made on the basis of whether the computed premium exceeds or is less than the provisional premium. A minimum premium of $500 is usually required.

Form A. This form is, in many respects, similar to form No. 1. It is designed to meet the requirements of smaller risks and may be used either for multiple location risks or the contract may be written to cover only a single location. The form follows the pattern of form No. 1 with respect to reporting and premium adjustments but differs in that average rates are not used. Instead of an average rate, the specific rate at each location is applied to the values at that location. The minimum premium is $200.

Form No. 2. This is a form designed to insure distillery risks. The form, in general, follows the pattern of form No. 1. The minimum premium, as in the case of form No. 1, is $500.

Form No. 4. This form, at one time known as the "class floater," is a coinsurance form used by business establishments that have small amounts of inventory located on the premises of a large number of different distributors. Because of the nature of the stock and the method of handling the accounts, it is not convenient to cover the various locations under a reporting form because of the difficulty and the detail involved in securing adequate monthly reports. Small consignments of this nature may be covered by the class floater. Locations need not be specified, but a limit of liability that is relatively small is established for any one place. The contract does not cover at the principal place of business. An average rate is used as with form No. 1, though there is no minimum premium requirement.

Form No. 5. This is a nonreporting coinsurance form providing blanket coverage on property at two or more locations. Under this form a limit of liability is established for each location. This limit fixes the maximum liability for the location but does not necessarily conform to actual or estimated values. The limit of liability may be altered at any time with the consent of the insurer. The premium is computed under this form by multiplying the amount of the contract by the contract rate. Either 90 percent or 100 percent coinsurance is required. As in the case of form No. 1, an average rate is used and the minimum premium is $500.

To recapitulate, forms No. 1, No. 2, and No. 5 require a minimum premium of $500 annually for all contributing insurance. In the event that insurance against loss by windstorm, sprinkler leakage, explosion, riot, or other peril is written on an insurer or insurers not carrying fire insurance, the rules require a $500 per annum minimum premium applicable to each peril. Contracts written for a three-year term under form No. 1 provide for a minimum deposit and final adjusted premium of not less than $1,500 for all contributing insurance. Form No. 1 and form No. 2 are both multiple location and reporting forms. Form No. 5 is a multiple location form but not a reporting form. Form No. 4 is not a reporting form but covers unspecified locations. Form A is a reporting form and may cover as a multiple location form or it may cover in a single location. All multiple location forms with the exception of form No. 4 contemplate coverage at specified locations. Form No. 4 covers unspecified locations within a designated geographical area.

Features Common to All Multiple Location Reporting Forms. It is the intent of reporting forms to follow fluctuating values to the end that whenever a loss occurs full insurance to value will be provided. The insurer obligates itself in this respect, but to make the contract effective there are certain obligations which the insured must meet, and to do this it is essential that he have a full comprehension of the features that distinguish the reporting forms from specific insurance. The following items are especially important: the reporting requirement, penalties for noncompliance, provisional amount of insurance, liability limits, effect of specific insurance, and premium adjustment.

Reporting Requirement. The value reporting clause obligates the insured to report in writing to the insurer not later than 30 days after the last day of each calendar month: (1) the exact location of all property covered, (2) the total actual cash value of insured property at each location, and (3) specific insurance in force.

Penalties for Noncompliance. Failure on the part of the insured to make the required report limits the obligation of the insurer for no more than the amounts included in the last report filed prior to a loss less specific insurance. This penalty is very serious, since if the insured, with sharply increasing values, neglects to make a report, he must abide by the values of his last report. The form also contains an "honesty clause" similar to that found in certain of the inland marine contracts. This clause provides that if the last reported value prior to a loss is less than the actual cash value at the time the report is made, then the insurer is liable for any loss only in the proportion that the value reported bears to the actual value. Briefly, if an insured reports a $50,000 value where there is $100,000 actual value and sustains a $10,000 loss, the insurer is liable only for $5,000. The insured reported 50 percent of actual values, so the insurer pays 50 percent of a loss subject to contract limits.

Provisional Amount of Insurance. Since it cannot be known at the outset the full amount of insurance coverage that the contract will provide, the forms are written with a provisional amount of insurance and a deposit premium is collected at the time by applying the rate to the provisional amount. The minimum provisional amount is determined by taking the total of the average values at all locations less the amount of specific insurance to be permitted by endorsement. The minimum provisional amount can never be less than the highest limit of liability at any one location, except that for form No. 1 for seasonal risks the minimum provisional amount may be less than the highest limit at one location. Manufacturing risks in which the nature of the raw stock normally prevents continuous operation during the entire year are classified as seasonal risks. Form No. 2 provides both for a provisional amount and a provisional rate. The premium for all forms is adjusted at the end of the contract term on the basis of actual values reported. In form No. 2 this procedure is followed as in the case of the other reporting forms, except in form No. 2 the rate is recomputed at the end of the contract term, and this recomputed rate is applied to the reported values to determine the final premium adjustment.

Liability Limits. Reporting forms provide a limit of liability which is to be distinguished from the provisional amount of insurance. It is the intention of the contract to cover fluctuating values, but in order to exercise some underwriting control the insurer establishes a limit to its liability. Where two or more locations are involved, a separate limit is established for each location. The limit of liability applies not with respect to each contract but to all contributing insurance. If reports are made showing values in excess of liability limits, premiums are collected for the full values reported, but if the values exceed the liability limits established, they remain the limit of recovery. Hence, if values are ever determined to be in excess of liability limits, steps should be taken immediately to have the limits increased. It is not an uncommon practice to forestall this necessity to write the coverage with liability limits established considerably higher than actual anticipated requirements.

Effect of Specific Insurance. Where specific insurance is written and it is considered in the computation of the final premium, the insured is obligated either to continue specific insurance in force upon expiration or to increase the limit of liability immediately under the reporting form if the values require it. Multiple location coverages are always excess over specific insurance. Limits of liability for multiple location coverages are always determined by subtracting specific insurance from peak values. If substantial amounts of specific insurance are allowed to expire without a corresponding increase in the limits of liability, the insured may find himself with inadequate protection.

Premium Adjustment. In effecting the final premium adjustment, three factors are considered: total monthly values reported, specific insurance, and minimum premiums. An average of the total monthly values reported for the term of the contract is determined, and if the premium on this average at the applicable rate exceeds the provisional premium, the insured is required to pay for the excess. If the premium is less than the provisional premium, the insurer is obligated to return any excess paid. In calculating total monthly values, permitted specific insurance at any location, if reported, is deducted from the value reported at that location and the remaining value is considered. The final adjusted premium in any case must equal the minimum premium. For all forms but form A, this is $500, and in the case of form A the minimum premium is $200.

Covering Chain Enterprises. Property suitable for coverage under the multiple location forms includes contents only and excludes buildings. Insurable items include merchandise, machinery, supplies, furniture, and the insured's interest in betterments. Such items as furniture and fixtures and machinery can be written only in connection with merchandise. Either form No. 1 or form A adapt themselves to mercantile establishments operating on a chain basis. Both forms are similar in many respects. While the forms are not restricted to the coverage of chain mercantile establishments, they are admirably adapted to the purpose. Form No. 1 designed for the larger risks will be described, and then the more important differences between form No. 1 and form A will be pointed out.

There are three items of coverage: item A covers stock, material, and supplies; item B covers furniture, fixtures, and machinery; item C covers improvements and betterments. Unlike the usual fire form that describes the coverage by items, separate amounts are not carried under each item. Instead the amount of insurance covers blanket on the three items, if one or both of the items other than the first are included, by inserting the word "and" in the space provided in the form. The wording of the coverage, as it appears in the form, is as follows:

Item A On Stock, Materials and Supplies consisting principally of ______________________________

____

including packages for or containing the same, usual or incidental to the business of the insured;

and on property described in Items B and C, but in no event unless the word "*and*" is inserted in the blank space immediately opposite such item;

Item B __________ Furniture, Fixtures and Machinery, but excluding machinery while located on the premises of any manufacturing plant owned or controlled by the insured;

Item C __________ Improvements and Betterments to buildings, except to buildings owned by the insured or while located on the premises of any manufacturing plant owned or controlled by the insured. This Company agrees to accept and consider the insured in the event of loss in the position of sole and unconditional owner of such Improvements and Betterments, any contract or lease the insured may have made to the contrary notwithstanding;

the property of the insured, or held in trust, or on consignment, or held by the insured and for which the insured may be liable in the event of loss, all while contained in any building, shed or structure or in cars, vehicles or in the open on the premises or within 100 feet of the buildings, within the limits of ______________________________

____

____

The average rate as determined is subject to discounts for favorable experience and size. A provisional amount of insurance is written covering at the inception date of the contract, but the actual coverage is dependent upon the monthly reports and the limits of liability for each location. The contract indicates what percentage of all contributing insurance it covers, and a limit of liability for each location on the basis of all contributing insurance is provided in the contract. For example, a contract written for a provisional amount of insurance of $100,000 might before expiration be covering for $200,000. There might be three other insurers each with equivalent amounts of insurance. In this case the limit of liability for the insurer would be 25 percent of the total contributing insurance. The liability of the insurer is limited to this percentage of any loss, and it never exceeds the percentage of the total limit prescribed for each location. There is provision in the form to cover automatically newly acquired locations. A limit of liability must be established for these locations, and they are covered only if the location is declared when the contract goes into effect or in the monthly reports. Liability limits are listed as follows:

Limits of Liability. This policy being for ....% of the total contributing insurance, liability of this company is limited to the same percentage of any loss and in no event to exceed the same percentage of each of the following limits, but no insurance attaches under any one or more of the following limits unless a definite amount is specified as a limit and inserted in the blank immediately opposite the location item:

Limit of Liability for all Contributing Insurance	*Location Street Address and City*
$......	at ....
$......	at ....
$......	at ....
$......	at ....
$......	at ....
$......	at any other location declared in the inception of this insurance.
$......	at any other location acquired if included in the next succeeding monthly report of values as provided in the Value Reporting clause.

When any location is a manufacturing, processing, or finishing plant, the limit of liability shall apply over the area within all structures, in cars or vehicles and in the open at the plant site, and outside thereof, if within 100 feet of any structure thereon, unless a specific limit of liability is provided at one or more designated structures at such a location in which event the limit of liability over the remainder of such a location shall be that provided for "any other location declared" if declared at inception; or if acquired, that provided "at any other location acquired."

Form A follows the pattern of form No. 1. Form No. 1 may be written if two or more locations are covered. Form A may cover a single location. The major difference between the two forms is to be found in the use of an average rate in the case of form No. 1, whereas specific rates that apply at each location are used for form A. It is apparent that form No. 1 applies if the premium for the risk and the number of locations are such as to warrant rate credits. There is a difference with respect to specific insurance. Since under form A specific rates at each location apply, there is no limitation as to the amount of specific insurance permitted. In the case of form No. 1 where average rates apply, specific insurance is permitted only where necessary to protect values in excess of the contract liability limits and when disclosed by written endorsement on the contract. Under both forms the coverage is excess over specific insurance.

Certain of the other features of reporting forms such as the value reporting clause, full reporting clause, and premium adjustment clause, are applicable to these forms. These forms are not by any means limited to chain mercantile establishments. They are adapted to almost any kind of risk where there are fluctuating values, with the exception of property on distillery premises. Distillery risks are specifically excluded, since there is a special form for this type of insurance. Endorsements for attachment to form No. 1 to make the coverage adaptable to special needs have been prepared. Potatoes on farms are covered on the basis of either average daily values or average weekly values. Forms are available to cover commercial poultry enterprises, fish canneries in Alaska, and hops on farms, among others. The variations from the standard form made in the special endorsements are designed to adapt the coverage more nearly to the needs of the particular business or industry to be covered.

Insurance of Distilled Spirits. Form No. 1 was originally used to cover whiskey and other stocks of distilled liquors. Because of the sharp fluctuations in values, as well as the concentration of values in distilling risks, form No. 1 was found not adequate to meet the needs of policyholders. Because of the values involved, it was not always possible to make a satisfactory adjustment between the liability to be carried by the reporting form and the specific insurance. With the reporting form designed to take care of fluctuating values in excess of specific insurance, difficulty developed when the liability limit established for one or more locations was insufficient to cover the swings in value. When all liability possible was assigned to the reporting form, it frequently became necessary to make adjustments in the amount of specific insurance to the end that total coverage would reflect fluctuating values. To have coverage under a reporting form and still find it necessary to make adjustment in specific coverages was not a happy situation for either the insured or the insurers. This is particularly the case since the average rate depends upon values at risk above specific coverage, and with fluctuating specific insurance the average rate might reflect to the disadvantage of either insured or insurer.

To meet the requirements of the situation a new distilled spirits form, known as form No. 2, has been prepared and covers only on distillery premises. Form No. 1 and form No. 5 now exclude coverage on distillery premises. The form grants permission for unlimited specific insurance and provides for the calculation of the final earned premium after the expiration of the contract based on the actual values and specific insurance reported during the term of the contract. Unlike the other reporting forms there is no coverage for furniture, fixtures, machinery, or betterments. The contract covers only stock materials and supplies consisting principally of distilled liquors and their packages. Property held in trust or on consignment or for which the insured may be liable in the event of loss is covered while contained in any building, shed, or structure on distillery property. It is also covered in blending and bottling plants or in cars, vehicles, or in the open on premises included in the coverage or within 100 feet of such premises.

As in the case of other reporting forms, the contract is written at the outset covering for a provisional amount of insurance. The deposit premium, as in the other forms, is based on this amount. This form differs in that the rate used is provisional and the initial premium is accordingly provisional. The rate used in determining the final earned premium is the final average rate calculated at the expiration of the contract based on the total values at risk adjusted on the basis of full values reported with credit for such specific insurance as is provided.

Market Value Clauses. These clauses provide for loss adjustment on the basis of market values rather than on the basis of cost to the insured. Distilled spirits are ordinarily so covered. With respect to bottled distilled spirits, the market value clause provides that the actual cash value shall be the market price at the time and place of loss less all discounts and uninsured expenses to which such distilled spirits would have been subject had no loss occurred. Bulk distilled spirits, including natural spirits, are likewise covered with the proviso that actual cash value shall be deemed to be the bulk market value of the insured spirits at the time and place of loss less discounts and uninsured expenses. The clause also assumes the obligation of paying loss incurred by the insured due to liability assumed on account of taxes or duties.

While market value clauses are used largely for the insuring of distilled spirits or wines, they are not limited to this class of risk. The justification for the clause is to be found in the length of processing time to bring wines and liquors to a marketable stage. The insured, if indemnified at cost, could not replace his stock on the market except at the going market price. It is felt that indemnity calls for the defining of actual cash value as the market value at time and place of loss. Stocks other than liquors may be covered by the use of a market value clause, provided the stock insured is of a kind which is bought and sold at an established market exchange where the market prices are posted and quoted.

Manufacturer's Selling Price Clause. This clause, like the market value clauses, covers the element of profits. Unlike the market value clauses that cover stocks of merchandise, the manufacturer's selling price clause is used to insure finished goods manufactured by the insured. When the clause is attached to the contract, it provides that actual cash value of the insured goods shall be that price at the factory for which the goods could have been sold had no loss occurred. This value includes freight and handling charges, if any. As before, discounts and unincurred expenses are deducted. The price does include markup for wholesale distribution and retail sales. The clause provides indemnity for loss or damage to finished goods manufactured by the insured in the amount for which he could have sold the goods and not, as would have been the case without the endorsement, for an amount representing cost of production.

Insuring Small Consigned Stocks. Form No. 4 is designed for this purpose. This form provides insurance without specific mention of locations and without requiring regular reports within a designated territory indicated in the contract. Insurers usually limit their commitments on this type of contract to a sum not in excess of $2,500 on any one loss. If the exposure is greater than this, it is expected that the account will lend itself to one of the regular reporting forms.

The contract is designed primarily for business establishments that consign small amounts of merchandise to gas filling stations, repair shops, tire stores, and similar firms. Locations and amounts of merchandise in each location are small but vary so constantly that the floater seems to be the only satisfactory method of providing the coverage.

There are two items in the form: item A covers stock, materials, and supplies; and item B covers furniture, fixtures, and machinery. Property of the insured or held in trust or on consignment or property of others held by the insured for which the insured may be liable in the event of loss is covered. Machinery while located on the premises of any manufacturing plant owned or controlled by the insured is excluded. The contract does not cover property in transit or property at the insured's principal places of business. It is definitely the intention not to provide marine coverage, nor is it the intent to cover the insured at his regular place of business where values are within the realm of his knowledge and can be specifically covered. The contract contains the same clause to be found in other multiple location forms making the cover excess over specific insurance. From a premium volume standpoint, this form is insignificant as compared to forms No. 1 and No. 5. It is designed for a specialized function and not subject to the premium adjustments applicable to the other forms.

Commercial Poultry Enterprises. Indicative of the extent of the specialization to which reporting covers may be carried is the limit of liability endorsement for commercial poultry enterprises. This endorsement is attached to form No. 1. The form establishes a limit of liability for any one building, as well as a limit for each acquired location. Because the value of poultry, particularly growing birds, changes so rapidly, a limit is established for each bird on an age basis. These limits are set up in the contract in a table, a copy of which is shown in Table 25–1.

TABLE 25–1

TABLE OF LIMITS OF LIABILITY PER BIRD

Age Limits	*Layers*	*Broilers*	*Breeders*	*Others*
Day old	$	$	$	$
Two weeks old	$	$	$	$
Four weeks old	$	$	$	$
Six weeks old	$	$	$	$
Eight weeks old	$	$	$	$
Ten weeks old	$	$	$	$
Twelve weeks old	$	$	$	$
Fourteen weeks old	$	$	$	$
Sixteen weeks old	$	$	$	$
Eighteen weeks old	$	$	$	$
Twenty weeks old	$	$	$	$
Older	$	$	$	$

The poultry endorsement form follows to some extent the inland marine form with respect to values. This form is indicated where transportation coverage is not required but where valuations fluctuate to such an extent that a reporting form is required to keep insurance protection adequate.

The Nonreporting Coinsurance Form. The usefulness of the reporting multiple location forms for keeping insurance coverages adjusted to values might well prompt the question as to the usefulness of a form that does not automatically cover increases in value. The answer is to be found in the fact that certain insureds have a reasonably stable aggregate value at risk at all locations but sharp fluctuations in values from one location to another. A calendar manufacturer might well have large amounts of paper in storage early in the year. By the end of the year the paper would have passed through the process of manufacture, and just before delivery date there would be large values of the finished product in storage. Small chains that do not report monthly inventories but do have aggregate values that fluctuate only slightly find a use for form No. 5. Again where specialized equipment having a fixed value is moved from location to location, form No. 5 provides coverage.

Under form No. 5, since increased values are not automatically covered and since there is a coinsurance clause when values increase, additional insurance must be provided to keep the coverage complete and avoid making the insured a coinsurer. The contract does cover at newly acquired locations subject to the limit of liability indicated in the contract. Since the contract is not a reporting form, no provision is made for reporting newly acquired locations, nor is any such report required. The insurer does not leave itself open to any unremunerated exposure in this respect. Since the coinsurance clause applies to the aggregate of all values and where newly acquired locations increase values, additional insurance is indicated. It follows that if a new location is acquired and property moved to that location from another location without any change in the aggregate value of the merchandise, coverage is automatically provided and no additional insurance is required.

With the exception of the coinsurance clause which is inserted in the contract in lieu of the requirement to make periodic reports, form No. 5 and form No. 1 are alike in all other essentials. They are interchangeable with respect to properties covered. In other words, an insured who covers his business under form No. 1 may change to form No. 5, or the reverse may be true. Both forms require two or more locations, retain a minimum premium of $500, and the same rate procedure with respect to average rate and discounts is followed.

Deficiency of Insurance. Because of the values involved in the insurance of wines and liquors, a special form was required. The form provides for specific insurance without limitation. Where the values are very great and particularly where they are concentrated, it is not always possible to secure an adequate amount of insurance coverage. To meet such a situation it is provided with respect to form No. 2 that the deficiency of insurance endorsement may be attached. To use the form the insured is required to furnish evidence, satisfactory to the sponsoring rating bureau, of his inability to procure full insurance. This evidence includes a statement signed by the insured that every reasonable effort to secure adequate insurance has been made without success within a period of 30 days. The deficiency of insurance endorsement is not limited to use with form No. 2 in insuring liquors but may be authorized in connection with any risk where it can be shown that the insured cannot adequately provide insurance for full values.

In the adjustment of a loss and in the computation of premiums, deficiency of insurance is treated as permitted specific insurance. This means that in the event of a loss the deficiency of insurance is liable for that proportion of loss that the deficiency of insurance bears to 100 percent of the actual cash value of the property less any specific insurance. In other words, the multiple location form covers in excess of specific insurance. The deficiency of insurance contributes to the multiple location contract liability on a pro rata basis. In the calculation of the annual premium, credit is given for the amount of deficiency insurance in exactly the same manner that credit is given for permitted specific insurance. The deficiency of insurance clause requires the reporting of full values, but no premium is charged for values in excess of the limit of liability provided in the contracts. In the absence of a deficiency of insurance clause, the insured is obligated to report full values and pay a premium on them, even though the values are in excess of the limit of liability.

Size of Risk and Rate Economies. A prime objective of the multiple location idea was the development of reporting and automatic pickup forms to eliminate the necessity of canceling and rewriting or endorsing contracts where the values at various locations fluctuate. The plan contemplated rates that would be developed by obtaining the published tariff rate for each specific location, weighing it by the reported values at the respective locations and thereby producing a national average rate.[5] As time went on, the concept of an average rate was changed to the end that consideration was given to factors applicable to the individual risks. Competition made its appearance, and to achieve a competitive rate reduction in regulated areas, substantial discounts were allowed in unregulated areas. This had the effect of creating unfair rate discrimination notwithstanding the appearance of compliance with the law.

Present rating laws forbid the charging or fixing of rates for any class or risk that are excessive, discriminatory, inadequate, or unreasonable. While not all insurers were in agreement as to the exact nature of the credits to be allowed in rating large multiple location risks, there was a general agreement on the proposition that the risks did show savings that should be reflected in the rate structure. The chief point of disagreement centered over the allowance of experience, debits, or credits. It was argued that the basic principle of fire rate making required the measurement in advance of fire hazards and other contributing hazards against a predetermined standard. To allow credits or debits on the basis of the experience of an individual risk amounts to superimposing such credits or debits upon a specific rate which has already measured the risk.[6] There is no point of

[5] State of New York Insurance Department, *Decision: New York Fire Insurance Rating Association and Interstate Underwriters' Board in Connection with Multiple Location Risks*, p. 2. See also National Association of Insurance Commissioners, *Report of Committee on Rates and Rating Organizations*, June 9, 1948.

[6] It has been argued that because casualty insurers have successfully developed experience rating that the idea may be carried into the field of fire insurance. Those who oppose the idea contend there is a fundamental difference. It is pointed out that experience rated casualty coverages bear the common characteristic of small but frequent general losses that may be reduced by prevention activities. The fire business, it is argued, offers no such assurance. Amounts at risk may be very large, and loss may originate from hazards over which the insured has no control. On the

disagreement, however, with the contention that multiple location underwriting would effect savings that in turn should be handed on to the insured. Commissions are generally lower on this class of business. Savings are reported in administration. For example, it is less expensive to write one contract for from 100 to 2,000 or more locations than it would be to write a separate contract for each location. Comparable economies have been noted in accounting, statistical maintenance, collection expense, credit reports, and underwriting. There are some additional expenses, such as the establishment of a special department, but it has been conceded that the net result of multiple location underwriting is a savings. In a sizable risk there may be some savings attributable to dispersion of risk and efficiency of management in loss prevention work.

Multiple location rate adjustments apply only to that portion of the basic annual premium which is in excess of $1,000. By preserving the first $1,000 of premium without discount, the application of rate adjustment commences at a point where economies in handling the business make themselves felt. It is apparent that not all multiple location risks are large enough to reflect inherent characteristics as to warrant premium credits from the basic annual premium produced by the application of specific rates. In the case of some of the reporting forms with a limited number of locations, the premium is based upon the limits of liability computed at the full tariff coinsurance rate applying to each location and not upon average values and average rates. The convenience of the single contract covering each location with insurance automatically following values and automatically extending to newly acquired locations is the appeal to the insured.

Multiple location rating is held not to be unfairly discriminatory as against individual risks. It is held that various insureds comprising a group possess sufficient similarity to be grouped together for rating purposes with differences from insureds noneligible under the plan. One of the purposes of insurance rating is to provide discrimination as to classes. It is only unfair discrimination that is forbidden.[7] On the

---

other hand, experience shows that there are certain risks that consistently develop better loss records over the years than do other risks that are in all respects similar from an underwriting standpoint. It is argued that management, good housekeeping, and other factors where overall management is unified, and there is a sizable premium and a spread of risks between locations will permit an application of experience credits to the particular risks. Those who advocate experience credits recognize that there are certain fire insurance risks to which they may be applied without abandoning the basic idea of insurance which provides for the contribution of the many who suffer no losses to the few who do suffer losses.

[7] State of New York Insurance Department, *Decision: In the Matter of Appeal by Members of the America Fore Group; Members of the Loyalty Group; Members of the Aetna Life Group; Members of the Hartford Group; and the New York Underwriters Insurance Company, from a Decision of the New York Fire Insurance Rating Organization, under Section 184, Par. 11, of the New York Insurance Law;*

other hand, to withhold a merited discount from a sizable group of policyholders, it is pointed out, is tantamount to maintaining an excessive rate level.[8]

MERCHANDISE FLOATER CONTRACT

This form is, in fact, a combination of a multiple location form with one or more inland marine forms for property in transit and in incidental storage. Coverage is also provided for property at premises of insured but not owned, leased, or controlled by him. Property on premises of bailees or processors may be covered.

The contract is a two-part form. One part deals with the transportation requirements of the insured together with such other additional inland marine exposures as are required. These will vary with different risks and the contract may be adjusted to meet the needs of the individual insured. The other part of the contract deals with the fire reporting requirements of the insured. Any one of the reporting forms previously described may be incorporated in the contract.

Some underwriters feel that all reporting contracts should be written with transportation insurance. The coverages that may be included in the marine section of the contract, depending upon the needs of the insured, are: (1) contractor's equipment, (2) deferred payment merchandise, (3) furrier's customers insurance, (4) garment contractors, (5) installation risks, and (6) processing risks, to mention but a few.

Rates for this form are computed separately for the fire coverage under the multiple location part of the contract and for the transportation coverages under the marine section. The already established rating procedures for both parts of the contract are followed.

This form lends itself to business establishments whose operations are not extensive enough to make use of the manufacturer's output contract in the light of the minimum premium requirement of $5,000. The form can be adopted to virtually any business with fluctuating stocks and transportation insurance requirements. Manufacturers, wholesalers, jobbers, and distributors are particularly mentioned as business organizations to which the form has an appeal.

PATENT PROTECTION INSURANCE

Patent protection contracts are written by property and liability insurers and are designed to protect patentees against infringement of their patents and to defend suits against patentees for alleged infringe-

---

and Proceedings for Review of a Decision of the New York Superintendent of Insurance, under Section 186-b, of the New York Insurance Law; and Proceedings to Review Rate Filing, under Section 186, Par. 3, of the New York Insurance Law, p. 39.

[8] *Ibid.*, p. 40.

ments of the patents of others. There are two forms of contracts issued, known as (1) protective contracts, and (2) defensive contracts.

The protective contract covers legal expenses of suits brought by the policyholder against infringers of their patent or trademark. The insured has a claim under the contract whenever he discovers an infringement of his patent. Upon notice to the insurer, a settlement is attempted on a basis that will satisfy the contract holder but in the event that this proves impossible, the contract holder is authorized to secure an attorney approved by the insurer and enter suit against the infringer. The costs of the suit up to the face of the contract are paid by the insurer.

Defensive contracts cover legal expenses of defense of suits brought against the insured for alleged infringements of patents or trademarks of others and also pay damages if any are awarded against the insured. Such a contract may be extended to cover not only the insured but his customers and any others who may be liable to suit by reason of the use of the patent or trademark owned by the insured. A certificate of protection is issued by the insurer to each customer named in the contract. Contracts also may be written covering damages only by excluding legal expenses.

The underwriting of patent insurance to some degree is similar to that followed in a real estate title search. The underwriting insurer requires that a comprehensive investigation be made by a competent patent counsel and a written opinion rendered before the insurer passes on the risk. Upon request of the party desiring protection, the insurer obtains in advance an estimate of the cost of the required legal opinion from patent counsel. When the application for insurance is filed, the applicant deposits a check to cover the cost of the infringement opinion. If the opinion indicates the risk to be an insurable one, it is customary to allow a credit of 15 percent on the annual premium to apply against the cost of the opinion. If the opinion indicates the risk is not an insurable one, the applicant is charged the exact cost of obtaining the infringement opinion from patent counsel, and he is furnished with a copy. The owner of the patent has the benefit of expert opinion if the contract is issued to the effect that the patent was in all respects legally granted and the patentee holds a valid claim to its benefits.

Defense contracts for product and process protection may be written. The product or process contract is issued to manufacturers and merchants and defends them against loss growing out of the charges of infringement of patents because of manufacture, sale, or use of the protected product or process.

A valuable feature of the defense contract is found in the fact that it may be written to cover decrees, judgments, or awards but excluding legal expenses, even after the manufacturer has been notified of an alleged infringement of patents. This is particularly valuable because the business of a manufacturer might be all but destroyed if his customers learned that suits were pending against him, the outgrowth of threats of competitors. In such an instance, the insurer would not, of course, obligate itself to assume the expenses of litigation, because this would represent a sure loss. It is willing, after due investigation, to assume the responsibility to pay damages which may be awarded against the insurer. The protection may be written not only to cover the insured but, as in the case of other defense contracts, his customers as well.

Among the more important conditions of the patent contract is the requirement that the insured forward by registered mail any charge of infringement made against the insured and give the insurer all information available touching upon the charge of infringements, as well as all information with respect to the party claiming infringement. The insurer has the right to negotiate with the party alleging infringement in an effort to compromise or settle the claim, but no final agreement may be entered into that is not satisfactory to the insured. In the event of suit, the insured is obligated to turn over to the insurer or its designated counsel every notice, demand, summons, subpoena, pleading, or other papers filed in such suit immediately upon receipt by the insured. He must turn over to the insurer complete control of the defense of the suit to the extent of the limit of liability. The insured may, if he elects to do so, select patent counsel, but this must be with the consent and approval of the insurer. In the event that the insured is charged with infringement, even though no suit has actually been filed, the insured is obligated upon request to supply to the insurer all cooperation and assistance that may enable it to defend or settle any claim for infringement. The insured may not negotiate with any party making a claim for infringement, looking to the settlement of a claim; nor may the insured agree or attempt to agree to any settlement of such claim prior to a final decree in the court of last resort having jurisdiction of the cause of action without the written consent of the insurer. Nor may the insurer settle in like circumstances without the written consent of the insured.

Patent protection and product and process protection are highly specialized forms of insurance and are not ordinarily offered, except through specialists carrying on a business in the field. The business is comparatively new, and there has been a tendency in recent years to discontinue writing protective contracts. Some organizations have discontinued them altogether.

FOR DISCUSSION

1. There is no requirement for an unearned premium reserve for a manufacturer's output contract. Why?

2. The manufacturer's output contract is said to provide an admirable installment premium payment plan. How?
3. The manufacturer's output contract is a continuous contract. It covers virtually all forms of personal property away from the manufacturing plant of the insured. In the case of newly acquired properties, what steps are necessary, if any, to effect coverage?
4. In the manufacturer's output contract, no amount of insurance is stated. What limits are there to the amount of coverage?
5. The manufacturer's output contract is said to follow the marine philosophy with respect to perils. Explain.
6. A manufacturer's output contract differs from the more usual insurance practice in the field of property insurance in two particulars. Name them.
7. There are two theories that are said to justify a reduction in premium for multiple line packaging of coverages: (*a*) packaging encourages more insurance to value, and (*b*) it eliminates selection against the insurer. Do you believe either or both of these theories to be valid? Discuss.
8. D contends that general cover reporting forms lend themselves only to covering risks in large communities where there is a concentration of fluctuating values. Do you think this to be true?
9. X wishes to cover (*a*) stock, (*b*) furniture and fixtures, and (*c*) improvements and betterments under a single reporting form. Is this possible?
10. B is opposed to carrying insurance on a reporting form because this form obligates him to making a monthly inventory. Is this true?
11. What differences in coverage, if any, are provided by form 1 and form A?
12. On December 1 the X department store purchased a reporting form contract and correctly reported its values at $100,000. Shortly after the Christmas stock began to arrive and on December 20 with a stock of $190,000, it had a total loss. How much will be collected with a contract having a limit of $250,000?
13. B covers his merchandise with a form A contract having a $50,000 limit. Two months after the inception date of the contract, B suffers a $40,000 loss. If he had made no report of values, to what extent would the insurance cover?
14. It has been stated that under certain of the reporting forms manufacturing profit on goods manufactured by the insured may be covered. Is this not in direct contrast to the practice generally in the fire insurance field? How can it be justified?
15. B reported values of $10,000 under his reporting form on June 1. He had actual values of $25,000. Shortly after the next reporting date, but before a report was made, a fire occurred with a resulting $10,000 loss. The loss exactly equaled the last report of values, and a premium was paid thereon. A sound value of $20,000 was shown at the time of

the loss. X claims the insured may collect $5,000. Y claims he may collect $10,000. Neither figure is correct. Give the correct figure and explain how you arrive at it.

16. B, an insured, with a large stock in a warehouse has been carrying specific insurance at the location. He changes the amounts from time to time to reflect changes in values. He is advised, however, that by this process there is danger of waste of overinsurance. Before changing to form A reporting coverage, what are some of the factors he should consider?
17. The manufacturer's output contract may be written with a deductible. If a $5,000 deductible amount is used, what effect has this on the normal loss rate in the final annual rate to be used for premium computation?
18. May the manufacturer's output contract be written if specific insurance coverage is provided on certain of the properties of the insured?
19. The manufacturer's output contract is an all risks contract in contrast to broad forms of insurance that provide coverage on a named perils basis. How does the burden of proof with respect to the establishment of loss differ under the two types of coverage?
20. In the case of a multiple location form where full values are not reported what would be the liability of the insurer in the following situation: (*a*) last value reported $75,000, (*b*) value at time of loss $80,000, (*c*) value at time of last report $100,000, and (*d*) loss $60,000?
21. B has a reporting form with a limit of liability at the place of loss of $50,000. The last value received was $25,000. For two months no further values were reported. The value at the time of loss was $48,000. The loss was $45,000. What is the liability of the insurer?
22. After a multiple location reporting form has been correctly written there are three things that must be kept in mind in order that the insured may not be penalized at time of loss. Name them.

CHAPTER · 26

Institutional Contracts

Institutions such as churches, hospitals, schools, governmental units, and other nonprofit organizations, like homes and business establishments, have a need for insurance protection against a large number of risks. Traditionally this protection has been afforded by a number of monoline contracts in such areas as fire and allied lines, liability, and marine insurance. Although these contracts are still in use, the trend today is toward the packaging of insurance protection for institutions through appropriate multiple line insurance contracts. These contracts plus the public and institutional property program will now be analyzed.

TYPES OF INSURANCE NEEDED BY INSTITUTIONS

Most institutions have a need for such insurance coverages as fire and extended coverage, public liability, automobile, theft, workmen's compensation and employers liability, glass, boiler, and fidelity bonds. In some circumstances construction bonds may be appropriate, and such coverages as rain insurance, water damage insurance, extra expense insurance, rent or rental value insurance, and replacement cost insurance may be of particular significance. Some institutions—particularly those of the nonprofit type—may be exempt in some states from coverage under a workmen's compensation law. Nevertheless, many states permit nonprofit organizations to elect to bring their employees under the law, and if this is done, workmen's compensation insurance is appropriate. On the health insurance side, disability insurance, hospitalization insurance, medical expense insurance, and surgical insurance may all be essential.

Some Considerations in Insuring Churches. Certain types of church property may require particular attention from the point of view of insurance. Valuable paintings, statuary, stained glass windows, silver, and other objects of considerable value may be (although not necessarily) insured separately. Property such as motion-picture projectors and tape recorders may be used away from the premises. Likewise, silver or gold chalices, candelabra, patens, and other property of this type may be kept in vaults and transported to the church when needed. Care must be given to adequate insurance for this property under all situations, including in transit. There may be special needs for liability insurance—particularly if the church operates a school or a summer camp. Similarly, Sunday school picnics and other activities may be held away from the church grounds, and thus give rise to additional liability insurance problems. There may even be a question about whether a church may be held liable for injuries, although recent court decisions appear to grant less and less immunity to churches and related institutions.

Problems in Insuring Schools. From the standpoint of financial loss to physical property, the needs of schools do not differ substantially from the needs of other institutions. In the area of liability insurance some special problems arise for governmentally supported schools. In the common law, it has long been held that the state can do no wrong, and as a consequence, the majority of the courts have held that "school districts as agents of the state, could not be held liable for the acts of their officers and employees."[1] This principle has not been uniformly applied to educational institutions, and a number of modifications have occurred in the various states through appropriate legislation. Statutes have been passed in Alaska, California, Connecticut, Maryland, Minnesota, New Jersey, New York, North Carolina, Oregon, Washington, and Wisconsin that modify the common-law rule in a number of ways. One state, Illinois, has abolished school district immunity altogether. In those states where immunity still exists or has been only partially abolished, four exceptions to general immunity have often been recognized by the courts: (1) Negligence arising out of proprietary functions (such a function might be charging for a summer recreational program or renting school facilities to other schools or organizations); (2) injuries arising as a result of the creation or maintenance of a nuisance; (3) active or positive wrong; and (4) taking or damaging private property for public use unless adequate compensation has been offered for the property.

Injuries to school children and others occur on school premises in laboratories, playgrounds, and classrooms, as well as in school buses. Damage suits have been brought against school districts for a large number of reasons: (1) actions by students alleging injuries caused by the negligence of the school district; (2) injuries from automobile accidents; (3) chemistry experiments; (4) injuries caused by fences

[1] See *Fire, Casualty, and Surety Bulletins* (Cincinnati, Ohio: The National Underwriter Company, 1966) Miscellaneous Fire Section. The discussion in this chapter is based on facts presented in this source.

or walls; (5) lack of supervision; (6) accidents caused by machinery; (7) injuries arising from manual or vocational training; (8) injuries from objects on play areas; (9) injuries from unprotected excavations; (10) playground accidents; (11) injuries arising out of heating equipment and incinerators; (12) accidents as a result of games, sports, swimming pools, and similar physical education activities; (13) accidents arising out of defective entrances, hallways, lavatories, and other areas of the building or buildings.[2] As far as school property is concerned, the law does not usually make a distinction among pupil injuries, injuries to employees, and injuries to members of the public. Further, " 'the law of master and servant' is not applied by the courts. The reason is that the relationship is created not for the private advantage of any individual or group—but rather to promote the general welfare through the education of children—a sovereign function to be exercised under the immunity of the sovereign from liability."[3]

In view of the variability that exists among the various political jurisdictions in regard to the extent of the liability of public educational institutions for injuries arising out of alleged negligence, one of the first problems that faces these institutions is the determination of whether they are liable at all and, if so, to what degree. For example, unless there is a statute holding to the contrary, school board members, trustees, and similar persons are not required to assume personal liability for negligence for their official actions. Teachers and other school personnel typically do not have the same kind of immunity and may be sued for negligent supervision and other causes. Once the nature of the liability has been established, some determination must be made about the desirability of purchasing insurance, and if the decision is to insure, what kind of insurance should be purchased and in what amounts? Closely related to this question is the one dealing with the legality of using public funds for the purchase of liability insurance. Presumably, this expenditure is inappropriate if the educational institution is immune from law suits alleging negligence on the part of the school and its personnel.

PUBLIC AND INSTITUTIONAL PROPERTY PROGRAM[4]

The public and institutional property program is available in most states and is under the jurisdiction of fire insurance rating organizations. It may be used with the special multiperil contract. There is no

---

[2] *Ibid.*

[3] *Ibid.*

[4] *Ibid.* Changes occurred in this program in January, 1967.

requirement that this program be used exclusively. Instead, it is optional for hospitals, churches, schools, colleges, and municipal, county, and state installations. It is available in those situations where an annual mimimum premium of $500 is developed for all perils and where the institution conforms to rather detailed eligibility rules.

Structure of the Contract. The basic form (form No. 1) used in the public and institutional property program has seven major sections: (1) amount of insurance, plus a statement about substitute coinsurance and waiver of inventory and appraisement clauses; (2) insuring agreement and definitions of coverage; (3) other insurance clauses; (4) exclusions; (5) deductible clause; (6) conditions; (7) extended coverage endorsement. The basic form is written on a named period basis and covers fire and extended coverage of perils. There is a special extended coverage form that places the insurance on an all risk basis, if this type of coverage is desired.

Insuring Agreement and Property Covered. The insuring agreement includes all property owned by the insured subject to certain limitations and exclusions. Included also is legally imposed liability in the event the insured has negligently lost the personal property of others and any prior-to-loss liability assumed by the insured for the personal property of others. Bulletins and manuscripts, improvements and betterments, and consequential loss applicable to specific types of property are all covered. There is a debris removal clause, and permission is granted for alterations, repairs, and additions.

Extensions of Coverage. The basic coverage provided by the contract is extended to include personal property away from the premises. The amount of the coverage is 1 percent of the amount of fire insurance or $5,000, whichever is less. Additional insurance in the amount of 1 percent of fire insurance or $5,000, whichever is less is provided on the personal property of employees. There is a $500 limit of recovery. Another extension of coverage provides additional insurance on newly acquired property within the state. The amount of coverage is 5 percent of fire insurance or $100,000, whichever is less. The percentages quoted here are somewhat larger if a special multiple peril contract is involved. Additional insurance is also provided on valuable papers. The coverage is for the "cost of research or other expense necessary to replace or restore accounts, abstracts, drawings, card index systems, or other records which fall within the general coverage of the contract, including film, tape, wire, and other recording media."[5] Replacement cost insurance is optional. It may be applied to personal as well as real property.

Exclusions. The contract contains a number of exclusions. Some

[5] *Ibid.*

of these apply to the property covered and others to the perils insured against. Among types of property excluded are land values; automobiles; aircraft; cost of excavations; grading or filling; brick, stone, or concrete foundations; growing crops; motor boats; sailboats; lawns, trees, shrubs, and plants; piling, piers, pipes, flues, and drains that are underground; and self-propelled vehicles and machines except motorized equipment not licensed for use on public ways but used on the premises. The perils excluded are represented by the electrical apparatus clause, the nuclear clause, and the various exclusions specified in connection with each of the extended coverage perils.

Deductibles. There is a deductible clause in the basic coverage that applies to all perils except fire and lightning. The amount of the deductible is $100, and it is applied separately to buildings and their contents and separately to personal property left in the open. The aggregate deductible is $1,000 per occurrence. The deductible is mandatory.

Endorsements and Miscellaneous Provisions. Endorsements other than the extended coverage endorsement may be attached to contracts covering public and institutional property. Two endorsements that are often used are the vandalism and malicious mischief endorsement and the sprinkler leakage endorsement. Similarly, business interruption and other time element coverages may be added.

There is no coinsurance clause in the contract. Substituted for it is an amount of insurance clause. The insured must submit a sworn statement of values, and this statement must be revised each year. The amount of the insurance is determined by taking 90 percent of the sworn values. This particular clause has its own expiration date, and if expiration occurs, losses are treated as if a 90 percent coinsurance clause were in effect.

An aspect of the public and institutional property program that is of considerable value is the inspection requirement. The insured is required to conduct inspections, and the premises are also inspected by a rating organization. The emphasis on prevention constitutes an effort to minimize losses and thus improve the experience under the program.

Eligibility. A special problem in institutional coverage centers around the question of the eligibility of particular institutions to participate in a program such as the one here described. Eligible institutions include almshouses, asylums, orphanages, infirmaries, soldiers' homes, churches, convents, chapels, monasteries, parish houses, and synagogues. Schools, colleges, and universities are eligible regardless of whether they are public or private. City halls, community buildings, armories, police and fire department houses, libraries, park properties, museums, state houses, and capitol buildings are also eligible. Hospitals and like institutions must be owned or occupied by governmental units such as states or counties or by non-profit organizations like fraternal societies or religious organizations.

INSTITUTIONAL MULTIPLE LINE PACKAGE CONTRACT[6]

The special multiperil contract discussed in Chapter 24 may be easily adapted to the insuring of institutions, and the institutional package contract is an extension of the special multiperil program. This program does not eliminate the public and institutional property plan. The package normally carries a 15 percent discount.

Structure of the Contract and Types of Form. The institutional version of the special multiple peril contract is structured much like the contract used for commercial property. There are two sections, the first of which relates to property coverages, and the second to liability.

Section I. The basic form for Section I carries the title, "Special Multi-Peril Institutional Property Form, Section I—Property Coverage." This form provides the basic fire and extended coverage protection. Vandalism and malicious mischief may be added by endorsement, and so may sprinkler leakage. If an institution wants all risk coverage on buildings, a special institutional property form may be used. This form covers business personal property on an all risk basis.

Optional Property Forms and Endorsements. As in the case of other types of contract, there are a number of forms and endorsements that may be added to the contract to enlarge the types of property covered or to provide for particular perils or situations. Illustrations of these endorsements are: replacement cost endorsement for personal property; business interruption insurance on either a gross earnings form subject to 50 percent, 60 percent, 70 percent, or 80 percent coinsurance or a loss of earnings—no coinsurance form; tuition fees endorsement; crime coverage supplement; church theft endorsement; musical instruments floater; glass insurance; camera floater; and fire arts coverage.

Section II. Section II is the liability coverage and is labeled "Special Institutional Form Section II—Liability Coverage." Coverage C is the liability insuring agreement and coverage D is medical payments. All general liability hazards are covered by the basic form. Product liability coverage may be deleted by endorsement if the insured wishes. Further, the insured need not take the medical payments coverage.

Mandatory Features of the Contract. As is true with package

---

[6] *Ibid.* Commercial multi-peril section.

contracts generally, the institutional package has certain mandatory features. Physical damage insurance (fire and extended coverage) must be carried on buildings and personal property. If the insured is a tenant, only personal property need be carried. Liability insurance is also required. It is written on an occurrence basis and has certain minimum limits, which are a single limit of $25,000 or "optionally, $25,000 per person, $25,000 per occurrence for bodily injury and $25,000 per occurrence for property damage, with a $25,000 aggregate limit where an aggregate applies."[7] When an institutional package is written for a governmental risk (federal, state, or local), there is a mandatory endorsement that states the ineligible exposures (such as streets and amusement parks) and clarifies whether playgrounds, schools, colleges, and hospitals that are governmentally operated are covered.

Eligibility. Like the public and institutional property program, not all institutions are eligible for the institutional package contract. Basically, this contract covers buildings used mainly by such non-profit organizations as schools, churches, charitable groups and governmental bodies. The following institutions are not eligible: chatauquas, camps, camp meeting grounds, amusement parks, private nursing homes operated for profit, public housing project, and penitentiaries, prisons, or other penal institutions. The Salvation Army, Volunteers of America, Goodwill Industries, or similar organizations are not eligible "if occupancy includes (1) manufacturing of any kind; (2) sales, storage, processing or repair of clothing or furniture; (3) paper or rag storage or sorting; or (4) supplying food or lodging to itinerants." In general, locations where a substantial amount of manufacturing takes place are ineligible, as are locations containing a sizable quantity of radioactive material. This latter restriction may raise some question about coverage for universities and hospitals.

INDEPENDENT PACKAGE CONTRACT FOR CHURCHES AND RELATED INSTITUTIONS[8]

The independent package contract that is to be reviewed in this section is one that may be used for churches and church-related schools and colleges and similar institutions. Like many of the other package contracts that have been discussed in this book, this contract in addition to declarations has two sections, the first of which refers to physical damage to and loss of use of property and the second to liability.

Declarations. The declarations appear on two pages of the con-

[7] *Ibid.*

[8] *Ibid.*, Company Coverages. The discussion in this section is based on a contract for non-profit institutions given in this source. The quotations are from that contract.

tract. There is space for the policy number, certificate number, and for the name and address of the insured. Space is also provided for stating the limits of liability of the various coverages. Under Section I, some eight coverages are listed, including real and personal property (coverages A and B); loss of income (coverage C); additional expense (coverage D); fine arts and other valuable articles and equipment (coverage E); comprehensive glass (coverage F); theft (either including or excluding) monies and securities (coverage G); and space for other forms (coverage H). Coverages E, F, G, and H involve special forms, and for E and F, possibly schedules. There are three coverages listed under Section II as follows: limit of liability for personal injury and property damage for each occurrence (coverage I); aggregate limit of liability for products hazard (coverage J); and medical payments (including volunteer workers), which is coverage K. There is also space for making statements about deductible clauses, coinsurance clauses, and for listing the mortgagee. On the second page of the declarations over half a page is provided for further statements about location and description of property.

Section I—Physical Damage to and Loss of Use of Property. Section I has five subsections which are: (1) coverages; (2) extensions of coverage; (3) perils insured against; (4) perils excluded; and (5) conditions.

Coverages. Coverage A includes "real property, building service equipment and supplies, except as hereinafter provided, used and located as specified on page one, or temporarily elsewhere." Coverage B, which relates to personal property, reads as follows:

> Personal property of the Insured of a business, professional, or institutional nature, except as provided under Coverage A, and such personal property of officers or partners not otherwise insured; personal property of others in the care, custody, or control of the Insured for which the insured is legally liable; and the Insured's use interest in improvements and betterments to buildings not owned by the insured; all while used and located as specified on page one or within 100 feet thereof.

If a peril insured against causes damage to building or equipment and if this, in turn, brings about a change in temperature or humidity, the resulting damage is covered under the contract. Accounts, bills, deeds, and property of this type are covered only to the extent of the cost of blank books and the cost of transcribing, although an extension of coverage allows $5,000 for "expenses necessarily incurred in the reproduction of valuable papers and records," which is in addition to any amounts that might be payable under coverage B. The following types of property are excluded from coverage under A and B: (1) land, trees, shrubs, plants, lawns, and growing crops, although the contract later extends coverage in the amount of $1,000 on "trees, shrubs, plants, and lawn against fire, lightning, explosion, riot, civil commotion, or aircraft—but for not more than $250 on any one tree, shrub, or plant, including expenses in removing debris;" (2) excavations, grading, or filling; (3) money, securities, animals, and aircraft (with certain exceptions); and (4) "personal property in which parties other than the insured also have an insurable interest when the insured's interest in such property is covered by insurance under any other policy."

Coverage C agrees to make financial provision for loss of income "during the period of recovery"[9] that results from the interruption of operations at the described location and caused by loss to real or personal property as defined by coverages A and B. Income for the purpose of this coverage is total revenue from the "net sales of goods or services, and the rental or lease of property to others less the cost of goods and service supplies sold, and services purchased (from other than employees) for resale which do not continue under contract." When the loss of income involves the opening date of a school or college, the period of recovery is governed by the following contractual provision:

a) The period of recovery is defined as and limited to the length of time, commencing with the date of damage to the property covered hereunder, and ending on the day preceding the beginning of the first school year following the date that the damaged or destroyed property could, with the exercise of due diligence and dispatch, be restored, but not limited by the expiration date of this policy.

b) If the period of time as provided in paragraph (*a*) ends on a date within 30 days immediately preceding the beginning of the first school year, the period of liability for loss is extended to end on the day preceding the beginning of the second school year.

c) The words "beginning of school year," however modified, shall mean the opening date of school in the fall as prescribed in the school catalogue.

There is a further requirement that the insured must resume operations as soon as possible and, if necessary, make use of substitute facilities.

The additional expense that might necessarily be associated with continuing operations as a result of a real or personal property loss is provided for under coverage D. Additional expense is defined as "the excess of the total cost of conducting operations during the period of recovery over and above the total cost of such operations during the

---

[9] Period of recovery is defined "as and limited to only such length of time as would be required with the exercise of due diligence and dispatch to rebuild, repair, or replace that part of the property which has been damaged or destroyed commencing with the date of such damage or destruction, but not limited by the expiration date of this policy."

same period had no loss occurred." Excluded from this computation are loss of income and the cost to repair or replace the damaged property. If in an effort to reduce an additional expense loss, the cost of repair or replacement is increased beyond the normal cost, this extra cost is taken into account. Consideration is also given to the "salvage value of property obtained for temporary use during the period of recovery."

Extension of Coverage. There are seven extensions of coverage in Section I. Two of these—the extension for trees, shrubs, and plants and for the expenses of reproducing valuable papers and records—have already been discussed. The other extensions are: (1) Fifteen percent of the amount of insurance under coverages A and B for property newly acquired within the state, in an amount not to exceed $100,000, which coverage shall cease "180 days from the date of acquisition or on the expiration date of this policy, whichever first occurs." (2) Coverage for personal property in transit or located on a temporary basis elsewhere. The amount of this coverage is $10,000. (3) Additional expense is provided in the amount of $1,000. (4) Five percent of the amounts of insurance under coverages A and B, or $5,000, whichever amount is smaller, may be used to cover the personal property of employees while such property is within the buildings covered under the contract. There is a limit of $500 in respect to any one employee, and if other insurance contracts cover this type of loss, this extension is inapplicable. (5) The last extension relates to dwellings not used for mercantile or farming purposes and provides that "ten percent of the actual cash value of any dwelling . . ." may be applied to each of the following: "(*a*) private structures pertaining to the dwelling; (*b*) rental value of the dwelling or its private structures, whether rented or not, subject to all policy conditions applicable to coverage C. . . ."[10]

Perils. Nine perils are listed in the contract as being insured against. They are: fire and lightning; windstorm and hail; explosion; sonic boom, vandalism and malicious mischief; riot and civil commotion; aircraft and vehicles; smoke; and removal. Each of the perils, with two or three exceptions, is subject to limitations. For example, the bursting of steam boilers is not regarded as an explosion, and glass (other than glass building blocks) is not covered under vandalism and malicious mischief. Two deductible clauses are included as a part of the perils section of the contract. Neither of these clauses is applicable unless so stated in the declarations. The amount of the deductible must be specified on page one of the contract, and under the first clause it may not exceed $500 in the aggregate in any one occurrence.

[10] *Ibid.* A dwelling is defined as "a residential building occupied by not more than four families (excluding janitor's or servant's quarters) nor over five rooms rented or held for rent."

Also, under the first clause the deductible applies "separately to each building or structure, including contents therein, and separately to personal property in the open." The second deductible clause is less limited than the first and states that "the amount specified on page one shall be deducted from the amount of loss in any one occurrence resulting from the perils insured against." In addition to the exclusions that were made part of the definition of perils, the contract contains a war risk exclusion; a nuclear clause; a nuclear exclusion; an electrical apparatus clause; and a neglect, theft, and order of civil authority clause.

Conditions. Sixteen conditions are specified in the contract as relating to Section I. Included are a basis of loss payment (coverages A and B), basis of loss payment (coverage C), privileges granted, debris removal, benefit to bailee, loss clause, requirements in case loss occurs, appraisal, abandonment, when loss is payable, suit, impairment of recovery, company's options, subrogation, mortgagee interests and obligations, and the mortgagee clause.

Under basis of loss payment (coverages A and B) such items as actual cash value, improvements and betterments, replacement cost, payment to others, coinsurance, and waiver of inventory are discussed. The replacement cost clause applies only to real property and is similar to the clause found in the homeowners' forms. Under privileges granted, the insured among other things is given permission "to construct additions and to make alterations and repairs to the buildings at the location described on page one, and to erect new buildings and structures at such location." The insured may also make repairs needed to protect the property from further damage and to include the cost of these repairs as a part of the amount of loss. Permission is also given for the property to be vacant or unoccupied without limit of time except as a limit is imposed under the peril of vandalism and malicious mischief. As is typical under most contracts insuring personal property, the insurance "shall not inure, directly or indirectly, to the benefit of any carrier or bailee." The other conditions are similar to those found in most contracts insuring property.

Optional Aspects of the Contract. As was suggested in the discussion of declarations, the contract may be enlarged by the adding of endorsements. For example, stained glass may be insured under the fine arts and scheduled property form and this schedule may be used to obtain all risks protection of certain property. Endorsements may also be used to provide replacement cost coverage for contents and to extend the perils insured against. The broad perils endorsement has a more liberal electrical apparatus clause and also broadens coverage of damage from vehicles and aircraft.

Section II—Liability. The liability section of the contract contains three coverages, only one of which will be discussed here. This coverage is coverage I, liability for personal injury and property damage. The basic insuring agreement is:

This company agrees with the named insured to pay on behalf of the Insured all sums which the insured shall become legally obligated to pay as damages because of personal injury, including death at any time resulting therefrom, sustained by any person or injury to or destruction of tangible property, including the loss of use thereof, caused by an occurrence. . . .

This statement is followed by the usual defense, settlement, and supplementary payments clause. A territorial limitation is placed on the coverage with the statement that "this section of the policy applies only to occurrences or accidents which happen during the policy period within the United States of America, its territories or possessions, or Canada."

Definitions. There are some seven definitions that form part B of Section II. The word "insured" includes:

Any person or organization named as an insured, also the following additional insureds: (1) any clergyman, vestryman, warden, member of the board of governors, executive officer, director or trustee of the organization while acting within the scope of his duties as such; (2) any church organization authorized by the Insured named on such certificate with respect to its operations on the premises described on such certificate; (3) the diocese or other major organizational or canonical authority.

Since the liability coverage is on an occurrence basis, the definition of the word "occurrence" is of some importance. An occurrence is:

either an accidental happening during the coverage period or a continuous or repeated exposure to conditions which unexpectedly and unintentionally causes personal injury or injury to or destruction of tangible property during the coverage period. All injury or damages arising out of such exposure to substantially the same general conditions shall be considered as arising out of one occurrence.

The definition of "personal injury" is quite broad and includes: "(*a*) bodily injury, sickness, disease, disability, including death at any time resulting therefrom, or if arising out of the foregoing, mental anguish and mental injury; (*b*) invasion of privacy, false arrest, false imprisonment, wrongful eviction, wrongful entry, wrongful detention, malicious prosecution, or, if arising out of the foregoing humiliation; (*c*) libel, slander, defamation of character." Other words or phrases that are defined are "automobile," "elevator," "products hazard," and "contract."

Exclusions. There are 14 exclusions listed that apply to liability. They cover such items as the nuclear exclusion, liability attached to the use of automobiles away from the premises, and obligations under workmen's compensation laws. Two of these exclusions are of particular interest to churches and schools. The first of these exclusions states that Section II does not apply: "to injury, sickness, disease, death or destruction" due to (except to a college, school, or camp by the named insured, with respect to the operation of infirmaries having facilities for lodging and treatment, public clinics, or hospitals): "(*a*) the rendering or failure to render: (1) medical, surgical, dental, X-ray or nursing service or treatment, or the furnishing of food or beverages in connection therewith; (2) any service or treatment conducive to health or of a professional nature; (*b*) the furnishing or dispensing of drugs or medical, dental, or surgical supplies or appliances; (*c*) the handling of or performing of autopsies on dead bodies; (*d*) the rendering or failure to render any cosmetic, tonsorial, massage, physiotherapy, chiropody, hearing aid, optical or optometrical services or treatment."

The second exclusion places a limitation on the applicability of the provision under defense, settlement, and supplementary payments that agrees to pay expenses for immediate medical and surgical aid. The contract does not apply to "(*a*) the Insured's pupils, while engaged in any athletic activities, including calisthenic drills and gymnasium classes, which are directed or organized by the Insured or by any person acting on behalf of the insured; (*b*) campers."

Conditions. Eleven conditions are applicable to the liability section of the contract. They carry the general headings of limits of liability, severability of interests, notice of occurrence or accident, notice of claim or suit, assistance and cooperation of the insured, premium, action against company, changes, assignment, subrogation, and waiver of eleemosynary defense. Two of these conditions are of particular interest to the subject matter of this contract—severability of interests and waiver of the eleemosynary defense.

Under severability of interests, the contract states that the term, "the insured" is "used severally and not collectively." There are two exceptions to this statement. The term is used collectively in respect to "(*a*) liability assumed by the Insured under any contract or agreement to the extent that such liability is an extension of the liability imposed upon the Insured by statutory or common law, or (*b*) Condition 1 (limits of liability), and Condition D (other insurance)." There is a further statement to the effect that the inclusion of more than one insured does increase the insurers' total liability beyond the limits stated in the declarations. The condition relating to eleemosynary institutions is fairly lengthy. The insurer agrees not to use the "immunity of the Insured named on the applicable certificate as an eleemosynary institution" as a defense unless the insured so requests. The insurer also states that the waiver of the defense of immunity will not serve to increase the insurer's liability under the contract beyond the limits of liability stated in the declarations. There is a further statement that even though immunity is used as a defense for the named insured, the applicable insurance "to the extent to which it would otherwise have been available to such Insured, shall apply to those additional Insureds" that are named in the definition of the word insured. It is understood that the insurer will retain all defenses other than that of immunity in suits against such insureds.

Medical Payments. The last part of Section II of the contract is labeled "medical payments." The insuring agreement reads:

To pay all reasonable expenses incurred within one year from the date of the accident for necessary medical, surgical and dental services, including prosthetic devices, and necessary ambulance, hospital, nursing and funeral services, to or for each person who sustains bodily injury, sickness or disease, caused by accident and arising out of the ownership, maintenance or use of premises and ways immediately adjoining, by the Insured named in the declarations as the organizational body or the Insured named on the applicable certificate, or operations of such insureds.

This agreement is subject to some seven exclusions and to two conditions that apply directly to it.

Other Conditions. There are ten conditions that apply to the entire contract. The items included are liberalization clause, time of attachment, annual payment of premium, other insurance, assignment, inspection and audit, concealment, fraud, cancellation, conformity with statute, and declarations. These conditions are similar to those contained in many property insurance contracts. Under cancellation the insurer agrees to give a ten days' written notice instead of the five days found in some contracts.

FOR DISCUSSION

1. A "loss of income" coverage may be important for many institutions. How is "loss of income" determined by the insurer in the event a claim is made under this part of the contract?
2. To what extent are lawns, trees, plants, and shrubs covered in insurance contracts that are applicable to institutions? What are the limitations placed on coverage of this type and why?
3. Why is a "fine arts and other valuable articles and equipment endorsement" often recommended for churches? Are there other endorsements that you would suggest in recommending coverages for churches?
4. To what extent do institutions of the type considered in this chapter have a products hazard?
5. In an institutional contract the following statement is made under the heading "Waiver of Inventory": "In the event that the aggregate claim for any loss is both less than $10,000 and less than 5 percent of the total amount of insurance on the described property at the time

such loss occurs, no special inventory or appraisement of the undamaged property shall be required, provided, however, that nothing herein shall be construed to waive the application of the Coinsurance Clause." Explain the foregoing statement.

6. A problem of some importance in the institutional field is the question of the legal liability of charitable institutions. The courts in the various states have differed on this question. What is the common-law rule and to what extent has it been modified by statute and by judicial decision?
7. To what extent are the supervisory boards of public school districts immune from liability suits alleging negligence in the performance of their duties?
8. What is meant by the public and institutional property program? How is it implemented? What, if any relationship does it have to the special multiperil program?
9. The public and institutional property program employs an amount of insurance clause. What is this clause? Does it have any relationship to coinsurance?
10. Instead of the blanket coverage of the basic public and institutional property form an insured may take a schedule form. In what ways does the schedule form differ from the blanket form? In which situations is the schedule form particularly useful?
11. Name and discuss the seven major sections of the public and institutional Form No. 1.
12. Discuss the eligibility rules for writing the public and institutional plan. What generalization would you make about eligibility requirements?
13. What are the differences between the special extended coverage endorsement as it is used with the public and institutional plan and its use with other classes of business?
14. What are the mandatory coverages of the special multiperil program as it relates to institutions? What are the property forms that may be added to the contract?
15. Compare the institutional special multiperil program with the apartment house, mercantile, motel, hotel, offices, and processing or service programs.

CHAPTER · 27

Service and Professional Contracts

The increasing complexity of human affairs has led to a considerable expansion in the number of persons who offer services to the public based upon special knowledge and skill acquired through professional study. Traditionally physicians and lawyers have offered their specialized knowledge and skill to members of the public on a fee-for-service basis. Since the turn of the century many other professions such as accounting, architecture, engineering, and insurance have become increasingly important, and practitioners in these fields have acquired professional degrees and designations. In turn, these professionals have offered their skill to individuals who have relied on the advice they have received. Legally, professional persons are required to maintain certain standards of care, and they may become obligated to pay damages in the event they are negligent or perform in a manner not consistent with the standards of their chosen field.

Over the years members of the public have become more aware of and insistent upon adequate performance on the part of professionals, and an increasing amount of space has been given in the press and other media to damage suits based on malpractice. A concomitant of this activity has been an increasing interest on the part of bar associations in offering postgraduate seminars for their members dealing with proper methods and procedures in the preparation and trial of malpractice cases.[1]

A matter of concern to many professional persons has been the high awards that juries have often made to persons who have in some manner been injured through negligent or careless performance or advice. The size of the awards is influenced by many factors, including cost of living changes and the difficulty in estimating the monetary value of injuries. Juries are often sympathetic with injured persons and seemingly are inclined toward higher and higher awards.

---

[1] See William F. Martin, "Medical Malpractice," *Insurance Counsel Journal*, Vol. XXXIII (April, 1966), pp. 266–76.

An indication of the magnitude of the settlements as they apply to the medical profession may be obtained by referring to Table 27–1.

TABLE 27–1

HIGHEST NATIONWIDE VERDICTS AND SETTLEMENTS IN MALPRACTICE SUITS

Amount	*State*	*Cause of Suit*	*Malpractice Alleged*
$1,086,666	Maryland	Paralysis	Error in surgery on spine.
725,000	Pennsylvania	Loss of jaw, Facial cancer	Failure to remove radioactive contrast media.
700,000	California	Paralysis	Failure to detect subdural hematoma.
443,124	Washington	Paralysis	Nonemergency hip-pinning on poor risk surgical patient.
334,046	California	Aplastic anemia	Failure to determine drug sensitivity.
300,000	New York	Paralysis	Failure to treat cardiac arrest promptly.
290,000	Oregon	Paralysis	Failure to diagnose subdural hematoma.
260,000	California	Death	Use of general anesthesia for removing small cyst on neck.
160,000	Florida	Death	Error in surgery for hematoma of scrotum.
160,000	Illinois	Loss of leg	Improper treatment of fracture, tight cast.

SOURCE: W. F. Martin, "Medical Malpractice," *Insurance Counsel Journal*, Vol. XXXIII (April, 1966), p. 270. Used by permission.

Although this table is not intended as a complete tabulation, it nevertheless provides a rather dramatic example of the amount of money that may be awarded to the plaintiff in suits alleging malpractice. The risk faced by the professional person is complicated further by a three-year statute of limitations which, in the case of infants, may extend to 24 years, since the statute does not start running until the infant is 21.

One way that a professional person may meet the need for protection against the financial obligation that may arise from a malpractice suit is through insurance. For quite some time the insurance industry has sold malpractice liability insurance, although for many years it was available to a limited number of professions—mainly medical, dental, and allied fields. Today insurance is available to almost every profession in which the practitioner makes his specialized knowledge and skill available to the public.[2] In the medical and allied fields the alleged damage is mainly bodily injury, whereas in the case of lawyers, insurer representatives, and similar persons it is property damage.

[2] See *Fire, Casualty, and Surety Bulletins* (Cincinnati, Ohio: The National Underwriter Company, 1967), Dmpl—1.

The need for separate contracts covering professional liability arises out of the fact that professional claims are excluded in the usual kind of liability contracts. The comprehensive personal liability contract, for example, excludes from coverage "the rendering of any professional service or the omission thereof." A great variety of contracts covering the professional risk is available, and most of these contracts are nonstandard, although standard provisions are now available for physicians', surgeons', and dentists' liability contracts, as well as for druggists and hospitals. There are endorsements for each contract, and a professional liability manual is available for each. There is also a miscellaneous professional liability manual and endorsements covering chiropodists, chiropractors, nurses, laboratories, opticians, optometrists, and technicians of various types. Contracts are available for lawyers, accountants, and engineers, and errors and omissions insurance covers insurance agents, abstracters, and similar professional undertakings. With the advent of multiple line insurance, package contracts have been developed—particularly in the medical field—that provide not only for the liability exposure, but for possible property losses that may arise in connection with operating an office. Equipment may be lost or damaged in many ways, and buildings may be destroyed from a variety of perils.[3]

PROFESSIONAL PACKAGE CONTRACT[4]

The professional package contract is designed to provide in one instrument the property and liability coverages needed by such professionals as physicians, surgeons, dentists, and optometrists. The contract follows the usual pattern and is divided into declarations, statement of coverages, and insuring agreements including exclusions, and general conditions. Space is provided for the adding of endorsements. As might be expected in a professional contract, the declarations page, in addition to providing space for limits of liability and premiums, also leaves blanks for a statement of where the insured received his professional degree and the date and year. The insured is also asked to list the county, state, and national professional societies of which he is a member.

The coverages section of the contract is divided into three parts; the first part provides professional liability coverage, the second, profes-

[3] Professional monoline insurance contracts available to medical and allied personnel were analyzed in Chapter 17 and will not be considered in detail here. The emphasis in this chapter will be on multiple line contracts and such specialized contracts as lawyers professional liability, errors and omissions insurance, and contracts for accountants, architects, and engineers.

[4] The contract selected for analysis is one appropriate to the medical and allied professions. It is not a standard contract and is an independent as opposed to a bureau-type contract.

sional office premises liability coverage, and the third, coverage for professional equipment.

The first part of the insuring agreement for professional liability reads as follows:

[Insurer] agrees to pay on behalf of the insured all sums which the insured shall become legally obligated to pay as damages because of injury arising out of:

a) malpractice, error or mistake of the insured, or of a person for whose acts or omissions the Insured is legally responsible except as a member of a partnership, in rendering or failing to render professional services, or

b) acts or omissions of the Insured as a member of a formal accreditation or similar professional board or committee of a hospital or professional society,

committed during the policy period in the practice of the Insured's profession described in the Declarations.

Following this statement provision is made for defense, settlement, and supplementary payments of the type that is typical in all liability insurance contracts. The insured in this part of the coverage is defined as the person named in the declarations as the insured and does not include persons associated with the insured. There are two exclusions applicable to part one: "(*a*) to any use of X-ray apparatus for therapeutic treatment unless such is specifically declared in Item 4 of the declarations . . . and (*b*) to liability of the Insured as proprietor, superintendent or executive officer of any hospital, sanitarium, clinic with bed and board facilities, laboratory, or business enterprise."

Part II of the coverages section is essentially an owners', landlords', and tenants' contract for the professional office premises. The insuring agreement in this part of the contract includes bodily injury and property damage liability coverage in those situations where the insured is held legally responsible for injuries arising out of the ownership, maintenance or use of property for office purposes. Medical payments are included apart from legal liability. The expenses must be incurred within one year from the date of accident and arise out of the ownership, maintenance, or use of the premises. The usual defense, settlement, and supplementary payments statement is included as a part of the agreement. The word "insured" includes, in addition to the named insured, "any organization or proprietor with respect to real estate management for the named insured. It is aso provided that the word "insured" is used severally and not jointly, although this fact does not increase the insurer's liability. There is a geographical clause that limits coverage to the United States, its territories, and Canada. There are eleven exclusions applicable to Part II. Eight of these apply to both liability and medical payments, one to liability only, and two to medical payments. The protection provided in Part I of the contract is excluded under Part II. Additionally, the ownership, maintenance, and use of vehicles, such as automobiles, away from the premises is excluded as in the operation of elevators on the premises. Contractual liability with certain exceptions, such as an agreement, is not included. The insurer is not liable for accidents covered under workmen's compensation, unemployment, or nonoccupational disability laws, nor is it responsible for accidents arising from goods or products manufactured or sold or otherwise handled by the insured, if these have been "relinquished to others and are used away from the office premises." The final exclusion under the liability and medical payments coverage is:

To any of the following insofar as any of them occur on or from premises owned by or rented to the named insured and injure or destroy buildings or property (1) the discharge, leakage or overflow of water or steam from plumbing, heating, refrigerating, or air-conditioning systems, stand pipes for fire hose or industrial or domestic appliances, or any substance from automatic sprinkler systems, (2) the collapse, or fall of tanks or the component parts or supports thereof which form a part of the automatic sprinkler systems, or (3) rain or snow admitted directly to the building interior through defective roofs, leaders or spouting, or open or defective doors, windows, skylights, transoms, or ventilators.

The remaining exclusions will not be detailed but they are not particularly restrictive and do not seriously limit coverage.

Equipment coverage (Part III) constitutes a separate contract and insures the "medical, surgical, and dental equipment and instruments (including tools, materials, supplies, and scientific books) owned and used by the Insured in the medical or dental profession. At the option of the Insured, property so described but belonging to others and used by the Insured in his profession shall be included as covered hereby." Radium, furniture, and fixtures are not included in the property insured. Part III is an all risks contract subject to six specific exclusions. These exclusions include such items as depreciation, inherent vice, breakage of glass, loss or damage to electrical apparatus except by fire, war, and nuclear reaction, radiation, or radioactive contamination. A coinsurance clause is applicable to equipment coverage and states that the insurer will be liable "in the event of loss for no greater proportion thereof than the amount hereby insured bears to 80 percent of the actual value of the property insured hereunder at the time when such loss shall happen." There are 14 conditions that apply to Part III and their headings are: misrepresentation and fraud, notice of loss, examination under oath, settlement of claims, no benefit to the bailee, subrogation, reinstatement, pair or set, parts, sue and labor, action against the insurer, appraisal, civil authority clause, and conformity to statute. Since these conditions were discussed earlier in the text, they will not be elaborated on here.

The professional package is concluded by a listing of ten general conditions. There is also a professional office furniture and fixtures endorsement and an extension of coverage endorsement, found in most property contracts and includes, among other things, statements about subrogation, assignment, cancellation, other insurance, and notice of injury.

ERRORS AND OMISSIONS INSURANCE

In the professional field, aside from malpractice coverages which involve bodily injury, there are certain liability coverages designed to indemnify the insured for loss the outgrowth of errors or omissions attributable to negligence for which he may be held legally liable. Investments involving very large sums of money are made relying upon the decisions of professional practitioners. Architects, engineers, conveyancers, representatives of insurers, and other professional persons have need for errors and omissions insurance. In real estate transactions the opinion of the attorney passing title and the services of the surveyor laying out the property on the face of the earth could involve the owners of a project in tremendous loss if the work of either proved to be faulty or inadequate. The responsibility of the legal profession in connection with the issuance of new securities has become tremendous. The law now requires the publication of material facts bearing upon the status of a company issuing securities, and it is the underwriters, and not the corporation issuing the securities, that are liable for faults and misleading statements. In connection with the construction of a large project where land values are important, an error on the part of a surveyor could involve the owners or other interested parties in great loss. The deed might convey a property free and clear of all encumbrances; but if the property is improperly located by the surveyor and part of a structure is built on land belonging to somebody else, the consequences are readily apparent.

The contracts written for surveyors and attorneys are highly specialized contracts and are not contracts readily obtainable, as are the standardized coverages that have obtained almost universal acceptances. The "attorney's policy," when written, is tailored to the particular needs of the individual or firm that is covered. High limits are provided because, if there is to be a loss at all, it will probably involve large values. The "surveyor's policy" is written primarily to strengthen the hand of the surveyor so that he can supply at the time he undertakes a project a guarantee of the accuracy of his work. The contract provides indemnity to: mortgagee or holder of a trust deed;

the owner of the property or the owner of an interest; and a title company insuring such holder or owner with respect to title to, or to an interest in, the premises in question.

LAWYERS LIABILITY INSURANCE

Lawyers liability insurance has been available for a number of years and is similar to other forms of professional liability insurance including errors and omissions insurance. Malpractice by lawyers does not involve bodily injury but rather is concerned with property losses that may occur because of acts or omissions of attorneys. The structure of the contract is much like that of the physician's, surgeon's, and dentist's liability contract and has the usual parts consisting of declarations, insuring agreements, exclusions, and conditions. Some of the significant aspects of the insuring agreements and exclusions will be reviewed.

Insuring Agreements and Related Matters. There are two insuring clauses in the lawyers liability insurance contract. The first of these clauses, coverage A, is the individual insuring clause, and the second, coverage B, is the partnership insuring clause. Both clauses are important, since attorneys often practice on a partnership basis and individual interests as well as partnership interests must be covered. In both coverages the insuring agreement states that liability protection is provided "because of any act or omission of the insured, or of any other person for whose acts or omissions the insured is legally responsible, and arising out of the performance of professional services for others in the insured's capacity as a lawyer."[5] Words such as accident, malpractice, error, or mistake are not used and the coverage is very broad. The insuring agreements do not contemplate that both coverage A and coverage B will apply in a single situation. Under coverage A it is stated that this coverage does not apply "if one or more claims arising out of the same professional service are made (1) jointly or severally against two or more members of the partnership or against any member of the partnership and the partnership, (2) against the partnership or (3) against the insured solely because he is a member of the partnership."[6] A similar statement appears under coverage B. The fiduciary exposure is covered and is applicable to lawyers who serve as attorneys for fiduciaries.

The contract covers acts or omissions that occurred during the term of the contract even though the contract may not be in force at the time the claim is paid. Past errors, those occurring before the insurance contract is entered into, are covered, if "at the time the insurance went into force, the insured 'did not know or could not

[5] See *Fire, Casualty, and Surety Bulletins, op. cit.,* Dmpl 1.

[6] *Ibid.,* Dmpl 3.

have reasonably foreseen that such acts or omissions might be expected to be the basis of a claim or suit'. . . and provided the claim is made during" the term of the contract.

Exclusions and Limitations. There are not many exclusions and limitations in the lawyers professional contract. A limitation that is put on the insurer, contrary to the provisions of most liability contracts, is that it may not make a settlement unless the insured gives consent in writing. As is true with other types of professional liability insurance there is an effort to avoid damaging the reputation of the professional through some type of compromise settlement. Five specific exclusions are listed in the contract. They are (1) "dishonest, fraudulent, criminal, or malicious act or omission of any insured partner or employee"; (2) "claims made by an employer against an insured who is a salaried employee of that employer"; (3) "liability for bodily injury to, or sickness, disease or death of any person, or to injury or destruction of any tangible property, including loss of its use"; (4) "any loss sustained by the insured as beneficiary or distributee of a trust or estate";[7] and (5) the broad nuclear energy exclusion.

Limits on Amount of Insurance. The basic limits for lawyers liability insurance are $5,000 per claim and $15,000 in the aggregate. Stating a liability per claim means that more than one person may be involved in a claim and there is no limit per person.

ACCOUNTANTS LIABILITY

An accountant in the practice of his profession, as is the case with other professionals, is required to exercise due care and may be sued for damages, if he has allegedly been negligent, or if he acted in bad faith or dishonestly in relation "to one with whom he is in privity or with whom he has direct contractual relations."[8] He may not be held liable for mistakes that are essentially errors in judgment. It must be shown that the accountant failed to exercise the "knowledge, skill, and judgment usually possessed by members of that profession in a particular locality."[9] Court decisions have consistently held that where privity does not exist the accountant has no liability in negligence to third parties. Thus, if a third party receives a balance sheet prepared by an accountant for his client and if the third party relies on the information therein, the accountant is not liable for any losses that the third party may sustain because of alleged negligence in constructing the statement. This doctrine is somewhat in conflict with

[7] *Ibid.*, Dmpl 4.

[8] Frederick A. Carroll, "Accountant's Third Party Liability," *Insurance Counsel Journal*, Vol. XXXIII (April, 1966), p. 252.

[9] *Ibid.*

other situations, such as product liability, where the manufacturer may be held responsible even though he is not bound by contract to the ultimate consumer. There is some indication that the privity rule in accounting may give way to the more general concept of liability illustrated by the legal rules associated with losses arising from negligently manufactured products. If so, the risk facing the accountant will be considerably increased.

Accountants Professional Liability Contract. Accountants liability contracts are not standard and no attempt will be made here to summarize all of the variations that exist. Instead the main divisions of an illustrative contract will be discussed. This contract is made up of declarations, insuring agreements, exclusions, and conditions.

Declarations. There are five items in the declarations. The first is space for the name and address of the insured; the second is a statement about the term of the contract; the third is space for stating the services rendered by the insured to clients; the fourth provides space for stating the average number of the insured's staff at the home office for the past year and the "location of all Branch Offices and average number of staff at each for the past year"; and the fifth is space for listing limits of liability and premiums. The premium for the contract is payable annually and "is based upon the average number of the Insured (if an individual) or partners (if a partnership) and employees of the insured engaged in the business of the insured as Accountants, Auditors, and Tax Counsellors at its Home Office and Branch Offices during the year prior to the Policy Period or the previous year in case a policy is continued."

Insuring Agreements. The insuring agreement of the accountants liability contract reads as follows:

To insure the Insured or the Insured's estate against direct pecuniary loss and expense arising from any claim made during the Policy Period, or within the claim notification period specified in Condition 1, by reason of legal liability for damages caused or alleged to have been caused by the Insured or by any partner or employee of the Insured in the performance of professional services for others, including but not limited to breach of contract, or services performed or advice given in relation to matters of taxation, prior to the termination of this Policy

a) through neglect, error, or omission,

b) through dishonesty, misrepresentation or fraud, except if made or committed by the Insured or any partner thereof with affirmative dishonesty or actual intent to deceive or defraud,

c) through libel, slander or defamation of character, except (1) if committed in bad faith or in willful violation of any statute or ordinance, (2) loss and expense due to criminal libel or criminal slander by the Insured, or by any partner or employee of the Insured.

In addition to the specific insuring agreement quoted above, there are five sections, that with this agreement, make up the part of the contract labeled "insuring agreements." These sections are defense; predecessors; claims or suits against employees; delegated work; and limit of liability, insured, joint insured. As is typical in liability insurance contracts, the insurer agrees to defend the insured even if the suit is groundless. The insuring and defense agreements may be extended under "predecessors" to apply to "such claims or suits arising from acts of predecessors in business or of any partner or employee thereof." The same two agreements are also extended to include claims or suits against employees, if the latter are charged with neglect, error, or omission in the course of their duties while performing professional services for others. Sometimes work is delegated to other accounting organizations. In this situation the word "employee" is extended to include any owner, partner, or employee of the organization performing delegated tasks.

Exclusions and Conditions. There is only one exclusion listed in the contract and that relates to nuclear energy. Eleven conditions appear on the last page of the contract. They are notices of information relating to claims; settlement of claims; insured to assist with evidence; subrogation of rights, salvage; termination of insurance; reduced amount of insurance, restoration; amendments, alterations, and changes in policy; assignment of interest; conflicting statutory provisions; action against company; other insurance; and declarations.

The insured is required to give written notice in the event of an occurrence that may give rise to a claim and, if suit is brought, to forward the summons to the insurer. The latter must be notified during the contract period or within 30 days of its expiration. The 30-day period may be extended, without the consent of the insurer, to one but not to exceed three years by the payment of an additional premium. If insurance is purchased to replace the expired contract in whole or in part, the extended insurance terminates and the insurer agrees to return the unearned premium. Under settlement of claims the insured must not admit liability nor make any settlement except at his own cost unless he has the written consent of the insurer. The insurer, in turn, agrees not to settle any claim or suit without the written consent of the insured. As in other liability contracts the insured, if the insurer so requests, is required to assist in the securing of information and evidence and in general to cooperate with the insurer in the defense of any claim or suit.

The contract may be terminated in any one of three ways. The insured may cancel the insurance by surrendering the contract to the insurer or by sending written notice in which the insurer is advised as to when the cancellation is to become effective. The insurer may terminate the contract by sending a written notice to the insured, which states when the cancellation is to be effective but this must not be less than 30 days after notice is given. If the insured retires from business, the contract is automatically terminated. There are the usual arrangements for the return of premium.

Most of the other conditions are similar to those found in other contracts and do not require specific discussion. Condition 11 emphasizes that the statements made in the declarations are the agreements of the insured and his representations and they are made a part of the contract.

ARCHITECTS AND ENGINEERS LIABILITY[10]

The illustrative contract of architects and engineers liability insurance here considered is in three parts: declarations, insuring agreements, and conditions. There are exclusions in the contract but these are made a part of the section on "insuring agreements" and are not listed as a separate part of the contract.

Declarations. The declarations section of the contract has seven items in which the usual kind of information about name, address, term of contract, and limits of liability are requested. Also, space is provided for stating the number of partners or officers; architects, draftsmen, engineers, and inspectors; surveyors, and all other technical personnel employed by the insured; and office employees.

Insuring Agreements. Item I of the insuring agreements is labelled "coverage" and reads as follows:

> To pay on behalf of the insured all sums which the insured shall become obligated to pay by reason of the liability imposed upon the insured by law for damages resulting from any claim made against the insured arising out of the performance of professional services for others in the insured's capacity as Architects and/or Engineers, and caused by any error, omission or act of the insured or of any person employed by the insured, or of any others for whose acts the insured is legally liable.

Immediately following the statement on coverage the insurer agrees to defend suits and to make certain settlements.

> As respects such insurance as is afforded by this policy the Company shall:
>
> *a*) defend any suit or Arbitration Proceedings against the insured alleging such error, omission or act and seeking damages on account thereof, even if such suit is groundless, false or fraudulent; but the Company shall have the right to make such investigation and negotiation of any claim or suit as may be deemed expedient by the

---

[10] The contract considered in this section is not standard and is offered as an example of the type of architects and engineers liability insurance that is available from at least one insurer.

Company. The Company, however, shall not make settlement or compromise any claim or suit without the written consent of the insured.

b) pay all premiums on bonds to release attachments for an amount not in excess of the limit of liability of this policy, all premiums on appeal bonds required in any such defended suit, but without any obligation to apply for or furnish such bonds, all costs taxed against the insured in any such suit, all expenses incurred by the Company, all interest accruing after entry of judgment until the Company has paid, tendered or deposited in court such part of such judgment as does not exceed the limit of the Company's liability thereon.

c) pay expenses incurred by the insured for such immediate medical and surgical relief to others as shall be imperative at the time of each occurence.

d) reimburse the insured for all reasonable expenses, other than loss of earnings, incurred at the Company's request.

Except amounts paid in settlement of any legal liability insured under Insuring Agreement 1, which liability shall be governed by the limit of liability stated in the Declarations, the Company agrees to pay the amounts incurred under this insuring agreement in addition to the limit of liability stated in the Declarations.

The definition of the insured includes persons or firm listed in Item 1 of the declarations and also includes "any partner, executive officer, director, stockholder, or employee while acting within the scope of his duties as such." If the named insured dies or becomes insane or becomes insolvent or bankrupt the contract applies to the named insured's legal representatives.

There are territorial limitations in the contract. Only "errors, omissions, or acts which occur within the United States of America, its territories or possessions, or Canada during the policy period" are covered, and "then only if claim is first made against the insured during the policy period. The contract goes on to state that

This policy is extended to cover, any loss or losses under any prior policy which shall be discovered after the expiration of the time limited in said prior policy for the discovery of loss thereunder and provided such loss or losses are discovered during the policy period of this policy and before the expiration of the time limited in this policy for the discovery of loss hereunder: Provided that such loss or losses would have been recoverable under said prior policy had it continued in force: and provided further that the errors, omissions, or acts causing such loss or losses be such as are covered under this policy.

Ten exclusions are stated under Item V of the insuring agreements. Loss caused intentionally is not covered nor is any liability under a workmen's compensation law. Other claims not covered are: those arising out of ownership, maintenance, use or repair of any property "or the conduct of any business enterprise that is wholly or partly owned, operated, or managed by the insured"; claims "for bodily injury, sickness, disease or death, injury to, or destruction of property resulting from any error, omission or act of the Named Insured, his agents, or employees, not arising out of the customary and usual performance of professional services for others in the insured's capacity as Architect and/or Engineer and including the failure or omission on the part of the insured to effect or maintain insurance, or any required bonds"; claims with respect to ownership, maintenance, or use of any aircraft, boat, or automobile or vehicles of any kind. Liability assumed by contract is not covered nor are claims arising because of the insolvency of the insured. Claims arising from activities "in connection with Fair and/or Exhibition grounds, other than in connection with permanent structures, the making of boundary surveys, surveys of the subsurface condition, and ground testing" are excluded unless a specific endorsement is placed on the contract. Again, unless specifically endorsed there is no coverage for claims "arising from activities in connection with tunnels and/or bridges which exceed 150 feet in length, and/or dams." There is also a nuclear energy exclusion.

Fourteen conditions appear at the end of the contract. They are: limit of liability, notice of claim or suit, arbitration procedure, assistance and cooperation of the insured, settlement, action against company, other insurance, subrogation, severability of interests, changes, assignment, cancellation, terms of contract conformed to statute, and a statement that the declarations are made a part of the contract.

COMPARISON WITH OTHER LIABILITY CONTRACTS[11]

Insurance contracts that cover professional liability have certain features (apart from the type of activity covered) that are different from the usual kind of liability insurance. These differences have been pointed out in the preceding discussion, but it may be useful to summarize them here. First, there is only one insuring clause that relates specifically to the type of liability that is contemplated under the contract. Second, no limit per accident (or occurrence) is stated, nor is the limit specified as bodily injury or property damage. Limits are stated on a per claim basis and there is an aggregate limit for each year of coverage. Third, claims may not be settled out of court without the consent of the insured. Fourth, professional liability insurance is not regarded as a substitute for other types of liability

---

[11] See *Fire, Casualty, and Surety Bulletins.*

insurance. A professional person may well need liability insurance in addition to that relating to the practice of his profession.

FOR DISCUSSION

1. Distinguish between a limit per claim and a limit per person. Why is the former type of statement preferred in professional liability insurance?
2. Discuss the arguments for and against extending accountants liability to cover third parties.
3. Discuss the ways in which professional liability insurance differs from the usual forms of liability insurance.
4. In what ways is the scope of professional liability insurance contracts limited?
5. A was sitting in a barber chair, although the barber had not yet started to cut his hair. Because of some structural defect the chair collapsed and A was injured. Would the barber be covered by a professional liability insurance contract? Would your answer be different if A had been injured by slipping on the floor?
6. Why is it common in professional liability insurance contracts to state that the insurer may not settle a malpractice case outside of court unless it has the written consent of the insured?
7. To what extent may the liability and other insurance needs of professional persons be handled through a single package contract?
8. When was professional liability insurance first developed? Were there limits on the types of professional services covered?
9. How do you account for the increase in the number of damage suits entered against professional men? What are the trends in the amounts of the award?
10. It is often stated that the usual type of lawyers liability insurance contract provides very broad coverage. Is this statement justified? Would you limit it in any way? Are there any problems that have arisen or may arise because of the way the insuring clause reads?

PART V

OPERATIONAL PROBLEMS OF THE PROPERTY AND LIABILITY INSURER

CHAPTER · 28

Types of Insurer and Problems of Organization

The principle of insurance requires some entity or instrumentality for carrying out the purpose of indemnity. An insurance plan, in order to give security, must provide for the accumulation of capital or other loss-paying funds in advance of the loss or make some satisfactory provision for the raising of loss-paying funds when or if losses occur.

The ownership of the capital of insurers in modern practice falls into two classifications and is responsible for a dividing of insurers into two major divisions. There is, first, the group of insurers who place their owners' capital in jeopardy. The second group consists of those insurers who group the losses of those they insure, paying them out of the contributions of the insureds and sharing the savings in insurance costs (dividends) as the case may be. The capital of the insureds of this second group is not at risk except to the extent that the contracts provide for assessment. The most important representative of the first group of insurers is to be found in the stock insurers, while the mutuals of the different types are the outstanding examples of the second class. Historically noncapital insurance developed as assessment insurance; most of this insurance today is not conducted on an assessment basis. Many of the insurers that do write on the assessment basis do not have any savings to share and do not pay "dividends." Rather, they usually collect assessments for the purpose either of paying past losses or accumulating a fund for the future.

CLASSIFICATION OF INSURERS

Insurers may be divided into six groups: (1) stock insurers, (2) mutuals, (3) Lloyd's, (4) reciprocals or interinsurers, (5) state insurers, and (6) self-insurers. The first four of these groups are commercial insurers in that they are not state owned or supported and must earn enough from sales of insurance contracts to at least pay losses and expenses of operation. Stock insurers and mutuals are organized as corporations and are as prevalent in life as in nonlife insurance. Reciprocals and Lloyd's organizations are almost unknown in the life insurance field.

By distinguishing between types of mutual insurers and types of Lloyd's associations, commercial insurers may be classified as follows:

1. Stock insurers.
2. Underwriters at Lloyd's.
3. Underwriting groups known as "Lloyd's associations."
4. Assessment mutuals.
5. Advance premium mutuals.
6. Reciprocal exchanges or interinsurance associations.

Additionally, consideration must be given to state funds and self-insurance. Premiums written for the various types of commercial property and liability insurance organizations in 1965 in terms of percentage of total follows: stock insurers, 72 percent; mutuals, 26 percent; and reciprocals and Lloyd's, 2 percent.

Features Common to Stock and Mutual Insurers. Stock and mutual insurers together write 98 percent of the aggregate of all insurance in this country written by commercial insurers. The stock and mutual systems are active competitors for business. Before noting the differences in these two types of insurer, it will be helpful to consider the features that are common to both.

Both stock and mutual organizations write the various forms of property and liability insurance. They may also engage in multiple line underwriting if they qualify to do so under the state laws. Both stock insurers and mutual insurers are subject to the general corporation and insurance laws of the states in which they operate. In the long run both types of insurer pay their losses out of the premiums collected from the insureds. Both are corporations, and the policy is a contract issued by the corporation to the insured. Charters are issued to both types of insurer, and both are regulated by the state insurance laws. The laws under which both stock insurers and advance premium mutuals operate set up minimum financial requirements for organization or admission. Requirements necessary for both plans for doing business are set out in detail. Generally these laws require both stock and mutual insurers to comply with the same reserve, investment, contract form, and other regulatory laws. As in the case of stock insurers, mutuals are subject to rigorous supervision by the various state insurance departments.

After losses have been paid from premiums collected, both stock and mutual insurers may, if they elect to do so, set up part of what is left as a surplus to serve as a cushion to absorb or help to absorb sizable or shock losses. In the case of both stock and mutual insurers, premiums collected and held in the form of a reserve or surplus are invested. The investment income is added to the premium income and used for the payment of losses and expenses and to increase surplus to meet increasing demand for broader coverages and coverage of larger limits. Both forms of organization undertake to reduce the loss experience through a careful selection of risks. Both are interested in loss prevention and risk improvement.

Mutuals. A mutual insurer is an insurance corporation without capital stock, owned by its policyholders collectively, who have the right to vote in the election of its directors. There are approximately 2,281 mutual property and liability insurers operating in the United States. Of these mutuals, 786 are of the advance premium type. Mutuals are organized under general laws for the purpose of providing insurance for their policyholders at cost. Every policyholder is a member of the company. There are no stockholders. The mutual policyholder-members elect the board of directors. The board elects the executive officers who manage the firm. The mutual corporation assumes the hazards of its policyholder-members. As a consideration for the assumption of this risk, each policyholder-member, except in the case of certain farm mutuals, pays or agrees to pay a premium in advance and, where their contracts so provide, a specified assessment where premium contributions are inadequate. Where the premiums in a given period are more than adequate to meet losses, expenses of carrying on the business, and a contribution to a reserve for contingencies (where it is the company practice), the excess is returned to policyholders. This return is called a "dividend." or unabsorbed premium.

The mutual insurer, thus, is a nonprofit organization, designed and operated to provide insurance protection at the lowest reasonable net cost.[1] It has sometimes been stated that mutual insurance is insurance at cost. If, by this, it is meant that the policyholder in a mutual insurer must receive his insurance at cost, measured only by the losses and expenses incurred while the contract is in force, the statement is not strictly accurate. If a mutual insurer were obliged to distribute as dividends during a contract term all the premium income in excess of losses and expenses, it would never be in a position to accumulate surplus and contingency reserves to meet anticipated emergencies and growth requirements. The mutual insurer has no access to the capital funds market for growth capital. Neither is the insurer in any sense a partnership, nor can policyholders either during the term their contracts are in force or afterwards compel distribution of surplus, contingency reserves, or any other form of safety fund the insurer

[1] *Statement submitted on behalf of the American Mutual Alliance to the Committee on Ways and Means, U.S. House of Representatives,* March 15, 1951, p. 4.

may have accumulated.[2] The rights of the policyholders in a mutual insurer are limited to the terms of their insurance contracts. Whatever rights the policyholders have to the assets of the insurer are set forth in the contract.[3]

Mutual insurance divides itself into numerous classes. Some of the local farm mutuals confine their activities to a limited area, collecting no advance premiums and levying assessments at stated intervals. A number of farm mutuals operate on the advance premium basis and cover a considerable territory. General-writing mutual insurers do business on the advance premium basis, operating over a wide area, many of them extending their activities throughout the United States. Their methods of operation vary; but they can be divided into three general groups, the division being based upon the method of handling premiums. Insurers in the first group, exemplified by organizations such as the Factory Mutuals, require assureds to deposit with them large premiums, estimated from past experience to be in excess of all loss and expense requirements. At the end of the contract period, deductions are made for expenses and actual losses paid, and the balance is returned or credited to the assured. Insurers in the second group base their rates on loss and expense experience. Their rates approximate those of stock insurers. The premium charged is equal to or less than that charged by stock insurers; and any balance above expenses, losses, and reserve requirements and a reasonable contribution to surplus is returned to the assured as a dividend. Mutuals in the third group charge rates substantially lower than those used by the stock insurers. These rates reflect the experience of the insurer, and no dividend return is contemplated.

Advance premium mutual insurers issue two types of contract: assessable and nonassessable. Up to a certain point of financial stability, they must provide for limited assessment liability. Assessment liability is usually limited to one additional premium.[4] The laws of the

---

[2] *Pelelas* v. *Caterpillar Tractor Company*, 113 Fed. (2d) 629. The surplus of a mutual insurer is determined by finding the amount by which its assets exceed statutory reserves or other liabilities. If the insurer sets aside a part of the surplus to be distributed as dividends, the remaining amount may be set up as contingency or safety fund.

[3] As has been stated: "The plaintiff says he does not depend for his rights upon the policy. . . . If the plaintiff depends upon anything but his rights under the contract contained in the policy, he depends upon something that does not exist." *Andrews* v. *Equitable Insurance Society*, 124 Fed. (2d) 788.

[4] In the early days of assessment mutuals the insurer sometimes required the insured to sign a note and deposit it with the insurer. This note was in a multiple of the premium charged for the contract. A general rule placed the amount of the note at four times the premium. The notes were held as part of the assets of the insurer and could be called upon in the event of an emergency on an unusually large loss. As time went by the insurers tended to accumulate a reserve out of premium payments,

various states authorize the issuance of nonassessable contracts by any mutual insurer that has a surplus of stated amount, usually equivalent to the capital required for a stock insurer.[5] The larger advance premium mutual insurers have met this statutory requirement and have gone on a nonassessable basis.[6] Policyholders whose contracts so provide are subject to assessment to meet losses and expenses when the resources of the insurer have been exhausted. In the case of a mutual insurer operated on an assessment basis, all the policyholders are liable for assessment for losses that occur between the inception date and termination date of the contract as long as the contract is in force.

A number of states have laws permitting or requiring the establishment of guaranty capital by mutual insurers. Guaranty capital is essentially a loan or advancement of money by individuals who are to receive interest under certain prescribed regulations. Thus, investment in guarantee capital is essentially a debt obligation. Many states have authorized the establishment of "guaranty funds" or "guaranty surplus funds" out of surplus rather than through the advancement of outside money by individuals. In some states a mutual insurer may establish a guaranty fund by a segregation of surplus or by a sale of guaranty fund certificates. In Massachusetts a guaranty fund may be so established in lieu of other guaranty capital in certain cases. Approximately half the states have guaranty capital or guaranty fund laws which provide for the fund's protection and use as well as its distribution under certain circumstances. In a number of states a guaranty fund is a prerequisite to the writing of nonassessable contracts by mutual insurers, just as in other states the requirement is a maintained surplus in a certain stated amount or in an amount equal to the capital of a similar stock insurer.

Farm Mutuals. There are approximately 1,495 farm mutual insur-

---

and this was set aside to meet unusual losses and made the requirement of a note no longer necessary. The accumulation of an adequate reserve with the elimination of the need for an assessment was followed by the issuance of the contracts that were on their face nonassessable.

[5] The right of a mutual insurer to issue nonassessable contracts has been established by the decisions of many courts. In *Union Insurance Company* v. *Hoge*, 21 Howard Reports 35 (1858), the United States Supreme Court held that because of the elimination of the assessment feature: "It has never been supposed that the mutual principle has been there abrogated."

[6] The term "advance premium cooperatives" is applied to insurers whose operations are similar to mutual insurers. Originally, these insurers confined their operations to a single county, but some of them have qualified to transact business in several states. These insurers usually charge premiums determined by rates filed with the State Insurance Department and may pay dividends, though in practice they charge lower rates rather than pay dividends. While these insurers historically were organized to operate on an assessment basis, they may qualify to issue nonassessable contracts. Many of these insurers still operate on a direct assessment principle within a limited territory.

ers doing business in the United States.[7] A few years ago the number was considerably greater, but the trend has been in the direction of fewer and larger insurers. Those now in business have grown larger and stronger, and the total volume of business written by farm mutuals has increased as the actual number of insurers in business has decreased.

Farm mutual insurers have little in common other than that they were organized to protect the property of their members. Some write fire insurance only, while others write such risks as windstorm and hail damage to growing crops. Not all insurers writing fire insurance provide extended cover protection which includes the hazards of windstorm, explosion, riot, smoke, aircraft, and vehicle damage. A substantial number of these insurers do provide this insurance. In some areas where the crops are specialized, mutual insurers have been organized to write hail insurance. Some of the insurers are old, extending their operations back over a hundred years, and others are comparatively new. Some limit their operations to a single town or county, while others operate on a statewide basis. Farm mutual contracts are written with both a limited and an unlimited assessment liability.

Class Mutuals. There are mutual insurers that were organized to insure primarily certain kinds of businesses such as factories and milling and grain operations; others insure lumber and allied lines, hardware and kindred risks, drugstores, and numerous other classifications. Because these insurers were organized to insure selected risks of a definite class, they are known as "class mutuals." While many of these insurers have expanded their operations to the end that they may be regarded as general-writing insurers, many still give emphasis to the special line contemplated when they were organized, and with respect to them, the term "class mutual" is still used. The factory mutuals and the mill mutuals are examples of the class mutual category. The history of these organizations and the basic facts concerning them were considered in Chapter 2.

Stock Insurers. The stock insurers operating in the United States are either corporations organized in the United States or corporations that are organized abroad. In the United States a corporation organized to write insurance under the laws of a particular state is considered a domestic insurer by that state but is usually termed "foreign" by all other states. The term "alien" is generally applied to those insurers incorporated in some foreign country.

---

[7] A farm mutual is a mutual insurer that always has written more than 50 percent of its risks on farm property. The oldest genuine farm mutual fire insurer in the United States is said to date from 1823 and was founded by eleven Quaker farmers in Crosswicks, New Jersey. John Bainbridge, *Biography of an Idea* (Garden City, N.Y.: Doubleday & Co., Inc., 1952), p. 156.

The stock insurers have for their purpose the conduct of one or several of the different classes of the insurance business. Strict laws govern their operation; and they are obliged to satisfy the designated authorities as to their capital, reserve fund, assets, and investments. The contracts (policies) they issue are written for a definitely stated consideration (premium), and so far as the insured is concerned the transaction has no interest for him beyond indemnification in the event he suffers loss. He receives no benefit (dividend) usually from the earnings of the insurer and pays no assessment or additional premium if losses exceed income.

Stock insurers are organized as profit-making ventures. The capital subscribed by the stockholders serves as a fund, in addition to the premium payments, out of which losses are to be paid. Additions made to the surplus serve the same purpose. Stock insurers assume risks with the profit element in view and fix their rates accordingly.[8]

The insured dealing with the stock insurer is entitled to, and expects, no return as a result of the operations of the business. He has paid his premiums for protection, and at the end of the contract term the entire premium belongs to the insurer. On the other hand, the insured cannot be called upon for assessments to meet the losses of the other insureds, nor is he in any way dependent upon other insureds for the payment of his losses. Unlike the assessment mutual insurer where the contingent liability of all persons holding similar contracts serves to guarantee that funds will be forthcoming to pay losses of policyholders, stock insurers, as well as mutuals, are required by law to have on hand at all times a sufficient fund in cash or prescribed securities to discharge in full every liability which they have assumed or incurred.[9] As in the case of mutual insurers, stock insurers expect in the long run to pay losses out of premium income. In order to commence business, they must have a guarantee fund made up of capital stock and surplus. At the outset both capital stock and surplus are contributed by stockholders. While the surplus may be increased from time to time out of earnings, as business judgment dictates, at the outset, when a stockholder subscribes to shares in the insurer he is also

---

[8] Many stock insurers have explored the possibilities of writing participating contracts in the field of property insurance. Special participating contracts have been written by stock life insurers affording policyholders much the same type of contract as that offered by the mutual insurers, with the difference that control of the stock insurers rested with the stockholders. Stock insurers in the property field have heretofore not made a practice of writing participating contracts, although more insurers are now doing so. Steps were taken in some jurisdictions to secure legislative authority to permit stock insurers to share earnings with policyholders without changing to a mutual basis. Virtually all stock insurance, however, still continues to be written on a nonparticipation basis; that is, the premium pays for the protection and is considered fully earned. There is neither liability for assessment nor provision for a dividend predicated upon favorable experience.

[9] *Aetna Insurance Company* v. *Hyde*, 315 Mo. 113.

required at the same time to make a contribution to surplus. Additions that are from time to time made to surplus are designed to increase the stability of the insurer and enhance its capacity with respect to the size of lines it will carry.

The stock insurer and the mutual insurer are required to keep intact at all times assets sufficient to discharge all liabilities in full. If because of a catastrophe, or as the result of poor management, or for any other reason the capital and surplus of the insurer fall below an amount that is required to cover the outstanding maximum liability of the insurer, in order for the insurer to remain in business the stockholders must at once repair the deficiency. By virtue of careful state supervision of the affairs of the insurer, it is expected to be in a cash or sufficiently liquid position at all times to meet any obligation that it has assumed under its contracts. It is, therefore, the stockholders of a stock insurer who in the long run assume the hazards against loss. The stockholders choose the directors who manage the business. Policyholders have no interest or voice in management nor any expectation with regard to profits or responsibility with regard to losses. Policyholders in stock and mutual insurers make a contract with the insurer without regard to any other policyholder. Premiums are paid solely in consideration for their own insurance. The premium paid to the insurer becomes at once its property. The insured has no interest in the ultimate disposition of the premium after it has been paid the insurer as long as the insurer follows statutory requirements with respect to reserve and remains solvent and able at all times to meet contractual obligations. In other words, the policyholders expect no profit or dividend, nor do they expect to be called on for an assessment or otherwise to fortify capital if insurance underwriting develops unfavorably for the insurer.

Since risks assumed by stock insurers are written with a profit element in view, rates are fixed with this end in mind. Stock insurance provides protection without a contingent liability of any sort. The stock insurer is a business organization that assumes risks for pay. The funds the insurer keeps on hand for the purpose belong in the long run to the stockholders. It is fundamental that in return for the security of stock insurance, provision must be made in the rate for compensating the capital.

The facilities of some stock insurers are worldwide in their scope and are being adjusted continually to meet changing conditions. In the United States stock insurers generally write their business through local agents, allowing them a commission on the business.

Underwriters at Lloyd's (London). Lloyd's of London is a corporation organized to supervise the activities of a group of insurance underwriters.[10] It is unquestionably one of the greatest insurance

[10] Question is sometimes raised as to whether the apostrophe is to be used in connection with the spelling of the name of this institution when there is no

institutions in the world. Taking its name from the coffee house of Edward Lloyd, where underwriters assembled to transact business and pick up news, the organization traces its origin to the latter part of the 17th century and, hence, becomes the oldest insurance organization in existence. Lloyd's as an organization is generally conceded to date from 1771. In that year the merchants and brokers who were making use of the facilities at Lloyd's Coffee House entered into their first formal agreement, and the following year a committee of Lloyd's was set up to govern the affairs of the subscribers in their capacity as underwriters. Lloyd's carried on in the capacity of a private association until 1871. In that year Parliament passed the Lloyd's Act incorporating the members of the association into a single corporate body with perpetual succession and a corporate seal. The act of incorporation made little change in the methods of doing business, though it did give the society recognition as a corporate body with certain statutory powers set forth in the act. The act recognized that it was the purpose of the underwriters to carry on a marine insurance business. Provision was made to protect the interest of the underwriters with respect to shipping and among other things provided for the collection and publication of pertinent information. From time to time further acts of Parliament have extended the powers of the Lloyd's corporation, and in 1911 the objects of the society were enlarged by removing any restriction limiting them to the business of marine insurance. The Act of 1911 set forth the objects of Lloyd's as follows: (1) the carrying on by members of the Society of the business of insurance of every description including guarantee business, (2) the advancement and protection of the interests of members of the Society in connection with the business carried on by them as members of the Society and in respect of shipping and cargoes and freight and other insurable property or insurance interests or otherwise, and (3) the doing of all things incidental or conducive to the fulfilment of the objects of the Society.

The corporation does not itself write insurance. The insurance is carried by individual underwriters on much the same basis as the original underwriters assumed risks in the days of Lloyd's Coffee House, but under conditions more carefully regulated and restricted. Since it is the individual underwriters who are responsible with respect to the insurance carried, it is not strictly correct to indicate a risk is insured with Lloyd's but rather it should be stated that the risk

---

possessive implication. The name is sometimes found to be spelled *Lloyd's* and sometimes *Lloyds*. The latter spelling is now held *not* to be correct. While it is conceded that originally the apostrophe found its way into the name when reference was made to Lloyd's Coffee House, it is now true that through statutory enactment official sanction is given to the use of the apostrophe, even though the word is not used as a possessive. Acts of Parliament, when the association was incorporated, used the apostrophe, and the spelling continues in subsequent enactments. See E. Golding and D. King-Page, *Lloyd's* (New York: McGraw-Hill Book Co., Inc., 1952), p. 30.

is carried by the underwriters "at Lloyd's." Lloyd's as a corporation is never liable on a contract. It does supervise the conditions under which its members may issue contracts; it undertakes to provide collective protection for the commercial and maritime interest of its members; and it maintains an agency for the collecting and disseminating of important information related to shipping and marine insurance.

Membership at Lloyd's is said to consist of about 2,700 underwriting members. These members in turn form groups termed "syndicates." The underwriting members of a syndicate are known as "Names," and the business of the syndicate is placed in the hands of an agent called an underwriting agent and usually known as "the underwriter." The membership of a syndicate may vary from a few members to as many as a hundred. Business is placed by brokers who circulate among underwriters offering the risks they have to place. Each underwriter signs a slip carried by the broker indicating the amount for which he will commit his syndicate. When the slip is full, that is, when the total required insurance is underwritten, a contract is prepared and sent to Lloyd's contract signing office. At this office the syndicates that have committed themselves to the risk are made parties to the contract and the contract is signed by a clerk, the official seal of Lloyd's is affixed, and the contract is then ready for delivery.

The Names never underwrite in a partnership capacity. Each underwriter or each member of a syndicate is liable only for that share of loss for which he obligates himself. Never is one member, or underwriter, liable for the losses of other members either on a contract or in a syndicate. The contract itself precludes any possibility of a partnership liability by providing that each of the underwriters assumes liability "each for himself and not for another."[11] Since each underwriter operates as an individual, all of his resources must, of necessity, be available for the payment of losses. It also means that all his resources may be called upon to liquidate other business ventures. Since this is the case, it is conceivable that unfortunate business ventures, entirely apart from insurance underwriting, might seriously deplete a Name's assets. To preclude this possibility, all insurance premiums are placed in the trust fund and held for the purpose of liquidating the insurance claims. The policyholders have a preferred claim under the deed of trust for insurance premiums paid in connection with the underwriting activities. The deed of trust, on the other hand, does not in any way minimize the overall liability of the underwriter with respect to his other assets.[12]

---

[11] The rule against partnerships operating as underwriters is very old. The Act of 1720, which established the Royal Exchange and the London Assurance, prohibited other insurance by any corporation, partnership, or firm. Only individual underwriters were exempt from this prohibition against marine underwriting.

[12] An American trust fund was established in the United States, August 28, 1939, and provides that all premiums and claims due to or by Lloyd's underwriters under

The governing authorities of Lloyd's require periodic audits to assure the solvency of each underwriter and his ability to meet his underwriting obligations. There is nothing comparable to our state regulation. Lloyd's does publish figures dealing with income and losses, but while experts go over the detailed investments and transactions of insurers in this country, they have no such opportunity with regards to Lloyd's as a whole or with regard to the individual underwriters and syndicates. An insured dealing with Lloyd's deals only in credibility and confidence. American insurance interests are not prepared to admit that the self-regulation practiced by Lloyd's is the equal of the American supervisory system.

The organization of Lloyd's is frequently compared to that of our New York Stock Exchange. Just as the New York Stock Exchange does not deal in securities, so the corporation of Lloyd's does not write insurance. The analogy holds good in the control exercised over its members. A member of the New York Stock Exchange may be suspended for unethical operations, inability to meet obligations, and the like, and Lloyd's exercises similar control over its members. The "Committee of Lloyd's" is composed of 12 men, and this group may expel an underwriter who breaks any of the rules of the corporation. A three-fourths vote of the members of the committee can expel a member for unethical practices.

Lloyd's writes all types of property insurance, although the predominating classification consists of marine coverages. Its business operations extend to all parts of the globe, and the organization maintains contacts with its business through agents, subagents, and representatives authorized to adjust and pay claims. It is a source of great pride to Lloyd's that during its long history an underwriter has never defaulted in the payment of a claim.

American Lloyd's Organizations. Groups of individual underwriters have been formed in the United States to provide insurance patterned after the underwriting procedure of the underwriters at Lloyd's of London. Because of the similarity of the method of doing business, these organizations are known as "Lloyd's groups."

In the American groups, contrary to the practice in Lloyd's of London, the business is conducted by an attorney-in-fact who assumes risks for the individual underwriters, issues the contracts, determines upon rates, and is otherwise responsible for all the detail of the business. Individual underwriters commit themselves for a given percentage of any risk assumed or a given amount of liability upon any desired number of risks, but as a general rule the total liability is definitely

---

policies issued in American dollars shall be paid in or out of Lloyd's American trust fund. The trust deed requires that all premiums in respect to U.S. dollar insurance be deposited with the City Bank Farmers Trust Company of New York as trustees.

limited by a specified maximum. The number of underwriters who operate in a given group may be as small as five or as large as five hundred. Most exchanges require a minimum deposit of $1,000 from each underwriter.

The American groups do not enjoy the long-established reputation of the English organization. On the other hand, they are subject to the American insurance regulatory system. This has become of increasing significance in recent years. Since Lloyd's groups consist of underwriters, each of whom assumes a part of the risk, one of the chief problems in connection with appraising the stability of such a group is to be found in the difficulty of knowing the financial condition of each subscriber to the contract. There has been some tendency on the part of insureds to associate the name of Lloyd's with the London organization. There is no connection between the American groups and the underwriters at Lloyd's of London.

Lloyd's Not Mutual Organizations. Lloyd's, composed of a group of unincorporated individuals who join together to assume risks, are not mutual organizations, nor are they in any sense cooperative organizations. The members of these associations place their own capital at risk (in this respect they are like incorporated stock insurers) and issue their contracts for a cash premium on a nonassessable basis. The insurers have no privity of interest with the insured, and the capital standing ready out of which the losses are to be paid is in no way owned by the insured. While the Lloyd's underwriters are free to write any form of insurance they wish, the original London organization was in its inception primarily a group of marine underwriters, and this represents still the major portion of its business. Nevertheless, many forms of risk have been carried by Lloyd's that find no regular classification among insurers and include protection against almost any conceivable insurable contingency.

Reciprocals. Reciprocal exchanges carry on their business by making provision for the policyholders to be the insurers of the group and to underwrite the risks of the exchange as individual underwriters, or subscribers, as they are more frequently termed. The plan is effectively mutual in its operation but is not mutual in the true sense because the individual subscribers in their capacity as underwriters assume their liability as individuals, and the form of agreement most generally used provides that this liability shall be several and not joint. The funds of one subscriber may not be diverted to liquidate claims of other subscribers, and the stability of an exchange or the financial responsibility behind a given contract can be determined only by ascertaining the financial responsibility of each individual underwriter on the risk.

Reciprocal exchanges do not incorporate, nor do they operate as partnerships. The policyholders, or subscribers, appoint a manager to whom is entrusted the responsibility of carrying on the business; he derives his authority from a power of attorney and is in turn known as an "attorney-in-fact." The power of attorney is the basis of the underwriting agreement made by the subscribers.

There is no partnership liability on the part of one subscriber to the other. It is usual in the power of attorney that each signer agrees to assume a definitely established underwriting liability, and such liability is "several and not joint with any other subscriber." The power of attorney usually further provides that no subscriber shall be or become liable for any default, failure, or neglect on the part of any other subscriber. Thus, if one subscriber defaults or is unable to meet his liabilities, the funds of the other subscribers can not be used to pay a loss, even though the attorney-in-fact has such funds in his possession.

Some reciprocal exchanges provide an advisory committee which has control of the investment policy and custody of all funds over the amounts immediately necessary for paying the expenses of the business. This committee maintains control over the attorney-in-fact, since through a majority vote of its members he may be replaced. Typically the members of the advisory committee are selected from the largest of the insurers; therefore, their interests and those of the insurers are expected to be identical. The control exercised by such a committee is regarded as a vital element in the plan. Otherwise, the attorney-in-fact would have placed in his hands authority so broad that it might tend to invite abuse.

State Insurance. When a state or nation performs the functions of an insurer, the insurance so provided is termed "government insurance." In this form of insurance enterprise the government manages the project and assumes the liability for payment of claims. State insurance falls into two general categories. The first embraces those projects of a social nature, such as the provision of old age pensions, unemployment insurance, and maternity benefits. The second classification includes the writing of insurance by the state in competition with, or to the exclusion of, privately owned insurers.

In competition with private enterprise, perhaps the most progress has been made in this country by state insurers in the field of workmen's compensation. That this is in effect a form of social insurance may to a degree account for the willingness of some states to participate. Compensation insurance, as written by the state, is carried on through a state fund. In the beginning the state sets up a fund which is augmented by premium payments and drawn upon to settle losses. Any profit remaining after the settlement of claims is returned to the policyholders. Adequate premiums must be charged, since the credit of the state is usually not pledged. Some states have made for themselves a monopoly of the compensation business, while others have entered the field as free and open competitors of privately owned and operated insurers.

The operation of state funds has met with varying degrees of success. In some instances they have functioned to the entire satisfaction of all parties concerned; in others there has been some question as to their efficiency, while in some cases the experience has been decidedly unsatisfactory. Indicative of the difficulties involved when competition is lacking, there is a tendency toward inefficiency; and when competition is permitted, the governmental insurance office is hardly in a position to compete effectively in the race, because it lacks the business organization and trained staff of the well-established insurers. State insurers, moreover, are frequently obliged to assume risks that a privately operated insurer would scarcely consider. A final difficulty or deterrent factor to state insurance, considered by many to be of great importance, is to be found in the possibility of insurance projects becoming involved in political upheavals.

Self-Insurance. The plan by which an individual or concern sets up a private fund out of which to pay losses is termed "self-insurance." Where self-insurance can be successfully carried out, there is no doubt that it furnishes the least expensive of all the possible forms. The fund, as it accumulates, belongs to the insured, and he can invest it as he may deem prudent. He pays no commissions to agents, and other costs of operation are reduced to a minimum. No fees are required by the state. Benefits to be derived from care reflect directly to the owner-insurer.

If the owner of a large plant exposed to loss from a single fire cancels all outstanding insurance and instead deposits the annual insurance premium in a fund to meet losses as they occur, it is sometimes said that he is insuring himself. While such a procedure is ordinarily included in the category of self-insurance, it is not insurance at all. There is no hedge, no shifting of the burden of risk. It is merely a gambling chance that no serious loss will occur—at least until the fund has reached a figure sufficient to meet it.

On the other hand, the setup of a chain store company with 1,000 retail outlets widely distributed geographically and much alike physically lends itself readily to a self-insurance plan. If an insurance premium is charged to each store, a fund sufficient to meet any loss that might occur at one time will rapidly accumulate. If each individual store of the chain has an extremely rapid stock turnover and low inventory, the loss to a single store will in no case be great. It will not in any instance be sizable enough to cripple or handicap the business seriously.

To institute a plan of self-insurance there must be a wide distribution of risks subject to the same hazards. The number of the greatest corporations in the country, with a wide distribution of property, who insure their property in commercial insurers and forego the temptation to build up funds of their own even in the face of years of favorable experience affords evidence that comparatively few organizations have an ideal setup for this plan. Certainly no company or individual with a limited number of risks should attempt to use it. Unless a fund is created and operated in accordance with insurance principles, it cannot be said that a business firm or individual is self-insuring. Other methods of meeting risk, not involving a transfer to professional risk takers (insurers) or a formed self-insurance fund, are noninsurance methods and may or may not be effective ways of meeting risk. Many large self-insurers and noninsurers transfer part of their risks through the purchase of excess insurance and thus combine ways of dealing with risk. Governmental units sometimes make use of self-insurance in protecting property because their buildings are often spread over a wide area. Nevertheless, there are situations where transfer to an insurer is to be preferred. If a building burns on a state university campus, for example, a private insurer, assuming the insurance is in order, will provide funds for rebuilding almost immediately, whereas to secure funds through governmental channels may take a considerable period of time.

INTERNAL ORGANIZATION OF INSURERS

Although property and liability insurers differ in terms of the nature of the ownership of the firm, the vast majority of insurers in the United States are organized as stock or mutual corporations and there is a great deal of similarity in the manner in which they conduct their affairs. A board of directors is elected by either the policyholders (mutual insurer) or the stockholders (stock insurer), and the board is responsible for appointing the officers of the firm. Operational complexities often arise in that large insurers may have a number of wholly or partially owned subsidiaries and may do business in all of the states in the United States as well as in some foreign countries. Decentralization is often advisable and the typical, large insurer will have regional offices in major geographical areas, as well as branch offices in smaller areas within a region. Various administrative as well as selling responsibilities are delegated to these offices in order to increase the efficiency of the total organization.

The administrative responsibilities of the home office are discharged by the creation of departments corresponding to lines of business, such as fire, marine, and casualty (although some insurers are now doing away with such divisions) or by function such as sales, underwriting, and legal or by some combination of these basic organizational principles. Overall administrative responsibility is assumed by the chairman of the board and the president and they are assisted by a number of vice presidents and persons with managerial titles. It is not uncommon to find vice presidents in charge of inland marine operations; automobile-casualty; fidelity and related fields; fire, homeowners, and personal lines; ocean marine; group disability and group life. In addition there is often a vice president and general counsel; vice president and actuary; vice presidents in charge of personnel; claims; marketing; organizational planning; and investments. If the insurer operates on a nationwide basis, there may well be vice presidents in charge of regional operations. There are fairly large staffs in support of each of the departments. The diversity of titles reflects the multiple line character of modern property and liability insurers.

Comparatively recently large insurers have established departments of research and product development. These departments have been responsible for the development of new types of contract especially in the field of commercial packages. They have also undertaken marketing research studies and have renewed their interest in risk analysis. In all departments the use of recent developments in the computer field is bringing about changes in the processing of applications, in the keeping of records, in future planning, and in research and development.

FOR DISCUSSION

1. If the power of attorney of a reciprocal exchange provides that the liabilities of subscribers shall be several and not joint, what does this mean?
2. In the event that an underwriter or syndicate at Lloyd's of London should contest a claim, what steps are necessary for the insured to establish his claim? Should he sue the Lloyd's Corporation, an American agent, or must he proceed to sue each individual underwriter in an English court?
3. May a resident of this country buy insurance in an alien insurer if that insurer is not licensed to do business in the United States?
4. Reciprocals, as they are operated today, in an effort to cut the cost of doing business to an irreducible minimum, centralize power of management in the hands of an attorney-in-fact. The powers of the attorney-in-fact, as conferred by a power of attorney signed by all who join the group, are sometimes very broad. Such limitations as are provided often are not made the subject of inquiry by prospective insureds, and it often happens that an insured under a reciprocal contract is unaware of the extent of the rights he has conferred and the obligations he has assumed. Indicate the dangers inherent in the plan.
5. In your opinion, may individuals or unincorporated associations lawfully engage in the business of insurance? In what category would they fall?
6. It has been suggested that the provisions of the American trust

agreement made by Lloyd's were designed to provide additional security for American insureds with Lloyd's underwriters. This is only partly true. What, in your opinion, is the primary reason for the American trust?

7. It is stated in the text that underwriters at Lloyd's of London write all kinds of property insurance. Would you expect this statement to apply to each syndicate and underwriter as well? Give reasons for your answer.
8. Some of the farm mutual fire insurers operate on what is known as the "post loss assessment plan." Explain.
9. The fact that the reciprocal exchange is not of itself a business entity leaves each subscriber with respect to his premium payments much in the same position as a depositor who has opened a checking account in a bank. Explain.
10. What significance has the term "foreign" in the business of insurance?
11. In what class of insurers is the major volume of insurance business written?
12. Distinguish between a stock and a mutual insurer.
13. Distinguish between (*a*) pure assessment mutuals, (*b*) deposit premium mutuals, and (*c*) general-writing mutuals.
14. Outline the plan of London Lloyd's.
15. Discuss the points of similarity and the differences between Lloyd's London and the American Lloyd's group.
16. The text states that the liability of a member of a reciprocal association is several and not joint. Explain the difference between the operation of a reciprocal and a mutual with respect to the distribution of financial resources held by the organization for the payment of losses.
17. Is Lloyd's London a mutual organization?
18. Is there any similarity between the Lloyd's plan and the reciprocal plan?
19. Discuss the shortcomings of a plan of self-insurance for a state and for a municipality.
20. In your opinion, is self-insurance ever feasible? If so, in what circumstances?
21. The prime motivating reason for self-insurance is a savings in cost. On the theory that insurance premiums are a direct charge in full against corporate net profit, some buyers regard premium reduction by self-insurance as money saved for profits. Give the fallacy of the reasoning behind such a conclusion.
22. A press notice indicated that one of the largest coal mining companies in Pennsylvania that had been for many years a self-insurer was having difficulty in placing $19.5 million fire coverage and $16 million business interruption. Why would the fact that the company had been a self-insurer create difficulties when corporate insurance was sought?

CHAPTER • 29

Associations of Insurers

The technical nature of the insurance business with its consequent need for interinsurer data, for educating employees and the public, for cooperation in the underwriting of large risks, and for the prevention of loss and for other interinsurer services has resulted over the years in the development of a large number of associations of insurers that have as a common goal cooperative action in the improvement of insurer operation and in the effectiveness with which insurance meets the needs of the insuring public. The *Insurance Almanac*[1] lists somewhat over 200 organizations in the field of property and liability insurance that operate on a national or regional level and in some manner rely on insurer cooperation for their existence, or, if not directly supported by insurers, at least have as their purpose or one of their purposes the dissemination of information about insurance and insurers. There are over 250 state organizations listed in the *Almanac*, and about 60 local groups.

Insurer associations may be classified in many ways. In addition to a classification based on geographical area, it is possible to distinguish associations by whether they represent and are supported by stock insurers, mutual insurers, reciprocals, or some other type of insurer organization. Within each of these groups the associations can be classified according to purpose or function.[2] Some associations are educational or professional in aim, and their activities center on the education of existing and prospective practitioners of the insurance art. Others are primarily rating bureaus and are concerned with the collection of data for rate-making purposes and with the designing of insurance forms. Still others are underwriting associations or agents' and brokers' organizations or associations primarily concerned with public relations, prevention, salvage, or some type of service.

[1] The *Insurance Almanac* (New York: Underwriter Printing and Publishing Co., 1965).

[2] Some associations cut across organizational lines and may serve all types of insurer.

NATIONAL AND REGIONAL ASSOCIATIONS

The national and regional insurer associations are perhaps the best known of the various associations and the range of their activities covers a wide variety of fields. Some of these activities will be reviewed in order better to understand the significance of insurer cooperation.

Rating Organizations. Rate making in the field of property and liability insurance is largely a function of organizations set up and maintained by insurers, and the rates promulgated by these organizations (or bureaus) are used by all insurers that participate in these cooperative ventures.[3] The first efforts to set up regional rate-making organizations met with bitter opposition. Public hostility reached a high pitch, and opposition was voiced on the ground that cooperative action was monopolistic and contrary to the public interest. As an outgrowth of this opposition, various state legislatures undertook to prohibit cooperative rate making by the enactment of bills that came to be known as "anticompact laws." It soon became apparent to those entrusted with the regulation of insurers that there devolved upon them an important duty that must be given precedence over the problem of securing rate reductions through the operation of unrestrained competition. Recognition of the importance of safeguarding the solvency of insurers was the first step in the direction of ending competitive rates and the establishment of cooperative rate-making agencies. Bills soon appeared in the state legislatures authorizing the association of insurers in the making of rates. Rate-making bureaus are now provided for by legal authority or requirement in several states as a means for regulating competition and stabilizing the business of insurance. Many insurers believe there is waste in duplication of any attempt on the part of each insurer to work out individual rates.

Headquarters for the various organizations are located at strategic points throughout the country. The matter of rate making is more centralized in some instances than in others. The exact nature of the organization depends on the need of the particular type of insurance. Organizations in some cases have jurisdiction over a limited territory, and branch offices sufficient to meet the territory's needs are located in important congested areas. On the other hand, some rate-making organizations operate on a national basis. In this latter category are to be found most automobile, inland marine, and casualty rating organizations. Fire insurance rates are usually made by state bureaus, though in a few instances a single bureau has jurisdiction over more than one

[3] Not all insurers use bureau rates and independent filing of rates with the state insurance authorities is possible. However, most insurers still rely on rating organizations. See Chapter 34.

state. Rate manuals and tariffs are published, usually by the bureau having jurisdiction over their own names. Corrections are furnished from time to time to member or subscribing insurers and their representatives.

National Bureau of Casualty Underwriters. Organized in 1910 as the Workmen's Compensation and Service Information Bureau, this group in 1911 absorbed the Bureau of Liability Insurance Statistics, which had been founded in 1896. The National Bureau of Casualty Underwriters is an unincorporated association of stock insurers. It is also voluntary and nonprofit. Affiliation with the bureau may be on a membership basis or a subscriber basis. There are some 76 insurers that are members, and approximately 200 additional insurers subscribe to the rating service. Membership is open to "any stock company engaged in casualty insurance."[4] This definition encompasses multiple line insurers, since they write many forms of "casualty" insurance. Subscribers need not be stock insurers and the only requirement is that they write "any kind of insurance within the jurisdiction of the Bureau."[5] Voting privileges are extended to members but not to subscribers, although subscribers may be invited to meetings of general interest.

Since the bureau is a national organization, it is "officially recognized as a rating or advisory organization under the rate regulatory laws of all of the states and the District of Columbia and Puerto Rico."[6] Although the bureau has its home office in New York City, it is cognizant of local problems and has six regional branch offices. These offices are located in San Francisco (Pacific Coast Branch), Seattle (Pacific Northwest Branch), Austin (Southwestern Branch), Atlanta (Southeastern Branch), Portland, Maine (Northeastern Branch), Chicago (Midwestern Branch), and Washington (District of Columbia Branch). The scope of the bureau's operation on a national basis is modified to some extent by the requirements of the insurance laws of the various states. North Carolina has "a local statutory automobile liability insurance rating bureau"[7] to which all insurers must belong. Therefore, the National Bureau's license in North Carolina does not include automobile liability insurance. Virginia, Texas, and Louisiana are other examples of states in which rate making in varying degrees is locally controlled. In Massachusetts the rates for compulsory automobile liability insurance are the responsibility of the Commissioner of Insurance. In workmen's compensation the bureau exercises varying degrees of responsibility depending

[4] *National Bureau of Casualty Underwriters* (pamphlet published by the bureau), p. 2.

[5] *Ibid.*

[6] *Ibid.*, p. 15.

[7] *Ibid.*

somewhat on the state and the type of workmen's compensation law.

The bureau is supervised by a committee of 15 member-insurers called the executive committee. Elections are held annually, and procedures have been adopted to insure representation of all members. Member-insurers are divided into four groups according to premium volume. The first group is made up of the six member-insurers with the largest premium volume. The second group also has six members; the third group consists of eight insurers; and the fourth group is comprised of the remaining members. The executive committee always has five members from the first group, four from the second, four from the third, and two from the fourth. In addition to the executive committee, there are a number of standing committees appointed by the executive committee, and there are also a general manager and a constitutional secretary. These two positions are elective and are filled each year by vote of the membership. The standing committees are "actuarial, law and statistical committees, and the automobile, boiler and machinery, burglary, general liability, glass, multiple line, and nuclear energy rating committees."[8] The practical work of the bureau is accomplished through divisions that correspond to the insurance lines represented by the rating committees. The rating committees and the divisions are responsible "for determining proper underwriting rules, classifications of risks, manual rates, coverages, minimum premiums, and rating plans for their respective kinds of insurance."[9]

Cooperation with other rating organizations is a significant aspect of the bureau's work. The continued growth of multiple line insurance, for one thing, has created the need to work with other organizations in the development of multiple line contracts because of the problems associated with the overlapping jurisdiction of rating bureaus. The National Bureau cooperated in the development of an automobile package and has had considerable influence in developing a certain amount of standardization in various insurance contracts.

Multi-Line Insurance Rating Bureau. Founded in 1963, the Multi-Line Insurance Rating Bureau has as a major function the development of rates and premiums for multiple line insurance coverages. It also has the responsibility for filing these rates with the various state insurance departments. The filings may be for member or subscriber insurers and for the multiple line coverages authorized by them. Other functions of the bureau are to engage in research and data collection, "to furnish information, statistics, recommendations, services and advice to members and subscribers and act as their agent to such extent as they may authorize."[10] Research as to forms and cover-

[8] *Ibid.*, p. 3.

[9] *Ibid.*

[10] See the *Insurance Almanac, op. cit.*, p. 207.

ages is handled by the Fire Insurance and Actuarial Association. The officers of the bureau consist of a chairman, vice chairman, and treasurer, who represent insurers. The other officers are a general manager, general counsel, and two secretaries.

The bureau replaces an older organization known as the Multiple Peril Insurance Rating Organization that was organized to deal directly with the multiple line concept and provide rates for multiple peril contracts without resorting to the necessity of putting together a rate based upon the known perils involved. The rating organization approaches the multiple peril premium on much the same basis that the ocean marine underwriter approaches the premium for sea perils, by assuming it to be indivisible with respect to specific perils. There is no separate charge in the ocean marine rate for all the various sea perils covered. The premium covers the voyage subject to certain exceptions. The same is true with respect to fire and lightning in the fire insurance contract. There is no separate premium for fire and another charge for lightning. By maintaining records for risks in the multiple peril category, separate hazards are not considered but all are grouped in a single risk. Thus the philosophy of multiple peril rating contemplates loss data by risk and not by peril. The bureau undertakes to maintain a statistical basis for the promulgation of rates that is free from dilution with results that are not comparable.

National Council on Compensation Insurance. Formerly the National Council on Workmen's Compensation Insurance, the present organization was founded in 1922, and its membership consists of insurers (stock, mutual, reciprocal, state fund) that write workmen's compensation insurance. The objectives of the council are: "(1) the making or rates for workmen's compensation and employers' liability insurance; (2) the collection and tabulation of statistics bearing thereon; (3) the development of rating plans and systems that will not only measure the hazard of each risk but will produce the greatest possible accident prevention effect, and (4) the administration of such rates and rating systems in the interests of the insured, the carrier and the public generally."[11] The affairs of the council are mainly handled by two committees which are the governing committee and the rates committee. The officers of the council consist of a general manager, assistant general manager, secretaries, secretary-treasurer, assistant secretaries, statistician, and comptroller. Its headquarters are in New York City.

Crop-Hail Insurance Actuarial Association. This group was established in 1947 by 62 fire insurers organized as stock companies. When first organized, the Crop-Hail Insurance Actuarial Association did not have the authority to act as a rating bureau but rather was

[11] *Cyclopedia of Insurance in the United States* (Paterson, N.J.: Index Publishing Co., 1965), p. 441.

intended "as a statistical and advisory organization to state fire insurance rating bureaus giving advice as to crop-hail insurance rates and forms."[12] Subsequently, by amendment of the association's constitution (1953), it gained the authority to act as a national rating organization and later (1959) was authorized to rate "rain insurance on public events, business ventures, and private proceedings."[13]

The association conducts its affairs in a manner similar to other rate-making organizations. There is a manager of the association and over 50 salaried employees, as well as an executive committee, which has responsibility for policy matters, and an actuarial and forms committee. Additionally there is a research committee appointed by the executive committee, a priority committee, and a rain insurance committee. A somewhat unique feature of the association is that it has 18 regional committees, which afford a means of making local contact throughout the United States. These committees make recommendations to the association about their geographical areas.

The association's headquarters is in Chicago, and there are now over 100 members and subscribers made up largely of fire insurers organized on a stock basis. Operating expenses are met by assessing the supporting insurers annually. The amount paid by each insurer depends on premiums written.

Inland Marine Insurance Bureau. Headquartered in New York City, the Inland Marine Insurance Bureau was founded in 1945 as a nonprofit rating bureau supported by stock insurers. A major purpose of the bureau is the gathering and analysis of statistical data, which in turn will be used to establish such items as rates, underwriting rules, and risk classifications. The bureau also provides the opportunity for members to discuss rating and related matters and to exchange views. It also is interested in preventing unfair discrimination and in promoting the best possible underwriting practices. The officers consist of a general manager, an assistant general manager, and counsel.[14]

Transportation Insurance Rating Bureau. The Transportation Insurance Rating Bureau has its headquarters in Chicago and is an association of mutual insurers. It was organized in 1946 and is the successor organization to the Mutual Marine Conference and the Mutual Aircraft Conference. The bureau files rates, rules, and forms for members and subscribers in the inland marine, aircraft hull, and multiple line fields. With the exception of Missouri it is licensed in all of the states. It is also authorized to operate in the District of Columbia and Puerto Rico. The purposes of the bureau are similar to the Inland Marine Insurance Bureau. It has a special interest in prevention

---

[12] R. J. Roth, "The Rating of Crop-Hail Insurance."

[13] *Ibid.*, p. 111.

[14] See Chapter 13.

and works with the National Safety Council and the National Fire Protection Association. The chief officers of the bureau are the chairman of the executive committee and the manager.

Southeastern Underwriters Association.[15] The Southeastern Underwriters Association, a nonprofit association, has its headquarters in Atlanta and was organized in 1882. It is a regional organization and serves the states of Alabama, Florida, Georgia, North Carolina, South Carolina, and Virginia. Its members are fire insurers organized on a capital stock basis. There are now 104 member insurers and 329 subscribers. The subscriber insurers are not limited to stock insurers but include mutual and reciprocal insurers as well. The association is primarily a rating bureau but it also provides engineering services to its members and subscribers. The officers consist of a president, vice president, manager, a number of secretaries, and a treasurer.[16]

Other Rating Organizations. There are a number of organizations other than the ones analyzed here that serve as rating bureaus on a national or regional basis. Among these organizations are New England Insurance Rating Bureau, Aviation Insurance Rating Bureau, Nuclear Insurance Rating Bureau, Factory Mutual Rating Bureau, Mutual Insurance Rating Bureau, Middle Department Association of Fire Underwriters, National Automobile Underwriters Association, Pacific Fire Rating Bureau, The Surety Association of America, and Western Actuarial Bureau. Brief descriptions of these organizations may be found in the *Insurance Almanac*.

Underwriting Organizations. Of increasing importance to the marketing of insurance are insurer organizations that through cooperation provide a strong domestic market for the insuring of risks of a magnitude that might not otherwise be undertaken by individual insurers. The American Hull Insurance Syndicate, which was discussed in Chapter 11, is an example of an organization with sufficient capacity to insure ships that represent very high values. The American Marine Insurance Syndicate for Insurance of Builder's Risks is another example of cooperative effort to provide adequate capacity to protect builders of ships and others with an insurable interest. In the nonmarine field the Cotton Insurance Association, Mutual Atomic Energy Liability Underwriters, Nuclear Energy Liability Insurance Association, Nuclear Energy Property Insurance Association, and Oil Insurance Association are illustrative of the organizations that serve to enlarge the insurance market.

Cotton Insurance Association. The Cotton Insurance Association was established in 1905 with headquarters in Atlanta, Georgia. It has branch offices in Memphis, Tennessee; Fresno, California; Dallas,

[15] See Chapter 34.

[16] For a listing of presidents of the association from 1882 until the present time, see *Cyclopedia of Insurance in the United States, op. cit.*, pp. 359–60.

Texas; Houston, Texas; Montgomery, Alabama; Raleigh, North Carolina; Columbia, South Carolina; and Phoenix, Arizona. The association issues insurance contracts "on cotton under per bale form for buyers, shippers, spinners, compresses, warehouses and railroads."[17] The contracts are issued through the association on any "one of its member insurers on their affiliated insurers or underwriters."[18] The principal officers of the association are a chairman, manager, and assistant manager.

Mutual Atomic Energy Liability Underwriters. Headquartered in Chicago, the Mutual Atomic Energy Liability Underwriters is an "underwriting syndicate of six mutual casualty insurers."[19] This syndicate is the agency that writes primary nuclear energy liability insurance contracts for business, industry, and research organizations. It also serves as a reinsurer for the Nuclear Energy Liability Insurance Association. The underwriters in turn cede 100 percent of all insurance and reinsurance to the American Mutual Reinsurance Company. This company then retrocedes to 102 members of the Mutual Atomic Energy Reinsurance Pool. The contracts that are issued provide "liability protection against radiation liability hazards arising out of or pertaining to (*a*) nuclear reactor installations designed for experimental, testing or power purposes, and (*b*) operations or facilities related or incident thereto."[20]

Nuclear Energy Liability Insurance Association. The Nuclear Energy Liability Insurance Association with headquarters in New York City is a syndicate of insurers organized on a stock basis and is the stock counterpart of the Mutual Atomic Energy Liability Underwriters. Its purposes and contracts are similar to those of the underwriters. Insurance is provided by the cooperating insurers on a several rather than a joint basis. The officers consist of a general manager, a secretary-treasurer, and a general counsel.

Other Underwriting Organizations. The associations selected for analysis by no means exhaust the underwriting organizations that operate on a national basis. The Nuclear Energy Property Insurance Association, which is a "voluntary, nonprofit unincorporated association of 154 stock insurers,"[21] provides through its members property insurance protection against nuclear hazards. Other organizations are the United States Aviation Insurance Group, the Building Owners Federation of Mutual Insurance Companies, the Cotton Fire and Marine Underwriters, the Crop Insurance Group, the Excise Bond Underwriters, the Farm Underwriters Association, the Foreign Credit

---

[17] See the *Insurance Almanac, op. cit.*, p. 195.

[18] *Ibid.*

[19] *Ibid.*, p. 207.

[20] *Ibid.*, p. 208.

[21] *Ibid.*

Insurance Association, Railroad Insurance Underwriters, Rain and Hail Insurance Bureau, and the Tugboat Underwriting Syndicate. All of these organizations play a significant role in enlarging insurance capacity.

Reinsurance Organizations. In addition to direct writing associations there are organizations that provide reinsurance by dividing liability among member-insurers. Among the associations operating on a national basis are the Mutual Reinsurance Bureau; American Cargo War Risk Reinsurance Exchange; Associated Lumber Mutuals; Coastwise, Great Lakes, and Inland Hull Association (reinsurance and coinsurance); Excess and Casualty Reinsurance Association; Furriers' Customers Reinsurance Syndicate; and the Mutual Atomic Energy Reinsurance Pool.

The Mutual Reinsurance Bureau may be taken as an illustration of how the associations just mentioned conduct their business. The bureau was organized in 1921 by the "Federation of Mutual Fire Insurance Companies and the National Association of Mutual Insurance Companies for the purpose of providing authorized mutual capacity and reinsurance throughout the United States on a multiple-line basis."[22] Pro rata and excess of loss contracts are written and automatic reinsurance is provided. The bureau holds an annual meeting, and there are the usual officers, including an account executive.

Educational Organizations. The insurance business has long been interested in educational and training activities designed to provide the background needed by employees and related personnel for the successful pursuit of an insurance career. These activities have taken many forms. Insurers have often cooperated with colleges and universities in their insurance courses and departments. They have also developed extensive in-company programs, and the larger insurers have directors of education, who in turn have a number of persons assisting them. Another activity has centered around cooperation with other insurers in the support of organizations that have as a major purpose the advancement of insurance in a professional sense. These organizations in some instances are primarily professional societies, such as the American Risk and Insurance Association, whose educational function is limited to publications of journals and the holding of meetings and seminars. In other instances they combine a professional purpose with examinations for membership and a prescribed course of study. Examples of these organizations are the Casualty Actuarial Society and, in the life insurance field, the Society of Actuaries. In some situations the organizations are not properly classified as professional societies or as societies actively engaged in giving courses or setting examinations. Instead they serve to support research and teach-

[22] *Ibid.*, p. 210.

ing and accomplishment in insurance in general. Organizations of this type are the Charles W. Griffith Memorial Foundation for Insurance Education, the Harry J. Loman Foundation, and the Commission on Insurance Terminology.

In the property and liability insurance field the following organizations are among the major associations that are directly related in varying degrees to insurance education: American Risk and Insurance Association; American Institute for Property and Liability Underwriters, Inc.; American Marine Insurance Forum; American Academy of Actuaries; Casualty Actuarial Society; College of Insurance; Commission on Insurance Terminology; Committee on Interpretation of the Nation-Wide Marine Definition; Conference of Mutual Casualty Companies, Inc.; Conference of Special Risk Underwriters; the Charles W. Griffith Memorial Foundation for Insurance Education, which, among its other activities, administers the Insurance Hall of Fame; Insurance Underwriters Association of the Pacific; Insurance Institute of America; the Harry J. Loman Foundation; and The Society of Chartered Property and Casualty Underwriters. A few of these associations will be discussed briefly in order to provide additional information on their organization and purpose.

The American Institute for Property and Liability Underwriters, Inc. This organization was formed in 1942 primarily as a result of a resolution passed in 1940 by the American Association of University Teachers of Insurance (now the American Risk and Insurance Association). This resolution endorsed "in principle the establishment of professional standards for property and casualty insurance" and expressed "willingness to cooperate in an advisory capacity with representatives of the insurance institution in attainment of this goal."[23] A first step in the formation of the American Institute for Property and Liability Underwriters, Inc. was a meeting with representatives of the following insurance associations: the American Mutual Insurance Alliance; the Association of Casualty and Surety Executives; the National Association of Insurance Agents; the National Association of Mutual Insurance Agents; the National Association of Insurance Brokers; and the National Board of Fire Underwriters (now a part of the American Insurance Association). As a result of this meeting and reports of committees that were appointed, the American Institute of Property and Liability Underwriters was incorporated as a nonprofit institution.

The purposes of the institute as recommended by the founding committees have been stated in the following way; the new institution should be "formed for the purpose of:

[23]The facts about the American Institute are based on the *Announcement* of that organization for 1965–66. The quotation is from page 7. The insurer associations that are listed are also from page 7.

1. Establishing educational standards and administering them so that properly qualified property and casualty underwriters might be recognized with a professional designation.
2. Encouraging and fostering the training of students in educational institutions and under competent instructors for the career of professional property and casualty underwriters; and
3. Cooperating with educational institutions in property and casualty insurance education.[24]

The aims of the institute are carried out through a number of specific activities. The main one is that of professional certification, which is accomplished through the administration of a series of five examinations, as well as an investigation of the "business reputation and moral character of the candidates."[25] The professional designation that is given is that of Chartered Property and Casualty Underwriter (C.P.C.U.). The institute actively encourages agents, brokers, and others in their efforts to acquire professional competence, and, although it does not offer any courses, it does encourage study groups designed to help the student prepare for examinations.

The educational program prescribed by the institute covers property and liability insurance, as well as the related areas of economics, government and business, business law, management, accounting, and finance. The first examination covers insurance principles and practices; the second, analysis of insurance functions; the third, economics and government and business; the fourth, insurance and business law; and the fifth, management, accounting, and finance. Before the candidate may take the examinations, he must demonstrate that he is a high school graduate or has had equivalent work. Also, before receiving the C.P.C.U. designation the candidate must, in addition to passing the examinations, fulfill certain experience requirements. There are examination centers in all of the states, as well as in a number of foreign countries. Reading lists and other materials are available to students who are preparing for the examinations.

In addition to its officers the institute is governed by a board of trustees made up mainly of persons holding high office with various insurers. There is a registration committee, an executive committee, and an examination committee, as well as a council of educational advisers. Various insurers and insurance associations provide financial support through contributions.

Insurance Institute of America, Inc. Founded in 1909 in Philadelphia, Pennsylvania, it is the "oldest continuously functioning national educational body" in the field of property and liability insurance.[26] It is administered jointly with the American Institute of Property and

[24] *Ibid.*, p. 8.

[25] *Ibid.*

[26] See *Announcement,* 1965–66 (Bryn Mawr, Pa.: Insurance Institute of America).

Liability Underwriters and the officers of the two organizations are identical. The Insurance Institute of America, Inc., supports three major programs: the program in general insurance, the program in insurance adjusting, and the program in risk management. There are advisory committees, made up mainly of representatives of insurers, for the programs in risk management and insurance adjusting and an examination committee for the program in general insurance.

The general insurance program involves three examinations, one in the general principles of insurance, one in the principles of fire, marine, and allied lines, and one in the principles of casualty insurance and surety bonding. If the examinations are completed successfully, the candidate is awarded a certificate in general insurance. The program in insurance adjusting consists of six parts: part 1 covers the principles of insurance and property loss adjusting; part 2, the principles of insurance and liability claim adjusting; part 3, the principles of fire, marine, and allied lines insurance; part 4, the principles of casualty insurance and surety bonding; part 5, property insurance adjusting; and part 6, liability insurance adjusting. Successful completion of the examinations covering each of these parts leads to a diploma in insurance loss and claim adjusting. The program in risk management is conducted with the cooperation of the American Society of Insurance Management, Inc., and, like the program in adjusting, is in six parts. The subject matter areas that are covered are the general principles of insurance; principles of fire, marine, and allied lines; principles of casualty insurance and surety bonding; principles of risk management; practices in risk management; and management and finance. The first three parts of this series are identical to the first three parts of the general insurance program. Successful completion of the program leads to a diploma in risk management.

Insurance Underwriters Association of the Pacific. A regional rather than a national organization it is the oldest insurance educational association in the United States and the second oldest in the world. It was founded in 1876 in Virginia City, Nevada, by a group of fire adjusters. The Insurance Underwriters Association of the Pacific Association conducts insurance classes and has done so continuously since 1905. In addition to classes the association provides a forum "for the consideration and discussion of problems."[27] Until recently it maintained an insurance library, which was founded in 1878. The association held its first annual meeting in San Francisco in 1877. There have been annual meetings since then.

College of Insurance. An outgrowth of the School of Insurance that had been operated for many years by the Insurance Society of New York, the College of Insurance was organized in February, 1962.

[27] *Proceedings of the 83rd Annual Meeting* (San Francisco, Calif.: Insurance Underwriters Association of the Pacific, 1959).

The college is a degree-granting institution and awards the B.B.A. degree (Bachelor of Business Administration). In order to receive the degree the student must earn 128 credits, approximately half of which must result from liberal arts courses. There are both day and evening divisions and extension work is offered in Westchester County, New York, and on Long Island and in East Orange, New Jersey. A notable aspect of the day division is the work-study program in which the student alternates study in the college with work in insurance offices. There are a number of certificate programs including one in multiple line insurance. Also, an M.B.A. program was recently established.

Casualty Actuarial Society. Although the present name of the organization was not adopted until 1921, the Casualty Actuarial Society was established in 1914. Its original name was the Casualty Actuarial and Statistical Society of America. In its early years the society was mainly concerned with actuarial problems in workmen's compensation and in sickness and disability insurance, but now, as a result of amending the bylaws in 1960, it has an interest in a variety of technical problems in all lines of insurance other than life. The society is composed of Fellows and Associates. Both of these membership grades are reached through passing of associateship and fellowship examinations. The society now has a membership of approximately 400 persons,[28] and publishes a journal called the *Proceedings.*

American Academy of Actuaries. Four actuarial societies cooperated in founding this new organization, the American Academy of Actuaries, which was organized in Montreal, Canada, in 1965. They were the Society of Actuaries, the Casualty Actuarial Society, the Conference of Actuaries in Public Practice, and the Fraternal Actuarial Association. In stating the reasons for organizing a new society the founding group stated that "at present there are no legal provisions, federal or state, that specify the technical education and experience required to qualify a man as an actuary."[29] It is planned that the academy will have only one class of membership and that all qualified actuaries will belong. It is one of the aims of the organization to have its members recognized legally as qualified actuaries and to this end a charter is being sought from Congress. Membership in the academy will be extended automatically to the existing senior members of the four parent actuarial societies. Others, including the junior members of these organizations, must apply for membership.

American Risk and Insurance Association. In December, 1932, the American Risk and Insurance Association was organized as the American Association of University Teachers of Insurance. It adopted its present name in 1961. There were ten charter members who founded the society primarily for the purposes of (1) providing

[28] See *Cyclopedia of Insurance in the United States, op. cit.,* p. 513.

[29] *National Underwriter,* November 12, 1965, p. 58.

a way for college and university teachers of insurance to exchange ideas about insurance curricula and other problems relating to the teaching of insurance and (2) promoting fundamental and applied insurance research. The association was organized originally as an independent section of the American Economics Association and for many years held its annual meetings at the same time and in the same place as that organization. Since 1963, the American Risk and Insurance Association has been meeting independently. One of the principal activities of the association is the publication of the *Journal of Risk and Insurance*, which appears quarterly and contains articles of interest to all persons engaged in insurance and insurance research. For many years membership in the association was limited to academic persons. In 1947 associate memberships were created and these were intended for persons and institutions engaged in the insurance business. At present (1966) there are approximately 400 academic members, 900 nonacademic members, and 200 institutional members in the association.

Commission on Insurance Terminology. A standing committee of the American Risk and Insurance Association, the Commission on Insurance Terminology was established in 1958. The commission is made up of six committees[30] and meets annually, although the separate committees may meet more often. The commission's main interest is in encouraging a more effective use of insurance words and phrases by publishing definitions of words that are generally agreed upon by insurance educators and practitioners. Through this process it is hoped that the present confusion in insurance language will be lessened.

The Charles W. Griffith Memorial Foundation for Insurance Education. In 1947 the Charles W. Griffith Memorial Foundation for Insurance Education was established in honor of a young Columbus, Ohio, insurance agent who lost his life in World War II. It is supported by insurers, insurance associations, and agencies, and by individuals. The activities of the foundation include "awarding of scholarships at Ohio colleges, development of research projects, publication of qualified insurance materials, stimulation of student interest in campus insurance societies, career guidance in many insurance fields, cooperation for the Annual Insurance Conference held at The Ohio State University, sponsorship of the Insurance Hall of Fame, and encouraging better insurance public relations and understanding through improved insurance education."[31]

Producers Organizations. Although producers organizations, defined as associations of agents or brokers, are not technically asso-

---

[30] For the names of these committees, see page 11.

[31] See *Announcement of the Griffith Memorial Foundation* (Columbus, Ohio: Griffith Memorial Foundation).

ciations of insurers, they are organizations closely related to the interests of insurers and are composed of persons who sell insurance contracts and who represent, except for brokers,[32] a large number of insurers. On a national (and/or regional) level the following associations have been formed to represent the interests of agents: National Association of Insurance Agents, Inc.; National Association of Mutual Insurance Agents; National Insurance Producers Conference; National Association of Casualty and Surety Agents; American Association of Managing General Agents, and the Northwest General Agents Association. The insurance brokers have as their organization the National Association of Insurance Brokers, Inc. Some of the facts about three or four of these organizations will serve to point up some of their functions.

National Association of Insurance Agents, Inc.[33] This group is the oldest of the producers organizations (property and liability) and was founded in Chicago in 1896. A group of 20 agents met at the Great Northern Hotel in September of that year and drew up plans for an association of agents. Today there are over 36,000 members of the association. The first name selected for the organization was the National Association of Local Fire Insurance Agents. The principal officers of the association are the president, vice president, executive secretary, and treasurer. There are also a number of committees, having titles of agency management, casualty, educational, fidelity and surety, finance, local board and membership, metropolitan and large lines agents, property, rural agents, safety, and technical conference that help with the work of the organization including the executive committee, which has a general supervisory function. The first president of the association was A. G. Simrall of Covington, Kentucky. The person who was perhaps most responsible for the idea of such an association was R. S. Brannen of Denver, Colorado.

The primary purpose of the National Association of Insurance Agents, Inc. has been to "uphold the principle of capital stock insurance, as well as the American Agency System, which system is defined to be 'the production of insurance premiums and the servicing of insurance contracts by insurance agents operating solely on a commission basis on their own account as independent contractors, who maintain their own offices separate and apart from any production office maintained by an insurance company.' "[34] The aims of the Association have been carried out through a large number of activities including the publication of the *American Agency Bulletin.* The association has taken stands on such problems as the ownership of

[32] Brokers represent the insured. See Chapter 31.

[33] See W. H. Bennett, *The History of the National Association of Insurance Agents* (Cincinnati, Ohio: National Underwriter Co., 1955).

[34] See the *Insurance Almanac, op. cit.*, p. 213.

expirations, agents licensing laws, bank agencies, automobile dealers as insurance agents, and the governmental supervision of insurance. There are representatives of the association in Washington, D.C. and a column entitled "Window on Washington" appears regularly in the *Bulletin*. The association has long had an interest in education and since 1940 there has been an educational director, who is responsible for supervising the association's educational work.

The National Association has four regional or territorial conferences (associations). A fifth conference, the Rocky Mountain Territories Conference, was disbanded in 1962. The Eastern Agents Conference encompasses the states of Connecticut, Delaware, Maine, Maryland, Massachusetts, New Hampshire, New Jersey, New York, Pennsylvania, Rhode Island, and Vermont. Organized in 1938 the Far West Agents Conference has headquarters in Berkeley, California, and is made up of representatives from Alaska, Arizona, California, Idaho, Hawaii, Nevada, Oregon, Montana, Utah, and Washington. The Southern Agents Conference was started in 1943 and includes the area represented by West Virginia, Virginia, North Carolina, South Carolina, Georgia, Florida, Alabama, Mississippi, Louisiana, Arkansas, Tennessee, Washington, D.C., and Puerto Rico. The Midwest Territorial Conference, which was organized in 1949, has as one of its purposes that of providing "a vehicle for reviewing forms and coverages with the various agency stock insurance companies in the area of the Western Actuarial Bureau.[35] It covers the states of Illinois, Indiana, Iowa, Kansas, Kentucky, Michigan, Missouri, Nebraska, North Dakota, Ohio, Oklahoma, South Dakota, and Wisconsin.

National Association of Mutual Insurance Agents. Organized in 1931, the National Association of Mutual Insurance Agents has headquarters in Washington, D.C. It is in many ways the mutual counterpart of the National Association of Insurance Agents. Among the purposes of the Association of Mutual Agents is that of promoting "the public benefits of mutual insurance sold and serviced by local independent mutual agents."[36] Other purposes[37] are to encourage a high standard of ethics, to oppose state or federal insurers, and to promote friendship and cooperation among mutual agents. In general the association tries to support the interests of mutual agents, and if necessary, to champion their rights. As is the case with the National Association of Insurance Agents, the Mutual Association has an interest in education and supports educational activities, including regional or state institutes or seminars designed to instruct agents in various phases of insurance.

---

[35] *Ibid.*, p. 206.

[36] *Ibid.*, p. 214.

[37] This list is not complete. For a more detailed discussion see *ibid.*, p. 215.

National Association of Casualty and Surety Agents. Headquartered in New York City, the National Association of Casualty and Surety Agents was started in 1913. The officers consist of a president, vice president, secretary, and treasurer. There is also an executive secretary. One function of the association is to promote good public relations and cooperation with other agencies. It is also interested in strengthening private enterprise and maintaining competition in the insurance market. Fields of insurance that are represented are casualty, surety, fire, and marine. The executive committee of 12 persons is made up of insurer representatives from various parts of the United States.

National Association of Insurance Brokers. This association was established in 1934 and since that time has played a significant role in supporting the interests of insurance brokers throughout the United States. The National Association of Casualty and Surety Agents keeps abreast of insurance legislation both state and national and works with the National Association of Insurance Commissioners. It publishes a weekly newsletter and, in general, serves a public relations function as this relates to informing the public about the duties and functions of insurance brokers. The association also presents the views of brokers "before company bureaus, boards, and governmental agencies."[38] The organization of the association is much like that of the National Association of Insurance Agents.

Public Relations and Related Organizations. There are a number of insurer organizations, some of which have been in existence since the latter part of the 19th century, that are not rating bureaus or are not primarily concerned with educating insurance personnel or are not concerned with providing a specific service such as adjusting. These organizations, rather, were established to promote the interests of insurance generally or in specific fields and may be broadly classified as public relations organizations. Among such organizations are the Insurance Information Institute, American Mutual Insurance Alliance, National Association of Mutual Insurance Companies, American Reciprocal Insurance Association, Association of Mill Elevator Mutual Insurance Companies, and the National Federation of Grange Mutual Insurance Companies. A few of the facts about the organization and purposes of the Insurance Information Institute, the National Association of Mutual Insurance Companies, and the American Mutual Alliance will be reviewed.

Insurance Information Institute.[39] Organized in 1959 with headquarters in New York City, the Insurance Information Institute is a "public information and public education agency." It is supported by

[38] The *Insurance Almanac, op. cit.,* p. 213.

[39] The facts in this section are from a brochure of the Insurance Information Institute.

194 insurers organized as stock companies. In addition it receives support from the American Insurance Association, Fire Insurance Research and Actuarial Association, Inland Marine Insurance Bureau, Inland Marine Underwriters Association, Multi-Line Insurance Rating Bureau, National Automobile Underwriters Association, National Bureau of Casualty Underwriters, and the Surety Association of America. The activities of the institute cover all lines of insurance with the exception of life, accident, and health. Although the Institute is primarily responsible for supplying public relations services to the organizations supporting it, it also provides public relations services to the Association of Texas Fire and Casualty Companies, General Adjustment Bureau, National Automobile Theft Bureau, National Insurance Actuarial and Statistical Association, Underwriters Adjusting Company, and Underwriters Salvage Company of New York. These organizations are supported in turn by many of the insurers who support the institute. The institute has four regional offices, one in Chicago (Midwestern), one in San Francisco (Pacific), one in Atlanta (Southeastern), and one in Dallas (Southwestern).

The objectives of the institute correspond in many ways to the objectives of the public relations function generally. Public relations has been defined as "the planned effort of a business organization or other institution to integrate itself into the society in which it exists."[40] This definition implies that public relations goes beyond publicity or promotion and includes the threefold purpose of evaluation, counseling, and communication. The objectives and purposes of the institute are both general and specific. The general objectives are: "(1) to achieve improved public understanding of the business of property and liability insurance; (2) to broaden public recognition of the social and economic import of insurance; and (3) to increase public acceptance of the policies, practices, and services of the insurance business."[41] Among the specific objectives are the creation of an awareness among insurer representatives of the importance of the insurance function in the economy and the need to represent it effectively; the establishment of lines of communication among insurers, agents, and brokers; the advancement of the public understanding of the principles of property and liability insurance; the encouragement among educators of the necessity to provide students with a basic understanding of insurance; the establishment of the institute as an "authoritative and reliable source of information concerning property, liability, surety, and inland marine insurance"; the helping of insurers with their public relations problems; and the establishment of a satisfactory relationship with regulatory authorities.

---

[40] J. C. Bateman, *The Public Relations Function in our Society* (New York: Insurance Information Institute, 1964), p. 3.

[41] From a brochure of the Insurance Information Institute.

The objectives of the institute are implemented through a number of activities which include the publication of the *Journal of Insurance Information*, the preparation of instructional aids for distribution to schools, the holding of seminars for insurance teachers in colleges and universities, and the distribution of speeches and articles dealing with insurance to persons who might have a particular interest in them. An important aspect of the institute is its multiple line orientation and its consequent interest in many aspects of property and liability insurance.

Western Insurance Information Service. A regional organization with objectives similar to the Insurance Information Institute but limited to the business of casualty insurance, the Western Insurance Information Service was organized in 1952. It operates in the Western states of Arizona, California, Colorado, Idaho, Montana, Nevada, New Mexico, Oregon, Utah, Washington, and Wyoming. Among its purposes is to "promote and encourage a widespread, dedicated dissemination to the general public of unbiased insurance information . . ."[42] The home office of the service is in Los Angeles, California, with branch offices in San Francisco, California, and Seattle, Washington. The officers consist of the chairman of the executive committee, president, vice president, secretary-treasurer, and assistant secretary-treasurer.

National Association of Mutual Insurance Companies. One of the oldest of the national insurance organizations and the oldest in the field of mutual insurers, the National Association of Mutual Insurance Companies was founded in 1895. It now has a membership of about 1,300 mutual fire and casualty insurers, nearly three fourths of which are county, township, or farmers mutuals. The objectives of the association are "(1) to maintain cooperation between companies and associations of these companies; (2) to gather information to promote the interest of all mutual insurance; (3) to help eliminate hazards and cooperate in the prevention of losses; (4) to encourage uniform enactment of mutual insurance laws; (5) to publicize the association and its members; and (6) to establish, conduct, and maintain departments, bureaus, services, and publications."[43] Although the objectives of the association are not solely those of public relations, many of the activities deal with promoting the interests of the member-insurers.

The association has three elected officers consisting of the president, vice president, and treasurer. The appointed officers are a secretary and two assistant secretaries. There are 15 persons on the board of directors. There are association committees on communications, education, and training, loss prevention, and membership. Addition-

---

[42] The *Insurance Almanac, op. cit.*, p. 231.

[43] *Yearbook* (National Association of Mutual Insurance Companies, 1962), p. 23.

ally, there are conference sections with the titles, casualty conference, crop-hail conference, farm fire conference, farm windstorm conference, and fire and allied lines conference. There are also state associations in 30 states and four affiliated mutual organizations which are the Eastern Federation of Mutual Insurance Companies, Federation of Mutual Fire Insurance Companies, Mutual Fire Insurance Association of New England, and National Federation of Grange Mutual Insurance Companies.

American Mutual Insurance Alliance. This group was established in 1922 as an association of "major mutual property-casualty" insurers. The headquarters of the American Mutual Insurance Alliance are in Chicago with branches in New York City, Boston, Washington, D.C., San Francisco, Atlanta, and Denver. Although its objectives are not solely public relations, it does have a public relations director and is interested in the general welfare and cooperation of mutual insurers and in promulgating the advantages of insurance offered by mutuals. Other objectives include research and the furtherance of insurance education; cooperation with governmental authorities in matters of the regulation of insurance and ethical behavior of those associated with the insurance industry; and the use of mutual insurance in foreign trade. The president, vice president, and treasurer are from large mutual insurers. The routine operations of the alliance are supervised by a general manager. The alliance publishes the *Journal of American Insurance* five times a year. The articles deal with a variety of topics of interest to the insuring public. A recent issue, for example, contained articles on the traffic accident problem, slum areas, fee courts for traffic offenses, power mowers, health insurance, and the federal crop indemnity program. In recent years each issue has contained a brief statement about one of the state insurance commissioners.

Other Organizations with a Public Relations Function. There are other organizations such as the National Federation of Grange Mutual Insurance Companies, the American Reciprocal Insurance Association, and the National Association of Independent Insurers that have a general interest in public relations as a part of their program. The Chamber or Commerce of the United States, although not an organization of insurers, has an interest in insurance and often takes a position in insurance matters affecting the public. Speakers bureaus represent another type of public relations activity that exists among insurers.

Service Organizations. There is a large group of insurer organizations that were established primarily to provide certain services to insurers or to establish a way to bring persons together whose interests are largely in the services area. Among areas that are to be examined here are prevention, adjusting, and purchasing. Salvage organizations are considered in a later chapter.[44] Examples of organizations that do not fit in these particular classifications but are essentially service in character are the Standard Forms Bureau and the Insurance Data Processing Center.

Prevention. Among the organizations with a primary interest in prevention are Mill Material Fire Protection Bureau, Cotton Warehouse Inspection Service, Factory Insurance Association, American Society of Safety Engineers, Association of Mutual Insurance Engineers, Factory Mutual Companies, National Fire Protection Association, the Society of Fire Protection Engineers, and Insurance Institute for Highway Safety. By way of illustration three of these organizations will be discussed briefly.

American Society of Safety Engineers. The American Society of Safety Engineers was founded in 1911 and has headquarters in Chicago. The organization is not made up solely of insurers but many insuring organizations participate in the affairs of the group.

Representatives of insurers are currently among the principal officers. Among the purposes of the organization is the application of the principles of safety engineering to the prevention of accidents and the protection of property. The society does not limit its interests to safety as related to property and liability insurance. It also is interested in problems relating to the conservation of health and prolongation of life.

National Fire Protection Association. Founded in 1896 with headquarters in Boston, Massachusetts, the National Fire Protection Association is one of the oldest organizations in the field of prevention. Insurers take an active interest in the association, although membership includes industrial and commercial organizations, public officials including fire chiefs and fire marshals, public utilities, and colleges. Any individual interested in the objectives of the association may join. The association has over 100 technical committees that establish standards of fire protection. Among the publications of the association is the *Fire Journal* and the *Handbook of Fire Protection.* The affairs of the organization are under the direction of a general manager.

Factory Insurance Association. The Factory Insurance Association, a nonprofit organization, was organized in 1890 and has headquarters in Hartford, Connecticut. The association is supported by 68 leading fire insurers organized as stock companies. In addition to the national office, there are three regional offices, one in the East, one in the Midwest, and one on the Pacific Coast. The association is "a service organization providing specialized insurance and complete fire protection engineering services for highly protected risks in the continental United States."[45] The association has a large staff of inspectors

[44] See Chapter 33.

[45] See *Cyclopedia of Insurance in the United States, op. cit.,* p. 314.

and engineers and also maintains underwriting and adjustment facilities. The organization operates under the direction of a general manager.

Adjusting. The General Adjustment Bureau, Inc., the Hail Insurance Adjustment and Research Association, and the Underwriter Adjusting Company are major insurer organizations in the adjustment field. Of these organizations perhaps the General Adjustment Bureau, Inc. is the best known.

General Adjustment Bureau, Inc. The General Adjustment Bureau was founded in 1906. Its headquarters are in New York City. It is a national loss adjusting organization, although it has not always operated on a national basis. Only during the last 36 years of its history has the bureau been national in scope. It is supported by approximately 300 property and liability insurers organized on a stock basis. The work of the bureau is carried out through geographical departments, each of which has a general manager. The Eastern Department is responsible for Connecticut, Delaware, Washington, D.C., Maine, Maryland, Massachusetts, New Hampshire, New Jersey, New York, Pennsylvania, Rhode Island, Vermont, and West Virginia. The Pacific Coast Department covers the states of Alaska, Arizona, California, Colorado, Hawaii, Idaho, Montana, Nevada, Oregon, Utah, Washington, and Wyoming. The Southeastern Department covers Alabama, Florida, Georgia, Kentucky, Mississippi, North Carolina, South Carolina, Tennessee, and Virginia. The Southwestern Department covers Arkansas, Kansas, Louisiana, Missouri, New Mexico, Oklahoma, and Texas. The Western Department is responsible for operations in Illinois, Indiana, Iowa, Michigan, Minnesota, Nebraska, North Dakota, Ohio, South Dakota, and Wisconsin.

There are over 750 branch offices located in the various states with staffs equipped to handle all types of losses and claims arising out of property and liability insurance contracts. The bureau has a large staff, numbering in the thousands, of highly skilled adjusters who adjust losses for insurers. The officers of the bureau consist of the chairman of the board, a vice chairman, president, executive vice president, other vice presidents, secretary-treasurer, and other secretaries. There are also a claims counsel, a director of education and research, and similar positions. The regional executives are assisted by departmental executives, general adjusters, and field adjusters.

The purposes of the bureau are:[46]

1. To examine, appraise, report upon, adjust and audit claims and losses arising under policies or contracts of insurance issued by fire, marine, casualty, and other classes of insurers and such other types

[46] See *Eastern Underwriter,* December 12, 1958, p. 72. The quotation is from this source.

and classes of claims and losses as from time to time may be authorized by the Board of Directors.
2. To inspect property damage by fire and other perils, to institute supervisory measures to protect and salvage property having remaining value and utility and to direct the disposition thereof.
3. To promote greater efficiency and to develop correct practices in the adjustment of such claims and losses.
4. To promote and maintain public good will between the insurers served and their policyholders.
5. To acquire and disseminate information relative to the causes of losses, the handling of salvage, and other matters pertinent to claims and loss adjustments.
6. To secure, develop, and promulgate pertinent data and information on conditions of interest to the business of insurance and to instruct, train, and educate adjusters in the various aspects of handling claims and losses.

By way of summary it may be said that the main purpose of the bureau is to "adjust all classes of property losses and to settle liability claims on behalf of its shareholders."[47]

The concept of an adjustment organization arose out of the similarity of claims that were presented to fire insurers. It was reasoned that a separate organization with trained adjusters to handle claims for many insurer could operate more efficiently than would be the case if each insurer attempted to maintain a large staff of its own.

Purchasing. There are many purchasing problems that are common to all types of property and liability insurers and to the persons in those organizations who are responsible for this activity. The Fire and Casualty Insurance Purchasing Forum, which was founded in 1957, serves as a way for member organizations to exchange information. Currently (1966), the officers of the forum include a president, vice president, secretary, and treasurer representing the Atlantic Companies, the Continental Insurance Company, the Great American Insurance Company, and the Reliance Insurance Companies.

American Insurance Association. The American Insurance Association with headquarters in New York City, began operations on January 1, 1965. This organization is multiple line in character and arises out of the merger of three older organizations: National Board of Fire Underwriters, Association of Casualty and Surety Companies, and the former American Insurance Association. This new organization is supported by approximately 200 insurers organized on a stock basis.

The association has branch offices in Chicago, San Francisco, and Washington, D.C. It is a service organization with some of the serv-

[47] *Ibid.*

ices available to nonmembers as well as to noninsurance organizations. The fire and accident prevention program is an example of a service available to business and the general public. The services to members fall into four general categories: legislative and legal, claims and loss adjusting, investigative services, and engineering and safety. Some of these services are also available to nonmembers on a subscription basis. Officers of the association include a chairman of the board, vice-chairman, president, vice president, secretary-treasurer, and general counsel.

The formation of this organization is an important step in the direction of the multiple line approach to property and liability insurance.

Professional Organizations. Professional organizations are related in many ways to educational organizations and their functions somewhat overlap. The professional organizations considered here are ones that do not formally operate an educational program designed to prepare candidates for a professional designation. Rather their interest is to advance a particular professional field through general meetings and perhaps publications.[48]

The Society of Chartered Property and Casualty Underwriters. Formed in 1944, the Society of Chartered Property and Casualty Underwriters is an organization of persons holding the C.P.C.U. designation. Its objectives relate primarily to the fostering of a higher level of education for insurance producers and others involved in property and liability insurance. It also fosters high professional standards among its members and in insurance generally. The society also publishes a journal.

Insurance Company Education Directors Society. Many insurers conduct their own in-company educational programs under the supervision of a director of education. In 1953, a number of insurers cooperated in forming the Insurance Company Education Directors Society. Currently (1966) the officers of the society represent such insurance firms as Nationwide Insurance Company, Crum and Forster, and State Auto Group. The society now has approximately 220 members involving some 100 insurers that maintain training programs for their employees. The purposes of the society relate to professional development and growth "through research and exchange of ideas related to education and training."[49]

National Association of Casualty and Surety Executives. The merger of the Board of Casualty and Surety Underwriters and the International Association of Casualty and Surety Underwriters

---

[48] The American Risk and Insurance Association might well be listed under "Professional Organizations." Because of its close relationship to education, it was discussed under "Educational Organizations."

[49] The *Insurance Almanac, op. cit.*, p. 199.

resulted in the organization of National Association of Casualty and Surety Executives in 1911. The officers are representatives of insurers and among their purposes is that of promoting "good will, harmony, confidence, and cooperation generally between the members."[50]

National Association of Insurance Commissioners. Founded in New York City in 1871 under the name of the National Convention of Insurance Commissioners, the association assumed its present name in 1935. This organization holds annual meetings to discuss problems of common interest to the state commissioners. The association has been active and influential since its inception in promoting uniformity among the states in insurance supervisory matters and in recommending desirable insurance legislation to state legislatures.

Other Professional Organizations. There are many other professional organizations in the insurance field in addition to those just described. Although producers organizations have been considered separately, they are essentially professional in character. Other organizations of a professional type are the Association of Average Adjusters in the United States, Association of Insurance Attorneys, National Association of Independent Insurance Adjusters, Society of Insurance Accountants, the National Association of Insurance Women, International Association of Insurance Counsel, and the National Association of Public Adjusters.

Other Organizations. There are a number of organizations that play a substantial role in the insurance world that are not easily classified under any of the preceding headings. Examples are the Fire Insurance Research and Actuarial Association; Insurance Accounting and Statistical Association; the National Insurance Actuarial and Statistical Association; the Honorable Order of the Blue Goose, International, which is a fraternal association; and the International Association of Industrial Accident Boards and Commissions. Also there are insurance-related organizations such as the A.F.C.O. Credit Corporation, which is a premium financing organization and is subscribed to by more than 560 fire and casualty insurers, and the National Association of Credit Management. Another organization with an insurance interest is the American Management Association. This organization, although not an association of insurers, has an insurance section with a primary interest in risk management. For purposes of illustration three of these organizations will be considered at greater length.

Fire Insurance Research and Actuarial Association. The Fire Insurance Research and Actuarial Association was organized in 1954 as the Inter-regional Insurance Conference. It assumed its present name in 1963. It is an association of fire insurers that are organized on a stock basis. Currently (1966), the chairman of the board, vice-

---

[50] *Ibid.*, p. 211.

chairman, and treasurer are from the Fund American Companies, Crum and Forster Group, and the Hanover Insurance Group. The general day by day supervision of the association is the responsibility of a general manager. Although the association was formed by stock insurers, other insurers may participate through a subscribership arrangement. The executive committee is the main standing committee. The *Cyclopedia of Insurance in the United States* lists five principal objectives of the association. They are (1) to assist fire and allied lines rating bureaus in the conduct of their affairs; (2) to help in the coordination of the activities of the insurers and organizations served to the end that the national character of insurance will be recognized and unjustifiable "variations in insurance contracts and rating practices nationwide" will be avoided; (3) to provide a central facility for discussion and study of problems of the member and subscriber organizations; (4) to conduct research and prepare studies that are consistent with the objectives of the associations; (5) "to furnish to members and subscribers, to rating and advisory organizations, and to others, information, statistics, recommendations, research and actuarial services and other assistance. . . ."

Insurance Accounting and Statistical Association. The Insurance Accounting and Statistical Association was founded in 1928 as the Round Table Assembly. It adopted its present name in 1932. The association is all lines in character and many life, property, liability, accident, and health insurers are members. It is international in its interests, and has as one of its main purposes the development of modern theory and practice in relation to insurance accounting and statistics. The members have annual conferences at which topics of interest to the various branches of the insurance business are discussed.

National Insurance Actuarial and Statistical Association. The National Insurance Actuarial and Statistical Association is one of the most recent of the insurer organizations and was formed in 1965 for the purpose of providing "a statistical and actuarial facility for collecting and processing statistics in accordance with 'modern actuarial methods.' "[51] Although the association is not a rating bureau, it does assist such bureaus as well as insurers in developing and supporting rating plans. The organization is multiple line in character, although most of its activity has been in the area of fire and allied lines. The association is also interested in research, and in developing and improving techniques of data collection and analysis.

STATE ASSOCIATIONS

State associations of insurers tend to follow a pattern similar to that found at the national level, although the emphasis is on associations of

[51] The *Insurance Almanac, op. cit.*, p. 219.

agents (stock and mutual) and on inspection and rating (mainly fire) organizations. In addition to these organizations many states have insurance information associations, associations of independent adjusters, and a variety of other groups representing many interests. The nature of these latter organizations is suggested to some extent by their names. Some of these organizations are the Marine Underwriters of Southern California, the California Insurance Federation, Inc., the Casualty Insurance Association of California, Surety Underwriters Association of Northern California, Surety Underwriters Association of Northern California, Surplus Line Association of California, Mariners Club of Connecticut, Board of Underwriters of Hawaii, Illinois Automobile Assigned Risk Plan, Iowa Insurance Institute, Insurance Federation of Massachusetts, Insurance Executives Association of Michigan, and the Missouri State Fire Prevention Association. Some of the state associations of insurance agents are affiliates of national organizations. Similarly the Alabama Inspection and Rating Bureau is a branch of the South-Eastern Underwriters Association.

Some of the state fire insurance rating organizations are fairly elaborately organized. For example, the New York Fire Insurance Rating Organization, which was founded in 1922, has a Metropolitan Division, an Albany Division, a Buffalo Division, a Rochester Division, and a Syracuse Division. Each division has a manager and an appropriate staff. In North Carolina there is the North Carolina Automobile Rate Administrative Office, the members of which must be all insurers that are licensed to write automobile liability insurance in North Carolina.

The Casualty Insurance Companies Serving Massachusetts is illustrative of a state organization whose principal function is public relations. This association serves as a public relations organization for most of the insurers that write casualty insurance in Massachusetts.[52] There are other state associations that have a public relations function but do not specialize in quite the same way as the Massachusetts organization.

LOCAL ASSOCIATIONS

Local associations of insurers are usually headquartered in large cities and serve to bring together persons and organizations interested in insurance. Many of these local groups are agents or brokers associations and a number of them have been in existence for many years. Apart from producers' organizations there are groups such as the Casualty and Surety Club of Baltimore, Boston Board of Fire Underwriters, Chicago Board of Underwriters, Insurance Board of Colum-

[52] See *ibid.*, p. 242.

bus, Surety Underwriters Association of the City of New York, Insurance Board of St. Louis, and the Board of Marine Underwriters of San Francisco. This list does not include all of the local associations that might be named, but should serve to give some idea of the range of the interests represented.

There are some local associations that have a special interest in insurance education and related activities and serve a major role in this capacity. Examples are the Insurance Library Association of Atlanta, Insurance Library Association of Boston, Insurance Society of Chicago, Insurance Society of New York, Inc., and the Insurance Society of Philadelphia. Perhaps the best known of these groups is the Insurance Society of New York, which in addition to conducting the College of Insurance, also maintains a large insurance library. This library has over 80,000 books and pamphlets dealing with insurance and is open to the public. The insurance library of Boston has over 30,000 volumes, and the one in Chicago has over 10,000. All of these associations have educational interests and often sponsor courses to prepare students for various insurance designations.

FOR DISCUSSION

1. Discuss the reasons for the establishment of the large number of insurer organizations that are now prevalent in the United States. To what extent is there a duplication of function?
2. Discuss the problems associated with trying to classify insurer organizations.
3. Write a short history of rating organizations.
4. Discuss the arguments for and against rate-making bureaus. Why should there be both state and national bureaus? Looking toward the future, do you believe rating organizations will become more or less important to insurer operations? Why?
5. When was the National Bureau of Casualty Underwriters formed? Describe the organizational structure of the bureau. What are the functions of the various committees?
6. List the insurer associations, described in the text, that have been formed since 1960. Do these associations have any common characteristics? If so, what are they?
7. The Southeastern Underwriters Association is one of the oldest rating bureaus in the United States. Describe the nature of its organizations. It is often referred to in discussions of the governmental supervision of insurers. What is its significance in the history of governmental regulation of the insurance business?
8. Why do many insurers participate in associations that were organized for underwriting purposes? Name five of these associations and discuss their significance in insurance marketing.

9. Discuss professional and educational associations in the property and liability insurance field. What is the significance of these organizations in terms of the advancement of insurance as a professional undertaking? What is the role of colleges and universities in insurance instruction?
10. Write a brief history of the American Risk and Insurance Association. What were the main reasons for founding this society and who were the charter members?
11. List the major insurance producer organizations that operate on a national basis. What are some of the reasons for the founding of these organizations? What role do they currently play on the national scene?
12. One of the most recent of the insurer organizations is the American Insurance Association. What organizations did it replace? What are some of its most important functions?
13. Read the latest issue of the major journals published by insurer organizations discussed in this chapter. Select one of them and review several of the articles in it.
14. Which of the insurer organizations discussed in this chapter were founded between 1860 and 1900? Between 1900 and 1940? Since 1940? What trends, if any, do you observe?
15. By 1975 do you believe there will be more or fewer insurer associations than now exist? Why?

CHAPTER · 30

Rates

All property and liability insurance rates other than nonfiled marine are computed by rate-making organizations and are promulgated for the use of insurers (see Chapter 29), although it is possible for insurers to reject rates computed by organizations and to file independently. These rates are subject to approval by the insurance commissioners of the various states, typically on a prior approval basis, although California, for example, has a rating law that does not require approval in advance of use. Every effort is made to make insurance rate making as systematic and exact as possible, although judgment still enters into rate determinations, particularly in the areas of fire and marine insurance. Ideally an insurance rate should be computed in such a way that it produces, when applied to a large class of risks having the same characteristics, just enough income to pay the losses that occur to the group, as well as the expenses of operation that may be attributed to the group, plus whatever may be necessary for contingencies, and in the case of stock insurers, a reasonable profit.[1] In practice it is not always possible to compute an ideal rate. Classifications, for various reasons, may not be precisely homogeneous. Further, every rate is a forecast, since the costs that are to be covered by the rate occur in the future, and it cannot be known in advance (with absolute accuracy) what these costs will be. An effort is made to identify the factors that determine costs and to combine these in such a way, often with the help of statistical methods, that as accurate a rate as is possible, within the limitations of the methods used, will be produced.

DEFINITIONS

Before discussing specific rate-making procedures in the field of property and liability insurance, it is necessary to define some of the

[1] A. H. Mowbray and R. H. Blanchard, *Insurance* (5th ed.; New York: McGraw-Hill Book Co., Inc., 1961), p. 372.

terms that are used in the mathematics of insurance pricing. By the word "rate" is meant price per unit of exposure. The units to which the rate is to be applied vary somewhat depending upon the type of insurance being considered. In fire insurance the rate is applied to each $100 of the face amount of insurance; in the bodily liability part of automobile insurance the rate is per automobile for certain defined basic limits. The total selling price of the insurance contract is the premium and is obtained by multiplying the number of exposure units by the rate.

The types of rating methods employed in property and liability insurance may be classified as individual, class, and merit. Individual rating is a procedure whereby an effort is made to determine the expected value of losses and expenses on an individual basis. Although a determination of a unique premium for each individual might seem ideal, there are a number of theoretical and practical difficulties with this method and it is little used. Class rating is based on a procedure whereby individuals assumed to have similar expected values of losses and expenses are grouped together. Since usually no two risks present exactly the same expected value of losses and expenses, some inequity may be introduced by this procedure. A further complication is introduced by the fact that in practice the subdivision of risks into classes is done on the basis of characteristics of the insureds and the property being covered. This procedure may not always produce insureds with similar expected values of losses and expenses.[2]

In those branches of the insurance business commonly classified as "casualty lines," rate computations often involve the determination of a pure premium as a first step. The class rate given in the rating manual (manual rate) reflects both losses and expenses and is the rate on which the selling price of the contract is based. The pure premium is the part of the premium intended to provide for losses, and the selling price is determined by loading the pure premium for expenses.[3] Finally, the selling price determined for the group may be modified by the credibility of the experience. In fire insurance a distinction is not made between the part of the premium relating to losses and the part for expenses. The class rate in this branch of the business is not determined by dividing the experience into two parts.

In class rating, as a practical matter, complete homogeneity within classes is rarely attained, and it is recognized that variations of risk quality within classes may exist. Merit rating, or the procedure whereby quality differences are measured for purposes of modifying the class rate, has been introduced as a way of introducing greater

---

[2] See C. A. Williams, Jr., *Price Discrimination in Property and Liability Insurance* (Minneapolis: University of Minnesota Press, 1959), pp. 15–23.

[3] Another procedure for computing premiums is the loss-ratio method which, for a permissible fixed loss ratio, is equivalent to the pure premium approach.

equity into the rate-making process. Merit rating may be subdivided into (1) schedule rating and (2) experience rating. Schedule rating is based on the physical characteristics of the risk and is primarily used in computing fire insurance rates for certain types of property. The class rate is modified depending on whether the particular risk is expected, because of special characteristics, to produce better than or worse than the average experience for the class. Experience rating is based on a statistical record and may be prospective or retrospective in form. Prospective experience rating, which is usually called "experience rating," produces a modification based on the past statistical record (often three years). Retrospective rating is used to modify a rate after the risk has been insured for a given time interval and the actual experience has been observed. It is most often used in connection with experience rating and is superimposed on it.[4]

PROPERTY INSURANCE RATES WITH SPECIAL REFERENCE TO FIRE INSURANCE

Class rating is used in property insurance for dwellings; certain standard types of mercantile and service properties; extended coverage; homeowner's contracts; filed marine classifications; and automobile physical damage. It is used with modifications in such areas as burglary and robbery insurance, sprinkler leakage insurance, and water damage insurance. Rating in fire insurance will be discussed at some length as an example of property insurance rating involving both class and schedule rates.

Fire Insurance. Fire insurance rating combines statistical data with an approach to each risk on an individual basis. No claim can be made to an invincible plan that will provide an accurate rate for every building in relation to all other buildings. What has been accomplished is the establishment of rating systems that fairly and within workable limits appraise the hazards for individual risks and fix a reasonable rate on the basis of this appraisal.[5]

The effort to eliminate, as far as possible, the element of judgment and substitute therefore a set of scientifically determined working rules has had the effect of making the problem of rate determination

[4] G. F. Michelbacher, *Multiple-Line Insurance* (New York: McGraw-Hill Book Co., Inc., 1957) pp. 107–11.

[5] This point was touched upon by Commissioner W. Ellery Allyn of Connecticut at a meeting of the New York Chapter of the National Insurance Buyers Association. He is reported to have stated that ". . . much of the learned discussion about scientific pinpointing of a rate within fractions of a percentage is so much eyewash." There are two important factors that must be ever present. The rate must be adequate if solvency of the insurers is to be protected, and it must be equitable as between insureds. These objectives are accomplished in the fire insurance rating systems, at the same time keeping them within the legal limitation touching upon the prohibition with respect to excess.

for a sizable structure a complicated and technical procedure. The average insurance agent is not equipped to make, or will he presume to make, a rate analysis. This work is assigned to highly trained experts who have qualified by education and experience for this branch of the business. Notwithstanding the technical nature of the work, the agent and the insured may take the make-up of the rate when the work is completed by the rating authority and, upon inspection, determine where it will be profitable to eliminate hazards for which charges are made and thereby reduce the rate.

Class and Specific Rates Distinguished. Fire insurance rates, as promulgated by the rating bureaus, fall into one of two categories: (1) class, and (2) specific. Class rates are sometimes known as "minimum rates" and specific rates as "tariff rates." The terms "minimum" and "class" are used interchangeably, as are the terms "tariff" and "specific." The term customarily used in the community is frequently the outgrowth of local custom, though not infrequently all of the terms find acceptance.[6]

Class rates apply to all properties that fall within a given category or classification. Classifications are defined according to differentials with respect to major features of (*a*) construction, (*b*) occupancy, and (*c*) class of fire protection. The construction classification concerns itself with whether the building is frame or masonry. Occupancy is considered in connection with dwelling risks and concerns itself primarily with the number of families. With respect to fire protection, towns and cities in each state are grouped into classes, and all communities falling within a particular class take the same rates. The outstanding example of class rating is to be found in detached dwelling houses. Class rates are promulgated to apply to all dwellings not subject to some special hazard. Class-rated dwellings are subdivided into groups in accordance with construction, with a rate assigned to each class. The rate also varies as to the classification of the city or town and the number of families occupying the property. In addition to class-rated dwellings, some jurisdictions apply class rates to buildings such as churches, apartment buildings, and others where the elements of construction and occupancy are similar enough to permit a ready grouping into rate classes.

When class rates do not apply, the rate is said to be "specific." Specific rates are promulgated by the rating bureaus for mercantile, manufacturing properties, and all types of business establishments. Public buildings and schools are likewise so rated. Specific rates are determined by the application to the particular risk of a schedule or formula designed to measure the relative quantity of fire hazard with respect to the particular risk. The system is known as "schedule

[6] Tariff rates in some parts of the United States may mean class rates. To avoid confusion, in this chapter the terms "class" and "specific" will be used.

rating." Specific rates are published in groupings by town, city, and street and each building with its contents is individually rated.

Schedule Rating. Schedule rating is a plan by which hazards with respect to any particular risk are measured. A schedule has been defined as ". . . an empirical standard for the measurement of relative quantity of fire hazard."[7] It undertakes to produce an equitable tariff of fire insurance costs. The schedule rate is a development of the recognition of the differences in hazards with respect to different risks. Schedule rating takes into consideration the various items contributing to the peril of fire. Among these are the construction of the building under consideration and its occupancy with a view to determining which features either enhance or minimize the probability of loss. Credits and charges representing departures from standard conditions as to building construction, occupancy, protection, and exposure are incorporated in the schedules. Thus, a schedule rate is the sum of all charges less the sum of its credits, and the schedule itself constitutes a standard for the measurement of the fire hazard. The rate produced by the application of a schedule is a numerical expression of the relative quantity of fire hazard expressed in the terms of the standard.

It may be pointed out that schedule rating has not by any means solved the fire insurance rating problem. A schedule, of itself, is an arbitrary and empirical standard. As among several or many risks using the same schedule, equity and uniformity as among insureds may be obtained. Where several different schedules are in use, and each produces a different result with respect to a given risk, the question may properly be asked as to whether the schedule in use is producing a rate that meets the objective of the rating laws. It would appear that in a territory where different schedules are in use and each produces a different result, not all can be correct.[8] It is also true that

---

[7] Jay S. Glidden, *Analytic System for the Measurement of Relative Fire Hazard, an Explanation* (Chicago: Jay S. Glidden, 1916), p. 17. Mr. Glidden was the author of this explanation of the Analytic System, but it was copyrighted by J. V. Parker. The Analytic System for the Measurement of Fire Hazard, that is, the rating instrument itself, was originally copyrighted by A. F. Dean in 1902, then by J. V. Parker, and is now copyrighted by the Western Actuarial Bureau.

[8] One rating organization used a total of 128 different schedules, according to the report of an examination made by a state insurance department. The report points out that for some classes different schedules were used in different areas under the jurisdiction of the bureau. In the report of the examination it is stated: "A review of the requirements of the schedules showed that in many cases there was duplication; in other cases it was difficult to determine which schedule should be used; and it was also noted that the use of each schedule would produce a different rate." The examination report cites examples of classes where different schedules might be used stating: "No instances were noted where schedules were improperly applied. However, it is the opinion of your examiners that this association employs far too many schedules and that the number should be reduced, where practical, by modifying the major schedules for occupancies."

even though the schedule in effect produces an equitable rate, unless risks are resurveyed periodically to pick up changes and hazards, faults of management, occupancy, construction, and exposure which otherwise would not be known, the promulgated rate, in spite of the accuracy of the schedule, may be defective.

The two most widely used schedules are known as the universal mercantile schedule and the analytic system. The first of these found early acceptance in the East, and the second, introduced by A. F. Dean late in the 19th century, found wide acceptance in the West. The analytic system is now widely used throughout the country; it is more generally known as the Dean schedule, taking its name from the author of the plan. The several schedules are basically different in their fundamental analysis of the factors affecting insurance risks, but they are alike in that they establish an arbitrary point from which to build up the rate and are based upon the various physical hazards of the risk. A schedule of additions and reductions is computed and the difference applied to the arbitrary point of departure.

Grading Cities and Towns. Fire protection provided by towns and cities is known as "public or municipal protection." Municipal protection is an important consideration in all schedule rating. The American Insurance Association has prepared a grading schedule for cities and towns of the United States based upon an analysis of conditions in more than five hundred cities.[9] The American Insurance Association does the grading for large cities, and the local fire insurance rating organization helps with the smaller cities and towns and may do grading on cities as large as 70,000. The schedule takes into consideration not only the natural and structural conditions that have a bearing on the hazards but also the status of laws designed to control unsatisfactory conditions. The schedule is based upon a maximum of 5,000 points of deficiency divided in accordance with the relative importance of each factor under consideration. The relative value of the deficiency points is as follows:

Water supply	1,700 points
Fire department	1,500 points
Fire alarm	550 points
Building laws	200 points
Fire prevention	350 points
Structural conditions	700 points
	5,000 points

On the basis of the application of the foregoing schedule, cities, and towns are classified as follows:

[9] National Board of Fire Underwriters (now the American Insurance Association), *Standard Schedule for Grading Cities and Towns of the United States with Reference to Their Fire Defenses and Physical Conditions* (New York, 1942).

Class	*Points of Deficiency*
First	0– 500
Second	501–1,000
Third	1,001–1,500
Fourth	1,501–2,000
Fifth	2,001–2,500

Class	*Points of Deficiency*
Sixth	2,501–3,000
Seventh	3,001–3,500
Eighth	3,501–4,000
Ninth	4,001–4,500
Tenth	A city or town receiving more than 4,500 points; or without a water supply and having a fire department grading tenth class; or with a water supply and no fire department; or with no fire protection.

Not all buildings in a particular municipality receive the same town grading classification. The classification of the town will apply to all risks under normal protection in the town, but specifically rated risks that are exceptionally far from any fire station, or not served by the normal water supply, may have a lower classification.

In preparing the schedule, the American Insurance Association has taken into consideration the effect of climatic conditions upon fire losses. It is recognized that in cold climates there is a heating hazard as well as a hazard growing out of the difficulty of fire apparatus in responding quickly and operating efficiently in cold weather. In hot, dry climates there is increased combustibility, and fires may be readily spread by high winds. Likewise, earthquakes, tornadoes, hurricanes, cyclones, blizzards, floods, and other unusual conditions contribute to the conflagration hazard. For those weather conditions that are more or less common to the whole country, there is no deficiency provided in the schedule. When climatic conditions are abnormal in these sections, an additional deficiency is applied, based on available data of the United States Weather Bureau. Additional deficiencies are applied when there is a danger that forest fires may spread to destroy a city or when tornadoes, hurricanes, and cyclones are common and may result in numerous fires or the interruption of fire service. Blizzards and severe snowstorms that impede operation of the fire department; earthquakes of such intensity as to injure buildings, water mains, and cause numerous fires; mine cave-ins affecting extensive areas; and floods which cover part of the district considered or cause wide detours of fire apparatus—all warrant the application of an additional deficiency. The additional deficiency is added to the deficiency determined by application of the schedule proper. It is apparent, therefore, that weather is an important factor in determining basic rates and, more than this, it is a factor over which the insured can exercise no control. The introduction of the weather factor is evidence of the care exercised in grading cities and towns.

If some seriously unfavorable climatic condition occurs once every ten years, it is regarded as "seriously frequent," and if it happens once in 20 years, "moderately frequent."

The ten grades of protection thus determined are used as the basis of schedule applications to specific rates. They are also used to determine class rates on dwelling house property. In New England the grade is determined as follows:

American Insurance Association Grading Classification	*Minimum-Rate Grade*
1, 2	A
3, 4	B
5, 6	C
7, 8	D
9	E
10	F

From the foregoing, it is evident that the control of the basis rate in many communities falls only indirectly within the control of the individual. As far as he can throw the weight of his influence, co-operating with other citizens, civic-minded bodies, mercantile associations, and the local city government with a view to securing the approval of conditions that reduce or eliminate fire hazards, he can contribute to a lower community rate.

Universal Mercantile Schedule. This schedule in the past found wide acceptance in some modified form in many eastern and in some southern states. It was designed to rate mercantile risks, and because it was designed to be applicable to all such risks, it was termed the "universal" schedule. Noting this characterization, one commentator has stated: "Somebody said it is referred to as the 'universal' schedule because it is the universal practice to tamper with it wherever it is in use."[10] Nevertheless this system has served as a pattern for a large number of schedules designed to measure the relative hazards of risk in particular classifications.

This plan of rating takes as its point of departure a standard build-

[10] Eugene F. Gallagher, *Fire Insurance Rating Problems* (Detroit: Planet Insurance Co., 1945), p. 5.

ing in a standard city. A standard city is described as one having wide level streets, gravity water works, adequate fire and police protection, and building conditions meeting a rigid set of requirements. A standard building, although not fireproof, represents the ideal for ordinary construction. The schedule makes use of (*a*) a basis rate, and (*b*) a key rate. One is developed from the other. When the key rate is determined, this serves as the basis for determining the specific rate to be promulgated by the rating bureau for any particular building. The basis rate is the rate of the standard building in a standard city. Charges, known as "deficiency charges," are made for deviations from a standard city. Deductions from the basis rate are made for exceptionally good features of environment. The key rate is the rate of a standard building in a given city. It is intended to measure the average rate of a standard building in the community under consideration. The specific rate that applies to the particular building is found by making adjustments to the key rate. If there are any deficiences in the structure or any unusually favorable features, the key rate is modified accordingly. For all unfavorable features, additions are made to the key rate, and deductions are made for the favorable features. Thus, by computing charges based upon a schedule of specific hazards, the rate for a standard building in the particular city in question is converted into the rate for the building under examination.

The Rate Makeup. As the first step in schedule rating, a survey is made. On the basis of the findings, the final rate is computed. The forms used are not identical in all jurisdictions but are generally alike in principle. To find a rate for a particular building, using the universal mercantile schedule, the charges for the various hazards and credits for protective devices or exceptionally good features are applied to the key rate of the city or town. In connection with the occupancy of the structure, there are two charges. The first of these is included in computing the building rate, and the other is a differential added to the building rate to determine the rate for contents. Schedules are adapted to the particular class of property to be rated. Corrections to the key rate are flat charges. This works out as follows:

Key rate		0.50
Charges:		
Frame	0.60	
Roof (shingles)	0.10	
Nonstandard stairway	0.10	
Nonstandard heat	0.10	0.90
Building rate		1.40

The effect of increasing the base rate under such a system does not increase the final rate proportionately. To increase the 0.50 rate by 25 percent to 0.625 will give a final building rate of 1.53. Actually to get a 25 percent increase over the 1.40 rate, the final rate should be 1.75. Under this system of flat charges and credits the entire level is not susceptible to changes in the basis rate.[11]

The Analytic System (the Dean Schedule). The analytic system for the measurement of the relative fire hazard is fundamentally different from the universal mercantile system; yet from the insured's point of view the two schedules are similar in that their charges and credits are added to a basis rate.

Perhaps the outstanding difference between the two schedules is to be found in the method of applying charges and credits. With the exception of certain after-charges for untidiness and carelessness, which represents flat sums added to the rate, all charges for other hazards deemed to be inherent in the risk are made in terms of a percentage of the basis rate. This practice is based upon certain fundamental assumptions. The basic concept of the system is that every factor involved is not an absolute, but is related to the other factors involved and thus modified by interaction between all pertinent factors. For example, an open staircase is charged a higher rate increment in a community with poor municipal fire protection and welding is charged a higher rate increment in a frame building than in a masonry building. It is assumed that every risk absorbs a ratio of the hazards to which it is exposed and that, by the same reasoning, it transmits a ratio of absorbed hazards. The risk itself radiates hazard inherent to it. The ratio of radiated, absorbed, and transmitted exposure is modified by the structure of the building, clear space intervening, and fire department protection. Because of these assumptions that hazards are radiated, transmitted, and absorbed as ratios, adjustments are made as percentages rather than flat charges. This is in contrast to the universal mercantile system in which flat charges are made for defects in the building as compared with standard, although certain unusual features in the building may permit a final credit in terms of percentages. Because of the wide acceptance of the analytic system and the underlying philosophy, certain of the important features of the schedule will be considered.

Elements of Risk. The analytic system defines a risk as a building or other structure together with its occupancy or occupancies. There are four features or elements of risk. These are: (*a*) structure, (*b*) occupancy, (*c*) exposure, and (*d*) protection.

Buildings are classified into A, B, or D construction. Buildings of

---

[11] The universal mercantile schedule while using flat amounts in adjusting the key rate with respect to features of construction allows adjustments for occupancy, protective devices, and management charges to be applied to the key rate on a percentage basis. Provision is also made for deductions from the rate in percentages for exceptionally good features of construction. *Standard Universal Schedule for Rating Mercantile Risks,* January, 1902, p. 5.

fireproof construction receive the A designation, those of brick and stone construction are class B, and class D includes buildings of frame construction. The schedule does not state in so many words that a standard building is thus and so but simply provides charges or credits from departure from the standards for individual items.

Occupancy is recognized as a prime factor among the causes of fire. A building itself does not cause fire, (except possibly for defects in electrical or heating systems), but its ability to resist fire will prove a contributing or deterring factor after a fire occurs. Even in the case of buildings damaged or destroyed by a fire spreading from another building, the cause of the loss may be traced to occupancy in the exposing risk. The analytic system carefully classifies and analyzes occupancy features as causes of fire.

Full consideration is given to the exposure factor. That fires originating in one building spread to another has long been recognized by fire insurance underwriters. On the basis of analysis it has been found that the hazard of exposure as a cause of fire ranks second to that of occupancy.

The classifications established under the standard grading schedule of the American Insurance Association are used as a basis for rating public protection. In addition to public protection, the property owner may provide private protection by means of fire hose, fire extinguishers, watchman's service, sprinkler systems, and the like. Credits are incorporated in the rating plan that give recognition to private protection.

Principle of Relativity. One of the outstanding advantages evidenced through the use of the analytic system is found in its recognition of what has been termed the "principle of relativity." The sum total of all the hazards that contribute to a particular risk are all a proportionate part of the risk. It is the recognition of this important principle that brought about the use of percentages to effect charges and credits rather than the use of flat charges as had been the case with respect to schedules prior to the analytic system.[12] The same percentages apply with respect to given hazards whenever they are found.

The analytic system makes use of the principle of relativity with respect to (*a*) the risk itself, (*b*) place, and (*c*) time.

---

[12] The philosophy underlying relativity as applicable to the fire hazard has thus been expressed by Mr. Dean: "The sum of fire hazard in every risk is made up by its parts and its environments, and the relativity of its parts, as well as its relativity as a whole to other risks, is shown by the fact that its hazard can be demonstrated quantitatively only by the laws of average, through which it is made a sharer with an indefinite number of other risks. There is, perhaps, nothing amenable to measurement in which relativity is more in evidence than in what we term fire hazard, for this relativity literally confronts us at every turn. The fact cannot be too strongly emphasized that in fire hazard we are dealing with relations." Quoted by Jay S. Glidden, *op. cit.*, p. 17.

With respect to the risk itself, assuming a large number of buildings of a given construction, occupancy, and protection, a loss ratio will develop during a given period. It is assumed under the law of large numbers that with respect to any risk the relativity between the whole and its part does not change, and the relativity between its parts is constant. In 100,000 buildings of like construction it may be assumed that nonstandard heat, elevators, nonstandard well holes, cornices, and the different types of occupancies will each make a proportionate contribution to the total loss cost. The charge for each is not a flat charge but a proportion of the whole. This has led in the analytic schedule to the practice of making charges and credits percentages of the base rate. This is illustrated as follows: Assume a frame building in a fifth-class Maine community. We might develop the following building rate:

	Charges	
Basis rate		$0.61
Height	10%	
Basement	15	
Area	10	
Roof	20	
Interior finish	20	
Open stairway	20	
Occupancy	100	
Total percentage charges	195%	
	1.95 × 0.61 =	1.19
		$1.80
Less fire extinguisher credit, 5%		0.09
Individual building rate		$1.71

Since all charges in the schedule become percentages of the basis rate and since all factors that contribute to a risk are relative, the schedule adapts itself as well to one location as to another. If it is found that the loss ratio in one state differs from that of another, the corresponding difference in rate required can be effected by a change in the basis rate. Thus there is relativity of place. To increase the rates in a given state 25 percent, it is only necessary to increase the basis rate by that amount. Since the individual charges and credit are percentages of the basis rate, the entire rate structure moves proportionately as the basis rate is changed. Like a ship that moves up and down with the tide as a complete unit, the entire rating structure in the analytic system may be moved in one direction or the other by an adjustment in the basis rate. Assume in a given state rates were to be increased 25 percent over those used in the area for the computation of the $1.71 rate just computed. No change need be made in the charges and credits. The basis rate is increased 25 percent from 0.61 to 0.76. Now our problem works out as follows:

	Charges	
Basis rate		$0.76
Height	10%	
Basement	15	
Area	10	
Roof	20	
Interior finish	20	
Open stairway	20	
Occupancy	100	
Total percentage charges	195%	
	1.95 × 0.76 =	1.48
		$2.24
Less fire extinguisher credit, 5%		0.11
Individual building rate		$2.13

This can be checked. The old rate of $1.71 increased 25 percent gives a new rate of $2.13. Of course, in actual rating practice old rates are not increased on a flat percentage basis. The rate structure is increased by increasing the basis rate, and this increase is reflected in new rates on the basis of charges and credits attributable to the risk at the time the new rate is made.[13]

The same relationship may be applied with respect to time. A substantial change in loss cost from the period on which the rates are based may require an increase or decrease in premium income. As before, this can be effected by a change in the basis rate. A movement of the basis rate one way or the other provides for an adjustment of premium income without any distortion of the relative contribution to the total made by each hazard of every risk. It makes no difference whether the necessity for a change in rate level grows out of different loss costs developed in different geographical areas or different loss costs that develop in the same area but in different periods of time. Because of the operation of the principle of relativity, the procedure for adjusting premium income levels is the same. In other words, by moving the basis rate in one direction or the other, the entire rate structure may be adjusted upward or downward without in any way affecting the relativity established by the system with respect to the risk itself.

The Basis Rate. A principal point of difference between the analytic system and the universal mercantile schedule lies in the determination of the basis rate. Instead of attempting to establish a basis rate for a standard risk in a standard city, the Dean schedule gives

[13] This calculation is based on the New England edition of the analytic system which is different in several respects from the edition used in the Middle West. The system used in New England is a modification of the older and parent system developed by Mr. Dean. Although the theory of rate adjustment by shifting the basis rate is satisfactory, in practice the specific re-rating of many thousands of risks takes considerable time. In this sense the analytic system lacks responsiveness to the need for quick adjustment of general rate levels.

consideration to the degree of fire protection and efficiency of fire-fighting facilities as represented by the classifications established under the standard grading schedule of the American Insurance Association. After these classifications have been adopted by the individual rating bureau, the analytic system makes use of them in connection with the establishment of a basis rate.

The basis rate is used as the beginning point in the calculation of the rate for any particular property. It is determined by (*a*) the construction of the building; (*b*) the class of exterior fire protection; and (*c*) in the case of B and D buildings, the height of the building. Basis tables are prepared for each state or rating territory, and the tables used are determined by the underwriting experience in the territory involved. Percentage charges are added to the basis rate to secure the specific rate of the property under consideration. These charges reflect conditions of the building construction and occupancy. Credits are subtracted for protective features and superior structural conditions. The exposure hazard is recognized, and charges are added for any unsafe condition which can readily be corrected by management.

Logic of the Basis Rate. The first fire insurance rates that were quoted on a class rate basis were, in fact, basis rates. With the advent of schedule rating and the analysis of risks to the end that charges or credits could be made for specific hazards, there always remained with respect to every risk an unanalyzed portion. This portion, sometimes referred to as "the residium of unanalyzed hazard," actually constituted a basis rate, since it was to this rate that other charges were added.

In connection with the Dean schedule, there is actually no difference between the charge in a schedule termed a "basis rate" and the other charges, except that the basis rate includes only those factors which of themselves are too obscure or unimportant to be separately scheduled. Any factor that can be identified as a hazard has a relative value attached to it. This applies to such features as floor openings, occupancy, height of building, and structure. To the remaining indefinite or unidentifiable factors a lump-sum charge is attached, and this is the basis rate.

The Master Basis Table. The schedule provides for standard basis tables for each of the three classes of construction. The fireproof tables, as is to be expected, have the lowest rates, the brick table rates are intermediate, and the frame table is the highest. Tables are divided into ten columns, each column representing a class in the standard grading schedule of the American Insurance Association.

The master basis table assumes that a city in the tenth class, as determined by the standard grading schedule will have a rate of $1.00. On the basis of experience the relative rate for a building located in a first-class is determined. Then, the relative value of the protection among all the other classes is established. Table 30–1 is a master basis table for A buildings designed as a medium for the derivation of standard basis tables. These are the tables necessary to produce the level of rates deserved for any given territory and are obtained by taking ratios of the master basis table.[14]

TABLE 30–1

MASTER BASIS TABLE, A CONSTRUCTION

Class of Exterior Fire Protection	*1*	*2*	*3*	*4*	*5*	*6*	*7*	*8*	*9*	*10*
With no starred occupancies.....	0.4989	0.5039	0.5090	0.5142	0.5194	0.5246	0.5299	0.5520	0.9200	1.0000

At this point it is necessary to consider the impact of occupancies on the master basis table. Occupancies are divided into two classes: (*a*) ordinary, and (*b*) starred. All occupancies not classified as starred are considered as ordinary. Starred occupancies, sometimes known as "starred risks," are those having rapidly burning qualities to the end that for these risks the value of municipal protection is relatively less than is the case with ordinary risks.

It is axiomatic with fire fighters that the first five minutes may determine the extent of the loss. Obviously, fires in certain risks will get beyond control in a much shorter time than others. In those risks where combustion is so rapid that fire may be expected to assume large proportions before the arrival of a fire apparatus, damage, once a fire starts, may be expected to be extensive. In those risks where the fire department can hardly be expected to reach the fire while it is still in the incipient stages, credit for municipal protection is less than is the case with the ordinary risk. The rate adjustment for starred risks is effected by the use of higher basis rates. Table 30–2 is the master basis table with starred occupancies included.

TABLE 30–2

MASTER BASIS TABLE, A CONSTRUCTION

Class of Exterior Fire Protection	*1*	*2*	*3*	*4*	*5*	*6*	*7*	*8*	*9*	*10*
With no starred occupancies.....	0.4989	0.5039	0.5090	0.5142	0.5194	0.5246	0.5299	0.5520	0.9200	1.0000
With starred occupancies......	0.6101	0.6147	0.6194	0.6240	0.6287	0.6335	0.6383	0.6580	0.9400	1.0000

[14] This table, as well as others used in this chapter, is reproduced from the *Analytic System for the Measurement of Relative Fire Hazard*. Definitions, as well as other explanatory matter, such, for example, as the combustibility and damageability classifications, are drawn directly from the same source. This material, copyrighted by the Western Actuarial Bureau, is used with permission.

The basis rate in the tenth class is 1.0000 for both classes of occupancy. This means that for starred risks the value of exterior fire protection is relatively less than for other risks and this decreased value has been recognized by increases in the basis rate under all classes of exterior fire protection except class 10. Where the basis rate in the first class with no starred occupancies is 50 percent of the tenth class rate with starred occupancies, it becomes 61 percent. Starred occupancies are indicated in the alphabetical occupancy list with an asterisk (*), and it is from this marking that the name "starred risk" is derived. The principal point of difference between the tenth-class rates for A buildings with or without starred occupancies is to be found in the effect of exterior fire protection. When exterior fire protection is of recognizable value (first to ninth classes), there is a difference in the basis rate. Under the tenth class, the basis rates are the same, since the exterior fire protection is not of recognizable value to any occupancy.

The master basis tables for A, B, and D construction differ in makeup. The A basis table makes no reference to height, and the D basis table makes no deduction for lack of basement nor any additional charge for subbasement. It is necessary in giving consideration to the construction of the master basis table for B building to notice not only the height of buildings but the matter of basements. Basis rates in the case of B and D buildings are increased for each additional story over one. If there is no basement, the basis rate is reduced in the case of B buildings but increased for subbasement. A table thus derived giving consideration to height of buildings and the presence or absence of basements is reproduced as Table 30–3 and is the master basis table for B buildings.

The master basis table thus derived is called the "100 table." This grows out of the fact that $1.00 is the point of departure in the

TABLE 30–3

MASTER BASIS TABLE, B CONSTRUCTION

Class of Exterior Fire Protection	*1*	*2*	*3*	*4*	*5*	*6*	*7*	*8*	*9*	*10*
Height:										
1 story	0.5428	0.578	0.6133	0.6532	0.6931	0.7381	0.7831	0.8628	0.9425	1.00
2 stories	0.5699	0.6069	0.644	0.6858	0.7277	0.775	0.8223	0.906	0.9896	1.05
3 "	0.597	0.6358	0.6747	0.7185	0.7624	0.8119	0.8615	0.9491	1.0367	1.10
4 "	0.635	0.6763	0.7176	0.7642	0.8109	0.8636	0.9163	1.0095	1.1027	1.17
5 "	0.6898	0.7346	0.7795	0.8302	0.8809	0.9586				
6 "	0.7598	0.8296								
Add for each additional story	0.12	0.12	0.12	0.12	0.12	0.12	0.12	0.12	0.12	0.12
Subtract if no basement	0.0271	0.0289	0.0307	0.0326	0.0346	0.0369	0.0291	0.0431	0.0471	0.05
Add for each subbasement	0.0271	0.0289	0.0307	0.0326	0.0346	0.0369	0.0291	0.0431	0.0471	0.05

tenth-class town. It is called the "master table" because it is from this table that others are derived. Derived tables are designated by the percentage of the 100 table that they represent. We may have a 95 table or a 60 table or any other table, depending upon the percentage of the master table used for its derivation. Table 30–4 is a 40 table and will serve as an illustration. The starting point of the table is 0.40 and that figure in the table is 40 percent of the corresponding figure in the master basis table shown in Table 30–3.

TABLE 30–4

BASIS TABLES FOR BUILDINGS OF B CONSTRUCTION
Table No. 40

Class of Exterior Fire Protection	*1*	*2*	*3*	*4*	*5*	*6*	*7*	*8*	*9*	*10*
Height:										
1 story	0.217	0.231	0.245	0.261	0.277	0.295	0.313	0.345	0.377	0.40
2 stories	0.228	0.243	0.258	0.274	0.291	0.31	0.329	0.362	0.396	0.42
3 "	0.239	0.254	0.27	0.287	0.305	0.325	0.345	0.38	0.415	0.44
4 "	0.254	0.271	0.287	0.306	0.324	0.345	0.367	0.404	0.441	0.468
5 "	0.276	0.294	0.312	0.332	0.352	0.383				
6 "	0.304	0.332								
Add for each additional story	0.048	0.048	0.048	0.048	0.048	0.048	0.048	0.048	0.048	0.048
Subtract if no basement	0.011	0.012	0.012	0.013	0.014	0.015	0.016	0.017	0.019	0.02
Add for each subbasement	0.011	0.012	0.012	0.013	0.014	0.015	0.016	0.017	0.019	0.02
Increase for*	30%	27½%	25%	22½%	20%	17½%	15%	10%	Use tenth class basis	

* Asterisk refers to starred occupancies.

To carry the illustration one step further Table 30–5 is an illustration of a 25 table. Since this is designed for buildings of A tios, separate rates for stories above the first are not required. This table will be recognized as representing 25 percent of Table 30–2.

TABLE 30–5

BASIS TABLES FOR BUILDINGS OF A CONSTRUCTION

Class of Exterior Fire Protection	*1*	*2*	*3*	*4*	*5*	*6*	*7*	*8*	*9*	*10*
With no starred occupancies	0.125	0.126	0.127	0.129	0.130	0.131	0.132	0.138	0.230	0.250
With starred occupancies	0.153	0.154	0.155	0.156	0.157	0.158	0.160	0.164	0.235	0.250

Standard basis tables are direct proportions of the master basis table. The number attached to the table represents the percentage of the 100 table that is developed. The rating bureau with jurisdiction establishes a basis rate for each community. In order to do this the bureau establishes a general level for the entire state based on the examination of the underwriting experience for the state, and then the basis rate for an individual community is determined by its classification under the standard grading schedule.

Hazard Factors in Occupancy. Occupancy as it contributes to the start of fire or its spread is an important feature of the analytic system. While a number of fires spread from exposure, and this feature is considered by the system, a very large proportion of all fires are due to the hazards of occupancy alone. Exposure fires are, for the most part, due to hazards of occupancy in the building of origin.

The system recognizes three general classes of occupancy. These are (*a*) mercantile, (*b*) industrial, and (*c*) miscellaneous. Mercantile occupancies include all risks in which the principal business consists of the sale or storage of merchandise. Both wholesale and retail establishments are included. Industrial risks comprise those in which the principal business consists of the production of materials or the manipulation of materials in the manufacture, packing, or shipping of merchandise. The miscellaneous category consists of occupancies classified as neither mercantile nor industrial.

The analytic system recognizes that the cause that starts a fire is quite a different factor from the medium that spreads it. The consequences of a fire vary with the nature of the occupancy. The factors of hazard found in occupancies are recognized to be: (*a*) causes, (*b*) media, and (*c*) effects. Causes are defined as the things which originate combustion. Media are the substances on which the causes act with reference to their latent energy or combustibility. Effects are defined as the relative susceptibility of media to damage as the direct of indirect results of fire commonly known as "damageability."

The system rates causes as cumulative and media as climacteric. A furnace may start a fire but does not contribute to the combustion that follows. A furnace, therefore, located in a building is rated as a cause of fire regardless of the number of occupancies in a building. In the case of multiple-occupancy buildings, each occupancy may carry the charge attributable to a furnace. While the furnace does not contribute to the combustion that follows, it is recognized to be more hazardous in proportion to the combustibility of the materials by which it is surrounded. This means that two identical furnaces located in two different plants might call for different charges. This would be the case if one furnace were located in a mattress factory and another located in a plant manufacturing cement blocks. Combustibility is recognized as a form of latent energy. Since transfers of energy are from bodies having more to those having less, it follows that the media of the highest combustibility will be significant in determining the charge applicable to the basis rate.

In applying these principles, the schedule recognized that where there are several causes that may originate a fire, a charge for each should appear in the rate. That is what is meant when it is stated that causes are cumulative. On the other hand, with respect to media, if there are several occupancies, the highest only appears in the rate. This means that in a building where there are varying degrees of combustibility and several are low and one is high, it would not be logical to take the sum of the ratings and apply them to the basis rate. If iron pipes were stored in one end of a warehouse and flammable plastics in another part of the same building, the plastics charge would govern and not the sum of the charges for pipes and plastics. The system uses only the highest charge for combustibility regardless of the number of occupancies in the building being rated.

An important feature of the schedule is the alphabetical occupancy list. In the construction of this list, occupancy hazards that have a common denominator with respect to a particular class of risks have been incorporated in the charges to be found there. A part of a page from the alphabetical occupancy list for the purpose of illustration is reproduced as Table 30–6. Reference to the list is frequently all that is necessary to secure the proper occupancy changes. In other instances, there are features of occupancy that do not lend themselves to inclusion in the occupancy list, and these items are treated separately elsewhere in the schedule.

The columns in the alphabetical occupancy list headed "B" indicate the charges to be applied to buildings rated under rules for both A and B construction. The columns headed "D" indicate the charges to be applied to buildings rated under the rules for D construction. In columns "B" and "D" column 1 is the column in cause and column 2 the column of combustibility or ignitibility. Charges in column 1 are cumulative in each building, but the highest charge only in column 2 enters the rate. The third column labeled "D" measures damageability.

Classification of Causes. Causes, or the features of occupancy which originate combustion, are divided in the schedule into the following groups: (*a*) traffic, (*b*) labor, (*c*) motive power, (*d*) heat producing and utility devices, (*e*) miscellaneous hazards, (*f*) special features of hazard, and (*g*) unclassified hazards.

Traffic is the hazard involved in the regular transaction of business connected with the sale of merchandise. Labor is the hazard involved in the production of materials or the manipulation of materials in their manufacture.

Motive power embraces the hazard of electric motors or generators and internal combustion engines. Heat producing and utility devices include the hazards of furnaces, kettles, dry heat boxes, dry rooms, enameling and japanning ovens, lumber dry kilns, and similar devices in which materials are dried or processed in heated rooms or compartments. Miscellaneous hazards include various processes and devices, such as metal working, painting, upholstering, woodworking, and the storage and use of highly volatile combustibles, to name but a few in this group. Special features of hazard are those attached to a number of processes and devices or the storage of materials, which as a rule are found in certain occupancies. The final category, unclassified hazards, embraces a group that are not readily included in the other groups noted. These include assemblage, recreational, and habitational occupancies, including offices and others not subject to definite analysis.

TABLE 30–6

SPECIMEN PAGE FROM ALPHABETICAL OCCUPANCY LIST

		B		*D*		*Damage-*
		1	*2*	*1*	*2*	*ability*
685	**Corset Parlors,** C.1					D3
688	**Corset Stocks,** C.2	5%	10%	40%		D3
	1. Labor (sewing), power, heat, etc., charge according to combustibility.					
690	**Cosmetics Stocks,** C.2	5%	10%	40%		D3
691	**Costumers' Stocks** (for sale or hire), C.3	10%	20%	50%	20%	D4
	1. Labor (sewing), power, heat, etc., charge according to combustibility.					
694*	**Cotton Batting Stocks,** C.4	40%	80%	80%	60%	D3
697	**Cotton Brokers' or Factors' Offices** (with samples), C.3	10%	20%	50%	20%	D3
	(If without samples, see Offices.)					
700	**Cotton Mills** (knitting and weaving only): See Knitting and Weaving Mills.					
703	**Cotton Stocks** (baled):					
	a. Not more than 20 bales, C.3	10%	20%	50%	20%	D2
	b. Not more than 100 bales, C.3½	20%	40%	70%	40%	D2
	c.*More than 100 bales, C.4	40%	80%	80%	60%	D2

Source: *Analytic System* (Chicago: Western Actuarial Bureau, 1965). Copyright, 1921, by J. V. Parker; 1952, by R. D. Hobbs; 1955 and 1965, by Western Actuarial Bureau.

With respect to certain occupancies, the charge for causes is incorporated in column 1 of the Alphabetical Occupancy List. This is not always the case. The basic occupancy charge for mercantile occupancies does not contemplate the additional hazard of labor in connection with industrial processes. The basic occupancy charge for industrial occupancies does not contemplate the additional hazard of traffic connected with the sale of merchandise. Tables are provided for making the necessary charges for features of occupancy when they are not already incorporated in column 1 of the Alphabetical Occupancy List.

Analysis and Classification of Combustibility. In rating a risk the rater is not obliged to classify the occupancy. By reference to the alphabetical occupancy list, it is possible to determine the combustibility of any listed occupancy. If, by chance, it should develop that any particular occupancy is not listed, its classification is determined by comparison with a similar occupancy. Notwithstanding, it is enlightening to consider the basis of classification.

In effecting classification, consideration is given to: the facility with which the substance will ignite or take fire, the rapidity of its combustion when started, and the intensity of combustion as indicated by quantity. Giving due consideration to the difficulty of establishing separate groups or classifications, the system recognizes five grades of combustibility that are inherent in the substances themselves. These are C.1, slow-burning or incombustible; C.2, moderate-burning; C.3, free-burning; C.4, intense burning; and C.5, flash-burning. It is apparent that Class C.1 comprises materials having the lowest fire hazard, while the greatest hazard is to be found in C.5. These five grades, with two intermediate grades, have been set up in the following nine classifications designed to provide for the various gradations of hazards.

Slow-burning or Incombustible (C.1). This includes merchandise or materials which do not in themselves constitute an active fuel for spread of combustion.

Moderate-burning (C.2). This includes merchandise or materials which burn moderately in themselves but may contain small quantities of a higher grade of combustibility.

Free-burning (C.3). This includes merchandise or materials which burn freely, constituting an active fuel.

Intermediate A (C.3½). This grade is not susceptible of definition by quality but is used principally for quantity, being available for large open stocks of grade C.3 and for moderate quantities of grade C.4. It is also used for some grades of C.7 (unclassifiable).

Intense-burning (C.4). This includes merchandise or materials that burn with great intensity and industrial risks which as a result of industrial processes produce debris which burns with great intensity but is not so finely divided as to cause flash fires or explosions.[15] It is also frequently available as a quantitative grade for storage of materials which belong to other classes.

Intermediate B (C.4½). This grade includes merchandise and materials which burn with great intensity and are difficult to extinguish. This grade is also used quantitatively for large risks of lower classes.

Flash-burning (C.5). This grade includes merchandise and materials that burn with an intensity equal to or greater than C.4 and, in addition, give off flammable or explosive vapors at ordinary weather

[15] Merchandise that legitimately belongs to this class is so dangerous that it is seldom found except in negligible quantities or in protective packages of a lower grade of combustibility; hence, grade C.4 is seldom used for mercantile stocks.

temperatures, or that spontaneously ignite through exposure to air or moisture.

Indefinite (C.6). This includes merchandise or materials the hazard of which, through uncertainty as to their nature, can be determined only through inspection and classification and stipulations made by the insured.[16]

Unclassifiable (C.7). This class embraces merchandise or materials that cannot be identified with any of the preceding classes, or that, if so classifiable by their physical characteristics, have a known record that discredits them because of their tendency to combustion, either spontaneous or because of an undiscovered hazard. On the other hand, a few risks of this class, for reasons that cannot be definitely determined, have an apparently favorable record. Class C.7 also embraces a number of special hazards. Risks of Class C.7 are necessarily graded by judgment.

The system recognizes that packages, wrappings, display shelving, or, in some cases, the materials used for packing will affect combustibility and, hence, influence classification. The same is true with respect to debris resulting from unpacking. Classification is also influenced by either quantity or density of arrangement, or both. When large quantities are crowded in premises such as warehouses or industrial risks, this will tend to increase the grade of combustibility. On the other hand, there are situations where highly combustible materials in small quantities are regarded as inconsequential. This is the case with respect to matches, oils, or chemicals found in stocks of groceries, general merchandise, or retail drugstores. There are other situations, such as when an industrial process on a small scale is carried on in the open in connection with the regular mercantile stock. If the material in process, including debris, is in such a quantity as not to be regarded as negligible, the combustible materials in process may determine the classification to the end that the grade of combustibility will be higher than a regular stock of similar nature. When a variety of materials is used in processing, grading is governed by the most combustible material unless this material is so small in quantity or kept under such conditions that it may be considered negligible as a factor of hazard. Mixed stocks, consisting of two or more distinct classes in quantities sufficient to determine the character and extent of combustion, are classed by the contents of highest combustibility.

Damageability. The analytic system gives consideration to the effect of fires as either (*a*) direct, or (*b*) resultant. Direct effects are those caused by the actual combustion of the substances themselves or by change in their molecular structure caused by the heat of adjacent

[16] Risks of this class necessarily take one of the regular grades (C.1–C.5, inclusive), the grade being subject to modification when stipulations eliminate dangerous substances and processes.

combustion. Resultant effects are those that are incidental to fires, caused either by the efforts to suppress combustion or to remove merchandise from burning premises or by effects of adjacent combustion other than heat. The most usual resultant effects of fire are from smoke, water, dampness, change of temperature, and breakage.[17] As in the case of combustibility, damageability may be determined by reference to the alphabetical occupancy list for the occupancies named therein. For occupancies that may for some reason or other have not found their way into the list, the basis of classification is helpful. There are five grades of damageability with three intermediate grades. These are:

Low (D.1). This includes merchandise that is largely immune to resultant effects, being material affected only by the direct effect of fire. Heavy hardware, granite ware, cement in bulk, and heavy iron and steel stocks are included in this classification.

Intermediate A (D.1½). This includes merchandise that is but slightly subject to direct and resultant effects, consisting of combined stocks of D.1 and D.2 or D.3. Also stocks of D.1, D.2, or D.3 which may have their damageability raised or reduced by nature of the materials entering into their manufacture or by nature of their containers. Packaged dry goods in warehouses, sugar storage, and heavy wholesale grocery stocks not including such items as oils, cigars or matches, carpets and rugs, rough heavy leather stocks, and lead pipe and sheet lead stocks indicate the nature of this classification.

Middling (D.2). This includes merchandise that is but moderately affected by direct and resultant effects. Examples of this classification are retail grocery stocks, battery stocks, wholesale dry goods, boots and shoes, and bottle and hollow glassware stocks.

Intermediate B (D.2½). This includes merchandise that is subject to considerable damage by direct or resultant effects, consisting of combined stocks of D.2, D.3, and small quantities of D.4. Also stocks of D.2 or D.3 which may have their damageability raised or reduced by nature of the materials entering into their manufacture or by nature of their containers. Fancy leather goods, clothing stocks, barber supply stocks, druggist sundries, and jewelry and plated ware stocks fall into this category.

High (D.3). This includes merchandise that is easily damageable by direct or resultant effects. Musical merchandise, books and stationery school supplies, bakeries, eggs, broom corn stocks, and silks and notions are to be found in this group.

Intermediate C (D.3½). This includes merchandise that is subject to heavy damage by direct or resultant effects, consisting of

[17] Merchandise that is highly susceptible to damage may have its damageability materially reduced by protective packages, and this is taken into account in the classification.

combined stocks of D.3 and D.4. Also included are stocks of D.3 or D.4 which may have their damageability raised or reduced by nature of the materials entering into their manufacture or by nature of their containers. An example is furniture repair stocks.

Extra High (D.4). This includes merchandise that is liable to heavy damage from slight causes, either direct or resultant ("total loss risks"). As noted, here are to be found types of merchandise that a fire would completely destroy, such as artificial flowers, florists' stocks, contents of greenhouses, decalcomania stocks, cigars, cigarettes, works of art, fireworks, and celluloid in process.

Indefinite (D.5). This consists of mixed or changeable stocks of differing degrees of damageability of which the average damageability should be established by personal estimate. General storage warehouses and department stores serve to illustrate this group.

In the alphabetical occupancy list under the column marked "Damageability," the relative susceptibility of each occupancy is represented by one of the symbols in the classifications just given. Unlike the basic occupancy charge for combined occupancies belonging to two or more distinct classes of combustibility where the highest combustibility classification applies to any of the contents of such occupancy, with respect to damageability for occupancies having contents belonging to two or more distinct classes, damageability is determined by an average of the charges.

The Contents Table. Under normal circumstances, contents can be expected to be more susceptible to damage than buildings. It follows, therefore, that the rate on contents will be higher than the rate on buildings. This difference between the hazard of the buildings and the hazard of contents is said to be the "contents differential." It is the amount added to the building rate in order to obtain the contents rate.

The location of stock may have a bearing on damageability. Location is reflected in the rates only in buildings of B construction. Both A construction and D construction give the same charge regardless of the location in the building. Merchandise in buildings of B construction located on the first floor is regarded in a more favorable position than merchandise in basement or on upper floors. The differential is also dependent on the value of the fire department protection to a given class of contents. The differential increases with the value of fire protection. Under the higher grades of protection it is expected there will be a greater difference in the amount of loss on contents than is the case where for the lack of protection the damage to both buildings and contents may be expected to be severe. The increased differential does not result in a higher contents rate than would develop for a similar risk under lower grades of municipal protection but rather produces a rate on contents where the difference between building and contents rates is both actually and relatively greater than is the case with lower grades of protection.

A table, known as a "Contents Table," is prepared that shows the amount to be added to the occupied building rate to obtain the rate of contents. The table represented by Table 30–7 is a 70 contents table for buildings of B construction. For purposes of comparison, the master contents table to be found in the schedule is reproduced as Table 30–8. The designation "Contents Table No. 70" means that the table shows amounts that are 70 percent of the master contents table.

Exposure Charges. In both the universal system and the analytic system of rating, charges incorporated in the rates are dependent, among other factors, upon the construction of adjoining buildings, the distance between risks which affect each other, protection, and the hazards of the exposing risk. That part of the rate attributable to adjoining properties is termed an "exposure charge."

In the mercantile system the charges are flat, as in the case of other charges. In the analytic system charges for exposures are based on the assumption that every risk absorbs a ratio of the hazard to which it is exposed and that, by the same reasoning, it transmits a ratio of absorbed hazards. Finally, the risk itself radiates hazards inherent to it. This gives rise to the three following classifications: (*a*) radiated exposure, (*b*) absorbed exposure, and (*c*) transmitted exposure. Radiated exposure consists of the proportion of its own hazard a risk radiates toward exposed risk. Absorbed exposure consists of the proportion of exposure hazard absorbed by an exposed risk. Transmitted exposure consists of the proportion of the hazard a risk absorbs on one side and transmits to a risk on another side. The ratio of radiated, absorbed, and transmitted exposures is modified by the structure of the facing walls, clear space intervening, and fire department protection. This relationship is illustrated by the use of three rectangles, each representing a building, each of which exposes the other. In Figure 30–1, the arrows indicate the direction in which the exposure is radiated. The arrowhead is to be found in the building that absorbs the exposure and the feathered end in the building which radiates the exposure. Where broken lines appear, exposures are represented as having been transmitted through an intermediate risk.

The individual rate of a building is the rate as computed by the rules for A, B, or D construction and includes all charges for structural or protective features; it does not include any charges for exposure, or after-charges. The exposed rate of a building is the rate after all charges for exposure have been added. The amount determined from the schedule to be added to the building rate is the "exposure load" of the building. An exposure load is also computed for contents. The exposure charge for building and contents may be and generally is the same. Exceptions exist, as in the case of wall damage exposure which applies to building rate but not to contents rate makeup.

After-Charges. After-charges, sometimes called "condition charges," are the only factors in the analytic system represented by

TABLE 30–7
CONTENTS TABLE NO. 70
Buildings of B Construction

Location of Contents	D1.	D1½.	D2.	D2½.	D3.	D3½.	D4.	
First Class Protection				(Deduct .11 for *)				
Basement	$0.30	$0.39	$0.47	$0.57	$0.66	$0.76	$0.85	B
Ground floor	**.22**	**.30**	**.38**	**.47**	**.55**	**.65**	**.74**	1
Second floor	.30	.39	.47	.57	.66	.76	.85	2
Third floor	.35	.44	.53	.63	.72	.83	.93	3
Fourth floor	.41	.50	.59	.69	.79	.90	1.01	4
Fifth floor	.46	.55	.65	.76	.86	.97	1.09	5
Sixth floor	.50	.61	.71	.82	.92	1.04	1.16	6
Seventh floor	.55	.67	.77	.88	.99	1.12	1.24	7
Eighth floor and higher	.61	.72	.83	.95	1.06	1.19	1.32	8
Second Class Protection				(Deduct .11 for *)				
Basement	$0.29	$0.37	$0.45	$0.55	$0.64	$0.74	$0.83	B
Ground floor	**.21**	**.29**	**.36**	**.45**	**.53**	**.62**	**.71**	1
Second floor	.29	.37	.45	.55	.64	.74	.83	2
Third floor	.34	.43	.51	.61	.70	.81	.90	3
Fourth floor	.39	.48	.57	.67	.77	.88	.98	4
Fifth floor	.44	.54	.63	.74	.84	.95	1.06	5
Sixth floor	.49	.60	.69	.80	.90	1.02	1.13	6
Seventh floor	.55	.65	.75	.86	.97	1.09	1.21	7
Eighth floor and higher	.60	.71	.81	.92	1.04	1.16	1.29	8
Third Class Protection				(Deduct .11 for *)				
Basement	$0.28	$0.36	$0.43	$0.53	$0.62	$0.71	$0.81	B
Ground floor	**.20**	**.28**	**.35**	**.43**	**.51**	**.60**	**.69**	1
Second floor	.28	.36	.43	.53	.62	.71	.81	2
Third floor	.33	.41	.50	.60	.69	.78	.88	3
Fourth floor	.39	.47	.55	.65	.75	.85	.96	4
Fifth floor	.43	.53	.62	.72	.82	.93	1.04	5
Sixth floor	.48	.58	.69	.78	.89	1.00	1.11	6
Seventh floor and higher	.54	.64	.74	.85	.95	1.07	1.19	7
Fourth Class Protection				(Deduct .11 for *)				
Basement	$0.27	$0.34	$0.41	$0.50	$0.59	$0.69	$0.78	B
Ground floor	**.19**	**.26**	**.33**	**.41**	**.49**	**.57**	**.67**	1
Second floor	.27	.34	.41	.50	.59	.69	.78	2
Third floor	.32	.40	.48	.57	.66	.76	.85	3
Fourth floor	.37	.46	.53	.63	.73	.83	.93	4
Fifth floor	.42	.51	.60	.69	.79	.90	1.01	5
Sixth floor and higher	.48	.57	.66	.76	.85	.97	1.09	6
Fifth Class Protection				(Deduct .10 for *)				
Basement	$0.26	$0.33	$0.40	$0.48	$0.57	$0.66	$0.75	B
Ground floor	**.18**	**.25**	**.31**	**.39**	**.47**	**.55**	**.64**	1
Second floor	.26	.33	.40	.48	.57	.66	.75	2
Third floor	.31	.39	.46	.55	.64	.74	.83	3
Fourth floor	.36	.44	.52	.62	.71	.81	.90	4
Fifth floor and higher	.41	.50	.57	.67	.77	.88	.98	5
Sixth Class Protection				(Deduct .09 for *)				
Basement	$0.24	$0.31	$0.37	$0.46	$0.54	$0.63	$0.71	B
Ground floor	**.17**	**.22**	**.28**	**.36**	**.44**	**.53**	**.60**	1
Second floor	.24	.31	.37	.46	.54	.63	.71	2
Third floor	.29	.36	.43	.52	.61	.70	.79	3
Fourth floor	.34	.42	.49	.59	.68	.78	.87	4
Fifth floor and higher	.40	.48	.55	.64	.74	.85	.95	5
Seventh Class Protection				(Deduct .08 for *)				
Basement	$0.22	$0.29	$0.35	$0.43	$0.52	$0.60	$0.69	B
Ground floor	**.15**	**.21**	**.26**	**.34**	**.41**	**.50**	**.57**	1
Second floor	.22	.29	.35	.43	.52	.60	.69	2
Third floor	.28	.34	.41	.50	.58	.67	.76	3
Fourth floor and higher	.33	.40	.47	.56	.65	.75	.84	4
Eighth Class Protection				(Deduct .06 for *)				
Basement	$0.20	$0.25	$0.31	$0.39	$0.47	$0.55	$0.63	B
Ground floor	**.12**	**.17**	**.22**	**.29**	**.36**	**.44**	**.52**	1
Second floor	.20	.25	.31	.39	.47	.55	.63	2
Third floor	.25	.31	.36	.45	.53	.62	.71	3
Fourth floor and higher	.30	.36	.43	.52	.60	.69	.78	4
Ninth Class Protection			(For * use 10th Class Charges)					
Basement	$0.17	$0.22	$0.26	$0.34	$0.42	$0.50	$0.57	B
Ground floor	**.09**	**.13**	**.18**	**.25**	**.32**	**.39**	**.46**	1
Second floor	.17	.22	.26	.34	.42	.50	.57	2
Third floor and higher	.22	.27	.32	.41	.48	.57	.65	3
Tenth Class Protection								
Basement	$0.15	$0.19	$0.23	$0.31	$0.39	$0.46	$0.53	B
Ground floor	**.07**	**.11**	**.14**	**.21**	**.28**	**.35**	**.42**	1
Second floor	.15	.19	.23	.31	.39	.46	.53	2
Third floor and higher	.20	.25	.29	.37	.45	.53	.61	3
	D1.	**D1½.**	**D2.**	**D2½.**	**D3.**	**D3½.**	**D4.**	

Source: *Analytic System*—Copyright, 1921, by J. V. Parker; 1952, by R. D. Hobbs; 1955, 1965 by Western Actuarial Bureau. Used with permission.

TABLE 30–8
MASTER CONTENTS TABLE
Buildings of B Construction

Location of Contents.	**D1.**	**D1½.**	**D2.**	**D2½.**	**D3.**	**D3½.**	**D4.**	
First Class Protection					(Deduct .16 for *)			
Basement	$0.43	$0.55	$0.67	$0.81	$0.94	$1.08	$1.22	B
Ground floor	**.32**	**.43**	**.54**	**.67**	**.79**	**.93**	**1.06**	1
Second floor	.43	.55	.67	.81	.94	1.08	1.22	2
Third floor	.50	.63	.76	.90	1.03	1.18	1.33	3
Fourth floor	.58	.71	.84	.99	1.13	1.29	1.44	4
Fifth floor	.65	.79	.93	1.08	1.23	1.39	1.55	5
Sixth floor	.72	.87	1.01	1.17	1.32	1.49	1.66	6
Seventh floor	.79	.95	1.10	1.25	1.42	1.60	1.77	7
Eighth floor and higher.	.87	1.03	1.18	1.35	1.52	1.70	1.88	8
Second Class Protection					(Deduct .16 for *)			
Basement	$0.41	$0.53	$0.64	$0.78	$0.91	$1.05	$1.18	B
Ground floor	**.30**	**.41**	**.52**	**.64**	**.76**	**.89**	**1.02**	1
Second floor	.41	.53	.64	.78	.91	1.05	1.18	2
Third floor	.48	.61	.73	.87	1.00	1.15	1.29	3
Fourth floor	.56	.69	.81	.96	1.10	1.25	1.40	4
Fifth floor	.63	.77	.90	1.05	1.20	1.36	1.51	5
Sixth floor	.70	.85	.98	1.14	1.29	1.46	1.62	6
Seventh floor	.78	.93	1.07	1.23	1.39	1.56	1.73	7
Eighth floor and higher.	.86	1.01	1.15	1.32	1.49	1.66	1.84	8
Third Class Protection					(Deduct .15 for *)			
Basement	$0.40	$0.51	$0.62	$0.75	$0.88	$1.02	$1.15	B
Ground floor	**.29**	**.40**	**.50**	**.62**	**.73**	**.86**	**.99**	1
Second floor	.40	.51	.62	.75	.88	1.02	1.15	2
Third floor	.47	.59	.71	.85	.98	1.12	1.26	3
Fourth floor	.55	.67	.79	.93	1.07	1.22	1.37	4
Fifth floor	.62	.75	.88	1.03	1.17	1.33	1.48	5
Sixth floor	.69	.83	.96	1.12	1.27	1.43	1.59	6
Seventh floor and higher	.77	.91	1.05	1.21	1.36	1.53	1.70	7
Fourth Class Protection					(Deduct .15 for *)			
Basement	$0.38	$0.49	$0.59	$0.72	$0.84	$0.98	$1.11	B
Ground floor	**.27**	**.37**	**.47**	**.59**	**.70**	**.82**	**.95**	1
Second floor	.38	.49	.59	.72	.84	.98	1.11	2
Third floor	.45	.57	.68	.81	.94	1.08	1.22	3
Fourth floor	.53	.65	.76	.90	1.04	1.18	1.33	4
Fifth floor	.60	.73	.85	.99	1.13	1.29	1.44	5
Sixth floor and higher..	.68	.81	.94	1.08	1.22	1.39	1.55	6
Fifth Class Protection					(Deduct .14 for *)			
Basement	$0.37	$0.47	$0.57	$0.69	$0.81	$0.94	$1.07	B
Ground floor	**.26**	**.35**	**.44**	**.56**	**.67**	**.79**	**.91**	1
Second floor	.37	.47	.57	.69	.81	.94	1.07	2
Third floor	.44	.55	.65	.78	.91	1.05	1.18	3
Fourth floor	.51	.63	.74	.88	1.01	1.15	1.29	4
Fifth floor and higher..	.59	.71	.82	.96	1.10	1.25	1.40	5
Sixth Class Protection					(Deduct .13 for *)			
Basement	$0.34	$0.44	$0.53	$0.65	$0.77	$0.90	$1.02	B
Ground floor	**.24**	**.32**	**.40**	**.52**	**.63**	**.75**	**.86**	1
Second floor	.34	.44	.53	.65	.77	.90	1.02	2
Third floor	.42	.52	.61	.74	.87	1.00	1.13	3
Fourth floor	.49	.60	.70	.84	.97	1.11	1.24	4
Fifth floor and higher..	.57	.68	.78	.92	1.06	1.21	1.36	5
Seventh Class Protection					(Deduct .12 for *)			
Basement	$0.32	$0.41	$0.50	$0.62	$0.74	$0.86	$0.98	B
Ground floor	**.22**	**.30**	**.37**	**.48**	**.59**	**.71**	**.82**	1
Second floor	.32	.41	.50	.62	.74	.86	.98	2
Third floor	.40	.49	.58	.71	.83	.96	1.09	3
Fourth floor and higher.	.47	.57	.67	.80	.93	1.07	1.20	4
Eighth Class Protection					(Deduct .09 for *)			
Basement	$0.28	$0.36	$0.44	$0.56	$0.67	$0.79	$0.90	B
Ground floor	**.17**	**.24**	**.31**	**.42**	**.52**	**.63**	**.74**	1
Second floor	.28	.36	.44	.56	.67	.79	.90	2
Third floor	.36	.44	.52	.64	.76	.89	1.01	3
Fourth floor and higher.	.43	.52	.61	.74	.86	.99	1.12	4
Ninth Class Protection				(For * use 10th Class charges)				
Basement	$0.24	$0.31	$0.37	$0.49	$0.60	$0.71	$0.82	B
Ground floor	**.13**	**.19**	**.25**	**.35**	**.45**	**.56**	**.66**	1
Second floor	.24	.31	.37	.49	.60	.71	.82	2
Third floor and higher..	.31	.39	.46	.58	.69	.81	.93	3
Tenth Class Protection								
Basement	$0.21	$0.27	$0.33	$0.44	$0.55	$0.66	$0.76	B
Ground floor	**.10**	**.15**	**.20**	**.30**	**.40**	**.50**	**.60**	1
Second floor	.21	.27	.33	.44	.55	.66	.76	2
Third floor and higher..	.28	.35	.41	.53	.64	.76	.87	3
	D1.	**D1½.**	**D2.**	**D2½.**	**D3.**	**D3½.**	**D4.**	

Source: *Analytic System*—Copyright, 1921, by J. V. Parker; 1952, by R. D. Hobbs; 1955, 1965, by Western Actuarial Bureau. Used with permission.

flat instead of percentage charges. They represent hazards that are temporarily present in the risk and are features of the risk that lend themselves readily to correction. Hence, they are not in a real sense a proportionate part of the risk that would in the usual course be measured by a percentage charge.[18]

After-charges are made for faults of management or for objectionable hazardous conditions. The unsafe arrangement of a heating apparatus would call for an after-charge, since this hazard is a matter of the condition of the plant and is not concerned with the presence of the plant itself. Unsafe arrangements of occupancy hazards, poor housekeeping, rubbish, or the improper handling of waste are all features that call for an after-charge. If there is any punitive feature in the system, the after-charge may be considered such. This is true since the condition of the risk that calls for the after-charge can in the ordinary course be corrected, and from the standpoint of both the insured and the insurer, the correction of the defect and the removal of the charge are desired objectives.

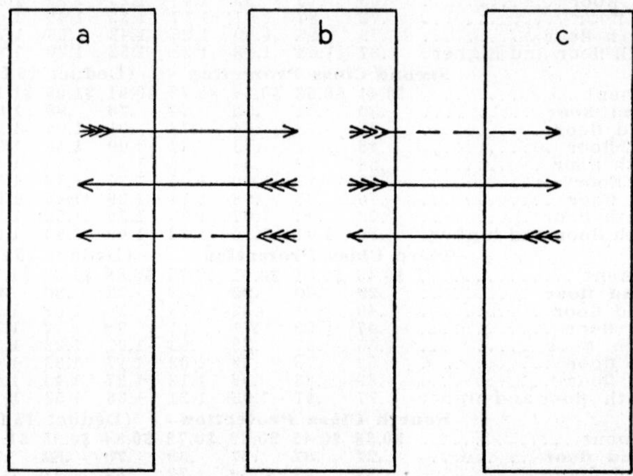

FIG. 30–1. Diagrammatic illustration of radiated, absorbed, and transmitted exposures.

A list of hazards calling for after-charges together with the charges, therefore, are a part of the system. After-charges for A buildings may be as low as 1/10 of 1¢ and generally are considerably lower than those applied to B or D buildings. These charges are sometimes as high as $1. In some adaptations of the system after-charges have been made as high as $4. After-charges apply in addition to specific charges, if any, for safe or approved arrangement, unless charges for unsafe or unapproved arrangement have already been covered. Since after-charges

[18] After-charges are not peculiar to the analytic system of schedule rating. They are a part of all schedules. After-charges are noticed at this point to give emphasis to the fact that in the analytic system after-charges are flat sums where all other charges and credits are percentages of the basis rate.

are not always quoted in the schedule as specific amounts but are frequently quoted as, for example, "1¢ to 25¢" or "5¢ to $1.00," it is apparent that in the application of after-charges the element of judgment is an important factor. Because of this in the application of after-charges there is found a possible source of variation among raters using the system. Not all raters are in agreement as to the need for a charge in a particular situation nor for the exact amount to be charged for the degree of hazard involved.

With respect to the element of judgment that may creep in through the application of after-charges or the suggestion that after-charges may be punitive, and, hence, excessive, this should not be held as a criticism of this system of rating. Actually the features that bring about after-charges should be removed. If they are removed, there can be no question of inequity, since there will be no after-charge. More serious, perhaps, is criticism that the after-charge feature in a rate has not always been brought to the attention of the insured, or, if it has, not with sufficient force. The recommendation has been made that where there are charges for correctable features in a risk, some method, originating with the rating authority, should be developed for notifying the insured. It has also been suggested that if, after notification, conditions are not remedied, the rate when published should contain some special designation indicating that an after-charge has been included in the rate structure of the risk. Such a promulgation would place an insurance agent or broker or any other person having access to tariffs on notice that the rate contains an after-charge that may be removed if the hazardous condition calling for the charge is corrected.

Coordination of the Tables. Certain of the salient features of the analytic system may now be reviewed. In order to determine a rate, reference is made, first, to the applicable basis table. Assuming a building of B construction four stories high, located in a class 5 town, by referring to Table 30–4, we find a basis rate of 0.324. Next, reference is made to the alphabetical occupancy list. A page from this list is reproduced in Table 30–6. Assuming the occupancy of the building about to be rated is syrup and sugar stocks, it is found that this is listed as item 2106 in the occupancy list. Columns 1 and 2 under the "B" caption apply with respect to A and B construction. Columns 1 and 2 under the "D" heading apply to D construction. Since interest attaches to a B construction building, column 1 and 2 charges for item 2106 are 3 percent and 5 percent of the basis rate, respectively. It will be recalled that the charge in column 1 is concerned with causes of fire and the charge in column 2 has to do with combustibility.

In the discussion of causes and combustibility, in the case of multiple occupancies, causes are cumulative, while with respect to media the highest combustibility prevails. This works out as follows. Assume in a single building there is a slaughterhouse, a smokehouse, and a soap factory. Referring to the alphabetical occupancy list, it is seen that a slaughterhouse to be starred risk with column 1 and 2 ratings to be 200 percent and 80 percent, respectively. The smokehouse charges for smoking in compartments are 55 percent and 40 percent, respectively. In the case of a soap manufacturing risk, column 1 and 2 charges are 65 percent and 40 percent. These are applied as follows:

	Column 1	*Column 2*
Slaughterhouse	200%	80%
Smokehouse	55	40
Soap factory	65	40
Total column 1 charges	320	
Add highest column 2 charge	80	
	400%	

Thus, we give cognizance to the cumulative feature of column 1 charges and to the charge for highest combustibility in column 2. The charge for the three occupancies just indicated would be 400 percent of the basis rate.

When the column 1 and column 2 charges have been determined, reference may be made to the third column of the alphabetical occupancy list under the caption "Damageability." The symbol in this column is used to determine the charge to be added to the unexposed building rate in order to obtain the rate for contents. This feature of the rate takes into consideration damageability and the location of the contents in the building under each class of fire protection. In the case of the syrup and sugar storage risk, the applicable damageability symbol to be D.1½. Next, referring to the contents table, "Contents Table No. 70," that appears in Table 30–7, it is found that for a Class B building with fifth-class protection, four floors and basement, the charge is 0.35. This is found by taking an average of the D.1½ contents charges for basement, first, second, third, and fourth floors. This average represents the contents differential applying to the entire building. This figure is not a percentage charge but an amount in cents that is added to unexposed building rate. In rating a building the structural charges and occupancy charges are added together and applied to the basis rate, and from this are subtracted first the credit of superior structural features and then the credit for protective features. This produces the unexposed building rate to which is added exposures and after-charges to produce the final building rate.

Multiple Location Rating Plans. A multiple location rating plan is in effect a modification of fire rating for a special group of risks. An example of the procedures used in this type of rating will be briefly considered.

Calculation of Final Annual Average Rates. The calculation of the annual average rate to reflect expense savings, dispersion of risks, and efficiency of management in loss prevention work involves three steps: (1) credits based on size of the premium, (2) credits based on number of locations, and (3) decreases in credits for an unfavorable loss ratio.

The first step in determining a final average rate is taken by applying to the average values in the application of the basic average rate. This gives a basic annual premium. A total of the basic annual premium for all contributing insurance is found. This gives the premium subject to credit. Credits ranging from 9 percent to 20 percent are allowed based on the size of premium and these credits are applicable to that portion of the premium over $1,000. These credits are computed to reflect expense savings, dispersion of risk, and efficiency of management in loss prevention work.

The next step involves credits based on the number of locations and the maximum percentage of net average value at any one location. The credits are determined from two tables constructed for that purpose. The indicated percentage derived from the table is applied to that amount of premium subject to credit in excess of $1,000. Which of the two tables is used is determined by the fire loss frequency of the insured. An insured having a record of low fire loss frequency will receive higher credits than a policyholder with more numerous losses.

The total credits developed on the basis of premium size and number of locations comprise the total credits allowed under the plan. There is a third and final step in the rate calculation. The credits determined are decreased where the fire loss ratio for the experience period exceeds 50 percent. This reduction is determined by entering a table based on the fire loss ratio and the number of fire losses. The net dollar credit is divided by the premium subject to credit to convert the net dollar credit to a percentage. The basic average annual rate is reduced by this percentage to determine the net average annual rate. The figure thus obtained is the rate to be used in premium calculations. This plan is used for Form No. 1, No. 2, and No. 5. This is determined by using the class floater rates applicable to the property which is the subject of the insurance. In the case of Form No. 1, No. 2, and No. 5 eligible for credits, the rates developed by the plan are used for computing the final premium charge. Form No. 2 differs from the others in that the final average rate is computed at the end of the contract term and replaces a provisional rate used at the inception of the coverage.

Application for Average Rate. The average rate applicable to the properties located in the various states is the responsibility of the rating bureau having jurisdiction. Since the value of a multiple location coverage derives from the fact that the insurance may cover across state lines, the plan provides for the development of a uniform average rate applicable to all properties of the insured. To effect this, provision is made for the cooperation and assistance of all rating bureaus concerned. One rating bureau is appointed to be known as the "sponsoring rating bureau." The insured designates a broker or agent to represent him. The broker so designated selects an insurer to negotiate with the sponsoring bureau. An application is filed containing all the essential data, and upon receipt of this application the sponsoring rating bureau calculates the final average rate in accordance with the plan based on property at all locations in all states in which the plan is approved and then promulgates the average rate so found as the rate for its own territory. The sponsoring rating bureau then sends to the filing insurer or its authorized representative, a certificate known as the "Final Average Rate Certification."

The filing insurer then takes steps to supply a certified copy or a photo copy of the certification to each interested rating bureau. The rating bureaus receiving the certification are then in a position so that each may promulgate the rates appearing in the certificate for its own territory. The rules provide that the filing insurer or its authorized representative will furnish a copy of the application and rate computation to any interested rating bureaus.

Pending the promulgation of an average rate, a filing insurer may itself calculate average rates for temporary use. Such rates are termed "tentative rates" and are used only to issue contract pending promulgation of final average rates. When a tentative rate is used, the contract is so endorsed and a provision is made that when the final average rates are promulgated by the bureau having jurisdiction they will be applied and become effective from the commencement date of the contract. If, during a contract term, conditions become materially changed, a new average rate based upon such changed conditions is promulgated by the rating bureau having jurisdiction, and the new average rate applies from its effective date even to contracts already in force.

RATING FOR LIABILITY AND RELATED INSURANCE COVERAGES

Class rating procedures are used for such liability lines as owners', landlords', and tenants' liability, manufacturers and contractors liability, products liability, auto liability, workmen's compensation, boiler insurance, and fidelity lines. Modifications of class rates based on statistical experience is common in automobile, workmen's compensation, general liability and fidelity lines. Workmen's compensation insurance will be used in this section as an example of experience modification procedures. The basic workmen's compensation rate is arrived at through the use of territorial and occupational class coding and related statistical data. Experience is then used to modify the basic class rate.

Experience Rating Plan. As was explained earlier in this chapter, experience rating bases its findings upon the past experience of the particular risk under consideration. For the purpose of experience rating, the experience of the particular risk is compiled. If the accident history shows a cost below normal for the class, a credit in the rate is allowed, while an unfavorable experience results in a debit. This credit is applied to the manual rate to find the new or adjusted rate. When the risk is very large, manual rates may be referred to, but experience will, in effect, almost absolutely be the sole basis for composing the rate. Such risks are said to be self-rated. To qualify for experience rating, the risk must produce a designated minimum premium figured at manual rates. The most common minimum premium for experience rating is $750. The usual experience period is the three years preceding the last contract period. There are now five retrospective rating plans available, but generally these plans are not considered at the $1,000 premium level.

The term "standard premium" is used to designate that premium determined by applying manual rates to the employer's payroll modified by either experience rating or schedule rating. In those instances where the annual standard premium exceeds $1,000, the insured has available to him four plans from which to choose that will further modify the premium charge. These include the premium discount plan and five retrospective rating plans.

The Premium Discount Plan. Workmen's compensation rating plans recognize that certain factors that enter into the premium charge do not increase proportionately as the premium increases. The principal factors considered are: losses; claim expense; engineering and accident prevention; administration and payroll audit expenses; acquisition costs; and taxes. Under the premium discount plan a definite portion of the first $1,000 of premium is allocated for insurer expenses and acquisition costs. As the size of the risk increases, certain insurer expenses and acquisition costs are graded down. It is the purpose of the plan, as the premium increases, to give credit for those expenses that do not increase proportionately. The first $1,000 of premium is standard. Premium in excess of $1,000 is grouped in brackets, and a discount applied. The discount is greater in the higher brackets. The net effect of this plan is to provide a reduction from the standard premium as the premium increases in amount. The theory upon which these premiums are computed is sometimes referred to as the "principle of graded expense."

The premium discount plan, in contrast to the retrospective plans, does not provide for a modification of the premium as a result of current loss experiences. It does take into consideration past experience, since the discount is applied to the standard premium, which, in turn, is modified by experience rating. The discounts are applied for the purpose of reflecting a lower ratio of expenses and acquisition cost to premiums in the higher brackets. The net effect is to provide a lower premium than would be the case if the standard rates applied uniformly to the entire payroll.

Retrospective Rating Plans. These plans differ from the premium discount plans in that under the premium discount plan there is no modification for current loss experience, while this is the distinguishing feature of the restrospective plans. These plans are not separate and apart from experience rating but are, in effect, supplementary. While experience rating looks definitely to the past to determine the rate for the future, retrospective rating permits the insured to influence his premium by his current performance. It is, in fact, an arrangement for giving consideration to future experience at the time the contract is written. Instead of assuming that the future will equal the past, retrospective rating gives consideration in its final charge to the actual experience during the contract term. Measured from the inception date of the contract, it is an arrangement whereby at a future date a premium will be computed based upon the losses which actually occurred during the contract period. It is apparent that at the inception date of the contract the actual anticipated experience can only be estimated. Under the retrospective plan, if the experience is particularly good, a credit reflects to the insured in his premium charge. If the experience is unsatisfactory, the cost to the insured is reflected in an increased premium. For the protection of the insured, upper limits to the cost are established; and for the protection of the insurer, lower limits are established. The term "cost plus" has sometimes been applied to this rating plan.

The retrospective plan provides for the determination of a basic premium, which is a percentage of the standard premium, developed by applying the regular manual or experience rates to the reported payroll of the insured. This basic premium provides for the agent's commission, home office expenses, audit, and safety inspection expenses, and since the insurer guarantees the cost will not exceed an upper limit, there is a small charge for insurance. This insurance charge or loading, as it is termed, provides actually for losses that develop in excess of the maximum premium. There is no charge in the basic premium for claims expense or premium tax. These are computed when the losses are determined. Loss expense is added to the amount of actual losses when the final premium is determined. The losses plus loss expense produce an amount known as the "converted loss figure." The converted loss figure plus the basic premium is increased by the amount of tax required in the particular state. This practice limits loss expense and taxes to actual dispersements on the particular risk and precludes any overcharge that might lurk in an estimate.

In actual operation the plan provides for three premiums: (1) minimum retrospective premium, (2) maximum retrospective premium, and (3) retrospective premium. The plan provides that the insured shall pay, in any case, the premium known as the "minimum retrospective premium." He is protected in that he never may be called upon to pay more than the maximum retrospective premium. The premium he will pay will probably fall somewhere between the two; this is known as the "retrospective premium" and is determined by adding to the basic premium the losses incurred, modified to provide for taxes and claim adjustment expenses. Under the plan, the premium charged may be the minimum retrospective premium, and this is considerably less than the manual rate. It may be more than the minimum retrospective premium, depending upon the experience of the risk, but the possibility of excessive losses is cut off by the provision that the premium may never exceed the maximum retrospective premium.

The retrospective rating plan gives the insured the same credit for decreasing administration and acquisition expenses as does the premium discount plan. In addition, however, the retrospective rating plan reflects current losses in the current premium charge. This is, in fact, a protected profit-sharing plan. With a good experience, the insured shares the profits. With an unfavorable experience, he shares the losses. The amount of loss in any year is subject to a definite limit. From the standpoint of the insured, this is particularly attractive because he gets immediate credit for such care as he may exercise in reducing his loss experience. From the point of view of the insurer, it is equally attractive because anything that will stimulate activity on the part of the insured to cut his losses will in the long run reflect to the benefit of the insurer.

There are five forms of retrospective rating known as plans A, B, C, D, and J. These plans are alike in principle but vary in detail, principally with reference to the fixing of the maximum and minimum premiums. In addition, several states have adopted retrospective plans of their own. All of the plans, however, are alike in that they aim to have the current premium predicated upon the loss experience of the current year.

RATE DETERMINATION IN MULTIPLE LINE INSURANCE

With the enactment of legislation permitting property and liability insurers to write all forms of insurance except life, the first move in the direction of multiple line underwriting evidenced itself in contracts that were, in fact, combinations of already existing coverages. It was but a step to develop all risks coverages that provided the protection formerly obtainable only by the purchase of several contracts and afforded in addition coverage for gaps in protection in areas where the individual contracts did not extend.

All risks protection called for a new approach to rating. Broad coverages could be afforded only at prohibitive cost when pieced together peril by peril. To meet the requirements of this new approach to rating, a rating organization geared to the multiple peril concept was essential. The Multi-Line Insurance Rating Bureau (formerly the Multiple Peril Insurance Rating Organization) was organized to deal with the rating aspects of multiple line insurance. Research as to forms and coverage is handled by the Fire Insurance Research and Actuarial Association. The rating bureau has the responsibility for providing rates for multiple line contracts without resorting to the necessity of putting together a rate based upon the known perils involved.

The rating organization approaches the multiple peril premium on much the same basis that the ocean marine underwriter approaches the premium for sea perils, by assuming it to be indivisible with respect to specific perils. There is no separate charge in the ocean marine rate for all the various sea perils covered. The premium covers the voyage subject to certain exceptions. The same is true with respect to fire and lightning in the fire insurance contract. There is no separate premium for fire and another charge for lightning. By maintaining records for risks in the multiperil category, separate hazards are not considered but all are grouped in a single risk. It is expected that the form will result in a demonstrable savings in premiums. Where the risk is large and where favorable underwriting factors evidence themselves, the savings can be appreciable.

The philosophy of multiple peril rating as carried on by the Multi-Line Insurance Rating Bureau contemplates loss data by risk and not by peril. The organization undertakes to maintain a statistical basis for the promulgation of rates free from dilution with results that are not comparable. For risks that the rating bureau promulgates rates, the arbitrary division of a unit premium among many hazards and among many statistical plans would defeat the objective. In order to keep costs reasonable and to avoid distortion with respect to the risks for which single premium rates are promulgated, the bureau has established a statistical plan to record underwriting results developed by the type of risk for which it promulgates rates. The plan is not a cut-rate insurance program for large risks. It is rather an undertaking to provide multiple line coverage on the basis of an experience developed by risks that are comparable.

The manufacturer's output contract is a multiple perils contract.

These contracts are to be distinguished from multiple location coverages that provide automatic insurance protection on reporting or coinsurance forms but are written on a named perils basis with rates applicable to the perils covered.

Rating of the Manufacturer's Output Contract.[19] The manufacturer's output contract has been selected as an example of multiple line rating. It is also an example of the role played by judgment in the determination of insurance rates.

Rating Procedure. Each risk insured under a manufacturer's output contract is specifically rated. Any insurer who is a member or subscriber to the Multi-Line Insurance Rating Bureau may submit a proposal for rating on a form provided by the organization. The data submitted are held confidential and will not be divulged except: if required by law, and after the rates for a risk have been promulgated. In this second instance a copy of the data used in determining rates may be obtained on request by any member or subscriber that is an insurer on the risk at the time the rate is made.

The rate is divided into two portions: normal loss rate, and major loss rate. The normal loss rate is designed to provide for all loss occurrences of $5,000 or under and the first $5,000 of losses over $5,000. The major loss rate is designed to provide for such portion of all loss occurrences as exceeds $5,000 each. In other words, losses less than $5,000 or the first $5,000 of losses that exceed that figure are in the normal loss category. If a loss exceeds $5,000, that part of the loss in excess of $5,000 is covered in the computations by the major loss rate. Normal losses do not include the amount of loss excluded by a deductible.

The normal loss rate is subject to substantial debits and credits based on the risk's experience on losses of less than $5,000. There are no experience modifications to the major loss rate which is derived from industry classification rates. They are modified by schedule to reflect hazards of the individual risk by a system of deficiency points requiring the analysis of eleven different factors affecting the risk.

Normal Loss Experience Modification. In computing the rate designed to provide for normal loss occurrences, reference is made to an industry classification. A copy from a page of the manual is reproduced in Table 30–9. There are six classifications, and a normal loss rate and a major loss rate are assigned to each. For the purposes of determining the normal loss experience modification, consideration is given to losses which have occurred covered by the type of insurance. The manual provides that the experience periods used shall be either the number of immediately preceding successive years during which the account has been insured under this type of contract, or the

[19] See Chapter 25 for an analysis of the provisions of this contract.

number of immediately preceding successive years prior to the existence for the account of this type of contract for which complete and credible value and loss data are available. The experience data must be for a period not less than nine months nor for a period longer than three years.

To secure the experience modification, expected normal losses are found by applying a normal loss rate found in the rate section to

TABLE 30–9

INDUSTRY CLASSIFICATION

Classification	*Group No.*
Abrasives, industrial, including abrasive paper and cloth	II
Acetate plastic products	II
Acids	II
Adding machines	II
Agricultural machinery	III
Air frames	II
Airplane engines	II
Alcohol, paints, varnish, turpentine	IV
Alkaline and saline products	II
Aluminum ware	I
Ammunition, matches, and explosives	VI
Animal products, including glue, fertilizer, gelatines	IV
Appliances, electrical	II
Asbestos	II
Asphalt and tar products, other than roofing, including creosote	II
Automobile	I
Automobile body, including trailer bodies	II
Automobile engine	II
Automobile parts and sub-assemblies, including radiators, wheels, lighting, ignition or starting apparatus, carburetors	II
Aviation instruments and related products, including propellors, instrument assemblies, synthetic training devices other than electronic devices	III
Bagging products, cordage, rope, and twine	III
Bags, paper	III
Bags, leather	III
Baked products, including crackers, cake, and macaroni	III
Ball and roller bearings	III
Barrels, metal—cans and containers	II
Baskets, wooden	V
Batteries and carbon	III
Bearings, ball and roller	III
Bedding, including mattresses, box springs, pillows, quilts, and cushions	V
Beer	II
Belting, industrial	I
Beverages, N.O.C., including beer and malt products	II

reported values. A concern manufacturing abrasives by reference to the rating classification finds itself in Group II. Reference then to a table will give an expected normal loss rate. By applying this rate to reported values, a figure representing expected normal losses is obtained. Normal losses for the experience period are tabulated. The modification of the normal loss rate is then computed based on a formula.

Where the actual normal losses are less than the expected losses the experience credit is computed as follows:

$$\text{Credit} = \frac{N}{36}\left(1 - \frac{A}{E}\right)$$

Where:
N = number of months in the experience period,
A = normal losses incurred in the experience period, and
E = expected losses.

Where the actual normal losses are more than the expected losses the formula becomes:

$$\text{Debit} = \frac{N}{36}\left(\frac{A}{E} - 1\right).$$

The debit or credit thus obtained is used to modify the normal loss rate. It follows that the modification provides a rate adjustment reflecting the experience with respect to normal losses, that is, losses under $5,000. The normal loss rate is also subject to minima based on the amount of deductible involved, and a maximum of $1.00.

Major Loss Rate. The major loss rate is not subject to modification on the basis of experience. While it is felt that the insured may have some control over small losses, the contributing factors to major losses are such that they do not lend themselves to experience credits. Industry classification rates are provided. They are expressed in a term that represents a range for each industry classification group. Within the range the rating organization establishes the final rate through the application of a point system. The major loss rate for industry Group II is quoted as 0.15–1.00. This means that the major loss rate for an industry in this classification may be as low as 0.15, but it may not exceed $1.00. Just where it falls between the two depends upon modifications added to the minimum major loss rate determined by the application of a deficiency point system.

The deficiency points take into consideration hazards of individual risk and are determined from the schedule shown in Table 30–10 on the basis of data revealed by the proposal and by reports of inspection.

There is a table of major loss rate modifications. When all the deficiency points applicable to a risk have been determined, reference to the table will indicate the change in cents that is to be added to the minimum loss rate for the applicable industry group shown in the rate section. This provides the major loss rate which must not exceed the maximum shown in the rate section.

Final Rate. The final rate is the sum of the modified normal loss rate and the modified major loss rate. A monthly rate is quoted. This is determined by dividing the annual rate by 12. A monthly rate is used since a month is the usual reporting period. If the reporting period is modified by endorsement to substitute other periods in place of a month, the rate applicable to such a period is determined by dividing the annual rate by the number of reporting periods in a year. The reporting period may not be longer than a quarter.

The contract may be written with a deductible. The deductible will affect the rate by having an effect on the losses used to calculate the normal loss rate and it will also affect the minimum normal loss rate.

TABLE 30–10

DEFICIENCY POINT SCHEDULE

Item	*Deficiency Points*
A. Disaster exposure, as evidenced by concentration of large values at few locations and wide variations from average value per location	0–750
B. Climatic hazards, as evidenced by high exposure in regions of severe hazard not contemplated in the industry classification rate	0–750
C. Special occupancy hazards, as evidenced by mixed occupancies, processing activities at storage locations, traffic and other internal exposures to fire, explosion, water damage, and theft	0–1,000
D. Lack of private protection, as evidenced by relative absence of automatic sprinklers, fire and theft alarm systems, and other loss prevention precautions	0–2,500
E. Inadequate public protection, as evidenced by concentration of values in unprotected areas or poorly protected areas	0–1,500
F. External exposure, not contemplated in industry rate	0–500
G. Construction—large values in frame buildings, or buildings with notable deficiencies	0–1,000
H. Combustibility and susceptibility not usual to commodities associated with the industry, e.g., unusual packaging, portion of output in more damageable goods, etc.	0–500
I. Arrangement of specific insurance to produce selection not contemplated by industry rate	0–500
J. Transit or floating equipment exposures greater than those contemplated in industry rate, including subrogation restrictions on goods in transit or bailment	0–1,000

FOR DISCUSSION

1. B is the owner of a building carrying a fire rate of 1 percent. C advises him to investigate his rate with a view to securing its reduction. B contends that such a reduction is out of the question, that fire rates are arbitrarily promulgated, and from them there is no appeal. Is this correct?
2. B owns a large building in a mercantile district occupied by several tenants. His insurance has been in force for several years and has been renewed each year by his agent. X, a new agent, secures a line and notes that the rate has remained unchanged for several years.

What immediate steps should he take to determine whether the rate is correct or not?

3. When it is said that fire spreads in almost geometrical proportion, what significance has this statement for the purposes of fire rate making?
4. The suggestion has sometimes been made that schedule rating is too complex and not readily understood by the purchaser of insurance who is indeed definitely an interested party. It is pointed out that certain broad classes, such as dwellings and farms, are class rated. Without advocating entirely the elimination of charges and credits, the suggestion has been made that a simple schedule taking into consideration the more evident hazards might well serve the purposes of all concerned. Do you think this to be the case? Discuss.
5. The question may present itself as to the accuracy of any rating, if it is conceded that there are no statistical data upon which to rely as a basis for computing the various charges and credits that comprise the schedule. Actually, the individual charges which make up the rates are to a large extent estimates based upon experience. Does this not mean that schedule rates and, in the last analysis, judgment rates are subject to the errors of judgment of the rate maker?
6. A problem in fire insurance rating, as well as a problem for municipal authorities, is to be found in the construction of a large mercantile building such as a supermarket in a small community. The fire department is geared to a semirural area without any substantial concentration in values. What suggestions would you make toward the elimination of this difficulty?
7. If an insurance rate is adequate to the risk, as all promulgated rates are presumed to be, why do underwriters prefer certain classes of risk and shun or limit their line with respect to others? In your opinion, are the high-rated or low-rated risks preferable? Why?
8. B is planning the construction of a sizable building. His insurance adviser has suggested submitting the plans and specifications to the fire insurance rating bureau before construction commences. What advantage can accrue if B follows the suggestion?
9. A criticism of schedule rating, but not of the system, is to be found in the failure on the part of rating authorities to make periodic inspections of risks. How may an individual insured overcome the unfavorable impact of this situation upon his individual rates?
10. Schedule rating today has but one object and that is to measure the hazards of fire. This was not always the situation. There was a time when individual charges substantially higher than the hazard warranted found their way into insurance rates. Can you think of a logical reason for this practice? Would you regard it as sound schedule rating?
11. How is it possible by the application of a schedule to arrive at different rates for the same property depending upon the amount of insurance carried, i.e. (*a*) a coinsurance rate, and (*b*) a flat rate?

12. The X department store has recently installed a department carrying furs. A large part of the stock is stored in a fireproof vault. The store covers its stock under one item in the form with a 90 percent coinsurance clause. Recommend a change.
13. What is an average rate, and how is it found?
14. A brick warehouse is located adjacent to a dilapidated wooden structure, and the owner accordingly finds an exposure charge in the rate. He has no control over the adjacent hazard. Is there any way he may reduce or eliminate the exposure charge?
15. X has installed a large number of fire extinguishers in his plant. Inquiry reveals that he is receiving no credit therefor in his fire rate, while Y, with a similar plant, enjoys a substantial reduction in rate. Can you advise X?
16. The Gem Theater has just been completed, and an application for a fire rate filed. It is now discovered that a substantial charge is included in the rate because the building was constructed with wooden laths. Wherein did the owners fail concerning this rate?
17. You are the city manager of X city. It has been brought to your attention that the janitor of the high school has fastened back the fire-proof doors leading to the stair wells. Will this affect the fire rate and why?
18. The city of X has adopted a building code recommended by the American Insurance Association. In discussing the community's deficiency points under the grading schedule, the authorities find that no credit has been given for the adoption of the satisfactory code, although the rating authorities are fully aware of its existence. Why?
19. If there were two cities with identical fire departments, explain how it would be possible for one city to have more deficiency points than another.
20. A case is reported where fire insurance underwriters were called upon to insure a collection of fine Egyptian statues. An inspection brought to light the fact that each statue was six feet high and weighed a ton or more. They were made of stone and housed in a fireproof building. From your knowledge of schedule rating, giving consideration to building construction and occupancy, would you expect a high or low rate? As an underwriter would you be willing to retain a large or small line before reinsurance?
21. Discuss the computation of rates in liability insurance.

CHAPTER • 31

Marketing and Underwriting

The basic principles upon which the idea of insurance is founded[1] assume that a large number of units exposed to risk will be brought together. It is also assumed that a sufficient spread of risk will be obtained in order to assure an independence of events and to avoid the problems associated with catastrophe. A primary object of any insurer is to achieve sales of sufficient volume (and adequately distributed geographically) to encourage stability in operations; to provide income to pay for losses, expenses, and contingencies; and to earn a profit for stockholders, in the event the insurer is organized as a stock corporation. Whether insurance operations are profitable in the long run will often depend not only on volume and distribution of sales but also on the quality of the risks assumed, as well as with the skill with which the entire insurance operation is managed. Since marketing and underwriting (risk selection) assume such a major role in the success of an insurer, they will be considered at some length in this chapter.

MARKETING

The marketing division of an insurer is responsible for the production of business and ordinarily encompasses sales, advertising and public relations, and research and development. Most insurers have a senior officer in charge of marketing, and he is responsible for the general supervision of sales and related operations.

In insurance terminology "market" is used to indicate both the area of distribution and the available source of the different insurance coverages.[2] In the first instance, reference might be made to persons in

[1] See Chapter 1.

[2] A market, in a strict sense, is a meeting of people who have as their purpose the transaction of business by means of private purchase and sale. By extension, the term has come to mean either the region in which a commodity can be sold or the group of persons who might be expected to purchase. It has come as well to mean the place of purchase. Thus, we have the stock market, the grain market, or for that matter the local market for the purchase of foods.

the middle-salary brackets as a market for sports liability insurance. Large industrial organizations are a market for the different types of catastrophe coverages. The second and more restricted use of the term applies it to the place or source for the purchase of different forms of coverage. It may be said, for instance, that the market for war risk marine coverages would probably disappear with the outbreak of a major war, or again that Lloyd's is a market for certain unusual and special risks.

The insurance buyer has little difficulty in placing ordinary risks—that is in finding a market. As a risk tends to involve special features, the limitations of the market evidence themselves. The significant point to understand about insurance markets is that the more usual coverages, such as fire insurance and automobile insurance are obtainable in every community through a local agency or an insurer representative. For other coverages, and this fact is particularly true of some of the more hazardous lines that are not written in volume, the market is more limited. It is true that almost every measurable hazard is insurable. It does not follow that every agent has the facilities for placing every insurable hazard. The failure of one agency to place a line should not be construed as evidence of insurability. Familiarity with the market and ability to place unusual lines are evidences that the agent or broker is well informed and keeping abreast of developments in his field.

Sales. In insurance the selling function is handled in a manner that is quite different from most other businesses in the sense that sales of insurance contracts are typically made by persons who are not employees of the insurer.[3] Rarely do insureds come in contact with the officers of the insurer, and seldom, with exceptions to be discussed later, is insurance purchased over the counter through retail establishments or through offices of the insurer. In most cases the contact between insured and insurer is made through an agent who is paid by the insurer that he represents.

Sales Organization. Insurers are termed direct-writing or agency organizations, depending on their production plan. Direct-writing (or direct selling) insurers employ a "distribution system under which the insurer negotiates contracts with the insured only through the insurer's employees." Agency insurers appoint local representatives in the communities in which they do business and pay the agents a commission on all business which they originate. Insurer representatives may

---

[3] Property and liability insurers operating on a direct-writing basis and factory mutuals are exceptions to this statement, but this kind of operation is not typical in the insurance business. In the case of the individual insurer, such as the underwriters at Lloyd's, the applicant for insurance does not deal directly with the underwriter, but through the intermediary of a broker. In county mutuals the policyholders are often active in selling insurance.

work under the independent agency system or the exclusive agency system. The independent system may be defined as a "distribution system operating through agents, brokers or others who sell and service property and liability insurance only on a commission or fee basis as independent contractors and who have agreements with one or more insurers which recognize ownership of policy records and expiration data in such independent contractors." The exclusive agency system is "a distribution system operating through agents under agreements which limit representation to one insurer, or several insurers under common management, and which reserve to the insurer the ownership of policy records and expiration data."[4] Insurers are able to write on a nationwide basis and secure a diversified classification of risks economically through the utilization of duly appointed representatives.

The applicant for insurance makes contact with the insurer through one or more of the following: (*a*) agent; (*b*) solicitor; (*c*) broker; and (*d*) service representative.

Agent. The agent is an insurer representative, and the authority under which he operates is delegated through the medium of an agency contract. An agent may be a natural person, a partnership, or a corporation. The significant feature of the agency relationship is to be found in the fact that the agent is appointed and authorized by an insurer to act as its representative with authority to solicit, negotiate, and effect contracts of insurance in its behalf.[5]

In the process of appointing the agent to represent insurers, three types of agency system have developed: (*a*) the direct reporting system; (*b*) the general agency system, and (*c*) the branch office system. By far the greater number of agents fall in the first category. These are the local agents appointed in the various communities to represent the insurers. They write contracts in their local offices and send copies to the home offices. They are the point of contact between the insurer and the insured. In many instances they adjust losses and otherwise service the account of the insured. Under the general agency system the country is divided into territories and the insurer designates the general agent to supervise all the business written in that territory. The general agent operates as an independent business organization, pays its own expenses, and maintains a staff adequate to service the subagents reporting to it. Subagents operate on much the same basis as the reporting agent, except that they report to the general agent rather than to the insurer. Frequently the general agent performs services for its subagent, such as writing contracts and

[4] The definitions in this paragraph are from the *Bulletin of the Commission on Insurance Terminology*, Vol. I, No. 4 (October, 1965), pp. 3–4.

[5] "Agents Qualification and Licensing Law," draft of May 16, 1950, *Proceedings of the National Association of Insurance Commissioners*, 1950, p. 338.

helping solicit new business, that tend to keep the subagent in close contact with his general agent. Under the branch office system there is a branch office manager appointed by the insurer who is a direct employee of the insurer and is compensated on a salary basis. The home office directs all the operations of the agency and governs its policy. The branch office is, in fact, an extension of the home office of the insurer. Branch offices deal with brokers and agents but are not themselves agents. The employees of the branch offices are all salaried employees and do not operate on a commission basis.

Solicitor. A solicitor is an individual authorized by an insurance agent or broker to solicit contracts of insurance. He acts only on behalf of one agent or broker. He does not have authority to bind the insurer with respect to risks but, in connection with his business activities, is authorized to collect premiums. The solicitor transacts business in the name of the agent or broker by whom he is employed, and the employer is responsible for his acts or omissions within the scope of his employment.

Broker. Like the agent, a broker may be a person, partnership, or corporation. The broker acts on behalf of the insured. He is an independent contractor and is remunerated, usually, on a commission basis. His principal function is to assist the applicant for insurance in placing risks. The broker has been termed an anomaly in that he serves the insured, yet is paid by the insurer. The difference between the broker and the agent will be considered later. The broker serves as an intermediary between the applicant for insurance and the insurer. The broker is not an agent but deals with agents on behalf of the applicant for insurance. He is not the employee of an insurer but operates independently on his own behalf.[6]

In the United States there are a number of large brokerage firms that operate on a national and even international basis and for the most part represent business firms. One of these brokerage firms has been in business since 1845, has 26 offices throughout the world, as well as correspondents in most of the world's principal cities. Firms of this type are able to represent their clients in the buying of all types of insurance and have their offices organized according to the main branches of insurance such as property and liability and life,

[6] The position of the broker in the insurance transaction has been expressed as follows: "There is no such thing as buying adequate business insurance *ready-made*. This is one of the many reasons why every corporation should use a competent insurance broker. The broker is essentially a buyer—not a salesman. He is unbiased and independent. He represents only the insured, sits on his side of the desk, helps him negotiate contracts and settle claims—at all times giving impartial advice. His compensation is a brokerage paid by the seller—the insurance company." (From an advertisement of Johnson and Higgins, Insurance Brokers, *Business Week,* July 26, 1941, p. 6.)

and they have specialists in each of these fields. In recent times considerable emphasis has been placed on employee benefit planning and most of the larger brokerage firms are able to give expert advice on pension plans, group life insurance, disability benefits, medical plans, profit sharing plans, thrift plans, and variable annuity plans. Additionally, help is given in all areas in such matters as risk analysis, claim analysis, fire prevention and safety engineering, loss adjustment, and in the continuing supervision of the insurance program.

Field Representative. Many insurers employ representatives on a salary basis to work with and assist agents in writing specialized lines. Such employees are termed "service representatives," "field representatives," "fieldmen," or sometimes "special agents" and may help an agent to effect insurance with the insurer employing the representative. General agents employ service representatives to work with and assist agents in soliciting and effecting insurance in one or in all the insurers represented by the general agent. Insurer officers, managers, or general agents of insurers employed on a salary basis are not included in the category of service representatives. The special agent is assigned to a geographic area which may be as large as a state or it may be a much smaller area such as a county or even smaller unit. Field agents of the general type should be distinguished from specializing agents or fieldmen who handle one particular type of insurance and who are assigned to much larger areas than is uaually the case for the special agent. With the advent of multiple line underwriting, the special agent's responsibility is greater than ever and he must have a thorough knowledge of many lines of insurance. He must also have the qualities that will enable him to supervise agents effectively, since part of his responsibility is to make sure that agents render the kind of service that is contemplated by the insurers that they represent.

The American Agency System. As the independent insurance agency system has developed in this country, the insurance agent operates as an independent businessman. The system has come to be known as the "American agency system." Most of the property and liability insurance business as it is carried on in the United States is handled through insurance agencies operating under this system. The property and liability insurance agent, in soliciting insurance business, does not hold himself out to represent any particular insurer; rather he solicits business on behalf of the agency. When he secures an order for insurance coverage, it is usually the agent, and not the applicant for insurance who determines the insurer in which the business will be placed. To be sure, it is not unusual for the applicant for insurance to indicate a preference for an insurer, and it may be because of the wish to insure with a particular insurer that a particular agent is sought out. For the most part the applicant for insurance places himself in the hands of the agent, or in the hands of a broker who in turn deals through the agent, and the agent or broker serves in a professional capacity as an insurance adviser.

The constitution of the National Association of Insurance Agents describes the American agency system as a method for producing insurance premiums and servicing insurance contracts by insurance agents operating solely on a commission basis. These agents operate on their own account as independent contractors who maintain and own offices separate and apart from any production office maintained by an insurer. The insurers who operate through the agencies appoint the members of these agencies to represent them. It will be recalled that an agent may, and usually does, represent several insurers. Agencies may specialize on some particular phase of the business, though it is usual for a property insurance agent to represent property and liability insurance generally and write all classes of property and liability insurance. Larger agencies may organize departments with specialists who confine their activities to a particular field.

The fact that, for the most part, it is the agent who selects the insurer to carry the insurance for his customers has led to the general acceptance of the idea that the record of expirations and the value of the good will of the agency belongs solely to the agency.[7] Because of this fact an insurance agency has a resale value that has come to be well recognized.[8]

Broker of Record. With the development of the professional concept of insurance underwriting, agents and brokers are more and more being called upon to assume responsibilities with respect to the planning of insurance programs. In the interest of convenience this often requires consultations with the various representatives of rating authorities. In the interest of maintaining some order with respect to

[7] The question of ownership of expirations was determined by the Yonkers case (*National Fire Insurance Company* v. *Sullard*, 89 N.Y. Supp. 934; 97 App. Div. 233), where it was held that because of the method by which a local agency is operated, allowing the agent to represent several insurers and to determine the insurers to carry the business of applicants, it is a good will value in such an agency that is subject to sale and that the ownership of expirations belongs to the agencies and not to each individual insurer to whom business has been allocated. In another case (*Heyl* v. *Emery & Kaufman, Ltd.*, 204 F. [2d] 137) it was held that because the agent does not solicit on behalf of any particular insurer, it is generally held that the information obtained in such solicitation and in the preparation of the contracts is gathered by the agent at his own expense, and the expirations are the property of the agent.

[8] Notwithstanding the fact that courts have recognized the ownership of renewals as belonging to the agent as an established part of the agency system, it has been the custom among careful agents to see that a clause governing this point is inserted in all agency agreements. A form of contract between the agent and the insurer containing a clause vesting title to all expirations in the agent is the accepted form of contract in use today. However, such a contract is not in universal use, and where the matter is not covered by contract, there is a considerable area of uncertainty. The National Association of Insurance Agents has strongly recommended that all agency contracts definitely cover the matter of title to expirations.

the distribution of rating information, rules have been set in the agents' jurisdictions with respect to the persons to whom such information will be given.[9]

Generally, the owner of a property, or a person having an insurable interest in a property, or one of their duly accredited representatives, when they are not engaged in the insurance business, may always obtain rating information concerning these properties. An insurer that is a member of the rating organization may secure this information upon submitting evidence that it is writing insurance on the risk. Rating information is supplied to local agents, licensed brokers, or subscribing insurers without an existing insurance interest when they are authorized by the owner of the property to receive it. Access to rating surveys is granted to agents or brokers only when authorized by the owner. This authorization is addressed to the rating bureau and must usually conform to the bureau's requirements with respect to its content. The letter must be written on the letterhead of the owner. If the owner has no printed letterhead, it is required that this fact be stated in the letter. If the owner is a firm or corporation, the handwritten signature of the authorized official in his official capacity must appear.

A broker-of-record letter may give to the holder authority to receive rating information without making this authority exclusive. When a broker or agent holds such a letter, the rating bureau will supply information requested. If a letter of authority is outstanding but not exclusive, an exclusive-agent or broker-of-record letter is subsequently filed in favor of another person. This has the effect of canceling all other outstanding letters.

Typically when a property owner makes arrangements with an agent or broker to study his insurance problems, the agent or broker is usually designated as the exclusive representative of the insured. The agent or broker-of-record letter supplied him is placed on file at the rating bureau and remains in effect until canceled or until it expires upon filing of a subsequent letter.

Rating organizations are always prepared to discuss with builders or architects the alterations of buildings or the construction of new buildings with a view to pointing out hazards and discussing rating problems. They also are willing to discuss with real estate agents the impact on the rate of any change or tendency. If persons in any of these categories require further detailed information, they are expected to supply credentials authorizing the rating bureau to supply

---

[9] The expression "rating information" has been defined to include: (*a*) information concerning the application of schedules, rates, charges, and credits; (*b*) consultation concerning improvements in risk and changes in hazard or rate; (*c*) makeup of rates; (*d*) access of rating surveys; (*e*) estimates of rate; and (*f*) all matters related to any of the foregoing subjects.

this information. Where builders, real estate operators, or architects require detailed rating information, the usual source is through the agent and he, in turn, secures this from the rating bureau acting under an agent or broker-of-record letter.

Rating agencies also may provide that the insured's authorized representatives may delegate, by letter of authority only, some other person to act in his behalf. This procedure is usually adopted when an agent or broker has been designated by the insured but the agent or broker in turn wishes to make use of an insurer representative to assist him in his negotiations. To simplify the procedure with respect to these negotiations between the insurer representative and the rating bureau, the agent may delegate by letter the insurer representative to act in his behalf.

Excess Line Broker. There are brokers who specialize in placing excess lines or lines that are otherwise difficult to place. In some instances the brokers are obliged to seek a market such as that afforded by Lloyd's of London, and in other instances the business is placed for a premium, higher than locally established rates, with insurers that have not been licensed to do business in a particular state and are known as "nonadmitted insurers."[10] Where capacity is a problem there is usually some feature of the risk that tends to make underwriters limit the amount that they will carry for their various insurers. In the case of burglary, for example, a large warehouse containing readily movable valuable items, such as cameras and television sets, with limited burglary alarm and watchmen service may call for the assistance of the excess line broker in handling so much of the risk as the local market is unable to absorb.

The market for excess lines may include insurers with a home office in the United States, or it may include foreign markets such as London, Canada, or South America. Domestic nonadmitted insurers are those chartered in one of the states but not licensed in all states. The insurer is nonadmitted with respect to those states in which it is not licensed. Foreign insurers may or may not be admitted, or they may be licensed in one or more states and not in others. The nonadmitted character of much of the market handling excess line business

[10] The type of risk that usually is placed by the excess line broker might include liability coverage on motorcycle and automobile racing, fireworks displays, amusement parks, aviation shows, and circuses. Short-term use and occupancy insurance covering from a day to several months is also handled in many instances by the excess line broker. Also it frequently happens that a new risk is carried in whole or in part by the market represented by excess line brokers during an early period of uncertainty. As time passes and the nature of the risk becomes clearer, more and more of it is absorbed by the local market. Finally, there are lines fraught with great uncertainty where the amount of insurance required taxes the facilities of the ordinary markets. In this category is found products liability coverage of new and untried products, such as cosmetics and medicinal products, that might with failure bring about catastrophic claims.

tends to invite the careful scrutiny of the prospective insured. The excess line broker may not always deal with the insured directly but may be sought out by the insured's broker. Much of the line may be placed in the local market with an accommodation line placed by the broker with nonadmitted insurers.[11]

Legal Problems Associated with Insurer Representation. The relationship between the insurer and its representatives is one based on contract and involves not only the law of contracts but the law of agency as well. The basic legal concepts applying to agency relationships should be carefully considered.

Operation of the Law of Agency. To the extent that the business of insurance is conducted by corporations, agents are essential. Thus, the law of agency is closely associated with the business of insurance, and virtually every transaction carried on by an insurer with the public makes use of the agency relationship. "An agent is defined as one who acts for another by authority from him; one who undertakes to transact some business or manage some affair for another by authority and on account of the latter."[12] Agency involves three parties: (1) the principal, (2) the agent, and (3) the third party. When a principal authorizes a second party to create, to modify, or to terminate contractual relations between himself and a third party, an agency relationship has been created. Anyone who may act for himself may also act as an agent, although contracts which delegate authority to an agent must, as in the case of contracts in general, have a legal object as their purpose.

To create an agency relationship, it is not necessary that the agreement be reduced to writing. Authorization may be written or oral, and no particular formalities are essential. To this general rule there is one exception: When the purpose of the agency can be fulfilled only by the signing of a formal document under seal, the agency must be created under seal. The agent is then said to possess a "power of attorney." The use of a power of attorney is essential for the agent authorized to execute bonds. As a matter of practice, it is the custom

---

[11] It is assumed that the originating broker will satisfy himself with respect to the financial position, adjusting facilities and practices, and general attitude toward claims of the insurer with which he places excess lines. It will be poor consolation to the insured, if he discovers the relationship to be an unsatisfactory one after a loss. It is always desirable that excess lines be placed, as far as it is possible to do so, with insurers licensed in the state where the business is placed. If this is impossible, the insured should carefully check the broker's sources of information in order to become satisfied personally with the financial responsibility of the insurer in question as well as its reputation.

It is sometimes possible to secure a "service of suit" clause in contracts obtained in a foreign market. Such a clause is quite customary in contracts obtained in the English market. By virtue of the clause, suit may be served on local representatives of the insurer and action may be brought against it in courts having local jurisdiction.

[12] *Moreland* et al. v. *Mason, Sheriff* et al., 260 Pac. 1035.

to appoint agents by means of a carefully worded document known as an "agency agreement." The powers of the agent are set forth, as well as his obligations. Frequently an engraved certificate, known as a "commission of authority," is delivered to the agent, and this is often framed and hung in a conspicuous position in his office.

Agent Represents the Insurer. It is a fundamental principle of agency that the agent cannot represent at the same time both the principal and the third party. It has been established as a matter of law that agents of insurers authorized to procure applications for insurance and to forward them to insurers for acceptance are deemed the agents of the insurer and not of the policyholder in whatever they do in preparing the applications. If an application is made by an agent of the insurer and the facts have been fully and correctly stated to him and later they have been misstated in the application, the contents of the application are not regarded as the statement of the applicant, even though signed by him. The knowledge of the agent is regarded as knowledge of the insurer, and it is sufficient if the applicant for insurance correctly stated the facts to the agent."[13]

When this principle was established by the courts, plans were made by insurers to insert a provision in the contract that the application, by whomsoever made, was to be deemed the act of the insured and not of the insurer. An effort was made under the terms of the contract to make the insurance agent who prepared an application an agent of the insured and not of the insurer. On this point, the courts stated: "There is no magic in mere words to change the real into the unreal. A device or words cannot be imposed upon a court in place of an actuality of fact."[14] It would be a stretch of legal principles to hold that a person dealing with an agent, apparently clothed with authority to act for his principal in the matter in hand, could be affected by any notice given after the negotiations were completed. A relationship

---

[13] Touching upon this point, it has been stated: "This rule is rendered necessary by the manner in which business is now usually done by the insurers. They supply these agents with printed blanks, stimulate them by the promise of liberal commissions, and then send them abroad in the community to solicit insurance. The companies employ them for that purpose, and the public regard them as the agents of the companies in the matter of preparing and filling up these applications—a fact which the companies perfectly understand. The parties who are induced by these agents to make applications for insurance rarely know anything about the general officers of the company or its constitution and by-laws, but look to the agent as its full and complete representative in all that is said or done in regard to the application. And in view of the apparent authority with which the companies clothe these solicitors, they have a perfect right to consider them such. Hence where an agent to procure and forward applications for insurance either by his direction or direct act, makes out an application incorrectly, notwithstanding all the facts are correctly stated to him by the applicant, the error is chargeable to the insurer and not to the insured." *Kausal* v. *Minnesota Farmers' Mut. Fire Ins. Ass'n.*, 31 Minn. 17, 16 N.W. 430, 47 Am. Rep. 776.

[14] *Ibid.*

between the insurance agent and the applicant was, to all intents and appearances, one of agency and third party. The courts held that by issuing a contract after the negotiations were completed, a clause in that contract could not have the effect of transposing the agent of one party into the agent of another.[15] The insurer is charged with knowledge acquired by his agent in negotiating a contract of insurance, not because he has consented to be so charged, nor because he has authorized his agent to bind him, but rather he is bound solely through the legal consequence of the agency relationship.[16]

In the circumstances, it may be stated that the weight of authority holds that an agent of the insurer who fills out and receives an application for insurance represents the insurer; and the insurer is charged with any knowledge the agent may have from the applicant, and the insurer is estopped from denying liability for any breach of which it had knowledge in such a manner.

Agency by Estoppel or Ratification. Even though no agency relationship has been established, if one party permits another to hold himself out to be his agent or acts in a manner that would reasonably allow a third party to assume that an agency relationship exists, then the party who appears to be the principal is estopped from denying the existence of an agency, and the relationship thus created is said to be an agency by estoppel. To such an agency, the term "ostensible" is frequently applied.

The operation of this principle as applied in the field of insurance may be found in a situation in which an agency relationship has been canceled but supplies, contracts, and forms have been left with the agent. If the agent issues a contract, even without authority but on the forms and contracts in his possession, the public will have no reason to suspect that he is not, in fact, an agent, and the insurer cannot deny

---

[15] To this end, in the previously cited case it is stated: "To be efficacious, such notice should be given before the negotiations are completed. The application precedes the policy, and the insured cannot be presumed to know that any such provision will be inserted in the latter. To hold that by a stipulation, unknown to the insured at the time he made the application, and when he relied upon the fact that the agent was acting for the company, he could be held responsible for the mistakes of such agent, would be to impose burdens upon the insured which he never anticipated. Hence we think that if the agent was the agent of the company in the matter of making out and receiving the application, he cannot be converted into the agent of the insured by merely calling him such in the policy subsequently issued. Neither can any mere form of words wipe out the fact that the insured truthfully informed the insurer, through its agent, of all matters pertaining to the application at the time it was made. We are aware that in so holding we are placing ourselves in conflict with the views of some eminent courts. But the conclusion we have reached is not without authority to sustain it, and is, we believe, sound in principle and in accordance with public policy."

[16] John P. Crowley, "Insurance-Misrepresentation—Extent to Which Insurer Can Limit Agent's Authority," *University of Cincinnati Law Review,* Vol. XX, No. 3 (May, 1951), p. 421.

liability to a holder who has purchased such a contract in good faith.

Sometimes an agent may hold himself out as having authority when no such authority exists. This might be the result of attempt at deliberate misrepresentation but is usually the outgrowth of misunderstanding or misinformation. An agent may have authority to issue bonds within a certain limit and, mistaking his authority, might attempt to issue a bond in a higher limit. Contracts entered into between a presumed agent and a third party, when the agent is without authority and there is no element of estoppel, will not bind the supposed principal. If, on the other hand, the principal ratifies the act of the unauthorized agent, the agreement becomes binding from the inception of the original agreement.

If definite formalities are required to grant the agent authority, such as power of attorney, the same formalities are necessary in order to effect ratification. In other circumstances, ratification may be expressed or implied from any act, expression, or conduct which would make clear the intent of the principal to adopt the transaction. Thus, the expression of approval or the acceptance of the partial or complete performance on the part of the principal, or the promise of performance, will constitute a ratification. To bring a suit based on the agreement in question has the same effect.

Secret Limitations Not Binding on Third Party. A principal may from time to time modify or limit the powers of his agent. The agent is responsible to the principal and bound by any limiting instructions. The same is not true in the case of the third party who has no knowledge of the limitations. He is under no obligation to search with a view to determining the existence of limiting instructions. If the third party has notice of limiting instructions, he is bound by them; otherwise, third parties are not affected if, in their dealings with an agent, he acts within the apparent scope of his authority. In the field of insurance, this finds application in the case of prohibited risks. Most insurers supply their agents with a list of risks upon which they are unwilling to be committed or upon which they will accept only limited lines. The lists of all insurers are not uniform. The third party—that is, the purchaser of insurance—is not obligated to determine what risks a particular insurer has instructed its agent to decline but is fully protected if he orders a contract from an agent in good faith upon a particular risk and it is delivered by the agent. When an agent writes a contract on a prohibited risk and notice of the issuance of the contracts reaches the insurer, if the insurer takes no steps to cancel the contract, it extends the authority of the agent to write that risk by ratification. If a loss occurs before the insurer has an opportunity to take steps to relieve itself from the risk, the insurer has a right of action against the agent for the amount of the loss but is bound to the third party for the full amount of the loss, always assuming that the contract was purchased in good faith and that the policyholder had no knowledge that the agent was lacking in authority because of limiting instructions.

Additional Comments on Agency Contracts. The agency contract is a unilateral agreement and the insurer is not required to perform under the contract until business has been placed with it. Earlier in this chapter it was emphasized that the agent is not required to place business in whole or in part with any particular insurer and has the right to select the insurer and to divide business among insurers at his discretion. The agent in effect solicits business for himself. In addition to these basic facts about the fundamental nature of the agency contract, this agreement should contain specific reference to the ownership of expirations, commission rates, profit sharing, and the protection of rights in the event of agency termination. In connection with agency dissolution it is of some importance to have a specific agreement about how unexpired contracts are to be handled. Ordinarily such contracts may be reinsured or allowed to continue until expiration.[17]

Agent and Broker Distinguished. Since the agent is a representative of the insurer, the authority under which he operates is delegated through an agency contract. The significant feature of the agency relationship is to be found in the fact that the agent is appointed and authorized by the insurer to act as its representative with authority to solicit, negotiate, and effect contracts of insurance in its behalf.

The broker is a middleman between the insured and the agent of the insurer. In a strict sense he is a buyer and represents only the insured. It is his function to assist the applicant for insurance in negotiating contracts and settling claims. In the early days when the broker made his first appearance in the insurance business, it was contended that he rendered no service, since he did for the insured only what insurer officers were ready and willing to do. Men of ability and integrity made their livelihood from this occupation, and their value to the insurer was finally recognized and admitted. By informing themselves of rates, forms, and other technical features of the business, they became increasingly useful to the insured; and since they secured their remuneration in the form of a commission from the insurer, their service to the insured had the additional attraction of being free. Brokers are now recognized intermediaries between the insurer and the insured.

There is sometimes some confusion on the part of the uninformed insured dealing with a broker because they do not differentiate between an insurance broker and an agent. The insurance agent is

---

[17] See G. S. Hanson and W. E. Jordan, "Some Thoughts on Agents' Contracts," *American Agency Bulletin,* Vol. LXII (May, 1965), pp. 40–48.

acting under specific and delegated authority from the insurer and is authorized to bind the insurer within the limits of his delegated authority. The broker has no such authority and in most jurisdictions is recognized as the agent of the insured. This doctrine has been modified in some states by statutes that specifically provide that, for the purposes of collecting premiums and delivering contracts, the broker is an agent of the insurer but for all other purposes is an agent of the insured.

Part of the confusion concerning the status of the broker grows out of the fact that while the service he renders is designed primarily for the insured, he receives no compensation from the insured but is remunerated on a commission basis by the insurer with whom he places the business. Also it should be pointed out that a given individual may act as both agent and broker. The simplest illustration is to be found in the case of an agent who commits his own insurers for part of a line and acts as broker in placing through another agency any excess his own insurers are not able to handle.

Because the broker is held to represent the policyholder, the insured is bound by the acts of the broker with respect to the negotiations between insurer and insured. Fraudulent acts of the broker are binding on the insured when perpetrated in his behalf. As in other agency relationships, the insured as principal is charged with the broker's knowledge. Any misrepresentation or breach of warranty perpetrated by the broker makes the insured responsible, as if he committed the acts. The same rule holds concerning mistakes. A mistake in issuing orders for coverage or accepting a contract that does not meet the requirements of the insured is the responsibility of the insured and not the issuing insurer. Notice of cancellation may be given to the broker and effectively terminate coverage. The broker may serve as the agent of the insured to substitute one contract for another and otherwise negotiate with the insurer for protection for the account of the insured.

It is important to understand clearly that the broker on his own authority cannot make insurance effective. He is not a party to an insurance contract as an insurer. He negotiates insurance contracts on behalf of third parties who are insureds but never on behalf of the insurer from which he derives his remuneration.[18]

---

[18] Notwithstanding the fact that the insurance broker is held to represent the applicant for insurance and not the insurer, it is generally held that the payment of an insurance premium to a broker is payment to the insurer. On this point Section 121 of the insurance law of the state of New York reads: "Any insurer which delivers in this state to any insurance broker a contract of insurance pursuant to the application or request of such broker, acting for an insured other than himself, shall be deemed to have authorized such broker to receive on its behalf payment of any premium which is due on such contract at the time of its issuance or delivery or which becomes due thereon in not more than 90 days thereafter."

Advertising and Public Relations. The advertising and public relations department of property and liability insurers is responsible for the preparation and dissemination of various types of advertising. This department also advises agents on their advertising and publicity problems and in general seeks to improve the public image of insurance. Virtually every type of advertising media is used including national magazines, trade journals, newspapers, radio, television, and a variety of descriptive brochures. Advertising by the insurer is also aimed at helping the agent or broker in his efforts to sell the insurer's product, and often serves to supplement the advertising the agent or broker may do on a local basis. A variety of themes is used in advertising campaigns. The financial strength and stability of insurers are often emphasized, as well as the services provided by the insurer. Other themes center around loss and accident prevention and the quality and special features of the product. New types of coverage and new packages are often described in descriptive brochures and/or in magazines. In some instances advertising agencies assist the insurer in its advertising efforts.

The growth of advertising expenditures from the years immediately following World War II through 1964 has varied considerably among the largest property and liability insurers. Those insurers operating on a direct selling basis or on an exclusive agency basis showed the greatest increase in advertising expenditures with one of these firms showing a 3,200 percent increase. These insurers also showed large increases in net premiums written, although the percentage increase in advertising expenditures was larger by a considerable amount. Comparison of figures of advertising expenditures and net premiums written for the years 1949 through 1964 for ten of the largest property and liability insurers shows increases in advertising expenditures varying from 197 percent to 3,200 percent and increases in net premiums written varying from 51 percent to 1,398 percent, although it did not necessarily follow that those insurers who spent least on advertising also experienced the smallest gains in net premiums written.

Research and Development. Research and development departments are fairly new in the organizational structure of insurers and many insurers do not have departments or divisions for this activity. There is an increasing amount of interest, however, in research and related activities, and product development and marketing research divisions are assuming new importance. Similarly the research elements in underwriting, statistical systems, personnel, and various product lines of insurance are being emphasized.

Impetus to product development was given by the widespread acceptance of package contracts and the resultant need to develop new packages to meet the demand primarily of commercial insurance buyers. Closely related to the problem of package design and marketing are problems of underwriting, rating, adjustment, and other matters that surround the development of a new product. Product development is not confined to package contracts. Demands for new types of protection, for a superior product, and for changes and innovations needed in existing lines form a significant aspect of the work of the research division.

Market researchers employed by insurers are primarily interested in market potentials and market shares. Assessment of market potentiality requires a study of changing trends in the size of the population and in the changing distribution of such characteristics of the population as income, age, occupation, and family size. Specific lines of insurance may be affected by particular characteristics of sociological change. For example, trends in new construction are of concern to surety underwriters and such items as auto registrations, population growth, safety engineering, and legislation regarding financial responsibility are important to the success of automobile insurance. Closely related to the problem of market potential is the problem of market shares. Many insurers have made extensive studies of their share of the market in the geographical areas in which they operate and this information is utilized in planning sales campaigns and in assessing their overall marketing performance.

Other Marketing Methods and Problems. The American agency system tends to be the dominant form of sales organization in the property and liability insurance business, with direct selling and exclusive agency systems being the main alternatives. Although these systems have been successful, underwriting losses, narrowing profit margins, and a variety of competitive pressures including price competition have led to the introduction of new proposals for marketing the insurance product. Credit card insurance, wrap-up plans, and group property and liability insurance are among the proposals that have been made and in some instances implemented in a limited way.[19]

Credit Cards. Retail stores, hotels, filling stations, and airports to name a few types of organization now offer insurance to their customers and in the case of retail stores and filling stations the insurance may be purchased through the use of credit cards. The type of insurance sold in this manner is mainly life and accident insurance, although in the early 1960's the Standard Oil Company of Indiana introduced automobile insurance. A next step for oil companies appears to be selling fire and homeowner's insurance to persons who hold their credit cards. The oil companies do not sell insurance at

---

[19] It is not assumed that revision of the marketing system will solve all of the insurers' financial problems. Reduction of selling expense through different types of marketing is only one of a number of factors to be considered.

service stations but rely on mail campaigns directed at holders of credit cards.

Among the advantages alleged for credit card insurance is that contracts are offered at lower prices than comparable contracts sold by insurance agents. One reason for this is that the group insurance technique is used. Billing costs are also reduced, since the bill for insurance can simply be added to the statement for gasoline or retail goods. This type of selling seems to be permitted by most states, although the Texas insurance commissioner does not allow credit card insurance. In Texas an insurance premium must be collected by licensed agents, and corporations in Texas cannot be licensed to sell insurance.[20]

Wrap-up Plans. A wrap-up plan is one in which a number of insurance contracts that might be applicable to a particular situation are merged into one overall contract with one insurer. An example would be workmen's compensation for a large construction project. In a typical case separate workmen's compensation contracts might be purchased by the subcontractors as well as the primary contractor. A "wrap" workmen's compensation contract would provide one contract for the entire project.

The major advantage of the wrap-up procedure that is cited by its proponents is that it saves money through the elimination of brokerage commissions particularly where the contract is sold by direct writing mutual or stock insurers. Further, premium discounts, dividends, and similar items accrue to the organization for whom the construction is taking place. Another advantage of the wrap-up plan is that many hold-harmless agreements and other contractual modifications may be eliminated. It has been charged by opponents of the wrap-up plan that it is unfairly discriminatory. The Supreme Court of Connecticut in a case involving the Connecticut Yankee Atomic Power Company agreed that the contract was discriminatory unless "all large construction projects received the same treatment."[21]

Group Property and Liability Insurance. Group underwriting has had widespread acceptance in the field of life and health insurance but has never been applied to property and liability insurance except on a very limited basis.[22] In the past, efforts to introduce group property insurance have not met with general acceptance. In 1965, the AFL–CIO supported a bill in the Oregon legislature that sought to authorize group property and casualty insurance. The bill did not pass. Had it done so, group fire, marine, casualty, surety, credit, and

---

[20] See *The Wall Street Journal,* Friday, April 16, 1965, p. 7.

[21] See the *New York Times,* December 5, 1965.

[22] Recently (1966) it was reported that the Continental-National-American Companies wrote automobile insurance on a payroll deduction plan for Montgomery Ward and Company.

livestock insurance would have been permitted on groups of ten or more. Individual contracts would have been made available to those persons leaving the group. In 1966, the State of Illinois approved a filing of a large insurer for a group plan covering firms with 1,000 or more employees. This filing provided for individual automobile contracts with premiums to be paid by payroll deduction. Supporters of the group concept believe that recent interest in group property and liability insurance derives from a need on the part of consumers for distributional efficiencies that are reflected in cost.

One of the specific arguments for group property insurance is that it would lead to lower sales and administrative expenses and in particular to much lower commissions; that savings in expenses would be substantial and might exceed 30 percent in some lines. Commissions would probably be in the neighborhood of 2½ percent. Another argument in favor of the group plan is that traffic safety programs might well be more effective when aimed at groups. Further, in the group situation there is an opportunity for balancing poor risks against good. Against group property insurance are the arguments that it might lead to unfair discrimination in pricing (and thus be illegal), that individual differences in risks would be masked, that hiring practices might be affected (younger persons might be poorer automobile risks), that the choice of coverage would be left up to the corporation, that the policyholder would not get proper service, that dividends would accrue to the employer, and that economic power would be placed in the hands of large consumer groups. While the arguments pro and con are being debated, experimentation continues, and initial steps have been taken in the direction of mass merchandising.

UNDERWRITING

Historically the word "underwriter" was synonymous with the word "insurer." But with the development of corporate insurers the role of the underwriter changed, and today the underwriting departments of insurers are responsible for the selection but not the insuring of risks. Basically the underwriter must determine which risks will be accepted by the insurer and the basis on which these risks will be insured. He must aim for a distribution of business that will prove to be profitable and which will provide suitable volume and spread of risk.

Organization of Underwriting Departments. The shift to multiple line underwriting by many insurers, and, on the consumer side, the increasing importance of the risk management function, with its stress on an analysis of all the pure risks facing a business firm, and the resultant emphasis on account selling, has brought about many changes in the organizational structure of insurers. At a time when monoline contracts were the rule, underwriting was largely specialized by line of business, and there were fire underwriters, marine underwriters, and other specialists. Today underwriters have the responsibility for accepting risks where a number of lines of insurance may be involved.

Although no one pattern of underwriting organization is universal, a number of insurers have divided the underwriting function between personal lines and commercial lines and have senior executives in charge of commercial lines and personal lines departments. One large insurer has its underwriting division divided into four departments—commercial lines, personal lines, special account, and underwriting administration. There is also an underwriting consultant on such matters as boards, bureaus, and syndicates. The commercial lines vice president has responsibility for the commercial aspects of such lines as liability, accident and health, inland marine, boiler and machinery, and fidelity and burglary, as well as for research and development. The personal lines vice president has responsibility for research and development as well as for the underwriting and control of all personal lines. The special accounts vice president is responsible for accounts where the annual premium produced for a particular risk exceeds a substantial figure. The secretary in charge of underwriting administration serves a coordinating function for the other departments and is concerned with underwriting procedures, rating and forms administration, training, and underwriting personnel.

The principles involved in the home office underwriting organization are carried out in regional office and branch office organization. In each regional office there is a regional underwriting manager and under his supervision a commercial lines manager, a personal lines manager, and a special account manager. These persons have the same type of responsibilities on a somewhat less comprehensive scale as their counterparts at the home office. Each branch office has a branch underwriting manager who carries out assigned responsibilities but there are not separate commercial lines and personal lines managers.

The Relationship of the Agent to Underwriting. The agent in property and liability insurance, in contrast to the life insurance agent, has the power in many situations to bind the insurer and to issue contracts and forms in accordance with instructions given to him. These instructions include information on prohibited risks, on those risks that are questionable, and on those risks that the insurer is willing to accept without much question. There are also instructions dealing with the amount of insurance that the insurer will write on any one risk. He also receives instruction about which risks must be submitted to regional or home offices. Thus, the agent performs an initial underwriting function and his skill in selecting business is a major factor in determining underwriting results.

Functions of the Underwriter. The functions of the underwriter may be classed under three general headings: (1) acceptability of the risk, (2) basis of acceptance, and (3) checking results.[23]

Acceptability of the Risk. The acceptability of a risk is determined by checking the risk against a large number of factors known to be related to loss potential. Perhaps these factors can best be illustrated by a consideration of the items that are reviewed in underwriting particular types of risk, although some of the procedures are applicable regardless of type of risk. The starting place for fire insurance underwriting is the daily report which gives the name of the insured, the location of the property, amount of liability, kind of coverage, type of building construction, nature of the occupancy, nature of the property, the coinsurance percentage, if any, encumbrances on the property, and the name of the producer. The items contained on the daily report often provide all of the information ordinarily needed for the uncomplicated types of risk. Similarly the report can provide clues for the necessity of additional information. Where the building is located, whether it is brick, frame, or of some other type of construction, and whether it is a family home, a mercantile establishment, or a manufacturing plant, and whether there are encumbrances on the property make considerable difference in the terms on which the risk is to be accepted or rejected. In situations where additional information appears to be necessary the underwriter might check on credit ratings, reports of physical inspection including such items as housekeeping, condition of the building, and other related factors. Also a Sanborn map might be checked to determine the nature of the exposure. The decision reached need not be solely one of acceptance or rejection. A risk may be accepted subject to recommendations, or a part of it may be accepted, or it may be referred to someone in a supervisory capacity.

The underwriter needs to be aware of moral hazard as well as the physical hazard that may result from the type of construction or the use of the building or its age, physical condition, and nature of upkeep. Danger signals for moral hazard may appear in a number of ways. An effort, for example, on the part of the prospective insured to overinsure or an unusual number of claims may indicate that the insured may not be a good risk. Closely connected with moral hazard is morale hazard which may be reflected in the personal attitudes of the property owner or manager. The nature of the fire protection

---

23 See Edward W. Brouder, *Insurance World* (New Haven: Yale Daily News, 1956), pp. 78–79.

afforded by the city or town where the property is located is of considerable importance to underwriting. Cities and towns are classified into ten categories or classes. In making this classification such items as the type of fire department, nature of water supply, fire alarm system, level of pay of the fire department, and local ordinances are taken into account. The exposure of the building both internally and externally is another factor to check. Tenants may be a problem, and on the external side surrounding buildings may increase the hazard. Where insurance on contents is involved such factors as ignitability, combustibility, and damageability should be checked.[24]

Another example of factors to be considered in underwriting may be taken from the field of contract bonds. Construction on both a public and private basis has increased greatly over the last decade creating a need for bonds. Failures of contractors often lead to large financial losses and careful underwriting is needed if the insurer's surety experience is to be favorable. R. W. Schmitt has indicated that ten factors should be assessed before deciding to accept a particular loss. These factors are: "(1) experience, ability, and integrity of the contractor; (2) financial resources and progress; (3) credit standing; (4) character and extent of work to perform; (5) incomplete work on hand; (6) adequacy of the contract price; (7) terms of the contract and the bond; (8) the amount of work to be subcontracted and to whom; (9) the sufficiency of the plant and equipment; and (10) the adequacy of the contractor's insurance program."[25] Most of these factors do not require a great deal of explanation. Adequate working capital and net worth are essential if the contractor is to be in a position to absorb losses that might occur from an inadequate contract price and if he is to carry the labor and material costs of the job, as well as the usual overhead costs. Facts about the work to be bonded should be carefully considered. Whether the contract is a direct contract or a subcontract, the price, the terms of payment, special hazards, and the location of the work are all related to the acceptability of the risk. The underwriter should ask for a schedule of all jobs in progress or to be undertaken by the contractor. This information is needed in order to assess whether the contractor is overextended.

An example of a field where underwriting is fairly informal is that of marine insurance, but in spite of informality, there are specific factors that are taken into account. The quality of the management is a factor, as well as the quality of the officers and crew and their attitudes toward upkeep and toward insurance. Sea routes, season of

---

[24] See John Adam, Jr., "Underwriting in Fire Insurance," in the *Property and Liability Insurance Handbook* (Homewood, Ill.: Richard D. Irwin, Inc., 1965).

[25] See R. W. Schmitt, "Underwriting Contract Bonds," *National Underwriter*, October 15, 1965.

the year, and meteorological conditions are also considered. If cargo is involved, the type of packing, labor conditions, possibility of pilferage, time to go through customs, weather conditions, and the peculiarities and characteristics of particular commodities are among the factors to be reviewed. In some areas such as tugboats and rowboats the underwriting is done by experts.

Perhaps enough examples have been given to illustrate that wherever the underwriting of property and liability insurance is undertaken the physical hazard as well as the moral hazard must be carefully reviewed. The nature of the physical hazard will depend on the type of property involved and whether it is in a fixed location or in transit. The protection available to guard against loss as well as possible sources of loss, are important for practically all lines of insurance. In judging acceptability the underwriter is called upon to weigh a large number of factors that are related to loss potential, and his success in terms of a favorable loss ratio will depend on the judgment and skill he uses in selecting business.

Basis of Acceptance. Although a risk may be acceptable, a standard contract may not be desirable and may have to be changed. Some complicated situations may require special rating plans and forms, and the underwriter must be aware of the need for a sufficient premium. Line limits should be observed and it is the responsibility of the underwriter to avoid excessive exposure. Where necessary, reinsurance should be used to avoid exceeding the maximum exposure that the insurer is willing to assume.

Checking Results. After underwriting decisions have been made it is part of the duty of the underwriter to check the results of his work by following up on the experience of the risks that have been accepted. There are a number of reasons for doing this. A particular risk may develop poor experience, and an entire class of risk may deteriorate as a result of adverse economic and social conditions. Conditions in particular geographical areas may change in such a way as to change the quality of business in those areas. Agencies change over time, and it may be necessary to review ways of improving a deteriorating situation. The underwriting division should review loss experience periodically and take whatever action might be needed to reclassify risks and to rerate them.[26]

Engineering. There are a number of risks where the application of engineering techniques to safety programs and other methods of loss control have a great deal of influence on the subsequent loss experience of the risk. Aiena has suggested that "Many risks are retained by an insurance company or an agency and many are newly acquired by the same parties primarily because of the company engi-

[26] Brouder, *op. cit.*, p. 79.

neer, the quality of his service and his understanding of the risk."[27] Workmen's compensation insurance is an example of an area where loss control can reduce the premium paid substantially, and the desirability of the risk may depend on the effective help of the insurer's engineering department.

FOR DISCUSSION

1. Discuss the functions of the marketing division of property and liability insurers. In what ways do the marketing divisions of insurers resemble similar divisions in manufacturing enterprises? In what ways do they differ?
2. Discuss what is meant by an insurance "market." To what extent do problems of market capacity arise in the insurance business?
3. How does the selling function in property and liability insurance differ from the way sales are handled in other types of business?
4. Distinguish between an agent and a broker. What is meant by a broker of record?
5. Give examples of insurers that may be classified as direct writers and of insurers that operate under the exclusive agency system. What are the distinguishing features of each type of sales organization?
6. What types of risk are usually placed by an excess line broker? What is meant by the expression "nonadmitted insurer"?
7. Agency involves three parties. List the parties and relate them to property and liability insurance. Must an agency relationship be in written form?
8. There are three types of agency system—direct reporting, general agency, and branch office. Describe each of these systems and comment on the extent to which each is used in the property and liability insurance business. How does an insurer decide on which system to use?
9. What is meant by agency by estoppel or ratification?
10. "When our office is asked to prepare a quotation on a given risk, we go well beyond such normal items as policy coverages, limits of liability, competitive premiums and 'basic factors.' We also must satisfy ourselves that the company being presented has the engineering and claims facilities necessary to handle the risk."[28] What is the relationship of engineering to underwriting?
11. Write a brief report on the history of the word "underwriting" as it has been used in the insurance business.
12. Discuss the functions of the property and liability insurance underwriter. What has been the impact of multiple line legislation on the underwriting function?

---

[27] S. W. Aiena, "'Engineering' the Big Risk," *Journal of Insurance Information*, September–October, 1966, p. 45.

[28] *Ibid.*, p. 43.

13. What is meant by account selling? To what extent has this concept been reflected in the organization of the underwriting divisions of property and liability insurers?
14. One of the functions of an underwriting division is to follow-up on the results of underwriting decisions. Why is this follow-up important?
15. Write a brief history of the American agency system. Include in your presentation a discussion of its current role in insurance sales.

CHAPTER · 32

Finance

With state commissioners carefully scrutinizing the financial position of insurers, their ability to pay can rarely be expected to become a matter of question. Selection of an insurer by an applicant for insurance is to a large degree influenced by the agent or broker. It is probably true that in a majority of cases the agent or broker makes the choice.

Where the applicant for insurance participates in the selection of an insurer, he is more often concerned with its underwriting and adjustment reputation than he is with an appraisal of its financial strength. The average buyer is usually satisfied if he limits his purchases of insurance to well-known and recognized insurers and places his business with an agent or broker of outstanding reputation. There are occasions when it becomes important to know something of the financial strength of the insurer. Officers of lending institutions are called upon to review insurance programs, and capacity and underwriting practices of insurers may become a matter for review. Where financial strength is to be determined from statement figures, perhaps in no other business is the searcher for factual material obligated to contend with as many obscurities.

RATIOS

Insurance rates are based on averages. The insurance underwriter undertakes to select his risks to the end that his experience will at least equal the average and will be better than the average if possible. If the losses in a given period are less than allowed for in the rate, and expenses do not exceed the allowance, there will result a profit for the insurer.

For the purpose of convenience the insurance industry uses the terms "loss ratio" and "expense ratio." The loss ratio is the percentage of losses to premiums. For most analytical purposes the preferred ratio is incurred losses to earned premiums. The expense ratio is the percentage of the premium used to pay all costs of acquiring, writing, and servicing business. With each class of business there is a breaking point beyond which the loss ratio cannot go if the business is to remain profitable. In some years the loss ratio in a class may be very profitable, while in other years the insurer may lose money in the class. The breaking point is determined by deducting from 100 percent a percentage that will represent all the expenses, including commissions, taxes, office rent, and all other business expenses. The aggregate of these items represents the premium charge as the word was originally understood. If, for instance, a given insurer, in underwriting a given class of business, has an expense ratio of 45 percent, then so long as the loss ratio is maintained under 55 percent, the insurer will make an underwriting profit. Once the insurer has a loss ratio in excess of 55 percent, even though it represents a substantial margin less than the total premium income, the insurer is suffering an underwriting loss on this class of business.

The difference between 100 percent and the expense loading percentage is known as the "permissible loss ratio." Briefly, the permissible loss ratio is that percentage of the premium dollar remaining after the deduction of allowances for all expenses, for profit, and for contingencies and conflagration hazards. It is a convenience, and its use simply means that as long as the loss ratio does not exceed the permissible loss ratio the operations of the insurer are on a profitable basis. In other words, the amount of the premium dollar necessary to pay all expenses and allow for a reasonable profit is computed and the balance is available for the payment of losses. If losses exceed this balance, they will encroach upon profits; and if they exceed this balance by more than the allowance for profits, the insurer will show an underwriting loss.

Significance of Underwriting Ratios for a Given Year. Two main assumptions of rate making are: (*a*) it is likely that the average loss ratio of the future will be equal to that of the past, and (*b*) there is a probability that the loss ratio will change to a marked degree from year to year corresponding to random annual fluctuations in the number and size of claims. On the basis of the loss experience for a determinable period in the immediate past, the loss to be expected in the future is calculated, and this loss is likewise distributed over a period of years. Once the size of the estimated future loss has been determined, it is expressed in a uniform fixed annual premium. In the insurance business, in the absence of a change in the risk or hazards, the premium rates remain the same from year to year. This is so even though the loss ratio for the particular class may fluctuate from year to year. In other words, an insurer may have a good or profitable year in a given class. A good year may be followed by a poor or unprofitable year. On the whole the years must average out to be reasonably profitable over a period, if the rate calculations are, in fact, adequate.[1]

Whether the earnings for a single year are in line with an established or typical trend in the industry can be determined by reference to published statements of aggregates. These tables indicate aggregate loss ratios by lines as well as by types of carrier. Aggregates of the various underwriting ratios are available in order that a marked deviation from an established trend in the industry is easy to observe. The availability of loss ratios by line enables a more careful analysis of a particular insurer than is to be obtained by reference to total aggregates. This is true since the insurer under observation may have a predominant part of its business in one or several lines and with respect to many lines write no business whatsoever.

RESERVES

In the balance sheet of any property and liability insurer, two types of reserves may appear. They are either: (*a*) statutory, or (*b*) voluntary. Statutory reserves are those required by law and include unearned premium reserves and reserves for losses. Voluntary reserves are those set up by the insurer to make provision for special situations and unforeseen contingencies.

Voluntary reserves should be distinguished from statutory reserves in that voluntary reserves are in a strict sense a part of the surplus. They represent a cutting off of part of the surplus and earmarking it for some special situation or contingency. Voluntary reserves are not liabilities in the sense that unearned premium reserves are so considered. They constitute a part of the stockholders' equity. The statutory reserves represent a liability. This liability is reduced by return premiums, reinsurance, or when premiums are transferred as earned to the surplus of the insurer.

Voluntary reserves are sometimes classified as: (*a*) those set aside for matured but unpaid obligations, and (*b*) those set aside to meet obligations that have not yet matured. In the first category are to be found such items as reserves for taxes, reserves for dividends voted, and claim reserves in excess of statutory requirements. In the second category are to be found any voluntary reserves set up to provide for

[1] An underwriting loss in a given year may not be particularly significant and is not necessarily evidence of poor underwriting. It is the underwriting experience over a period sufficiently long to evidence a trend that is important. When a stock company or a mutual, writing nonassessable contracts, covers a number of risks and receives the premium, there is no further income regardless of how great or how small the loss figure for the contract may be. Insurance underwriters undertake to select their risks with a view to minimizing losses but it is not within the realm of possibility in any given year deliberately to establish an aggregate amount of losses. Losses, therefore, from year to year fluctuate. The income from premiums on a given class of business remains constant but the losses on that class may be equivalent to the expected average or be greater or less.

unseen contingencies such as sums set aside to provide for catastrophes or sums designed to absorb unfavorable investment fluctuations.

Unearned Premium Reserve Requirements. It is the practice for the states to require insurers to set up as a liability a reserve equivalent to the portion of the gross premiums on contracts in force corresponding to the period the contract yet has to run to expiration.[2] This is required because it is held that the full amount of the premium should not be allocated without restriction to the insurer until protection for the full contract period has been afforded. In addition, with respect to most contracts, the insured may elect to cancel his coverage at any time during the contract term and demand a return premium. Finally, because the insurer is obligated at any time during the contract term to provide protection for the balance of the term, a fund must be available to reinsure all unexpired risks in the event that for any reason this becomes necessary or desirable. Basically, the reserve requirement amounts to the establishment of an accounting practice that will make available funds from premium income for the proper settlement of claims or payment of losses only as the premiums are earned and, at the same time, account for income received but not yet earned.

The reserve is carried on the books of the insurer as a liability and is computed on the gross premium. The reserve at all times must equal the unearned portions of gross premiums charged on all outstanding contracts. Reserve calculations are based on the assumption that a premium is earned pro rata as the period covered by the contract runs out. Specifically, in the case of a three-year contract, the day the contract goes into effect, the entire premium becomes a part of the reserve and is a liability on the books of the insurer. At the end of one month, $\frac{1}{36}$ of the premium is regarded as earned, and a like amount is earned each month thereafter as long as the contract remains in force. Thus, in the case of a three-year contract with a term premium of \$300 written to be effective on June 30 of a given year, at the end of that year the insurer would be credited with an earned premium of \$50 and would carry in the reserve an unearned premium of \$250. During the next year, a full year's premium would be considered earned, that is, \$100, and \$150 would remain as unearned premium in the reserve. This procedure is carried out during the entire contract term until the end of the three years. The entire premium is earned, and there is nothing left from the premium in the reserve. This works out as follows:

---

[2] The only exception to this requirement is to be found in the case of certain types of mutual insurers operating on an intrastate basis and usually confining their operations within a small local area. In the case of these local mutuals, the reserve requirement may vary. The requirement will depend upon the assessment liability provided in the contract. In all other instances the reserve is established by law.

End of:	Earned Premium	Unearned Premium
First calendar year	$ 50	$250
Second calendar year	150	150
Third calendar year	250	50
Policy term	300	0

While the state laws require that 100 percent of the premiums received for new business shall be set up in the unearned premium reserve, the insurers are not obligated to compute reserves on the basis of every contract written as noted in the example just cited. Obviously, this would be a tremendous task. In the interest of simplifying accounting, it is assumed that during a given year there is a steady flow of business. Some contracts are written immediately after the beginning of the year, and others are written just before the close of the year. Insurers in such circumstances are allowed to assume that all the business of a given year is written as of the mid-period. This means that if $1 million in premiums is written during a given year, for a term of one year, the insurer will be allowed to take credit for half that amount at the end of the year as earned premium for the contracts written on January 1. For the contracts written on December 31, it will have earned none. Averaging all the contracts written for the year, the 50 percent of the net premium is regarded as earned.[3] It can be seen that with an insurer with an increasing volume of new business, allocating reserve on the foregoing basis will provide an amount less than contemplated. The same is true in the case of a newly organized insurer. In filing its annual statement the insurer is required to indicate the basis of its computations. If the reserve is calculated on the basis of an annual fraction, and if because of a rapidly increasing volume of business, or for any other reason, the annual fraction basis provides a reserve less than the statutory requirement, the insurer will be required to make new computations on another basis. Where annual fractions have proved inadequate, an unearned premium reserve computed on a semimonthly, monthly, bimonthly, or semiannual pro rata basis may be required. Computers have now made it possible for some insurers to use the daily method.

Whatever periods are used for computing the reserve, it is apparent

[3] With respect to two-year contracts written in a given year, the same rule applies. It would be assumed that at the end of the calendar year six months' premium would be earned out of the 24, or ¼ of the total premium collected. In the case of a three-year contract, ⅙ of the premium is earned, meaning that ⅚ of the premium collected must be set up as an unearned premium reserve. In the case of a four-year contract, ⅛ is earned the first year, and in the case of a five-year contract, 1⁄10 is earned. Here again it means that in the case of a four-year contract, ⅞ of the premium must be set up as an unearned premium reserve, and in the case of a five-year contract, 9⁄10 of the premium must be set up. Thus, if an insurer were to write in a given year $1 million in premiums on five-year business, at the end of the year the unearned premium requirement would be $900,000.

that only as time goes on is the unearned premium reserve released as earned premium. It is obvious then that the unearned premium reserve absorbs premium income as it is paid into the insurer and only as the term for which the contract is written expires does the premium income pass to the asset side of the insurer statement. Generally speaking, portions of newly written premiums are credited to the underwriting account of the insurer at predetermined intervals.

Ownership of the Reserve. While the law requires that unearned premiums be set up as a reserve and from an accounting standpoint they are regarded as a liability, this reserve is not in any way segregated in the insurer funds. There are no special assets identifiable as constituting the reserve. The courts have held it to be the exclusive property of the insurer, and the right of the insured to recover a part of his premium is a mere incident of the contract. It is sometimes stated that the unearned premium reserve is held in the nature of a trust. While this may be so, it is not a trust fund in the true sense, and that portion of the assets of the corporation which represent the reserve is held by the courts to be as much the property of the corporation as that portion which represents the contributions of the stockholders or funds derived from other sources. This point assumes significance when consideration is given to income derived from the investment of insurer assets.

Premiums as collected are mingled with all the other assets of the insurer. As they are paid, they become the property of the insurer. With respect to unearned premiums or any other assets of the insurer, the insured has no preferred claim. Under the terms of his contract he has a contractual right to indemnity in case of loss, or in the event of the cancellation of his contract he has a similar right to the refund of the unearned portion of his premium. In the case of liquidation because of impairment of the financial structure of the insurer by reason of insufficient assets, the policyholder is in no better position with respect to the distribution of the reserve than are all other creditors.

Equity in the Unearned Premium Reserve. The unearned premium reserve is based on the full amount of the premium paid by the insured. Deductions are not allowed for expenses. Losses are paid from earned premium, and future losses are expected to be paid from that part of the unearned premium reserve that becomes, with the passage of time, earned premium. Since the gross premium provides for both pure premium and loading, the pure premium is expected to be adequate to pay all losses. The loading represents the expense items transferred from surplus, and since they have already been paid they will not be paid again. This amount in the unearned premium reserve for all practical purposes amounts to a loan from surplus, even though it cannot be so carried in the statement.

The amount of the reserve must equal the aggregate amount that the insurer would be obligated to return to its policyholders for the unexpired terms of contracts in force should every contract be canceled at the statement date. It follows that since the premiums must, of necessity, be sufficiently large to pay both losses and expenses, and since no credit has been taken in the reserve for expenses, a well-managed insurer must have equity in the unearned premiums. This equity should closely approximate the percentage of the premium allocated to expenses. In other words, when a contract is written, if the commission is 25 percent and all other expenses increase the total percentage of expense to 35 or 45 percent, then it is to be presumed that at all times the insurer has a corresponding equity in the reserve.

In the case of emergency, where the surplus account is being depleted, either because of losses, an expanding volume of business, or for any other reason, the equity in the reserve may be realized through reinsurance. If the insurer reinsures part of its outstanding liability, the reinsurer ordinarily allows as commission the acquisition costs of the business. A reserve is no longer required for the reinsured business, and the equity in the reserve in the form of a commission is transferred to surplus. Even though this equity remains locked up in the unearned premium reserve, consideration is given it in measuring the net worth of an insurer.[4]

Loss Reserves. Whenever a loss is reported to an insurer, a reserve is immediately set up in an amount estimated to be adequate to settle the claim. In the case of fire losses, loss reserves do not constitute a serious problem. Protracted settlements are not the usual thing, and a reasonable estimate of the value of a fire claim immediately following a loss is not at all difficult. In the field of liability insurance the situation is quite different. With respect to liability claims, in particular, there is considerable uncertainty from the outset with respect to the amount that will be required for a settlement. If the claim is contested, the litigation may extend over a period of years. With respect to automobile insurance claims in some states the courts are a year or two behind. For all these pending claims a reserve fund must be established by the insurers.

When a claim is reported to a property and liability insurer, its adjusters determine first whether there is liability and then make an

---

[4] Equity in the unearned premium differs with the line of insurance, and with any given line it will fluctuate from year to year. A reasonable estimate of the workmen's compensation is placed at 20 percent. This is low because of the custom of estimating premiums and collecting part of a premium following an audit. On fidelity and surety business the equity may be as high as 50 percent. A reasonable estimate fixes the equity for fire insurers at 40 percent and for casualty insurers at 35 percent. However, with increasing emphasis now being placed on multiple line underwriting and package contracts, equity by line of insurance is of less importance.

appraisal of the extent of loss or damage. The reserve must equal statutory requirements, but if the insurer estimate of the "value of the claim" exceeds the statutory requirements, the insurer estimate prevails.

In the early days of property and liability insurance the insurer estimate was the sole basis for fixing the amount of the reserve. The tendency to underestimate the value of claims tended to produce inadequate reserves. Statutes were enacted designed to correct the situation. With a view to increasing the amount of the reserves, an average value method was adopted. When this method, too, proved unsatisfactory, new statutes were enacted providing for the formula and loss ratio plan now in use.

The statutes require that loss reserves with respect to property and liability claims shall be carried, less losses paid, for a minimum of three years after a premium is earned. The reserves are based on an assumed loss ratio of 60 percent. The statutory reserve, then, for contracts issued during the last three calendar years is 60 percent of the earned premium less any amount paid for losses and loss expenses. The reserve thus calculated is called the "remainder reserve." This remainder reserve is compared with the insurer's estimate of the value of each claim. If the insurer's estimate is greater than the remainder reserve, this latter figure represents the amount required. The same rule holds with respect to workmen's compensation insurance with the difference that the assumed final loss ratio is 65 percent. Average values are used for suits pending under contracts written three or more years prior to the statement date. A value of $850 is assigned to suits outstanding for a period of three years. An increasing value is assigned with each passing year until a value of $1,500 is assigned for each outstanding suit pending against contracts written ten or more years prior to the statement date. The total required reserves is the sum of insurer estimates or total suit liability, whichever is the greater, for contracts written three or more years plus the remainder reserves for the last three years or the insurer estimates of the value of the claims, whichever is the greater. Where loss reserves are established on the basis of the insurer's estimate of the value of each claim, the reserves so established are known as "case basis" loss reserves.

The seeker for information concerning the stability of an insurer, when appraising the loss reserve, has only the information afforded in the annual statement upon which to rely. Access to claim files, actual number of outstanding claims, and other supporting data are available to the examiners of the state insurance department when an actual examination is in process. The insurance department may call for a supplemental report in any instance that it elects to do so. Members of the public are compelled to rely solely upon the data that appear in the annual statement. Fortunately this is sufficiently adequate to give a very substantial amount of information and to permit the drawing of reasonably accurate conclusions.

A sudden increase in loss reserves on a given class of business might raise the question as to whether reserves in previous years were too low. If, on the other hand, loss reserves appear to be unreasonably low in the light of previous years' loss experience, this is again the occasion for inquiry. Fortunately, the annual report gives adequate data for determining whether loss reports have been underestimated in the past or whether such a practice is of recent development. The data will also show when steps have been taken to correct a previously unfortunate situation. A comparison of the incurred losses as they appear in the annual statement for different years will indicate whether the insurer is generous in making its estimates or is making inadequate estimates of loss reserve. If the case reserves carried for a given year as shown in the statement are lower than the payments made on those claims as determined by the figures for a subsequent year, this is indication that the reserve for the year under question was inadequate. The significance of determining whether reserves for previous years are inadequate is to be found only as it reflects insurer policy. Inadequate reserve for previous years reflects "water over the dam." If the losses exceeded reserves but they are paid, and the surplus even though reduced is adequate, then the past experience of the insurer has no immediate bearing upon present condition. If the insurer has been in the habit of inadequately establishing reserves for losses, there is a rebuttable presumption that the practice is still in vogue. It is to be presumed that any apparent discrepancy in the reserve will be picked up by the insurance department and the insurer will be required to increase loss liability. An insurer that has been in the habit of underestimating or very closely figuring the loss reserve may still be expected to provide a reserve that is something less than generous.[5]

In appraising claim reserves it is customary to recognize both the impact of inflation and the constant upward trend in awards. Past experience with respect to certain types of claims will not always measure the award that can be expected from a present-day jury. The

---

[5] Indicative of the nature of property and liability loss reserves and the necessity for their revision from time to time is the obligation now placed on workmen's compensation insurers with respect to permanent and total disability. The insurer is obligated to set up reserves covering anticipated payments during the entire lifetime of the injured party. It is the practice of the insurer writing the line to establish reserves on the basis of a full life expectancy where permanent disability is involved. A person who is paralyzed because of an injury to the spine may be expected to live a full life span. The compensation insurer is obligated to pay medical, hospital, nursing bills, and similar items. If a moderately young man is injured and obligated to spend the rest of his life hospitalized, his hospital, nursing, and doctor bills may run as high as $15,000 a year. Over a period of 20 years this will call for an outlay of $300,000. A change in the cost of medical expenses will be reflected immediately in the amount of required reserve.

trend has evidenced itself not only in the case of personal injury liability claims but also in the field of workmen's compensation. In the case of medical costs in the compensation field, protracted recoveries are an important factor and, with increased medical costs, an upward revision of reserve account is as often an absolute necessity.[6]

The policy with respect to the establishment of these loss reserves has an important bearing upon the financial strength of the insurer. If the reserve is generous, over a period of time the insurer has an equity in this reserve at the cost of affecting unfavorably the figure representing underwriting profit. If the loss reserve is inadequate for the year in which it is too closely trimmed, the insurer will show an exaggerated underwriting profit. This shortage in reserve must ultimately be made up when the claims mature with a payment of the loss. The insurer that invariably makes a generous appraisal of the cost of its pending claims, for the purposes of the reserve, is in a stronger position financially than its less generous competitor, even though its loss ratio makes a less favorable showing.[7]

Equity in Loss Reserve. Where the statutory loss reserve provides for an amount consistently in excess of the loss experience of a property and liability insurer, there will from time to time be transferred back to surplus an amount equal to the difference between actual experience and statutory reserves. If the insurer sets up its own estimate on a case basis and actual experience closely coincides with the case basis estimate, then the estimate at any time of the amount of surplus recoverable from the reserve for losses is the difference between the insurer's case basis estimate and the statutory requirement.

At one time it was necessary to adjust property and liability underwriting results on a case basis where experience was less than statutory reserves to obtain an adjusted underwriting earnings figure. Annual convention statements now show underwriting earnings computed on a case basis, so that it is no longer necessary to adjust an earnings

---

[6] State supervisory officials recognize that an underreserved claim condition might conceal an extremely weak insurer position, if not actually conceal insolvency. Any transfer of substantial amounts from claim reserves to surplus on the part of a property and liability insurer, particularly if the surplus appeared to be getting low and the transfer were made with the appearance of bolstering the surplus position, would be carefully scrutinized by state supervisory authorities.

[7] Some insurers in setting up their own appraisal of loss reserve use average values. This is particularly the case with respect to compensation insurance and in the field of automobile insurance. In any field where the number of claims is large, an average value of each claim may be determined based upon the experience of the insurer tempered with judgment. Where such a practice is in vogue, the average value of a claim is determined upon and this is multiplied by the number of loss notices receive in the period under consideration. From this total amount is deducted losses paid to date on notices received during the period. This plan precludes individual judgment with respect to each case, but where the number of cases is sufficiently large, averages based on experience provide reasonably accurate approximations.

figure based on a statutory reserve to secure a picture of true underwriting earnings on a case basis. Although in the property and liability statement the term "statutory earnings" still finds a place, the figure that appears is actually a case basis earnings figure. For the purpose of determining equity capital or liquidating value, it is still necessary to adjust statutory loss reserves on a case basis when experience coincides with the case basis and this reserve is less than the statutory requirements.

OPERATIONAL RESULTS

The underwriting profits or losses represent the underwriting results for an insurer computed on a basis established by the statutes. In computing an underwriting profit (or loss), three factors are considered: (*a*) earned premiums, (*b*) incurred losses, and (*c*) incurred expenses. It is necessary briefly to consider the meaning of these factors.

Insurers by law are required to set up the proportionate premiums unearned as a liability. The insurer is not allowed to take credit for any of the premiums received until they become earned and are then removed from the reserve. It is only the earned premiums that may be taken into consideration in computing the underwriting profit. The logic of this is apparent. The insurer cannot spend a liability, and only when a premium becomes "earned" may it be devoted to loss payments.

Incurred losses are to be distinguished from losses paid. There is always some time lag between the occurrence of a loss and its adjustment. Sometimes the lag involves a considerable period of time if the loss is a difficult one to adjust or if, for any reason, liability is questioned. Incurred losses constitute a liability, and for this reason it is the incurred losses that are taken into consideration in computing the loss ratio rather than paid losses. The impact of the incurred losses on insurer's position in contrast to the paid losses may be illustrated by the happening of a catastrophe. Take, for example, the great Texas City explosion. There was no question concerning the liability of the insurers, but if a financial statement were taken a few days after the explosion and only paid losses were taken into consideration, the impact of the disaster would not appear at all as affecting the loss ratio. Any severe losses that develop near the end of the year will probably not be paid until the following year. To reflect these losses in the current year, a reserve is set up to pay them and they are deducted from income as incurred losses.

Expenses are ordinarily paid in the year in which they are incurred. There are items such as federal, state, and other taxes which may be incurred in one year but are not payable until sometime during the following year. Reserves are set up to meet expenditures of this sort, where they are not paid in the year in which they are incurred, and to the extent that such reserves are established, they are considered in determining the underwriting exhibit for the year.

To determine the earned premium for a given year, the net premiums written for the year are added to the unearned premium figure for December 31 of the previous year. From the total of these two items is deducted the unearned premium figure for the end of the year under consideration. Thus:

Premiums representing new business	$.....
Unearned premium end of previous year	.....
Total	$.....
Less unearned premium at end of year under consideration	.....
Earned premium for the year	$.....

The logic of this procedure is apparent. Certain of the unearned premiums at the end of the previous year will become earned during the year under consideration. All of the premiums paid for new business are unearned at the time they go on the books. For the purpose of this computation both items are regarded as unearned and totaled. By deducting the calculated unearned premiums at the end of the year under observation, there is a difference which must represent earned premiums for the year.

To determine the statutory underwriting profit or loss, expenses incurred are added to losses and loss adjustment expenses incurred. Thus:

Expenses incurred	$.....
Losses and loss expenses incurred	.....
Incurred losses and expenses	$.....

Statutory underwriting profit or loss is the difference in the two preceding results. Briefly then underwriting profit or loss is determined by deducting from earned premiums incurred losses and expenses.

Adjusted Underwriting Profit. The statutory underwriting profit or loss is determined by finding the difference between earned premium and incurred losses and expenses. The statutory results thus determined do not give an accurate picture of the true operating results of an insurer. This can be illustrated by means of an example.

Assume in a given year that new business written was such as to make necessary the increase in the unearned premium reserve of the insurer by the amount of $1 million. In order to set up that reserve, there would have to be transferred from surplus an amount equivalent to the cost of placing the business on the books of the insurer. Assume the business to be fire insurance and the cost of placing the business on the books to be 40 percent of the premium. This would mean there would of necessity be transferred from surplus the amount of $400,000. With the passing of time if the losses on the business did not exceed 60 percent of the premium, then in due course the 40 percent transferred from surplus to reserve would be again returned to surplus. This transfer, however, is not lost to the insurer. This means that for any given year in order to secure the adjusted underwriting profit the statutory underwriting result is adjusted by adding any increase or deducting any decrease in the equity in the unearned premium reserve.[8]

To illustrate the determination of adjusted underwriting profits, the following example may be considered. Assume a property and liability insurer writes $120,000 in fire premiums on three-year business in a year with $36,000 in acquisition costs. If this amount is written so that premium income is evenly distributed throughout the year, there will be required at the end of the year in the unearned premium fund the amount of $100,000. This is the situation of an insurer with a cash income of $120,000 required to set up an unearned premium reserve of $100,000 and spend $36,000 to get the business. This means for each $120,000 income on three-year business, the insurer must spend in expenses or allocated reserve $136,000. This reduces the surplus at once by $26,000. Now assuming a 50 percent loss ratio, the insurer will sustain out of the $20,000 in earned premiums the first year fire losses of $10,000. In addition to expenses of $36,000 attributable to acquisition costs, there will be 10 percent additional expenses chargeable to administration. This may be set up as follows:

Premium income		$120,000
Less unearned premiums		100,000
Earned premiums		$ 20,000
Losses incurred	$10,000	
Expenses incurred	48,000	
Total losses and expenses		58,000
Statutory underwriting loss		$ 38,000

This statutory underwriting loss will reduce the surplus account by the amount of the loss in the year that it develops. If, with the passing of time, the business expires and it is found that the losses do not exceed 50 percent of the premium as it is earned, the underwriting loss will gradually turn to a profit. When one half of the premium is earned, the following situation is indicative of the trend:

---

[8] In the case of fire insurance this equity is generally calculated as 40 percent of the reserve, while with respect to some other types of property and liability insurance a figure of 35 percent is used.

Premium income		$120,000
Less unearned premiums		60,000
Earned premiums		$ 60,000
Losses incurred	$30,000	
Expenses incurred	48,000	
Total losses and expenses		78,000
Statutory underwriting loss		$ 18,000

From the foregoing it can be seen that the statutory underwriting loss becomes less as the contract approaches expiration. At the outset, to determine the actual profit, termed the "adjusted underwriting profit," the equity in the reserve is added to the statutory result. This works out as follows, using the figures for the end of the first year:

Statutory underwriting loss	$38,000
Equity in unearned premium	40,000
Adjusted underwriting profit	$ 2,000

From the foregoing it appears that the insurer, instead of losing $38,000, actually earned $2,000. This represented a retained profit of 10 percent of the earned premium and 1.7 percent of the premium income.

Use of Ratios to Determine Underwriting Profit. An alternative method for determining the adjusted underwriting profit is to be found by combining the statutory loss ratio with an expense ratio based on expenses incurred to premiums written.

The statutory loss ratio represents the ratio of losses incurred including loss adjustment expenses to earned premiums. This ratio gives the most accurate possible determination of loss experience. It is presumed that the loss experience determined by the ratio will be reflected in additional increments of premium as they are earned. It is possible to determine, at the outset, within very close limits, what the expenses will be for the entire contract term. By taking the loss ratio on an incurred-earned basis and the expense ratio on incurred-written basis, it is possible to make a reasonably accurate appraisal of the profit or loss position of the insurer for a given year.

In the example given the premium written amounted to $120,000 with incurred expenses of $48,000. This produces an expense ratio on an incurred-written basis of 40 percent. Losses the first year amounted to $10,000. With earned premiums of $20,000 this represents a statutory loss ratio of 50 percent. Adding the loss ratio and expense ratio thus obtained, the total is less than 100 percent. This indicates a profit of 10 percent on the earned premium. Since the earned premium is $20,000, the ratios indicate an underwriting profit of $2,000. This is the same figure derived by correcting the statutory underwriting loss by adding to it the equity in the unearned premium. Carrying out the same procedure at the point where the earned premium amounted to $60,000, we have here a statutory underwriting loss of $18,000. Taking 40 percent of the unearned premium of $60,000 and applying it to the statutory underwriting loss, we arrive at an underwriting profit of $6,000. This again is 10 percent of $60,000, the amount of the earned premium at this point.

Investment Income. While the business of insurance concerns itself primarily with underwriting risks, an important activity is the investment and reinvestment of funds in the possession of the insurer. From this source every insurer derives an important part of its income.

Insurers hold funds which in total represent the capital stock account, the surplus, the unearned premium reserve, reserve for losses, and other special or contingency reserves that the insurer may establish. All these amounts represent in the aggregate a very substantial sum. The proceeds derived from their investment are an important source of income.

While the laws of the various states impose restrictions on the nature of insurer investments, there is sufficient leeway to permit a considerable variation among insurers with respect to the yield from this source. The nature of the investment program is a factor for consideration when the financial stability and loss paying ability of an insurer are under consideration. It is sufficient here to make the point that an insurer carries on a business having two important phases: (*a*) underwriting, and (*b*) investment. Both branches of the business require specialized skills. The investment profits and the underwriting profits are each separate and distinct. The income from both underwriting and investment flow together to show the final income figures upon which adjusted profits, as contrasted to underwriting profits, are based.

Arguments have been advanced that investment income from funds representing the unearned premium reserve should be credited to the underwriting account. This credit would tend to swell underwriting results to the end that an underwriting profit could be obtained with a lower rate. The loading in the premium for profit would be lessened. Since the unearned premium reserve represents funds advanced by the policyholder, this argument at first thought seems to be a valid one. There are numerous objections, however. The theoretical one is to be found in the fact that although the unearned premium reserve represents the unearned portion of the premium paid by the policyholder, it is also true that a substantial amount of this reserve represents prepaid expense transferred from surplus. In order that the reserve be maintained intact, funds from the surplus have been transferred to the reserve.

In the case of insurers organized as stock companies the surplus belongs to the stockholders, and actually the money advanced from it might be considered in the nature of a loan. If this were the case and interest on the unearned premium reserve were to be credited to the underwriting account, it would be equally logical that the unearned premium reserve pay to the surplus interest on the money advanced. Stockholders would be entitled to an income on their equity in the reserve. If interest on the unearned premium reserve is credited to the underwriting account and then underwriting, in turn, has to pay interest on the capital that has been advanced from the reserve, to a very large degree one item cancels out the other. If the insurer were to be liquidated, the stockholders' equity, that is, the capital, surplus, special reserves, and equity in the unearned premium reserve, would be available to the stockholders to invest. The income from these investments would belong to the stockholders without any consideration for underwriting profits or losses. The fact that the capital is placed at risk for the purpose of securing an underwriting profit, it is argued, should not preclude the owners of the capital from obtaining the investment income that they are entitled to in any case.

It has been a long-standing practice of the insurance business to invest the entire underwriting profit in the business. This has the effect of creating an additional factor of safety and at the same time enlarging the facilities for underwriting. Dividends, when they are paid, are as a matter of general practices restricted to a part of the interest derived from investment. The addition of the underwriting profits to surplus, together with a portion of the investment income, has tended to promote a steady growth of the insurance industry over the years and to lend strength and stability to the insurers.[9]

Net Operating Earnings. Insurers have two separate and distinct sources of income: one derived from premiums on contracts, and another derived from interest on capital and surplus. These two sources of income represent the operation of two separate departments of the insurer. When added together they give the net operating earnings of the insurer before federal income taxes. With taxes

---

[9] In discussing insurance results, reference is sometimes made to what is termed "trade profits." Using trade profits as a basis, the loss ratio thus determined is said to be a "loss ratio on a trade basis." Trade profits are determined by taking the aggregate income of an insurer for a given period and charging against that income expenses, including loss adjustment expenses and incurred losses. It is a statement of the excess of income in a given period over aggregate expenditures. An insurer writing a large volume of business with the premium account sharply expanding is in a position to show a very substantial profit on a trade basis and, hence, on the same basis, a favorable loss ratio. This figure is virtually worthless for the purposes of appraising the strength and underwriting accomplishments of an insurer. It has been termed at best "enthusiastic bookkeeping." Whatever may be the purpose of citing a trade profit or a favorable loss ratio on a trade basis, such figures are hardly acceptable as evidence of the successful operations of the underwriting division. See, for example, Roger Kenney, *Fundamentals of Fire and Casualty Insurance Strength* (2d ed.; Dedham, Mass.: Kenney Insurance Studies, 1953), p. 54.

deducted, the result reflects the net operating earnings for the year. This works out as follows:

Adjusted underwriting profit	$....
Net investment income	....
Net operating earnings before taxes	$....
Less federal income taxes	....
Net operating earnings after taxes	$....

Net operating earnings are the adjusted underwriting results plus net investment income. It will be recalled that investment income does not reflect captial gains or losses. Realized or unrealized gains from investments are reflected from year to year in the surplus account. Market fluctuations do not influence the operating account.

SURPLUS

The impact of new business on surplus can best be illustrated by giving consideration to the situation of a new insurer just embarking upon business. When the first contracts are written and the reserve fund established, expenses and disbursements attributable to the acquisition of the business must be paid. Since the insurer is new and has no earned surplus, in order that capital may not be impaired, it is necessary for the stockholders to pay in a surplus. This is the custom with a new stock insurer. Not only must the stockholders contribute the capital but they must pay in enough surplus to permit the insurer to engage in business until an earned surplus sufficient for its needs can be acquired. This usually requires a period of years.

After the insurer has been established, the principle remains the same. As the insurer grows and makes a profit, part or all of the profit from underwriting is used to augment the originally paid-in surplus to the end that the insurer may be in a position to expand its business. The extent of an insurer's business is very definitely limited by its available surplus. No matter how strong the insurer, or how long it has been in business, every new contract depletes surplus in favor of reserve, and when there is no longer an available surplus the insurer must curtail new business or take steps to augment the reserve.

Policyholders' Surplus. This figure represents the net assets of an insurer computed by deducting from total assets all balance sheet liabilities. This means that the unearned premium reserve finds no place in this figure either in its entirety or through consideration of the equity in the reserve.

The policyholders' surplus represents free funds immediately available for insurer purposes but more particularly available for the payment of losses. It includes funds paid in as capital, paid-in and earned surplus, and special reserves that may be set aside, such as a reserve for dividends.

The policyholders' surplus is a significant figure. Because it is the fund immediately available for the payment of losses, it must be maintained in securities that are readily marketable. At the same time these securities must be of a type that do not lend themselves to violent market fluctuations. Consideration of the policyholders' surplus resolves itself into three factors: amount, liquidity, and stability.

The One to One Fire Insurance Ratio. The policyholders' surplus is the factor of safety upon which the insurer operates. Since the measure of potential losses is to be found in the unearned premium reserve, the safety factor to be found in the policyholders' surplus is not dependent upon its size but on its relationship to potential losses, that is, to the unearned premium reserve. A relationship established between the policyholders' surplus and the unearned premium reserve will give some indication of the stability of the insurer.

In the field of fire insurance an ideal situation is presumed to exist when the policyholders' surplus and the unearned premium reserve are equal. This constitutes the one to one ratio so widely used as a point of departure for appraising the financial strength of an insurer. Where the policyholders' surplus exceeds the unearned premium reserve, the insurer enjoys a preferred rating and falls in the blue-chip category. Where the policyholders' surplus falls as low as 75 percent of unearned premiums, the insurer may be doing well but its financial strength is something less than ideal. As the ratio of policyholders' surplus to unearned premium reserve drops, a situation is reached in which one hand washes the other and there is little capacity for expansion and somewhat less than ideal strength to withstand catastrophic losses. Insurers with a policyholders' surplus below 50 percent of unearned premiums who are writing only a fire business would probably require additional paid-in surplus from the stockholders if they elected to expand and write other lines by carrying on a multiple line business.

Insurers that elect to build up a strong ratio of policyholders' surplus to unearned premium reserve do this frequently in the full knowledge that the business carried on indicates no immediate requirement for an impregnable position. There have been periods where unprofitable underwriting, falling security prices, and catastrophic losses have appeared all within a period of a year or two.[10] It is the insurer with the strong ratio of policyholders' surplus to unearned premium reserve that meets such situations with equanimity.

---

[10] For example, the period of 1946–47 was a year of unprofitable underwriting. This period witnessed catastrophes such as San Antonio, Texas, in 1946; Texas City, Texas, in 1947; and the Florida Gulf Coast catastrophe of 1947. Coupled with these developments there was a falling stock market. A three-way pressure such as this is welcomed by no insurance underwriter, but the prudent underwriter foresees and prepares for it.

The Two for One Casualty Ratio. In insurers writing fire insurance the unearned premium reserve is the largest liability item. Few fire losses entail long periods of investigation. The extent of a fire loss can usually be determined promptly and settlement with the insured made without delay. Because of this fact claim reserves are comparatively small. In other forms of property and liability insurance the reverse is often true. By their very nature workmen's compensation and liability claims may entail a considerable period for settlement and may, in lines such as workmen's compensation, involve payments to an injured person for a lifetime. Such claim reserves run high. On the other hand, in some cases a substantial part of the premium is collected at the end of the contract term following an audit. The premium collected after the expiration of the contract pays for a part of the liability exposure but never appears in the unearned premium reserve. The unearned premium reserve for an insurer doing business of this type is not an accurate measure of potential liability. In seeking such a measure net premium income for a year was determined to be the best substitute for unearned premium. Unearned premium reserve represents potential liability for contracts in force. Net premiums for a year must be based on a previous year and may not accurately represent current conditions. They are reasonably close and for all practical purposes have proved to be satisfactory. Using net premiums for a year as a measure of potential liability it has been found, on the basis of experience, that if claims are adequately reserved $2 of premium may safely be written for each dollar of policyholders' surplus. This provides the casualty two for one ratio. When the premium volume begins to exceed $2 for each $1 of policyholders' surplus this may serve as a warning for a close scrutiny of the insurer's operations. While it may be found in the case of an insurer with a consistently low loss ratio over a long period that the two for one rule need not necessarily establish a limit for safe underwriting its use as a rule of thumb invites attention to the fact that the insurer may possibly be assuming excessive liability on the basis of its financial structure. It places a burden upon the insurer to show otherwise.[11]

There is a considerable diversity of opinion in the property and liability field with respect to the application of this ratio. Various alternative suggestions have been made. Some of these give increasing emphasis to the importance of loss reserves. It is suggested that if a careful check is maintained to see that the loss reserves are adequate at all times, the two for one ratio of premiums to policyholders' surplus

[11] The two for one rule probably stems from an old New York law that provided that a stock casualty insurer could not at any time pay cash dividends on its capital stock unless, after providing for such dividends, its surplus to policyholders was at least equal to 50 percent of the net premiums written during the next preceding calendar year. While the rule is not now a matter of law, it still serves as an important thumb rule for determining the financial stability of casualty insurers.

need no longer prevail. Such a check would be made by periodically comparing losses actually paid with the sum reserved for them.

It has been suggested, as well, that if a figure representing the aggregate of the full amount of the loss reserves plus 65 percent of the unearned premium reserve is represented in the investment portfolio by liquid assets such as United States government bonds or cash, then the necessity no longer exists for maintaining the two for one ratio. This plan is, in fact, an invasion of the unearned premium reserve to provide a cushion for loss payments. Just as in the case of the unearned premium reserve for fire insurance, the unearned premium reserve in other forms of property and liability insurance is not available for loss payments until the premiums become earned and the underwriting profit is transferred to surplus. Without entering into the various arguments pro and con with respect to the two for one ratio as a measure for the strength of a multiple line insurer, for the purchaser of insurance it provides a safe guide. It may be too strict, and to this extent complete reliance upon it may not do full justice to all insurers. This is particularly the case with respect to certain insurers that, over a long period of time, can show a record of conservative underwriting and unusually satisfactory loss ratios. Admitting that there may be much to be said on both sides, no matter what may be said against the rule it can be stated that by means of its use any error in judgment that the policyholder makes will be in his own favor. In other words, it is a safe rule.

Liquidity. Property and liability insurance underwriters know from experience that over the period of a year there will be a constant call for loss payments. They also know that they live constantly under the threat of catastrophic losses that bring about without notice demands for additional payments running to millions. This being the case, sufficient assets must be available that can readily be turned into cash to meet claim payments as they mature whatever their character.

The investment policy of the insurer, then, is to be scrutinized as a basis for determining its liquidity. A strong position is indicated when high-grade bonds, cash, and current premium balances in the aggregate cover all liabilities except the policyholders' surplus. This means that the insurer should have a diversified investment list of high-grade securities equal to the sum of the unearned premium reserve plus loss reserve. This relationship is also sometimes referred to as a one to one ratio.

Providing liquidity to cover the unearned premium reserve and loss reserves puts the insurer in a position immediately to pay all losses for which reserves are set up and to pay return premiums if there should be a sudden demand for the cancellation of all outstanding contracts. This last eventuality could hardly be expected, but closely akin to the payment of return premiums is the ability to reinsure. Should the insurer through impairment of surplus, because of catastrophic losses, elect to reinsure all or part of its outstanding liability, a liquid financial position smooths the way for the transaction.[12]

ADDITIONAL CONSIDERATIONS IN FINANCIAL STRENGTH

While there are some very successful insurers that have confined their activities to a limited geographical area and write but one type of insurance, it is nevertheless an evidence of stability if an insurer can show a substantial spread of liability. This is accomplished through geographic distribution of risks, and distribution of underwriting exposure through variation in types of risk.

Fire insurance underwriters learned early the painful way that a local concentration of risks might have disastrous consequences. It is now regarded as representing sound underwriting practices for an insurer writing the various forms of property and liability insurance to distribute its liability as widely as possible. For example, the windstorm that struck the Northeast in November, 1950, affected more than a quarter of a million policyholders. Catastrophes occur with surprising frequency, but usually the loss is confined within a limited area. The insurer with the greatest geographic distribution of risks suffers the least proportionately from these catastrophic losses. Obviously, an insurer concentrating its line in an area hit by a catastrophe is in an unenviable position. Granting that widespread geographic distribution is not an absolute essential to soundness, where present, it is an important factor for favorable consideration.

Variation with respect to the different types of lines written tends to cancel an unfavorable loss experience in one field with a favorable experience in another. Immediately following the end of World War II the casualty business that had theretofore experienced a lean period turned favorable. At the same time the fire business which had behind it a number of especially good years began to show an increasingly narrow margin of underwriting profit. Within the property and liability field there are compensating lines. For example, the automo-

[12] Aggregate assets of property and liability insurers are published showing the relative amounts invested in United States government bonds, municipal and state bonds, and in stock. By reference to these aggregates it is possible to determine whether a particular insurer conforms closely to the average of all insurers, or if it varies, whether the variation is in the direction of conservatism or the opposite. It is also possible by reference to these aggregates to determine whether the holdings in real estate for home office purposes and real estate acquired from foreclosed mortgages are reasonable. With respect to the individual insurer, the unearned premium reserve and the reserve for losses should always be covered by assets immediately convertible into cash.

bile business may reflect an unfavorable experience while general liability lines are profitable. In the fire business if extended cover business shows a loss due to a multiplicity of small windstorm claims in a catastrophe area, this experience may be offset by profits in the fire business and allied lines. With a wide distribution in types of risk the underwriting experience of the insurer is not tied to the unfavorable showing of a particular line in any given period.

Market Position of Insurer Stock. An indirect approach to the financial health of an insurer is to be found in the market action of the insurer stock. There are brokers who are specialists in this field who are constantly following insurer experiences with a view to recommending stock purchases as an investment.

The approach of the investor and the purchaser of insurance is not in all respects identical; figures that are of significance to the investor may be of less interest to the applicant for insurance. Notably in this category is the figure representing liquidating value. The insured has little interest in liquidating value, though this figure is of considerable interest to a stockholder. The stockholder is also interested in dividend policies and to that end earnings allocated to dividends. The policyholder may obtain from the combined appraisal of all stockholders as represented by market action of the stock a reasonably reliable measure of financial stamina.

There are market influences that reflect on a group of securities as a whole or on the entire market. A falling market or an advancing market in insurance stocks is not in itself significant with respect to an individual stock. If a stock over a considerable period moves continuously against the trend, this development warrants attention. A protracted sinking spell for a given stock constitutes a very definite warning.

Size as a Factor. Financial strength and the size of an insurer are not necessarily equivalents. This being the case, the size of an insurer is not a controlling factor in its selection. This is not to say that the factor of size is not a consideration.

It is possible to find a large insurer with assets running to a very substantial figure in excess of liabilities and, at the same time, upon examination to find the investment account something less than ideal. A medium-sized insurer might show a relatively strong preponderance of assets over liabilities and an investment portfolio of predominantly government bonds or other readily marketable investments. One insurer may be writing lines that are unprofitable, while the contrary may be the case with another insurer. It is sufficient here to indicate the necessity of making a determination of acceptability on factors other than size.

Size does have some values that must be taken into consideration. Some small insurers do not have the facilities for servicing accounts that are available to the larger insurers. This same situation holds true with respect to medium-sized insurers; and some large insurers do not have the same facilities in all areas. Claim adjustment offices and investigators immediately available to handle claims on a nationwide basis may be the determining feature to influence a choice. By the same token, well-managed insurers themselves limit their lines to geographic areas in which they have established well-staffed servicing offices.

Ratings have been assigned to insurers based on total admitted assets. Reference to the Spectator's factual financial appraisals indicates ratings from AAAA for an insurer with total admitted assets over $100 million to a B minus rating for an insurer whose assets are less than a quarter of a million.

RULES APPLICABLE TO MUTUAL INSURERS

Up to this point the discussion with respect to insurer finances has been limited to stock insurers. By means of this plan it was possible to obviate the necessity of continued repetition with respect to technical differences between stock and mutual insurers.

The rules for determining the strength of the two types of insurer are identical, though the organization of the balance sheets is slightly different. There is no capital stock account in the mutual statement. In the stock insurer the paid-in capital is part of the surplus to policyholders. In the mutual insurer the surplus to policyholders has the same significance as it has with the stock insurer, though the amounts in the fund may have different tags in the financial statement.

Assume a stock insurer with a policyholders' surplus of $1 million consisting of $500,000 paid-in capital and $500,000 surplus and a mutual insurer writing nonassessable contracts with a surplus of $1 million. Assume, in both instances, the unearned premium reserve is $1 million. The balance sheet of both insurers will show total assets of $2 million. Assuming that over the past five years the business of both insurers has shown consistent underwriting profit, the question for determination now is, on the basis of the figures, which of the two insurers is the stronger?

In both cases the ratio of policyholders' surplus to unearned premium reserve is one to one. On the basis of this test the financial strength of the insurers is identical. From this point on, the other tests for strength and acceptability of the insurer are applied. It makes no difference whether the insurer is mutual or stock with respect to the application of the tests. The only difference is to be found in the point of departure where policyholders' surplus is determined from a financial statement that provides no entry for a capital stock account.[13]

RECAPITULATION

Consideration has been given to the various concepts essential to the understanding of the financial statement of an insurer. It may now prove profitable to summarize their application.

First. Consideration may be given to the size of the insurer as represented by the total assets figure on the statement. Size is important as a basis for determining whether the insurer is sufficiently diversifying its risks both as to lines and to location. Size is also a factor in considering the impact of catastrophe or conflagration losses. Size will have a bearing upon the quality of the services an insurer can supply. Size of itself is not the determining factor in selection.

Second. Apply the test ratio of policyholders' surplus to unearned premium; one to one in fire insurance and in some other forms of property and liability insurance and in multiple line insurance a two to one ratio of premium to policyholders' surplus.

Third. Examine the list of investments and determine to what extent the policyholders' surplus is covered by readily marketable securities. If the insurer carries securities subject to wide market fluctuation or of a nonliquid category such as real estate, determine to what extent all liabilities are covered by liquid assets.

Fourth. Study the loss ratio over a period of five years. If it has been continuously unfavorable, compare it with published aggregates to determine whether the experience represents an industry trend or an unfavorable insurer position.

Fifth. Notice whether the insurer concentrates on a single or a few lines or writes a sufficiently diversified number of lines to expect that favorable experience in one group may cancel out losses in another.

Sixth. Notice the geographic areas in which the insurer operates with a view to determining the impact of catastrophes.

Seventh. Investigate the adequacy of loss reserves by checking over the actual payments of the past few years against reserves maintained.

[13] Mention may be made here of the Factory Mutual Group and the system of premium deposits under which it operates. These deposits are far in excess of the estimated net premium required for a risk, and any excess over loss requirements and business expenses is returned as a dividend. Deposits may equal ten times the annual premium requirement, and dividend returns over a period of years have been 90 percent or higher. Because of this unique method of doing business, the unearned premium reserve in Factory Mutual statements is unusually large. It does not measure the exposure to loss, as in the case of other insurers, until adjusted by giving consideration to the excess of the deposit premium over actual premium requirements.

Eighth. Check the number of claims with suits pending. A large number of suits suggests generous loss reserves.

Ninth. Check insurer dividend practices. Particularly determine whether any part of underwriting profits is used for dividends. Is a portion of earnings set aside each year for surplus?

All of these tests serve to throw light on the position of the insurer under consideration. They do not all apply with equal force to all insurers. Some insurers with large outstanding claims will have a very substantial loss reserve. This must be maintained liquid at all times. The fire insurer with all claims paid will need only to keep policyholders' surplus or unearned premium reserve, whichever is the larger, covered by immediately marketable securities. A favorable loss ratio may justify something less than the one to one ratio of surplus to reserve. All of the tests are significant, and while something less than ideal with respect to one test may not be an adequate ground for rejecting an insurer, a finding of serious impairment with respect to any one will prompt caution, and in the case of doubt, rejection.

FOR DISCUSSION

1. The question sometimes presents itself as to what constitutes the stockholders' equity in an insurer. Notably, this is the case when attempts are made to determine the amount of earnings that represent a fair return on invested capital. How would you arrive at the concept of equity capital?
2. It has sometimes been stated that the unearned premium reserve added to the policyholders' surplus will give a measure of the strength of an insurer. There is a fallacy in the reasoning behind this statement. Can you detect it?
3. If the financial standing of an insurer is under scrutiny, there are some simple tests that may be readily applied to its reinsurance program. Entirely aside from the stability of the reinsuring insurers, there is the question of the practices of the ceding insurer. Can you think of any devices by which a weak insurer could temporarily use reinsurance, apparently to bolster its financial position?
4. In appraising the financial position of an insurer, it is necessary to know that the reinsurance facilities of which the insurer makes use are in all respects sound. If the state supervisory authority allows reinsurance, is this not satisfactory evidence of the soundness of reinsurance? Discuss.
5. In the case of an unearned premium reserve computed on a monthly basis, what would be the earned premium on a contract written on an annual basis on July 1? A contract written 30 days later, on July 31, and for the same term, would have a month less to run from inception date. Compare the unearned premium reserve requirements.
6. The amount of surplus places a definite limitation on the amount of business that an insurer may accept. Explain.

7. Insurance premiums as collected are mingled with the other assets of the insurer. It has been asserted that the insurer does not actually own these premiums because they are subject to the risks taken until the contracts expire by limitations. Is this correct?
8. This statement is frequently made: "The unearned premium reserve in a solvent insurer is not available for the payment of losses." True or false? Explain.
9. If the loss experience for a given insurer is markedly unfavorable for a year or two, in the light of the trend in the industry, as indicated by the published aggregates, this may give occasion for inquiry but it is not necessarily indicative of unsound operations. Explain.
10. Can you justify the statement that rather than being a measure of strength the unearned premium reserve is a measure of potential loss?
11. One of the tests to determine whether an insurer is showing favorable underwriting results is to compare its operations with aggregates of other insurers writing similar lines. Where would you expect to secure dependable information to use in making such a comparison?
12. Why is it necessary or desirable to set up a reserve for matured but unpaid obligations? Why would it not be preferable to liquidate the obligations as they mature?
13. Are investment earnings a significant factor in current rate-making procedures? What arguments can you offer in defense of your position?
14. It has been stated that if average earnings of insurers from investments were included in the rate structure, conservative companies would be penalized. Why?
15. In an ordinary merchandising enterprise, profits are determined by taking aggregate income for a given period and charging expenses of operations. Profit results when the income from sales is in excess of the cost of merchandise plus the cost of doing business. Why is this type of accounting acceptable for a merchandising firm but not for an insurer?
16. In the conclusion of a Report to the Subcommittee of the National Association of Insurance Commissioners appointed to study the question of reinsurance, it is stated: "Reinsurance is an indispensable tool in the continued operation of the insurance business, and is usually transacted in an atmosphere of genuine good faith and mutual trust. It is unfortunate that it has been misused by a few companies." (*Proceedings of the National Association of Insurance Commissioners,* 1950, p. 473.) How can an insurer of doubtful financial worth deliberately misuse reinsurance to give a false sense of security?
17. Not infrequently, statements are published showing the combined assets of a group of insurers. Such presentations are interesting and frequently informative. Any tabulation of aggregate capital and surplus of insurers where one is the subsidiary of another represents a certain amount of duplication. Why is this so? Why is it significant to

give attention to the financial position of the insurer in the group that is to issue the contract rather than to rely on a group consolidated statement?

18. It is stated in the text that the aggregate of expense items such as commissions, taxes, office rent, and the like represents the premium charge as the word was originally understood. Explain.
19. In the text there is the suggestion that if an aggregate of the full amount of loss reserves plus 65 percent of the unearned premium reserve is retained liquid this should provide adequate security for a multiple line insurer. Explain the reasoning and particularly explain the logic of the 65 percent figure.

CHAPTER • 33

Adjustment of Losses

Insurance contracts written by multiple line and other property and liability insurers are typically indemnity contracts intended (within the limits of the contract) to make the insured whole in regard to financial loss suffered as the result of the happening of an insured event. In those cases where the contract is not one of indemnity there is nevertheless an agreement to pay a specified sum designed to replace the value of a lost asset or, as in the case of life insurance, to pay a cash amount regardless of value. All of these contracts contain conditions, limitations and exclusions, and the settlement of loss or damage is subject to the limitations of the agreement entered into by the insurer and the insured. The effectiveness of insurance as a way of meeting risk is often measured, particularly by the insured, in terms of the extent to which the contract with the insurer results in a satisfactory settlement in terms of the dollar-value of the lost property. Perhaps no aspect of insurance is as much misunderstood or gives rise to more problems in public relations than that of adjustment of losses. In this chapter the principles and problems of adjustment will be considered, as well as some of the procedural details.

CLAIMS VERSUS LOSSES

There is a distinction between a claim and the fact of loss. A claim has been defined as "a demand by an individual or corporation to recover under a policy of insurance for loss which may come within that policy or may be a demand by an individual against an insured for damages covered by a policy held by him. . . ."[1] Not all claims are valid in that the loss may not be one contemplated by the contract or in some instances the claim may be fraudulent. A loss may be defined as "The basis for a claim for indemnity or damages under the

[1] L. E. Davids, *Dictionary of Insurance* (Paterson, N.J.: Littlefield, Adams & Co., 1959), p. 44.

terms of an insurance policy. . . ."[2] Thus, loss implies a reduction in value of property which may be brought about by destruction from physical elements such as fire, windstorm, and similar forces or loss through legally imposed damages. A further implication is that losses may be sustained by the insured or by third parties, as in the case of liability losses. Losses to property may be placed in three categories: losses to real property; losses to personal property; and losses involving rights of possession or use.

TYPES OF ADJUSTER

The word "adjuster" is in certain ways a misnomer in that it does not describe the work involved in responding to and working out a settlement of claims. It has been suggested that "claimsman" would be more appropriate and would avoid some misunderstanding on the part of the public about the work of an adjuster. Other terms that are sometimes used are "investigator," "claim auditor," or "claim agent."[3] In spite of the merit of the suggestion that a new word be used, the word "adjuster" will be used in this chapter, since it is the one commonly employed in insurance to describe the work of a person who settles claims, and "adjustment" will refer to the process involved in reaching a decision about a claim including its final disposition.

There are three types of adjuster—staff, public, and independent.

Staff Adjusters. A staff adjuster is a full-time employee of the insurer and is responsible for processing claims for his employer. He may, and sometimes does, have a legal background. He is also responsible for observing trends in claim amounts and for observing the economic, political, and sociological forces that affect the settlement of claims. In order to settle claims as efficiently as possible, insurers frequently have adjusters working out of field offices. Thus one large insurer has over 700 claim service offices in the principal cities of the United States. Some 3,200 full-time salaried claims representatives and supervisors work out of these offices.

Public Adjuster. A public adjuster is a person with professional knowledge about claim processing and settlement, who may be retained by the insured to represent him in the settlement of loss. Thus, the public adjuster represents the insured and his interests and is not associated with insurers.

Independent Adjuster. An independent adjuster is a person who is available to help various insurers with problems associated with the adjustment of claims. He is not an employee of any particular

---

[2] *Ibid.*, p. 130.

[3] James H. Donaldson, *Casualty Claims Practice* (Homewood, Ill.: Richard D. Irwin, Inc., 1964), p. 2.

insurer and works as an independent contractor. He is paid on a fee basis. An independent adjuster may be a sole proprietor or an employee of a firm that specializes in claims work. Of particular interest in this regard are the insurer-owned adjustment bureaus who handle claims for member-insurers and for other insurers on approval of the board of directors.[4]

The Role of the Agent and Other Producers. Although agents are not formally regarded as adjusters and in no sense give full time to this aspect of insurance work, they nevertheless play an important role in claims settlement. In some instances they may be given the responsibility for the entire adjustment of relatively small claims and may be the only contact the insured has with the insurer. Even in those instances where the agent does not have the responsibility for settling the loss, he is often relied upon by the insured as the person who will see that the insured's interests are properly represented and assist the insured in filling out forms and helping him comply with other contractual requirements.

Legally the agent is the representative of the insurer, but in practice his role is a dual one and he cannot avoid considering the interests of his clients. It has been argued that the "possibility of loss is the only reason for the sale of insurance,"[5] and at the time the contract is entered into the point of view should be that of the loss. The agent (or other producer) can do much to prepare the way for a satisfactory adjustment in the event of loss, if he understands the contract that is being sold and explains it carefully to the prospective insured. Exclusions, limitations, and other aspects of the contract that may be misunderstood should be pointed out at the time the contract is entered into. Additionally, the producer should be aware of changes in property values, increases in hazard, and similar matters that occur during the term of the insurance and that may affect settlement in the event of loss, and bring these to the attention of the insured.

FUNCTIONS AND RESPONSIBILITIES OF THE ADJUSTER

The responsibility falling on the adjuster is a heavy one, since he must undertake to effect a settlement that will be agreeable to both the insured and the insurer. He must dispose of claims promptly and fairly within the provisions of the contract, but not settle too liberally and thus be unfair to other insureds and unnecessarily raise loss costs. At the same time he cannot be niggardly, causing the insured to feel that he has been badly treated, and thus create the impression of sharp

[4] See page 729.

[5] Prentice B. Reed, William M. Mortimer, B. L. Jones, Ray G. Bachman, *Loss Adjusting* (New York: Underwriter Printing & Publishing Co., 1947), p. xii.

practices on the part of the insurer. Adjusters are responsible for settling property and liability losses amounting to nearly $9 billion each year. Legally, the adjuster is a fiduciary agent and he must be loyal to the interests of the insurer, may not represent adverse interests, and may not profit from his role as a fiduciary except for the agreed upon fee for his work.[6]

Work of the Adjuster. The work of the adjuster has been described by various authors. Donaldson, for example, has classified the adjuster's work by placing it in three categories: investigation and negotiation, evaluation, and termination.[7] The task of investigation and negotiation begins with a presentation of a claim to the insurer by the insured. The adjuster will normally not have first-hand information about the fire, automobile accident, loss of cargo at sea, or whatever event is the subject matter of the claim. It will be necessary for him to establish the validity of the claim by contacting the insured, talking with witnesses, examining the property, reviewing the contract, and taking whatever other steps are necessary to acquire full information about the facts and circumstances surrounding the claim. Once the merit of the claim has been established, the adjuster will need to arrive at some decision about the value of the lost or damaged property based on accepted principles of valuation. The final or terminating phase of the adjustment process involves the acceptance or rejection of the insured's claim by the adjuster and his recommendations for further action. Normally, when a claim is rejected no further action is taken unless the insured reopens the case.

Additional light on the procedural aspects of adjustment may be obtained by considering the work of the adjuster in terms of the typical provisions of property and liability insurance contracts as they relate to procedures to be followed in the event of loss.

Checking the Contract. Once notice of loss has been received, the adjuster must check for coverage, which means that he must determine whether the contract is in force and whether the property that was destroyed, lost, or damaged was covered by the contract. After coverage has been established, the adjuster must then proceed to adjust the loss in accordance with the terms of the contract.[8]

Status of Contract. The existence of a contract or binder covering the loss must be determined and the effective dates reviewed. Unless such a contract exists and unless the loss has occurred during the term of the contract, there is no basis for further consideration of a claim.

[6] Donaldson, *op. cit.*, p. 3.

[7] *Ibid.*, pp. 4–5. Although this classification was developed for liability insurance, essentially the same procedure is followed in property insurance.

[8] The material in the next two paragraphs is based on the steps in adjustment outlined by Prentice B. Reed, *Adjustment of Property Losses* (New York: McGraw-Hill Book Co., Inc., 1953).

The adjuster must also be certain that a cancellation has not occurred bringing the agreement between the insured and the insurer to an end.

Property Covered. Although a contract may be in force, it does not automatically follow that the property that is the subject of the claim is covered. The adjuster must determine whether the property that has been lost, damaged, or destroyed is the property described in the contract or some part thereof. In some contracts, certain types of property are specifically excluded and a claim involving such property should be rejected. Closely related to the indentification of property is the determination of the interest of the insured in it. Since, typically, settlement under property contracts must not exceed the insurable interest of the insured, and since this interest must be demonstrated at time of loss, it is essential that the adjuster determine the facts about insurable interest. Likewise, interests of other parties such as mortgagees must be considered.

Possible Voidance of Contract and Other Limiting Conditions. There are a number of legal rules and contractual provisions that serve to limit insurance coverage quite apart from questions of whether specific property is covered. Misrepresentation of material facts or circumstances and concealment of such facts will void the contract as will any act of fraud. Increases in hazard not communicated to the insurer will limit its liability as will changes in occupancy. Questions of waiver and estoppel will also have an effect on the nature of the adjustment and the subsequent liability of the insurer.

Perils Insured Against. Since no insurance contract covers all possible perils, a prime consideration for the adjuster is whether the cause of loss was a peril insured against under the terms of the contract. If the agreement is on a named perils basis, the cause of loss must be one of the perils listed. If the agreement is an all risks type, then the cause of loss must not be from a specifically excluded peril, if the insurer is to be expected to respond. The insuring agreement of the contract should be checked, along with the exclusions, to determine the nature of the coverage from the standpoint of the perils covered.

Other Contractual Matters that are Related to Loss Settlement. It is common for property and liability contracts to contain a number of provisions that are related to loss settlement and may play a fairly large role in matters of loss adjustment. Examples are: limits of liability clauses in liability contracts, apportionment clause, notice of accident or loss, notice of suit, notice of action against the insurer, assistance and cooperation of the insured, assignment, and subrogation. All of these concepts have been discussed in earlier chapters of the text[9] and it is sufficient here to point out their relationship to the adjust-

[9] See, for example, Chapters 5 and 17.

ment process. Other clauses that should be looked for are coinsurance and related provisions, which may have a significant effect on the final settlement.

Problems of Value. Since property and liability insurance contracts are, generally speaking, contracts of indemnity, questions surrounding the value of what was lost or destroyed are inherent in any settlement. It is possible that no concept in insurance gives rise to more difficulty than the concept of insurable value. The insured is likely to believe that he should receive the amount it would take to replace the damaged property with new materials even though the typical property insurance contract agrees to only the cash value at the time of loss, which is generally interpreted to mean replacement cost less depreciation. If the insured does not expect replacement value, he may assume that the value of the property is its original cost. Still another concept of value is that of market price, and the insured may believe that this price should form the basis of a proper settlement. Thus, four concepts of value often emerge during the adjustment process: original cost, market, replacement new, and actual cash value. Of these concepts only replacement new and actual cash value are contemplated in insurance contracts.

Although replacement cost insurance is available, an example being the replacement cost provisions of the homeowner's contract, historically property insurance contracts have been, and still are, written on an actual cash value basis. Insurance written on this basis always involves a deduction for depreciation.[10] Since difficulties may arise in the course of settlement, the typical property insurance contract contains provisions for appraisal and for the option to rebuild or replace with material of like kind and quality. These provisions have been discussed in Chapter 6.

Salvage. Salvage is an aspect of the adjustment process that plays a large role in many settlements. It may be defined as the procedure wherein lost or damaged property is recovered for the purpose of reducing the amount of loss, although it should be pointed out that the word "salvage" is used variously in the insurance business. It can refer to property that was not destroyed by a given peril, to damaged property that will be offered for sale, or to the money received as a result of the sale of damaged property. In marine insurance salvage has the connotation of the cost of saving endangered property, while in suretyship it refers to money obtained from a principal as an offset to a settlement that a surety may have made to an obligee.[11]

The relationship of salvage to loss adjustment may vary. In some

---

[10] See Emmett J. Vaughan, "What is Insurable Value," *American Agency Bulletin*, Vol. LXIII (September, 1965), pp. 13–15.

[11] Davids, *op. cit.*, p. 185.

cases, the insured may be allowed to keep the damaged property and the insurer will pay the sound value; in other instances, the insurer may take the damaged property. Another possibility is for the insurer and the insured to agree to a sale of the damaged property with an understanding that the proceeds would be used to help pay the claim. In situations where salvage is a substantial factor in loss settlement, the adjuster may seek the help of salvors, persons or firms who are skilled in dealing with property that has been lost or damaged by one or more perils. A salvor may enter the adjustment process at various stages, depending on the judgment of the adjuster and, in some cases is not consulted until an agreement on sound value has been reached by the insured and the insurer.[12]

Salvors may help adjusters in a variety of ways. They may act as advisers on the actual cash value of the damaged property, they may help in preserving property, or they may be asked to sell salvage. When property is turned over to a salvor for protection or sale, formal agreements may be entered into that state the conditions surrounding the transfer. The importance of this activity is illustrated by the fact that stock property and liability insurers in certain instances own salvage companies. Two of these salvage firms are the Underwriters Salvage of New York and Underwriters Salvage of Chicago.

Education of the Adjuster.[13] Although some states have licensing requirements for adjusters, there is no specific type of educational background that is universally required. Insurers often seek prospective adjusters by recruiting on college campuses, and many adjusters are college graduates. On-the-job supervision and study programs are used as ways of providing specific knowledge skills, along with workshops, college insurance classes, and correspondence courses.

If the work of the adjuster is considered in terms of the variety of losses that may be incurred in the whole property-liability field (marine, fire and related perils, inland marine, casualty, and other lines), the amount and variety of knowledge that an adjuster must have are very large. Although adjusters are not necessarily lawyers (in some insurance firms, 20 to 30 percent of the adjusters may be), the need for some legal knowledge is apparent in dealing with contracts in all forms of insurance, in obtaining facts in liability cases,

---

[12] Reed, *op. cit.,* p. 397.

[13] In the early 1960's the Insurance Institute of America established a series of six examinations dealing with property and liability insurance loss and claims adjusting. Successful completion of these examinations leads to a diploma in insurance loss and claim adjusting. The syllabi for these examinations cover such topics as: procedural aspects of adjusting property and liability losses, building loss estimated, claims handling procedures, the human factor in insurance claim adjusting, personal property losses, books and records, salvage, casualty claims practice, and medical aspects of loss adjustment.

and in seeking evidence of damage, to name a few areas. More specifically, such branches of the law as the law of torts, law of contracts, law of agency, law of products, law of automobiles, law of admiralty, and the law of evidence may be related to a particular adjustment. Additionally, the adjuster may need some knowledge of medicine in dealing with workmen's compensation and other aspects of insurance that have medical implications. Knowledge of building construction and materials used by builders is helpful in settling property losses, as well as knowledge of merchandise and other types of inventory. Even though the adjuster would normally consult specialists in fields in which he is no expert, it is nevertheless valuable for him to have enough knowledge in a variety of fields in order to utilize the advice of specialists effectively.

FURTHER CONSIDERATION OF THE ADJUSTMENT PROCESS

The principles and procedures for the adjustment of losses are fairly general in their application and apply in broad terms regardless of the branch involved in a particular loss settlement. Just as underwriting has become increasingly multiple line, so has adjusting become general rather than specialized and the old boundaries between lines of insurance are beginning to vanish. Current educational programs now emphasize multiple line adjusting and the necessity for the adjuster to know the problems associated with adjusting losses caused by a variety of perils. Since the types of loss vary among the various fields of insurance, some of the details of loss settlement will differ (although the theory is the same), depending on whether the loss involves destruction by fire, windstorm, a liability suit, or some other types of property-liability claim.

Requirements of the Insured in the Event Loss Occurs. The standard fire insurance contract and other property and liability contracts contain provisions that place certain responsibilities on the insured in the event loss occurs. Some of these provisions have already been reviewed in connection with the analysis of insurance contracts. Some others of these provisions will now be reviewed.

Lines 90 through 122 of the standard fire insurance contract[14] contain a complete statement of the responsibility of the insured in the event of a loss from one of the perils insured against. The first requirement is for the insured to give immediate written notice to the insurer. (This requirement is general and applied to all types of insurance.) He must then (2) protect the property from further damage; (3) provide an inventory of destroyed, damaged, and un-

---

[14] See page 141 and the discussion on page 142.

damaged property, including detail on costs, actual cash value, and amount of loss claimed; and (4) submit a proof of loss within 60 days (unless the insurer extends the time through a written memorandum). Figure 31–1 shows a form to be used in submitting a proof of loss. This form provides space for recording the types of information required by the standard contract in lines 101 through 110. (The

Form recommended by the National Board of Fire Underwriters June, 1950

SWORN STATEMENT IN PROOF OF LOSS

$__________ AMOUNT OF POLICY AT TIME OF LOSS

__________ POLICY NUMBER

__________ DATE ISSUED

__________ AGENCY AT

__________ DATE EXPIRES

__________ AGENT

To the__________
of__________
At time of loss, by the above indicated policy of insurance you insured__________

against loss by__________to the property described under Schedule "A," according to the terms and conditions of the said policy and all forms, endorsements, transfers and assignments attached thereto.

1. Time and Origin: A__________loss occurred about the hour of____o'clock____M.,
STATE KIND
on the____day of__________19____. The cause and origin of the said loss were:__________

2. Occupancy: The building described, or containing the property described, was occupied at the time of the loss as follows, and for no other purpose whatever:__________

3. Title and Interest: At the time of the loss the interest of your insured in the property described therein was__________ No other person or persons had any interest therein or incumbrance thereon, except:__________

4. Changes: Since the said policy was issued there has been no assignment thereof, or change of interest, use, occupancy, possession, location or exposure of the property described, except:__________

5. Total Insurance: The total amount of insurance upon the property described by this policy was, at the time of the loss, $__________, as more particularly specified in the apportionment attached under Schedule "C," besides which there was no policy or other contract of insurance, written or oral, valid or invalid.

6. The Actual Cash Value of said property at the time of the loss was . . . . $__________

7. The Whole Loss and Damage was . . . . $__________

8. The Amount Claimed under the above numbered policy is . . . . $__________

The said loss did not originate by any act, design or procurement on the part of your insured, or this affiant; nothing has been done by or with the privity or consent of your insured or this affiant, to violate the conditions of the policy, or render it void; no articles are mentioned herein or in annexed schedules but such as were destroyed or damaged at the time of said loss; no property saved has in any manner been concealed, and no attempt to deceive the said company, as to the extent of said loss, has in any manner been made. Any other information that may be required will be furnished and considered a part of this proof.

The furnishing of this blank or the preparation of proofs by a representative of the above insurance company is not a waiver of any of its rights.

State of__________ __________

County of__________ __________Insured

Subscribed and sworn to before me this______day of__________19____

__________Notary Public

UNIFORM STANDARD Form No. 3904-A (OVER)
PRINTED IN U.S.A.

FIG. 31–1.

reverse side of the form, which contains space for providing the kind of information required in Schedules A, B, and C, is not reproduced here.) The insured must give data on time and origin of the loss, occupancy, title and interest, changes, actual cash value, other insurance, amount of loss and damage, and amount claimed. In addition the insured may be called upon to "furnish a copy of all the descriptions and schedules in all policies and, if required, verified plans and specifications of any building, fixtures or machinery destroyed or damaged." The insured also agrees to exhibit remains of property, submit to examination under oath, and "produce for examination all books of account, bills, invoices and other vouchers, or certified copies thereof if originals be lost, at such reasonable time and place as may be designated by this Company or its representative, and shall permit extracts and copies thereof to be made." After proof of loss has been submitted, the insurer agrees on its part to pay the amount of the loss for which it is liable 60 days after it receives the statement of proof and ascertainment of the amount of loss is made either by agreement between insurer and insured or by an appraisal procedure as outlined in the contract.

The requirements placed on the insured in inland marine contracts in the event of loss are similar to those found in the fire insurance contract, although in some ways are not as detailed. A typical inland marine contract provides that the insured must give written notice of loss as soon as practicable to either the insurer or its agent and also file a proof of loss within ninety days. Examination under oath may be required of the insured and he may be called upon, if within his power, to cause his employees, members of his household, and others to submit to similar examination. The insured may also be called upon to "produce for examination all writings, books of account, bills, invoices, and other vouchers."

Marine insurance contracts are less specific about the duties of the insured in the event of loss, although the sue and labor clause places responsibility on the insured to make every effort to preserve the venture in the event loss occurs. The Open Cargo contract states that "It is necessary for the Assured to give prompt notice to these Assurers when they become aware of an event for which they are 'held covered' under this policy and the right to such cover is dependent on compliance with this obligation." There is an additional statement that says "In case of loss, such loss to be paid not later than thirty days after proof of loss and proof of interest in the property hereby insured (the amount of the premium, if unpaid, being first deducted). Proofs of loss to be authenticated by the agents of the Assurers, if there be one at the place such proofs are taken." There are other clauses in the open cargo contract that relate to the adjustment process (e.g., constructive total loss clause, partial loss, breakage and leakage, and general average clause), but they do not place specific duties on the insured.

There are a number of clauses in a typical liability insurance contract that relate specifically to the insured and his responsibilities in the event of loss. Under the heading "Notice of Accident" is the statement that: "When an accident occurs written notice shall be given by or on behalf of the insured to the company or any of its authorized agent as soon as practicable. Such notice shall contain particulars sufficient to identify the insured and also reasonably obtainable information respecting the time, place, and circumstances of the accident, the names and addresses of the injured and of available witnesses." Under "Notice of Claim or Suit—Coverages A, B, and D," there is the statement, "If claim is made or suit is brought against the insured, the insured shall immediately forward to the company every demand, notice, summons or other process received by him or his representative." Other clauses that refer to duties of the insured, are assistance and cooperation of the insured—Coverages A, B, and D; medical reports; proof and payment of claim; action against company (for the specific coverages to which this clause would be applicable).

Although the specific requirements placed on the insured when loss occurs vary somewhat from contract to contract depending on the perils involved, all property and liability contracts have provisions that call for the insured to assist in the adjustment process through giving immediate notice, filing proof of loss, and in other ways furthering the process of settlement.

Adjustment Procedures for Specific Lines of Insurance. The procedures followed by adjusters in settling losses for fire, marine, liability, and other lines of insurance are complicated and detailed and are the subject matter of separate treatises. A systematic discussion of the details in a general survey of adjustment is impractical, although some of the problems can be indicated.[15]

In situations where losses occur to fixed property (fire and related losses) the principal problem is usually to determine the value of the loss. This leads to the need for estimating building losses which requires a detailed inspection of the damaged dwelling, taking measurements, taking photographs, and making sketches. It is also necessary to make a detailed list of damaged items. The procedures needed for a successful determination of the amount of loss and its value are

[15] For comprehensive discussions of particular lines of insurance see Reed, *op. cit.;* Corydon I. Johns, *An Introduction to Liability Claims Adjusting* (Cincinnati: National Underwriter Co., 1965); J. H. Donaldson, *op. cit.;* Harold S. Daynard, *Transportation Insurance Claims* (New York: Roberts Publishing Corp., 1961); Neil Carter, *Guide to Workmen's Compensation Claims* (New York: Roberts Publishing Corp., 1965); and L. J. Buglass, *Marine Insurance Claims American Law and Practice* (Cambridge, Md.: Cornell Maritime Press).

acquired through experience and a detailed study of building construction and repair. Damage to buildings often involves damage to contents and the need for descriptions of missing items, cost data, possibility of repair, and other items. Also involved is protection against further damage and a knowledge of ways of effectively carrying out the needed protection.

Typically fire and allied lines contracts cover property in a fixed location while the spirit of inland marine contracts is that they provide coverage for property while it is in transit.[16] Often the property covered is not described in the contract, and a problem for the adjuster is to determine whether the property for which claim is made really existed. Evidence of the existence of property may take the form of sales receipts, bills of sale, or similar records. In the personal property floater, for example, unscheduled personal property is listed in categories such as silverware and pewter, clothing, books, and similar designations. Certain property, such as jewelry, watches, and furs may be scheduled and described in the contract and a value agreed upon. Some contracts cover the property of others while in the care of the insured, and this property is an unknown factor at the time the contract is entered into.

Limitations on the amount of coverage may exist for certain types of property, as illustrated by the "limitations" section of the personal property floater. In that section "unscheduled personal property ordinarily situated throughout the year at residences other than the principal residence of the insured" is covered to an amount not to exceed 10 percent of the amount of insurance listed on the first page of the contract as being the coverage for unscheduled personal. In a typical personal property floater the insurer is not liable for more than $250 for any one loss of unscheduled jewelry, watches, or furs. Dollar limitations are also placed on money, numismatic property, notes, securities, philatelic property, accounts, bills, and similar property. Another factor that may determine whether property is covered and place limitations on recovery is the terms of sale. Thus, merchandise sold f.o.b. is the responsibility of the consignee once it is loaded on a transport conveyance.

Because of the nature of the property covered, and because mysterious disappearance may be the basis for a claim in some contracts, it is essential that the adjuster investigate claims very promptly. Unless action is prompt, the facts surrounding the loss may be difficult to establish and the insurer may not have a very satisfactory basis for claim settlement.

---

[16] This statement is not intended to overlook the fact that in homeowner's contracts both fixed property and personal property in transit is covered and that the dwelling and contents form attached to fire contracts provides some in-transit coverage.

All risk contracts tend to be typical in inland marine insurance and the adjuster has not so much the task of checking whether loss was covered by a specific peril that has been insured against, but whether loss was caused by an excluded peril. Since all risk coverage is broader, typically, than that found in named peril contracts, more types of loss would be covered and adjustment may be more complicated. The insuring conditions of a contract such as the jewelers' block are fairly involved and require detailed checking by the adjuster.

Although the general approach to adjusting liability insurance losses is not unlike that used in property insurance, the type of skills needed are for the most part different, since losses mainly take the form of third-party claims for damages due to an alleged legal responsibility on the part of the insured. The adjuster of the liability claim should have a substantial knowledge of the law of torts and of the statutory modifications of this law, as well of the law of contracts. Additionally he should know the law of bailments, law of products, and the law surrounding automobiles. Since he may be called upon to settle claims involving medical malpractice familiarity with the physician's duty to his patient, standards of care, operating room responsibility, and other aspects of medical practice is essential. Since a legal trial may be necessary in settling a case, the basic facts about the law of evidence are also needed.

As in other types of adjustment a thorough investigation of the facts surrounding the accident is a first step. If an automobile accident is the subject for investigation, the adjuster will need to get such critical evidence as a statement from the adverse driver, statement from the claimant, and photograph of the scene of the accident. Evidence should also be obtained from disinterested witnesses and various official reports such as police reports, fire department reports, and traffic court proceedings may be needed. In the case of injuries to persons medical reports should be reviewed. Claims evaluation and settlement also require detailed knowledge about the nature of damages, special and general damages, duty of the claimant to establish damages, and the various measures of damages.

Workmen's compensation insurance, although closely related to liability insurance in that personal injuries are involved, poses a number of special problems. The workmen's compensation laws of the various states are legal remedies and impose liability for work injuries regardless of fault. Workmen's compensation insurance contracts undertake to pay compensation in accordance with statutory provisions. A basic test that is applied is whether the injury arose out of and in the course of employment. Investigations are needed to determine the facts, and hearings are often needed when differences arise as to the interpretation of the facts. Knowledge of the special claims and medical problems that arise is needed if adequate settlements are to be arrived at.

Marine insurance may involve property as well as liability losses and satisfactory adjustments involve a knowledge of marine law and of many of the specific terms that apply to marine undertakings. General average situations form a special case and these losses are settled in accordance with maritime law, even though insurers may ultimately pay the losses. General average adjusters are specialists and their training is accomplished differently from the training of insurance adjusters generally. Marine insurance adjusters operate in a complex field where investigations of losses may be hampered by lack of witnesses, and where knowledge of practices and customs may be acquired only through long experience.

Apportionment. Special problems in loss settlement may arise when more than one insurance contract covers a particular loss. A typical provision is property and liability insurance contracts about apportionment is that the insurer will "not be liable for a greater proportion of any loss than the amount hereby insured shall bear to the whole insurance covering the property against the peril involved, whether collectible or not."[17] This rule is not difficult to apply if all the contracts covering the same property read exactly the same way. If the contracts are not concurrent, that is, do not read alike, then problems often arise that require special procedures. Some of these procedures will be illustrated with examples.

Historically there were four rules that found application in cases of nonconcurrent apportionments: the Page rule, the Cromie rule, the Kinne rule, and the limit of liability rule. The first three rules are no longer used. The limit of liability rule is now the only one that is generally employed in property insurance apportionment. If there were no coinsurance clause, reduced rate contribution clause, or reduced rate average clause in the contract, the Page Rule was used in situations where specific insurance covered certain property that was also covered by blanket insurance that, in turn, covered other property as well and the loss was to the property covered by specific insurance; the Cromie rule was applicable to situations similar to the preceding one except that the loss involved not only specific insurance, but also other property included under blanket insurance. The Kinne rule was used for nonconcurrences not covered by the Page or Cromie rules. Because of their historical importance the first three rules will be briefly discussed. The limit of liability rule will be more fully considered.

The Page rule stated that "the full amount of the blanket insurance

---

[17] Some contracts read that the proportion is taken of all valid and collectible insurance.

contributed with the full amount of the specific insurance to pay the loss."[18]

Example: There is blanket insurance covering stock and machinery in the amount of $2,000 and specific insurance covering stock in the amount of $1,000. A loss of $750 occurs to the stock only. How much of the loss does each type of insurance pay?

Solution:

Blanket insurance	$2,000	
Specific insurance	1,000	
Total Insurance	$3,000	
Blanket insurance pays ⅔ × $750		$500
Specific insurance pays ⅓ × $750		$250
Insured receives		$750

The Cromie rule stated that "The blanket insurance first pays the loss on property which it alone covers, and thereafter its remainder contributes with the specific insurance on the property covered by both."[19]

The Kinne rule was the most complicated of the various rules of apportionment and is best explained by outlining the steps that were to be taken in solving a problem through the use of this rule.

Principle: The correct method of applying the principle has been formulated in the following:

First: Ascertain the non-concurrence of the various policies and classify the various items covered into as many groups as the non-concurrence demands, whether of property, location of ownership.

Second: Ascertain the loss on such groups of items separately.

Third: If but a single group is found with a loss upon it, the amounts of all policies covering the group contribute pro rata.

Fourth: If more than one group has sustained a loss, and such loss on one or more groups be equal to or greater than the total of blanket and specific insurance thereon, then let the whole amounts of such insurance apply to the payment of loss on such groups.

Fifth—Apportionment: If more than one group has sustained a loss, and such loss be less than the totals of unexhausted blanket and specific insurance thereon, then apportion the amount of each policy covering blanket on such groups, to cover specifically on such groups in the same proportion that the sum of the losses on such groups bears to the loss on each individual group. (Note: When a group is covered by one or more blanket policies, it would be well to see at once if an apportionment as above on that group would equal the loss, as, in case it will not, it will show without further calculation that the whole amount of loss on such

[18] See *Catastrophe Loss Adjustment Procedure* (New York: National Board of Fire Underwriters, 1952), p. 77. The examples of the Page and limit of liability rules are from this publication, as is the statement of the Kinne rule.

[19] *Ibid.* An example of this rule may be found in this reference.

group must be met by such policies pro rata, and the remainder only apportioned. In such cases, carrying out Step 6 simply accomplishes by a longer process what here is indicated.

Sixth—Reapportionment: If the loss on any group or groups is then found to be greater than the sum of the now specific insurance as apportioned, add sufficient to such specific insurances to make up the loss on the group taking the amount of the deficiency from the now specific insurance of the heretofore blanket amounts previously covering the new deficient groups, which cover on groups having an excess of insurance, in the proportion that their sum bear to the individual amounts. (Note: Very rarely are new deficiencies created by the reapportionment, but if so, simply repeat Step 6.)

Seventh: Cause the amounts of all the now specific insurances to severally contribute pro rata to pay the partial losses, and it will be found that the whole scheme has resulted in the claimant being fully indemnified in accordance with the various contracts and on a basis which preserves the equities between the companies throughout."[20]

A numerical example of the Kinne rule will not be worked out here, although illustrations may be found in various places.[21]

The limit of liability rule may be stated as follows:

The sound value of and loss on property covered by each class or kind of insurance having been determined, first find the limit of liability under each class or kind of insurance, whether a single policy or group covering concurrently. The limit of liability will be (*a*) the amount of insurance or (*b*) the amount of loss, or (*c*) the coinsurance, reduced rate contribution, or average clause limit.[22] Whichever is smallest is the limit as it is the greatest amount for which insurance is liable. Next add the limits as above determined. If the total exceeds the whole loss, each group will then pay that proportion of the whole loss which its limit bears to the sum of all limits. If the sum of the limits of liability is less than the whole loss, it is evident that payment by each company must be on the basis of its maximum individual limit of liability on the principle that the greatest possible collectible loss is due the insured.

Example:[23] Assume the following set of facts:

	Value	*Loss*	*Average Clause (%)*
Stock..............	$ 8,504.95	$ 8,504.95	$ 3,000 specific insurance, 80%
Machinery..........	9,287.72	8,050.00	$ 9,000 specific insurance, 80%
			$28,000 blanket, stock, and machinery, 90%
Totals........	$27,792.67	$16,554.95	$40,000.

[20] *Ibid.*, p. 78.

[21] See, for example, *ibid.*, pp. 79–80.

[22] See Chapter 4 for a discussion of coinsurance and average clauses.

[23] National Board of Fire Underwriters (now American Insurance Association), *op. cit.*, p. 81.

Determine the apportionment based on the limit of liability rule.

Solution: The loss would be apportioned as follows:

	Apportionment	*Limit of Liability*	*Pays*
Specific insurance of stock	$ 3,000.00		
Average clause computation:			
$\frac{3,000}{80\% \text{ of } \$8,504.95} \times \$8,504.95$	3,750.00		
Loss on stock	8,504.95		
The smallest of these amounts is the limit of liability		$ 3,000.00	$ 2,048.01
Specific insurance on machinery	9,000.00		
Average clause computation:			
$\frac{9,000}{80\% \text{ of } 19,287.72} \times 8,050.00$	4,695.35		
Loss on machinery	8,050.00		
The smallest of these amounts is the limit of liability		4,695.35	3,205.37
Blanket insurance on stock and machinery	28,000.00		
Average clause computation:			
$\frac{28,000}{90\% \text{ of } 27,792.67} \times 16,554.95 = 18,531.61$			
Loss on stock and machinery is	16,554.95		
The smallest of these amounts is the limit of liability		16,554.95	11,301.57
Totals		$24,250.30	$16,554.95

The examples just cited are among the more complicated kinds of problem associated with adjustment of loss, but by no means exhaust the problems that arise. Situations involving deductibles in one contract and not in another, and coinsurance in one contract, but not in all are examples of other problems for which procedures have been worked out. The apportionment clause, explained in Chapter 8, is another example of rules to be followed in apportioning losses caused by extended coverage perils.

Loss Valuation. Earlier in this chapter the meaning of actual cash value and other valuation concepts was discussed. Although in theory cash value of property at the time of loss is easy to determine, in practice a number of circumstances may make valuation very difficult. The location, character, and condition of real property may affect the ease with which it can be repaired or replaced and whether this replacement or repair can be undertaken at reasonable cost. Badly located buildings, ones that are obsolete, and ones that were badly designed in the first place may not be fairly valued for insurance purposes unless these factors are taken into account. In the case of *McAnarney* v. *Newark Fire Insurance Co.*, the courts recognized the fact that obsolescence should be considered in determining actual cash value and since that time this factor has been recognized in valuation procedures.

Personal property, whether in use as in the case of household furniture or for sale such as stocks of commodities, may present valuation problems similar to those found in dealing with real property. Furniture that has been properly cared for and that is still useful is fairly easy to value, but obsolete and no longer used furniture may present difficulties. Antiques, articles of sentimental value, and objects that cannot be replaced can be troublesome to the adjuster from a valuation standpoint. Similarly, machinery used in manufacturing and various inventories of commodities may become obsolete and arguments may arise as to the usefulness and value of materials that are no longer appropriate or needed in a rapidly changing world. The adjuster must have considerable knowledge and skill in arriving at value decisions in these circumstances.[24]

Catastrophe Loss Adjustment Procedure. Some losses may be adjusted by the local agent (see page 832), and larger losses are adjusted by insurers representatives or professional adjusters. At one time, when a loss occurred that involved several insureds, there was a tendency toward competitive adjustment. The agent who was able to effect an adjustment for an insured who had suffered a loss before neighboring losses were adjusted felt that he had enhanced the reputation of his agency. Morever, agents tended to seek the service of adjusters who had a reputation toward generosity. Sometimes agents brought pressure upon company representatives to effect a prompt and sometimes generous adjustment in the interest of agency service. The situation was neither healthy nor in the long run was it a happy one for anyone.

The insurance business today recognizes that the most important service it can render is the prompt adjustment of losses. It also recognizes that more harm results to the business than any possible gain to an individual agent or insurer if efforts are made to effect adjustments for less than the amount of the loss. It has become equally recognized that it is not in the interest of either the agent or the business to permit competitive adjusting. In support of this position, when several losses occur in a given building or neighborhood, it is the general practice to assign all losses to the same adjusters. This being the case, one assured may not claim preferential treatment and, more important, an aggrieved insured may not attribute his grievance to the fact that the adjuster assigned to him was less fair than the one who adjusted his neighbor's loss.

In the case of catastrophes, where thousands of loss claims reach insurers in the course of a single day, special problems are created.

---

[24] See Reed, Mortimer, Jones, and Bachman, *op. cit.*, pp. 11–21.

Even in the case of a multiplicity of small losses, anything in the nature of prompt adjusting practice is simply beyond the capacity of the average agent.

The American Insurance Association classifies as a catastrophe any disaster, involving stock fire insurers and losses estimated at $1 million or over. The basic catastrophe plan for the settling of losses arising out of a disaster was developed by the Actuarial Bureau of the former National Board of Fire Underwriters and the first catastrophe reported under that plan was the Amarillo, Texas, tornado of May 15, 1949. The association assigns serial numbers to a catastrophe when it is reported and, where the circumstances seem to require, establishes a supervisory office to act as a clearing house for adjustments. Experience has shown that catastrophe losses occur at frequent intervals. These usually involve a multiplicity of a windstorm and hail loss, and there is always the probability that a conflagration caused by fire or earthquake may happen. It is to be prepared in advance for immediate action and to make available the benefit of past experience with catastrophe that the association has formulated its plan. The catastrophe plan undertakes to marshal all available resources to the end that all losses will be settled promptly and that all who suffer loss will be treated equally.

Most (probably all) catastrophe plans are patterned after the basic plan established by the National Board of Fire Underwriters (now a part of the American Insurance Association). This plan is described in a booklet that provides information on the duties and responsibilities of the American Insurance Association and of adjusters and fieldmen, when catastrophe losses must be adjusted.

Guiding Principles. Difficult problems often arise in adjustment and apportionment of losses when two or more overlapping contracts are involved and these problems have become somewhat more complex by the advent of multiple line contracts. In order to provide some help in these circumstances the Association of Casualty and Surety Companies, the Inland Marine Underwriters Association, the National Automobile Underwriters Association, the National Board of Fire Underwriters, the National Bureau of Casualty Underwriters, and the Surety Association of America recommended that their members and subscribers follow certain guiding principles. The principles were to be applicable to losses and claims occurring after November 1, 1963, but were not to apply to retrospectively rated contracts except for retrospective rated boiler-machinery fire contracts. The insurance classifications to which the principles apply are casualty, fire, inland marine, and fidelity.

The statement of guiding principles covers general principles, general conditions, and illustrative problems. The general principles are in two sections, the first deals with insurance covering the same property and the same interest, and the second deals with insurance covering the same property and different interests. A number of situations are set forth and statements are made about when a contract shall be primary or excess. In cases where contribution applies, "whether or not deductibles are involved, contribution shall be on the basis of the limit of liability rule."[25]

There are nine general conditions. Item 2, which deals with contribution states: " 'Contribution,' " unless otherwise as specified on in General Principle I–G, shall be on the basis of the applicable limit of liability under each respective policy or group of concurrent policies as though no other insurance existed. . . ." The statement then continues with a listing of the requirements for the limit of liability rule (see page 845). The remainder of the general conditions are too extensive to summarize here but their content may be obtained by reading the complete statement.[26]

INSURER ORGANIZATION FOR ADJUSTMENT

Property and liability insurers typically have a division in the home office that is entitled "claims" or "claim and loss" or some equivalent title. This division is usually headed by a vice president or someone of comparable rank. The claims division will usually have departments that have the responsibility for dealing with loss problems and such related activities as salvage and subrogation. Historically it was not unusual for separate departments to be based on lines of insurance, but the trend today is toward a more general type of organization. The organization of field offices follows much the same pattern, with regional and branch offices having claims departments. A headquarters division that is closely related to adjustment is the legal department. This department often acts in an advisory capacity to assist the claims department in matters of contract interpretation and other matters of law. The legal division often has considerable responsibility for settling liability losses, and some large insurers maintain a separate legal staff as a part of the claims division. Staff attorneys are not always used in the defense of lawsuits, and there are times when outside attorneys are hired to try liability cases.

The local adjuster is the person who comes in contact with the insured and may be a staff adjuster or he may be an independent adjuster who has been assigned to the case.[27] The latter type is often

---

[25] There is an exception stated in the general principles. See pages 74 and 75 for a more complete discussion of the guiding principles.

[26] See *Fire, Casualty, and Surety Bulletins* (Cincinnati, Ohio: The National Underwriter Company) Multiple Line Section.

[27] For definitions see pages 831 and 832.

used in areas where the insurer may find it impractical to maintain staff personnel, or in situations involving catastrophic losses where a large number of adjusters may be needed in order to handle claims efficiently. How much responsibility for loss adjustment is extended to the field staff often varies with insurers and with their philosophy concerning the decentralization of administrative functions.

CLAIM TRENDS

The amount paid by insurers for losses under insurance contracts is increasing year by year. Part of this increase results from the general expansion of the economy and part from an increase in accident rates, in delinquencies of various kinds, in hospitalization, in damage suits, and in many other sources of loss. Although insurance rates have increased in many areas in response to adverse experience, underwriting losses continue and the property and liability insurance business is faced with a continuing inadequacy of premiums in a number of lines.

In the field of property insurance, experience under multiperil contracts has not been especially favorable, partly because of the difficulty in computing premiums for such contracts, partly because of strong competition among large multiple line insurers and a resultant tendency to depress rate increases, and partly because of an increase in such crimes as arson, vandalism, robbery, and theft. There also appears to be an increase in claims consciousness on the part of many insureds.

The problem of the increasing dollar amount of claims is perhaps most acute in the field of liability insurance. Juries are increasingly liberal, and the costs of litigation are high. A number of reasons have been cited by students of this problem for the high costs of litigation and settlement. Some lawyers feel that the legal system increasingly provides many advantages for the plaintiff and that liability is imposed on whichever party is best able to discharge it. In the area of manufactured products the concept of strict liability applies with the result that more and more cases appear to be settled in favor of the plaintiff. In liability claims the basis for determining the amount of the loss is usually to compute the time lost and the wages that might have been earned if the accident had not occurred. Increasing living costs and increasing salaries mean that liability claim evaluations are correspondingly increased. Medical costs have also increased, and injuries of various types may lead to substantial medical expenses. Many liability claims are handled under a contingent fee arrangement. In fact, in only one state (Maine) is this type of fee illegal. Such arrangements often lead to higher claims costs. All of these factors, and perhaps others, have led to a fairly pessimistic attitude on the part of many insurers toward the claims problem.

If the insurance business is to continue to operate effectively, there is need for greater emphasis on loss prevention on the part of insureds, as well as better attitudes toward fairness in loss settlements on the part of many segments of the insuring public.

FOR DISCUSSION

1. "Difficult at any time, the problem of claims adjustment is multiplied a thousand times when an area is hit by a major catastrophe, a hurricane, tornado, or explosion. Handicapped by a shortage of manpower and clerical help in an emergency, quite possibly faced with a breakdown of mail and telephone service, agents and adjusters must cooperate to handle thousands of claims promptly and courteously."[28] What procedures are available to expedite the handling of losses of catastrophic proportions?
2. What has been the impact of multiple line legislation on loss adjustment?
3. Distinguish between claims and losses.
4. Comment on the appropriateness of the word "adjuster" and of the expression "adjustment of losses." What words or expressions would you prefer, if any?
5. Distinguish among staff adjusters, public adjusters, and independent adjusters and comment on the role of the agent and other producers in the adjustment of losses.
6. Donaldson has placed the work of the adjuster into three categories: investigation and negotiation, evaluation, and termination. Explain the duties of the adjuster in each of the three stages of his work.
7. What are the state licensing requirements for adjusters? What types of educational preparation are available to adjusters? Evaluate current programs.
8. How are general average losses adjusted?
9. How is the value of property that has been destroyed or damaged determined? What is meant by actual cash value? Replacement value? Market value? What effect does obsolescence have on value determinations?
10. One definition of "salvage" is that it is the procedure wherein lost or damaged property is recovered for the purpose of reducing the amount of loss. In what other ways is the word "salvage" used in the insurance business?
11. What influence might the Interstate Commerce Act, various state statutes, and the common law have on the settlement of transportation insurance claims?
12. Select an insurer that operates on a national basis. Summarize the claims organization of that insurer by drawing an appropriate organi-

[28] Stuart V. d'Adolf, "I. When Disaster Strikes . . . ," *American Agency Bulletin*, Vol. LXIII (September, 1965), p. 16.

zation chart. Comment on the effectiveness of the claims organization of the insurer that you have selected.

13. Discuss the need for specialists in the adjusting of particular types of loss.
14. What are some of the problems facing insurers today in loss adjustment? What has been the impact of these problems on rates?

CHAPTER · 34

Governmental Supervision

Very early in its history insurance as a commercial enterprise became the object of varying degrees of public supervision and support. Governmental interest in insurance took two forms. First, the government sought to regulate the activities and practices of insurers and their agents, and second, in a number of instances, and in comparatively recent times, the government became an insurer. Both types of intervention had as a major purpose the securing to the public the advantages of insurance in a manner that would provide maximum benefit and security at the lowest cost. The extent of governmental participation in the affairs of insurance has varied considerably over time and, also, geographically. The earliest insurance codes were quite limited, and in countries such as Great Britain insurance regulation is not nearly as detailed as in the United States. On the other hand, the role of the government as an insurer has been quite common in Europe for many years and has only fairly recently, and in a limited way, been a part of governmental activity in the United States.

In property and liability insurance in the United States neither the federal nor the state governments has assumed the role of insurer except in times of war or for special purposes such as crop insurance or workmen's compensation insurance.[1] Rather the principal role of the government has been the supervision of the activities of nongovernmental insurers.

Insurance as interstate commerce is subject to regulation by Congress. As a matter of practice, because of affirmative action by Congress inviting state regulation, the business of insurance is regulated by the states. The effect of the congressional action is to make the standards of applicable state laws determine the legality of insurance practices within the state. The business is subject to the federal

[1] This statement with appropriate changes applies for the most part to life insurance, too, although in the life field such programs as Federal Old Age and Survivors' Insurance and National Service Life Insurance represent a large concentration of assets.

antitrust laws and to certain other federal regulating statutes dealing with interstate commerce to the extent that the states fail to provide adequate regulation. The federal antitrust laws continue to govern in all jurisdictions in respect to situations involving coercion, intimidation, and boycott.

A number of reasons have been advanced by authors of insurance books for the pattern of supervision and control that has emerged in the United States.[2] Among these reasons are the complexity of the product of insurers, the serious consequences of insurer insolvency, the fact that beneficiaries of insurance contracts are often not parties to the contract, the long-term nature of many insurance agreements, the dependence of insurance costs on the happening of future events, the ineffectiveness of competition as a regulatory measure, and the feeling that the product of the insurer should be available to anyone in need of insurance protection.

The product of the insurer is the insurance contract (as well as the service offered by the insurer to the insured). This document is complicated both as to form and language and is difficult for noninsurance trained persons to understand. In some instances archaic language is retained because it has withstood judicial interpretation, and its meaning is known in at least a legal sense. Because of the various complexities involved, the insurance layman needs to be protected against unfair and misleading contracts. He also needs assurance that insurer representatives are competent and that their advice and other services rendered by the insurer can be relied upon.

Not all insurance contracts are for the sole benefit of the named insured. Workmen's compensation contracts redound to the benefit of the injured employee, and liability contracts not only cover insureds other than the person or corporation named in the contract, but are also primarily of benefit to third parties. Since these beneficiaries typically have no voice in the making of the contract or in its continuance, their interest can be protected only through the intervention of laws designed to offer protection to the beneficiary.

Insurance contracts are typically long-term agreements. This fact is especially true in life insurance, but is also relevant in the property and liability field where three-year contracts subject to renewal are not uncommon. Performance on the part of the insurer depends on the happening of some event which may not occur at all, or may occur sometime in the future. It is important for the insured to know

---

[2] See, e.g., Charles C. Center and Richard M. Heins (eds.), *Insurance and Government* (New York: McGraw-Hill Book Co., Inc., 1962), pp. 15–19; C. F. Michelbacher, et al, *Multiple-line Insurance* (New York: McGraw-Hill Book Co., Inc., 1957), pp. 525–28; and Spencer L. Kimball, *Insurance and Public Policy* (Madison, Wis.: University of Wisconsin Press, 1960), pp. 6–7. The material considered here is based on these references.

that the insurer will be able to pay claims regardless of when they occur. Closely related to the long-term nature of the contract is the fact that insurance costs are incurred in the future and at the time the contract is issued only an estimate can be made of the losses and expenses that will be applicable. There needs to be some assurance that the premiums collected will, in the aggregate, be adequate in amount to meet future obligations. It is also necessary that the premiums collected not be excessive and that discrimination among insureds be prevented.

Competition is often thought of as a means of guaranteeing efficiency of operation and it has been argued that close supervision of insurance would be unnecessary if insurers competed freely. There is considerable historical evidence to suggest that unlimited competition in the setting of rates leads, in insurance at least, to inadequacy of rates and to subsequent insolvency of the firm. This argument has seemed especially true of property and liability insurance and has been instrumental in bringing about rate regulation.

In many ways insurance takes on the characteristics of a public utility. Not only is it supervised by the government but there is a growing feeling that insurance protection, for example, in the automobile field, should be made available to all of those persons who require it. Insurers have long operated on the basis that they could accept or reject any or all risks. In fact, successful operation often depends on how carefully risks are selected. Any modification of these practices usually leads to further governmental supervision and control.

Although all of the reasons for governmental supervision of insurance that have been discussed above are important, the primary objective of supervision is solvency. Solvency means that not only must insurers be in a position to meet all obligations as they mature, but the financial structure of the insurer must be such that the insurer will be able at all times to meet incurred obligations. To meet obligations as they mature, the insurer must have on hand sufficient funds to pay all claims in accordance with the terms of the contract. To meet incurred obligations the insurer must have on hand funds at all times adequate when augmented by additional premiums and earned interest, to meet any anticipated future obligations. To this end, it is basic that the premium charged be sufficient to produce funds to cover all the obligations of the insurer and, at the same time, provide that the premiums charged bear a relationship to the risk against which insurance is provided.

Equity is of almost equal importance with solvency as a major purpose of regulation. Much of the activity involved in the approval of property insurance rates is aimed at the need for equitable treatment of insureds. Complaint bureaus, licensing laws, approval of contract forms are further examples of the desire of the state to insist on equity. Mayerson has argued that equity has three components, which are reasonableness, impartiality, and fairness. The first of these components refers to equity as it relates to the entire group of policyholders; the second to problems of equity between two policyholders; and the third to the fair treatment of one insured.[3] These criteria were illustrated in the discussion on rate making. It should not be assumed that the approval of rates is the only place where equity is of importance. Marketing practices, claim practices, advertising, and other activities also involve problems relating to equity.

The relationship of the government to a business institution such as insurance may be looked at in a somewhat different way. It may be viewed at the "ways in which the public policy of our society . . . impinged upon the insurance enterprise." Kimball identifies five areas of insurer operation in which the government has a basic interest. (1) Validation of the insurance enterprise; (2) creation of an adequate insurance fund; (3) protection of the insurance fund; (4) distribution of the fund; and (5) impact on the larger society.[4] These areas encompass the major reasons for the regulatory activity of the government. The extent to which insurance is acceptable legally as a social institution depends on the rules established for entering the business, and their relative severity or leniency. Likewise the legal limits within which the business may operate helps to determine the extent to which insurance needs may be met. Once an insurance firm is in operation the government has an interest in the ways in which money is collected, conserved, and distributed. This interest is basically concerned with the solvency of the firm and its ability to meet its contractual obligations. That insurance has an impace on the larger society has recently been dramatically demonstrated by the large accumulations of money that insurance firms invest in various of societies' enterprises. The extent to which insurers may effectively participate in capital depends to a considerable extent on public policy in respect to the investment of insurance funds. Insurers can affect society in other ways. Efforts to reduce risk through prevention is an example of the role an insurer may play in improving societal conditions.

HISTORICAL CONSIDERATIONS

The current system of governmental supervision in the United States can best be understood in terms of the historical development of insurance as a social and business institution. Insurance as a business

[3] Allen L. Mayerson, "An Inside Look at Insurance Regulations," *Journal of Risk and Insurance*, Vol. XXXII, No. 1 (March, 1965), pp. 53.

[4] Kimball, *op. cit.*, p. 6.

enterprise started in Europe and later spread throughout the world. The relationship of the government to this development has done much to shape the characteristics of present-day insurers.

European Precedents. Since insurance as a business started in the cities of northern Italy[5] at the beginning of the 14th century, it is not surprising that the earliest records of insurance supervision date from the insurance codes of several northern Mediterranean cities. In 1401 an insurance statute was passed in Genoa which provided for the taxation of insurance. This law was followed in 1435 by legislation in Barcelona, which was considerably more extensive than the earlier taxation statute. Among the provisions of this law were restrictions on insurance brokers including regulation of fees. The next insurance legislation of importance was enacted in Florence in 1523. This statute created an administrative agency that was given authority to regulate insurance. The city magistrates appointed commissioners and these persons among other things could fix premium rates. A review of this early legislation shows that many aspects of modern regulation parallels the type of control exercised over insurance almost from the beginning of its commercial operation.[6]

In England efforts were made in the 16th century to regulate insurance, but it appears that the legislation of that time was not particularly effective. Patterson[7] concludes that "Down to 1870 England made no restrictions upon the way in which an insurer should conduct his business, apart from the statutes against wagering and similar statutes governing judicial controversies." Legislation passed in 1870 established certain financial requirements for life insurers, including the filing of a financial statement with the Board of Trade. Two statutes, the "Assurance Companies Act of 1909" and the "Industrial Assurance Act of 1923" represent efforts to establish comprehensive regulation of insurers; however, this legislation in many respects was not as thorough as that found in the United States. Considerable reliance is still placed on the integrity of the individual firm and on the ability of the firm to engage in sound management.

REGULATION OF INSURANCE IN THE UNITED STATES

It was not until after the Civil War that the regulation of insurers in the United States became fairly general and it was not until the first decade of the 20th century that regulation became fairly effective.

---

[5] Edwin W. Patterson, *The Insurance Commissioner in the United States* (Cambridge: Harvard University Press, 1927), p. 514.

[6] *Ibid.*, p. 515.

[7] *Ibid.*, p. 517.

During the colonial period there were no domestic insurers other than those operating on an individual basis or as mutual organizations and there were only two of the latter type. This lack of activity was due at least partly to the Act of Parliament of 1719, which gave charters to two British stock insurers and which prohibited the forming of other stock insurers in England or any of its possessions.[8]

Following the Revolutionary War and the establishment of independence, stock insurers were formed as were additional mutual insurers. The role of the government from a regulatory viewpoint was limited mainly to the granting of charters by the legislatures of the various states and to occasional statutes providing for the taxation of premiums or for the limitation of the activities of foreign insurers. From the beginning of the United States, statutes affecting insurance were state laws and the federal government evidenced little interest in controlling the activities of insurers or their agents.

Until the middle of the 19th century the various states did not take a particularly active interest in insurance regulation. From roughly 1800 to 1850, the principal type of supervision, apart from the statutes mentioned above, consisted of laws requiring that periodical financial reports be filed with designated officials. It was expected that these reports would be made public and would form a way for the citizen to judge the solvency of insurers. These laws did not prove very effective in terms of curbing insolvency or unfair practices and the states then moved in the direction of the establishment of independent administrative agencies headed by a commissioner or an officer with a similar title.

Until 1851, when New Hampshire established a board of insurance commissioners, the supervision of insurance activities (to the extent that it existed) within a state was the responsibility of a variety of state officials, very often the secretary of state or the treasurer. The New Hampshire board was appointed on a full-time basis, consisted of three persons appointed by the governor, and had the responsibility for personally examining insurers. This board was replaced by a single commissioner in 1869. A number of states followed the lead of New Hampshire and appointed insurance boards. Among these states were Massachusetts, Rhode Island, Florida, and Tennessee. These boards did not prove fully effective in the substantial task of supervising insurance and the next step in administration and control was the establishment of a separate office headed by a single commissioner or superintendent. Thirteen of these offices were created since 1900.[9]

The first state to place administrative control in the hands of a single official was New York, which created the office of superintend-

---

[8] *Ibid.*, p. 522.

[9] *Ibid.*, p. 537.

ent of insurance in 1859. Subsequently all states established insurance departments presided over by an official who was most often designated commissioner of insurance. For the most part, those states not using this title called the insurance supervisory official the "superintendent" or "director" of insurance. In three states insurance is combined with banking and the person in charge is called the "commissioner of insurance and banking." The commissioner is typically an appointed official, selected by the governor, and subject to the approval of the state senate, or in three states to an executive council. In four instances the appointment may be by the governor without approval. In a minority of states the commissioner is elected by the populace. In general the various state statutes do not specify any particular qualifications for the office, and the commissioners have a variety of backgrounds. An important development from the standpoint of insurance supervision was the establishment of the National Association of Insurance Commissioners. This organization was founded in 1870 and was first called the National Convention of Insurance Commissioners. Although this group has no legal authority it has done much to promote high standards of supervision and to encourage uniformity of reporting among the states.[10]

The history of insurance supervision is closely related to the passing of insurance statutes and the establishment of administrative departments. Although these aspects of regulation are primary, it is also true that, over the years, judicial interpretation and the findings of various committees and commissioners have had a profound effect on the course of governmental supervision and control. A number of decisions and investigations have been related to property and liability insurance and deserve to be considered in some detail.

Paul* v. *Virginia. From the beginning of constitutional government in the United States, it was assumed that the states had the right to regulate insurance. The constitution nowhere mentioned insurance and it appeared that the federal government was not concerned with it. The validity of this idea was put to the test in 1869 when the Supreme Court heard the case of *Paul* v. *Virginia.* This case arose originally as a result of a dispute between Samuel Paul and the Commonwealth of Virginia. Although Paul was a resident of Virginia, he represented a number of insurers that were domiciled in New York State. There was a Virginia statute that required that foreign insurers obtain licenses before transacting business in Virginia and there was also a requirement that a security deposit be made. It was also necessary for an agent representing out-of-state insurers to obtain a license to sell.[11]

---

[10] *Ibid.*, pp. 29–56. See also Chapter 29 of this text.

[11] E. W. Sawyer, *Insurance as Interstate Commerce* (New York: McGraw-Hill Book Co., Inc., 1945), p. 33. The facts in this case are based on Sawyer's discussion.

Paul and the insurers he represented were willing to comply with all of the demands of the Virginia statute except for the deposit of security. Licenses were denied because of the failure to make the required deposit. Notwithstanding Paul attempted to sell insurance, was arrested, and convicted of violation of law. The matter was taken to court, and after appeal finally reached the Supreme Court of the United States. Paul's defense was "(1) that the business of insurance was commerce; (2) that insurance written by nonresident insurance companies on risks in Virginia was commerce among the several states, and (3) that the Virginia statute amounted to regulation of commerce among the several states which was invalid because power to regulate such commerce was placed in Congress by the Constitution."[12] The Supreme Court upheld the validity of the Virginia statute and Justice Field in his decision declared that selling an insurance contract was not a transaction of commerce and that such contracts could not be considered articles of commerce. The net result of this decision was that from 1869 to 1944 the regulation of insurance was held to be a matter entirely in the hands of the several states.

A number of cases followed *Paul* v. *Virginia*, most notable of which were *Hooper* v. *California* and *New York Life Insurance Company* v. *Deer Lodge County*. In the first case on the validity of the California law prohibiting the sale of insurance to a resident of the state, if the contract was to be issued by an insurer not incorporated in California, or one that had not filed the proper bond.[13] The second case tested a Montana statute that imposed a tax on insurers based on "the excess of premiums over losses and expenses incurred within the State."[14] In both cases the state statutes were upheld and it appeared that state regulation of insurance was firmly established.

Merritt Committee. In the years following the Civil War, the business of insurance developed rapidly and with this growth a number of problems arose. Alleged abuses, including unfair treatment of insureds, were levied against insurers. Legislative investigations were undertaken. In the life insurance field the most notable investigation was that undertaken by Senator Armstrong in 1906, which resulted in important statutory revisions and closer supervision of life insurance. The Armstrong Investigation was followed in 1911 by the study made by the Merritt Committee dealing mainly with fire insurance. The committee was formed on July 8, 1910. The chairman selected by the group was Edwin A. Merritt, Jr., a member of the New York Legislature. There were four members of the committee in addition to Merritt, as well as legal, actuarial, and accounting

---

[12] *Ibid.*, p. 34.

[13] *Ibid.*, p. 35.

[14] *Ibid.*, p. 36.

consultants. The committee held public sessions on 42 days. The charge to the committee was as follows:

> To investigate as speedily as possible, all corruptions and corrupt practices shown to exist by the evidence of the recent investigation before the Senate of the State of New York; all matters indicating corrupt practices in connection with legislation which have developed in the recent investigation conducted by the Superintendent of Insurance; the business methods, operation, management, supervision and control of all insurance companies other than those doing life insurance business, including fire insurance exchanges and state local boards of fire underwriters and the relations of such companies, exchanges and boards with legislation, including industrial life insurance; any specific charges, verified upon knowledge of corrupt practices or official misconduct in connection with legislation or the legislature, or with any matter or proceeding before any state department, board, body or officer; and any other matters pertaining to the conduct of the business of the state and its officers which, in the judgment of the committee, warrants investigation, to the end that such remedial legislation may be enacted or changed or method in the conduct of public business may be adopted as will prevent a recurrence of any abuse or evils disclosed.[15]

The final report of the committee was submitted on February 1, 1911, and was in three parts. Part I consisted of the "Introduction and General Outline of the Business," Part II was "An Analysis, Based upon Evidence Received, of the Problems of Fire Insurance," and Part II consisted of "Recommendations."

The committee was aware of the complicated nature of its undertaking and organized it work on the following plan:

The companies and their relation to the State—State supervision.
Statistics regarding the amount and character of the fire insurance business.
The organizations among the companies.
The principles involved in the furnishing of fire insurance indemnity.
The interior organization of a company—its officers and agents.
The actual detailed work of a company—getting and doing business.
The settlement of losses—adjusting.
The theory of rating.
Rating organizations.
The New York Fire Insurance Exchange.
The Suburban Fire Insurance Exchange.
The Underwriters' Association of New York State—the Upstate Association.
Factory Mutual Insurance Companies.
Miscellaneous Mutual Insurance Companies.
Town and County Co-operative Insurance Companies.

---

[15] *Hearings Before the Subcommittee on Antitrust and Monopoly of the Committee on the Judiciary United States Senate*, 86th Cong., 1st Sess., Part 5, pp. 2791–92.

Interinsurance Associations.
Lloyds.
Local agents and their problems—the expense problem.
Brokers.
Complaints by the insured and the answers thereto by the companies.
Fire prevention.[16]

Each of these topics was considered but the greatest emphasis was given to rating. Problems of competition, schedule rating, anticompact laws, discrimination among classes, classification, and combined loss experience were discussed at length. Additionally there was consideration of taxation, valued-policy laws, the coinsurance clause, agents, brokers, and commissions.

The committee made recommendations on the following 14 topics: valued policy, coinsurance, anticompact and rating exchanges, state license law, antirebate law, conflagration hazard, mutual companies, Lloyds and interinsurers, standard policy, amendments affecting county and town cooperative insurance companies, surplus lines, state fire marshal law, classification of loss experience, and building codes. Space does not permit full discussion of each recommendation. The committee recommended against valued contracts, anticompact laws, and rebating. It favored coinsurance, licensing of agents and brokers, admission of mutual insurers of other states, no change in the standard fire insurance contract, the enactment of a state fire marshal law, urged the legislature to consider a state building law along with better building codes, and approved the idea of interinsurance exchanges. In many of the areas of recommendation legislation was prepared and submitted for approval.

Southeastern Underwriters. From the time of the Merritt investigation until 1944 there were no major investigations of the property and liability business by governmental or other committees, although the Temporary National Economic Committee had investigated the life insurance business in the 1930's, and there were no court decisions during that time that brought about major changes in the way the insurance business was conducted. This relatively tranquil state was shattered on June 5, 1944, when the Supreme Court handed down its decision in the case of the *United States* v. *Southeastern Underwriters Association et al.* The Southeastern Underwriters Association was a rate-making organization whose membership consisted of 200 stock fire insurers and 27 individuals doing business in six Southern states. This group was charged with alleged violations of the Sherman Antitrust Act and the case was tried in the district court. The indictment was that the group had attempted "to restrain interstate trade and commerce by fixing and maintaining arbitrary and

[16] *Ibid.*, p. 2794.

non-competitive premium rates on fire and specified allied lines . . ." and had tried "to monopolize trade and commerce in the same lines of insurance in and among the same states."[17] There was evidence that the Southeastern Underwriters had engaged in such tactics as boycott and other forms of coercion in its effort to control the fire-insurance business in the Southeastern part of the United States.

The case was taken ultimately to the Supreme Court, which ruled in a 4–3 decision that insurance was commerce and could be controlled by Congress. This decision reversed the long-standing opinion to the contrary and created an entirely new situation in insurance regulation. Among the immediate consequences of this decision was the fact that federal statutes such as the Sherman Act, the Clayton Act, the Robinson-Patman Act, the Federal Trade Commission Act, the National Labor Relations Act, the Fair Labor Standards Act, and the Merchant Marine Act were now applicable to the operations of insurers. Additionally, questions were raised as to whether the states could continue to tax out-of-state insurers and whether the states could in other ways regulate insurers operating on an interstate basis. These concerns were stressed by the dissenting justices, who also pointed out that the states, relying on a precedent of some 76 years, had well-developed regulatory systems, which, for the most part, were operating satisfactorily.

Since there were no federal statutes specifically regulating insurance, considerable confusion existed as to the form federal regulation might take assuming that Congress intended to enter this field. Sawyer[18] argued that Congress had three alternatives: (1) no action, which would mean that the states could continue their regulatory activities, assuming that they did not interfere with such federal laws as the Sherman Act; (2) a federal system of regulation designed to control the interstate aspects of insurer operation, and (3) a system of federal help to the states in the sense of trying to strengthen state laws and to bring them into conformity with congressional intent. The states had alternatives of continuing along the same lines as before or making some effort to revise their regulatory systems, assuming that the revision would be within constitutional limits and not in contravention of federal law. Insurers were much interested in the form that any revised system of regulation might take and were divided in their attitudes toward revision of the system of regulation that had been in existence for many years. There were some insurers that favored federal regulation, some preferred to continue as before, and others believed that no action should be taken and were willing to wait and see what kind of system evolved as a result of the Southeastern

---

[17] Sawyer, *op. cit.*, p. 42. See also Chapter 29 of this text.

[18] *Ibid.*, p. 53.

Underwriters' decision. It is probably fair to say that most insurers, especially the smaller ones, did not want federal regulation and preferred supervision by the various states. Their reasons centered around the fact that many forms of insurance were influenced by local conditions and were best understood by local authorities.[19]

In order further to clarify congressional intent and to resolve some of the problems that had arisen from the decision of the Supreme Court, Congress passed Public Law 15 on March 9, 1945. The text of the law begins with these words: "That the Congress hereby declares that the continued regulation and taxation by the several states of the business of insurance is in the public interest, and that silence on the part of the Congress shall not be construed to impose any barrier to the regulation or taxation of such business by the several states."[20] Although the states were largely given the right to continue to regulate insurance without fear that then existing federal statutes would supersede state laws, the law contained certain provisos. One of these restrictions was that after January 1, 1948, the Sherman Act, the Clayton Act, and the Federal Trade Commission Act would apply to insurers to the extent that state laws did not provide similar regulations. Congress further emphasized that, although a moratorium had been granted, this delay did not apply to any "agreement to boycott, coerce, or intimidate, or act of boycott, coercion, or intimidation."[21] Likewise, the National Labor Relations Act, the Fair Labor Standards Act, and the Merchant Marine Act were to apply immediately to insurers.

O'Mahoney Committee. Although Public Law 15 served to introduce a certain amount of order into a difficult situation, doubts about the future course of regulation remained. On the part of federal agencies, as well as Congress, there was continuing concern about the effectiveness of state regulation and whether state laws were adequate for the task. In 1958, the Subcommittee on Antitrust and Monopoly of the Committee on the Judiciary, later to be known as the O'Mahoney Committee, undertook an investigation of the ocean marine and aviation insurance fields, as well as certain general aspects of state rate regulation. The committee was concerned with possible violations of the antitrust laws because marine and aviation insurance are often written by associations of insurers. It was also concerned with the fact that property and liability insurers continued to rely heavily on rate-making organizations. The final report of the committee, published in 1960, consisted of some nine volumes and represented a thorough review of a fairly limited segment of the insurance

[19] *Ibid.*, p. 54.

[20] *Ibid.*, pp. 64–65.

[21] *Ibid.*, p. 65.

business. The committee found a considerable amount of concentration in aviation and marine insurance in the sense that a very few groups appeared to dominate the business. It was also critical of various aspects of state regulation. One result of the work of the committee was the introduction of a bill by Senator O'Mahoney, which undertook to bring about more competition in rate making. The bill was to apply only to the District of Columbia and was not intended to apply to all of the states. Apart from this effort to introduce reform into rate making, the work of the committee has not resulted in widespread changes in insurance regulation. Nevertheless the interest of Congress in the insurance business appears to be a continuing one and important changes may ultimately be brought about.

PATTERN OF REGULATION

With the main facts of the history of insurance regulation in mind, it is useful to review the structure of the insurance departments of the several states, since these organizations are still responsible for insurance supervision. As might be expected, a multiplicity of laws leads to considerable diversity among the states and it is not easy to describe a typical insurance department. The description that follows is based on New York statutes, since practice in that state illustrates a fairly comprehensive effort to regulate insurance in an area where there is a concentration of large insurers and where a large volume of business is transacted. Moreover, the policies and practices of the New York department have been followed in varying degrees by most of the other states.

Departmental Organization. The statutes provide for a superintendent of insurance who has general administrative responsibility for the department of insurance and for administering the insurance statutes. In New York (as in many other states) he is appointed by the governor with the advice and consent of the senate. His term of office parallels that of the governor who appointed him, although he may continue to serve until his successor has been appointed. He has the authority to appoint a first and other deputies, as well as clerks, examiners, and other employees. In New York there are six deputy superintendents four of whom are in the New York office and two at Albany. In addition to the deputies there are chiefs of bureaus who are responsible for various aspects of the work of the insurance department. Among the bureaus are life, property, rating, complaint, audit and training, legal, research, administrative services, and welfare fund. There is also a chief actuary and a chief real estate appraiser. The superintendent is required to submit a report to the legislature each year in which he reviews the insurance business for the preceding year; summarizes official regulations; presents a financial statement; lists the number and kinds of insurers authorized to do business in the state along with a statement about assets, liabilities, and premiums written; summarizes changes in insurers in regard to organization, admission to the state, and similar matters; reviews the facts in regard to liquidation, rehabilitation, or conservation proceedings; and summarizes amendments to the insurance law.[22] A seven-member insurance board is authorized by statute and has the authority to advise the superintendent and to make recommendations on matters submitted to it. The superintendent of insurance serves as chairman of the board and the other members are appointed by the governor with the advice and consent of the senate.

Procedural Matters. An important aspect of the superintendent's responsibility involves the promulgation of regulations; the giving of notices of proposed actions; the holding of hearings; receiving and reviewing annual statements from insurers; as well as any special reports; conducting examinations of insurers; and receiving the rating services of other states. The insurance statutes are fairly detailed in setting forth the rules to be followed in regard to these matters. Two of these items, the annual statement and examinations, should be considered at greater length, since they play a considerable role in the work of the insurer, as well as in the work of the insurance department.

Annual Statement. An annual statement is required by law from every insurer doing business in a state. The term "insurer" includes fraternal societies, pension funds, and similar organizations, if the latter are required by law to report to the superintendent or commissioner or are in any way subject to his jurisdiction. The form may vary as to type of insurer and from state to state.

The first page of a typical annual statement for property and liability insurers provides a place for the name of the insurer and a listing of the principal officers and the directors or trustees, as well as a place for a sworn statement of the accuracy of the report. The next two pages provide for a listing of assets, liabilities, surplus, and other funds. Some seven pages of the form are devoted to underwriting and investment exhibits. The titles of some of the tables are: statement of income (underwriting and investment); capital and surplus account; interest, dividends, and real estate income; capital gains and losses on investments; premiums written and premiums earned; premiums in force; losses paid in incurred; unpaid losses and loss adjustment expenses; and general expenses. The underwriting and investment exhibits are broken down by line of business, including such items as fire, extended coverage, earthquake, homeowners' multiple peril, commer-

[22] Based on Paul R. Taylor (ed.), *Insurance Law of the State of New York* (Albany, N.Y.: Williams Press, Inc., 1950), p. 8.

cial multiple peril, burglary, theft, and others. It is not unusual for 25 or 30 lines of business to be included in the statement. Gross premiums (after return premiums), in the premiums written and premiums earned exhibit are divided into direct business, reinsurance assumed, and reinsurance ceded.

Three exhibits provide for an analysis of assets, of nonadmitted assets, and a reconciliation of ledger assets. In addition to listing the amounts of bonds, stocks, and similar items, separate schedules are provided for listing the securities and recording the book value, market value, and actual cost. Space is also available for listing the amount of dividends. There are schedules for listing all real estate owned and sold and mortgages owned. Another schedule contains the details on collateral loans. The nonadmitted assets for which a listing must be made are such items as company's stock owned; loans on company's stock; deposits in suspended banks, less estimated amount recoverable, agents' balances or uncollected items over three months due; bills receivable, past due, taken for premiums; excess of bills receivable, not past due, taken for risks over the unearned premiums thereon; equipment, furniture, and supplies; bills receivable, not taken for premiums; loans on personal security, endorsed or not; and other itemized assets, which may be nonadmissable, such as salvage and subrogation (individuals). The reconciliation of ledger assets involves an accounting for the increase in ledger assets from such sources as net premiums written, interest and other income, sale of assets, and other income items, and the decrease in assets brought about by net losses paid, expenses paid, and other disbursement items. The amount of ledger assets of the previous year plus (or minus) the increase (or decrease) yields the ledger assets for the current year and should correspond to the figure given in Exhibit I. The figure for net admitted assets should correspond to the figure for total assets given on page two of the statement.

One page of the annual statement is given over to general interrogatories and a wide variety of questions are asked. Examples of the queries are: "Does the company issue both participating and non-participating policies?" "What interest, direct or indirect, has this company in the capital stock of any other insurance company?" "Does the company own any securities of a real estate holding company or otherwise hold real estate indirectly?" "What provision has this company made to protect itself from an excessive loss in the event of a catastrophe under a workmen's compensation contract without limit of loss?" "Does the company keep a complete permanent record of the proceedings of its board of directors and all subordinate committees thereof?"

The final exhibit before the various schedules is an exhibit of premiums and losses. The various lines of business are listed and space is provided for recording direct premiums written, direct premiums earned, dividends paid or credited to policyholders on direct business, direct losses paid (minus salvage), and direct losses incurred.

The annual statement blank closes with space for twenty schedules labeled A through T. Certain of these schedules (A through D) were mentioned in a previous paragraph as dealing with investments. The other schedules are for the following items: reinsurance ceded (and related matters); reserve for credit losses; rates of dividends in effect for participating contracts; direct or indirect payments of more than $100 (exclusive of expenses paid in connection with settlement of losses, claims, and salvage under policy contracts) in connection with any matter, measure, or proceeding before legislative bodies, officers, or departments of government during the year (with certain exceptions); list of payments in excess of $500 to any officer, director, or employee, excluding salary and other compensation and reimbursement of expenditures for transportation and similar items for auditors, inspectors, special agents, claims investigators and adjusters; list of banks in which insurer funds were deposited and the amounts of such deposits; list of losses by line of business other than bodily injury liability and workmen's compensation claims; reserve for unpaid bodily injury liability losses and workmen's compensation losses; unlisted assets; and exhibit of premiums written allocated by states and territories.

Examinations. The superintendent (or commissioner) is authorized and required to examine insurers and other organizations under his supervision and doing business in or authorized to do business in his state as often, according to New York law, as he deems expedient but "of every domestic life insurance company, every cooperative life and accident insurance company, every domestic casualty insurance company, every domestic surety company, and every authorized domestic fraternal benefit society, at least once in every three years; and of every other authorized domestic insurance company or authorized domestic insurer and every rating organization at least once in every five years."[23] The supervisory official is required to indicate to the insurer the scope of the examination and a copy of the examination order must be submitted to the insurer upon demand. The insurer is required to co-operate in the examination and make appropriate files and documents available; if examination is refused by an insurer, this fact is regarded as grounds for revocation or refusal of a license. Provisions are made for filing and publishing reports of examination. Each insurer examined has a right to a copy of the report and is also required to withstand the expenses of the examination.

Organization and Licensing of Insurers. The statutes require

[23] *Ibid.*, p. 14.

that no person or firm of any kind may do an insurance business in a state without first obtaining a license. Licenses issued to domestic insurers are for indefinite terms and terminate when the business ceases to exist. Foreign and alien insurers are licensed for a term of years subject to renewal. The commissioner has the power to refuse or revoke a license, but only after observing proper procedure for a hearing and review. Certain types of insurers are exempt from licensing and certain other requirements to the extent specified in the law.

Insurance statutes are quite specific in terms of the requirements to be met in organizing an insurance business. The rules vary somewhat depending on whether the organization is mutual or stock or some type of organization not classified in the usual way. All states specify a minimum capital and surplus which an insurer must have in order to do business in the state. These minima vary and in some states may be too low. An organization wishing to organize as a stock property insurer in New York State, and willing to limit its business to a few casualty lines may start with a capital and surplus of $150,000. A stock multiple line insurer in New York State would need a capital and surplus of $1,500,000.[24] Mutual insurers are typically not required to meet the same minima as stock insurers and in some states may be admitted with assets as low as $50,000, although in addition the mutual organization must have a minimum number of policyholders varying from 20 to 1,000 depending on the state and type of business.[25] Any person or groups of persons wishing to start an insurance business must make application to the superintendent or commissioner of his (or their) state prior to entry and to the commissioner of each additional state he (or they) wish to enter.

Assets, Investments, and Deposits. The New York insurance law, as is the case with most insurance statutes, has a lengthy section dealing with rules applicable to accounting for the assets and liabilities of insurers. Admitted and nonadmitted assets are defined, types of required reserves are specified, investments and their valuation and any limitations imposed are discussed. Likewise, deposits required of insurers are specified and the responsibility of the superintendent or commissioner is outlined.

Among admitted assets are cash; investments meeting the requirements of the insurance law; premium notes; premiums in the course of collection that are not more than 90 days past due; installment

---

[24] A. L. Mayerson, "An Inside Look at Insurance Regulation," *Journal of Risk and Insurance*, XXXII (March, 1965), p. 62. The minima in New York apply not only to organizing a domestic insurer but apply as well to licensing and renewal of both domestic and nondomestic insurers to do or to continue to do business in New York State.

[25] *Ibid.* The differences between stock and mutual requirements are mostly confined to local county mutual type organizations.

premiums; notes; reinsurance recoverable by a ceding insurer (with some limitations); deposits or equities "recoverable from underwriting associations, syndicates and reinsurance funds, or from any suspended banking institutions. . ."; and other assets. In the latter two categories the superintendent may admit these assets to the extent that they are available for the recovery of losses. The types of asset listed above are the only ones that may be used in determining the financial condition of the insurer. Nonadmitted assets are such items as goodwill, trade names, agency plants, and other intangible assets; prepaid or deferred charges (with some exceptions); advances to officers and employees (with some exceptions); stock of the insurer; furniture, fixtures, automobiles, and similar items; checks returned as unpaid, and the amount by which "the aggregate bank value of investments carried in the ledger assets of such insurer exceeds the aggregate value thereof"[26] as determined by the law. The manner in which these items are reported was discussed previously.

Insurance statutes generally require that certain liabilities, labeled "reserves," are to be maintained. Specifically listed are loss or claim reserves, valuation reserves, and unearned premium reserves. The nature and importance of these reserves have been elaborated in an earlier chapter.

Investment regulations are quite complex and can only be briefly summarized here. Except for life insurance contract loans, all investments and loans must be approved by the board of directors of the insurer or by a committee of directors that has been authorized to supervise this aspect of the business. In general insurers cannot participate in the underwriting of securities in advance of their sales nor can they buy their own common stock. Insurers may not make loans to officers or directors or guarantee financial obligations of these persons.

Certain classes of securities are specified for minimum capital investments. The New York law reads as follows:

> Before investing any of its funds in any other classes of securities or types of investments, every domestic insurer shall, to the extent of an amount equal in value to the minimum capital required by law for a domestic stock corporation authorized to transact the same kinds of insurance, invest its funds only in securities of the classes described in this section which are not in default as to principal or interest. . . . Minimum capital requirements of such an insurer shall consist of the following classes of securities and not less than sixty percent of the total amount of the required minimum capital investments shall consist of the classes specified in paragraphs (*a*) and (*b*) following:
>
> *a*) Bonds or other evidences of indebtedness of the United States of America or of any of its agencies when such obligations are

[26] Taylor (ed.), *op. cit.*, p. 57.

guaranteed as to principal and interest by the United States of America.

b) Bonds, or stocks or other evidences of indebtedness which are direct obligations of the state of New York or of any county, district or municipality thereof.

c) Bonds or other evidences of indebtedness which are direct obligations of any state of the United States.

d) Mortgage loans or deeds of trust as specified in paragraphs (*a*) or (*c*) of subsection six of section eighty-one, on property located in this state.[27]

The statute continues by describing the nature of the required reserve investments. Investments representing the amount of the legal reserve may be made in the following types of securities: government obligations, corporate obligations, preferred or guaranteed stocks or shares, trustees' or receivers' obligations, acceptances and bills of exchange, mortgage loans, real estate, foreign securities, stock and evidences of indebtedness of housing companies, stock of a federal home loan bank, obligations issued or guaranteed by the international bank for reconstruction and development, and shares of a savings and loan association or building and loan association. In the case of some of these investments, such as real estate, there are various limitations and a detailed reading of the law is necessary for a complete understanding of the restrictions. There are additional restrictions for life insurers.

Foreign insurers are required to deposit securities of a specified type and amount with the commissioner of the state in which they wish to do business or with the commissioner in the state of domicile. Alien insurers must deposit securities with the appropriate state officers if they wish to do business in the United States. These deposits are for the protection of policyholders and creditors in this country.

Sales Representatives and Adjusters. The New York law, as is true of most states, requires that no one be permitted to sell insurance or act as an adjuster unless he has an appropriate license. The commissioners of the various states are responsible for administering the statutory provisions relating to licensing. Licenses have to be renewed annually or at the end of some specified term in some states, while in others they are good until revoked, even though an annual fee may be required. The license in the case of insurance agents is regarded as owned by the insurer and an agent must have a license for each insurer he represents. The law prescribes the penalties for acting without a license and also outlines the requirements that must be met in order to obtain a license.

Since agents, brokers, and adjusters deal directly with the public, and since they are legally held to the same standards of care as are

[27] *Ibid.*, pp. 65–66.

other professional persons, the question of their competence is an important one. Most states take the matter of licensing fairly seriously and require the passing of an examination before a license is issued. In New York State a prospective agent must submit a written application and provide the information required by the superintendent. Additionally, the insurer to be named in the license must submit a certificate saying that the applicant is competent and trustworthy and will be appointed to sell "such kind or kinds of insurance business as is specified in the written application, if the license applied for is issued by the superintendent."[28] After the application and certificate have been filed, the applicant must take a written examination at such time and place as is determined by the superintendent. The nature of the examination depends on the type of license being sought. A fee is charged to each person applying for the examination.

There are similar requirements for brokers, although they are somewhat more extensive including the necessity of taking courses in a degree-conferring college or university.

Any person, corporation, or association wanting to act as an independent or public adjuster must seek a license. The type of license awarded depends on the kinds of insurance claims that the prospective adjuster wants to investigate. Certain persons do not need to acquire a license to be an adjuster such as a licensed attorney in the state in question or an adjuster of maritime losses. Written examinations are required of the applicant and must be passed before a license will be issued.

Approval of Contracts. An important responsibility of the commissioner of insurance is the approval of contract forms and no such forms may be used until approval has been secured. Except for the basic fire insurance contract, there are no standard contracts in the sense that a particular form must be used without change, although in some states (e.g. Texas), no deviation is permitted from any filed form. There are some contracts, particularly in life and health insurance, that must contain certain standard provisions as required by law although the wording need not be identical for all insurers. In view of these facts it is possible for insurers to use varying language and to add provisions subject to the commissioners' approval. Insurance departments look at proposed contract forms very carefully to be sure that the language used is not misleading, that exclusions are not unreasonable, that the benefits promised are not subject to deceptive provisions.

Rates. Property and liability insurance rates are subject, in general, in every state, to the approval of the insurance commissioner.

---

[28] *Ibid.*, p. 98.

The section of the New York insurance law that relates to rates and rating organizations begins as follows: "The purpose of this article is to promote the public welfare by regulating insurance rates to the end that they shall not be excessive, inadequate, unfairly discriminatory or otherwise unreasonable and to authorize and regulate cooperative action among insurers in rate making and in other matters within the scope of this article."[29] Rating organizations must be licensed by the insurance department and their activities are subject to administrative review. Before a license will be issued the prospective organization must file with the commissioner a statement of intention, articles of association, and list of insurers that have agreed to participate as members. These organizations are subject to examination by the commissioner and their licenses may be revoked if they fail to comply with insurance department orders and regulations. Most states do not permit insurers to use rates until such time as the commissioner has approved them. The commissioner is under obligation to review filings "as soon as reasonably possible." The rating organization or the insurer filing independently must support the filing with appropriate information, which may include statistical data as well as statements based on experience and judgment. The statutes provide for hearings in the event that discriminatory, inadequate, or excessive rates have been found to exist.

Other Responsibilities of the Commissioner. Although the responsibilities previously considered are probably among the most important that the commissioner and the insurance department assume, they by no means exhaust the variety of activities that come within the scope of insurance supervision. Nor has the discussion of these activities indicated all of the matters included in the insurance statutes. The more extensive statutes, such as New York's, have articles dealing with specific types of insurance such as life, accident, health, casualty and surety, stock and mutual fire and marine insurers, reciprocal insurers and Lloyd Underwriters, title insurers, and fraternal benefit societies. These articles provide definitions of the type of insurance involved and other details of specific interest to a particular branch of the business. There are also articles dealing with merger, consolidation, and conversion of insurers; rehabilitation, liquidation, conservation, and dissolution of insurers; and taxes and fees.

As a result of Public Law 15, the insurance commissioners have responsibility for problems relating to insurance marketing, such as advertising, and for supervision of antitrust activities. Although there do not seem to be many problems of an antitrust nature currently visible, there is always a possibility that these problems may arise.

---

[29] *Ibid.*, p. 182.

PROBLEMS AND TRENDS IN REGULATION

Although the several states continue to regulate insurers operating within their jurisdictions and although the system seems to be stable and fairly effective, there is still some feeling among insurers, insureds, and the governmental authorities that the problem of regulation has still not been settled. There are two problems that are perhaps of primary importance: whether insurers should be regulated by the state or by the federal government or by some combination of the two; and the extent to which insurance rates and solvency standards should be regulated by any governmental authority.

State versus Federal Regulation. That insurance is affected with a public interest is now seldom questioned, and its regulation has long been accepted. Until the decision in the Southeastern Underwriters' case, it was assumed that such regulation was left exclusively to the states. One of the consequences of this case was the reversal of this assumption and the subsequent debate of the merits of federal versus state regulation.

Insurers have tended to favor state regulation for a number of reasons. Part of their support stems from the fact that this type of regulation has worked reasonably well and that the public generally (with perhaps, a few exceptions) has been protected from the consequences of the insolvency of insurers. There is also a feeling that regulation by the states permits more flexibility than would otherwise be the case and is more adaptable to local needs. This argument is particularly persuasive for property and liability insurers operating essentially on a statewide rather than interstate basis. There seems to be some support, too, for the notion that consumers can be more effectively heard if regulation is essentially local. Another argument for the continuation of state regulation is that the National Association of Insurance Commissioners has been effective in encouraging uniformity of practice among the states.

Against state regulation is the argument that insurance statutes are far from uniform throughout the United States and that in some areas considerable laxness has been allowed to exist. Even when legal provisions are similar, interpretations often vary. Some would argue that strong insurance laws exist in far too few states. Further, lack of uniformity in state requirements has led to a considerable amount of special procedure which is expensive and burdensome to insurers, especially those operating in all or virtually all of the states. Another problem with state regulation is that it is perhaps too easy for insurers domiciled in a particular state to lobby for special-interest legislation.

Exclusive federal regulation has been advocated by some as a way of overcoming the alleged difficulties associated with state regulation.

It has been argued that the federal government has greater power to uphold satisfactory standards and could achieve uniformity in terms of reports to be filed, forms to be issued, and in other ways eliminate the inefficiency associated with the present system. This type of uniformity cannot be achieved in the same way by the National Association of Insurance Commissioners, since this organization does not have legal authority. Federal regulation could do much to lift educational standards for agents, adjusters, and other insurance personnel, and could operate more effectively in the interest of the consumer. The federal government could, it is argued, be more effective than the states in the field of antitrust activities, rate regulation, and regulation of advertising, to name areas in which it has been particularly strong in relation to other businesses.

On the negative side, it should be pointed out that uniformity can bring about a certain amount of rigidity and might well not be responsive to local needs. It is also possible that in areas where insurers operate on a strictly local basis that the federal government would not be able to regulate certain aspects of the insurance business and state governments, of necessity, would have to participate. Thus, federal regulation would be superimposed on state regulation and would increase the costs of regulation to the public. Also, federal regulation might well result in difficult bureaucratic and political problems that would frustrate the efficient conduct of insurers.

The arguments in the debate concerning federal versus state regulation have not been resolved and discussion continues. The present system is one involving both state and federal supervision although the federal government has elected through Public Law 15 to exercise an indirect and passive role. Whether this type of system, wherein the states have almost the entire responsibility for supervision, will continue, depends to a large extent on the degree to which the states are able to demonstrate their ability to regulate insurance in a manner acceptable to Congress.

Rate Regulation. Perhaps no aspect of insurance supervision has been more throughly and inconclusively debated than that of rate regulation. The problem is complicated by the fact that the degree of rate regulation varies with type of insurance and with the state exercising the supervision. Life insurance rates, for example, do not have to be approved in any state and the same is true for ocean marine insurance. Rate approval is a matter that applies to property and liability insurance, particularly to the fire and casualty branches. Historically rate approval and the preparation of property insurance rates by rating bureaus came about as a result of alleged abuses of rate competition. The insolvency of a number of insurers was believed to be due to inadequate rates, and this result led to a desire for rate approval by the states. The National Board of Fire Underwriters (now a part of the American Insurance Association) was founded in 1866 largely for the purpose of establishing uniform rates.[30] Over the years the difficulties encountered with bureau rates and attendant problems led to the Southeastern Underwriters' case and to a reconsideration of the whole problem of rate making.

Today, state rate-regulatory laws vary. In most states bureau rates are not mandatory and insurers may file independently. Exceptions to this generalization are found in Texas, North Carolina, Louisiana, and Massachusetts for certain types of insurance, where all insurers must adhere to the same rate. Most states will not permit the use of rates until they have been approved by the commissioner, although some states, notably California, have no-prior-approval laws. One result of the variation is that compliance becomes difficult and confused, and insurers operating on an interstate basis have the added burden of meeting a multiplicity of requirements.[31]

The current practice relating to rate regulation is based on the Commissioners-All-Industry Bills, which have now been enacted in all states, although not all jurisdictions have enacted both the fire and marine and the casualty and surety bills. Some dissatisfaction has arisen with this solution to the problem for a number of reasons. Additional administrative burdens have been placed on commissioners and procedural problems have sometimes caused insurers difficulties in responding to varying circumstances. Excessiveness or inadequacy of rates has not been defined in rating laws and this fact has led to additional confusion and uncertainty. Further, separate fire and casualty laws have introduced complications in rating package contracts.

No completely satisfactory solution to rate regulation has been found. Those insurers who favor independent action in rate making believe that the emphasis on insolvency as a result of inadequate rates has been misplaced and that the failure of insurers results from "management excesses and incompetence."[32] It is not likely that self-regulation of insurers in this important area will eventuate, but continued discussion and search for an adequate solution will no doubt continue.

TAXATION OF INSURERS

One of the earliest forms of governmental supervision of insurance in the United States was the levying of premium taxes. Every state

[30] Center and Heins, *op. cit.*, p. 31.

[31] Uniform rates among the states would be discriminatory, since loss data show a considerable amount of variation from state to state even for the most detailed classification rating plans.

[32] *Ibid.*, p. 89.

now levies such taxes, usually 2 percent of the premiums received by insurers, and in addition there are various taxes and fees related to licensing and examination procedures. The states use the funds collected through taxes to support the costs of insurance departments, although they are by no means used exclusively for this purpose.

In comparatively recent times federal income taxes have been imposed on insurers. Stock insurers pay the usual corporate income tax on net underwriting profit plus net investment income. Mutual insurers and reciprocals, as a result of the Revenue Act of 1962, are taxed in much the same manner as stock insurers, although the taxing formula for mutuals and reciprocals provides for a "protection-against-loss-account." The need for this account arises from a provision in the law permitting a deferral of a comparatively small proportion of taxable income to be used over a five year period in the event underwriting losses exceed investment income.

FOR DISCUSSION

1. Discuss the extent to which government (federal or state or both) has entered into insurance as an insurer.
2. Describe in some detail the administrative arrangements and the benefits offered under the following insurance programs: federal crop insurance, old age and survivors' insurance, unemployment insurance, and Wisconsin state life insurance.
3. State the arguments that are usually given for regulating insurance. Discuss these arguments critically in terms of their basic merit, as well as in terms of comparative regulatory systems in other countries.
4. Summarize the history of insurance regulation in the United States and discuss in detail the events in this history that have had the greatest impact on insurers and their development.
5. List the arguments for and against federal regulation of insurance. To what extent does the federal government now participate in the supervision of insurance in the United States?
6. Summarize the following legal cases and state their relevance to insurance supervision. *Paul* v. *Virginia*, *Hooper* v. *California*, and *New York Life Insurance Company* v. *Deer Lodge County*.
7. What are the duties and responsibilities of the state insurance commissioners?
8. Distinguish among the following items: assets, nonadmitted assets, and ledger assets.
9. What are the main differences between the accounting methods used by insurers and those used by manufacturing firms?
10. Distinguish between prior-approval and no-prior-approval rate regulatory laws. What are the advantages and disadvantages of each?

What are the arguments for not regulating insurance rates at all?

11. What are the statutory reserves in property and liability insurance and what purpose do they serve? How are they computed and what problems arise for the insurer as a result of the way in which these reserves are determined?
12. The Subcommittee on Antitrust and Monopoly of the Committee on the Judiciary has announced plans for continuing its investigation of property insurance. Which aspects of this field will be studied and what are the objectives of this review?

BIBLIOGRAPHY

BIBLIOGRAPHY

BOOKS

ARGYLL, GEORGE DOUGLAS CAMPBELL, EIGHTH DUKE OF ARGYLL. *The Reign of Law.* 5th ed. London: Alexander Strahan, 1867.

BAINBRIDGE, JOHN. *Biography of An Idea.* Garden City, N.Y.: Doubleday and Co., Inc., 1952.

BENNET, W. H. *The History of the National Association of Insurance Agents.* Cincinnati, Ohio: The National Underwriter Co., 1955.

BICKELHAUPT, D. L. *Transition to Multiple-Line Insurance Companies.* Homewood, Ill.: Richard D. Irwin, Inc., 1961.

BRAINARD, C. H. *Automobile Insurance.* Homewood, Ill.: Richard D. Irwin, Inc., 1961.

BUGLASS, L. J. *Marine Insurance Claims American Law and Practice.* Cambridge, Maryland: Cornell Maritime Press, 1963.

BULAU, A. E. *Footprints of Assurance.* New York: The Macmillan Company, 1953.

BURKE, E. *Philosophical Enquiry into the Origin of Our Ideas of the Sublime and Beautiful.* (ed. J. T. BOULTON). New York: Columbia University Press, 1958.

CABELL, H. *The Fire Insurance Contract.* Indianapolis: The Rough Notes Co., 1922.

CARTER, NEIL. *Guide to Workmen's Compensation Claims.* New York: The Roberts Publishing Corporation, 1965.

CENTER, CHARLES C., AND HEINS, RICHARD M. (eds.). *Insurance and Government.* New York: McGraw-Hill Book Company, Inc., 1962.

JOHNS, CORYDON I. *An Introduction to Liability Claims Adjusting.* Cincinnati: The National Underwriter Company, 1965.

CRIST, G. W., JR. *Corporate Suretyship.* 2d ed. New York: The McGraw-Hill Book Company, 1950.

Cyclopedia of Insurance in the United States. Paterson, N.J.: The Index Publishing Co., 1965.

DAVIDS, L. E. *Dictionary of Insurance.* Paterson, N.J.: Littlefield, Adams, & Co., 1959.

DAYNARD, H. S. *Transportation Insurance Claims.* New York: The Roberts Publishing Corporation, 1961.

DONALDSON, JAMES H. *Casualty Claims Practice*. Homewood, Ill.: Richard D. Irwin, 1964.

Examination of Insurance Carriers. New York: The New York State Insurance Department, 1953. Vol. I.

Fire, Casualty, and Surety Bulletins. Cincinnati: National Underwriter Co.

GALLAGHER, EUGENE F. *Fire Insurance Rating Problems.* Detroit: Planet Insurance Co., 1945.

GLIDDEN, J. S. *Analytic System for the Measurement of Relative Fire Hazard and Explanation.* Chicago: J. S. Glidden, 1916.

GOLDING, E., AND KING-PAGE, B. *Lloyd's.* New York: McGraw-Hill Book Co., Inc., 1952.

A History of the Insurance Company of North America. Philadelphia: Press of Review Publishing and Printing Company, 1885.

Insurance Almanac, The. New York: The Underwriter Printing and Publishing Company, 1965.

JEVONS, W. STANLEY. *The Principles of Science.* London: Macmillan & Co., Ltd., 1874.

KENNEY, ROGER. *Fundamentals of Fire and Casualty Insurance Strength.* 2d ed. Dedham, Mass.: Kenney Insurance Studies, 1953.

KIMBALL, S. L. *Insurance and Public Policy*. Madison: University of Wisconsin Press, 1960.

LONG, J. D., AND GREGG, D. W. (eds.). *Property and Liability Insurance Handbook*. Homewood, Ill.: Richard D. Irwin, Inc., 1965.

MEHR, R. S., AND HEDGES, B. A. *Risk Management in the Business Enterprise*. Homewood, Ill.: Richard D. Irwin, Inc., 1963.

MICHELBACHER, G. F., ET AL. *Multiple-Line Insurance*. New York: McGraw-Hill Book Company, 1957.

MOWBRAY, A. H., AND BLANCHARD, R. H. *Insurance.* 5th ed. New York: McGraw-Hill Book Company, Inc., 1961.

PARK, J. A. *A System of the Law of Marine Insurance with Three Chapters on Bottomry, on Insurance on Lives, and on Insurance Against Fire*. 3d ed. Dublin: James Moore, 1742.

PATTERSON, E. W. *Cases and Materials on Insurance*. 3d and 4th eds. Brooklyn, N.Y.: The Foundation Press, Inc., 1962.

PATTERSON, E. W. *The Insurance Commissioner in the United States.* Cambridge, Mass.: Harvard University Press, 1927.

PIERCE, J. E. *Development of Comprehensive Insurance for the Household*. Homewood, Illinois: Richard D. Irwin, Inc., 1958.

REED, PRENTICE B. *Adjustment of Property Losses*. New York: McGraw-Hill, 1953.

REED, PRENTICE B., *et al.* *Loss Adjusting*. New York: The Underwriter Printing and Publishing Co., 1947.

TAYLOR, PAUL R. (ed.). *Insurance Law of the State of New York.* Albany, N.Y.: Williams Press, Inc., 1950.

Richards, G. *Laws of Insurance.* 4th ed. New York: Baker, Voorhis & Co., 1932.

Sawyer, E. W. *Insurance as Interstate Commerce.* New York: McGraw-Hill Book Company, Inc., 1945.

Trennery, C. P. *The Origin and Early History of Insurance.* London: P. S. King & Sons, Ltd., 1926.

Walford, C. *Insurance Cyclopedia.* London: Charles and Edwin Layton, 1871. Vol. II.

Willett, A. H. *The Economic Theory of Risk and Insurance.* New York: Columbia University Press, 1961.

Williams, C. A., Jr. *Price Discrimination in Property and Liability Insurance.* Minneapolis: The University of Minnesota Press, 1959.

Williams, C. A., Jr., and Heins, R. M. *Risk Management and Insurance.* New York: McGraw-Hill Book Co., 1964.

Young, K. *Social Psychology.* New York: A. A. Knopf, Inc., 1930.

ARTICLES AND BROCHURES

"Agents Qualification and Licensing Law," *Proceedings of the National Association of Insurance Commissioners,* 1950.

Announcement of the Griffith Memorial Foundation. Columbus, Ohio: Griffith Memorial Foundation.

Arina, S. W. " 'Engineering' the Big Risk," *The Journal of Insurance Information,* (September–October, 1966).

Bateman, J. C. "The Public Relations Function in our Society," New York: The Insurance Information Institute, 1964.

Beveridge, William, Sir. *Insurance for All and Everything, the New Way.* Series VII (London, 1924).

Bulletin of the Commission on Insurance Terminology, Vol. I, No. 4 (October, 1965).

Business Week. July 26, 1941.

Carroll, Frederick A. "Accountant's Third Party Liability," *Insurance Counsel Journal,* XXXIII (April, 1966).

Catastrophe Loss Adjustment Procedure. New York: National Board of Fire Underwriters, 1952.

Cristy, James. "Selling Insurance to Risk Managers," *The National Insurance Buyer,* XIII (September, 1966).

d'Adolf, Stuart V. "I. When Disaster Strikes . . . ," *American Agency Bulletin,* LXIII (September, 1965).

Eastern Underwriter. December 12, 1958.

Friedman, Milton, and Savage, L. J. "The Utility Analysis of Choices Involving Risk," The Journal of Political Economy, Vol. LVI, No. 4 (August, 1948).

Harnett, B., and Thornton, J. U. "Insurable Interest in Property," *Columbia Law Review,* (December, 1948).

Hearings Before the Subcommittee on Antitrust and Monopoly of the Committee on the Judiciary, United States Senate. 86th Cong., 1st sess., Part 5.

Insurance Facts. New York: Insurance Information Institute.

Insurance World. New Haven, Conn.: Yale Daily News, 1956.

IVRY, DAVID A. "The Corporate Insurance Manager and Employee Benefit Plans," *The Journal of Insurance*, XXXIII (March, 1966).

MARTIN, W. P. "Medical Malpractice," *Insurance Counsel Journal*, XXXIII (April, 1966).

MATTHEWS, DEAN E. "Is Farm Market Untapped?" *American Agency Bulletin*, Vol. 63, No. 8 (April, 1966).

MAYERSON, ALLEN L. "An Inside Look at Insurance Regulations," *The Journal of Risk and Insurance*, XXXII, No. 1 (March, 1965).

NATIONAL ASSOCIATION OF INSURANCE COMMISSIONERS. *Report of Committee on Rates and Rating Organizations*, June 9, 1948.

NATIONAL BOARD OF FIRE UNDERWRITERS. *Standard Schedule for Grading Cities and Towns of the United States with Reference to Their Fire Defenses and Physical Conditions*, New York, 1942.

NATIONAL BUREAU OF CASUALTY UNDERWRITERS. Pamphlet published by the Bureau.

National Underwriter, The. November 12, 1965.

Proceedings of the 83rd Annual Meeting. San Francisco: Insurance Underwriters Association of the Pacific, 1959.

ROTH, R. J. "The Rating of Crop-Hail Insurance."

Sample Insurance Policies for Property and Liability Coverages. New York: Insurance Information Institute, 1966.

SCHMITT, R. W. "Underwriting Contract Bonds," *The National Underwriter*, October 15, 1965.

Standard Universal Schedule for Rating Mercantile Risks. January, 1902.

State Workmen's Compensation Laws. Washington, D.C.: U.S. Department of Labor, Bureau of Labor Standards, Bulletin #212, Revised 1964.

VAUGHAN, EMMETT J. "What Is Insurable Value?" *The American Agency Bulletin*, Vol. LXIII (September, 1965).

Wall Street Journal, The. Friday, April 16, 1965.

Yearbook. National Association of Mutual Insurance Companies, 1962.

APPENDIXES

THE CONTRACTS and forms reproduced in this section are those not ordinarily contained in published kits of contracts and to which some reference has been made in the text.

APPENDIX A

Appendix A—Earthquake or Volcanic Eruption Endorsement

UNIFORM STANDARD

FORM No. 53
(Edition Feb. '59)

EARTHQUAKE OR VOLCANIC ERUPTION ENDORSEMENT FOR DWELLING PROPERTY

(FOR ATTACHMENT ONLY TO A FIRE INSURANCE POLICY WRITTEN SUBJECT TO THE EXTENDED COVERAGE ENDORSEMENT, DWELLING BUILDING(S) AND CONTENTS - BROAD FORM OR DWELLING BUILDING(S) SPECIAL FORM)

In consideration of the premium for this coverage shown on the first page of this policy, and subject to provisions and stipulations (hereinafter referred to as "provisions") herein and in the policy to which this endorsement is attached, including riders and endorsements thereon, the coverage of this policy is extended to include direct loss by **Earthquake or Volcanic Eruption.**

This endorsement does not increase the amount or amounts of insurance provided in the policy to which it is attached.

If this policy covers on two or more items, the provisions of this endorsement shall apply to each item separately.

Substitution of Terms: In the application of the provisions of this policy, including riders and endorsements (but not this endorsement), to the perils covered by this Earthquake or Volcanic Eruption Endorsement, wherever the word "fire" appears there shall be substituted therefor the peril involved or the loss caused thereby, as the case requires.

Exclusions: This Company shall not be liable under this endorsement for any loss caused directly or indirectly by explosion, fire, lightning, or flood of any nature, or by tidal wave, whether or not the same be caused by or be attributable to Earthquake or Volcanic Eruption.

Deductible Clause: This Company shall be liable only when loss to property covered hereunder exceeds 2% of the actual cash value in any one occurrence and then only for its proportion of such excess. If, however, the insured makes claim under the terms of the Replacement Cost Coverage Clause, if any, of this policy (as applicable to buildings) this Company shall be liable only when loss exceeds 2% of the full replacement cost and then only for its proportion of such excess.

The provisions of this Loss Deductible Clause shall not apply to insurance covering Rental Value or Additional Living Expense.

Earthquake—Defined and Limited: Each loss by Earthquake shall constitute a single claim hereunder; provided, if more than one earthquake shock shall occur within any period of seventy-two hours during the term of this endorsement, such earthquake shocks shall be deemed to be a single earthquake within the meaning hereof. This Company shall not be liable for any loss caused by any earthquake shock occurring before the effective date and time of this endorsement, nor for any loss occurring after the expiration date and time of this policy.

Apportionment Clause: This Company shall not be liable for a greater proportion of any loss less the amount of deductible from Earthquake or Volcanic Eruption than (1) the amount of insurance under this policy bears to the whole amount of fire insurance covering the property, or which would have covered the property except for the existence of this insurance, whether collectible or not, and whether or not such other fire insurance covers against Earthquake or Volcanic Eruption; (2) nor for a greater proportion of any loss less the amount of deductible than the amount hereby insured bears to all insurance, whether collectible or not, covering in any manner such loss, or which would have covered such loss except for the existence of this insurance; except if any type of insurance other than fire extended to cover Earthquake or Volcanic Eruption applies to any loss to which this insurance also applies, or would have applied to any such loss except for the existence of this insurance, the limit of liability of each type of insurance for such loss, hereby designated as "joint loss", shall first be determined as if it were the only insurance, and this type of insurance shall be liable for no greater proportion of joint loss than the limit of its liability for such loss bears to the sum of all such limits. The liability of this Company (under this endorsement) for such joint loss shall be limited to its proportionate part of the aggregate limit of this and all other insurance of the same type. The words "joint loss", as used in the foregoing, mean that portion of the loss in excess of the highest deductible, if any, to which this endorsement and other types of insurance above referred to both apply.

Nuclear Exclusion: Loss by nuclear reaction or nuclear radiation or radioactive contamination, all whether controlled or uncontrolled, is not insured against by this endorsement, whether such loss be direct or indirect, proximate or remote, or be in whole or in part caused by, contributed to, or aggravated by earthquake or volcanic eruption as insured against by this endorsement.

Provisions Applicable Only when this Endorsement is attached to a Policy Covering Additional Living Expense, Rents or Consequential Loss: When this Endorsement is attached to a policy covering Additional Living Expense, Rents or Consequential Loss, the term "direct," as applied to loss means loss, as limited and conditioned in such policy, resulting from direct loss to described property from Earthquake or Volcanic Eruption.

Form No. 53. (2-59)

CAUTION

WHEN THIS ENDORSEMENT IS ATTACHED TO ONE FIRE POLICY, THE INSURED SHOULD SECURE LIKE COVERAGE ON ALL FIRE POLICIES COVERING THE SAME PROPERTY.

APPENDIX B

Appendix B—Special Extended Coverage Endorsement

UNIFORM STANDARD **FORM NO. 61S**
(Edition Sept. '61)

SPECIAL EXTENDED COVERAGE ENDORSEMENT

(With Respect To Any Item(s) Of This Policy To Which This Endorsement Applies, The Extended Coverage Endorsement (if any) Attached To This Policy Is Superseded By This Endorsement)

1. COVERAGE: In consideration of the premium for this coverage, and subject to provisions herein and in the policy to which this endorsement is attached including endorsements thereon, THIS POLICY IS EXTENDED TO INSURE AGAINST ALL OTHER RISKS OF DIRECT PHYSICAL LOSS, EXCEPT AS HEREINAFTER PROVIDED.

2. DEDUCTIBLE:

The sum of $100 shall be deducted from the amount of loss resulting from any peril other than (1) windstorm or hailstorm, or (2) fire, lightning, aircraft, vehicles, smoke, explosion, riot or civil commotion. This deductible shall apply separately to each building or structure.

This Deductible shall not apply to insurance covering Business Interruption, Tuition Fees, Extra Expense, Rent or Rental Value or Leasehold Interest.

3. EXCLUSIONS:

This Policy does not Insure Against Loss—

A. By wear and tear, deterioration, rust or corrosion, mould, wet or dry rot; inherent or latent defect; smog; smoke, vapor or gas from agricultural or industrial operations; mechanical breakdown, including rupture or bursting caused by centrifugal force; settling, cracking, shrinkage, bulging or expansion of pavements, foundations, walls, floors, roofs or ceilings; animals, birds, vermin, termites or other insects; unless such loss results from a peril not excluded in this policy. If loss by a peril not excluded in this policy ensues, then this Company shall be liable for only such ensuing loss.

B. Caused by, resulting from, contributed to or aggravated by earthquake, volcanic eruption, landslide or any other earth movement; unless loss by fire or explosion not excluded in this policy ensues, and then this Company shall be liable for only such ensuing loss.

C. Caused by, resulting from, contributed to or aggravated by any of the following—

(1) flood, surface water, waves, tidal water or tidal wave, overflow of streams or other bodies of water, or spray from any of the foregoing, all whether driven by wind or not:

(2) water which backs up through sewers or drains;

(3) water below the surface of the ground including that which exerts pressure on or flows, seeps or leaks through sidewalks, driveways, foundations, walls, basement or other floors, or through doors, windows or any other openings in such sidewalks, driveways, foundations, walls or floors;

unless loss by fire or explosion not excluded in this policy ensues, and then this Company shall be liable for only such ensuing loss.

D. By theft of any property which at the time of loss is not an integral part of a building or structure (except direct loss by pillage and looting occurring during and at the immediate place of a riot or civil commotion), unless loss by a peril not excluded in this policy ensues from theft or attempted theft, and then this Company shall be liable for only such ensuing loss.

E. By unexplained or mysterious disappearance of any property, or shortage disclosed on taking inventory; or caused by any wilful or dishonest act or omission of the Insured or any associate, employee or agent of any Insured.

F. By vandalism, malicious mischief, theft or attempted theft, if the described building(s) had been vacant beyond a period of 30 consecutive days immediately preceding the loss, unless loss by a peril not excluded in this policy ensues, and then this Company shall be liable for only such ensuing loss.

G. Occasioned directly or indirectly by enforcement of any local or state ordinance or law regulating the construction, repair or demolition of buildings or structures.

This Policy does not Insure Against Loss to—

H. Plumbing, heating, air conditioning or fire protective systems or other equipment or appliances, or for loss by leakage or overflow from such systems, equipment or appliances, caused by or resulting from freezing while the described building(s) is vacant or unoccupied, unless the Insured shall have exercised due diligence with respect to maintaining heat in the building(s) or unless such systems, equipment and appliances had been drained and the water supply shut off during such vacancy or unoccupancy.

I. Steam boilers, steam pipes, steam turbines or steam engines, caused by any condition or occurrence within such boilers, pipes, turbines or engines (except direct loss resulting from explosion of accumulated gases or unconsumed fuel within the firebox, or combustion chamber, of any fired vessel or within the flues or passages which conduct the gases of combustion therefrom); and this policy does not insure against loss by explosion of steam boilers, steam pipes, steam turbines or steam engines, if owned by, leased by or operated under the control of the Insured, or for any ensuing loss except by fire or explosion not excluded in this policy, and then this Company shall be liable for only such ensuing loss.

J. Hot water boilers or to other equipment for heating water, caused by any condition or occurrence within such boilers or equipment, other than an explosion.

K. Electrical appliances, devices, fixtures or wiring, caused by artificially generated electrical currents, unless loss by fire or explosion not excluded in this policy ensues, and then this Company shall be liable for only such ensuing loss.

L. Glass, unless caused by fire, lightning, wind, hail, aircraft, vehicles, discharge from fire protective or building service equipment, explosion, riot or civil commotion, and then only to the extent that such perils are insured against in this policy.

M. Fences, pavements, swimming pools and related equipment, retaining walls, bulkheads, piers, wharves or docks, when covered under this policy, caused by freezing or thawing, impact of water craft, or by the pressure or weight of ice or water whether driven by wind or not.

N. Metal smokestacks nor, when outside of buildings, to cloth awnings, signs, radio or television antennas including their lead-in wiring, masts or towers, caused by ice, snow or sleet, nor by wind or hail unless liability therfor is assumed in the form attached to this policy or by endorsement hereon.

O. Lawns, trees, shrubs or plants, when covered under this policy, unless caused by fire, lightning, aircraft, explosion, riot or civil commotion, and then only to the extent that such perils are insured against in this policy.

P. The interior of buildings, caused by rain, snow, sand or dust, whether driven by wind or not, unless: (1) the building(s) shall first sustain an actual damage to roof or walls by the direct action of wind or hail and then this Company shall be liable for loss to the interior of the building(s) as may be caused by rain, snow, sand or dust entering the building(s) through openings in the roof or walls made by direct action of wind or hail; or (2) such loss results from fire, lightning, aircraft, vehicles, explosion, riot or civil commotion, vandalism or malicious mischief, to the extent that such perils are insured against in this policy

Q. Buildings or structures in process of construction, including materials and supplies therefor, when covered under this policy, unless caused by fire, lightning, wind, hail, aircraft, vehicles, smoke, explosion, riot or civil commotion, vandalism or malicious mischief, and then only to the extent that such perils are insured against in this policy.

R. Any property undergoing alterations, repairs, installations or servicing, including materials and supplies therefor, if directly attributable to the operations or work being performed thereon, unless loss by a peril not excluded in this policy ensues, and then this Company shall be liable for only such ensuing loss.

THE PROVISIONS PRINTED ON THE BACK OF THIS ENDORSEMENT ARE HEREBY REFERRED TO AND MADE A PART HEREOF.

Appendix B—Special Extended Coverage Endorsement (Continued)

War Risk Exclusion (This clause applies to all perils except fire and lightning, which perils are otherwise provided for in this policy): This Company shall not be liable for loss caused directly or indirectly by (a) hostile or warlike action in time of peace or war, including action in hindering, combating or defending against an actual, impending or expected attack, (1) by any government or sovereign power (de jure or de facto), or by any authority maintaining or using military, naval or air forces; or (2) by military, naval or air forces; or (3) by an agent of any such government, power, authority or forces, it being understood that any discharge, explosion or use of any weapon of war employing nuclear fission or fusion shall be conclusively presumed to be such a hostile or warlike action by such a government, power, authority or forces; (b) insurrection, rebellion, revolution, civil war, usurped power, or action taken by governmental authority in hindering, combating or defending against such an occurrence.

Nuclear Exclusion (This clause applies to all perils except fire and lightning, which perils are otherwise provided for in the Nuclear Clause attached to this policy): Loss by nuclear reaction or nuclear radiation or radioactive contamination, all whether controlled or uncontrolled, or due to any act or condition incident to any of the foregoing, is not insured against by this policy, whether such loss be direct or indirect, proximate or remote, or be in whole or in part caused by, contributed to, or aggravated by any of the perils insured against by this policy.

4. **OTHER PROVISIONS:**

A. This endorsement does not increase the amount(s) of insurance provided in this policy.

B. If this policy covers on two or more items, this endorsement shall apply separately to each item to which this endorsement applies.

C. A claim for loss under this endorsement, except as provided under Exclusions F. and H., shall not be barred because of change of occupancy, nor because of vacancy or unoccupancy.

D. The term "riot or civil commotion", as used in Sections 2, 3.D., 3.L., 3.O., 3.P., and 3.Q., shall include direct loss by acts of striking employees of the owner or tenant(s) of the described buildings while occupied by said striking employees and shall also include direct loss from pillage and looting occurring during and at the immediate place of a riot or civil commotion.

5. **APPORTIONMENT:** This Company shall not be liable for a greater proportion of any loss less the amount of deductible, if any, from any peril or perils insured against by this endorsement than (1) the amount of insurance under this policy bears to the whole amount of fire insurance covering the property, or which would have covered the property except for the existence of this insurance, whether collectible or not, and whether or not such other fire insurance insures against the additional peril or perils insured against hereunder, nor (2) for a greater proportion of any loss less the amount of deductible, if any, than the amount hereby insured bears to all insurance whether collectible or not, covering in any manner such loss, or which would have covered such loss except for the existence of this insurance; except if any type of insurance other than fire extended to cover additional perils or windstorm insurance applies to any loss to which this insurance also applies, or would have applied to any such loss except for the existence of this insurance the limit of liability of each type of insurance for such loss, hereby designated as "joint loss," shall first be determined as if it were the only insurance, and this type of insurance shall be liable for no greater proportion of joint loss than the limit of its liability for such loss bears to the sum of all such limits. The liability of this Company (under this form) for such joint loss shall be limited to its proportionate part of the aggregate limit of this and all other insurance of the same type. The words "joint loss," as used in the foregoing, mean that portion of the loss in excess of the highest deductible, if any, to which this form and other types of insurance above referred to both apply.

6. **PROVISIONS APPLICABLE ONLY WHEN THIS ENDORSEMENT IS ATTACHED TO A POLICY COVERING BUSINESS INTERRUPTION, TUITION FEES, EXTRA EXPENSE, RENT OR RENTAL VALUE, LEASEHOLD INTEREST OR OTHER CONSEQUENTIAL LOSS:** The term "direct," as applied to loss, means loss, as limited and conditioned in such policy, resulting from direct loss to described property from the peril(s) insured against; and while the business of the owner or tenant(s) of the described building(s) is interrupted by a strike at the described location, this Company shall not be liable for any loss due to interference by any person(s) with rebuilding, repairing or replacing the property damaged or destroyed or with the resumption or continuation of business.

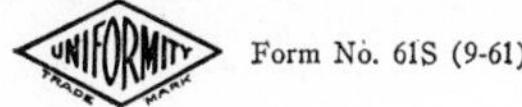

Form No. 61S (9-61)

CAUTION

WHEN THIS ENDORSEMENT IS ATTACHED TO ONE FIRE POLICY, THE INSURED SHOULD SECURE LIKE COVERAGE ON ALL FIRE POLICIES COVERING THE SAME PROPERTY.

APPENDIX C

Appendix C—Office Contents Special Form

COINSURANCE CONTRACT

OCSF 1
(Ed. 11-61)

OFFICE CONTENTS SPECIAL FORM

Insurance attaches only to those items described on the first page of this policy for which an amount is shown in the space provided therefor and for not exceeding said amount.

All provisions of this form shall apply separately to each item of insurance covered, except as otherwise specifically provided.

I. INSURING AGREEMENT

In consideration of the provisions, stipulations and agreements, and payment of premium as provided herein, this Company insures the Insured named on the face of the policy against all risks of direct physical loss of or to the property covered, except as provided elsewhere in this policy.

II. PROPERTY COVERED

This policy covers: Business Personal Property of the Insured usual to the office occupancy of the Insured including furniture, fixtures, equipment and supplies, or similar property of others held by the Insured for which the Insured is liable, all while in the premises, except as provided elsewhere in this policy.

This Coverage shall also include:

1. Tenants Improvements and Betterments (meaning the Insured's use interest in fixtures, alterations, installations or additions comprising a part of the building occupied but not owned by the Insured and made or acquired at the expense of the Insured exclusive of rent paid by the Insured, but which are not legally subject to removal by the Insured).
2. Expense incurred in the removal of all debris of the property covered hereunder which may be occasioned by loss by a peril insured against. The total amount recoverable under this policy shall not exceed the total limit of liability stipulated for each item herein.

III. PROPERTY SUBJECT TO LIMITATIONS

A. The following property is subject to these additional limitations:

1. Glass, glassware, statuary, marbles, bric-a-brac, porcelains and other articles of a fragile or brittle nature are covered against loss by breakage only if directly caused by the "specified perils". This limitation shall not apply to lenses of photographic or scientific instruments.

2. Neon, automatic and electric signs at the described location(s) are covered, but only against loss by the "specified perils" other than vandalism and malicious mischief.

3. Steam boilers, steam pipes, steam turbines and steam engines are not covered against loss caused by bursting, rupture, cracking or explosion originating therein (other than explosion of accumulated gases or unconsumed fuel within a fire box or combustion chamber).

4. Machines and machinery are not covered against loss caused by rupture, bursting or disintegration of their rotating or moving parts resulting from centrifugal or reciprocating force.

B. The term **"specified perils"** appearing in this section shall mean direct loss by fire, lightning, aircraft, explosion, riot, civil commotion, smoke, vehicles, windstorm or hail to property contained in any building, vandalism and malicious mischief, leakage or accidental discharge from automatic sprinkler systems.

IV. EXTENSIONS OF COVERAGE

A. Off-Premises
Coverage under this policy includes loss to property covered while temporarily away from the premises (not exceeding thirty consecutive days), but within the 48 contiguous states of the United States of America, the District of Columbia and in transit within and between such places, and in transit between such places and Canada, for up to 10% of the amount specified for all contributing insurance but not exceeding $10,000 in any one occurrence.

B. Extra Expense
Coverage under this policy includes the extra expense necessarily incurred by the Insured to continue normal office operations which are interrupted as a result of loss by a peril insured against to the property covered hereunder, while in the premises, or to the building containing the same, but only for the period of time required with the exercise of due diligence and dispatch to restore normal operations. The liability of this Company under this extension shall be 10% of the amount specified for all contributing insurance but not exceeding $1,000 in any one occurrence.

C. Currency, Money and Stamps
Coverage under this policy includes loss of currency, money and stamps in the premises, or while being conveyed outside the premises by the Insured, or by an employee of the Insured. The liability of this Company under this extension shall not exceed $250 in any one occurrence.

D. Personal Effects
The Insured may apply up to 5% of the amount specified for all contributing insurance to cover loss to the following:

1. Business Personal Property belonging to officers and partners, if not otherwise insured;
2. Personal Effects, the property of the Insured or others in the premises of the Insured, if not otherwise insured;

caused by fire, lightning, aircraft, explosion, riot, civil commotion, smoke, vehicles, windstorm or hail, vandalism and malicious mischief, leakage or accidental discharge from automatic sprinkler systems. At the option of this Company, losses to property of others covered under this extension may be adjusted with and payable to the Insured.

E. Valuable Papers and Records
Coverage under this policy includes the extra expenses necessarily incurred in the reproduction of books of account, manuscripts, drawings, card index systems and other business records, all the property of the Insured. The liability of this company under this extension shall not exceed $500 in any one occurrence.

F. Theft Damage to Buildings
This policy includes loss (except by fire or explosion) to that part of the building(s) occupied by the Insured and containing property covered, and to equipment therein pertaining to the service of the building directly resulting from theft (including attempt thereat), provided the Insured is the owner of such building or equipment or is liable for such damage, but in no event shall this coverage apply to glass (other than glass building blocks) or to any lettering or ornamentation thereon.

The provisions of this Section do not increase the limits of liability or the amounts recoverable as specified or provided for elsewhere in this policy. In no event shall this company be liable for more than its pro-rata share of the limits of liability set forth in the foregoing extensions of coverage.

V. EXCLUSIONS

A. This policy does not cover the following:

1. Property for sale; samples or merchandise in the care, custody or control of salesmen away from the premises.

2. Currency, money, stamps, bullion, notes, securities, deeds, accounts, bills, evidences of debt, letters of credit and tickets, except to the extent provided for in Section IV;

3. Property shipped by mail from the time it passes into the custody of the Post Office Department.

4. Fur, fur garments, jewelry and watches, watch movements, jewels, pearls, precious and semi-precious stones, gold, silver, platinum and other precious alloys or metals;

5. Property which is more specifically insured in whole or in part under this or any other contract of insurance.

6. Animals, pets, aircraft, watercraft including motors, equipment and accessories (except rowboats and canoes, while out of the water and on the described premises) and automobiles including self-propelled vehicles and machines, except motorized equipment not licensed for use on public thoroughfares and operated principally on the premises of the Insured.

B. This policy does not insure against loss caused by:

1. Earthquake, volcanic eruption, landslide or other earth movement; unless loss by fire or explosion ensues, and then only for such ensuing loss. This exclusion does not apply to property in transit;

2. Unexplained or mysterious disappearance of property (except property in the custody of carriers for hire); or shortage of property disclosed on taking inventory;

3. Actual work upon or installation of property covered, latent defect, failure, breakdown or derangement of machines or machinery, faulty materials or workmanship; unless loss by fire or explosion ensues and then only for such ensuing loss;

4. Electrical injury or disturbance caused by electrical currents artificially generated unless loss by fire ensues, and then only for such ensuing loss;

5. Delay, loss of market, interruption of business, nor consequential loss of any nature;

6. Inherent vice, wear and tear, marring or scratching, gradual deterioration, moths, vermin, dampness or dryness of atmosphere, changes in temperature, rust or corrosion;

7. Theft (including attempt thereat) from any private passenger type automobile, station wagon, motorcycle, or motorscooter, occurring while such vehicle is unattended, unless the property is contained in a fully enclosed and securely locked body or compartment and theft results from forcible entry, evidenced by visible marks. This exclusion shall not apply to property in the custody of carriers for hire;

8. Voluntary parting with title or possession of any property by the Insured or others to whom the property may be entrusted (except by carriers for hire) if induced to do so by any fraudulent scheme, trick, device or false pretense;

9. Any fraudulent, dishonest or criminal act done by or at the instigation of any Insured, partner or joint adventurer in or of any Insured, an officer, director or trustee of any Insured; pilferage, appropriation or concealment of any property covered due to any fraudulent, dishonest or criminal act of any employee while working or otherwise, or agent of any Insured, or any person to whom the property covered may be entrusted, other than any carrier for hire;

10. Rain, snow or sleet to property in the open (other than property in the custody of carriers for hire);

11. Any legal proceeding;

12. Enforcement of any local or state ordinance or law regulating the construction, repair, or demolition of building(s) or structure(s) unless such liability is otherwise specifically assumed by endorsement hereon;

C. This Company shall not be liable for loss caused by:

1. hostile or warlike action in time of peace or war, including action in hindering, combating, or defending against an actual, impending or expected attack, (a) by any government or sovereign power (de jure or de facto), or by any authority maintaining or using military, naval or air forces; or (b) by military, naval or air forces; or (c) by an agent of any such government, power, authority or forces, it being understood that any discharge, explosion or use of any weapon of war employing nuclear fission or fusion shall be conclusively presumed to be such a hostile or warlike action by such a government, power, authority or forces;

2. insurrection, rebellion, revolution, civil war, usurped power, or action taken by governmental authority in hindering, combating or defending against such an occurrence, seizure or destruction under quarantine or customs regulations, confiscation by order of any government or public authority, or risks of contraband or illegal transportation or trade.

This exclusion does not apply to fire and lightning, such exclusion being otherwise provided for on Page 2 of this policy.

D. **NUCLEAR EXCLUSION:** Loss by nuclear reaction or nuclear radiation or radioactive contamination, all whether controlled or uncontrolled, or due to any act or condition incident to any of the foregoing, is not insured against by this policy, whether such loss be direct or indirect, proximate or remote, or be in whole or in part caused by, contributed to, or aggravated by any of the perils insured against by this policy; and nuclear reaction or nuclear radiation or radioactive contamination, all whether controlled or uncontrolled, is not "explosion" or "smoke."

(This clause applies to all perils insured against hereunder except the perils of fire and lightning, which are otherwise provided for in the Nuclear Clause elsewhere in this policy).

E. **WATER EXCLUSION:** This policy does not insure against loss caused by, resulting from, contributed to or aggravated by any of the following:

1. flood, surface water, waves, tidal water or tidal wave, overflow of streams or other bodies of water, or spray from any of the foregoing, all whether driven by wind or not;

2. water which backs up through sewers or drains;

3. water below the surface of the ground including that which exerts pressure on or flows, seeps or leaks through sidewalks, driveways, foundations, walls, basement or other floors, or through doors, windows or any other openings in such sidewalks, driveways, foundations, walls or floors;

unless loss by fire or explosion ensues, and this Company shall then be liable only for such ensuing loss; but these exclusions shall not apply to property in due course of transit or to loss arising from theft.

VI. COINSURANCE CLAUSE

This Company shall not be liable for a greater proportion of any loss less the amount of deductible, if any, of or to the property described herein than the amount of insurance bears to the percentage specified on the first page of this policy of the actual cash value of the property covered under Section II, at the time such loss shall happen, nor for more than the proportion which this policy bears to the total contributing insurance thereon.

In the event that the aggregate claim for any loss is both less than ten thousand dollars ($10,000) and less than five percent (5%) of the total amount of contributing insurance upon the property described herein at the time such loss occurs, no special inventory or appraisement of the undamaged property shall be required, provided, however, that nothing herein shall be construed to waive the application of the first paragraph of this clause.

This clause shall apply separately to each item of insurance covered.

Cost of removal of debris shall not be considered in the determination of actual cash value when applying the Coinsurance Clause.

This clause shall not apply to Section IV, Extensions of Coverage.

Appendix C—Office Contents Special Form (Concluded)

VII. DEDUCTIBLE CLAUSE

Each loss shall be adjusted separately and from the amount of each such adjusted loss the sum of $50 shall be deducted or, if there is contributing insurance, this Company's pro-rata share thereof. When loss is between $50 and $500, this Company shall be liable for 111% of loss in excess of $50; and when loss is $500 or more, this deductible shall not apply. This deductible shall not apply to loss by fire, lightning, aircraft, explosion, riot, civil commotion, smoke, vehicles, windstorm or hail to property contained in any building, vandalism and malicious mischief, leakage or accidental discharge from automatic sprinkler systems, burglary or robbery; loss of or to property in transit while in the custody of carriers for hire; or loss resulting from collision, upset or overturn of a motor vehicle.

VIII. VALUATION

Subject to the provisions and stipulations of this policy the following valuations of property are established:

A. Property of Others — the amount for which the Insured is liable but in no event to exceed actual cash value.

B. Tenants Improvements and Betterments —

1. If repaired or replaced within a reasonable time after loss, at the expense of the Insured, the actual cash value of the damaged or destroyed property;
2. If not repaired or replaced within a reasonable time, after loss, that proportion of the original cost of the damaged or destroyed property which the unexpired term of the lease or rental agreement, whether written or oral, in effect at the time of loss bears to the period(s) from the date(s) such Improvements or Betterments were made to the expiration date of the lease;
3. If repaired or replaced at the expense of others for the use of the Insured, there shall be no liability hereunder.

C. Books of account, manuscripts, drawings, and other records (except film, tape, wire or other recording media), card-index systems for not exceeding the cost of blank books, blank cards and other materials.

D. Film, tape, wire or other recording media for not exceeding the cost of unexposed or blank film, tape, wire or other recording media.

E. All other property at actual cash value.

IX. SPECIAL AGREEMENTS

A. **PREMISES:** The unqualified word "premises" means the interior of that portion of any building at the location(s) designated in this Policy occupied as an office by the Insured.

B. **LOSS CLAUSE:** Any loss hereunder shall not reduce the amount of this policy.

C. **EXAMINATION OF RECORDS:** Any duly authorized representative of this Company, shall be permitted at all reasonable times to inspect the property covered hereunder and to examine the Insured's books, records and such policies as relates to any property covered hereunder. This inspection or examination shall not waive nor in any manner affect any of the terms or conditions of this policy.

D. **OTHER INSURANCE:** If there is available to the Insured, or any other interested party, any insurance, whether collectible or not, which would apply in the absence of this policy, the insurance under this policy shall apply only as excess insurance over such "Other Insurance".

E. **CONTRIBUTING INSURANCE:** Contributing insurance shall mean insurance written in the name of the Insured and upon the identical plan, terms, conditions and provisions contained in this policy and shall not be deemed to be other insurance.

F. **PERMITS AND USE:** Except as otherwise provided permission is hereby granted:

1. for any building to be and remain vacant or unoccupied without limit of time;
2. for existing and increased hazards and for any change in occupancy or use of the premises.

G. **NO CONTROL:**

This insurance shall not be prejudiced:

1. by any act or neglect of the owner of any building if the Insured is not the owner thereof, or by any act or neglect of any occupant (other than the Insured) of any building, when such act or neglect of the owner or occupant is not within the control of the Insured, or
2. by failure of the Insured to comply with any warranty or condition contained in any form or endorsement attached to this policy with regard to any portion of the premises over which the Insured has no control.

H. **PROTECTIVE SAFEGUARDS:** It is a condition of this insurance that the Insured shall maintain so far as is within his control such protective safeguards as were in effect at the time of attachment of this insurance. Failure to maintain such protective safeguards shall suspend this insurance, only as respects the location or situation affected, for the time of such discontinuance.

I. **PROTECTION OF PROPERTY:** In case of loss, it shall be lawful and necessary for the Insured, his or their factors, servants and assigns, to sue, labor, and travel for, in and about the defense, safeguard and recovery of the property insured hereunder, or any part thereof, without prejudice to this insurance, nor shall the acts of the Insured or the Company, in recovering, saving and preserving the property insured in case of loss be considered a waiver or an acceptance of abandonment. The expenses so incurred shall be borne by the Insured and the Company proportionately to the extent of their respective interests.

J. **NUCLEAR CLAUSE:** The word "fire" in this policy or endorsements attached hereto is not intended to and does not embrace nuclear reaction or nuclear radiation or radioactive contamination, all whether controlled or uncontrolled, and loss by nuclear reaction or nuclear radiation or radioactive contamination is not intended to be and is not insured against by this policy or said endorsements, whether such loss be direct or indirect, proximate or remote, or be in whole or in part caused by, contributed to, or aggravated by "fire" or any other perils insured against by this policy or said endorsements; however, subject to the foregoing and all provisions of this policy, direct loss by "fire" resulting from nuclear reaction or nuclear radiation or radioactive contamination is insured against by this policy.

K. **NO BENEFIT TO BAILEE:** This insurance shall in no wise inure directly or indirectly to the benefit of any carrier or other bailee.

L. **SUBROGATION:** In the event of any payment under this policy, the Company shall be subrogated to the Insured's rights of recovery therefor against any person, organization or government, and the Insured shall execute and deliver instruments and papers and do whatever else is necessary to secure such rights.

M. **IMPAIRMENT OF RECOVERY:** Except as noted below, this Company shall not be bound to pay any loss if the Insured shall have impaired any right of recovery for loss to the property insured; however it is agreed that:

1. as respects property while on the premises of the Insured, permission is given the Insured to release others in writing from liability for loss prior to loss, and such release shall not affect the right of the Insured to recover hereunder, and
2. as respects property in transit, the Insured may, without prejudice to this insurance, accept such bills of lading, receipts or contracts of transportation as are ordinarily issued by carriers containing a limitation as to the value of such property.

N. **LIBERALIZATION CLAUSE:** If during the period that insurance is in force under this policy, or within 45 days prior to the inception date thereof, on behalf of this Company there be adopted, or filed with and approved or accepted by the insurance supervisory authorities, all in conformity with law, any changes in the form attached to this policy by which this form of insurance could be extended or broadened without increased premium charge by endorsement or substitution of form, then such extended or broadened insurance shall inure to the benefit of the Insured hereunder as though such endorsement or substitution of form had been made.

O. **CONFORMITY WITH STATUTE:** In any state requiring a standard form of fire policy, insurance hereunder on values and properties in such state shall attach and cover in accordance with the terms and conditions of such standard fire policy.

APPENDIX D

Appendix D—Commercial Property Coverage—Reporting Form

COMMERCIAL PROPERTY COVERAGE

C.P.C. No. 2
(Ed. 9-60)

REPORTING FORM

I. INSURING AGREEMENT

In consideration of the provisions, stipulations and agreements, and payment of premium as provided herein, this Company insures the Insured named on the face of the policy against all risks of direct physical loss of or to the property covered, except as provided elsewhere in this policy.

II. LIMITS OF LIABILITY

This policy being for ______% of the total contributing insurance, liability of this Company is limited to the same percentage of any loss resulting from one occurrence, regardless of whether one or more perils contribute to such loss, and in no event to exceed the same percentage of each of the following limits, but no insurance attaches under any of the following items unless a specific limit is inserted in the blank immediately opposite the item or subitem:

LIMIT(S) OF LIABILITY FOR ALL CONTRIBUTING INSURANCE

A. Property at locations owned, leased, operated, regularly used or specifically declared by the Insured, except property covered under Sections B or C.

Location — Street Address, City & State

$______________ at ______________________________
$______________ at ______________________________
$______________ at ______________________________
$______________ at ______________________________
$______________ at ______________________________
$______________ at ______________________________
$______________ at ______________________________
$______________ at ______________________________
$______________ at any other location declared at the inception of this insurance.
$______________ at any new location acquired if included in the next succeeding monthly report of values as provided in Section XII B.

B. Property at locations not owned, leased, operated or regularly used by the Insured, except property covered under Sections A or C.

$______________ at any one such location. (Maximum limit permitted is $10,000.)

C. Property in the following situations:

1. $______________ on property in transit (other than property in the care, custody or control of salesmen) on any one vehicle owned, operated or leased by the Insured.
2. $______________ on property in the care, custody or control of any salesman away from the Insured's premises.
3. $______________ in any one loss, disaster or casualty as respects property in the custody of carriers for hire or transit other than as provided in 1 and 2 above.

III. PROPERTY COVERED

The policy covers:

A. Personal property usual to the conduct of the Insured's business, consisting principally of ______________________________

the property of the Insured, or similar property of others held by the Insured for which the Insured is liable except as provided elsewhere in this policy;

B. Tenants Improvements and Betterments (meaning the Insured's use interest in fixtures, alterations, installations or additions comprising a part of a building occupied but not owned by the Insured and made at the expense of the Insured, but which are not legally subject to removal by the Insured).

IV. MINIMUM PREMIUM

The minimum premium for all contributing insurance shall be $________.

V. LOCATION

"Location", as used in this policy, means the area in or on the premises containing the property covered and within 100 feet of such premises.

VI. TERRITORIAL LIMITS

This policy covers while the property is within the 48 contiguous states of the United States of America, the District of Columbia, and in transit within and between such places, and between such places and the Dominion of Canada.

VII. DEDUCTIBLE

Each loss shall be adjusted separately and from the amount of each such adjusted loss the sum of $50 shall be deducted or if there is contributing insurance, this Company's pro-rata share thereof. This deductible shall not apply to loss by fire lightning, aircraft, explosion, riot, civil commotion, smoke, vehicles, windstorm or hail to property contained in any building, vandalism and malicious mischief, leakage or accidental discharge from fire protective sprinkler systems, burglary or robbery; loss of or to property in transit while in the custody of carriers for hire; or loss resulting from collision, upset or overturn of a motor vehicle.

Appendix D—Commercial Property Coverage—Reporting Form (Continued)

VIII. EXTENSIONS OF COVERAGE

Coverage under this policy includes:

A. Expense incurred in the removal of debris of property covered occasioned by loss insured against in this policy, but this Company shall not be liable for expense occasioned by the enforcement of any state or municipal law or ordinance which necessitates the demolition of any portion of a building or removal of contents thereof which has not suffered damage, nor for more than the amount for which this Company would be liable, exclusive of debris removal expenses, if all of the property covered at the location where the loss occurred were destroyed;

B. Loss (except by fire or explosion) to that part of the building(s) occupied by the Insured and containing property covered, and to equipment therein pertaining to the service of the building directly resulting from theft (including attempt thereat), provided the Insured is the owner of such building or equipment or is liable for such damage, but in no event shall this coverage apply to glass (other than glass building blocks) or to any lettering or ornamentation thereon;

C. The contingent interest of the Insured in shipments sold by the Insured on "Free on Board" or "Freight Allowed" terms, providing any loss recoverable under this policy is not collectible from the purchaser or any other insurance that would have attached if this policy had not been issued.

The provisions of this Section do not increase the limits of liability or the amounts recoverable as specified or provided for elsewhere in this policy applicable to the property covered where the loss occurs.

IX. PROPERTY SUBJECT TO LIMITATIONS

A. The following property is subject to these additional limitations:

1. (a) Fur and fur garments are covered, for not exceeding loss in the aggregate of $1,000 in any one occurrence for all contributing insurance. This limitation shall not apply to loss by the "specified perils";

(b) Jewelry and watches, watch movements, jewels, pearls, precious and semi-precious stones, gold, silver, platinum and other precious alloys or metals are covered, for not exceeding loss in the aggregate of $1,000 in any one occurrence for all contributing insurance. This limitation shall not apply to jewelry and watches valued at $25 or less per item or to loss by the "specified perils".

2. Patterns, dies, molds, models and forms are covered, for not exceeding loss in the aggregate of $1000 in any one occurrence for all contributing insurance.

3. Live animals, birds and fish are not covered except when held for sale or sold but not delivered, and then only against death or destruction directly resulting from or made necessary by the "specified perils".

4. Shrubs and plants are not covered, except when held for sale or sold but not delivered, or when used for decorative purposes within buildings and then only against direct loss by the "specified perils".

5. Glass, glassware, statuary, marbles, bric-a-brac, porcelains and other articles of a fragile or brittle nature are covered against loss by breakage only if directly caused by the "specified perils". This limitation shall not apply to bottles or similar containers of property for sale, or sold but not delivered, nor to lenses of photographic or scientific instruments.

6. Neon, automatic and electric signs not held for sale are covered only against loss by the "specified perils" other than vandalism and malicious mischief.

7. Steam boilers, steam pipes, steam turbines and steam engines are not covered against loss caused by bursting, rupture, cracking or explosion originating therein (other than explosion of accumulated gases or unconsumed fuel within a fire box or combustion chamber).

8. Machines and machinery are not covered against loss caused by rupture, bursting or disintegration of their rotating or moving parts resulting from centrifugal or reciprocating force.

B. The term "specified perils" appearing in this section shall mean direct loss by fire, lightning, aircraft, explosion, riot, civil commotion, smoke, vehicles, windstorm or hail to property contained in any building, vandalism and malicious mischief, leakage or accidental discharge from automatic sprinkler systems.

X. EXCLUSIONS

A. This policy does not cover the following:

1. Property sold by the Insured under conditional sale, trust agreement, installment payment or other deferred payment plan, after delivery to customers;

2. Property shipped by mail from the time it passes into the custody of the Post Office Department;

3. Property while waterborne, except ferry operations incidental to other modes of transportation;

4. Automobiles, motor trucks, trailers, semi-trailers, motorcycles, motorscooters; similar vehicles licensed for highway use; watercraft (including motors, equipment and accessories) while afloat; aircraft.

This exclusion does not apply to the following when held for sale or sold but not delivered:

a. Motorcycles and motorscooters;

b. Trailers designed for use with private passenger vehicles for general utility purposes or carrying boats.

5. Currency, money, stamps, bullion, notes, securities, deeds, accounts, bills, evidences of debt, letters of credit and tickets;

6. Trees, lawns or growing crops (including nursery stock).

B. This policy does not insure against loss caused by:

1. Earthquake, landslide or other earth movement; unless loss by fire or explosion ensues, and then only for such ensuing loss. This exclusion does not apply to property in transit;

2. Unexplained or mysterious disappearance of property (except property in the custody of carriers for hire); or shortage of property disclosed on taking inventory;

3. Actual work upon or installation of property covered, latent defect, failure, breakdown or derangement of machines or machinery, faulty materials or workmanship; unless loss by fire or explosion ensues and then only for such ensuing loss;

4. Electrical injury or disturbance to electrical appliances, devices, fixtures or wiring caused by electrical currents artificially generated unless loss by fire ensues, and then only for such ensuing loss;

5. Delay, loss of market, interruption of business, nor consequential loss of any nature;

6. Inherent vice, wear and tear, marring or scratching, gradual deterioration, moths, vermin, dampness or dryness of atmosphere, changes in temperature, rust or corrosion;

7. Theft (including attempt thereat) from any private passenger type automobile, station wagon, motorcycle, or motorscooter, occurring while such vehicle is unattended, unless the property is contained in a fully enclosed and securely locked body or compartment and theft results from forcible entry, evidenced by visible marks. This exclusion shall not apply to property in the custody of carriers for hire;

8. Voluntary parting with title or possession of any property by the Insured or others to whom the property may be entrusted (except by carriers for hire) if induced to do so by any fraudulent scheme, trick, device or false pretense;

9. Any fraudulent, dishonest or criminal act done by or at the instigation of any Insured, partner or joint adventurer in or of any Insured, an officer, director or trustee of any Insured; pilferage, appropriation or concealment of any property covered due to any fraudulent, dishonest or criminal act of any employee while working or otherwise, or agent of any Insured, or any person to whom the property covered may be entrusted, other than any carrier for hire;

10. Rain, snow or sleet to property in the open (other than property in the custody of carriers for hire);

11. Any legal proceeding;

C. This Company shall not be liable for loss caused by:

1. hostile or warlike action in time of peace or war, including action in hindering, combating, or defending against an actual, impending or expected attack, (a) by any government or sovereign power (de jure or de facto), or by any authority maintaining or using military, naval or air forces; or (b) by military, naval or air forces; or (c) by an agent of any such government, power, authority or forces;

2. insurrection, rebellion, revolution, civil war, usurped power, or action taken by governmental authority in hindering, combating or defending against such an occurrence, seizure or destruction under quarantine or customs regulations, confiscation by order of any government or public authority, or risks of contraband or illegal transportation or trade.

This exclusion does not apply to fire and lightning, such exclusion being otherwise provided for on Page 2 of this policy.

D. **NUCLEAR EXCLUSION:** Loss by nuclear reaction or nuclear radiation or radioactive contamination, all whether controlled or uncontrolled, or due to any act or condition incident to any of the foregoing, is not insured against by this policy, whether such loss be direct or indirect, proximate or remote, or be in whole or in part caused by, contributed to, or aggravated by any of the perils insured against by this policy; and nuclear reaction or nuclear

Appendix D—Commercial Property Coverage—Reporting Form (Continued)

radiation or radioactive contamination, all whether controlled or uncontrolled, is not "explosion" or "smoke."

(This clause applies to all perils insured against hereunder except the perils of fire and lightning, which are otherwise provided for in the Nuclear Clause elsewhere in this policy).

E. **WATER EXCLUSION:** This policy does not insure against loss caused by, resulting from, contributed to or aggravated by any of the following:

1. flood, surface water, waves, tidal water or tidal wave, overflow of streams or other bodies of water, or spray from any of the foregoing, all whether driven by wind or not;
2. water which backs up through sewers or drains;
3. water below the surface of the ground including that which exerts pressure on or flows, seeps or leaks through sidewalks, driveways, foundations, walls, basement or other floors, or through doors, windows or any other openings in such sidewalks, driveways, foundations, walls or floors;

unless loss by fire or explosion ensues, and this Company shall then be liable only for such ensuing loss; but these exclusions shall not apply to property in due course of transit or to loss arising from theft.

XI. VALUATION

Subject to the provisions and stipulations of this policy the following valuations of property are established:

A. Property of Others—the amount for which the Insured is liable including the value of services performed by the Insured prior to the time of loss, but in no event to exceed actual cash value.

B. Tenants Improvements and Betterments —

1. If repaired or replaced within a reasonable time after loss, at the expense of the Insured, the actual cash value of the damaged or destroyed property;
2. If not repaired or replaced within a reasonable time after loss, that proportion of the original cost of the damaged or destroyed property which the unexpired term of the lease or rental agreement, whether written or oral, in effect at the time of loss bears to the period(s) from the date(s) such Improvements or Betterments were made to the expiration date of the lease;
3. If repaired or replaced at the expense of others for the use of the Insured, there shall be no liability hereunder.

C. Books of record, manuscripts, drawings, and other records (except film, recording tape or wire), card index systems for not exceeding cost of blank books, blank cards and other materials plus the actual cost of labor in transcribing or copying such records.

D. Film, recording tape or wire, except stocks held for sale for not exceeding the cost of unexposed film or blank tape or wire.

XII. REPORTING PROVISIONS

A. **PROVISIONAL AMOUNT CLAUSE:** The amount of insurance provided for hereunder is provisional and is the amount on which the Provisional Premium is based, it being the intent of this insurance to insure hereunder the total actual cash value of the property described herein subject to the Limits of Liability for All Contributing Insurance. Any loss in excess of the limits stated in this policy shall be borne by the Insured, notwithstanding the requirement that premium is to be adjusted on the basis of full values reported.

B. **VALUE REPORTING CLAUSE:** As respects property covered under Section IIA, the Insured shall report in writing to this Company not later than thirty(30) days after the last day of each calendar month, the exact location of all property covered and the total actual cash value of such property at each location as of the last day of each month. As respects property covered under Section IIB, the Insured shall report in writing to this Company not later than thirty (30) days after the last day of each calendar month, the total aggregate actual cash value of such property at all such locations as of the last day of each month. At the time of any loss, if the Insured has failed to file with this Company reports of values as above required, this policy, subject otherwise to all its terms and conditions, shall cover only at the locations and for not more than the amounts included in the last report of values filed prior to the loss, and further, if such delinquent report is the first report of values herein required to be filed, liability shall be limited to 90% of the amount for which this Company would otherwise be liable.

C. **FULL REPORTING CLAUSE:** As respects property covered under Section IIA, liability under this policy shall not in any case exceed that proportion of any loss hereunder which the last value reported prior to the loss at the location where the loss occurs bears to the total actual cash value at that location on the date for which such report was made; and liability for loss hereunder occurring at any new location acquired since the last report (except as provided in the Value Reporting Clause) shall be apportioned in a like manner, except that the proportion used shall be the relation that the values reported prior to the loss at all locations bear to the total actual cash values at all such locations on the date for which such report was made.

As respects property covered under Section IIB, liability under this policy shall not in any case exceed that proportion of any loss hereunder which the last value reported prior to the loss bears to the total aggregate actual cash value on the date for which such report was made.

D. **ADJUSTMENT OF PREMIUM:** The premium named in this policy is provisional only. The actual premium consideration for the liability assumed hereunder shall be determined at the expiration or cancellation of this policy by the following method:

1. An average of the total values reported as respects property covered under Section IIA and B during the period for which the adjustment is being made shall be calculated, and if the premium on such average values at the rate applying to this policy during such period exceeds the provisional premium, the Insured shall pay to the Insurer an additional premium for such excess; and, if such premium is less than the provisional premium, the Insurer shall refund to the Insured any excess paid.
2. The actual premium consideration shall in no event be less than this policy's proportion of the Minimum Premium stated elsewhere in this form.

(OVER)

Appendix D—Commercial Property Coverage—Reporting Form (Concluded)

XIII. SPECIAL AGREEMENTS

A. **LOSS CLAUSE:** Any loss hereunder shall not reduce the amount of this policy.

B. **EXAMINATION OF RECORDS:** Any duly authorized representative of this Company, shall be permitted at all reasonable times to inspect the property covered hereunder and to examine the Insured's books, records and such policies as relate to any property covered hereunder. This inspection or examination shall not waive nor in any manner affect any of the terms or conditions of this policy.

C. **NUCLEAR CLAUSE:** The word "fire" in this policy or endorsements attached hereto is not intended to and does not embrace nuclear reaction or nuclear radiation or radioactive contamination, all whether controlled or uncontrolled, and loss by nuclear reaction or nuclear radiation or radioactive contamination is not intended to be and is not insured against by this policy or said endorsements, whether such loss be direct or indirect, proximate or remote, or be in whole or in part caused by, contributed to, or aggravated by "fire" or any other perils insured against by this policy or said endorsements; however, subject to the foregoing and all provisions of this policy, direct loss by "fire" resulting from nuclear reaction or nuclear radiation or radioactive contamination is insured against by this policy.

D. **OTHER INSURANCE:** If there is available to the Insured, or any other interested party, any insurance, whether collectible or not, which would apply in the absence of this policy, the insurance under this policy shall apply only as excess insurance over such other insurance.

E. **CONTRIBUTING INSURANCE:** Contributing insurance shall mean insurance written in the name of the Insured and upon the identical plan, terms, conditions and provisions contained in this policy and shall not be deemed to be other insurance.

F. **PERMITS AND USE:** Except as otherwise provided permission is hereby granted:

1. for any building to be and remain vacant or unoccupied without limit of time;
2. for existing and increased hazards and for any change in occupancy or use of the premises.

G. **NO CONTROL:**
This insurance shall not be prejudiced:

1. by any act or neglect of the owner of any building if the Insured is not the owner thereof, or by any act or neglect of any occupant (other than the Insured) of any building, when such act or neglect of the owner or occupant is not within the control of the Insured, or
2. by failure of the Insured to comply with any warranty or condition contained in any form or endorsement attached to this policy with regard to any portion of the premises over which the Insured has no control.

H. **PROTECTIVE SAFEGUARDS:** It is a condition of this insurance that the Insured shall maintain so far as is within his control such protective safeguards as were stipulated in the application for this insurance or for which credit in rate has been granted. Failure to maintain such protective safeguards shall suspend this insurance, only as respects the location or situation affected, for the time of such discontinuance.

I. **PROTECTION OF PROPERTY:** In case of loss, it shall be lawful and necessary for the Insured, his or their factors, servants and assigns, to sue, labor, and travel for, in and about the defense, safeguard and recovery of the property insured hereunder, or any part thereof, without prejudice to this insurance, nor shall the acts of the Insured or the Company, in recovering, saving and preserving the property insured in case of loss be considered a waiver or an acceptance of abandonment. The expenses so incurred shall be borne by the Insured and the Company proportionately to the extent of their respective interests.

J. **NO BENEFIT TO BAILEE:** This insurance shall in no wise inure directly or indirectly to the benefit of any carrier or other bailee.

K. **SUBROGATION:** In the event of any payment under this policy, the Company shall be subrogated to the Insured's rights of recovery therefor against any person, organization or government, and the Insured shall execute and deliver instruments and papers and do whatever else is necessary to secure such rights.

L. **IMPAIRMENT OF RECOVERY:** Except as noted below, this Company shall not be bound to pay any loss if the Insured shall have impaired any right of recovery for loss to the property insured; however it is agreed that:

1. as respects property while on the premises of the Insured, permission is given the Insured to release others in writing from liability for loss prior to loss, and such release shall not affect the right of the Insured to recover hereunder, and
2. as respects property in transit, the Insured may, without prejudice to this insurance, accept such bills of lading, receipts or contracts of transportation as are ordinarily issued by carriers containing a limitation as to the value of such goods or merchandise.

M. **LIBERALIZATION:** If, during the period that insurance is in force under this policy, or within 45 days prior to the inception date thereof on behalf of this Company there be filed with and approved or accepted by the insurance supervisory authorities, in conformity with law, any forms, endorsements, rules or regulations by which this insurance could be extended or broadened, without additional premium charge, by endorsement or substitution of form, then such extended or broadened insurance shall inure to the benefit of the Insured hereunder as though such endorsement or substitution of form had been made.

N. **CONFORMITY WITH STATUTE:** In any state requiring a standard form of fire policy, insurance hereunder on values and properties in such state shall attach and cover in accordance with the terms and conditions of such standard fire policy.

APPENDIX E

Appendix E—Commercial Property Coverage—Non-Reporting Form

COMMERCIAL PROPERTY COVERAGE
NON-REPORTING FORM
(COINSURANCE CONTRACT)

C.P.C. No. 1
(Ed. 9-60)

I. INSURING AGREEMENT

In consideration of the provisions, stipulations and agreements, and payment of premium as provided herein, this Company insures the Insured named on the face of the policy against all risks of direct physical loss of or to the property covered, except as provided elsewhere in this policy.

II. LIMITS OF LIABILITY

This policy being for ______% of the total contributing insurance, liability of this Company is limited to the same percentage of any loss resulting from one occurrence, regardless of whether one or more perils contribute to such loss, and in no event to exceed the same percentage of each of the following limits, but no insurance attaches under any of the following items unless a specific limit is inserted in the blank immediately opposite the item or subitem:

LIMIT(S) OF LIABILITY FOR ALL CONTRIBUTING INSURANCE

A. Property at locations owned, leased, operated, regularly used or specifically declared by the Insured, except property covered under Sections B or C.

Location — Street Address, City & State

$______________ at ______________________________

$______________ at ______________________________

$______________ at ______________________________

$______________ at ______________________________

$______________ at ______________________________

$______________ at ______________________________

$______________ at ______________________________

$______________ at ______________________________

B. Property at locations not owned, leased, operated or regularly used by the Insured, except property covered under Sections A or C.

$______________ in the aggregate at all such locations not to exceed $__________ at any one location. (Maximum limit permitted at any one location is $10,000.)

C. Property in the following situations:

1. $______________ on property in transit (other than property in the care, custody or control of salesmen) on any one vehicle owned, operated or leased by the Insured.
2. $______________ on property in the care, custody or control of any salesman away from the Insured's premises.
3. $______________ in any one loss, disaster or casualty as respects property in the custody of carriers for hire or in transit other than as provided in 1 and 2 above.

III. PROPERTY COVERED

The policy covers:

A. Personal property usual to the conduct of the Insured's business, consisting principally of ______________________________

the property of the Insured, or similar property of others held by the Insured for which the Insured is liable, except as provided elsewhere in this policy;

B. Tenants Improvements and Betterments (meaning the Insured's use interest in fixtures, alterations, installations or additions comprising a part of a building occupied but not owned by the Insured and made at the expense of the Insured, but which are not legally subject to removal by the Insured).

IV. COINSURANCE PERCENTAGE

The coinsurance percentage referred to in Section XIII is ______________%.

V. MINIMUM PREMIUM

The minimum premium for all contributing insurance shall be $75 when the policy is written for one year and $150 when written for a term of three years.

VI. LOCATION

"Location", as used in this policy, means the area in or on the premises containing the property covered and within 100 feet of such premises.

VII. TERRITORIAL LIMITS

This policy covers while the property is within the 48 contiguous states of the United States of America, the District of Columbia, and in transit within and between such places, and between such places and the Dominion of Canada.

VIII. DEDUCTIBLE

Each loss shall be adjusted separately and from the amount of each such adjusted loss the sum of $50 shall be deducted or, if there is contributing insurance, this Company's pro-rata share thereof. This deductible shall not apply to loss by fire, lightning, aircraft, explosion, riot, civil commotion, smoke, vehicles, windstorm or hail to property contained in any building, vandalism and malicious mischief, leakage or accidental discharge from fire protective sprinkler systems, burglary or robbery; loss of or to property in transit while in the custody of carriers for hire; or loss resulting from collision, upset or overturn of a motor vehicle.

(OVER)

IX. EXTENSIONS OF COVERAGE

Coverage under this policy includes:

A. Expense incurred in the removal of debris of property covered occasioned by loss insured against in this policy, but this Company shall not be liable for expense occasioned by the enforcement of any state or municipal law or ordinance which necessitates the demolition of any portion of a building or removal of contents thereof which has not suffered damage.

B. Loss (except by fire or explosion) to that part of the building(s) occupied by the Insured and containing property covered, and to equipment therein pertaining to the service of the building directly resulting from theft (including attempt thereat), provided the Insured is the owner of such building or equipment or is liable for such damage, but in no event shall this coverage apply to glass (other than glass building blocks) or to any lettering or ornamentation thereon.

C. The contingent interest of the Insured in shipments sold by the Insured on "Free on Board" or "Freight Allowed" terms, providing any loss recoverable under this policy is not collectible from the purchaser or any other insurance that would have attached if this policy had not been issued.

The provisions of this Section do not increase the limits of liability or the amounts recoverable as specified or provided for elsewhere in this policy.

X. PROPERTY SUBJECT TO LIMITATIONS

A. The following property is subject to these additional limitations:

1. (a) Fur and fur garments are covered, for not exceeding loss in the aggregate of $1,000 in any one occurrence for all contributing insurance. This limitation shall not apply to loss by the "specified perils";

(b) Jewelry and watches, watch movements, jewels, pearls, precious and semi-precious stones, gold, silver, platinum and other precious alloys or metals are covered, for not exceeding loss in the aggregate of $1,000 in any one occurrence for all contributing insurance. This limitation shall not apply to jewelry and watches valued at $25 or less per item or to loss by the "specified perils".

2. Patterns, dies, molds, models and forms are covered, for not exceeding loss in the aggregate of $1,000 in any one occurrence for all contributing insurance.

3. Live animals, birds and fish are not covered except when held for sale or sold but not delivered, and then only against death or destruction directly resulting from or made necessary by the "specified perils".

4. Shrubs and plants are not covered, except when held for sale or sold but not delivered, or when used for decorative purposes within buildings and then only against direct loss by the "specified perils".

5. Glass, glassware, statuary, marbles, bric-a-brac, porcelains and other articles of a fragile or brittle nature are covered against loss by breakage only if directly caused by the "specified perils". This limitation shall not apply to bottles or similar containers of property for sale, or sold but not delivered, nor to lenses of photographic or scientific instruments.

6. Neon, automatic and electric signs not held for sale are covered only against loss by the "specified perils" other than vandalism and malicious mischief.

7. Steam boilers, steam pipes, steam turbines and steam engines are not covered against loss caused by bursting, rupture, cracking or explosion originating therein (other than explosion of accumulated gases or unconsumed fuel within a fire box or combustion chamber).

8. Machines and machinery are not covered against loss caused by rupture, bursting or disintegration of their rotating or moving parts resulting from centrifugal or reciprocating force.

B. The term "specified perils" appearing in this section shall mean direct loss by fire, lightning, aircraft, explosion, riot, civil commotion, smoke, vehicles, windstorm or hail to property contained in any building, vandalism and malicious mischief, leakage or accidental discharge from automatic sprinkler systems.

XI. EXCLUSIONS

A. This policy does not cover the following:

1. Property sold by the Insured under conditional sale, trust agreement, installment payment or other deferred payment plan, after delivery to customers;

2. Property shipped by mail from the time it passes into the custody of the Post Office Department;

3. Property while waterborne, except ferry operations incidental to other modes of transportation;

4. Automobiles, motor trucks, trailers, semi-trailers, motorcycles, motorscooters; similar vehicles licensed for highway use; watercraft (including motors, equipment and accessories) while afloat; aircraft.

This exclusion does not apply to the following when held for sale or sold but not delivered:

a. Motorcycles and motorscooters;
b. Trailers designed for use with private passenger vehicles for general utility purposes or carrying boats.

5. Currency, money, stamps, bullion, notes, securities, deeds, accounts, bills, evidences of debt, letters of credit and tickets;

6. Trees, lawns or growing crops (including nursery stock).

B. This policy does not insure against loss caused by:

1. Earthquake, landslide or other earth movement; unless loss by fire or explosion ensues, and then only for such ensuing loss. This exclusion does not apply to property in transit;

2. Unexplained or mysterious disappearance of property (except property in the custody of carriers for hire); or shortage of property disclosed on taking inventory;

3. Actual work upon or installation of property covered, latent defect, failure, breakdown or derangement of machines or machinery, faulty materials or workmanship; unless loss by fire or explosion ensues and then only for such ensuing loss;

4. Electrical injury or disturbance to electrical appliances, devices, fixtures or wiring caused by electrical currents artificially generated unless loss by fire ensues, and then only for such ensuing loss;

5. Delay, loss of market, interruption of business, nor consequential loss of any nature;

6. Inherent vice, wear and tear, marring or scratching, gradual deterioration, moths, vermin, dampness or dryness of atmosphere, changes in temperature, rust or corrosion;

7. Theft (including attempt thereat) from any private passenger type automobile, station wagon, motorcycle, or motorscooter, occurring while such vehicle is unattended, unless the property is contained in a fully enclosed and securely locked body or compartment and theft results from forcible entry, evidenced by visible marks. This exclusion shall not apply to property in the custody of carriers for hire;

8. Voluntary parting with title or possession of any property by the Insured or others to whom the property may be entrusted (except by carriers for hire) if induced to do so by any fraudulent scheme, trick, device or false pretense;

9. Any fraudulent, dishonest or criminal act done by or at the instigation of any Insured, partner or joint adventurer in or of any Insured, an officer, director or trustee of any Insured; pilferage, appropriation or concealment of any property covered due to any fraudulent, dishonest or criminal act of any employee while working or otherwise, or agent of any Insured, or any person to whom the property covered may be entrusted, other than any carrier for hire;

10. Rain, snow or sleet to property in the open (other than property in the custody of carriers for hire);

11. Any legal proceeding;

C. This Company shall not be liable for loss caused by:

1. hostile or warlike action in time of peace or war, including action in hindering, combating, or defending against an actual, impending or expected attack, (a) by any government or sovereign power (de jure or de facto), or by any authority maintaining or using military, naval or air forces; or (b) by military, naval or air forces; or (c) by an agent of any such government, power, authority or forces;

2. insurrection, rebellion, revolution, civil war, usurped power, or action taken by governmental authority in hindering, combating or defending against such an occurrence, seizure or destruction under quarantine or customs regulations, confiscation by order of any government or public authority, or risks of contraband or illegal transportation or trade.

This exclusion does not apply to fire and lightning, such exclusion being otherwise provided for on Page 2 of this policy.

Appendix E—Commercial Property Coverage—Non-Reporting Form (Continued)

D. **NUCLEAR EXCLUSION:** Loss by nuclear reaction or nuclear radiation or radioactive contamination, all whether controlled or uncontrolled, or due to any act or condition incident to any of the foregoing is not insured against by this policy, whether such loss be direct or indirect, proximate or remote, or be in whole or in part caused by, contributed to, or aggravated by any of the perils insured against by this policy; and nuclear reaction or nuclear radiation or radioactive contamination, all whether controlled or uncontrolled, is not "explosion" or "smoke."

(This clause applies to all perils insured against hereunder except the perils of fire and lightning, which are otherwise provided for in the Nuclear Clause elsewhere in this policy).

E. **WATER EXCLUSION:** This policy does not insure against loss caused by, resulting from, contributed to or aggravated by any of the following:

1. flood, surface water, waves, tidal water or tidal wave, overflow of streams or other bodies of water, or spray from any of the foregoing, all whether driven by wind or not;

2. water which backs up through sewers or drains;

3. water below the surface of the ground including that which exerts pressure on or flows, seeps or leaks through sidewalks, driveways, foundations, walls, basement or other floors, or through doors, windows or any other openings in such sidewalks, driveways, foundations, walls or floors;

unless loss by fire or explosion ensues, and this Company shall then be liable only for such ensuing loss; but these exclusions shall not apply to property in due course of transit or to loss arising from theft.

XII. VALUATION

Subject to the provisions and stipulations of this policy the following valuations of property are established:

A. Property of Others — the amount for which the Insured is liable including the value of services performed by the Insured prior to the time of loss, but in no event to exceed actual cash value.

B. Tenants Improvements and Betterments —

1. If repaired or replaced within a reasonable time after loss, at the expense of the Insured, the actual cash value of the damaged or destroyed property;

2. If not repaired or replaced within a reasonable time, after loss, that proportion of the original cost of the damaged or destroyed property which the unexpired term of the lease or rental agreement, whether written or oral, in effect at the time of loss bears to the period(s) from the date(s) such Improvements or Betterments were made to the expiration date of the lease;

3. If repaired or replaced at the expense of others for the use of the Insured, there shall be no liability hereunder.

C. Books of record, manuscripts, drawings, and other records (except film, recording tape or wire), card index systems for not exceeding cost of blank books, blank cards and other materials plus the actual cost of labor in transcribing or copying such records.

D. Film, recording tape or wire, except stocks held for sale for not exceeding the cost of unexposed film or blank tape or wire.

E. All other property at actual cash value.

XIII. COINSURANCE CLAUSE

As respects property covered under Section II A, this Company shall not be liable for a greater proportion of any loss at the location where the loss occurs than the Limit of Liability for All Contributing Insurance at such location bears to the percentage (as set forth in Section IV) of the value as set forth in Section XII of all property covered at that location at the time of loss.

As respects property covered under Section II B, this Company shall not be liable for a greater proportion of any loss at the location where the loss occurs than the aggregate Limit of Liability for All Contributing Insurance at all such locations bears to the percentage (as set forth in Section IV) of the value established in Section XII of all property covered at all such locations at the time of loss.

In the event the aggregate claim for any loss is both less than Ten Thousand Dollars ($10,000) and less than Five Percent (5%) of the Limit of Liability for All Contributing Insurance applicable to the property involved at the time such loss occurs, no special inventory or appraisement of the undamaged property shall be required, provided, however, that nothing herein shall be construed to waive the application of the preceding paragraphs of this clause.

This Coinsurance Clause shall not apply to property covered under Section II C.

Appendix E—Commercial Property Coverage—Non-Reporting Form (Concluded)

XIV. SPECIAL AGREEMENTS

A. **LOSS CLAUSE:** Any loss hereunder shall not reduce the amount of this policy.

B. **EXAMINATION OF RECORDS:** Any duly authorized representative of this Company, shall be permitted at all reasonable times to inspect the property covered hereunder and to examine the Insured's books, records and such policies as relate to any property covered hereunder. This inspection or examination shall not waive nor in any manner affect any of the terms or conditions of this policy.

C. **NUCLEAR CLAUSE:** The word "fire" in this policy or endorsements attached hereto is not intended to and does not embrace nuclear reaction or nuclear radiation or radioactive contamination, all whether controlled or uncontrolled, and loss by nuclear reaction or nuclear radiation or radioactive contamination is not intended to be and is not insured against by this policy or said endorsements, whether such loss be direct or indirect, proximate or remote, or be in whole or in part caused by, contributed to, or aggravated by "fire" or any other perils insured against by this policy or said endorsements; however, subject to the foregoing and all provisions of this policy, direct loss by "fire" resulting from nuclear reaction or nuclear radiation or radioactive contamination is insured against by this policy.

D. **OTHER INSURANCE:** If there is available to the Insured, or any other interested party, any insurance, whether collectible or not, which would apply in the absence of this policy, the insurance under this policy shall apply only as excess insurance over such "Other Insurance".

E. **CONTRIBUTING INSURANCE:** Contributing insurance shall mean insurance written in the name of the Insured and upon the identical plan, terms, conditions and provisions contained in this policy and shall not be deemed to be other insurance.

F. **PERMITS AND USE:** Except as otherwise provided permission is hereby granted:

1. for any building to be and remain vacant or unoccupied without limit of time;
2. for existing and increased hazards and for any change in occupancy or use of the premises.

G. **NO CONTROL:**

This insurance shall not be prejudiced:

1. by any act or neglect of the owner of any building if the Insured is not the owner thereof, or by any act or neglect of any occupant (other than the Insured) of any building, when such act or neglect of the owner or occupant is not within the control of the Insured, or
2. by failure of the Insured to comply with any warranty or condition contained in any form or endorsement attached to this policy with regard to any portion of the premises over which the Insured has no control.

H. **PROTECTIVE SAFEGUARDS:** It is a condition of this insurance that the Insured shall maintain so far as is within his control such protective safeguards as were stipulated in the application for this insurance or for which credit in rate has been granted. Failure to maintain such protective safeguards shall suspend this insurance, only as respects the location or situation affected, for the time of such discontinuance.

I. **PROTECTION OF PROPERTY:** In case of loss, it shall be lawful and necessary for the Insured, his or their factors, servants and assigns, to sue, labor, and travel for, in and about the defense, safeguard and recovery of the property insured hereunder, or any part thereof, without prejudice to this insurance, nor shall the acts of the Insured or the Company, in recovering, saving and preserving the property insured in case of loss be considered a waiver or an acceptance of abandonment. The expenses so incurred shall be borne by the Insured and the Company proportionately to the extent of their respective interests.

J. **NO BENEFIT TO BAILEE:** This insurance shall in no wise inure directly or indirectly to the benefit of any carrier or other bailee.

K. **SUBROGATION:** In the event of any payment under this policy, the Company shall be subrogated to the Insured's rights of recovery therefor against any person, organization or government, and the Insured shall execute and deliver instruments and papers and do whatever else is necessary to secure such rights.

L. **IMPAIRMENT OF RECOVERY:** Except as noted below, this Company shall not be bound to pay any loss if the Insured shall have impaired any right of recovery for loss to the property insured; however it is agreed that:

1. as respects property while on the premises of the Insured, permission is given the Insured to release others in writing from liability for loss prior to loss, and such release shall not affect the right of the Insured to recover hereunder, and
2. as respects property in transit, the Insured may, without prejudice to this insurance, accept such bills of lading, receipts or contracts of transportation as are ordinarily issued by carriers containing a limitation as to the value of such goods or merchandise.

M. **LIBERALIZATION:** If during the period that insurance is in force under this policy, or within 45 days prior to the inception date thereof on behalf of this Company there be filed with and approved or accepted by the insurance supervisory authorities, in conformity with law, any forms, endorsements, rules or regulations by which this insurance could be extended or broadened, without additional premium charge, by endorsement or substitution of form, then such extended or broadened insurance shall inure to the benefit of the Insured hereunder as though such endorsement or substitution of form had been made.

N. **CONFORMITY WITH STATUTE:** In any state requiring a standard form of fire policy, insurance hereunder on values and properties in such state shall attach and cover in accordance with the terms and conditions of such standard fire policy.

APPENDIX F

Appendix F—Radioactive Contamination Assumption Endorsements

UNIFORM STANDARD **FORM NO. 152**
(Edition Jan. '61)

RADIOACTIVE CONTAMINATION ASSUMPTION ENDORSEMENT "A"
(LIMITED COVERAGE)

In consideration of the premium for this coverage, and subject to the provisions herein and in the policy to which this endorsement is attached including endorsements thereon, the provisions of this policy, including other endorsements, are hereby modified and this policy is extended to insure against direct loss by sudden and accidental radioactive contamination, including resultant radiation damage to the property covered, resulting directly from any peril(s) insured against by this policy, provided such radioactive contamination arises out of material on the Insured's premises at the location(s) described in this policy, and provided, at the time of such loss, there is neither a nuclear reactor capable of sustaining nuclear fission in a self-supporting chain reaction, nor any new or used nuclear fuel which is intended for or which has been used in such a nuclear reactor, on the Insured's premises at the location(s) described.

This endorsement does not increase the amount(s) of insurance provided in the policy to which it is attached.

If this policy covers on two or more items, the provisions of this endorsement shall apply separately to each item to which this endorsement applies.

APPORTIONMENT: This Company shall not be liable for a greater proportion of any loss less the amount of deductible, if any, from radioactive contamination insured against in this endorsement than (1) the amount of insurance under this policy bears to the whole amount of fire insurance covering the property, or which would have covered the property except for the existence of this insurance, whether collectible or not, and whether or not such other fire insurance covers against radioactive contamination, nor (2) for a greater proportion of any loss less the amount of deductible, if any, than the amount hereby insured bears to all insurance whether collectible or not, covering in any manner such loss, or which would have covered such loss except for the existence of this insurance; except if any type of insurance other than fire applies to any loss to which this insurance also applies, or would have applied to any such loss except for the existence of this insurance, the limit of liability of each type of insurance for such loss, hereby designated as "joint loss," shall first be determined as if it were the only insurance, and this type of insurance shall be liable for no greater proportion of joint loss than the limit of its liability for such loss bears to the sum of all such limits. The liability of this Company (under this endorsement) for such joint loss shall be limited to its proportionate part of the aggregate limit of this and all other insurance of the same type. The words "joint loss," as used in the foregoing, mean that portion of the loss in excess of the highest deductible, if any, to which this endorsement and other types of insurance above referred to both apply.

PROVISIONS APPLICABLE ONLY WHEN THIS ENDORSEMENT IS ATTACHED TO A POLICY COVERING BUSINESS INTERRUPTION, TUITION FEES, EXTRA EXPENSE OR RENTS: When this endorsement is attached to a policy covering Business Interruption, Tuition Fees, Extra Expense or Rents, the term "direct loss" in this endorsement means loss, as limited and conditioned in such policy, resulting from direct damage to described property from the peril insured against; and, while the business of the owner or tenant(s) of the described building(s) is interrupted by a strike at the described location, this Company shall not be liable for any loss owing to interference by any person(s) with rebuilding, repairing, replacing or decontaminating the property damaged or destroyed or with the resumption or continuation of business.

Form No. 152 (1-61)

CAUTION

WHEN THIS ENDORSEMENT IS ATTACHED TO ONE POLICY, THE INSURED SHOULD SECURE LIKE COVERAGE ON ALL POLICIES COVERING THE SAME PROPERTY.

Appendix F—Radioactive Contamination Assumption Endorsements (Continued)

UNIFORM STANDARD | **FORM NO. 153** (Edition Jan. '61)

RADIOACTIVE CONTAMINATION ASSUMPTION ENDORSEMENT "B"

(BROAD COVERAGE)

In consideration of the premium for this coverage, and subject to the provisions herein and in the policy to which this endorsement is attached including endorsements thereon, the provisions of this policy, including other endorsements, are hereby modified and this policy is extended to insure against direct loss by sudden and accidental radioactive contamination, including resultant radiation damage to the property covered, provided such radioactive contamination arises out of material on the Insured's premises at the location(s) described in this policy, and provided, at the time of such loss, there is neither a nuclear reactor capable of sustaining nuclear fission in a self-supporting chain reaction, nor any new or used nuclear fuel which is intended for or which has been used in such a nuclear reactor, on the Insured's premises at the location(s) described.

This endorsement does not increase the amount(s) of insurance provided in the policy to which it is attached.

If this policy covers on two or more items, the provisions of this endorsement shall apply separately to each item to which this endorsement applies.

APPORTIONMENT: This Company shall not be liable for a greater proportion of any loss less the amount of deductible, if any, from radioactive contamination insured against in this endorsement than (1) the amount of insurance under this policy bears to the whole amount of fire insurance covering the property, or which would have covered the property except for the existence of this insurance, whether collectible or not, and whether or not such other fire insurance covers against radioactive contamination, nor (2) for a greater proportion of any loss less the amount of deductible, if any, than the amount hereby insured bears to all insurance whether collectible or not, covering in any manner such loss, or which would have covered such loss except for the existence of this insurance; except if any type of insurance other than fire applies to any loss to which this insurance also applies, or would have applied to any such loss except for the existence of this insurance, the limit of liability of each type of insurance for such loss, hereby designated as "joint loss," shall first be determined as if it were the only insurance, and this type of insurance shall be liable for no greater proportion of joint loss than the limit of its liability for such loss bears to the sum of all such limits. The liability of this Company (under this endorsement) for such joint loss shall be limited to its proportionate part of the aggregate limit of this and all other insurance of the same type. The words "joint loss," as used in the foregoing, mean that portion of the loss in excess of the highest deductible, if any, to which this endorsement and other types of insurance above referred to both apply.

PROVISIONS APPLICABLE ONLY WHEN THIS ENDORSEMENT IS ATTACHED TO A POLICY COVERING BUSINESS INTERRUPTION, TUITION FEES, EXTRA EXPENSE OR RENTS: When this endorsement is attached to a policy covering Business Interruption, Tuition Fees, Extra Expense or Rents, the term "direct loss" in this endorsement means loss, as limited and conditioned in such policy, resulting from direct damage to described property from the peril insured against; and, while the business of the owner or tenant(s) of the described building(s) is interrupted by a strike at the described location, this Company shall not be liable for any loss owing to interference by any person(s) with rebuilding, repairing, replacing or decontaminating the property damaged or destroyed or with the resumption or continuation of business.

Form No. 153 (1-61)

CAUTION

WHEN THIS ENDORSEMENT IS ATTACHED TO ONE POLICY, THE INSURED SHOULD SECURE LIKE COVERAGE ON ALL POLICIES COVERING THE SAME PROPERTY.

APPENDIX G

Appendix G—Business Interruption Coverage

UNIFORM STANDARD

FORM NO. 19C

(Edition Apr. '65)

BUSINESS INTERRUPTION FORM NO. 4

Gross Earnings Form for Manufacturing or Mining Risks

Insurance attaches to this item(s) only when "Business Interruption," a specific amount and a contribution percentage are specified therefor in this policy, and, unless otherwise provided, all provisions and stipulations of this form and policy shall apply separately to each such item.

1. This policy covers against loss resulting directly from necessary interruption of business caused by damage to or destruction of real or personal property, except finished stock, by the peril(s) insured against, during the term of this policy, on premises occupied by the Insured and situated as herein described.

2. In the event of such damage or destruction this Company shall be liable for the ACTUAL LOSS SUSTAINED by the Insured resulting directly from such interruption of business, but not exceeding the reduction in Gross Earnings less charges and expenses which do not necessarily continue during the interruption of business, for only such length of time as would be required with the exercise of due diligence and dispatch to rebuild, repair or replace such part of the property herein described as has been damaged or destroyed, commencing with the date of such damage or destruction and not limited by the date of expiration of this policy. Due consideration shall be given to the continuation of normal charges and expenses, including payroll expense, to the extent necessary to resume operations of the Insured with the same quality of service which existed immediately preceding the loss.

3. **Resumption of Operations:** It is a condition of this insurance that if the Insured could reduce the loss resulting from the interruption of business,

(a) by complete or partial resumption of operation of the property herein described, whether damaged or not, or

(b) by making use of other property at the location(s) described herein or elsewhere, or

(c) by making use of stock (raw, in process or finished) at the location(s) described herein or elsewhere,

such reduction shall be taken into account in arriving at the amount of loss hereunder.

4. **Expenses Related to Reducing Loss:** This policy also covers such expenses as are necessarily incurred for the purpose of reducing loss under this policy (except expense incurred to extinguish a fire) and such expenses, in excess of normal, as would necessarily be incurred in replacing any finished stock used by the Insured to reduce loss under this policy; but in no event shall the aggregate of such expenses exceed the amount by which the loss otherwise payable under this policy is thereby reduced. Such expenses shall not be subject to the application of the Contribution Clause.

5. **Gross Earnings:** For the purposes of this insurance "Gross Earnings" are defined as the sum of:

(a) Total net sales value of production,

(b) Total net sales of merchandise, and

(c) Other earnings derived from operation of the business,

less the cost of:

(d) Raw Stock from which such production is derived,

(e) Supplies consisting of materials consumed directly in the conversion of such raw stock into finished stock or in supplying the service(s) sold by the Insured,

(f) Merchandise sold, including packaging materials therefor, and

(g) Service(s) purchased from outsiders (not employees of the Insured) for resale which do not continue under contract.

No other costs shall be deducted in determining Gross Earnings.

In determining Gross Earnings due consideration shall be given to the experience of the business before the date of damage or destruction and the probable experience thereafter had no loss occurred.

6. **Contribution Clause:** In consideration of the rate and form under which this policy is written, this Company shall be liable, in the event of loss, for no greater proportion thereof than the amount hereby covered bears to the Contribution (Coinsurance) percentage specified on the first page of this policy (or endorsed hereon) of the Gross Earnings that would have been earned (had no loss occurred) during the 12 months immediately following the date of damage to or destruction of the described property.

7. **Finished Stock:** This Company shall not be liable for any loss resulting from damage to or destruction of finished stock nor for the time required to reproduce said finished stock.

8. **Interruption by Civil Authority:** This policy is extended to include the actual loss as covered hereunder during the period of time, not exceeding 2 consecutive weeks, when, as a direct result of the peril(s) insured against, access to the premises described is prohibited by order of civil authority.

9. **Special Exclusions:** This Company shall not be liable for any increase of loss resulting from:

(a) enforcement of any local or state ordinance or law regulating the construction, repair or demolition of buildings or structures; or

(b) interference at the described premises, by strikers or other persons, with rebuilding, repairing or replacing the property or with the resumption or continuation of business; or

(c) the suspension, lapse or cancellation of any lease, license, contract or order unless such suspension, lapse or cancellation results directly from the interruption of business, and then this Company shall be liable for only such loss as affects the Insured's earnings during, and limited to, the period of indemnity covered under this policy;

nor shall this Company be liable for any other consequential or remote loss.

When this form is attached to a policy covering the perils of windstorm and hail, this Company shall not be liable for any Business Interruption loss resulting from damage to or destruction of metal smokestacks by windstorm or hail, unless otherwise provided for by endorsement hereon and premium paid therefor.

THE PROVISIONS PRINTED ON THE BACK OF THIS FORM ARE HEREBY REFERRED TO AND MADE A PART HEREOF.

NOTE TO AGENTS: Other clauses, such as Special Conditions Applicable to Coal Mining Property, Automatic Sprinkler Clause or Watchman and Clock Clause, to be added as provided in the rules.

10. **Pro Rata Clause:** The liability under this policy shall not exceed that proportion of any loss which the amount of insurance hereunder bears to all insurance, whether collectible or not, covering in any manner the loss insured against by this policy.

11. **Definitions:** The following terms wherever used in this policy shall mean:
   (a) "Raw Stock": material in the state in which the Insured receives it for conversion by the Insured into finished stock.
   (b) "Stock in Process": raw stock which has undergone any aging, seasoning, mechanical or other process of manufacture at the location(s) herein described but which has not become finished stock.
   (c) "Finished Stock": stock manufactured by the Insured which in the ordinary course of the Insured's business is ready for packing, shipment or sale.
   (d) "Merchandise": goods kept for sale by the Insured which are not the product of manufacturing operations conducted by the Insured.
   (e) "Normal": the condition that would have existed had no loss occurred.

12. **Loss Clause:** Any loss hereunder shall not reduce the amount of this policy.

13. **Work and Materials Clause:** Permission granted for such use of the premises as is usual or incidental to the occupancy as described herein.

14. **Electrical Apparatus Clause (This Clause Void as to Windstorm Insurance):** This Company shall not be liable for Business Interruption loss resulting from electrical injury or disturbance to electrical appliances or devices (including wiring) caused by electrical currents artificially generated unless fire ensues, and if fire does ensue this Company shall be liable only for its proportion of Business Interruption loss caused by such ensuing fire.

15. **Alterations and New Buildings Clause:** Permission granted to make alterations in, or to construct additions to, any building described herein and to construct new buildings on the described premises. This policy is extended to cover, subject to all its provisions and stipulations, loss resulting from damage to or destruction of such alterations, additions or new buildings while in course of construction and when completed or occupied, provided that, in the event of damage to or destruction of such property (including building materials, supplies, machinery or equipment incident to such construction or occupancy while on the described premises or within one hundred (100) feet thereof) so as to delay commencement of business operations of the Insured, the length of time for which this Company shall be liable shall be determined as otherwise provided herein but such determined length of time shall be applied and the loss hereunder calculated from the date that business operations would have begun had no loss occurred.

If any building herein described is protected by automatic sprinklers, this permit shall not be held to include the reconstruction or the enlargement of any building so protected, without the consent of this Company in writing. This permit does not waive or modify any of the terms or conditions of the Automatic Sprinkler Clause (if any) attached to this policy.

16. **Liberalization Clause:** If during the period that insurance is in force under this policy, there be adopted in this state by the fire insurance rating organization on behalf of this Company, any forms, endorsements or rules by which this insurance could be extended or broadened, without additional premium charge, by endorsement or substitution of such form or endorsement, then such extended or broadened insurance shall inure to the benefit of the Insured hereunder as though such endorsement or substitution of form had been made.

17. **Subrogation Clause:** It is hereby stipulated that this insurance shall not be invalidated should the Insured waive in writing prior to a loss any or all right of recovery against any party for loss occurring to the property described herein.

18. **Nuclear Clause:** The word "fire" in this policy or endorsements attached hereto is not intended to and does not embrace nuclear reaction or nuclear radiation or radioactive contamination, all whether controlled or uncontrolled, and loss by nuclear reaction or nuclear radiation or radioactive contamination is not intended to be and is not insured against by this policy or said endorsements, whether such loss be direct or indirect, proximate or remote, or be in whole or in part caused by, contributed to, or aggravated by "fire" or any other perils insured against by this policy or said endorsements; however, subject to the foregoing and all provisions of this policy, loss by "fire" resulting from nuclear reaction or nuclear radiation or radioactive contamination is insured against by this policy.

19. **SPECIAL CONDITIONS APPLICABLE TO MINING RISKS:** The following additional conditions (a) and (b) are applicable only to Mining Risks:
   (a) This insurance does not extend to cover any loss caused by the peril(s) insured against occurring in mine or mines or by the disturbance of any property underground, unless as a result of such peril(s) any superstructure above ground is damaged or destroyed, and then only for the loss that would be occasioned during the time required to repair or replace such structure or structures.
   (b) This policy applies only to the buildings and machinery that contribute to the production of the mining plant. Commissaries, commissary warehouses and dwellings, including contents of such buildings, are excluded unless specifically provided for herein.

Form No. 19C (4-65)

UNIFORM STANDARD | **FORM NO. 19G** (Edition Mar. '59)

BUSINESS INTERRUPTION FORM NO. 3

Gross Earnings Form for Mercantile or Non-Manufacturing Risks

Attached to and forming part of Policy No..

of the...NAME OF INSURANCE COMPANY...

issued at its..........CITY OR TOWN..STATE..............Agency. Dated..19.......

1. Subject to all its provisions and stipulations, this policy covers only against loss resulting directly from necessary interruption of business caused by damage to or destruction of real or personal property by the peril(s) insured against, during the term of this policy on premises occupied by the Insured as..

....

....

and situated..

.......................HERE GIVE STREET NUMBER, OR LOT OR BLOCK NUMBER OR TOWNSHIP, SECTION AND RANGE.......................

....

City or Town of..State of..

2. In the event of such damage or destruction this Company shall be liable for the ACTUAL LOSS SUSTAINED by the Insured resulting directly from such interruption of business, but not exceeding the reduction in Gross Earnings less charges and expenses which do not necessarily continue during the interruption of business, for only such length of time as would be required with the exercise of due diligence and dispatch to rebuild, repair or replace such part of the property herein described as has been damaged or destroyed, commencing with the date of such damage or destruction and not limited by the date of expiration of this policy. Due consideration shall be given to the continuation of normal charges and expenses, including payroll expense, to the extent necessary to resume operations of the Insured with the same quality of service which existed immediately preceding the loss.

3. **Resumption of Operations:** It is a condition of this insurance that if the Insured could reduce the loss resulting from the interruption of business,
(a) by complete or partial resumption of operation of the property herein described, whether damaged or not, or
(b) by making use of merchandise or other property, at the location(s) described herein or elsewhere,
such reduction shall be taken into account in arriving at the amount of loss hereunder.

4. **Expenses Related to Reducing Loss:** This policy also covers such expenses as are necessarily incurred for the purpose of reducing loss under this policy (except expense incurred to extinguish a (fire), but in no event shall the aggregate of such expenses exceed the amount by which the loss under this policy is thereby reduced. Such expenses shall not be subject to the application of the Contribution Clause.

5. **Gross Earnings:** For the purposes of this insurance "Gross Earnings" are defined as the sum of:
(a) Total net sales, and
(b) Other earnings derived from operations of the business,
less the cost of:
(c) Merchandise sold, including packaging material therefor,
(d) Materials and supplies consumed directly in supplying the service(s) sold by the Insured, and
(e) Service(s) purchased from outsiders (not employees of the Insured) for resale which do not continue under contract.
No other costs shall be deducted in determining Gross Earnings.
In determining Gross Earnings due consideration shall be given to the experience of the business before the date of damage or destruction and the probable experience thereafter had no loss occurred.

6. **Contribution Clause:** In consideration of the rate and form under which this policy is written, this Company shall be liable, in the event of loss, for no greater proportion thereof than the amount hereby covered bears to..........................% (INSERT 50, 60, 70, 80 OR 90) of the Gross Earnings that would have been earned (had no loss occurred) during the 12 months immediately following the date of damage to or destruction of the described property.

THE PROVISIONS PRINTED ON THE BACK OF THIS FORM ARE HEREBY REFERRED TO AND MADE A PART HEREOF.

UNIFORMITY TRADE MARK Form No. 19G (3-59) ....Agent.

NOTES TO AGENTS:

1. Sprinklered Risks.—If policy covers risk equipped with automatic sprinklers, the Automatic Sprinkler Clause must be attached.

2. Watchman's Clause.—If policy covers risk where credit has been allowed for watchman's service, the Watchman's Clause must be attached.

Appendix G—Business Interruption Coverage (Continued)

7. **Interruption By Civil Authority:** This policy is extended to include the actual loss as covered hereunder, during the period of time, not exceeding 2 consecutive weeks, when as a direct result of the peril(s) insured against, access to the premises described is prohibited by order of civil authority.

8. **Special Exclusions:** This Company shall not be liable for any increase of loss which may be occasioned by any local or state ordinance or law regulating construction or repair of buildings or structures, nor by the suspension, lapse or cancellation of any lease or license, contract or order, nor for any increase of loss due to interference at the described premises by strikers or other persons with rebuilding, repairing or replacing the property or with the resumption or continuation of business; nor shall this Company be liable for any other consequential loss or remote loss.

9. **Pro Rata Clause:** The liability under this policy shall not exceed that proportion of any loss which the amount of insurance hereunder bears to all insurance, whether collectible or not, covering in any manner the loss insured against by this policy.

10. **Definition of "Normal":** The condition that would have existed had no loss occurred.

11. **Loss Clause:** Any loss hereunder shall not reduce the amount of this policy.

12. **Work and Materials Clause:** Permission granted for such use of the premises as is usual or incidental to the occupancy as described herein.

13. **Electrical Apparatus Clause (This Clause Void as to Windstorm Insurance):** This Company shall not be liable for Business Interruption loss resulting from electrical injury or disturbance to electrical appliances or devices (including wiring) caused by electrical currents artificially generated unless fire ensues, and if fire does ensue this Company shall be liable only for its proportion of Business Interruption loss caused by such ensuing fire.

14. **Alterations and New Buildings Clause:** Permission granted to make alterations in, or to construct additions to, any building described herein and to construct new buildings on the described premises. This policy is extended to cover, subject to all its provisions and stipulations, loss resulting from damage to or destruction of such alterations, additions or new buildings while in course of construction and when completed or occupied, provided that, in the event of damage to or destruction of such property (including building materials, supplies, machinery or equipment incident to such construction or occupancy while on the described premises or within one hundred (100) feet thereof) so as to delay commencement of business operations of the Insured, the length of time for which this Company shall be liable shall be determined as otherwise provided herein but such determined length of time shall be applied and the loss hereunder calculated from the date that business operations would have begun had no loss occurred.

If any building herein described is protected by automatic sprinklers, this permit shall not be held to include the reconstruction or the enlargement of any building so protected, without the consent of this Company in writing. This permit does not waive or modify any of the terms or conditions of the Automatic Sprinkler Clause (if any) attached to this policy.

15. **Liberalization Clause:** If during the period that insurance is in force under this policy, there be adopted in this state by the fire insurance rating organization on behalf of this Company, any forms, endorsements or rules by which this insurance could be extended or broadened, without additional premium charge, by endorsement or substitution of such form or endorsement, then such extended or broadened insurance shall inure to the benefit of the Insured hereunder as though such endorsement or substitution of form had been made.

16. **Subrogation Clause:** It is hereby stipulated that this insurance shall not be invalidated should the Insured waive in writing prior to a loss any or all right of recovery against any party for loss occurring to the property described herein.

17. **Nuclear Clause:** The word "fire" in this policy or endorsements attached hereto is not intended to and does not embrace nuclear reaction or nuclear radiation or radioactive contamination, all whether controlled or uncontrolled, and loss by nuclear reaction or nuclear radiation or radioactive contamination is not intended to be and is not insured against by this policy or said endorsements, whether such loss be direct or indirect, proximate or remote, or be in whole or in part caused by, contributed to, or aggravated by "fire" or any other perils insured against by this policy or said endorsements; however, subject to the foregoing and all provisions of this policy, loss by "fire" resulting from nuclear reaction or nuclear radiation or radioactive contamination is insured against by this policy.

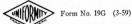

Form No. 19G (3-59)

11. **Loss Clause:** Any loss hereunder shall not reduce the amount of this policy.

12. **Alterations and Repairs Clause:** Permission granted to make alterations in, or to construct additions to, any building described herein. This policy is extended to cover, subject to all its provisions and stipulations, loss resulting from damage to or destruction of such alterations or additions to any building described herein while in course of construction and when completed or occupied, provided that, in the event of damage to or destruction of such property (including building materials, supplies, machinery or equipment incident to such construction or occupancy while on the described premises or within one hundred (100) feet thereof) so as to delay commencement of business operations of the Insured, the length of time for which this Company shall be liable shall be determined as otherwise provided herein but such determined length of time shall be applied and the loss hereunder calculated from the date that business operations would have begun had no damage or destruction occurred.

If any building herein described is protected by automatic sprinklers, this clause shall not be held to include the reconstruction or the enlargement of any building so protected, without the consent of this Company in writing. This clause does not waive or modify any of the terms or conditions of the Automatic Sprinkler Clause (if any) attached to this policy.

13. **Electrical Apparatus Clause:** This Company shall not be liable for any loss of earnings resulting from any electrical injury or disturbance to electrical appliances, devices, fixtures or wiring caused by electrical currents artificially generated unless fire ensues and, if fire does ensue, this Company shall be liable only for its proportion of loss of earnings caused by such ensuing fire.

14. **Liberalization Clause:** If during the period that insurance is in force under this policy, or within 45 days prior to the inception date thereof, on behalf of this Company there be adopted, or filed with and approved or accepted by the insurance supervisory authorities, all in conformity with law, any changes in the form attached to this policy by which this form of insurance could be extended or broadened without increased premium charge by endorsement or substitution of form, then such extended or broadened insurance shall inure to the benefit of the Insured hereunder as though such endorsement or substitution of form had been made.

15. **Nuclear Clause:** The word "fire" in this policy or endorsements attached hereto is not intended to and does not embrace nuclear reaction or nuclear radiation or radioactive contamination, all whether controlled or uncontrolled, and loss by nuclear reaction or nuclear radiation or radioactive contamination is not intended to be and is not insured against by this policy or said endorsements, whether such loss be direct or indirect, proximate or remote, or be in whole or in part caused by, contributed to, or aggravated by "fire" or any other perils insured against by this policy or said endorsements; however, subject to the foregoing and all provisions of this policy, loss by "fire" resulting from nuclear reaction or nuclear radiation or radioactive contamination is insured against by this policy.

16. **Work and Materials Clause:** Permission granted for such use of the premises as is usual or incidental to the occupancy as described herein.

Form No. 19F (10-61)

UNIFORM STANDARD **FORM NO. 19H**
(Edition Apr. '65)

ORDINARY PAYROLL EXCLUSION ENDORSEMENT
(FOR USE ONLY WITH BUSINESS INTERRUPTION FORMS 19C OR 19G)

In consideration of the rate charged and substitution of the following Contribution Clause in lieu of the Contribution Clause contained in the form attached to this policy, this Company shall not be liable for any ordinary payroll expense as hereinafter defined.

Contribution Clause: In consideration of the rate and form under which this policy is written and this endorsement, this Company shall be liable, in the event of loss, for no greater proportion thereof than the amount hereby covered bears to the Contribution (Coinsurance) percentage specified (not less than 80%) on the first page of this policy (or endorsed hereon) of the Gross Earnings that would have been earned (had no less occurred) during the 12 months immediately following the date of damage to or destruction of the described property, less the same percentage of ordinary payroll expense for that 12 months period.

Definition of Ordinary Payroll Expense: The entire payroll expense for all employees of the Insured, except officers, executives, department managers, employees under contract and other important employees.

All other provisions and stipulations of this policy remain unchanged.

UNIFORM STANDARD **FORM NO. 19R**
(Edition Oct. '61)

ENDORSEMENT EXTENDING THE PERIOD OF INDEMNITY
(FOR USE WITH BUSINESS INTERRUPTION FORMS)

Attached to and forming part of Policy No...
of the..................................NAME OF INSURANCE COMPANY..................................
issued at its........CITY OR TOWN........................STATE........................Agency. Dated........................19.......

In consideration of $........................ additional premium, this policy is extended to cover the Actual Loss Sustained by the Insured resulting directly from the interruption of business, as covered by this policy for such additional length of time as would be required with the exercise of due diligence and dispatch to restore the Insured's business to the condition that would have existed had no loss occurred, commencing with the later of the following dates:

1. the date on which the liability of this Company for loss resulting from interruption of business would terminate if this endorsement had not been attached to this policy; or
2. the date on which repair, replacement or rebuilding of such part of the building(s), structure(s), machinery, equipment, or furniture and fixtures of the property herein described as has been damaged or destroyed is actually completed;

but in no event for more than........................consecutive calendar days from said later commencement date.

The liability under this endorsement shall not exceed that proportion of any loss which the amount of insurance under this policy bears to all insurance, whether collectible or not, covering in any manner the loss insured against by this policy, whether or not all such insurance includes this or a similar extension of coverage.

In all other respects, the terms and conditions of this policy and the form attached thereto remain unchanged and are applicable to this extension of coverage.

Form No. 19R (10-61) ....Agent.

UNIFORM STANDARD **FORM NO. 19J**
(Edition Apr. '65)

ORDINARY PAYROLL — LIMITED COVERAGE ENDORSEMENT
(FOR USE ONLY WITH BUSINESS INTERRUPTION FORMS 19C OR 19G)

In consideration of the rate charged and substitution of the following Contribution Clause in lieu of the Contribution Clause contained in the form attached to this policy, the liability of this Company for ordinary payroll expense, as hereinafter defined, is limited to such expense which must necessarily continue during the interruption of business for not exceeding 90* consecutive calendar days immediately following the date of damage to or destruction of the described property.

Contribution Clause: In consideration of the rate and form under which this policy is written and this endorsement, this Company shall be liable, in the event of loss, for no greater proportion thereof then the amount hereby covered bears to the Contribution (Coinsurance) percentage specified (not less than 80%) on the first page of this policy (or endorsed hereon) of the Gross Earnings that would have been earned (had no less occurred) during the 12 months immediately following the date of damage to or destruction of the described property, less the same percentage of ordinary payroll expense for the portion of that 12 months period which follows the 90* days specified above.

Definition of Ordinary Payroll Expense: The entire payroll expense for all employees of the Insured, except officers, executives, department managers, employees under contract and other important employees.

All other provisions and stipulations of this policy remain unchanged.

NOTE TO AGENTS: *The 90-day limit may be increased as provided in the rules.

UNIFORM STANDARD

FORM NO. 19V
(Edition July '61)

CONTINGENT BUSINESS INTERRUPTION INSURANCE

Attached to and forming part of Policy No...

of the.............................NAME OF INSURANCE COMPANY.............................

issued at its......CITY OR TOWN..............................STATE..................Agency. Dated...................................19........

Amount $..................................

1. Subject to all its provisions and stipulations, this policy covers only against loss resulting directly from necessary interruption of business conducted on premises occupied by the Insured as..and situated...

HERE GIVE STREET NUMBER, OR LOT OR BLOCK NUMBER OR TOWNSHIP, SECTION OR RANGE

....

City or Town of..State of.......................................
caused by damage to or destruction of any of the real or personal property hereinafter described and referred to as CONTRIBUTING PROPERTY(IES) and which is not operated by the Insured, by the peril(s) insured against during the term of this policy, which wholly or partially prevents the delivery of materials to the Insured or to others for the account of the Insured and results directly in a necessary interruption of the Insured's business.

2. In the event of such damage or destruction this Company shall be liable for the ACTUAL LOSS SUSTAINED by the Insured resulting directly from such interruption of business, but not exceeding the reduction in Gross Earnings less charges and expenses which do not necessarily continue during the interruption of business, for only such length of time as would be required with the exercise of due diligence and dispatch to rebuild, repair, or replace such CONTRIBUTING PROPERTY(IES) as has been damaged or destroyed, commencing with the date of such interruption of the Insured's business and not limited by the date of expiration of this policy. Due consideration shall be given to the continuation of normal charges and expenses, including payroll expense, to the extent necessary to resume operations of the Insured with the same quality of service which existed immediately preceding the loss.

DESCRIBED CONTRIBUTING PROPERTY(IES)
(Not Operated by the Insured)

Name and Describe Occupancy and Location (Street, City and State) of Supplier(s) of Materials

....

....

....

....

....

....

....

....

The following extension of coverage shall apply only if the word "AND" is inserted in the blank space provided therefor, immediately preceding the extension of coverage, but not otherwise.

..........................all other CONTRIBUTING PROPERTIES not operated by the Insured, wherever located within the Continental United States and not elsewhere, but in no event shall this Company be liable for loss caused by damage to or destruction of any CONTRIBUTING PROPERTY not specifically named and described herein, for an amount exceeding one-half of one per cent (½ of 1%) of the amount of this policy for any one month of interruption of the Insured's business, or proportionate part thereof for periods of less than one month, subject in all other respects to the provisions and stipulations of this policy; provided further that wherever the term "DESCRIBED CONTRIBUTING PROPERTY(IES)" is used in this form it shall include all contributing properties to which this insurance extends, whether or not specifically named and described herein.

3. **Resumption of Operations:** It is a condition of this insurance that if the Insured could reduce the loss resulting from the interruption of business,

(a) by complete or partial resumption of operation of his business, or
(b) by making use of any other available source of materials, or
(c) by making use of stock (raw, in process or finished) at the location(s) operated by the Insured and described herein or elsewhere,

such reduction shall be taken into account in arriving at the amount of loss hereunder.

The Insured shall also use his influence to induce the CONTRIBUTING PROPERTY(IES) to make use of any other machinery, equipment, supplies or location available in order to resume operations and delivery of materials to the Insured and shall cooperate with the CONTRIBUTING PROPERTY(IES) to this effect in every way, but not financially unless such expenditure shall be authorized by this Company.

4. **Contribution Clause:** In consideration of the rate and form under which this policy is written, this Company shall be liable, in the event of loss, for no greater proportion thereof than the amount hereby covered bears to..............................% (INSERT 50, 60, 70 OR 80) of the Gross Earnings of the Insured, dependent upon or affected by delivery of all materials from the DESCRIBED CONTRIBUTING PROPERTY(IES) to the Insured or to others for the account of the Insured, that would have been earned (had no loss occurred) during the 12 months immediately following the date of interruption of the Insured's business.

THE PROVISIONS PRINTED ON THE BACK OF THIS FORM ARE HEREBY REFERRED TO AND MADE A PART HEREOF.

UNIFORMITY TRADE MARK Form No. 19 V (7-61) ....Agent.

5. **Expenses Related to Reducing Loss:** This policy also covers such expenses as are necessarily incurred for the purpose of reducing loss under this policy and such expenses, in excess of normal, as would necessarily be incurred in replacing any finished stock used by the Insured to reduce loss under this policy; but in no event shall the aggregate of such expenses exceed the amount by which the loss under this policy is thereby reduced. Such expenses shall not be subject to the application of the Contribution Clause.

6. **Gross Earnings:** For the purposes of this insurance "Gross Earnings" are defined as the sum of

(a) Total net sales value of production,

(b) Total net sales of merchandise, and

(c) Other earnings derived from operation of the business,

less the cost of:

(d) Raw Stock from which such production is derived,

(e) Supplies consisting of materials consumed directly in the conversion of such raw stock into finished stock or in supplying the service(s) sold by the Insured,

(f) Merchandise sold, including packaging materials therefor, and

(g) Service(s) purchased from outsiders (not employees of the Insured) for resale which do not continue under contract.

No other costs shall be deducted in determining Gross Earnings.

In determining Gross Earnings due consideration shall be given to the experience of the Insured's business before the date of interruption and the probable experience thereafter had no loss occurred.

7. **Interruption By Civil Authority:** This policy is extended to include the actual loss as covered hereunder during the period of time, not exceeding 2 consecutive weeks, when, as a direct result of the peril(s) insured against, access to the premises of the DESCRIBED CONTRIBUTING PROPERTY(IES) is prohibited by order of civil authority.

8. **Special Exclusions:** This Company shall not be liable for any increase of loss which may be occasioned by any local or state ordinance or law regulating construction or repair of buildings or structures, nor by the suspension, lapse or cancellation of any lease or license, contract or order, nor for any increase of loss due to interference at the premises of the CONTRIBUTING PROPERTY(IES) by strikers or other persons with rebuilding, repairing or replacing the property or with the resumption or continuation of business, nor for any loss of selling commissions due to damage to or destruction of any manufacturing property(ies), the products of which the Insured has contracted to sell in whole or in part, which prevents delivery of such products to the Insured's customers under such contracts; nor shall this Company be liable for any other consequential loss or remote loss.

9. **Pro Rata Clause:** The liability under this policy shall not exceed that proportion of any loss which the amount of insurance hereunder bears to all insurance, whether collectible or not, covering in any manner the loss insured against by this policy.

10. **Definitions:** The following terms wherever used in this policy shall mean:

(a) "Raw Stock": material in the state in which the Insured receives it for conversion by the Insured into finished stock.

(b) "Stock in Process": raw stock which has undergone any aging, seasoning, mechanical or other process of manufacture at the location(s) operated by the Insured and herein described but which has not become finished stock.

(c) "Finished Stock": stock manufactured by the Insured which in the ordinary course of the Insured's business is ready for packing, shipment or sale.

(d) "Merchandise": goods kept for sale by the Insured which are not the product of manufacturing operations conducted by the Insured.

(e) "Normal": the condition that would have existed had no interruption of the Insured's business occurred as a result of damage to or destruction of the CONTRIBUTING PROPERTY(IES) by the peril(s) insured against.

11. **Loss Clause:** Any loss hereunder shall not reduce the amount of this policy.

12. **Electrical Apparatus Clause:** This Company shall not be liable for any Contingent Business Interruption loss resulting from damage to the described CONTRIBUTING PROPERTY(IES) resulting from any electrical injury or disturbance to electrical appliances, devices, fixtures or wiring caused by electrical currents artificially generated unless fire ensues and, if fire does ensue, this Company shall be liable only for its proportion of Contingent Business Interruption loss caused by such ensuing fire.

13. **Liberalization Clause:** If during the period that insurance is in force under this policy, or within 45 days prior to the inception date thereof, on behalf of this Company there be adopted, or filed with and approved or accepted by the insurance supervisory authorities, all in conformity with law, any changes in the form attached to this policy by which this form of insurance could be extended or broadened without increased premium charge by endorsement or substitution of form, then such extended or broadened insurance shall inure to the benefit of the Insured hereunder as though such endorsement or substitution of form had been made.

14. **Nuclear Clause:** The word "fire" in this policy or endorsements attached hereto is not intended to and does not embrace nuclear reaction or nuclear radiation or radioactive contamination, all whether controlled or uncontrolled, and loss by nuclear reaction or nuclear radiation or radioactive contamination is not intended to be and is not insured against by this policy or said endorsements, whether such loss be direct or indirect, proximate or remote, or be in whole or in part caused by, contributed to, or aggravated by "fire" or any other perils insured against by this policy or said endorsements; however, subject to the foregoing and all provisions of this policy, loss by "fire" resulting from nuclear reaction or nuclear radiation or radioactive contamination is insured against by this policy.

15. **Alterations and New Buildings Clause:** Permission granted to make alterations in or to construct additions to any building at the CONTRIBUTING PROPERTY(IES) and to construct new buildings on such premises. This policy is extended to cover, subject to all its provisions and stipulations, loss resulting from damage to or destruction of such alterations, additions or new buildings while in course of construction and when completed or occupied, provided that, in the event of damage to or destruction of such property (including building materials, supplies, machinery or equipment incident to such construction or occupancy while on the described premises or within one hundred (100) feet thereof) so as to delay commencement of business operations of the Insured, the length of time for which this Company shall be liable shall be determined as otherwise provided herein but such determined length of time shall be applied and the loss hereunder calculated from the date that business operations would have begun had no damage or destruction occurred.

If any building herein described is protected by automatic sprinklers, this permit shall not be held to include the reconstruction or the enlargement of any building so protected, without the consent of this Company in writing. This permit does not waive or modify any of the terms or conditions of the Automatic Sprinkler Clause (if any) attached to this policy.

Form No. 19V (7-61)

UNIFORM STANDARD **FORM NO. 20**
(Edition Mar. '59)

BUSINESS INTERRUPTION PREMIUM ADJUSTMENT ENDORSEMENT

(For Use Only with Business Interruption Forms Nos. 19C, 19G or 19V without either the Ordinary Payroll Exclusion Endorsement or the Ordinary Payroll — Limited Coverage Endorsment)

Attached to and forming part of Policy No...

of the.........................NAME OF INSURANCE COMPANY.........................

issued at its..............CITY OR TOWN..............STATE..............Agency. Dated..............19.........

1. The intent of this endorsement being to convert the insurance provided by this policy to a premium adjustment form, the premium consideration therefor is provisional and this policy is hereby amended to the extent set forth in the terms and conditions of this endorsement. In all other respects the policy remains unchanged.

2. **Limits of Liability:** (a) This policy being for the amount of $.............................., being...........................% of the limit of liability of all business interruption insurance covering the loss insured against by this policy (whether or not such insurance is written subject to the terms and conditions of this endorsement), the liability under this policy shall in no event exceed the same percentage of any loss or the amount of this policy.

(b) In consideration of the provision for premium adjustment hereunder and based upon that percentage of "Gross Earnings" which is specified as......................% in the Contribution Clause attached to this policy, liability under this policy shall in no event exceed this policy's proportion of the said percentage of "Gross Earnings" that would have been earned (had no loss occurred) during the twelve months immediately following date of damage to or destruction of the described property.

3. **Full Reporting Clause:** Liability under this policy shall in no event exceed that proportion of any loss hereunder, which the last reported value received by this Company prior to the date of damage or destruction bears to the actual value during the period covered by such report.

4. **Other Insurance:** This insurance does not attach nor become operative if at the time of damage or destruction there is in force other insurance (whether collectible or not) that is not written upon the same plan, terms, conditions and provisions as contained in the forms and endorsements, including this endorsement, attached to this policy, until the liability of such other insurance has been exhausted.

5. **Value Reporting Clause:** It is a condition of this insurance that the Insured shall submit reports to this Company upon forms (sample printed on reverse side hereof) prescribed by this Company, in accordance with the following requirements:

(a) On the effective date of this endorsement, a report showing the "Gross Earnings" as defined in this policy, except that such report shall cover the Insured's latest preceding fiscal year for which such figures are available.

(b) Within 120 days after the close of each of the Insured's succeeding fiscal years, a report similar to that described above covering the preceding fiscal year.

(c) Within 120 days after the expiration or cancellation of this policy by this Company, a similar report except that such report shall cover from the close of the Insured's last fiscal year to, or beyond, the expiration or cancellation date of this policy.

6. **Premium Adjustment Clause:** (a) The premium under this policy being provisional shall be adjusted after receipt of the final report as required by the terms and conditions of this endorsement.

(b) If the effective date of this endorsement is subsequent to the effective date of this policy, the premium applicable to the period preceding the effective date of this endorsement shall be considered as fully earned and no adjustment shall be made thereon.

(c) If there has been any change in the percentages referred to in Paragraph 2 of this endorsement or in the rates named in this policy during the term of this endorsement, the final adjusted premium hereunder shall be determined by applying the method prescribed herein to each period that elapsed between the effective dates of such changes.

(d) All reported values applying only in part to such periods as are prescribed for premium computation hereunder shall be prorated to each such period.

(e) All reported values applying during periods covered by this endorsement shall be adjusted to the percentage specified in the Contribution Clause, and shall then be further adjusted to this policy's percentage of said limit of liability of all business interruption insurance, as indicated in Paragraph 2 of this endorsement. The total earned premium for this policy shall be determined by adding the premium, if any, applicable to the period preceding attachment of this endorsement to the premium developed by applying the proper proportion of the rates named in this policy to the values for each period covered by this endorsement.

(f) In consideration of the privileges and conditions of this endorsement, if the total earned premium under this policy as developed by the above method is less than the provisional premium paid, this Company shall refund to the Insured the excess paid, but in no event shall the total premium retained under this policy be less than $50.00.

(g) If the Insured fails to submit any report of values when and as required herein or if, at the request of the Insured, the policy is cancelled on a short rate basis, the terms and conditions of this endorsement shall cease to apply and no adjustment of premium shall be made under this endorsement.

7. **Verification of Values:** This Company or its duly appointed representative, shall be permitted at all reasonable times during the term of this policy, or within a year after its expiration, to inspect the property described hereunder and to examine the Insured's books, records and such policies as relate to any property described hereunder. This inspection or examination shall not waive or in any manner affect any of the terms or conditions of this policy.

UNIFORMITY TRADE MARK Form No. 20 (3-59) ....Agent.

NOTE TO AGENTS: A sample of the form of report required hereunder is printed on the reverse side hereof and such form (Uniform Form No. 20A) must in all cases be used in making reports. Full responsibility for accuracy and promptness of reports rests entirely with the Insured.

SAMPLE REPORT OF VALUES UNDER BUSINESS INTERRUPTION PREMIUM ADJUSTMENT ENDORSEMENT

(To be used only in conjunction with Premium Adjustment Endorsement)

DATE..........

TO .... POLICY No..........
Insurance Company

INSURED..........

LOCATION..........

REPORT OF VALUES FROM.......... TO..........

....
Agent/Broker Address

A. Total annual net sales value of production from Manufacturing Operations; and total annual net sales from Merchandising or Non-Manufacturing Operations, (Gross sales less discounts, returns, bad accounts and prepaid freight, if included in sales) - - - $..........

B. **Add** other earnings (if any) derived from operation of the business:..........
1. Cash Discounts Received - - - - - - - - - - - ....
2. Commissions or Rents from Leased Dept's. - - - - - - - - ....
3. ....

C. Total ("A." plus "B.") - - - - - - - - - - - - - - $..........

D. **Deduct cost of:**
1. Raw stock from which such production is derived - - - - - - - - - $..........
2. Supplies consisting of materials consumed directly in the conversion of such raw stock into finished stock or in supplying the service(s) sold by the Insured - - - - - - - - - $..........
3. Merchandise sold, including packaging materials therefor - - - - - - - - - $..........
4. Service(s) purchased from outsiders (not employees of the Insured) for resale which do not continue under contract - - - - - - - $..........
5. Total Deductions - - - - - - - - - - - - - $..........

E. GROSS EARNINGS ("C" Minus "D") - - - - - - - - - - - $..........

The fiscal year ends each..........
Date

I certify the foregoing is a true and correct report of values as required under the policy indicated above for the period indicated above.

....
Insured Named in Policy

BY..........

TITLE..........

NOTE: The above form is shown here for purposes of illustration but should not be filled out. In making actual reports use the corresponding separate form, Uniform Form No. 20A.

UNIFORMITY TRADE MARK Form No. 20 (3-59)

UNIFORM STANDARD

FORM NO. 19F
(Edition Oct. '61)

EARNINGS INSURANCE FORM

Monthly Limitation Form for Mercantile or Non-manufacturing Risks

1. Insurance attaches to this item(s) only when "Earnings" are specified in this policy and when a specific amount(s) is indicated therefor. All provisions and stipulations of this form and policy shall apply separately to each such item.

2. When this policy covers EARNINGS, this Company shall be liable for the ACTUAL LOSS SUSTAINED by the Insured resulting directly from necessary interruption of business caused by damage to or destruction of real or personal property by the peril(s) insured against, during the term of this policy, on the premises described, but not exceeding the reduction in Earnings less charges and expenses which do not necessarily continue during the interruption of business, for only such length of time as would be required with the exercise of due diligence and dispatch to rebuild, repair or replace such part of the property herein described as has been damaged or destroyed, commencing with the date of such damage or destruction and not limited by the date of expiration of this policy. Due consideration shall be given to the continuation of normal charges and expenses, including payroll expense, to the extent necessary to resume operations of the Insured with the same quality of service which existed immediately preceding the loss.

3. This Company shall not be liable for more than 25% of the amount specified for this item in any 30 consecutive calendar days.

4. **Resumption of Operations:** It is a condition of this insurance that if the Insured could reduce the loss resulting from the interruption of business,

(a) by complete or partial resumption of operation of the property herein described, whether damaged or not, or

(b) by making use of merchandise or other property at the location(s) described herein or elsewhere,

such reduction shall be taken into account in arriving at the amount of loss hereunder.

5. **Expenses to Reduce Loss:** This policy also covers such expenses as are necessarily incurred for the purpose of reducing loss under this policy (except expense incurred to extinguish a fire), but in no event shall the aggregate of such expenses exceed the amount by which the loss under this policy is thereby reduced.

6. **Earnings:** For the purpose of this insurance "Earnings" are defined as the sum of:
(a) Total net profit, (b) Payroll expenses, (c) Taxes, (d) Interest, (e) Rents, and (f) All other operating expenses earned by the business.

7. **Interruption by Civil Authority:** This policy is extended to include the actual loss as covered hereunder during the period of time, not exceeding 2 consecutive weeks, when, as a direct result of the peril(s) insured against, access to the premises described is prohibited by order of civil authority.

8. **Special Exclusions:** This Company shall not be liable for any increase of loss which may be occasioned by any local or state ordinance or law regulating construction or repair of buildings or structures, nor by the suspension, lapse or cancellation of any lease or license, contract or order, nor for any increase of loss due to interference at the described premises by strikers or other persons with rebuilding, repairing or replacing the property or with the resumption or continuation of business; nor shall this Company be liable for any other consequential loss or remote loss.

9. **Pro Rata Clause:** The liability under this policy shall not exceed that proportion of any loss which the amount of insurance hereunder bears to all insurance, whether collectible or not, covering in any manner the loss insured against by this policy.

10. **Definition of "Normal":** The condition that would have existed had no loss occurred.

THE PROVISIONS PRINTED ON THE BACK OF THIS FORM ARE HEREBY REFERRED TO AND MADE A PART HEREOF.

Form No. 19F (10-61)

NOTES TO AGENTS:

1. **Sprinklered Risks.—If policy covers risk equipped with automatic sprinklers, the Automatic Sprinkler Clause must be attached.**

2. **Watchman's Clause.—If policy covers risk where credit has been allowed for watchman's service, the Watchman's Clause must be attached.**

3. **NO CHANGE OR ALTERATION IN THIS FORM WILL BE PERMITTED EXCEPT BY ENDORSEMENT, COPY OF WHICH MUST BE SENT TO COMPANY.**

Appendix H—Rental Value Insurance Contribution Form

UNIFORM STANDARD

FORM NO. 158
(Edition Mar. '64)

RENTAL VALUE INSURANCE CONTRIBUTION FORM

Insurance attaches to this item(s) only when "Rental Value" is specified in this policy and when a specific amount(s) is indicated therefor, and, unless otherwise provided, all provisions and stipulations of this form and policy shall apply separately to each such item.

1. When this policy covers Rental Value, this Company shall be liable for the ACTUAL LOSS SUSTAINED by the Insured resulting directly from necessary untentability, caused by damage to or destruction of the building(s) or structure(s) as furnished and equipped by the Insured, on the described premises by the peril(s) insured against during the term of this policy, but not exceeding the reduction in Rental Value less charges and expenses which do not necessarily continue during the period of untenantability, for only such length of time as would be required with the exercise of due diligence and dispatch to rebuild, repair or replace such part of the property herein described as has been damaged or destroyed, commencing with the date of such damage or destruction and not limited by the date of expiration of this policy.

2. **Expenses to Reduce Loss:** This policy also covers such expenses as are necessarily incurred for the purpose of reducing loss under this policy (except expense incurred to extinguish a fire), but in no event shall the aggregate of such expenses exceed the amount by which the loss otherwise payable under this policy is thereby reduced. Such expenses shall not be subject to the application of the Contribution Clause.

3. **Rental Value:** For the purposes of this insurance "Rental Value" is defined as the sum of:
   (a) The total anticipated gross rental income from tenant occupancy of the described property as furnished and equipped by the Insured, and
   (b) The amount of all charges which are the legal obligation of the tenant(s) and which would otherwise be obligations of the Insured, and
   (c) The fair rental value of any portion of said property which is occupied by the Insured.

In determining Rental Value due consideration shall be given to the rental experience before the date of damage or destruction and the probable experience thereafter had no loss occurred.

4. **Contribution Clause:** In consideration of the rate and form under which this policy is written, this Company shall be liable, in the event of loss, for no greater proportion thereof than the amount hereby covered bears to the Contribution (Coinsurance) percentage specified on the first page of this policy (or endorsed hereon) of the Rental Value that would have been earned (had no loss occurred) during the 12 months immediately following the date of damage to or destruction of the described property.

5. **Interruption by Civil Authority:** This policy is extended to include the actual loss as covered hereunder during the period of time, not exceeding 2 consecutive weeks, when, as a direct result of the peril(s) insured against, access to the premises described is prohibited by order of civil authority.

THE PROVISIONS PRINTED ON THE BACK OF THIS FORM ARE HEREBY REFERRED TO AND MADE A PART HEREOF.

Form No. 158 (3-64)

Appendix H—Rental Value Insurance Contribution Form (Continued)

6. **Special Exclusions:** This Company shall not be liable for any increase of loss resulting from:
   (a) Enforcement of any local or state ordinance or law regulating the construction, repair or demolition of buildings or structures; or
   (b) Interference at the described premises by strikers or other persons with rebuilding, repairing or replacing the property or with the reoccupancy of the premises; or
   (c) The suspension, lapse or cancellation of any lease, license, contract or order unless such suspension, lapse or cancellation results directly from the untenantability of the premises, and then this Company shall be liable for only such loss as affects the Rental Value of the premises during, and limited to, the period of indemnity covered under this policy;

nor, shall this Company be liable for any other consequential or remote loss.

7. **Pro Rata Clause:** The liability under this policy shall not exceed that proportion of any loss which the amount of insurance hereunder bears to all insurance, whether collectible or not, covering in any manner the loss insured against by this policy.

8. **Loss Clause:** Any loss hereunder shall not reduce the amount of this policy.

9. **Alterations and New Buildings:** Permission granted to make alterations in or to construct additions to any building described and to construct new buildings on the described premises. This policy is extended to cover, subject to all its provisions and stipulations, loss of Rental Value resulting from damage to or destruction of such alterations, additions or new buildings while in course of construction and when completed or occupied, provided that, in the event of damage to or destruction of such property (including building materials, supplies, machinery or equipment incident to such construction or occupancy while on the described premises or within one hundred (100) feet thereof) so as to delay restoration to a tenantable condition, the length of time for which this Company shall be liable shall be determined as otherwise provided herein but such determined length of time shall be applied and the loss hereunder calculated from the date that the property would have been tenantable had no damage or destruction occurred.

This clause does not waive or modify any of the conditions of the Automatic Sprinkler Clause, if any, attached to this policy.

10. **Electrical Apparatus Clause:** This Company shall not be liable for any loss resulting from any electrical injury or disturbance to electrical appliances, devices, fixtures or wiring caused by electrical currents artificially generated unless fire ensues and, if fire does ensue, this Company shall be liable only for its proportion of loss caused by such ensuing fire.

11. **Liberalization Clause:** If during the period that insurance is in force under this policy, or within 45 days prior to the inception date thereof, on behalf of this Company there be adopted, or filed with and approved or accepted by the insurance supervisory authorities, all in conformity with law, any changes in the form attached to this policy by which this form of insurance could be extended or broadened without increased premium charge by endorsement or substitution of form, then such extended or broadened insurance shall inure to the benefit of the Insured hereunder as though such endorsement or substitution of form had been made.

12. **Nuclear Clause:** The word "fire" in this policy or endorsements attached hereto is not intended to and does not embrace nuclear reaction or nuclear radiation or radioactive contamination, all whether controlled or uncontrolled, and loss by nuclear reaction or nuclear radiation or radioactive contamination is not intended to be and is not insured against by this policy or said endorsements, whether such loss be direct or indirect, proximate or remote, or be in whole or in part caused by, contributed to, or aggravated by "fire" or any other perils insured against by this policy or said endorsements; however, subject to the foregoing and all provisions of this policy, loss by "fire" resulting from nuclear reaction or nuclear radiation or radioactive contamination is insured against by this policy.

Form No. 158 (3-64)

APPENDIX I

Appendix I—Water Damage Coverage

WATER DAMAGE POLICY — FORM H

No. WD

TYPE OF COMPANY

RENEWAL OF NUMBER

SPACE FOR COMPANY NAME, INSIGNIA, AND LOCATION

Insured's Name and Mailing Address

SPACE FOR PRODUCER'S NAME AND MAILING ADDRESS

Inception (Mo. Day Yr.) Expiration (Mo. Day Yr.) Years

SPECIMEN

It is important that the written portions of all policies covering the same property read exactly alike. If they do not, they should be made uniform at once.

INSURANCE IS PROVIDED AGAINST ONLY THE PERIL OF "WATER DAMAGE" AND FOR ONLY THOSE COVERAGES INDICATED BELOW BY A PREMIUM CHARGE.

LIMIT OF LIABILITY	RATE	PREMIUM IF PAID IN FULL AT INCEPTION	PREMIUM IF PAID IN INSTALLMENTS: AMOUNT DUE AT INCEPTION	AND AMOUNT DUE AT EACH SUBSEQUENT ANNIVERSARY	Coverage(s) Provided (Insert Name of Each)
$	$	$	$	$	PROPERTY DAMAGE
$	XXXXXXX	$	$	$	LIABILITY IMPOSED BY LAW
$	$	$	$	$	
XXXXXXX	XXXXXXX	$	$	$	CHEMICAL REFRIGERANT LEAKAGE
XXXXXXX	XXXXXXX	$	$	$	UNDERGROUND WATER SUPPLY MAINS AND FIRE HYDRANTS
	TOTAL(S)	$	$	$	

$ TOTAL PREMIUM FOR POLICY ON INSTALLMENT BASIS

Item No.	Limit of Liability	Per Cent of Co-Insurance Applicable	Amount of Deductible	DESCRIPTION AND LOCATION OF PROPERTY COVERED
1.-	$			

Subject to Form No(s). INSERT FORM NUMBER(S) AND EDITION DATE(S) **attached hereto.**

Agency at

Countersignature Date

Agent

IN CONSIDERATION OF THE PROVISIONS AND STIPULATIONS HEREIN OR ADDED HERETO AND OF the premium above specified, this Company, for the term of *years specified above* from *inception date shown above* At Noon (Standard Time) to *expiration date shown above* At Noon (Standard Time) at location of property involved, to an amount not exceeding the amount(s) above specified, does insure *the insured named above* and legal representatives, to the extent of the actual cash value of the property at the time of loss, but not exceeding the amount which it would cost to repair or replace the property with material of like kind and quality within a reasonable time after such loss, without allowance for any increased cost of repair or reconstruction by reason of any ordinance or law regulating construction or repair; and without compensation for loss resulting from interruption of business or manufacture, nor in any event for more than the interest of the insured, against all **DIRECT LOSS BY "WATER DAMAGE" AND BY REMOVAL FROM PREMISES ENDANGERED BY "WATER DAMAGE", EXCEPT AS HEREINAFTER PROVIDED,** to the property described herein while located or contained as described in this policy, or pro rata for five days at each proper place to which any of the property shall necessarily be removed for preservation from "Water Damage", but not elsewhere.

Assignment of this policy shall not be valid except with the written consent of this Company.

This policy is made and accepted subject to the foregoing provisions and stipulations and those hereinafter stated, which are hereby made a part of this policy, together with such other provisions, stipulations and agreements as may be added hereto, as provided in this policy.

OTP 426-O-C UNIFORM PRINTING & SUPPLY DIV.

Appendix I—Water Damage Coverage (Continued)

"Water Damage" Wherever in this policy the term "Water Damage" occurs, it shall be held to mean (a) the accidental discharge, leakage or overflow of water or steam from within the following source or sources: plumbing systems (excluding sprinkler systems), plumbing tanks for the storage of water for the supply of a plumbing system, heating systems, elevator tanks and cylinders, standpipes for fire hose (except when supplied by a sprinkler system), industrial or domestic appliances and refrigerating or air conditioning systems; (b) the accidental admission of rain or snow directly to the interior of the building through defective roofs, leaders or spouting, or through open or defective doors, windows, skylights, transoms or ventilators.

Damage by Tanks Except as herein provided this policy shall also cover direct loss caused by collapse or fall of a tank or any component part or support thereof, which forms a part of the plumbing system; such loss being considered as incidental to and part of the loss caused by "Water Damage".

Damage to Source of Loss This policy shall not cover damage to any system, tank, appliance, or contents thereof, or part of a building which is the source of such damage.

Perils not included This Company shall not be liable for loss by "Water Damage" or collapse or fall of a tank caused directly or indirectly by: (a) flood, surface water, waves, tidal water or tidal wave, overflow of streams or other bodies of water, or spray from any of the foregoing, all whether driven by wind or not; (b) water which backs up through sewers or drains; (c) water below the surface of the ground including that which exerts pressure on or flows, seeps or leaks through sidewalks, driveways, foundations, walls, basement or other floors, or through doors, windows or any other openings in such sidewalks, driveways, foundations, walls or floors; (d) gases, fumes or vapors (other than steam); (e) any failure, however caused, of refrigerating or air conditioning systems or equipment to maintain proper temperatures; (f) fire; (g) lightning; (h) windstorm, cyclone, tornado or hurricane; (i) earthquake; (j) blasting; (k) explosion (including explosion of refrigerating and air conditioning systems); (l) explosion or rupture of steam boilers or fly wheels; (m) riot; (n) civil commotion; (o) hostile or warlike action in time of peace or war, including action in hindering, combating or defending against an actual, impending or expected attack, (1) by any government or sovereign power (de jure or de facto), or by any authority maintaining or using military, naval or air forces; or (2) by military, naval or air forces; or (3) by an agent of any such government, power, authority or forces, it being understood that any discharge, explosion or use of any weapon of war employing nuclear fission or fusion shall be conclusively presumed to be such a hostile or warlike action by such a government, power, authority or forces; (p) insurrection, rebellion, revolution, civil war, usurped power, or action taken by governmental authority in hindering, combating or defending against such an occurrence; (q) order of any civil authority; (r) neglect of the insured to use all reasonable means to save and preserve the property at and after a "Water Damage"; (s) nor shall this Company be liable for loss by theft.

Uninsurable and excepted property This policy shall not cover: (a) accounts, bills, currency, deeds, evidences of debt, money or securities; (b) bullion or manuscripts (unless specifically named hereon in writing); (c) buildings or contents of buildings in process of construction or reconstruction unless entirely enclosed and under permanent roof with all outside doors and windows permanently in place; (d) open structures; (e) articles, materials or other personal property, not otherwise specifically excluded hereunder, outside of enclosed buildings.

Unless otherwise provided in writing added hereto, this Company shall not be liable for "Water Damage" loss:

(a) while a building at the location(s) described herein, whether intended for occupancy by owner or tenant, is vacant or unoccupied;

(b) caused directly or indirectly by breakage of or leakage from underground water supply mains or fire hydrants;

(c) caused directly or indirectly by discharge or leakage of the chemical refrigerant from any refrigerating or air conditioning system;

(d) occurring during and resulting from the making of repairs, alterations or extensions involving a wall or support(s) of a floor or roof or the installation of or change in any of the sources of loss enumerated in this policy at the location(s) described herein, after a period of fifteen consecutive days from the beginning of such operations.

Concealment, fraud This entire policy shall be void if, whether before or after a loss, the insured has wilfully concealed or misrepresented any material fact or circumstances concerning this insurance or the subject thereof, or the interest of the insured therein, or in case of any fraud or false swearing by the insured relating thereto.

of this policy, refund the excess of paid premium above the customary short rates for the expired time. This policy may be cancelled at any time by this Company by giving to the insured a five days' written notice of cancellation with or without tender of the excess of paid premium above the pro rata premium for the expired time, which excess, if not tendered, shall be refunded on demand. Notice of cancellation shall state that said excess premium (if not tendered) will be refunded on demand.

Mortgagee interests and obligations If loss hereunder is made payable, in whole or in part, to a designated mortgagee not named herein as the insured, such interest in this policy may be cancelled by giving to such mortgagee a ten days' written notice of cancellation.

If the insured fails to render proof of loss such mortgagee, upon notice, shall render proof of loss in the form herein specified within sixty (60) days thereafter and shall be subject to the provisions hereof relating to appraisal and time of payment and of bringing suit. If this Company shall claim that no liability existed as to the mortgagor or owner, it shall, to the extent of payment of loss to the mortgagee, be subrogated to all the mortgagee's rights of recovery, but without impairing mortgagee's right to sue; or it may pay off the mortgage debt and require an assignment thereof and of the mortgage. Other provisions relating to the interests and obligations of such mortgagee may be added hereto by agreement in writing.

Pro rata liability This Company shall not be liable for a greater proportion of any loss than the amount hereby insured shall bear to the whole insurance covering the property against the peril involved, whether collectible or not.

Requirements in case loss occurs The insured shall give immediate written notice to this Company of any loss, protect the property from further damage, forthwith separate the damaged and undamaged personal property, put it in the best possible order, furnish a complete inventory of the destroyed, damaged and undamaged property, showing in detail quantities, costs, actual cash value and amount of loss claimed; **and within sixty days after the loss, unless such time is extended in writing by this Company, the insured shall render to this Company a proof of loss,** signed and sworn to by the insured, stating the knowledge and belief of the insured as to the following: the time and origin of the loss, the interest of the insured and of all others in the property, the actual cash value of each item thereof and the amount of loss thereto, all encumbrances thereon, all other contracts of insurance, whether valid or not, covering any of said property, any changes in the title, use, occupation, location, possession or exposures of said property since the issuing of this policy, by whom and for what purpose any building herein described and the several parts thereof were occupied at the time of loss and whether or not it then stood on leased ground, and shall furnish a copy of all the descriptions and schedules in all policies and, if required, verified plans and specifications of any building, fixtures or machinery destroyed or damaged. The insured, as often as may be reasonably required, shall exhibit to any person designated by this Company all that remains of any property herein described, and submit to examinations under oath by any person named by this Company, and subscribe the same; and, as often as may be reasonably required, shall produce for examination all books of account, bills, invoices and other vouchers, or certified copies thereof if originals be lost, at such reasonable time and place as may be designated by this Company or its representative, and shall permit extracts and copies thereof to be made.

Appraisal In case the insured and this Company shall fail to agree as to the actual cash value or the amount of loss, then, on the written demand of either, each shall select a competent and disinterested appraiser and notify the other of the appraiser selected within twenty days of such demand. The appraisers shall first select a competent and disinterested umpire; and failing for fifteen days to agree upon such umpire, then, on request of the insured or this Company, such umpire shall be selected by a judge of a court of record in the state in which the property covered is located. The appraisers shall then appraise the loss, stating separately actual cash value and loss to each item; and, failing to agree, shall submit their differences, only, to the umpire. An award in writing, so itemized, of any two when filed with this Company shall determine the amount of actual cash value and loss. Each appraiser shall be paid by the party selecting him and the expenses of appraisal and umpire shall be paid by the parties equally.

Company's options It shall be optional with this Company to take all, or any part, of the property at the agreed or appraised value, and also to repair, rebuild or replace the property destroyed or damaged with other of like kind and quality within a reasonable time, on giving notice of its

Appendix I—Water Damage Coverage (Continued)

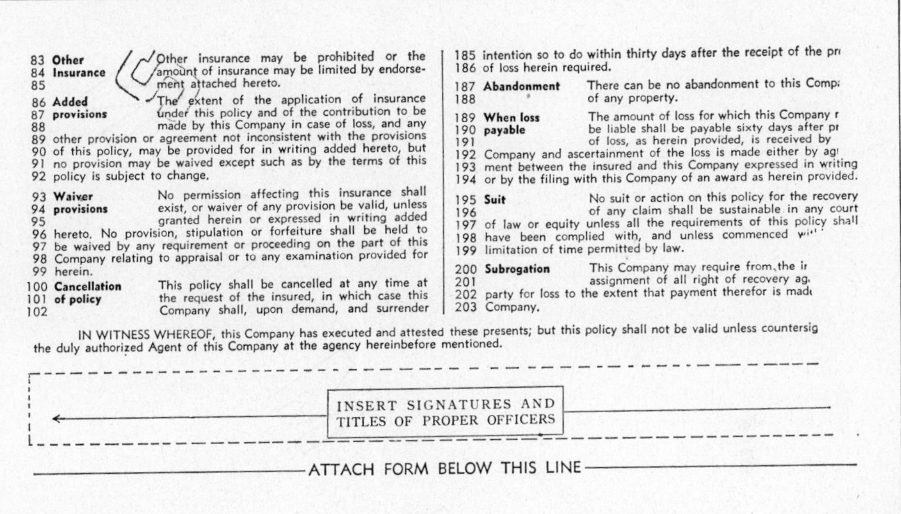

Other Insurance Other insurance may be prohibited or the amount of insurance may be limited by endorsement attached hereto.

Added provisions The extent of the application of insurance under this policy and of the contribution to be made by this Company in case of loss, and any other provision or agreement not inconsistent with the provisions of this policy, may be provided for in writing added hereto, but no provision may be waived except such as by the terms of this policy is subject to change.

Waiver provisions No permission affecting this insurance shall exist, or waiver of any provision be valid, unless granted herein or expressed in writing added hereto. No provision, stipulation or forfeiture shall be held to be waived by any requirement or proceeding on the part of this Company relating to appraisal or to any examination provided for herein.

Cancellation of policy This policy shall be cancelled at any time at the request of the insured, in which case this Company shall, upon demand, and surrender

intention so to do within thirty days after the receipt of the pr of loss herein required.

Abandonment There can be no abandonment to this Comp of any property.

When loss payable The amount of loss for which this Company r be liable shall be payable sixty days after pr of loss, as herein provided, is received by Company and ascertainment of the loss is made either by ag ment between the insured and this Company expressed in writing or by the filing with this Company of an award as herein provided.

Suit No suit or action on this policy for the recovery of any claim shall be sustainable in any court of law or equity unless all the requirements of this policy shall have been complied with, and unless commenced wi limitation of time permitted by law.

Subrogation This Company may require from the ir assignment of all right of recovery ag party for loss to the extent that payment therefor is mad Company.

IN WITNESS WHEREOF, this Company has executed and attested these presents; but this policy shall not be valid unless countersig the duly authorized Agent of this Company at the agency hereinbefore mentioned.

INSERT SIGNATURES AND TITLES OF PROPER OFFICERS

ATTACH FORM BELOW THIS LINE

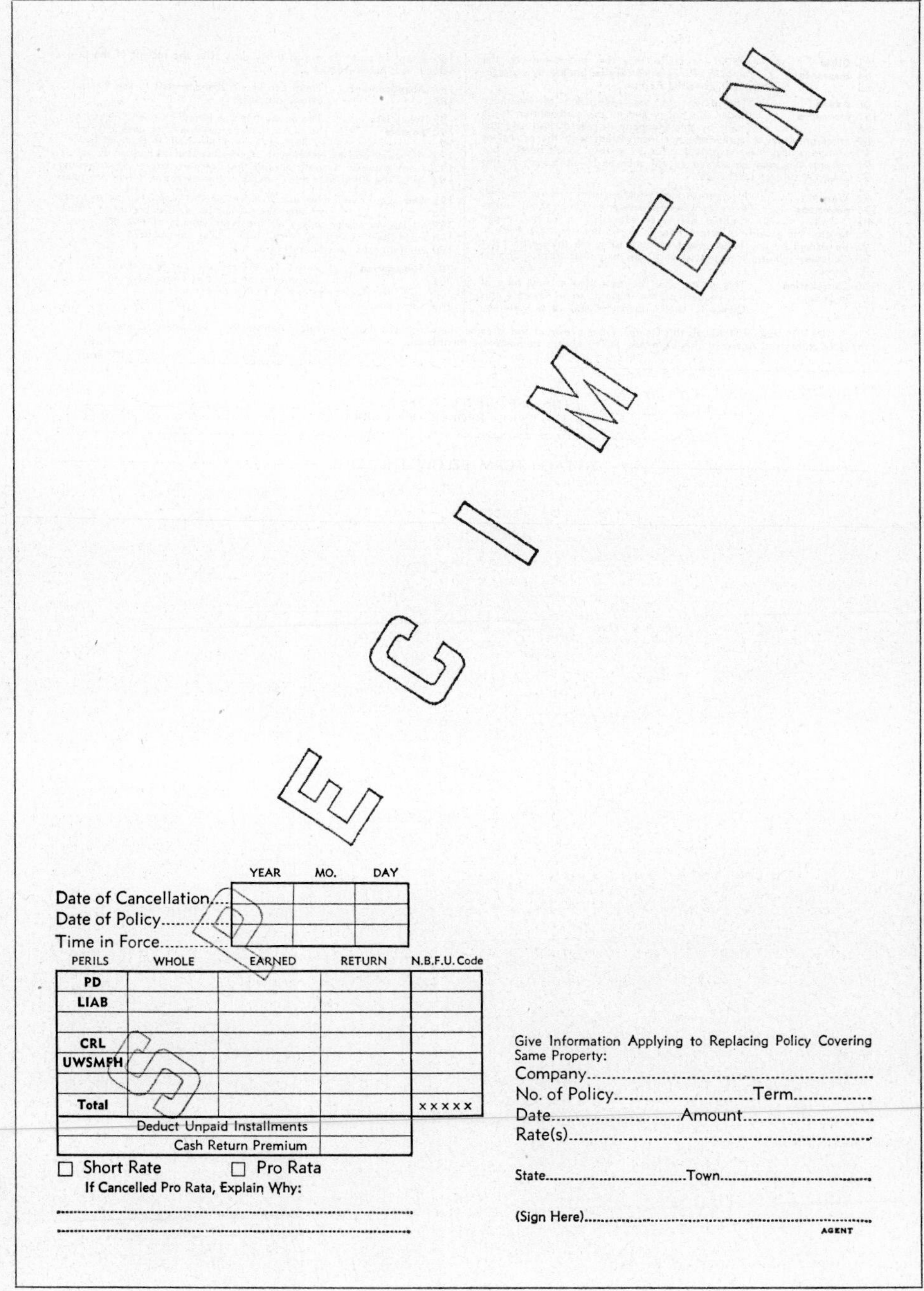

	YEAR	MO.	DAY
Date of Cancellation			
Date of Policy			
Time in Force			

PERILS	WHOLE	EARNED	RETURN	N.B.F.U. Code
PD				
LIAB				
CRL				
UWSMFH				
Total				x x x x x
Deduct Unpaid Installments				
Cash Return Premium				

☐ Short Rate ☐ Pro Rata

If Cancelled Pro Rata, Explain Why:

....

....

Give Information Applying to Replacing Policy Covering Same Property:

Company..

No. of Policy....................Term..............

Date....................Amount......................

Rate(s)...

State....................Town..........................

(Sign Here)..
AGENT

W. D. 602
(Ed. 1963)

WATER DAMAGE LIABILITY IMPOSED BY LAW FORM

For Use ONLY With Water Damage Policy—Form H

Insurance attaches only to the item(s) specifically described in this policy for which a specific limit of liability and premium for **Liability Imposed by Law** are shown. As to such item(s) the insuring clause in the policy is hereby amended to cover ONLY the liability of the Insured imposed upon him by law excluding all direct loss to the property of the Insured.

DESCRIPTION OF COVERAGE

The Company agrees with the named Insured to pay on behalf of the Insured all sums which the Insured shall become legally obligated to pay as damages because of injury to or destruction of property owned by others, including the loss of use thereof, (except property in the portion of a building occupied by the Insured) caused by "Water Damage," and arising out of the ownership, maintenance or use of the described premises, subject to the provisions herein. The limit of liability stated in this policy is the limit of the Company's liability for all damages as the result of any one occurrence.

SPECIAL PROVISIONS APPLICABLE TO THIS COVERAGE

This insurance applies only to occurrences during the policy period.

The inclusion herein of more than one Insured shall not operate to increase the limit of the Company's liability.

This insurance is subject to all the provisions and stipulations of this policy (except those entitled "Uninsurable and Excepted Property," "Mortgagee Interests and Obligations," "Requirements in Case Loss Occurs," "Appraisal," "Company's Options," "Abandonment," "When Loss Payable" and "Suit") and to the following:

1. Defense, Settlement, Supplementary Payments: As respects the insurance afforded by the other terms hereof the Company shall:

(a) Defend any suit against the Insured alleging such injury or destruction and seeking damages on account thereof, even if such suit is groundless, false or fraudulent; but the Company may make such investigation, negotiation and settlement of any claim or suit as it deems expedient;

(b) Pay all premiums on bonds to release attachments for an amount not in excess of the applicable limit of liability stated herein, all premiums on appeal bonds required in any such defended suit, but without any obligation to apply for or furnish any such bonds;

(c) Pay all expenses incurred by the Company, all costs taxed against the Insured in any such suit, and all interest accruing after entry of judgment until the Company has paid, tendered or deposited in court such part of such judgment as does not exceed the limit of the Company's liability thereon;

(d) Reimburse the Insured for all reasonable expense, other than loss of earnings, incurred at the Company's request.

The amounts incurred hereunder, except settlements of claims and suits, are payable by the Company in addition to the applicable limit of liability stated herein.

2. Other Provisions:

(a) The Insured shall cooperate with the Company and, upon the Company's request, shall attend hearings and trials and shall assist in effecting settlements, securing and giving evidence, obtaining the attendance of witnesses and in the conduct of suits. The Insured shall not, except at his own cost, voluntarily make any payment, assume any obligation or incur any expense.

(b) No action shall lie against the Company unless, as a condition precedent thereto, the Insured shall have fully complied with all the terms hereof and of the policy, nor until the amount of the Insured's obligation to pay shall have been finally determined either by judgment against the Insured after actual trial or by a written agreement of the Insured, and the claimant and the Company.

(c) Any person or organization or the legal representative thereof who has secured such judgment or written agreement shall thereafter be entitled to recover hereunder to the extent of the insurance afforded hereunder.

(d) Nothing contained herein or in the policy shall give any person or organization any right to join the Company as a co-defendant in any action against the Insured to determine the Insured's liability. Bankruptcy or insolvency of the Insured or of the Insured's estate shall not relieve the Company of any of its obligations hereunder.

(e) In the event of any payment under this policy the Company shall be subrogated to all the Insured's rights of recovery therefor against any person or organization and the Insured shall execute and deliver instruments and papers and do whatever else is necessary to secure such rights. The Insured shall do nothing after loss to prejudice such rights.

(f) Assignment of interest under this policy shall not bind the Company until its consent is endorsed hereon; if however, the named Insured shall die or be adjudged bankrupt or insolvent within the policy period, this policy, unless cancelled, shall, if written notice be given to the Company within sixty days after the date of such death or adjudication, cover the named Insured's legal representative as the named Insured.

(g) Notice to any agent or knowledge possessed by any agent or by any other person shall not effect a waiver or a change in any part of this policy or estop the Company from asserting any right under the terms of this policy nor shall the terms of this policy be waived or changed, except by endorsement issued to form a part of this policy.

SPECIAL CONDITIONS APPLICABLE TO THIS COVERAGE

(A) NOTICE OF OCCURRENCES: When a "Water Damage" occurs, written notice shall be given by or on behalf of the Insured to the Company or any of its authorized agents as soon as practicable. Such notice shall contain particulars sufficient to identify the Insured and also reasonably obtainable information respecting the time, place and circumstances of the occurrence, the names and addresses of the interested parties and of available witnesses.

(B) NOTICE OF CLAIM OR SUIT: If claim is made or suit brought against the Insured, the Insured shall immediately forward to the Company every demand, notice, summons or other process received by him or his representative.

EXCLUSIONS APPLICABLE TO THIS COVERAGE

1. This insurance does not apply to liability assumed by the Insured under any contract or agreement.

2. Nuclear Exclusion: Loss by nuclear reaction or nuclear radiation or radioactive contamination, all whether controlled or uncontrolled, or due to any act or condition incident to any of the foregoing, is not insured against by this policy, whether such loss be direct or indirect, proximate or remote, or be in whole or in part caused by, contributed to, or aggravated by "Water Damage" as insured against by this policy.

DEFINITION & LIMITATION APPLICABLE TO THIS COVERAGE

1. DEFINITION

Definition of Insured: The unqualified word "Insured" includes the named Insured and also includes any partner, executive officer, director or stockholder thereof while acting within the scope of his duties as such.

2. LIMITATION

Other Insurance: If the Insured has other insurance against a loss covered hereunder the Company shall not be liable for a greater proportion of such loss than the applicable limit of liability stated herein bears to the total applicable limit of liability of all valid and collectible insurance against such loss.

DEFERRED PREMIUM PAYMENT

Deferred Premium Payment: If the Insured elects to pay the premium in equal annual payments as indicated on the first page of this policy, the premium for this policy is hereby made so payable, provided that no payment shall be less than the minimum premium applicable.

If the Insured is in default of any such premium payment and this Company elects to cancel this policy, notice of cancellation shall be in accordance with the provisions of this policy, but in such case any portions of the premium previously paid shall be earned by this Company.

W. D. 601
(Ed. 1963)

WATER DAMAGE — PROPERTY DAMAGE FORM

(For use ONLY with Water Damage Policy—Form H)

SECTION I

Insurance attaches only to those items specifically described in this policy for which a specific amount is shown, and, unless otherwise provided, all conditions of this form and the provisions of the policy to which it is attached shall apply separately to each item covered.

Any loss hereunder shall not reduce the amount of this policy.

If this policy is cancelled at the request of the Insured, the total premium retained by the Company shall be not less than the minimum set forth in customary short rate table.

SECTION II—DESCRIPTION OF COVERAGE

Building Coverage: When the insurance under this policy covers "Building(s)," such insurance shall include all additions and extensions attached thereto; all permanent fixtures, machinery and equipment forming a part of and pertaining to the service of the building; personal property of the Insured as landlord used for the maintenance or service of the described building(s).

Stock Coverage: When the insurance under this policy covers "Stock," such insurance shall include merchandise, materials and stock supplies of every description.

Contents, Except Stock, Coverage: When the insurance under this policy covers "Contents, Except Stock," such insurance shall include furniture; fixtures; machinery; equipment; and personal property of every description except stock.

All Contents Coverage: When the insurance under this policy covers "All Contents," such insurance shall include all property described in "Stock Coverage" and "Contents, Except Stock, Coverage."

Note: Signs, storm doors and sash, awnings and screens, the property of the Insured, in, on or attached to building(s) or elsewhere on the described premises are covered as follows: (1) as part of "Building Coverage" if the Insured is the owner of the building; (2) as part of "Contents, Except Stock, Coverage" if the Insured is not the owner of the building.

Furniture and Fixtures Coverage: When the insurance under this policy covers "Furniture & Fixtures," such insurance shall cover furniture and fixtures usual and incidental to the occupancy of the Insured, while contained in the building(s), additions and extensions located as described in this policy. This insurance does not cover property appertaining to the service of the building(s), additions and extensions and used in the maintenance thereof.

Machinery Coverage: When the insurance under this policy covers "Machinery," such insurance shall cover machinery usual and incidental to the occupancy of the Insured, while contained in the building(s), additions and extensions located as described in this policy. This insurance does not cover property appertaining to the service of the building(s), additions and extensions and used in the maintenance thereof.

Property of Employees or Members of the Firm Coverage: When the insurance under this policy covers "Property of Employees or Members of the Firm," the coverage shall be limited to such property while contained in the building(s), additions and extensions located as described in this policy.

Improvements and Betterments Coverage: (Applies only when the Insured is not the building owner.) When the insurance under this policy covers "Improvements and Betterments," such insurance shall cover the Insured's use interest in Improvements and Betterments to the described building.

1. The term "Improvements and Betterments" wherever used in this policy is defined as fixtures, alterations, installations, or additions comprising a part of the described building and made or acquired at the expense of the Insured exclusive of rent paid by the Insured, but which are not legally subject to removal by the Insured.

2. The word "Lease" wherever used in this policy shall mean the lease or rental agreement, whether written or oral, in effect as of the time of loss.

3. In the event Improvements and Betterments are damaged or destroyed during the term of this policy by the perils insured against, the liability of this Company shall be determined as follows:

   (a) If repaired or replaced at the expense of the Insured within a reasonable time after such loss, the actual cash value of the damaged or destroyed Improvements and Betterments.

   (b) If not repaired or replaced within a reasonable time after such loss, that proportion of the original cost at time of installation of the damaged or destroyed Improvements and Betterments which the unexpired term of the lease at the time of loss bears to the period(s) from the date(s) such Improvements and Betterments were made to the expiration date of the lease.

   (c) If repaired or replaced at the expense of others for the use of the Insured, there shall be no liability hereunder.

Underground Water Supply Mains and Fire Hydrants Coverage: (This Coverage void unless premium is inserted therefor on the first page of this policy.) This policy is extended to also include the peril of accidental discharge or leakage of water from underground water supply mains and fire hydrants, not including, however, any branch piping installed to supply any sprinkler system, and, WITH RESPECT TO SUCH PERIL ONLY, the exclusion of loss from water below the surface of the ground including that which exerts pressure on or flows, seeps or leaks through sidewalks, driveways, foundations, walls, basement or other floors, or through doors, windows or any other openings in such sidewalks, driveways, foundations, walls or floors shall not apply.

Chemical Refrigerant Leakage Coverage: (This Coverage void unless premium is inserted therefor on the first page of this policy.) This policy is extended to also include the peril of accidental discharge or leakage of the chemical refrigerant from any refrigerating or air conditioning system, and, WITH RESPECT TO SUCH PERIL ONLY, the exclusion of loss by gases, fumes or vapors (other than steam) shall not apply.

Extension of Coverage: When the insurance under this policy covers personal property, it also covers the interest of the Insured in and legal liability for similar property belonging in whole or in part to others, and held by the Insured, while contained in the building(s), additions and extensions located as described in this policy.

Limitation of Coverage: This policy limits coverage;

(a) On books of account, drawings, card index systems and other records (except film, recording tape or wire,) for not exceeding cost of blank books, blank cards and other materials plus cost of labor for actually transcribing or copying such records;

(b) On film, recording tape or wire (except stock) for not exceeding the cost of unexposed film or blank tape or wire.

Property Not Covered: This policy does not cover personal property in which parties other than the Insured also have an insurable interest, when the Insured's interest in said property is otherwise covered by insurance.

Nuclear Exclusion: Loss by nuclear reaction or nuclear radiation or radioactive contamination, all whether controlled or uncontrolled, or due to any act or condition incident to any of the foregoing, is not insured against by this policy, whether such loss be direct or indirect, proximate or remote, or be in whole or in part caused by, contributed to, or aggravated by "Water Damage" as insured against by this policy.

SECTION III

Deductible Clause: (This Clause void unless amount of deductible is inserted on the first page of this policy.) In consideration of the reduced premium at which this policy is written, this Company shall not be liable unless the Insured shall sustain a loss in excess of the amount of deductible inserted on the first page of this policy, and then only for its pro rata share of such excess.

THE PROVISIONS PRINTED ON THE BACK OF THIS FORM ARE HEREBY REFERRED TO AND MADE A PART HEREOF.

Appendix I—Water Damage Coverage (Concluded)

Coinsurance Clause: (This Clause applies only when a percentage of Coinsurance is specified on the first page of this policy or by endorsement hereon.) This Company shall not be liable for a greater proportion of any "Water Damage" loss or damage to the property described herein than the sum hereby insured bears to the percentage(s) specified in the first page of this policy (or endorsed hereon) of the actual cash value of said property at the time such loss shall happen, nor for more than the proportion which this policy bears to the total "Water Damage" insurance thereon.

In the event that the aggregate claim for any "Water Damage" loss is both less than $2,500 and less than two per cent (2%) of the total amount of "Water Damage" insurance upon the property described herein at the time such loss occurs, no special inventory or appraisement of the undamaged property shall be required, provided, however, that nothing herein shall be construed to waive application of the first paragraph of this clause.

SECTION IV

Deferred Premium Payment: If the Insured elects to pay the premium in equal annual payments as indicated on the first page of this policy, the premium for this policy is hereby made so payable, provided that no payment shall be less than the minimum premium applicable.

If the Insured is in default of any such premium payment and this Company elects to cancel this policy, notice of cancellation shall be in accordance with the provisions of this policy, but in such case any portions of the premium previously paid shall be earned by this Company.

SECTION V—OTHER PROVISIONS

Liberalization Clause: If, during the period that insurance is in force under this policy, or within 45 days prior to the inception date thereof, on behalf of this Company there be adopted, or filed with and approved or accepted by the insurance supervisory authorities, all in conformity with law, any changes in the form attached to this policy by which this form of insurance could be extended or broadened without increased premium charge by endorsement or substitution of form, then such extended or broadened insurance shall inure to the benefit of the Insured hereunder as though such endorsement or substitution of form had been made.

Apportionment: This Company shall not be liable for a greater proportion of any loss less the amount of deductible, if any, from "Water Damage" than (1) the amount of insurance applicable under this policy bears to the whole amount of "Water Damage" written under the same type of insurance, terms and conditions covering the property, or which would have covered the property except for the existence of this insurance, whether collectible or not; nor (2) if any type of insurance other than "Water Damage" insurance written under the same type of insurance, terms and conditions applies to any loss to which this insurance also applies, or would have applied to any such loss except for the existence of this insurance, the limit of liability of each type of insurance for such loss, hereby designated as "joint loss," shall first be determined as if it were the only insurance, and this type of insurance shall be liable for no greater proportion of joint loss than the limit of its liability for such loss bears to the sum of all such limits. The liability of this Company (under this policy) for such joint loss shall be limited to its proportionate part of the aggregate limit of this and all other insurance of the same type. The words "joint loss," as used in the foregoing, mean that portion of the loss in excess of the highest deductible, if any, to which this insurance and other types of insurance above referred to both apply.

Control of Property: This insurance shall not be prejudiced by any act or neglect of any person (other than the named Insured,) when such act or neglect is not within the control of the named Insured.

Divisible Contract Clause: If this policy covers two or more buildings or the contents of two or more buildings, the breach of any condition of the policy in any one or more of the buildings covered or containing the property covered shall not prejudice the right to recover for loss occurring in any building covered or containing the property covered, where at the time of loss a breach of condition does not exist.

Subrogation Clause: This insurance shall not be invalidated should the Insured waive in writing prior to a loss any or all right of recovery against any party for loss occurring to the property described herein.

Debris Removal Clause: This insurance covers expenses incurred in the removal of all debris of the property covered hereunder which may be occasioned by loss caused by "Water Damage." However, the total liability under this policy for both loss to property and removal of debris shall not exceed the amount of insurance applying under this policy to the property damaged or destroyed. This Company shall not be liable for more than the proportion of such debris removal expense as the amount of insurance under this policy bears to the total amount of insurance on the property covered hereunder, whether or not all such insurance includes this clause.

Unless liability is otherwise specifically assumed by endorsement attached hereto, this Company shall not be liable for debris removal expense occasioned by the enforcement of any state or municipal law or ordinance which necessitates the demolition of any portion of a building covered hereunder which has or has not suffered damage by "Water Damage."

Debris removal expense shall not be considered in the determination of actual cash value in the application of the Coinsurance Clause, if any, made a part of this policy.

APPENDIX J

Appendix J—Builders Risk Coverage

UNIFORM STANDARD

FORM NO. 17
(Edition Feb. '62)

BUILDERS' RISK FORM

Attached to and forming part of Policy No..

of the.. NAME OF INSURANCE COMPANY ....

issued at its.............. CITY OR TOWN .... STATE ....Agency. Dated..............................19..........

1. This policy being for the Amount of $.............................., being..............% of the total amount of contributing insurance, covers on the..............................story..............................roof..............................

building or structure, while in course of construction, including foundations, additions, attachments, and all permanent fixtures (except as limited in Paragraph 3 (below) belonging to and constituting a part of said building or structure, to be occupied as

....

all while situated..

.... HERE GIVE STREET NUMBER, OR LOT OR BLOCK NUMBER OR SECTION, TOWNSHIP AND RANGE ....

....

City } of..............................State of..............................,
Town }

subject to the following provisions and stipulations.

2. This policy also covers materials and supplies incident to the construction of said building or structure and when the 80% or higher Coinsurance Clause applies, this policy also covers:

(a) temporary structures; and
(b) when not otherwise covered by insurance, builders' machinery, tools and equipment owned by the Insured or similar property of others for which the Insured is legally liable;

all forming a part of or contained in said building or structure, temporary structures, or on vehicles, or in the open; only while on the premises described or within 100 feet thereof.

3. When this form is attached to a policy covering the perils of windstorm and hail, it is a condition of this policy that cloth awnings and metal smokestacks are not covered against loss by windstorm or hail unless the 80% or higher Coinsurance Clause applies.

4. **Loss Payable Clause:** Loss, if any, to be adjusted only with the Insured named herein and payable to the Insured and

....

as their respective interests may appear, subject, nevertheless, to all the provisions and stipulations of the policy.

5. **Occupancy Clause:** It is a condition of this insurance that the premises shall not be occupied without obtaining the consent of this Company endorsed hereon; except that machinery may be set up and operated solely for the purpose of testing the same without prejudice to this policy.

6. **Coinsurance Clause (This Clause Void unless Percentage is Inserted therein):** In consideration of the rate and (or) form under which this policy is written, it is expressly stipulated and made a condition of this contract that the Insured shall at all times maintain contributing insurance on each item of property covered by this policy to the extent of at least..............% of the actual cash value at the time of the loss, and that failing to do so, the Insured shall to the extent of such deficit bear his, her or their proportion of any loss.

In the event that the aggregate claim for any loss is less than 2% of the total amount of insurance upon the property described herein at the time such loss occurs, the Insured shall not be required to furnish any inventory of the undamaged property to establish the actual cash value referred to in the Coinsurance Clause provided, however, that nothing herein shall be construed to waive the application of the Coinsurance Clause.

If this policy be divided into two or more items, the foregoing conditions shall apply to each item separately.

THE PROVISIONS PRINTED ON THE BACK OF THIS FORM ARE HEREBY REFERRED TO AND MADE A PART HEREOF.

Form No. 17 (2-62) ....Agent.

Note to Agents: When it is desired to eliminate from coverage foundations which are below the under surface of the lowest basement floor, etc., or other Coinsurance exclusion, as permitted by the published rules, the form may be so endorsed.

7. **Liberalization Clause:** If during the period that insurance is in force under this policy, or within 45 days prior to the inception date thereof, on behalf of this Company there be adopted, or filed with and approved or accepted by the insurance supervisory authorities, all in conformity with law, any changes in the form attached to this policy by which this form of insurance could be extended or broadened without increased premium charge by endorsement or substitution of form, then such extended or broadened insurance shall inure to the benefit of the Insured hereunder as though such endorsement or substitution of form had been made.

8. **Nuclear Clause:** The word "fire" in this policy or endorsements attached hereto is not intended to and does not embrace nuclear reaction or nuclear radiation or radioactive contamination, all whether controlled or uncontrolled, and loss by nuclear reaction or nuclear radiation or radioactive contamination is not intended to be and is not insured against by this policy or said endorsements, whether such loss be direct or indirect, proximate or remote, or be in whole or in part caused by, contributed to, or aggravated by "fire" or any other perils insured against by this policy or said endorsements; however, subject to the foregoing and all provisions of this policy, direct loss by "fire" resulting from nuclear reaction or nuclear radiation or radioactive contamination is insured against by this policy.

9. **Debris Removal Endorsement (This endorsement applies only to items of insurance covering direct property loss):** This insurance covers expenses incurred in the removal of all debris of the property covered hereunder which may be occasioned by loss caused by any of the perils insured against in this policy. However, the total liability under this policy for both loss to property and removal of debris shall not exceed the amount of insurance applying under this policy to the property damaged or destroyed. This Company shall not be liable for more than the proportion of such debris removal expense as the amount of insurance under this policy bears to the total amount of insurance on the property covered hereunder, whether or not all such insurance includes this clause.

Unless liability is otherwise specifically assumed by endorsement attached hereto, this Company shall not be liable for debris removal expense occasioned by the enforcement of any state or municipal law or ordinance which necessitates the demolition of any portion of a building covered hereunder which has or has not suffered damage by any of the perils insured against.

If this policy covers on two or more items, this clause shall apply to each item separately.

Debris removal expense shall not be considered in the determination of actual cash value in the application of the Coinsurance Clause, if any, made a part of this policy.

10. **Subrogation Clause:** It is hereby stipulated that this insurance shall not be invalidated should the Insured waive in writing prior to a loss any or all right of recovery against any party for loss occurring to the property described herein.

11. **Loss Clause:** Any loss hereunder shall not reduce the amount of this policy.

12. **Electrical Apparatus Clause:** This Company shall not be liable for any loss resulting from any electrical injury or disturbance to electrical appliances, devices, fixtures or wiring caused by electrical currents artificially generated unless fire ensues and, if fire does ensue, this Company shall be liable only for its proportion of loss caused by such ensuing fire.

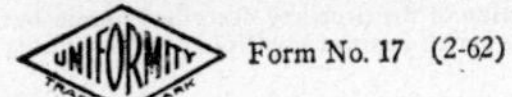

Form No. 17 (2-62)

UNIFORM STANDARD **FORM NO. 17A**
(Edition Feb. '62)

BUILDERS' RISK REPORTING FORM

Attached to and forming part of Policy No. ....
of the .... NAME OF INSURANCE COMPANY ....
issued at its .... CITY OR TOWN .... STATE .... Agency. Dated .... 19.....

1. This policy being for the Provisional Amount of $.........., being ....% (hereinafter referred to as "this Company's percentage") of the total amount of contributing insurance, covers on the ....story .... roof ....
building or structure, while in course of construction, including foundations, additions, attachments, and all permanent fixtures belonging to and constituting a part of said building or structure, to be occupied as ....
....
all while situated ....
.... HERE GIVE STREET NUMBER, OR LOT OR BLOCK NUMBER OR SECTION, TOWNSHIP AND RANGE ....
....
City / Town } of .... State of ....,
subject to the following provisions and stipulations.

2. This policy also covers temporary structures, materials, equipment and supplies of all kinds incident to the construction of said building or structure and, when not otherwise covered by insurance, builders' machinery, tools and equipment owned by the Insured or similar property of others for which the Insured is legally liable, all forming a part of or contained in said building or structure, temporary structures, or on vehicles, or in the open; only while on the premises described or within 100 feet thereof.

3. **Loss Payable Clause:** Loss, if any, to be adjusted only with the Insured named herein and payable to the Insured and
....
as their respective interests may appear, subject, nevertheless, to all the provisions and stipulations of the policy.

4. **Limit of Liability:** The limit of liability for all contributing insurance is $.......... and the liability of this Company shall not exceed this Company's percentage of such limit.

5. **Amount of Insurance Clause:** The provisional amount of insurance is for the purpose of determining the premium. The actual amount of insurance hereunder shall equal this Company's percentage of the total value of the property described herein but this Company shall not be liable for any loss in excess of this Company's percentage of the stated limit of liability notwithstanding the requirement that the premium shall be adjusted on the basis of full values reported.

6. **Value Reporting Clause:** It is a condition that the Insured shall report monthly to this Company the total value of the property covered. Within thirty days after inception of this policy the Insured shall select a day of the month as of which the first and all succeeding monthly reports shall be made; each of such reports to this Company shall be due within thirty days after the day of the month selected.

At the time of any loss, if the Insured has failed to file with this Company reports of values as above required, this policy shal. cover for not more than this Company's percentage of the amount stated in the last report of values filed prior to the loss. In the event no initial report, as above required, has been made within 60 days, this policy shall cover for not more than the provisional amount.

THE PROVISIONS PRINTED ON THE BACK OF THIS FORM ARE HEREBY REFERRED TO AND MADE A PART HEREOF.

Form No. 17A (2-62) .... Agent.

NOTES TO AGENTS: 1. The Provisional Amount of Insurance to be inserted at top of form should be not less than this Company's percentage of 100% of the values to be covered at inception of policy.

2. When it is desired to eliminate from coverage foundations which are below the under surface of the lowest basement floor, etc., or other Coinsurance exclusions, as permitted by the published rules, the form may be so endorsed.

Appendix J—Builders Risk Coverage (Continued)

7. **Full Reporting Clause:** Liability under this policy shall not in any case exceed that proportion of any loss hereunder which the last reported value filed prior to the date of the loss bears to the actual value on the date for which the report was made.

8. **Premium Adjustment Clause:** The premium named in this policy is provisional only. The actual premium consideration for the liability assumed hereunder shall be determined as follows: Upon receipt of each report of value, this policy shall be endorsed to the amount of this Company's percentage of the value reported; additional or return premium being computed on a pro rata basis to the expiration date of the policy from the date midway between the dates of the current and the preceding report.

9. **Verification of Values:** This Company or its duly appointed representative, shall be permitted at all reasonable times during the term of this policy, or within a year after its expiration, to inspect the property covered hereunder and to examine the Insured's books, records and such policies as relate to any property covered hereunder. This inspection or examination shall not waive or in any manner affect any of the terms or conditions of this policy.

10. **Occupancy Clause:** It is a condition of this insurance that the premises shall not be occupied without obtaining the consent of this Company endorsed hereon; except that machinery may be set up and operated solely for the purpose of testing the same without prejudice to this policy.

11. **Electrical Apparatus Clause:** This Company shall not be liable for any loss resulting from any electrical injury or disturbance to electrical appliances, devices, fixtures or wiring caused by electrical currents artificially generated unless fire ensues and, if fire does ensue, this Company shall be liable only for its proportion of loss caused by such ensuing fire.

12. **Liberalization Clause:** If during the period that insurance is in force under this policy, or within 45 days prior to the inception date thereof, on behalf of this Company there be adopted, or filed with and approved or accepted by the insurance supervisory authorities, all in conformity with law, any changes in the form attached to this policy by which this form of insurance could be extended or broadened without increased premium charge by endorsement or substitution of form, then such extended or broadened insurance shall inure to the benefit of the Insured hereunder as though such endorsement or substitution of form had been made.

13. **Subrogation Clause:** It is hereby stipulated that this insurance shall not be invalidated should the Insured waive in writing prior to a loss any or all right of recovery against any party for loss occurring to the property described herein.

14. **Debris Removal Clause (Limited Coverage):** This policy is extended to cover expense incurred in the removal of debris of the property covered hereunder occasioned by loss caused by any of the perils insured against but the total liability of this Company for the sum of:

"A" the amount of loss hereunder exclusive of debris removal expense, and

"B" the amount of debris removal expense,

shall not exceed this Company's proportion of 100% of the amount for which all contributing insurance would be liable, exclusive of debris removal expense, if all of the property covered hereunder at the location where the loss occurs were destroyed.

This Company shall not be liable for loss occasioned by the enforcement of any state or municipal law or ordinance which necessitates the demolition of any portion of a building or removal of contents thereof which has not suffered damage by any of the perils insured against in this policy.

This extension of coverage does not increase the limits of liability provided in this policy.

Debris removal expense shall not be considered in the determination of the values under this policy.

15. **Nuclear Clause:** The word "fire" in this policy or endorsements attached hereto is not intended to and does not embrace nuclear reaction or nuclear radiation or radioactive contamination, all whether controlled or uncontrolled, and loss by nuclear reaction or nuclear radiation or radioactive contamination is not intended to be and is not insured against by this policy or said endorsements, whether such loss be direct or indirect, proximate or remote, or be in whole or in part caused by, contributed to, or aggravated by "fire" or any other perils insured against by this policy or said endorsements; however, subject to the foregoing and all provisions of this policy, direct loss by "fire" resulting from nuclear reaction or nuclear radiation or radioactive contamination is insured against by this policy.

Form No. 17A (2-62)

UNIFORM STANDARD

FORM NO. 17 C
(Edition Feb. '62)

BUILDERS' RISK COMPLETED VALUE FORM

Attached to and forming part of Policy No. ....
of the .... NAME OF INSURANCE COMPANY ....
issued at its .... CITY OR TOWN .... STATE .... Agency. Dated .... 19......

1. This policy being for the Provisional Amount of $.................., being ....% of the total amount of contributing insurance, covers on the ....story ....roof building or structure, while in course of construction, including foundations, additions, attachments, and all permanent fixtures belonging to and constituting a part of said building or structure, to be occupied as ....

....

all while situated ....

.... HERE GIVE STREET NUMBER, OR LOT OR BLOCK NUMBER OR SECTION, TOWNSHIP AND RANGE ....

City / Town } of .... State of ....,
subject to the following provisions and stipulations.

2. This policy also covers temporary structures, materials, equipment and supplies of all kinds incident to the construction of said building or structure and, when not otherwise covered by insurance, builders' machinery, tools and equipment owned by the Insured or similar property of others for which the Insured is legally liable, all forming a part of or contained in said building or structure, temporary structures, or on vehicles, or in the open; only while on the premises described or within 100 feet thereof.

3. **Loss Payable Clause:** Loss, if any, to be adjusted only with the Insured named herein and payable to the Insured and

....

as their respective interests may appear, subject, nevertheless, to all the provisions and stipulations of the policy.

4. **Occupancy Clause:** It is a condition of this insurance that the premises shall not be occupied without obtaining the consent of this Company endorsed hereon; except that machinery may be set up and operated solely for the purpose of testing the same without prejudice to this policy.

5. The amount of insurance stated in this policy is provisional. It is a condition of this Insurance, wherein the rate and premium are based on an average amount of liability during the period of construction, that at any date while this policy is in force, the actual amount of insurance hereunder is that proportion of the provisional amount that the actual value of the described property on that date bears to the value at the date of completion, but shall not in any case exceed the provisional amount.

In consideration of the reduced rate at which this policy is written, it is a condition of this insurance that in the event of loss, this Company shall be liable for no greater proportion thereof than the provisional amount of insurance under this policy bears to the value of the described property at date of completion.

If this policy be divided into two or more items, the foregoing shall apply to each item separately.

6. **Loss Clause:** Any loss hereunder shall not reduce the amount of this policy.

7. **Electrical Apparatus Clause:** This Company shall not be liable for any loss resulting from any electrical injury or disturbance to electrical appliances, devices, fixtures or wiring caused by electrical currents artificially generated unless fire ensues, and, if fire does ensue, this Company shall be liable only for its proportion of loss caused by such ensuing fire.

8. **Liberalization Clause:** If during the period that insurance is in force under this policy, or within 45 days prior to the inception date thereof, on behalf of this Company there be adopted, or filed with and approved or accepted by the insurance supervisory authorities, all in conformity with law, any changes in the form attached to this policy by which this form of insurance could be extended or broadened without increased premium charge by endorsement or substitution of form, then such extended or broadened insurance shall inure to the benefit of the Insured hereunder as though such endorsement or substitution of form had been made.

9. **Nuclear Clause:** The word "fire" in this policy or endorsements attached hereto is not intended to and does not embrace nuclear reaction or nuclear radiation or radioactive contamination, all whether controlled or uncontrolled, and loss by nuclear reaction or nuclear radiation or radioactive contamination is not intended to be and is not insured against by this policy or said endorsements, whether such loss be direct or indirect, proximate or remote, or be in whole or in part caused by, contributed to, or aggravated by "fire" or any other perils insured against by this policy or said endorsements; however, subject to the foregoing and all provisions of this policy, direct loss by "fire" resulting from nuclear reaction or nuclear radiation or radioactive contamination is insured against by this policy.

10. **Debris Removal Endorsement (This endorsement applies only to items of insurance covering direct property loss):** This insurance covers expenses incurred in the removal of all debris of the property covered hereunder which may be occasioned by loss caused by any of the perils insured against in this policy. However, the total liability under this policy for both loss to property and removal of debris shall not exceed the amount of insurance applying under this policy to the property damaged or destroyed. This Company shall not be liable for more than the proportion of such debris removal expense as the amount of insurance under this policy bears to the total amount of insurance on the property covered hereunder, whether or not all such insurance includes this clause.

Unless liability is otherwise specifically assumed by endorsement attached hereto, this Company shall not be liable for debris removal expense occasioned by the enforcement of any state or municipal law or ordinance which necessitates the demolition of any portion of a building covered hereunder which has or has not suffered damage by any of the perils insured against.

If this policy covers on two or more items, this clause shall apply to each item separately.

Debris removal expense shall not be considered in the determination of actual cash value in the application of the Coinsurance Clause, if any, made a part of this policy.

11. **Subrogation Clause:** It is hereby stipulated that this insurance shall not be invalidated should the Insured waive in writing prior to a loss any or all right of recovery against any party for loss occurring to the property described herein.

Form No. 17 C (2-62) .... Agent.

Note to Agents: When it is desired to eliminate from coverage foundations which are below the under surface of the lowest basement floor, etc., or other Coinsurance exclusion, as permitted by the published rules, the form may be so endorsed.

APPENDIX K

Appendix K—Errors and Omissions Form

UNIFORM STANDARD **FORM NO. 63**
(Edition Jan. '60)

ERRORS AND OMISSIONS FORM

Attached to and forming part of Policy No...

of the..NAME OF INSURANCE COMPANY...

issued at its..........CITY OR TOWN..STATE...........................Agency. Dated..........................19........

ALL TERMS, PROVISIONS AND CONDITIONS HEREIN SET FORTH, INCLUDING THOSE ON THE BACK OF THIS FORM, ARE MADE A PART OF THIS POLICY.

....Agent.

Subject to the provisions and stipulations applying to Section I and Section II, this policy covers,

$..............................being the limit of this Company's liability, with respect to the property specified in any one mortgage, under Section I; or under Section II; or under both Sections I and II, and any loss hereunder shall not reduce said limit of this Company's liability.

Insurance as provided herein attaches only with respect to the interest of the named Insured, specified by the insertion of the estimated average number of mortgage loans that will be in force during the term of this policy in each of the following categories:

..............................mortgage loans owned by the named Insured;

..............................mortgage loans serviced by the named Insured for the account of others;

..............................Total.

PROVISIONS APPLICABLE TO SECTION I AND SECTION II

(a) Subject to the limit of liability, the loss which would have been insured against, must occur within the policy period regardless of when the precedent error or accidental omission may have occurred.

(b) The Insured shall make every reasonable effort:

(1) to require, procure and maintain valid insurance payable to itself as mortgagee against those risks and perils which the Insured customarily requires its mortgagors to furnish, and

(2) with respect to insurance otherwise included in a policy so furnished, to maintain insurance against those risks and perils customarily insured against by the mortgagor, in amounts and under terms and conditions accepted by the mortgagor and by the Insured.

(c) This insurance covers only errors or accidental omissions with respect to policies of insurance as above set forth in connection with real property located in the United States of America and Puerto Rico.

(d) This insurance shall not contribute with other insurance unless written under the identical terms, conditions and provisions contained in this policy.

(e) None of the terms of the standard fire insurance policy, to which this form is attached, shall apply to the insurance afforded hereunder except the provisions as to concealment, fraud and cancellation of policy.

(f) **Nuclear Clause:** The word "fire" in this policy or endorsements attached hereto is not intended to and does not embrace nuclear reaction or nuclear radiation or radioactive contamination, all whether controlled or uncontrolled, and loss by nuclear reaction or nuclear radiation or radioactive contamination is not intended to be and is not insured against by this policy or said endorsements, whether such loss be direct or indirect, proximate or remote, or be in whole or in part caused by, contributed to, or aggravated by "fire" or any other perils insured against by this policy or said endorsements; however, subject to the foregoing and all provisions of this policy, direct loss by "fire" resulting from nuclear reaction or nuclear radiation or radioactive contamination is insured against by this policy.

(g) **Nuclear Exclusion**—(This clause applies to all perils insured against hereunder except the perils of fire and lightning, which are otherwise provided for in the Nuclear Clause attached to this policy): Loss by nuclear reaction or nuclear radiation or radioactive contamination, all whether controlled or uncontrolled, or due to any act or condition incident to any of the foregoing, is not insured against by this policy, whether such loss be direct or indirect, proximate or remote, or be in whole or in part caused by, contributed to, or aggravated by any of the perils insured against by this policy; and nuclear reaction or nuclear radiation or radioactive contamination, all whether controlled or uncontrolled, is not "explosion" or "smoke".

(h) Exclusions: This Company shall not be liable for loss resulting from:

(1) any occurrence taking place more than ten (10) days after the Insured had knowledge that an error or accidental omission had occurred;

(2) or caused by, contributed to or aggravated by any of the following:

(a) flood, surface water, waves, tidal water or tidal wave, overflow of streams or other bodies of water, or spray from any of the foregoing, all whether driven by wind or not;

(b) water which backs up through sewers or drains;

(c) water below the surface of the ground including that which exerts pressure on or flows, seeps or leaks through sidewalks, driveways, foundations, walls, basement or other floors, or through doors, windows or any other openings in such sidewalks, driveways, foundations, walls or floors;

unless loss by fire or explosion ensues, and this Company shall then be liable only for such ensuing loss.

PROVISIONS APPLICABLE TO SECTION I

A. INSURING AGREEMENT

(1) Subject to the limit of liability, and the exclusions and conditions applying to Section I, this Company agrees to indemnify the Insured against loss to the Insured's mortgagee interest (including the Insured's mortgagee interest in any legal fiduciary capacity) in real property arising by reason of error or accidental omission in the operation of the Insured's customary procedure in requiring, procuring and maintaining valid insurance against the risks and perils described below: (a) payable to itself as mortgagee on such real property; and, (b) on such real property during and after foreclosure by the Insured or when sold under a conditional sales agreement or other instrument where title remains with the Insured; if, by reason of such error or accidental omission, requisite insurance is not in force at the time of loss.

(2) If the Insured services mortgages under a written contract or agreement with one or more principals and the number of such mortgages is included in the estimate above, this insurance covers as though the Insured owned the mortgage interest under mortgages serviced for the account of others, and any payments hereunder shall be made jointly to the named Insured and the owner of the mortgage.

B. RISKS AND PERILS

(1) All risks and perils against which the Insured customarily requires its mortgagors to provide policy(ies) of insurance covering real property.

C. EXCLUSIONS

(1) This Company shall not be liable for loss resulting from:

(a) Earthquake, landslide or other earth movement unless loss by fire or explosion ensues, and this Company shall then be liable only for such ensuing loss;

(b) Any error in judgment as to amount, form, conditions or provisions of insurance;

(c) Any risks or perils other than those which the Insured customarily requires its mortgagors to provide insurance against to protect the mortgagee interest(s);

(d) Any hostile or warlike action in time of peace or war, including action in hindering, combating or defending against an actual, impending, or expected attack, (1) by any government or sovereign power (de jure or de facto), or by any authority maintaining or using military, naval or air forces; or (2) by military, naval or air forces; or (3) by an agent of any such government, power, authority or forces, it being understood that any discharge, explosion or use of any weapon of war employing nuclear fission or fusion shall be conclusively presumed to be such a hostile or warlike action by such a government, power, authority or forces; insurrection, rebellion, revolution, civil war, usurped power, or action taken by governmental authority in hindering, combating or defending against such an occurrence;

(e) An order of any civil authority except acts of destruction at the time of and for the purpose of preventing the spread of fire, provided that such fire did not originate from any of the perils excluded in paragraph (d).

D. LIMITATIONS

(1) The liability of this Company, within the limit specified above, shall not exceed the smallest of the following:

(a) The amount of the actual direct loss to the property damaged or destroyed, determined in accordance with the conditions of the policy(ies) of insurance which would have covered the loss had no error or accidental omission occurred, less the amount due the Insured under all other insurance on such property;

(b) The amount that would be due from that part of the insurance procured, maintained or customarily required by the Insured (under terms and conditions customarily accepted by the Insured) which, because of error or accidental omission, is lacking;

(c) The amount of the Insured's mortgagee interest;

(d) The amount represented by no greater proportion of any loss than the limit specified above bears to the whole amount of any errors and omissions insurance, whether collectible or not.

E. CONDITIONS

(1) **Assistance of Insured:** It is a condition of this insurance that the Insured shall in every way assist in all matters pertaining to coverage hereunder.

(2) **Requirements in Case Loss Occurs:** The Insured shall give written notice to this Company of any loss as soon as practicable after notice thereof has been received by the Insured. Such notice shall contain particulars regarding the time, place and circumstances of the loss as are available at the time. Within sixty (60) days after the loss, unless such time is extended in writing by this Company, the Insured shall render to this Company a proof of loss, signed and sworn to by the Insured, stating the knowledge and belief of the Insured as to the following: the time and origin of the loss, the interest of the Insured and of all others in the property, the actual cash value of each item thereof and the amount of loss thereto, all encumbrances thereon, all contracts of insurance, whether valid or not covering any of said property, by whom and for what purpose the damaged or destroyed building was occupied at the time of loss. The Insured, as often as may be reasonably required, shall submit to examinations under oath by any person named by this Company, and subscribe to the same; and as often as may be reasonably required, shall produce for examination all books of account, bills, invoices and other vouchers, or certified copies thereof if originals be lost, at such reasonable time and place as may be designated by this Company or its representative, and shall permit extracts and copies thereof to be made.

(3) **Appraisal:** In case the Insured and this Company shall fail to agree as to the amount of loss, then on the written demand of either, each shall select a competent and disinterested appraiser and notify the other of the appraiser selected within twenty (20) days of such demand. The appraisers shall first select a competent and disinterested umpire; and failing for fifteen (15) days to agree upon such umpire, then, on request of the Insured or this Company, such umpire shall be selected by a judge of a court of record in the state in which the Insured is located. The appraisers shall then appraise the loss, stating separately the loss to each item; and failing to agree, shall submit their differences, only, to the umpire. An award in writing so itemized, of any two when filed with this Company shall determine the amount of loss. Each appraiser shall be paid by the party selecting him and the expenses of appraisal and umpire shall be paid by the parties equally.

(4) **When Loss Payable:** The amount of loss for which this Company may be liable shall be payable sixty (60) days after proof of loss, as herein provided, is received by this Company and ascertainment of the loss is made either by agreement between the Insured and this Company expressed in writing or by the filing with this Company of an award as herein provided.

(5) **Suit:** No suit or action on this policy for the recovery of any claim shall be sustainable in any court of law or equity unless all the requirements of this policy shall have been complied with, and unless commenced within twelve (12) months next after date of discovery of the error or accidental omission.

(6) **Subrogation:** Whenever the payment to the Insured by this Company and other Companies equals the balance due under the mortgage, or when the payment of this Company and other Companies is less than such balance due under the mortgage and this Company by itself, or with others, elects to pay the Insured the balance due on the mortgage (after deducting any amount recoverable from this and other insurance), it is a condition of this insurance that the Companies having and exercising subrogation rights shall, as their interest may appear, thereupon receive full assignment of the mortgage and all securities held as collateral for the mortgage debt.

(7) **Abandonment:** There can be no abandonment to this Company of any property.

Appendix K—Errors and Omissions Form (Concluded)

PROVISIONS APPLICABLE TO SECTION II

A. INSURING AGREEMENT

(1) Subject to the limit of liability, and the exclusions and conditions applying to Section II, this Company agrees with the named Insured to pay on behalf of the Insured all sums which the Insured shall become legally obligated to pay as damages in any mortgagee, mortgage fiduciary or mortgage servicing agency capacity arising by reason of error or accidental omission in the operation of the Insured's customary procedure in procuring and maintaining valid insurance against the risks and perils described below for the benefit of the mortgagor in amounts and under terms and conditions customarily accepted by the mortgagor; and this Company shall:

(a) Defend any suit against the Insured alleging such liability as covered hereunder and seeking damages on account thereof, even if such suit is groundless, false or fraudulent; but this Company may make such investigation, negotiation and settlement of any claim or suit as it deems expedient;

(b) Pay all premiums on bonds to release attachments for an amount not in excess of the applicable limit of liability, all premiums on appeal bonds required in any such defended suit, but without any obligation to apply for or furnish any such bonds;

(c) Pay all expenses incurred by this Company, all costs taxed against the Insured in any such suit and all interest accruing after entry of judgment until this Company has paid or tendered or deposited in court such part of such judgment as does not exceed the limit of this Company's liability thereon;

(d) Reimburse the Insured for all reasonable expenses, other than loss of earnings, incurred at this Company's request; and the amounts so incurred, except settlements of claims and suits, are payable by this Company in addition to the applicable limit of liability in any one loss or occurrence.

(The unqualified word "Insured" includes the named Insured and also includes any executive officer, director or trustee thereof while acting within the scope of his duties as such.)

B. RISKS AND PERILS

All risks and perils against which the mortgagor customarily obtains policies of insurance except policies of title, life, sickness or accident insurance.

C. EXCLUSIONS

(1) This insurance does not cover any liability imposed upon the Insured by law resulting from:

(a) Any error in judgment as to amount, form, conditions or provisions of insurance to protect the mortgagor;

(b) Any risk or peril other than those customarily insured against by the mortgagor.

D. CONDITIONS

(1) **Cooperation of the Insured:** It is a condition of this insurance that the Insured shall cooperate with this Company and, upon this Company's request, shall attend hearings and trials and shall assist in effecting settlement, securing and giving evidence, obtaining the attendance of witnesses and in the conduct of suits, but the Insured shall not, except at his own cost, voluntarily make any payment, assume any obligation or incur any expense. Upon this Company's request, the Insured shall give to this Company a signed statement of facts containing all available information deemed necessary by this Company to determine and define its liability and rights under this insurance.

(2) **Notice of Claim or Suit:** If claim is made or suit is brought against the Insured, the Insured shall immediately forward to this Company every demand, notice or summons or other process received by him or his representative.

(3) **Action Against Company:** No action shall lie against this Company unless as a condition precedent thereto, the Insured shall have fully complied with all the terms of Section II, nor until the amount of the Insured's obligation to pay shall have been finally determined either by judgment against the Insured after actual trial or by written agreement of the Insured, the claimant and this Company. Any person or organization or the legal representative thereof who has secured such judgment or written agreement shall thereafter be entitled to recover under this insurance to the extent afforded thereby. Nothing contained in this insurance shall give any person or organization any right to join this Company as a co-defendent in any action against the Insured to determine the Insured's liability. Bankruptcy or insolvency of the Insured or of the Insured's estate shall not relieve this Company of any of its obligations hereunder.

(4) **Subrogation:** In the event of any payment under this policy, this Company shall be subrogated to all the Insured's rights of recovery therefor against any person or organization and the Insured shall execute and deliver instruments and papers and do whatever else is necessary to secure such rights. The Insured shall do nothing after loss to prejudice such rights.

Form No. 63 (1-60)

APPENDIX L

Appendix L—Replacement Cost Endorsement

UNIFORM STANDARD **FORM NO. 158R**
(Edition Feb. '64)

REPLACEMENT COST ENDORSEMENT

This endorsement applies only to those items of this policy which, on the first page thereof, are specified as being covered hereunder.

1. In consideration of One Dollar ($1.00) and the following Coinsurance Clause being made a part of this policy to apply only to the item(s) to which this endorsement applies, which Coinsurance Clause supersedes and replaces the Coinsurance Clause, if any, otherwise applicable to such item(s), the provisions of this policy applicable only to such item(s) are amended to substitute the term "replacement cost" for the term "actual cash value" wherever it appears in this policy, thereby eliminating any deduction for depreciation, subject, however, in all other respects to the provisions of this endorsement and of the policy to which this endorsement is attached.

2. This endorsement shall not apply to manuscripts; or to paintings, etchings, pictures, tapestries, statuary, marbles, bronzes, antique furniture, rare books, antique silver, porcelains, rare glassware and bric-a-brac, or other articles of art, rarity or antiquity.

3. This Company shall not be liable under this policy including this endorsement for any loss —
   (a) Occasioned by enforcement of any local or state ordinance or law regulating the construction, repair or demolition of buildings unless such liability has been specifically assumed under this policy;
   (b) Unless and until the damaged property is actually repaired or replaced by the Insured, on the same premises and with due diligence and dispatch.

4. **COINSURANCE CLAUSE:** In consideration of the rate and (or) form under which this policy is written, it is expressly stipulated and made a condition of this contract that the Insured shall at all times maintain contributing insurance on each item of property, the replacement cost of which is covered by this policy, to the extent of at least the percentage specified on the first page of this policy of the replacement cost (without deduction for depreciation) at the time of the loss, and that failing to do so, the Insured shall to the extent of such deficit bear his, her or their proportion of any loss.

In the event that the aggregate claim for any loss is less than 2% of the total amount of insurance upon the property described herein at the time such loss occurs, the Insured shall not be required to furnish any inventory of the undamaged property to establish the value referred to in the Coinsurance Clause provided, however, that nothing herein shall be construed to waive the application of the first paragraph of this clause.

If this policy be divided into two or more items, the foregoing conditions shall apply to each item separately.

5. The Insured may elect first to make claim under this policy in accordance with its provisions, disregarding this endorsement, except that the foregoing Coinsurance Clause applicable to the replacement cost of said property, shall apply; and the Insured may make further claim for any additional liability brought about by this endorsement in accordance with its provisions, provided this Company is notified in writing within 180 days after loss of the Insured's intent to make such further claim.

6. This Company's liability for loss under this policy including this endorsement shall not exceed the smallest of the following amounts (a), (b) or (c)—
   (a) The amount of this policy applicable to the damaged or destroyed property;
   (b) The replacement cost of the property or any part thereof, identical with such property on the same premises and intended for the same occupancy and use;
   (c) The amount actually and necessarily expended in repairing or replacing said property or any part thereof on the same premises.

7. **APPORTIONMENT CLAUSE:** This Company shall not be liable under this policy including this endorsement for a greater proportion of any loss than the amount of this policy applying to the property to which this endorsement applies bears to the total amount of insurance on such property against the peril involved, whether or not such other insurance includes the extension of coverage provided under this endorsement,and whether such other insurance is collectible or not.

8. If the coverage on property under this policy be divided into two or more items, all of the foregoing shall apply separately to each item to which this endorsement applies.

Form No. 158R (2-64)

NOTES TO AGENTS: **1. The items to which this endorsement applies must be clearly indicated on the face of the policy.**
2. This endorsement applies only to building items except as permitted by the published rules.

INDEXES

Index of Legal Cases

Index

J

K

L